Frommer's
France

24th Edition

By Jane Anson, Anna E. Brooke,
Mary Anne Evans, Lily Heise,
Sophie Kevany, Mary Novakovich,
Tristan Rutherford, Louise Simpson,
Kathryn Tomasetti, Victoria Trott,
Simon Willmore

FrommerMedia LLC

Published by
FROMMER MEDIA LLC

Copyright © 2019 FrommerMedia LLC, New York, NY. All rights reserved. No part of this publication may be reproduced, stored in a retrieval system or transmitted in any form or by any means, electronic, mechanical, photocopying, recording, scanning or otherwise, except as permitted under Sections 107 or 108 of the 1976 United States Copyright Act, without the prior written permission of the Publisher. Requests to the Publisher for permission should be addressed to Support@FrommerMedia.com.

Frommer's Complete Guide to France 2019, 24th Edition

ISBN 978-1-62887-398-6 (paper), 978-1-62887-399-3 (e-book)

Editorial Director: Pauline Frommer
Editor: Melinda Quintero
Production Editor: Kelly Dobbs Henthorne
Cartographer: Liz Puhl
Page Compositor: Heather Pope
Photo Editor: Meghan Lamb

For information on our other products or services, see www.frommers.com.

Frommer Media LLC also publishes its books in a variety of electronic formats. Some content that appears in print may not be available in electronic formats.

Manufactured in China

5 4 3 2 1

HOW TO CONTACT US

In researching this book, we discovered many wonderful places—hotels, restaurants, shops, and more. We're sure you'll find others. Please tell us about them, so we can share the information with your fellow travelers in upcoming editions. If you were disappointed with a recommendation, we'd love to know that, too. Please write to: Support@FrommerMedia.com

FROMMER'S STAR RATINGS SYSTEM

Every hotel, restaurant and attraction listed in this guide has been ranked for quality and value. Here's what the stars mean:

★   Recommended
★★   Highly Recommended
★★★   A must! Don't miss!

AN IMPORTANT NOTE

The world is a dynamic place. Hotels change ownership, restaurants hike their prices, museums alter their opening hours, and buses and trains change their routings. And all of this can occur in the several months after our authors have visited, inspected, and written about, these hotels, restaurants, museums, and transportation services. Though we have made valiant efforts to keep all our information fresh and up-to-date, some few changes can inevitably occur in the periods before a revised edition of this guidebook is published. So please bear with us if a tiny number of the details in this book have changed. Please also note that we have no responsibility or liability for any inaccuracy or errors or omissions, or for inconvenience, loss, damage, or expenses suffered by anyone as a result of assertions in this guide.

CONTENTS

LIST OF MAPS

ABOUT THE AUTHORS

Jane Anson has lived in France since 2003. She is author of "Bordeaux Legends" (Abrahms 2013), "Wine Revolution" (Quarto 2017), "The Club of Nine" (Katz Publishing 2016), "Angelus" (Editions de la Martiniere 2016), and translator for Lynch Bages & Cie (Glenat 2015). Anson is contributing writer of the "Michelin Guide to the Wine Regions of France" (Michelin Publications, March 2010) and more than a dozen guidebooks on France and Japan.

Anna E. Brooke moved to Paris in 2000 and hasn't looked back since. British-born, she is now a full-fledged bohemian, juggling life between freelance travel writing, screenwriting, and songwriting. She has authored seven guides for Frommer's and is a Paris expert for the U.K.'s best-selling *Sunday Times Travel Magazine.*

Mary Anne Evans bought a house in a remote part of the Auvergne after leaving university and began exploring France in a Renault 4 van. Her delight in discovering both the best of and the off-beat in French cities and the countryside remains as strong as ever. She has written books on Japanese prints and guitars, guides to Belgium and Stockholm and to London for Gault Millau and gayot.com, articles on Finland and Sweden, and many articles on France for tripsavvy.com. Visit her at her website, maryannesfrance.com.

Lily Heise left behind her native Canada in 2000 to pursue her love of French joie de vivre in Paris. She writes on travel and romance for a variety of international and local publications. She is also the author of two lively books on searching for love in Paris, "Je T'Aime, Me Neither," and "Je T'Aime…Maybe?" and shares further romantic travel tips at www.jetaimemeneither.com. She also would like to thank Emily Dilling for her advice on the Loire.

Sophie Kevany was born in Washington, D.C., and has lived and worked in Ireland, France, South Africa, and Peru. She is a freelance journalist, writer, and researcher. Over the last 20 years she has written for a range of news agencies and publications including Agence France Presse (AFP), Dow Jones, Decanter, and Wine Business International. Most recently she has launched a communications and strategy company, Client Planet, for plant-based and vegan businesses.

Mary Novakovich is an award-winning travel writer and journalist and a member of the British Guild of Travel Writers based in Hertfordshire, England. She has been writing extensively about France and her other countries for 20 years for *The Independent, The Guardian, The Daily Telegraph, France Magazine, Sunday Times Travel Magazine,* the BBC, CNN, and Lonely Planet, among others. She also has written guidebooks for Frommer's, Berlitz, and Insight Guides.

Tristan Rutherford has been a freelance writer for more than a decade. His lucky first assignment took him to Nice, and he's been based there ever since. He has visited some 70 countries and written about 30 of them for *The Independent* and the Sunday *New York Times Travel* magazine. Tristan also lectures on travel journalism at London's Central Saint Martins.

Louise Simpson fell in love with all things French as a teenager on holidays to her family home in Dordogne and as a French student at Cambridge University. Since moving to France nearly two decades ago, she has authored a dozen travel guides to France and is the hotel correspondent for Telegraph Travel on Central and Southern France. She also has written for *FT Weekend, The Independent,* and *The Spectator* in the U.K., as well as for Zagat and Google in the U.S. and as a food columnist for Monaco Life. Louise lives in London and Monaco.

Kathryn Tomasetti, U.S.-born and Italian-raised, writes travel and food features for a variety of publications including *The Guardian* and *Delicious.* Her holiday photos—snapped from as far afield as China, Albania, and Chile—have been published by *National Geographic* and *Time Out.* Kathryn's favorite places in Provence are the pavement cafes of Avignon and the art-filled city of Arles. She resides in Nice.

Victoria Trott is an award-winning freelance travel journalist who specializes in France. A graduate in French and Spanish, she writes for a range of international publications. Her most exciting discovery in this update was that you can get a glass of champagne for 5€ in Reims.

Simon Willmore's career in travel writing began when he moved to Grenoble in 2008—when he should have been studying for his Master's in Engineering. Since retraining as a journalist, he has coauthored four guide books for Rough Guides, blogged for National Geographic Traveller, and written a technology column in a national women's magazine. He is currently the editorial director of Travel Daily and a board member of the British Guild of Travel Writers. Follow him on Twitter: @SiWillmore.

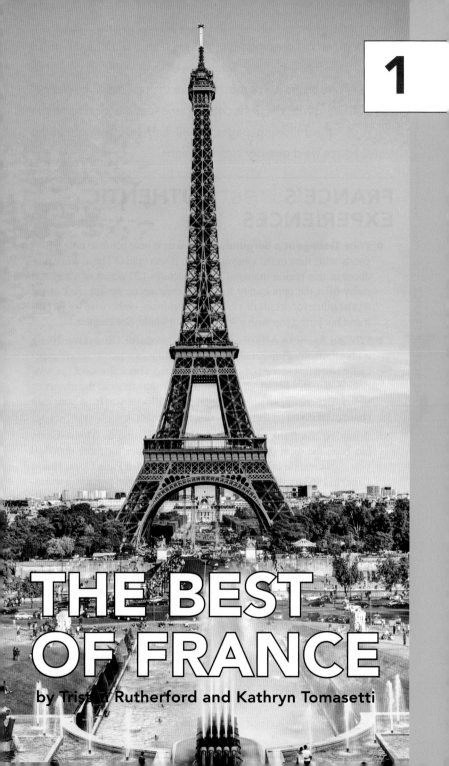

THE BEST OF FRANCE

by Tristan Rutherford and Kathryn Tomasetti

F rance presents visitors with an embarrassment of riches—you may find yourself overwhelmed by all the choices. We've tried to make the task easier by compiling a list of our favorite experiences and discoveries. In the following pages, you'll find the kind of candid travel advice we'd give our closest friends.

FRANCE'S best AUTHENTIC EXPERIENCES

o **Wine Tastings at a Burgundy Vineyard:** Where better to taste a Burgundy wine than in the vineyard where it was made? The average producer in this region manages just 8 hectares (20 acres) of vines and many offer the opportunity to sample their nectar on site. Ask at the tourist office for details of visits for individuals—otherwise we recommend booking a trip with a specialist tour guide. See chapter 11.

o **Whiling Away an Afternoon in a Parisian Cafe:** There is something quintessentially Parisian about doing nothing in a public space, especially when that space is a cafe. You can read a book, look out the window, chat with a friend, sip some wine, or simply ponder the mysteries of life. Better still, no one will attempt to dislodge you from your cafe chair, even if you sit there for hours. See chapter 4.

o **Breaking the Bank at Monte-Carlo:** The **Casino de Monte-Carlo** has been the most opulent place to have a flutter for more than 150 years. Its creation by architect Charles Garnier (of Paris Opera House fame) in 1863 transformed Monaco from a provincial port into a world-class tourist destination. Expect frescoed ceilings and wealthy, well-dressed clientele from as far afield as China and Russia. See p. 632.

o **Ogling the Pomp of the Pope's Medieval Party Pad:** Those medieval popes knew a thing or two about interior design. Avignon's **Palais des Papes,** or Pope's Palace, is a moneyed medley of Gothic architecture and vast banqueting halls. The Châteauneuf-du-Pape papal vineyards just north of Avignon still produce some of the most noted wine in France. See p. 498.

o **Eating Boeuf Bourgignon:** Burgundy is as well known for its gastronomy as its wine. One of its most famous dishes is *boeuf bourgignon,* ideally made with Charolais beef (from the famous white cows which originated in the Charolais area near Mâcon) slow cooked with onions and mushrooms in a regional red wine. See chapter 11.

PREVIOUS PAGE: **Eiffel Tower seen from Jardins du Trocadéro**

An outdoor cafe in Paris

- **Buying Your Daily Bread:** That cute little boulangerie just down the street? Depending on where you are, there's likely to be another—or several—a short stroll away. The daily baguette run is a ritual for many French people. Get your coins ready (1€, give or take 10 centimes) and join the queue. To really fit in, ask for your baguette chewy (*pas trop cuite*), or crusty (*bien cuite*).

- **Shopping at a Market:** Markets are one of the best ways to explore French towns like a local. We recommend the open-air market in **Arles** (p. 517), one of Provence's most authentic destinations. A colorful line of vendors sells olives, fresh bread, cheese, and local ham underneath the city ramparts, a few blocks from the town's Roman amphitheater. Alternatively, French covered markets are time machines—visiting

Fresh bread at a French bakery

one is like taking a trip back through the centuries. Bordeaux's vast **Marché des Capucins** offers not just good things to take home, but

A couple strolling along the Seine, Paris

great things to eat on site from various stands, including Chez JeanMi, where you can enjoy oysters straight out of nearby Arcachon Bay, or the newly-opened Café Laiton, where owner Gaëlle serves up freshly brewed cups of Columbian, Brazilian, and Kenyan coffees, along with some delicious pastries, at the entrance to the market. And in the Rhône Valley, local gourmands crowd the covered market of Lyon's **Les Halles** to stock up on high-quality Lyonnaise specialties, from creamed fish *quenelles* to sweet *bugnes*—either round and doughnut-like, or flat and crunchy. See p. 502.

o **Shucking Fresh Oysters:** The French adore oysters and there's no better place to get the freshest than in Cancale, Brittany. Today everyone has access to these jewels of the sea—once a favorite of King Louis XIV—perfectly paired with a crisp white wine down by the old port. See chapter 8.

o **Strolling along the Seine:** The lifeblood of the City of Light, the Seine is at the center of Paris's history, which becomes obvious when you stroll along its banks. Just about every major monument can be seen from here, including the **Eiffel Tower, Notre-Dame,** and the **Louvre.** And now that many of Seine's embankments have become pedestrian-only, promenading along them is a delight. See chapter 4.

o **Château-hopping through the Loire Valley:** An excursion to the châteaux dotting the valley's rich fields and forests will familiarize you with the French Renaissance's architectural aesthetics and the intrigues of the kings and their courts. Visit the main castles, such as **Chambord** or **Chenonceau,** and then stop in at some lesser-visited ones, like **Chaumont** or **Valençay.** See chapter 6.

- **Touring the Villages along France's Oldest "Wine Road"** (Alsace-Lorraine): More than 60 villages line the famous Alsatian wine road. Enjoy their medieval town squares and half-timbered houses while stopping in at the local vineyards. See chapter 10.

- **Taking a Trip on a Gabarre down the Dordogne River** (Dordogne): *Gabarres* are traditional flat-bottomed boats that used to ply the shallow Dordogne, taking goods from one town to the next. Today they are used for guided river cruises, offering tourists a unique way to experience this unspoiled waterway. See p. 769.

- **Wandering through Europe's Greatest Fortress City** (Languedoc-Roussillon): Carcassonne was built for war with its fortifications, imposing citadel, and double ring of defensive walls. But even its massive towers didn't keep it safe from conquest and re-conquest during the endless feuds of catholic vs heretics and medieval power politics. Its inevitable decline was reversed in the 19th century with a massive restoration, and today Carcassonne is one of the great sites of Europe. See p. 670.

- **Skiing Chamonix** (The French Alps): The place where skiing came to the masses—and French skiing came to the world, during the 1924 Winter Olympics. More affordable than nearby Megève or Courchevel, this is the people's ski resort and party town. See p. 486.

- **Getting Bubbly at the Moët et Chandon Champagne Cellars** (Champagne Country): Go straight to the source to learn the secrets of one of the world's most prestigious Champagne houses. The tour includes an explanation of the *méthode Champenoise* as well as anecdotes about illustrious clients including Napoleon Bonaparte. In Epernay, 90-min. from Paris by train, this also makes for a great rainy-day Plan B. See p. 353.

FRANCE'S best RESTAURANTS

- **Le Grand Véfour** (Paris): There aren't many restaurants where you can both savor an exquisite meal and eat it in a room where Napoléon Bonaparte once dined. Tucked under an arcade at the Palais Royal, Le Grand Véfour has fed everyone from Cocteau to Colette amid magnificent 18th-century decor—now it's your turn. See p. 146.

- **Le Domaine des Hauts de Loire,** between Blois and Amboise (Loire): For more than 20 years, Rémy Giraud has been wowing locals and weary château-hoppers at his double-Michelin-starred restaurant. The menu showcases seasonal and regional ingredients, such as Aquitaine caviar on pecan shortbread or crispy Gatinais quail with celery cream. See p. 239.

- **La Roche le Roy,** Tours (Loire): The finest in Touraine cuisine is delicately prepared at this award-winning 18th-century manor. Maximilien

Bridier adds contemporary flair to traditional dishes like *meunière* of Saint Pierre fish drizzled in Persian lime. See p. 243.

o **Didier Méril,** Dinard (Brittany): Savor the best catches and flavors of Brittany at this well-loved local restaurant set in a picturesque stone building overlooking the beautiful Bay of Prieuré. See p. 315.

o **L'Atlantide,** Nantes (Brittany): The most inventive take on Breton cuisine can be sampled at this sleek panoramic restaurant dominating the city and the Loire River. Tantalize your palate with Chef Jean-Yves Guého's creative delights of ginger-glazed veal sweetbreads or ravioli of merlan in a lemongrass broth. See p. 337.

o **Auberge de l'Ill,** north of Colmar (Alsace): For over 100 years the Haeberlin family have tempted gastronomes to their exceptional restaurant. They've maintained their three Michelin stars since 1967 with dishes like fillet of venison coated with grilled buckwheat and herb Kasknepfla and served with wild mushrooms and spicy beetroot compote. See p. 384.

o **Chez Yvonne,** Strasbourg (Alsace): Sink your teeth into some of the region's best sausage and choucroute at this charming winstub, a favorite with the locals since 1873. See p. 370.

o **L'Escargot,** Carcassonne (Languedoc-Roussillon): Serving great—and great-value—tapas, this bistro and wine bar is the place for a light lunch on the terrace. Try snails, Iberico ham, caramelized foie gras, and patatas bravas, and you're set up for an afternoon walking around the ramparts of the fortified city. See p. 673.

o **La Planque de l'Evêque,** Albi (Languedoc-Roussillon): You'll find it difficult to discover a more idyllic spot than this restaurant that looks out to the spectacular red brick cathedral. Make the short journey across the river for a south of France feast of red mullet with confit tomatoes and tapenade, chicken supreme with mushroom risotto, and a chestnut crème brûlée. See p. 679.

o **Ostalamer,** Saint-Jean-de-Luz (The Basque Country): Sample *chipirones à la plancha* with a side order of incredible views over the Atlantic at this wonderful restaurant in the Basque region. See p. 712.

o **Pressoir d'Argent,** Bordeaux (Bordeaux): One of the best restaurants in a city that is increasingly packed full of great places to eat, the Pressoir d'Argent is overseen by Gordon Ramsay and has a brilliant wine list that goes way beyond simply Bordeaux. See p. 724.

o **La Couronne,** Rouen (Normandy): Julia Child enjoyed her first-ever French meal at this traditional Norman restaurant. A bustling *auberge* in business for more than 6 centuries—and pulling in plenty of celebrity diners along the way—La Couronne makes the most of this region's hearty produce, from *côte de boeuf* (rib steak) to aged Camembert cheeses. See p. 273.

- **Marché aux Poissons,** Trouville (Normandy): This fish market's dozen seafood stalls perch on the banks of the Touques River. Each one will happily plate up your own unique *plateau de fruits de mer* (seafood platter): Take your pick of fresh oysters, lobsters, scallops and more, then dig in at one of the market tables. Be sure to order a glass of Normandy's famous cider (*cidre*), a delicate, fermented version of apple juice that is a refreshing alcoholic tipple. See p. 285.

- **Café de la Table Ronde,** Grenoble (The French Alps): Founded in 1739, this is the second oldest cafe in France; only the well-touted Procope in Paris is older. The delicious fondue Savoyarde is the epitome of French alpine cuisine. See p. 481.

- **Auberge du Père-Bise,** Talloires (The French Alps): Helmed by Jean Sulpice, who received two Michelin stars at his Val Thorens restaurant, here the rich and famous enjoy dishes such as foie gras mousse on the shore of Lake Annecy. See p. 477.

- **L'Assiette Champenoise,** Reims (Champagne Country): This three-Michelin-star restaurant was voted 13th best restaurant in the world by La Liste 2018. See p. 347.

- **Maison Lameloise,** Chagny (Burgundy): Burgundian cuisine with a Modern French touch is the reason to visit this three-Michelin star restaurant in the heart of the vineyards. See p. 425.

- **Régis et Jacques Marcon,** (Rhône Valley): On a plateau overlooking the Mézenc hills, this three-Michelin-starred restaurant abounds in local flavors such as Puy lentils, chestnuts, and mushrooms grown in the nearby pinewoods. This outstanding restaurant has created a village empire that now includes a cooking school, bakery, hotel, and spa. See p. 464.

- **Oustau de Baumanière,** Les Baux (Provence): The cinematic setting of the ancient fortress of Les Baux had troubadours singing in its streets during the Middle Ages. Today it is no less romantic. Several picturesque hideaways are tucked into the hills surrounding the village, including this double-Michelin-starred gem housed in a 16th-century farmhouse. See p. 517.

- **L'Atelier Jean-Luc Rabanel,** Arles (Provence): Fixed-price tasting menus—no à la carte allowed—are becoming increasingly popular. If you're ready to put yourself in the hands of one of France's most talented chefs, try Jean-Luc Rabanel's sublime creations. This culinary genius cultivates most of his organic ingredients himself. See p. 523.

- **La Merenda,** Nice (Riviera): Utterly unpretentious, this snug bistro doesn't take reservations or credit cards. But it remains one of the Riviera's top spots for sampling traditional Niçois cuisine. Try slow-cooked beef *daube, petits-farcis* (stuffed vegetables), and *pissaladière,* a pizza-like local flatbread topped with caramelized onions. See p. 610.

○ **Le Louis XV,** Monaco (Riviera): Superchef Alain Ducasse oversees this iconic restaurant—regularly rated as one of the finest in the world—located in Monte-Carlo's Hôtel de Paris. Dining is extravagant, with fare steeped in lavish ingredients, from white truffles to foie gras, and served in an ornate, golden dining room. Yet many dishes of elegant simplicity are equally magnificent. Best for serious epicureans. See p. 636.

FRANCE'S best HOTELS

○ **Hôtel Caron de Beaumarchais** (Paris): This adorable inn re-creates the ambience of 18th-century Paris, when the hotel's namesake, the author of "The Barber of Seville," was cavorting in the neighborhood. Rooms are covered in fine reproductions of period fabrics and furnished with antique writing tables, ceiling fixtures, and paintings—a bit of Old France right in the middle of trendy Marais. See p. 131.

○ **Relais St-Germain** (Paris): A luxurious mix of past and present makes this hotel a romantic and modern haven, just steps from the bustle of Boulevard St-Germain. Run by the same management as the famous restaurant Le Comptoir du Relais (downstairs), this beautiful spot makes the perfect gourmet getaway. See p. 140.

○ **Château d'Artigny,** south of Tours (Loire): Complete your castle experience by staying at one of the Loire's most regal château-hotels. You really will feel like a king, bedding down in Louis XV–style rooms and relaxing in the hotel's luxurious spa. See p. 244.

○ **Le Manoir Les Minimes,** Amboise (Loire): Regional charm and character shine through at this reasonably priced manor, a perfect base for exploring the château country. Tucked behind its high walls, it has many rooms facing the river, while others offer glimpses of the royal château of Amboise. See p. 235.

○ **Grand Hôtel Barrière de Dinard,** Dinard (Brittany): Relive the era of grand Victorian seaside resorts at one of the period's finest hotels. This luxurious hotel-casino features modern comforts, chic dining facilities, and stunning views of the bay. See p. 315.

○ **Manoir du Stang,** near Quimper (Brittany): Surround yourself in the charms of Brittany at this enchanting 16th-century stone manor. Tucked away in the Fouesnant Forest yet only a 10 min. drive to the coast, it's the perfect countryside retreat in western France. See p. 322.

○ **Cour du Corbeau,** Strasbourg (Alsace): One of the oldest hotels in France, this 17th-century inn combines the historic character of thick wooden beams and sainted-glass windows with stylish contemporary furnishings and amenities. See p. 369.

- **Clos St-Vincent,** between Strasbourg and Colmar (Alsace): Admire the vineyards of Alsace directly from your private terrace at this refined hotel along the country's oldest wine route. See p. 377.

- **Alchimy,** Albi (Languedoc-Roussillon): For a small restaurant with rooms and a very large wow factor, book at Alchimy in Albi, designed by two top interior designers. Rooms are a mix of bold colors, mirrors, striking art, and one-off objects. The glass-vaulted restaurant with columns and terracotta-colored walls is fast becoming Albi's top place to eat (and certainly to be seen at). See p. 678.

- **Hôtel de la Cité,** Carcassonne (Languedoc-Roussillon): Go medieval at this hotel in Carcassonne, which looks over the ramparts and to the distant mountains. Wood paneling, friezes, and four-poster beds take you back to its origins. But there's also a heated pool, a top restaurant, and every 21st-century mod con you could wish for. See p. 672.

- **Le Pavillon,** St-Emilion (Bordeaux): A luxurious *chambres d'hotes* in the beautiful medieval village of St-Emilion. Six rooms focus on luxury and carefully chosen details, with prices that remain the same year-round and include breakfast plus a bottle of wine. See p. 729.

- **Hotel de Bouilhac,** Montignac (Dordogne): Not just lovely, but great value too. This hotel is located near the new Lascaux caves exhibition, one of the must-visit attractions in southwest France. See p. 762.

- **Hôtel Parc Beaumont,** Pau (The Basque Country): Some of Pau's best accommodation, with good-sized beds, balconies, and beautiful views over the park. The hotel's Jeu de Paume restaurant is particularly recommended. See p. 696.

- **Hotel Le Normandy,** Deauville (Normandy): This legendary hotel, built in 1912 is a giant fairy-tale concoction that overlooks the seafront. With spacious rooms and a glass-ceilinged indoor pool, it's favored by smart Parisian families. See p. 282.

- **Le Strato,** Courchevel (The French Alps): The height of decadence: this Small Luxury Hotels of the World property is the place to be seen in the French skiing place to be seen: Courchevel 1850. It's not rare for guests to arrive by private helicopter. See p. 485.

- **Hôtel Ermitage,** Evian-les-Bains (The French Alps): Both part of the Evian Resort, these two properties occupy the hillside rolling down towards Lac Léman. True to the area's luxurious heritage, spa treatments and expensive meals are the order of the day. See p. 470.

- **Le Champ des Oiseaux,** Troyes (Champagne Country): Step back into the middle ages at this half-timbered four-star hotel which has been elegantly renovated by master craftsmen. See p. 357.

- **Le Cep,** Beaune (Burgundy). Old-fashioned service and luxury are what you'll find at this historic five-star hotel and spa in Burgundy's wine capital. See p. 423.

o **Château de Bagnols,** (Rhône Valley): Surrounded by Beaujolais vineyards, this fairy-tale Renaissance castle comes complete with a drawbridge, moat, fortifications, extensive formal gardens, and a spa. In 2017, this Relais & Châteaux hotel celebrated its 800th anniversary with the winning of a Michelin star for its restaurant. See p. 453.

o **Mama Shelter,** Marseille (Provence): The work of legendary designer Philippe Starck, this contemporary hotel is located in the hip cours Julien neighborhood. On the ground floor, there's a courtyard pastis bar, perfect for sampling the city's favorite aperitif. See p. 540.

o **Château Saint-Martin,** Vence (Riviera): Perched on a hilltop just 20 min. from Nice, Château Saint-Martin is one of the Riviera's most splendid hotels. The gardens are sprinkled with wildflowers; the infinity pool quite literally goes on forever; and a truly exquisite spa is onsite. Lucky guests can gaze at the Mediterranean from bed. See p. 596.

o **Hôtel Belles-Rives,** Juan-les-Pins (Riviera): Once a vacation villa to Zelda and F. Scott Fitzgerald, the Hôtel Belles-Rives still maintains a flamboyant, 1920s feel. Sip a sundowner on the hotel's sea-facing terrace, or try waterskiing at the hotel's aquatic club, the very spot where the sport was invented a century ago. See p. 583.

undiscovered **FRANCE**

o **Cycling in the Countryside:** The country that hosts the Tour de France offers thousands of options for bike trips, all of them ideal for leaving the crowds far behind. You're even welcome to take your bike aboard most trains in France, free of charge. For cycling through Provence's vineyards and past pretty hilltop villages, check out **Le Luberon à Vélo**'s downloadable routes. See p. 510.

o **Hunting for Antiques:** The 18th- and 19th-century French aesthetic was gloriously different from that of England and North America. Many objects bear designs with mythological references to the French experience. France has some 13,000-plus antiques shops throughout the country. Stop where you see the sign antiquaire or brocante.

o **Cruising France's Rivers:** Floating slowly down one of France's major rivers is a superb way to see hidden corners of the countryside. Most luxury barge cruises offer daily excursions, elegant dinners on deck, and bicycles for solitary exploration. See chapter 20.

o **Reveling in St-Etienne-du-Mont:** One of the prettiest in Paris, this stunning church that sits atop the highest point in Paris's Latin Quarter is often left off the tourist itinerary. A delightful mix of late-Gothic and Renaissance styles, the church has a 16th-century chancel boasting the city's only rood screen, a magnificent work with decorations inspired by the Italian Renaissance. See p. 116.

Antiques market in Nice

o **Going Underground at Touraine's Troglodyte Caves:** Admire art, sample regional wine, and even stay the night underground in the Loire's Touraine region, home to France's largest concentration of Troglodyte caves. See p. 252.

o **Returning to the Time of the Crusades** (Loire): See the history behind the foolhardy Crusades at the 12th-century Abbey of Fonte-vraud. It's one of the largest medieval monasteries in Europe as well as the final resting place of most of the Plantagenets. See p. 259.

o **Peeking at Crypt Murals** Auxerre (Burgundy): The overused term "hidden gems" is appropriate to describe Auxerre's two crypt murals because that is exactly what they are. Underneath the remains of the Abbaye Saint-Germain are a series of religious wall murals dating from the 9th century, the oldest so far found in France. Those at the nearby Cathédrale Saint-Etienne go back to the 11th century and are famous for depicting a rare image of Christ on a horse. See p. 409.

o **Discovering Secret Beaches between Monaco and Roquebrune-Cap-Martin** (Riviera): The Riviera's rippling coastal path turns up plenty of hidden surprises. Head east out of Monaco, passing the Monte-Carlo Beach Hotel. The trail then meanders along the Mediter-ranean shoreline. Aleppo pines and fig trees part to reveal the tiniest turquoise coves. Pack your swimming suit. See p. 630.

o **Tracing the Trenches:** While Normandy usually attracts most visitors interested in war history, the western front of World War I carved its way through Eastern France. Many moving battlefield sites and memo-rials are located near Verdun. See p. 296.

Beach at Roquebrune-Cap-Martin in the French Riviera

o **Marveling at France's "Stonehenge"** (Brittany): The seaside resort of Carnac is home to the largest megalithic site in the world. A visit might not answer how these massive stones got turned upright, but it will certainly leave you pondering the mysteries and theories surrounding this curious site. See p. 328.

o **Exploring the Glamorous Château des Milandes** (Dordogne): This splendid Renaissance castle was the former home of singer/dancer Josephine Baker. Learn about her fascinating life and visit rooms furnished as they were when she lived there, then take a stroll in the gardens. See p. 769.

o **Meandering through Traboules in Vieux Lyon** (Rhône Valley): Hidden behind brown-painted doorways lie flower-ringed courtyards and vaulted masonry ceilings. You'll discover many architectural gems on a 2-hr. tour around Vieux Lyon's medieval *traboules*—corridors connecting two streets through a building or courtyard. See p. 437.

o **Rambling the Sentier des Ocres de Roussillon** (Provence): Located in the heart of the Luberon, Roussillon once possessed some of the world's most important ochre quarries. Today this landscape is just as brilliantly hued and can be explored via a picturesque hiking trail. See p. 510.

o **Greeting the Morning** (Languedoc-Roussillon): Stay in Cordes-sur-Ciel, wake up at dawn and walk to the ramparts to watch the sun rise over the medieval city "in the sky." Cordes is the most spectacular medieval bastide around Albi but it's overrun by visitors during peak months, so this way you'll have the fairytale village to yourself. See p. 680.

- **Sampling Champagne's Art Treasures** (Champagne Country): The south of the Champagne region has some little-known gems that will delight art lovers. The Musée d'Art Moderne in Troyes, housed in an atmospheric former bishops' palace, has an exquisite collection of modern art from 1850–1960. Two new museums opened in 2017 in this area: Auguste Renoir's family home in Essoyes, and the Musée Camille Claudel in Nogent-sur-Seine, which celebrates the talent of Auguste Rodin's student and lover. See p. 359.

FRANCE'S best FOR FAMILIES

- **Climbing the Heights of Mont-St-Michel** (Normandy): Straddling the tidal flats between Normandy and Brittany, this Gothic marvel is the most spectacular fortress in northern Europe. Said to be protected by the archangel Michael, much of it stands as it did during the 1200s. As of 2014, however, a brand-new pedestrian path connects the visitor center to Mont-St-Michel itself. You can now stroll, bike, or trot (in a horse-drawn carriage) across to the fortress. See chapter 7.

- **Getting Medieval in the Hilltop Town of Les Baux** (Provence): The age-old hilltown of **Les Baux** commands views over hundreds of miles of Provençal countryside. The film-set location, including the hilltop

Monumental Mont-St-Michel, Normandy

ruins of its "ghost village," plus a volley of great restaurants, have made it a retreat for France's rich and famous. Kids will love its car-free medieval streets and awesome views, not to mention the daily display of a siege engine catapult. See p. 514.

o **Visiting the new Lascaux IV** (Dordogne): Opened in January 2018, the latest replica reveals far more of the cave than previous ones and uses a range of digital technology (including a very clever tablet guide) to take visitors back 20,000 years. From the outside, Lascaux IV is perfectly blended into the natural landscape. It is particularly good for children—and afterwards you can take them to nearby Le Thot Zoo to see live animals like those on the Lascaux walls. See p. 760.

o **Making the Most of Modern Art in Antibes** (French Riviera): The **Musée Picasso** (Picasso Museum) in Antibes highlights some of the most accessible art in France. The Spanish painter set up shop in the atmospheric old quarter of Antibes's Château Grimaldi some 70 years ago. In such relaxed surroundings, children can appreciate the color, vibrancy, and playfulness that made Picasso one of the greats of the 20th century. The far-out sculptures and sunny views of the surrounding coastline will please non-art fans, too. See p. 586.

o **Joining the Cowboys in the Camargue** (Provence): Riding a sturdy Camarguais horse and with a local cowboy to guide you, make your way through the marshes of these beautiful, remote wetlands. Spot pink flamingos and watch the *gardians* with their large felt hats rounding up black bulls bred for the bullrings of the south. If the children don't ride, then slow boats, bicycles, and jeeps make great alternatives. See chapter 14.

o **Sailing along a Canal** (Burgundy): Burgundy has France's largest network of waterways. As well as the navigable rivers of the Yonne, Saône, and Seille, seven canals were built between the 17th and 19th century to link the rivers Seine, Loire, and Rhône. Hire your own boat or take an organized trip passing châteaux and vineyards, going through tunnels, over aqueducts, and up or down staircase locks. See chapter 11.

o **Getting a Chocolate Education** (Rhône Valley): The trials of finding a museum suitable for children are solved upon discovering the cacao-infused wonders of La Cité du Chocolat. All five senses are used in the interactive exhibits that entertain little ones with the rich experience of chocolate making and tasting. See p. 549.

o **Exploring the Calanques** (Provence): The **Parc National des Calanques** is a stunning series of limestone cliffs and tumbling fjords that stretch along the coast for some 30km (18 miles) southeast of Marseille. Serious hikers can trek the Calanques' rocky promontories. Families with children can take in the coastline from aboard one of the many tour boats that depart from Marseille's port. See p. 547.

The American Cemetery at Colleville-sur-Mer, Normandy

- **Walking through a Real Fairy Tale** (Loire): The whole region of the Loire offers kids the chance to live out their fairy-tale fantasies. Step right into a storybook at the **Château d'Ussé,** the inspiration for "Sleeping Beauty." See p. 258.

- **Remembering Fallen Heroes on Normandy's D-Day Beaches:** On June 6, 1944, the largest armada ever assembled departed on rough seas and in dense fog from southern England. For about a week, the future of the civilized world teetered between the Nazi and Allied armies. Today the entire family can immerse itself in the past with superb interactive exhibits, such as the personal tales detailed at the **Normandy American Visitor Center.** Kids can then run wild on the windswept sands below. See p. 297.

- **Playing in the Jardin des Plantes** (Paris): A splendid place for a picnic, this historic botanical garden is a quiet oasis in the Latin Quarter, where families can relax and tiny travelers can enjoy the playground, hothouses, and green spaces. When playtime is over, everyone can wander over to the small zoo or the adjoining natural-history museum. See p. 114.

- **Stargazing at Cité des Sciences et de l'Industrie** (Paris): Set amid the vast Parc de la Villette in the 19th arrond., this huge museum of science and industry includes a planetarium, an Imax theater, and even an authentic 1950s submarine that kids can climb into. But the biggest draw is the Cité des Enfants, a supremely kid-friendly collection of hands-on exhibits and displays. See p. 110.

- **Hameau Duboeuf,** Romanèche-Thorins (Burgundy): To the south of Mâcon is the Beaujolais wine area and the "wine hamlet," created by wine merchant Georges Duboeuf, is the place to go for the whole

15

family to learn about this particular drink from its origins to the present day. Kids will love "flying" over the Mâconnais countryside and playing crazy golf, while adults can enjoy a tasting or two. See p. 427.

o **Pioneering à la Francaise,** Ungersheim (Alsace): Enter a rebuilt historic Alsatian hamlet at the Ecomuseum near Colmar. Kids will adore the country-style houses. They may take in a horse-and-cart ride and observe the costumed "villagers" at work. See p. 395.

o **Understanding Cavemen in the Ardèche** (Rhône Valley): This double attraction at Le Grand Site de L'Aven d'Orgnac fills wet days as the limestone cave is at its most beautiful when it rains. The neighboring archaeological museum offers child-friendly exhibits and 3-D animations that will leave visitors of all ages with a palpable idea of how prehistoric humans lived. See p. 462.

o **Bicycling around the Bassin d'Arcachon (Bordeaux):** Over 200 km (125 miles) of cycling routes around Arcachon Bay take you through beaches, oyster villages, and pine forests, with over 35 places to hire bicycles along the way. As it's fairly flat the whole way, it's perfect for cycling with young families. See p. 730.

o **A surf lesson in Anglet, St-Jean-de-Luz or Biarritz:** The beaches as you head down towards the Spanish border offer brilliant surfing opportunities. Book a lesson rather than just paddling out solo, as the waves and currents of the Atlantic can be strong. Or get a body board and splash around in the shallows. See p. 705.

FRANCE'S best BEACHES

o **Plage de Deauville** (Normandy): Coco Chanel used the chic resort of Deauville to propel herself to stardom and then added greatly to the town's sense of glamour. Revel in the sun-kissed sense of style and nostalgia with a stroll along the elegant Les Planches boardwalk, which skirts the edge of Deauville's silky, sandy, parasol-dotted *plage* for 2km (1.25 miles). See p. 280.

o **Plage de Pampelonne** St-Tropez (French Riviera): Any blonde feels like Brigitte Bardot in sunny St-Tropez. And the scantily clad satyrs and nymphs splashing in the surf at Plage de Pampelonne can perk up the most sluggish libido. The real miracle here is that the charm of this 5km (3-mile) crescent of white sand still manages to impress, despite its celebrity hype and hordes of A-list visitors. See p. 558.

o **Paloma Plage** Cap Ferrat (French Riviera): Tucked into one of Cap Ferrat's sheltered bays, petite Paloma Plage is part chic beach club and part family-friendly stretch of pebbly shoreline. In the afternoon, fragrant Aleppo pines shade much of the beach. See p. 617.

o **Plage de Arromanches-les-Bains** (Normandy): This immense beach is dotted with the mammoth, otherworldly remains of Winston, a prefabricated port essential for the D-day landings. At low tide, the sandy expanse is firm (you can push a stroller or cycle along it!) and truly vast, rendering it ever-popular with families. See p. 297.

Villefranche-sur-Mer on the Côte d'Azur, French Riviera

o **Calanque d'En Vau** (Provence): Nestled into the heart of Parc National des Calanques, Calanque d'En Vau wouldn't look out of place in the tropics. Imagine an ice-white pebbly sands and transparent turquoise waters. Sitting at the base of limestone cliffs, it's accessible only on foot (for experienced hikers), by kayak or boat. See p. 547.

o **Plage des Marinières** Villefranche-sur-Mer (French Riviera): A seemingly endless sweep of honey-hued sand, this popular beach sits at the base of a giant sun-kissed bay. It's perfect for families, as the sea shelves slowly and waves are seldom. See p. 615.

o **Plage de la Garoupe** Cap d'Antibes (French Riviera): The sun rises at dawn over the Cap d'Antibes' most mythical beach. Views pan out over Antibes to the Alps beyond; beach bars serve chilled rosé behind. And a coastal footpath around the secluded peninsula starts to your right. What more could you possibly want? See p. 582.

o **Plages de Dinard** (Brittany): The poshest *plage* along Brittany's Emerald coast, this historic seaside resort features 10 easy-access beaches, the best being la plage du Prieuré. See p. 314.

o **Plage des Grand-Sables** Belle-Ile-en-Mer (Brittany): Gorgeous beaches line the wild coast of Quiberon peninsula near Carnac. Take the ferry out to Belle-Ile and set your towel down on the nice sandy beach of Grand-Sables. The tropical waters will make you doubt you're in France. See p. 325.

FRANCE'S best FREE THINGS TO DO

o **Visiting a Municipal Museum:** Paris has 14 municipal museums and you won't pay a single centime to get into their permanent collections. This includes the Musée d'Art Moderne (MAM), the Petit Palais, the Maison de Victor Hugo, and the Musée Zadkine.

o **Wandering through a Market:** If you want to get a sense of what Paris really is like, poke around one of the many *marches* sprinkled around the city. Not only does it make for great people-watching, but at many markets you can also find tempting morsels to eat on site.

o **Taking in the sweeping cityscape from the Temple of the Sibyl, a 19th-century belvedere in Parc des Buttes Chaumont:** There's no charge for entering this picturesque park, filled with sloping, tree-shaded lawns, a waterfall and a lake; just take the bridge to the rocky outcrop it sits upon and bring your camera. See p. 111.

o **Getting Lost in Loches** (Loire): The medieval village of Loches is perfect for wandering around. Its tiny cobblestone lanes, arched bridges over the river, and scenic views of church and castle towers don't cost a cent. See p. 250.

o **Reveling in the Tour de Normandie, Bernay to Bayeux** (Normandy): Join the party for four days in June when this classic car race zooms through Normandy's historic towns. In the 150 or so municipalities along the route, each town will put on festivities, with the drivers themselves dressed up in the fashion of their vehicle's bygone era. See p. 291.

o **Getting Festive at Medieval Fairs** (Normandy): The Middle Ages come to life in the summer as many of Normandy's picturesque towns put on lively medieval festivals. The biggest and most spectacular of the region's medieval fairs is in Bayeux every July. Costumed performers fill the streets alongside market stalls, medieval games for kids, and colorful jousters. See p. 29.

o **Beachcombing in Brittany:** The whole of the Breton coastline makes for phenomenal touring. Hike, bike, or drive from the northern Emerald coast with its sparkling waters to the wilder western seaboard with its rocky bays and Atlantic waves. See chapter 8.

o **Admiring the Hôtels Particuliers in Dijon** (Burgundy): Dijon has more than 100 townhouses built for wealthy families between the 15th and 18th centuries. Some of the finest examples can be seen on rue des Forges including Hôtel Chambellan (no. 34) and the ornately decorated Maison Maillard (no. 38), both of whose courtyards can be visited for free (enter via the open passageways). See chapter 11.

o **Staring up at Sculptural Heavens** Strasbourg (Alsace): You'll be awe-struck at the facade of Strasbourg cathedral, the tallest Gothic building in Europe. Entrance is free. Though the cathedral's towers and astronomical clock come with a fee, these additional sites are gratis on the first Sunday of each month. See p. 366.

o **Driving the La Route des Crêtes,** near Colmar (Alsace): The countryside of Alsace makes for beautiful driving. If you've done the wine road, head uphill along la Route des Crêtes for the best panoramic views of the valley and the Vosges mountains beyond. See p. 385.

The Royal Apartments in medieval Loches, Loire Valley

- **Ogling the Orchids in Lyon** (Rhône Valley): Housed within the grounds of France's largest city-based public park, Lyon's Botanical Garden is completely free. One may explore over 6,000 plants ranging from orchids to cacti and carnivorous flowers. You'll also find deer wandering freely around the surrounding Parc de la Tête d'Or with its broad tree-lined avenues and lakeside setting. See p. 440.

- **Admiring the Rose Window in Lyon's Cathedral** (Rhône Valley): It's hard not to be moved by the multi-colored brilliance of Primatiale St-Jean's 14th-century rose window. Come before sunset as the light filters through the stained glass of this west-facing window to find the nave bathed in an ethereal white light. See p. 436.

- **Photographing Provence's Fields of Lavender:** Sure, we've all seen those shots of iridescent Provençal hills cloaked with purple lavender. But it's another thing entirely to get out and snap these stunning— and fragrant—fields in person. Lavender's peak blooming season is usually between mid-June and mid-July; the area around Plateau de Valensole is particularly vibrant. See chapter 14.

- **Hiking the Caps** (Riviera): The Riviera's *sentier du littoral* is an almost continuous coastal footpath that winds its way along the country's seductive southern shores. Leave the coastal hubbub behind and spend a day wandering between the wealthy private mansions and the sparkling sea on Cap Ferrat or Cap d'Antibes. See chapter 15.

- **Wandering the Streets of Sarlat-la-Canéda** (Dordogne): A medieval jewel, this perfectly preserved town is a warren of pretty, narrow streets opening onto picturesque plazas, ideal for random explorations and discoveries. It's best to get there early in the summer months, as things can get busy. See p. 763.

o **Visiting a Wine Estate** (Bordeaux): More and more châteaux are open to visitors and offering interesting tours that even cater to children. Most of them offer tours and tastings for free, but it might be worth paying for one of the more organized visits. See p. 732.

o **The Routes Touristiques du Champagne** (Champagne Country): Wind your way through the back roads and villages of Champagne along this 70-km (45-mile) drive. In addition to hillside vineyards, woods, and Marne River views, you'll pass dozens of independent Champagne houses, some open for drop-in tastings. See p. 350.

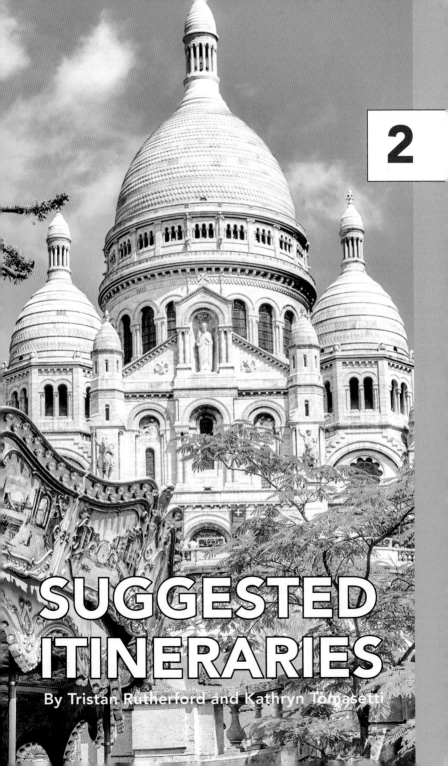

2

SUGGESTED ITINERARIES

By Tristan Rutherford and Kathryn Tomasetti

W hen the Frommer's guidebooks were first launched, founder Arthur Frommer cautioned his readers, "You can get lost in France." It's still an apt warning—and promise—today. For those with unlimited time, one of the world's great pleasures is getting "lost" in France, wandering at random, making new discoveries off the beaten path. Few of us have this luxury, however, and so here we present 1- and 2-week itineraries to help you make the most of your time.

France is so treasure-filled that you could barely do more than skim the surface in a week. So relax and savor Paris, Mont-St-Michel, Chardonnay, or Cannes—among other alluring destinations—saving the rest for another day. You might also review Chapter 1, "The Best of France," to find out what experiences or sights have special appeal to us and then adjust your itineraries to suit your particular travel plans.

The itineraries that follow take you to some major attractions and some charming off-the-beaten-track towns. The pace may be a bit breathless for some visitors, so feel free to skip a town or sight if you'd like to give yourself some chill-out time. You're on vacation, after all. Of course, you might also use these itineraries merely as a jumping-off point to develop your own custom-made trip.

THE REGIONS IN BRIEF

Although France's 547,030 sq. km (211,209 sq. miles) make it slightly smaller than the American state of Texas, no other country has such a diversity of sights and scenery in such a compact area. A visitor can travel through the north's flat, fertile lands; the Loire Valley's green hills; the east's Alpine ranges; the Pyrénées; and the southeast's Mediterranean coast. Even more noteworthy are the cultural and historical differences of each region.

Destinations in France are within easy reach from Paris and each other. **French National Railroads (SNCF)** offers fast service to and from Paris. For example, the highlights of Normandy and the Loire Valley (the château country) are just 1 or 2 hr. from Paris by train. You can travel from Paris to Cannes on the Riviera in 5 hr.—or fly down in 45 min.

You can motor along nearly 71,000km (about 44,020 miles) of French roads, including a good number of well-maintained superhighways. But do your best to drive the secondary roads too: Nearly all of France's scenic splendors are along these routes.

A "grand tour" of France is nearly impossible for the visitor who doesn't have a lifetime to explore. If you want to get to know a province, try to devote at least a week to a specific region. Note that you'll probably have a more rewarding trip if you concentrate on getting to know two or three areas at a leisurely pace rather than racing around trying to see everything! To help you decide where to spend your time, we've summarized the highlights of each region for you.

PARIS & ILE DE FRANCE   The Ile de France is an island only in the sense that rivers—with odd-sounding names such as Essonne, Epte, Aisne, Eure, and Ourcq—and a handful of canals delineate its boundaries (about an 81km/50-mile radius from the center of Paris). France was born in this temperate basin, where the attractions include **Paris, Versailles, Fontainebleau, Notre-Dame de Chartres,** and **Giverny.** Despite industrialization (and Disneyland Paris), many pockets of charm remain, including the forests of Rambouillet and Fontainebleau, and the artists' hamlet of Barbizon. For more information, see chapters 4 and 5.

THE LOIRE VALLEY   This area includes two ancient provinces, Touraine (centered on **Tours**) and Anjou (centered on **Angers**). It was beloved by

Château de Sully-sur-Loire, Loire Valley

royalty and nobility, flourishing during the Renaissance until Henry IV moved his court to Paris. Head here to see the most magnificent castles in France. Irrigated by the Loire River and its many tributaries, the valley produces many superb wines. For more information, see chapter 6.

NORMANDY   This region will forever be linked to the 1944 D-day invasion. Some readers consider a visit to the D-day beaches the most emotionally worthwhile part of their trip. Normandy boasts 599km (371 miles) of coastline and a maritime tradition. It's a popular weekend getaway from Paris, and many hotels and restaurants thrive here, especially around the casino town of **Deauville.** Normandy's great attractions include **Rouen**'s cathedral, medieval **Bayeux,** the fishing village of **Honfleur,** and the abbey at **Mont St-Michel.** For more information, see chapter 7.

BRITTANY   Jutting into the Atlantic, the westernmost region of France is known for its rocky coastlines, Celtic roots, frequent rain, and ancient dialect, akin to the Gaelic tongues of Wales and Ireland. Many French vacationers love the seacoast (rivaled only by the Côte d'Azur) for its sandy beaches, cliffs, and relatively modest—by French standards—prices. **Quimper** is Brittany's cultural capital, whereas **Carnac** is home to ancient Celtic dolmens and burial mounds. For more information, see chapter 8.

CHAMPAGNE COUNTRY   Every French monarch since A.D. 496 was crowned at **Reims,** and much of French history is linked with this holy site. In the path of any invader wishing to occupy Paris, Reims and the Champagne district have seen much bloodshed, including the World War I battles of the Somme and the Marne. Industrial sites sit among patches of forest, and vineyards sheath the steep sides of valleys. The 126km (78-mile) road from Reims to Vertus, one of the **Routes du Champagne,** takes in a trio of winegrowing regions that produce 80 percent of the world's bubbly. For more information, see chapter 9.

BURGUNDY   Few trips will prove as rewarding as several leisurely days spent exploring Burgundy, with its splendid old cities such as **Dijon.** Besides its famous cuisine (*boeuf* and *escargots à la bourguignonne*), the district contains, along its Côte d'Or, hamlets whose names (Mercurey, Beaune, Puligny-Montrachet, Vougeot, and Nuits-St-Georges) are synonymous with great wine. For more information, see chapter 11.

ALSACE-LORRAINE   Between Germany and the forests of the Vosges is the most Teutonic of France's provinces: Alsace, with cosmopolitan **Strasbourg** as its capital. Celebrated for its cuisine, particularly its *foie gras* and *choucroute,* this area is home to villages with half-timbered designs and the oldest wine road in France. Lorraine, birthplace of Joan of Arc, witnessed many battles during the world wars, though its capital **Nancy,** remains elegant and holds the beautiful place Stanislas. The much-eroded peaks of the Vosges forest, the closest thing to a wilderness in France, offer lovely hiking. For more information, see chapter 10.

Village of Vergisson surrounded by vineyards, Burgundy

THE FRENCH ALPS   This area's resorts rival those of neighboring Switzerland and contain incredible scenery: snowcapped peaks, glaciers, and Alpine lakes. **Chamonix** is a famous ski resort facing **Mont Blanc,** western Europe's highest mountain. **Courchevel** and **Megève** are chicer. During the summer, you can enjoy such spa resorts as **Evian** and the restful 19th-century resorts ringing **Lake Geneva.** For more information, see chapter 13.

THE RHÔNE VALLEY   This fertile area in eastern France follows the curves of the River Rhône from Beaujolais wine country in the north towards the borders of Provence in the south. The district is thoroughly French, unflinchingly bourgeois, and dedicated to preserving the gastronomic and cultural traditions that have produced some of the most celebrated chefs in France. Only 2 hr. by train from Paris, the region's cultural centerpiece, **Lyon,** is France's "second city." Wine lovers will enjoy contrasting the aromatic red wines of **Beaujolais** with the robust red wines of the Northern Rhône or mythical appellations such as Côte Rôtie and Hermitage. Gourmands should travel to **Valence** to dine with France's only Michelin-starred female chef or to Bresse's ancient capital, **Bourg-en-Bresse,** which produces the world's finest poultry. Try to visit the medieval villages of **Pérouges** and **Vienne,** 27km (17 miles) south of Lyon; the latter is known for its Roman ruins. For more information, see chapter 12.

LANGUEDOC-ROUSSILLON   Languedoc may not be as chic as Provence, but it's less frenetic and more affordable. **Roussillon** is the rock-strewn French answer to Catalonia, just across the Spanish border. Also appealing are **Toulouse,** the bustling pink capital of Languedoc; and the "red city" of **Albi,** birthplace of Toulouse-Lautrec. **Carcassonne,** a marvelous walled city with fortifications begun around A.D. 500, is the region's highlight. For more information, see chapter 16.

Mont Blanc reflected in Cheserys Lake, French Alps

PROVENCE One of France's most popular destinations stretches from the southern Rhône River to the Italian border. Long frequented by starving artists, *la bourgeoisie,* and the downright rich and famous, its premier cities are **Aix-en-Provence,** associated with Cézanne; **Arles,** famous for bullfighting and Van Gogh; **Avignon,** the 14th-century capital of Christendom; and **Marseille,** a port city established by the Phoenicians that today is the melting pot of France. Quieter and more romantic are villages such as **St-Rémy-de-Provence, Les Baux,** and **Gordes.** To the west, the **Camargue** is the marshy delta formed by two arms of the Rhône River. Rich in bird life, it's famous for its grassy flats and such fortified medieval sites as **Aigues-Mortes.** For more information, see chapter 14.

THE FRENCH RIVIERA (CÔTE D'AZUR) The resorts of the fabled Côte d'Azur (Azure Coast) still evoke glamour: **Cannes, St-Tropez, Cap d'Antibes,** and **Juan-les-Pins.** July and August are the most buzzing months, while spring and fall are still sunny but way more laid-back. **Nice** is the biggest city and most convenient base for exploring the area. The Principality of **Monaco** only occupies about 2 sq. km (.75 sq. miles) but has enough sights, restaurants, and opulence to go around. Along the coast are some sandy beaches, but many are pebbly. Topless bathing is common, especially in St-Tropez, and some of the restaurants are citadels of conspicuous consumption. Dozens of artists and their patrons have littered the landscape with world-class galleries and art museums. For more information, see chapter 15.

THE BASQUE COUNTRY Since prehistoric times, the rugged Pyrénées have formed a natural boundary between France and Spain. The Basques, one of Europe's most unusual cultures, flourished in the valleys here. In the 19th century, resorts such as **Biarritz** and **St-Jean-de-Luz** attracted the French aristocracy; the empress Eugénie's palace at Biarritz is now a hotel. Four million Catholics make annual pilgrimages to the city of Lourdes. In the villages and towns of the Pyrénées, the old folkloric traditions, permeated with Spanish influences, continue to thrive. For more information, see chapter 17.

BORDEAUX & THE ATLANTIC COAST Flat, fertile, and frequently ignored by North Americans, this region includes towns pivotal in French history (**Poitiers, Angoulême,** and **La Rochelle**), as well as wine- and liquor-producing villages (**Cognac, St-Emilion,** and **Sauternes**) whose names are celebrated around the world. **Bordeaux,** the district's largest city, has an economy based on wine merchandising and showcases grand 18th-century architecture. For more information, see chapter 18.

THE DORDOGNE & THE LOT The splendid Dordogne River valley has been a favorite vacation spot since Cro-Magnon peoples were painting bison on cave walls in **Lascaux.** Today visitors flock to the valley to marvel at prehistoric sites near **Les Eyzies-de-Tayac** and to ramble through exquisite villages like **Sarlat-le-Canéda** and **Beynac-et-Cazenac.** The land of truffles and foie gras, Périgord has long been famed as a gastronomic Mecca, while nearby **Cahors** is celebrated for its rich red wine. For more information, see chapter 19.

FRANCE ITINERARIES
1 WEEK IN PARIS & NORMANDY

If you budget your days carefully, one week provides enough time to visit the major attractions of Paris, such as the **Musée du Louvre** (the world's greatest art gallery), the **Eiffel Tower,** and **Notre-Dame.** After two days in Paris, head for the former royal stamping grounds of **Versailles,** followed by Normandy (an easy commute from Paris), visiting such highlights as the **D-day beaches,** the cathedral city of **Rouen** (where Joan of Arc was burned at the stake), the tapestry of **Bayeux,** and the incredible monastery of **Mont-St-Michel.**

DAYS 1 & 2: arrive in Paris ★★★

Take a flight that arrives in Paris as early as possible on **DAY 1.** Check into your hotel and hit the nearest cafe for a pick-me-up café au lait and a croissant. Since you are probably still groggy with jet lag, limit intellectual activity and head to the **Eiffel Tower ★★★** for a literal overview of the city (see time-saving tips, p. 120). After coming back to Earth, take the RER Line C to **place St-Michel** and find lunch in the **Latin Quarter ★★★** (avoiding tourist-trap eateries around rue de la Huchette). If jet lag is a problem, now is the time to return to the hotel and take a nap. Continue, refreshed, to the **Ile de la Cité** and marvel at the stained glass of the **Ste-Chapelle ★★★** and the heavenly vaulted arches of the Cathedral of **Notre Dame ★★★** (p. 77).

Now take a break from cultural icons and enjoy some shopping or sit in a cafe and enjoy the sunset in the trendy—and beautiful—**Marais ★★★** neighborhood, before scouting out a restaurant for dinner (if you have the wherewithal you can visit one of the many small-ish museums in this area). Walk off your meal with a romantic stroll along the **quays of the Seine** and enjoy the magical nighttime lighting of the iconic monuments along the river's banks.

On **DAY 2,** get an early start and head for the **Louvre ★★★** (p. 82). Spend at least a couple hours soaking in its many artistic wonders (and don't forget to see the **Mona Lisa**). Recover with a stroll and a sit in the **Tuileries Garden ★★★**, and perhaps a picnic. Continue strolling to the **place de la Concorde ★★★** and admire the Egyptian obelisk, then peer down the **Champs-Elysées ★★** and see the **Arc de Triomphe ★★★** in the distance. End the day poking around the delightful **St-Germain ★★★** neighborhood, where you can visit a church (St-Germain-des-Prés or St-Sulpice), check out famous cafes (Les Deux Magots, Café de Flore), or shop until you drop. Enjoy one of the many nearby restaurants and then scope out Parisian nightlife.

DAY 3: a day trip to Versailles ★★★

Bid *adieu* to Paris and take the RER Line C to the Versailles/Rive Gauche station. You can spend a full day at **Versailles** (p. 183) and see the château, meander in the gardens, and visit Marie Antoinette's domain. Or else just go for the palace highlights, which should take around 3 hr. and, includes the Grands and Petits Appartements, the glittering Hall of Mirrors, the Opéra Royal, the Royal Chapel, and the gardens.

Versailles

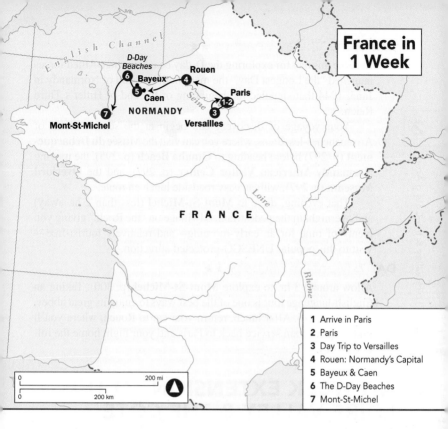

D-Day
Beaches
6
Bayeux
Rouen
4
5
Caen
Paris
1-2
7
NORMANDY
Versailles
Mont-St-Michel
3

English Channel

Seine

Loire

FRANCE

Rhône

0   200 mi
0   200 km

1 Arrive in Paris
2 Paris
3 Day Trip to Versailles
4 Rouen: Normandy's Capital
5 Bayeux & Caen
6 The D-Day Beaches
7 Mont-St-Michel

DAY 4: Normandy's capital of Rouen ★★

Take an early train to Rouen and check in to one of the city's great hotels. Spend at least 2 hr. exploring the city's ancient core, especially its **Cathédrale Notre-Dame** (p. 270), immortalized in paintings by Monet. Stand at the **place du Vieux-Marché** (p. 269), where Joan of Arc was executed for heresy in 1431, and visit the **Eglise St-Maclou** (p. 271), a 1432 church in the Flamboyant Gothic style. After lunch, rent a car for the rest of your trip and drive to **Giverny**—it's only 60km (37 miles) southeast of Rouen. At Giverny, visit the **Claude Monet Foundation** (p. 278), returning to your hotel in Rouen for the night.

DAY 5: Bayeux ★★ & Caen ★

Even after a leisurely breakfast, you can easily be in the city of Caen by late morning, with plenty of time to visit **Abbaye aux Hommes** (p. 288), founded by William the Conqueror. After a hearty Norman lunch in Caen, continue west to the city of **Bayeux** to view the celebrated **Musée de la Tapisserie de Bayeux** (p. 293). Stay overnight in Bayeux.

DAY 6: the D-Day beaches ★★

Reserve this day for exploring the D-day beaches where Allied forces launched "the Longest Day," the mammoth invasion of Normandy in June, 1944 that signaled the beginning of the end of Hitler's Third Reich.

Your voyage of discovery can begin at the seaside resort of Arromanches-les-Bains, where you can visit the **Musée du Débarquement** (p. 297) before heading to **Omaha Beach** (p. 295), the moving **Normandy American Visitor Center** (p. 297), and the **Overlord Museum** (p. 297), with an easy roadside lunch en route.

That evening, drive to **Mont-St-Michel** (less than 2 hr. away) and overnight in the pedestrianized village on "the Rock," giving you plenty of time for an early-morning—and relatively tourist-free—visit to this popular UNESCO-protected attraction.

DAY 7: Mont-St-Michel ★★★

Allow around 3 hr. to explore **Mont-St-Michel** (p. 300). Taking an English-language tour is one of the best ways to enjoy its great abbey, founded in 966. After lunch, return your car to Rouen, where you'll find frequent train service back to Paris and your flight home the following day.

A 1-WEEK EXTENSION TO THE LOIRE VALLEY & THE CÔTE D'AZUR

If you have two weeks to explore France, you'll have time to visit several regions—not only Paris, but also the best of the Loire Valley châteaux, the most history-rich town of Provence (Avignon), and several resorts on the Riviera, taking in the beaches, art galleries, and even the Principality of Monaco.

For **days 1 through 7,** follow the "1 Week in Paris & Normandy" itinerary, above.

DAY 8: Orléans, gateway to the Loire Valley ★

Leave Paris on an early train to **Orléans** (trip time: 1 hr., 10 min.; p. 216). Rent a car here and drive west to the **Château de Chambord** (p. 227), the largest château in the Loire Valley, representing the apogee of the French Renaissance architectural style. Allow 2 hr. for a visit. Back on the road again, continue southwest to the **Château de Blois** (p. 223), called "the Versailles of the Renaissance" and a virtual illustrated storybook of French architecture. Stay overnight in Blois.

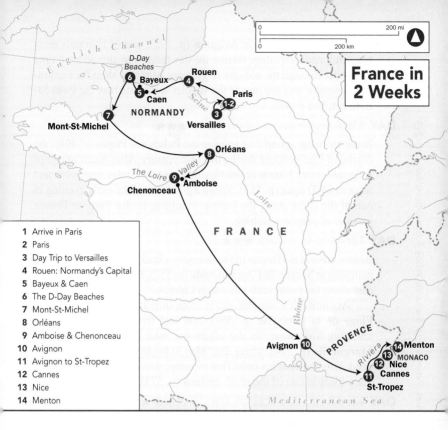

DAY 9: Amboise ★★ & Chenonceau ★★★

In the morning, continue southeast from Blois to **Amboise,** where you can check into a hotel for the night. Visit the 15th-century **Château d'Amboise** (p. 232), in the Italian Renaissance style, and also **Clos-Lucé** (p. 233), last residence of Leonardo da Vinci. In the afternoon, drive southeast to the **Château de Chenonceau** (p. 236), famous for the French dames who have occupied its precincts, including Diane de Poitiers (mistress of the king) and Catherine de Médicis (the jealous queen). You can spend a couple of hours at the château before driving back to Amboise for the night.

DAY 10: Avignon, gateway to Provence ★★★

From Amboise, get an early start and drive east to Orléans to return your rental car. Then take an early train from Orléans to Paris's Gare d'Austerlitz, then the Métro or a taxi to the Gare de Lyon, and hop on a TGV bound for Avignon (2.5 hr.).

Check into a hotel in **Avignon** (p. 492), one of Europe's most beautiful medieval cities. Before the day fades, you should have time to wander through the old city to get your bearings, shop for Provençal souvenirs, and see one of the smaller sights, such as the **Pont St-Bénézet.** See p. 496.

DAY 11: Avignon to St-Tropez ★★★

In the morning, spend 2 hr. touring the **Palais des Papes** (p. 498), the capital of Christendom during the 14th century. After lunch in one of Avignon's cozy bistros or cobblestoned outdoor cafes, rent a car and drive to **St-Tropez** (p. 553). Spend a good part of the early evening in one of the cafes along the harbor, indulging in that favorite French pastime of people-watching.

DAY 12: chic Cannes ★★★

Before leaving St-Tropez in the morning, check out the Impressionist paintings at **Musée de l'Annonciade** (p. 557). Drive 50km (31 miles) east along the coast until you reach Cannes.

Assuming it's summer, get in some time at the beach, notably at **Plage de la Croisette** (p. 567), and feel free to wear your most revealing swimwear. In the afternoon, take the ferry to **Ile Ste-Marguerite** (p. 574), where the "Man in the Iron Mask" was imprisoned. You can visit his cell. That evening, you may want to flirt with Lady Luck at one of the plush **casinos** (p. 573).

DAY 13: Nice, capital of the Riviera ★★★

It's only a 32km (20-mile) drive east from Cannes to **Nice,** the Riviera's largest city. After checking in to a hotel (the most affordable options along the Riviera), stroll through **Vieille Ville** (p. 594), the Old Town. Enjoy a snack of *socca,* a round crepe made with chickpea flour that vendors sell steaming hot in the **cours Saleya market.** Then head for the **promenade des Anglais** (p. 601), the wide boulevard along the waterfront. In the afternoon, head for the famed hill town of **St-Paul-de-Vence,** only 20km (12 miles; p. 590) to the north. You can wander its ramparts in about 30 min. before descending to the greatest modern-art museum in the Riviera, the **Fondation Maeght** (p. 591).

Continue on to **Vence** (p. 594) for a visit to the great Henri Matisse's artistic masterpiece, **Chapelle du Rosaire** (p. 595). From there, it's just 24km (15 miles) southeast back to Nice, where you can enjoy dinner at a typical Niçois bistro.

DAY 14: Nice to Menton ★★

While still overnighting in Nice, head east for the most thrilling drive in all of France, a trip along the **Grande Corniche** highway, which stretches 31km (19 miles) east from Nice to the little resort of **Menton** (p. 638) near the Italian border. Allow 3 hr. for this trip.

The Mediterranean Sea at Nice, French Riviera

Highlights along this road include **Roquebrune-Cap Martin** and **La Turbie** (p. 624). The greatest view along the Riviera is at the **Eze Belvedere,** at 1,200m (3,936 ft.). Return to Nice by dinnertime and prepare for your flight home in the morning.

FRANCE FOR FAMILIES

France offers many attractions for kids. Our suggestion is to limit the bustle of **Paris** to two days, and then spend a day wandering the spectacular grounds and glittering interiors of **Versailles,** two days in **Disneyland Paris,** and two days on the **Riviera.**

DAYS 1 & 2: Paris ★★★

On **DAY 1**, spend the morning at the **Luxembourg Gardens ★★★** (p. 116), where your offspring can go wild at the huge playground, sail toy boats in the fountain, ride a pony, or just run around and have fun. Parents can take turns sneaking off to visit nearby attractions like the **Panthéon ★** (p. 115), **Musée Zadkine ★★** (p. 118), and **St-Etienne-du-Mont ★★** (p. 116), or just find peace and quiet in a **Latin Quarter** cafe. Then walk down to **St-Germain-des-Prés ★★** (p. 116) and visit the church before lunch. For a post-prandial visit, try 17th-century **St-Sulpice ★★** church (p. 120), which contains paintings by Delacroix, and then hop the no. 87 bus to the **Champs de Mars** and visit the **Eiffel Tower ★★★** (p. 120). After that, everyone will probably be pooped and ready to relax with **a boat ride on the Seine**, which departs near the tower.

On **DAY 2,** start the day at the **Jardin des Plantes ★★**, where you can choose between the **Muséum National d'Histoire Naturelle ★★** (p. 114), the **Ménagerie ★** (a small zoo; p. 114), and a playground. A fun boxwood labyrinth is at the top of the hill. Lunch at the nearby Jardin des Pâtes (p. 160). Once stomachs are filled, head over to **Notre Dame ★★★** (p. 77), and if your kids are old enough (and the line is not too long), climb the 422 steps to the first level of the cathedral's towers, where a collection of gruesome gargoyles frames a beautiful view. Now hop the metro to Abbesses station (line #12) on the **Butte Montmartre ★★★** to see the sunset from the esplanade in front of the **Basilique du Sacré-Coeur ★★** (p. 105). Even if your kids don't appreciate the view, they will enjoy the ride in the **funicular** that you take to get there. Up on the esplanade, you'll find plenty of room to run around, and lots of buskers for entertainment. If that doesn't work, there is always the merry-go-round at **place des Abbesses ★** (p. 105) when you head back down to your hotel.

DAY 3: Versailles ★★★

Tear yourself away from the glories of Paris for a day at the **Château de Versailles** (p. 186). Take the RER Line C to the Versailles/Rive Gauche station. Hopefully, your kids will be old enough to appreciate that they are wandering around a royal palace and seeing where the king and queen slept. If not, they might enjoy running around or riding a bike through the park or rowing a boat on the Grand Canal. You can buy a picnic lunch in Paris and enjoy it on the grounds, or else purchase a sandwich at one of the stands placed in discreet corners of the garden. See p. 184 for tips on how to avoid the lines.

DAYS 4 & 5: Disneyland Paris ★

Do it for the kids—they've put up with three days of grown-up stuff (or at least that's how they'll see it). Allow a full day to see the highlights of **Disneyland Paris** (p. 210), plus part of another day to either absorb some secondary adventures or take in **Walt Disney Studios** (p. 211). You can probably see the main park, with all its classic areas (**Main Street, U.S.A., Frontierland, Tomorrowland,** and so on) on the first day, and visit **Walt Disney Studios,** the second day, leaving early enough to get back to Paris. Stay overnight in one of the many onsite hotels, which range from ridiculously expensive to only slightly so (choose from oodles of attractive package deals). The RER commuter express train A takes you from Etoile in Paris to Marne-la-Vallée/Chessy in 45 min.

DAY 6: Nice ★★★

Fly to Nice, capital of the French Riviera. If you flew Air France transatlantic, Nice can often be attached as a low-cost extension of your round-trip fare.

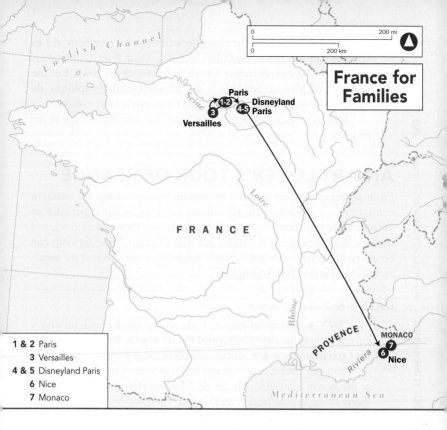

In Nice, you can check into your hotel for 2 nights, as the city has the most affordable hotels on the coast. Set out to explore this old city. There's always a lot of free entertainment in summer along Nice's seafront boardwalk, the **promenade des Anglais** (p. 601), and the people-watching on the Riviera—particularly on the beach—is likely to leave your kids wide-eyed.

In the afternoon, journey to the evocative hill town of **St-Paul-de-Vence** (p. 590). Children delight in touring the ramparts, strolling along the pedestrian-only rue Grande, or exploring the sculpture garden at the **Fondation Maeght** (p.591), one of France's greatest modern-art museums.

Return to Nice for the evening and take your kids for a stroll through the Old Town, dining as the sun dips over the Mediterranean.

DAY 7: Monaco ★★

While still based in Nice, head for the tiny Principality of Monaco, which lies only 18km (11 miles) east of Nice.

Children will enjoy the changing-of-the-guard ceremony at **Les Grands Appartements du Palais** (p. 630), where Prince Albert married South African swimmer Charlene Wittstock in 2011. But the best part of Monaco for kids is the **Musée Océanographique de Monaco** (p. 631), home to sharks and other exotic sea creatures.

Return to Nice that night and prepare for your flight home in the morning.

AN ART LOVER'S TOUR OF FRANCE

From contemporary art in Paris to modern masters along the southern coast, France is a country infused with art. Aficionados can experience an unforgettable trip taking in Paris (2 days), Aix-en-Provence (1 day), and then the Riviera between St-Tropez and Nice (4 days). Museum visits can be interspersed with wonderful meals, sunbathing, and stops at the area's architectural and artistic highlights.

DAYS 1 & 2: Paris ★★★

Start **DAY 1** of your art tour of Paris with a quick check of what's currently on in the city: The **Grand Palais** ★★ (p. 98) and the **Musée du Luxembourg** ★★★ all host excellent temporary exhibitions.

You can attend a show at any of these venues or begin your day at the newly renovated **Musée de Montmartre** ★★ (p. 106), formerly home to both Renoir and Utrillo. Then hop onto the Métro and head south to the **Jardin du Luxembourg** ★★★. After a leisurely stroll in the gardens, head over to tiny **Musée Zadkine** ★★ dedicated to sculptor Ossip Zadkine and located in the artist's former house and atelier. Take a minute to rest in the pretty little garden. Enjoy a leisurely lunch at one of the neighborhood's many bistros. Round out the afternoon by taking in a cutting-edge contemporary exhibition at the wacky **Palais de Tokyo** ★★ (p. 103), overlooking the Seine and Eiffel Tower.

On **DAY 2,** spend the morning admiring the modern art on display at the **Centre Pompidou** ★★ (p. 88). After lunching at one of the many nearby restaurants, amble over to the **Marais** (p. 88), and either cruise the art galleries, or visit the **Musée Picasso Paris** ★★★ (p. 94), set in the sumptuous 17th-century mansion, L'Hôtel Salé.

Mid-afternoon, jump aboard one of the many TGV trains heading south to Aix-en-Provence. The journey takes around 3 hr., leaving you plenty of time to enjoy a typical Provençal dinner upon arrival.

DAY 3: Aix-en-Provence ★★

Paul Cézanne is Aix's most celebrated son. Begin your day at his **Atelier** (p. 527), almost perfectly preserved as it was when the great

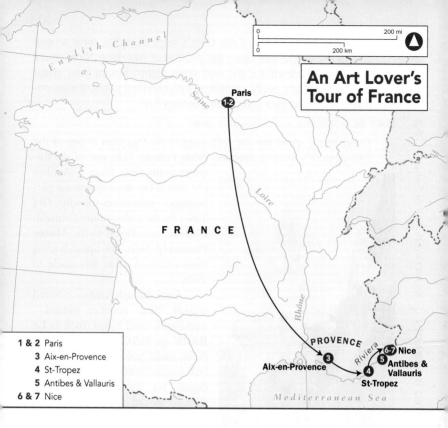

artist worked here more than a century ago. There are regularly scheduled English-language tours of the site. Afterward, a visit to the city's famed **Musée Granet** (p. 527)—one of the region's most superb modern-art museums—is a must.

Aix's plane-tree-shaded **cours Mirabeau** is almost a work of art in itself. Be sure to drop into **Brasserie Les Deux Garçons** (p. 526), where Cézanne used to drink and debate with the famous French writer Emile Zola.

After lunch, rent a car and drive to **St-Tropez** (p. 553). Warm evenings are best enjoyed strolling the port's pretty quays or taking in the million-dollar panoramas from the hilltop **Citadelle** (p. 556).

DAY 4: St-Tropez ★★★

Since the 1890s, when painters Signac and Bonnard discovered St-Tropez, artists and their patrons have been drawn to the French Riviera. Spend the morning appreciating the **Musée de l'Annonciade's** (p. 557) Impressionist paintings, many of them depicting St-Tropez and the surrounding coast.

After lunch in one of the town's sidewalk cafes, drive around 100km (62 miles) east along the coast until you reach Nice, where you'll base yourself for the next three nights. Return your rental car—traffic-heavy roads, combined with excellent public transportation, render your own vehicle unnecessary here.

DAY 5: Antibes & Vallauris ★★

Today you'll spend the day following in the footsteps of one of the 20th-century's modern masters: Pablo Picasso. Take one of the frequent trains from Nice to Antibes (20 min.). On the edge of the picturesque, pedestrian-friendly Old Town sits the 14th-century Grimaldi Château, now home to the **Musée Picasso** (p. 586). The Spanish artist lived and worked in this castle in 1946.

Clock tower in Aix-en-Provence

Stroll through Antibes' covered market, then—appetite piqued—stop into a small bistro, such as **Le Rustic** (p. 588), for a light lunch. Next, make your way to Antibes' bus station, where frequent buses depart for Vallauris (35 min.). Picasso moved to this hilltop village during the 1950s, reviving the local ceramic-making industry and personally producing thousands of pieces of pottery. Visit Picasso's mammoth paintings in the **Musée National Picasso La Guerre et La Paix** (p. 578), the artist's tribute to pacifism.

Make your way back to Nice (it's quickest to simply reverse your route). Spend the evening strolling the promenade des Anglais or wandering the city's atmospheric Old Town.

DAYS 6 & 7: Nice ★★★

Outside of Paris, Nice is home to more museums than any other city in France. Begin your **DAY 6** citywide explorations in the neighborhood of Cimiez, where both the famed **Musée Matisse** (p. 605) and the **Musée National Message Biblique Marc Chagall** (p. 605) are located. It's possible to walk between the two (around 15 min.) but be sure to hit the Matisse Museum first—then it's downhill all the way to see Chagall's ethereal artworks.

If it's summertime, spend a couple of hours picnicking on the beach or relaxing with a glass of wine in one of the city's many sidewalk cafes. Mid-afternoon, make your way over the **Musée Masséna** (p. 603), where a combination of local art and history gives visitors a peek at the ritzy French Riviera of the past.

Use your final day to make a day trip to the hilltop village of **St-Paul-de-Vence** (p. 590), 20km (12 miles) to the north. Wander the St-Paul-de-Vence's ramparts for 30 min., before descending to the world-class modern art on display at the **Fondation Maeght** (p. 591). En route back to Nice, stop into the **Musée Renoir** (p. 614) in Cagnes-sur-Mer, which comprises the artist's former home and gardens. Note that you can either rent a car for the day or access both St-Paul-de-Vence and Cagnes-sur-Mer via frequent buses from Nice.

Spend your final night in Nice savoring a hearty Niçois dinner, paired with plenty of local wine.

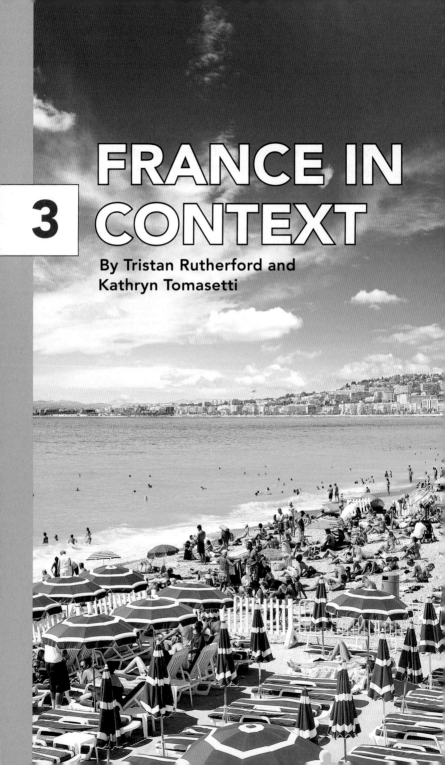

FRANCE IN CONTEXT

3

By Tristan Rutherford and
Kathryn Tomasetti

T he civilization and culture of France—not to mention the French way of life—makes the country easily the most visited in the world. The savoir-faire of its people lures travelers from across the globe to a country that covers an area smaller than Texas. Yet despite France's size, each region is so intriguing and varied that you may immerse yourself in one province so deeply that you'll never have time to see what's on the other side. You'd be surprised how many people do just that. Perhaps more than any other country in the world, France is a land to be savored. Ideally, France is discovered slowly by car or along the country's magnificent rail network, which lets you stop whenever and wherever you wish.

No European country, not even Britain, Italy, or Spain, can beat France in its pageantry of personalities. Its colorful characters range from Madame de Pompadour to Charles de Gaulle, from Jean-Luc Godard to Gustave Flaubert, from Catherine de Médici to Joan of Arc, from Emperor Napoleon to footballer Zinedine Zidane. You'll be introduced to some of these figures in the pages ahead. Seeing where they lived, worked, loved, and became legends is part of the experience of visiting France.

This guide is meant to help you decide where to go in France, but ultimately the most gratifying experience will be your own serendipitous discoveries—sunflowers, a picnic in a poppy field, an hour spent chatting with a small winemaker—whatever it is that stays in your memory for years to come.

FRANCE TODAY

France remains one of the world's most hyped and written-about destinations. It can inspire a masterpiece—and has on countless occasions. Even the cantankerous James McNeill Whistler would allow his masterpiece, a portrait of his mother, to hang in no other city save Paris.

Although not large by North American standards (about the size of Britain and Germany combined), France is densely packed with attractions, both cultural and recreational. Even better, it's permeated with cool and known for its *joie de vivre*.

As for style, it has always been foolhardy to try to compete with the French on their terms. The theatrical backdrops of the sometimes-silly

FACING PAGE: **Promenade des Anglais, Nice**

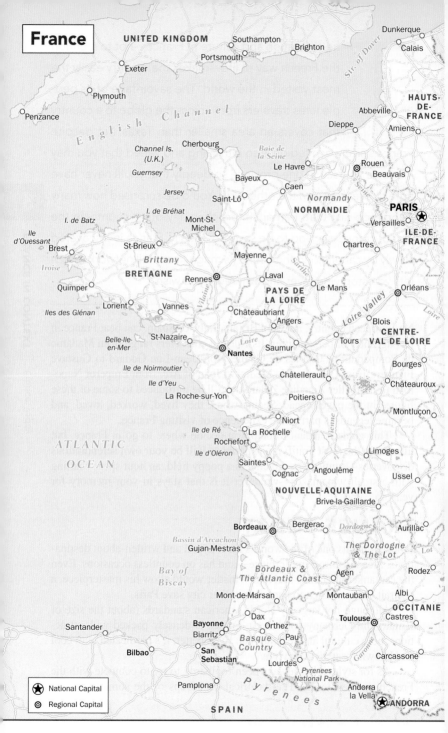

Gallic monarchs have been interpreted by latter-day aesthetes as history's crowning achievement when it comes to conspicuous displays of wealth and prestige.

In politics and ideology, France has long been a leader and remains so today. Fueled by Enlightenment writings, whose most articulate voices were French, the 1789 Revolution toppled Europe's most deeply entrenched regime and cracked the foundations of dozens of other governments. In 1968 the revolutionaries were on the streets again: the original political spring.

Newcomers have commented (often adversely) on the cultural arrogance of the French. But despite its linguistic and cultural rigidity, France has received more immigrants and political exiles than any other European country. Part of this derives from France's status as one of Europe's least densely populated nations per square mile, and part of it from the tendency of the French to let others be until their actions become dangerous or obnoxious, not necessarily in that order.

If you're a first-timer, everything in France, of course, is new. But if you've been away for a long time, expect changes. Taxi drivers in Paris may no longer correct your fractured French but address you in English—and that's tantamount to a revolution. Part of this derives from the country's interest in music, culture, and films from foreign countries, and part from France's growing awareness of its role as a leader of a united Europe.

Yet France has never been more concerned about the loss of its unique identity within a landscape that has attracted an increasing number of immigrants from its former colonies. Many worry that France will continue to lose the battle to keep its language strong, distinct, and unadulterated by foreign slang or catchwords (and good luck with banning such terms as *l'email* and *le week-end*). But as the country moves deeper into the millennium, foreign tourists spending much-needed cash are no longer perceived as foes or antagonists. *Au contraire:* France welcomes the world to its palaces, parks, beaches, and UNESCO World Heritage sites. And if those tens of millions of guests spend a few euros—and soak up a little local culture while they're here—that's all to the good.

THE HISTORY OF FRANCE

EARLY GAUL   When the ancient Romans considered France part of their empire, their boundaries extended deep into the forests of the Paris basin and up to the edges of the Rhine. Part of Julius Caesar's early reputation came from his defeat of King Vercingetorix at Alésia in 52 B.C., a victory he was quick to publicize in one of the ancient world's literary masterpieces, "The Gallic Wars." In that year, the Roman colony of Lutetia (Paris) was established on an island in the Seine (Ile de la Cité).

As the Roman Empire declined, its armies retreated to the flourishing colonies that had been established along a strip of the Mediterranean

The Roman Arena in Arles, Provence

coast—among others, these included Orange, Arles, Antibes, and Marseille, which today retain some of the best Roman monuments in Europe.

As one of their legacies, the Roman armies left behind the Catholic Church, which, for all its abuses, was the only real guardian of civilization during the anarchy following the Roman decline. A form of low Latin was the common language. This slowly evolved into the archaic French that the more refined language is based upon today.

THE CAROLINGIANS   From the wreckage of the fall of the Roman Empire emerged a new dynasty: the Carolingians. One of their leaders, Charles Martel, halted a Muslim invasion of northern Europe at Tours in 743 and left a much-expanded kingdom to his son, Pepin. The Carolingian empire eventually stretched from the Pyrénées to a point deep in the German forests, encompassing much of modern France, Germany, and northern Italy. The heir to this vast land was Charlemagne. Crowned emperor in Rome on Christmas Day in 800, he returned to his capital at Aix-la-Chapelle (Aachen) and created the Holy Roman Empire. Charlemagne's rule saw a revived interest in scholarship, art, and classical texts, defined by scholars as the Carolingian Renaissance.

THE MIDDLE AGES   When the Carolingian dynasty died out in 987, the hectic, migratory Middle Ages officially began. Invasion by Hungarians, Vikings, and the English (who ruled half the country) lent France a cosmopolitan, if fractured, air. Politically driven marriages among the ruling families more than doubled the size of the territory controlled from Paris, a city that was increasingly recognized as the country's capital. Philippe II (reigned 1179–1223) infiltrated more prominent families with his genes than anyone else in France, successfully marrying members of his family into the Valois, Artois, and Vermandois. He also managed to win Normandy and Anjou back from the English. Louis IX (St. Louis) emerged as the 13th century's most memorable king, though he ceded most of the hard-earned military conquests of his predecessors back to the English.

The 14th century saw an increase in the wealth and power of the French kings, an increase in general prosperity, and a decrease in the power of the feudal lords. The death of Louis X without an heir in 1316 prompted more than a decade of scheming and plotting before the eventual emergence of the Valois dynasty.

France's burgeoning wealth and power was checked by the Black Death, which began in the summer of 1348. The rat-borne plague killed an estimated 33 percent of Europe's population, decimating the population of Paris and setting the stage for the exodus of the French monarchs to safer climes in such places as the Loire Valley. A financial crisis, coupled with a series of ruinous harvests, almost bankrupted the nation.

During the Hundred Years' War, the English made sweeping inroads into France in an attempt to grab the throne. At their most powerful, they controlled almost all of the north (Picardy and Normandy), Champagne, and parts of the Loire Valley. The peasant-born charismatic visionary Joan of Arc rallied the dispirited French troops as well as the timid *dauphin* (crown prince), whom she managed to have crowned as Charles VII. As threatening to the Catholic Church as she was to the English, she was declared a heretic and burned at the stake in Rouen in 1431. The place of her demise is now sited in the city's marketplace.

THE RISING POWER By the early 17th century, France was a modern state. Few vestiges of feudalism remained. In 1624, Louis XIII appointed a Catholic cardinal, the duc de Richelieu, as his chief minister. Amassing enormous power, Richelieu virtually ruled the country until his death in 1642. His sole objective was investing the monarchy with total power, and in trying to attain this goal he committed a series of truly horrible acts, paving the way for the eventual absolutism of a dynasty of future despotic rulers.

Although he ascended the throne when he was only 9, Louis XIV was the most powerful monarch Europe had seen since the Roman emperors. The estimated population of France at this time was 20 million, as opposed to 8 million in England and 6 million in Spain. French colonies in Canada, the West Indies, and America (Louisiana) were stronger than ever. The mercantilism that Louis's brilliant finance minister, Colbert, implemented was one of the era's most important fiscal policies, hugely increasing France's power and wealth. The arts flourished, as did a sense of aristocratic style that's remembered with a bittersweet nostalgia today. Louis's palace of Versailles is the perfect monument to the most flamboyantly consumptive era in French history.

Louis's territorial ambitions so deeply threatened the other nations of Europe that they united to hold him in check. France entered a series of expensive and demoralizing wars that, coupled with high taxes and bad harvests, stirred up much civil discontent. England was viewed as a threat both within Europe and in the global rush for lucrative colonies. The rise of Prussia as a militaristic neighbor posed an additional problem. Fresh political ideas from abroad unsteadied the status quo.

THE REVOLUTION & THE RISE OF NAPOLEON Meanwhile, the Enlightenment was training a new generation of thinkers for the struggle against absolutism, religious fanaticism, and superstition. On August 10, 1792, troops from Marseille, aided by a Parisian mob, threw the dimwitted Louis XVI and his tactless Austrian-born queen, Marie Antoinette, into prison. After months of bloodshed and bickering among violently competing factions, the two thoroughly humiliated monarchs were executed.

France's problems got worse before they got better. In the ensuing bloodbaths, both moderates and radicals were guillotined in full view of a bloodthirsty crowd that included voyeurs like Dickens's Madame Defarge, who brought her knitting every day to place de la Révolution (later renamed place de la Concorde) to watch the beheadings. Only the militaristic fervor of Napoleon Bonaparte could reunite France and bring an end to the revolutionary chaos. A political and military genius who appeared on the landscape at a time when the French were thoroughly sickened by

Chapel of Saint Louis des Invalides, Paris, site of Napoleon's tomb

the anarchy following their revolution, he restored a national pride that had been severely tarnished. He also established a bureaucracy and a code of law that has been emulated in other legal systems around the world. In 1799, at the age of 30, he entered Paris and was crowned first consul and master of France. Soon after, a decisive victory in his northern Italian campaign solidified his power at home.

Alas, Napoleon's victories made him overconfident—and made the rest of Europe clamor for his demise. Just as he was poised on the verge of conquering the entire continent, Napoleon's famous retreat from Moscow during the winter of 1812 reduced his formerly invincible army to tatters. As a plaque in the Lithuanian town of Vilnius once told the tale: "napoleon bonaparte passed this way in

1812 with 400,000 men"—and on the other side are the words "napoleon bonaparte passed this way in 1812 with 9,000 men." Napoleon was then decisively beaten at Waterloo by the combined armies of the English, Dutch, and Prussians. Exiled to the British-held island of St. Helena in the South Atlantic, he died in 1821, probably the victim of a prison poisoner.

THE BOURBONS & THE SECOND EMPIRE In 1814, following the destruction of Napoleon and his dream of Empire, the Congress of Vienna redefined the map of Europe. The Bourbon monarchy was reestablished, with reduced powers for Louis XVIII, an archconservative. After a few stable decades, Napoleon I's nephew, Napoleon III, was elected president in 1848. Appealing to the property-protecting instinct of a nation that hadn't forgotten the violent upheavals of less than a century before, he initiated a repressive right-wing government in which he was awarded the totalitarian status of emperor in 1851. Steel production was begun, and a railway system and Indochinese colonies were established. New technologies fostered new kinds of industry, and the bourgeoisie flourished. The baron Georges-Eugène Haussmann radically altered Paris by laying out the grand boulevards the world knows today.

As ever, intra-European conflict knocked France off its pedestal once again. In 1870, the Prussians—a rising power in the German east—defeated Napoleon III at Sedan and held him prisoner with 100,000 of his soldiers. Paris was besieged and occupied, an inglorious state for the world's greatest city. After the Prussians withdrew, a violent revolt ushered in the Third Republic and its elected president, Marshal MacMahon, in 1873. Peace and prosperity slowly returned, France regained its glamour, a mania of building occurred, the Impressionists made their visual statements, and writers like Flaubert redefined the French novel into what today is regarded as the most evocative in the world. As if as a symbol of this period, the Eiffel Tower was built as part of the 1889 Universal Exposition.

THE WORLD WARS International rivalries, lost colonial ambitions, and conflicting alliances led to World War I, which, after decisive German victories for two years, degenerated into the mud-slogged horror of trench warfare. Mourning between 4 and 5 million casualties, Europe was inflicted with psychological scars that never healed. In 1917, the United States broke the European deadlock by entering the war.

After the Allied victory, grave economic problems, plus the demoralization stemming from years of fighting, encouraged the growth of socialism and communism. The French government demanded every centime of reparations it could wring from a crushed Germany, humiliating the country into a vengeful spiral that would have repercussions two decades later.

The worldwide Great Depression of 1929 devastated France. Poverty and widespread bankruptcies weakened the Third Republic to the point where successive coalition governments rose and fell (although a number of expatriate writers, among them Ernest Hemingway and F. Scott Fitzgerald, enjoyed the dollar exchange rate and relative freedoms while they could). The crises reached a crescendo on June 14, 1940, when Hitler's armies arrogantly marched down the Champs-Elysées, and newsreel cameras recorded French people openly weeping. Under the terms of the armistice, the north of France was occupied by the Nazis, and a puppet French government was established at Vichy under the authority of Marshal Pétain. The immediate collapse of the French army is viewed as one of the most significant humiliations in modern French history. In Europe, Britain was left to counter the Nazi threat alone.

Pétain and his regime cooperated with the Nazis in unbearably shameful ways. Not the least of their errors included the deportation of more than 75,000 French Jews to German work camps. Pockets of resistance fighters *(le maquis)* waged small-scale guerrilla attacks against the Nazis throughout the course of the war. Charles de Gaulle, the irascible giant who is forever associated with the politics of his era, established himself as the head of the French government-in-exile.

The scene was radically altered on June 6, 1944, when the largest armada in history—a combination of American, British, and Canadian troops—successfully established a beachhead on the shores of Normandy. Paris rose in rebellion even before the Allies arrived. On August 26, 1944, de Gaulle entered the capital as head of the government. The Fourth Republic was declared even as pockets of Nazi snipers continued to shoot from scattered rooftops throughout the city.

THE POSTWAR YEARS   Plagued by the bitter residue of colonial policies that France had established during the 18th and 19th centuries, the Fourth Republic witnessed the rise and fall of 22 governments and 17 premiers. Many French soldiers died on foreign battlefields as once-profitable colonies in North Africa and Indochina rebelled. After suffering a bitter defeat in 1954, France ended its occupation of Vietnam and freed its former colony. It also granted internal self-rule to Tunisia and Morocco.

Algeria was to remain a greater problem. The advent of the 1958 Algerian revolution signaled the end of the much-maligned Fourth Republic. De Gaulle was called back from retirement to initiate a new constitution, the Fifth Republic, with a stronger set of executive controls. To nearly everyone's dissatisfaction, de Gaulle ended the Algerian war in 1962 by granting the country full independence. The sun had finally set on most of France's far-flung empire.

In 1968, major social unrest and a violent coalition hastily formed between the

> ### Impressions
>
> *The left which does nothing, achieves nothing. The right, which did nothing and doesn't propose anything, achieves nothing. So we are moving forward.*
>
> — Emmanuel Macron,
> current French President

nation's students and blue-collar workers eventually led to the collapse of the government. De Gaulle resigned when his attempts to placate some of the marchers were defeated. The reins of power passed to his second-in-command, Georges Pompidou, and his successor, Valérie Giscard d'Estaing, both of whom continued de Gaulle's policies emphasizing economic development and protection of France as a cultural resource to the world.

THE 1980S, 1990S, & TURN OF THE CENTURY In 1981, François Mitterrand was elected the first Socialist president of France since World War II (with a close vote of 51 percent). In almost immediate response, many wealthy French decided to transfer their assets out of the country, much to the delight of banks in Geneva, Monaco, and the Cayman Islands. Though reviled by the rich and ridiculed for personal mannerisms that often seemed inspired by Louis XIV, Mitterrand was reelected in 1988. During his two terms, he spent billions of francs on his *grands projets* (like the Louvre pyramid, Opéra Bastille, Cité de la Musique, and Grande Arche de La Défense), although unemployment and endemic corruption remained.

On his third try, on May 7, 1995, Jacques Chirac won the presidency with 52 percent of the vote and immediately declared war on unemployment. But his popularity soon faded in the wake of unrest caused by an 11.5 percent unemployment rate and a stressed economy struggling to meet entry requirements for the European Union that France had signed up for three years before.

Financial crisis or not, in May 1996 thousands of Parisian workers took to the streets, disrupting passenger train service to demand a work-week shorter than the usual 39 hours. Most French now work a 35-hour week and retire at 60 years old.

In 1999, France joined with other European countries in adopting the euro as its standard of currency. The new currency accelerated the creation of a single economy comprising over 500 million Europeans, although the ability of several fiscally wayward states to borrow at preferential rates has led to a sovereign debt crisis that remains today. Nonetheless, the European Union now boasts a combined gross national product approaching 17€ trillion ($23 million), a shade larger than that of the United States.

Although Chirac steadied the ship—and most French today think he ran a decent presidency—in 2005 a rotten core was exposed. Decades of pent-up resentment felt by the children of African immigrants exploded into an orgy of violence and vandalism. Riots began in the suburbs of Paris and spread around the country. Throughout France, gangs of youths battled the French police, torching schools, cars, and businesses. Rioting followed in such cities as Dijon, Marseille, and Rouen. Most of the rioters were the sons of Arab and black African immigrants, Muslims living in a mostly Catholic country. The reason for the protests? Leaders of the riots claimed they live "like second-class citizens," even though they are French citizens. Unemployment is 30 percent higher in the ethnic ghettos of France.

Against a backdrop of discontent regarding issues of unemployment, immigration, and healthcare, the charismatic Nicolas Sarkozy swept into the presidential office in May 2007. Sarkozy, the combative son of a Hungarian immigrant, promised to reinvigorate ties with France's traditional ally, the United States. He even made a summer vacation trip to New England directly after his election.

In the ensuing years, Sarkozy found time to divorce a wife and take a beautiful new bride. A glamorous model-turned-singer, Carla Bruni, became first lady of France in 2008. The tabloids had a field day with Bruni, whose former lovers include Mick Jagger and Donald Trump.

> ### Impressions
>
> *Above 1 million euros ($1.25 million), the tax rate should be 75 percent because it's not possible to have that level of income.*
> —François Hollande, former French President

Outside of politics, the French looked at Sarkozy's personal life with ridicule. His marriage to Bruni and his holidays with the rich and famous earned him the title of the "bling bling president." In a show of how divided France was over his administration, he lost the 2012 presidential election by a whisker to Socialist challenger François Hollande.

Hollande promised a government of hard-working technocrats. Alas, "Monsieur Normal" proved anything but. A series of gaffes—including employing a minister with a secret Swiss bank account to superintend France's endemic tax evasion—made him, in 2014, the least popular president since polling began, with a disapproval rating of 75 percent. Soaring unemployment hasn't helped either. Nor has his decision to raise taxes (in particular his infamous 75 percent tax rate for those who earn more than a million) in order to boost the economy.

The nail in Hollande's claim to run a scandal free administration came when president's private life once again became front-page news. Not content with family ties to his first girlfriend, the socialist politician Ségolène Royale, or his former mistress-turned-First Lady, Valérie Trierweiler, he embarked on another relationship with actress Julie Gayet. His method of courting Miss Gayet (which essentially involved turning up to her apartment on the back of his bodyguard's scooter wearing a motorcycle helmet) was deemed tacky by the French press. That said, Hollande's handling of the atrocities that rocked Paris and Nice in 2015 and 2016, where hundreds of civilians were killed in France's worst terrorist attacks, was broadly praised.

Such a backdrop rendered the 2017 presidential election the most contentious yet. Hollande's socialist party was in perpetual hysteria. The right wing fronted its usual cast of old, white leaders before deciding on

François Fillon. The veteran fought his campaign alongside charges of gross embezzlement—namely the payment of hundreds of thousands of euros of state funds to his wife and children for little or no work. The centrist path was left wide open for Emmanuel Macron, who was elected in May 2017 at the tender age of 39.

Far from appearing a political lightweight, Macron has led a charge to reinvent France's ailing economy. Fights have been picked—and won—with the powerful unions, who insist on maintaining the country's prized 35-hour week. The President's next task is to trim the French state. A Herculean task, given that some 50 percent of taxpayers work for the government. With the UK spiraling from Brexit, and Germany in political disarray, Macron hopes to count himself the de facto leader of Europe.

Better still, Macron aims to avoid the scandals that have tarnished every French leader since the 1960s. He seems ever-besotted with his school sweetheart, Brigitte. The fact the couple fell in love when she was his teacher (Brigitte is 25 years Macron's senior) has only recently ceased to raise eyebrows across the land.

Politics aside, France still leads the world in tourism and culture. New museum and transport openings abound, and annual visitor numbers could top 90 million in 2018. The nation's successful hosting of the EURO2016 soccer championship proved France to be a nation united in its pursuit of sporting and cultural endeavor. In 2024, the Paris Olympics—events of which will be held nationwide—should crown the world's most visited nation.

ART

France's manifold art treasures range from Rodin's *The Thinker* to Monet's Impressionist *Water Lilies*; its architecture encompasses Roman ruins and Gothic cathedrals as well as Renaissance châteaux and postmodern buildings like the Centre Pompidou. This brief overview is designed to help you make sense of it all.

Impressions
In France you cannot not have lunch. If you stopped the French from having lunch, you will have a second revolution, I can tell you. —Christian Louboutin, shoe designer

A fine place to start is Paris's **Louvre** (p. 77). The world's greatest museum abounds with Renaissance works by Italian, Flemish, and German masters, including **Michelangelo** (1475–1564) and **Leonardo da Vinci** (1452–1519). Da Vinci's ***Mona Lisa*** (1503–05), the most famous painting on the planet, hangs here.

Back in the early 19th century, the **romantics** felt that both the ancients and the Renaissance had gotten it wrong and that the Middle

Ages was the place to be. They idealized romantic tales of chivalry and the nobility of peasantry. Some great artists and movements of the era, all with examples in the **Louvre,** include **Theodore Géricault** (1791–1824), who painted *The Raft of the Medusa* (1819), which served as a model for the movement; and **Eugène Delacroix** (1798–1863), whose *Liberty Leading the People* (1830) was painted in the romantic style.

Decades later, the **Impressionists** adopted a free, open style, seeking to capture the *impression* light made as it reflected off objects. They painted deceptively loose compositions, using swift, visible brushwork and often light colors. For subject matter, they turned to landscapes and scenes of modern life. You'll find some of the best examples of their works in the **Musée d'Orsay** (p. 124).

Impressionist greats include **Edouard Manet** (1832–83), whose groundbreaking *Luncheon on the Grass* (1863) and *Olympia* (1863) helped inspire the movement with their harsh realism, visible brush strokes, and thick outlines; **Claude Monet** (1840–1926), who launched the movement officially in an 1874 exhibition in which he exhibited his Turner-inspired *Impression, Sunrise* (1874), now in the **Musée Marmottan** (p. 102); **Pierre-Auguste Renoir** (1841–1919), known for his figures' ivory skin and chubby pink cheeks; **Edgar Degas** (1834–1917), an accomplished painter, sculptor, and draftsman—his pastels of dancers and bathers are particularly memorable; and **Auguste Rodin** (1840–1917), the greatest Impressionist-era sculptor, who crafted remarkably expressive bronzes. The **Musée Rodin** (p. 126), Rodin's former Paris studio, contains, among other works, his *Burghers of Calais* (1886), *The Kiss* (1886–98), and *The Thinker* (1880).

The smaller movements or styles of Impressionism are usually lumped together as "post-Impressionism." Again, the best examples of these turn-of-the-20th-century works are exhibited at the **Musée d'Orsay,** though you'll find pieces by Matisse, Chagall, and the cubists, including Picasso, in the **Centre Pompidou** (p. 88) and the key museums of Nice, Rouen, Avignon, and Marseille. Important post-Impressionists include **Paul Cézanne** (1839–1906), who adopted the short brush strokes, love of landscape, and light color palette of his Impressionist friends; **Henri de Toulouse-Lautrec** (1864–1901), who created paintings and posters of wispy, fluid lines anticipating Art Nouveau and often depicting the bohemian life of Paris's dance halls and cafes; **Vincent van Gogh** (1853–90), who combined a touch of crazy Japanese influence with thick, short strokes; **Henri Matisse** (1869–1954), who created **fauvism** (a critic described those who used the style as *fauves,* meaning "wild beasts"); and **Pablo Picasso** (1881–1973), a Málaga-born artist who painted objects from all points of view at once, rather than using such optical tricks as perspective to fool viewers into seeing "cubist" three dimensions.

FRANCE IN POPULAR CULTURE

Books

For a taste of French culture before you travel, we recommend you load a half-dozen titles on your iPad or Kindle. Simon Schama's "Citizens" is the pick of the bunch for a history of the French Revolution. Moving into the 20th century, "Paris Was Yesterday, 1925–1939," is a fascinating collection of excerpts from Janet Flanner's "Letters from Paris" column in the *New Yorker,* while "On Paris" comprises a newly bound series of essays by Ernest Hemingway, written for the *Toronto Star* between 1920 and 1924. Two unusual approaches to French history are Rudolph Chleminski's "The French at Table," a funny and honest history of why the French know how to eat better than anyone and how they go about it; and "Parisians: An Adventure History of Paris" by Graham Robb, entertaining historical snippets that range from the French Revolution through the 1968 riots. More recently, "Chocolat" by Joanne Harris illustrates the tension between tradition and modernity in rural France by way of the nation's favorite treat.

And travel? Well, since 1323, some 10,000 books have been devoted to exploring Paris. One of the best is "Paris: Capital of the World," by Patrice Higonnet. This book takes a fresh social, cultural, and political look at the City of Light, exploring Paris as "the capital of sex" and, in contrast, the "capital of art." In "The Flâneur: A Stroll Through the Paradoxes of Paris," Edmund White wants the reader to experience Paris as Parisians do. Hard to translate exactly, a *flâneur* is someone who wanders, loafs, or idles. And for the frequent visitor, Jean-Christophe Napais's "Quiet Corners of Paris: Unexpected Hideaways, Secret Courtyards, Hidden Gardens" is sure to turn up plenty of undiscovered gems.

Representing the city's most fabulous era are "A Moveable Feast," Ernest Hemingway's recollections of Paris during the 1920s, and Morley Callaghan's "That Summer in Paris: Memories of Tangled Friendships with Hemingway, Fitzgerald and Some Others," an anecdotal account of the same period. Another great read is "The Autobiography of Alice B. Toklas," by Gertrude Stein.

For a fictional tour of the 19th century, pick up "Madame Bovary," by Gustave Flaubert. The carefully wrought characters, setting, and plot attest to Flaubert's genius in presenting the tragedy of Emma Bovary; Victor Hugo's "Les Misérables," a classic tale of social oppression and human courage set in the era of Napoleon I; and "Selected Stories," by the master of the genre, Guy de Maupassant.

Films

The world's first movie was shown in Paris on December 28, 1895. Its makers were the Lumière brothers, who scared an audience to death with images of a train moving towards the audience seats. Later, Charles Pathé and Léon Gaumont were the first to exploit filmmaking on a grand scale.

The golden age of the French silent screen on both sides of the Atlantic was 1927 to 1929. Actors were directed with more sophistication, and technical abilities reached an all-time high. The film "Hugo" (2011), directed by Martin Scorsese, is a heart-warming tale set against the film industry's transformation during this period. And despite its mind-numbing length, Abel Gance's masterpiece "Napoleon" (1927) is also sweepingly evocative. Its grisly battle scenes are easily as chilling as any war film made today.

In 1936, the Cinémathèque Française was established to find and preserve old (usually silent) French films. By that time, an average of 130 films a year was made in France, by (among others) Jean Renoir, Charles Spaak, and Marcel Carne. This era also brought such French luminaries as Claudette Colbert and Maurice Chevalier to Hollywood.

After World War II, two strong traditions—*film noir* and French comedy—offered viewers new kinds of genre, like Jacques Tati's side-splitting "Les Vacances du Monsieur Hulot" ("Mr. Hulot's Holiday"). By the mid-1950s, French filmmaking ushered in the era of enormous budgets and the creation of such frothy potboilers as director Roger Vadim's "And God Created Woman," which helped make Brigitte Bardot a celebrity around the world, contributing greatly to the image in America of France as a kingdom of sexual liberation.

By the late 1950s, counterculture was flourishing on both sides of the Atlantic. François Truffaut, widely publicizing his auteur theories, rebelled with a series of short films (like "The 400 Blows" in 1959). Other contemporary directors included Jean-Luc Godard ("A Bout de Soufflé"), Alain Resnais ("Muriel"), Agnès Varda ("Le Bonheur"), Jacques Demy ("Les Parapluies de Cherbourg"), and Marguerite Duras ("Detruire, Dit-elle").

Many American films were filmed in Paris (or else used sets to simulate Paris). Notable ones have included the classic "An American in Paris," starring Gene Kelly, and "Moulin Rouge," starring Ewan McGregor as a Parisian artist. "Last Tango in Paris," with Marlon Brando, was one of the most controversial films set in Paris. Woody Allen's acclaimed "Midnight in Paris" was the most recent film to celebrate the City of Light. The film features beautiful shots of the city and includes cameos of iconic figures who lived in Paris in the 1920s. The big French movie of 2014 was another Allen number, "Magic in the Moonlight." This romantic comedy stars Colin Firth and Emma Stone against the sun-kissed backdrop of the French Riviera.

One French film that continues to enchant is Jean-Pierre Jeunet's "Amélie," with its beautiful scenes shot in Montmartre. More recently, "La Vie en Rose" earned Marion Cotillard an Oscar in 2008 for her performance as "The Little Sparrow," Edith Piaf.

Music

Music and France have gone together since the monks in the 12th century sang Gregorian chants in Notre-Dame. Troubadours with their ballads traveled all over France in the Middle Ages. In the Renaissance era, **Josquin des Prez** (c. 1440–1521) was the first master of the High Renaissance style of polyphonic vocal music. He became the greatest composer of his age, a magnificent virtuoso. **Jean-Baptise Lully** (1632–87) entertained the decadent court of Versailles with his operas. During the reign of Robespierre, **Claude-Joseph Rouget de Lisle** (1760–1836) immortalized himself in 1792 when he wrote "La Marseillaise," the French national anthem. Regrettably, he died in poverty.

The rise of the middle class in the 1800s gave birth to both grand opera and opéra comique. Both styles merged into a kind of lyric opera, mixing soaring arias and tragedy in such widely popular hits as Bizet's "Carmen" in 1875 and St-Saën's "Samson et Dalila" in 1877.

During the romantic period of the 19th century, foreign composers moving to Paris often dominated the musical scene. **Frédéric Chopin** (1810–49) was half French, half Polish. He became the most influential composer for piano and even invented new musical forms such as the ballade. **Félix Mendelssohn** (1809–47) had to fight against anti-Semitism to establish himself with his symphonies, concerti, and chamber music.

At the dawn of the 20th century, music became more impressionistic, as evoked by **Claude Débussy** (1862–1918). In many ways, he helped launch modernist music. His "Prélude à L'Après-midi d'un Faune" in 1894 and "La Mer" in 1905 were performed all over Europe. From Russia came **Igor Stravinsky** (1882–1971), who made *Time* magazine's list of the 100 most influential people of the 20th century. He achieved fame as a pianist, conductor, and composer. His "Le sacre du printemps" (The Rite of Spring), with its pagan rituals, provoked a riot in Paris when it was first performed in 1913.

A revolutionary artist, **Yves Klein** (1928–62) was called a "neo-Dada." His 1960 "The Monotone Symphony" with three naked models became a notorious performance. For 20 minutes, he conducted an orchestra on one note. Dying of a heart attack at the age of 34, Klein is considered today an enigmatic postmodernist. **Pierre Boulez** (1925–2016) developed a technique known as integral serialism using a 12-tone system pioneered in the 1920s. As director of the IRCAM institute at the Centre Pompidou from 1970 to 1992, he influenced young musicians around the world.

France took to American jazz like no other country. Louis Armstrong practically became a national hero to Parisians in the 1930s, and in 1949 Paris welcomed the arrival of Miles Davis. **Stéphane Grappelli** (1908–97), a French jazz violinist, founded the Quintette du Hot Club de France, the most famous of all-string jazz bands. **Django Reinhardt** (1910–53) became one of the most prominent jazz musicians of Europe, known for such works as "Belleville" and "My Sweet."

Some French singers went on to achieve world renown, notably **Edith Piaf** (1915–63), "The Little Sparrow" and France's greatest pop singer. Wherever you go in France, you will hear her "La Vie en Rose," which she first recorded in 1946. Born in 1924, **Charles Aznavour** remains an eternal favorite. He's known for his unique tenor voice with its gravelly and soulful low notes. **Jacques Brel** (1929–78), a singer-songwriter, saw his songs interpreted by everybody from Frank Sinatra to David Bowie. A popular chanson singer, **Juliette Gréco** (b. 1927) became known as "the High Priestess of Existentialism" on Paris's Left Bank and was beloved by Jean-Paul Sartre. She dressed all in black and let her long, black hair hang free before coming to Hollywood and becoming the mistress of mogul Darryl Zanuck.

Among rock stars, the French consider **Johnny Halladay** (1943–2017) their equivalent of Elvis Presley. He scored 18 platinum albums, selling more than 100 million records, and a million Frenchmen took to the streets to mourn his passing in 2017. Another pop icon is **Serge Gainsbourg** (1928–91). He was a master of everything from sexy rock to jazz and reggae. Upon his death, President François Mitterrand called him "our Baudelaire, our Apollinaire." In the late 1990s, a dreamy French house music secured international notoriety with bands such as **Air** and **Daft Punk.** More recently, chart-topping indie band **The Dø** performed another first—headlining the French album charts with songs sung entirely in English.

Artists with immigrant backgrounds often are the major names in the vibrant French music scene of today, with influences from French Africa, the French Caribbean, and the Middle East. Along with rap and hip-hop, these sounds rule the nights in the boîtes of France's biggest cities. **Khaled** (b. 1960), from Algeria, has become known as the "King of Raï." The most influential French rapper today is **MC Solaar** (b. 1969); born in Senegal, he explores racism and ethnic identity in his wordplays.

EATING & DRINKING IN FRANCE

As any French person will attest, French food is the best in the world. That's as true today as it was during the 19th-century heyday of the master chef Escoffier. A demanding patriarch who codified the rules of French cooking, he ruled the kitchens of the Ritz in Paris, standardizing the complicated preparation and presentation of *haute cuisine.*

However, at the foundation of virtually every culinary theory ever developed in France is a deep-seated respect for the *cuisine des provinces* (also known as *cuisine campagnarde*). Ingredients usually included only what was produced locally, and the rich and hearty result was gradually developed over several generations of *mères cuisinières.* Springing from

Vineyards on the hills of Hermitage in the Rhône wine region

an agrarian society with a vivid sense of nature's cycles, the cuisine provided appropriate nourishment for bodies that had toiled through a day in the open air. The movement is alive and well today with a tradition for eating locally produced—or *zero km*—foods.

Despite the availability of top-quality ingredients across the country, regional cuisine is more sought after than ever before. Try salmon, lark pâté, goat's milk cheese, partridge, rillettes, herb-flavored black pudding, and fine white wines from the Loire Valley. Not forgetting sole, brill, mackerel, turbot, mussels, and big fat lobsters from the Normandy coast, often bathed in the region's rich butter sauce. Just don't forget the Camembert for dessert.

Gourmets, not just beach lovers, should go to the Riviera. Bouillabaisse, an exquisite fish soup said to have been invented by Venus, is Marseille's best-known dish. Riviera specialties include *daube* (slow-cooked beef stew), *soupe au pistou* (vegetable soup with basil), and *salade Niçoise* (traditionally made with tomatoes, olives, radishes, scallions, peppers, and tuna or anchovies). All are best served with a glass of ice-cold *rosé* in the afternoon sun.

And Paris? At the center of the country's gastronomic crossroads, it tops the lot. The city literally has thousands of restaurants to choose from. The best of them are listed in this book or discussed on websites likes **Chowhound** (www.chow.com) and **Time Out** (www.timeout.fr). Beef from Lyon, lamb from the Auvergne, crêpes from Brittany, and *cassoulet* from southwest France are served up in abundance. This city of 10 million gastronomes has also become a mecca for creative foreign fare. Until you've eaten sashimi, bibimbap, ceviche, and gourmet burgers in Paris, you haven't lived.

To accompany such cuisine, let your own good taste—and your wallet—determine your choice of wine. Most wine stewards, called *sommeliers,* are there to help you in your choice, and only in the most dishonest of restaurants will they push you toward the most expensive selections. Of course, if you prefer only bottled water, or perhaps a beer, or even a cider in Normandy, then be firm and order your choice without embarrassment.

Some restaurants include a beverage in their menu rates *(boisson compris)*, either as part of a set tasting menu in ritzy restaurants or as part of a fixed-price formula in cheaper establishments. Some of the most satisfying wines we've drunk in France came from unlabeled house bottles or carafes, called *vin de la maison.* In general, unless you're a real connoisseur, don't worry about labels and vintages. When in doubt, you can rarely go wrong with a good Burgundy or Bordeaux. As a rule of thumb, expect to spend about one-third of the restaurant tab on wine.

WHEN TO GO

The best time to visit France is in the spring (Apr–June) or fall (Sept–Nov), when things are easier to come by, from Métro seats to good-tempered waiters. The weather is temperate year-round. July and August are the worst for crowds but best for beaches. That's when Parisians desert their city, leaving it to the tourists.

France's weather varies from region to region. Despite its latitude, Paris never gets very cold. Normandy is a little fresher—and foggier—but the Mediterranean boasts one long summer, with the French Riviera soaking up 300 days of sun per year. Provence dreads *le mistral* (an unrelenting wind), which most often blows in the winter for bouts of a few days at a time but can also last up to two weeks.

Paris's Average Daytime Temperature & Rainfall

	JAN	FEB	MAR	APR	MAY	JUNE	JULY	AUG	SEPT	OCT	NOV	DEC
Temp. °F	38	39	46	51	58	64	66	66	61	53	45	40
Temp. °C	3	4	8	11	14	18	19	19	16	12	7	4
Rainfall (in.)	3.2	2.9	2.4	2.7	3.2	3.5	3.3	3.7	3.3	3.0	3.5	3.1
Rainfall (cm)	8.1	7.4	6	6.9	8.1	8.9	8.4	9.4	8.4	7.6	8.9	7.9

France Calendar of Events

JANUARY

Monte Carlo Motor Rally (Le Rallye de Monte Carlo). The world's most venerable car race. Mid-January. www.acm.mc

FEBRUARY

Carnival of Nice. Parades, music, fireworks, and "Les Batailles des Fleurs" (Battles of the Flowers) are all part of this celebration. The climax is the burning of the Carnival king effigy. Late February to early March. www.nicecarnaval.com

MARCH

International Ready-to-Wear Fashion Shows (Le Salon International de Prêt-à-Porter). Tapis Rouge, 67 rue du Faubourg St-Martin, Paris. See what you'll be wearing next season. Early March; also held late September. www.capsuleshow.com

APRIL

Foire du Trône, on the Reuilly Lawn of the Bois de Vincennes, 12e, Paris. This mammoth fun fair operates daily from noon to midnight. Early April to late May. www.foiredutrone.com

International Garden Festival, Château de Chaumont, Amboise (Loire). An international competition showcasing the best in garden design. Mid-April to mid-October. www.domaine-chaumont.fr

International Marathon of Paris. Runners from around the world compete along the Champs-Elysées. Early April. www.parismarathon.com

Vin'Estival, Mâcon. France's largest wine tourism festival allows visitors to learn about and taste the wines of the Mâconnais and Beaujolais regions. There is also a competition to find France's best Grand Vin. www.vinestival.com

MAY

Cannes Film Festival (Festival International du Film). Movie madness transforms this Mediterranean town into a media circus. Admission to films and parties is by invitation. Other films play 24 hours a day. Mid-May. www.festival-cannes.com/fr/

Normandy Impressionist Festival. New region-wide event that showcases the

Port Le Vieux of Cannes, home of the Cannes Film Festival

area's favorite painters (Monet, Manet, Signac) in museums across Normandy, held every 2 to 3 years; last one was in 2016. April to September. www.normandieimpressionniste.eu

Monaco Formula 1 Grand Prix. The world's most high-tech cars race through Monaco's narrow streets in a blizzard of hot metal and ritzy architecture. Late May. www.formula1.com

Coupes Moto Légende, Dijon. Thousands of motorcyclists, including well-known names, descend upon Dijon to race their vintage bikes around the Prenois track. Late May. www.coupes-moto-legende.fr

Festival de St-Denis. A celebration of music in the burial place of the French kings, a grim early Gothic monument in Paris's northern suburb of St-Denis. Late May to late June. www.festival-saint-denis.com

French Open Tennis Championship, Stade Roland-Garros, 16e, Paris. The French Open features two weeks of men's, women's, and doubles tennis on hot, red, dusty clay courts. Late May to early June. www.rolandgarros.com

JUNE

Prix du Jockey Club and Prix Diane-Longines, Hippodrome de Chantilly. Thoroughbreds from as far away as Kentucky and Dubai compete in this race. On race days, dozens of trains depart from Paris's Gare du Nord for Chantilly, where racegoers take free shuttle buses to the track. Early to mid-June. www.france-galop.com

Paris Air Show. France's military-industrial complex shows off its high-tech hardware. Fans, competitors, and industrial spies mob Le Bourget Airport. Next event mid-June 2015. www.paris-air-show.com

Catalpa Festival, Auxerre. This 3-night world music festival takes place in various venues around town including the atmospheric surrounds of the cloister of the Abbaye Saint-Germain. www.lesilex.fr

French Formula 1 Grand Prix. The classic track at Le Castellet near Toulon, where previous winners have included Jackie Stewart and Alain Prost, became the new home of the French Grand Prix in 2018. Mid-June. www.formula1.com

Les 24 Heures du Mans Voitures. Racing cars blast around the clock at this venerable circuit. Also hosts the huge September motorcycle rally. Mid-June. www.24h-lemans.com

Festival Chopin, Paris. Everything you've ever wanted to hear by the Polish exile, who lived most of his life in Paris. Piano recitals take place in the Orangerie du Parc de Bagatelle, 16e. Mid-June to mid-July. www.frederic-chopin.com

Gay Pride Parade, place du 18 Juin 1940 to place de la Bastille, Paris. A week of expositions and parties climaxes in a parade patterned after those in New York and San Francisco. Late June. www.gaypride.fr

JULY

Fêtes Médiévales, Bayeaux. The Middle Ages come to life as many of Normandy's picturesque towns put on lively medieval festivals. The biggest and most spectacular is in Bayeux. Costumed performers fill the streets alongside market stalls, medieval games for kids, and colorful jousters. First weekend of July. www.bayeux.fr

Les Chorégies d'Orange, Orange. One of southern France's most important lyric festivals presents oratorios, operas, and choral works in France's best-preserved Roman amphitheater. Early July to early August. www.choregies.fr

Les Nocturnes du Mont-St-Michel. This sound-and-light tour meanders through the stairways and corridors of one of Europe's most impressive medieval monuments. Early July to late August. www.ot-montsaintmichel.com

Colmar International Festival, Colmar. Classical concerts are held in public buildings of one of the most folkloric towns in Alsace. Early July. www.festival-colmar.com

A Bastille Day (July 14) parade, Paris

Tour de France. The world's most hotly contested bicycle race sends crews of wind-tunnel–tested athletes along an itinerary that detours deep into the Pyrenees, Alps, Provence, and Normandy. The finish line is on the Champs-Elysées. First 3 weeks of July. www.letour.fr

Festival d'Avignon. This world-class festival has a reputation for exposing new talent to critical scrutiny and acclaim. The focus is usually on avant-garde works in theater, dance, and music. Last three weeks of July. www.festival-avignon.com

Bastille Day. Celebrating the birth of modern-day France, the nation's festivities reach their peak with country-wide street fairs, fireworks, and feasts. In Paris, the day begins with a parade down the Champs-Elysées and ends with fireworks at Montmartre. July 14.

Paris Quartier d'Eté. For four weeks, music rules around the city. Two-dozen French and international performances take place at unusual venues like the Musée de Cluny, the Gare du Nord, and the Parc de Belleville. Mid-July to mid-August. www.quartierdete.com

Nice Jazz Festival. The most prestigious jazz festival in Europe. Concerts begin in the afternoon and go on until late at night (sometimes all night) in place Masséna and the Jardin Albert 1er, overlooking Nice's promenade des Anglais. Mid-July. www.nicejazzfestival.fr

Festival d'Aix-en-Provence. A musical event *par excellence,* with everything from Gregorian chants to operas composed on synthesizers. Recitals are in the medieval cloister of the Cathédrale St-Sauveur. Expect heat, crowds, and loud sounds. July. www.festival-aix.com

Réncontre d'Arles. The prettiest town in Provence hosts a city-wide photography festival. Prepare to be wowed. July to September. www.rencontres-arles.com

Festival de Cornouaille, Quimper. An annual weeklong celebration of Breton culture. The festivities include parades in traditional costume and Celtic and Breton concerts throughout the city. Late July. www.festival-cornouaille.com

AUGUST

Festival Interceltique de Lorient, Brittany. Celtic verse and lore are celebrated in the Celtic heart of France. The 150 concerts include classical and folkloric musicians, dancers, singers, and painters. Traditional Breton pardons (religious processions) take place in the once-independent maritime duchy. Early August. www.festival-interceltique.com

Musical Gatherings (Les Rencontres Musicales), Vézelay. Four days of classical music concerts held in several venues including the magnificent basilica. www.rencontresmusicalesdevezelay.com

Deauville American Film Festival. The likes of Clooney, Pitt, and Travolta jet in for a yearly celebration of movies, glitz, and glamour. First week September. www.festival-deauville.com

La Villette Jazz Festival. Some 50 concerts are held in churches, auditoriums, and concert halls in the Paris suburb of La Villette. Past festivals have included Kenny Garrett, Jamie Callum, and other international artists. Early to mid-September. www.jazzalavillette.com

Festival d'Automne, Paris. One of France's most famous festivals is also one of its most eclectic, focusing mainly on modern music, ballet, theater, and art. Mid-September to mid-January. www.festival-automne.com

Festival de la Loire, Orléans (Loire). The Loire River and its banks come alive with sails, music, and food during the largest boat festival in Europe. Late September, every other year; next in 2019. www.orleans.fr

Paris Auto Show, Parc des Expositions, Porte de Versailles, 15e, Paris. This biennial showcase for European car design comes complete with glitzy attendees, lots of hype, and the latest models. Mid-October; next in 2018. www.mondial-automobile.com

Prix de l'Arc de Triomphe, Hippodrome de Longchamp, 16e, Paris. France's answer to England's Ascot is the country's most prestigious horse race, culminating the equine season in Europe. Early October. www.evenements.france-galop.com/en

Armistice Day, nationwide. In Paris, the signing of the document that ended World War I is celebrated with a military parade from the Arc de Triomphe to the Hôtel des Invalides. November 11.

Dijon Gastronomy Fair (Foire gastronomique de Dijon). One of France's biggest food fairs attracts around 600 exhibitors and 200,000 visitors each year. www.dijon-congrexpo.com

Hospices de Beaune Wine Auction (Vente des vins des Hospices de Beaune). Three days of wine tastings, street entertainment and a half marathon culminating in the world-famous charity wine auction. www.beaune-tourisme.fr

Boat Fair (Le Salon Nautique de Paris). Europe's major exposition of what's afloat, at Porte de Versailles. One week in early December. www.salonnautiqueparis.com

Fête de Lumières, Lyon. In honor of the Virgin Mary, lights are placed in windows throughout the city. Early December. www.fetedelumieres.lyon.fr

Fête de St-Sylvestre (New Year's Eve), nationwide. In Paris, this holiday is most boisterously celebrated in the Latin Quarter. At midnight, the city explodes. Strangers kiss, and boulevard St-Michel and the Champs-Elysées become virtual pedestrian malls. December 31.

Getting Tickets

Visitors can purchase tickets for almost every music festival, soccer game, or cultural event in France online. Try the official website first, or log onto **Fnac** (www.fnactickets.com), France's largest music chain, which offers both a digital reservation service as well as in-store ticket booths.

RESPONSIBLE TRAVEL

From pioneering eco-friendly *autopartage* (car-sharing) programs to an unabashed enthusiasm for *biodynamique* wines, the French have embraced sustainability. In an age when environmental, ethical, and social concerns are becoming ever more important, France's focus on green principles—whether through traditional markets, carbon-neutral public transport, or all-natural outdoor adventure—offers visitors and residents alike plenty in the way of sustainable tourism.

In 2007, Paris mayor **Bertrand Delanoë** introduced the **Vélib'** scheme (https://www.velib-metropole.fr), a public bicycle "sharing" program. With tens of thousands of bicycles and bike-rental stations spread throughout the city, it is a fast and inexpensive way to get around. Similar schemes are in place in many other major French cities, including Nice, Avignon, Aix-en-Provence, Rouen, Lyon, Bordeaux, and Marseille.

Also under Delanoë's guidance, a similar car-sharing program called the **Autolib'** (www.velib-metropole.fr) was launched in Paris in 2011. More than 5,000 eco-friendly and exhaust-free public cars now slip silently around the Parisian streets; passes for their use can be purchased by the hour, day, month, or year. Nice followed suit in 2012 with **Auto Bleue** (www.auto-bleue.org). Nearly 200 electric cars with a range of 100km (62 miles) now ply the streets. More importantly, the scheme's 50 recharging points serve as charging depots for an increasing number of resident-owned electric cars. Similar systems now exist across France, like **AutoCool** (www.bordeaux.citiz.coop) in Bordeaux.

In order to crisscross France's vast countryside, many French ditch their cars and opt instead for travel on a **TGV** (www.tgv-europe.com). This network of high-speed trains is powered by SNCF, France's government-owned rail company, which is dedicated to becoming completely carbon-neutral. TGVs run from Paris's hub to cities throughout the country, including Nantes, Rouen, Lyon, Dijon, Rennes, Avignon, Aix-en-Provence, Nice, and Marseille.

Many hotels in France have undertaken measures to preserve the environment, and those that have are awarded with a green label. Look for hotels with the title of *La Clef Verte* (Green Key; www.laclefverte.org). The label rewards hotels that take a more environmental approach to water, energy, and waste, and help raise the awareness of their guests. Even if you don't stay at a green hotel, you can still do your bit: Turn off the air-conditioning when you leave the room, request that your sheets aren't changed every day, and use your towels more than once. Laundry makes up around 40 percent of an average hotel's energy use.

When planning your travels, it's equally important to consider the impact your visit will have on the environment. France's rippling vineyards, **Grande Randonnée (GR)** hiking trails, and pristine coastline all make for enchanting (and eco-friendly) escapes.

Responsible tourism also means leaving a place in the same condition you found it. You can do this by not dropping litter and respecting the color-coded garbage bin system. Support the local economy and culture by shopping in small neighborhood stores and at open-air markets that showcase the seasonal harvest of local, often organic *(bio)* producers. Look out for organic and *biodynamique* (biodynamic) wines, frequently sold at wine shops and farmers' markets, too. And given the myriad of tiny, family-run restaurants scattered throughout France's cities, towns, and countryside, it's all too easy to dig into a home-cooked meal.

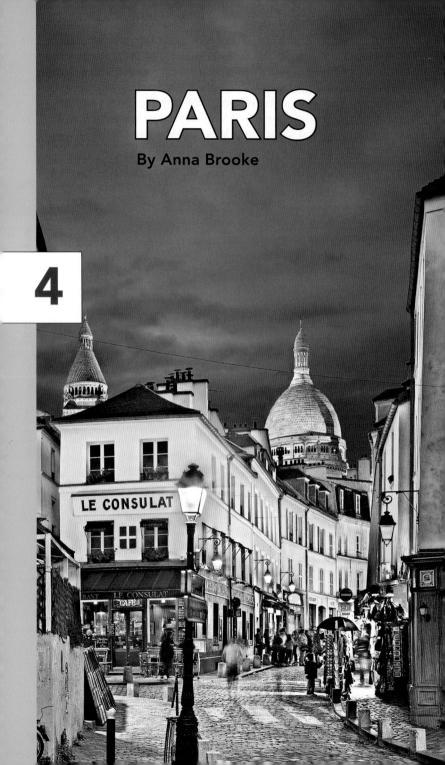

PARIS

By Anna Brooke

4

he name "Paris" conjures up such a potent brew of images and ideas that it's sometimes hard to find the meeting point between myth and reality. But the city's graceful streets, soaked in history, really are as elegant as they say, its monuments and museums as extraordinary; and a slightly world-weary, *fin-de-siècle* grandeur really is part of day-to-day existence. Paris is much more than a beautiful assemblage of buildings, however; it is the pulsing heart of the French nation.

Where to begin? With so many wonderful things to see, it's easy to get overwhelmed in the City of Light. If you are here for only a few days, you'll probably be spending most of your time in the city center, the nucleus of which is the Ile de la Cité. The **top neighborhoods** on most short-term visitors' hit parade are the 1st through 8th arrondissements (see "City Layout," below), which includes the Ile de la Cité, the Louvre area, the Champs Elysées, the Eiffel Tower, the Latin Quarter, the Marais, and St-Germain. **If you have a bit more time,** you should explore some of the outlying neighborhoods, like Montmartre in the 18th arrondissement, and the funky, eastern areas of Menilmontant, Belleville, Canal St-Martin, and Bastille, as well as the elegant, museum-rich depths of the 16th arrondissement. Whether you're here for a few days or longer, this chapter is designed to give you the essential information you need to create a Paris itinerary that's just right for you.

ESSENTIALS & ORIENTATION

Arriving

BY PLANE

Paris has two international airports: **Aéroport d'Orly (ORY),** 18km (11 miles) south of the city (for both airports: www.aeroportsdeparis.fr; © **00-33-1-70-36-39-50** from abroad, or **39-50** from France), and **Aéroport Roissy-Charles-de-Gaulle (CDG),** 30km (19 miles) northeast. If you are taking Ryanair or another discount airline that arrives at **Beauvais** (BVA; www.aeroportbeauvais.com; © **08-92-68-20-66**), be advised that this airport is located about 70km (40 miles) from Paris.

CHARLES DE GAULLE AIRPORT (ROISSY) **By commuter train:** The quickest way into central Paris is the **RER B** (www.ratp.fr), suburban trains that leave every 10 to 15 min. between 4:50am and 11:50pm

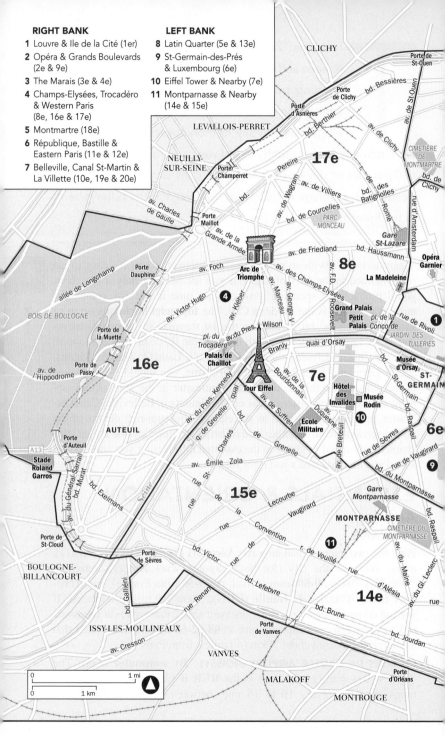

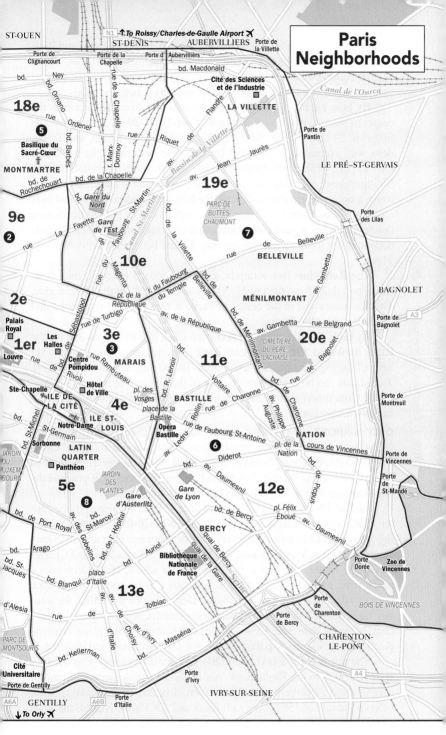

(midnight on weekends). It takes about 40 min. to get to Paris, and RER B stops at several Métro stations including Châtelet-Les-Halles, Saint-Michel-Notre-Dame, and Luxembourg. A single ticket costs 10.30€ and you can buy it from the machines in the stations at both terminals.

By bus: Le Bus Direct operates three routes from the airport to the center of Paris (www.lebusdirect.com; ℰ **08-10-81-20-01** .12€/min.): The first (line 2) stops at Port Maillot, Charles de Gaulle–Etoile, and Trocadéro, with a terminus at the Eiffel Tower; the second (line 3) links CDG to Orly airport; while the third stops at Gare de Lyon with a terminus at Gare Montparnasse. All stops have good Métro connections. Depending on the route, a one-way trip costs 12€ to 21€ adults and children ages 4 and over (children 3 and under travel free), and e-tickets can be bought in advance online (valid for a year from purchase); trips take about 1 hr., 10 min., depending on traffic. Buses leave every 30 min. between roughly 6am and 11pm.

The **Roissybus** (www.ratp.fr; ℰ **34-24**) departs every 20 min. from the airport daily from 6am to 12:30am and costs 12€ for the 70-min. ride. The bus leaves you in the center of Paris, at the corner of rue Scribe and rue Auber, near the Opéra.

By taxi: The flat rate for a **taxi** from CDG into the city is 54€ for the Right Bank and 59€ for the Left Bank, not including supplements (1€/item of luggage, 20 percent extra 5pm–10am, Sun, and bank holidays). Taxi stands can be found outside each of the airport's terminals. Alternatively, Uber functions in France, with flat rates of 45€ to 50€ in an uberX car (www.uber.com).

ORLY AIRPORT   Orly has two terminals: Orly Sud (south) and Orly Ouest (west). To get to the center of Paris, take the 8-min. monorail **Orly-Val** to the RER station "Antony" to get **RER B** into the center. Combined travel time is about 40 min. Trains run between 6am and 11:30pm, and the one-way fare for the OrlyVal plus the RER B is 9.30€.

Le Bus Direct operates one route (line 1) from the airport to the center of Paris (www.lebusdirect.com; ℰ **08-10-81-20-01,** .12€/min.), leaving from both Orly terminals every 20 min. between 6am and 11:30pm, stopping at Gare Montparnasse, the Eiffel Tower, Trocadéro, and Charles de Gaulle–Etoile. The fare is 12€ one-way for adults, 7€ children ages 4 to 11 (free for kids 3 and under). E-tickets can be bought in advance online (valid for a year from purchase). Depending on the traffic, the journey takes about 1 hr. The **Orlybus** (www.ratp.fr), which leaves every 15 min. between 6am and 12:30am, links the airport with place Denfert-Rochereau, a 30-min. trip that costs 8.30€ for both adults and children.

The flat rate for a **taxi** from Orly to central Paris is 34€ to the Left Bank and 39€ to the Right Bank, not including supplements (1€/item of luggage, and 20 percent extra 5pm–10am, Sun, and bank holidays). Uber offers a flat rate of 35€ for the Left Bank and 40€ for the Right Bank in an uberX car (www.uber.com; also see p. 73).

BEAUVAIS AIRPORT   Buses leave about 20 min. after each flight has landed, and, depending on the traffic, take about 1 hr., 15 min. to get to Paris. The bus drops you at Porte Maillot (Métro: Porte Maillot). To return to Beauvais, you need to be at the bus station at least 3 hr. before the departure of your flight. A one-way ticket costs 17€.

BY TRAIN

Paris has six major train stations: **Gare d'Austerlitz** (13th arrond.), **Gare de Lyon** (12th arrond.), **Gare Montparnasse** (14th arrond.), **Gare St-Lazare** (8th arrond.), **Gare de l'Est** (10th arrond.), and **Gare du Nord** (10th arrond.). Each station can be reached by bus or Métro. *Warning:* As in most major cities, the stations and surrounding areas can be seedy and frequented by pickpockets. Be alert, especially at night. To buy train tickets, visit www.oui.sncf, call ✆ **36-35** (.40€/min.), or go to a desk in one of the stations.

BY BUS

Most long-haul buses arrive at the **Eurolines France** station on the eastern edge of the city, 23 av. du Général-de-Gaulle, Bagnolet (www.eurolines.fr; ✆ **08-92-89-90-91** in France .35€/min.; other countries **01-41-86-24-21;** Métro: Gallieni).

BY CAR

While I wouldn't recommend driving in Paris, renting a car and driving around France before or after your Paris trip can be a lovely way to see the country. All of the major car-rental companies have offices here, but you'll often get better deals if you reserve before you leave home. **AutoEurope** (www.autoeurope.com) is an excellent source for discounted rentals.

Even better may be **AutoSlash.com** which applies discount codes to rentals from all of the major multinational firms, which can mean big savings. It also monitors prices, so if a rate drops, it re-books you automatically. You pay for the rental at the counter, not in advance.

Getting Around Town

For everything you ever wanted to know about the city's public transport, visit the **RATP** (www.ratp.fr; ✆ **34-24**). Paris and its suburbs are divided into six travel zones, but you'll probably only be concerned with zones 1 and 2, which cover the city itself.

RATP tickets are valid on the Métro, bus, and RER. You can buy tickets over the counter (if you are lucky—ticket booths are an endangered species) or from machines at most Métro/RER entrances. A **single ticket** costs 1.90€ and a *carnet* of 10 tickets costs 14.90€. Children 4 to 9 years old pay half price; kids 3 and under ride free. Tourists can benefit from a **Paris Visite** pass, which offers unlimited travel in zones on bus, Métro, and RER, and discounts on some attractions. Think hard about how much you are going to use your pass however, as you'll probably end up walking a lot, and in the end a cheaper *carnet* of 10 tickets might do the trick. A 1-day Paris Visite adult pass for zones 1 to 3 costs 12€, a 2-day pass 19.50€, a 3-day pass 26.65€, and a 5-day pass 38.35€. Each day begins at midnight and finishes at midnight the following day. It is also possible to buy more expensive passes for zones 1 to 5, which will also get you to the airport. For a slightly cheaper 1-day pass, try a **Mobilis** ticket, which offers unlimited travel in zones 1 up to 5; a pass for zones 1 and 2 costs 7.50€. For travelers 25 and under, look for the **Ticket Jeunes,** a 1-day ticket that can be used on a Saturday, Sunday, or bank holiday and provides unlimited travel in zones 1 to 3 for 4.10€, or zones 1 to 5 for 5.25€.

BY MÉTRO OR RER (SUBWAY)

The city's first Métro, or subway, was at the apex of high tech when it was inaugurated on July 19, 1900. Today, more than a century later, it still functions very well. Aside from the occasional strike or work slowdown, the Métro is usually efficient and civilized, especially if you avoid rush hour (7:30–9:30am and 6–8pm). It's generally safe at night (although you might want to think twice about using it to get to more isolated parts of the city); the service shuts down between midnight and 1am weekdays, and at 2am on Friday, Saturday, and pre-holiday evenings. The **RER** (pronounced "ehr-euh-ehr") is the suburban train network that dashes through the city making limited stops; it closes down around the same time at the Métro (without the weekend bonus hour). The downsides are to the RER trains are: (a) They don't run as often as the Métro, and (b) they're hard to figure out since they run on a different track system and the same lines can have multiple final destinations.

Important: Make sure to hold on to your ticket; you'll need it to get *out* of the turnstile on the way out.

BY BUS

Buses can be an efficient way to get around town, and you'll get a scenic tour to boot. The majority run from 6:30am to 9:30pm (a few operate until 12:30am), with reduced service on Sundays and holidays. You can use Métro tickets on the buses or you can buy tickets directly from the driver (2€). Tickets need to be validated in the machine next to the driver's cabin. After the bus and Métro services stop running, head for the **Noctilien** night bus (www.transilien.com/static/noctilien). The 47 lines crisscross the city and head out to the suburbs every half-hour or so from 12:30 to 5:30am. Tickets cost the same as for the regular bus.

BY TRAM

Over the past few years, Paris has added eight new tramway lines, with extensions and new lines in progress. They connect Paris with its suburbs; within Paris they run along the outer circle of boulevards that trace the city limits. Tickets are the same price as the Métro.

vélib': A GREAT WAY TO CYCLE AROUND PARIS

Since July 2007, when the mayor's office inaugurated the **Vélib'** (vel-LEEB) system of low-cost bike rentals, Parisians have been pedaling up a storm. Traffic be dammed: It's fun to ride around town, drop off your bike near your destination, and not have to worry about locking it up. And since the launch of Vélib-Metropole in 2018 (an updated, broader service), it's just got easier, thanks to the addition of a number of electric bikes, and pedal bikes that are 30 percent lighter—though the prices have gone up. The way it works is this: You buy a 1- or 7-day subscription (5€ or 158€ respectively) online or from the machine at one of hundreds of bike stands, which gives you the right to as many half-hour rides as you'd like for 1 or 7 days. If you want to go over a half-hour, you pay 1€ for your extra half-hour, 2€ for the half-hour after that one, and 4€ for the third half-hour on. Use of electric bikes costs 1€ extra. The bikes are fitted with a V-Box, a smart computer system set between the handle bars, which enables you to lock and unlock the bikes. It also lets you leave your bike in a full station; follow the instructions and park it top to tail with another bike. At time of writing, the English website (www.velib-metropole. fr) wasn't up and running, but when it is, it should meticulously explain how everything works, and there's a number you can call for assistance (☎ **01-76-49-12-34**). The big catch, however, is that to use the machines you must have a credit or debit card with a chip in it. This can be a problem for North American tourists, so I advise either getting a TravelEx "cash passport" with money on it (www. travelex.com), or, even easier, just buy your subscription ahead of time online (make sure you have your secret code to punch in on the stand).

Helmets are not provided, so if you're feeling queasy about launching into traffic, bring one along. The city has an ever-increasing number of bike lanes, and success has been such that new ones are being added. ***Note:*** Cyclists no longer always have the right to ride in the bus lanes; check for road signs. One more ***tip:*** Before you ride, download the app on your phone, so you don't waste precious time looking for a place to check in or check out.

BY TAXI

Changing the taxi landscape in France (much to the disdain of regular taxi drivers) is **Uber** (www.uber.com). Just download the smart phone app and enter your credit-card details. Once you're logged on, you enter your location and your destination. No money changes hands, and the cost of your journey is precalculated according to its "real" distance, so you're not penalized if you have to make a detour. While you wait, the screen shows the whereabouts of your taxi in real time, as well as the car's number plate, the driver's name, and his/her photo. For central Paris, you rarely have to wait more than 5 min. for an Uber to arrive. Generally speaking, it's cheaper than standard taxis as well.

If you don't use Uber, you can hail taxis in the street, but not all will stop (only hail those with a full green or white light), or look for a taxi stand, which resembles a bus stop and usually sports a blue taxi sign. Once inside, you'll have to pray that your driver is skilled in dodging Parisian traffic, which is horrendous.

Calculating fares is a complicated business. When you get in, the meter should read 2.60€. Then, the basic rates for Paris *intramuros* ranges from 1.06€ to 1.56€ per kilometer, depending on the day of the week and the hour. There's a minimum fare of 7€; if you have more than four people in your party, you'll also be charged 4€ for each additional passenger. You'll also be charged 1€ for each suitcase you put in the trunk. The saving grace here is that the distances are usually not huge, and barring excessive traffic, your average crosstown fare should fall between 15€ and 25€ for two without baggage. Tipping is not obligatory but rounding up or a .50€ to 1€ tip is customary.

It's often easier to call a cab then to hail one on the street: Contact **Taxi G7** (www.taxisg7.fr; ✆ **36-07** at .15€/min.). Avoid minicabs or unlicensed taxis.

BY BICYCLE

Cycling in Paris has been revolutionized by the hugely successful **Vélib'** bike rental scheme (the name comes from *vélo* meaning bicycle and *liberté* meaning freedom) launched in 2007. It takes a little effort for a tourist to sign up, but it's worth it to see Paris from two wheels (see box below).

Alternatively, you can rent a bike from **Paris à vélo, c'est sympa!**, 22 rue Alphonse Baudin, 11th arrond. (https://parisvelosympa.fr; ✆ **01-48-87-60-01**; Métro: St-Sébastien-Froissart or Richard Lenoir). Rentals cost 20€ for half a day and 30€ for a full day, but they do require 250€ or a passport as a deposit.

ON FOOT

If you have the time and the energy, the best mode of transport in this small and walkable city is your own two feet. You can cross the center of town (say from the place St-Michel to Les Halles) in about 20 min. This is the best way to see and experience the city and take in all the little details that make it all so wonderful.

BY CAR

Driving is *not* recommended in Paris, but the auto-adventurous may want to try tooling around in a small electric car through **Autolib'** (www.autolib.eu; ✆ **01-58-34-44-10**), the recent outgrowth of the popular Velib' bicycle rental program (see above). A similar concept to its cycling cousin, the scheme involves short-term electric car rental. To register you can go to one of the Autolib' parking spaces or to the Autolib' information center

(5 rue Edouard VII, 9th arrond.) with your driving license, a valid form of ID, and a credit card, or you can simply register online. A 1-day subscription is free, but you pay 9.50€ per 30 min. A year is 120€ plus 4.66€ per 20 min., and 0.23€ per extra minute. You are given a badge that you then pass over a sensor at a rental station to unlock the car. Unplug it from the charger and drive away. To return it, you must find a spot at an Autolib' station and plug in your car.

Visitor Information

A good place to start any information quest is at the Paris Tourist Office, 25 rue des Pyramides, 1st arrond. (www.parisinfo.com; ⓒ **01-49-52-42-63;** Métro: Pyramides). There's always a multilingual person on the other end of the line when you call (if you'd prefer not to spring for an international call, surf to their comprehensive website). The Tourist Office has several branches sprinkled around the city; check the website for addresses and hours.

City Layout

One of the nice things about Paris is that it's relatively small. It's not a sprawling megalopolis like Tokyo or London; in fact, Paris *intramuros,* or inside the long-gone city walls, numbers a mere 2.22 million habitants, and, excluding the large exterior parks of Bois de Vincinnes and the Bois de Boulogne, measures about 87 sq. km (34 sq. miles). (The suburbs, on the other hand, are sprawling, but chances are you won't be spending much, if any, time there.) Getting around is not difficult, provided you have a general sense of where things are.

The city is vaguely egg shaped, with the Seine cutting a wide upside-down "U"-shaped arc through the middle. The northern half is known as the **Right Bank,** and the southern, the **Left Bank.** To the uninitiated, the only way to remember is to face west, or downstream, so that the Right Bank will be to your right, and the Left to your left.

If you can't get your banks straight, don't worry, because most Parisians don't talk in terms of Right or Left Bank, but in terms of ***arrondissements,*** or districts. The city is neatly split up into 20 official arrondissements, which spiral out from the center of the city. The lower the number, the closer you'll be to the center, and as the numbers go up, you'll head toward the outer limits. Though their borders don't always correspond to historical neighborhoods, they do chop up the city into easily digestible chunks, so if you know what arrondissement your destination is in, your chances of finding it easily go way up. Your chances will be even better if you have a good map. Even if you're only in the city for a week, it's worthwhile to invest in a purse-size map book (ask for a "Paris par Arrondissement" at bookstores or larger newsstands), which costs around 8€.

[FastFACTS] PARIS

ATMs/Banks ATMs can be found all over the city. For currency exchange, look for **Travelex** (www.travelex.fr) counters at Paris airports, and Gare de l'Est and Montparnasse train stations.

Dentists & Doctors To download a list of English-speaking dentists and doctors in Paris, visit the U.S. Citizens Services page on the U.S. Embassy website (https://fr.usembassy.gov/) and click on "Medical Assistance." You can also reach U.S. Citizens Services by phone at (℃ **01-43-12-22-22.**

Hospitals Paris has excellent public hospitals; visit www.aphp.fr for locations and details on specialties. Private hospitals with English-speaking staff: **American Hospital of Paris,** 63 bd. Victor Hugo, 92200 Neuilly-sur-Seine (www.american-hospital.org; (℃ **01-46-41-25-25**) and **Institut Hospitalier Franco-Britannique,** 3 rue Barbès or 4 rue Kleber, Levallois

(www.ihfb.org/en; (℃ **01-47-59-59-59**).

Emergencies For an ambulance, call (℃ **15.** For the police, call (℃ **17.** Emergency services: (℃ **112.** You can also call the fire brigade (*Sapeurs-Pompiers*; (℃ **18**), who are trained to deal with all kinds of medical emergencies, not just fires.

Lost & Found **Bureau des Objets Trouvés,** 36 rue des Morillons, 15e (℃ **34-30,** .06€/min.). If you lose something in the Métro or on a train, contact the station on the line where you lost the object.

Mail & Postage Every arrondissement has a post office (**La Poste;** www.laposte.fr; (℃ **36-31**). Most are open Monday to Friday 8:30am to 8pm, Saturday 8am to 1pm; the main post office (52 rue du Louvre; Métro: Louvre-Rivoli) is open Monday to Saturday 7:30am to 6am and Sunday 10am to 6am. Stamps are also sold in *tabacs* (tobacconists).

Pharmacies Pharmacies are all over the city; look for the green neon cross above the door. Most are closed Sundays; both the **Pharmacie les Champs,** 84 av. des Champs-Elysées ((℃ **01-45-62-02-41**) and the **Pharmacie Européene,** 6 pl. de Clichy ((℃ **01-48-74-65-18**) are open daily 24 hr.

Safety In general, Paris is a safe city and it is safe to use the Métro at any time, though it's best to avoid the RER late at night. **Beware of pickpockets,** especially in tourist areas and the Louvre; organized gangs will even use children as decoys. Avoid walking around the less safe neighborhoods (Barbès-Rochechouart, Strasbourg St-Denis, Châtelet-Les-Halles) alone at night and never get into an unmarked taxi.

Toilets Paris is full of gray-colored, street toilet kiosks, which are a little daunting to the uninitiated, but free, and are automatically washed and disinfected after each use.

EXPLORING PARIS

With more than 130 world-class museums to visit, scores of attractions to discover, extraordinary architecture to gape at, and wonderful neighborhoods to wander, Paris is an endless series of delights. Fortunately, you can have a terrific time even if you don't see everything. In fact, some of your best moments may be simply roaming around the city without a plan. Lolling on a park bench, dreaming over a drink at a sidewalk cafe, or noodling around an unknown neighborhood can be the stuff of some of your best travel memories.

One of Notre-Dame's famous gargoyles looks out on the roofs of Paris

The following pages highlight the best that Paris has to offer, from iconic sights known the world over to quirky museums and hidden gardens, from medieval castles to galleries celebrating the most challenging contemporary art.

The Right Bank

LOUVRE & ILE DE LA CITÉ (1ST ARRONDISSEMENT)

This is where it all started. Back in the city's misty and uncertain beginnings, the Parisii tribe set up camp on the right bank of the Seine and started hunting on the **Ile de la Cité.** Many centuries later, the **Louvre** popped up, first as a fortress, then a royal palace and now one of the world's mightiest museums. The city's epicenter packs in a high density of must-see monuments and museums, but don't miss the opportunity for aimless strolling, in the magnificent **Tuileries Gardens,** say, or over the **Pont Neuf.** *Note:* For simplicity's sake, the entire Ile de la Cité has been included in this section, though technically half of it lies in the 4th arrondissement.

Cathédrale de Notre-Dame ★★★ CATHEDRAL   This remarkably harmonious ensemble of carved portals, huge towers, and flying buttresses has survived close to a millennium's worth of French history and served as a setting for some of the country's most solemn moments. Napoléon crowned himself Emperor here, Napoléon III was married here, and the funerals of some of France's greatest generals (Foch, Joffre, Leclerc) were held here. In August 1944, the liberation of Paris from the Nazis was commemorated in the cathedral, as was the death of General de Gaulle in 1970.

Construction on the cathedral began in 1163 and lasted more than 200 years. The building was relatively untouched up until the end of the 17th century, when monarchs started meddling with its windows and architecture. By the time the Revolutionaries decided to convert it into a "Temple of Reason," the cathedral was already in sorry condition—and the pillaging that ensued didn't help. The interior was ravaged, statues were smashed, and the cathedral became a shadow of its former glorious self.

We can thank the famous Hunchback himself for saving Notre-Dame. Victor Hugo's novel "The Hunchback of Notre Dame" drew attention to the state of disre-

Cathédrale de Notre-Dame

pair, and other artists and writers began to call for the restoration of the edifice. In 1844 Louis-Phillipe hired Jean-Baptiste Lassus and Viollet-le-Duc to restore the cathedral, which they finished in 1864.

Begin your visit at **Point Zéro,** just in front of the building on the parvis (the esplanade). This is the official center of Paris and the point from which all distances relative to other French cities are calculated. Before you are three enormous **carved portals** depicting (from left to right) the Coronation of the Virgin, the Last Judgment, and scenes from

---

Views from the Two Towers

The lines are long and the climb is longer, but the view from the **rooftop balcony** at the base of the cathedral's towers is possibly the most Parisian of all views. After trudging up some 422 steps (in narrow winding staircases—not for small children or anyone with mobility concerns) you'll be rewarded with a panorama that not only encompasses the Ile de la Cité, the Eiffel Tower, and Sacré-Coeur, but is also framed by a collection of photogenic **gargoyles.** One of the most famous is the **Stryga,** a horned and winged beasty holding his head in his hands, pensively sticking his tongue out

at the city below. On a cloudy day the vista is beautifully moody, especially from the summit of the **south tower,** from which you get an endless view of Paris. Come in the morning before the crowds get thick and avoid weekends. And don't be surprised if you see a bee buzzing nearby; there are hives on the roof (www.tours-notre-dame-de-paris.fr; ℂ **01-53-40-60-80;** 10€ adults, 8€ under 26, free under 18; Apr–June and Sept daily 10am–6pm; July–Aug Mon–Fri 10am–6pm, Sat–Sun 10am–11pm; Oct–Mar 10am–5:30pm).

the lives of the Virgin and St. Anne. Above is the **Gallery of the Kings of Judah and Israel**—thought to be portraits of the kings of France, the original statues were chopped out of the facade during the Revolution; some of the heads were eventually found in the 1970s and now are in the Musée National du Moyen Age/Thermes de Cluny (p. 115).

Upon entering the cathedral, you'll be immediately struck by two things: the throngs of tourists clogging the aisles, and, when you look up, the heavenly dimensions of the pillars holding up the ceiling. Soaring upward, these delicate archways give the impression that the entire edifice is about to take off into the sky. Up there in the upper atmosphere are three remarkable stained-glass **rose windows.** The north window retains almost all of its 13th-century stained glass; the other two have been heavily restored. An impressive **treasury** is filled with relics of various saints including the elaborate cases for the **Crown of Thorns,** brought back from Constantinople by Saint Louis in the 13th century. The crown itself is not on display; however, it can be viewed, along with a nail and some pieces of the Holy Cross, on the first Friday of the month (3pm), every Friday during Lent (3pm) and Good Friday (10am–5pm). For a detailed look at the cathedral, take advantage of the **free guided tours in English** (Wed–Thurs 2pm, Sat 2:30pm) or rent an **audio guide** for 5€.

When you leave, be sure to take a stroll around the outside of the cathedral to admire the other portals and the famous flying buttresses.

pl. du Parvis Notre-Dame, 4th arrond. www.notredamedeparis.fr. ℭ **01-53-10-07-02.** Free admission to cathedral; treasury 4€ adults, 2€ students and seniors, 1€ ages 6–12, free for children 5 and under. Cathedral: Mon–Fri 8am–6:45pm; Sat–Sun 8am–7:15pm. Treasury: daily 9:30am–6pm. Métro: Cité or St-Michel. RER: St-Michel.

Conciergerie ★ HISTORIC SITE

Despite looking like a turreted, fairy-tale castle, the Conciergerie is in fact a dark relic of the Revolution—a famous prison that commemorates the Reign of Terror, when murderous infighting between the various revolutionary factions engendered panic and paranoia that led to tens of thousands of people being arrested and

Soaring pillars and stained glass, Notre-Dame

The Conciergerie illuminated at night

executed. Many of the Revolution's most pivotal characters spent their final days here before making their way to the guillotine, including Marie Antoinette.

Though it's been a prison since the 15th century, the building itself is actually what remains of a 14th-century royal palace built by Philippe le Bel. The enormous **Salle des Gens d'Arms,** with its 8.4m-high (28-ft.) vaulted ceiling, is an impressive reminder of the building's palatial past. As for the prison, though the cells have been outfitted with displays and re-creations of daily life (including Marie Antoinette's cell), it's a little difficult to imagine what it was like in the bad old days. However, the **Cours des Femmes** (the women's courtyard) virtually hasn't changed since the days when female prisoners did their washing in the fountain. In a curious attempt to spice up its offerings, the site has recently been hosting contemporary art exhibits.

2 bd. du Palais, 1st arrond. www. paris-conciergerie.fr. ⟡ **01-53-40-60-80.** Admission 9€ adults; 7€ ages 18–25; free for children 17 and under. Daily 9:30–6pm. Métro: Cité, Châtelet, or St-Michel. RER: St-Michel.

Jardin des Tuileries ★★★ GARDENS   This exquisite park spreads from the Louvre to the place de la Concorde. What you see today is based on the design by 17th-century master landscape artist André Le Nôtre— the man behind the gardens of Versailles. Le Nôtre's elegant geometry of flowerbeds, parterres, and groves of trees made the Tuileries Gardens the ultimate stroll for the era's well-to-do Parisians. It continues to delight both tourists and locals in the 21st century.

During World War II, the furious fighting that went on here damaged many statues. Little by little in the postwar years, the garden put itself back together. Seventeenth- and eighteenth-century representations of various gods and goddesses were repaired, and the city added new works by modern masters such as Alberto Giocometti, Jean Dubuffet, and Henry Moore. Rodin's *The Kiss* and *Eve* are here, as well as a series of 18 of Maillol's curvaceous women, peeking out of the green **labyrinth** of hedges in the Carousel Gardens near the museum.

Pulling up a metal chair and sunning yourself on the edge of the large **fountain** in the center of the gardens (the **Grande Carrée**) is a delightful respite for tired tourists after a day in the Louvre; tots will enjoy playing with one of the wooden **toy sailboats** that you can rent from a stand (3€/30 min.).

Near pl. de la Concorde, 1st arrond. ℂ **01-40-20-90-43.** Free admission. Daily Apr–May 7am–9pm; June–Aug 7am–11pm; Sept 7am–9pm; Oct–Mar 7:30am–7:30pm. Métro: Tuileries or Concorde.

MAD ★★ MUSEUM   Possessing some 150,000 items in its rich collection, the MAD (standing for Musée des Arts Décoratifs) is a fascinating museum that offers a glimpse of history through the prism of decorative objects, with a spectrum that ranges from medieval traveling trunks to Philippe Starck stools. The collection is organized in more or less chronological order, so on your journey you will pass by paintings from the First Italian Renaissance, through a room filled with exquisite 15th-century intarsia ("paintings" made out of intricately inlaid wood), before gaping at huge, intricately carved 17th-century German armoires. Other highlights include a tiny room covered in gilded woodwork from an 18th-century mansion in Avignon, a stunning Art Nouveau dining room, and fashion designer Jeanne Lanvin's decadent, purple Art Deco boudoir. While the objects themselves are beautiful, the link between style and historic context is illuminating; the endless curlicues of the rococo style, which perfectly reflected the excesses of Louis XV's court, for example, gives way to more puritanical neoclassicism, which developed during the Enlightenment, when unrestrained frivolity began to look degenerate.

A statue grouping in the Jardin des Tuileries

Two other collections worthy of your time are the Publicité/Graphisme collection, which takes on the history of advertising, and the Mode/Textile fashion displays. While the former will mostly be of interest to those who are in the biz, the latter hosts a terrific range of works from famous couture houses like Jean-Paul Gaultier and Dior. Another intriguing addition is a collection of wallpaper through the ages—the earliest of which dates from 1864 and depicts a bucolic hunting scene. *Note:* The visit starts on the third, not the first, floor.

Palais du Louvre, 107 rue de Rivoli, 1st arrond. http://madparis.fr. *(C)* **01-44-55-57-50.** Admission 11€ adults; 8.50€ ages 18–25; free for children 17 and under. Tues–Sun 11am–6pm. Métro: Louvre–Palais-Royal or Tuileries.

Musée de l'Orangerie ★★ MUSEUM   Since 1927, this former royal greenhouse has been the home of Monet's *Nymphéas,* or **water lilies,** which he conceived as a "haven of peaceful meditation." Two large oval rooms are dedicated to these masterpieces, in which Monet tried to replicate the feeling and atmosphere of his garden at Giverny. He worked on these enormous canvases for 12 years, with the idea of creating an environment that would soothe the "overworked nerves" of modern men and women.

The other highlight here is the Guillaume collection, an impressive assortment of late-19th- and early-20th-century paintings. The first light-filled gallery displays works by Renoir and Cezanne. The rest of the collection includes slightly sinister landscapes by Rousseau, enigmatic portraits by Modigliani, distorted figures by Soutine, as well as some kinder, gentler Picassos (*Les Adolescents* bathed in pink and rust tones).

Jardin des Tuileries, 1st arrond. www.musee-orangerie.fr. *(C)* **01-44-77-80-07.** Admission 9€ adults; 6.50€ ages 18–25; free for children 17 and under. Wed–Mon 9am–6pm. Métro: Concorde.

Musée du Louvre ★★★ MUSEUM   The best way to thoroughly visit the Louvre would be to move in for a month. Not only is it one of the largest museums in the world, with more than 35,000 works of art displayed over 60,000 sq. m (645,835 sq. ft.), but it's packed with enough masterpieces to make the Mona Lisa weep. Rembrandt, Reubens, Botticelli, Ingres, and Michelangelo are all represented here; subjects range from the grandiose (Antoine-Jean Gros's gigantic *Napoleon Bonaparte Visiting the Plague-Stricken in Jaffa*) to the petite (Vermeer's tiny, exquisite *Lacemaker*). You can gape at a diamond the size of a golf ball in the royal treasury, or marvel over exquisite bronze figurines in the vast Egyptian section.

Today, the building is divided into three wings, Sully, Denon, and Richelieu, each one with its own clearly marked entrance, found under I.M. Pei's glass pyramid. Get your hands on a museum map (the museum's website has an excellent interactive map), choose your personal "must-sees," and plan ahead. There's no way to see it all, but mercifully, the museum is well organized and has been very reasonably arranged into color-coded sections. If you're really in a rush or you just want to get an

The Louvre at dusk, with I.M. Pei's famous pyramid

overall sense of the place, you can take the introductory guided tour in English (1 hr., 30 min.; Wed–Mon except the first Sun of the month 11am and 2pm; 12€).

The museum's three biggest stars are all located in the Denon wing. La Joconde, otherwise known as the *Mona Lisa,* now has an entire wall to herself, making it easier to contemplate her enigmatic smile. Another inscrutable female in this wing is the *Venus de Milo,* who was found on a Greek island in 1820. The *Winged Victory of Samothrace,* another magnificent Greek sculpture, stands at the top of a majestic flight of stairs, her powerful body pushing forward as if about to take flight. This headless deity originally overlooked the Sanctuary of the Great Gods on the island of Samothrace.

Because a complete listing of the Louvre's highlights would fill a book, below is a decidedly biased selection of my favorite areas:

13TH- TO 18TH-CENTURY ITALIAN PAINTING   A few standouts in the immense Italian collection include the delicate fresco by Botticelli called *Venus and the Three Graces Presenting Gifts to a Young Woman,* Veronese's enormous *Wedding Feast at Cana,* and of course, the *Mona Lisa.* The Divine Miss M is in a room packed with wonders, including several Titians and Tintorettos. Once you've digested this rich meal, stroll down the endless Grande Galerie, past more da Vincis (*Saint John the Baptist, The Virgin of the Rock*), as well as works by Raphael, Caravaggio, and Gentileschi.

GREEK & ROMAN SCULPTURE   While the *Venus de Milo* and the *Winged Victory of Samothrace* are not to be missed, the Salle des Caryatides (the room itself is a work of art) boasts marble masterworks like *Artemis* hunting with her stag and the troubling *Sleeping Hermaphrodite,* an alluring female figure from behind—and something entirely different from the front.

The Louvre Museum

THE GALERIE D'APOLLON   The gold-encrusted room is an excellent example of the excesses of 17th-century French royalty. Commissioned by Louis XIV, aka "The Sun King," every inch of this gallery is covered with gilt stucco sculptures and flamboyant murals invoking the journey of the Roman sun god Apollo (ceiling paintings are by Charles Le Brun). The main draw here is the collection of crown jewels. Among necklaces bedecked with quarter-sized sapphires and tiaras dripping with diamonds and rubies is the jewel-studded crown of Louis XV and the pearl-and-diamond diadem of Empress Eugenie.

THE EGYPTIANS   This is the largest collection outside of Cairo, thanks in large part to Jean-François Champollion, the 19th-century French scientist and scholar who first decoded Egyptian hieroglyphs. Sculptures, figurines, papyrus documents, steles, musical instruments, and of course, mummies, fill numerous rooms in the Sully Wing, including the colossal statue of Ramses II and the strangely moving Seated Scribe. He gazes intently out of intricately crafted inlaid eyes: A combination of copper, magnesite, and polished rock crystal create a startlingly life-like stare.

LARGE-FORMAT FRENCH PAINTINGS   Enormous floor-to-ceiling (and these are high ceilings!) paintings of monumental moments in history cover the walls in these three rooms. The *Coronation of Napoléon* by Jacques-Louis David depicts the newly minted Emperor crowning Josephine, while the disconcerted pope and a host of notables look on. Farther on are several tumultuous canvases by Eugène Delacroix, including *Liberty Guiding the People,* which might just be the ultimate expression of French patriotism.

Leaping over the Louvre Line

Don't want to wait in line for tickets to the Louvre? The easiest option is to buy tickets in advance online (in English) at **www.ticketlouvre.fr** and print them out. Or try **www.fnactickets.com**; you can print out your tickets, get them mailed to you, or pick them up at any French branch of the Fnac bookstore chain. If you are of an improvisational bent and prefer to pick up tickets at the entrance, you have four ways to avoid the lines that often snake around the glass pyramid entryway. Either:

1) Enter directly from the Palais Royal–Musée du Louvre metro stop.

2) Take one of the two staircases on either side of the Arc du Carrousel in the Tuileries Gardens that lead directly down to the ticketing area.

3) Buy your ticket from the Civette du Carousel tobacconist in the Carousel du Louvre shopping center (99 rue de Rivoli) where there's never a wait.

4) Go for late-night opening (after 6pm on Wed and Fri when the museum closes at 9:45pm), usually a quiet time to visit.

Note: When visiting the museum, **watch your wallets and purses—** there has been an unfortunate increase in pickpockets; organized groups even use children to prey on unsuspecting art lovers.

1st arrond. Main entrance in the glass pyramid, cour Napoléon. www.louvre.fr. ℂ **01-40-20-50-50.** Admission 15€ adults; free for children 17 and under. Sat–Mon and Thurs 9am–6pm; Wed and Fri 9am–9:45pm. Métro: Palais-Royal–Musée du Louvre.

Palais Royal ★★ HISTORIC SITE/GARDEN   The gardens and long arcades of the Palais Royal are not only a delight to stroll through, they were also witness to one of the most important moments in French history. Built by Cardinal Richelieu, the lavish palace eventually came into the hands of a certain Duke Louis Philippe d'Orleans at the end of the 18th century. An inveterate spendthrift, the young lord soon found himself up to his ears in debt. To earn enough money to pay off his creditors, he came up with the shockingly modern idea of opening the palace gardens to development, building apartments on the grounds. The bottom floor of the galleries, which make up three sides of the enclosure you see today, were let out as shops, cafes, and boutiques. Gambling houses and bordellos sprang up between the shops and cafes, and the gardens became the central meeting place for revolutionaries. Things came to a head on July 12, 1789, when Camille Desmoulins stood up on a table in front of the Café de Foy and called the people to arms—2 days later, the mob would storm the Bastille, igniting the French Revolution. In more recent times, the palace was taken over by various government ministries, and the apartments were rented to artists and writers, including Colette and Jean Cocteau.

Today the shops in the arcades are very subdued, and very expensive—mostly high-end designer clothes, and pricey restaurants, including the legendary Grand Véfour (p. 146). The *cour d'honneur* on the south end is filled with black-and-white-striped columns by Daniel Buren; though most Parisians have now gotten used to this unusual installation, when it was unveiled in 1987 it caused almost as much of a stir as Camille Desmoulins did on that fateful day.

Rue St-Honoré, 1st arrond. Free admission to gardens and arcades; buildings closed to public. Daily 7:30am–dusk. Métro: Palais Royal–Musée du Louvre.

Place Vendôme ★★ SQUARE   In 1686, Louis XIV decided the time had come to design a magnificent square, at the center of which would stand a statue of His Royal Highness. Though the statue is long gone, this is still one of the classiest squares in the city. The work of Jules Hardouin-Mansart, this über-elegant octagonal ensemble of 17th-century buildings today is the home of the original Ritz Hôtel, as well as the world's most glitzy jewelry makers. When Napoléon took over, he erected a huge Roman-style column honoring his glorious army (yes, once again), this time documenting its victory at Austerlitz. A long spiral of bas-reliefs recounting the campaign of 1805 march up the Colonne de la Grande Armée, crowned by a statue of the Emperor himself.

Enter by rue de Castiglione, 1st arrond. Métro: Tuileries or Concorde.

Sainte-Chapelle ★★★ CHURCH   A wall of color greets visitors who enter this magnificent chapel. Stained-glass windows make up a large part of the upper level of the church, giving worshippers the impression of standing inside a jewel-encrusted crystal goblet. What isn't glass is elaborately carved and painted in gold leaf and rich colors: vaulting arches, delicate window casings, and an almost Oriental wainscoting of arches and medallions. The 15 windows recount the story of the Bible, from Genesis to the Apocalypse, as well as the story of St-Louis, who was responsible for the chapel's construction. During the Crusades, Louis IX (who was later canonized) brought home some of the holiest relics in Christendom from Constantinople: the crown of thorns and a piece of the Holy Cross. Such a treasure required an appropriately splendid chapel in the royal palace, and thus the chapel was built (the relics are now in the treasury of Notre-Dame). The record is not clear, but the architect may have been the illustrious Pierre de Montreuil, who worked on the cathedrals of St-Dennis and Notre-Dame. What is sure is that the mysterious architect was brilliant: He managed to support the structure with arches and buttresses in such a way that the walls of the upper chapel are almost entirely glass.

The **lower chapel,** which was meant for the servants, has a low, vaulted ceiling painted in blue, red, and gold and covered with fleur-de-lys motifs. Up a small staircase is the **upper chapel,** clearly meant for the royals. This masterpiece suffered both fire and floods in the 17th century

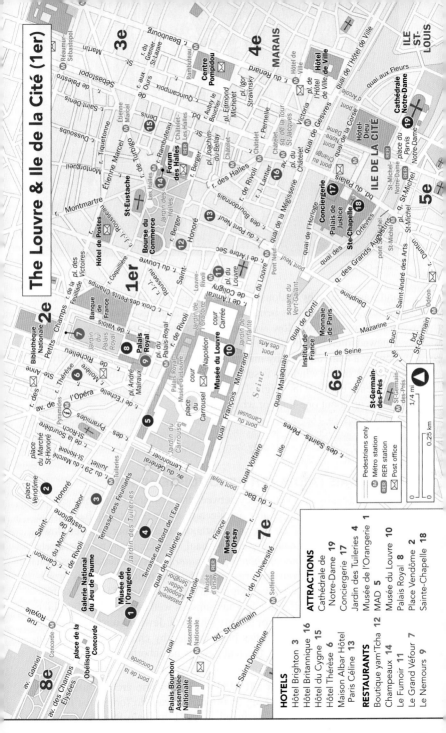

The Louvre & Ile de la Cité (1er)

3e

4e

MARAIS

ILE ST-LOUIS

Centre Pompidou

Cathédrale Notre-Dame 19

ILE DE LA CITÉ

5e

Conciergerie 17

Palais de Justice

Ste-Chapelle 18

Forum des Halles 14

St-Eustache

Bourse du Commerce

1er

Banque de France

Bibliothèque Nationale 7

2e

Palais Royal 8, 9

Musée du Louvre 10

6e

St-Germain-des-Prés

Monnaie de Paris

Institut de France

Seine

Musée d'Orsay

7e

Galerie National du Jeu de Paume

Musée de l'Orangerie 1

place Vendôme 2

place de la Concorde

Obélisque

8e

Palais Bourbon Assemblée Nationale

N

1/4 mi

0.25 km

— Pedestrians only

Ⓜ Metro station

RER RER station

⊠ Post office

HOTELS
Hôtel Brighton 3
Hôtel Britannique 16
Hôtel du Cygne 15
Hôtel Thérèse 6
Maison Albar Hôtel
Paris Céline 13

RESTAURANTS
Boutique yam'Tcha 12
Champeaux 14
Le Fumoir 11
Le Grand Véfour 7
Le Nemours 9

ATTRACTIONS
Cathédrale de
Notre-Dame 19
Conciergerie 17
Jardin des Tuileries 4
Musée de l'Orangerie 1
MAD 5
Musée du Louvre 10
Palais Royal 8
Place Vendôme 2
Sainte-Chapelle 18

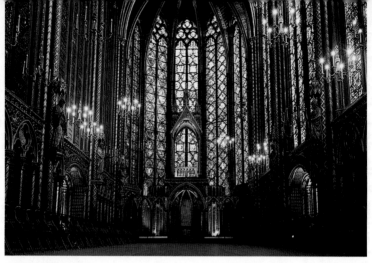

Sainte-Chapelle

and was pillaged by zealous Revolutionaries in the 18th. By the mid–19th century, the chapel was being used to store archives—2m (6.5 ft.) of the bottom of each window was removed to install shelves. Fortunately, renewed interest in medieval art eventually led to a conscientious restoration by a team advised by master restorer Viollet-le-Duc. The quality of the work on the windows is such that it is almost impossible to detect the difference between the original and the reconstructed stained glass (which makes up about one-third of what you see).

Palais de Justice, 4 bd. du Palais, 1st arrond. www.sainte-chapelle.fr. ℂ **01-53-40-60-80.** Admission 10€ adults; 8€ ages 18–25; free for children 17 and under. Mar–Oct daily 9:30am–6pm; Nov–Feb daily 9am–5pm. Métro: Cité, St-Michel, or Châtelet–Les Halles. RER: St-Michel.

LE MARAIS (3RD & 4TH ARRONDISSEMENTS)

Home to royalty and aristocracy between the 14th and 17th centuries, the Marais still boasts remarkable architecture, some of it dating back to the Middle Ages. One of the few neighborhoods that was not knocked down during Baron Haussmann's urban overhaul, the Marais has narrow streets still lined with magnificent *hôtels particuliers* (that is, mansions) as well as humbler homes from centuries past. The **Pompidou Center** is probably the biggest and most well-known attraction, but the Marais also harbors a wealth of terrific smaller museums, as well as the delightful **place des Vosges.** The remnants of the city's **historic Jewish quarter** are found on rue des Rosiers, which has been invaded by chic clothing shops in recent years. These days, the real Jewish neighborhood is in the 19th arrondissement.

Centre Pompidou ★★ MUSEUM   The bizarre architecture of this building provokes such strong emotions, it's easy to forget that there is something inside. It was designed in 1971 by Italo-British architects

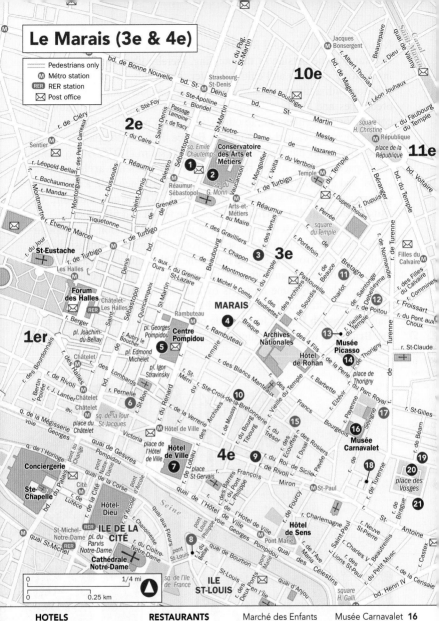

Le Marais (3e & 4e)

Pedestrians only
Ⓜ Métro station
RER RER station
☒ Post office

2e

10e

11e

3e

MARAIS

1er

4e

ILE DE LA CITÉ

ILE ST-LOUIS

0   1/4 mi
0   0.25 km

HOTELS
Hôtel Caron de
  Beaumarchais **9**
Hôtel de la Bretonnerie **10**
Hôtel Jeanne d'Arc
  le Marais **18**
Jules et Jim **3**
Pavillon de la Reine **19**

RESTAURANTS
Benoit **6**
Big Love Caffé **12**
Breizh Café **13**
Café des Musées **17**
La Brasserie de
  l'Isle Saint-Louis **8**
L'As du Fallafel **15**

Marché des Enfants
  Rouges **11**

ATTRACTIONS
Centre Pompidou **5**
Gaîté Lyrique **1**
Hôtel de Ville **7**
Maison de
  Victor Hugo **21**

Musée Carnavalet **16**
Musée de l'Art et
  Histoire du Judaïsme **4**
Musée des Arts
  et Metiers **2**
Picasso Paris **14**
Place des Vosges **20**

89

Renzo Piano and Richard Rogers, whose concept was to put the support structure on the outside of the building, thereby liberating space on the inside for a museum and cultural center. The result was a grid-like exoskeleton with a tubular escalator inching up one side and huge multicolored pipes and shafts covering the other. To some, it's a milestone in contemporary architecture; to others, it's simply a horror. Either way, it's one of the most visited structures in France. For the Pompidou is much more than an art museum. Its some 100,000 sq. m (1,076,390 sq. ft.) of floor space includes a vast **reference library,** a **cinema archive,** bookshops, and a **music institute,** as well as a performance hall, a **children's gallery,** and areas for educational activities. The actual museum, the **Musée National d'Art Moderne,** is on the fourth and fifth floors.

Because the museum collection is in constant rotation, it's impossible to say what you're likely to see on your visit, but the emphasis is generally on works from the second half of the 20th century, with a good dose of surrealism, Dada, and other modern movements from the first half. It includes relatively tame abstracts by **Picasso** and **Kandinsky** to **Andy Warhol**'s multiheaded portrait of Elizabeth Taylor to a felt-wrapped piano by **Joseph Beuys.** Just outside of the front of the center is the **Atelier Brancusi,** where the sculptor's workshop has been reconstituted in its entirety.

Centre Pompidou

Don't miss the view from the top floor—a wonderful opportunity to gaze at the city's higgledy-piggledy rooftops. Even if you don't visit the museum, you can buy a ticket to the top for 5€. Or you can admire it from within **Georges** (http://restaurantgeorgesparis.com/), the museum's oh so chic rooftop cafe/restaurant, which flaunts decor just as avant-garde as the artworks inside the museum. The staff are a little snooty however.

pl. Georges-Pompidou, 4th arrond. www.centrepompidou.fr. ⓒ **01-44-78-12-33.** Admission 14€–13€ adults; free for children 17 and under; admission varies depending on exhibits. Wed–Mon 11am–10pm. Métro: Rambuteau, Hôtel de Ville, or Châtelet–Les Halles.

Gaîté Lyrique ★ CULTURAL CENTER   One of the newer additions to the city's cultural scene, this gallery space/concert hall/educational center is devoted to exploring mixed-media and digital art forms. Set in an abandoned 19th-century theater (hence the name), the building has been transformed to host rotating exhibits that range from music and multimedia performances to design, fashion, and architecture to new media—there's even an interactive room dedicated to video games.

3 bis rue Papin, 3rd arrond. www.gaite-lyrique.net. ⓒ **01-53-01-52-00.** Admission and opening hours may vary according to the exhibitions and events. Tues–Sat 2–8pm and Sun noon–6pm. Métro: Réaumur Sébastopol.

Hôtel de Ville ★ HISTORIC SITE   No, it's not a hotel. This enormous Neo-Renaissance wedding cake is Paris's city hall, and you can't go inside the official parts of the building, though it does host regular art exhibits on subjects linked to Paris's history, usually for free (access is through the back entrance on rue Lobau). But even if you can't get in to see the sumptuous halls and chandeliers, you will be able to feast on the lavish exterior, which includes 136 statues representing historic VIPs of Parisian history. Since the 14th century, this spot has been an administrative seat for the municipality; the building you see before you dates from 1873, but it is a copy of an earlier Renaissance version that stood in its place up until 1870, when it was burned down during the Paris Commune. The vast square in front of the building, which used to be called the place du Grève, was used for municipal festivals and executions, and it was also the stage for several important moments in the city's history, particularly during the Revolution: Louis XVI was forced to kiss the new French flag here, and Robespierre was shot in the jaw and arrested here during an attempted coup. Today the square is host to more peaceful activities: There's usually a merry-go-round or two to captivate the little ones, and in winter an **ice-skating rink** is sometimes set up.

29 rue de Rivoli, 4th arrond. www.paris.fr. ⓒ **01-42-76-43-43.** Free admission. Métro: Hôtel-de-Ville.

Maison de Victor Hugo ★ MUSEUM   The life of Victor Hugo was as turbulent as some of his novels. Regularly visited by both tragedy and triumph, the author of "The Hunchback of Notre Dame" lived in several apartments in Paris, including this one on the second floor of a corner house on the sumptuous place des Vosges. From 1832 to 1848, he lived here with his wife and four children. When Napoleon III seized power in 1851, this passionate advocate of free speech declared the new king a traitor of France. Fearing for his life, Hugo left the country and lived in exile until 1870 when he triumphantly returned and was elected to the senate. By the time he died in 1885 he was a national hero; his funeral cortege through the streets of Paris is the stuff of legend, and his body was one of the first to be buried in the Panthéon. The small museum's collection charts this dramatic existence through the author's drawings, manuscripts, notes, furniture, and personal objects, which are displayed in rooms that recreate the ambiance of the original lodgings. *Note:* Closed for renovations until April 2019.

6 pl. des Vosges, 4th arrond. www.maisonsvictorhugo.paris.fr. © **01-42-72-10-16.** Free admission to the permanent collections. Tues–Sun 10am–6pm. Métro: St-Paul, Bastille, or Chemin-Vert.

Musée d'Art et Histoire du Judaïsme ★★ MUSEUM Housed in the magnificent Hôtel de Saint Aignan, this museum chronicles the art and history of the Jewish people in France and Europe. It features a superb collection of objects of both artistic and cultural significance (a splendid Italian Renaissance torah ark, a German gold-and-silver Hanukkah menorah, a 17th-century Dutch illustrated torah scroll, documents from the Dreyfus trial), which is interspersed with texts, drawings, and photos telling the story of the Jews and explaining the basics of both Ashkenazi and Sephardic traditions. The final rooms include a collection of works by Jewish artists, including Modigliani, Soutine, Lipchitz, and Chagall. In recent years, this museum has hosted some terrific temporary exhibits on offbeat subjects like the (Jewish) origins of Superman, Radical Jewish Culture, and the Walter Benjamin archives. Be prepared for airportlike security at the entrance.

71 rue du Temple, 3rd arrond. www.mahj.org. © **01-53-01-86-53.** Admission 9€ adults; 6€ ages 18–25; free for children 17 and under. Mon–Fri 11am–6pm; Sat–Sun 10am–6pm. Métro: Rambuteau or Hôtel de Ville.

Musée Carnavalet ★★★ MUSEUM *Note:* The museum closed for extensive renovations in December 2016 and is expected to remain closed until end 2019/early-2020.

The Pont Neuf

Since it has recently had a makeover, it does indeed look brand-spanking *neuf* (new), even though it is, in fact, the oldest bridge in Paris. The bridge was an instant hit when it was inaugurated by Henri IV in 1607: Ample sidewalks, and the fact that it was the first bridge sans houses, made it a delight for pedestrians. It still is, especially if you ignore the cars and just take in the lovely views.

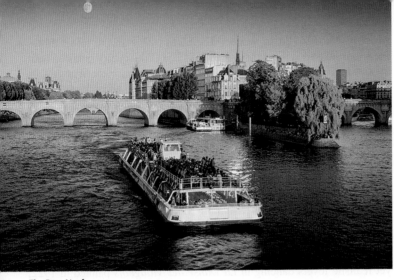

The Pont Neuf

Paris has served as a backdrop to centuries' worth of dramatic events, from Roman takeovers to barbarian invasions, from coronations to decapitations to the birth of the modern French republic. These stories and others are told at this fascinating museum through objects, paintings, and interiors. The collection is displayed in two extraordinary 17th-century mansions—works of art in their own right. Starting with a prehistoric canoe from 4600 B.C. and continuing into the 20th century, the history of Paris is illustrated with items as diverse as Gallo-Roman figurines, Napoleon's toiletry kit, and an 18th-century portrait of Benjamin Franklin painted when he was the U.S. ambassador to France.

16 rue des Francs-Bourgeois, 3rd arrond. www.carnavalet.paris.fr. ✆ **01-44-59-58-58.** Free admission for permanent collection except during certain temporary exhibits. Tues–Sun 10am–6pm. Métro: St-Paul or Chemin Vert.

Musée des Arts et Métiers ★ MUSEUM

Here's a museum for the techies in your crowd. With a collection that runs from astrolabes to supercomputers, this place is a goldmine for geeks of all ages. The goodies are organized into seven categories: scientific instruments, materials, construction, communication, energy, mechanics, and transportation. Learn how the metric system was born, what the first waterwheels looked like, and how the machine age got up to speed. See cyclotrons, gasometers, and microscopes. Probably the most famous item on display is Foucault's original pendulum, which still gracefully demonstrates the rotation of the Earth, just like it does in Umberto Eco's eponymous novel. The museum is housed in the ancient abbey of St-Martin-des-Champs.

60 rue Réaumur, 3rd arrond. www.arts-et-metiers.net. ✆ **01-53-01-82-00.** Admission 8€ adults; 5.50€ students; free for children 17 and under. Tues–Wed and Fri–Sun 10am–6pm; Thurs 10am–9:30pm. Métro: Arts et Métiers.

Musée Picasso Paris ★★★ MUSEUM   This shrine to all things Picasso is housed in the stunning Hôtel Salé, a 17th-century mansion built by salt-tax farmer Pierre Aubert, whose position gave the mansion its name—Salé means "salty." This unique institution valiantly strives to make sense of the incredibly diverse output of this prolific genius: Some 400 carefully selected paintings, sculptures, collages, and drawings are presented in a more or less chronological and thematic order, no small task when dealing with an artist who experimented with every style, from neoclassicism to surrealism to his own flamboyantly abstract inventions. Impressionist portraits (*Portrait of Gustave Coquiot*, 1901), Cubist explorations (*Man with Guitar*, 1911), mannerist allegories (*The Race*, 1922), and deconstructionist forms (*Reclining Nude*, 1932) make up only part of his oeuvre, which has been estimated to include some 50,000 works. Not only that, Picasso often worked in wildly different styles during the same period, sometimes treating the same subjects. For example, the rounded yet realistic lovers dancing in *La Danse des Villageois* painted in 1922, hang next to two forms in a blaze of color representing *The Kiss* painted in 1925. There's also a sampling of the somewhat disturbing portraits of the many women in his life, including portraits of Dora Maar and Marie-Thérèse, both painted in 1937. On the top floor is Picasso's private collection, which includes works by artists he admired like Courbet and Cézanne, as well as paintings by his friends, who included masters like Braque and Matisse.

All in all, what you see on the walls is less than 10 percent of the 5,000 works in the museum's collection; the presentation rotates every couple of years. Unless you enjoy waiting in long lines exposed to the elements, **buy your ticket in advance online;** you'll usually walk right in with your e-ticket.

5 rue de Thorigny, 3rd arrond. www.museepicassoparis.fr. ℃ **01-85-56-00-36.** Admission 12.50€ adults; free for children 17 and under. Tues–Fri 10:30am–6pm; Sat–Sun 9:30am–6pm. Métro: St-Paul or Chemin Vert.

Place des Vosges ★★★ PLAZA   Possibly the prettiest square in the city, this beautiful spot combines elegance, greenery, and quiet. Nowhere in Paris will you find such a unity of Renaissance-style architecture; the entire square is bordered by 17th-century brick townhouses, each conforming to rules set down by Henri IV himself, under which runs arched arcades. The square's history dates back to a mishap in 1559, when the site was occupied by a royal palace. During a tournament, feisty King Henri II decided to fight Montgomery, the captain of his guard. A badly aimed lance resulted in Henri's untimely death; his wife, Catherine de Medicis, was so distraught she had the palace demolished. His descendant, Henri IV, took advantage of the free space to construct a royal square. Over the centuries, a number of celebrities lived in the 36 houses, including Mme de Sévigny and Victor Hugo. Today the homes are for the

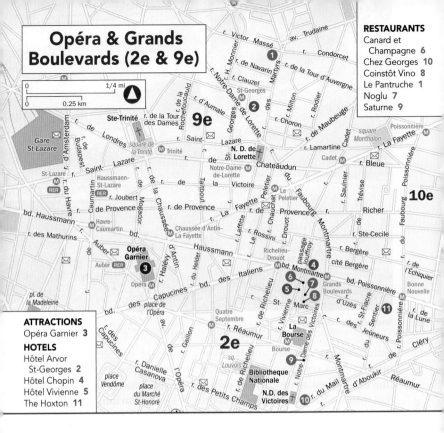

Opéra & Grands Boulevards (2e & 9e)

rich, as are the chic boutiques under the arcades, but the lawns, trees, fountains, and playground are for everyone.

4th arrond. Métro: St-Paul.

OPÉRA & GRANDS BOULEVARDS (2ND & 9TH ARRONDISSEMENTS)

The grandiose **Opéra Garnier** reigns over this bustling neighborhood, which teems with office workers, tourists, and shoppers scuttling in and around the Grands Magasins (the big department stores) on boulevard Haussmann. Which may account for why there are perhaps more opportunities for outstanding retail experiences here than for cultural ones.

Opéra Garnier ★★ OPERA HOUSE   Flamboyant, extravagant, and baroque, this opulent opera house is a splendid example of Second Empire architectural excess. Corinthian columns, loggias, busts, and friezes cover the **facade** of the building, all topped by a gold dome. The interior is no less dramatic. The vast **lobby,** built in a spectrum of different-colored marble, holds a spectacular double staircase that sweeps up to the different levels of the auditorium, as well as an array of glamorous

Interior, Opéra Garnier

antechambers, galleries, and ballrooms that make you wonder how the opera scenery could possibly compete. Mosaics, mirrors, gilt, and marble line these grand spaces, whose painted ceilings dance with fauns, gods, and nymphs. The main event, of course, is the **auditorium,** which might seem a bit small, considering the size of the building. In fact, it holds not even 2,000 seats. The beautiful **ceiling** was painted with colorful images from various operas and ballets by Marc Chagall in 1964.

All of this (with the exception of the Chagall ceiling) sprang from the mind of a young, unknown architect named Charles Garnier, who won a competition launched by Napoléon III. Though the first stone was laid in 1862, work was held up by war, civil unrest, and a change in regime; the Palais Garnier was not inaugurated until 1875. Some contemporary critics found it a bit much (one called it "an overloaded sideboard"), but today it is generally acknowledged as a masterpiece of the architecture of the epoch.

And what about that phantom? Gaston Leroux's 1911 novel, "The Phantom of the Opera," clearly was inspired by the building's **underground lake,** which was constructed to help stabilize the building and is used today by Paris' firebrigade for underwater training.

You can visit the building on your own, but you might want to take advantage of the **guided visits in English** (15.50€ adults, 8.50€ children under 10; Sept–June Wed, Sat–Sun 11:30am and 2:30pm; July–Aug daily 11:30am and 2:30pm). Either way, your visit will be limited to the lobby, the surrounding foyers, the museum, and if there's not a rehearsal in progress, the auditorium—sorry, you won't get to see the lake. Or simply **buy tickets to a show.**

Corner of rue Scribe and rue Auber, 9th arrond. www.operadeparis.fr. ℂ **08-92-89-90-90** (.34€/min.). Admission 11€ adults; 8€ students and ages 12–25; free for children 11 and under. Oct to mid-July daily 10am–4:30pm; mid-July to Sept 10am–5:30pm. Métro: Opéra.

CHAMPS-ELYSÉES, TROCADÉRO & WESTERN PARIS (8TH, 16TH & 17TH ARRONDISSEMENTS)

Decidedly posh, this is one of the wealthiest parts of the city in both per-capita earnings and cultural institutions. While the **Champs-Elysées ★★** is more glitz than glory, the surrounding neighborhoods offer high-end shops and restaurants as well as some terrific museums and concert halls. This is also where you will find grandiose architectural gestures, like the **Arc de Triomphe** and the **place de la Concorde,** which book-end the Champs, and the **Grand Palais** and **Petit Palais,** leftovers from the legendary 1900 Universal Exposition.

Arc de Triomphe ★★★ MONUMENT   If there is one monument that symbolizes "La Gloire," or the glory of France, it is this giant triumphal arch. Crowning the Champs-Elysées, this mighty archway both celebrates the military victories of the French army and memorializes the sacrifices of its soldiers. Over time, it has become an icon of the Republic and a setting for some if its most emotional moments: the laying in state

Champs-Elysées at night, leading to the Arc de Triomphe

Arc de Triomphe

of the coffin of Victor Hugo in 1885, the burial in 1921 of the ashes of an unknown soldier who fought in World War I, and General de Gaulle's pregnant pause under the arch before striding down the Champs-Elysées to the cheering crowds after the Liberation in 1944.

It took a certain amount of chutzpah to come up with the idea to build such a shrine, and sure enough, it was Napoléon who instigated it. In 1806, still glowing after his stunning victory at Austerlitz, the Emperor decided to erect a monument to the Imperial Army along the lines of a Roman triumphal arch. Unfortunately, the Empire came to an end before the arch was finished, and construction dragged on until 1836 when it was completed by Louis-Philippe.

The arch is covered with bas-reliefs and sculptures, the most famous of which is the enormous *Depart of the Volunteers* of 1792, better known as the Marseillaise, by François Rude. Just above is one of the many smaller panels detailing Napoleonic battles—in this case, Aboukir— wherein the Emperor trods victoriously over the Ottomans. At the base of the arch is the Tomb of the Unknown Soldier, over which a flame is relit every evening. The inscription reads ici repose un soldat français mort pour la patrie, 1914–1918 ("Here lies a French soldier who died for his country").

Don't try crossing the vast traffic circle to get to the arch; take the underpass near the Métro entrances. The panorama from the rooftop terrace is quite impressive; you will see the 12 boulevards that radiate from the star-shaped intersection (hence the moniker "Etoile"), most of which are named after Napoleonic battles. Out front is the long sweep of the Champs-Elysées, ending at place de la Concorde, behind which lurks the pyramid of the Louvre. In the other direction you will get a good gander at the modern Grande Arche de la Défense, a huge, hollow cubelike building that could fit Notre-Dame under its arch.

pl. Charles de Gaulle–Etoile, 8th arrond. www.paris-arc-de-triomphe.fr. ℭ **01-55-37-73-77.** Admission 12€ adults; 9€ ages 18–24; free for children 17 and under. Apr–Sept daily 10am–11pm; Oct–Mar daily 10am–10:30pm. Métro: Charles-de-Gaulle–Etoile.

Grand Palais ★★ HISTORIC SITE/MUSEUM Built for the 1900 Universal Exhibition, this giant exhibition hall spans a total area of 72,000 sq. m (775,000 sq. ft.), with the biggest glass roof in Europe—an elegant lighting solution, since the building was constructed prior to electricity.

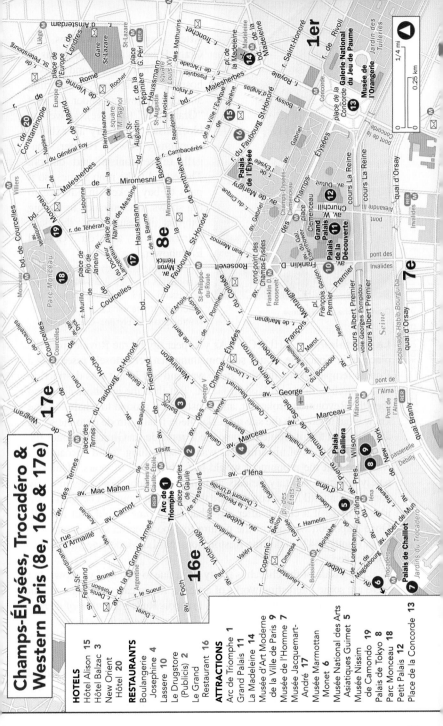

Champs-Élysées, Trocadéro & Western Paris (8e, 16e & 17e)

HOTELS

Hôtel Alison **15**
Hôtel Balzac **3**
New Orient
Hôtel **20**

RESTAURANTS

Boulangerie
Josephine **4**
Lasserre **10**
Le Drugstore
(Publicis) **2**
Le Grand
Restaurant **16**

ATTRACTIONS

Arc de Triomphe **1**
Grand Palais **11**
La Madeleine **14**
Musée d'Art Moderne
de la Ville de Paris **9**
Musée de l'Homme **7**
Musée Jacquemart-
André **17**
Musée Marmottan
Monet **6**
Musée National des Arts
Asiatiques Guimet **5**
Musée Nissim
de Camondo **19**
Palais de Tokyo **8**
Parc Monceau **18**
Petit Palais **12**
Place de la Concorde **13**

Grande Arche de la Défense

After years of renovations, the Grand Palais is now as gorgeous as it was when it opened, and today it hosts a changing array of sporting and cultural events under the vast "Grand Nef" (or nave), as well as blockbuster temporary art exhibits (previously Edward Hopper, Chagall, Impressionists, and others). These tend to be mob scenes, so it pays to buy tickets in advance to big shows. The entrance to the big exhibits is usually at the side entrance, 3 av. du Général Eisenhower.

pl. Clemenceau, 8th arrond. www. grandpalais.fr. ⓒ **01-44-13-17-17.** Admission and opening hours vary according to the exhibitions and events. Métro: Champs-Elysées–Clémenceau.

La Madeleine ★ CHURCH   As you peer up the rue Royale from the place de la Concorde, you'll see something that very closely resembles a Roman temple. When the first stone was laid in 1763, it was destined to be a church with a neoclassical facade. But then the architect died, and then the Revolution broke out, and construction ground to a halt. No one knew what to do with the site until Napoléon finally strode onto the scene and declared that it would become the Temple de La Gloire, to honor the glorious victories of his army. He wanted something "solid" because he was sure that the monument would last "thousands of years." Unfortunately for him, military defeats and mounting debt would again delay construction until Napoléon decided that maybe it wouldn't be such a bad idea to make it a church after all—that way Rome would foot the bill. Once Napoléon was out of the picture for good, inertia sunk in again. It wasn't until 1842, under the Restoration, that La Madeleine was finally consecrated.

The inside of the church is pretty dark, due to a lack of windows, but there are some interesting works of art here, if you can make them out in the gloom. On the left as you enter is François Rude's *Baptism of Christ;* farther on is James Pradier's sculpture *La Marriage de la Vierge.*

pl. de la Madeleine, 8th arrond. www.eglise-lamadeleine.com. ⓒ **01-44-51-69-00.** Free admission. Daily 9:30am–7pm. Métro: Madeleine.

Musée d'Art Moderne de la Ville de Paris ★ MUSEUM   Housed in a wing of the massive Palais de Tokyo, this municipal modern-art museum covers ground similar to that of the Pompidou Center but on a smaller scale. Though several big names are represented (Picasso, Rouault, and Picaba, to name a few), in general these are not their best-known works; highlights include a room dedicated to surrealism (the personal collection of André Breton) and a series of paintings by Delaunay and Léger. The contemporary section, from 1960 on, covers seriously abstract movements like Fluxus and Figuration. In recent years, the collection has acquired several new works from the 1980s on, but for the most recent cutting-edge ideas, you are probably better off at the Palais de Tokyo museum (see below) in the wing next door. There's also a huge room covered with brilliant wall murals by Raoul Dufy (*La Fée Electricité*), as well as another vast room with two enormous versions of *La Danse* by Matisse.

11 av. du Président-Wilson, 16th arrond. www.mam.paris.fr. © **01-53-67-40-00.** Free admission to permanent collections. Tues–Sun 10am–6pm (Thurs during exhibitions until 10pm). Métro: Iéna or Alma-Marceau.

Musée de l'Homme ★★ MUSEUM   The primitive art housed in this museum once inspired Picasso. Today, it is a state-of-the-art anthropology museum showcasing the richness of human culture and the evolution of mankind. In true existential Sartre fashion, this is where you come to reflect on the hard questions: What does it mean to be human? Where do we come from? And where are we headed—especially in the light of climatic change? The answer is there's no one answer, but it's great thinking about it as you work your way around the exhibits—everything from a Cro-Magnon skull to André Pierre Pinson's anatomical waxworks (fabulous, intricate examples of anatomy from the French Enlightenment and a gallery of 19th-c. busts designed to illustrate the diversity of human beings). The building itself is a showpiece. Set in the Passy wing of the Palais de Chaillot—built for the 1937 World Fair on the site of the former 1878 Trocadéro Palace—it is an Art Deco treasure filled with natural light, thanks to rows of floor-to-ceiling windows that look out onto the most famous icon of all, the Eiffel Tower. For the best views, head to **Café Lucy,** an ultra-modern cafeteria on the 2nd floor.

17 pl. du Trocadéro, 16th arrond. www.museedelhomme.fr. © **01-44-05-72-72.** Admission 10€ adults; 7€ students and children 13–25; free for children 12 and under. Wed–Mon 10am–6pm. Métro: Trocadéro.

Musée Jacquemart-André ★★★ MUSEUM   The love-child of a couple of passionate art collectors, this terrific museum takes the form of a 19th-century mansion filled with fine art and decorative objects. Not only is the collection superb, but it is also of a blissfully reasonable size—you can see a wide range of beautiful things here without wearing yourself to a frazzle.

Nélie Jacquemart and Edouard André devoted their lives to filling this splendid dwelling with primarily 18th-century French art and furniture. The paintings of Fragonard, Boucher, and Chardin are in evidence, as is an impressive assortment of Louis XV– and Louis XVI–era decorative objects. The many superb portraits include *Comte Français de Nantes* by David. The couple also amassed a number of 17th-century Dutch paintings, including a jaunty *Portrait of a Man* by Frans Hals, and Rembrandt's evocative *Pilgrims at Emmaus.*

The peripatetic couple, who traveled frequently in search of new items for their collection, also took an interest in Renaissance Italian art; though at the time considered "primitive" by most art fans, that didn't stop them from snapping up Quattrocento masterpieces like Botticelli's *Virgin and Child.* The Italian collection (on the second floor) is the most awe-inspiring part of the museum; not only are there works by masters like Bellini, Uccello, and Mantegna, they are presented in an intimate space with excellent lighting. You feel like you are walking into a jewel box. Enjoy a light lunch or tea in the lovely tea room.

158 bd. Haussmann, 8th arrond. www.musee-jacquemart-andre.com. ✆ **01-45-62-11-59.** Admission 13.50€ adults; 10.50€ students and children 7–17; free for children 6 and under. Daily 10am–6pm. Métro: Miromesnil or St-Philippe-du-Roule.

Musée Marmottan Monet ★★ MUSEUM   Boasting the world's largest collection of Monets, this museum offers an in-depth look at this prolific genius and some of his talented contemporaries. Among the dozens of Monet canvases is the one that provided the name of an entire artistic movement. Pressed to give a name to this misty play of light on the water for the catalog for an 1874 exposition that included Cézanne, Pissarro, Renoir, and Degas, Monet apparently said, "put 'impression.'" The painting, *Impression, Sunrise,* certainly made one, as did the show—thereafter the group was referred to as the Impressionists. Monet never stopped being fascinated with the interaction of light and water, be it in a relatively traditional portrait of his wife and daughter against the stormy sea in *On the Beach at Trouville,* or in an almost abstract blend of blues and grays in *Charing Cross Bridge.* Monet often painted the same subject at different times of the day, as in his famous series on the Cathedral of Rouen, one of which is here: *Effect of the Sun at the End of the Day.* Fans of the artist's endless water lily series will not be disappointed; the collection includes dozens of paintings of his beloved garden in Giverny.

Paintings by Renoir, Sisley, Degas, Gauguin, and other contemporaries can be seen in the light-filled rooms on the upper floor, as well as works by one of the only female members of the group, Berthe Morisot, who gets an entire room devoted to her intimate portraits and interiors.

2 rue Louis-Boilly, 16th arrond. www.marmottan.com. ✆ **01-44-96-50-33.** Admission 11€ adults; 7.50€ ages 8–24; free for children 7 and under. Tues–Wed and Fri–Sun 10am–6pm; Thurs 10am–9pm. Métro: La Muette. RER: Bouilainvilliers.

Musée National des Arts Asiatiques Guimet ★★ MUSEUM Founded in 1889 by collector and industrialist Emile Guimet, today this vast collection of Asian art is one of the largest and most complete in

Europe. Here you'll find room after room of exquisite works from Afghanistan, India, Tibet, Nepal, China, Vietnam, Korea, Japan, and other Asian nations. You could spend an entire day here, or you could pick and choose regions of interest (displays are arranged geographically); the free audio guide is a good bet for finding standouts and providing cultural context. Highlights include a Tibetan bronze sculpture (*Hevajra and Nairâtmya*) of a multiheaded god embracing a ferocious goddess with eight faces and 16 arms; a blissfully serene stone figure of a 12th-century Cambodian king (*Jayavarman VII*) and superb Chinese scroll paintings, including a magnificent 17th-century view of the Jingting mountains in autumn. A few minutes' walk from the museum is the **Panthéon Bouddhique,** also known as the Hôtel d'Heidelbach, 19 av. d'Iéna (⌀ **01-40-73-88-00;** free admission; Wed–Mon 10am–5:30pm), an old mansion and tea ceremony venue where Guimet's collection of Buddhist art from Japan is on display.

6 pl. d'Iéna, 16th arrond. www.guimet.fr. ⌀ **01-56-52-53-00.** Admission to permanent collection 11.50€ adults; 8.50€ ages 18–25; free for children 17 and under. Wed–Mon 10am–6pm. Métro: Iéna.

Musée Nissim de Camondo ★★ MUSEUM   In 1914 Count Moïse de Camondo built a mansion in the style of the Petit Trianon at Versailles and furnished it with rare examples of 18th-century furniture, paintings, and art objects. After the count's death in 1935, the house and everything in it was left to the state as a museum. This little-visited museum is a delight—the count's will stipulated that the house be left exactly "as is" when it was transformed into a museum, as a result you can wander through salons filled with gilded mirrors, inlaid tables, and Beauvais tapestries; a fully equipped kitchen; and a gigantic tiled bathroom—all in the same configuration as when Camondo and his family lived there. A special room displays the Buffon service, a remarkable set of Sèvres china decorated with a myriad of bird species, reproductions of drawings by the renowned naturalist, the Count of Buffon. Be sure to pick up a free English audio guide. The museum's latest addition is a hip restaurant/bar, **Le Camondo** (http://lecamondo.fr/), set in the mansion's former garage with tables that spill out onto an umbrella-shaded courtyard. It's a wonderful spot for lunch or dinner on a warm day.

63 rue de Monceau, 8th arrond. http://madparis.fr. ⌀ **01-53-89-06-40.** Admission 9€ adults; 6.50€ ages 18–25; free for children 17 and under. Wed–Sun 10am–5:30pm. Métro: Villiers.

Palais de Tokyo ★★ MUSEUM/PERFORMANCE SPACE   If you're traveling with cranky teenagers who've had enough of La Vieille France, or if you're also sick of endless rendezvous with history, this is the place to come for a blast of contemporary madness. This vast art space not only offers a rotating bundle of expositions, events, and other happenings, but it's also one of the only museums in Paris that stays open until midnight.

While some might quibble over whether or not the works on display are really art, there's no denying that this place is a lot more fun than its stodgy neighbor across the terrace (the Musée d'Art Moderne de la Ville de Paris, p. 100). Without a permanent collection, the Palais de Tokyo hosts continuous temporary exhibits, installations, and events, which include live performances and film screenings. The center is now one of the largest sites devoted to contemporary creativity in Europe. It's also somewhat of a food destination thanks to three hip restaurants, **Monsieur Bleu, Les Grandes Verres,** and **Le Readymade.**

13 av. du Président-Wilson, 16th arrond. www.palaisdetokyo.com. ℂ **01-81-97-35-88.** Admission 12€ adults; 9€ ages 18–25; free for children 17 and under. Wed–Mon noon–midnight. Métro: Iéna.

Parc Monceau ★★ PARK/GARDENS   Marcel Proust used to laze under the trees in this beautiful park, and who could blame him? The lush lawns and leafy trees of this verdant haven would brighten the spirits of even the melancholiest writer. Located in a posh residential neighborhood and ringed by stately mansions, this small park, commissioned by the duke of Chartres in 1769, is filled with *folies,* faux romantic ruins, temples, and antiquities inspired by exotic faraway places. Don't be surprised to stumble upon a minaret, a windmill, or a mini-Egyptian pyramid here. The most famous *folie* is the **Naumachie,** a large oval pond surrounded in part by Corinthian columns. You'll find a sizeable **playground** in the southwest corner, as well as a **merry-go-round** near the north entrance.

35 bd. de Courcelles, 8th arrond. Free admission. 8am–sundown. Métro: Monceau or Villiers.

Petit Palais ★★ MUSEUM   The collection may not be exhaustive, and you may not see any world-famous works, but you will enjoy a wonderful mix of periods and artists at this small-ish municipal fine arts museum, whose chronology stretches from the ancient Greeks to World War I. The paintings of masters like Monet, Ingres, and Rubens are displayed here, as well as the Art Nouveau dining room of Hector Guimard, and the exquisite multilayered glass vases of Emile Gallé. Those interested in earlier works will find Greek vases, Italian Renaissance majolica, and a small collection of 16th-century astrolabes and gold-and-crystal traveling clocks. Intricately carved ivory panels and delicately sculpted wood sculptures stand out in the small Medieval section, and a series of rooms dedicated to 17th-century Dutch painters like Steen and Van Ostade is considered one of the best collections of its kind in France (after the Louvre). Refresh yourself after your visit at the cafe in the gorgeous inner courtyard.

av. Winston Churchill, 8th arrond. www.petitpalais.paris.fr. ℂ **01-53-43-40-00.** Free admission to permanent collection. Tues–Sun 10am–6pm (Fri until 9pm). Métro: Champs-Elysées Clémenceau.

Place de la Concorde ★★★ PLAZA   Like an exclamation point at the end of the Champs-Elysées, the place de la Concorde is a magnificent arrangement of fountains and statues, with a 3,000-year-old Egyptian obelisk (a gift to France from Egypt in 1829) at its center. Looking at it today, it is hard to believe that this magnificent square was once bathed in blood, but during the Revolution, it was a grisly stage for public executions. King Louis XVI and his wife, Marie-Antoinette, both bowed down to the guillotine here, as did many prominent figures of the Revolution, including Danton, Camille Desmoulins, and Robespierre. Once the monarchy was back in place, the plaza hosted less lethal public events like festivals and trade expositions.

In 1835 the *place* was given its current look: Two immense fountains, copies of those in St. Peter's Square in Rome, play on either side of the obelisk; 18 sumptuous columns decorated with shells, mermaids, and sea creatures each hold two lamps; and eight statues representing the country's largest cities survey the scene from the edges of the action. On the west side are the famous **Marly Horses,** actually copies of the originals, which were suffering from erosion and have since been restored and housed in the Louvre. On the north side of the square are two palatial buildings that date from the 18th century: On the east side is the **Hôtel de la Marine,** and on the west side is the **Hôtel Crillon,** where in 1778, a treaty was signed by Louis XVI and Benjamin Franklin, wherein France officially recognized the United States as an independent country and became its ally.

Note: Cars tend to hurtle around the obelisk like racers in the Grand Prix; if you feel compelled to cross to the obelisk and you value your life, find the stoplight and cross there.

8th arrond. Métro: Concorde.

MONTMARTRE (18TH ARRONDISSEMENT)

Few places in this city fill you with the urge to belt out sappy show tunes like the *butte* (hill) of Montmartre. Admiring the view from the esplanade in front of the oddly Byzantine **Basilique du Sacré-Coeur,** you'll feel as if you've finally arrived in Paris, and that you now understand what all the fuss is about. Ignore the tour buses and crowds mobbing the church and the hideously touristy **place du Tertre** behind you and wander off into the warren of streets towards the **place des Abbesses** ★ or up **rue Lepic,** where you'll eventually stumble across the **Moulin de la Galette** and **Moulin du Radet,** the two surviving windmills of the 30 that were once on this hill.

Basilique du Sacré-Coeur ★★ CHURCH   Poised at the apex of the hill like a *grande dame* in crinolines, this odd-looking 19th-century basilica has become one of the city's most famous landmarks. After France's defeat in the Franco-Prussian War, prominent Catholics vowed to build a church consecrated to the Sacred Heart of Christ as a way of making up for whatever sins the French may have committed that had made God so angry at them. Since 1885, prayers for humanity have been continually chanted here (the church is a pilgrimage site, so dress and behave accordingly). Inspired by the Byzantine churches of Turkey and Italy, this multi-domed confection was begun in 1875 and completed in 1914, though it wasn't consecrated until 1919 because of World War I. The white stone was chosen for its self-cleaning capabilities: When it rains, it secretes a chalky substance that acts as a fresh coat of paint. Most visitors climb the 300 stairs to the **dome,** where the splendid city views extend over 48km (30 miles).

35 rue Chevalier de la Barre, 18th arrond. www.sacre-coeur-montmartre.com. © **01-53-41-89-00.** Free admission to basilica; joint ticket to dome and crypt 9€ adults, 5.50€ ages 4–16, free for children 3 and under. Basilica daily 6am–10:30pm; dome and crypt May–Sept daily 9:30am–8pm and Oct–Apr 9:30am–5pm. Métro: Abbesses; take elevator to surface and follow signs to funicular.

Musée de Montmartre ★★ MUSEUM   The main reason to visit this small museum is to get an inkling of what Montmartre really was like back in the days when Picasso, Toulouse-Lautrec, Van Gogh, and so on were painting and cavorting up here on the *butte*. While there are few examples of the artists' works here, plenty of photos, posters, and even films document the neighborhood's famous history, from the days when its importance was mainly religious, to the gory days of the Paris Commune, and finally to the artistic boom in the 19th and 20th centuries. Next to an original poster of Jane Avril by Toulouse-Lautrec, for example,

Sacré-Coeur at sunrise

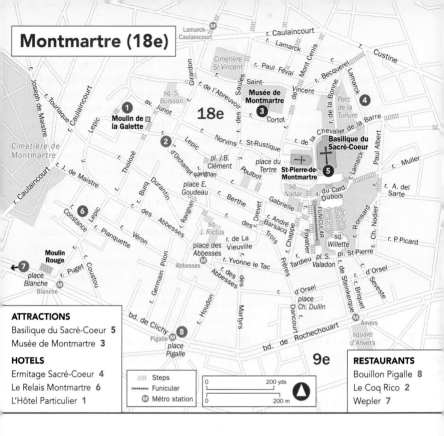

Montmartre (18e)

ATTRACTIONS
Basilique du Sacré-Coeur **5**
Musée de Montmartre **3**

HOTELS
Ermitage Sacré-Coeur **4**
Le Relais Montmartre **6**
L'Hôtel Particulier **1**

Steps
Funicular
Métro station

0   200 yds
0   200 m

RESTAURANTS
Bouillon Pigalle **8**
Le Coq Rico **2**
Wepler **7**

you'll see a photo of the real Jane Avril, as well as other Montmartre cabaret legends like Aristide Bruant and La Goulue. The 17th century house
that shelters the museum was at various times the studio and home of
Auguste Renoir, Raoul Dufy, Susan Valadon, and Maurice Utrillo. Surrounded by gardens and greenery it offers a lovely view of the last scrap
of the Montmartre vineyard. There's a great cafe too, **Café Renoir,** set in
a winter garden with a terrace that sprawls out towards lawns.

12 rue Cortot, 18th arrond. www.museedemontmartre.fr. ☏ **01-49-25-89-37.** Admission 9.50€ adults; 7.50€ ages 18–25; 5€ ages 10–17; free for children 9 and under.
Oct–Mar daily 10am–6pm; April–Sept 10am–7pm. Métro: Lamarck-Caulaincourt.

RÉPUBLIQUE, BASTILLE & EASTERN PARIS (11TH & 12TH ARRONDISSEMENTS)

While you can't really point to any major tourist attractions in this area,
this is a nice part of town for eating (thanks to a plethora of neo-bistros),
and aimless wandering, especially if you are a) in search of youth-
oriented nightlife, b) in search of youth-oriented clothing shops, or c) a
history buff. The French Revolution was brewed in the workshops of the
Faubourg St-Antoine and ignited at the **place de la Bastille.**

Parc Zoologique de Paris ★★ ZOO   This lush, ecologically correct animal reserve invites visitors to five regions of the world, from the plains of Sudan to Europe, via Guyana, Patagonia, and Madagascar. Going for quality instead of quantity, the zoo may not have room for elephants and bears, but it does introduce visitors to animals they might not be familiar with, like the fossa, a catlike carnivore from Madagascar, or the capybara, a giant South American rodent. There is also a good sampling of zoo favorites like lions, baboons, penguins, and a troupe of giraffes—if you are lucky you can get an up-close look while the latter lunch in the giraffe house. The enclosures are well adapted to their inhabitants, so much so that at times it's hard to see them. But if you are patient you'll spy wolves peeking out of the foliage, or a bright red tomato frog gripping a vine. There are more than 1,000 animals in all, yet the zoo is human-sized—you can see the whole thing in a couple of hours. Don't miss the huge aviaries, one of which is home to a large flock of flamingos.

Parc de Vincennes, 12th arrond. www.parczoologiquedeparis.fr. © **01-44-75-20-10.** Admission 20€ adults; 17€ students 12–25; 15€ children ages 3–11; free for children 2 and under. Mid-Oct to mid-Mar Wed–Mon 10am–5pm; mid-Mar to mid-Oct Mon–Fri 10am–6pm, Sat–Sun and school holidays 9:30am–7:30pm.

Place de la Bastille ★   The most notable thing about this giant plaza is the building that's no longer here: the Bastille prison. Now an enormous traffic circle where cars careen around at warp speed, this was once the site of an ancient stone fortress that became a symbol for all that was wrong with the French monarchy. Over the centuries, kings and queens condemned rebellious citizens to stay inside these cold walls, sometimes with good reason, other times on a mere whim. By the time the Revolution started to boil, though, the prison was barely in use; when the angry mobs stormed its walls on July 14, 1789, there were only seven prisoners to set free. Still, the destruction of the Bastille came to be seen as the ultimate revolutionary moment; July 14 is still celebrated as the birth of the Republic. Surprisingly, the giant bronze column in the center honors the victims of a different revolution, that of 1830.

12th arrond. Métro: Bastille.

La Promenade Plantée ★★ WALKING TRAIL   Transformed from an unused train viaduct, this beautiful aerial garden walkway runs from the place de la Bastille to the Bois de Vincennes. The 4.5km (2.8-mile) pedestrian path runs along flower gardens, tree bowers, rose trellises, and fountains and takes you over the 12th arrondissement, past the Gare de Lyon, and through the Reuilly Gardens. At ground level along av. Daumesnil, the brick archways now shelter the **Viaduct des Arts,** a series of galleries and workshops that show off the work of highly skilled artisans.

Enter by the staircase on av. Daumesnil just past the Opéra Bastille, 12th arrond.

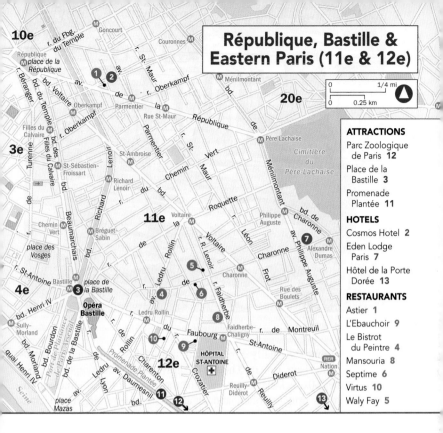

República, Bastille &
Eastern Paris (11e & 12e)

ATTRACTIONS

Parc Zoologique
de Paris **12**

Place de la
Bastille **3**

Promenade
Plantée **11**

HOTELS

Cosmos Hotel **2**

Eden Lodge
Paris **7**

Hôtel de la Porte
Dorée **13**

RESTAURANTS

Astier **1**

L'Ebauchoir **9**

Le Bistrot
du Peintre **4**

Mansouria **8**

Septime **6**

Virtus **10**

Waly Fay **5**

BELLEVILLE, CANAL ST-MARTIN & LA VILLETTE (10TH, 19TH & 20TH ARRONDISSEMENTS)

One of the most picturesque attractions in this area is the **Canal St-Martin** itself, which crosses a formerly working-class neighborhood that is now inhabited by an arty mix of regular folk and *bobos* (bourgeois bohemians). The Belleville neighborhood is home to one of the city's bustling **Chinatowns,** as well as many artists' studios.

Cimetière du Père-Lachaise ★★★ CEMETERY   It's hard to believe that a cemetery could be a top tourist attraction, but this is no ordinary cemetery. This hillside resting place is wonderfully green and romantic, with huge leafy trees and narrow paths winding around the graves, which include just about every French literary or artistic giant you can imagine, plus several international stars. Proust, Moliére, La Fontaine, Colette, Delacroix, Seurat, Modigliani, Bizet, Rossini are all here, as well as Sarah Bernhardt, Isadora Duncan, Simone Signoret, and Yves Montand (buried side-by-side, of course), not to mention Oscar Wilde, whose huge

Père-Lachaise Cemetery

stone monument is usually covered with lipstick kisses. Even the Lizard King, Jim Morrison, is here. Though the grave itself is unexceptional, the tomb of the '60s rock star is possibly the most visited in the cemetery. In 1971, battling drug, alcohol, and legal problems, the singer/musician came to Paris; 4 months later, he was found dead in a Parisian bathtub, at age 27.

A map is essential. You can find one at the newsstand across from the main entrance, on the website, or at the visitor's booth.

16 rue de Repos, 20th arrond. www.pere-lachaise.com. Free admission. Mon–Fri 8am–6pm; Sat–Sun 8:30am–6pm (Nov to early Mar until 5pm). Métro: Père-Lachaise or Philippe Auguste.

Cité des Sciences et de l'Industrie ★★ MUSEUM   This gigantic science-and-industry museum began life as an immense slaughterhouse. During construction in the 1960s, it was touted as the most modern of its kind. It turned out to be the center of a corruption scandal and was quickly abandoned when the city's abattoirs were transferred elsewhere. After years of head-scratching, the building was finally turned into this terrific museum, which includes a planetarium, a 3-D movie theater, and a multimedia library, not to mention a real live submarine. The heart of the museum is Explora, two huge floors of interactive exhibits and displays, as well as excellent temporary exhibits. On the ground floor, parents will be delighted to find the Cité des Enfants (separate admission: 12€ adults, 9€ under 25 for 1 hr., 30 min.; see website for hours; reservations essential, particularly during French school vacations), which has separate

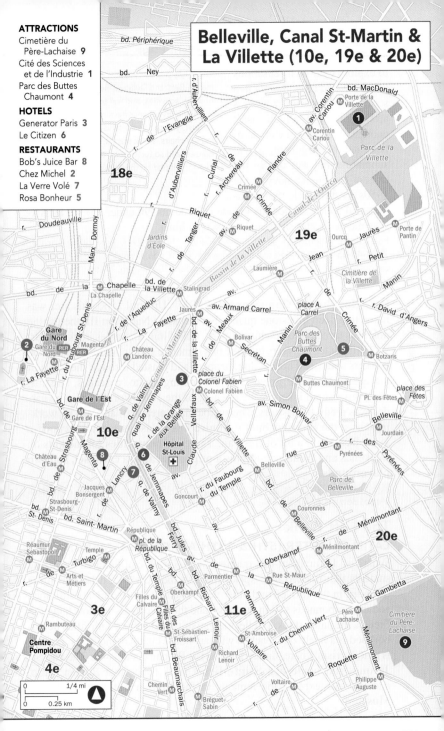

Belleville, Canal St-Martin & La Villette (10e, 19e & 20e)

programs for 2- to 7-year-olds and 7- to 12-year-olds. Kids get to explore their own sensations and the world around them in a series of hands-on activities and displays. If all this isn't enough, outside you can clamber into the Argonaut, a real submarine that was one of the stars of the French navy in the 1950s, or dip inside the gigantic metal sphere, called the Geode (12€ adults, 9€ under 25), an IMAX-type movie theater showing large screen films.

> **Paris Plage**
>
> The wildly popular initiative of Paris's former mayor, Bertrand Delanoë, has brought tons of sand, activities, and fun to the banks of the Seine. Every year from mid-July to mid-August, you can find a sandy beach with lounge chairs, snack stands, concerts, dances, and so forth along the edge of the Right Bank and on the Bassin de la Villette.

Parc de La Villette, 30 av. Corentine-Cariou, 19th arrond. www.cite-sciences.fr. ℂ **01-40-05-70-00.** Varied ticket packages 12€–24€ adults; 6€–15€ under 25; free for children 2 and under. Tues–Sat 10am–6pm; Sun 10am–7pm. Métro: Porte de La Villette.

Parc des Buttes Chaumont ★ PARK   Up until 1860, this area was home to a deep limestone quarry, but thanks to Napoléon III, the gaping hole was turned into an unusual park, full of hills and dales, rocky bluffs, and cliffs. It took 3 years to make this romantic garden; more than a 1,000 workers and a 100 horses dug, heaped, and blasted through the walls of the quarry to create green lawns, a cooling grotto, cascades, streams, and even a small lake. By the opening of the 1867 World's Fair, the garden was ready for visitors. The surrounding area was, and still is, working-class; the Emperor built it to give this industrious neighborhood a green haven and a bit of fresh air. There are **pony rides** for the kids on weekends and Wednesdays, plus a **puppet theater,** a **carousel,** and **two playgrounds.**

Rue Botzaris, 19th arrond. May 1–Sept 30 7am–11pm; Oct 1–Apr 30 7am–8pm. Métro: Botzaris or Buttes Chaumont.

The Left Bank

LATIN QUARTER (5TH & 13TH ARRONDISSEMENTS)

What's so Latin about this quarter? Well, for several hundred years, the students that flocked here spoke Latin in their classes at the **Sorbonne** (founded in the 13th c.) and other nearby schools. The students still flock and the Sorbonne is still in business, and though classes are now taught in French, the name stuck. Intellectual pursuits aside, this youth-filled neighborhood is a lively one, packed with art-house cinemas and cafes. History is readily visible here, dating back to the Roman occupation: The **rue St-Jacques** and **boulevard Saint-Michel** mark the former Roman cardo, and you can explore the remains of the **Roman baths** at the **Cluny Museum.**

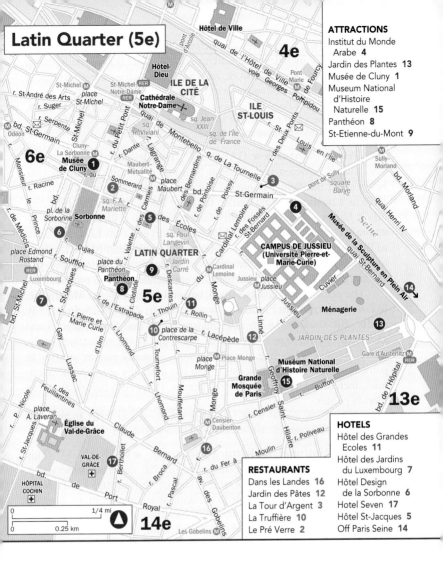

Latin Quarter (5e)

Institut du Monde Arabe ★★ MUSEUM In an age when Arab culture is all over the headlines, this is a good place to come to find out what the phrase actually means. The building, designed by architect Jean Nouvel 1987, is worth the price of admission. The south facade, which has a metallic latticework echoing traditional Arab designs, includes 30,000 light-sensitive diaphragms that regulate the penetration of light by opening and closing according to how bright it is outside. After a major overhaul, this museum, which used to be devoted solely to Islamic art, has now expanded its mission to include the many facets of the Arab world, specifically the 22 countries that helped create this institution in 1987. The collection includes beautiful examples of traditional calligraphy, miniatures, ceramics, woodwork, and carpets, as well as scientific objects, textiles, and illuminated manuscripts.

1 rue des Fossés St-Bernard, 5th arrond. www.imarabe.org. ✆ **01-40-51-38-38.** Admission to permanent collections 8€; 4€ 25 and under. Tues–Fri 10am–6pm, Sat–Sun 10am–7pm. Métro: Jussieu, Cardinal Lemoine, Sully-Morland.

Jardin des Plantes ★★ GARDENS   This delightful botanical garden, tucked between the Muséum National d'Histoire Naturelle (see below) and the Seine, is one of my favorite picnic spots. Created in 1626 as a medicinal plant garden for King Louis XIII, in the 18th century it became an internationally famed scientific institution thanks to naturalist, mathematician, and biologist Georges-Louis Leclerc, Count of Buffon, with the help of fellow-naturalist Louis-Jean-Marie Daubenton. Today the museums are still part academic institutions, but you certainly don't need to be a student to appreciate the lush grounds.

The garden also harbors a small, but well-kept zoo, the **Ménagerie, le Zoo du Jardin des Plantes** ★ (www.mnhn.fr; ✆ **01-40-79-56-01;** 13€ adults, 10€ students 18–26 and children 4–16, free for children 3 and under; daily 9am–6pm). Created in 1794, this is the oldest zoo in the world. Because of its size, the zoo showcases mostly smaller species, in particular birds and reptiles, but it also has a healthy selection of mammals, including rare species like red pandas, Przewalski horses, and even Florida pumas.

Rue Geoffroy-St-Hilaire, 5th arrond. www.jardindesplantes.net. ✆ **01-40-79-56-01.** Free admission to gardens. 8am–dusk. Métro: Gare d'Austerlitz.

Muséum National d'Histoire Naturelle ★★ MUSEUM   This natural-history museum was established in 1793 under the supervision of two celebrated naturalists, the Count of Buffon and Louis Jean-Marie Daubenton. This temple to the natural sciences contains a series of separate museums, each with a different specialty. The biggest draw is no doubt the **Grande Galerie de l'Evolution,** where a sort of Noah's ark of animals snakes its way around a huge hall filled with displays that trace the evolution of life and man's relationship to nature. Another interesting hall, the **Galerie de Minérologie et de Geologies,** includes a room full of giant crystals. For dinosaurs, saber-toothed tigers, ancient humans, and thousands of fossilized skeletons, repair to the **Galeries de Paléontologie et d'Anatomie Comparée.** A recent **Galerie des Enfants** has hands-on interactive displays for the little tykes.

36 rue Geoffrey, 5th arrond. www.mnhn.fr. ✆ **01-40-79-54-79.** Admission to each gallery 9€–12€ adults; 6€–9€ students, seniors 60 and older, and children ages 4–13. Wed–Mon 10am–6pm. Métro: Jussieu or Gare d'Austerlitz.

Musée National du Moyen Age/Thermes de Cluny (Musée de Cluny) ★★ MUSEUM   Ancient Roman baths and a 15th-century mansion set the stage for a terrific collection of Medieval art and objects at this museum. Built somewhere between the 1st and 3rd centuries, the baths (visible from bd. St-Michel) are some of the best existing examples of Gallo-Roman architecture. They are attached to what was once the palatial home of a 15th-century abbot, whose last owner, a certain Alexandre du Sommerard, amassed a vast array of Medieval masterworks. When he died in 1842, his home was turned into a museum and his collection put on display. Sculptures, textiles, furniture, and ceramics are on display, as well as gold, ivory, and enamel work. Of the several magnificent tapestries the biggest draw is the late-15th-century *Lady and the Unicorn* series, one of only two sets of complete unicorn tapestries in the world (the other is in New York City).

Among the many sculptures displayed are the famous severed heads from the facade of Notre-Dame. Knocked off their bodies during the furor of the Revolution, 21 of the heads of the Kings of Judah were found by chance in 1977 during repair work in the basement of a bank. Other treasures include Flemish retables, Visigoth crowns, bejeweled chalices, wood carvings, stained-glass windows, and beautiful objects from daily life, like hair combs and game boards.

6 pl. Paul Painlevé, 5th arrond. www.musee-moyenage.fr. ✆ **01-53-73-78-00.** Admission 8€ adults; 6€ ages 18–26; free for children 17 and under. Wed–Mon 9:15am–5:45pm. Métro/RER: Cluny–La Sorbonne or St-Michel.

Panthéon ★★ CHURCH/MAUSOLEUM   High atop the "montagne" (actually a medium-size hill) of St-Geneviève, the dome of the Panthéon is one of the city's most visible landmarks. This erstwhile royal church has been transformed into a national mausoleum—the final resting place of luminaries such as Voltaire, Rousseau, Hugo, and Zola, as well as Marie and Pierre Curie, and—since 2015—four World War II heroes of the Résistance. Initially dedicated to St-Geneviève, the church was commissioned by a grateful Louis XV, who attributed his recovery from a serious illness to the saint. The work of architect Jacques-Germain Soufflot, who took his inspiration from the Pantheon in Rome, it must have been magnificent—the vast interior was clearly created with a higher power in mind. However, during the Revolution its sacred mission was diverted toward a new god—the Nation—and it was converted into a memorial and burial ground for Great Men of the Republic. This meant taking down the bells, walling up most of the windows, doing away with religious statuary and replacing it with works promoting patriotic virtues. The desired effect was achieved—the enormous empty space, lined with huge paintings of great moments in French history, resembles a cavernous tomb. The star attraction in the nave is **Foucault's Pendulum** (named after the French physicist Léon Foucault, who invented it in 1851), a simple device—a heavy ball suspended on a long wire above markers—that proves the rotation of the Earth. And since major restoration work, visitors can once again climb the Panthéon's lofty dome (the highest spot in Paris until the Eiffel Tower was erected in 1889) to see the city unfurl in a hig-gledy-piggledy sprawl of gray rooftops. It's a breathtaking sight, spread-ing all the way out past the Eiffel Tower to the high-rises of Paris's out-of-town business district, La Defense.

pl. du Panthéon, 5th arrond. www.paris-pantheon.fr. ℂ **01-44-32-18-00.** Admission 9€ adults; 7€ ages 18–25; free for children 17 and under (and under 26 from EU countries). Dome 2€ extra. Apr–Sept daily 10am–6:30pm; Oct–Mar daily 10am–6pm. Dome Apr–Oct only. Métro: Cardinal Lemoine. RER: Luxembourg.

St-Etienne-du-Mont ★★ CHURCH One of the city's prettiest churches, this ecclesiastical gem is a joyous mix of late Gothic and Renaissance styles. The 17th-century facade combines Gothic tradition with a dash of classical Rome; inside, the 16th-century chancel sports a magnificent **rood screen** (an intricately carved partition separating the nave from the chancel) with decorations inspired by the Italian Renais-sance. Book-ended by twin spiraling marble staircases, this rood screen is the only one left in the city. A pilgrimage site, this church was once part of an abbey dedicated to St-Geneviève (the city's patron saint), and stones from her original sarcophagus lie in an ornate shrine here. That's about all that is left of her—the saint's bones were burned during the Revolution and their ashes thrown in the Seine. The remains of two other great minds, Racine and Pascal, are buried here.

1 pl. St-Geneviève, 5th arrond. www.saintetiennedumont.fr. ℂ **01-43-54-11-79.** Free admission. Mon 6:30am–7:30pm; Tues, Thurs, Fri 8:45am–7:45pm; Wed 8:45am–10pm; Sat–Sun 8:45am–noon and 2:30pm–7:45pm. Métro: Cardinal Lemoine or Luxembourg.

ST-GERMAIN-DES-PRÉS & LUXEMBOURG (6TH ARRONDISSEMENT)

In the 20th century, the St-Germain-des-Prés neighborhood became asso-ciated with writers like Jean-Paul Sartre, Simone de Beauvoir, Albert Camus, and the rest of the intellectual bohemian crowd that gathered at **Café de Flore** or **Les Deux Magots** (p. 166). But back in the 6th century, a mighty abbey founded here ruled over a big chunk of the Left Bank for 1,000 years. The French Revolution put a stop to that, and most of the original buildings were pulled down. Remains of both epochs can still be found in this chic and artsy neighborhood, notably at the 10th-century church **St-Germain-des-Prés,** and the surviving bookstores and publish-ing houses that surround it.

Jardin du Luxembourg ★★★ GARDENS Rolling out like an exotic Oriental carpet before the Italianate Palais du Luxembourg, this vast expanse of fountains, flowers, lush lawns, and shaded glens is the perfect setting for a leisurely stroll, a relaxed picnic, or a serious make-out session, depending on who you're with. At the center of everything is a fountain with a huge basin, where kids can sail toy wooden sailboats (3€/30 min.) and adults can sun themselves in the green metal chairs at the

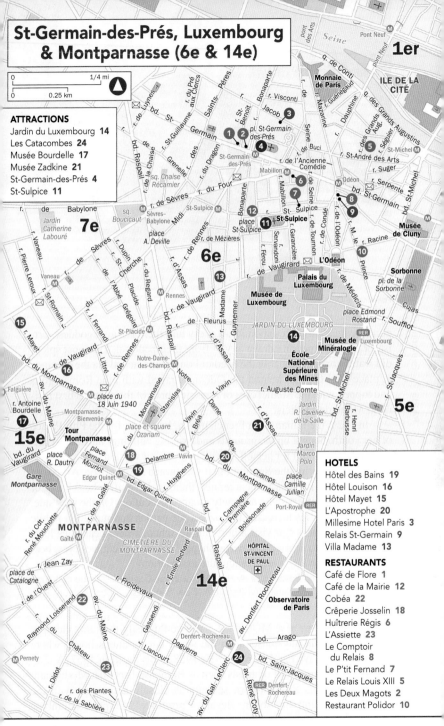

St-Germain-des-Prés, Luxembourg & Montparnasse (6e & 14e)

1er

ILE DE LA CITÉ

ATTRACTIONS
Jardin du Luxembourg **14**
Les Catacombes **24**
Musée Bourdelle **17**
Musée Zadkine **21**
St-Germain-des-Prés **4**
St-Sulpice **11**

HOTELS
Hôtel des Bains **19**
Hôtel Louison **16**
Hôtel Mayet **15**
L'Apostrophe **20**
Millesime Hotel Paris **3**
Relais St-Germain **9**
Villa Madame **13**

RESTAURANTS
Café de Flore **1**
Café de la Mairie **12**
Cobéa **22**
Crêperie Josselin **18**
Huîtrerie Régis **6**
L'Assiette **23**
Le Comptoir du Relais **8**
Le P'tit Fernand **7**
Le Relais Louis XIII **5**
Les Deux Magots **2**
Restaurant Polidor **10**

Fontaine de Observatoire, Luxembourg Gardens

pond's edge. Sculptures abound: At every turn there is a god, goddess, artist, or monarch peering down at you from their pedestal. The most splendid waterworks is probably the Medici Fountain (reached via the entrance at place Paul Claudel behind the Odéon), draped with lithe Roman gods and topped with the Medici coat of arms, in honor of the palace's first resident, Marie de Medicis.

In 1621, the Italian-born French queen, homesick for the Pitti Palace of her youth, bought up the grounds and existing buildings and had a Pitti-inspired palace built for herself as well as a smaller version of the sumptuous gardens. During the Revolution, it was turned into a prison. American writer Thomas Paine was incarcerated there in 1793 after he fell out of favor with Robespierre; he narrowly escaped execution. On the plus side, the Revolutionaries increased the size of the garden and made it a public institution. Visitors can visit a horticulture school where pear trees have been trained into formal, geometric shapes, as well as beehives (yes, beehives) maintained by a local apiculture association.

Entry at pl. Edmond Rostand, pl. André Honnorat, rue Guynemer, or rue de Vaugirard, 6th arrond. www.senat.fr/visite/jardin. Daily 8am–dusk. Métro: Odéon. RER: Luxembourg.

Musée Zadkine ★★ MUSEUM   You could easily miss the alleyway that leads to this tiny museum in the small but luminous house where Ossip Zadkine lived and worked from 1928 to his death in 1967. A contemporary and neighbor of artists such as Brancusi, Lipchitz, Modigliani, and Picasso, this Russian-born sculptor is closely associated with the Cubist movement; his sober, elegant, "primitive" sculptures combine abstract geometry with deep humanity. Be sure to visit the artist's workshop, tucked behind the tranquil garden. *Note:* Due to the museum's small size, during temporary exhibits you'll have to pay to enter the permanent collection (which is usually free).

100 bis rue d'Assas, 6th arrond. www.zadkine.paris.fr. © **01-55-42-77-20.** Free admission to permanent collections; temporary exhibits: 7€ adults, 5€ visitors over 60, 3.50€ ages 14–26, free for children 13 and under. Tues–Sun 10am–6pm. Métro: Notre-Dame des Champs or Vavin.

St-Germain-des-Prés ★★ CHURCH   The origins of this church stretch back over a millennium. First established by King Childebert in 543, who constructed a basilica and monastery on the site, it was built, destroyed, and rebuilt several times over the centuries. Nothing remains of the original buildings, but the bell tower dates from the 10th century and is one of the oldest in France. The church and its abbey became a major center of learning and power during the Middle Ages, remaining a force to be reckoned with up until the French Revolution, when all hell broke loose: The abbey was destroyed, the famous library burned, and the church vandalized. Restored in the 19th century, the buildings have regained some of their former glory, though the complex is a fraction of its original size.

Much of the interior is painted in a range of greens and golds—one of the few Parisian churches to retain a sense of its original decor. The heart of King Jean Casimir of Poland is buried here, as are the ashes of the body of René Descartes (his skull is in the collections of the Musée de l'Homme, p. 101). On the left as you exit you can peek inside the **chapel of St-Symphorien,** where during the Revolution over 100 clergymen were imprisoned before being executed on the square in front of the church. The chapel was restored in the 1970s and decorated by contemporary artist Pierre Buraglio in 1992.

Classical music concerts are regularly held in the church on Thursday and Friday evenings. (Tickets and information are at www.fnac tickets.com.) On the last Sunday of the month, afternoon organ recitals are free.

Attention Bored Kids & Tired Parents

Frazzled parents take note: the Jardin de Luxembourg has lots of activities for kids who need to blow off steam. First off, there is the extra-large **playground** (1.20€ adults, 2.50€ children 11 and under) filled with all kinds of things to climb on and play in. Then there are the wonderful wooden **sailboats** (3€/30 min.) to float in the main fountain, as well as an ancient **carousel** (2.50€, next to the playground) and **pony rides** (3€-6€). At the **marionette theater** (6.40€ each for parents and children; Wed, Sat, Sun, and school vacation days; shows usually start after 3pm, Sat–Sun additional show at 11am), you can see Guignol himself (the French version of Punch) in a variety of French-language puppet shows.

3 pl. St-Germain-des-Prés, 6th arrond. www.eglise-sgp.org. ✆ **01-55-42-81-10.** Free admission. Daily 8am–7:45pm. Métro: St-Germain-des-Prés.

St-Sulpice ★★ CHURCH   After years of renovations, the scaffoldings have finally come off the majestic facade of this enormous edifice. Construction started in the 17th century over the remains of a medieval church; it took over a hundred years to build, and one of the towers was never finished. Inside, the cavernous interior seems to command you to be silent. Tucked into the chapels that line the church are several important works of art. The most famous of them are **three masterpieces by Eugène Delacroix,** *Jacob Wrestling with the Angel, Heliodorus Driven from the Temple,* and *St-Michael Vanquishing the Devil* (on the right just after you enter the church). Jean-Baptiste Pigalle's statue of the *Virgin and Child* lights up the Chapelle de la Vierge at the farthest most point from the entrance. A bronze line runs north–south along the floor; this is part of a **gnomon,** an astronomical device set up in the 17th century to calculate the position of the sun in the sky. A small hole in one of the stained-glass windows creates a spot of light on the floor; every day at noon it hits the line in a different spot, climbing to the top of an obelisk and lighting a gold disk at winter equinox.

pl. St-Sulpice, 6th arrond. ✆ **01-42-34-59-98.** Free admission. Daily 7:30am–7:30pm. Métro: St-Sulpice.

EIFFEL TOWER & LES INVALIDES (7TH ARRONDISSEMENT)

The Iron Lady towers above this stately neighborhood, where the very buildings seem to insist that you stand up straight and pay attention. Stuffed with embassies and ministries, you'll see lots of elegant black cars with smoked glass cruising the streets, as well as many a tourist eyeing the **Eiffel Tower** or the golden dome of **Les Invalides** and scurrying in and out of some of the city's best museums, like the **Musée du Quai Branly, Musée d'Orsay,** and **Musée Rodin.**

Eiffel Tower ★★★ MONUMENT   In his wildest dreams, Gustave Eiffel probably never imagined that the tower he built for the 1889 World's Fair would become the ultimate symbol of Paris and, for many, of France. Originally slated for demolition after its first 20 years, the Eiffel Tower has survived more than a century and is one of the most visited sites in the nation. No less than 50 engineers and designers worked on the plans, which resulted in a remarkably solid structure that despite its height (324m/1,063 ft., including the antenna) does not sway in the wind.

But while the engineers rejoiced, others howled. When the project for the tower was announced, a group of artists and writers, including Guy de Maupassant and Alexandre Dumas, published a manifesto that referred to it as an "odious column of bolted metal." Others were less diplomatic:

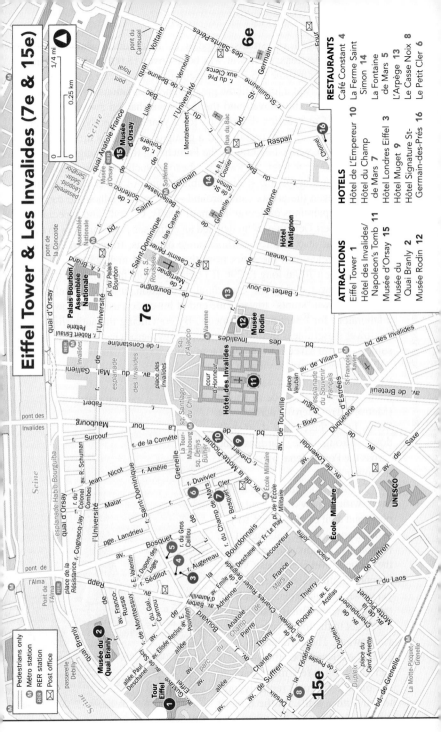

Eiffel Tower & Les Invalides (7e & 15e)

RESTAURANTS
Café Constant 4
La Ferme Saint Simon 14
La Fontaine de Mars 5
L'Arpège 13
Le Casse Noix 8
Le Petit Cler 6

HOTELS
Hôtel de L'Empereur 10
Hôtel du Champ de Mars 7
Hôtel Londres Eiffel 3
Hôtel Muget 9
Hôtel Signature St-Germain-des-Prés 16

ATTRACTIONS
Eiffel Tower 1
Hôtel des Invalides/ Napoleon's Tomb 11
Musée d'Orsay 15
Musée du Quai Branly 2
Musée Rodin 12

Pedestrians only
Ⓜ Métro station
RER RER station
⊠ Post office

0   0.25 km
0   1/4 mi

121

Novelist Joris-Karl Huysmans called it a "hole-riddled suppository." Despite the objections, the tower was built—over 18,000 pieces of iron, held together with some 2.5 million rivets. In this low-tech era, building techniques involved a lot of elbow grease: The foundations, for example, were dug entirely by shovel, and the debris was hauled away in horse-drawn carts. Construction dragged on for 2 years, but finally, on March 31, 1889, Gustave Eiffel proudly led a group of dignitaries up the 1,710 steps to the top, where he unfurled the French flag for the inauguration.

Over 100 years later, the tower has become such an integral piece of the Parisian landscape that it's impossible to think of the city without it. Over time, even the artists came around—the tower's silhouette can be found in the paintings of Seurat, Bonnard, Duffy, Chagall, and especially those of Robert Delaunay, who devoted an entire series of canvases to the subject. It has also inspired a whole range of stunts, from Pierre Labric riding a bicycle down the stairs from the first level in 1923 to Philippe Petit walking a 700m-long (2,296-ft.) tightrope from the Palais de Chaillot to the tower during the centennial celebration in 1989. Eiffel performed his own "stunts" towards the end of his career, using the tower as a laboratory for scientific experiments. By convincing the authorities of the tower's usefulness in studying meteorology, aerodynamics, and other subjects, Eiffel saved it from being torn down.

The most dramatic view of the tower itself is from the wide esplanade at the Palais de Chaillot (Métro: Trocadéro) across the Seine. From there it's a short walk down through the gardens and across the Pont d'Iena to the base of the tower.

The first floor just had a makeover, with a new restaurant, displays and a bit of glass floor, so you can pretend you are walking on air. Personally, I think the view from the second level is the best; you're far enough up to see the entire city, yet close enough to clearly pick out the monuments. But if you are aching to get to the top, an airplanelike view awaits. The third level is, mercifully, enclosed, but thrill-seekers can climb up a few more stairs to the outside balcony (entirely protected with a grill). At the time of writing the base of the tower was

Eiffel Tower

A Workout & a Bargain at the Eiffel Tower

No need to go to the gym after marching up the 704 steps that lead you to the second floor of the Eiffel Tower. Not only will you burn calories, but you'll save money: At 10€ adults, 5€ ages 12 to 24, and 2.50€ ages 4 to 11, this is the least expensive way to visit. Extra perks include an up-close view of the amazing metal structure and avoiding long lines for the elevator.

being surrounded by bulletproof glass walls as part of a plan to protect visitors from terror attacks. Don't be alarmed: It's precautionary and not the sign of an imminent danger, and you'll still be able to walk underneath for free once you've passed the security checks—though build in extra time for passing the check points. The construction of the wall marks the beginning of a 15-year modernization plan that aims to improve access to the tower in general and provide shelter for visitors in bad weather. And of course, Paris wouldn't be Paris without the tower, so the monument will remain open throughout the work.

Champ de Mars, 7th arrond. www.tour-eiffel.fr. © **01-44-11-23-23.** Lift to 2nd floor 16€ adults, 8€ ages 12–24, 4€ ages 4–11; lift to 2nd and 3rd floors 25€ adults, 12.50€ ages 12–24, 6.30€ ages 4–11; stairs to 2nd floor 10€ adults, 5€ ages 12–24, 2.50€ ages 4–11; stair to 2nd floor and lift to the top 19€ adults, 9.50€ ages 12–24, and 4.80€ ages 4–11. Free for children 3 and under. Early July to early Sept daily 9am–12:45am; early-Sept to early-July daily 9:30am–11:45pm; Sept to mid-June stairs open only to 6:30pm. Métro: Trocadéro or Bir Hakeim. RER: Champ de Mars–Tour Eiffel.

Hôtel des Invalides/Napoléon's Tomb ★★ MUSEUM This grandiose complex houses a military museum, church, tomb, hospital, and military ministries, among other things. Commissioned by Louis XIV, who was determined to create a home for soldiers wounded in the line of duty, it was built on what was then the outskirts of the city. The first war veterans arrived in 1674—between 4,000 and 5,000 soldiers would eventually move in, creating a mini-city with its own governor. An on-site hospital was constructed for the severely wounded, which is still in service today.

As you cross the main gate, you'll find yourself in a huge courtyard, the *cour d'honneur,* once the site of military parades. The surrounding buildings house military administration offices and the **Musée de l'Armée,** one of the world's largest military museums, with a vast collection of objects testifying to man's capacity for self-destruction. The most impressive section is **Arms and Armor,** a panoply of 13th- to 17th-century weaponry. Viking swords, Burgundian battle axes, 14th-century blunderbusses, Balkan *khandjars,* Browning machine guns, engraved Renaissance serpentines, musketoons, grenadiers—if it can kill, it's enshrined here. There is also a huge wing covering the exploits of everyone from **Louis XIV** to **Napoléon III,** another on the two **World Wars,** and a shrine to **Charles de Gaulle.** Also onsite is the **Musée des Plans et Reliefs,** a somewhat dusty collection of scale models of fortresses and battlefields.

The **Eglise du Dôme** is split in two, the front half being the light-filled Soldier's Church, decorated with magnificent chandeliers and a collection of flags of defeated enemies. On the other side of the glass partition the **Tomb of Napoléon** lies under one of the most splendid domes in France. Designed by Hardouin-Mansart, it took over 2 decades to build. The interior soars 107m (351 ft.) up to a skylight, which illuminates a brilliantly colored cupola. Ethereal light filters down to an opening where you can look down on the huge porphyry sarcophagus, which holds the emperor's remains, encased in five successive coffins (one tin, one mahogany, two lead, and one ebony). Surrounding the sarcophagus are the tombs of two of Napoléon's brothers, his son, and several French military heroes. Don't blame the over-the-top setting on Napoléon; the decision to transfer his remains to Paris was made in 1840, almost 20 years after his death. Tens of thousands crowded the streets to pay their respects as the coffin was carried under the Arc de Triomphe and down the Champs-Elysées to Les Invalides, where it waited another 20 years until the tomb was finished.

pl. des Invalides, 7th arrond. www.invalides.org. (✆) **01-44-42-37-72.** Admission to all the museums, the church, and Napoléon's Tomb: 12€ adults; free for children 17 and under. Apr–Oct daily 10am–6pm; Nov–Mar daily 10am–5pm. Métro: Latour-Maubourg, Varenne, or Invalides. RER: Invalides.

Musée d'Orsay ★★★ MUSEUM   What better setting for a world-class museum of 19th-century art than a beautiful example of Belle Epoque architecture? In 1986, the magnificent Gare d'Orsay train station, built to coincide with the 1900 World's Fair, was brilliantly transformed into an exposition space. The huge, airy central hall lets in lots of natural light, which is artfully combined with artificial lighting to illuminate a collection of treasures.

The collection spans the years 1848 to 1914, a period that saw the birth of many artistic movements, but today it is best known for the emergence of Impressionism. All the superstars of the epoch are here, including Monet, Manet, Degas, and Renoir, not to mention Cézanne and Van Gogh.

The top floor is the home of the most famous Impressionist paintings, like Edouard Manet's masterpiece, *Le Déjeuner sur l'Herbe.* Though Manet's composition of bathers and friends picnicking on the grass draws freely from those of Italian Renaissance masters, the painting shocked its 19th-century audience, which was horrified to see a naked lady lunching with two fully clothed men. Manet got into trouble again with his magnificent *Olympia,* a seductive odalisque stretched out on a divan. There was nothing new about the subject; viewers were rattled by the unapologetic

Musée d'Orsay

look in her eye—this is not an idealized nude, but a real woman, and a tough cookie to boot.

The middle level is devoted to the post-Impressionists, with works by artists like Gauguin, Seurat, Rousseau, and Van Gogh, like the latter's *Church at Auvers-sur-Oise,* an ominous version of the church in a small town north of Paris where he moved after spending time in an asylum in Provence. This was one of some 70 paintings he produced in the two months leading up to his suicide.

1 rue de la Légion d'Honneur, 7th arrond. www.musee-orsay.fr. ② **01-40-49-48-14.** Admission 12€ adults; 9€ ages 18–25; free for children 17 and under. Tues–Wed and Fri–Sun 9:30am–6pm; Thurs 9:30am–9:45pm. Métro: Solférino. RER: Musée d'Orsay.

Musée du quai Branly ★★★ MUSEUM   It's just a few blocks from the Eiffel Tower, but this museum's wildly contemporary design has forever changed the architectural landscape of this rigidly elegant neighborhood. Its enormous central structure floats on a series of pillars, under which lies a lush garden, separated from the noisy boulevard out front by a huge glass wall. However you feel about the outside, you cannot help but be impressed by the inside: The vast space is filled with exquisite examples of the traditional arts of Africa, the Pacific Islands, Asia, and the Americas. Designed by veteran museum-maker Jean Nouvel, this intriguing space makes an ideal showcase for a category of artwork that too often has been relegated to the sidelines of the museum world.

This magnificent collection is displayed in a way that invites you to admire the skill and artistry that went into the creation of these diverse objects. Delicately carved headrests from Papua New Guinea in the form of birds and crocodiles and intricately painted masks from Indonesia vie for your attention. Look at and listen to giant wooden flutes from Papua New Guinea, displayed with an on-going recording. A selection of "magic stones" from the island nation of Vanuatu includes smooth abstract busts reminiscent of Brancusi sculptures. A fascinating collection of Australian aboriginal paintings segues into the Asian art section, and the journey continues into Africa, starting with embroidered silks from Morocco and heading south through magnificent geometric marriage cloths from Mali and wooden masks from the Ivory Coast. The Americas collection includes rare Nazca pottery and Inca textiles, as well as an intriguing assortment of North American works, like Haitian voodoo objects and Sioux beaded tunics.

37 quai Branly and 206 and 218 rue de Université, 7th arrond. www.quaibranly.fr. ✆ **01-56-61-70-00.** Admission to permanent exhibitions 10€ adults, free children 17 and under. Tues–Wed and Sun 11am–7pm; Thurs–Sat 11am–9pm. Métro: Alma-Marceau. RER: Pont d'Alma.

Musée Rodin ★★★ MUSEUM   There aren't many museums that can draw thousands of visitors who never even go inside. But the grounds of this splendid place are so lovely that many are willing to pay 4€ just to stroll around. Behind the Hôtel Biron, the mansion that houses the museum, is a formal garden with benches, fountains, and even a little cafe. Of course, it would be foolish *not* to go inside and drink in the some of the 6,600 sculptures in this excellent collection (don't worry, not all are on display), but it would be equally silly not to take the time to admire the large bronzes in the garden, which include some of Rodin's most famous works. Take, for example, *The Thinker.* Erected in front of the Panthéon in 1906 during a political crisis, Rodin's first public sculpture soon became a Socialist symbol and was quickly transferred here by the authorities, under the pretense that it blocked pedestrian traffic. Other important outdoor sculptures include the *Burghers of Calais, Balzac,* and the *Gates of Hell,* a monumental composition that the sculptor worked on throughout his career.

Indoors, marble works prevail, although there are also works in terracotta, plaster, and bronze, as well as sketches and paintings on display. The most famous of the marbles is *The Kiss,* which was originally meant to appear in the *Gates of Hell.* In time, Rodin decided that the lovers were too happy for this grim composition, and he explored it as an independent work. As usual with Rodin's works, the critics were shocked by the couple's overt sensuality, but not as shocked as they were by the large, impressionistic rendition of *Balzac,* exhibited at the same salon, which critic Georges Rodenbach described as "less than a statue than a strange monolith, a thousand-year-old menhir." The museum holds hundreds of works, many of them legendary, so don't be surprised if after a while your vision starts to blur. That'll be your cue to head outside and enjoy the garden.

Gardens at the Musée Rodin

79 rue de Varenne, 7th arrond. www.musee-rodin.fr. ℭ **01-44-18-61-10.** Admission 10€ adults; 7€ ages 18–25; free for children 17 and under. Tues and Thurs–Sun 10am–5:30pm, Wed 10am–8:30pm. Métro: Varenne or St-Francois-Xavier.

MONTPARNASSE (14TH & 15TH ARRONDISSEMENTS)

Even though it had its heart ripped out in the 1970s when the original 19th-century train station was torn down and the ugly Tour Montparnasse was erected, this neighborhood still retains a redolent whiff of its artistic past. Back in the day, artists like Picasso, Modigliani, and Man Ray hung out in cafes like **Le Dôme, La Coupole, La Rotonde,** and **Le Sélect,** as did a "Lost Generation" of English-speaking writers like Hemingway, Fitzgerald, Faulkner, and Joyce. Today the famous cafes are mostly filled with tourists, but you can still find quiet corners. Amazingly, **La Ruche,** the legendary artists' studio from the Golden Years, is still standing (http://laruche-artistes.fr). And of course, if you don't want to look at the Tour Montparnasse you should take the lift to the 56th-floor observation deck and marvel at the 360° views of Paris (17€ adults, 9.50€ ages 4 to 11, free for children 3 and under), or sip a cocktail in its panoramic bar, Ciel de Paris (www.cieldeparis.com).

Les Catacombes ★ CEMETERY/HISTORIC SITE   Definitely not for the faint of heart, the city's catacombs are filled with the remains of millions of ex-Parisians, whose bones line the narrow passages of this mazelike series of tunnels. In the 18th century, the Cimetière des Innocents, a centuries-old, overpacked cemetery near Les Halles, had become so foul and disease-ridden that it was finally declared a health hazard and closed. The bones of its occupants were transferred to this former quarry,

Les Catacombes

which were later joined by those of other similarly pestilential Parisian cemeteries.

In 1814, the quarry stopped accepting new lodgers. Rather than leaving just a hodge-podge of random bones, they organized them in neat stacks and geometric designs, punctuating the 2km (1.25 miles) with sculptures and epigrammatic sayings carved into the rock. The one at the entrance sets the tone: stop—here is the empire of death. The visit will be fascinating for some, terrifying for others; definitely not a good idea for claustrophobics or small children. You'll want to wear comfortable shoes and bring a sweater of some sort, as it's cool down here (around 57°F/14°C).

1 av. du Colonel Henri Rol-Tanguy, 14th arrond. www.catacombes.paris.fr. ⓒ **01-43-22-47-63.** Admission 13€ adults; 11€ ages 18–26; free for children 17 and under. Tues–Sun 10am–8:30pm (last entry 7:30pm). Métro and RER: Denfert-Rochereau.

Musée Bourdelle ★ MUSEUM   This quaint museum is a testament to the sculptor Antoine Bourdelle, whose work went far beyond the 10 years he spent as Rodin's assistant. A renowned teacher who influenced an entire generation of sculptors, including Alberto Giacometti and Aristide Maillol, Bourdelle was one of the pioneers of 20th-century monumental sculpture. Proud, muscular centaurs, gods, and goddesses stride across these rooms, as well as monuments to famous people. You can also visit the sculptor's studio. **Audio guides** in English (5€) are a big help here.

18 rue Antoine-Bourdelle, 15th arrond. www.bourdelle.paris.fr. ⓒ **01-49-54-73-73.** Free admission to the permanent collection. Tues–Sun 10am–6pm. Métro: Montparnasse-Bienvenüe.

WHERE TO STAY

Paris has more than 1,500 hotels, from palaces fit for a pasha to tiny family-run operations whose best features are their warm welcome and personal touch. Over the last few years, a plethora of new establishments have opened too, many with exquisite, modern decor. In theory, you should be able to find something in line with your budget, timeframe, and personal tastes. But even if you can't find the hotel of your dreams in the list below, don't despair—at the end of this section I list a few alternative lodging options, including bed-and-breakfasts and short-term apartment rentals.

The Right Bank

LOUVRE & ILE DE LA CITÉ (1ST ARRONDISSEMENT)

The area surrounding the Louvre is littered with hotels, some of which are dreadfully overpriced. Yes, if you only are in town for 1 day or 2, a central locale is key, since time is of the essence. But if you have a little more time, you'll find much more comfortable lodgings, at the same or lower prices, a 10-min. walk away.

Expensive

Hotel Brighton ★★ Did someone say "view"? How about a panorama of the Louvre and the Tuileries gardens from your bed? While not every room in this gracious hotel has the jackpot view, those in the "deluxe" and "executive" categories do, and all have a subdued, classic look with elegant fabrics draping windows and tasteful decorative touches. This classy establishment, under the arcades of the rue de Rivoli may not be not quite as grand as the Meurice, just down the block, but it is about one-third the price. Understandably, rooms with views book up early, so plan ahead.
218 rue de Rivoli, 1st arrond. www.paris-hotel-brighton.com. ℂ **01-47-03-61-61.** 61 units. 249€–450€ double; 352€–460€ suite. Métro: Tuileries. **Amenities:** Bar; concierge; laundry service; room service; tea room; free Wi-Fi.

Maison Albar Hôtel Paris Céline ★★ This spankingly chic hotel housed in the former HQ of couture house Céline is sandwiched between Pont Neuf and the brand new Canopée (covered mall) in Les Halles shopping district. And boy is it a sight to behold: It's all elegant 1920s-style furniture that melts into wavy cream fabrics and light-filled windows offering classic street views. For a special treat, book the 1923 room on the top floor, with its 180-degree, floor-to-ceiling vistas over Paris' rooftops. Or nab a table at Odette, the hotel's gourmet bistro specialized in sharing platters. To cap off a day's sight-seeing, the spa awaits with its indoor pool and Jacuzzi too.
23/25 rue du Pont Neuf, 1st arrond. www.maison-albar-hotel-paris-celine.com. ℂ **01-44-88-92-60.** 60 units. 275€–496€ double; from 510€ suite. Métro: Châtelet, Louvre Rivoli or Pont Neuf. **Amenities:** Restaurant; bar; concierge; laundry service; room service; free Wi-Fi and iPads.

Moderate

Hôtel Britannique ★★   When you step into the salon off the lobby here, you'll be tempted to immediately throw yourself into one of the plush armchairs and order a cup of tea. Decidedly British in decor and atmosphere, the immaculate, soundproofed rooms are comfortably and conservatively furnished, with gentle swaths of drapery hanging over the bed and windows. Rooms facing the street are the most pleasant, with large windows that offer views of the Théâtre du Châtelet across the street; rooms on the courtyard are larger though and can be made into triples if needed. Also available are adjoining rooms for families and one suite that sleeps four. A good value, considering the quality of the lodgings and the central location.

20 av. Victoria, 1st arrond. www.hotel-britannique.fr. ✆ **01-42-33-74-59.** 39 units. 102€–191€ double; 291€–409€ for suite up to 4 people. Métro: Châtelet. **Amenities:** Bar; room service after 6pm; free Wi-Fi.

Hôtel du Cygne ★   Chock-full of exposed beams and stone walls, this 17th-century building has been carefully restored, and the simple lodgings receive ongoing tender-loving care. Most rooms are predictably small but cheerfully decorated, with fresh white walls, floral bedspreads, and the owner's personal touch. If you can handle the climb to the top floor, you'll be rewarded with a roomy suite that sleeps three. The hotel is located near Les Halles and the Montorgueil neighborhood (very hip at night). There is no elevator.

3–5 rue du Cygne, 1st arrond. www.hotelducygne.fr. ✆ **01-42-60-14-16.** 18 units. 60€–119€ double; 147€–167€ suite. Métro: Etienne Marcel. RER: Les Halles. **Amenities:** Free Wi-Fi.

Hôtel Thérèse ★★   Just a few steps from the Palais Royal and the Louvre, these warm, cozy lodgings combine old-fashioned Parisian charm with modern Parisian chic. Soft grey/teal blues highlight a creative decor that complements the building's age instead of fighting it. Comfy sofas invite you to relax in the lobby, whose stylish look includes mirrors, bookcases, and unique lighting fixtures. The comfort factor extends to the rooms, many of which have very high ceilings, interesting drapery fabrics, and upholstered headboards.

5–7 rue Thérèse, 1st arrond. www.hoteltherese.com. ✆ **01-42-96-10-01.** 40 units. 180€–370€ double. Métro: Palais-Royal or Pyramides. **Amenities:** Concierge; library/bar; free Wi-Fi.

LE MARAIS (3RD & 4TH ARRONDISSEMENTS)

Centuries ago, this neighborhood was a swamp *(marais)*, but now it's merely swamped with stylish boutiques, restaurants, and people who seem to have just stepped out of a hair salon. Stunning 16th- and 17th-century mansions house terrific museums; the narrow streets harbor clothing stores, cool bars, clubs, and the remnants of the city's historic Jewish quarter. The 4th arrond. is the city's main LGBTQ district and draws the most tourists thanks to picturesque spots like **place des Vosges** (p 94), while the 3rd arrond. has a fashionista vibe, and a great set of restaurants and coffee shops.

Expensive

Pavillon de la Reine ★★★   Just off place des Vosges, the "Queen's Pavilion" harkens back to the days when the magnificent square was home to royalty. Set back from the hustle and bustle of the Marais, this heavenly hideaway feels intimate, like a lord's private hunting lodge in the country. The decor is a suave combination of subtle modern and antique: The dark period furniture blends with rich colors on the walls and beds; choice objects and historic details abound. Several deluxe duplexes have staircases leading to cozy sleeping lofts.

28 pl. des Vosges, 3rd arrond. www.pavillon-de-la-reine.com. ℭ **01-40-29-19-19.** 56 units. 302€–550€ double; from 600€ suite. Métro: Bastille. **Amenities:** Bar; concierge; fitness room; laundry service; room service; sauna; spa; free Wi-Fi.

Moderate

Hôtel Caron de Beaumarchais ★   In the 18th century, Pierre Auguste Caron de Beaumarchais—author of "The Barber of Seville"—lived near here, and this small hotel celebrates both the playwright and the magnificent century he lived in. Delightful details give you a taste of what life was like back in the day: Walls are covered in high-quality reproductions of period fabrics; rooms are furnished with authentic antique writing tables; and period paintings and first-edition pages of "The Barber of Seville" hang on the walls. A pianoforte that dates from 1792 stands in the lobby, next to an antique card table set up for a game. You half expect Pierre Auguste himself to come waltzing through the door.

12 rue Vieille-du-Temple, 4th arrond. www.carondebeaumarchais.com. ℭ **01-42-72-34-12.** 19 units. 145€–245€ double. Métro: St-Paul or Hôtel de Ville. **Amenities:** Free Wi-Fi.

Hôtel de la Bretonnerie ★★   This popular and affordable hotel, located smack in the middle of the Marais, has a remarkably high charm factor. Rooms feature exposed beams, period prints, and high ceilings, as well as large windows that let in light from either the small street or the courtyard. Romantics on a budget will appreciate the rooms with four-poster beds; those who need to stretch out will enjoy the spacious junior suites and duplexes. The enthusiastic manager is passionate about her work and the service is excellent.

22 rue Sainte Croix de la Bretonnerie, 4th arrond. www.hotelbretonnerie.com. ℭ **01-48-87-77-63.** 29 units. 119€–185€ double; 200€–240€ junior suites and duplexes for up to 4 people. Métro: Hôtel de Ville. **Amenities:** Computer in lobby; free Wi-Fi.

Inexpensive

Hôtel Jeanne d'Arc le Marais ★★   With a prime location, comfortable rooms, and great prices, it's no wonder this hotel books up months in advance. It's located in the lower Marais, right next to the leafy place du Marché St-Catherine. While definitely not luxurious, the rooms are in excellent shape, decked out in warm colors and (in some cases) vintage-style prints; several have been given a more modern makeover and new bathrooms. Families will be interested in the reasonably priced quads as well as the two adjoined rooms on the sixth floor.

3 rue de Jarente, 4th arrond. www.hoteljeannedarc.com. © **01-48-87-62-11.** 35 units. 109€–169€ double; 180€ triple; 220€ quad. Métro: St-Paul. **Amenities:** Computer in lobby; free Wi-Fi.

Jules et Jim ★★   The entrance to this gem of a hotel is so discreet you could walk right past it. Find your way inside and you're in for a treat: A cobbled courtyard with an outdoor fireplace merges into a low-key cocktail bar with vintage-inspired furniture, while the rooms—all ultra-comfortable—flaunt hip decor such as white walls with clever back lighting and beautiful wall art. Some have bathrooms with floor-to-ceiling windows; others, on the upper floors, provide panoramic rooftop views. For those needing extra room the duplex suite is resplendent in dark woods and retro-chic furniture (but its staircase is not child-proof).

11 rue des Gravilliers, 3rd arrond. www.hoteljulesetjim.com. © **01-44-54-13-13.** 23 units. 220€–310€ double; 400€ duplex for up to 4 people. Métro: Arts et Métiers. **Amenities:** Cocktail bar; free Wi-Fi.

CHAMPS-ELYSÉES, TROCADÉRO & WESTERN PARIS (8TH, 16TH & 17TH ARRONDISSEMENTS)

Affordable lodgings are scarce in this opulent environment, especially near the Champs and the Arc de Triomphe, where high prices often have more to do with location than the quality of the lodging. But here are a few that are worth checking out.

Expensive

Hôtel Balzac ★★★   Chandeliers and rich fabrics await you in the lobby of these luxurious lodgings, built for the director of the Paris Opéra in 1853. Just a few steps away from the Champs-Elysées, this classy townhouse features spacious rooms with huge beds, high thread-counts, and swags of chiffon and velour around the bed and windows. The ambiance is classic and very French, with antiques, high ceilings, and subtle colors. Visiting dignitaries can opt for a Royal or Presidential Suite with views of the Eiffel Tower; junior and "regular" suites feature separate sitting areas and dressing rooms. There's an interior courtyard where you can enjoy a drink on a plush sofa; if you're itching to get out, Louis Vuitton and Fouquet's are just around the corner. If you want luxury on a small, personal scale, this is an excellent choice; the service is impeccable and polite, and the hotel is small enough to still feel intimate. Pierre

Gagnaire, a Michelin three-star gourmet pleasure palace, is in the same building.

6 rue Balzac, 8th arrond. www.hotelbalzac.com. © **01-44-35-18-00.** 69 units. 271€–600€ double; from 450€ suite. Métro: George V. Parking 25€. **Amenities:** Restaurant; bar; business center; concierge; dry cleaning; room service; free Wi-Fi.

Moderate

Hôtel Alison ★★   While the lobby decor at this comfortable, family-run hotel hasn't changed since at least 1982 (think Almodóvar movies), it's impeccably clean and shiny, as are the relatively spacious rooms. No matter what you feel about beige walls and chocolate carpets, you should be pleased with the generally high level of comfort here, and the location is excellent: around the corner from the Madeleine and a short stroll to the Champs Elysées and the place de la Concorde.

21 rue de Surène, 8th arrond. www.hotel-alison.com. © **01-42-65-54-00.** 34 units. 129€–185€ double; 185€–205€ triple; 230€ family suite. Métro: Madeleine or Concorde. **Amenities:** Bar; free Wi-Fi.

Inexpensive

New Orient Hôtel ★★★   This lovely hotel, which offers comfortable rooms with high ceilings, 19th-century moldings, and antique headboards and armoires, may not be on top of the Champs Elysées, but it's not far, and it is close to stately Parc Monceau and a quick trot to the Saint Lazare train station. The friendly owners, inveterate flea market browsers, have refinished and restored the antique furniture themselves. Rooms (many of which have small balconies) are in tip-top shape, and bathrooms sparkle. Though there's an elevator, you'll have to negotiate stairs to get to it.

16 rue de Constantinople, 8th arrond. www.hotelneworient.com. © **01-45-22-21-64.** 30 units. 115€–192€ double; 165€–212€ family room for 4. Métro: Villiers, Europe, or St-Lazare. **Amenities:** Computer in lobby; free Wi-Fi.

OPÉRA & GRANDS BOULEVARDS (2ND & 9TH ARRONDISSEMENTS)

This area offers a lovely mix of hip bars and restaurants and old-time Paris, with museums for a dose of culture and old covered passages for stepping back in time. What the area lacks in big monuments, it makes up for with lower room rates and a more neighborhood-y feel.

Moderate

Hôtel Arvor Saint Georges ★★   Located in the charming "New Athens" neighborhood, where 19th-century Romantics like George Sand and Frédéric Chopin lived and worked, these spiffy lodgings offer an arty yet relaxed atmosphere, where fresh white walls show off modern photography and Daniel Buren graphics. Rooms are a little small, but simple and chic, with white walls, a splash of color, and a distinctive table or armchair. The airy lobby, with large windows and bookshelves is an invitation to kick back and read or sip a cup of tea. A tasty breakfast is served here or outside in the flower-filled patio. The friendly staff will give you a map of their favorite nearby restaurants; you can also check out the hotel's blog, which offers lots of tips (mostly in French) from real, live Parisians (www.jadooore.com).

8 rue Laferrière, 9th arrond. www.hotelarvor.com. ✆ **01-48-78-60-92.** 30 units. 149€–206€ double; 189€–269€ suite. Métro: St-Georges. **Amenities:** Bar; free Wi-Fi.

The Hoxton ★★★ Set in a sumptuous 18th-century mansion, this place oozes class, from the cobblestone atrium and trendy brasserie to the cocktail bar dressed up in granny-tastic floral wallpaper. Rooms are just as lovely, mixing fun, mid-century-style furnishings with elegant classics such as chevron timber floors and typical Parisian moldings. Plus, you won't have to pay a fortune for minibar drinks as they're sold at high-street prices, a rarity in Paris. More perks? Free breakfast, delivered to your room each morning, and complimentary international calls. Oh, and you'll be staying in one of the city's most up-and-coming areas too, smack bang in the Sentier (a foodie hot spot) by Grands Boulevards, home to theaters and bars.

30-32 rue du Sentier, 2nd arrond. https://thehoxton.com/paris/paris/hotels. ✆ **01-85-65-75-00.** 172 units. 119€–579€ double. Métro: Bonne Nouvelle or Grands Boulevards. **Amenities:** Restaurant; cocktail bar; room service; minibar; free Wi-Fi.

Inexpensive

Hôtel Chopin ★ Nestled at the back of the delightful Passage Jouffroy, this budget hotel has remarkably quiet rooms considering its location in the middle of the rush and bustle of the Grands Boulevards. The staircase is a little creaky (you have to climb a flight to get to the elevator), and the decor is nothing to write home about, but the rooms are clean and colorful and the bathrooms are spotless. Rooms on the upper floors get more light; many have nice views of Parisian rooftops.

10 bd. Montmartre or 46 passage Jouffroy, 9th arrond. www.hotel-chopin.com. ✆ **01-47-70-58-10.** 36 units. 96€–130€ double; 145€ triple. Métro: Grands Boulevards or Richelieu-Drouot. **Amenities:** Free Wi-Fi.

Hôtel Vivienne ★★★ Right around the corner from Passage des Panoramas, this family-run hotel offers comfortable, renovated, spotless lodgings at terrific prices. About half the hotel is decorated in a classic, if old-fashioned style; other rooms have been given a modern makeover. A few rooms have balconies with space for a small table; some have connecting doors, and there are some large suites that are great for families. If you don't mind sharing a toilet, several doubles go for 72€. The location is excellent, near bars, theaters, and restaurants, plus it's a short walk to the Métro and a 10-min. stroll to the Palais Royal. If you are a light sleeper, ask for a room facing the courtyard as the street can be a little noisy.

40 rue Vivienne, 2nd arrond. www.hotel-vivienne.com. ✆ **01-42-33-13-26.** 44 units. 86 €–160€ double; 148€ suite. Métro: Grands Boulevards or Richelieu–Drouot. **Amenities:** Free Wi-Fi.

MONTMARTRE (18TH ARRONDISSEMENT)

Once you leave behind the tourist hordes that invade the Sacré-Coeur and place du Tertre, you'll find a neighborhood of lovely little lanes and small houses, harkening back to the days when Picasso and the boys were at the Bateau Lavoir. Just one thing to consider: Although Montmartre is utterly charming, and filled with cafes and eateries, it's on the northern edge of the city, so you'll need to budget extra time to get back down the hill to the center of town (20 min. on foot to Opéra, 35 min. to the Louvre).

Expensive

L'Hôtel Particulier ★★   If your vision of Montmartre involves secret little cobbled lanes and old townhouses with tree-filled gardens, this chic, arty hotel is for you. To get to it, you must buzz in from the street, then take a narrow, private path—Passage de la Sorcière (aka the "witch's alley")—to an elegant former mansion. Each of the five suites was designed by a different artist: One evokes a fancy bordello, with jewel-studded velvet walls; another has psychedelic floral wallpaper and stunning views over the garden; all are sumptuous. For extra pizazz, the loftlike, top-floor suite is awash in natural light and flaunts an open bathroom with a clawfoot bathtub. Into food? You may want to consider dining in: The hotel's on-site restaurant, **Mandragore,** offers exquisite French dishes with a modern twist, and serves afternoon tea (Wed–Sun) in an *olde-worlde* courtyard—a glorious treat on a sunny day.

23 av. Junot (Pavillon D), 18th arrond. www.hotel-particulier-montmartre.com. ✆ **01-53-41-81-40.** 5 units. 390€–590€ suite. Métro: Lamarck Caulincourt. **Amenities:** Restaurant; bar; garden; laundry service; room service; Wi-Fi (free).

Moderate

Le Relais Montmartre ★★   These comfortable lodgings include small but impeccable rooms decked out in light, warm colors and a classic decor. Nothing particularly hip or stylish here, just quality accommodations in tasteful floral prints, plus reliable service. The one decorative quirk: exposed beams on the ceilings in shades of lavender and blue. The hotel is on a peaceful little side street, right around the corner from a delicious stretch of food shops on Rue Lepic. There are connecting rooms for families and a lovely little patio for breakfasting in good weather.

6 rue Constance, 18th arrond. www.hotel-relais-montmartre.com. ✆ **01-70-64-25-25.** 26 units. 158€–259€ double; 210€–289€ triple. Métro: Blanche. **Amenities:** Concierge; laundry service; iPad for guests; free Wi-Fi.

Inexpensive

Ermitage Sacré-Coeur ★★★   Built in 1890 by a rich gentleman for his mistress, this beautifully preserved townhouse has been lovingly converted into an intimate hotel. It may not offer room service (although a complimentary breakfast is served in your room) or much by way of amenities, but the ambience is unique. Tucked behind the Sacré-Coeur, this small mansion still feels like a private home. In fact, it virtually is: The

Canipel family has run these unconventional lodgings for more than 40 years. Each of the five rooms is decorated in period prints and draperies, with beautiful antique bedsteads and armoires. The hotel has no elevator. The Canipels also rent nearby studios and apartments that sleep one to four.

24 rue Lamarck, 18th arrond. www.ermitagesacrecoeur.fr. ✆ **01-42-64-79-22.** 5 units. 110€–120€ double; 130€ triple; 140€ quad. Breakfast included. No credit cards. Métro: Lamarck-Caulaincourt. Parking 25€. **Amenities:** Free Wi-Fi.

RÉPUBLIQUE, BASTILLE & EASTERN PARIS (11TH & 12TH ARRONDISSEMENTS)

Encompassing the recently overhauled place de la République, as well as the historic place de la Bastille, this area is a good choice for both budget travelers and creatures of the night—it includes the bars and clubs of the Oberkampf and Charonne neighborhoods and is close to the Marais. It's also one of the most exciting areas for restaurants, housing a plethora of small, chef-driven neo-bistros that draw foodies from across town.

Moderate

Eden Lodge Paris ★★★ Hidden from the street in the back of a beautiful garden, this modern wooden structure combines environmental awareness with extremely comfortable lodgings. With only five rooms and a free breakfast, some might call this a bed and breakfast instead of a hotel. The warm smell of larch wood (the construction material) hits your nose when you enter the lobby, a glassed-in atrium with a staircase leading up to the rooms. Quality insulation, LED lighting, solar panels, and zero-carbon output give these lodgings its ecological creds, as well as self-cleaning tiles that absorb air-pollution. There's no skimping on comfort though: Rooms are chic, warm, and minimalist, with vintage-look furniture and high-tech Japanese toilets. A microwave and refrigerator are available for guests in the breakfast room, which is open all day. Bicycles on hand, as well as a 500 sq. m- (5,381 sq. ft.-) garden for communing with nature.

175 rue de Charonne, 11th arrond. www.edenlodgeparis.net. ✆ **01-43-56-73-24.** 5 units. 225€–250€ double; 350€–390€ suite. Breakfast included. Métro: Alexandre Dumas. **Amenities:** Free Wi-Fi.

Inexpensive

Cosmos Hotel ★★ Just around the corner from the animated Oberkampf neighborhood, this budget option is one of the best deals in town. The modern rooms are generally spotless; aside from a few nicks on the walls, everything from the bed linens to the floor covering looks spanking new. And such a deal: only 74€ to 84€ for a double. Furthermore, the staff is friendly and helpful. The only downside: Weekend nights can be noisy as people spill out of the busy bars and cafes nearby.

35 rue Jean-Pierre Timbaud, 11th arrond. www.cosmos-hotel-paris.com. ✆ **01-43-57-25-88.** 36 units. 74€–84€ double; 96€ triple; 100€ quad. Métro: Parmentier. **Amenities:** Free Wi-Fi.

Hôtel de la Porte Dorée ★★   True, it's a little out of the way, but these lovely lodgings are well worth the Métro fare. Soothing neutral tones, antique headboards, high ceilings, wood floors, and original curlicue moldings are all part of the package at this hotel, owned by a friendly Franco-American couple. The hotel goes the extra mile for both the environment (ecologically correct policies) and babies (toys, playpens, and even potty seats available). And you'll pay less for all this than you will for something utterly basic in the center of town. What's more, it is right next to the verdant Bois de Vincennes, where you can rent bikes or picnic. The nearby Métro will get you to the city center in about 15 min.

273 av. Daumesnil, 12th arrond. www.hoteldelaportedoree.com. ℂ **01-43-07-56-97.** 43 units. 85€–129€ double; 125€–195€ triple. Métro: Porte Dorée. **Amenities:** Babysitting; bicycles; free Wi-Fi.

BELLEVILLE, CANAL ST-MARTIN & LA VILLETTE (10TH, 19TH & 20TH ARRONDISSEMENTS)

When historic arty neighborhoods like Saint-Germain and Montmartre became too expensive for up-and-coming artists, many immigrated to these more proletarian neighborhoods, giving the area a funky, bohemian feel. Even though it's gentrifying, Belleville is still known for artists' studios, while dozens of hip cafes and restaurants have popped up along the Canal St-Martin and the Bassin de la Villette. The young and adventurous will appreciate this part of town, but others may find it too much of a commute to the main sights.

Moderate

Le Citizen ★★   Maybe it's the smiling young staff in jeans, or the ecological ethos, but there's something alternative in the air at this adorable boutique hotel on the Canal St-Martin. While the rooms are on the small side, they are light and airy, with lots of blonde wood and clean lines; all look out on the tree-lined canal. When you check in, you'll be handed an iPad loaded with information and apps on Paris. The minibar and a delicious buffet breakfast are included in your room rate.

96 quai de Jemmapes, 10th arrond. www.lecitizenhotel.com. ℂ **01-83-62-55-50.** 12 units. 180€–270€ double; 280€–330€ suite; 480€ apartment. Breakfast included. Métro: Jacques Bonsergent. **Amenities:** Free minibar; iPad; room service; free Wi-Fi.

Inexpensive

Generator Paris ★★   A 20-min. walk from Gare du Nord (the Eurostar terminal) and 5 min. from the picturesque quays and bars of Canal St-Martin, this trendy establishment (opposite Oscar Niemeyer's iconic French Communist party's HQ) blurs the lines between hotel and hostel by offering both private rooms and dormitories (for up to 10 people). It also offers perks that many of the city's standard hotels can't provide: namely, a roof-top bar with views onto the Sacré Coeur and a Métro-themed basement "club" with a fab cocktail happy hour. Breakfast is served in a light-filled cafe overlooking a small urban garden. The bright dorms are filled with young, mostly English-speaking travelers, but the more expensive private rooms attract a more demanding set of mature clients with extras like terraces. Female-only dorms are available.

9-11 pl. du Colonel Fabien, 10th arrond. https://generatorhostels.com. ✆ **01-70-98-84-00.** 199 units. 19€–50€ per person in dormitories; 78€–150€ double. Métro: Colonel Fabien. **Amenities:** Cafe; bar; in-room lockers; laundromat; towel rental; free Wi-Fi.

The Left Bank

LATIN QUARTER (5TH & 13TH ARRONDISSEMENTS)

Central and reasonably priced, the Latin Quarter is a long-time favorite for travelers in search of affordable accommodations. As a consequence, a few corners of this famously academic neighborhood are overrun with tourists and trinket shops. The streets immediately surrounding the place St-Michel (especially around rue de la Huchette) are where you'll find the worst tourist traps, both hotel and restaurant-wise; better prices and quality are to be had in the quieter and more authentic areas around the universities, a little farther from Notre-Dame but still within easy walking distance.

Moderate

Hôtel Design De La Sorbonne ★★   In the thick of the student quarter facing La Sorbonne, this cozy boutique hotel combines comfort with an unusual, but classy decor. Period furniture is covered in lively green, blue, and dark brown stripes; colorful wall fabrics put a modern spin on Victorian patterns, and excerpts from French literary classics are woven into the carpets. Each room has a desk with an iMac for guest's use. As pretty as they are, the rooms are small, and some have bathrooms that are downright tiny. If you need space, opt for a deluxe with a bathtub or the large room on the top floor with a view of the Sorbonne and the Pantheon.

6 rue Victor Cousin, 5th arrond. www.hotelsorbonne.com. ✆ **01-43-54-58-08.** 38 units. 130€–370€ double; 200€–400€ top floor double. Métro: Cluny–La Sorbonne. RER: Luxembourg. **Amenities:** Free Wi-Fi.

Hôtel Saint-Jacques ★★   The spacious rooms in this delightful hotel retain lots of architectural details from its Belle Epoque past. Most of the ceilings are adorned with masses of curlicues, and some have restored 18th-century murals to gaze at while you laze in bed. Modern reproductions of famous French paintings hang on the walls; Second Empire–themed murals decorate the lobby and breakfast room. The romantic decor has a light, feminine feel, all shades of light blue, cream, and gray—considerably more inviting than when the hotel served as a set for the Audrey Hepburn/Cary Grant classic "Charade." Service is especially friendly here.

35 rue des Ecoles, 5th arrond. www.paris-hotel-stjacques.com. ✆ **01-44-07-45-45.** 26 units. 137€–326€ double; 217€–312€ triple. Métro: Maubert-Mutualité. RER: St-Michel–Notre-Dame. **Amenities:** Bar; babysitting; concierge; laundry service; loaner computer; free Wi-Fi.

Hotel Seven ★★★   Weird and wonderful, this luxury concept hotel seems made for lovers in search of a night to remember. Mirrors and transparent showers abound here, as do huge beds, theatrical lighting and large sofas. Rooms are romantically space-age, with mobiles, pinpoint lights and in-room transparent double showers, while the suites go all out: "Sublime" is all white with a round double bed under a feathery ceiling; "The Black Diamond" features a faux crocodile headboard and a black bathtub studded with Swarovski synthetic diamonds. Most have "levitation" beds, which are suspended horizontally from the wall, as well as Nespresso machines, iPod docks, and fluffy bathrobes. The hotel is a bit out of the way, at the southern end of the Latin Quarter.

20 rue Berthollet, 5th arrond. www.sevenhotelparis.com. ℭ **01-43-31-47-52.** 35 units. 135€–252€ double; 337€–575€ suite. Métro: Les Gobelins. **Amenities:** Bar; concierge; laptop loans; massages by appointment; room service; wine cellar; free Wi-Fi.

Off Paris Seine ★★★   Feel like taking a cruise but don't want to leave the city? Try Paris' first floating hotel, docked on the banks of the Seine at the foot of the Gare d'Austerlitz. Once inside, you'll feel like you're on a trendy ocean liner, especially when you are having a drink on one of the two decks that overlook the water. On warm days, you can even paddle in a narrow pool that separates the bar areas. The chic cabinlike rooms are small but well thought out; it's worth paying for a Seine-side room so you can gaze at the lights that reflect on the river at night. There's no room service per se, but if you pay at the bar in advance, you can have goodies delivered to your room.

20–22 Port d'Austerlitz, 13th arrond. www.offparisseine.com. ℭ **01-44-06-62-65.** 58 units. 139€–239€ double; 250€–400€ suite. Métro: Gare d'Austerlitz or Gare de Lyon. **Amenities:** Bar; free Wi-Fi.

Inexpensive

Hôtel des Grandes Ecoles ★★★   Tucked into a private garden on the slope of the Montagne St-Geneviève, this hotel makes you feel as if you have just walked out of Paris and into the countryside. A path leads to a flower-bedecked interior courtyard, where birds chirp in the trees; the reception area adjoins an inviting breakfast room. The spotless rooms are filled with country-style furniture, with crocheted bedspreads and framed etchings of flowers completing the look. The calm is such that the hotel has nixed TVs. What's more, this unique ambience comes at a reasonable price. Families will appreciate the six large suites that can sleep four.

75 rue de Cardinal-Lemoine, 5th arrond. www.hotel-grandes-ecoles.com. ℭ **01-43-26-79-23.** 51 units. 135€–165€ double; 180€ family room. Parking 30€. Métro: Cardinal Lemoine or pl. Monge. **Amenities:** Free Wi-Fi.

Hôtel des Jardins du Luxembourg ★★   Just around the corner from its glorious namesake, this is an excellent hideaway for a romantic honeymoon or cozy retreat. The building's claim to fame is that Sigmund Freud stayed here on his first visit to Paris; perhaps this has something to do with the 1930s and 1940s touches to the decor. The Art Deco ambience of the lobby and lounge invites deep reflection or at least a nice rest in one of the plush armchairs; for full relaxation, indulge in a visit to the sauna. While the standard rooms are quite pretty, with curly wrought-iron headboards and puffy comforters, the superior rooms, which cost only 10€ more, have nicer views, small balconies, snazzy bathrooms, and designer-fabric-covered walls.

5 impasse Royer-Collard, 5th arrond. www.les-jardins-du-luxembourg.com. ✆ **01-40-46-08-88.** 26 units. 116€–185€ double. Métro: Cluny–La Sorbonne. RER: Luxembourg. **Amenities:** Bar; free Wi-Fi.

ST-GERMAIN-DES-PRÉS & LUXEMBOURG (6TH ARRONDISSEMENT)

Sleek boutiques and restaurants abound in this legendary neighborhood; historic cafes and monuments lend plenty of atmosphere. Unlike some other Parisian neighborhoods, this one is lively even late at night; it is also centrally located and within walking distance of many top sights.

Expensive

Relais St-Germain ★★★ Fashioned from three adjoining 17th-century townhouses, this intimate hotel mixes old-world charm and jazzy modernity. Rooms are spacious, and even the smallest are equipped with a comfortable sitting area. The decor blends period furniture with modern prints, like the Louis XV armchair covered in zigzagged leather, or the 18th-century painting hung on a wall of mirrors. The effect is both stylish and deeply comforting. There are some extra stairs between floors, so if you have mobility issues, be sure to make that clear when you reserve. Guests have priority at the hotel restaurant, **Le Comptoir** (p. 161), where you might otherwise have a 6-month wait for a reservation. Book your room at least a month in advance.

9 carrefour de l'Odéon, 6th arrond. www.hotelrsg.com. ✆ **01-44-27-07-97.** 22 units. 295€–385€ double; 415€–460€ suite. Breakfast included if you reserve on the hotel's website. Métro: Odéon. **Amenities:** Restaurant; free Wi-Fi.

Villa Madame ★★ These sleek lodgings offer spacious, modern rooms in subdued tones with a large dose of Parisian elegance. Tranquil shades of beige and white are punctuated with red cushions and detailing, giving the light-filled rooms a calm appeal—perfect for relaxing after pounding the Parisian pavement. A few on the upper floors have balconies overlooking the neighborhood, which is just a short walk from the Jardin du Luxembourg; one large suite comes with a roomy terrace. Downstairs is a handicap-accessible room, as well as an interior courtyard where you can have breakfast or just lounge around with a drink in the evening surfing on the house iPad. When it's nippy out you can have tea by the fireplace in the salon.

44 rue Madame, 6th arrond. www.hotelvillamadameparis.com. ✆ **01-45-48-02-81.** 28 units. 199€–333€ double; 370€–525€ suite. Métro: Rennes or St-Sulpice. **Amenities:** Bar; concierge service; laundry service; room service; free Wi-Fi.

Moderate

Hôtel Louison ★★ Hovering on the invisible border between the Montparnasse and Saint-Germain neighborhoods, this adorable hotel is a quick walk to the Luxembourg Gardens and the delights of the Bon Marché department store. While maintaining the original detailing and mood of this 19th-century building, the period decor is spiced up with contemporary colors and textures, like a gold and purple version of traditional *toile de jouy* wallpaper, or old-fashioned stripes cheered up with lush velvet pillows and contemporary headboards. Off the lobby, a cozy reading room is available for quiet pursuits and discussion; nearby the breakfast room is open all day with a microwave for guests who want to heat up a quick bite. Connecting rooms are available for families, as well as a furnished apartment for rent by the week or the month.

105 rue de Vaugirard, 6th arrond. www.louison-hotel.com. ℂ **01-53-63-25-50.** 42 units. 149€–199€ double; 199 triple. Métro: Duroc or Falguière. Parking 38€. **Amenities:** Concierge; guest iPad; laundry service; free Wi-Fi.

Millesime Hôtel ★★ These cozy lodgings defy their historic surroundings with a set of modern, chic rooms in soothing shades of beige and grey. A 21st-century take on Parisian elegance that includes unusual wood headboards and soft flannel upholstery, the decor is contemporary without being overbearing. If you need to work or write, desks are unusually functional here, especially in the superior doubles and suites. Sip your post-sightseeing drinks in the small bar, or if the weather is nice, on the pretty courtyard patio.

15 rue Jacob, 6th arrond. www.millesimehotel.com. ℂ **01-44-07-97-97.** 20 units. 160€–280€ double; 310€–450€ suite. Métro: St-Germain-des-Prés. **Amenities:** Bar; concierge; mobile phones; room service; free Wi-Fi.

Inexpensive

Hotel Mayet ★★ The lobby of this young-at-heart hotel sports two murals, one by American graffiti artist JohnOne and the other by his French counterpart André. Rooms are snug but colorful, with white walls and touches of bright orange. The hotel has a lighthearted North African theme, with paintings of camels in the desert and vintage photos of beautiful Moroccan movie stars. This family-run enterprise also has an apartment for rent next door that sleeps four with a kitchen and washer-dryer.

3 rue Mayet, 6th arrond. www.mayet.com. ℂ **01-47-83-21-35.** 23 units. 102€–200€ double; 154€–240€ triple. Métro: Duroc. **Amenities:** Bar; free Wi-Fi.

EIFFEL TOWER & NEARBY (7TH ARRONDISSEMENT)

For some reason, many visitors to Paris clamor for hotels that are right near the Eiffel Tower, perhaps under the mistaken impression that this is a central location. It isn't. Still, there's no denying that this extremely posh area is beautiful, and there is something magical about wandering out of your hotel in the morning and seeing the Eiffel Tower looming in the background.

Expensive

Hôtel Signature St-Germain-des-Près ★★★   After undergoing a complete overhaul, the erstwhile Hôtel Lindberg has been reborn as a delightful boutique hotel. The new decor boasts interiors that are both stylish and welcoming. Bright colors on the walls blend harmoniously with subdued bedsteads and linens; mid-century reproduction furniture and faux antique phones take the edge off sleek modern lines. The "Prestige" rooms cost more but are especially roomy (30 sq. meters/323 sq. ft.). In addition to particularly attentive service, this hotel is also blessed with an excellent location for shopping addicts: it's just down the street from Bon Marché.

5 rue Chomel, 7th arrond. www.signature-saintgermain.com. ☎ **01-45-48-35-53.** 26 units. 180€–350€ double; 380€ triple; 500€ 2-room connecting family suite. Métro: Sèvres-Bablylone or St-Sulpice. **Amenities:** Concierge; free Wi-Fi.

Moderate

Hôtel de L'Empereur ★★   All the rooms facing the street in this perfectly manicured hotel (run by the same meticulous management as the Hôtel Muguet; see below) have swell views of the nearby golden dome of Les Invalides, which hovers over the tomb of Napoleon (hence the name of the hotel). The best views are from the fifth and sixth floors. If views aren't your priority, consider the larger rooms facing the courtyard, which get lots of light and less street noise and are less expensive. The plush rooms are decorated with a modern take on Empire style. The hotel has connecting rooms for families.

2 rue Chevert, 7th arrond. www.hotelempereur.com. ☎ **01-45-55-88-02.** 31 units. 180€–210€ double; 200€ triple; 330€ quad. Métro: Ecole Militaire. **Amenities:** Concierge; guest computer; free Wi-Fi.

Hôtel Londres Eiffel ★★   From the moment you enter, you feel like you are in a private home. In fact, you may very well be welcomed by Samba, the hospitable owners' lovely golden retriever. Polished wood banisters lead up spiral staircases to narrow hallways and cozy rooms decorated with a personal touch. Walls are covered with fabrics printed with tasteful 19th-century kitsch motifs, furniture is 1940s style, and the comfort level is terrific. A few rooms have views of the Eiffel Tower. They book up early. Connecting rooms are available for families.

1 rue Augereau, 7th arrond. www.hotel-paris-londres-eiffel.com. ☎ **01-45-51-63-02.** 30 units. 165€–275€ double; 330€ triple. Métro: Ecole Militaire. **Amenities:** Free Wi-Fi.

Hôtel Muguet ★★   Comfort is key at this personable hotel, where the conscientious staff has considered the smallest details of your stay. The lovely rooms are fitted with faux-antique furniture, big wood headboards hand-painted with a lily-of-the-valley *(muguet)* motif, and pretty new bathrooms with old-fashioned wooden washstands and mirror frames. Rooms are relatively large for Paris, and the triples are downright spacious. Five doubles have a great view of the Eiffel Tower, three others of Les Invalides; needless to say, these book up months in advance. The others, which are equally comfy and less expensive, look out on either the quiet street or the airy courtyard.

11 rue Chevert 7th arrond. https://hotelparismuguet.com. © **01-47-05-05-93.** 43 units. 165€–280€ double; 250€–350€ triple. Métro: Varenne or La Tour Maubourg. **Amenities:** Computer and printer in lobby; free Wi-Fi.

Inexpensive

Hôtel du Champ de Mars ★★   An adorable and affordable little inn right around the corner from the food shops of rue Cler—what more could you ask for? Owners Françoise and Stéphane Gourdal offer all of their comfortable doubles at one great price: 130€. The impeccably maintained rooms are decorated with the kind of care people generally reserve for their own homes: thick cotton bedspreads, framed etchings, and warm colors. The friendly staff includes a delightful cocker spaniel named Cannelle.

7 rue du Champ de Mars, 7th arrond. www.hotelduchampdemars.com. © **01-45-51-52-30.** 25 units. 130€ double. Métro: Ecole Militaire. **Amenities:** Laptop; free Wi-Fi.

MONTPARNASSE & NEARBY (14TH & 15TH ARRONDISSEMENTS)

Montparnasse is more centrally located than it might seem—it's right on the border of St-Germain and close to the Luxembourg gardens. Also, the train station is a major transit hub for a bundle of Métro lines and bus routes. Though the utterly unaesthetic Tour Montparnasse now casts a shadow over this ancient artists' haunt (Henry Miller, Man Ray, Chagall, Picasso . . .), the little streets in the surrounding area are still full of personality.

Inexpensive

L'Apostrophe ★   Honoring the area's literary history (nearby writers' haunts include La Coupole and the Closerie des Lilas), this "poem hotel" is dedicated to the beauty and mystery of writing. The decor is a little off the wall, but very tastefully so, starting with an impressive silhouette of a tree on the hotel's facade. Rooms are themed: "Caligraphy" has Chinese characters set on royal blue walls; "Musique" features stenciled sheet music and instruments. Larger rooms include a Jacuzzi bathtub right in the room.

3 rue de Chevreuse, 6th arrond. www.apostrophe-hotel.com. © **01-56-54-31-31.** 16 units. 88€–176€ double; 195€–353€ double with a Jacuzzi. Métro: Vavin. **Amenities:** Bar; free Wi-Fi.

Hôtel des Bains ★★★   With cute, comfortable rooms and excellent rates, this friendly hotel is one of the best deals on the Left Bank, especially for families. It offers several good-sized, two-room suites for up to four people. Doubles are amply sized as well, with high ceilings; the largest ones face the pretty courtyard. The decor is simple but nicely accessorized with objects and artwork from the nearby Sunday art market. The elevator stops at a landing between floors, which have a few stairs.

33 rue Delambre, 14th arrond. www.hotel-des-bains-montparnasse.com. © **01-43-20-85-27.** 42 units. 110€ double; 135€–170€ suites for up to 4 people. Métro: Vavin, Edgar Quinet, or Montparnasse. **Amenities:** Free Wi-Fi.

Alternative Accommodations

Hotels are all very well and good, but for some, nothing beats staying in a private home or apartment, particularly if you are a family on a budget. Fortunately for travelers with an independent streak, several Parisian options are available including short-term rentals, bed-and-breakfasts, and "aparthotels," that is, short-term apartments with some hotel services.

SHORT-TERM RENTALS

Dozens of agencies offer hundreds of apartments smack in the center of the City of Light. Though the rates for two people are sometimes (but not always) significantly less than what you'd pay at a hotel, the advantages are many, not the least of which is the fact that you can cook some of your meals at home and save yourself a ton of time and money. Other benefits are privacy, independence, and a chance to see what it's like to live like a Parisian, even if it's just for a week.

If you are more than two, and especially if you are traveling *en famille,* the benefits can be huge. Family suites and/or adjoining rooms are rare in Parisian hotels, so you'll often end up paying for two doubles— somewhere around 250€ to 500€ per night—whereas you could rent a one-bedroom apartment with a foldout couch and/or extra bed in the living room for anywhere from 600€ to 2,000€ per week, or 85€ to 285€ per night.

So how should you book? While established agencies like the ones listed below come with more services and guarantees, rates also tend to be more expensive than Internet rental platforms like **Airbnb.com, Flipkey. com, Homeaway.com,** and **VRBO.com,** as many of the rentals listed on these sites are done by the owners directly, so there's no middle man to pay. Agencies justify their costs by having cleaning staff, all-inclusive rates, and an office you can call when something goes wrong. They also can vet all of their apartments to make sure they are legal and that there is no funny business on the owners' side. That said, when this book went to print, Airbnb-style rentals, where individual apartment owners use the website to rent short-term, were legal in France, *as long as the apartment is the renter/owner's primary residence.* And there is no denying that thousands of people happily use Airbnb and similar sites and find great accommodations for very reasonable rates. The problem is that hugely popular sites like Airbnb cannot check up on every owner, so you cannot be entirely sure that your rental is legal.

Bottom line: If you want to minimize risk and are willing to pay more for it, go with a well-established agency like **Parisian Home** (www.

parisianhome.com; ✆ **01-45-08-03-37**), **France Lodge** (www.france lodge.fr; ✆ **01-56-33-85-85**), **Paris Attitude** (www.parisattitude.com; ✆ **01-42-96-31-46**), or **Paris Appartements Services** (www.paris-appartements-services.com; ✆ **01-40-28-01-28**). **Apartments Actually** (http://apartmentsactually.com) also has some stunning properties in the Marais. In most cases, you will deal directly with the agency (not the owners), and the minimum stay is usually 4 days to 1 week.

BED & BREAKFASTS

Though bed-and-breakfasts *(chambres d'hôtes)* are extremely common in the French countryside, in the big city, where privacy and anonymity are treasured, the idea of strangers living in one's home generally fills Parisians with horror. This is a city where despite the high rents, roommates are virtually unheard of.

A terrific way to find a quality B&B is to visit the city's official B&B website: Hôtes Qualité Paris (www.hotesqualiteparis.fr). A partnership with Paris's most well-established and trusted B&B agencies, the site offers a wide range of rooms for about 50€ to 140€ per person per night, based on double occupancy. A couple of other recommended agencies are:

○ **Alcôve & Agapes** (www.bed-and-breakfast-in-paris.com; ✆ **07-64-08-42-77**)

○ **Good Morning Paris** (www.goodmorningparis.fr; ✆ **01-47-07-28-29**)

APARTHOTELS

Mostly designed for business travelers, these utilitarian lodgings are a cross between a hotel and an apartment. Short on charm, *aparthotels* are decidedly practical, as each unit comes with a kitchenette as well as hotel services such as fresh towels, dry cleaning, and a reception desk. Rates are generally higher than short-term rentals, but you do have the comfort of knowing you are dealing with a large company (if that makes you comfortable), with standardized apartments, organized websites, and customer service.

The best-known *aparthotel* company is **Citadines** (www.citadines. com; ✆ **01-41-05-79-05**), which offers clean, comfortable units in excellent locations around the city. The cheapest rentals are the studios with pull-out beds, which range from about 110€ to 320€ a night depending on the season and location.

WHERE TO EAT

Everywhere you look in Paris, someone is doing their best to ruin your waistline. *Boulangeries* (bakeries) with buttery croissants and decadent pastries lurk on every street corner; open-air markets tempt the senses; and restaurants with intriguing menus sprout up on every block.

Fortunately, you don't have to have a king-size budget to dine like royalty. Sure, there are those world-famous, multistarred restaurants that everyone has heard about. But recently, a whole new crop of "neo-bistros" has emerged, offering high-quality eats for a fraction of what you would pay in a gourmet palace. One outgrowth of this movement is the obsession with "noble" ingredients—high-quality, regional products, often from a small-scale farm or artisan, often organic, and always in keeping with the oldest and best traditions.

Note: Restaurants tend to be small in Paris, and when it comes to reservations, size matters. To be sure to get a table, reserve ahead for most of the restaurants listed below under the "Expensive" or "Moderate" categories.

The Right Bank

LOUVRE & ILE DE LA CITÉ (1ST ARRONDISSEMENT)

Dining near the Louvre can be an expensive and frustrating affair; it's rife with overpriced, mediocre tourist restaurants boasting menus in at least five languages. If you poke around some of the smaller streets however, you'll discover plenty of little restaurants where you can eat well and affordably. That said, if you are ready to spend, gourmet opportunities abound.

Expensive

Le Grand Véfour ★★★ CLASSIC FRENCH   Channel centuries of history at this illustrious restaurant, where Napoléon, Danton, Hugo, Colette, and Cocteau all once dined. Thanks to Guy Martin, chef and owner for the past decade, the food is as memorable as the magnificently preserved 18th-century salon: Signature dishes like Prince Rainier III pigeon and truffled oxtail parmentier share the menu with new creations with contemporary flavors like sumac and star anise. The desserts are incredible, especially the *palet* (a thick biscuit) with milk chocolate and hazelnuts, served with caramel and sea-salt ice cream. Reserve at least 2 weeks in advance and note that the lunch fixed-price menu is a third of the price of the fixed-price dinner.

17 rue de Beaujolais, 1st arrond. www.grand-vefour.com. ✆ **01-42-96-56-27.** Main course 88€–126€; fixed-price lunch 115€ or dinner 315€. Mon–Fri 12:30–1:45pm and 8–9:45pm. Closed Aug. Métro: Louvre–Palais-Royal or Pyramides.

Moderate

Champeaux ★ MODERN BRASSERIE   This is another one of multi-Michelin-starred-chef Alain Ducasse's ventures: a vintage-chic, train-station-inspired neo-brasserie set under the *canopée* (roof) of the new Halles shopping center. The place takes its name from a circa-1800s restaurant that once stood near Les Halles, and the menu also harks back to days gone by: onion soup, black pudding with apple salad, and the house specialty, soufflé, which comes in both sweet and savory varieties (think lobster, cheese, or caramel). Last order for food is at 11pm; after that, you'll have to make do with the excellent cocktails! Snacks such as *croque-monsieur* and cold meat platters are served all afternoon.

La Canopée, Forum des Halles, porte Rambuteau, 1st arrond. www.restaurant-champeaux.com. ✆ **01-53-45-84-50.** Main course 16€–26€; afternoon snacks from 12€. Sun–Wed 11:30am–midnight and Thurs–Sat until 1am. Métro: Les Halles. RER: Châtelet–Les Halles.

Le Fumoir ★★ FRENCH-SCANDINAVIAN   With its high ceilings, subdued lighting, and large windows, this understatedly hip spot is a good place to regroup. During the day (except at lunchtime) dawdling is encouraged: Magazines and newspapers are available at the front entry, and a small lending library/book exchange is in the back room. At night, well-dressed 30-somethings crowd around the magnificent wood bar—which in a former life stood in a Philadelphia speakeasy—as they wait for their

---

Dining After Hours

There aren't many restaurants that stay open until the wee hours of the Parisian night, but a few stalwarts are around Les Halles. **Le Tambour,** 41 rue de Montmartre, 2nd arrond. (✆ **01-42-33-06-90;** Métro: Les Halles), serves reliable dishes like steak-frites (main course 16€–20€) from noon to 5:30am every day in a dining room filled with kitschy Paris memorabilia. Nearby, **Au Pied de Cochon,** 6 rue Coquillière, 1st arrond. (www. pieddecochon.com; ✆ **01-40-13-77-00;** **Métro: Les Halles),** is a brasserie open 24/7 that specializes in pork and more pork (main course 22€–50€). Au Pied du Cochon also has some good seafood dishes and a restorative onion soup is ideal at 4am after a night on the town. For a late-night beef fix, head to **La Tour de Montlhéry–Chez Denise** (until 5am), where the steak is as juicy as it is huge.

table. You'll eat well here too: The offerings might include Nordic poached cod with smoked potato purée or a very French and very tender lamb navarin (stew) with fresh peas. On Sundays, there's a 27€ brunch complete with pancakes and eggs Benedict, and on Sunday nights, the Swedish chef (Henrik Andersson) returns to his roots with an all-Swedish menu.

6 rue de l'Amiral Coligny, 1st arrond. www.lefumoir.com. ℃ **01-42-92-00-24.** Main course 13€–28€; fixed-price menu lunch 24€–28€ or dinner 35€–39€. Daily 11am–2am (lunch noon–3pm; dinner 7:30–11pm). Métro: Louvre-Rivoli.

Inexpensive

Boutique yam'Tcha ★★★ FRENCH-ASIAN STREET FOOD Book a table at renowned chef Adeleine Grattard's Michelin-starred restaurant yam'Tcha and you'll certainly have a fabulous meal (121 rue St. Honore, 1st arrond.; ℃ **01-40-26-08-07**; from 65€ tasting menu; reserve 2 months in advance). Grattard works miracles with simple ingredients such as lobster, seabass, truffles, and pork. But her second place near the Louvre—a duel take-out *bao* bar (steamed Taiwanese buns) and tearoom—lets you taste her cooking for a fraction of the price. The bar section is a window open to the street, where foodies queue for bao buns filled with delectables such as smoked tofu or crab with vegetables, plus unexpected mixes like stilton and cherries. The tearoom, run by Grattard's Hong Kong-born husband Chi Wah Chan (a veritable tea guru who pairs teas with dishes in the same way sommeliers pair wines) serves excellent main courses such as Peking soup and fish tartare, both for around 14€.

4 rue Sauval, 1st arrond. www.yamtcha.com. ℃ **01-40-26-06-06.** Bao buns 5€–7€; main course 8€–14€. Wed–Fri noon–6pm; Sat noon–8pm. Métro: Louvre-Rivoli.

OPÉRA & GRANDS BOULEVARDS (2ND & 9TH ARRONDISSEMENTS)

Buzzing with cafes and theaters back in the 19th century, the long-overlooked Grand Boulevards have come back to life, especially near the Opéra and the hip part of the 9th arrondissement that borders Montmartre. Less trendy, but also less expensive, the little streets around the Bourse (the French stock exchange) have a wide range of restaurant options, especially at lunchtime. The covered passages that crisscross parts of the 2nd arrondissement also harbor some excellent dining options.

Expensive

Chez Georges ★★ TRADITIONAL FRENCH   A step back in time, this is how Parisian restaurants were before cuisine became nouvelle, or vanilla infusions were allowed to touch a fish dish. The room is crowded and lively, the cooking old-fashioned and delicious. Many of the customers are regulars who work in nearby offices. The handwritten menu features beautifully well-executed classics like filet of sole, *pot-au-feu* (beef simmered with vegetables), and sweetbreads with morels. Save room for the profiteroles at dessert.

1 rue du Mail, 2nd arrond. ℰ **01-42-60-07-11.** Main course 22€–43€. Mon–Fri noon–2:30pm and 7–11pm. Closed Aug and the last week of Dec. Métro: Bourse.

Saturne ★★★ MODERN FRENCH   There are not very many glass-roofed restaurants in Paris, and even fewer with a kitchen like this one. The chef's Scandinavian roots are evident in the decor, with its sleek blonde wood and white walls. But it's what's on the plate that makes it so hard to get a table here: exquisite combinations of flavors and textures, described on the menu as a list of ingredients. Resembling works of contemporary art, dishes might combine gnocchi, chestnuts, and truffles, or guinea hen with purple artichokes and spring garlic, and could be followed with a concoction of carrots, citrus, and olives. At lunch you can choose from a menu of three or six dishes; at dinner, it's one fixed-price six-course menu for one and all.

17 rue Notre-Dame-des-Victoires, 2nd arrond. www.saturne-paris.fr. ℰ **01-42-60-31-90.** Fixed-price lunch 45€–85€ or dinner 85€ (150€ with wine). Mon–Fri noon–2pm and 8–10:30pm. Closed first 3 weeks of Aug & end-Dec to early-Jan. Métro: Bourse.

Moderate

Canard et Champagne ★★ MODERN BISTRO   Tucked away in the old-world Passage des Panoramas, this delightful spot attracts the eye with a giant wall mural of French actor Louis de Funès (in his iconic role as Mr. Septime in the 1966 movie "Le Grand Restaurant"), then reels patrons in with fabulous duck dishes—foie gras, *confit de canard,* and *magret*—all washed down with hand-picked champagne from the region's best small producers. The concept is fabulous, especially since it won't break the bank: The set menus, which include two or three courses and up to three glasses of champagne, start at 32€. Reserve in advance or arrive early (noon for lunch, 7pm for dinner).

57 passage des Panoramas, 2nd arrond. http://frenchparadox.paris. ✆ **09-81-83-95-69.** Fixed-price lunch 18€–21€ or dinner 26€, including champagne 32€–62€. Tues–Sun noon–midnight. Closed 2 weeks in Aug. Métro: Bonne Nouvelle.

Coinstôt Vino ★★ WINE BAR   What's in a name? In this case, an amalgam of French and Italian words for "corner bistro" and "wine," which pretty much sums things up. This tiny place, which sits on the corner of two covered alleyways in the lovely Passage des Panoramas, has a generous and excellent selection of wines. While much of the menu is top-quality nibbles to enjoy while you savor your wine, like oysters, plates of smoked ham, pâté, and cheese, there are also a few *plats du jour* (daily specials) like grilled sea bass and steak with mushrooms. In season, the oysters come from Utah Beach, of Normandy landings fame. A pizza chef was recently imported from Italy, and you can sample his excellent wares with your glass of *vino.*

26 bis passage des Panoramas, 2nd arrond. https://lecoinstotvino.com. ✆ **01-44-82-08-54.** Main course 15€–25€; fixed-price lunch 17€–20€. Mon–Fri noon–2pm and 6–11pm; Sat 6–11pm. Closed first 3 weeks of Aug and last week of Dec. Métro: Grands-Boulevards or Bourse.

Le Pantruche ★★ TRADITIONAL FRENCH/BISTRO   The name is old-fashioned slang for Paris, but this little bistro has a decidedly modern feel to it. Another case of a runaway chef from Michelin-starred restaurants, Le Pantruche offers deliciously updated bistro fare like braised sweetbreads with carrots in a licorice glaze, or suckling pig with pears, celery root, and chestnuts. It's hard to resist dessert when chocolate ganache or Grand Marnier soufflé are on the menu. Definitely reserve ahead, as the fixed-price menus are a terrific value and the tiny dining room fills quickly.

3 rue Victor Massé, 9th arrond. www.lepantruche.com. ✆ **01-48-78-55-60.** Lunch main course 14€–25€; dinner main course 21€–25€; fixed-price lunch 20€ or dinner 35€. Mon–Fri 12:30–2:30pm and 7:30–9:30pm. Closed first 3 weeks of Aug. Métro: Pigalle.

Inexpensive

Noglu ★★ GLUTEN-FREE   Hidden down one of the foodiest covered passageways in Paris—the Passage des Panoramas—this tiny restaurant is where gluten-intolerant people bring their friends, quite simply because the home-cooked gluten-free food is so tasty you don't have to have a food allergy to appreciate it. Dishes might include cod with lentils, vegetable lasagna, and warm chocolate cake. Though not vegetarian per se, Noglu always has meat- and fish-free dishes on the menu. If you're in a hurry, the takeout section (just opposite) is a handy address to have up your sleeve, and doubles as a tiny cafe—the perfect spot for afternoon coffee and cake. There are now two new addresses elsewhere in Paris too:

In the Marais (38 rue Saintonge, 3rd arrond.) and on the Left Bank (69 rue de Grenelle, 7th arrond.).

16 passage des Panoramas, 2nd arrond. www.noglu.fr. ℂ **01-40-26-41-24.** Main course 11€–13€; fixed-price lunch 18€ –24€; Sat brunch 24€. Mon noon–2:30pm; Tues–Sat noon–2:30pm and 7:30–10:30pm. Closed 2 weeks in Aug. Métro: Bonnes Nouvelles.

LE MARAIS (3RD & 4TH ARRONDISSEMENTS)

You should have no trouble finding good things to eat in the Marais. Between its working-class roots and its more recent makeover, it offers a wide range of choices, from humble falafel joints to trendy brasseries.

Expensive

Benoit ★★ TRADITIONAL FRENCH This historic bistro had already hosted a century's worth of Parisian notables when Alain Ducasse took the helm in 2005. The dining room is still lined with mirrors, zinc, and tiles, while the classic menu has been given an extra dash of pizzazz. Dishes like escargots in garlic butter and brill braised with Jura wine share the stage with roasted milk-fed lamb from the Pyrenées and sautéed scallops *grenobloise.* The sommelier will help you navigate the huge wine list.

20 rue St-Martin, 4th arrond. www.benoit-paris.com. ℂ **01-42-72-25-76.** Main course 26€–54€; fixed-price lunch 39€. Daily noon–2pm and 7:30–10pm. Closed first 3 weeks of Aug. Métro: Hôtel-de-Ville.

La Brasserie de l'Isle Saint-Louis ★ TRADITIONAL BRASSERIE Owned by the same family for three generations, this lovely, old-fashioned brasserie serves healthy portions of classic Alsatian dishes, like choucroute garni—a small mountain of sauerkraut topped with slices of ham, sausage, and other smoked meats—in a relaxed atmosphere. Or try other classic brasserie fare like a tender entrecote (rib steak) or a breaded fillet of haddock. The decor is rustic without being kitsch. Despite the location, many of the diners are regulars. Eating's not a requirement; if you want, you can just enjoy a Mutzig (Alsatian beer) on the terrace and soak up a splendid view of the buttresses of Notre-Dame. Service is "nonstop."

55 quai de Bourbon, 4th arrond. www.labrasserie-isl.fr. ℂ **01-43-54-02-59.** Main course 19€–32€. Thurs–Tues noon–11pm. Closed in Aug. Métro: Pont Marie.

Moderate

Café des Musées ★★ TRADITIONAL FRENCH/BISTRO Weary culture vultures who've just finished the Picasso Museum will appreciate this bustling corner cafe with its appealing sidewalk tables. This is not just any old corner cafe, mind you, but one where the inventive chef works wonders with bistro classics like steak frîtes and *andouillette* (tripe sausage) as well as lighter fare like fresh vegetable casserole with basil oil, or shrimp with Thai curry. If you're here early enough (8am–11:30am), it's a top spot for breakfast too: think hot drink, pastry and fruit juice for 8€.

49 rue de Turenne, 3rd arrond. ℂ **01-42-72-96-17.** Main course 12€–26€. Daily noon–3pm and 7–11pm. Closed mid-Aug to early Sept. Métro: St. Paul or Chemin Vert.

Inexpensive

L'As du Fallafel ★ FALAFEL/ISRAELI   This Marais institution offers, without a doubt, one of the best falafels in Paris. True, falafel joints are scarce in this city, but that doesn't take away from the excellence of these overstuffed beauties, brimming with cucumbers, pickled turnips, shredded cabbage, tahini, fried eggplant, and those crispy balls of fried chickpeas and spices. Wash it down with an Israeli beer. Service is fast and furious, but basically friendly—be prepared to deal with hordes of tourists and locals at lunch. Closed Friday afternoon and all day Saturday.

34 rue des Rosiers, 4th arrond. ℂ **01-48-87-63-60.** Main course 8€–150€. Sun–Thurs 11am–midnight; Fri 11am–3pm. Métro: St. Paul.

Biglove Caffé ★ ITALIAN   Jars of preserved fruit line the walls, and hams hang from the ceiling—yes, you're still in Paris, but this place sure feels like Napoli. It tastes like it, too. For breakfast patrons tuck into pancakes with buffalo ricotta and passion fruit, for brunch a highlight is eggs benedict with 24-month-matured parma ham, and most any other time of day, pizza reigns supreme (the gluten-free versions are just as good), as does pasta. Whatever you choose, everything is made with only the choicest and freshest of ingredients, many of them direct from "petits producteurs" (small producers) in Italy. Set in a frighteningly hip part of the northern Marais, it is a popular place. Biglove doesn't take reservations, so if you come for brunch, arrive as early as possible—especially on weekends when this neighborhood is a brunch hotspot.

30 rue Debelleyme, 3rd arrond. ℂ **01-42-71-43-62.** Main course 10€–16€. Daily 9am–4:30pm and 7–10:30pm. Métro: Filles de Calvaire.

Breizh Café ★★ CREPERIE   After heading to Japan, where he found both a wife and professional success, Chef Bertrand Larcher started opening hugely popular creperies, first in Tokyo and then back in the home country. His Paris version is a warm and modern space that offers friendly service and great food. Jump straight in with a savory buckwheat *galette*, crisp and nutty and filled with high-quality organic ingredients, such as farm fresh eggs, Bordier butter, and seasonal produce. Try an artisanal cider, and save room for a sweet crepe, drizzled with chocolate or salted butter caramel. It gets very crowded here, so reserve ahead.

109 rue Vieille du Temple, 3rd arrond. www.breizhcafe.com. ℂ **01-42-72-13-77.** Main course 9€–15€. Mon–Fri 11:30am–11pm; Sat 10am–11pm and Sun until 10pm. Closed last 3 weeks in Aug. Métro: Filles du Calvaire.

Marché des Enfants Rouge ★★ STREET FOOD   On rue de Bretagne, this quaint, 400-year-old food market (the oldest in Paris) is a bustling, fragrant labyrinth of ready-to-eat food stalls hawking everything from Caribbean curries to couscous, sushi, and pasta. A hugely popular spot (if the queues are anything to go by) is Alain Miam Miam's organic crêpe stand, which serves made-to-order paninis and pancakes dripping in tasty cheese and ham. This is also where you'll find some of the best burgers in town: Burger Fermier makes the bread on-site, slathers the burgers in French cheese such as cider-infused Tomme, and only uses hand-picked beef from a farm in northern France. Come late afternoon and you can join the post-shopping crowd over a glass of wine.

39 rue de Bretagne, 3rd arrond. http://marchedesenfantsrougesfr.com. No phone. Main course 7.50€–16€. Tues–Sat 8am–8:30pm; Sun 8:30am–5pm. Métro: Saint Sébastien-Froissart.

CHAMPS-ELYSÉES, TROCADÉRO & WESTERN PARIS (8TH, 16TH & 17TH ARRONDISSEMENTS)

Mobbed with tourists, oozing with opulence, the Champs-Elysées is a difficult place to find a good meal, unless you are willing to spend a lot of money. Mediocre chain restaurants abound on the grand avenue itself, and tacky joints mingle with frighteningly expensive gourmet palaces on the surrounding side streets.

Expensive

Le Grand Restaurant ★★★ MODERN FRENCH Chef Jean-François Piège is—in my humble opinion—the most exciting chef in France right now. His ultra-modern take on traditional "bourgeois" cuisine is playful, delicious, and wholly unlike anything you'll taste anywhere else. Book ahead for a table in his swish, grey dining room (decked in concrete walls and geometric ceiling panels that wouldn't look amiss in Kubrick's "2001: A Space Odyssey"), then sit back for a rollercoaster ride of haute cuisine: shellfish-stuffed potato with caviar, Parmesan-infused spaghetti with truffles and fall-off-your-fork pork, and a delightful bergamot-flavored custard cream to finish. Don't be fooled by the simplicity of the descriptions; Piège's cooking is as complex as it is satisfying. His place is near the Élysée palace, so don't be surprised if you spot politicians out for a business meal—though Piège's devoted fans are never far away.

7 rue d'Aguesseau, 8th arrond. www.jeanfrancoispiege.com. © **01-53-05-00-00.** Main course 68€–155€; fixed-price lunch 85€ or dinner 216€ and 266€. Mon–Fri 12:30–2pm and 7:30–9pm. Closed 3 weeks in Aug and last week in Dec. Métro: Concorde or Madeleine.

Lasserre ★★★ GOURMET FRENCH André Malraux, Salvador Dalí, Audrey Hepburn, Marlene Dietrich—the list of celebrities who have dined at this legendary restaurant is understandably long. What famous person wouldn't want to eat in this superb dining room, where the ceiling opens when the weather is willing? The room is elegance incarnate, with walls decked in bold toile de jouy-like bird scenes, and tables laden with fine porcelain and silver knickknacks. Famous chef Michel Roth has recently brought new life to the classic menu, adding his own subtle creations, such as lobster roasted with chestnuts and honey, and served with saffron gnocchi, or sweet and sour duck with citrus-glazed turnips. Reserve at least 2 weeks ahead. Dinner jackets required for men.

17 av. Franklin D. Roosevelt, 8th arrond. www.restaurant-lasserre.com. © **01-43-59-02-13.** Main course 90€–130€; fixed-price lunch 60€–90€ and 190€ or dinner 190€. Thurs–Fri noon–2pm; Tues–Sat 7–10pm. Closed mid-July through Aug. Métro: Franklin Roosevelt.

Moderate

Le Drugstore (Publicis) ★★ MODERN BRASSERIE You won't find toothpaste at this "drugstore," whose name comes from a former 1950s incarnation that consisted of a warren of shops, restaurants, and services "à l'americaine." This ultra-modern, oh-so-chic complex has replaced the funky original but kept the multi-use concept intact with shops, restaurants, and a cinema. The Brasserie is the most accessible eating option—a cozy expanse with an incredible view of the Champs and the Arc de Triomphe from its terrace. The food is high-end casual, featuring gourmet hamburgers, grilled fish, steak tartare, and fillet of sole delivered by a young and beautiful wait staff. Meals are served non-stop until 2am, a good bet for a late-night meal after sampling nearby nightlife. Up early? Aa long daily breakfast menu is available from 8am to 11:30am too.

133 av. des Champs Elysées, 8th arrond. www.publicisdrugstore.com. © **01-44-43-77-64.** Main course 19€–39€; Mon–Fri 8am–2am. Sat–Sun 10am–2am. Métro: Charles de Gaulle–Etoile.

Inexpensive

Boulangerie Joséphine ★ BAKERY/SANDWICHES This terrific bakery near the Arc de Triomphe has a nice outdoor terrace and a pretty upstairs dining room that fills quickly with local office workers and businesspeople. You can buy sandwiches and salads (and desserts, of course) to go, or sit down and sample one of the excellent daily specials, like stuffed vegetables, roast chicken, or osso bucco. Also open for breakfast from 8am.

69 av. Marceau, 8th arrond. www.josephine-boulangerie.com. © **01-47-20-49-62.** Main course 5€–15€. Mon–Fri 8am–8pm. Métro: Charles de Gaulle–Etoile.

MONTMARTRE (18TH ARRONDISSEMENT)

When you get away from the tourist traps of place du Tertre, you start to understand why this neighborhood is a favorite with the artsy-hipster set. And where there's art, you are bound to find an artist in the kitchen.

Moderate

Le Coq Rico ★★★ ROTISSERIE At the top of the Butte de Montmartre, this popular rotisserie is where renowned chef Antoine Westerman proves that poultry can go way beyond the nugget. When raised in the right conditions (in the open-air, with space and with nutritious food), poultry can be just as delicious as the finest cut of beef. On the menu are such delicacies as guinea fowl in a hazelnut crumb, succulent whole duck from the Dombes region (to share) and tantalizingly juicy Challans chicken—the lot accompanied by crispy, hand-cut fries or macaroni and cheese. The desserts are worth leaving space for, too: lemon crumble, caramelized brioche with poached pears and beer ice-cream, and one of the best chocolate mille-feuille (layers of pastry and chocolate) in town.

98 rue Lepic, 18th arrond. http://en.lecoqrico.com. ℰ **01-42-59-82-89.** Main course 22€–41€; whole birds to share 85€–98€. Daily noon–2:30pm and 7pm–midnight. Métro: Abbesses or Lamarck-Caulincourt.

Wepler ★★ FRENCH BRASSERIE   Picasso and Modigliani used to hang out at this venerable brasserie on place de Clichy, as did writer Henry Miller, who made it his headquarters. "I knew it like a book," he wrote. "The faces of the waiters, the managers, the cashiers, the whores, the clientele, even the attendants in the lavatory, are engraved in my memory as if they were illustrations in a book which I read every day." Today the atmosphere is quite sedate, but it's still a wonderful place to sit and watch the world go by, and the prices are accessible enough that it is still frequented by artists and writers. The menu is classic brasserie (steak tartare, shellfish platters, poached haddock in *beurre blanc*) but with a light, gourmet touch. If you don't want a big meal, ask for the less expensive cafe menu, which features delicate omelets, a *plat du jour,* and meal-size salads served on the covered terrace.

14 pl. de Clichy, 18th arrond. www.wepler.com. ℰ **01-45-22-53-24.** Main course 18€–30€; fixed-price lunch or dinner 26.50€–38€. Daily 8am–12:30am. Métro: place de Clichy.

Inexpensive

Bouillon Pigalle ★★ TRADITIONAL FRENCH   The word *bouillon* refers to the workers' restaurants, found all over Paris back in the 19th century. The idea was to offer good food at modest prices, a concept that still speaks to working Parisians some 100 years later, if the line out the door of this brand-new, 300-seater joint is any indication. You come here to tuck into classics like leeks in vinaigrette, beef bourguignon, and chocolate eclairs at prices so low (think 1.90€ for a starter, 10€ for a main and less than 4€ for dessert), you wonder how they make a profit. The menu covers a wide variety of traditional dishes like steak with fries or rum baba. Service is fast and furious, but it's all part of the atmosphere, which is something that belongs to another time and place. It takes no reservations, so be prepared to wait.

22 boulevard de Clichy, 18th arrond. www.bouillonpigalle.com. ℰ **01-42-59-69-31.** Main course 8.50€–11€. Daily noon–midnight Métro: Pigalle.

RÉPUBLIQUE, BASTILLE & EASTERN PARIS (11TH & 12TH ARRONDISSEMENTS)

Home to a mix of working-class families, hipsters, and *bobos* (bourgeois bohemians), the area between République and Nation is diverse, young, and fun. This might be why there are so many good restaurants around here. It's also a good neighborhood for discovering the flavors of Africa in restaurants featuring dishes from France's former colonies.

Expensive

Septime ★★★ MODERN FRENCH   With its seafood tapas bar next door **(Clamato)** and its tiny wine bar across the street **(Septime la Cave),** Septime has done more to gentrify this stretch of the 11th arrond. than years of town planning ever could. People cross the entire city for a table in Bertrand Grébaut's retro-chic neo-bistro (including Beyoncé, Jay Z, and Gwyneth Paltrow), reserving months in advance. But that's not why you should come. The progressive, seasonal dishes—anything from line-caught squid with mustard and leek sauce to pigeon with beetroot and Morello cherries—are consistently delicious, and the menus change daily according to what's freshest in the produce market. If you can't score a dinner reservation, try lunchtime. And if all else fails, nip next door to Clamato, where fabulous small plates of crab fritters, clams, or trout roe are washed down with lip-smacking wine that starts for as little as 5.50€ a glass. You won't be disappointed.

80 rue de Charonne, 11th arrond. www.septime-charonne.fr. ✆ **01-43-67-38-29.** Fixed-price lunch 42€ or dinner 80€. Tues–Fri 12:15–2pm and 7:30–10pm; Mon 7:30–10pm. Closed Aug. Métro: Charonne or Ledru-Rollin.

Moderate

Astier ★★ TRADITIONAL FRENCH/BISTRO   This beautiful old restaurant has kept its polished wood and checked tablecloths, as well as its classic menu. Wild boar terrine, rabbit in mustard sauce, rib steak with anchovy toasts, pike *quenelles* (a sort of elegant dumpling) and *tarte tatin* (apple tart) are menu regulars, plus the legendary cheese tray. It's a postcard version of a Paris bistro, minus the surly waiters. The fixed-price menu is your best bet, as the main courses can get pricey on their own.

44 rue Jean-Pierre Timbaud, 11th arrond. www.restaurant-astier.com. ✆ **01-43-57-16-35.** Main course 22€–26€; fixed-price lunch or dinner 35€–45€. Daily 12:15–2:15pm and 7–10:30pm. July–Aug closed Sat and Mon lunch, and Sun. Métro: Parmentier or Oberkampf.

Mansouria ★★ MOROCCAN   Generally accepted as the queen of Moroccan cooking (she's published half a dozen cookbooks), Fatéma Hal rules supreme in the kitchen of this elegant restaurant. Naturally, it offers a wide variety of delicious couscous dishes, garnished with fragrant broths and grilled meats, but the real treat here are the tagines, or stews, like the one with chicken and walnut-stuffed figs, or another with lamb, eggplant, and preserved lemons. One dish, La Mourouzia, is prepared from a 12th-century recipe featuring lamb seared in real *ras al hanout*—an intense mixture of 27 spices—and stewed in honey, raisins, and almonds.

11 rue Faidherbe, 11th arrond. www.mansouria.fr. ✆ **01-43-71-00-16.** Main course 18€–26€; fixed-price dinner 28€–55€. Mon 7:30–10:30pm; Tues–Sat noon–2pm and 7:30–11pm. Métro: Faidherbe-Chaligny.

Virtus ★★★ BISTRO   This discreet little place, tucked away on a gentrifying street in a residential part of the 12th arrond., draws food-savvy locals with impressively executed dishes like scallops in hazelnut butter, succulent roast lamb with peas, and lip-smacking passion fruit mousse with yogurt ice-cream. The descriptions sound simple, but the result is wonderfully complex, with layers of flavors that explode in your mouth. A good time to visit is lunchtime, when the 17€ menu (dish of the day and a plate of cheese) is an absolute steal. If you come along for dinner, you're in for a wonderful six-course ride with the obligatory tasting menu, which may include delights like asparagus with strawberries and burrata, and pollack in anchovy emulsion—the lot washed down with wine served by the resident sommelier who may well double as your waiter.

29 rue de Cotte, 12th arrond. www.virtus-paris.com. ℭ **09-80-68-08-08.** Main course 18.50€–35€; fixed-price dinner 59.50€. Tues–Sat noon–2pm and 7–10pm. Closed part of Aug. Métro: Ledru Rollin.

Inexpensive
L'Ebauchoir ★ MEDITERRANEAN   In an unlikely corner of the 12th arrondissement, this neighborhood hangout offers a great selection of bistro cooking at reasonable prices. High ceilings, sunny yellow walls, and wooden fixtures create a friendly atmosphere for Mediterranean-inspired dishes like roast lamb with sweet garlic, polenta, and olives, or grilled bonito with a peach and preserved lemon salad. Vegetarian options might include eggplant and feta with olives and fresh capers. Serving one of the few reasonable three-course lunches (14€), this place is jammed at noontime, so try to reserve.

43 rue des Citeaux, 12th arrond. www.lebauchoir.com. ℭ **01-43-42-49-31.** Main course dinner 19€–24€; fixed-price lunch 14€–26€. Mon 8–11pm, Tues–Fri noon–2:30pm and 8–11pm, Fri–Sat noon–2:30pm and 7:30–11pm. Closed 1 week mid-Aug. Métro: Faidherbe Chaligny or Reuilly Diderot.

Waly Fay ★★ SENEGALESE   Take a gastronomic voyage to West Africa at this popular restaurant that has introduced umpteen Parisians to delicious Senegalese cuisine. A former French colony, Senegal has absorbed culinary influences from France, as well as its northern neighbors in the Magreb. Cool music and candlelight set the scene for some of the best poulet yassa (chicken marinated in lime and onions) in Paris; there also several versions of n'dolé, spinach-like leaves cooked with peanut sauce and mixed with shrimp, fish, or meat. Less adventurous eaters might like the marinated brochettes, which are grilled over a wood fire. Fill out the meal with a side order of fried plantains or *atéké* (manioc). The terrific selection of rums here are well-suited to cocktail hour.

6 rue Godefroy Cavalgnac, 11th arrond. www.walyfay.com. ℭ **01-40-24-17-79.** Main course 13€–28€; fixed-price lunch 14€–18€. Daily noon–3pm and 7–11:30pm.

4

BELLEVILLE, CANAL ST-MARTIN & LA VILLETTE (10TH, 19TH & 20TH ARRONDISSEMENTS)

One of the last strongholds of Paris's bohemian set, here you can find both gourmet bistros and funky cheap eats, as well as a good number of wine bars that serve both nibbles and the fruit of the vine.

Moderate

Chez Michel ★★ BRETON/SEAFOOD   Prices have barely budged in a decade at this popular restaurant, where chef Thierry Breton improvises on recipes from back home (Brittany), including lots of seafood dishes, like cotriade, a Breton fish stew, or fresh crab salad. A massive oven has been installed in the dining room itself, cooking up slow-cooked specialties like braised lamb. For dessert, try the copious rice pudding or the awe-inspiring Paris-Brest (a choux pastry filled with praline cream).

10 rue de Belzunce, 10th arrond. www.restaurantchezmichel.fr. ℂ **01-44-53-06-20.** Fixed-price lunch 29€–35€ or dinner 38€. Mon–Fri 11:45am–2pm and 6:45–11pm. Closed Aug. Métro: Gare du Nord.

Rosa Bonheur ★ TAPAS   This unconventional space is named after an unconventional 19th-century painter/sculptress. It's a restaurant and tapas bar, but it's also a sort of off-the-wall community center, hosting various expositions and events—it even has its own chorus and soccer team. Located in an old *buvette* (refreshment pavilion) inside the Parc des Buttes Chaumont, dating from the Universal Exposition of 1900, the restaurant boasts a sprawling terrace and one of the best panoramic views in town. A huge crowd gathers to drink and nibble tapas outside or sample dishes from the creative menu. An indoor play area and kids' menu make this a good family option.

2 allée de la Cascade, 19th arrond. www.rosabonheur.fr. ℂ **01-42-00-00-45.** Tapas 6€–9€; main course 16€–22€. Thurs–Sun noon–midnight. Closed first 2 weeks in Jan. Métro: Botzaris.

Le Verre Volé ★ WINE BAR/MODERN FRENCH   The sun is shining, the leafy trees are posing prettily along the Canal St-Martin, and you are walking over one of the pretty footbridges that curve over the water. All that's missing is a table and a glass of wine. Luckily, this wine bar/restaurant is on hand to delight you with its vast selection. You could share a plate of sliced smoked meats and sausage, the usual accompaniment to a glass of red, or explore the menu, which might include a slice of milk-fed veal or mullet ceviche. Then select a bottle of wine from the shelves that line the walls and enjoy it (for a nominal corkage fee) in this informal, if crowded, setting.

67 rue de Lancry, 10th arrond. www.leverrevole.fr. ℂ **01-48-03-17-34.** Main course 16€–23€. Daily 12:30–2pm and 7:30–10:30pm. Métro: Jacques Bonsergent.

Inexpensive

Bob's Juice Bar ★ VEGETARIAN   Hip Parisians are tripping all over themselves to try "smoossies" (that is, smoothies) these days, and some of the best can be found at this terrific vegetarian restaurant, which has muffins, bagels, soups, and other delicious goodies. The brainchild of Marc Grossman (alias "Bob"), an erstwhile New Yorker, this may not be the most authentically French experience, but it certainly is a tasty one. Sit down or take out here, or try the larger **Bob's Kitchen** in the Marais (74 rue des Gravilliers, 3rd arrond.) or in the famous Shakespeare & Company bookshop cafe (37 rue de la Bûcherie, 5th arrond.).

15 rue Lucien Sampaix, 10th arrond. www.bobsjuicebar.com. ✆ **09-50-06-36-18.** Smoothies 4€–5€; main course 5€–8€. Mon–Fri 8am–3pm and Sat 8:30am-4pm. Métro: Jacques Bonsergent.

The Left Bank

LATIN QUARTER (5TH & 13TH ARRONDISSEMENTS)

Steer clear of the unbearably touristy area around rue de la Huchette and the often mediocre restaurants on rue Moufftard. Venture farther afield, where innovative restaurateurs have been cultivating a knowledgeable clientele of professors, professionals, and food savvy locals.

Expensive

La Tour d'Argent ★★ CLASSIC FRENCH   Sure, you come here for the pressed duck (the signature dish—each duck has been numbered since 1890), but the real reason to come to the "Silver Tower" is to sample its history, its view, and its incredible service. Five or six different waiters will visit your table at one time or another, accomplishing various tasks (opening wine bottles, pulling out your chair, and even leading you to the bathroom) with utmost professionalism and not a hint of snobbery. They then discreetly disappear into the rich decor as you gaze through the huge windows that give you a first-class view of Notre-Dame's flying buttresses. By the time you've finished your meal (which still merits its one Michelin star), you feel like a pasha. The fixed-price lunch is a good way to enjoy this singular experience without ruining your budget. Be sure to reserve at least a week in advance; jackets required for men at dinner.

15–17 quai de la Tournelle, 5th arrond. www.latourdargent.com. ✆ **01-43-54-23-31.** Main course 70€–140€; fixed-price lunch 105€ or dinner 280€–350€. Tues–Sat noon–1pm and 7–9pm. Closed in Aug. Métro: St-Michel or Maubert-Mutualité.

La Truffière ★★ CLASSIC FRENCH   An atmospheric 17th-century dining room near the Seine, with exposed stone walls and wooden beams is the setting for the sort of French cuisine you crave for when you think of Paris. Hint: langoustines, suckling lamb, ultra-ripe cheeses, and the black diamonds (truffles) that the restaurant takes its name from, all prepared with panache by talented chef Christophe Poard. If you're into wine, you'll be hard-pressed to find a better restaurant: There are some 3,200 bottles on the menu. Thank goodness for the sommelier who takes into account both your budget and the dishes you've ordered. Tasting menus costs up to 125€ in the evening, so the 40€ lunch menu is one of the best deals in town.

4 rue Blainville, 5th arrond. www.la-truffiere.fr. © **01-46-33-29-82.** Main dishes 62€–95€; fixed-price lunch 40€ or dinner 68€–180€. Daily noon–2pm and Tues–Sat 7–10:30pm. Closed Aug. Métro: place Monge or Cardinal Lemoine.

Moderate

Dans les Landes ★★ SOUTHWESTERN FRENCH/TAPAS Chef Julien Duboué takes inspiration from his homeland and neighboring Basque country to create luscious tapas to be enjoyed with (many) glasses of great regional wines. Fried chipirions (small squid), polenta with smoked duck breast, Basque-style mussels—the list is long and tempting. It's packed at night, so get here early or reserve a table.

119 bis rue Monge, 5th arrond. http://dansleslandes.fr. © **01-45-87-06-00.** Tapas 9€–29€. Mon-Fri noon–2:30pm and 7–11pm; Sat–Sun noon–4pm and 7–11pm. Closed last week of Dec, first week of Jan, and 3 weeks in Aug. Métro: Censier-Daubenton.

Le Pré Verre ★★ MODERN FRENCH/ASIAN FUSION This crowded and convivial gourmet wine bar offers dishes that are a scrumptious blend of traditional French and exotic ingredients—not particularly flashy or trendy or even spicy, just deliciously unexpected. One of the signature dishes is a meltingly tender *cochon de lait* (milk-fed pork) served with a smooth cinnamon-infused sauce and a delectably crunchy mass that turns out to be cabbage. The weekday lunch menu is a particularly great deal: You get an appetizer, a main dish, a glass of wine, and coffee for 14.90€.

8 rue Thenard, 5th arrond. www.lepreverre.com. © **01-43-54-59-47.** Main course 20€; fixed-price lunch 14.90€ or dinner 28€ and 35€. Tues–Sat noon–2pm and 7:30–10:30pm. Closed last week of Dec. Métro: Maubert-Mutualité or Cluny–La Sorbonne.

Inexpensive

Jardin des Pâtes ★ PASTA/VEGETARIAN This light-filled restaurant specializes in pasta. But this is no ordinary pasta—not only are the rice, wheat, rye, and barley noodles made fresh every day, but the organic flour that goes into them is ground daily on the premises. The focus on wholesome ingredients is menu-wide; even the ice cream is 100 percent natural. While you won't find the usual Italian sauces, you will find original creations like rye pasta with ham, cream, sweet onions, white wine, and Comté cheese or barley pasta with fresh salmon, leeks, seaweed, and crème fraîche. Vegetarians have lots of choices here, and the relaxed atmosphere makes it a good place to bring (well-behaved) kids. Pastas are made to order, so don't be in a hurry.

4 rue Lacépède, 5th arrond. www.restaurant-lejardindespates.fr. © **01-43-31-50-71.** Main course 13€–15€. Daily noon–2:30pm and 7–11pm. Métro: place Monge.

ST-GERMAIN-DES-PRÉS (6TH ARRONDISSEMENT)

Saint Germain is a mix of expensive eateries that only the lucky few can afford and stalwart holdouts from the days when poverty-stricken intellectuals and artists frequented the Café de Flore. Though the Marché St-Germain has been transformed into a type of mall, the restaurants hugging its perimeter offer a wide range of possibilities.

Expensive

Le Relais Louis XIII ★★★ CLASSIC FRENCH   This acclaimed restaurant pays homage to traditional French cuisine at its most illustrious. No tonka beans or reduced licorice sauce here—Chef Manuel Martinez trains his formidable skills on classic sauces and time-honored dishes like sea-bass quenelles and roast duck, though he's not opposed to topping off the meal with a little lemon-basil sherbet. Signature dishes include lobster and foie gras ravioli, or braised sweetbreads with wild mushrooms. The atmospheric dining room, crisscrossed with exposed beams and ancient stonework, makes you wonder if the Three Musketeers might tumble through the doorway bearing your mille feuille with bourbon vanilla cream.

8 rue des Grands-Augustins, 6th arrond. www.relaislouis13.fr. ✆ **01-43-26-75-96.** Main course 58€–59€; fixed-price lunch 65€ or dinner 95€–145€. Tues–Sat 12:15–2:30pm and 7:15–10:30pm. Closed 1st week Jan, 1st week May, and all of Aug. Métro: Odéon or St-Michel.

Moderate

Le Comptoir ★★★ TRADITIONAL FRENCH/BISTRO   The brainchild of super-chef Yves de Camdeborde, this small and scrumptious bistro is still bringing in the crowds almost a decade after it opened. During the day, it serves relatively traditional fare, say, a slice of lamb with thyme sauce or maybe the *panier de cochonaille,* a basket of the Camdeborde family's own brand of smoked meats. On weeknights, it's a temple to haute cuisine, with a five-course tasting menu. You'll need to reserve several weeks in advance for this meal (or have a room in the adjoined Relais Saint Germain hotel, p. 140), which changes every night and is

4

PARIS | Where to Eat

nonnegotiable—the chef decides what you are going to eat (though allergies are of course taken into account). There are no reservations at lunch or on the weekends, when the bistro menu is served from noon to 11pm, so arrive early or be prepared to wait.

9 carrefour de l'Odéon, 6th arrond. www.hotel-paris-relais-saint-germain.com. ✆ **01-44-27-07-50.** Main course weekends and weekdays 17€–32€; fixed-price dinner weeknights 65€. Daily noon–11pm. Métro: Odéon.

Huîtrerie Régis ★ OYSTERS/SEAFOOD   Like oysters on the half shell? Good, because that's pretty much all they have here: delicious bivalves that come straight from the Marennes-Oléron region on France's Atlantic coast. The brief and to-the-point menu gives you a choice of various sizes and grades of oysters, as well as sea urchins, clams, and shrimp. You'll have to order at least a dozen oysters to sit down in the tiny restaurant; considering the price, you may as well order a *formule,* or fixed-price menu, which include various combinations of oysters, wine, and coffee. These oysters are fresh, oceany mouthfuls of flavor that deserve a good glass of Sancerre.

3 rue de Montfaucon, 6th arrond. www.huitrerieregis.com. ✆ **01-44-41-10-07.** Oysters per dozen 26€–65€; fixed-price lunch or dinner 30€–40€. Mon–Fri noon–2:30pm and 6:30–10:30pm; Sat and Sun noon–10:45pm. Closed mid-July to mid-Sept. Métro: Mabillon or St-Germain.

Le P'tit Fernand ★★ TRADITIONAL FRENCH/BISTRO   This tiny slice of a restaurant packs a flavorful punch. Red-checked tablecloths provide a homey background for excellent bistro dishes like thick steak with a confit of shallots and creamy mashed potatoes, or duck magret (breast) served with morello-cherry sauce. You could start with a nice light beet and rhubarb gazpacho or go nuts and order the homemade terrine of foie gras. Whatever it is, it will be executed with loving care and quality ingredients, which is why this restaurant has a devoted clientele.

7 rue Lobineau, 6th arrond. ✆ **01-40-46-06-88.** Main course 18€–26€. Daily noon–2pm and 7–11:30pm. Métro: Mabillon.

Inexpensive

Restaurant Polidor ★ TRADITIONAL FRENCH/BISTRO   An unofficial historic monument, Polidor is not so much a restaurant as a snapshot of a bygone era. The decor has not changed substantially for at least 100 years, when Verlaine and Rimbaud, the bad boys of poetry, would come here for a cheap meal. In the 1950s, it was dubbed "the College of Pataphysics" by a rowdy group of young upstarts that included Max Ernst, Boris Vian, and Eugene Ionesco; André Gide and Ernest Hemingway were reputed regulars. The menu features hefty bistro standbys like boeuf bourguignon and *blanquette de veau* (veal stew), but you'll also find lighter fare like salmon with basil or chicken breast with morel sauce. These days, the artsy set has moved elsewhere; you'll probably be sharing the long wooden tables with other tourists, along with a dose of locals. Though the food is not particularly memorable, the ambience is unique.

41 rue Monsieur-le-Prince, 6th arrond. www.polidor.com. ✆ **01-43-26-95-34.** Main course 14€–25€; fixed-price menu 22€–35€. Daily noon–2:30pm; Mon–Sat 7pm–12:30am and Sun 7–11pm. Métro: Odéon.

EIFFEL TOWER & NEARBY (7TH ARRONDISSEMENT)

Crowded with ministries and important people, this neighborhood is so grand, you half expect to hear trumpets blowing each time you turn a corner. Though it's a rather staid neighborhood, a few streets are fairly lively, namely rue Cler, a pretty market street, and rue St-Dominique, home to some of the best restaurants on this side of the Seine.

Expensive

L'Arpège ★★★ MODERN FRENCH   This is probably the only Michelin-three-star restaurant where vegetables are the stars. You can still find meat on the menu, but it takes a back seat to carrots, turnips, sweet peas, or whatever other lovely plant life is in season. The pristine produce comes from Chef Alain Passard's farm and is often picked the same day it's served. The menu comes in two sections: the "grand crus" of the vegetable garden, and the "memory" dishes: milk-fed lamb from the Aveyron with wild celery, or fresh fish from Brittany with lovage and sweet peas. Don't miss the *tarte aux pommes bouquet de roses* (tart composed of apple ribbons rolled into tiny rosettes). Reservations are required at least 2 weeks in advance.

84 rue de Varenne, 7th arrond. www.alain-passard.com. ✆ **01-47-05-09-06.** Main course 82€–175€; fixed-price lunch 175€ or tasting menu (lunch and dinner) 320€ and 420€. Mon–Fri noon–2:30pm and 7–10:30pm. Métro: Varenne.

La Ferme Saint Simon ★★★ TRADITIONAL FRENCH   Off the beaten track, down a quiet side street, this gourmet restaurant feels like a secret, attracting only those in the know—generally ambassadors from the nearby embassies and other locals. The menu treats classic dishes with kindness and care, giving each a dash of delicious originality. We've been impressed with the roast monkfish with bacon, horseradish and turnip, the rib of beef in red wine sauce, and the frogs' legs in parsley sauce—and for dessert, the out-of-this-world chocolate soufflé.

6 rue de Saint Simon, 7th arrond. www.fermestsimon.com. ✆ **01-45-48-35-74.** Main course 29€–84€; fixed-price lunch 39€. Mon–Fri noon–2:30pm; Mon–Sat 7–10pm. Métro: Ru du Bac or Solférino.

Moderate

Le Casse Noix ★★ TRADITIONAL FRENCH/BISTRO   The result of yet another great chef realizing his bistro dreams, this relaxed restaurant offers high-caliber food in a casual, affordable setting. The decor is nostalgic and the traditional French cooking is sincere and generous, featuring dishes like roast pork shoulder Ibaïona with olive puree, or a classic *petit salé* (lentils with smoky ham). About a 10-min. walk from the Eiffel

Tower, this is a good bet for those looking for a bit of authenticity in an otherwise very touristy neighborhood. At dinnertime, the fixed-price menu is *obligatoire*, so no à la carte ordering. Lunch is more flexible.

56 rue de la Fédération, 15th arrond. www.le-cassenoix.fr. ℂ **01-45-66-09-01.** Main course at lunch 19€–23€; fixed-price lunch or dinner 34€. Mon–Fri noon–2:30pm and 7–10:30pm. Closed Aug and between Christmas and New Year. Métro: Dupleix.

La Fontaine de Mars ★★ BISTRO/SOUTHWESTERN FRENCH Red and white checks are everywhere at this old-school bistro: on the tablecloths, the wicker chairs, and even the curtains. A venerable institution since it first opened in 1908, its low-key classy decor and traditional menu attracted the attention of President Obama, who made a surprise visit here with his wife Michele in 2009. The kitchen turns out reliable and succulent southwestern French dishes like cassoulet, foie gras, and duck breast with black cherry sauce. Starters include *escargots* (snails) and *oeufs au Madiran* (eggs baked with red wine and bacon), and the dessert list is full of classics such as île flottante, crème brûlée, and dark chocolate mousse.

129 rue St-Dominique, 7th arrond. www.fontainedemars.com. ℂ **01-47-05-46-44.** Main course 17€–49€. Daily noon–3pm and 7:30–11pm. Métro: Ecole Militaire.

Inexpensive

Café Constant ★★ TRADITIONAL FRENCH/BISTRO Of the three Christian Constant restaurants on this street, this one is the most relaxed; you may find the master himself at the bar smoking a cigar here during his off-hours. The menu features modern versions of French comfort food like tangy poached cod with aioli, melt-in-your-mouth beef *daube* (stew) with carrots, or steak with shallots and creamy potato puree. The weekday lunch *formule* is a two-course meal (chef's choice) for 18€, a terrific deal for this level of quality. If you are hankering for a meal off-hours, between 3pm and 5pm you can select a dish from a more limited menu. No reservations.

139 rue Saint-Dominique, 7th arrond. www.maisonconstant.com. ℂ **01-47-53-73-34.** Main course 16€–29€; fixed-price lunch 18€–26€. Daily 7am–11pm. Métro: Ecole Militaire.

Le Petit Cler ★ TRADITIONAL FRENCH/BISTRO   A mini-version of La Fontaine de Mars (see above), this cute little cafe tumbles out on to the rue Cler pedestrian market street and serves food of the same high quality as its upscale big sister, but simpler, and at a lower price. While you won't find as many red and white checks, you will find classic cafe fare (steaks with sautéed potatoes, omelets, and tartines—open-faced grilled sandwiches) as well as a daily special, which might be roast chicken (Sunday) or fresh fish (Friday). You can also get a good continental breakfast here.

29 rue Cler, 7th arrond. www.lepetitcler.com. ℂ **01-45-50-17-50.** Main course 11€–18€. Daily 8am–11:30pm. Closed 2 weeks in Aug. Métro: Ecole Militaire

MONTPARNASSE & NEARBY (14TH & 15TH ARRONDISSEMENTS)

The famous cafes and brasseries (Le Dôme, Le Select, La Coupole, and Closerie des Lilas) where struggling writers and artists like Picasso, Hemingway, and Chagall once hung out make for atmospheric spots, but there are plenty of other good options, from Breton creperies near the train station to a bundle of new gourmet bistros farther south.

Expensive

Cobéa ★★ MODERN FRENCH   Chef Philippe Bélissent invents concoctions that are as delicate and refined as the dining room in this pretty little house: Perfectly cooked veal with fava beans and polenta; freshly caught John Dory; or pigeon with artichokes and olives might show up on the mix-and-match menu. The concept at dinner is as follows: There is one menu, from which you decide whether you'd like to try four (75€), six (95€), or eight (115€) courses. Service is impeccable.

11 rue Raymond Losserand, 14th arrond. www.cobea.fr. ℂ **01-43-20-21-39.** Fixed-price lunch 50€–70€ or dinner 85€–120€. Tues–Sat 12:15–1:15pm and 7:15–9:15pm. Closed mid-Feb to early-Mar and Aug. Métro: Gaîté or Pernety.

Moderate

L'Assiette ★★ TRADITIONAL FRENCH   There's a whiff of the Belle Epoque in this old-fashioned dining room, which has its share of mirrors and ceiling ornaments. The menu appeals to culinary nostalgia as well, with dishes like homemade cassoulet, pike quenelles (long and delicate fish dumplings) with Nantua sauce, as well as escargots and homemade foie gras for starters. For dessert, indulge in crème caramel made with salted butter or profiteroles with chocolate sauce. The restaurant also hosts workshops for tea-lovers, where you can explore the secrets of gourmet teas (more information at www.thesdelassiette.com).

181 rue du Château, 14th arrond. www.restaurant-lassiette.com. ℂ **01-43-22-64-86.** Main course 25€–38€; fixed-price lunch 23€. Wed–Sun noon–2:30pm and 7:30–10:30pm. Closed Aug. Métro: Gaîté.

CAFE SOCIETY: PARIS'S top cafes

Cafe life is an integral part of the Parisian scene, and it simply won't do to visit the capital without joining in. Here are a few ideas for your own personal cafe tour. **Tip:** Coffee or other drinks at the bar often cost half of what they do at a table.

Café de Flore ★ Every great French intellectual and artist seems to have had their moment here: Apollinaire, André Breton, Picasso, Giacometti, and of course, Simone de Beauvoir and Jean-Paul Sartre, who virtually lived here during World War II. The atmosphere today is less thoughtful and more showbiz, but it's still worth an overpriced cup of coffee just to come in and soak it up. 172 bd. St-Germain, 6th arrond. www.cafedeflore.fr. *℃* **01-45-48-55-26.** Daily 7am–2am. Métro: St-Germain-des-Prés.

Café de la Mairie ★ What could be nicer than sitting outdoors at a sidewalk cafe on the place St-Sulpice? Indoors, it's a 1970s archetype: Formica bar, boxy chairs, and an odd assortment of pensioners, fashion victims, students, and would-be novelists. 8 pl. St-Sulpice, 6th arrond. *℃* **01-43-26-67-82.** Mon–Fri 7am–2am, Sat 8am–2am, Sun 9am–2am. Métro: Mabillon or St-Sulpice.

Le Bistrot du Peintre ★ Artists, hipsters, and other fauna from the bustling rue de Charonne area flock to this popular spot, which sports an authentic Art Nouveau interior with the original peeling paint. 116 av. Ledru-Rollin, 11th arrond. www.bistrotdupeintre.com. *℃* **01-47-00-34-39.** Daily 7am–2am. Métro: Ledru-Rollin.

Les Deux Magots ★ The literary pedigree here is impressive: Poets Verlaine and Rimbaud camped out here, as did André Gide and Albert Camus. Sartre and de Beauvoir moved in postwar and stayed for decades. The outdoor terrace is pleasant early in the morning before the crowds awake. 6 pl. St-Germain-des-Prés, 6th arrond. www.lesdeuxmagots.fr. *℃* **01-45-48-55-25.** Daily 7:30am–1am. Métro: St-Germain-des-Prés.

Le Nemours ★ Cuddled up in a corner next to the Comedie Française, this beautiful cafe has a great terrace stretching out onto the place Colette. The ideal spot for taking a load off after a day at the nearby Louvre. 2 pl. Colette. *℃* **01-42-61-34-14.** Mon–Fri 7am–midnight, Sat 8am–midnight, Sun 9am–8:30pm. Métro: Palais Royal–Musée du Louvre.

Inexpensive

Crêperie Josselin ★★ CREPERIE   This is one of the best of the dozens of crêperies concentrated near the Montparnasse train station. The cooks working the griddle know exactly how to achieve the lacy, golden edges of a perfect galette, and they are not shy with the butter. Josselin's specialty is the "couple," a double crepe that uses two of these lacy confections in one dish. It's delicious but filling; if you are not starving ask the waiter to make it a "simple." Tradition demands that this meal be accompanied by a bowl of hard cider (low alcohol content; for adults only). The easy prices, continuous service, and wide range of flavor combinations make this a great option for children as well. Closed on Monday, but you can wander down to No. 59, Le Petit Josselin, its sister restaurant (closed Sun).

67 rue du Montparnasse, 14th arrond. ℰ **01-43-20-93-50.** Main course 7€–11€; fixed-price menu 11€. No credit cards. Tues–Fri 11:30am–3pm and 6–11pm; Sat–Sun noon–11pm. Métro: Montparnasse-Bienvenüe.

SHOPPING

Vuitton, Chanel, Baccarat—the names of famous French luxury brands roll around the tongue like rich chocolate. But while it's fun to window-shop at Cartier, few of us can actually afford to buy anything there. Guess what? Neither can most Parisians. Thus, there's so much more shopping to explore than those big-box luxury stores on the Champs-Élysées. Seek out the small boutiques by up-and-coming designers, lesser-known but fab chocolate stores, and hip yet inexpensive French chain stores where you can throw together a look in minutes. Paris is shopaholic heaven, if you know where to go to find your *bonheur* (happiness).

Business Hours

In general, shops are open from 9 or 10am to 7pm; some are closed on Monday, and most are closed on Sunday. Unfortunately, that means that the stores are jam-packed on Saturday, so don't say I didn't warn you.

Some smaller, family-run operations sometimes still close between noon and 2pm for lunch, but most stores stay open all day. Many larger stores and most department stores stay open late (that is, until 9pm) one night a week (called a *nocturne,* usually a Thursday). For food and toiletry emergencies, tiny minimarkets (called *alimentations*) stay open late into the night daily. ***Note:*** Many shops close down for 2 or 3 weeks in July or August, when the vacation exodus empties out major portions of the city.

Great Shopping Areas

STREETS FOR BARGAIN HUNTING

You can find clothes and knickknacks at significantly reduced prices at discount shops, which tend to conglomerate on certain streets. **Rue d'Alésia** (14th arrond., Métro: Alésia) is lined with outlet stores *(déstock)* selling discounted wares, including designer labels like Sonia Rykiel; and **Rue St-Placide** (6th arrond., Métro: Sèvres-Babylone) has both outlet stores and discount shops like Mouton à Cinq Pattes (p. 171).

MIDRANGE SHOPPING HUBS

Several areas have high concentrations of chain and midrange stores where you can get a lot of shopping done in a small area. They are: **Rue de Rennes** (6th arrond.; especially near the Tour Montparnasse); **Les Halles** (1st arrond.; the Forum des Halles underground mall is still open during the reconstruction of Les Halles above; don't ignore the many nearby shops above); **Rue de Rivoli** (1st arrond., btw. rue du Pont Neuf and Hôtel de Ville); and **Grands Magasins** (9th arrond.)—be sure to look in the little streets that weave around the Printemps and Galeries Lafayette department stores (see below).

CHIC BOUTIQUE-ING

Paris has an endless number of darling boutiques, ranging from funky to fantastic. A few of the best streets for boutique shopping or simply *lèche-vitrine* (window shopping) are: **Rue des Abbesses** (18th arrond.; Métro: Abbesses), for affordable chic and the shops of hip, young startup designers; **Rue de Charonne** (11th arrond.; Métro: Bastille), a youth-oriented street that has recently taken a turn upscale with a dose of hip boutiques; **Rue des Francs Bourgeois** (4th arrond.; Métro: St-Paul), for a cornucopia of fashionable/cool stores, most of which are open on Sunday; and **Rue Etienne Marcel** (2nd arrond.; Métro: Etienne Marcel), next to the in-vogue Montorgueil pedestrian zone, with stylish boutiques galore.

THE SKY'S THE LIMIT

If you don't look at price tags and are always searching for the ultimate everything, Paris does not disappoint. For centuries, Paris has been the capital of luxury goods, many of them for sale on **avenue Montaigne** (8th arrond.; Métro: Franklin D. Roosevelt), with breathtakingly expensive designer flagships like Dior and Chanel; the **place Vendôme** (1st arrond.; Métro: Concorde or Tuileries), with eye-popping jewelry shops (Cartier, Boucheron, and so on); and **Rue du Faubourg St-Honoré** (8th arrond.; Métro: St-Philippe du Roule), with deeply elegant boutiques filled with choice morsels of designer goods.

Markets: Food & Flea

Marchés (open-air or covered markets) are small universes unto themselves where nothing substantial has really changed for centuries. These markets are great local spots to hunt for fresh food or browse flea-market finds.

FOOD MARKETS

Paris's food markets are noisy, bustling, joyous places where you can buy fresh, honest food. Following is a short list of food *marchés;* you can find more on Paris tourism website (https://en.parisinfo.com; type search "food and specialist markets"). *Note:* Unless you see evidence to the contrary, don't pick up your own fruits and vegetables with your hands. Wait until the vendor serves you.

Marché d'Aligre ★★★ (also called Marché Beauveau, place d'Aligre, 12th arrond.; outdoor market Tues–Sun 9am–1pm, covered market Tues–Sat 9am–1pm and 4–7:30pm, Sun 9am–1:30pm; Métro: Ledru Rollin or Gare de Lyon): One of the city's largest markets, this sprawling affair invades a whole neighborhood, with both outdoor stalls and a covered market.

Marché Batignolles ★★ (bd. Batignolles, btw. rue de Rome and place Clichy, 17th arrond.; Sat 9am–3pm; Métro: Rome): A terrific, all-organic Saturday market with fresh regional produce and close proximity to pretty sidewalk cafes for an after-marché coffee.

Marché Raspail ★★ (bd. Raspail, btw. rue de Cherche-Midi and rue de Rennes, 6th arrond.; Tues and Fri 7am–2:30pm; organic Sun 9am–3pm; Métro: Rennes): Stretching several blocks down the center divider of a wide avenue, this outdoor market makes a delicious gourmet stroll.

FLEA MARKETS

Marché aux Puces de la Porte de Vanves ★★ (av. Georges-Lafenestre, 14th arrond.; www.pucesdevanves.fr; Sat and Sun 7am–2pm; Métro: Porte de Vanves): This weekend event sprawls along two streets and is the best flea market in Paris—dealers swear by it. Look for old linens, vintage Hermès scarves, toys, ephemera, costume jewelry, perfume bottles, and bad art. Get there early—the best stuff goes fast.

Marché aux Puces de Paris St-Ouen-Clignancourt ★ (Porte de Clignancourt, 18th arrond.; www.marcheauxpuces-saintouen.com; Sat 9am–6pm, Sun 10am–6pm, Mon 11am–5pm; Métro: Porte de Clignancourt): At the northern edge of the city, this claims to be the world's largest antiques market. It was once a bargain-hunter's dream, but prices now often rival those of antiques dealers. Hard-core browsers will get a kick out of wandering the serpentine alleyways of this Parisian medina. *Note:* Beware of pickpockets.

Shopping A to Z
ANTIQUES & COLLECTIBLES

L'Objet qui Parle ★★ This delightful and quirky shop sells a jumble of vintage finds, including framed butterflies, teapots, furniture, chandeliers, crockery, hunting trophies, religious paraphernalia, and old lace. Great for souvenir shopping. 86 rue des Martyrs, 18th arrond. ℂ **06-09-67-05-30.** Métro: Abbesses.

Village St-Paul ★★ When you pass through an archway on rue St-Paul, you come upon a lovely villagelike enclosure, the remnant of a centuries-old hamlet that was swallowed up by the city. Today, it's a village of antiques dealers and design shops, selling everything from old bistro chairs and vintage lingerie to Brazilian eco-furniture and Iranian kilim rugs. www.levillagesaintpaul.com. No phone. Métro: St-Paul.

BEAUTY & PERFUME

The Different Company ★★ This independent perfume house makes its own unique fragrances with mostly natural materials. Signature scents include Osmanthus, Sel de Vétiver, and Rose Poivrée, but let your nose lead the way when you visit the store. 10 rue Ferdinand Duval, 4th arrond. www.thedifferentcompany.com. ℂ **01-42-78-19-34.** Métro: St-Paul.

Sale Mania

Despite recent changes to the laws that restricted sales to certain times of the year, stores still follow the traditional sale (soldes) seasons. Twice a year, around the second week in January and the second week in July (specific dates are plastered all over the city), retailers go hog-wild and slash prices; the rest of the year sale prices don't dip down much below 30 percent. When opening day finally arrives, chaos ensues. There are good deals to be had but try to avoid the first days of havoc and especially the weekends.

Editions de Parfums Fréderic Malle ★★   This chic temple to the nose offers a superb range of original fragrances. Sample M. Malle's wares in special "smelling columns," round, phone-booth-like tubes where you can experience aromas like Noir Epice and Lipstick Rose. The three other stores are at 140 av. Victor Hugo in the 16th arrondissement, 13 rue des Francs Bourgeois in the 4th, and 21 rue du Mont Thabor in the 1st. 37 rue de Grenelle, 7th arrond. www.fredericmalle.com. ✆ **01-42-22-76-40.** Métro: Rue du Bac.

Make Up Forever ★   This French cosmetics company, which trains professional makeup artists, also runs this boutique where you can buy products and get a **makeup lesson** (25 min. for 25€; 60 min. for 60€; call to reserve). Two other locations are at 5 rue de la Boétie in the 8th arrondissement, and 52 ter rue des Vinaigriers in the 10th. 5 rue des Francs Bourgeois, 4th arrond. www.makeupforever.fr. ✆ **01-42-71-23-19.** Métro: St-Paul.

BOOKS

The Abbey Bookshop ★   Canadians will be happy to find a cozy store that specializes in Canadian authors, as well as other English-language literature. You'll have to squeeze in between the piles of books, but this is a relaxed, welcoming place with good readings and events, including hikes in nearby forests. 29 rue de la Parcheminerie, 5th arrond. www.facebook.com/abbeybookshop. ✆ **01-46-33-16-24.** Métro: St-Michel.

Galignani ★★   This old-fashioned shop has thrived since 1810. Owned by the literary Gagliani family, whose ancestor used one of the first print-ing presses back in 1520, the store is filled with a terrific range of both French and English books, with a special emphasis on French classics, modern fiction, sociology, and fine arts. 224 rue de Rivoli, 1st arrond. www.galignani.com. ✆ **01-42-60-76-07.** Métro: Tuileries.

Shakespeare & Company ★★★   This venerable shrine is a must on any Parisian literary tour. Run by George Whitman for some 60 years before he passed away in 2011 at 98, today it is helmed by his daughter, Sylvia, who was named for Sylvia Beach (who founded the original book-shop in 1919). Many a legendary writer has stopped in over the decades for tea; many an aspiring author has camped out in one of the back rooms

(Whitman liked to think of this store as a "writer's sanctuary"). Today, Whitman's presence is still felt at this historic bookshop, which sells used and new books. Check the website for ongoing readings and other events. 37 rue de la Bûcherie, 5th arrond. www.shakespeareandcompany.com. ✆ **01-43-25-40-93.** Métro/RER: St-Michel–Notre-Dame.

CLOTHING & ACCESSORIES

Abou d'Abi Bazar ★★ Here's a store with mostly casual clothes, multiple brands, and rotating collections—in other words, great one-stop boutique shopping. There are two other locations: 33 rue de Temple in the Marais, and 15 rue Soufflot, near the Panthéon in the 5th. 59 rue des Francs Bourgeois 4th arrond. www.aboudabibazar.com. ✆ **01-40-33-24-59.** Métro: Rambuteau.

Antoine & Lili ★★ Hot pink is the signature color at this wacky store, where the gaily painted walls are hung with oodles of colorful objects from around the world. The women's clothes are innovative and fresh yet wearable and come in a range of bright colors. It has five other branches in town; check the website for addresses. 95 quai de Valmy, 10th arrond. www.antoineetlili.com. ✆ **01-40-37-41-55.** Métro: Jacques-Bonsergent.

French Trotters ★ Airy and spacious, this Marais emporium is the flagship store for this temple of urban chic. While the original store (which is still open, 30 rue de Charonne, 11th arrond.) featured both hot local French labels and the store's own brand of relaxed *branchitude* (hipness), this one sells all that plus housewares, books, and stationary. Terrific styles for both men and women. 128 rue Vieille du Temple, 3rd arrond. www.frenchtrotters.fr. ✆ **01-44-61-00-14.** Métro: Saint Sébastien–Froissart or Files du Calvaire.

Children

Botoù ★★ If you're looking for something funky for your children's feet, this is where to head. These cool and colorful shoes will make your kids look like they live in this fun and hip neighborhood (SoPi), with everything from goldfish-print sneakers to chick-yellow ankle boots. 20 rue Milton, 9th arrond. http://botou.fr. ✆ **09-83-82-06-58.** Métro: Notre-Dame-de-Lorette.

Marie Puce ★★ A little softer and gentler, Marie offers easy elegance for tots who need to dress up (at least a little) but can't stand frills. Most of the clothing here is 100 percent Made in France. 60 rue du Cherche Midi, 6th arrond. www.mariepuce.com. ✆ **01-45-48-30-09.** Métro: Sèvres-Babylone or St-Placide.

Discount

Mouton à Cinq Pattes ★ Sift through the packed racks of designer markdowns and you just might find Moschino slacks or a Gaultier dress at a fabulous price. If you do, grab it fast—it might not be there tomorrow. The store at no. 8 is women's apparel only; no. 18 serves both sexes, and a third store at 138 bd. St-Germain is just for men. 8 and 18 rue St-Placide, 6th arrond. www.moutonacinqpattesparis.com. ✆ **01-45-48-86-26.** Métro: Sèvres-Babylone.

Lingerie

Fifi Chachnil ★★★   A boudoir-boutique tucked into a courtyard, this is where young French movie stars go to find retro-sexy-fun-posh underthings with a decidedly girly feel. Prices are steep, but the experience and the lingerie are unique. It has one other pink and fluffy boutique: 34 rue de Grenelle in the 7th. 68 rue Jean-Jacques Rousseau, in the courtyard, 1st arrond. www.fifichachnil.com. © **01-42-21-19-93.** Métro/RER: Les Halles.

Orcanta ★   This chain has a great selection of name brands (such as Lise Charmel, Chantal Thomas, and Huit) and usually at least a rack or two of discounted items. More locations listed on the website. 60 rue St-Placide, 6th arrond. www.orcanta.fr. © **01-45-44-94-44.** Métro: St-Placide.

CONCEPT STORES

Over the last few years, these hard-to-categorize stores with eclectic collections have popped up in several parts of the city. These are good places to hunt for that atypical gift you've been seeking.

Bü ★   A cross between Colette (see below), Ikea, and an upscale hardware store, this new and enigmatically named store (it's French, not Scandinavian) has reasonably priced housewares, stationary, leather handbags, luggage, and toys, as well as regional edibles. 45 rue Jussieu, 5th arrond. www.bu-store.com. © **01-40-56-33-22.** Métro: Jussieu or Cardinal-Lemoine.

Colette ★★   What can you say about a store that sells both Hermès scarves and knitted hot dogs? This shopping phenom offers both high style and high concept—basically, if it's utterly cool and happening, they sell it. Karl Lagerfeld jeans, heart-shaped sunglasses, psychedelic nail polish, designer toilet brushes, and so forth. 213 rue St-Honoré, 1st arrond. www.colette.fr. © **01-55-35-33-90.** Métro: Tuileries.

Les Parisettes ★   Looking for a Paris souvenir that isn't (too) tacky? Metro-map serviettes say? Or your own model Paris bus? Well roll up to this fun store, where every shelf is lined exclusively with Paris-themed jewelry, accessories, kitchenware, and quirky games and stationary all made by French and Parisian designers. 10 rue Gramme, 15th arrond. http://lesparisettes.com/. © **01-75-43-23-65.** Métro: Dupleix or Avenue Emile Zola.

DEPARTMENT STORES

Le Bon Marché ★★★   Founded in the mid-1800s, this was one of the world's first department stores. Despite its name (*bon marché* means affordable), this is the most expensive of Paris' *grand magasins.* It is also the most stylish, with beautiful displays and fabulous clothes of every imaginable designer label, both upscale and midrange. Right next door is its humongous designer supermarket, **La Grande Epicerie Paris** (see "Specialty Groceries," below). 24 rue de Sèvres, 7th arrond. www.lebon marche.com. © **01-44-39-80-00.** Métro: Sèvres–Babylone.

Galeries Lafayette ★★ The biggest of the *grand magasins* (department stores) sports an over-the-top Art Nouveau dome under which oodles of fashionable goodies are displayed for style-conscious shoppers. A bit less expensive than its more glamorous rival next door (see "Printemps," below), it's also so huge that you can usually find just what you are looking for. It has everything from luxury labels to kids' stuff, not to mention books, stationary, wine, and a gourmet shop. 40 bd. Haussmann, 9th arrond. https://haussmann.galerieslafayette.com/en. ✆ **01-42-82-34-56.** Métro: Chausée d'Antin–Lafayette.

Galeries Lafayette

Printemps ★★ The glistening domes of this 19th-century building bring to mind a grand hotel on the French Riviera. High fashion gets priority here; four of the seven floors of women's wear are devoted to designer labels. If you can't handle the crowds inside, you can always enjoy the famed *vitrines,* or **window displays,** outside. Better yet, ride to the top of Printemps Beauté/Maison and enjoy the splendid **panoramic view;** it even has a cafe at the top where you can lunch. 64 bd. Haussmann, 9th arrond. www.printemps.com. ✆ **01-42-82-50-00.** Métro: Havre-Caumartin or St-Lazare.

FOOD & DRINK
Chocolate
A La Mère de Famille ★ Founded in 1761, this piece of Parisian history (rumor has it the original owner hid the mother superior of the nearby convent from raging revolutionaries during the Terror) has committed its soul to candies and chocolates à l'ancienne. You'll find classic chocolates as well as old-fashioned bonbons like *berlingots,* lemon drops, caramels, and jellied fruits. There are nine other locations. 35 rue du Faubourg Montmartre, 9th arrond. www.lameredefamille.com. ✆ **01-47-70-83-69.** Métro: Grands Boulevards.

Patrick Roger ★★ This cutting-edge chocolate boutique could easily be mistaken for a jewelry shop. Here you can sample chocolates with names like "Insolence" (almond and chestnut) and "Zanzibar" (thyme and lemon), as well as candied fruits, nougat, and other delicacies. Five other stores in the city. 108 bd. St-Germain, 6th arrond. www.patrickroger.com. ✆ **01-43-29-38-42.** Métro: Odéon.

Specialty Groceries

Fauchon ★   Some (like me) find it overhyped and overpriced; others think it's heaven on Earth. Founded in 1886, this tea-room-cum-luxury-food-emporium has been wowing the crowds for over a century, and the crowds are certainly still coming. Today you can find Fauchon everywhere from Hamburg to Ho Chi Min City. The multi-storied, multi-function establishment includes a restaurant, a *pâtissier,* a *boulangerie,* a gourmet delicatessen, and a wine cellar. 30 pl. de la Madeleine, 8th arrond. www.fauchon.com. ✆ **01-70-39-38-02.** Métro: Madeleine.

La Grande Epicerie Paris ★★   This humongous gourmet grocery mecca, an outgrowth of Le Bon Marché department store (see above) stocks every gourmet substance you could possibly imagine, and many that you couldn't. Sculpted sugar cubes, designer mineral waters, truffled balsamic vinegar, pink salt from the Himalayas—need I go on? It also has an excellent (if expensive) takeout department for picnic items. A second address has opened at 80 rue de Passy in the 16th arrond. 38 rue de Sèvres, 7th arrond. www.lagrandeepicerie.fr. ✆ **01-44-39-81-00.** Métro: Sèvres-Babylone.

Wines

Before you start planning to stock your wine cellar back home, consider this sad truth: Most non–EU countries won't let you bring back much more than a bottle or two. Your best bet is to drink up while you're here.

Les Domaines Qui Montent ★   This association of some 150 wine producers offers a vast selection of wines that come from small, independent vineyards where the emphasis is on quality and *terroir,* not quantity. An on-site wine bar also serves meals. There are several other locations, including at 136 bd. Voltaire in the 11th arrondissement and on the corner of rue Ballu and rue Vintimille in the 9th. 22 rue Cardinet, 17th arrond. www.lesdomainesquimontent.com. ✆ **01-42-27-63-96.** Métro: Courcelles or Wagram.

Legrand Filles et Fils ★★   More than just a wine store, this fabulous place is where you can learn everything there is to know about the sacred grape. 1 rue de la Banque, 2nd arrond. www.caves-legrand.com. ✆ **01-42-60-07-12.** Métro: Bourse.

JEWELRY

Bijoux Blues ★★   Hand-crafted, unique jewelry at reasonable prices made in an atelier in the Marais—who could ask for more? Designs are fun and funky, yet elegant. Pieces can be custom-designed. 30 rue St-Paul, 4th arrond. www.bijouxblues.com. ✆ **01-48-04-00-64.** Métro: St-Paul.

White Bird ★   If you are looking for a unique engagement ring or present for your sweetheart, this is a good bet. It has a terrific selection of jewelry made by talented, independent craftspeople/designers. 38 rue du Mont Thabor, 1st arrond. www.whitebirdjewellery.com. ✆ **01-58-62-25-86.** Métro: Concorde.

STATIONERY

L'Art du Papier ★★   This delightful stationery store has a fabulous selection of colored papers and envelopes, as well as ink-stamps, sealing wax, and the essentials for hobbies like calligraphy and "le scrapbooking." It has three other locations: 16 rue Daunou in the 2nd arrondissement, 197 bd. Voltaire in the 11th, and 17 av. de Villiers in the 17th. 48 rue Vavin, 6th arrond. www.art-du-papier.fr. ✆ **01-43-26-10-12.** Métro: Vavin.

ENTERTAINMENT & NIGHTLIFE

Paris blooms at night; its magnificent monuments and buildings become even more beautiful when they're cloaked in their evening illuminations. The already glowing Eiffel Tower bursts out in twinkling lights for the first 5 minutes of every hour. While simply walking around town can be an excellent night out, the city is also a treasure trove of rich evening offerings: bars and clubs from chic to shaggy, sublime theater and dance performances, top-class orchestras, and scores of cinemas and art-film houses.

With few exceptions, the city's major concert halls and theaters are in action between September and June, taking off during the summer months during the annual vacation exodus. On the upside, summer is the time for several wonderful music festivals, including the **Festival Chopin** and **Jazz à La Villette** (p. 63), many of which take place in Paris's lovely parks and gardens.

GETTING TICKETS   You can get tickets in person at **Fnac,** the giant bookstore/music chain that has one of the most comprehensive box offices in the city (a central location open daily is at Galerie du Claridge, 74 av. des Champs-Elysées; follow the signs to the "Billeterie"). You can also **order your tickets online in English** at www.fnactickets.com or by phone at ✆ **08-92-68-36-22** (.40 €/min.). **Ticketmaster.fr** offers a similar service where you can buy tickets either online (www.ticketmaster.fr) or by phone (✆ **08-92-39-01-00,** .45€/min.).

Finding Out What's On

Paper magazine listings are dwindling, but for up-to-the-minute dates and schedules for what's happening in music, theater, dance, and film, you can still pick up the **weekly "l'Officiel des Spectacles"** (1€), a comprehensive listing of weekly events. also has a weekly pull-out listings guide, complete with reviews. Both come out on Wednesdays and are available at any newsstand.

Online, "**Pariscope**" has excellent listings (www.pariscope.fr), as do "**l'Officiel des Spectacles**" (www.offi.fr) and "**Télérama**" (www.telerama.fr). All three sites are in French only. By the way, if you see a sign at a theater or on an events website that says *location,* that means "box office," not location.

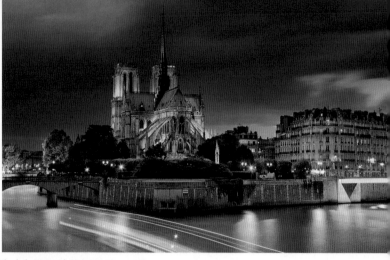
Ile de la Cité with Notre-Dame at night

   Discount hunters can stand in line at one of the city's three **half-price ticket booths,** all run by **Le Kiosque Théâtre** (www.kiosqueculture.com). One is in front of the Montparnasse train station, another on the west side of the Madeleine (facing 15 pl. de la Madeleine, exit rue Tronchet from the Madeleine Métro stop), and a third in the center of place des Ternes (17th arrond.) The first two are open from Tuesday to Saturday (12:30–7:30pm) and Sun (12:30–3:45pm), while Ternes' is open just Tuesday to Saturday (12:30–2:30pm and 3–7:30pm). Half-price tickets for same-day performances go on sale here at 12:30pm. Don't dawdle—by noon the line is long. **BilletRéduc,** www.billetreduc.com (in French), also has plenty of ticket discounts.

Theater

Paris has hundreds of theaters, many of which have nightly offerings. Although most of it is in French, you can find a few English-language shows (see "Entertainment in English," below). Of course, avant-garde shows combining dance, theater, and images really need no translation.

Comédie-Française ★★   Established by Louis XVI in 1680, this legendary theater is the temple of classic French theater (Corneille, Racine, Molière), though in recent decades the troupe has branched out into more modern territory. In addition to the gorgeous main theater **(Salle Richelieu),** the company presents its offerings in its two other theaters: the medium-size **Théâtre du Vieux Colombier** (21 rue du Vieux Colombier, 6th arrond.; ✆ **01-44-39-87-00;** Métro: St-Sulpice or Sèvres–Babylone) and the smaller **Studio-Théâtre** (Galerie du Carrousel du Louvre, under the Pyramid, 99 rue de Rivoli, 1st arrond.; Métro: Palais Royal–Musée du Louvre). pl. Colette, 1st arrond. www.comedie-francaise.fr. ✆ **01-44-58-15-15.** Métro: Palais-Royal–Musée du Louvre.

Théâtre National de Chaillot ★★   Dance and theater are on equal footing at this beautiful Art Deco theater in the Palais de Chaillot, where contemporary choreographers and theater directors share a jam-packed program. There is a lot of blurring of lines here between the two disciplines; dance programs often include video and text, and theater productions often incorporate the abstract. 1 pl. du Trocadéro, 16th arrond; www. theatre-chaillot.fr. ✆ **01-53-65-30-00.** Métro: Trocadéro.

Opera, Dance & Classical Concerts

Philharmonie de Paris ★★★   Hovering over La Villette like a visiting spaceship, this mega venue seats 2,400 spectators and serves as the new home of the Orchestre de Paris. Yet another creation of über-architect Jean Nouvel (this time in partnership with Harold Marshall and with input from Yasuhisa Toyota), this silvery apparition also encompasses a music museum and other performance spaces in the adjacent **Philharmonie 2** building (the former Cité de la Musique), as well as a nifty cafe and restaurant. The season includes symphonic and choral concerts, as well as a good dose of the offbeat and unexpected, like a silent film accompanied by the music of Philip Glass, or a weekend of dance and music dedicated to African women. 221 av. Jean-Jaurès, 19th arrond. philharmoniedeparis.fr/en. ✆ **01-44-84-44-84.** Métro: Porte de Pantin.

Opéra Comique/Salle Favart ★★   For a lighter take on opera, try this architectural puff pastry filled with operettas and (French) musicals. Created in 1714 for theatrical performances that included songs, the Opéra Comique endured several fires before finally settling down in a beautiful 19th-century theater complete with huge chandeliers. An excellent opportunity to enjoy both history and music in a splendid setting. 5 rue Favart, 2nd arrond. www.opera-comique.com. ✆ **08-25-01-01-60** (.15€/min.). Métro: Richelieu–Drouot or Quatre-Septembre.

Opéra de Paris ★★★   This mighty operation includes both the **Palais Garnier** (pl. de l'Opéra, 9th arrond.; p. 96), an attraction in itself, and the **Opéra Bastille** (2 pl. de la Bastille, 12th arrond.) a slate-colored

---

Entertainment in English

English-language shows are rare, and comics even more so, but a long-standing gig in town is worth a detour. At press time, the best place to go for a good giggle was **"How to Become a Parisian in One Hour"** (playing at Théâtre des Nouvautés; details at www.oliviergiraud.com), a terrific one-person

show written by Olivier Giraud, a Frenchman who spent several years in the U.S. Also check out the website www.theatre inparis.com, which sells tickets to the above, along with French shows that have English subtitles—anything from the latest musicals to a Victor Hugo play.

behemoth that has loomed over the place de la Bastille since 1989. The company has since split its energies between the two venues. In theory, more operas are performed at the Bastille, which has more space and top-notch acoustics, and the Garnier, home of the **Ballet de l'Opéra de Paris,** focuses more on dance, but the reality is you can see either at both. www.operadeparis. fr. © **08-92-89-90-90** (.35€/min.); from outside of France: © **+33 (0)1-71-25-24-23.**

Cabaret

Some visitors feel they simply haven't had the true Paris experience without seeing a show at the Moulin Rouge or the Lido, even though there is nothing particularly Parisian, or even French, about them these days. Today's audiences are more likely to arrive in tour buses than touring cars, and the shows are more Vegas than Paris. What you will see here is a lot of scenic razzmatazz and many sublime female bodies, mostly *torse nue* (topless).

The Crazy Horse ★ This temple to "The Art of the Nude" presents an erotic dance show with artistic aspirations. Be advised that unlike the other shows, this one is known for what the girls *aren't* wearing. The performers, who slither, swagger, and lip-synch with panache, have names like Zula Zazou and Nooka Karamel. ***Note:*** While it has no dining on site,

The Moulin Rouge

it has dinner-show packages with nearby restaurants. 12 av. George V, 8th arrond. www.lecrazyhorseparis.com. ℂ **01-47-23-32-32.** 105€ show only; from 125€ show and champagne; show plus dinner packages 185€–225€. Métro: George V or Alma Marceau.

Moulin Rouge ★   When it opened in 1889, the Moulin Rouge was the talk of the town, and its huge dance floor, multiple mirrors, and floral garden inspired painters like Toulouse-Lautrec. Times have changed—today's Moulin Rouge relies heavily on lip-synching and pre-recorded music, backed up by dozens of befeathered Doriss Girls, long-legged ladies who prance about the stage. Be prepared for lots of glitz and not much else. 82 bd. Clichy, pl. Blanche, 18th arrond. www.moulinrouge.fr. ℂ **01-53-09-82-82.** 87€–210€ show alone; 190€–420€ show with dinner. Métro: Blanche.

Jazz Clubs

Paris has been a fan of jazz from its beginnings, and many legendary performers like Sidney Bechet and Kenny Clark made the city their home. Still a haven for jazz musicians and fans of all stripes, Paris offers dozens of places to duck in and listen to a good set or two. Here are a few of the best:

Baiser Salé ★★   On a street lined with famous jazz clubs, this one holds its own with a lineup that shows off jazz in all its diversity. Some of the biggest Franco-African jazz stars, like Richard Bona and Angelique Kidjo, got their start here, and the program still highlights the best in African, Caribbean, and Asian, as well as French jazz. Regular jam sessions are on Sundays and Mondays. 58 rue des Lombards, 1st arrond. www.lebaiser sale.com. ℂ **01-42-33-37-71.** Cover free to 25€, depending on the act. Métro: Châtelet.

New Morning ★★★   If you are looking for big names and hot acts, look no further. This place has incredible lineups, including jazz giants, pop legends, and international superstars, as well as top-grade local talent. This relatively large club (the room holds 300) fills up quickly, and no wonder: This truly is one of the best jazz venues in town, and the top ticket price is only around 30€. 7 rue des Petites-Ecuries, 10th arrond. www. newmorning.com. No phone. Cover 18€–28€. Métro: Château-d'Eau.

Le Sunset/Le Sunside ★★   One of several famous jazz clubs on the rue des Lombards (and it's a short street!), this one has a split personality. Le Sunset Jazz, is dedicated to electric jazz and international music, whereas le Sunside is devoted to acoustic jazz for the most part. Some of the hottest names in French jazz appear here regularly (Jacky Terrasson, Didier Lockwood) along with a new crop of international stars. 60 rue des Lombards, 1st arrond. www.sunset-sunside.com. ℂ **01-40-26-46-60.** Tickets 15€–30€. Métro: Châtelet.

The Bar Scene

Paris may not be the 24-hr. party city some other international capitals claim to be, but it has plenty of places to sip, flirt, and be merry. In general, bars stay open until around 2am.

Andy Wahloo ★★ A play on the name of the famous pop artist, this is a tiny temple to 1970s North African culture and kitsch. Sip your drink beneath a silk-screened Moroccan coffee ad and listen to some of the best Algerian raï around. 69 rue des Gravilliers, 3rd arrond. www.andywahloo-bar.com. ✆ **01-42-71-20-38.** Métro: Arts et Métiers.

Le Bar du Plaza Athénée ★★ Knock yourself out and order a shockingly expensive drink at this classy, historic joint, which simply drips with glamour and fabulousness. The bar itself literally glows (it's lit from inside), fashioning an even more luminous aura around the sleek patrons. Hotel Plaza-Athénée, 25 av. Montaigne, 8th arrond. www.plaza-athenee-paris.fr. ✆ **01-53-67-66-65.** Métro: Alma-Marceau.

Experimental Cocktail Club ★ If you're looking for a sophisticated spot to spot stars, you've come to the right place. Known, not surprisingly, for its gourmet cocktails, this cosmopolitan lounge has the feel of a retro speakeasy. 37 rue St-Sauveur, 2nd arrond. http://www.experimentalevents.com/paris/. ✆ **01-45-08-88-09.** Métro: Sentier.

WINE BARS

Le Baron Rouge ★ This neighborhood institution spills out onto a corner that it shares with the sprawling Marché d'Aligre, a giant outdoor and covered market. It only has a few tables, but most people stand at the counter or outside, glass in hand, especially during market hours. It's a little rough-and-tumble getting your drink order in at the bar. 1 rue Théophile Roussel, 12th arrond. ✆ **01-43-43-14-32.** Métro: Ledru-Rollin.

Le Perchoir ★★★ Take in a fabulous view of eastern Paris from this rooftop bar, which has been so successful it has spawned a passel of other high-altitude nightspots on top of buildings in the Marais, Buttes Chaumont, and other hip parts of the city (check website for locations). Sip a cocktail on an outdoor sofa and gaze at the Sacré-Coeur, or flirt at the tented bar; if you want to sit down, come early before the crowd arrives. 14 rue Crespin du Gast, 11th arrond. www.leperchoir.tv. ✆ **01-48-06-18-48.** Métro: Ménilmontant.

The Club Scene

If you want to go out to a *boîte de nuit* (nightclub), you'll have plenty to choose from in Paris. Keep in mind that the French love their fashion, so dressing to impress is obligatory—sneakers will rarely get you past the line outside. Most clubs don't really get going until at least 11pm, if not later.

NIGHTCLUBS

Nouveau Casino ★★   This former movie theater is now a giant dance club with live music, a huge bar that vaguely resembles an iceberg, hanging chandeliers, and a terrific program that includes all sorts of avant-garde dance music and bands with names like Flatbush Zombies and Moon Safari Club. 109 rue Oberkampf, 9th arrond. www.nouveaucasino.net. ℂ 01-43-57-57-40. Métro: St-Maur, Parmentier, or Ménilmontant.

Showcase ★   This unusual club is actually under a bridge. Seriously. Set in an old boat hangar beneath the Pont Alexandre III, it has incredible views of the Seine and atmospheric spaces lined with original stone walls and archways. Music-wise, expect high-quality electro, techno, hip-hop, and house. Port des Champs-Élysées under the Pont Alexandre III. www.showcase.fr. No phone. Métro: Invalides.

GAY & LESBIAN BARS & CLUBS

Paris has a vibrant gay nightlife scene, primarily centered around the **Marais.** Pick up one of the magazines devoted to the subject—like **"Qweek"** (www.qweek.fr)—for free in gay bars and bookstores. Also look for **"Têtu"** magazine at newsstands—it has special nightlife sections.

Le 3w Kafe ★   The most popular lesbian bar in the Marais, this is a good place to come to find company. Downstairs, a DJ spins on weekends, when there's dancing. Men can only enter the premises if accompanied by a woman. 8 rue des Ecouffes, 4th arrond. ℂ 01-48-87-39-26. Métro: St. Paul.

Le Cox ★   You'll know it when you get here; it's where the crowd is spilling out onto the sidewalk. This place still gets big crowds, even though it's been here for years; people come for the bar as well as the great DJs. The clientele is a pleasant mix, everything from hunky American tourists to sexy Parisians. 15 rue des Archives, 4th arrond. www.cox.fr. ℂ 01-42-72-08-00. Métro: Hôtel de Ville.

Open Café ★   More relaxed and more diverse than neighboring Le Cox, this cafe-bar has a busy sidewalk terrace that's usually full both day and night. Everyone from humble tourists to sharp-looking businessmen to TV stars hang out here. 17 rue des Archives, 4th arrond. www.opencafe.fr. ℂ 01-42-72-26-18. Métro: Hôtel-de-Ville.

5

SIDE TRIPS
FROM PARIS

By Anna Brooke

W hether you are escaping Paris for the day or embarking on an adventure to another part of France, plenty of wonderful destinations are just 1 hr. from the capital. Royal castles like **Versailles, Vaux-le-Vicomte,** and **Fontainebleau,** as well as the forest of **Rambouillet,** and even **Disneyland** are all within the borders of the Ile-de-France, which is not an island but a region encompassing Paris and its outer environs (also known as Greater Paris). Just outside its borders but still within easy reach are Monet's famous gardens at **Giverny** and the stained-glass windows of the cathedral of **Chartres.**

Your main problem will be deciding where to go. If you've never been there, your first choice should probably be the château and gardens of **Versailles.** They're close by, easily accessible by train, and truly mind-blowing. **Chartres** would be my second choice, for its breathtaking Gothic cathedral, winding streets, and half-timbered houses. After that, it's a toss-up. If castles are your game, **Fontainebleau** and **Vaux-le-Vicomte** should be high on your list. Fans of Claude Monet will love exploring the gardens at **Giverny,** and families with kids in tow will appreciate **Disneyland Paris.**

VERSAILLES ★★★

21km (13 miles) SW of Paris; 71km (44 miles) NE of Chartres

The grandeur of the Château of Versailles is hard to imagine until you are standing in front of it. Immediately, you start to get an idea of the power (and ego) of the man who was behind it, King Louis XIV. One of the largest castles in Europe, it is also forever associated with another, less fortunate king, Louis XVI and his wife Queen Marie Antoinette, who were both forced to flee when the French Revolution arrived at their sumptuous doorstep. The palace's extraordinary gardens, designed by the legendary landscape architect André Le Nôtre, are almost worth the visit on their own.

Don't feel you have to see everything—for many, a visit to the palace is enough culture, and a nice relaxing stroll/picnic/nap in the park is a great way to finish off the day. If you can't handle crowds but you still want to get a taste of life during the Ancien Régime, you could just visit

Marie Antoinette's Estate—you'll miss the palace, but you'll get to revel in a beautiful garden and see the pretty Trianons, hamlet, and other small buildings.

Essentials

ARRIVING Take the **RER C** (www.transilien.fr; 30 min. from the Champs de Mars station) to **Versailles Rive Gauche–Château de Versailles.** Make sure the final destination for your train is Versailles Rive Gauche and *not* Versailles Chantier, which will leave you on the other end of town, a long walk from the Château. Even worse, the Versailles Chantier trains actually run in the opposite direction, touring all around Paris before arriving at Versailles, which will add 1 hr. or so to your journey. Assuming you've taken the right train, it's about a 5-min. walk from the train station to the Château. For a little more (4.45€ adults), you can also take the **SNCF** Transilien suburban train (www.transilien.fr; 45 min.) from the Gare St-Lazare station to **Versailles-Rive Droite,** and then walk about 10 min. to the Château (around 45 min. total). This is a great option if you plan to picnic in the palace grounds, as you'll go down Rue du Maréchal Foch, past a U Express supermarket (no. 45) and Marché Notre Dame (p. 192), the town's main market, where you can fill up on French delights. Glass is permitted in the park, so don't feel you have to skimp on wine!

Unless you have a **Paris Visite** or other pass that includes zones 1 to 4, you will need to buy a special ticket (one-way fare 3.65€ adults; 1.80€ children ages 4–10; free for 3 and under); a regular Métro ticket will not suffice. Another option is to buy a one-day **Mobilis** pass for zones 1 to 4 (12.40€), which gives you unlimited travel in those zones for the day. You can buy a ticket from any Métro or RER station; the fare includes a free transfer to the Métro.

TICKETS If you are made of tough stuff and want to see everything, you can buy the all-inclusive, 1- or 2-day **Château Passeport,** which grants you access to the main château, the gardens, the Trianon Palaces, and the

---

Two Line-jumping Tactics

Versailles is so popular you will not be alone, so grin and bear it. But there are two little-known ways to avoid the lines at the entrance and waltz straight in. **The first:** reserve a 90-min. guided tour in English (7€ on top of your entry ticket; free for children 9 and under). You will be given a time slot and enter the château via a different door to the masses so you shouldn't have to wait. Once the tour is over, you're free to roam the rest of the palace and gardens. **The second:** go for breakfast in world-famous chef Alain Ducasse's new restaurant Ore, set inside the palace. Open from 9am you can buy a breakfast/passport ticket for 40€ (that's 20€ for fabulous pastries, eggs, and sausages) then head straight into the palace without even seeing the snaking lines outside.

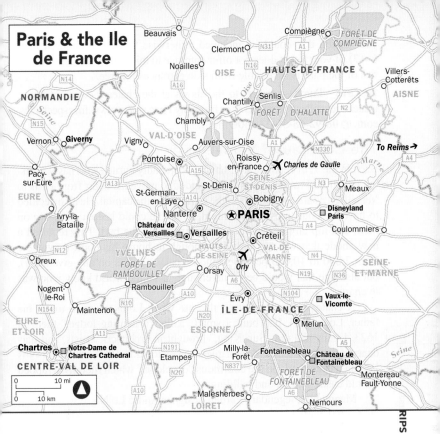

Paris & the Ile de France

Beauvais

Compiègne — FORÊT DE COMPIÈGNE

Clermont

Noailles

OISE

HAUTS-DE-FRANCE

Villers-Cotterêts

NORMANDIE

Chantilly

Senlis

FORÊT D'HALATTE

AISNE

Chambly

VAL-D'OISE

Vernon — Giverny

Vigny

Auvers-sur-Oise

Pontoise

Roissy-en-France — Charles de Gaulle

To Reims →

Pacy-sur-Eure

St-Germain-en-Laye

St-Denis

SEINE-ST-DENIS

Meaux

Ivry-la-Bataille

Nanterre

Bobigny

PARIS

Disneyland Paris

Château de Versailles — Versailles

Créteil

Coulommiers

Dreux

YVELINES

FORÊT DE RAMBOUILLET

HAUTS-DE-SEINE

VAL-DE-MARNE

Orly

SEINE-ET-MARNE

Nogent-le-Roi

Rambouillet

Orsay

Maintenon

Évry

ÎLE-DE-FRANCE

Vaux-le-Vicomte

Melun

Chartres — Notre-Dame de Chartres Cathedral

CENTRE-VAL DE LOIR

Etampes

Milly-la-Forêt

Fontainebleau

Château de Fontainebleau

0   10 mi
0   10 km

Malesherbes

FORÊT DE FONTAINEBLEAU

Montereau-Fault-Yonne

Nemours

LOIRET

Marie Antoinette Estate (1 day Nov–Mar 20€ adults, Apr–Oct including *Les Grandes Eaux Musicales* 27€ adults; 2 days Nov–Mar 25€, Apr–Oct 30€; free for children 17 and under). If you are merely human, you can buy a **ticket to just the Palace** (18€ adults; free 17 and under) or **just the Trianons and Marie Antoinette's Estate** (12€). A **Paris Museum Pass** will get you into everything except *Les Grandes Eaux Musicales* (Apr–Oct), so you'll have to buy a separate ticket to get into the gardens (9.50€).

VISITOR INFORMATION **Château de Versailles,** en.chateauversailles.fr; ✆ **01-30-83-78-00; Versailles Tourist Office,** 2 bis av. de Paris (www.versailles-tourisme.com; ✆ **01-39-24-88-88**).

EVENING SHOWS From mid-June to mid-September, there are spectacular **fountain night shows** (24€ adults; 20€ children ages 6–17) where you stroll around the gardens and enjoy illuminated fountains, music, and fireworks.

DAYTIME SHOWS From April to October on weekends and Tuesdays, fountains play to Baroque music throughout the gardens closest to the castle, otherwise known as *Les Grandes Eaux Musicales* (depending on your ticket, this could be included, otherwise 9.50€; 8€ children ages 6–17). If your ticket does not offer entrance to this part of the gardens, the rest of the park is accessible from side entrances for free.

TICKETS   Purchase tickets to the shows at the château, online at www. chateauversailles-spectacles.fr or from any Fnac store (www.fnacspectacles. com; ✆ **08-92-68-36-22,** .40€/min.).

The Château of Versailles

Back in the 17th century, after having been badly burned by a nasty uprising called Le Fronde, Louis XIV decided to move his court from Paris to Versailles, a safe distance from the intrigues of the capital. He also decided to have the court move in with him, where he could keep a close eye on them and nip any new plots or conspiracies in the bud. This required a new abode that was not only big enough to house his court (anywhere from 3,000 to 10,000 people would be palace guests on any given day), but also one that would be grand enough to let the world know who was in charge.

A château was already on the site when Louis came to town; his father, Louis XIII, had built a small castle, "a hunting lodge," there in 1623. Louis, aka the "Sun King," brought in architects, artists, and gardeners to enlarge the castle and give it a new look. In 1668, architect Louis Le Vau, began work on the enormous "envelope," which literally wrapped the old castle in a second building.

Meanwhile, legendary garden designer André Le Notre was carving out formal gardens and a huge park out of what had been marshy countryside. Thousands of trees were planted, and harmonious geometric designs were achieved with flower beds, hedges, canals, and pebbled pathways dotted with sculptures and fountains.

Construction involved as many as 36,000 workers and ground on for years; in 1682 the King and his court moved in, but work went on right through the rest of his reign and into that of Louis XV. Louis XVI and his wife, Marie Antoinette, made few changes, but history made a gigantic one for them: On October 6, 1789, an angry mob of Parisians marched on the palace and the royal couple was forced to return to Paris. Versailles would never again be a royal residence.

The palace was ransacked during the Revolution, and in the years after it fell far from its original state of grace. Napoleon and Louis XVIII did what they could to bring the sleeping giant back to life, but by the early 1800s, during the reign of Louis-Philippe, the castle was slated for demolition. Fortunately for us, this forward-thinking king decided to invest his own money to save Versailles for future generations, and in 1837 the vast structure was made into a national museum. Little by little, precious furniture and art objects were retrieved or re-created; paintings, wall decorations, and ceilings were restored. Not surprisingly, restoration is ongoing, so be prepared for the unexpected when you arrive. Even if a

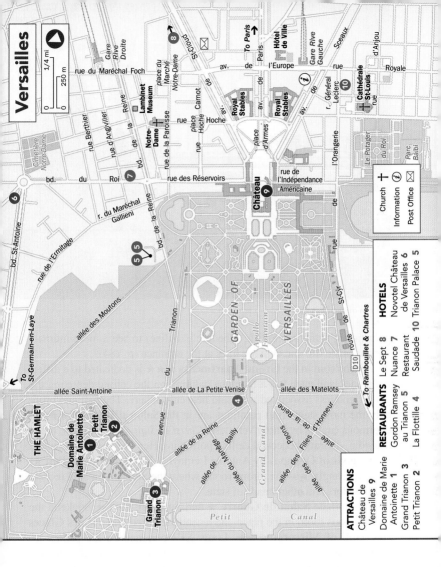

few areas are closed, the place is so huge that should you feel so inclined, you can still tour yourself into a 17th-century stupor.

TOURING THE PALACE

The "envelope," or the newer part of the building, includes a series of rooms called the **Grand Apartments,** used primarily for ceremonial events (a daily occurrence), the **Queen's Apartments,** and the **Galerie des Glaces.** These, along with the **King's Apartments,** and the **Chapel,** are the must-sees of the palace. If you have time and fortitude, you can take a **guided visit** to the royal family's private apartments (7€ on top of

Château of Versailles

your ticket, some in English; schedule is online) to see a more intimate look at castle life and skip the lines at the entrance (p. 184).

Each room in the **Grand Apartments ★★★** is dedicated to a different planet, and each has a fabulous painting on the ceiling depicting the god or goddess associated with said heavenly sphere. The first and probably the most staggering paintings are in the **Salon d'Hercule ★★**: an enormous canvas by Paolo Veronese, *Christ at Supper with Simon,* and a splendid, divinity-bedecked ceiling portraying Hercules being welcomed by the gods of Olympus by Antoine Lemoyne. The **Salon d'Apollon ★**, not surprisingly, was the throne room, where the Sun King would receive ambassadors and other heads of state.

The ornate **Salon de Guerre ★** and **Salon de Paix ★** bookend the most famous room in the place, the recently restored **Galerie des Glaces (the Hall of Mirrors) ★★★**. Louis XIV commanded his painter-in-chief, Charles Le Brun, to paint the 12m-high (40-ft.) ceiling of this 73m-long (240-ft.) gallery with representations of his accomplishments. This masterwork is illuminated by light from the 17 windows that overlook the garden, which are matched on the opposite wall by 17 mirrored panels. This splendid setting was the scene of a historic event in a more recent century: In 1919, World War I officially ended when the Treaty of Versailles was signed here.

The **Queen's Apartments ★★** include a gorgeous bedroom with silk hangings printed with lilacs and peacock feathers, which looks exactly as it did in 1789, when the Queen, Marie Antoinette, was forced to flee revolutionary mobs through a secret door (barely visible in the wall near her bed). The **King's Apartments ★★★** are even more splendiferous, though in a very different style: Here the ceilings have been left blank white, which brings out the elaborate white and gold decoration on the walls. The **King's bedroom ★★★**, hung from top to bottom with gold brocade, is fitted with a banister that separated the King from the 100 or so people who would watch him wake up in the morning.

You should also make sure to see the **Chapel ★★★**, a masterpiece of light and harmony by Jules Hardouin Mansart, where the kings attended mass. This lofty space (the ceiling is over 25m/82 ft. high) reflects both Gothic and Baroque styles, combining a vaulted roof, stained glass, and gargoyles with columns and balustrades typical of the early 18th century.

TOURING THE DOMAINE DE MARIE ANTOINETTE

Northwest of the fountain lies the **Domaine de Marie Antoinette ★★★** (if you don't have a Château passport or museum pass you'll pay a separate ticket to get in). It was here that the young queen sought refuge from the strict protocol and infighting at the castle. Her husband gave her the **Petit Trianon ★★**, a small manor that Louis XV used for his trysts, which she transformed into a stylish haven. She created an entire world around it, including a splendid **English garden ★**, several lovely pavilions, a jewel-like **theater ★★**, and even a small **hamlet ★** with a working farm and a dairy, where she and her friends would play cards and gossip,

The Hall of Mirrors, Versailles

or just stroll in the "country." Although the **Grand Trianon ★** is not really linked to the story of Marie Antoinette, it is worth a brief visit. Built by Louis XIV as a retreat for himself and his family, this small marble palace consists of two large wings connected by an open columned terrace from which there is a delightful **view ★** of the gardens. The furniture and decor dates from the Napoleonic era.

TOURING THE GARDENS & PARK

The entire 800-hectare (2,000-acre) park is laid out according to a precise, symmetrical plan. From the terrace behind the castle is an astounding **view ★★★** that runs past two parterres, down a central lawn (the Tapis Vert), down the **Grand Canal ★★** and seemingly on into infinity. Le Nôtre's masterpiece is the ultimate example of French-style gardens; geometric, logical, and in perfect harmony—a reflection of the divine order of the cosmos. A solar theme is reflected in the statues and fountains along the main axis of the perspective; the most magnificent of these is the **Apollo Fountain ★★★** where the sun god emerges from the waves at dawn on his chariot. On the sides of the main axis, near the castle, are a set of six groves, or **bosquets ★**, leafy mini-gardens hidden by walls of shrubbery; some were used as small outdoor ballrooms for festivities, others for intimate rendezvous out of reach of the prying eyes of the court. Today, you can **picnic, bike ride** (bikes can be rented next to the restaurant), or even **row a boat** on a sunny day.

One of many fountains in the gardens at Versailles

pl. d'Armes. www.chateauversailles.fr. ☎ **01-30-83-78-00.** Palace 18€ adults; Marie Antoinette's Estate 12€ adults; everything free for children 17 and younger. Entry to the park is free. Palace Apr–Oct Tues–Sun 9am–6:30pm; Nov–Mar Tues–Sun 9am–5:30pm. Marie Antoinette's Estate Apr–Oct Tues–Sun noon–6:30pm; Nov–Mar Tues–Sun noon–5:30. Garden and park: Apr–Oct 8am–8:30pm; Nov–Mar 8am–6pm.

Where to Stay

EXPENSIVE

Trianon Palace, a Waldorf Astoria Hotel ★★★ Versailles is close enough to Paris that you don't need to spend the night, but if you are celebrating something special or have bought the 2-day passport, this is one of the poshest hotels in the Ile de France. Elegant gardens and grounds, an indoor heated pool, 19th-century frills, luxurious rooms, and a one-star Michelin restaurant with a famous Scottish chef, **Gordon Ramsey au Trianon** (see below). A more low-key dining option is La Veranda, and if you need total relaxation, there's a Guerlain spa.

1 bd. de la Reine. www.trianonpalace.com. ✆ **01-30-84-50-00.** 199 units. 200€–600€ double; 350€–810€ junior suites; from 1,000€ suite. Parking 20€. **Amenities:** 2 restaurants; bar; concierge; indoor pool; spa; Wi-Fi (25€ per day).

MODERATE

Novotel Château de Versailles ★ A 15-min. walk north of one of the side wings of the château, this chain hotel, built in 1988, has a modern facade with columns and large windows. It's not too expensive and is a convenient choice for visitors to Versailles. All bedrooms have been recently renovated and sport a contemporary style.

4 bd. St-Antoine, Le Chesnay. www.novotel.com. ✆ **01-39-54-96-96.** 105 units. 90€–137 € double; 165€–185€ suite. Children 16 and under stay free in parent's room. Parking 11€. **Amenities:** Restaurant; bar; room service; free Wi-Fi.

Where to Eat

EXPENSIVE

Gordon Ramsay au Trianon ★★★ FRENCH/INTERNATIONAL The *enfant terrible* of chefs, Gordon Ramsay, has invaded Versailles and is king of the roost at this stylish restaurant inside the swanky Trianon Palace Hotel. He is a master at traditional French cooking done in a modern style and changes his menu frequently to take advantage of the best and the freshest in any season. No one does filet of turbot like Ramsay. But the same could be said of his pan-fried John Dory with crab cannelloni in basil emulsion. He stuffs delectable ravioli with langoustines, and you can toss a pork belly his way, and he'll create a culinary masterpiece for you. The service, the setting, everything here is a delight. The food is of the highest order—and so are the prices. In summer, you can dine under the canopy on the front terrace. Reservations required. ✆ **01-30-84-55-55.**

In the Hotel Trianon Palace, 1 bd. de la Reine. www.trianonpalace.com. ✆ **01-30-84-55-55.** Main course 74€–88€; fixed-price menu 148€. Fri–Sat noon–2pm; Tues–Sat 7–10:30pm. Closed 1 week in Jan and 1 week in Mar.

MODERATE

Restaurant Saudade ★ PORTUGUESE This little bistro has been in the same family since 1974, and though just 7 min. on foot from the palace, makes for an ideal lunch or dinner spot away from the maddening crowds. Sitting in a rustic-chic setting of exposed stone walls, wood floors and Chesterfield-style couches, tuck into lip-smacking Portuguese dishes like lamb stew with chorizo sausage, and hunky *feijoada*, a prawn and squid cassoulet. Wine with that? The Tapada de Villar Reserve is an intense, dry, spicy red that goes well with many of the meaty, garlicky dishes on the menu.

20 rue du Général Leclerc. www.saudade-versailles.com. © **01-30-21-23-43.** Fixed-price menu 25€–38€. Tues–Sun noon–2pm and 7–10pm.

INEXPENSIVE

La Flottille ★ FRENCH One of the few restaurants inside the château's grounds (at the head of the Grand Canal), it has a sweeping view over some of Europe's most famous landscaping. Both restaurant and snack-bar service are available. In warm weather, the traditional French cuisine is also served at outside tables. Reservations are recommended.

Parc du Château. www.laflotille.fr. © **01-39-51-41-58.** Main course 22€; fixed-price menu 28.50€–36€. Daily noon to château closing.

Nuance ★ MODERN FRENCH A cozy dining room, a modern menu, and reasonable prices are enough to keep locals crowding into this gourmet eatery, which is about a 10-min. walk from the Château of Versailles. Roast pork with honey and rosemary, sautéed scallops in a Thai bouillon, or a simple chicken brochette with curry sauce might be on the menu, depending on the season and your appetite.

10 bd. du Roi. www.restaurant-nuance.com. © **01-39-49-58-35.** Main course 20€–25€. Tues–Fri noon–1:30pm and 7:30–9:30pm, Sat 7:30–9:30pm.

Le Sept ★★ WINE RESTAURANT You'll want to reserve in advance for a table in this wine-lovers' spot, where hearty homemade dishes like duck terrine, entrecote, and apple tart are served alongside a choice of 200 wines, most of them biodynamic, sold at shop price, whether you eat in or take out. Le Sept's motto? Only serve quality, seasonal produce from traceable, hand-picked sources. And it shows: the beef (from an artisan farmer in Normandy) cuts like butter, and the small plates of cheese and cold meats are flavor explosions unto themselves. Reservations are required.

7 rue de Montreuil. © **01-39-49-55-27.** Main course 12€; fixed-price menus 15€–20€. Tues–Sat noon–2pm and 7–9:30pm.

Shopping

Founded by the Sun King himself, Louis XIV, **Marché Notre-Dame,** pl. du Marché Notre-Dame, is the major public market in Versailles, housed in a series of red-brick buildings. The present look dates from the 19th century. Indoor shops selling local cheeses, meats, and fresh fruits are open daily from 7am to 7pm, but the outdoor stalls in the center of the square flourish only on Tuesday, Friday, and Sunday, from about 9am to 2pm. It's best to go before noon; some of the stalls start shutting down in the early afternoon.

Close to the mammoth market, **Passage de la Geôle** (www.antiques-versailles.com; ✆ **01-30-21-15-13**) is open Friday to Sunday 10am to 7pm, housing antiques shops of furniture and objets d'art at "all prices."

Versailles Nightlife

O'Paris Pub, 15 rue Colbert, off place d'Armes (www.puboparis.com; ✆ **01-39-50-36-12**), is an Irish pub where you can order the best brews in town. A bit more upmarket, **Bar à Vins-Restaurant Le Ducis,** 13 rue Ducis (✆ **01-30-21-93-76**), provides a mellow atmosphere on a summer evening, with tables spilling onto a side street. A bottle of wine and a good companion should get you through an evening, enhanced perhaps by a plate of food selected from the chalkboard menu.

CHARTRES ★★★

88km (58 miles) SW of Paris; 76km (47 miles) NW of Orléans

You'll see it long before you see the actual town: the spire of the cathedral of Chartres rising above a sea of wheat fields. About 1 hr. from Paris, you can easily visit this stunning church and its inspiring stain-glassed windows and still have enough time to wander through the narrow streets of the old town.

Essentials

ARRIVING Direct **trains** leave from Paris' Gare Montparnasse and take about 1 hr. (16€ one-way). For information visit www.oui.sncf or call ✆ **36-35** (.40€/min.). If **driving** from Paris take A10/A11 southwest and follow signs to Le Mans and Chartres. The Chartres exit is marked.

VISITOR INFORMATION The **Office de Tourisme** in the Maison du Saumon, 8 rue de la Poissonerie (www.chartres-tourisme.com; ✆ **02-37-18-26-26**).

Exploring the Cathedral

With its carved portals and three-tiered flying buttresses, this cathedral would be a stunning sight even without its legendary **stained-glass windows**—though the world would be a drearier place. For these ancient glass panels are truly glorious: a kaleidoscope of colors so deep, so rich, and so bright, it's hard to believe they are some 700 years old. Meant as teaching devices more than artwork, the windows functioned as a sort of enormous cartoon, telling the story of Christ through pictures to a mostly illiterate populace. From its beginnings, pilgrims came from far and near to see a piece of cloth that believers say was worn by the Virgin Mary during Christ's birth. The **relic** is still here, but these days it's primarily a different sort of pilgrim that is drawn to Chartres: Over 1.5 million tourists come here every year.

A Romanesque church stood on this spot until 1194, when a fire burnt it virtually to the ground. All that remained were the towers, the Royal Portal, and a few remnants of stained glass. The locals were so horrified that they sprung to action; in a matter of only 3 decades a new cathedral was erected, which accounts for its remarkably unified Gothic architecture. This was one of the first churches to use buttresses as a building support, allowing the architect (whose name has been lost) to build its walls at twice the height of the standard Romanesque cathedrals and make space for its famous windows. The new cathedral, dedicated 1260, has miraculously survived the centuries with relatively little damage. The French Revolution somehow spared

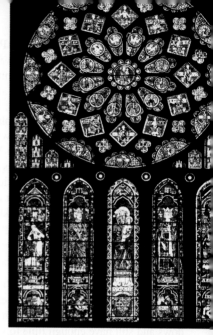

Stained glass rose window at Chartres Cathedral

the cathedral. During World War I and World War II, the precious windows were carefully dismounted piece by piece and stored in a safe place in the countryside.

The cathedral's **facade** ★★ is a remarkable assemblage of religious art and architecture. The tower to your right (the **Old Tower** or South Tower) is topped by its original sober Romanesque spire; that on your left (**New Tower** or North Tower) was blessed with an elaborate Gothic spire in the early 1500s, when the original burned down. Below is the **Royal Portal** ★★★, a masterpiece of Romanesque art. Swarming with kings, queens, prophets, and priests, this sculpted entryway tells the story of the life of Christ. You can **climb to the top of the New Tower** to take in the **view** ★ (call ✆ 02-37-21-22-07 in advance to reserve your time slot); just

---

Tours, Guided & Otherwise

For over 3 decades, Malcolm Miller has been studying the cathedral and giving terrific **guided tours in English.** The 75-min. tour Monday through Saturday usually begins at noon and sometimes

also at 2:45pm (10€ adults; 5€ students). No need to reserve; a sign inside the gift shop entrance indicates that day's tour schedule. You can also rent an audio guide (in English) for 6.20€.

remember to wear rubber-soled shoes, as the 300 steps are a little slippery after all these centuries.

As you enter the cathedral, the radiant colors of the **stained-glass windows ★★★** pierce the dim light. Three windows on the west side of the building, as well as the beautiful rose window to the south called **Notre Dame de la Belle Verière ★** date from the earlier 12th-century structure; the rest, with the exception of a few modern panels, are of 13th-century origins. The scenes depicted in glass, read from bottom to top, recount stories from the Bible as well as the lives of the saints. You will soon find yourself wondering how medieval artists, with low-tech materials, managed to create such vivid colors. The blues, in particular, seem to be divinely inspired. In fact, scientists have pierced at least part of the mystery: The blue was made with sodium and silica compounds that made the color stand up to the centuries better than other colors.

Another marvel is the **chancel enclosure ★★★**, which separates the chancel (the area behind the altar) from the ambulatory (the walkway that runs around the outer chapels). Started in 1514 by Jehan de Beauce, this intricately sculpted wall depicts dozens of saints in a recounting of the lives of the Virgin and Christ. Back in the ambulatory is the Chapel of the Martyrs, where the cathedral's cherished **relic** resides: a piece of cloth that the Virgin Mary apparently wore at the birth of Christ, which was a gift of Charles the Bald in 876.

Chartres also harbors a rare **labyrinth ★**, traced on the floor of the cathedral near the nave. A large circle, divided into four parts, is entirely filled by a winding path that leads to the center. *Note:* The cathedral asks that visitors not talk or wander around during mass, which is generally held in the late morning and early evening. You are welcome to sit in on services, of course.

16 Cloître Notre-Dame. www.chartres-cathedrale.fr. ℂ **02-37-21-22-07.** General admission to the cathedral is free, admission to the towers 6€ adults, 5€ adults 18–25, free for children 17 and under. Cathedral daily 8:30am–7:30pm (until 10pm Tues, Fri, and Sat in July & Aug).

Exploring the Old Town

Give yourself a little time to explore the medieval cobbled streets of the **Vieux Quartier (Old Town) ★**. The narrow lanes near the cathedral have several gabled houses, including the colorful facades of **rue Chantault,** one of which is 8 centuries old. Seek out rue du Bourg, where you'll find the famous **Salmon House** (which houses the tourist office) and some lovely sculptures (including a certain fish). In the lower town, you can stroll along the picturesque **Eure River** with its stone bridges and ancient wash-houses. If you go on a Saturday morning, a covered farmers market is in **place Billard** (until 1pm), the perfect place to grab some lunch supplies for the park behind the cathedral or along the river.

Musée des Beaux-Arts de Chartres ★ MUSEUM Housed in an impressive former Episcopal palace, this museum of fine arts boasts a collection covering the 16th to 20th centuries, including the work of masters such as Zurbarán, Watteau, and Soutine.

29 Cloître Notre-Dame. 🕾 **02-37-90-45-80.** May–Oct Thurs 10am–12:30pm and 2–8pm; Fri–Sat 10am–12:30pm and 2–6pm; the rest of the year, until 5pm. Admission free.

Where to Stay

Grand Monarque Best Western ★★ This appealing hotel occupies an imposing civic monument whose 600-year-old foundations and infrastructures were "gentrified" sometime in the 19th century with white stucco, neoclassical detailing, and touches of the baroque. Functioning as an inn since its original construction in the 15th century and expanded and improved many times since, the hotel remains under the direction of a local family. It attracts guests who enjoy its old-world charm—such as Art Nouveau stained glass and Louis XV chairs in the dining room—and those looking for a bit of pampering: amenities include two excellent restaurants (see "Le Georges," below) and a spa with a pool and a sauna.

22 pl. des Epars. www.bw-grand-monarque.com. 🕾 **800/528-1234** in the U.S., or 02-37-18-15-15. 60 units. 109€–185€ double; 179€–245€ suite. Parking 10€. **Amenities:** 2 restaurants; bar; room service; free Wi-Fi.

Jehan de Beauce Hostellerie ★★ Right by the train station, this grand old hotel has been revamped in an art-deco style. Many of the comfortably chic rooms have bold black-and-white 1920s-inspired patterned carpets and drapes; others are subtler, with wood headboards and a gold theme. The hotel is famed for its bar, Le Fitzgerald, where you can sip champagne and cocktails to the rhythm of jazz. There's also a wellness area with a sauna and a gym.

1 pl. Pierre Semard. www.jehandebeauce.fr. 🕾 **02-37-21-01-41.** 35 units. 120€–175€ double; 180€–280€ suite. Parking 9€. **Amenities:** Bar; 24-hr. room service; wellness area; free Wi-Fi.

Le Parvis ★ Overlooking the cathedral, this restaurant with five rooms is in a great spot if you don't mind the high-season crowds. The cozy guest rooms are each individually decorated; for instance, the Pénélope room is kitschy-modern with a circular bed, while the Les Louis suite features antique-style furnishings, an old-world fireplace, and fab views of the cathedral. The brasserie-style restaurant serves French classics and has a sidewalk terrace. The wee tea salon that doubles as a boutique selling regional produce.

5 rue du Cheval Blanc, 13 pl. de la Cathédrale. www. le-parvis-chartres.fr. 🕾 **02-37-21-12-12.** 5 units. 94€–128€ double. Breakfast included. **Amenities:** Restaurant; bar; tea room; free Wi-Fi.

Where to Eat

Esprit Gourmand ★★ CLASSIC FRENCH   This quaint little bistro on a narrow street near the cathedral has a lot going for it: friendly owners and well-executed French classics like braised lamb shank, veal blanquette and crème brûlée. Sweet tooth? Opt for the café gourmand, a coffee served with no less than four little dessert portions that might include panna cotta, chocolate mousse, banana trifle, and ice-cream. The dining room, outfitted in tile floors and wooden tables, is pleasantly low-key, but ask for a spot in the interior courtyard for some peace and quiet on a sunny day.

6 rue du Cheval Blanc. ✆ **02-37-36-97-84.** Main course 15€–20€. Wed–Sun noon–2pm and 7–10pm.

Le Georges ★★★ FRENCH   The most upscale and delicious dining experience in Chartres is in the Grand Monarque, a hotel with roots that date from the 15th century, when the site served food and drink (not as elegant as what you'll find today) to weary travelers and postal workers. Today's diners feast in a formal, high-ceilinged dining room outfitted in soft grays and browns. Menu items change with the seasons but might include savory portions of crispy langoustines with fennel and vanilla, freshly grilled scallops, or a superb beef Rossini. Another specialty is Pâté de Chartres, the local meat pie. Desserts are sumptuous, and the chef is known locally for his Grand-Marnier soufflé.

In the Grand Monarque Best Western, 22 pl. des Epars. ✆ **02-37-18-15-15.** Fixed-price menus 56€–98€. Tues–Sat noon–1:30pm; Tues–Sat 7–10pm.

Shopping

Your best shopping bet is place des Epars, a pedestrian area home to most of the apparel shops and even some haute couture boutiques. Many shops selling regional items line the narrow streets that fan southeast from the cathedral. Along rue Noël-Balay is a small mall with about 15 interesting shops, which can also provide a dry respite if it's raining.

At **Galerie du Vitrail,** 17 Cloître Notre-Dame (www.galerie-du-vitrail.com; ✆ **02-37-36-10-03**), you'll find a huge selection of stained glass. **Lassaussois Antiquités,** 17 rue des Changes (www.antiquites lassaussois.com; ✆ **02-37-21-37-74**), specializes in antique objets d'art and contemporary furnishings.

Chartres Nightlife

For an evening of theater or modern dance from September to June, try the **Théâtre de Chartres,** pl. de Ravennes (www.theatredechartres.fr; ✆ **02-37-23-42-79**). For dancing, go to **Le Privilège,** 1 pl. St-Pierre (www.leprivilege.fr; ✆ **02-37-35-52-02**), where you'll find a range of dance music from zouk to disco.

RAMBOUILLET

55km (34 miles) SW of Paris; 42km (26 miles) NE of Chartres

Once known as La Forêt d'Yveline, the **Forest of Rambouillet ★** is one of the loveliest forests in France. More than 19,000 hectares (46,930 acres) of greenery stretch from the valley of the Eure to the high valley of Chevreuse, the latter rich in medieval and royal abbeys. Lakes, copses of deer, and even wild boar are some of the attractions of this "green lung." Most people, however, come here to see the château, which you can visit when it's not in use as a "Camp David" for French presidents.

Essentials

GETTING THERE **Trains** depart from Paris's Gare Montparnasse every 30 min. throughout the day for a 35-min. ride. Information and train schedules can be obtained by contacting the Transilien suburban train service (www.transilien.com). By **car,** take N10 southwest from Paris, passing Versailles along the way.

VISITOR INFORMATION The **tourist office** is at the Hôtel de Ville, pl. de la Libération (www.rambouillet-tourism.com; ✆ **01-34-83-21-21**).

Touring the Château de Rambouillet ★

Stately, elegant, and surrounded by formal French gardens and a park, the château is located in one of the most famous forests in France. While its origins lie deep in the Middle Ages, most of the facades were reconstructed in the 19th century, and the interiors date from the 16th. Superb woodwork is used throughout, and the walls are adorned with tapestries, many from the era of Louis XV. François I, the Chevalier king, died of a fever here in 1547 at age 52. When the château was later occupied by the comte de Toulouse, Rambouillet was often visited by Louis XV, who was amused (in more ways than one) by the comte's high-spirited wife. Louis XVI eventually acquired the château, but Marie Antoinette found it boring and called it "the toad." In his surprisingly modest boudoir are four panels representing the continents.

After the Revolution, the Bonaparte family moved in, leaving behind the emperor's ornate bathroom, decorated with Pompeian frescos. Before his final exile to the remote island of St-Helena, Napoleon insisted on spending a final night at Rambouillet, where he secluded himself with his meditations and memories.

In 1830, the elderly Charles X, Louis XVI's brother, abdicated the throne at Rambouillet as a mob marched on the château and his troops began to desert him. From Rambouillet, he embarked for a safe but controversial haven in England. Afterward, Rambouillet fell into private hands. At one time, it was a fashionable restaurant attracting Parisians by offering gondola rides. Napoleon III returned it to the Crown. In 1896, it was designated a residence for the presidents of the republic. In 1944, Charles de Gaulle lived here briefly before giving the order for what was

Rambouillet and its forests can provide a verdant interlude. If you've exhausted the idea of a ramble through the gardens that surround the château (or if they're closed because of a visit from the president of France), consider a visit to the **Rochers d'Angennes,** rocky hillocks that remain as leftovers from the Ice Age. To reach them, park your car on the D107, where you'll see a sign pointing to the **Rochers et Etang d'Angennes,** about 4km (2.5 miles) north of the hamlet of Epernon. Walk along a clearly marked trail through a pine forest before you eventually reach a rocky plateau overlooking the hills and a pond (*l'Etang d'Angennes*). Round-trip, from the site of your parked car to the plateau and back, your promenade should take between 30 and 45 min.

left of the French army to join the Americans in liberating Paris. In more recent years, major political figures like Boris Yeltsin, Nelson Mandela, and Hosni Mubarak have been château guests.

Two must-sees in the park include the **Queen's Dairy,** built for Marie Antoinette and sporting a romantic artificial grotto; and the **Shell Cottage,** a "humble" thatched cottage built for the Princess de Lamballe, whose interior is decorated with an astounding array of seashells, marble, and mother-of-pearl.

It takes about 2 hr. to see the château at Rambouillet.

Parc du Château. www.chateau-rambouillet.fr. ✆ **01-34-83-00-25.** Admission 9€ adults; 7€ students 18–25; free for children 17 and under. Apr–Sept Wed–Mon 10am–noon and 2–6pm; Oct–Mar Wed–Mon 10am–noon and 2–5pm.

Where to Eat

Orangerie des Trois Roys ★★ HAUTE FRENCH   Set in a former 17th-century girls' school, every corner of this chic restaurant oozes elegance—from the lounge's leather chesterfields and stained glass to the veranda's contemporary sculptures. On the plate expect equally refined delights like scrambled egg with foie gras and black truffles, poached blue lobster, and Grand Marnier soufflé. Also popular are the Charolais beef glazed in foie gras, and the lobster bisque pasta.

4 rue Raymond Poincaré. www.lorangeriedestroisroys.fr. ✆ **01-30-88-69-95.** Main course 29€–59€. Tues–Sat noon–2:30pm and 7:30-10:30pm.

Ty Bilig ★ CRÊPERIE   In the town's historic center, in an unlikely corner-building on the square opposite the entrance to the château's park, this no-frills crêperie is in a handy spot for a quick lunch or dinner. The interior is nothing to write home about with simple wooden furnishings and fake flowers on the tables, but the savory galettes and sweet crêpes are as tasty as they are cheap, and cider is served in classic Breton bowls. In summer a terrace sprawls out onto the cobbles in front.

13 pl. Félix Faure. ✆ **01-30-46-23-11.** Tues–Sat noon–2pm and 6:45pm–10pm. Main course 8€. Closed 1st week of Jan and 2 weeks in Aug.

5

SIDE TRIPS FROM PARIS

Rambouillet

FONTAINEBLEAU ★★★

60km (37 miles) S of Paris, 74km (46 miles) NE of Orléans

Napoleon called it "the house of the centuries; the true home of kings," and he had a point: Fontainebleau was a royal residence for more than 700 years. Elegant and dignified, this grand château carries the architectural imprint of many a monarch, in particular, Francis I, Henri IV, and Napoleon I. Surrounded by dense forest and verdant countryside, a trip out here is a relaxing green interlude to your Parisian trip.

Essentials

ARRIVING **Trains** to Fontainebleau leave from the Gare de Lyon (www.transilien.fr). The 40-min. trip costs 9€ for adults and 5.10€ for children ages 4 to 10 one-way. From the Fontainebleau–Avon train station take the local bus (line 1), direction Lilas, to the Château; the fare is 1.90€ one-way. Buses are timed to arrive with the train from Paris. If you're **driving** from Paris, take the A6 south, exit Fontainebleau.

VISITOR INFORMATION The **Office de Tourisme** is at 4 rue Royale, Fontainebleau (www.fontainebleau-tourisme.com; ✆ **01-60-74-99-99**), opposite the main entrance to the château.

Exploring Fontainebleau

Though kings were already living here by the 12th century, it was during the Renaissance that Fontainebleau really took on its regal allure. In 1528, inveterate castle-builder King François I decided to completely rebuild Fontainebleau and make it into a palace that would rival the marvels of Rome. He tore down most of the medieval castle and hired an army of architects and artisans to construct a new one. He also imported a passel of Italian painters, including Il Rosso and Primaticcio, whose style of painting, featuring frescoes in bright colors with sensuous (often nude) figures in mythological landscapes, became known as the School of Fontainebleau.

After François' death, work continued, but it wasn't until Henri IV arrived on the scene in the 17th century that there were more major transformations. Henri added several wings and a courtyard (the **Cour des Offices**), and invited a new clutch of artists, who established a second School of Fontainebleau. This time, the artists were of French and Flemish origins (Ambrose Dubois, Martin Fréminet, and others), and used oil paint and canvas instead of frescos. Louis XIV, preferring Versailles, didn't bother much with Fontainebleau, but both Louis XV and Louis XVI left their mark. Napoleon also made a lasting imprint on the castle's interior. Fontainebleau made an imprint on the Emperor as well: On April 20, 1814, he abdicated here, before being sent off to exile on the island of Elba.

The Forest of Fontainebleau is riddled with *sentiers* (hiking trails) made by French kings and their entourages who went hunting in the forest. A *Guide des Sentiers* is available at the tourist information center (p. 202, you can also download trail maps from their website). Bike paths also cut through the forest. You can rent bikes at **A La Petite Reine,** 14 rue de la Paroisse, a few blocks from the château (www.alapetitereine.com; ✆ **01-60-74-57-57;** 8€/hr., 15€ for a full day.)

TOURING THE CHÂTEAU

Most of what you'll want to see (and what I describe below) is in the **Grands Appartements.** The **Petits Appartements,** a series of rooms that were Napoleon's private residence, requires an additional ticket.

Your first stop will be the **Cour du Cheval Blanc ★★** at the entrance to the palace. It was in this grand square, which is surrounded by wings of the castle on three sides, that Napoleon said adieu to his faithful imperial guards. "Continue to serve France," he pleaded. "Her welfare was my only concern." The sumptuous **horseshoe staircase ★★** was contributed by Henri II. On the left, as you enter, is the **Chapelle de la Trinité ★.** When he was 7, Louis XIII climbed up the scaffolding to watch Martin Fréminet, his art instructor, paint the glorious ceiling. Linking the chapel with the royal apartments is the **Gallery of François I ★★★,** a stunning example of Renaissance art, whose walls are covered with exceptional frescos, moldings, and boiseries (carved woodwork). Throughout the gallery (and elsewhere in the castle) you will see the salamander, François' official symbol.

The other major must-see is the **Salle de Bal ★★★.** This 30m (98-ft.) long ballroom is a feast of light and color; the frescos by Primaticcio and Nicolo dell'Abate have been completely restored, and their rich hues radiate like they were painted yesterday. The monumental fireplace at the far end was designed by 16th-century architect Philibert Delorme.

The **Royal Apartments ★★** were decorated and redecorated by successive monarchs. Louis XIII was born in the **Salon Louis XIII ★,** a fact that is symbolized in the ceiling mural showing Love riding a dolphin. Though several different queens slept in the **Chambre de l'Impératrice ★★,** its current set-up reflects the epoch of Empress Josephine (Napoleon's first wife). The sumptuous bed, crowned in gilded walnut and covered in embroidered silk, was made for Marie Antoinette in 1787. The queen would never see it; the Revolution exploded before she could arrange a royal visit to the château. Napoleon transformed the Kings' bedroom into the **Salle du Trône ★,** or Throne Room. It's easy to imagine the emperor receiving his subjects up there in blue velvet, bookended by two huge Napoleonic standards.

The **Musée Napoléon 1er ★,** in the Louis XV wing, celebrates the life of the emperor with historic memorabilia and artwork relating to his

5

SIDE TRIPS FROM PARIS

Fontainebleau

reign, like the tent he slept in during military campaigns, and a remarkable mechanical desk. With an additional ticket, you can visit the **Musée Chinois de l'Impératrice,** which dates from 1863 and contains the Empress Eugénie's lavish collection of Oriental artefacts, some of which were given to her by the Embassy of Siam in 1861.

TOURING THE GARDENS

The formal gardens must have been beautiful when André Le Nôtre put his hand to them in the 17th century, but today, though well-kempt, they look a little arid. More lush is the **Garden of Diane ★**, a quiet spot of green on the north side of the castle created during the time of François I, which centers around a statue of the goddess surrounded by four dogs. The **English Garden ★**, complete with an artificial stream and lush groves of tall trees, was added by Napoleon. The vast **Carp Pond ★**, which extends directly from the south side of the **Cour de la Fontaine,** has a small island with a pavilion where an afternoon snack would be served to royal residents. Surrounding the gardens and its park is the enormous **Fontainebleau Forest ★★**, which, if you have the time, is definitely worth the visit (see box, below).

Pl. du Général-de-Gaulle. www.musee-chateau-fontainebleau.fr. ✆ **01-60-71-50-70.** Grands appartements & Musée Napoléon 1er 12€ adults, 10€ students 18–25; ticket to Musée Chinois de l'Impératrice 3€ adults; all admission free for children 17 and under. Apr–Sept Wed–Mon 9:30am–6pm; Oct–Mar Wed–Mon 9:30am–5pm.

Where to Stay

Hôtel Aigle-Noir ★★   This 18th-century mansion, once the home of Cardinal de Retz, is just down the street from the château. You'll pass through mighty gates and a grand courtyard before you enter the hotel, which is one of Fontainebleau's most elegant. Rooms are decked out with antiques and reproductions, walls are covered with period prints, and the staff will make you feel that you are one of the Cardinal's close friends. A Napoléon III-style bar completes the picture.

27 pl. Napoleon–Bonaparte. www.hotelaiglenoir.com. ✆ **01-60-74-60-00.** 53 units. 115€–340€ double; 240€–480€ suite. Parking 12€. **Amenities:** Bar; concierge; laundry service; room service; free Wi-Fi.

Hôtel de Londres ★★   With a historic 1850s-era facade, this hotel enjoys one of the best locations in town for anyone fascinated by the architecture of the château of Fontainebleau. It's directly in front of the cour des Adieux, site of Napoleon's farewell to his troops before his exile to Elba. It's been owned and managed by the same family for three generations. The well-maintained rooms are tastefully and cozily outfitted with a mix of modern and period furniture and have extra-long beds. Other than breakfast, no meals are served.

1 pl. du Général-de-Gaulle. www.hoteldelondres.com. ✆ **01-64-22-20-21.** 16 units. 138€–188€ double; 180€–350€ suite. Closed 1 week in Aug and Christmas through 1st week in Jan. **Amenities:** Bar; free Wi-Fi.

Le Clos Saint Honoré ★★★   A short walk from the château, in a converted 19th-century manor house, this wonderful *chambre d'hôtes* is a solid choice if you're looking for something more personable than a hotel. The six rooms are all understatedly elegant and overlook the tree-filled garden. The rooftop terrace is a luxury on a warm evening, when you can bring your own bottle of wine and wind down as the sun sets. The family suite includes a kitchen.

11 rue Saint Honoré. www.leclossaintehonore.com. ℂ **06-72-87-60-16.** 6 units. 70€–95€ double; 120€ suite. **Amenities:** Garden; free Wi-Fi.

Where to Eat

Auberge de la Croix d'Augas ★ SAVOYARD   This country inn is located 2.5km (1.5 miles) from the château in the forest of Fontainebleau. The decor and the menu resemble that of an Alpine chalet; Savoyard specialties like fondue, raclette, and tartiflette figure prominently here. Don't worry, if you aren't up for these cheese, potato, and ham-laden dishes—there are also pasta, fish, and steak choices. The rustic setting has lots of wood beams and a lovely terrace for outdoor dining in good weather.

Exit Fontainebleau on bd. de Maréchal Foch (rte. D606) to rte. D116, about 1km (.5 mile) into the forest. www.restaurant-fontainebleau.fr. ℂ **01-64-23-49-25.** Main course 9.90€–20.60€; fixed-price lunch 14.90€ or dinner 20.80€. Daily noon–2pm and 7:15–10pm.

L'Axel ★★★ MODERN FRENCH   If, after a few hours experiencing life in a castle you feel like treating yourself to a royal meal, this is the place. Widely hailed as a rising culinary star, chef Kunihisa Goto creates exciting French dishes with a dash of Japanese *je ne sais quoi*, like Wagyu steak with sweet potatoes and onions, or sea bass and oysters with crispy soybeans and truffles. Reservations are a must.

43 rue de France. www.laxel-restaurant.com. ℂ **01-64-22-01-57.** Main course 40€–90€; fixed-price lunch 35€–42€ or dinner 60€–110€. Apr–Oct Thurs–Sun 12:15–2pm and 7:30–9:30pm, Mon and Wed 7:30–9:30pm; Nov–Mar Thurs–Sun 12:15–2pm and 7:30–9:30pm, Wed 7:30–9:30pm.

Chez Bernard ★ TRADITIONAL FRENCH   The premier dining choice in Fontainebleau has a covered terrace overlooking the château and the cour des Adieux. Chef Bernard Crogiez's cuisine is meticulous, with an undeniable flair. Seasonal specialties come and go, but you can be sure to find baked snails in garlic cream sauce, roasted *magret* of duck with cassis sauce, *rognon de veau* (veal kidneys) with mustard sauce, and sautéed scallops à la Provençale. Reservations are required.

3 rue Royale. ℂ **01-64-22-24-68.** Main course 15€–29€; fixed-price lunch Mon–Fri 16€ or dinner 27€. Tues–Sun noon–2pm; Mon–Sat 7:30–9:30pm. Closed 2 weeks in Aug and 1 week in Dec.

VAUX-LE-VICOMTE ★★★

47km (29 miles) SE of Paris; 24km (15 miles) NE of Fontainebleau

This jewel of a castle comes with a story that reads like a Hollywood screenplay. Nicolas Fouquet, the château's original owner, was a brilliant finance minister and lover of arts and leisure. In the early 1700s he was the toast of Paris. His circle included France's top artists and intellectuals, drawn to his gorgeous home in the country. Unfortunately, Fouquet underestimated the jealousy of his superiors, in particular the young king, Louis XIV.

Things came to a head one fateful night in the summer of 1661. As Voltaire put it, "On August 17, at 6 in the evening, Nicolas Fouquet was the King of France; at two in the morning, he was nobody." Oblivious to the fact that the king was already fed up with his penchant for stealing the spotlight, Fouquet organized a stupendous party in his honor. He pulled out all the stops: There was a sumptuous meal, a play written and performed by Molière, and a fireworks display—no one had seen anything like it. Three weeks later, Fouquet was arrested on trumped-up charges of embezzlement. The king seized the castle, confiscated its contents, and hired its artists and architects to work on Versailles. Though writers like Madame de Sévigné and La Fontaine pleaded with the king on Fouquet's behalf, the once untouchable financial minister spent the rest of his life in prison.

Château de Vaux-le-Vicomte

Vaux by Candlelight

To give you just an inkling of what Vaux looked like on the evening of the famous party Fouquet threw for Louis XIV back in 1661, visit the castle when it's illuminated by candlelight. From May to mid-October on Saturday nights, some 2,000 candles burn from 7pm to midnight, when you can visit the castle's interior, stroll in the gardens, and enjoy a fireworks display with classical music (19.50€ adults, 17.50€ for children ages 6 to 16, free for children 5 and under). Top it off with a meal at the château's cafeteria, Le relais de l'Ecureuil (main course from 12€), or the gourmet garden restaurant, Les Charmilles (fixed-price menu from 59.60€).

Essentials

ARRIVING   Though it's close to Paris, Vaux-le-Vicomte is hard to reach by mass transit. By **car,** take the A4 east to the N104 south to Vert Saint-Denis, then the D82 east to Vaux-le-Vicomte. **Trains** run from Gare de l'Est to Verneuil l'Etang (35 min.; www.oui.sncf; ✆ **36-35** at .40€/min.; 8.40€ adults, 4.20€ children 4–10), but then you'll need to take a shuttle bus ("Châteaubus") from the Melun train station (7€ per person round trip; free for children 11 and under).

VISITOR INFORMATION   The nearest **tourist office** is in Melun, at 26 pl. Saint-Jean (www.melun-tourisme.fr; ✆ **01-64-52-64-52**).

Touring the Château

Though his reaction was extreme, Louis XIV's jealousy is not too hard to understand when you are standing in front of Vaux-le-Vicomte; the edifice is the epitome of 17th-century elegance. The castle was eventually released to Fouquet's widow, and has remained in private hands ever since. The ancestors of the current owners, Jean-Charles and Alexandre de Vogüé, bought the palace in 1875, when they started a much-needed program to restore Vaux to its original splendor. The restored château is now filled with splendid tapestries, carpets, and art objects.

One of its most impressive rooms was actually never finished: the oval **Grand Salon ★★,** which Fouquet never got a chance to paint or furnish. Here, you actually don't miss all the decorative trimmings; the bare white pilasters and detailed carvings have a classical beauty that stands on its own. For something more ornate, there is the **King's bedroom ★★;** this lavish ensemble of chandeliers, brocade, and painted ceiling (by Le Brun) was a model for the King's Apartments in Versailles. The **Salon des Muses ★** also gets a fabulous ceiling by Le Brun, as well as several fine tapestries covering its walls. To help imagine what Fouquet's dinner parties were like, take a stroll through the elaborately decorated **Salle à Manger ★** (dining room), where a table is set with stacks of rare fruits and gold candlesticks, and a sideboard displays a set of extraordinary majolica. You can see life on the other side of the banquet table downstairs in the **kitchen,** with its humbler servants' dining area.

The **gardens** ★★★ are almost as spectacular as the château. The carefully calculated geometry of the flowerbeds and alleyways makes this a study in harmony, even if you couldn't call them exactly natural. Nature is lurking close by, however—the entire ensemble is surrounded by seemingly endless forest. Just behind the castle are two enormous beds of boxwood trimmed into elaborate designs; Le Nôtre took his inspiration from the patterns in Turkish carpets. The far end of the gardens is crossed by a large **canal.** There you will also find a series of grottos, each sheltering a statue of a different river god. Finally, from the last basin, turn around and take in the lovely **view** ★ of the gardens with the château rising in the background.

77950 Maincy. www.vaux-le-vicomte.com. ☏ **01-64-14-41-90.** Admission 16.50€ adults; 13.50€ students, seniors, and children ages 6–16; free for children 5 and under. Mid-Mar to mid-Nov 10am–6pm. Closed mid-Nov to mid-Mar, except for certain days during the Christmas holidays.

Where to Stay & Eat

Auberge de Crisenoy ★★ MODERN FRENCH   You are more likely to find locals from Melun than fellow visitors at this *auberge,* and that's part of its charm. Behind the solid stone walls of a former private home, the two dining rooms (on separate floors), plus an additional 10 tables on a mezzanine, overlook a garden. The menu items are based on modern interpretations of French classics and change every three months. The best examples include foie gras with white grapes, toast, and compote of apples; *filet l'agneau* stuffed with onions, pears, and new onions; and well-seasoned cassoulet of snails and sweetbreads, served in a copper pot placed directly on the table.

23 Grande Rue, Crisenoy. ☏ **01-64-38-83-06.** Fixed-price lunch Tues–Fri 26€; fixed-price menu 32€ and 49€. Wed–Sat noon–1:30pm and 7:30–9pm; Sun noon–1:30pm. Closed 1 week at Christmas, 1 week in Mar, and 3 weeks in Aug. From Vaux-le-Vicomte, follow N36 toward Meaux for 2.5km (1.5 miles).

Château de Courtry ★   Unless you want to sleep in uninspiring Melun, your best overnight bet is to find a bed-and-breakfast, like this lovely little château. While the inside might not be quite as impressive as its noble exterior, the three guest rooms are quite comfortable, and your hosts also offer various meal possibilities, from brunch to gourmet picnics to candlelight dinner (8€–39€).

12 rue du Château, Sivry-Courtry, 6km (3.7 mi) from the château on the D215 and the D126. www.chateaudecourtry.com. ☏ **01-60-69-36-01** or 06-62-79-78-20. 3 units. 96€ double; 99€–102€ family room for up to 5 people. Breakfast included. **Amenities:** Meals for guests; free Wi-Fi (on ground floor only).

La Table de Saint Just ★★★ TRADITIONAL FRENCH   You're bound to be charmed while dining at this elegant 17th-century farmhouse, whose oak beams and exposed stone walls were once associated with the nearby **Château de Vaux-le-Pénil.** Menu items change with the seasons but may include foie gras with figs served with spice bread; lobster with green apples; scallops roasted with truffles; and roasted rack of lamb with moussaka of fresh vegetables.

11 rue de Libération, Ferme Saint Just, Vaux-le-Pénil. www.restaurant-latable-saintjust.com. ✆ **01-64-52-09-09.** Main course 35€–41€; fixed-price menu 54€ and 105€. Tues–Sat noon–1:30pm and 7:30–9pm. Closed 3 weeks in Aug, 2 weeks at Christmas, and 1 week at Easter. From Vaux-le-Vicomte, drive 5.5km (3.5 miles) west, following signs to Melun, then to Maincy, and then to Vaux-le-Pénil.

GIVERNY ★★

74km (46 miles) NW of Paris

In 1883, Claude Monet and his family moved to a tiny town north of Paris, where they rented a house that came with almost 1 hectare (2.5 acres) of land. He didn't know it then, but he would spend the rest of his life there, painting scenes from the fabulous garden that he would create out of the grassy slope behind his house. Today, the **Fondation Claude Monet à Giverny** is open to the public, and for a small fee, you too can wander in and out of the brilliant flower beds, lush bowers, and shady arbors that inspired this impressionist master.

Essentials

ARRIVING   Trains (SNCF; www.oui.sncf; ✆ **36-35** at .40€/min) leave every hour or two from the Gare St-Lazare train station to Vernon, the closest stop to Giverny, which is about 7km (4.5 miles) away. The trip takes around 45 min. and costs 12€ to 16.70€ one-way. From Vernon you can either take a shuttle bus (10€ round-trip) or rent a bike at the station (L'Arrivé de Giverny, ✆ **02-32-21-16-01;** 15€/day) and pedal there on the marked bike path.

If you're **driving,** take the Autoroute A14 to the A13 toward Rouen. Take exit 14 for Vernon/Bonnières and cross the Seine on to Bennecourt. From here, a direct road with signs leads to Giverny.

VISITOR INFORMATION   The **Office de Tourisme des Portes de l'Eure** is at 36 rue Carnot in Vernon (www.cape-tourisme.fr; ✆ **02-32-51-39-60**).

Exploring Giverny

When you enter this green haven, you'll quickly realize that Monet wasn't just a brilliant painter; he was also a gifted gardener. By the end of his life, the garden was just as much a work of art as the paintings, or perhaps they *were* the paintings. If you have already visited the Orangerie in Paris, and seen his magical Nympheas, or water lilies, spread across huge canvases in two oval-shaped rooms, in a way, you have already visited this garden; they were painted here, with the aim of faithfully recreating the feeling you would have if you were looking at the same flowers at Giverny.

Monet's garden and pond at Giverny

There are actually two gardens here: The first and closest to the house is the **Clos Normand ★★**, a French-style garden that is resolutely orderly and geometric, despite the riot of colors. Gladioli, larkspur, phlox, daisies, and asters clamor for your attention; irises and oriental poppies brighten the western lawn. Monet painted here, but his famous water lily series was born in the **Water Garden ★★★**. Monet bought this piece of property in 1893 with the intention of building a garden that resembled those in the Japanese prints he collected; the ornate **Japanese bridge ★** figures prominently in several of his canvases. Today the garden looks much as it did when Monet was immortalizing it. Willows weep quietly into the ponds, heather, ferns, azaleas, and rhododendrons carpet the banks. This garden was a sanctuary for the painter, who came here to contemplate and explore one of his favorite subjects: the complex interplay of water and light.

At **Monet's house ★** you can see the artist's living spaces as well as his **Japanese print collection.** Unfortunately, none of his paintings are on display.

Be advised that it will be virtually impossible to experience the gardens as Monet did—more or less alone. This is an extremely popular outing for both individuals and tour groups, so your best bet is to come on a slow day like Monday or Wednesday, and/or to arrive after 3pm, when the groups have left.

84 rue Claude-Monet. www.fondation-monet.com. ℂ **02-32-51-28-21.** Admission 9.50€ adults; 5.50€ students; free for children 6 and under. End of Mar to end of Oct daily 9:30am–6pm. Closed Nov to end of Mar.

Where to Stay & Eat

Cocotte et Bouchons ★ MODERN FRENCH   This pleasant, popular restaurant does a large percentage of its business with locals, despite its location on the main street of Vernon, just 4.8km (3 miles) southwest of the Claude Monet Foundation across the river in Giverny. The menu focuses on flavorful, French cuisine with a modern twist, with dishes that that might include cod in andouille de vire sauce (Normandy tripe sausage), salmon and scallop terrine, and even a burger with Roblochon cheese. Desserts—think chocolate profiteroles with orange ice-cream—are scrumptious, but if you're into cheese, make room for the Pont L'Evêque and apple rolls, crispy and delicious.

71 rue Carnot, Vernon. ℂ **02-32-64-10-44.** Main course 17€–20€; fixed-price menu 23€–29€. Wed–Sun 12:15–3pm; Wed–Sat 7–9pm. From the Claude Monet Foundation in Giverny, drive 5km (3 miles) southwest, crossing the Seine, and follow signs to Vernon.

Le Jardin des Plumes ★★   Top chef and local boy Eric Guerin turned this Anglo-Norman mansion into a chic yet comfy hotel and restaurant, offering colorful and fresh accommodations and excellent cuisine to Monet fans (and others). Half of the eight guest rooms are in the main house, the others are in a modern annex; some look out on a lovely garden. The restaurant shares the garden view; the exquisite fixed-price menus start at 48€.

1 rue de Milieu, a short walk from the gardens. ℂ **02-32-54-26-35.** www.lejardindes plumes.fr. 8 units. 195€–310€ double; 310€–370€ suite. Nov–Mar closed Mon–Tues; closed Jan. **Amenities:** Restaurant; free Wi-Fi.

La Musardière ★   A short walk from Monet's museum and gardens, this family-run hotel is in a former manor house. A scenic park filled with ancient trees surrounds the hotel and restaurant. The mansard-roofed building dates from 1880 and was around in Monet's time. Many of the antique features and architectural adornments are still in place. *Musardière* is French for a place for "idling or dawdling along," and that is just what you do here. Each medium-size guest room, attractively and comfortably furnished, has a small bathroom with tub or shower. The hotel also operates its own restaurant and crêperie, where fixed-price menus cost 26€ and 36€.

123 rue Claude-Monet. www.lamusardiere.fr. ℂ **02-32-21-03-18.** 10 units. 85€–99€ double; 125€–145€ suite. Free parking. Closed Nov to mid-Mar. **Amenities:** Restaurant; bar; free Wi-Fi.

Giverny's Other Sights

After you've explored the gardens, take a stroll along the main street up the cemetery to visit the **Monet family tomb.** To dig deeper into Impressionism, visit the **Musée des Impressionismes,** 99 rue Claude Monet (www.mdig.fr; ℂ **02-32-51-94-65;** 7.50€ adults, 5€ students, 3.50€ children ages 7–11 years old, free for children 6 and under; Apr–Oct 10am–6pm), which explores the high points of the movement, as well as what lead up to it and what came after.

DISNEYLAND PARIS ★

41km (25 miles) E of Paris

It might not be particularly French, but there's no denying that this is a fun place to visit—especially if you're traveling with kids. Once there, it's very hard not to resist getting swept up by the fun rides and the good cheer. There are two parks here, **Disneyland Paris** and **Disney Studios;** depending on your stamina, you can do them both in a day.

Essentials

ARRIVING   You could arrive by **TGV** (the French railway's high-speed train), but a less spectacular and less complicated option is to simply climb on the **RER A** (www.ratp.fr; 40 min.; 7.60€ adults, 3.80€ ages 4–10 one-way) and take it all the way to its terminus at Marne-la-Vallée–Chessy-Parc Disney (just make sure that this is the terminus—the RER A has multiple destinations). When you get out, you'll be about a 5-min. walk from the entrance. By **car,** head east on the A4 and take the Parcs Disney exit.

VISITOR INFORMATION   The **Disneyland Paris Guest Relations Office** is located in City Hall on Main Street, U.S.A. (www.disneyland paris.com; ℂ **08-25-30-05-00,** .15€/min.). For general tourist information for the region, visit the **Espace de Tourisme,** between the train station and Disney Village (www.tourisme77.fr; ℂ **01-60-43-33-33**).

ADMISSION   Admission varies depending on the season whether you buy tickets online or at the gate, but here's a general price guide: In peak season, a one-day park ticket (for either the main park or Walt Disney Studios) costs around 64€ for adults, 58€ for children ages 3 to 11, and is free for children 2 and under; a two-day park-hopper ticket is around 139€ for adults, 126€ for kids; and a three-day park-hopper ticket is around 169€ for adults, 156€ for kids. Oodles of special offers are available throughout the year, some that include transportation to and from Paris; check the website for details.

HOURS   Hours vary throughout the year, but often are 10am to 7pm with later closings in the summer. Check the website for exact hours.

Exploring Disney

The U.S. has Disneyland and Disney World; in France, you could call it Disney Universe. This giant resort has two parks: the classic **Disneyland,** complete with lots of new Star Wars rides, like Hyperspace Mountain and Path of the Jedi; and **Disney Studios,** where you can try your hand at cinematography or delve into the world of cartoons. But the parks are just the beginning of your excellent adventure in Marne-la-Vallée: There are also seven hotels, a golf course, tennis courts, and an ice skating rink, not to mention Disney Village, with its boutiques, restaurants, discotheque, cinema, and

IMAX theater. For the purposes of this guide, we'll just stick with parks. In general, Disneyland is a better choice for the under-7 crowd; though even the little ones will still get a kick out of the cartoon attractions at Disney Studios, like the 4-D *Rataouille* ride.

DISNEYLAND PARK

Isn't it comforting that some things never change? Here you are in France, and yet there is Frontierland, Adventureland, and Fantasyland, just the way you remember them back home. Okay, not exactly. For one thing, everyone's speaking French. And Japanese. And Bulgarian, Hindi, and Farsi. The success of this resort is its international appeal. When you enter the park, you'll step right into **Main Street USA,** that utopian rendition of early-20th-century America, complete with horse and buggies and barber-shop quartets. Here you'll find the **information center** as well as a train, which leaves from Main Street Station. The train, which does a circuit around the park, will whisk you off to **Frontierland,** where you'll find a paddle-wheel steamboat, a petting zoo, and the Lucky Nugget saloon, among other things. Next, you'll chug through **Adventureland,** with old favorites like the Swiss Family Robinson treehouse and the Pirates of the Caribbean, as well as newer attractions like Aladdin's Oriental Palace. Onward towards **Fantasyland** with Sleeping Beauty's Castle (Le Château de Belle au Bois Dormant), whizzing teacups, flying Dumbos, and "It's a Small World." Last stop is **Discoveryland,** home of the Star Wars Hyperspace Mountain and the submarine Nautilus, as well as "Buzz Lightyear's Laser Blast." Main Street has parades virtually every afternoon, and a spectacular light and fountain show, Disney Dreams, around closing time.

DISNEY STUDIOS

Though the primary draw here, of course, is Disneyland Park, Disney Studios makes an interesting alternative for older kids who have already done Disney and are up for something different. The main entrance to the studios, called the **Front Lot,** consists of Disney Studio 1, an elaborate sound stage complete with film props, shops, and restaurants. You then move inside the park, with its film-oriented attractions like **Disney Animation Studios,** where you can learn how cartoons are made, and the **Back Lot,** with its special effects and stunt shows.

Naturally, there are fun rides here, too, like the **Tower of Terror** (based on the classic "Twilight Zone" TV show), **Crush's Coaster** and the **Rock 'n' Rollercoaster** (featuring Aerosmith tunes). Smaller visitors will appreciate **Toy Story Playland,** where they can speed around on the **RC Racer** or soar through the skies on the **Toy Soldiers Parachute Drop.**

Where to Stay

You can easily make Disney a day trip from Paris—the transportation links are excellent—or you can spend a night . . . or two. Most overnight guests take a package that includes park entry, breakfast, and a couple of nights in a hotel. The per-night hotel prices listed below can range wildly, depending on the package you book, the number of days you stay, the time of year, and so on. Your best bet is to study the website or call the reservations service shared by the resort's seven theme hotels. If you'd like to reserve by phone, call ✆ **407/W-DISNEY** [934-7639] in North America, or ✆ **08-25-30-02-22**, (.15€/min.) in France. Otherwise, you can always reserve online at www.disneylandparis.com.

VERY EXPENSIVE

Disneyland Hotel ★★   Looking like a cartoon version of a Victorian resort, this giant pink pagoda is Disney's most luxurious hotel. Rooms are spacious and comfortable (at these prices they better be); many overlook Sleeping Beauty's Castle and Big Thunder Mountain. Some less desirable units open onto a parking lot, so specify when you reserve. There are extras galore here, including an indoor pool, multiple restaurants, and a spa.

www.disneylandparis.com. ✆ **01-60-45-65-89.** 495 units. From 620€ double; from 1,270€ suite. **Amenities:** 2 restaurants; bar; babysitting; café; health club w/indoor pool; room service; sauna; spa; free Wi-Fi.

EXPENSIVE

Newport Bay Club ★★   This gargantuan hotel on the edge of Lake Disney strives to resemble a New England harbor-front inn (ca. 1900). The yacht club atmosphere carries over to the nautically decorated blue and cream rooms, arranged in various shapes and sizes. Stay here and you're about 15 min. on foot from the park entrance.

www.disneylandparis.com. ✆ **01-60-45-55-00.** 1,093 units. 267€–502€ double; from 544€ suite. **Amenities:** 2 restaurants; bar; health club; indoor and outdoor pools; room service; sauna; Wi-Fi (15€ per day).

MODERATE

Hotel Cheyenne/Hotel Santa Fe ★   These two Old West–style lodgings stand side by side, vaguely resembling a movie set. The Cheyenne is a collection of western-looking two-story buildings along Desperado Street; the desert-themed Santa Fe is a clutch of 42 adobe-style pueblos. Kids will enjoy sleeping in a hotel that looks like a park attraction; parents will appreciate the indoor/outdoor playgrounds and kid-friendly atmosphere.

www.disneylandparis.com. ✆ **01-60-45-63-12** (Cheyenne) or **01-60-45-79-22** (Santa Fe). 2,000 units. 109€–369€ double. **Amenities:** Restaurant; bar; free Wi-Fi (in common areas only).

Where to Eat

You won't starve at Disneyland Paris, which offers some 70 restaurants and snack bars. You can live on burgers and fries or try one of the following upscale restaurants. One way or another, the bill will probably be higher than you bargained for. For all restaurant **reservations**, call ✆ **01-60-30-40-50.**

California Grill ★ CALIFORNIAN/FRENCH   For a meal with class, this is Disney's gourmet restaurant, tucked into the swank Disneyland Hotel. While it may not rival the gourmet palaces back in Paris, the menu features well-executed French classics, as well as a few "Californian" dishes like gourmet burgers and grilled vegetable platters. This is a quiet, mostly adult venue (though they do have nice children's menus). The restaurant is open only for dinner; reservations required.

In the Disneyland Hotel. ✆ **01-60-45-65-76.** Fixed-price menu 70€–130€; children's menu 36€. Daily 6:30pm–10:30pm.

Inventions ★ INTERNATIONAL   This may be the only restaurant in Europe where Disney characters go table-hopping. This is not *grande cuisine*, but the quality is much better than your average buffet, with dishes such as chilled asparagus, Italian prosciutto, or even escargot and bouillabaisse, plus lots of kid-friendly dishes from spaghetti to Buzz Lightyear éclairs.

In the Disneyland Hotel. ✆ **01-60-45-65-76.** Buffet 65€ adults; 35€ children ages 3–11. Daily 12:30–3pm and 6–10:30pm.

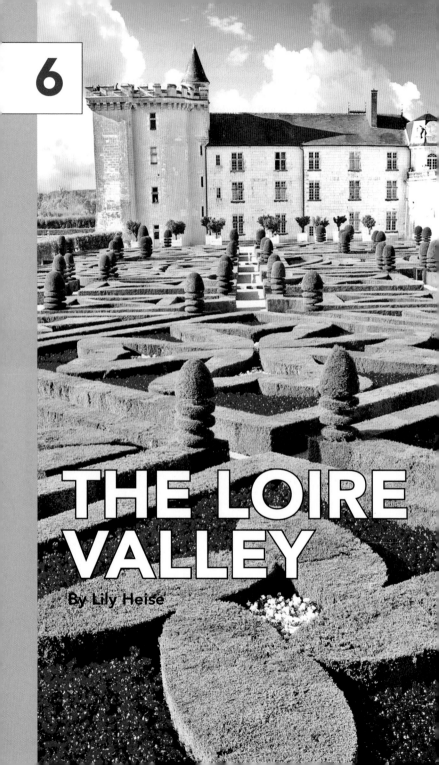

THE LOIRE VALLEY

By Lily Heise

J ust two hr. south of Paris, the Loire Valley enchants visitors with a stunning landscape of castles and vineyards straight out of a fairy tale. King François I and his Renaissance court left a spectacular cultural legacy, earning the entire valley a place on the World Heritage Site list. History buffs follow Joan of Arc from Orléans to Chinon; romantics fall in love with the storybook châteaux of Chenonceau, Azay-le-Rideau, and Ussé; garden lovers revel in the verdant paradise of Chaumont and Villandry; gastronomes tantalize their palates at Michelin-starred restaurants and rustic *auberges;* and outdoor adventurers can see it all by bike.

As its name would imply, the region's rolling hills and forests hug the winding Loire River, encompassing 800 sq. km (308 sq. miles) of land south of Ile-de-France, from the city of Orléans and extending west to Nantes on the Atlantic coast. Most visitors use Tours or Orléans as their starting point; however, the towns of Blois, Amboise, or Saumur make excellent bases for exploring the region.

Most visitors to the Loire arrive via Paris; there are about six direct trains daily from the TGV station at Charles de Gaulle airport to the Tours TGV station Saint-Pierre (1 hr., 40 min.; 39€–70€ one-way). At least one high-speed train (TGV) an hour runs to both Orléans and Tours, convenient starting points for anyone not renting a car directly in Paris.

You can also seek additional assistance planning your trip via the Loire Valley's **main regional tourist offices**: **Comité Régional de Tourisme du Centre-Val de Loire,** 37 av. de Paris, Orléans 45000 (www.valdeloire-france.com; © **02-38-79-95-28**) or through the various local tourist offices listed throughout the chapter.

ORLÉANS ★

119km (74 miles) SW of Paris; 72km (45 miles) SE of Chartres

Ever since **Joan of Arc** relieved the besieged city from the Burgundians and the English in 1429, the city has honored the "Maid of Orléans." This deliverance is celebrated every year on May 8, the anniversary of her victory. But even if you aren't in town for the celebration, it's impossible to overlook the city's affection for the warrior; her name adorns everything from streets and cafes to chocolates and candies. Though it suffered

FACING PAGE: **Château de Villandry, Loire Valley**

BIKING YOUR WAY THROUGH THE LOIRE

Trains serve some towns, but the best way to see this relatively flat region is by car or bike. Ten years and several million euros later, the vast program called **La Loire à Vélo ("The Loire on a Bike";** www.cycling-loire.com) has completed the 800km-long (496-mile) **Loire à Vélo trail,** so you can now safely pedal from Nevers to the sea on a dedicated bike path past châteaux, villages, and natural areas or easily bike from one château to another. The path was designed for low-key cycling and is linked to cycling-friendly hotels and bike-rental outfits along the way (look for the accueil vélo signs). More paths are added every year, and the trail will hook up to an even more massive project called **EuroVelo 6,** a cycling path that leads all the way to the Black Sea, at the far eastern edge of Europe.

La Loire à Vélo has partnered with various tourist offices and travel agencies to offer a range of bike-trip packages that include hotel, meals, bike rental, and baggage transport (very important if you don't want to haul extra weight). For more information, visit the "Organise your stay" tab on **www.cycling-loire.**

com. The website also has detailed information on dozens of bike-rental outfits along the route, as well as brochures and links to guidebooks on various sections of the path.

One of the better-known outfitters is **Detours de Loire,** 35 rue Charles Gille, Tours (www.locationdevelos.com; ✆ **02-47-61-22-23**), which has three other shops in Blois, Saumur, and Tours as well as 10 or so associated outlets up and down the Loire à Vélo circuit. This means that you can pick up your bike in one town and leave it in any partner outlet along the way without backtracking. If you are arriving in the Loire Valley by train, the four main shops are all located close to the town station. Prices for all-purpose bikes run from 15€ to 22€ per day, with discounts for multi-day rentals. A 300€ deposit (usually a credit card imprint) is required. Detours de Loire can also organize hotel-bike packages, deliver your bike to your hotel, and store your bags while you are pedaling. **Note:** Most outlets are open only from April/May to October, except for the outlet in Blois and Tours.

damage in World War II, the city's downtown still remains quaint, though it has gradually been losing its regional prominence to the more prosperous Tours to the southwest.

Essentials

ARRIVING   About two **trains** per hour arrive from Paris's Gare d'Austerlitz (1 hr., 10 min.; www.oui.sncf; ✆ **36-35** at .40€/min.; 10€– 25€ one-way); there are also a dozen connections from Tours (50–70 min.). The one-way fare from Tours to Orléans is about 21€. Orléans lies on the road between Paris and Tours. If you're **driving** from Paris, take A10 south; from Tours, take A10 north.

VISITOR INFORMATION   The **Office de Tourisme** is at 2 pl. de L'Etape (www.tourisme-orleans.com; ✆ **02-38-24-05-05**).

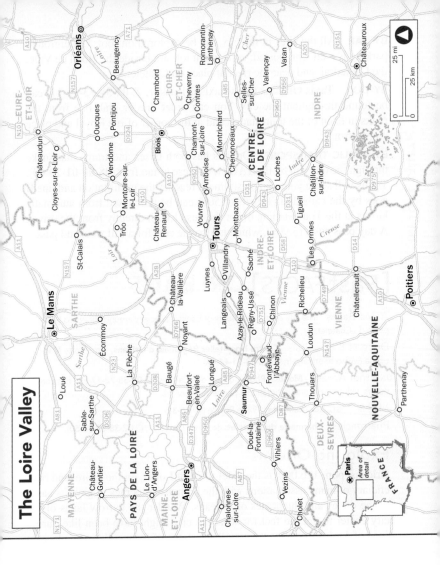

The Loire Valley

Getting Around

ON FOOT   Orléans's city center is small and many streets are pedestrianized. For short stays, it's easiest to explore the town on foot.

BY BICYCLE   Orléans has a Paris style bike-sharing scheme, **Vélo'+** (www.agglo-veloplus.fr). There are 360 bikes available at 35 stations around the city. You can register online (where you can also download a map of the city's bike stations) or directly at one of eight bike stands where credit cards are accepted; fees are 1€ per day.

BY CAR　All the sites in the city can be explored on foot. Underground parking is well sign-posted; convenient lots are beside the Hotel de Ville, the Cathedral, and near the river at place du Châtelet.

BY TAXI　**Taxis Orléans** (www.taxis-orleans.fr; ✆ **02-38-53-11-11**) can be found throughout the city. You can order one or grab one from the ranks in front of the train station and at the corner of rue Royal and place du Martroi.

BY PUBLIC TRANSPORT　Orléans has both buses and trams that snake through the city run by the **TAO** (www.reseau-tao.fr; ✆ **08-00-01-20-00**). Trams will serve your visit best; line A reaches the train station and line B goes by the cathedral. Tickets (1.50€) can be purchased from automatic kiosks at the Tram station, or for the bus (1.60€) directly from the driver. A day pass costs (3.90€), which is also the cost for a full weekend pass.

[FastFACTS] ORLÉANS

ATMs/Banks　The city center has plenty of banks, especially around shopping hub place du Châtelet.

Doctors & Hospitals　**Centre Hospitalier Régionale d'Orléans,** 1 rue Porte Madeleine (www.chr-orleans.fr; ✆ **02-33-51-44-44**).

Internet Access　**Mondial Phone,** 84 rue des Carmes (✆ **02-38-72-17-52**), has computers with Internet and international phone call services.

Mail & Postage　**La Poste,** 19 rue Royale (✆ **36-31**).

Pharmacies　**Pharmacie du Châtelet,** 38 Pl. du Châtelet (✆ **02-38-53-34-50**).

Exploring Orléans

Orléans, pop. 116,000, is the chief town of Loiret, on the Loire, and beneficiary of many associations with the French aristocracy. It gave its name to the dukes and duchesses of Orléans. Wander the narrow lanes of the city center to get the feel for what the city might have been like during Joan of Arc's time. Note the equestrian statue of Jeanne d'Arc on place du Martroi. From the square, you can walk past the elegant arched galleries on rue Royal (rebuilt in 18th-c. style) across pont George-V (erected in 1760). A simple cross marks the site of the Fort des Tourelles, which Joan of Arc and her men captured.

Cathédrale Ste-Croix ★ CATHEDRAL　Begun in 1287 after a Romanesque church here collapsed from old age, the cathedral was burned by the Huguenots in 1568. Henri IV laid the first stone of the present building in 1601; work continued until 1829. The cathedral boasts a 17th-century organ and woodwork from the early 18th century in its chancel, the masterpiece of Jules Hardouin-Mansart and other artists associated with Louis XIV.

Orléans

Pl. Ste-Croix. ☎ **02-38-77-87-50.** Free admission. May–Sept daily 9:15am–6pm; Oct–Apr daily 9:15am–noon and 2–6pm.

Eglise St-Aignan ★ CHURCH One of the most frequently altered churches in the Loire Valley, St-Aignan was consecrated in 1509 in the form you see today. It possesses one of France's earliest vaulted hall crypts, complete with polychromed capitals. Scholars of pre-Romanesque art are interested in its rare 10th- and 11th-century aesthetics. Above ground, the church's Renaissance-era choir and transept remain, but the Protestants burned the nave during the Wars of Religion. In a wood-carved shrine are the remains of the church's patron saint.

Pl. St-Aignan. No phone. Crypt can be visited only on a guided tour 4€; sign up at the tourist office.

Hôtel Groslot ★ HISTORIC HOME This brick Renaissance mansion was begun in 1550 and embellished in the 19th century. François II (the first husband of Mary, Queen of Scots) lived here during the fall of 1560 and died on December 5. It was here that his brother and successor Charles IX met his lovely Marie Touchet. Between the Revolution and the mid-1970s, it functioned as the town hall. Marriage ceremonies, performed by the town's magistrates, are still held here. The statue of Joan of Arc praying was the work of Louis-Philippe's daughter, Princesse Marie d'Orléans. In the garden, you can see the remains of the 15th-century Chapelle St-Jacques.

Pl. de l'Etape (northwest of the cathedral). ℰ **02-38-79-22-30.** Free admission. July–Sept Mon–Fri and Sun 9am–6pm and Sat 10am–8pm; Oct–June Mon–Fri 10am–noon and 2–6pm, Sat 10am–7pm, Sun 10am–6pm (occasionally closed Sat for weddings).

Musée des Beaux-Arts ★★ MUSEUM   The best art museum in the region, the fairly large collection is made up of mostly French, but also Italian, Dutch, and Flemish works from the 15th to 20th centuries. It includes some impressive treasures by Tintoretto, Boucher, Van Dyke, and Vélasquez as well as a variety of portraits, including one of Mme. de Pompadour by Drouais. The museum also holds one of the country's best collections of pastels with works by Quentin de la Tour and Chardin.

Pl. Saint-Croix. http://musees.regioncentre.fr/les-musees/musee-des-beaux-arts-d-orleans. ℰ **02-38-79-21-55.** Permanent collections 4€ adults, 2€ students; joint ticket including exhibitions and several other museums in town 6€ adults, 3€ students; free for children 18 and under and for all visitors on first Sun of the month. Tues–Sat 10am–6pm and Sun 1–6pm (Fri until 8pm).

Where to Stay

Best Western Hôtel d'Arc ★
Located minutes from the station and close to the city center, this hotel is a good option for a quick and convenient stopover in town. Built in the 1920s, the four-story building has an elegant Art Deco facade. The friendly staff makes you feel you're at a family run establishment and not a chain hotel. The bedrooms have classic appeal, the best being the Prestige rooms which have been recently updated with a more stylish decor and feature plush king-sized beds and private balconies. Light sleepers should request a courtyard side room as those facing busy rue de la République can be somewhat noisy.

37 ter rue de la République. www.lhotel darc.com. ℰ **02-38-53-10-94.** 35 units. 149€–250€ double. Parking 12€. **Amenities:** Room service; free Wi-Fi.

Street in Orléans

Sleep Like a King (or Queen)

As one of the most visited regions of France, it's not surprising to find a great variety of accommodation options. Sleep like a king or queen in one of the Loire's many châteaux hotels, from the medieval **Hostellerie Gargantua** (p. 257) to the opulence of the **Château** d'Artigny (p. 244) or the **Château de Marçay** (p. 257). The valley is dotted with thousands of unique *gîtes* (B&Bs) including medieval towers, houseboats, and even troglodyte caves. For details and reservations, go to http://en. gites-de-france.com.

Hôtel de l'Abeille ★★   If you're taking some time to get to know Orléans before embarking on château country this is the city's most charming hotel. Stepping into the foyer, you will be instantly transported back to the turn of the 20th century. In fact, the hotel dates from 1903 and has been run for four generations by the same family. The cozy Belle Epoque feel flows into the guest rooms, each decorated with vintage prints and antiques. Throughout the building are ornamental nods to both Napoleon, whose symbol was the bee and the namesake of the hotel, and Joan of Arc, the liberator of Orléans. Take a late afternoon break or morning coffee on its peaceful rooftop terrace.

64 rue Alsace-Lorraine. www.hoteldelabeille.com. ℂ **02-38-53-54-87.** 23 units. 88€–125€ double; 149€–200€ family suite. Parking 12€. **Amenities:** Bar; room service; free Wi-Fi.

Where to Eat

Chez Jules ★★ TRADITIONAL FRENCH   Yvan and Isabelle Cardinaux take the idea of "chez" to a whole new level with the warm welcome and delectable dishes at one of the best restaurants in town. Service and quality prevail; don't expect fine crystal and a maitre d'. The extremely reasonable menu features seasonal refined dishes such as roebuck with pumpkin mousse topped with chorizo shavings and half-roasted pigeon with ginger. To finish, try their legendary Roquefort cheese *tartine* with pear sorbet drizzled in pear liqueur. Reservations recommended.

136 rue de Borgogne. www.chezjulesorleans.fr. ℂ **02-38-54-30-80.** Main course 16€–22€; fixed-price lunch 19€ or dinner 25€–35€. Tues–Sat noon–2pm and 7–9:30pm. Closed 2–3 weeks in July.

De Sel et d'Ardoise ★ MODERN   For a break from snails and steak-frites, book a table at the city's most cutting-edge restaurant. Having trained under world famous Alain Passard at his Parisian three Michelin-starred l'Arpège, the young and talented Maxime Voisin is making his own mark on the French culinary scene right here in modest Orléans. The dining room and menu are both small, yet the menu is big on flavor. Dazzle your taste buds with his daily creations like cream of sweet potato topped with smoked cecina and timut pepper, leg of lamb on a bed of kasha and spelt cooked in Margoulette beer or rack of pork grilled with sage and served with melon. Reserve 2 weeks in advance.

44 rue du Faubourg Bannier. www.facebook.com/deseletdardoise. ☏ **02-34-50-23-40.** Main course 22€–25€; fixed-price lunch 23€ or dinner 25€. Tues–Sat noon–1pm, Tues and Thurs–Sat 7:30–9pm. Closed 1 week in June and mid-Aug to early Sept.

BEAUGENCY

150km (93 miles) SW of Paris; 85km (53 miles) NE of Tours

On the right bank of the Loire, the charming town of Beaugency boasts many medieval sites including a long 12th-century bridge with 23 arches, said to have been built by the Devil himself.

Essentials

ARRIVING If you're **driving** from Blois to Beaugency, take N152 northeast. About 20 **trains** per day run between Beaugency and either Blois or Orléans; each trip takes about 20 min., and the one-way fare is 6.40€. For railway information, visit www.oui.sncf or call ☏ **36-35** (.40€/min.). From Orléans, about four to eight **buses** a day go to Beaugency. For bus schedules and information, visit www.remi-centrevaldeloire.fr.

Exploring Beaugency

A major medieval event took place here: the 1152 annulment of the marriage of Eleanor of Aquitaine and her cousin, Louis VII. She then married Henry II of England, bringing southwestern France as her dowry, an act that set off the Hundred Years' War. This remarkable woman was the mother of Richard the Lion-Hearted. (The film "The Lion in Winter" dramatizes these events.)

The brooding and impressive 15th-century **Château Dunois** has historical links stretching back to almost-mystical medieval antecedents. The current castle was built by Jean d'Orléans, who fought alongside Joan of Arc in the siege of Orléans, on the foundations of an earlier 10th-century fortress that belonged to the lords of Beaugency, whose feudal power extended throughout the region. Astride the street (la rue du Pont) that leads to one of the château's secondary entrances, the **Voûte St-Georges (St. George's Vault)** is an arched gateway from the earlier château.

More medieval moodiness is on hand at **La Tour César,** a 36m-tall (118-ft.) castle keep remaining from an 11th-century citadel. It's a fine example of Romanesque military architecture, but the interior is in ruins.

Eglise Notre-Dame, pl. Saint-Fermin, a 12th-century abbey, was rebuilt after it was burned during the Wars of Religion (1562–98). You can still see traces of its original Romanesque architecture in the chancel and transept. Nearby, the 16th-century **Tour St-Fermin,** a bell tower with a panoramic view of the valley, is famous for bells that ring out a traditional tune three times a day.

The 10th-century **Eglise St-Etienne,** pl. du Martroi, is one of the oldest churches in France. Now deconsecrated, it is owned by the municipality and is open only for temporary exhibitions of painting and sculpture.

Where to Stay & Eat Nearby

For lunch in the center of Beaugency, the **Relais du Château,** 8 rue du Pont (www.lerelaisduchateau-beaugency.com; ✆ **02-38-44-55-10**), at the foot of the castle, serves up satisfying traditional dishes and a lunch menu from 16€.

La Tonnellerie ★★ Situated a short drive south of Beaugency, this 19th-century manor house makes for the perfect restful stay in the immediate area. Surrounded by a lush garden and filled with antiques, vintage artwork, and tasteful pastel wallpaper, the hotel feels straight out of a novel by Balzac or Flaubert. Nevertheless, its philosophies are firmly from the 21st century having obtained the European Eco-label certification in 2016 for their efforts towards environmental sustainability. This "green" approach is reinforced by their restaurant which serves a fresh take on regional classics using local, mainly organic ingredients (main course from 16€, fixed-price menus from 23€).

12 rue des Eaux-Bleues, Tavers, Beaugency 45190. www.latonnelleriehotel.com. ✆ **02-38-44-68-15.** 16 units. 88€–118€ double; 175€ suite; family rooms available. Closed Dec 15–Jan 31. Take A10, exit at Beaugency, and then take N152 to Beaugency/Tavers. **Amenities:** Restaurant; bar; bike rental; outdoor pool; free Wi-Fi.

Princess de la Loire Youth Hostel ★ The best bargain for bikers on a budget, this youth hostel near Beaugency offers the most reasonable accommodation in the whole of the Loire. Clean and bright, the hostel has dormitories with four to six beds, a common kitchen, and laundry facilities. Share your Loire touring routes with other travelers at the sociable barbecue and picnic areas. Bike rentals are available directly from the hostel or in town at the Détours shop near the train station.

152 rue de Châteaudun (2km/1.25 miles from Beaugency on the D925). www.hihostels.com/hostels/auberge-de-jeunesse-hi-beaugency-sur-loire. ✆ **02-38-44-61-31.** 116 beds. 22€ shared dormitory. Closed Oct to mid-March. **Amenities:** Bike rental; laundry room; shared kitchen; free Wi-Fi.

BLOIS

180km (112 miles) SW of Paris; 60km (37 miles) NE of Tours

The star attraction in this town of 52,000 is unquestionably the **Château de Blois,** but if time remains after a château visit, you may want to wander around the quaint historic core to get a feel for a real Loire Valley town.

Essentials

ARRIVING Several direct **trains** run from Paris's Gare de Austerlitz every day (1 hr., 30 min.; from 10€ one-way), and around a dozen depart from the Gare Montparnasse, which involves a change in Tours (around 1

> ## Lights, Sound, Action!
>
> Many of the Loire châteaux present *son-et-lumière* (sound and light) shows on summer nights. The **Château de Blois** hosts one of the best nightly from April to September (around 10–10:30pm; on Wed nights, the show is in English). As a taped lecture plays, colored lights and readings evoke the age in which the château was built. Admission 8.50€ adults, 7€ students, 5€ children 6 to 17, and free for children 5 and under (www.chateaudeblois.fr).

hr., 50 min.; 35€–65€). From Tours, trains run almost every hour (trip time: 40 min.), at a cost of 11.50€ one-way. For information and schedules, visit www.oui.sncf or call ✆ **36-35** (.40€/min.). From June to September, you can take a **bus** (www.tlcinfo.net; ✆ **02-54-58-55-55**) from the Blois train station to tour châteaux in the area, including Chambord, Chaumont, Chenonceau, and Amboise. If you're **driving** from Tours, take RN152 east to Blois, which runs along the Loire; if you want to get there fast, take the A10 autoroute. If you'd like to explore the area by **bike,** check out **Traineurs de Loire,** 1 rue Chemonton (http://traineurs-de-loire.com; ✆ **02-54-79-36-71**). Rentals start at 10€ per half day, 15€ per day, open April to October.

VISITOR INFORMATION The **Office de Tourisme** is at 23 pl. du Château (www.bloischambord.co.uk; ✆ **02-54-90-41-41**).

Exploring the Blois & the Château

Blois is a piece of living history, with cobblestone streets and restored white houses with slate roofs and redbrick chimneys. Some of its "streets" are mere alleyways originally laid out in the Middle Ages or lanes linked by a series of stairs. If you have time for **shopping,** head for the area around **rue St-Martin** and **rue du Commerce** for high-end clothing, perfume, shoes, and jewelry. On Saturday, a daylong **food market** is on place Louis XII and place de la République, lining several blocks in the center of town at the foot of the château.

Château de Blois ★★★ CASTLE   On the misty morning of December 23, 1588, Henri I, the duc de Guise, had just left a warm bed of one of Catherine de Médicis' ladies-in-waiting. His archrival, King Henri III, had summoned him, but when the duke arrived, only the king's minions were about. The guards approached with daggers. Wounded, the duke made for the door, where more guards awaited him. Staggering, he fell to the floor in a pool of his own blood. Only then did Henri III emerge from behind the curtains. "Mon Dieu," he reputedly exclaimed, "he's taller dead than alive!" The body couldn't be shown: The duke was too popular. Quartered, it was burned in a fireplace.

Château de Blois

The murder of the duc de Guise is only one of the events associated with the Château de Blois, begun in the 13th century by the comte de Blois. Blois reached the apex of its power in 1515, when François I moved to the château. For that reason, Blois is often called the "Versailles of the Renaissance," the second capital of France, and the "City of Kings." But Blois soon became a palace of exile. Louis XIII banished his mother, Marie de Médicis, to the château, but she escaped by sliding into the moat down a mound of dirt left by the builders.

If you stand in the courtyard, you'll find that the château is like an illustrated storybook of French architecture. The Hall of the Estates-General is a beautiful 13th-century work; Louis XII built the Charles d'Orléans gallery and the Louis XII wing from 1498 to 1501. Mansart constructed the Gaston d'Orléans wing between 1635 and 1637. Most remarkable is the François I wing, a French Renaissance masterpiece containing a spiral staircase with ornamented balustrades and the king's symbol, the salamander.

Blois. www.chateaudeblois.fr. ℂ **02-54-90-33-33.** Admission 10.50€ adults; 8€ students; 5€ children 6–17; free for children 5 and under. Additional fees for light shows and special events; joint tickets available. July–Aug daily 9am–7pm; Apr–June and Sept–Oct daily 9:15am–6:30pm; Nov–Mar daily 10:15am–5:30pm; closed Jan 1 and Dec 25.

Where to Eat & Stay

Assa ★★   Meaning "morning" in Japanese, this restaurant has dawned a new era for Loire cuisine. Since 2013, the efforts of chefs Fumiko and Anthony Maubert at this restaurant have paid off nicely in the form of a highly coveted Michelin star. Earning their chops at France's top restaurants, the couple has fused their talent and culinary backgrounds in their contemporary menus with an ever-present Japanese aura. Their delightful creations, with poetic names like "garden and nature in perfect harmony" and "sweet voyage," revolve around local and seasonal ingredients such as strawberries or mushrooms personally picked by the chefs, fresh *chèvre* straight from the cheese farm or sandre or trout from the Loire River, which the relaxed yet sophisticated dining room overlooks. Vegetarian menus also available.

189 quai Ulysse Besnard. www.assarestaurant.com. ℂ **02-54-78-09-01.** Main course 38€; fixed-price menu 49€–85€. Wed and Fri–Sun 12:15–1:30pm, Wed–Sat 7:30–9pm. Closed 2 weeks in Jan and end of Sept to mid-Oct.

Côté Loire–Auberge Ligérienne ★ Even though its decor is akin to a seaside resort, you won't feel lost at sea staying at this quaint hotel on the banks of the Loire. Only a 5-min. walk from the château, it's a great option for travelers touring the region without a car. There is plenty of character at this B&B-like inn, from the vintage maritime posters, pillows with sailboat motifs, and ancient building features from the 12th, 15th, and 16th centuries. Most rooms are rather large for the size of the establishment, though beware of the narrow staircase. A tiny restaurant (main course 18.50€; fixed-price lunch menu 22.50€ and dinner 32.50€; Tues–Sat noon–1:30pm and 7:30–9pm) on the ground floor is open to outside guests, with one of the owners doing double duty as chef. His love of the region shines in such culinary creations as savory blancmange with goat cheese and tomatoes confit or guinea fowl cooked in local Crémant de Loire sparkling wine.

2 pl. de la Grève. www.coteloire.com. ✆ **02-54-78-07-86.** 9 units. 62€–105€ double. Closed Jan to mid-Feb. **Amenities:** Restaurant; bar; free Wi-Fi.

Le Médicis ★★ TRADITIONAL FRENCH It's worth the short 1km (.5 mile) trip from the center of town to dine at this Michelin-starred restaurant and inn. It will be hard to choose from original dishes like lobster with Vouvray wine emulsion and seasonal vegetables, pigeon suprême with gnocchi of green peas and beans, or veal sweetbreads with spinach ravioli. Even more difficult will be selecting an accompanying bottle from an extensive wine list of over 300 labels. The inn also rents 10 elegant rooms; double rates are 79€ to 130€. Reservations are required.

2 allée François 1er. www.le-medicis.com. ✆ **02-54-43-94-04.** Main course 20€–40€; fixed-price menu 29€–45€. Tues–Sat noon–1:15pm and 7–9pm. Closed most of Jan and Nov–Mar Sun evening and Mon. Bus: 2.

L'Orangerie du Château ★★★ TOURAINE The king's blessing has been bestowed on this wonderful restaurant located in a former outbuilding of the castle, the perfect majestic lunch spot after a morning inside the château. The classic dining room is also bustling with local fans of chef Jean-Marc Molveaux. He passionately prepares scallop and vegetable tortellini, frogs' legs with watercress gnocchi and veal sweetbreads served with parsnip mousseline. There's even a special children's menu for *petits gourmands*. Your regal feast is made complete in summer when you can dine on the outdoor terrace facing the castle.

1 av. Jean-Laigret. www.orangerie-du-chateau.fr. ✆ **02-54-78-05-36.** Main course 25€–45€; fixed-price menu 40€–85€; children's menu 15€. Tues–Sat noon–1:30pm and 7:15–9:15pm. Closed 3 weeks from mid-Feb.

CHAMBORD ★★★

91km (118 miles) SW of Paris; 18km (11 miles) E of Blois

The Château de Chambord, the grandest of the region's castles, is the culmination of François I's two biggest obsessions: hunting and architecture. It's a must for any Loire castle itinerary.

Essentials

ARRIVING It's best to **drive** to Chambord. Take D951 northeast from Blois to Saint Dyé, turning on to the rural road to Chambord. You can also rent a **bicycle** in Blois and ride the 18km (11 miles) to Chambord or take a **tour** to Chambord from Blois in summer. From May to September, **Transports du Loir et Cher** (www.tlcinfo.net; ✆ **02-54-58-55-44**) operates bus service to Chambord.

Exploring the Château

The Château de Chambord ★★★ CASTLE   Built as a hunting lodge, this colossal edifice is a masterpiece of architectural derring-do. Some say Leonardo da Vinci had something to do with it, and when you climb the amazing double spiral staircase, that's not too hard to believe. The staircase is superimposed upon itself so that one person may descend and a second ascend without ever meeting. While da Vinci died a few

Château de Chambord at sunset

Interior, Château de Chambord

months before construction started in 1519, what emerged after 20 years was the pinnacle of the French Renaissance and the largest château in the Loire Valley. The castle's proportions are of exquisite geometric harmony, and its fantastic arrangement of turrets and chimneys makes it one of France's most recognizable châteaux.

Construction continued for decades; François I actually stayed at the château for only a few weeks during hunting season, though he ensured Chambord would forever carry his legacy by imprinting his "F" emblem and symbol, the Salamander, wherever he could. After he died, his successors, none too sure what to do with the vast, unfurnished, and unfinished castle, basically abandoned it. Finally, Louis XIII gave it to his brother, who saved it from ruin; Louis XIV stayed there on several occasions and saw to restorations, but not a single monarch ever really moved in. The state acquired Chambord in 1932, and restoration work has been ongoing ever since, which most recently involved the replanting of its 18th century formal gardens.

Four monumental towers dominate Chambord's facade. The three-story keep has a spectacular terrace from which the ladies of the court watched the return of their men from the hunt. Many of the vast rooms are empty, though several have been filled with an impressive collection of period furniture and objects, giving an idea of what the castle looked like when parts of it were occupied. The château lies in a park of more than 5,260 hectares (12,992 acres), featuring miles of hiking trails and bike paths, as well as picnic tables and bird-watching posts.

www.chambord.org. ℰ **02-54-50-40-00.** Admission 13€ adults; free for children 17 and under accompanied by an adult. Daily Apr–Sept 9am–6pm and Oct–Mar 9am–5pm.

CHEVERNY ★

192km (119 miles) SW of Paris; 19km (12 miles) SE of Blois

Unlike most of the Loire castles, Cheverny is the residence of the original owner's descendants, offering a rare glimpse into the normally very private life of French aristocrats.

Essentials

ARRIVING   Cheverny is 19km (12 miles) south of Blois, along D765. It's best reached by **car** or on a **bus tour** (Apr–Aug only) from Blois with **TLC Transports du Loir et Cher** (www.tlcinfo.net; ✆ **02-54-58-55-44**). Bus no. 4 leaves from the railway station at Blois once or twice per day; see the TLC website for the schedule. You can also take a **taxi** (✆ **02-54-78-07-65**) from the railway station at Blois.

Exploring the Château

Château de Cheverny ★ CASTLE   The family of the vicomte de Sigalas can trace its lineage from Henri Hurault, the son of the chancellor of Henri III and Henri IV, who built the château in 1634. Designed in classic Louis XIII style, it is resolutely symmetrical. Its elegant lines and sumptuous furnishings provoked the Grande Mademoiselle, otherwise known as the Duchess of Montpensier, to proclaim it an "enchanted castle."

   You, too, will be impressed by the antique furnishings, tapestries, and objets d'art. A 17th-century French artist, Jean Mosnier, decorated the fireplace with motifs from the legend of Adonis. The Guards' Room contains a collection of medieval armor; also on display is a Gobelin tapestry depicting the abduction of Helen of Troy. In the king's bedchamber, another Gobelin traces the trials of Ulysses. Most impressive is the stone stairway of carved fruit and flowers. To complete the regal experience, your arrival or departure might be heralded by red-coated trumpeters accompanied by an enthusiastic pack of hunting hounds.

www.chateau-cheverny.fr. ✆ **02-54-79-96-29**. Admission 11€ adults; 8€ students 24 and under and children 7–18; free for children 6 and under; additional fee for exhibits; boat and golf cart rentals also available. Daily Apr–Oct 9:15am–6:30pm; Nov–Mar 10am–5pm.

Where to Stay & Eat

The **Orangerie** on the castle grounds makes a nice option for a quick bite, serving a variety of snacks, lunch, and teatime fare.

St-Hubert ★ TRADITIONAL FRENCH   If you can't get invited to lunch by the château owners, your appetite can be pleasantly satisfied at this nearby excellent-value inn. It offers fixed-price menus of regional specialties such as Muscadet-infused rabbit terrine with pear compote; local free-range Touraine Géline chicken with pommes darphin (thick potato pancake), topped with a tomato caviar; and for "dessert" Ste.

Maure goat cheese or Sologne strawberry melba. While it's a far cry from the luxurious bedrooms of the castle, the St-Hubert offers economic **lodging** with 20 conservatively decorated rooms for 72€ to 81€ for a double. 122 rte. Nationale. www.hotel-sthubert.com. ✆ **02-54-79-96-60.** Main course 18€–26€; fixed-price menu 14.50€–34€; children's menu 12€. Daily noon–2pm and 7–9pm. Closed Sun night off-season.

VALENÇAY ★★

233km (144 miles) SW of Paris; 56km (35 miles) S of Blois

One of the Loire's most handsome Renaissance châteaux, Valençay combines the wonders of châteaux-hopping and family fun, and even has a special museum for car lovers.

Essentials

ARRIVING   Driving from Tours, take A85 east, turning south on D956 (exit 13 to Selles-sur-Cher) to Valençay. From Blois, follow D956 south.

Exploring the Château & Park

Château de Valençay ★★ CASTLE   Talleyrand acquired this château in 1803 on the orders of Napoleon, who wanted his minister of

Château de Valençay

Kitchen in Château de Valençay

foreign affairs to receive dignitaries in style. The d'Estampes family built
Valençay in 1520. The dungeon and west tower are of this period, as is the
main body of the building, but other wings were added in the 17th and
18th centuries. The effect is grandiose, all domes and turrets. The apartments are sumptuously furnished, mostly in the Empire style, but with
Louis XV and Louis XVI trappings as well. A star-footed table in the
main drawing room is said to have been the one on which the final agree-
ment of the Congress of Vienna was signed in June 1815 (Talleyrand represented France).

After your visit to the château, take a walk through the garden and
deer park. Kids will enjoy plenty of activities here, including a giant labyrinth, a miniature farm, a playground, and a golf cart circuit through the
forest. A few nights each summer the château and its grounds return to the
Renaissance, decked out with thousands of candles, costumed performers, and musical entertainment (see website for details).

Classic car enthusiasts' motors can get revved up at the **Musée de
l'Automobile de Valençay,** situated a mere 200m (656 ft.) from the château. The exhibit shows the evolution of the automobile with over 60
antique vehicles, including a rare tandem style pulley-operated Bédélia
(ca. 1914).

2 rue de Blois. www.chateau-valencay.fr. ℂ **02-54-00-10-66.** The Automobile
Museum is located at 12 av. de la Résistance (www.musee-auto-valencay.fr; ℂ **02-54-
00-07-74**). Admission for castle, automobile museum, and park 13€ adults; 10€ students; 4.50€ children ages 4–6; free for ages 3 and under. Daily mid-March to Apr
10:30am–6pm; May 10am–6pm; June 9:30am–6:30pm; July–Aug 9:30am–7pm; Sept
10am–6pm; Oct–Nov 9 10:30am–5pm.

AMBOISE ★★

219km (136 miles) SW of Paris; 35km (22 miles) E of Tours

Amboise is on the banks of the Loire in the center of vineyards known as Touraine-Amboise. The good news: This is a real Renaissance town. The bad news: Because it is so beautiful, tour buses overrun it, especially in summer. Other than the myriad of notable royal residences, the town has also played host to Leonardo da Vinci, who spent his last years here, and more recently, royal rocker Mick Jagger, lord of a nearby château.

Essentials

ARRIVING   About a dozen **trains** per day leave from both Tours and Blois. The trip from Tours takes 20 min. and costs 5.70€ one-way; from Blois, it takes 20 min. and costs 7.20€ one-way. Several conventional trains a day leave from Paris's Gare d'Austerlitz (trip time: about 2 hr., 15 min.), and several TGVs depart from the Gare Montparnasse, with a change to a regular train at St-Pierre-des-Corps, next to Tours (trip time: 1 hr., 30 min.). Fares from Paris start at 28€. For information, visit www.oui.sncf or call ✆ **36-35** (.40€/min.).

If you prefer to travel by bus, **Fil Vert Buses** (www.tourainefilvert.com), which operates out of Gare Routière in Tours, just across from the railway station, runs about six to eight **buses** every day between Tours and Amboise. The one-way trip takes about 45 min. and costs 2.40€.

If you're **driving** from Tours, take the D751, following signs to Amboise.

VISITOR INFORMATION   The **Office de Tourisme** is on quai du Général-de-Gaulle (www.amboise-valdeloire.com; ✆ **02-47-57-09-28**).

Exploring Amboise

Château d'Amboise ★★ CASTLE   On a rocky spur above the town, this medieval château was rebuilt in 1492 by Charles VIII, the first in France to reflect the Italian Renaissance.

Visitors enter on a ramp that opens onto a panoramic terrace fronting the river. At one time, buildings surrounded this terrace, and fêtes took place in the enclosed courtyard. The castle fell into decline during the Revolution, and today only about a quarter of the once-sprawling edifice remains. You first come to the Flamboyant Gothic **Chapelle de St-Hubert,** distinguished by its lacelike tracery, which holds the **tomb of Leonardo da Vinci,** who died in Amboise. Tapestries cover the walls of what's left of the château's grandly furnished rooms, which include the **Logis du Roi (King's Apartment).** The vast **Salle du Conseil,** book-ended by a Gothic and a Renaissance fireplace, was once the venue of the lavish fêtes. Exit via the **Tour des Minimes** (also known as the Tour des

The Loire at sunset from a bridge in Amboise

Cavaliers), noteworthy for its ramp that could accommodate horsemen and their mounts. The other notable tower is the Heurtault, which is broader than the Minimes, with thicker walls.

www.chateau-amboise.com. ⓒ **02-47-57-00-98.** Admission 11.50€ adults; 9.90€ students; 7.70€ ages 7–14; free for children 6 and under. Daily Jan 9am–12:30pm and 2–4:45pm; Feb 9am–12:30pm and 1:30–5pm; Mar 9am–5:30pm; Apr–June 9am–6:30pm; July–Aug 9am–7pm; Sept–Oct 9am–6pm; Nov 2–15 9am–5:30pm; Nov 16–Dec 31 9am–12:30pm and 2–4:45pm.

Château du Clos-Lucé ★ HISTORIC HOME/MUSEUM   Within 3km (1.75 miles) of the base of Amboise's château, this brick-and-stone building was constructed in the 1470s. Bought by Charles VII in 1490, it became the summer residence of the royals and also served as a retreat for Anne de Bretagne, who, according to legend, spent a lot of time praying and meditating. Later, François I installed "the great master in all forms of art and science," Leonardo himself. Da Vinci lived here for 3 years, until his death in 1519. Today the site functions as a small museum, where you can step back into the life and imagination of da Vinci. The manor contains furniture from his era; examples of his sketches; models for his flying machines, bridges, and cannon; temporary exhibits; and a Renaissance musical festival in late September (a nod to da Vinci's musical talents).

2 rue de Clos-Lucé. www.vinci-closluce.com. ⓒ **02-47-57-00-73.** Admission 15.50€ adults; 11.50€ students; 11€ children 6–18; 43€ family ticket (2 adults, 2 children); free for children 6 and under. Daily Jan 10am–6pm; Feb–June 9am–7pm; July–Aug 9am–8pm; Sept–Oct 9am–7pm; Nov–Dec 9am–6pm.

Where to Stay & Eat

For the best gastronomic restaurants in the area, see those in the hotels listed below.

Le Choiseul ★★★   Composed of three mansions dating from the 15th through 18th centuries and nestled on the banks of the Loire River, Le Choiseul is the best hotel in Amboise and serves its best cuisine. Its rooms are opulent with traditional charm and all the modern comforts of a luxury hotel. Be sure to explore the grounds, where an outdoor pool is surrounded by Italian sculptures; ask the staff about visiting the impressive Greniers de César troglodyte caves nearby.

New chef Mickaël Renard has brought his creativity and savoir-faire to the recently reinvented restaurant **Le 36** (open to nonguests). His refined menu of beautifully presented dishes might include sea elms with Jerusalem artichoke mousse and truffle juice or filet of duckling, with nougat, tender turnips, with orange sweet-and-sour sauce. Lunch ranges from 31€ to 38€, with dinner going for 52€ to 86€.

36 quai Charles-Guinot. www.le-choiseul.com and www.le36-amboise.fr (restaurant). ℱ **02-47-30-45-45.** 32 units. 200€–325€ double; 385€ suite. **Amenities:** Restaurant; bar; bikes; outdoor pool; room service; free Wi-Fi.

L'Ecluse ★ MODERN FRENCH   Escape the castle crowds at this charming new restaurant a few minutes' walk from all the action. Alongside the small Amasse River, this restaurant offers seating in the peaceful garden under the weeping willow or in the simple yet stylish dining room. Chef Mélanie Popineau has sourced the best local producers for her seasonal, creative dishes. You might find butternut squash soup with candied hazelnuts, chèvre tortellini and bacon, filet of stripped mullet atop potato mousse drizzled in truffle oil and tarragon-shallot reduction, cabbage stuffed with pheasant and foie gras, served with spätzle and sautéed oyster mushrooms and pheasant juice. Splurge on the regional cheese plate or the dark chocolate cake with homemade cocoa sorbet.

Rue Racine. www.ecluse-amboise.fr. ℱ **02-47-79-94-91.** Main course 6€–22€; fixed-price weekday lunch menu 19€ or evening 25€–39€; children's menu 18€. Tues–Sat noon–1pm and 7–9pm. Closed Dec 23–Feb 1.

Le Fleuray ★★   The welcome couldn't be warmer at this lovely ivy-covered manor house run by a family of English expatriates, a short drive from Amboise. With their cross-cultural approach, the Newingtons turned a rundown farmhouse into the perfect mélange of Anglo-Saxon comfort and French sophistication. This attention to detail is evident from the intimate foyer to the spacious guest rooms; several of which have private terraces. With peaceful surroundings and plenty to do on the extensive grounds, this is an excellent base for château touring and some family fun. The hotel also has an excellent restaurant serving food infused with regional and international flavors. Items on the fixed-price menus (29€–35€) might include roasted cod, with squash purée topped with hazelnuts and hollandaise of local organic red Miso of Hirai Akiko, duck from Sologne with celeriac mousseline, kale and red cabbage dropped in kumquat sauce or wild mushroom risotto topped with baby glazed onions and mature parmesan shavings.

Route D74, near Amboise. www.lefleurayhotel.com. © **02-47-56-09-25.** 26 units. 78€–166€ double. Free parking. From Amboise, take the D952 on the north side of the river, following signs to Blois; 12km (7.5 miles) from Amboise, turn onto D74, in the direction of Cangey. **Amenities:** Restaurant; bar; free bikes; golf course; Jacuzzi; massage; outdoor pool; room service; tennis court; free Wi-Fi.

Le Manoir Les Minimes ★★   In the shadow of the looming castle is this welcoming and reasonably priced hotel, set in a magical restored 18th-century mansion. Built on the foundations of an ancient convent, the hotel is made up of the main building, draped in wisteria, and a small annexed cottage, centered by a tranquil garden. Once inside, you feel like you've entered a fine aristocratic home, with tasteful furnishings and decorations chosen with a careful eye to detail. The most charming rooms are in the main building, especially those in the attic with their beautiful exposed beams (though tall guests might have trouble with the slanted ceilings). The rooms in the annex aren't as quaint but are more spacious. Many second- and third-floor rooms open to views of the Loire or the château. A few rooms only have a bathtub (with a shower head), which may not appeal to all guests.

34 quai Charles Guinot. www.manoirlesminimes.com. © **02-47-30-40-40.** 15 units. 139€–249€ double; 342€ suite. Free parking. **Amenities:** Wheelchair accessible room; bar; free Wi-Fi.

CHENONCEAUX ★★★

224km (139 miles) SW of Paris; 26km (16 miles) E of Tours

Chenonceau is one of the most remarkable castles in France. Its impressive setting, spanning a whole river, along with an intriguing history and renowned residents, make it many visitors' favorite château in the whole country. (*Note:* The village, whose year-round population is less than 300, is spelled with a final *x,* but the château isn't.)

Essentials

ARRIVING   About a dozen daily **trains** run from Tours to Chenonceaux (trip time: 30 min.), costing 7€ one-way. The train deposits you at the base of the château; from there, it's an easy walk. For information, visit www.oui.sncf or call © **36-35** (.40€/min.). If you're **driving,** from the center of Tours follow the signs to the D40 east, which will take you to the signposted turnoff for Chenonceaux.

Exploring the Château, Museum & Gardens

Château de Chenonceau ★★★ CASTLE   A Renaissance master-piece, the château is best known for the dames de Chenonceau, who once occupied it. Built first for Katherine Briçonnet, the château was bought in 1547 by Henri II for his mistress, Diane de Poitiers. For a time, this remarkable woman was virtually queen of France, infuriating Henri's dour wife, Catherine de Médicis. Diane's critics accused her of using magic to preserve her celebrated beauty and keep Henri's attentions from waning. Apparently, Henri's love for Diane continued unabated, and she was in her 60s when he died in a jousting tournament in 1559.

When Henri died, Catherine became regent (her eldest son was still a child), and one of the first things she did was force Diane to return the jewelry Henri had given her and abandon her beloved home. Catherine then added her own touches, building a two-story gallery across the bridge—obviously inspired by her native Florence. The gallery, which was used for her opulent fêtes, doubled as a military hospital in World War I. The gallery also played a crucial role in World War II, serving as the demarcation line between Nazi-occupied France and the "free" zone.

Gobelin tapestries, including one depicting a woman pouring water over the back of an angry dragon, and several important paintings by Poussin, Rubens, and Tintoretto adorn the château's walls. The chapel contains a marble Virgin and Child by Murillo, as well as portraits of Catherine de Médicis in black and white. There's even a portrait of the

Château de Chenonceau

stern Catherine in the former bedroom of her rival, Diane de Poitiers. In François I's Renaissance bedchamber, the most interesting portrait is that of Diane as the huntress Diana.

The château boasts some of the loveliest grounds of the whole Loire that include a maze, a vegetable garden, and a beautiful *jardin à la française*. At the end of your visit, stop in at the new Cave des Dômes, located near the Former Royal Stables, to sample wines produced in the vineyards surrounding the castle (extra fee applies).

www.chenonceau.com. © **02-47-23-90-07.** Admission 14€ adults; 11€ students and children 7–17; free for children 6 and under; admission for evening garden light show 5€ adults, free for children 6 and under. Daily July–Aug 9am–8pm; June and Sept 9am–7:30pm; Oct 9:30am–6:30pm; Nov 2–Nov 13 9:30am–6:30pm; Nov 14–Feb 12 9:30am–5pm; Feb 22–Mar 25 9:30am–5:30pm; Mar 26–May 9:30am–7pm.

Where to Stay & Eat

From March to November a gourmet lunch can be enjoyed at the **Orangerie** of the château; the grounds also have a tea salon, a snack bar, and picnic areas.

Auberge du Bon-Laboureur ★★　This inn, within walking distance of the château, is your best bet in town for a comfortable night's sleep and exceptional Loire Valley cuisine. A former coach house opened in 1786, the hotel authentically evokes the era with its tiled, turreted tower, ivy-covered walls and antique furniture. Spread across various buildings, guest rooms are generally spacious and some have fireplaces or open out onto the garden with private terraces. Dine like a *reine* at its Michelin-starred restaurant; its seasonal menu uses produce direct from the hotel's garden and may include green pea and langoustine *millefeuille*, with beet-root puree or preserved shoulder of lamb with garlic cream. The excellent value menu at lunch is 32€; dinner menus run from 54€ to 105€ and a vegetarian menu is also available.

6 rue du Dr. Bretonneau. www.bonlaboureur.com. © **02-47-23-90-02.** 27 units. 136€–285€ double; 340€–440€ suite. Closed mid-Nov to mid-Dec and Jan 7–Feb 14. **Amenities:** Restaurant; bar; spa; heated outdoor pool; room service; free Wi-Fi.

Au Gâteau Breton ★ TRADITIONAL FRENCH　A brief jaunt from the château, this restaurant is ideal for a casual lunch or tea. This pretty 18th-century inn was formerly a grocery store run by locals of neighboring Brittany. On a warm summer day opt for a table on one of it shady terraces or in its pretty garden adorned with flowers and statues. Worth-while dishes include homey favorites like local andouillette sausage, coq au vin, and their specialty poulet Tourangelle (sautéed chicken with mushroom and cream sauce).

16 rue du Dr. Bretonneau. www.restaurant-chenonceaux37.fr. © **02-47-23-90-14.** Main course 18€–26€; fixed-price menus 19€–34€; kids' menu 10.50€. May–Aug daily noon–2:30pm and 7–10pm; Apr–Sept Thurs–Tues noon–2:30pm and 7–10pm, Wed 7–10pm; Nov–Mar daily noon–2:30pm.

CHAUMONT-SUR-LOIRE ★★

200km (124 miles) SW of Paris; 40km (25 miles) E of Tours

The connections of this lesser-visited castle to Diane de Poitiers make it an excellent château to pair with a visit to the Château de Chenonceau. It is also a wonderful stop for garden enthusiasts.

Essentials

ARRIVING   Several **trains** a day travel to Chaumont from Blois (trip time: 10–15 min.) and Tours (about 40 min.). The one-way fare is 3.70€ from Blois, 8.80€ from Tours. The railway station serving Chaumont is in Onzain, a nice 2.4km (1.5-mile) walk north of the château. For train schedules and ticketing information, visit www.oui.sncf or call ✆ **36-35** (.40€/min.).

Exploring the Château & Garden

Château de Chaumont ★★ CASTLE   On the morning when Diane de Poitiers first crossed the drawbridge, the Château de Chaumont looked grim. Henri II, her lover, had recently died. The king had given her Chenonceau, but his angry widow, Catherine de Médicis, forced her to trade her favorite château for Chaumont, a comparatively virtual dungeon for Diane, with its medieval battlements, pepper-pot turrets and perch high above the Loire.

The château belonged to the Amboise family for 5 centuries. In 1465, when one of them, a certain Pierre, rebelled against the rule of Louis XI, the king had the castle burned to the ground as a punishment. Pierre and his descendants rebuilt for the next few decades. The castle's architecture spans the period between the Middle Ages and the Renaissance, and the vast rooms still evoke the 16th and 17th centuries. In the bedroom occupied by Catherine de Médicis, hangs a portrait of the Italian-born queen. The superstitious Catherine housed her astrologer, Cosimo Ruggieri, in one of the tower rooms (a portrait of him remains). He reportedly foretold the disasters awaiting her sons.

The château passed through the hands of various owners and was eventually acquired and restored by the eccentric Marie Say and Amédée de Broglie in the late 18th century, who also added elaborate stables, a farm, and gardens. Since 1992, the latter has hosted the **International Garden Festival,** a world-renowned gathering of cutting-edge landscape designers that lasts from mid-April to mid-October and is open to the public. Each year, a dozen different gardens are created, using thousands of different plants and innovative garden designs. More recently, the château has also been a site for contemporary art and photography exhibits; check the website for this year's program.

www.domaine-chaumont.fr. ✆ **02-54-51-26-26.** Admission to castle and festival Apr–Oct 18€ adults, 12€ children 12–18, 6€ children 6–11; rest of year castle admission 12€ adults, 7€ children 12–18, 4€ children 6–11; free for children 5 and under.

Daily Nov–Jan 10:30am–4:30pm; Feb–Mar from 10am; Apr–June and Sept 10am–6:30pm; July–Aug until 7pm; Oct until 6pm.

Where to Stay & Eat

From April to October, the château grounds are home to four places you can dine or snack, the best being the **Grand Velum** restaurant with refined dishes mainly using local or organic ingredients.

Le Domaine des Hauts de Loire ★★   A 3km (1.75 miles) drive from the Château de Chaumont, this is one of the finest château-hotels on the eastern Loire circuit. Perched on the north side of the Loire, this estate house was built by the owner of a Paris-based newspaper in 1840. He referred to it as his "hunting lodge," much in the lines of Louis XIII and his grand Versailles. Rooms are decorated in Louis Philippe or Empire style, each with its own individual touches such as vintage tiles or rustic wooden beams. Most are quite large; though those in the half-timbered annex that was originally the stables are less coveted. After your busy day of castle-hopping, enjoy a tranquil sunset stroll through the estate's sprawling park or pamper yourself in the new Clarins spa.

Its Michelin-two-starred restaurant is definitely a highlight. The creative menu may offer red mullet with grilled artichokes and smoked marrow or the decadent wild boar with truffle cream and quince purée. Main courses range from 56€ to 70€, with fixed-price menus ranging from 85€ to 165€ and a vegetarian menu at 75€. The hotel has recently added a new modern "Bistrot" for those looking for a more casual, though equally delicious, meal in the area.

Rte. d'Herbault. www.domainehautsloire.com. ② **02-54-20-72-57.** 31 units. 250€–399€ double; 595€–990€ suite. Closed Dec–Jan. **Amenities:** Restaurant; bar; spa; hammam; sauna; outdoor pool; room service; tennis court; free Wi-Fi.

TOURS ★

232km (144 miles) SW of Paris; 113km (70 miles) SW of Orléans

Though it doesn't have a major château, Tours (pop. 137,000), at the junction of the Loire and Cher rivers, is known for its food and wine. Many of its buildings were bombed in World War II, and 20th-century apartment towers have taken the place of castles. But the downtown core is quite charming, and because Tours is at the doorstep of some of the most magnificent châteaux in France, it makes a good base from which to explore.

Essentials

ARRIVING   As many as 14 high-speed TGV **trains** per day depart from Paris's Gare Montparnasse and arrive at St-Pierre des Corps station, 6km (3.75 miles) east of the center of Tours, in 1 hr. Free *navettes,* or shuttle buses, await your arrival to take you to the center of town (the Tours Centre train station). A limited number of conventional trains also depart from

Gare d'Austerlitz and arrive in the center of Tours, but these take twice as long (about 2.25 hr.). One-way fares range from 23€ to 72€. For information, visit www.oui.sncf or call ✆ **36-35** (.40€/min.). If you're **driving,** take highway A10 to Tours.

VISITOR INFORMATION   The **Office de Tourisme** is at 78–82 rue Bernard-Palissy (www.tours-tourisme.fr; ✆ **02-47-70-37-37**).

Getting Around

ON FOOT   Besides the TGV train station, which is in the suburb of St-Pierre des Corps, most other sites of interest in Tours are accessible on foot.

BY BICYCLE   Tours has safe and extensive bike paths. You can rent a bike at **Detours de Loire,** 35 rue Charles Gilles (www.locationdevelos.com; ✆ **02-47-61-22-23**), at a cost of 15€ per day. A deposit is required.

BY CAR   If you have a car for exploring the Loire, you can find a number of underground parking garages downtown. A convenient one is at the Tours Centre train station and another at rue Nationale and rue de la Préfecture. You can rent a car at **Avis** (www.avis.fr; ✆ **02-47-20-53-27**), located in the Tours Centre station, or **Europcar,** at the St-Pierre des Corps station (www.europcar.fr; ✆ **02-47-63-28-67**).

BY TAXI   The most extensive taxi network is **Taxis Tours** (www.taxis-tours.fr; ✆ **02-47-20-30-40**). Their hotline has some English-speaking operators or you can usually find a taxi in front of the train station.

BY PUBLIC TRANSPORT   Tours has both buses and a tram line, a network called **Le Fil Bleu,** 9 rue Michelet (www.filbleu.fr; ✆ **02-47-66-70-70**). Tickets (2€) can be purchased from automatic kiosks at a Tram station, from bus drivers or from their office.

[FastFACTS] TOURS

ATMs/Banks   The city center has plenty of banks, especially around place Gaston Paillhou or along rue Nationale.

Doctors & Hospitals   **Centre Hospitalier Régionale de Tours,** 2 bd. Tonnellé (www.chu-tours.fr; ✆ **02-47-47-47-47**).

Internet Access   Many cafes in the center have Wi-Fi. You can get online and savor a good cup of coffee at the cute modern coffee shop **Le Petit Atelier,** 61 rue Colbert (✆ **02-47-31-94-21**).

Mail & Postage   **La Poste,** 17 rue Nationale (✆ **36-31**).

Pharmacies   **Pharmacie du Centre,** 28 rue des Halles (✆ **02-47-05-65-20**).

Exploring Tours

Pilgrims en route to Santiago de Compostela in northwest Spain once stopped here to pay homage at the tomb of St-Martin, the "Apostle of Gaul" and bishop of Tours in the 4th century. One of the most significant

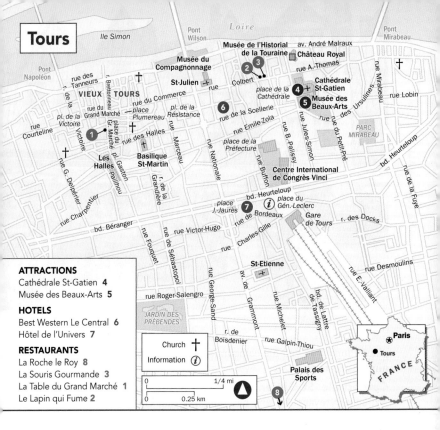

Tours

Ile Simon

Pont Wilson

Pont Mirabeau

Loire

av. André Malraux

Pont Napoléon

rue des Tanneurs

rue de la Victoire

VIEUX TOURS

rue du Commerce

rue du Grand Marché

pl. de la Victoire

place du Gr. Marché

pl. Gaston Paillhou

place Plumereau

pl. de la Résistance

rue des Halles

Musée du Compagnonnage

St-Julien

Colbert

Musée de l'Historial de la Touraine

Château Royal

rue A.-Thomas

place de la Cathédrale

Cathédrale St-Gatien

Musée des Beaux-Arts

rue de la Scellerie

rue Émile-Zola

rue Jules-Simon

rue du Petit-Pré

rue des Ursulines

rue Lobin

PARC MIRABEAU

bd. Heurteloup

rue de la Fuye

rue Courteline

Les Halles

Basilique St-Martin

rue Marceau

r. de la Grandière

place de la Préfecture

rue Nationale

rue Buffon

rue B.-Palissy

Centre International de Congrès Vinci

rue G. Delpérier

rue Charpentier

bd. Béranger

rue Fouquet

rue de Sébastopol

place J.-Jaurès

rue Victor-Hugo

rue de Bordeaux

bd. Heurteloup

place du Gén.-Leclerc

Gare de Tours

r. des Docks

rue Desmoulins

rue E.-Vaillant

rue Charles-Gille

JARDIN DES PRÉBENDES

rue Roger-Salengro

rue George-Sand

av. de Grammont

r. de Boisdenier

St-Etienne

rue Michelet

rue Galpin-Thiou

bd. de Lattre de Tassigny

Palais des Sports

Paris

Tours

FRANCE

ATTRACTIONS
Cathédrale St-Gatien **4**
Musée des Beaux-Arts **5**

HOTELS
Best Western Le Central **6**
Hôtel de l'Univers **7**

RESTAURANTS
La Roche le Roy **8**
La Souris Gourmande **3**
La Table du Grand Marché **1**
Le Lapin qui Fume **2**

Church

Information (i)

0   1/4 mi
0   0.25 km

conflicts in European history, the 732 Battle of Tours checked the Arab advance into Gaul. In the 15th century, French kings set up shop here and Tours became France's capital, a position it held for more than 100 years.

Most Loire Valley towns are rather sleepy, but Tours is where the action is, where streets and cafes bustle with a large student population. The heart of town is **place Jean-Jaurès.** The principal street is **rue Nationale,** running north to the Loire River. Head west along rue du Commerce and rue du Grand-Marché to Vieux Tours/Vieille Ville (old town). If you turn left on rue du Commerce toward the old town center, you can explore the streets and courtyards for regional specialties, books, toys, and crafts. A hotbed for antiques is east of rue Nationale (toward the cathedral), along **rue de la Scellerie.** Up rue Nationale toward the river are more shops and upscale boutiques and a small mall with chain stores.

Place Plumereau (often shortened to "place Plume"), a square of medieval buildings, houses a concentration of restaurants and bars. In the warmer months, the square explodes with tables that fill with people who like to people-watch (and be watched themselves). This is a good place to start if you're going out in the evening; otherwise, venture to the trendy bars on **rue Colbert,** which lies in the heart of Tours, midway between the

Place Plumereau, Tours

place Plumereau and the cathedral. Allow a morning, afternoon, or evening to see Tours.

Cathédrale St-Gatien ★ CATHEDRAL   This cathedral honors a 3rd-century evangelist and has a Flamboyant Gothic facade flanked by towers with bases from the 12th century. The lanterns date from the Renaissance. The choir is from the 13th century, with new additions built in each century through the 16th. Sheltered inside is the handsome 16th-century tomb of Charles VIII and Anne de Bretagne's two children. Some of the glorious stained-glass windows are from the 13th century.

5 pl. de la Cathédrale. ⟨⟩ **02-47-70-21-00.** Free admission. Daily 9am–7pm.

Musée des Beaux-Arts ★ ART MUSEUM   For an art fix in Tours, stop by this provincial museum, worth visiting just to see the lovely rooms and gardens of the former Archbishop's palace, with parts dating to the 12th century. Hanging on the walls are works by Rubens, Delacroix, Rembrandt, and Boucher; the sculpture collection spans Roman busts to moody Rodin.

18 pl. François Sicard. www.mba.tours.fr. ⟨⟩ **02-47-05-68-73.** Admission 6€ adults; 3€ seniors and students; free for children 12 and under. Wed–Mon 9am–12:45pm and 2–6pm. Bus: 3.

Where to Stay

Most visitors use Tours as a starting point for their Loire exploration. Staying in a small town or the countryside is ideal for discovering the region; see the suggestions throughout the chapter.

Best Western Le Central ★   If you're spending more time touring the sites of Tours or taking in an evening in town, this central hotel is a good headquarters. Despite being walking distance from the station and the cathedral, the surrounding greenery gives it an almost country feel. Parts of the building face a leafy garden, reducing street traffic noise, though it makes the hotel a little tricky to find. Many of its rooms have been recently refurbished and decor remains classic and conservative, their size makes them generous by French standards.

21 rue Berthelot. www.bestwestern.com. ✆ **800/528-1234** in the U.S. and Canada, or 02-47-05-46-44. 36 units. 99€–140€ double; 210€–350€ suite. Parking 10€. **Amenities:** Bar; babysitting; room service; free Wi-Fi.

Hôtel de l'Univers ★★   This grand old 19th-century hotel has recently undergone a much-needed facelift, returning to its former grandeur as top hotel in town. Its star-studded line of guests has included Rockefeller, Churchill, and Hemingway. Its midsize rooms are decorated in a stylish contemporary style in beiges and creams accented with splashes of vibrant color. The bathrooms have also been renewed with shower/tubs, some with Jacuzzi functions. If you don't have one in your room, make your way to the hotel's new wellness center with a Jacuzzi, heated pool and hammam. Its restaurant serves a good quality and value menu at 28€ if you don't venture out into the city. On weekdays, the hotel is popular with business travelers; on most weekends it offers greatly reduced rates.

5 bd. Heurteloup. www.oceaniahotels.com. ✆ **02-47-05-37-12.** 91 units. 200€–245€ double; 200€–300€ suite. Parking 15€. **Amenities:** Restaurant; bar; gym; hammam; heated indoor pool; room service; free Wi-Fi.

Where to Eat

Restaurants in Tours can be pricey, but you can keep costs low by dining at **La Souris Gourmande,** 100 rue Colbert (http://lasourisgourmande. com; ✆ **02-47-47-04-80**), where the chef is respected for the diversity of his cheese selection. You may be asked to join a communal table. Main courses cost 13€ to 15€. At the raffish but cheerful bistro **Le Lapin qui Fume,** 90 rue Colbert (www.aulapinquifume.fr; ✆ **02-47-66-95-49**), a fixed-price menu costs 10€ to 15€ at lunch and 15€ to 26€ at dinner and features standard bistro fare and, as the name suggests, rabbit.

La Roche le Roy ★★ MODERN FRENCH   Serious gastronomes need not tour the Tours dining scene; head straight to this tasty and tasteful restaurant set in a picturesque 18th-century manor south of the center. In 2016 chef Maximilien Bridier took over the helm, maintaining the establishment's commitment to tradition, sprinkled with a dash of modern elegance. His market-based menus could include sautéed frogs' legs served on a bed of artichokes and watercress, a *meunière* of local Saint Pierre fish with seasonal vegetables and shavings of Persian lime or farm-raised quail stuffed with foie gras and heirloom vegetables. Regular patrons needn't fret; the restaurant's famous Grand Marnier soufflé is still on the menu.

55 rte. St-Avertin. www.rocheleroy.com. © **02-47-27-22-00.** Main course 28€–35€; lunch menu 35€; dinner menu 60€–75€. Tues–Sat noon–1:30pm and 7:30–9:30pm. Closed 2 weeks in Feb and 3 weeks in Aug. From the center of town, take av. Grammont south (follow signs to St-Avertin–Vierzon).

La Table du Grand Marché ★ MODERN FRENCH   This little gem in the heart of Tours is an excellent value, creative bistro. The booths of its simple yet appealing dining room are packed with locals who come back time and time again for its refined seasonal menu. Chef Flavien Lelong gathers inspiration from near and far with such dishes as the local Touraine "burger" of *rillons* and *rillettes* (potted meats) topped with Saint Maure cheese and prune coulis, ray fish wings with black rice and grapefruit butter, or the gamey parmentier of hare and skewer of doe with blueberry sauce.

25 rue du Grand Marché. www.la-table-du-grand-marche.com. © **02-47-64-10-62.** Main course lunch 13€ and dinner 21€; fixed-price lunch 17€–20€ or dinner 36€. Wed–Sun 12:30–2pm and 7–10pm.

Where to Eat & Stay Near Tours

Château d'Artigny ★★★   If you want to have the utmost castle experience, this is the glitziest château-hotel in the valley. Nestled in a forest 1.5km (1 mile) west of the hamlet of Montbazon and 15km (9.25 miles) south of Tours, the château is newer than it looks, built in 1912 for the perfume and cosmetics king François Coty, who spared no cost for this perfect architectural beauty. Much of this character remains today, with fine antiques, Louis XV–style chairs, and various bronze and marble statuary. Only 31 units are in the main building; the others are in four annexes: a former chapel, gatehouse, mill, and staff dormitory. Each have their own charm, yet might not be what you're expecting so be careful when booking. Complete your château experience at the Artigny's regal restaurant **L'Origan** (lunch menu from 29€, dinner from 35€, vegetarian/gluten free options available).

Rte. des Monts (D17). www.artigny.com. © **02-47-34-30-30.** 58 units. 145€–335€ double; 415€–550€ junior suite; excellent special rates available online for advance bookings. From Tours, take N10 south for 11km (6.75 miles) to Montbazon, and then take D17 1.5km (1 mile) southeast. **Amenities:** Restaurant; bar; babysitting; bike rental; exercise room; outdoor heated pool; indoor pool; room service; sauna; spa; 2 tennis courts; free Wi-Fi.

Château de Beaulieu ★★   With a lack of special hotels inside Tours, it's well worth driving out to this lovely and reasonably priced 18th-century manor. Situated only 5km (3 miles) south of the city, the refined estate sits on a 3-hectare park. The grounds include fountains and a manicured French garden. A gracious double-curving stairway takes you to the welcoming reception hall. Guest rooms have elegant wooden furniture, fireplaces, and refitted bathrooms. The nine best rooms are in the main

If you aren't renting a car, several tour companies in Tours arrange full- and half-day visits to nearby castles that leave daily from the tourist office. **Acco-Dispo** (www.accodispo-tours.com; ✆ 06-82-00-64-51) offers good value small group tours visiting two to four châteaux and costing 24€ to 58€ per person. The price usually does not include meals or admission to the châteaux, but participation in the tour qualifies you for reduced group rates. **Quart de Tours** (www.quartdetours.com;

✆ 06-30-65-52-01) has a collection of more boutique minibus tours that include a three-course lunch at a traditional local restaurant and start from 124€ per person (including lunch and entrance tickets). You can reserve on the tourist office website (www.visaloire.com) or directly on the company websites. Keep in mind that less is sometimes more when it comes to castle viewing; after two or three, you may not be able to remember which was which.

château; the other 10 are in the nearby turn-of-the-20th-century pavilion. Before heading out on your castle touring, relax in the steam room or get a massage in their recently installed Magnolia spa. The restaurant is appreciated around the area for its inventive cuisine and extensive wine list (lunch menu 29€, dinner menu 45€–75€).

67 rue de Beaulieu, Joué-les-Tours. www.chateaudebeaulieu37.com. ✆ 02-47-53-20-26. 19 units. 137€–197€ double. From Tours, take av. de Grammont south, and turn right on bd. Winston Churchill and then left on av. de Pont Cher and right on rue de Beaulieu. **Amenities:** Restaurant; bar; bike rental; spa; free Wi-Fi.

Tours Nightlife

Long a student town, Tours has a lively young population. Much of the evening action centers around place Plumereau and **rue Colbert.** The twenty-something crowd gets early evening drinks and snacks at **Le Baron,** 11 rue des Ofèvres (www.facebook.com/BarLeBaronDeTours). You can keep the tempo of your night going with some live jazz at the friendly **Strapontin Café,** 23 rue de Châteauneuf (www.facebook.com/strapontin.cafe; ✆ 02-47-47-02-74).

In summer, many locals camp out at **La Guinguette,** a vast open-air "bar" by the Pont Wilson along the Loire River, much in the spirit of Paris Plages. The daytime activities extend nightly with concerts, dancing, food, drink, and games. It's open mid-May to end of September and note that some vendors only accept cash.

If you have the urge for more dancing, the hottest place in town is **L'Excalibur,** 35 rue Briçonnet (www.facebook.com/excalibur.tours; ✆ 02-47-64-76-78), with an electro beat and video system. A clientele of all ages, many from the surrounding countryside, heads to **Le Pyms,** 170 av. de Grammont (www.lepyms.com; ✆ 02-47-66-22-22), where one space plays '80s nostalgia and another contemporary electro.

VILLANDRY ★★★

253km (157 miles) SW of Paris; 32km (20 miles) NE of Chinon; 18km (11 miles) W of Tours; 8km (5 miles) E of Azay-le-Rideau

The Renaissance Château de Villandry should be at the top of the list for any garden lover. Its 16th-century-style *jardins* are celebrated throughout Touraine and amaze visitors from around the world with their beauty and faithful historic preservation.

Essentials

ARRIVING   Three daily **buses** operate from Tours from July to October only; the trip takes about 30 min. and costs 2.40€. For bus information, visit www.tourainefilvert.com or call ⓒ **02-47-05-30-49.** Villandry has no train service. The nearest connection from Tours is in Savonnières; the trip takes around 15 min. and costs 6.40€ one-way. For information, visit www.voyages-sncf.com or call ⓒ **36-35.** From Savonnières, you can walk along the Loire for 4km (2.5 miles) to reach Villandry, rent a **bike** at the station, or take a **taxi.** You can also **drive,** following D7 from Tours.

Exploring the Gardens & Château

Château de Villandry ★★★ CASTLE/GARDENS   Every square meter of the gardens is like a geometric mosaic. Designed on a trio of superimposed cloisters with a water garden on the highest level, the

Château de Villandry

gardens were restored by the Spanish doctor and scientist Joachim Carvallo, great-grandfather of the present owner. The grounds contain 17km (11 miles) of boxwood sculpture, which the gardeners cut to style in only 2 weeks each September. The borders symbolize the faces of love: tender, tragic (represented by daggers), and crazy (with a labyrinth that doesn't go anywhere). The arbors, citrus hedges, and walks keep six men busy full-time. The vegetable garden is being reverted to all-organic.

A feudal castle once stood at Villandry. In 1536, Jean le Breton, François I's finance minister and former ambassador to Italy, acquired the property and built the present château with influences of the Italian Renaissance. The buildings form a U and are surrounded by a moat. Near the gardens is a terrace from which you can see the small village and its 12th-century church. A tearoom, **La Doulce Terrasse** (© **02-47-50-02-10;** closed mid-Nov to mid-Feb), serves light dishes using vegetables from the garden and other local ingredients as well as fresh-baked bread and homemade ice cream. For a more gourmet meal, try **Le Cheval Rouge** (see below).

www.chateauvillandry.com. © **02-47-50-02-09.** Gardens and château 11€ adults, 7€ children 8–18; gardens only 7€ adults, 5€ children 8–18; free for children 7 and under. Gardens daily 9am–5 or 7:30pm, depending on the hour of sunset; château daily Feb–Oct and during the Christmas holidays 9am–4:30 or 6:30pm, according to a complicated seasonal schedule available online.

Where to Stay & Eat

Le Cheval Rouge ★ MODERN FRENCH   Next to the château, this is a surprising country restaurant serving up sophisticated versions of French classics. You may dine in the bright and welcoming dining room or a large enclosed terrace with individual tables shaded with umbrellas. The chef highlights local specialties in dishes like pork belly *rillons* with chestnuts and chanterelle mushrooms, bass poached in sparkling Vouvray wine, and quail roasted with grapes. On a hot day, finish off with the frozen soufflé with Cointreau. The inn also rents 45 rooms with contemporary appeal and furnishings. A double is 74€; the hotel also has several three to five bed family rooms renting for 84€ to 140€.

9 rue Principale. www.lecheval-rouge.com. © **02-47-50-02-07.** Main course 15€–18€; fixed-price menu 20€–36€. Daily noon–2:30pm and 7–9pm.

LANGEAIS ★

259km (161 miles) SW of Paris; 26km (16 miles) W of Tours

Dominating the town on a steep slope, this medieval fortress is one of the few châteaux actually on the Loire. Crossing over its drawbridge and through its massive towers takes you back 500 years to the start of the golden age of the Loire.

Essentials

ARRIVING   Several **trains** per day stop here en route from Tours or Saumur. One-way from Saumur is 8.30€; one-way from Tours is 5.70€. Transit time from both cities is around 20 min. For schedules and information, visit www.oui.sncf or call ℂ **36-35** (.40€/min.). If you're **driving** from Tours, take D952 southwest to Langeais.

Exploring the Château

Château de Langeais ★★ CASTLE   On December 6, 1491, 15-year-old Anne de Bretagne was wed to Charles VIII at Langeais, permanently attaching Brittany to France. The original castle was built in the 10th century when Fulk III (972–1040), Count of Anjou, sometimes called the "Black Falcon," seized Langeais from the Count of Blois. He erected the first keep, the ruins of which can still be seen. The present structure was built in 1465 in the late medieval style. The interior is well preserved and furnished, thanks to Jacques Siegfried, who not only restored it over 20 years, but also bequeathed it to the Institut de France in 1904.

The rooms recreate the ambience of a regal residence of the late Middle Ages, rich with ornamental fireplaces and tapestries. A remarkable 15th-century millefleurs tapestry decorates the Chambre de la Dame, and seven superb tapestries known as the "Valiant Knights" cover the walls of the Salle des Preux.

The Banquet Hall features a mantelpiece carved to resemble a fortress, complete with crenellated towers. The Wedding Hall includes a recreation of the marriage of Anne de Bretagne and Charles VIII with lavishly costumed wax figures. In the Luini Room is a large 1522 fresco by that artist, removed from a chapel on Lake Maggiore, Italy. It depicts Saint Francis of Assisi and Saint Elizabeth of Hungary with Mary and Joseph. Kids can learn medieval castle construction with interactive displays, or have some fun exploring the tree house and the two playgrounds.

www.chateau-de-langeais.com. ℂ **02-47-96-72-60.** Admission 9.80€ adults; 7.80€ students and ages 18–25; 5€ children 10–17; free for children 9 and under. Daily Apr–June and Sept to mid-Nov 9:30am–6:30pm; mid-Nov to Jan 10am–5pm; Feb–Mar 9:30am–5:30pm; July–Aug 9am–7pm.

AZAY-LE-RIDEAU ★★

261km (162 miles) SW of Paris; 21km (13 miles) SW of Tours

With its idyllic location and fairy-tale turrets, the Renaissance Château d'Azay-le-Rideau was deemed by neighboring writer Honoré de Balzac to be "a facetted diamond set in the Indre."

Essentials

ARRIVING   To reach Azay-le-Rideau, take the **train** from Tours or Chinon. From either starting point, the trip time is about 30 min.; the one-way fare is 5.30€ from Chinon, 5.90€ from Tours. For the same fare, the SNCF railway also operates a bus between Tours and Azay; the trip takes 50 min. For schedules and information, visit www.oui.sncf or call ⓒ **36-35** (.40€/min.). If you're **driving** from Tours, take D751 southwest to Azay-le-Rideau.

Exploring the Château

Château d'Azay-le-Rideau ★★ CASTLE   Its machicolated towers and blue-slate roof pierced with dormers give it a medieval air; however, its defensive fortress-like appearance is all for show. The château was actually commissioned in the early 1500s for Gilles Berthelot, François I's finance minister, and his wife, Philippa, who supervised its construction. They didn't have long to enjoy their elegant creation: In 1527, Berthelot was accused of misappropriation of funds and forced to flee, and the château reverted to the king. He didn't live here, but granted it to Antoine Raffin, one of his high-ranking soldiers. It became the property of the state in 1905.

Before you enter, circle the château and note the perfect proportions of this crowning achievement of the Renaissance in the Touraine. Check out its most fancifully ornate feature, the bay enclosing a grand stairway with a straight flight of steps. From the second-floor Royal Chamber, look out at the gardens. This lavish bedroom housed Louis XIII when he came through in 1619. The private apartments are lined with rich tapestries dating from the 16th and 17th centuries and feature examples of rare period furniture. The castle underwent extensive renovations completed mid 2017, giving the exteriors a much-needed facelift in addition to refurbishments to the interior and grounds.

www.azay-le-rideau.monuments-natio naux.fr. ⓒ **02-47-45-42-04.** Admission 10.50€ adults; 8.50€ youth 18–25; free for children 17 and under. Daily early July– late Aug 9:30am–11pm; first week of July and last days of Aug 9:30am–7pm; Apr– June and Sept 9:30am–6pm; Oct–Mar 10am–5:15pm.

Château d'Azay-le-Rideau in autumn

Where to Eat

L'Aigle d'Or ★★ TRADITIONAL FRENCH   In this practically one-horse town this isn't merely a watering hole. The tiny town of Azay holds one of the area's best value gastronomic gems. It might not look very special from the outside, which helps keep away the masses; however, the dining room's toasty fireplace and rustic wooden beams reveal its true character. For decades now chef Jean Luc Fèvre has been wowing guests with his signature filet of beef Chinon and his seasonal creations such as crab parmentier with shrimp cream, sandre fish stew with local Azay wine, or chilled peaches and raspberries with Chinon rosé wine sorbet. Treat yourself to the wine-pairing menu, a steal at only 72€ and featuring wines produced in the vicinity of the château.

10 av. Adélaïde-Riché. www.laigle-dor.fr. ℂ **02-47-45-24-58.** Main course 16€–27€; fixed-price lunch 22€–24€ or dinner 31€–59€. Mon–Tues and Thurs–Sat noon–1:30pm and 7:30–9pm, Sun noon–1:30pm. Closed second half of Nov and Jan to mid-Feb.

LOCHES ★★

258km (160 miles) SW of Paris; 40km (25 miles) SE of Tours

Forever linked to legendary beauty Agnès Sorel, Loches is an exquisite medieval village, situated on the banks of the Indre River.

Essentials

ARRIVING   Six to 10 **buses** run daily from Tours, run by the SNCF railway; the 50-to-70-min. trip costs 9.60€ one-way. For schedules, visit www.voyages-sncf.com or call ℂ **02-47-05-30-49.** If you're **driving** from Tours, take N143 southeast to Loches.

VISITOR INFORMATION   The **Office de Tourisme** is near the bus station on place de la Marne (www.loches-valdeloire.com; ℂ **02-47-91-82-82**).

Exploring Loches

Sitting high on a bluff overlooking the valley, the château and its satellite buildings form a complex called the **Cité Royale ★**. The House of Anjou, from which the Plantagenets descended, owned the castle from 886 to 1205. Its royal legacy continued with its occupation by the kings of France from the mid-13th century, until Charles IX became king in 1560.

Château de Loches ★★, 5 pl. Charles-VII (www.chateau-loches.fr; ℂ **02-47-59-01-32**), one of the region's best examples of medieval architecture, is remembered for the *belle des belles* (beauty of beauties) Agnès Sorel, who lived there in the 15th century. Maid of honor to Isabelle de Lorraine, Charles VII became so enamored by Agnès that he gifted his new mistress the château. She bore the king three daughters and wielded great influence over him until her mysterious death. She was immortalized on canvas posthumously by Fouquet as a nearly topless Virgin Mary–with a disgruntled Charles VII looking on. (The original is in Antwerp; the château has a copy.) The château also contains the oratory of Anne de

Bretagne, decorated with ermine tails. One of its outstanding treasures is a triptych of *The Passion* (1485) from the Fouquet school.

The massive 36 meter-high (118 feet) keep, or *donjon,* of the comtes d'Anjou was built in the 11th century and turned into a prison by Louis XI. The Round Tower contains rooms used for torture; a favorite method involved suspending the victim in an iron cage. In the 15th century, the duke of Milan, Ludovico Sforza, was imprisoned in the Martelet and painted frescoes on the walls to pass the time; he died here in 1508.

You can visit the château, the keep, and medieval garden without a guide daily. It's open April to September from 9am to 7pm, and October to March 9:30am to 5pm; in August the castle usually holds a medieval festival.

Tickets to the château and the dungeon cost 8.50€ for adults, 6.50€ for students and children 7 to 18. Children 6 and under enter free.

The tomb of Agnès Sorel rests nearby at the Romanesque **Collégiale St-Ours (Collegiate Church of St-Ours),** 1 rue Thomas-Pactius (℃ **02-47-59-02-36**), which was erected in the 11th and 12th centuries. Sculpted figures of saints and animals decorate the portal. Stone pyramids *(dubes)* surmount the nave; the carving on the west door is exceptional. The church is open daily from 9am to 7pm, except during mass; admission is free.

Finally, you may want to walk the ramparts and enjoy the view of the town, including a 15th-century gate and Renaissance inns.

Where to Stay & Eat

Hotel de France ★ Located in the medieval center of Loches, this charming hotel was a postal relay station until the mid–19th century. In 1932, three floors were added, converting it into an inn. Though the rooms have been upgraded and redecorated, the place keeps its classic provincial charm. The quietest rooms overlook the courtyard; however, the front rooms might be preferred for their balconies. This atmosphere is carried over into the excellent quality and value of the restaurant; guests and day-trippers can dine in the graceful dining room or in the peaceful paradise of the verdant courtyard (menus 18€–55€).

6 rue Picois. www.hoteldefrance-loches.com. ℃ **02-47-59-00-32.** 17 units. 58€–95€ double. Parking 5€. **Amenities:** Restaurant; bar; room service; free Wi-Fi.

Le Pet't Restau ★ FRENCH Don't be misled by its name, this restaurant might be "petit" in size, cost, and menu, however, it's "très grand" in flavor and finesse. Located in the historic center of Loches, you'll be greeted with *grand* friendliness as soon as you enter the bright and modern dining room. Matthieu will help you decide which local Loire wine to sample with your meal while in the kitchen Marie is applying her culinary passion to the best locally sourced ingredients. The menu may offer fish *rillettes* with homemade aïoli, chicken risotto with shiitake mushrooms or exotic pork filet mignon with lemongrass and coconut milk. They will also happily adapt their dishes for vegetarians, celiacs, and other dietary concerns.

6 Grande Rue. www.leptitrestau.fr. ℂ **02-47-19-85-32.** Main course 14€; fixed-price lunch menu 14€ or dinner 24€. Fri–Tues noon–2:30pm and 7–10pm and Wed noon–2:30pm. Closed 2 weeks mid–Feb.

SAUMUR

299km (185 miles) SW of Paris; 53km (33 miles) SE of Angers

Saumur lies in a region of vineyards, where the Loire separates to encircle an island. It makes one of the best bases for exploring the western Loire Valley. A small but thriving town, it doesn't entirely live off its past: Saumur produces some 100,000 tons per year of the mushrooms the French adore. Balzac left us this advice: "Taste a mushroom and delight in the essential strangeness of the place." The cool tunnels for the *champignons* also provide the ideal resting place for the region's celebrated sparkling wines. Enjoy both of these local favorites at a neighborhood cafe.

Essentials

ARRIVING **Trains** run frequently between Tours Centre and Saumur. Some 20 trains per day arrive from Tours (trip time: 30–40 min.); the one-way fare is 12.30€. From the station, take bus A into town. For schedules and information, visit www.oui.sncf or call ℂ **36-35** (.40€/min.). If you're **driving** from Tours, follow D952 or the A85 autoroute southwest to Saumur.

VISITOR INFORMATION The **Office de Tourisme** is on pl. de la Bilange (www.ot-saumur.fr; ℂ **02-41-40-20-60**).

Exploring the Area

Of all the Loire cities, Saumur remains the most bourgeois; perhaps that's why Balzac used it for his classic characterization of a smug little town in

Going Underground

As you drive along the Loire, something other than castles may catch your eye along the riverbanks. The region of Anjou holds the largest concentration of troglodyte caves in all of France. The beige limestone of the area was put to good use building the many châteaux, and the empty caverns from the excavated stone were not left abandoned.

Not surprisingly, the caves were first used to store bottles of the region's bubbly wine; more recently, however, many have been converted into homes, art galleries, and even restaurants. For a true troglodyte experience, stop in at the bustling and mainly underground artist town of **Turquant,** 10 km (6 miles) east of Saumur (www.turquant.fr).

Rock-carved troglodyte home near Saumur

"Eugénie Grandet." Saumur is also famous as the birthplace of the *couturière* Coco Chanel.

The men of Saumur are among the best equestrians in the world. Founded in 1768, the city's riding school, **Cadre Noir de Saumur** ★, av. de l'Ecole Nationale d'Equitation (www.cadrenoir.fr; ☎ **02-41-53-50-50**), is one of the grandest in Europe, rivaling Vienna's, enough so to be deemed a UNESCO World Heritage Site in 2011. The stables house some 350 horses. Mid-February to October, 1-hr. tours (8€ adults, 6€ children) run from 10 to 11:30am and 2pm to 4pm from Monday afternoon to Saturday afternoon. Tours depart about every 20 min. with two in English daily in high season at 10:45am or 3:15 pm. Some 48km (30 miles) of specialty tracks wind around the town—to see a rider carry out a curvet is a thrill. The performances peak during the **Carrousel de Saumur** ★★ on the third weekend in July.

Predating many of the region's other castles, the 12th-century **Château de Saumur** (www.chateau-saumur.com; ☎ **02-41-40-24-40**) was converted into the royal residence of Philippe II in the early 13th century. In 1410 it was immortalized in the September scene of the famous illuminated manuscript "Les Très Riches Heures" and, as you'll be able to see for yourself, it hasn't changed much since. The interior of the castle has displays recounting the history of the château as well as examples of tapestries, porcelain, furniture, and other decorative arts. Admission to the château museum from June to September is 7€ adults, 5€ children ages 7 to 16, free for children 6 and under; spring and autumn 6€ adults, 4€

children (mid-June to mid-Sept daily 10am–6:30pm; April to mid-June and mid-Sept to Oct Tues–Sun 10am–1pm and 2–5:30pm; closed Nov–Apr).

The area surrounding the town has become famous for its delicate sparkling wines. In the center of Saumur, you can wander the many aisles of **La Maison du Vin,** 7 quai Carnot (www.vinsvaldeloire.fr; *℗* **02-41-38-45-83**) and choose from a large stock direct from the surrounding vineyards.

An alternative is to travel east of Saumur to the village of **St-Hilaire,** where you'll find a host of vineyards. One of the better ones is **Veuve Amiot,** 21 rue Jean-Ackerman (www.veuveamiot.fr; *℗* **02-41-83-14-14**), where you can tour the wine cellars, taste different vintages, and buy bottles right in the showroom (daily 10am–1pm and 2–6pm; closed Sun in Jan–Feb).

Mushroom enthusiasts can learn about the cultivation of the local fungi first-hand at the **Musée du Champignon** (www.musee-du-champignon.com; *℗* **02-41-50-31-55**). Don't miss the October mushroom festival. Museum admission is 9€ adults, 7€ children under 18 (daily Feb to mid-Nov 10am–6pm and until 7pm Apr–Sept).

Where to Stay

Hôtel St-Pierre ★ Sophisticated Saumur style shines through at this reasonably priced hotel. In the shadows of the Eglise St-Pierre, this 500-year-old building has been brought up to 21st-century standards with creative care to every last detail. Guest rooms have been uniquely decorated with artistic touches and many showcase their architectural aspects such as stone fireplaces or thick wooden beams; the prestige rooms are the best and well worth the splurge. The small French town ambience is completed by listening to the tolling church bells while relaxing in the garden terrace.

Rue Haute-Saint-Pierre. www.saintpierresaumur.com. *℗* **02-41-50-33-00.** 14 units. 120€–200€ double; 250€–350€ suite. Free parking. **Amenities:** Babysitting; room service; free Wi-Fi.

Where to Eat

If you're just breezing through town or looking for a casual bite, try **Les Tontons** (http://lestontonshugo.wixsite.com/bistrotlestontons; *℗* **02-41-59-59-40**), a welcoming English-friendly bistro with great-value daily lunch specials and a fabulous local wine list. If you're visiting the equestrian center, you can rub shoulders with the riders at nearby **Le Carrousel** (www.le-resto-du-carrousel.com; *℗* **02-41-51-00-40**), showcasing a freshly renovated dining room and excellent regional cuisine available à la carte or in their reasonably priced menus of 15€ for lunch and from 22€ for dinner.

Le Gambetta ★★ MODERN FRENCH   For cuisine as chic as the city of Saumur, book a table at this avant garde address. The contemporary decor matches the inventive menu of Michelin-starred chef Mickael Pihours. He takes French cuisine far afield with wild turbot smoked with Oolong tea accompanied by parsnip soup, venison with truffle oil with porcini and bacon lasagna, and adventurous desserts such as pumpkin topped with Valrhona grand cru chocolate and caramel.

12 rue Gambetta. www.restaurantlegambetta.com. ℂ **02-41-67-66-66.** Main course 22€–32€; fixed-price lunch menu 29€, dinner 36€–100€. Tues and Thurs–Sun noon–2pm; Tues and Thurs–Sat 7–9pm. Closed 2 weeks in Jan, 3 weeks in Aug.

CHINON ★★

283km (175 miles) SW of Paris; 48km (30 miles) SW of Tours; 31km (19 miles) SW of Langeais

In the film "Joan of Arc," Ingrid Bergman identified the dauphin as he tried to conceal himself among his courtiers. This took place in real life at the Château de Chinon, one of the oldest fortress-châteaux in France. Charles VII centered his government at Chinon from 1429 to 1450. In 1429, with the English besieging Orléans, the Maid of Orléans prevailed upon the dauphin to give her an army. The rest is history. The seat of French power stayed at Chinon until the end of the Hundred Years' War.

Essentials

ARRIVING   The SNCF runs about seven **trains** and four **buses** every day to Chinon from Tours (trip time: 45 min. by train; 1 hr., 15 min. by bus); the one-way fare is 9.90€. For schedules and information, www.oui.sncf or call ℂ **36-35** (.40€/min.). Both buses and trains arrive at the train station, which lies at the edge of the very small town. If you're **driving** from Tours, take D751 southwest through Azay-le-Rideau to Chinon.

Visitor Information   The **Office de Tourisme** is at pl. Hofheim (www.azay-chinon-valdeloire.com; ℂ **02-47-93-17-85**).

Exploring Chinon & the Château

On the banks of the Vienne, the winding streets of Chinon are lined with many medieval turreted houses, built in the heyday of the court. The most typical street is **rue Voltaire,** lined with 15th- and 16th-century townhouses. At no. 44, Richard the Lion-Hearted died on April 6, 1199, from a wound suffered during the siege of Chalus in Limousin. The Grand Carroi, in the heart of Chinon, was the crossroads of the Middle Ages. For the best view, drive across the river and turn right onto quai Danton. From this vantage point, you'll be able to see the castle in relation to the town and the river.

Chinon is known for its delightful red wines. After you visit the attractions, stop for a glass on one of Chinon's terraced cafes or visit a few local vineyards.

IN PURSUIT OF THE grape

Chinon is famous for its wines, which crop up on prestigious lists around the world. Supermarkets and wine shops throughout the region sell them; families that have been in the business longer than anyone can remember maintain the two most interesting stores. At **Caves Plouzeau,** 94 rue Haute-St-Maurice (www.plouzeau.com; ☎ **02-47-93-32-11**), the 12th-century cellars were dug to provide building blocks for the foundations of the château. In the same family since 1929, it is currently being converted into a fully organic vineyard. You're welcome to climb down to the cellars (open for visits and wine sales Apr–Sept Tues–Sat 11am–1pm and 3–7pm and Oct–Mar Thurs–Fri 2–6pm, Sat 11am–1pm and 2–6pm).

The cellars at **Couly-Dutheil,** 12 rue Diderot (www.coulydutheil-chinon.com; ☎ **02-47-97-20-20**), are suitably medieval; many were carved from rock. This company produces largely Chinon wines (mostly reds); the popularity of its Bourgueil and St-Nicolas de Bourgueil has grown in North America in recent years. Tours of the caves and a *dégustation des vins* (wine tasting) and cost 4€ to 6€ per person. Tours held year-round 9am to noon and 1:45 to 5:30pm.

Château de Chinon ★★ CASTLE   The château, which was more or less in ruins, has recently undergone a massive excavation and restoration which has returned it (or mostly) to its former glory. After being roofless for 200 years, the apartments now have pitched and gabled slate roofs and wood floors, and the keep is once again fortified. The restoration, while not exact (due to the state of the original building), gives the overall impression of what the castle looked like around the time of Joan of Arc's visit. The buildings are separated by a series of moats, adding to its medieval look. A new building has been constructed on the foundations of the Fort of St-George, which serves as an entrance hall and museum, featuring new archeological finds discovered during the restoration, as well as objects and interactive displays that recount the story of Joan of Arc, Charles VII, and the history of the castle.

Btw. rue St-Maurice and av. Francois Mitterrand. www.forteressechinon.fr. ☎ **02-47-93-13-45.** Admission 8.50€ adults; 6.50€ students; free for children 6 and under. Daily May–Aug 9:30am–7pm; Mar–Apr and Sept–Oct 9am–6pm; Nov–Feb 9:30am–5pm.

Musée Rabelais–La Devinière ★ MUSEUM   The most famous son of Chinon, François Rabelais, the earthy humanist Renaissance writer, lived in town on rue de la Lamproie. (A plaque marks the spot where his father practiced law and maintained a home and office.) The museum in his honor, just outside the hamlet of Seuilly 5.5km (3.5 miles) west of Chinon, was an isolated cottage at the time of his birth. Spending the early years of his life here profoundly affected the writer, and the area served as inspiration for parts of his most famous work, "Gargantua." Exhibits are spread out on the three floors of the main building, in the dovecote and the wine cellars, each area dedicated to an aspect of Rabelais, his times, and his role in Chinon. It is still an active vineyard, producing 4,000 bottles of excellent wine that would do the writer proud.

La Devinière, just outside of Seuilly off the N751. www.musee-rabelais.fr. © **02-47-95-91-18.** Admission 5.50€ adults, 4.50€ students, free for children 6 and under. Daily Apr–June 10am–12:30pm and 2–6pm; July–Aug 10am–7pm; Sept 10am–12:30pm and 2–6pm; Oct–Mar Wed–Mon 10am–12:30pm and 2–5pm. From Chinon, follow road signs pointing to Saumur and the D117.

Where to Stay & Eat

Château de Marçay ★★★   Fairytale dreams come true without breaking the bank at this unique château-hotel. The reverie begins as you drive onto the grounds of this imposing medieval fortress surrounded by vineyards. The 21st century has made it to the interior with all the modern comforts. Guest rooms feature vintage floral prints and most rooms have massive exposed beams to augment the castle charm; the less-expensive rooms are located in the Pavillon des Vignes annex. The restaurant is one of the best in the region, where you can dine on regional seasonal specialties accompanied by the château's own wine (fixed-price menus at lunch 30€–35€ and dinner 48€–85€).

Marçay. www.chateaudemarcay.com. © **02-47-93-03-47.** 28 units. 195€–235€ double; 265€–332€ suite. Closed early Jan to early Mar, mid-Nov to mid-Dec. Take D116 for 7km (4.25 miles) southwest of Chinon. **Amenities:** Restaurant; bar; outdoor pool; room service; tennis court; free Wi-Fi.

Hostellerie Gargantua ★   This is the one of the most original economic hotels in all of the Loire. Located in the heart of town at the foot of the Château de Chinon, the castle-like 15th-century building used to be a courthouse where the father of writer François Rabelais (see "Musée Rabelais–La Devinière," above) worked as a lawyer. A highlight is its early Renaissance spiral staircase. The hotel has its quirks, but these are overruled by the large high-ceilinged guest rooms; most have canopy beds and some have stone fireplaces and/or views of the castle and all have been recently refreshed. Dine in its medieval hall, where you can sample some tasty local freshwater sandre prepared with Chinon wine, or duckling with dried pears and smoked lard.

73 rue Haute St. Maurice. www.hotel-gargantua.com. © **02-47-93-04-71.** 7 units. 65€–98€ double. Closed Dec. **Amenities:** Restaurant; bar; free Wi-Fi.

Les Années 30 ★ FRENCH   Tucked away on the oldest street in Chinon is the town's most cutting-edge cuisine. Set in an appealing 16th-century building the interior is decorated with paintings and photos from the 1930s, hence the restaurant's name. Its excellent-value menu could include such dishes as rabbit terrine with grapefruit mousse and ginger sorbet, or duck with cherry reduction and poached pear. The raspberry millefeuille with thyme ice cream is the perfect way to end a summertime lunch on the vine-draped terrace. Vegetarian menu available on request.

78 Rue Haute St Maurice. www.lesannees30.com. © **02-47-93-37-18.** Main course 16€–28€; fixed-price lunch weekdays 19.50€ or dinner 27€–45€. Thurs–Mon 12:15–2pm; Tues 7:30–10pm Jul–Aug. Closed June 10–Jul 1 and 2 weeks mid Nov–Dec.

USSÉ ★

295km (183 miles) SW of Paris; 14km (8.75 miles) NE of Chinon

The Château d'Ussé is truly a fairy-tale castle. At the edge of the dark forest of Chinon in Rigny-Ussé, it was the inspiration for Perrault's legend of "The Sleeping Beauty" ("La Belle au Bois Dormant").

Essentials

ARRIVING   The château is best visited by car or on an organized bus tour from Tours. If you're driving from Tours or Villandry, follow D7 to Ussé.

Exploring the Château

Château d'Ussé ★ CASTLE   Conceived as a fortress in 1424, this complex of steeples, turrets, towers, and dormers was erected at the dawn of the Renaissance on a hill overlooking the Indre River. The terraces, laden with orange and lemon trees, were laid out by the royal gardener Le Nôtre. When the need for a fortified château passed, the north wing was

Château d'Ussé

demolished to open up a greater view. The château was later owned by the duc de Duras and then by Mme. de la Rochejacquelin; its present owner, the marquis de Blacas, has opened many rooms to the public, most recently the private dining room and the dungeon. The visit begins in the Renaissance chapel, with its sculptured portal and handsome stalls. You then proceed to the royal apartments, furnished with tapestries and antiques. One gallery displays an extensive collection of swords and rifles. A spiral stairway leads to a tower with a panoramic view of the river and a waxwork Sleeping Beauty waiting for her prince to come.

www.chateaudusse.fr. © **02-47-95-54-05.** Admission 14€ adults; 4€ students and children 8–16; free for children 7 and under. Daily mid-Feb to Mar 10am–6pm; Apr–Aug 10am–7pm; and Sept–Nov 10am–6pm; closed the rest of the year.

FONTEVRAUD-L'ABBAYE ★★

304km (188 miles) SW of Paris; 16km (10 miles) SE of Saumur

The Plantagenet dynasty is buried in the Abbaye Royale de Fontevraud. The kings, whose male line ended in 1485, were also the comtes d'Anjou, and they wanted to be buried in their native soil. This regal patronage led to the building of one of Europe's largest medieval monastery complexes.

Essentials

ARRIVING   If you're **driving,** take D147 about 4km (2.5 miles) from the village of Montsoreau. In season, you can take a **bus** (Line 1) from Saumur; schedules vary according to school holidays—visit the bus company's website, www.agglobus.fr, to download the schedule or call © **02-41-51-11-87.** The one-way fare for the 30-min. trip is 1.40€.

Exploring the Abbey

Fontevraud-l'Abbaye ★★ ABBEY   In this 12th-century Romanesque church—with four Byzantine domes—lie the remains of two English kings and princes, including Henry II of England, the first Plantagenet king, and his wife, Eleanor of Aquitaine, the most famous woman of the Middle Ages. Her crusading son, Richard the Lion-Hearted, is also entombed here. The Plantagenet line ended with the death of Richard III at the 1485 Battle of Bosworth. The tombs fared badly during the Revolution, when mobs desecrated the sarcophagi and scattered their contents on the floor.

More intriguing than the tombs is the octagonal **Tour d'Evraud,** the last remaining Romanesque kitchen in France. Dating from the 12th century, the tower contains five of its original eight *apsides* (half-rounded indentations originally conceived as chapels), each crowned with a conically roofed turret. A pyramid tops the conglomeration, capped by an open-air lantern tower pierced with lancets. Robert d'Arbrissel, who spent much of his life as a recluse, founded the abbey in 1101. Aristocratic ladies occupied one part; many, including discarded mistresses of kings, had been banished from court. The four youngest daughters of Louis XV were educated here. Since 1975, the abbey has also functioned as a cultural center, offering expositions, concerts, and seminars.

www.abbaye-fontevraud.com. © **02-41-51-73-52.** Admission 11€ adults; 7.50€ students; free for children 8 and under. Daily Apr–Oct 9:30am–7pm; late Jan–Mar and Nov–Dec 10am–6pm; closed 3 weeks in Jan.

Where to Eat

La Licorne ★ MODERN FRENCH   Luckily the frugal monks' lifestyle of the Fontevraud Abbey isn't replicated at this nearby popular dining spot. Located on a walkway between the abbey and the parish church, this 18th-century bourgeois home exudes the grace of the *ancien régime.* However, the service isn't quite as regal and can be somewhat slow. So sit back and relax in its walled garden; the excellent-value menu is certainly worth the wait. It includes refined dishes such as poached sea bream stuffed with shellfish and quinoa grown in the region or royal Maine D'Anjou filet of beef draped in Saumur-Champigny red wine reduction, and such delectable desserts as local Alienor pastries.

Allée Ste-Catherine. www.lalicorne-restaurant-fontevraud.fr. © **02-41-51-72-49.** Main course 19€–39€; fixed-price lunch menu 19€ or dinner 26€–72€. Nov–Apr Tues–Sun noon–2pm and Tues and Thurs–Sat 7–9pm; May–Oct daily noon–2pm and 7–9pm. Closed last 2 weeks of Dec.

ANGERS ★★

288km (179 miles) SW of Paris; 89km (55 miles) E of Nantes

Once the capital of Anjou, Angers straddles the Maine River at the western end of the Loire Valley. Though it suffered extensive damage in World War II, it has been restored, blending provincial charm with a hint of sophistication. The bustling regional center is often used as a base for exploring the châteaux to the west. Young people, including some 30,000 college students, keep this vital city of 155,700 jumping until late at night.

Essentials

ARRIVING   High-speed **trains** make the 1.5-hr. trip every hour from Paris's Gare Montparnasse; the cost is 14€ to 80€ one-way. From Tours, about 10 trains per day make the 1-hr. trip; a one-way ticket is 10.70€ to 19€. The Angers train station is a convenient walk from the château. For schedules and information, visit www.oui.sncf or call © **36-35** (.40€/min.). From Saumur, there are direct **bus** connections (1.5 hr.); visit www.angoubus.fr or call © **08-20-16-00-49** (.15€/min.) for schedules. If you're **driving** from Tours, take the A85 autoroute west and exit at Angers Centre.

The **Office de Tourisme,** 7 pl. Kennedy (www. angersloiretourisme.com; ℭ **02-41-23-50-00**), is opposite the entrance to the château.

Exploring the Town

If you have time for shopping, wander to the pedestrian zone in the center of town. Its boutiques and small shops sell everything from clothes and shoes to jewelry and books. To satisfy your sweet-tooth stop in at **Benoit,** 2 rue Lices (www.chocolats-benoit.com; ℭ **02-41-88-94-52**). The best chocolate shop in Angers was passed from father to daughter and Anne-Francoise's new recipes have garnered her enough awards and renown to open boutiques in Paris and Lille.

Oenophiles will not be disappointed with the selection at the **Maison du Vin de l'Anjou,** 5 bis pl. Kennedy (www.vinsdeloire.fr; ℭ **02-41-17-68-20**), where you can learn about the area's vineyards and buy a bottle or two for gifts or a picnic.

Cathédrale St-Maurice ★★

CATHEDRAL The cathedral dates mostly from the 12th and 13th centuries; the main tower is from the 16th century. The statues on the portal represent everybody from the Queen of Sheba to David at the harp. The tympanum depicts Christ Enthroned. The stained-glass windows from the 12th through the 16th centuries have made the cathedral famous. The oldest one illustrates the martyrdom of St. Vincent; the most unusual is of St. Christopher with the head of a dog. The 12th-century nave, a landmark in cathedral architecture, is a work of harmonious beauty.

Pl. Freppel. ℭ **02-41-87-58-45.** Free admission; donations appreciated. Daily 9am–7pm.

Cathédrale St-Maurice, Angers

Château d'Angers ★★★ CASTLE

The château, dating from the 9th century, was the home of the comtes d'Anjou. The notorious Black Falcon lived here, and in time, the Plantagenets took up residence. From 1230 to 1238, the outer walls and 17 enormous towers were built, creating a fortress. King René favored the château, and during his reign, a brilliant court life flourished until he was forced to surrender to Louis XI. Louis XIV turned the château into a prison. In World War II, the Nazis used it as a munitions depot, and the Allies bombed it in 1944.

THE LOIRE VALLEY FOR KIDS

The Loire is a wonderful family holiday destination, and the highlights, of course, are the castles (**Valençay**, p. 263, **Langeais**, p. 248, and **Loches**, p. 250, being the best to include for children). But the two most frequently visited attractions for families are located at the same address: the **Aquarium du Val de Loire** (www.decouvrez-levaldeloire.com; *②* **02-47-23-44-44**) and the **Parc des Mini-Châteaux** (www.parcminichateaux.com; *②* **02-47-23-44-57**), 9.5km (6 miles) west of Amboise, near the village of Lussault-sur-Loire.

The **Parc des Mini-Châteaux** (daily early Apr–May 10:30am–7pm; June–Aug 10am–7pm/8pm; Sept–Nov 14 10:30am–6pm; closed mid-Nov to early Apr) holds replicas of France's most famous castles, built at ⅟₃₀ the size of the originals. Chambord, for example, is less than 3.5m (11 ft.) tall. It's all very patriotic—a sort of learning game that teaches French schoolchildren the glories of their

patrimoine (heritage) and collects some of the most celebrated architecture in Europe. Admission is 14€ adults, 10.50€ students and children ages 4 to 14, and free for children 3 and under; for a full day of fun get a discounted joint ticket with the Aquarium 22€ and 17€. The **aquarium** is home to some 10,000 freshwater and saltwater fish. Admission is 14€ adults, 10.50€ children ages 4 to 14 (daily Jan–Mar and Sept–Dec 10:30am–6pm; Apr–May 10:30am–7pm; June to late July 10am–7pm; and late July to mid-Aug 10am–8pm; closed 2 weeks in Nov and Jan).

The area also offers plenty of activities for outdoor adventures. Take a break from navigating the castles of the Loire by paddling it. **The Canoe Company** (www.canoe-company.fr; *②* **06-37-01-89-92**) rents canoes daily on both the Loire River at Rochecorbon and on the Cher at the foot of the Château de Chenonceau (from 14€ per person for 2 hr.).

Visit the castle to see the **Apocalypse Tapestries** ★★★. They weren't always so highly regarded—they once served as a canopy to protect orange trees and were also used to cover the damaged walls of a church. Woven in Paris by Nicolas Bataille from cartoons by Jean de Bruges around 1375 for Louis I of Anjou, they were purchased for a nominal sum in the 19th century. The series of 77 sections, illustrating the Book of St. John, stretches 100m (328 ft.).

A full visit should also include the ramparts, windmill tower, and 15th-century chapel. Once you've paid the entrance fee, you can take an hour-long guided tour focusing on the architecture and history of the château, or a tour devoted to the Apocalypse Tapestries. Both are available only in French; a self-guided tour with audio guide is available in English.

2 promenade du Bout-du-Monde. www.angers.monuments-nationaux.fr. *②* **02-41-86-48-77**. Admission 9€ adults; 7€ seniors and students 18–25; free for children 17 and under and to all on 1st Sun of the month. Sept–Apr daily 10am–5:30pm; May–Aug daily 9:30am–6:30pm.

Musée Jean Lurçat ★★ MUSEUM The town has four museums, but the most interesting is in the Ancien Hôpital St-Jean. Visitors to this hospital established in 1174 now come for its famous tapestry, *Le Chant du Monde (The Song of the World)*, created by Jean Lurçat between 1957 and 1966. This monumental work of 10 panels is a symphony of the artist's interpretation of the destiny of the world, from awe-inspiring space travel to the horrible apocalypses of war. Be sure to view the more than 60 tapestries the museum has on view and its 17th-century dispensary, equipped with shelves of earthenware jars and trivets. Don't miss the Romanesque cloister with its secret garden on your way out.

4 bd. Arago. www.musees.angers.fr. ℰ **02-41-24-18-45.** Admission 6€ adults, 3€ students, free for visitors 25 and under; joint ticket with the Château d'Angers 9.50€ adults. June–Sept daily 10am–6:30pm; Oct–May Tues–Sun 10am–noon and 2–6pm.

Where to Stay & Eat

La Salamandre ★★ CLASSIC FRENCH   Located in the Best Western Hotel d'Anjou, this elegant restaurant celebrates the king who put the Loire Valley on the map: François I. His symbol, the salamander, appears cleverly throughout the decor. Enjoy royal service and regal ambiance with its large wooden fireplace, and stately furniture and wallpaper. Its menus could feature traditional pot-au-feu soup à l'ancienne, or the more adventurous zucchini flower soufflé with lobster mousse, or you can't go wrong with the divine Anjou pigeon with truffles.

Built in 1846, the hotel (www.hoteldanjou.fr; ℰ **02-41-21-12-11**) continues on with the same royal themes. It rents 53 comfortable, spacious rooms that are slightly dated, though not as far back as the building itself (from 105€–195€).

In the Hotel d'Anjou, 1 bd. du Maréchal Foch. www.restaurant-lasalamandre.fr. ℰ **02-41-88-99-55.** Main course 24€–42€; fixed-price lunch 19€ or dinner 31€–68€. Daily noon–2pm and Mon–Sat 7:30–9:30pm.

L'Hôtel de France ★   Situated right across from the railway station, this comfortable 19th-century hotel is the best place to overnight in Angers. It has been in the careful hands of the Bouyer family since 1893. The spacious rooms are decorated in mainly cream and beige tones with smart classic furnishings. It is a common stopover for business travelers and room rates go up 15€ to 25€ per night during trade shows.

8 pl. de la Gare, Angers. www.hoteldefrance-angers.com. ℰ **02-41-88-49-42.** 55 units. 131€–152€ double; 189€ suite. Parking 7€. **Amenities:** Restaurant; bar; room service; free Wi-Fi.

Provence Caffè ★ PROVENÇAL   If you've had your fill of Loire specialties, come here for the flavors of Provence. From the outside, it doesn't look like much, but that helps keep it a good local secret. Recently revamped, the dining room is bright and modern, matching the fresh seasonal menu. The best tables are next to the windows, overlooking the pretty main town square. Chef Arnaud Le Calloch has a fondness for fish, covered in his red mullet salad with pistou or sea bream with ratatouille

A Toast with the Home-Brew—Cointreau

Another libation unique to Angers is Cointreau. Two confectioner brothers set out to create a drink of "crystal-clear purity." The result was Cointreau, a twice-distilled alcohol from the peels of two types of oranges, bitter and sweet. The factory has turned out the drink since 1849. Cointreau flavors such drinks as the cosmopolitan and the sidecar. Recent marketing campaigns, including one featuring seductress Dita Von Teese, have helped modernize the brand and today some 13 million bottles of Cointreau are consumed annually.

La Carée Cointreau, 2 bd. des Bretonnières (www.carre-cointreau.fr; © **02-41-31-50-50**), is in the suburb of St-Barthèlemy, a 10-min. drive east of the town center. If you call ahead to reserve, you can take a 1.5-hr.-long guided tour of the distillery and then visit the showroom, where you can sample and stock up on the fruity liqueur. Hours are variable; tours run on Saturdays only from October to April, and Tuesday through Saturday the rest of the year (10€–18€ adults depending on tastings, 4.50€ children 12–17, free for children 11 and under).

tart, yet carnivores fear not, you can sink your teeth into a succulent braised lamb shank with mashed potatoes topped with confit garlic and rosemary juice. To cleanse your palate, order a *Versinthe*, the lesser-known Provençal cousin to absinthe.

9 pl. du Ralliement. www.provence-caffe.com. © **02-41-87-44-15.** Main course 17€; fixed-price menu 19€–35€. Tues–Sat noon–2pm and 7–10pm.

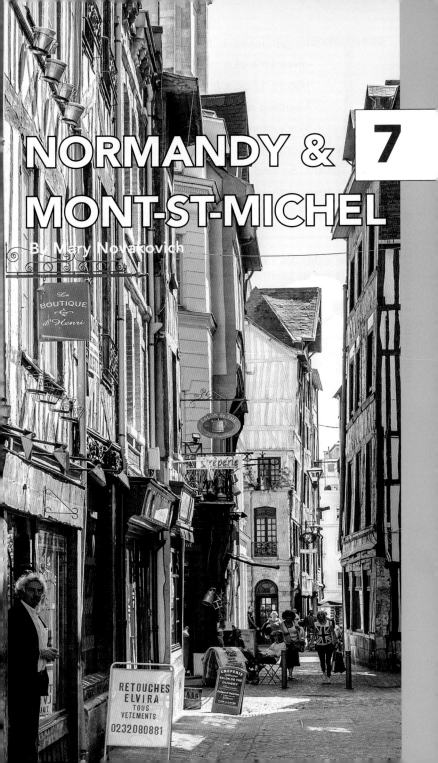

NORMANDY & 7
MONT-ST-MICHEL

By Mary Novakovich

The gentleness in Normandy's rich rolling landscape gives little clue to the region's long and turbulent history. Look a little closer, however, and you see haunting reminders of some of the Second World War's most dramatic and decisive battles. The Allied landings on Normandy's beaches in June 1944 changed the course of the Second World War. Although the embarkation beaches teem with visitors in the summer, they remain living memorials to bravery, determination, and ingenuity.

But these sights don't exclusively define the region either. Fashionable Deauville and its family-friendly neighbor Trouville have been drawing sun-seekers since the 19th century. As the age of the railway expanded during the Victorian era, so too did genteel seaside resorts that dot this stretch of France's northern coast.

Bayeux attracts lovers of history and art, many to see the extraordinary tapestry that recounts another battle that altered the course of history: the Norman Conquest. Honfleur is a place of arty pilgrimage, and Rouen's history and bustling restaurant scene attract foodies hungry for culture. At the western border is Mont-St-Michel, which has stood guard for a millennium and is linked to the coastline via a pedestrian bridge.

Head inland to savor the cream of Normandy produce: namely the pungent cheeses from Camembert, Pont l'Evêque, and Livarot. Instead of the vineyards that characterize the South of France, Normandy has apple orchards that produce the region's renowned cider and Calvados brandy.

ROUEN ★★

135km (84 miles) NW of Paris; 89km (55 miles) E of Le Havre

Normandy's capital buzzes from dawn 'til dusk, thanks to its busy port and lively university. Its agreeable atmosphere invites leisurely strolls along medieval lanes, where some of Normandy's most delicious produce sits temptingly in shop windows. Former celebrated residents of Rouen include writer Gustave Flaubert (who grew up along the city's enchanting cobbled streets), Claude Monet (who endlessly painted Rouen's Cathédrale de Notre-Dame), and Joan of Arc, who met her tragic end in the place du Vieux Marché, the Old Marketplace, in 1431.

Rouen suffered greatly during World War II when half of it was destroyed, mostly by Allied bombers. During the reconstruction of the old quarters, some of the almost-forgotten crafts of the Middle Ages were

PREVIOUS PAGE: **The streets of old Rouen**

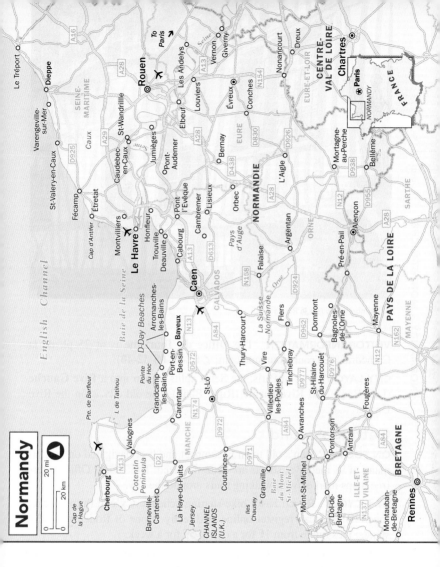

Normandy

English Channel

Baie de la Seine

revived. Today its metropolitan area is home to half a million people, with about 100,000 clustered in the large center.

Essentials

ARRIVING From Paris's Gare St-Lazare, **trains** leave for Rouen about once an hour (trip time: 1.5 hr.). The one-way fare is 22€, but you can get deals online for as little as 10€. The main station is a 10-min. walk to the city center. For rail information and schedules, visit www.oui.sncf or call ✆ **36-35** (.40€/min.). To **drive** from Paris, take A13 northwest to Rouen (trip time: 1.5 hr.).

Half-timbered houses in Rouen

VISITOR INFORMATION   The **Office de Tourisme** is at 25 pl. de la Cathédrale (en.rouentourisme.com; ✆ **02-32-08-32-40**).

CITY LAYOUT   As in Paris, the Seine splits Rouen into a **Rive Gauche** (Left Bank) and **Rive Droite** (Right Bank). The old city is on the Rive Droite.

Getting Around

ON FOOT   Rouen's old town is compact and best navigated on foot, as many of its medieval streets are pedestrianized. The Tourist Office offers free maps marked with walking tours around the city.

BY BICYCLE   Rouen has a bike-sharing scheme, **Cy'clic** (http://cyclic. rouen.fr). You can register online or directly at one of Rouen's 24 bike stands; fees range from 1€ for a day to 5€ for a week.

BY CAR   **Rouen Park** (www.rouenpark.com) details the city's five central public parking lots and their hourly prices. As prices average 15€ for 24 hr., having a car in Rouen can be expensive. Unless you plan to visit other areas, you won't be needing a car in Rouen itself.

BY TAXI   Les Taxi Blancs (✆ **02-35-61-20-50**).

BY PUBLIC TRANSPORT   Rouen's **Métro** (www.crea-astuce.fr) has two lines running north-south through the city, underground on Rive Droite and at street level on Rive Gauche. The most central stations in Rive Droite are Théâtre des Arts, Palais de Justice, and the train station, Gare-Rue Verte. Tickets cost 1.60€ and are on sale at automatic kiosks at each station.

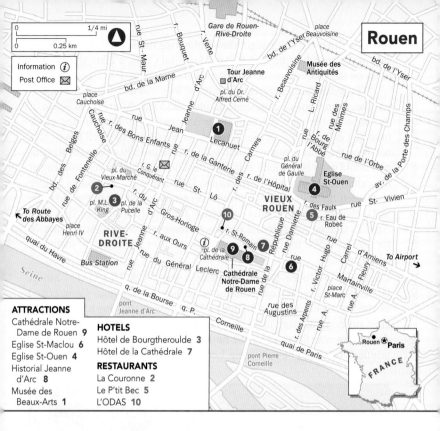

ATTRACTIONS
Cathédrale Notre-
    Dame de Rouen **9**
Eglise St-Maclou **6**
Eglise St-Ouen **4**
Historial Jeanne
    d'Arc **8**
Musée des
    Beaux-Arts **1**

HOTELS
Hôtel de Bourgtheroulde **3**
Hôtel de la Cathédrale **7**

RESTAURANTS
La Couronne **2**
Le P'tit Bec **5**
L'ODAS **10**

[Fast FACTS] ROUEN

ATMs/Banks   Dozens of banks are all around the city center, with 10 along rue Jeanne
d'Arc.

Doctors & Hospitals   **Centre Hospitalier Universitaire de Rouen** (www.chu-rouen.
fr; ☏ **02-32-88-89-90**).

Mail & Postage   **La Poste,** 112 rue Jeanne d'Arc (☏ **36-31**).

Pharmacies   **Grande Pharmacie du Centre,** 29 pl. Cathédrale (☏ **02-35-71-33-17**).

Exploring Rouen

The city's main sights—and the old town— are on the Right Bank of the
Seine. Visitors usually make a beeline for **place du Vieux Marché.** Their
first impression is often one of bafflement when they see the giant modernist Church of Ste-Jeanne in the place where Joan of Arc was executed
for heresy on May 30, 1431. Surrounded by medieval half-timbered restaurants and shops, the church's 1970s architecture comes as a bit of a
shock. But it somehow works, with its enormous stained-glass windows

and a swirling roof that nudges the neighboring market stalls. On the west side of the church is the Joan of Arc Memorial Cross, a 20m- (65 ft.-) tall cross on the spot where she was burned at the stake.

The pedestrianized "Street of the Great Clock"—**rue du Gros Horloge**— runs between Rouen's cathedral and place du Vieux Marché and is one of the hubs of the city. It's named for an ornate gilt Renaissance clock mounted on an arch over the street and is connected to a bell tower; this had been the clock's home until it was lowered in 1529 so that the Rouennais could get a closer look at it. You can climb the bell tower, stopping at the exhibition rooms along the way to learn about the structure's history and watch the bells in action. At the top are lovely views of the old town and cathedral. Open Tuesday to Sunday 10am to 1pm and 2 to 7pm from April to October, and from 2 to 6pm November to March. Admission 7€ for adults, 3.50€ for children ages 6 to 18, free for under 6, including audio guide.

Cathédrale Notre-Dame de Rouen ★★★ CATHEDRAL Monet immortalized Rouen's cathedral in more than 30 paintings. Consecrated in 1063, the cathedral, a symphony of lacy stonework, was reconstructed after suffering damage in World War II. Two towers distinguish it: **Tour de Beurre** was financed by the faithful who were willing to pay for the privilege of eating butter during Lent. Containing a carillon of 56 bells,

Cathédrale Notre-Dame de Rouen

Interior, Cathédrale Notre-Dame de Rouen

the 1877 **Tour Lanterne** rises to almost 150m (492 ft.), making its spire the tallest in France.

Inside, the cathedral's choir is a masterpiece, with 14 soaring pillars. Particularly interesting is the **Chapelle de la Vierge,** adorned with Renaissance tombs of the cardinals of Amboise. Also entombed here is the heart of Richard the Lion-Hearted. Along the south-facing side of the cathedral is an entrancing collection of statues of saints that had previously adorned the exterior.

Pl. de la Cathédrale. www.cathedrale-rouen.net. ✆ **02-35-71-51-23.** Free admission. Apr–Oct Mon 2–7pm and Tues–Sun 9am–7pm; Nov–Mar Mon 2–6pm, Tues–Sat 9am–noon and 2–6pm, Sun 2–6pm. Closed during Mass and some holidays. Metro: Palais de Justice.

Eglise St-Maclou ★★ CHURCH   St-Maclou was built in the Flamboyant Gothic style with a crenelated porch and cloisters. It's known for the 16th-century panels on its doors; look out for the Portail des Fontaines on the left. The church was built in 1200, rebuilt in 1432, and consecrated in 1521. Its lantern tower is from the 19th century, and its exterior was completely renovated in 2013.

Well worth a peek is the nearby **Aître Saint-Maclou,** 184 rue Martainville (✆ **02-76-08-81-13**). Half-timbered buildings, decorated with creepy skull motifs, mark the site of a cemetery dedicated to victims of the 1348 Great Plague. It now houses the regional Ecole des Beaux-Arts. From April to October it's open daily 9am to 6pm; from November to March it's open Saturday and Sunday 9am to 5pm, plus during French school holidays. Admission is free.

3 pl. Barthélémy. ✆ **02-35-08-69-00.** Free admission. Apr–Oct Sat–Mon 10am–noon and 2–6pm; Nov–Mar Sat–Mon 10am–noon and 2–5:30pm.

Historial Jeanne d'Arc ★★ MUSEUM   Set within the Archbishop's Palace behind the cathedral is France's largest site devoted to Joan of Arc. The palace's elaborate interior is an impressive setting for the story of the Maid of Orléans told in multimedia and interactive displays. These compelling exhibits do an excellent job in telling Joan's tragic story and subsequent trial, and you'll also see the room where she was condemned to death in 1431.

7 rue Saint-Romain. www.historial-jeannedarc.fr. ✆ **02-35-52-48-00.** Admission 9.50€ adults; 6.50€ for children 6–17; free for children 5 and under. Tues–Sun 10am–12:15pm and 12:45–7pm.

Musée des Beaux-Arts ★★★ MUSEUM   Featuring the second-largest collection of Impressionist paintings in France, this impressive fine arts museum displays more than 8,000 artworks ranging from medieval primitives to contemporary paintings. Within this handsome 19th-century building are works by Renaissance masters including Veronese, Velázquez, Caravaggio, and Rubens. Fans of Impressionism can marvel at paintings by Monet, Renoir, Sisley, and Pissarro, including several of

Monet's paintings of Rouen's cathedral. In 2016, the museum launched the popular idea of devoting a salon to works chosen by members of the public, which changes every year.

Esplanade Marcel Duchamp. http://mbarouen.fr. ℂ **02-35-71-28-40.** Free admission. Wed–Mon 10am–6pm.

Where to Stay

Hotel de Bourgtheroulde ★★   Ancient meets modern in dazzling style at Rouen's only five-star hotel. Step inside this 15th-century mansion by the place du Vieux Marché and you're immediately in one of the most modern and chicest hotel interiors in the region. The galleried Atrium Bar makes a bold statement with its soaring red ceiling and glass floor exposing the spa's enormous indoor pool below. No two rooms are alike: Some have sleek, minimalist decor while others go for the full traditional look with antique-style furnishings, exposed ceiling beams, and wood-paneled walls. In addition to an indoor pool, the **Spa du Drap d'Or** features a steam bath, sauna, a fitness room, and treatment rooms.

15 pl. de la Pucelle. www.hotelsparouen.com. ℂ **02-35-14-50-50.** 78 units. 184€– 290€ double; 369€–430]eu] suite. Parking 25€. **Amenities:** 2 bars; 2 restaurants; indoor pool; spa; free Wi-Fi.

Hôtel de la Cathédrale ★   It's hard to beat the location of this simple yet charming hotel: It's just off a pedestrian street midway between the cathedral and the Eglise St-Maclou. Some rooms have more dash than others, with pretty *toile de jouy* wallpaper, deep leather armchairs and exposed beams. The courtyard garden is just as charming and is a little haven in the summer. When it's too chilly to eat outside, the cozy breakfast room—with its beamed ceiling and inglenook fireplace—is a delightful alternative. Some of the public areas could do with sprucing up, though, and the hotel might not suit people with limited mobility.

12 rue St-Romain. www.hotel-de-la-cathedrale.fr. ℂ **02-35-71-57-95.** 26 units. 95€– 125€ double; 140€ triple; 160€ quadruple. Public parking 11€ nearby. **Amenities:** Breakfast room; free Wi-Fi.

Where to Eat

Don't be surprised to find plenty of fresh, succulent seafood in France's fourth largest port. Rouen lives up to its status as Normandy's capital in offering a superb selection of restaurants serving fantastic Norman cuisine. Restaurants are dotted all around the city, with many found in the antiques quarter near Eglise St-Maclou and, inevitably, in the old market square. Key local ingredients include fresh fish, rich cream, butter, and apples, which are on tantalizing display in the **daily market,** place du Vieux Marché (Tues–Sun 6:30am–1:30pm). A much larger **food market** is in the place St-Marc east of the cathedral (Tues, Fri, and Sat 6am–6pm, Sun 6am–1:30pm).

La Couronne ★★★ TRADITIONAL FRENCH   It calls itself France's oldest *auberge* and has been keeping travelers well fed since 1345 in its superb location on the place du Vieux Marché. Step upstairs and you'll see the photos of those who passed their way through this cocoon-like half-timbered house—everyone from Salvador Dalí to Patti Smith. Julia Child had her first-ever lunch in France here in 1948, and immediately swooned over the supremely buttery *sole meunière*, which you can have with oysters from the 65€ menu named after her. The Gourmet Harmony menu (49€) includes delicately braised turbot but save room for the cheese trolley and its 21 mouthwatering choices.

31 pl. du Vieux Marché. www.lacouronne.com.fr. ✆ **02-35-71-40-90.** Main course 25€–48€; fixed-price lunch menu 25€–75€ or dinner 37€–75€. Daily noon–2:30pm and 7–10:30pm.

L'ODAS ★★ FRENCH   In an interior as cool and contemporary as the cuisine, Olivier Da Silva—the ODAS of the restaurant's name—deliberately keeps his menu short in this laid-back Michelin-starred restaurant. A succulent John Dory fillet comes with a gentle coating of smoked butter and warmed oysters, while the scallop carpaccio starter has a wonderful caviar kick. The Sunday brunch at 55€ is especially indulgent, with touches of lobster and more caviar. If you're feeling adventurous, give the chef carte blanche to cook you what he wants. It's a compact space, so book ahead.

Passage Maurice Lenfant. http://lodas.fr. ✆ **02-35-73-83-24.** Main course 39€–41€; fixed-price menu 49€–135€. Tues–Sat noon–2pm and 7:30–9:30pm; Sat 7–10pm; Sun 10:30am–2:30pm.

Le P'tit Bec ★★ FRENCH   Gratin dishes are the specialty of this cheerful, friendly bistro. It's pure comfort food: try the Paysan—potatoes, ham, eggs, bacon, cream, and Emmental all baked to crispy goodness. Or an all-cheese extravaganza of camembert, goats' cheese, emmental, and Neufchâtel. The menu also has some French classics such as confit de canard.

182 rue Eau de Robec. www.leptitbec.com. ✆ **02-35-07-63-33.** Main course 11€– 15.50€. Mon–Wed noon–2:30pm; Thurs–Sat noon–2:30pm and 7–10:30pm.

Shopping

Rouen was once one of France's major producers of the fine decorative ceramic ware known as *faïence de Rouen.* For contemporary faïence, your best bet is **Faïencerie Augy,** 26 rue St-Romain (✆ **02-35-88-77-47**). Rouen is also an antiques capital, with dozens of vendors in the Old Town. The best hunting ground is along **rue Damiette,** and **rue St-Romain.** A **flea market** joins the food stalls in place St-Marc on Fridays and Saturdays. Other antiques shops worth visiting are **Galerie Bertran,** 108 rue Molière (✆ **02-35-98-24-06**), with a good selection of 18th- and 19th-century paintings, especially by School of Rouen Impressionists; and

On Normandy's Cider & Calvados Route

Normandy might not have the vineyards of other parts of France, but it does have endless apple orchards that produce the acclaimed Calvados brandy, refreshing alcoholic cider, and *pommeau*, a mixture of Calvados and apple juice. In the lush rolling hills of the Pays d'Auge east of Caen, producers open their half-timbered farms (mostly by appointment) to thirsty tourists eager to try the different varieties of apple nectar. Some of the region's most delightful villages lie on this 40km (25-mile) Route du Cidre (www.larouteducidre.fr), notably Cambremer

and Beuvron-en-Auge, the latter being one of the designated Most Beautiful Villages of France (www.les-plus-beaux-villages-de-france.org/en/beuvron-en-auge). In 2018, **Calvados Experience** (www.calvados-experience.com; ☎ **02-31-64-30-31;** 12.50€ adults, 8€ children 6–17, free for children 5 and under; Apr–Sept daily 9:30am–7pm, Oct–Mar daily 10am–1pm and 2–6pm) opened in Pont-l'Evêque. This entertaining museum uses multisensory displays to show how the apple brandy is made, and also offers tastings.

Etienne Bertran, 110 rue Molière (☎ **02-35-70-79-96**), with its collection of antique books.

Chocolate lovers are spoiled for choice, with delectable treats at **Le Cacaotier,** 5 rue Guillaume le Conquérant (www.lecacaotier.com; ☎ **02-35-62-71-06**) and **Auzou,** 163 rue du Gros Horloge (www.auzouchocolatier.fr; ☎ **02-35-70-59-31**).

Nightlife

Opéra de Rouen, 7 rue du Docteur Rambert (www.operaderouen.fr; ☎ **02-35-98-74-78**), schedules year-round ballet, opera, and classical music. A variety of concerts takes place at **Abbatiale Saint-Ouen,** place du Général-de-Gaulle. The former hangar **Le 106,** quai Jean de Béthancourt (www.le106.com; ☎ **02-32-10-88-60**), offers a jam-packed lineup of French and international pop and rock shows. Check the Tourist Office's website for the latest events.

Le Vicomté, rue de la Vicomté (☎ **02-35-71-24-11**), attracts everyone from the after-work crowd to clubbers, with five levels devoted to fun and food. The space has a club with live bands and DJs, classy fireside cocktail bar, restaurant, patio, and even a billiard room.

HONFLEUR ★★

201km (125 miles) NW of Paris; 63km (39 miles) NE of Caen

This exquisite fishing port dating from the 11th century has been the focus of artists for hundreds of years—native son Eugène Boudin, Gustave Courbet, and Claude Monet, to name but three. Stroll along the Vieux Bassin (old harbor) and you can still see art students with their sketchbooks trying to capture the enchanting light that dances off the white boats and glistening water. Impossibly tall 18th-century townhouses tower over the harbor, where cafes and restaurants crowd around the pleasure boats.

It's busy and, yes, full of tourists from all over the world. But it's such a beguiling place that it's worth putting up with the throngs. Time your visit so that you have lunch a bit early, about noon. Then you'll have the streets to yourself while everyone else is still eating.

The approach from the east is along the impressive Pont de Normandie bridge that spans the Seine River from Le Havre. And the Côte de Grace—the start of the alluring Côte Fleurie—meanders westwards from here, passing half-timbered Norman homes and ancient chapels en route to Trouville.

Essentials

ARRIVING There's no direct **train** service into Honfleur. From Paris, take one of the half-dozen or so daily trains from Gare St-Lazare to Trouville-Deauville (from 19€ one-way). Fares are cheaper if booked in advance online. From there, **Bus Verts du Calvados** (www.busverts.fr; © **08-10-21-42-14**) no. 20 or 50 makes the 25-min. ride to Honfleur; the one-way fare is 2.40€.

Sailboats in Honfleur harbor

To **drive** from Paris (trip time: 2–2.5 hr.; 20.80€ in tolls), take A13 west, then the A29 north in the direction of Le Havre. From Pont l'Evêque or other points southwest, D579 leads to Honfleur's major boulevard, rue de la République.

VISITOR INFORMATION   The **Office de Tourisme** is on quai Lepaulmier (www.ot-honfleur.fr; ℂ **02-31-89-23-30**).

Getting Around

ON FOOT   Honfleur is small enough to get around on foot. The **bus** service, **HO Bus** (www.hobus.fr), is used by locals mainly to come into town from the outskirts.

BY CAR   During high season, it can be difficult to find a place to park. The tourist board's website has a handy map detailing which areas are free and which car parks charge and their fees.

BY TAXI   Taxis Honfleur (ℂ **06-08-60-17-98**).

[Fast FACTS] HONFLEUR

ATMs/Banks   Half a dozen banks are along rue de la Foulerie, pl. Pierre Berthelot and rue des Longettes.

Mail & Postage   **La Poste,** 7 cours Albert Manuel (ℂ **36-31**).

Pharmacies   **Pharmacie du Dauphin,** 5 rue Dauphin (ℂ **02-31-89-10-80**).

Exploring Honfleur

Begin your tour of Honfleur by picking up a map from the Tourist Office. Each one is printed with three handy walking routes, all detailing points of interest around town. The "Footsteps of the Painters" map leads you to 14 panels of paintings by 19th-century artists around town. Stroll along the scenic quays, past the fishing boats and narrow, slate-roofed houses that line the **Vieux Bassin.** On the north side of the harbor, the former governor's house, the imposing **Lieutenance,** dates from the 16th century. Nearby is France's largest wooden church, **Eglise Ste-Catherine,** pl. Ste-Catherine (ℂ **02-31-89-11-83**), which was built by 15th-century shipbuilders. The church is open daily from 9am–7pm except during services and ceremonies.

See the village from a different perspective on one of the regular **boat trips** (www.promenade-en-bateau-honfleur.fr; 45–90 min.; 8€–11€) that depart from jetties east of the Vieux Bassin. The 45-min. ride on *La Calypso* explores the harbors that make up the port of Honfleur, while the 90-min. journey on *La Jolie France* takes you out into the Seine estuary.

Les Maisons Satie ★★ MUSEUM   It helps if you know even a little of the background to Erik Satie before you visit the wonderfully whimsical museum in the house where he was born in 1866. The composer, perhaps best known for his *Gymnopédies* piano compositions, was also part of the Surrealist and Dadaist crowd and was great friends with Picasso and Cocteau. So don't be surprised by the giant bizarre pear sculpture at the start of the tour, which is enhanced by the equally eccentric audio guide. *Tip:* You'll need to apply a little pedal power for one of the exhibits.

67 bd. Charles V. www.musees-honfleur.fr. © **02-31-89-11-11.** Admission 6.20€ adults; 4.70€ students 16–25; free for children 15 and under. May–Sept Wed–Mon 10am–7pm; Oct–Apr Wed–Mon 11am–6pm. Closed Jan–Feb 10.

Musée Eugène Boudin ★★ MUSEUM   Many Impressionists and other painters flocked to Honfleur in the 19th century, captivated by its light and water. You can see their works, including some by Monet, Courbet, Dufy, and Dubourg, in this handsome museum set in the former chapel of an Augustinian convent. But the star of the museum is Honfelur's native son, Eugène Boudin, whose pastels and paintings form part of an extensive permanent collection. In addition to local photographs (snapped between 1880–1920), Norman tourism posters, and antiques, the museum features a regularly changing roster of temporary exhibitions.

Rue de l'Homme de Bois. www.musees-honfleur.fr. © **02-31-89-54-00.** Admission 8€ adults; 6.50€ students and children 16 and over from July 1–Oct 16; 6€ and 4.50€ Feb 11–Jun 1 and Oct 16–Dec 31. Apr–Jul 6 and Sept Wed–Mon 10am–noon and 2–6pm; Jul–Aug 31 Wed–Mon 10am–6pm; Jan–Mar and Oct–Dec Mon and Wed–Fri 2:30–5:30pm and Sat–Sun 10am–2pm and 2:30–5:30pm. Closed Jan 8–Feb 2.

NaturoSpace ★★ MUSEUM   You'll feel as if you've landed in the tropics in this captivating "equatorial zoo". In this luxuriant space, you'll be surrounded by countless butterflies, birds, and exotic plants. More than 50 species from South America, Asia, Africa, and Oceania flutter through an indoor rainforest that is kept at steady temperature of 25°C (77°F). Visit in the morning to watch chrysalises crack open and butterflies make their first flight.

bd. Charles V. www.naturospace.com. © **02-31-81-77-00.** Admission 8.80€ adults; 6.80€ students and children 3–13; family package 34€. Daily Apr–Sept 10am–6:30pm; Oct–Nov and Feb–Mar 10am–5pm. Closed Nov 13–Dec 22 and Jan 9–Feb 2.

Where to Stay

Hotel l'Ecrin ★★   Step into the 18th century in this quietly grand three-star Norman manor house just a 5-min. walk from the Vieux Bassin. Cozy rooms, some with four-poster beds, have antique-style furnishings and plenty of chintz that hark back to the days of Louis XIV. The gardens are a wonderful place to relax and have breakfast, and it's unusual to find an outdoor pool so close to the center. The free parking is another bonus.

19 rue Eugène Boudin. www.hotel-ecrin-honfleur.com © **02-31-14-43-45.** 30 units. 120€–145€ double; 250€ suite. Free parking. **Amenities:** Outdoor pool; spa; free Wi-Fi.

Monet's Garden at Giverny

Claude Monet spent the last 43 years of his life in creative contentment in his house and sprawling gardens in the Normandy village of Giverny, 75km (47 miles) northwest of Paris. It's just as enchanting as when he lived there with his wife and eight children surrounded by colorful gardens and ponds decked with the water lilies and green Japanese bridge seen in so many of his paintings. Most people make the visit from Paris. However, direct trains from Rouen to Vernon (the nearest station) take about 40 min. and can cost as little as 7€ one-way when booked online in advance. From Vernon, you take a shuttle bus or bike to Giverny. See p. 268 for more information.

La Maison de Lucie ★★   This 18th-century townhouse is only about a 5-min. walk from the main port, but you really get a sense of being in a peaceful private house. The fact that it only has 12 rooms helps. There are open fires in the lounges and a friendly, warm welcome. Elegant, traditionally furnished rooms ring the internal courtyard while some rooms open directly into the garden; one has its own little terrace. The suite is in its own pavilion, with a fireplace and parquet floors adding to the luxurious feel. Check out an atmospheric vaulted cellar of the main house for a relaxing session in the hot tub.

44 rue des Capucins. www.lamaisondelucie.com. ✆ **02-31-14-40-40.** 12 units. 170€–200€ double; 250€–330€ suite. Parking 15€. **Amenities:** Spa 40€ for two; free Wi-Fi.

Les Maisons de Léa Hotel & Spa ★★★   Covered in ivy, this collection of 16th-century buildings in place Sainte-Catherine is one of the most romantic spots in Honfleur. You won't find two identical rooms within this converted salt warehouse, adjoining houses, and former school. Themes range from marine decor to soft floral fabrics and plump leather armchairs. Indulge in afternoon tea in the library or unwind in the spa's steam room. Intimate **Restaurant de Léa,** with vivid red walls and open fire, has refined, inventive dishes, including slow-cooked pork belly with Espelette peppers or poached cod with chard and a creamy risotto. Menus range from 30€ to 58€.

Pl. Sainte-Catherine. www.lesmaisonsdelea.com. ✆ **02-31-14-49-49.** 30 units. 160€–205€ double; 260€–305€ suite. **Amenities:** Restaurant; bar; spa; free Wi-Fi.

Where to Eat

Honfleur has its fair share of mediocre restaurants, especially along the Vieux Bassin. Too many cater to large groups on day trips, knowing that these patrons are unlikely to come back. If you're happy with a bowl of so-so mussels, then by all means take in the lively atmosphere of the harborside restaurants. If you want better quality food, then check out the back streets.

L'Envie ★★ FRENCH   This cheerful bistro opposite the tourist office offers no-nonsense, good-value, homemade French food in convivial surroundings. Start with local oysters or a creamy risotto made with celery and Spanish ham, before continuing with veal cooked Normandy style with a wonderfully rich sauce of Calvados, cream, and lots of butter.

14 pl. de la Porte de Rouen. © **02-14-63-13-64.** Main course 11.90€–20€; fixed-price menu 17.90€–27.90€. Thurs–Mon 11:30am–10pm and Tues 11:30am–2:30pm.

La Fleur de Sel ★★ FRENCH   Chef Vincent Guyon set up this classy restaurant in a handsome half-timbered townhouse in 1999, where he has been experimenting with his individual take on French cuisine. The menus change but could include a lighter-than-air mousseline of reblochon cheese and Iberico ham. Carnivores can feast on bone marrow with pigs' trotters, cèpes, and a mustard hollandaise. It's a small space, so book ahead.

17 rue Haute. www.lafleurdesel-honfleur.com. © **02-31-89-01-92.** Fixed-price menu 32€–75€. Wed–Sun 12:15–1:30pm and 7:15–9:30pm.

SaQuaNa ★★★ CONTEMPORARY FRENCH   Alexandre Bourdas has picked up two Michelin stars for his clever, exquisite cuisine that trades on his parentage (father from Normandy, mother from Aveyron) and a deep love of Japan. In a minimalist interior lined with exposed brick walls, Bourdas offers only two menus—one is five courses, the other eight—both of which regularly change. Fish is the focus: a John Dory filet comes with tempura kale, pumpkin purée, and a sharp Japanese ponzu sauce. Whichever menu you choose, save room for the copious desserts.

22 pl. Hamelin. www.alexandre-bourdas.com. © **02-31-89-40-80.** Fixed-price menu 90€–130€. Thurs–Sun 12:30–2:30pm and 7:30–9:30pm.

DEAUVILLE ★★★

206km (128 miles) NW of Paris; 47km (29 miles) NE of Caen

Deauville has been associated with the rich and famous since the Duc de Morny, Napoleon III's half-brother, founded it as an upscale resort in 1859. In 1913, it entered sartorial history when Coco Chanel launched her career here, opening a boutique selling tiny hats that challenged the fashion of huge-brimmed hats loaded with flowers and fruit. Chanel cultivated a tradition of elegance that dominates Deauville. It's classy, restrained, and understated—precisely the qualities that have been attracting well-heeled Parisians in overwhelming numbers since the early 20th century. They're the ones who unselfconsciously call Deauville the 21st arrondissement of Paris.

Essentials

ARRIVING   Five to nine daily **rail** connections run from Paris's Gare St-Lazare (trip time: 2–2.5 hr.); prices start at 14€ one-way. The rail depot lies midway between Trouville and Deauville, within walking distance of both resorts. **Bus Verts du Calvados** (www.busverts.fr; ✆ 08-10-21-42-14) serves the Normandy coast from Caen to Le Havre. To **drive** from Paris (trip time: 2.5 hr.), take A13 west to Pont L'Evêque, and then follow D677 north to Deauville.

VISITOR INFORMATION   The **Office de Tourisme** is at 112 rue Victor Hugo (www.deauville.fr; ✆ 02-31-14-40-00).

[FastFACTS] DEAUVILLE

ATMs/Banks   A half-dozen banks are clustered on and around rue Eugène-Colas.

Mail & Postage   **La Poste,** 20 rue Robert Fossorier (✆ 36-31).

Pharmacies   **Pharmacie de l'Horloge,** 14 pl. de Morny (✆ 02-31-88-20-47).

Getting Around

ON FOOT   Deauville is compact enough to get around on foot.

BY CAR   Streets in the town center can get busy, but free parking can be found about a 10-min. walk from the center.

BY TAXI   **Central Taxis** (✆ 02-31-87-11-11).

Exploring Deauville

Some of the architecture looks as if it had stepped out of a gothic fairy tale. The style is ostensibly Norman—lots of half-timbered buildings mostly in suitably muted shades. But then you see turrets sprouting here and there, with gables and balconies wedged into every nook and cranny. It's as if a French version of the Addams Family had a hand in designing some of these glorious confections. The overall effect is delightful, enhanced by the profusion of flowers in the public spaces. With its golf courses, casinos, deluxe hotels, La Touques and Clairefontaine racetracks, regattas, yacht harbor, polo grounds, and tennis courts, Deauville hums with upper-class patronage. Soak up the exclusive vibe with an afternoon spent people-watching, particularly along boutique-lined **rue Eugène-Colas, place Morny** (named for the resort's founder), and **place du Casino.**

Outdoor Activities

BEACHES   Deauville's boardwalk, **Les Planches,** is an impossibly pretty promenade running parallel to the town's 2km (1-mile) beach, **Plage de Deauville.** Beaux Arts and half-timbered Norman-inspired buildings line its edges. Deauville's distinctively primary-colored parasols dot the sands—even out of season. Visitors parade along the boardwalk past private bathing cabins, each one's entrance stenciled with the names of Hollywood film stars who have attended the Deauville American Film

Colored parasols on the beach at Deauville

Festival, which takes place in September. It's hard not to smile at some of the misspellings.

Access to every beach in Normandy is free, although beach clubs cover some stretches of sand. You can rent a beach umbrella for 12€ a day and a sun-lounger for 7€. Rent two sun-loungers and an umbrella for 16€ per half-day. A bathing cabin costs from 12€ a day. Parking costs from 2€ per hour in the public lots beside the sea.

The **Piscine Municipale,** bd. de la Mer (© **02-31-14-02-17**), is a large indoor seawater pool. Bathers pay from 3.50€ per person. You can buy the obligatory caps and trunks from machines if you don't have your own.

HORSE RACES/POLO　You can watch horses—either racing or competing at polo—most days from late June to early September. The grounds have a very festive, family-friendly atmosphere, with plenty of activities for children. The venues are the **Hippodrome de Deauville-La Touques,** 45 av. Hocquart de Turtot (www.france-galop.com; © **02-31-14-20-00**), in the heart of town near the Mairie de Deauville (town hall); and the **Hippodrome de Deauville Clairefontaine,** route de Clairefontaine (www. hippodrome-deauville-clairefontaine.com; © **02-31-14-69-00**), within the city limits, 2km (1 mile) west of the center. Entrance costs from 3.50€ for adults and is free for those 17 and under.

Where to Stay

Villa Augeval Hotel & Spa ★★　A flower-filled garden, a swimming pool, and two Norman-style villas greet you when you walk through the gate of the Villa Augeval. This tranquil three-star hotel is barely a 10-min. walk from the center, and it's also very close to the Hippodrome. The style is elegantly French, with furnishings recalling the 18th and 19th centuries, and a few of the rooms have whirlpool baths for an extra touch of luxury. The newer annex, the Trait de l'Union, has more spacious rooms, but most of the rooms will have balconies and the suite has a gorgeous loggia, lovely for relaxing and hearing the sounds of the horses in the nearby stables.

15 av. Hocquart-de-Turtot. www.augeval.com. © **02-31-81-13-18.** 42 units. 85€–239€ double; 115€–395€ suite. **Amenities:** Bar; babysitting; exercise room; outdoor pool; table tennis; room service; sauna and steam room 34€ for 30 min.; free Wi-Fi.

Hotel Le Normandy ★★★   Sprawling over an entire block, this legendary hotel built in 1912 is belle époque Norman-style half-timbering at its most grandiose. It's like a giant fairy-tale concoction of pale green and cream gables clustering around a courtyard and overlooking the seafront. Its spacious rooms are a riot of *toile de jouy* fabrics and wallpaper, giving it a French country style but with city comforts. Moneyed film buffs can stay in the voluptuous "Un Homme et Une Femme Suite," where Anouk Aimée and Jean-Louis Trintignant stayed while making the cult 1966 film "A Man and a Woman." Smart Parisian families relax in the glass-ceilinged indoor pool; the spa features a yoga studio.

38 rue Jean Mermoz. www.hotelsbarriere.com. © **02-31-98-66-22.** 271 units. 223€–647€ double; from 455€ suite. Parking 33€; 15€ per charge for electric vehicles. **Amenities:** Restaurant; bar; babysitting; spa; exercise room; heated indoor pool; room service; children's club; free bike rental; free Wi-Fi.

Where to Eat

As expected, Deauville has its share of fine-dining restaurants, and simply those that are touristy and overpriced, particularly along rue Eugène Colas. You also pay a premium to sit at one of the restaurants along the beachfront promenade Les Planches—the sea views don't come cheap.

La Cantine de Deauville ★ FRENCH   This bustling brasserie stands out from the touristy restaurants along Eugène Colas. Inside its industrial-chic interior are generous plates of hearty food, ranging from enormous burgers and steaks to hefty salads of chicken, foie gras, and poached eggs.

90 rue Eugène Colas. www.lacantinedeauville.fr. © **02-31-87-47-47.** Main course 15.50€–32€. Daily 9am–10pm (Fri–Sat until 10:30pm).

L'Essentiel ★★ FRENCH/ASIAN   South Korea meets northern France—with the odd Spanish touch—in this innovative restaurant run by a husband-and-wife chef team who won their first Michelin star in 2018. While the limited menu changes regularly, it could include veal loin jazzed up with pungent shiso leaves and spicy kosho juice. There aren't many tables, so book ahead.

29 rue Mirabeau. www.lessentiel-deauville.com. © **02-31-87-22-11.** Main course 28€–34€. Daily noon–2pm and 7:30–9:30pm (Sun until 9pm).

Le Garage à Deauville ★ FRENCH Choose from the classy interior or the sheltered terrace in this lively brasserie that's a 2-min. walk from the place de Morny. Seafood lovers can tuck into platters of *fruits de mer* or try the whole sea bream grilled à la plancha. Carnivores looking for a treat can share the massive côte de boeuf but save some space for the Grand Marnier soufflé.

118 av. de la République. www.restaurant-garage-deauville.fr ℂ **02-31-76-25-25.** Main course 14.50€–32€. Daily noon–3pm and 7–midnight.

Shopping

Luxury boutiques such as Hermès, Ralph Lauren, and Louis Vuitton cluster around the **place du Casino.** If you're looking for more inclusive and slightly more affordable shops, including a lovely Norman-style Printemps department store, take a stroll along **rue Eugène-Colas** and **place de Morny.**

To see Norman produce in all its glory, head for the **Marché Publique** (open-air market) in place du Marché beside place de Morny. In July, August, Easter, Christmas, and French school holidays, it's open daily 8am to 1pm. The rest of the year, market days are Tuesday, Friday, and Saturday, as well as Sunday from February to November. In addition to fruits, vegetables, poultry, cider, wine, and cheese, you'll find cookware, porcelain tableware, and cutlery.

Nightlife

The **Casino de Deauville,** rue Edmond Blanc (www.casinobarriere.com; ℂ **02-31-14-31-14**), has been one of France's foremost casinos since it opened in 1912. Over the years, the original Belle Epoque has expanded to include a theater, Le Brummel nightclub, three restaurants, two bars, and a huge collection of slot machines *(machines à sous)*. The casino distinguishes areas for slot machines from more formal zones containing such games as roulette, baccarat, blackjack, and poker. The slots are open daily 10am to 2am (to 3am Fri and 4am Sat) and have no dress code, although shorts are not allowed. The areas containing *les jeux de table* (table games) are open Monday to Thursday 7pm–2am (from 4pm Fri–Sun). Entrance is free, and you must present a passport or ID to gain admission.

Clubbers head for **Le Chic,** 14 rue Désiré-le-Hoc (ℂ **02-31-88-30-91**), a favorite with French actors and off-duty jockeys. Polo players frequent the perennially popular **Brok Café,** 14 av. du Général-de-Gaulle (ℂ **02-31-81-30-81**)—if you're keen to join them, make sure you hit this Cuban-style venue before midnight. For chilled-out live music and delicious tapas, check out **La Plancha,** 57 av. de la République (http://laplancha-deauville.com; ℂ **02-31-89-98-19**).

TROUVILLE-SUR-MER ★★★

206km (128 miles) NW of Paris; 47km (29 miles) NE of Caen

Hugging the eastern bank of the Touques River is Deauville's less fashionable—but no less fascinating—neighbor Trouville-sur-Mer. Deauville might have the chic boutiques, but Trouville has the soul of a working fishing port. Cross the Touques at the Pont des Belges (a short 10 to 15 min. walk) and you immediately see the change in atmosphere. The large fish market, Marché aux Poissons, is a hive of activity and teems with small cafes selling the freshest seafood. More restaurants line the quayside, which becomes even livelier every Wednesday and Sunday when the open-air food market sets up its stalls.

Essentials

ARRIVING **Trains** connect Trouville with Gare St-Lazare in Paris (see the "Deauville" section, earlier in this chapter). **Bus Verts du Calvados** (www.busverts.fr) links Trouville, Deauville, and the surrounding region with the rest of Normandy. For bus information, call the **Gare Routière** (✆ 08-10-21-42-14). Trouville and Deauville are also connected by ferry and footbridge. See "Exploring Trouville," below.

VISITOR INFORMATION   The **Office de Tourisme** is at 32 bd. Fernand-Moureaux (www.trouvillesurmer.org; ✆ 02-31-14-60-70).

[FastFACTS] TROUVILLE-SUR-MER

ATMs/Banks   Banks are along bd. Fernand Moureaux, rue Victor Hugo and Pl. Foch.

Mail & Postage   **La Poste,** 25 rue des Bains (✆ **36-31**).

Pharmacies   **Pharmacie Centrale du Port,** 138 bd. Fernand Moureaux (✆ **02-31-88-10-59**).

Exploring Trouville

The bustle of Trouville's quayside carries on into the narrow alleyways that wind behind the port. It's a pleasure to get lost here among the many restaurants and little shops that somehow squeeze into the haphazard collection of lanes. Eventually you'll come to the grand Victorian villas along **Les Planches,** the first seaside boardwalk on the Normandy coast, which dates back to 1867. In those days, artists and writers including Gustave Flaubert, Marguerite Duras, Claude Monet, and Eugène Boudin flocked to Trouville's beach, **Plage de Trouville,** captivated by the light and fresh air. Nowadays it's a firm favorite with families, with a giant children's play area, donkey rides, tennis courts, and the **Complexe Nautique** (✆ **02-31-14-48-10**), an indoor freshwater pool that gets very crowded in summer. The heated outdoor pool is open July and August. Depending on the season, bathers pay 3.30€ to 7.90€ per person. Hours July to August are daily 10am to 6:45pm; other times vary according to the French school holiday schedule.

If you want to cross over to Deauville, you can take the little foot ferry—Le Bac de Trouville Deauville—that trundles back and forth at high tide (daily Mar–Sept; weekends and holidays only Oct–Feb; 1.20€) or the pedestrian walkway (same charge). Or just walk south to the permanent bridge, the Pont des Belges, which spans the Touques. It's only a 10-to-15-min. walk between Deauville and Trouville. On the Trouville quayside, you can rent bikes of all shapes and sizes by the hour at **Les Trouvilllaises** (www.lestrouvillaises.com; © **02-31-98-54-11**).

Where to Stay

Les Cures Marines Trouville Hotel Thalasso & Spa ★★ Trouville's first five-star hotel occupies a palatial wing of the very grand belle époque casino built in 1912 in a prime seafront location. Its minimalist rooms and suites are cool and calming, many with views of the sea and some with terraces. The original thermal baths were replaced with a state-of-the-art thalassotherapy spa with two indoor seawater pools. Seafood is the star at the elegant 1912 restaurant, and the warm ambience of the Eugène bar is irresistible.

bd. de la Cahotte. www.lescuresmarines.com. © **02-31-14-26-00.** 103 units. 176€–576€ double; 378€–824€ suite. Closed Jan. Parking 20€. **Amenities:** Restaurant; bar; spa; exercise room; babysitting; free Wi-Fi.

Hotel Flaubert ★ Step out of this 1930s Norman-style three-star hotel and you're right on the beach. The friendly Flaubert is old-fashioned seaside charm at its best, with traditionally furnished rooms, some with exposed ceiling beams and New England-style wood paneling. Many of the rooms have balconies overlooking the beach, and it's worth the extra few euros to get a sea view. If you're a light sleeper, you might not want a room facing the street as it can get noisy in high season.

Rue Gustave Flaubert. www.flaubert.fr © **02-31-88-37-23.** 31 units. 129€–209€ double; 199€–299€ suite. Closed mid-Nov to mid-Feb. Parking 12€. **Amenities:** Bar; free Wi-Fi.

Where to Eat

Trouville's 60-odd restaurants are well served by the constant supply of seafood that comes into the port. It doesn't have the fine-dining scene of Deauville—nor, for the most part, its high prices. That doesn't mean it's particularly cheap, but you can find a delicious lunch in one of the many quayside bistros and cafes. A visit to the **Marché aux Poissons** is a must: browse its stalls and take your pick of whatever seafood is on offer—from oysters and tiny shrimps to whelks and scallops. Then get the stallholder to cook it for you. Grab a glass of chilled muscadet and perch on one of the high tables surrounding the market. One of the best stalls is **Poissonnerie Pillet-Saiter** (www.poissonnerie-pilletsaiter.fr; © **02-31-88-02-10**).

La Régence ★★ FRENCH   Don't let the wonderfully ornate Napoleon III interior distract you from one of Trouville's most elegant dining experiences. Seafood, not surprisingly, is the star—the lobster tanks give a clue. Highlights include the *pot au feu de la mer*, which puts the together the most succulent and freshest fish to have come from the market, as well as the lobster gratin with a saffron sauce.

132 bd. Fernand Moureaux. www.restaurant-laregence.fr ✆ **02-31-88-10-71.** Fixed-price menu 26€–56€. Daily noon–2pm and 7–10pm.

Les Mouettes ★ SEAFOOD/NORMAN   The writer Marguerite Duras counted Les Mouettes among her favorite Trouville restaurants. Set just behind the quayside, this former fishermen's hangout serves good-quality seafood and meat dishes. Specialties include *grand aïoli*— poached cod, mussels, and vegetables served with garlicky mayonnaise—as well as the full range of fantastically fresh seafood and shellfish.

11 rue des Bains. www.restaurants-trouville.com ✆ **02-31-98-06-97.** Main course 8.10€–46.60€; fixed-price menu 14.80€–30.80€. Daily 11:45am–2:45pm and 6:45–10pm.

Trouville Nightlife

Trouville's casino, **Casino Barrière de Trouville,** pl. du Maréchal-Foch (www.casinosbarriere.com; ✆ **02-31-87-75-00**), is smaller and less stuffy than Deauville's, and features two restaurants and a bar. Entrance to the slot machines is free. Entrance to the more formal area—with roulette, blackjack, and craps—costs 14€ per person. You must present a passport or ID card to gain admission and be 18 or over. The formal area is open Sunday through Friday 9:30pm to 3am and Saturday to 4am. Though the casino does not have a formal dress code as such, but you should dress smartly.

CAEN ★

238km (148 miles) NW of Paris; 119km (74 miles) SE of Cherbourg

Situated on the banks of the Orne, the port of Caen suffered great damage in the 1944 invasion of Normandy. Mercifully, though, the twin abbeys founded by William the Conqueror and his wife, Mathilda, were spared. Today much of Caen is both cosmopolitan and commercial, with a vibrant, welcoming vibe. The capital of Lower Normandy, it's home to a student population of 30,000 and several great museums; it also serves as a convenient base for exploring the surrounding coast.

Essentials

ARRIVING   From Paris's Gare St-Lazare, between 15 and 18 **trains** a day arrive in Caen (trip time: 2–2.5 hr.). Online fares start at 14€ one-way (www.oui.sncf; ✆ **36-35,** .40€/min.). To **drive** from Paris, travel west along A13 to Caen (drive time: 2.5–3 hr.).

VISITOR INFORMATION   The **Office de Tourisme** is on place St-Pierre in the 16th-century Hôtel d'Escoville (www.caen-tourisme.fr; ✆ **02-31-27-14-14**).

CITY LAYOUT   Downtown Caen stretches from Abbaye aux Dames in the east to Abbaye aux Hommes in the west. The pedestrianized rue St-Pierre bisects the town's main shopping district. The train station is southeast of the city center. The towering ramparts of the hilltop Château de Caen make an ideal spot to get your bearings.

Getting Around

ON FOOT   Caen's city center is small and much of it is pedestrianized. For short stays, it's easiest to explore the town on foot.

BY BICYCLE   Caen has its own bike-sharing scheme, **Twisto Vélo** (www.twist.fr). You can register online or directly at one of Caen's 17 bike stands; access starts at 1.50€ for the first 30 min., and 2€ per hour after that.

BY CAR   It's best to park your wheels and explore the city center on foot. The main parking lots in the center are behind the train station, three just south of the Château and one underground in front of the Château.

BY TAXI   **Taxis Abbeilles,** 54 pl. de la Gare (www.taxis-abbeilles-caen.com; ✆ **02-31-52-17-89**).

BY PUBLIC TRANSPORT   The **Twisto bus and tram network** (www.twisto.fr; ✆ **02-31-15-55-55**) crisscrosses the city. From January 2018 until at least late 2020, buses will replace trams while the tram network is being extended from its two lines to three. Tickets (1.50€) can be purchased from automatic kiosks at each station. A free electric shuttle bus goes through the center from Monday to Saturday 12:30 to 8pm.

> ### BYO Speedo
>
> France's municipal swimming pools require all bathers wear swimming caps. Men have to wear Speedo-style trunks. No baggy shorts allowed. Many pools sell these items on site, but when in doubt, pack your own.

[Fast FACTS] CAEN

ATMs/Banks   The city center has plenty of banks, including five on rue Jean Eudes.

Doctors & Hospitals   **Centre Hospitalier Universitaire de Caen,** av. De la Côte de Nacre (www.chu-caen.fr; ✆ **02-31-06-31-06**).

Mail & Postage   **La Poste,** 2 rue Georges Lebret (✆ **36-31**).

Pharmacies   **Pharmacie du Château,** 27 av. De la Libération (✆ **02-31-93-64-78**).

Exploring Caen

A fun way to visit Caen's major sites, including both Abbayes and the Château, is to follow the self-guided **William the Conqueror Circuit.** Maps can be picked up at the Tourist Office, which is the convenient start of the walking tour. You can download the map from the website and use the flash codes to get a free audio guide of the tour.

Abbaye aux Dames ★ RELIGIOUS SITE   William the Conqueror's wife Mathilda founded this abbey around 1060, which embraces Eglise de la Trinité and its Romanesque towers. Its spires were destroyed in the Hundred Years' War. The 12th-century choir houses the tomb of Queen Mathilda.

Pl. Reine Mathilde. ℰ **02-31-06-98-45.** Free admission. Daily 2–6pm. Free guided 1-hr. tour of choir, transept, and crypt (in French) daily 2:30 and 4pm.

Abbaye aux Hommes ★★ RELIGIOUS SITE   Founded by William the Conqueror in 1066 to ensure a papal pardon for marrying his distant cousin Mathilda, this abbey is next to the Eglise St-Etienne. During the Allied invasion, residents of Caen fled to St-Etienne for protection. Twin Romanesque towers 84m- (276 ft.-) tall dominate the church. A marble slab inside the high altar marks the site of William's tomb. The hand-carved wooden doors and an elaborate wrought-iron staircase are exceptional.

Esplanade Jean-Marie Louvel. ℰ **02-31-30-42-81.** Oct–Mar 4.50€ adults, 3.50€ students; Apr–Sept 7€ adults, 5.50€ students; free for children 17 and under. Obligatory tours (50–90 min.) July–Aug daily 11am, 1:30pm, and 4pm in English; 10:30am, noon, 2pm, 3pm, 4pm, and 5:30pm in French; Apr–June and Sept daily 10:30am, 2pm, and 4pm French only; Oct–Mar Mon–Fri 10:30am and 4pm, Sat–Sun no tours but cloisters may occasionally be open. During French school holidays, tours in French Sun 10:30am, 2pm, and 4pm; call in advance to schedule an English tour Mon–Fri.

Le Château de Caen ★★ CASTLE   This castle complex was built on the ruins of a fortress erected by William the Conqueror in 1060. As soon as the weather warms up, much of the population picnics in the surrounding grounds. Climb to the top of the extensive ramparts for sublime views over Caen. Within the medieval compound are two museums, as well contemporary sculptures. The **Musée de Normandie** (www.musee-de-normandie.caen.fr; ℰ **02-31-30-47-60**) displays local archaeological finds, along with a collection of regional sculpture, paintings, and ceramics. Admission is 3.50€ to 5.50€ depending on the exhibitions (free for visitors 25 and under), and it's open Monday to Friday 9:30am to 12:30pm and 2 to 6pm, Saturday 11am to 6pm (closed Nov–May Tues). Also within the walls is the **Musée des Beaux-Arts** (www.mba.caen.fr; ℰ **02-31-30-47-70**), a collection of Old Masters including Veronese, Tintoretto, and Rubens. Admission is free excluding temporary shows, which cost 3.50€ (free for visitors 25 and under). It's open June to October Monday to Friday 9:30am to 12:30pm and 2 to 6pm and Saturday and Sunday 11am–6pm (closed Nov–May Mon–Tues).

Esplanade de la Paix, rue de Geôle, av. De la Libération. musee-de-normandie. caen.fr.

Le Mémorial de Caen (Caen Memorial) ★★★ MONUMENT/MEMORIAL

This is not a museum to be rushed through, as it explores history from 1918 to the present day in engrossing and thought-provoking exhibits. It puts the 20th century in context by starting with the end of the First World War, leading to the horrors of the Second World War and beyond to the Cold War and the Berlin Wall. Civilian stories are told in heartbreaking detail, along with tales of courage and ingenuity of Allied soldiers. Not surprisingly, a large exhibition is dedicated to the D-Day landings, as well as the reopening of the headquarters used by German General Richter during the war. The museum's café is reasonably priced and a good spot to relax in between exhibitions.

Esplanade Général Eisenhower. www.memorial-caen.fr. © **02-31-06-06-45.** Admission 19.80€ adults, 17.50€ students and children 10–18; free to World War II veterans and children 9 and under. Feb–Mar 9am–6pm; Apr–Sept 9am–7pm; Oct–Dec 9:30am–6pm (closed Mon in Nov–Dec). Closed Jan.

Where to Stay

Best Western Hotel le Dauphin ★

You can't beat the location of this four-star hotel—it's just a few steps from the Château as well as Caen's pedestrianized center. It's made up of three separate buildings, one of which was built on the site of a 15th-century priory. It's a bit of a hodge podge, with some rooms featuring more contemporary furnishings while others have traditional 19th-century-style decor tucked into alcoves. The spa is a welcome place to relax, especially under the pulsating jets of the hydrotherapy pools.

29 rue Gémare. www.le-dauphin-normandie.com. © **02-31-86-22-26.** 37 units. 130€–230€ double. Parking free but limited. **Amenities:** Restaurant; bar; room service; spa; free Wi-Fi.

Le Clos St-Martin ★★

This stylish and cozy *chambres d'hôtes*, or bed-and-breakfast, has a mere four rooms set in a townhouse dating from the 16th and 17th centuries, so it's worth booking well ahead. Its three suites and one double room are romantically furnished with family antiques and oriental rugs, and three have atmospheric exposed ceiling beams. Breakfast is just as romantic, served in the warm dining room at individual candlelit tables.

18 bis pl. Saint Martin. www.leclosaintmartin.com. © **07-81-39-23-67.** 4 units. 105€–155€ double or suites, including breakfast. Public parking nearby. **Amenities:** Free Wi-Fi.

A Proustian Remembrance of "Balbec"

If you read Marcel Proust's "Remembrance of Things Past," you'll discover that the resort of "Balbec" was really Cabourg, 24km (15 miles) northeast of Caen. Guests can check into the **Grand Hôtel,** Les Jardins du Casino, promenade Marcel Proust, 14390 Cabourg (www.grand-hotel-cabourg.com; ℂ **02-31-91-01-79;** doubles from 155€–470€), a hold-over from the opulent days when it was first built in 1855. What used to be Marcel Proust's favorite room has been restored from a description in his novel. Film buffs will also recognize the Grand Hotel's dining room from the 2011 French hit comedy-drama "The Untouchables," with its majestic floor-length windows overlooking the sea.

The town of Cabourg (www.cabourg.net) is just as charming, its Victorian streets fanning out from the grand circle where the hotel stands. Beneath the hotel is the indoor municipal swimming pool, where locals flock when it's too cold to take to the huge stretch of sands in front of Promenade Marcel Proust. Every June, the beach becomes the setting for the Romantic Film Festival, when a giant screen shows dozens of romance-themed films over 5 days. The large covered market is worth a visit, too, on Wednesdays, Fridays, and weekends (daily in July and August), when farmers bring their fresh Normandy produce.

Where to Eat

A large student population helps make Caen's dining scene one of the most dynamic in Normandy. Sidewalk cafes and restaurants line rue du Vaugueux and the surrounding neighborhood, east of the Château.

A Contre Sens ★★ FRENCH/NORMAN Anthony Caillot's Michelin-starred and Asian-inflected cuisine is among the best in the city, and he gets more creative every year. Take your pick from the à la carte menu, which changes but include mouthwatering dishes such as twice-cooked pigeon or ravioli filled with foie gras and simmered in a boudin noir-flavored broth. His Intuition menu features up to seven courses that Caillot chooses for you. Reservations are highly recommended.

8 rue des Croisiers. www.acontresenscaen.fr. ℂ **02-31-97-44-48.** Main course 32€–36€; fixed-price lunch 26€–56€ or dinner 52€–64€. Wed–Sat noon–1:15pm; Tues–Sat 7:30–9:15pm.

Le Bouchon du Vaugueux ★★ FRENCH The husband-and-wife team that runs this warm little bistro has come up with a winning formula. The food is beautifully prepared with little fuss and a great deal of skill. The seasonal menu changes but could include a velvety soup of pumpkin and octopus, or a whole grilled sea bream with shrimps in a delicate sabayon sauce. Book ahead for a table in this small space.

12 rue Graindorge. www.bouchonduvaugueux.com. ℂ **02-31-44-26-26.** Fixed-price lunch 17€–25€ or dinner 23€–35€. Tues–Sat noon–2pm and 7–10pm.

Shopping

Caen has some excellent boutique-lined shopping streets, including **boulevard du Maréchal-Leclerc, rue St-Pierre,** and **rue de Strasbourg. Antiques** hunters should check out the shops along **rue Ecuyère.** The **market** at place Courtonne on Sunday morning sells secondhand goods.

For foodie souvenirs, **Chocolaterie Charlotte Corday,** 114 rue St-Jean (✆ **02-31-86-33-25**), has an irresistible collection of chocolate and other sweet goodies. Cheese-lovers can taste before they buy at the *bar à fromages* and boutique at **Fromagerie Conquérant,** 27 rue Guillaume le Conquérant (http://fromagerie-conquerant.com; ✆ **02-50-65-47-33**).

Nightlife

Take a walk down rue de Bras, rue St-Pierre, and rue Vaugueux to size up the action. **Au Verre Dit Vin,** quai Vendeuvre (www.auverreditvincaen.fr; ✆ **02-31-91-38-03**), is a cozy wine bar that offers good food along with a piano bar on Thursdays and live music on Fridays and Saturdays. For off-beat international gigs, head to **Le Cargö,** 9 cours Caffarelli, Port de Caen (www.lecargo.fr; ✆ **02-31-86-79-31**).

BAYEUX ★★

267km (166 miles) NW of Paris; 25km (16 miles) NW of Caen

Bayeux's alluring medieval heart was spared bombardment in 1944 and was the first town to be liberated—the day after D-Day, in fact. Its half-timbered houses, stone mansions, cobblestoned streets, and ancient watermills have remained more or less intact, making this immensely pleasant town a joy to explore. It does get busy in the summer—with the double whammy of the nearby D-Day beaches and the extraordinary historical document that is the Bayeux Tapestry—but it retains its agreeable Norman atmosphere and the sense that it exists beyond the tourist crowds.

Essentials

ARRIVING Nine **trains** depart daily from Paris's Gare St-Lazare. The 2.5-hr. trip to Bayeux costs from 18.50€ if booked in advance online (www.oui.sncf or call ✆ **36-35,** .40€/min.). To **drive** to Bayeux from Paris (trip time: 3 hr.), take A13 to Caen and E46 west to Bayeux.

VISITOR INFORMATION The **Office de Tourisme** is at 4 pl. Gauquelin Despallières (www.bayeux-bessin-tourisme.com; ✆ **02-31-51-28-28**).

SPECIAL EVENTS The town goes wild on the first weekend in July during **Fêtes Médiévales** (www.bayeux.fr; ✆ **02-31-92-03-30**); the streets fill with market stalls, medieval dress, and themed treats during two days of medieval revelry. In mid-June, Bayeux is the finishing point for the annual **Tour de Normandie** (www.tourdenormandie.com; ✆ **06-28-33-00-75**), a classic car race that winds through the Normandy countryside in elegant style.

Bayeux

[FastFACTS] BAYEUX

ATMs/Banks   Many banks are along rue Saint-Malo.

Mail & Postage   **La Poste** rue Larcher (© **36-31**).

Pharmacies   **Pharmacie St Martin,** 20 rue St Martin (© **02-31-92-00-22**).

Exploring Bayeux

This compact town is best explored on foot. At its heart in rue du Général de Dais is **Cathédrale Notre-Dame de Bayeux,** a Norman medieval structure consecrated in 1077 in the presence of William the Conqueror. It's open daily 8:30am to 7pm. Entrance is free, although guided visits are available for 5€ at 10am and 2:15pm in July and August.

Musée d'Art et d'Histoire Baron Gérard (MAHB) ★ MUSEUM Five thousand years of art history are on display in this well-designed museum in the ancient bishop's palace, which dates from the 11th to the 18th centuries. About 600 local archaeological finds mingle with 1,000 pieces of lacework and delicate porcelain, as well as more than 600 regional artworks created between the 15th and 20th centuries.

37 rue du Bienvenu. www.bayeuxmusuem.com © **02-31-92-14-21.** Admission 7.50€ adults; 5.50€ students and children; free for children 9 and under. May–Sept daily 9:30am–6:30pm; Feb–Apr and Oct–Dec daily 10am–12:30pm and 2–6pm. Closed Jan 8–31.

Musée de la Tapisserie de Bayeux ★★★ MUSEUM   This extraordinary tapestry—actually an elaborate embroidery on linen—is one of the sights of Bayeux that really shouldn't be missed, even if historians believe it was created in Kent, not France. Measuring 69m (226 ft.) long and 50cm (20 in.) wide, this masterpiece displayed in a 270-degree glass case that curves along a tunnel-like room. Throughout its 58 scenes, you discover the story of the conquest of England by William the Conqueror. The free audio guide is definitely worth following, as it provides fascinating details that you are likely to overlook. The devil is in the detail—in more ways than one—so look out for surprising depictions at the top and bottom of the cloth.

A separate part of the museum focuses on the creation of the Bayeux Tapestry, and its displays and scale models bring the Middle Ages to life. Plans are in the works to display the tapestry in Great Britain on a temporary basis from 2020.

Centre Guillaume le Conquérant, 13 bis rue de Nesmond. www.bayeuxmuseum. com. ℰ **02-31-51-25-50.** Admission 9.50€ adults, 5€ students, free for children 9 and under. Mar–Nov daily 9am–6:30pm (May–Aug until 7pm); Feb and Nov–Dec daily 9:30am–12:30pm and 2–6pm. Closed Jan 8–31.

Detail of the Bayeux Tapestry

Musée Memorial de la Bataille de Normandie ★ MUSEUM The Battle of Normandy (June 6–Aug 29, 1944) is told in compelling detail in this bunker-like building. Displays of beach landings, maps, tanks, and weapons recall the battle, during which Bayeux was among the first towns to be liberated. A 25-min. film shows of news clips from the period. The **Commonwealth Cemetery** across the street contains 4,144 graves of British soldiers who were killed during the battle.

bd. Fabian Ware. ☎ www.bayeuxmuseum.com. **02-31-51-46-90.** Admission 7.50€ adults, 5€ students and children, free for children 9 and under. May–Sept daily 9:30am–6:30pm; Oct–Apr daily 10am–12:30pm and 2–6pm. Closed Jan 8–31.

Where to Stay

Hôtel d'Argouges ★★ You step into a tranquil little world once you go through the hidden stone archway of this 18th-century mansion. Elegant rooms hark back to the 19th century with their antique-style furnishings, wood paneling, gilt mirrors, polished parquet floors, and period fireplaces. The garden is a delight, and a relaxing place for breakfast under the shade of the trees.

21 rue St-Patrice. www.hotel-dargouges.com. ☎ **02-31-92-88-86.** 28 units. 85€–205€ double; 170€–295€ suite. Free parking. **Amenities:** Breakfast room; bar; room service; free Wi-Fi.

Villa Lara ★★★ Five-star luxury meets intimate boutique hotel in Villa Lara, where they've found the right balance between refinement and relaxation. Some of its spacious rooms come with balconies and views of Bayeux's cathedral, but they all have elegant antique-style furnishings with plenty of brocade and velvet. The wood-paneled lounge is a cozy spot, complete with library and fireplace.

6 pl. du Québec. www.hotel-villalara.com. ☎ **02-31-92-00-55.** 28 units. 200€–420€ double; 380€–570€ suite. Free parking. **Amenities:** Breakfast room; gym; free Wi-Fi. Closed Dec–Feb.

Where to Eat

Bayeux has plenty of informal cafes offering quick snacks for visitors touring the D-Day beaches or just popping in to visit the tapestry. There are, however, a couple of special places worth checking out.

Au P'tit Bistrot ★ NORMAN In this cozy bistro by the cathedral, you'll find some unexpected—but delicious—flavors mixed into traditional Norman dishes. Although the menu changes regularly, you might find sea bream tartare with mango jam and coconut mousse, or perhaps pork shoulder slowly braised in cider. It's a small restaurant, so you might want to book ahead.

2 rue du Bienvenu. ☏ **02-31-92-30-08.** Fixed-price menus 16€–35€. Mon–Sat noon–2pm and 7–9:30pm.

Le Volet qui Penche ★★ NORMAN   Pierre-Henri Lemessier keeps his menu short and simple in this rustic bistro that's also a wine shop. It all depends on what Pierre-Henri has picked up at the market that day and could include a pastry pie filled with fish and a reduced white wine sauce, or pork filet mignon with garlic cream and the most decadent mashed potatoes. If you want a knowledgeable introduction to French wines, Pierre-Henri will suggest the best wines for your budget.

3 impasse de l'Islet. www.levoletquipenche.com. ☏ **02-31-21-98-54.** Fixed-price menu 19.50€. Mar–June and Sept–Dec Tues–Sat 10am–8:30pm; July–Aug also Mon; Jan Tues–Fri lunch only; closed Feb.

THE D-DAY BEACHES ★★

Arromanches-les-Bains: 272km (169 miles) NW of Paris, 11km (6.74 miles) NW of Bayeux; Grandcamp-Maisy (near Omaha Beach): 299km (185 miles) NW of Paris, 56km (35 miles) NW of Caen

A visit to the beaches, where the greatest invasion force of all time landed, is a must for anyone visiting Normandy's north coast. The 70th anniversary of the invasion in 2014 was the occasion for new museums, exhibitions, and events to mark this momentous event in modern history.

It was a rainy week in early June 1944 when the greatest armada ever was assembled along the southern coast of England. A full moon and cooperative tides were needed for the cross-Channel invasion. Britain's top meteorologist for the USAAF and RAF—Sir James Stagg—forecast a small window in the inclement weather. Over in France, Normandy's German occupiers lacked such a detailed weather forecast, so many Nazi officers drifted home for the weekend in the belief that no landing could take place soon.

Supreme Allied Commander Dwight D. Eisenhower believed Stagg's reports—and knew that further delays would hinder his element of surprise. With the British invasion commander, Field Marshal Montgomery, at his side, Eisenhower made the ultimate call.

At 9:15pm on June 5, the BBC announced to Normandy's French Resistance that the invasion was imminent by way of coded messages. The underground movement started dynamiting the region's railways to hinder German troop movement.

Before midnight, Allied planes began bombing the Norman coast. By 1:30am on June 6 ("the Longest Day", and what the French call *Jour-J*), members of the 101st Airborne were parachuting to the ground on German-occupied French soil. At 6:30am, the Americans began landing on the beaches, code-named Utah and Omaha. An hour later, British and

The beach at Arromanches, with the remains of Mulberry Harbour in the distance

Canadian forces made beachheads at Juno, Gold, and Sword, swelling the number of Allied troops in Normandy to a massive 135,000. That evening a joint beachhead had been formed and yet more troops, tanks, trucks, and other *matériel* poured into Normandy. The push to Paris—and Berlin—had begun.

Essentials

ARRIVING   A **car** is practically essential to explore the D-Day Beaches at leisure. Each monument, museum, and beach has plenty of parking.

   Bus Verts (www.busverts.fr; ✆ 08-10-21-42-14) runs buses from Bayeux to Arromanches (no. 74) and from Bayeux to Omaha Beach and the American Cemetery (no. 70) every few hours for 2.50€ per trip.

   Several group tours also cover the D-Day Beaches. From Bayeux, **Normandy Tours,** Hotel de la Gare (www.normandy-landing-tours.com; ✆ 02-31-92-10-70), runs a 4-to-5-hr. tour (in English) to Arromanches, Omaha Beach, the American Military Cemetery, and Pointe du Hoc for 67€ adults and 60€ students and seniors from April to October.

VISITOR INFORMATION   The **Office de Tourisme,** 2 rue Maréchal-Joffre, Arromanches-les-Bains (www.bayeux-bessin-tourisme.com; ✆ 02-31-22-36-45), is open daily year-round, but from January to February and November to December it's open only on Saturday and Sunday.

Reliving the Longest Day

Few places in the world have a more concentrated—or more moving—selection of sights than Normandy's D-Day Beaches. More than 30 memorials, cemeteries, and museums, which range from coastal batteries to museums dedicated to underwater military finds, are spread out along this 50km (31-mile) stretch of coast. The most spellbinding site for all nationalities is the **Normandy American Visitor Center ★★★**, behind Omaha beach at Colleville-sur-Mer (www.abmc.gov; ✆ **02-31-51-62-00**). The graves of 10,000 Allies who liberated mainland France lie within 70 hectares (173 acres) of manicured grounds above the cliffs. The visitor center retells the dramatic story of the American landings—and those of British, Canadian, Polish, Free French, and other allies—on the morning of June 6, 1944. Most dramatic are the personal tales, often told via video and interactive displays. Make certain you leave enough time for a good look at the exhibitions—they really are captivating. Admission is free. The cemetery is open daily 9am to 6pm from April 14 to September 15, and until 5pm the rest of the year. Public access to Omaha Beach itself is no longer available from the memorial, but other public paths are nearby.

The **Overlord Museum,** Colleville-sur-Mer (www.overlord museum.com; ✆ **02-31-22-00-55**), opened in summer 2013, half a mile uphill from the Normandy American Visitor Center. More than 10,000 pieces of *matériel* and 35 military vehicles are showcased in D-Day dioramas around a great hall. Admission is 7.80€ adults and 5.70€ students and children; free for children under 10. Open daily 10am to 5:30pm February to March, November and December; 10am to 6:30pm April, May, and Sept; 9:30am to 7pm June to Aug; closed January to February 11.

Farther west along the coast, you'll see the jagged lime cliffs of the **Pointe du Hoc.** A cross honors a group of American Rangers who scaled the cliffs using hooks to get at the gun emplacements. The pockmarked landscape has a lunar look, with giant craters showing where the bombs fell. Farther along the Cotentin Peninsula is **Utah Beach,** where the 4th U.S. Infantry Division landed at 6:30am. A U.S. monument commemorates their heroism.

Eastward along the coast in the British invasion sector is the seaside resort of **Arromanches-les-Bains.** A deep-water port was deemed essential to Allied success, so in June 1944, two mammoth prefabricated ports known as Mulberry Harbours were towed across the Channel. The one that landed in Arromanches was nicknamed Port Winston. "Victory could not have been achieved without it," Eisenhower later said. Indeed, in 10 months this "temporary" artificial harbor delivered 2.5 million men and countless vehicles into northern France. The wreckage is still visible just off the beach. Arromanches's **Plage Musée du Débarquement,** pl. du 6-Juin (www.musee-arromanches.fr; ✆ **02-31-22-34-31**), illuminates the scale of the D-Day landings through maps, models, a film, photos, and a diorama of the landing beaches. Admission is 8€ adults and 5.90€ students and children. Open May to August daily 9am to 7pm (until 6pm in Sept); February, November, and December 10am to 12:30pm and 1:30 to 5pm; March and October 9:30am to 12:30pm and 1:30 to 5:30pm; April 9am to 12:30pm and 1:30 to 6pm (closed Jan).

Eastward again through the British and Canadian invasion sectors is **Musée Gold Beach,** 2 pl. Amiral Byrd, Ver-sur-Mer (www.goldbeach musee.fr; ✆ **02-31-22-58-58**). The museum focuses on the heroism of Britain's RAF and Royal Navy and the meticulous Allied coordination that went into the D-Day landings. Admission is 4.50€ adults and 2.50€ students and children. From April to October, hours are daily 10:30am to 5:30pm (closed Tues Apr–June and Sept–Oct); open November to March only by appointment.

Just eastward along the coast in Courseulles-sur-Mer is the **Centre Juno Beach ★★**, voie des Français Libres (www.junobeach.org; ✆ **02-31-37-32-17**). This gem of a museum details Canada's entire war effort, with particular focus on the Battle of the Atlantic and the march through Germany. Outside the museum is a stark memorial to the Canadian dead of D-Day, their names inscribed simply on blue towers. Walk towards the beach and pause in front of the sculpture with the words to Paul Verlaine's poem "Chanson d'Automne": this was the code the BBC used to alert the French Resistance on June 5. Admission is 7€ adults and 5.50€ students and children, with reduced rates for visits only to the park or temporary exhibits. From April to September, hours are daily 9:30am to 7pm (Mar, Oct 10am–6pm; Feb, Nov, and Dec 10am–5pm; closed Jan and also June 5–6 2019 during the commemorations for the 75th anniversary of D-Day).

Normandy American Visitor Center and Cemetery, Omaha Beach

Where to Stay & Eat near the D-Day Beaches

Ferme de la Rançonnière ★★ Everything about this baronial manor house is awe inspiring, but the immensely warm welcome is anything but intimidating. Four stone mansions dating from the 13th to the 15th centuries and clustering around a large courtyard combine to form a wonderfully romantic, charming country hotel only a few miles south of the coast near Asnelles. The restaurant, with its exposed stone walls and beamed ceiling, is just as charming. Traditional Norman cuisine meets the sea, with dishes including slow-cooked pigs' cheeks and a duo of sea bass and scallops with cèpes. Fixed-price menus run between 32€ and 44€, with lunch at 16€. The restaurant is open to the public, and guests have the option of half board.

Route de Creully, Crépon. www.ranconniere.fr. ✆ **02-31-22-21-73.** 35 units. 60€–150€ double; 140€–265€ suite. Free parking. **Amenities:** Restaurant; bar; breakfast room; tennis; free Wi-Fi.

Hôtel de la Marine ★ This friendly three-star hotel is right on Gold Beach, where the British landed on D-Day. Individually decorated bedrooms have a simple, breezy style, but some have balconies and fabulous sea views. The restaurant, which also has a sea-facing terrace, focuses on fresh seafood—including big platters of *fruits de mer*—as well as hearty meat dishes. Main courses from 15€, with menus going from 25€ to 38€.

1 quai du Canada, Arromanches-les-Bains. www.hotel-de-la-marine.fr. ✆ **02-31-22-34-19.** 33 units. 89€–271€ double. Free parking. Closed Nov 12–Feb 10. **Amenities:** Restaurant; bar; free Wi-Fi.

La Marée ★ NORMAN This cozy waterfront restaurant has a superb selection of local shellfish including oysters, whelks and langoustines as well as beautifully cooked fish dishes including *sole meunière*. Meat-eaters can enjoy tender beef cheeks cooked slowly in a *daube*. When it's warm, you can eat by the water's edge.

5 quai Henri Chéron, Grandcamp Maisy. www.restolamaree.com. ✆ **02-31-21-41-00.** Fixed-price menus 17€–27€. Daily 12:30–2:30pm and 7–9:30pm; closed Sun evenings out of season. Closed Jan 1–Feb 3.

Mercure Omaha Beach ★ The attractive village of Port-en-Bessin and its rocky beach are only a 15-min. walk from this modern spa and golf hotel. With an outdoor pool, spa, and golf course, it's a convenient place to base yourself while touring the D-Day beaches. Streamlined rooms have business-like modern decor, but they're spacious and many have balconies. The hotel's **restaurant** has an impressive range of seafood and meat dishes, including roast lobster for two and a rib of Normandy beef. Main courses start at 14.50€.

Chemin du Colombier, Port-en-Bessin. www.hotel-omaha-beach.com. ✆ **02-31-22-44-44.** 74 units. 89€–215€ double. Free parking. **Amenities:** Restaurant; bar; breakfast room; gym; outdoor pool; spa; free Wi-Fi.

MONT-ST-MICHEL ★★★

324km (201 miles) W of Paris; 129km (80 miles) SW of Caen; 48km (30 miles) E of St-Malo

A UNESCO World Heritage Site, Mont-St-Michel is one of the most alluring spots on France's northern coast. The fortified island seems to float on a shifting bed of sand and sea. Once a bastion marking the border between Normandy and Brittany, then a place of monastic retreat, this Disney-like castle now attracts 3 million visitors every year. In high summer it's exceptionally busy but enthralling nevertheless.

Essentials

ARRIVING   The most efficient way to reach Mont-St-Michel is to **drive.** From Caen, follow A84 southwest towards Avranches, eventually taking the D43 and following signs to its end at Mont-St-Michel. Total driving time from Paris is about 3.5 hr.

There are no direct **trains** between Paris and Mont-St-Michel. One option is to take a local TER train from Paris's Gare St-Lazare to Caen, then another local TER train to Pontorson, where a 2.80€ shuttle bus ferries passengers directly to the visitor center. Another is to take a TGV (fast train) from Paris Montparnasse to Rennes in Brittany, from where a coach takes you to Mont-St-Michel for 15€ each way. For train information, visit www.oui.sncf or call ☏ **36-35** (.40€/min.).

Mont-St-Michel

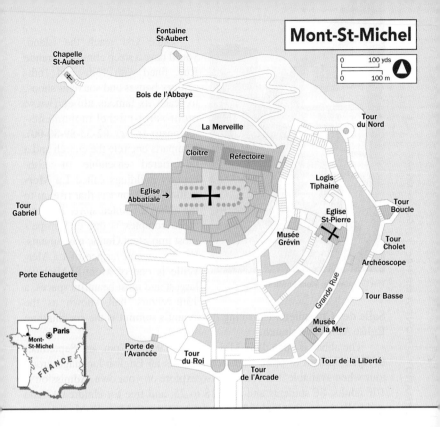

Mont-St-Michel

Fontaine
St-Aubert

Chapelle
St-Aubert

Bois de l'Abbaye

La Merveille

Tour
du Nord

Cloître   Réfectoire

Logis
Tiphaine

Eglise
Abbatiale

Tour
Gabriel

Tour
Boucle

Eglise
St-Pierre

Tour
Cholet

Musée
Grévin

Archéoscope

Porte Echaugette

Grande Rue

Tour Basse

Paris

Mont-
St-Michel

FRANCE

Porte de
l'Avancée

Tour
du Roi

Musée
de la Mer

Tour de la Liberté

Tour
de l'Arcade

VISITOR INFORMATION   The **Tourist Information Center** is Lieu-dit le Bas Pays, Beauvoir (www.bienvenuemontsaintmichel.com; ☎ **02-14-13-20-15**).

Exploring Mont-St-Michel

France's biggest tourist attraction outside of Paris has been undergoing major changes over the past few years. Before 2012, the causeway linking the island with the mainland was rammed with parked cars, and the bay was in danger of silting up. To restore Mont-St-Michel to its island status, the authorities built a **new approach** and banished cars to a parking lot by a visitor center. Free shuttle buses take visitors to the island 2.5km (1.5 miles) away. Parking costs 12€ for 24 hr., but is free if you stay less than 30 min.

Otherwise it's a 50-min. hike to the island across the shifting sands. Those with their own bike can pedal over. A ride across in a horse-drawn carriage costs 5.30€ per person. An additional **Office de Tourisme** is on the island itself, to the left of the gates (www.ot-montsaintmichel.com; ☎ **02-33-60-14-30**). Both tourist centers are open daily year-round.

The Grande Rue, Mont-St-Michel

Once you reach the island, you'll have a steep climb up Grande Rue, lined with 15th- and 16th-century houses and souvenir shops, to reach its famous **abbey** (www.mont-saint-michel.monuments-nationaux.fr; ✆ **02-33-89-80-00**). Ramparts encircle the church and a three-tiered ensemble of 13th-century buildings called **La Merveille** (The Wonder) that rise up to the abbey's pointed spire. This terraced complex is one of Europe's most important Gothic monuments. On the second terrace of La Merveille is one of Mont-St-Michel's largest and most beautiful spaces, a 13th-century hall known as the **Salle des Chevaliers.** Crowning the mount's summit is the spellbinding **Eglise Abbatiale** church.

The abbey is open daily May to August 9am to 7pm, and September to April 9:30am to 6pm. Entrance includes an English-language group tour when available, but you can also explore on your own. Admission is 10€ adults, 8€ students and ages 18 to 25, and free for children 17 and under. Be aware that high tides can delay access to Mont-St-Michel.

Most visitors are content to wander around the medieval ramparts. Those seeking a little more sightseeing may head to the **Musée de la Mer,** Grande Rue (✆ **02-33-89-02-02**), which showcases marine crafts throughout history and the ecology of the local tidal flats. Another museum worth visiting is the **Logis Tiphaine,** Grande Rue (✆ **02-33-89-02-02**), a 15th-century home originally under the control of the Duguesclin family. Both museums are open daily from 9:30am to 5pm (closed Wed and Thurs in Feb), and cost 9€ for adults, free for children 18 and under. You can buy a pass for 18€ that covers the cost of three museums.

For a different perspective of Mont-St-Michel, join one of the guided walks from the mainland to the island, tracing the original pilgrim route. **Chemins de la Baie** (www.cheminsdelabaie.com; ✆ **02-33-89-80-88**) takes groups on various barefoot walks across the sands. A one-way crossing costs 7.30€ and lasts 1 hr., 45 mins.; a crossing that includes a return by bus costs 12.60€ and is a 4-hr. round trip.

Where to Stay & Eat

If you plan to stay overnight on the island, be prepared to pay a premium. It is, however, an unforgettable experience, as you can explore the island in the evening in peace after the crowds have left. But **travel light:** the hotels are a long, mostly uphill walk from where the shuttle bus drops you off, and the cobblestoned streets don't make it easy to transport your luggage. And don't expect to have a late supper; most restaurants close soon after the day-trippers leave, apart from hotel restaurants. But there are advantages to staying overnight—particularly in the summer, when evening concerts are staged in the abbey and sound-and-light shows illuminate the island.

Auberge Saint-Pierre ★   You'll be sleeping in an official historic monument in this 15th-century half-timbered inn. While the rooms are on the small side, their exposed ceiling beams and half-timbered walls make them immensely comfortable and cozy. Rooms are divided between the Chapeau Blanc Logis, a secluded former fisherman's cottage a few minutes' (uphill) walk from the hotel, and the Logis, which has small terraces with gorgeous views. The restaurant is an impossibly romantic place, with an enormous fireplace and a little courtyard garden. Fixed-price menus cost from 18€ to 70€, which include lobster from neighboring Brittany, and the famously fluffy Mont-St-Michel omelet.

Grande Rue. www.auberge-saint-pierre.fr. ℂ **02-33-60-14-03.** 23 units. 222€–252€ double; 269€–304€ suite. **Amenities:** Restaurant; bar; free Wi-Fi.

Crêperie La Sirène ★ NORMAN   Set in a 15th-century building, this cheerful crêperie is a good choice for lunch. It specializes in savory buckwheat crepes known as galettes, which come stuffed with everything from mushrooms, eggs, and ham to gooey goat's cheese and potatoes. A sweet crepe makes a fine dessert, accompanied by Normandy cider.

Grande Rue. ℂ **02-33-60-08-60.** Main course 4.20€–8.90€. Daily 9am–10:30pm; closed Jan.

BRITTANY

By Lily Heise

8

"**L**ittle Britain," as it was called by the 4th- and 5th-century Celts who came to settle this northwestern peninsula, always seems apart from the rest of France. While this was once politically true (the region resisted conquer and incorporation into Charlemagne's Frankish empire, remaining an independent duchy until 1532), even today's Bretons hold fast to their traditions, and their independent spirit is undeniable. The original Breton language, with its roots in Welsh and Cornish, though once suppressed, has experienced a revival. The *Gwenn-ha-du*—the black-and-white Breton flag—still flies proudly in every town. This unique cultural identity, along with its wild coast, succulent seafood, rustic hamlets, and medieval fortresses make it one of the most authentic areas of France.

Brittany is home to some of the nicest towns in the country. You can't help but be charmed strolling the streets of the former fortress town of St-Malo or medieval Dinan. Quimper is the bastion of Breton culture and Nantes is becoming a cool outpost for Parisians.

The region is a perfect destination for nature or beach lovers with its promontories, coves, and traffic-free islands dotting the rocky coastline, some 1,207km (748 miles) long. The posh resort of Dinard satisfies the more glamorous sunbathers.

The British, just a channel-hop away, think of Brittany as a resort region. But the French typically go south to chase their sun. Therefore, you'll never run into huge tourist masses, yet popular beaches can get crowded in summer.

If you're coming from Mont-St-Michel, use St-Malo, Dinan, or Dinard as a base to explore northern Brittany. Visitors from the eastern Loire Valley can reach the coastline of southern Brittany in under 3 hr.

ST-MALO ★★★

414km (257 miles) W of Paris; 69km (43 miles) N of Rennes; 13km (8 miles) E of Dinard

Despite past lives as a fortress and the site of a monastery, St-Malo is best known for the *corsaires* who used it as a base during the 17th and 18th centuries. During wartime, a decree from the French king sanctioned the

FACING PAGE: **Port of Concarneau, Brittany**

seafaring mercenaries to intercept British ships and requisition their cargo. During peacetime, they acted as intrepid merchant marines, returning from Asia and the Americas with gold, coffee, and spices. Indeed, the sea is in the hearts of all *Malouins*, as natives of St-Malo are called—especially during the city's famous transatlantic sailing race, the *Route du Rhum*, which is held every four years and finishes in Guadeloupe.

Walking the ramparts and cobblestone streets, it's hard to imagine that 80 percent of St-Malo was destroyed in World War II. What you see today is thanks to a meticulous, decades-long restoration.

St-Malo encompasses the communities of St. Servan and Paramé, but most tourists head for the walled city, or *Intra-muros*. In summer, the Grande Plage du Sillon towards Paramé is dotted with sun-seekers; year-round it's sought after for its deluxe seawater spa. St. Servan's marina is adjacent to a large terminal where ferries depart for and arrive from the Channel Islands and England.

Essentials

ARRIVING   From Paris's Gare Montparnasse, about 14 TGV **trains** per day make the journey; a one-way ticket ranges from 44€ to 107€. Three of these trains are nonstop, making the journey in 2.25 to 2.75 hr.; transferring at Rennes takes 2.5 to 3 hr. For information, visit www.oui.sncf or call ☎ **36-35** (.40€/min.). If you're **driving** from Paris, take A13 west to Caen and continue southwest along N175 to the town of Miniac Morvan. From there, travel north on N137 directly to St-Malo. Driving time is 4 hr. from Paris.

VISITOR INFORMATION   The **Office de Tourisme** is on esplanade St-Vincent (www.saint-malo-tourisme.com; ☎ **08-25-13-52-00**).

SPECIAL EVENTS   The **Festival de la Musique Sacrée,** from mid-July to mid-August, stages evening concerts twice a week in the cathedral. The famous transatlantic yacht race, the **Route du Rhum** (www.routedurhum.com), departs from St-Malo every 4 years in November and 2018 marked its 40th birthday.

Getting Around

ON FOOT   With its layout and tiny one-way streets, its best to tour the city on foot.

BY BICYCLE   Many of the city's streets have bike lanes. You can rent bikes in St-Malo, Dinard, and Dinan and even have them delivered to your hotel from **Vélo Emeraulde** (www.velo-corsaire.fr; ☎ **06-58-02-24-61**). Rentals are 15€ daily for adults and 10€ for children (weekend/weeklong rates available).

BY CAR   Several parking lots are along Quai Saint-Vincent, but they fill up quickly in summer months. You can rent a car at the TGV train station

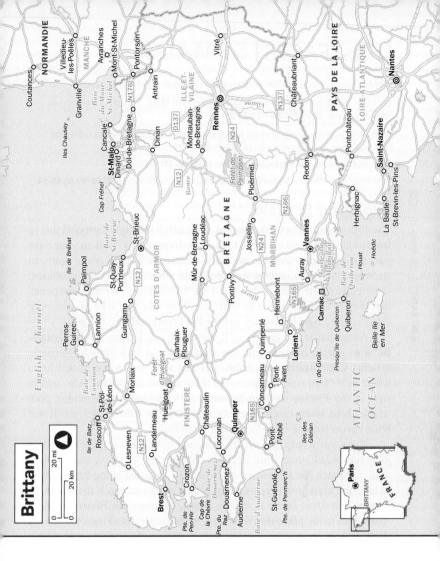

from **Europcar** (www.europcar.fr; ℰ **02-99-56-75-17**) or **Avis** (www.avis.fr; ℰ **02-99-40-18-54**).

BY TAXI Taxis are usually in front of the station or call **Saint Malo Taxi** (www.taxi-st-malo.com; ℰ **02-23-18-18-18**).

BY PUBLIC TRANSPORT The local bus service does not go into the old city but you can get a bus (line C1 or C2) from the station to the city walls; the network is run by **KSMA** (www.ksma.fr; ℰ **02-99-40-19-22**). Buy your one-way tickets (1.35€) directly from the bus driver.

[Fast FACTS] ST-MALO

ATMs/Banks   Several ATMs are around the cathedral or along rue Broussais.

Doctors & Hospitals   **Centre Hopitalier de Saint Malo,** 1 rue de la Marne (www.cht-ranceemeraude.fr; ✆ **02-99-21-21-21**).

Internet Access   Wi-Fi is readily available at cafes throughout town, including the quirky **Le Java,** 3 rue Sainte Barbe (✆ **02-99-56-41-90**).

Mail & Postage   **La Poste,** 6 pl. du Prieuré (✆ **36-31**).

Pharmacies   **Pharmacie des Cotes d'Emeraude,** 3 rue Broussais (✆ **02-99-40-85-54**).

Exploring St-Malo

The 15th-century **Porte St-Vincent**, with a Belle Epoque carrousel just in front of it, is the main entrance to St-Malo Intra-muros. Walk to your right past the restaurant terraces on place Chateaubriand—a portal leads to steps up to the **ramparts ★★★**. Built and rebuilt over several centuries, some parts of these walls date from the 14th century. Weather cooperating, they're an ideal place to start a walking tour and take in sweeping views of the English Channel and the **Fort National** (see below).

About halfway round, you'll see an islet called the **Ile du Grand-Bé ★★**; during low tide you can walk to it and visit French Romantic novelist **Chateaubriand's tomb.** His last wish was to be buried here, where he'd "hear only the sounds of the wind and the ocean." Also within sight is the **Piscine de Bon-Secours,** a 1930s outdoor swimming pool whose three walls catch receding seawater. On warm days you'll see brave divers leaping from its cement platform.

If it's too windy, get off the ramparts by descending the ramp that joins rue de la Crosse. Turn left onto rue de la Pie Qui Boit and follow it until you reach rue Broussais. Alternatively, continue along the ramparts (where the view just keeps getting better) until you reach the **Porte de Dinan.** The street below it, rue de Dinan, becomes rue Broussais. Both routes lead to the **place de Pilori** back in the center. Head back toward the Porte St-Vincent for the greatest concentration of shopping and dining options.

Cathédrale St-Vincent ★★★ CATHEDRAL   Transformation of a monastic church into this cathedral began in 1146. Over the centuries, various architects added Romanesque, Gothic, and Neoclassical elements—only to have the steeple knocked off and the transept destroyed during fierce fighting in 1944. It took nearly 30 years to restore the structure and its magnificent stained glass. A floor mosaic commemorates the 1535 blessing of St-Malo native Jacques Cartier before he set off to discover Canada. Cartier's tomb is here, along with that of René Duguay-Trouin, a legendary privateer so successful he was made a commander in the French navy.

12 rue St-Benoît. ✆ **02-99-40-82-31.** Free admission. Daily 10am–6pm.

Fort National, St-Malo

Fort National ★ HISTORIC SITE   Designed by famed military architect Sébastien de Vauban, construction of this fortress began in 1689. You can access it by walking 300m (984 ft.) over sand at low tide (heed the tidal information, or you may find yourself wading back). Thirty-five-minute guided tours take you into the dungeon and explain the fort's history; it's equally rewarding to wander on your own and enjoy the views of the bay.

Grande Plage de Sillon. www.fortnational.com. ✆ **06-72-46-66-26.** Tours: 5€ adults; 3€ ages 6–16; free for children 5 and under. Jun–Sept; hours depend on the tide. Call in advance or look to the fort itself (when the French flag is flying, it's open to visitors).

Musée d'Histoire de St-Malo ★★ MUSEUM   This museum is perfect for understanding the history and commercial importance of St-Malo. The buildings themselves, the keep and gatehouse of the Château de St-Malo, add to the experience. Exhibits use artifacts, ship models, and imagery to tell the stories of the city's most famous citizens—Chateaubriand, Jacques Cartier, and the privateers Duguay-Trouin and Surcouf. A section is reserved for photos of the extensive damage the city incurred during World War II.

Porte St-Vincent. ✆ **02-99-40-71-57.** Admission 6€ adults; 3€ ages 8–18; free for children 7 and under. Apr–Sep daily 10am–12:30pm and 2–6pm; Oct–Mar Tues–Sun 10am–noon and 2–6pm.

Beaches

Along the coast, stretches of sand intersperse with rugged outcroppings that suggest fortresses protect Brittany from Atlantic storms. Both the **Grande Plage du Sillon** and the **Plage de Bon Secours,** west of the city walls, are very popular. Situated between the two, the **Plage de l'Eventail** is small and especially rocky. Beach amenities are scarce, but Sillon does have lifeguards on duty in the summertime.

Where to Stay

While some hotels inside the city walls are up to snuff, others are a bit run down. An alternative is to stay along the Plage du Sillon and walk the 10 minutes into the historic center.

Hotel Alba ★   Facing the shimmering sea, this is the perfect beach-based hotel in St-Malo. You almost have the impression of staying on a boat, due to its proximity to the water; the smallish rooms gain in size thanks to their expansive views. Each is tastefully decorated in earthy tones, with modern, comfortable furnishings. The best rooms feature balconies and you can also choose from several family rooms. If you're not strolling on the beach at sunset, enjoy a drink on its terrace or its scenic bar.

17 rue des Dunes. www.hotelalba.com. ✆ **02-99-40-37-18.** 22 units. 99€–171€ double; 200€ family room. Free parking. **Amenities:** Bar; room service; free Wi-Fi.

Hôtel France et Chateaubriand ★★   To experience the 19th-century heyday of the Emerald coast, there's no better place than at the birthplace of one of its heroes: writer Chateaubriand. Located inside the walls of old St-Malo, the flowering courtyard feels as though you've stepped into the Romantic era. Common areas still have this bygone feeling; however, guestrooms have been brought into the 21st century, the best and most modern rooms being the *chambres supérieures*. Request a room with views of the ramparts or the sea. Sip cool cocktails in the chic bar or dine in the regal restaurant with gold-trimmed Corinthian columns.

12 pl. Chateaubriand. www.hotel-chateaubriand-st-malo.com. ✆ **02-99-56-66-52.** 80 units. 119€–219€ double; 218€–275€ family room. Parking 15€. **Amenities:** Restaurant; cafe; bar; babysitting; room service; free Wi-Fi.

Quic en Grogne ★   Ideally positioned on a quiet street close to shops and the beach, this is the perfect budget hotel *intra-muros*. The hotel finished a lengthy renovation in early 2014, giving it a fresh, contemporary feel. The small guestrooms have a subtle nautical theme while steering clear of kitsch. All bathrooms have been refitted; the more expensive ones have bathtubs. The best rooms look over a flowery courtyard. Breakfast is served in a glass-covered sunroom, and the hotel's convenient private parking allows guests to avoid the hassle of parking outside the ramparts.

8 rue d'Estrées. www.quic-en-groigne.com. ✆ **02-99-20-22-20.** 15 units. 94€-122€ double; 121€–136€ family room. Parking 13€. Closed end of Dec–Jan. **Amenities:** Free Wi-Fi.

Where to Eat

Satisfy your summer taste buds with the best ice cream in St-Malo at **Sanchez**, 9 rue Vieille Boucherie (www.sanchez-artisanglacier.fr; ℭ **02-99-56-67-17**). With over 120 flavors, it'll be hard to choose, but we love their signature flavor "Le péché Malouin."

For a formal meal, **Hôtel France et Chateaubriand** (see above) has one of the finest dining rooms in town.

La Brasserie du Sillon ★ SEAFOOD/FRENCH Outside the city walls you'll find St-Malo's most innovative restaurant. Set in a lovely stone building facing the Sillon beach, the interior is refined and the best tables overlook the sea. Dishes are beautifully presented, though on the pricey side *à la carte*; savings can be made with their great value fixed-priced menus. Savor specialties such as fisherman's *choucroute,* scallops in butter sauce or filet mignon of pork with chestnuts, or you might be easily tempted by 13 different *plateaux de fruit de mer,* overflowing with freshly caught shrimp, periwinkle snail, crab, and lobster.

3 Chaussée du Sillon. www.brasseriedusillon.com. ℭ **02-99-56-10-74.** Main course 17€–35€; fixed-price menus 22.50€–42€. Daily noon–2:30pm; Sun–Thurs 7–10pm; Fri–Sat 7–10:30pm.

Le Chalut ★★ SEAFOOD/FRENCH French for "fish-net," here's where you can reel in the freshest catches in town. The kitschy nautical decor keeps this 1-Michelin-starred pearl well hidden. Some of Chef Jean-Philippe Foucat's creations include red mullet filets with marinated capers and artichokes drizzled with orange oil, John Dory with asparagus and fresh coriander, scallops with ginger and celery mousse or turbot with regional white Paimpol beans and lobster cream. Save a little room for the Chivas whiskey soufflé with citrus and passion fruit caramel. Reservations required.

8 rue de la Corne-de-Cerf. www.facebook.com/le.chalut.authentique. ℭ **02-99-56-71-58.** Main course 20€–30€; fixed-price lunch 24€ or dinner 29€–59€. Wed–Sun noon–1:30pm and 7–9:30pm.

Shopping

If you're in St-Malo on Tuesday or Friday between 8am and 1pm and want to experience a great Breton market, head for the **Halle au Blé,** in the heart of the old city. You can't miss the bustle and the hawking of seafood, fresh produce, local dairy products, and baked goods.

Check out **Marin-Marine,** 5 Grand Rue (ℭ **02-99-40-90-32**), for men's and women's fashions including mariner's shirts and Breton wool sweaters. **Gauthier Marines,** 2 rue Porcon de la Barbinais (www. gauthiermarines.com; ℭ **02-99-40-91-81**), is a walk-in treasure chest of model ships, wooden sculpture, and marine-themed gift items.

lunch **ON THE HALF-SHELL**

If you're driving east from St-Malo to Mont-St-Michel, consider a stop in **Cancale ★★★**—a harbor town famous for its oysters since the 17th century, when Louis XIV had them delivered regularly to Versailles.

Head to the northernmost end of the Port de la Houle, just beyond the jetty, where you'll see a handful of blue and white covered stalls selling shellfish out of crates. Come armed with a baguette and half-bottle of muscadet (easily found on the port's main street) and order a dozen oysters to go. The sellers will shuck them immediately and hand them to you on a plastic plate. Find a spot on a bench or the rocks, slurp down your mollusks and toss the shells onto the sun-bleached pile below.

For a second course, pop in to the **Crêperie du port,** 1 pl. du Calvaire, 7 quai Thomas (✆ **02-99-89-60-66**), for inventive buckwheat *galettes* and dessert crepes.

Oysters at Cancale

Brittany's most revered chef and modern-day spice hunter, Olivier **Roellinger,** has an eponymous shop at 12 rue Saint-Vincent (www.epices-roellinger.com; ✆ **06-18-80-44-10**). His beautifully presented blends, made from spices found all over the world, are worth collecting. And just try leaving **Maison Larnicol,** 6 rue St Saint-Vincent (www.chocolaterielarnicol.fr; ✆ **02-99-40-57-62**), empty handed. It specializes in Breton sweets including baked goods, chocolates, and a variety of flavored caramels.

St-Malo Nightlife

For an evening of gambling, head to **Le Casino Barrière,** 2 chaussée du Sillon (www.casinosbarriere.com/en/saint-malo.html; ✆ **02-99-40-64-00**). You can also order dinner, sometimes accompanied by live music. You must present your passport.

For dancing, consider **L'Escalier,** La Buzardière (www.escalier.fr; ✆ **02-99-81-65-56**), open Thursday to Saturday midnight to 7am. The cover doesn't exceed 14€. You'll need wheels, as the club is in the countryside 5km (3 miles) east of town. It does have a free shuttle, however; for information and reservations call ✆ 06-85-31-27-64. **Le 109,** 3 rue des Cordiers (www.le-109.com; ✆ **02-99-56-81-09**), is a futuristic bar and dance club in a 300-plus-year-old vaulted cellar. It isn't as fashionable as L'Escalier but is accessible without a car. It's open Tuesday to Sunday 8pm to 3am; the price of your first drink (10€–12€) is considered the cover charge.

Popular pubs include **L'Aviso,** 12 rue du Point du Jour (www.facebook.com/BarLAVISO; ✆ **07-68-15-01-07**), offering 300 types of beer and Breton beer on tap, and **Pub Saint Patrick,** 24 rue Sainte-Barbe (✆ **02-99-56-66-90**), serving 50 different Irish whiskeys, along with Breton beer. Concerts are regularly scheduled at the latter.

DINARD ★★

417km (259 miles) W of Paris; 23km (14 miles) N of Dinan

Dinard (not to be confused with its inland neighbor, Dinan) sits on a rocky promontory at the top of the Rance River, opposite St-Malo. Once a small fishing community, by the late 19th century it was a favorite of the European jet set, thanks largely to wealthy British families who built grand Victorian villas along the coast.

Though its golden age has tarnished somewhat, Dinard is still one of France's best-loved resorts. It's also a destination for cinephiles, who flock to the film festival here every October.

Essentials

ARRIVING   If you're driving, take D186 west from St-Malo to Dinard. SNCF trains go only as far as St-Malo; from there, take bus no. 16A, which departs from the St-Malo rail station daily for the 30-min. ride to Dinard. The one-way fare is 4.40€. Buses arrive from many towns and cities in Brittany, including Rennes. Schedule and fare information is available via Illenoo (www.illenoo-services.fr; ✆ 08-25-13-81-30). Between April and October, Compagnie Corsaire, Gare Maritime de la Bourse, St-Malo (www.compagniecorsaire.com; ✆ 02-23-18-15-15), operates ferryboats from St-Malo to Dinard. The trip takes 10 min. and costs 5.20€ one-way. A taxi to Dinard from St-Malo is another option; it costs 25€

during the day, with a 50 percent surcharge after 7pm and on Sundays and holidays. For information, call ℂ 06-84-92-55-73.

VISITOR INFORMATION The Office de Tourisme is at 2 bd. Féart (www. ot-dinard.com; ℂ 08-21-23-55-00).

[Fast FACTS] DINARD

ATMs/Banks   Easy-access ATMs are on avenue Edouard VII and pl. Rochaid.

Doctors & Hospitals   **Centre Hopital Arthur Gardiner,** 1 rue Henri Dunant (http://centre-hospitalier.ehpadhospiconseil.fr; ℂ **02-99-16-88-88**).

Internet Access   Free Wi-Fi is available at the **Office de Tourisme** listed above.

Mail & Postage   **La Poste,** 8 pl. Rochaid (ℂ **36-31**).

Pharmacies   **Pharmacie Centrale Franca,** 15 bd. Féart (ℂ **02-99-46-22-68**).

Enjoying the Resort

Most visitors come to Dinard for the beach. It's a 10-min. walk from the town's historic core to the Pointe du Moulinet and encircles most of the old town with its haunting 19th-century villas and encompasses views as far away as St-Malo.

BEACHES & SWIMMING   Dinard's main beach is the Plage de l'Ecluse (La Grande Plage), the strip of sand between the peninsulas that defines the edges of the old town. Favored by families and vacationers, it's crowded on hot days. Smaller and more isolated is the Plage de St-Enogat (you pass through the village of St-Enogat on the 20-min. hike east from Dinard). The Plage du Prieuré, a 10-min. walk from the center, has a few trees that shade the sand. The beaches have a few restaurants, toilets, showers, changing cabins, rental boats, and lifeguards (in summer). Because of the big difference between high and low tides, the municipality has built swimming pool–style basins along the Plage de L'Ecluse and the Plage du Prieuré to catch the seawater.

The Piscine Olympique, boulevard du Président-Wilson, next to the casino (ℂ 02-99-46-22-77), is a covered, heated seawater pool open year-round. Entrance is 5€ for adults, 4€ for ages five to 17, and free for children four and under. From July to mid-September, it's open Monday to Friday 10am to 12:30pm and 3 to 7:30pm, weekends 10am to 12:30pm and 3 to 6:30pm. Hours vary the rest of the year according to the needs of school groups and swim teams (inquire at the tourist office). A swim cap (for everyone) and a speedo (for men) are required and available for purchase on site.

Where to Stay

Didier Méril (see "Where to Eat," below) also rents rooms.

Grand Hôtel Barrière de Dinard ★★   The glory of the Victorian era lives on at one of the Emerald coast's grandest hotels. Part of the Lucien Barrière luxury chain, this 1858 hotel epitomizes Second Empire style. A short walk from downtown, the majestic two-winged building overlooks the Vicomté bay. Luxury knows no bounds, from the spacious foyer to the deluxe pool and spa. Guestrooms have modern elegance, the balconies being a major plus. However, the perfect sea-views are best admired from the four balconies of the recently added 70 sq. m (753 sq. ft.) executive suite. In the evening you can savor succulent seafood in the regal restaurant or a cocktail in the swanky bar.

46 av. George V. www.lucienbarriere.com. ✆ **02-99-88-26-26.** 89 units. 244€–450€ double; from 655€ suite. Closed mid-Nov to early April. **Amenities:** Restaurant; bar; babysitting; kids' club; fitness center; indoor pool; room service; rooms for those with limited mobility; sauna; spa; free bike rental; free Wi-Fi.

Hôtel Printania ★   The keys to Breton hospitality are handed to you at this quaint hotel. Considered by its family-run management as a *musée-hôtel*, you will definitely feel at home here if you're looking for a warm, cultural experience right down to the staff dressed in folkloric costumes. Although recently upgraded, the hotel has retained its traditional charm and features solid wooden furniture, traditional floral wallpaper, and grandmother-style nautical antiques and artwork dating back to when it opened in 1920. Your room might even feature *lits clos*—Breton-style beds akin to ships' bunks. Don't worry, there are also modern flatscreen TVs and wireless Internet. It's only 5 minutes from the beach, which you can appreciate from the glassed-in terraces or great restaurant that, not surprisingly, serves up tasty local classics.

5 av. George-V. www.printaniahotel.com. ✆ **02-99-46-13-07.** 56 units. 98€–142€ double; 260€–332€ suite. Closed mid-Nov to mid-Mar. Parking 12€. **Amenities:** 3 restaurants; bar; free Wi-Fi.

Where to Eat

The Grand Hôtel Barrière de Dinard (see above) offers fine dining.

Didier Méril ★★ FRENCH/BRETON   The best meal in Dinard comes with the best views. Located right on the Bay of Prieuré, this historic stone building has been refurbished with designer furniture. This new-meets-old is carried over on Chef Didier Méril's refined menu with such dishes as cod with Avruga caviar and champagne butter and minced beef with foie gras cream and roasted duck drizzled with salty caramel. The wine list is equally impressive, with over 450 labels. If those aren't enough, the view of the bay from its summer terrace will certainly leave you awe-struck.

Above the restaurant are six stylish bedrooms and two suites for rent, some with sea views; rates range from 65€ to 320€.

1 pl. du Gen. de Gaulle. www.restaurant-didier-meril.com. ✆ **02-99-46-95-74.** Main course 20€–75€; fixed-price menu 31€–90€. Daily 12:15–2pm and 7:15–9:30pm.

La Passerelle du Clair de Lune ★ SEAFOOD   As its name indicates, this restaurant is located at one end of the Promenade du Claire de Lune, a perfect spot to enjoy the views of the sea and its excellent catches. The menu is a steal granted its location. The exotic hints in its decor are also sprinkled into the foie gras with kumquat chutney, Brittany lobster grilled with cocoa beans, or the steamed sea bass with smoked carrots and ginger sauce. On a hot summer night, finish off with the pineapple carpaccio with saffron cream.

3 av. George-V. www.la-passerelle-restaurant.com. © **02-99-16-96-37.** Main course 18€–28€; fixed-price menu 28€–39€. Daily noon–2:30pm and 7–9:30pm.

Shopping

For shops and boutiques, concentrate on rue du Maréchal-Leclerc, rue Levavasseur, and boulevard Féart. In the 15th-century house containing Galerie d'Art du Prince Noir, 70 av. George-V (© 02-99-46-29-99), you'll find paintings and sculptures by some of the most talented artists in France. The gallery is closed from October to April. Another worthwhile destination is L'Ancien Temple, 29 rue Jacques-Cartier (© 02-99-46-82-88), in a former Protestant church. The high-ceilinged showrooms feature upscale porcelain, stoneware, kitchen utensils, gift items, and fresh flowers.

Nightlife

Like many French beach resorts, Dinard has a casino. **Le Casino Barrière,** 4 bd. Du Président-Wilson (www.lucienbarriere.com; © **02-99-16-30-30**) is liveliest from Easter to late October with games including roulette, blackjack, and slot machines and two bars and a restaurant in-house. Hours are Sunday through Thursday from 11am to 2am, Friday and Saturday from 11am to 3am. Admission is free though you must present your passport; dress code is smart casual. An alternative is **La Suite,** 2 rue la Ville Biais, off of route du Barrage (www.facebook.com/lasuitedinard; © **02-99-46-46-46**), a nightclub and dance club on the outskirts with a loyal following thanks to a good wine selection and amiable ambience. It's open Thursdays through Saturdays, with varying cover charges and free shuttle-bus service to Dinard and St-Malo. According to its club rules, "Homosexuality is not a problem—but homophobia is."

In the evenings from June to September, tourists stroll the Promenade du Clair de Lune to admire specially illuminated buildings and gardens and hear all kinds of music performed outside.

DINAN ★★★

396km (246 miles) W of Paris; 52km (32 miles) NW of Rennes

Once a fortified stronghold of the Dukes of Brittany, Dinan is one of the prettiest and best-preserved towns in the region. It's noted for its *maisons à piliers,* medieval half-timbered houses built on stilts over the sidewalks.

For centuries the town has served as a hub of cultural and commercial activity, from the original merchants and traders to today's artists and craftspeople. The tourist bustle can make for a busy day, but it's hard not to be moved by a walk atop the ramparts or a visit to the basilica.

Essentials

ARRIVING Dinan has an SNCF train station, but service is infrequent. The trip from Rennes, with one stop, takes about 1 hr. and costs 15.70€. From St-Malo it takes about as long and costs 10€. Most rail passengers just transfer to one of the buses from the train stations for connection to Dinan. The trip time is almost the same, but tickets are 2€. For information on bus schedules visit www.tibus.fr or call ✆ 08-10-22-22-22. If you're driving from Dinard, take highway D166 south to Dinan.

VISITOR INFORMATION The Office de Tourisme is at 9 rue du Château (www.dinan-tourisme.com; ✆ 02-96-87-69-76).

SPECIAL EVENTS One of the biggest medieval festivals in the world, the Fêtes des Remparts (www.fete-remparts-dinan.com), is held the third weekend of July in even-numbered years. Mingle amongst the knights and maidens and enjoy authentic street entertainment, food, and crafts. Take in an archery competition or even a jousting match.

[FastFACTS] DINAN

ATMs/Banks   Several ATMs are in pl. Duclos or on rue Thiers.

Doctors & Hospitals   **Centre Hopitalier Dinan/St Brieuc,** av. Saint-Jean de Dieu (www.chdinanstbrieuc.fsjd.fr; ✆ **02-96-87-18-00**).

Internet Access   You can get free Wi-Fi while enjoying a crèpe or cider *en terrace* at the **Creperie Pizzeria d'Armor,** 15 pl. des Cordeliers (✆ **02-96-39-23-53**).

Mail & Postage   **La Poste,** 7 pl. Duclos (✆ **36-31**).

Pharmacies   **Pharmacie Centrale Gildas Morvan,** 8 pl. Duclos (✆ **02-96-39-07-10**).

Exploring Dinan

Dinan's ramparts, which include 14 watchtowers and four gates, extend for almost 3.5km (2 miles) around the town. The tourist office provides a printed walking guide.

An authentic and appealing street is the sloping rue du Jerzual, flanked with 15th-century dwellings and shops with craftspeople selling their wares. In the middle is the Porte du Jerzual, a 13th- and 14th-century gate—you can still see traces of its drawbridge in the stone. In the direction of the river the street becomes rue du Petit-Fort and leads to the town's small port and its Gothic style bridge.

Basilique St-Sauveur ★★ CHURCH   Built between the 12th and 16th centuries, this church has Romanesque, Gothic, Baroque, and Classical elements. A monument holds the heart of Bertrand du Guesclin, the beloved Breton knight who defended Dinard during the Hundred Years' War. Just behind the basilica, the terraced Jardin Anglais (English Garden) provides a panoramic view of the Rance Valley and direct access to the ramparts.

pl. St-Sauveur. *☎* **02-96-39-06-67.** Free admission.

Château Musée de Dinan ★ MUSEUM   Three medieval structures reunited in the 16th century form this fascinating municipal museum. The dungeon of this colossal 14th-century fortress was a residence for the Duke of Brittany before being converted into a jail. It contains displays on Dinan's history dating back to prehistory, and the chapel contains holy artifacts, furniture, and silver. The visit is worthwhile merely to see the castle interior.

rue du Château. *☎* **02-96-39-45-20.** Admission 4.70€ adults; 2.50€ ages 8–18 and students; free for children 7 and under. Apr–May and Sept–Dec daily 1:30–6:30pm; June and Sept daily 10am–6:30pm; Jul–Aug daily 10am–7pm. Closed Jan–late Mar.

Tour de l'Horloge ★ HISTORIC SITE   This structure boasts a clock made in 1498 and a bell donated by Anne de Bretagne in 1507. After the 158 steps you'll be rewarded with a view of Dinan from the 23m- (75-ft.-) belfry–one of only two intact belfries in all of Brittany. Its main bell is named after Anne—three smaller ones are engraved with the names Jacqueline, Françoise, and Noguette.

rue de l'Horloge. *☎* **02-96-87-58-72.** Admission 4€ adults; 2.50€ ages 8–18 and students; free for children 7 and under. Apr–May daily 2–6pm; June–Sept 10am–6:30pm.

Where to Stay

Hôtel Arvor ★★   The entrance to this former 14th-century Jacobin convent ushers you into the most romantic hotel in town. The building was first refurbished in the 18th century in a Renaissance style, and thankfully, again in 2011, bringing it up to 21st-century standards. Guestrooms carry on in an amorous ambiance with colorful drapery, plush armchairs and even some heart-shaped throw pillows. The rooms are rather spacious, in contrast to the small, though well-equipped bathrooms. Families will be able to spread out in their spacious duplex suite that sleeps six.

5 rue Pavie. www.hotelarvordinan.com. *☎* **02-96-39-21-22.** 22 units. 88€–140€ double. Parking 6€. Closed Jan. **Amenities:** Free Wi-Fi.

Hôtel d'Avaugour ★★   Set in a stone house just inside the ramparts, this is a perfect and comfortable base for exploring Dinan. The entire hotel is tastefully decorated in a contemporary style and the ground floor has recently been renovated, the additional windows now shedding

Medieval houses in Dinan

delicate daylight onto readers in the comfortable lounge. The guestrooms have simple yet plush furnishings with hints of Brittany in the decor. The verdant window views either showcase the surrounding historic buildings or the large and lovely backyard garden, where you can take tea in the afternoon.

1 pl. du Champs. www.avaugourhotel.com. © **02-96-39-07-49.** 24 units. 120€–205€ double; 235€–310€ suite. Closed Nov–Mar. **Amenities:** Free Wi-Fi.

Where to Eat

For a less formal meal, lighter eateries are on rue de la Poissonnerie. Stop in at busy Creperie Ahna, no. 7 (© 02-96-39-09-13), which has been run by the same family for four generations.

Fleur de Sel ★ FRENCH/BRETON   Enjoy some excellent surf and turf with a twist at this friendly local favorite. The small dining room successfully combines a contemporary look with classic Breton appeal, something which is also echoed on the menu. You'll find the likes of foie gras paired with candied pineapple and Tonka beans, meunière of flounder with buckwheat butter and grilled almonds or soft black noodles with crispy vegetables—all certainly served with a healthy dash of Brittany *fleur de sel*.

7 rue Sainte Claire. www.restaurantlafleurdesel.com. © **02-96-85-15-14.** Main course 14€–20€; fixed-price lunch 20€ or dinner 30€–42€; children's menu 18€. Tues–Sat noon–2:30pm and 7–10pm and Sun noon–2:30pm.

AN idyll ON AN ILE

The **Ile de Bréhat** is home to some 350 hearty folk who live most of the year in isolation—until the summer crowds arrive. The tiny island (actually two islands, Ile Nord and Ile Sud, linked by a bridge, Le Pont Vauban) is in the Gulf of St-Malo, north of Paimpol. A visit to Bréhat is an adventure, even to the French. The only settlement on the islands is Le Bourg, in the south. The only bona fide beach is a strip of sand at Guerzido.

Walking is the primary activity, and it's possible to stroll the footpaths around the island in a day. Cars, other than police and fire vehicles, aren't allowed. Tractor-driven carts carry visitors on an 8km (5-mile) circuit of Bréhat's two islands, charging 9€ for the 45-min. jaunt (it's 4€ for children 4–11, free for children 3 and under). A number of places rent bikes, but they aren't necessary.

The rich flora here astonishes many visitors, who arrive expecting a wind-swept island only to discover a more Mediterranean clime. Flowers abound in summer, though both the gardens and houses appear tiny because of the scarcity of land. At the highest point, Chapelle St-Michel, you'll be rewarded with a panoramic view.

The tourist office, pl. du Bourg, Le Bourg (www.brehat-infos.fr; ☏ **02-96-20-83-16**), is open Monday to Saturday mid-June to mid-September.

To reach Paimpol, **drive** west on D768 from Dinard to Lamballe, then take E50 west to Plérin and D786 north to Paimpol. To reach the island, take D789 4km (2.5 miles) north of Paimpol, where the peninsula ends at the Pointe de l'Arcouest. From Paimpol, 6 to 10 **Tibus** (www.tibus.fr; ☏ **08-10-22-22-22**) buses make the 10-min. run to the point for a one-way fare of 2€. Then catch one of the **ferries** operated by **Les Vedettes de Bréhat** (www.vedettesdebrehat.com; ☏ **02-96-55-79-50**). Ferries depart about every 30 min. in summer, around seven times per day in the off-season; the round-trip costs 10.30€ for adults, 8.80€ for ages 4 to 11, free for children 3 and under. Visitors in April, May, June, and September will find the island much less crowded than in July and August. Cars are not allowed on the ferry.

QUIMPER ★★

570km (353 miles) W of Paris; 205km (127 miles) NW of Rennes

Quimper, the town that pottery built, is the historic capital of Brittany's most traditional region, La Cornouaille. It takes its name from the Breton word *kemper*, the meeting of two rivers—in this case the Odet and the Steir. There's no better place to get a feel for southern Breton culture, whether during its annual festival or just trolling the *vieux centre* for Quimperware, the hand-painted *faience* that's symbolized Brittany for centuries. Modern-day Quimper is somewhat bourgeois, home to some 67,000 *Quimperois* who walk narrow streets spared from World War II damage.

Essentials

ARRIVING   Speedy TGV trains take only 3.5 to 4 hr. from the Montparnasse station in Paris. The one-way fare ranges from 30€ to 72€. For information, visit www.oui.sncf or call ✆ **36-35** (.40€/min.). If you're driving, the best route is from Rennes: Take E50/N12 west to just outside the town of Montauban, continue west along N164 to Châteaulin, and head south along N165 to Quimper.

VISITOR INFORMATION   The Office de Tourisme is on place de la Résistance (www.quimper-tourisme.com; ✆ 02-98-53-04-05).

SPECIAL EVENTS   For six days around the third week of every July, the **Festival de Cornouaille** celebrates Breton culture. The festivities include parades in traditional costume and Celtic and Breton concerts throughout the city. For information, contact the tourist office.

[FastFACTS] QUIMPER

ATMs/Banks   Several ATMs can be found on rue du Parc and rue René Madec.

Doctors & Hospitals   **Centre Hopitalier de Cornouaille,** av. Yves Thépot (www. ch-cournouaille.fr; ✆ **02-98-52-60-60**).

Internet Access   Free WIFI (and tasty snacks) are available at the cute **C.com C@fé**, 9 Quai du Port au Vin (✆ **02-98-95-81-62**).

Mail & Postage   **La Poste,** 37 bd. Amiral de Kerguélen (✆ **36-31**).

Pharmacies   **Pharmacie de la Cathédrale,** 24 pl. Saint-Corentin (✆ **02-98-95-00-20**).

Exploring Quimper

In some quarters, Quimper maintains its old-world atmosphere, with narrow medieval streets and footbridges spanning the rivers.

Cathédrale St-Corentin ★★ CATHEDRAL   Characterized by two towers that climb 75m (246 ft.), this cathedral was built between the 13th and 15th centuries. The twin steeples were added in the 19th. Inside, note the 15th-century stained glass—windows on the north side were funded by religious donors, those on the south by secular ones.

pl. St-Corentin. ✆ **02-98-95-06-19.** Free admission. Sept–Jun daily 9:45am–noon and 1:30–6:30pm; July–Aug daily 9:45am–6:30pm; closed during Sun morning services.

Musée Departemental Breton ★★★ MUSEUM   Located in the medieval Palais des Eveques de Cornouaille (Palace of the Bishops of Cornwall), next to the cathedral, this is a highlight of any visit to Quimper. Renovations over the last decade have revamped its displays of the archaeological and decorative history of the region. It is one of the best ways to learn about the customs and traditions of Brittany, illustrated in items of stained glass, sculpture, furniture, painting, and *faience*, in addition to four rooms showcasing quotidian and ceremonial Breton costumes.

1–3 rue Roi Gradlon. www.museedepartementalbreton.fr. ✆ **02-98-95-21-60.** Admission 5€ adults; 3€ ages 18–25; free for children 17 and under; free on weekends from Jan–May and Oct–Dec. Jun–Sept daily 9:30am–6pm; Tues–Fri 9:30am–5:30pm and Sat–Sun 2–5:30pm.

A sunny day in Quimper

Musée des Beaux-Arts ★★ MUSEUM   This museum is a nice cultural surprise along the mostly outdoorsy Brittany coast. First opened in 1872, it underwent renovations and extension work in the early 1990s. The collection features some impressive names including Rubens, Boucher, Fragonard, and Corot, in addition to a strong collection of the Pont-Aven school (Gaugin, Sérusier, Bernard, Lacombe, Maufra, Denis). A special tribute is also paid to Quimper native Mac Jacob, a Surrealist poet and painter.

40 pl. St-Corentin. www.mbaq.fr. © **02-98-95-45-20.** Admission 5€ adults; 3€ ages 12–26; free for children 11 and under. July–Aug daily from 10am–6pm; Mar–Jun and Sept–Oct Wed–Mon 9:30am–noon and 2–6pm; and Nov–Feb Mon and Wed–Sat 9:30am–noon and 2–5:30pm, Tues and Sun 2–5:30pm.

Where to Stay

Hôtel Kregenn ★   For a solid sleep in the center, this is your best option. Located on a quiet street a block from the river, this hotel is an excellent value for the money. Though a Best Western, the hotel is still family-run, with an exceptionally friendly staff. Guestrooms are relatively spacious and have a simple yet stylish decor. The interior garden-terrace is the place to retire for a relaxing break. A coffee or glass of wine can be had at the bar; however, breakfast, for 13€, is the only meal served.

11–15 rue des Réguaires. www.hotel-kregenn.fr. © **02-98-95-08-70.** 32 units. 109€–180€ double; 220€ suite. Parking 7€. Pets 15€. **Amenities:** Bar; limited room service; free Wi-Fi.

Manoir du Stang ★★   Hidden away in the Fouesnant Forest is one of Brittany's loveliest manor-hotels. Only 13km (8 miles) from Quimper, this refined 16th-century estate has changed hands only once in its 400-year history. The imposing stone walls and impeccably maintained grounds are proof of this test of time. The 10 hectares (25 acres) of natural woodland are perfect for idyll strolls, and golfers delight in teeing off at the neighboring 18-hole course. The lounge is cozy with a toasty fireplace and is furnished with antiques and patterned armchairs. Guestroom decor is a little old fashioned, but this adds to its homey Breton feel. There's no restaurant, but breakfast can be brought to your bed.

La Forêt-Fouesnant. www.manoirdustang.com. © **02-98-56-96-38.** 16 units. 105€–150€ double; 165€–195€ family room. Free parking. Closed end-Sept to late April. Drive 1.5km (1 mile) north of the village center and follow signs from N783; access is by private road. **Amenities:** Bar; free Wi-Fi.

Where to Eat

For a drink or meal at any time of the day, sit down at the stylish Café de l'Epée, 14 rue du Parc (© **02-98-95-28-97**). The oldest "brasserie" in Brittany, it dates back to 1830 and serves elegant bistro fare, and, of course, copious seafood options.

Ambroisie ★ BRETON/FRENCH   Breton cuisine at its best is prepared in this popular establishment in the heart of Brittany's cultural capital. For more than 25 years, Gilbert Guyon has honed his culinary arts, earning himself the only Michelin star in Quimper. His focus is in the kitchen; however, the dining room hasn't been neglected and has nice contemporary furniture and large paintings inspired by English painter Francis Bacon. Guyon's menu features modern takes on regional traditions such as his signature buckwheat galette with prawns. You might also like cocotte of duck cooked in cider or mussels with Breton artichokes. Pursue this local theme for dessert with an excellent selection of cheese straight from the farm or homemade fromage blanc sorbet.

49 rue Elie Fréron. www.ambroisie-quimper.com. © **02-98-95-00-02.** Fixed-price menu lunch 25€ or dinner 48€–65€; children's menu 15€. Tues–Sat 12:15–1:30pm and 7:15–9:15pm.

Shopping

Quimper's proximity to the rivers gave it plenty of access to clay; it's been known as a pottery town since the late 1600s. *Faience,* the French term for glazed earthenware (as opposed to porcelain, manufactured to be more delicate) is your go-to souvenir here. Quimperware is recognized for its bright, hand-painted motifs, often Breton figures, fruits, and flowers. One of the most popular designs is a male *Breton* or female *Bretonne,* both in profile and in traditional costume. Today this 19th-century motif is copyrighted and fiercely protected.

The best shopping streets are rue Kéréon and rue du Parc, where you'll find Breton products including pottery, dolls and puppets, clothing made from regional cloth and wool, jewelry, lace, and beautiful Breton costumes.

One site that produces stoneware is open for tours. From April to September, Monday to Friday 10am to 12:45pm and 1:45 to 4:30pm, five to seven tours per day depart from the visitor information center of La Faïencerie Henriot-Quimper, rue Haute, Quartier Locmaria (www.henriot-quimper.com; ✆ 02-98-90-09-36). Tours in English, French, or both last 40 to 45 min. and cost 5€ for adults, 2.50€ for children 8 to 14, and are free for children 7 and under. On site, a store sells the most complete inventory of Quimper porcelain in the world. You can invest in first-run (nearly perfect) pieces or slightly discounted "seconds," with almost imperceptible flaws. Everything can be shipped.

For more Breton pottery, as well as fine tablecloths, linens, and other household items, visit François le Villec, 4 rue Roi-Gradlon (www.armorlux.com; ✆ 02-98-95-31-54).

CONCARNEAU ★★

539km (334 miles) W of Paris; 93km (58 miles) SE of Brest

This port is a favorite of painters, who never tire of capturing the subtleties of the fishing fleet. It's also unique among the larger coastal communities because fishing, not tourism, is its main industry (Concarneau's canneries produce most of the tuna in France). Walk along the quays, especially in the evening, and watch the Breton fishers unload their catch; later, join them for a pint of cider in the taverns.

Essentials

ARRIVING　Concarneau does not have rail service. If you're driving, the town is 21km (13 miles) southeast of Quimper along D783. A **bus** runs from Quimper to Concarneau (trip time: 30 min.); the one-way fare is 2€. The bus from Rosporden, site of another SNCF railway station, runs about eight times per day (trip time: 20 min.) for a fare of 1€. For information call (✆ **08-10-81-00-29**).

VISITOR INFORMATION　The Office de Tourisme is on quai d'Aiguillon (www.tourismeconcarneau.fr; ✆ 02-98-97-01-44).

Exploring the Area

The town is built on three sides of a natural harbor whose innermost, sheltered section is the Nouveau Port. In the center of this is the heavily fortified Ville Close ★★, an ancient hamlet surrounded by ramparts, some from the 14th century. From the quay, cross the bridge and descend into the town. Souvenir shops have taken over, but don't let that spoil it. You can spend an hour wandering the alleys, gazing up at the towers, peering at the stone houses, and stopping in secluded squares.

For a splendid view of the port, walk the ramparts ★. They're open to pedestrians daily 10am to 7:30pm, with seasonal variations.

Also in the old town is a fishing museum, Musée de la Pêche ★, 3 rue Vauban (www.musee-peche.fr; ℗ 02-98-97-10-20). The 17th-century building displays ship models and exhibits chronicling the development of the fishing industry. Be sure to also tour the *Hemerica,* a restored fishing boat docked in the port and included in your entrance ticket. Admission is 5€ for adults, 3€ for students and free for children 18 and under. It's open February, March, November, and December Tuesday to Sunday 2 to 5:30pm, from April to June, September and October 10am to 6pm, and July to August 10am to 7pm. Closed January.

BEACHES   Concarneau's largest, most beautiful beach, popular with families, is the Plage des Sables Blancs, near the historic core. Within a 10-min. walk are the Plage de Cornouaille and two small beaches, the Plage des Dames and Plage de Rodel, where you'll find fewer families with children. The wide-open Plage du Cabellou, 5km (3 miles) west of town, is less crowded than the others.

SEA EXCURSIONS   Boat rides are usually fine between June and September but can be treacherous the rest of the year. The dazzling Glenans archipelago, 16km (10 miles) off the coast, is a must if you have the time and sea legs. It can be visited on excursions through **Vedettes de l'Odet** (www.vedettes-odet.com; ℗ 02-98-57-00-58), which runs several times per day from April to September and cost 39€ for adults, 21€ for children ages 4 to 12 and 7€ for children 3 and under. In midsummer, you can arrange deep-sea fishing with the captain of the Santa Maria (www.santa mariapeche.com; ℗ 06-62-88-00-87).

Where to Stay & Eat

La Coquille ★ SEAFOOD/TRADITIONAL FRENCH   Located right on the port, you can practically see your dinner being reeled in at the freshest venue in town. While it might not look sophisticated from the outside, the dining room features stone walls, ceiling beams, century-old oil paintings from the School of Pont-Aven, and a spectacular view of the harbor. Not surprisingly, you'll find a lot of seafood on the menu at La Coquille (the shell). The menu varies according to the latest catches. It could include scallops with algae butter, grilled lobster with Kari Gosse sauce or, to please the carnivores, filet of beef with red wine reduction sauce. The friendly staff will make you want to stay for dessert; try the "palette" of sorbets, inspired by the colorful local paintings on the walls. Reservations are a must in season.

1 quai du Moros, at Nouveau Port. www.lacoquille-concarneau.com. ℗ **02-98-97-08-52.** Main course 20€–48€; fixed-price lunch 15€–20€ or dinner 30€–46€. Thurs–Sat and Mon–Tues noon–2pm and 7–9pm; Wed and Sun noon–2pm. Closed 3 weeks late Oct to mid-Nov.

Les Sables Blancs ★★   Overlooking Concarneau's loveliest beach, you can't have a better seaside stay than at this boutique hotel. Recent renovations made to this 1960s building transformed it into a glass paradise. Every room has expansive windows facing the sea in addition to small private terraces. Most rooms are vastly white with only small hints of color in pillows or artwork; the never-ending sea is decoration enough. For some sophisticated surf and turf grab a table on the terrace or in the stylish dining room of the hotel's restaurant, Le Nautile with reasonably priced menus from 22€ to 39.50€.

Plage des Sables Blancs. www.hotel-les-sables-blancs.com. ☎ **02-98-50-10-12.** 16 units. 145€–270€ double; 270€–445€ suite. **Amenities:** Restaurant; free Wi-Fi.

PONT-AVEN ★★

522km (324 miles) W of Paris; 32km (20 miles) SE of Quimper; 16km (10 miles) S of Concarneau

Paul Gauguin loved this inland village, with its white houses flanking the River Aven on its gentle course to the Atlantic. It's also known for 15 *moulins,* or water mills, that once operated along the waterways. Only one of them is still functional, but the rest have been restored for historical and aesthetic purposes. With such picturesque surroundings, one might suspect Pont-Aven of being a tourist trap, but its modest, pleasant atmosphere endures.

Essentials

ARRIVING   If you're driving from Quimper, go southeast on N165 and follow signs into Pont-Aven. From Quimperlé, head west along D783 until N165 and follow signs. SNCF trains stop at Quimper, where you can transfer to between four and six daily buses to Pont Aven (trip time: 30 min.; one-way fare 2€). For bus information, call the Pont-Aven tourist office (see below). For train information visit www.oui.sncf or call ☎ **36-35** (.40€/min.).

VISITOR INFORMATION   The **Office de Tourisme** is at 5 pl. de l'Hôtel-de-Ville (www.pontaven.com; ☎ **02-98-06-04-70**).

Exploring the Area

Themed walking tours are available in the village, such as the artists' trail or the *promenade des moulins*—the tourist office can provide maps. You can also visit one of the shops that produce the famous *galette de Pont-Aven*, a round, butter-rich cookie that Bretons like to dunk in their coffee. Two of the oldest are Traou Mad, rue du Port (☎ 02-98-06-18-18) and **Penven**-Délices de Pont-Aven, 1 quai Théodore Botrel (☎ 02-98-06-02-75). Both offer tours of their nearby production facilities in July and August, Penven's are free and take place on Tuesday and Thursday at 11am.

The 16th-century Chapelle de Trémalo, lieu-dit Trémalo (☎ 02-98-06-01-68), is 1.2km (.75 mile) north of the town center. Here is the wooden crucifix that inspired two of Gauguin's best-known paintings,

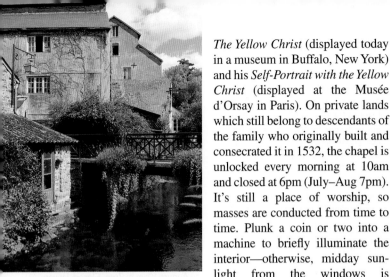

The Yellow Christ (displayed today in a museum in Buffalo, New York) and his *Self-Portrait with the Yellow Christ* (displayed at the Musée d'Orsay in Paris). On private lands which still belong to descendants of the family who originally built and consecrated it in 1532, the chapel is unlocked every morning at 10am and closed at 6pm (July–Aug 7pm). It's still a place of worship, so masses are conducted from time to time. Plunk a coin or two into a machine to briefly illuminate the interior—otherwise, midday sunlight from the windows is sufficient.

Picturesque Pont-Aven

Where to Stay & Eat

Hotel Les Mimosas ★   Wake up to views from a Gauguin painting at this friendly excellent value inn. Facing the river with its bobbing sailboats, the hotel has been recently redone in a smart contemporary look achieved with attractive flower print wallpaper and contemporary furnishings. Spend a little extra and you can have a room with a large terrace. The hotel also has a popular local restaurant serving mainly fish and seafood available in extremely reasonable menus ranging from 19€ to 25€. Or stop in after your day of sightseeing for their 10€ "apéro" special of a glass of wine and your choice of oysters, sausage, sardines or *terrine de campagne*.

22 square Théodore Botrel. www.lesmimosas-pontaven.com. ✆ **02-98-06-00-30.** 10 units. 69€–90€ double. Free parking. **Amenities:** Restaurant; free Wi-Fi. Restaurant Tues–Wed, Fri–Sat 12:30–2pm and 7:30–9pm; Thurs and Sun 12:30–2pm.

La Taupinière ★★ TRADITIONAL FRENCH   Skip the casual crêperies in town and make your way to this excellent seafood restaurant. Located in a lovely thatched cottage nestled in the woods on the outskirts of town, you'll be warmly received in the elegant yet homey dining room. Chef Guy Guillox, with four cookbooks under his belt, prepares local fresh catches with extreme finesse. If you're not tempted by his exquisite specialty of lobster prepared in a "thousand ways," then go for foie gras crème brûlée topped with crab or the Peking-style duck with butternut squash purée. The light as a feather chocolate and raspberry soufflé is the perfect way to cap off your heavenly gastronomic meal.

Route de Concarneau-Croissant Saint-André. www.la-taupiniere.fr. ✆ **02-98-06-03-12.** Main course 28€–50€; fixed-price menu 55€–100€. Wed–Sun 12:30–2pm and 7:30–9pm.

In the Footsteps of Gauguin

In the summer of 1886, Paul Gauguin arrived in the Breton village of Pont-Aven. Lesser-known artists, including Maurice Denis, Paul Sérusier, and Emile Bernard, soon followed. Breaking from mainstream Impressionism, the Pont Aven School—as the style of Gauguin and his 20 or so followers came to be known—emphasized pure colors, shunned perspective and shadowing, and simplified human figures. Both *The Yellow Christ* and *The Green Christ*, two of Gauguin's most memorable works, exemplify this method, also known as Synthetism.

The **Musée des Beaux-Arts de Pont-Aven,** pl. de l'Hôtel de Ville (www.musee pontaven.fr; © **02-98-06-14-43**), reopened in 2016 after extensive renovations providing a fresh look and double the exhibition space. The collections and permanent collection display key works of 19th-century painters that put this town on the map. Admission to the museum and exhibits is 8€ for adults, 6€ for students and free for children 17 and under. It's open February, March, November, and December Tuesday to Sunday 2 to 5:30pm, from April to June, September, and October 10am to 6pm, and daily July to August 10am to 7pm. Closed January.

CARNAC ★★

486km (301 miles) W of Paris; 37km (23 miles) SE of Lorient; 100km (62 miles) SE of Quimper

Aside from being a popular beach resort, Carnac is home to the largest megalithic site in the world. Spread out over 4km (2.5 miles), Les Alignements, as three fields of huge, upright stones are known, date back more than 6,000 years to Neolithic times. Scholars have debated their purpose for centuries, though most suggest they had astronomical or religious significance. One theory is that the stones marked burial sites. Another legend claims they are Roman soldiers turned to stone by the wizard Merlin. In all, the town contains 2,732 *menhirs,* some rising to heights of 20m (66 ft.).

Carnac's five beaches stretch over nearly 3km (1.75 miles). Protected by the Quiberon Peninsula, they back up onto sand dunes and shady forests. Carnac-Plage is a family resort and camping hotspot beside the ocean and along the waterfront boulevard de la Plage. The area is packed in July and August.

Essentials

ARRIVING   Driving is the most convenient way to get to Carnac. From Pont-Aven, travel southeast along N165, passing through Hennebont. At the intersection with D768, continue south along the signposted road to Carnac. From Nantes, take N165 northwest to Auray and then D768.

Links to Carnac by public transport are inconvenient, as there's no railway station. Train travelers leave the SNCF network at either Quiberon or Auray and take a bus into town. An additional option, available between June and August only, is to get off the train at Plouharnel-Carnac station, 3km (1.75 miles) from Carnac. For more information about bus transit from any of these hamlets, call ℰ 08-10-10-10-56.

VISITOR INFORMATION   The Office de Tourisme is at 74 av. des Druides (www.ot-carnac.fr; ℰ 02-97-52-13-52). It also offers free WIFI.

Exploring the Area

Out of fear of vandalism, the local tourist authorities have fenced in the megaliths and now allow visitors to wander freely among the *menhirs* only between October and March, when the park is open daily from 10am to 5pm, and when entrance is free. From April to September, the park can be visited only as part of a rigidly controlled 1-hr. guided tour, priced at 6€ per person (5€ for students or anyone between ages 18 and 24; under 18 are free). Tours are usually in French but, depending on the perceived need, may include some additional commentary in English. The only way to be sure is to call the visitor center, La Maison des Mégalithes, at ℰ 02-97-52-29-81, for a rundown on the tours arranged for the day of your intended visit. For more information, visit www.carnac.monuments-nationaux.fr.

At Carnac Ville, Musée de Préhistoire, 10 pl. de la Chapelle (www.museedecarnac.com; ℰ 02-97-52-22-04), displays collections from 450,000 B.C. to the 8th century. Admission is 6€ for adults, 3€ for ages 6 to 18, and free for children 5 and under. Hours are as follows: July and August Wednesday to Monday 10am to 6:30pm; April to June and September 10am to 12:30pm and 2 to 6pm, October 10am to 12:30pm and 2 to 5:30pm, and November to March 2 to 5:30pm.

Where to Stay & Eat

Auberge le Ratelier ★★ BRETON   A true taste of Brittany is savored at this converted farmhouse, situated a short stroll from the center of Carnac. The stone building is draped in vines and the interior is equally charming with rustic decor, a fireplace, and wooden beams. Due to its seaside location the menu showcases local seafood, particularly celebrated in its "trip around lobster" set menu. You can also enjoy non-fish dishes like smoked duck with Breton artichokes and Camembert toasts, or the saddle of rabbit stuffed with foie gras.

Upstairs, the inn has eight small, slightly old-fashioned but comfortable guest rooms with showers. They are a steal at 63€ to 73€.

4 chemin du Douët. www.le-ratelier.com. ℰ **02-97-52-05-04.** Main course 20€–35€; fixed-price menu 24€–53€. Daily noon–2pm and 7–9:30pm. Closed mid-Nov to mid-Dec and Jan.

Camping La Grande Métairie ★   A 5-min. drive from the center of Carnac is this family fun paradise. The large complex next to the Megaliths is surrounded by trees and is a short drive to the beach. Multiple

THE WILD, WILD coast

Follow the D768 south from Carnac over the isthmus connecting the mainland to **Quiberon,** with its crescent of white sand. You'll probably see weathered Breton fishers hauling in their sardine catch.

The entire **Côte Sauvage,** or Wild Coast, is rugged and dramatic, with waves breaking ferociously against the reefs. Winds, especially in winter, lash the dunes, shaving the short pines that grow here. On the landward side, the beach is calm and relatively protected.

A 45-min. ferry ride from Quiberon is **Belle-Ile-en-Mer,** an 83 sq. km (32 sq. miles) outpost of sand, rock, and vegetation. It feels blissfully isolated, despite a scattering of hotels and seasonal restaurants. Depending on the season, five to 15 **ferries** depart daily from Port Maria in Quiberon (✆ **08-20-05-61-56**). A round-trip ticket costs 33.65€ for adults, 21.90€ for ages 4 to 17, and free for children 3 and under. In summer, you must reserve space for your car, as well as for passengers. The ferry docks at **Le Palais,** a fortified 16th-century port that is the island's window to mainland France. The **Office**

de Tourisme is here, on Quai Bonnelle Le Palais (✆ **02-97-31-81-93**).

Excellent accommodation and dining can be found in **Port de Goulphar,** an inlet on the southern shore framed by cliffs. The standout is the 63-unit Relais & Châteaux property **Castel Clara** (www.castel-clara.com; ✆ **02-97-31-84-21**), with restful rooms, two heated swimming pools (one seawater), and extensive spa services. Ideal service and first-class cuisine add to the sense of peace. Depending on the season, and on the view from the room (sea or garden), rates range from 120€ to 385€ double, 335€ to 515€ suite. The hotel is closed from mid-November to mid-December.

A fitting souvenir are sardines from **La Belle-Iloise boutique** on the place de la République (www.labelleiloise.fr; ✆ **02-97-31-29-14**). Even if you don't like sardines, the attractive tins make unusual *objets*. The last cannery in Belle-Ile-en-Mer closed in 1975, but production continues in Quiberon, and Belle-Iloise boutiques can be found in most Breton towns.

Beach at Quiberon

activities onsite include a large pool complex, water slides, a tree adventure park, mini-golf, tennis, and more. They even have a little farm and a circus school. You can either pitch your own tent or rent a variety of equipped mobile homes or for something different, opt for one of their tree-houses perched safely in the branches.

Route des Alignements de Kermario–Kerlescan. www.lagrandemetairie.com. ✆ **02-30-26-02-29.** From 14€ tent lots; 96€–295€ mobile homes; discounts on weekly rates. Closed mid-Sept to Apr. **Amenities:** Restaurant; babysitting; bar; disco; grocery; Jacuzzi; outdoor pool; Wi-Fi in central bar (3€/hr.; 6€/day; 20€/week).

Château de Locguénolé ★★★   Crowning a small bay enveloped by a 120-hectare (297-acre) forest, this is the most graceful hotel in southern Brittany. Located near the town of Hennebont, 29km (18 miles) northwest of Carnac, the château has been in the same family for over two centuries, enough time to perfect this excellent combination of French elegance and maritime personality. While strolling the beautifully maintained gardens you can watch sailboats idly cruise by. The stately main building is filled with tasteful antiques, tapestries, and paintings. Guestrooms are very spacious; though the decor is a touch dated, this also adds to its charm. Rooms in the renovated 1720 Breton cottage annex are well appointed but lack the sea view. The elegant drawing room now serves as the hotel's Michelin-starred restaurant, the best place to enjoy local seafood and shellfish.

Rte. De Port-Louis en Kervignac. www.chateau-de-locguenole.com. ✆ **02-97-76-76-76.** 22 units. 178€–278€ double; 340€–440€ suite. Closed Jan to mid-Feb. From Hennebont, follow hotel signs, 4km (2.5 miles) south. **Amenities:** Restaurant; babysitting; outdoor pool; room service; 2 saunas; tennis; free bike rental; free Wi-Fi.

NANTES ★★★

385km (239 miles) W of Paris; 325km (202 miles) N of Bordeaux

Technically, Nantes (pop. 298,000) is outside of Brittany. In 1941, the Vichy Government transferred it from the region into a newly-created one, the Pays de la Loire. This administrative action did nothing to change Nantes' deeply Breton soul, however, and no guide to Brittany would be complete without its inclusion.

The capital of Brittany is Rennes (pop. 213,000), but when comparing the two cities, many agree that Nantes is more vibrant. It's best known for its busy port, which suffered great damage in World War II, and for the 1598 Edict of Nantes, which guaranteed religious freedom to Protestants (this was later revoked). During the Middle Ages, Nantes expanded from an island in the Loire to the northern edge of the river, where its center lies today. Many famous people, from Molière to Stendhal, have lived here.

Despite a lackluster reputation, Nantes is becoming a kind of Atlantic Coast Parisian annex for young *bobos* and families tired of the capital's rat race. Impressive revitalization is changing the city, as once-dreary industrial suburbs are being transformed into places you'd actually like to visit.

Essentials

ARRIVING The TGV train from Paris's Gare Montparnasse takes about 2 to 2.25 hr. to get to Nantes and costs range from 29€ to 77€. For information, visit www.oui.sncf or call ✆ **36-35** (.40€/min.). Nantes's Gare SNCF, 27 bd. de Stalingrad, is a 5-min. walk from the town center. If you're driving, take A11 for 385km (239 miles) west of Paris. The trip takes about 4 hr. Aéroport Nantes-Atlantique (✆ 02-40-84-80-00) is 12km (7.5 miles) southeast of town. Air France (www.airfrance.fr; ✆ 36-54 within France only) offers daily flights from Paris. A shuttle bus between the airport and the Nantes train station takes 25 min. and costs 9€. A taxi from the airport costs 30€ to 35€ and takes about 20 min.

VISITOR INFORMATION The Office de Tourisme is at 9 rue des Etats (www.nantes-tourisme.com; ✆ 08-92-46-40-44).

PASS NANTES Available at the airport, tourist office, and certain hotels, the pass allows you to enter museums and ride any of the city's public conveyances, including buses, trams, and some of the boats that cruise through town along the Erdre River. Adult passes cost 25€ for 1 day, 35€ for 2 days, and 45€ for 3 days; passes for families of four are a good value.

Getting Around

ON FOOT The downtown, cathedral, castle, and the island are accessible on foot and the central train station helps for visitors without wheels.

BY BICYCLE Nantes has a Paris-style bike-sharing program called Bicloo (www.bicloo.nantesmetropole.fr; ✆ 09-69-39-36-67). With 103 stations it's a great way to get around. You can register online at machines at most stations or at the tourist office. Fees are 1€ for a day pass or 5€ for a weekly pass.

BY CAR As the downtown core is highly pedestrianized, it's best to park your car; around the station are ideal official lots. Otherwise, another is at the cathedral. You can rent a car near the train station through Europcar, 325 rue Marcel Paul (www.europcar-atlantique.fr; ✆ **02-40-47-19-38**) or Hertz, rue Cornulier (www.hertz.fr; ✆ 02-40-35-78-00).

BY TAXI For an English-speaking service call Taxis Nantes or reserve online (www.taxisnantes.fr; ✆ **06-88-28-16-29**).

BY PUBLIC TRANSPORT Nantes has an extensive transit system of trams, buses, and ferries run by the **TAN** (www.tan.fr; ✆ 0**2-40-44-44-44**). A one-way ticket costs 1.60€ and can be purchased from a machine at tram stations or 2€ from the bus driver or an unlimited day pass is 5.40€.

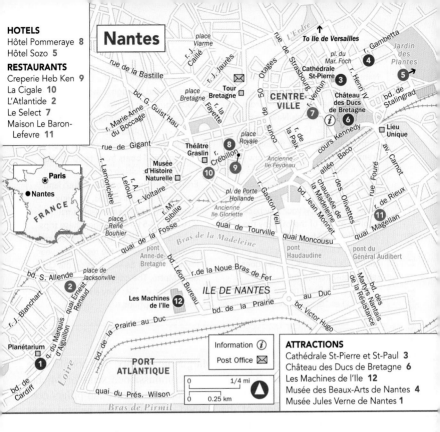

HOTELS
Hôtel Pommeraye 8
Hôtel Sozo 5

RESTAURANTS
Creperie Heb Ken 9
La Cigale 10
L'Atlantide 2
Le Select 7
Maison Le Baron-
Lefevre 11

Information (i)
Post Office ✉

ATTRACTIONS
Cathédrale St-Pierre et St-Paul 3
Château des Ducs de Bretagne 6
Les Machines de l'Ile 12
Musée des Beaux-Arts de Nantes 4
Musée Jules Verne de Nantes 1

[Fast FACTS] NANTES

ATMs/Banks   Easy-access ATMs are in front of the cathedral or around place Royale.

Doctors & Hospitals   **Centre Hopitalier Universitaire de Nantes,** 85 rue Saint-Jacques (www.chu-nantes.fr; ✆ **02-40-08-33-33**).

Internet Access   Free Wi-Fi is available at the tourist office or at many cafes in the downtown core like the hip cafe-bookshop **Les Bien-Aimés,** 2 Rue de la Paix (www.les-bien-aimes.fr; ✆ **02-85-37-36-01**).

Mail & Postage   **La Poste,** 2 pl. de Bretagne (✆ **36-31**).

Pharmacies   **Grand Pharmacie de Paris,** 17 rue Orléans (✆ **02-40-48-64-48**).

Exploring Nantes

Cathédrale St-Pierre et St-Paul ★★ CATHEDRAL   Begun in 1434, this cathedral wasn't finished until the late 19th century. Still, it managed to remain architecturally harmonious—a rare feat. Two square towers dominate the facade; more impressive is the 100m-long (328-ft.) interior. Its *pièce de résistance* is the Renaissance tomb of François II, duc

On the Rivers

Nantes might not be on the sea, but it's still highly connected to water with its two rivers: the Loire and the Erdre. You can hop on the Loire's **Navibus** public watertaxi and in 15 min. you disembark at the charming former fishing village of **Trentemoult**. You wouldn't know you were in the Nantes suburbs while strolling its narrow lanes lined with colorful three-story houses, artist studios, and secret gardens. On your way back, grab a coffee at one of the cafes by the ferry dock. The small ferries depart regularly from the Nantes Gare Maritime on the Quai de la Fosse; the journey goes for a regular bus/tram ticket.

The Erdre River, deemed by King François I as "the most beautiful river of France," empties into the Loire, hidden underground through downtown, but it pops above not far from la Tour de Bretagne. A visit to its **Ile de Versailles** offers various pleasures, namely its tranquil Japanese garden. In summer, you can rent small boats from its tip. Or better yet, take a leisure cruise along the Erdre to admire its beautiful plush landscape and graceful castles; **Bateaux Nantais** (http://bateaux-nantais.fr; ✆ **02-40-14-51-14**) arranges these trips which depart twice daily in summer (and several times weekly the rest of the year) just north of Ile de Versailles on the Quai de la Motte. The cruise lasts 1 hr., 45 min. and costs 13€; they also run lunch and dinner options.

de Bretagne, and his second wife, Marguerite de Foix. The couple were the parents of Anne de Bretagne, who commissioned sculptor Michel Colombe to create their final resting place. White walls and pillars contrast with the rich colors of the stained-glass windows; helpful signs explain the significance of most objects.

pl. St-Pierre. ✆ **02-40-47-84-64.** Free admission. Daily 8:30am–6:15pm. Crypt: Sat–Sun 3–6pm.

Château des Ducs de Bretagne ★★ CASTLE/MUSEUM   This enormous complex, seat of the Dukes of Brittany, was constructed in the 9th or 10th century, enlarged in the 13th century, destroyed, then rebuilt into its present shape by François II in 1466. The Duchesse du Berry, royal courtesan, was imprisoned here, as was Gilles de Retz (aka "Bluebeard"), one of France's most notorious mass murderers. The castle's rich inventory has been presented as a museum since the 17th century. About 30 rooms are devoted to the history of the port, displaying evocative objects such as scale models of the city during different eras. The museum charges admission, but you can visit the courtyard and stroll along the ramparts for free.

4 pl. Marc-Elder. www.chateau-nantes.fr. ✆ **08-11-46-46-44.** Ramparts free daily 8:30am–7pm (July–Aug until 8pm). Museum 5€ adults; 3€ students 25 and under; free for children 17 and under. Sept–June Tues–Sun 10am–6pm; July–Aug daily 10am–7pm. Closed public holidays.

Musée des Beaux-Arts de Nantes ★ MUSEUM   After a massive 6-year renovation, the city's fine arts museum reopened in 2016 with 30 percent more exhibition space and the addition of the Cube, a new building devoted to contemporary art. The vast body of its collection was amassed in the late 18th century by the Cacault brothers and features a fine array of paintings from the 12th to the late 19th centuries. The strong Italian representation (Perugino, Tintoretto, Gentileschi) is due to François Cacault's travels as a diplomat. The municipality added to this foundation with purchases of 19th-century works by Delacroix, Rousseau, Renoir, and Gauguin, in addition to modern and contemporary artists.

10 rue Georges Clemenceau. www.museedesbeauxarts.nantes.fr. *©* **02-51-17-45-00.** Admission 8€ adults; 4€ students ages 18–26; free for children 17 and under and all visitors on the 1st Sun Sept–June. Wed–Mon 11am–7pm (Thurs until 9pm).

Musée Jules Verne de Nantes ★ MUSEUM   Nantes's most historic figure is certainly the novelist Jules Verne ("Journey to the Center of the Earth," "Around the World in Eighty Days"). Born in Nantes in 1828, he sat for hours on end, looking out his window at the busy port, imagining the exotic destinations the ships had traveled from. His adventures best come to life not at the museum, but at Les Machines de L'Ile (see "Brittany for Kids" box at the end of the chapter). However, fans of the

The Jules Verne Museum, Nantes

author and young explorers will enjoy the museum's displays of memorabilia and artifacts inspired by his writings, from ink spots to a "magic" lantern with glass slides. Die-hard fans can seek out his former residence at 4 rue de Clisson in the Ile-Feydeau, though it is privately owned and not open to the public.

3 rue de l'Hermitage. www.julesverne.nantesmetropole.fr. ℂ **02-40-69-72-52.** Admission 6€ adults; 3.50€ students; 2.50€ children ages 7–17; free for ages 6 and under. Jul–Aug daily 10am–7pm; Sept–June Mon, Wed, Thurs, Fri, and Sun 2–6pm and Sat 10am–noon and 2–6pm.

Where to Stay

Hôtel Nantes Centre Passage Pommeraye ★ Situated in the heart of town, this is a convenient option for a reasonably priced overnight in Nantes. It's surrounded by a multitude of shops, restaurants, and the historic Passage Pommeraye. Acquired by Accor Hotels in 2017, the compact rooms have all been redone in a stylish light mauve, coral, and beige palette complemented with contemporary furnishings and high-quality beds and linen. Rooms on the street side have lovely views of town, yet can be noisy, so for a peaceful sleep request a room facing the courtyard.

2 rue Boileau. www.hotel-pommeraye.com. ℂ **02-40-48-78-79.** 50 units. 110€–170€ double; 150€–220€ suite. Small pets 5€. Parking 13€. **Amenities:** Restaurant; bar; room service; free Wi-Fi.

Hôtel Sozo ★★★ Located in a renovated 19th-century chapel across from the Jardin des Plants, this exceptional boutique hotel is more than just a place to lay your head, it's a philosophy. "Sozo" means creation and imagination in Japanese; the driving force behind the hotel's inception and its ongoing spirit. Guestrooms are small though extremely well appointed; each one features characteristics of the chapel from stained glass to pillars and arches. The room size matters less since the monumental foyer is the place to be. Enjoy a cocktail or take your turn at the grand piano, that is, unless it's already occupied by a famous musician—the hotel is a favorite for visiting artists and performers. They've also recently added in a new sensorial experience spa which includes a sauna, hammam, ice room, and sensory shower which emits real Breton sea mist.

16 Rue Frédéric Cailliaud. http://sozohotel.fr. ℂ **02-51-82-40-00.** 24 units. 192€–225€ double; 330€–450€ suite. Parking 10€. **Amenities:** Room service; spa (19 €); free Wi-Fi.

Where to Eat

You can't beat a traditional Breton crepe to satisfy hunger and the best in town have been flipped for the last 40 years at **Creperie Heb Ken,** 5 rue de Guérande (www.heb-ken.fr; ℂ **02-40-48-79-03**). Adventurous eaters should try the scallops with saffron sauce. Or for brunch, a light lunch, or afternoon tea surrounded by crystal chandeliers and stuffed animal heads with sunglasses, pop into the hip **Le Select,** 14 rue du Château (www.leselect.fr; ℂ **02-40-89-04-49**).

For a fancier *chocolat chaud* or *confit de canard,* settle in at the glitzy Belle Epoque brasserie **La Cigale,** 4 pl. Gralin (www.lacigale.com; ✆ **02-51-84-94-94**).

L'Atlantide ★★★ MODERN FRENCH   The panoramic view rivals the amazing culinary creativity at the best restaurant in Nantes. Situated on the 4th floor of the city's chamber of commerce building, the Jean-Pierre Wilmotte designed dining room has a wall of windows looking out onto the city and Loire River. Chef Jean-Yves Guého took his knives around the world before returning to his native Brittany. His travels have influenced his innovative menu, which may include ravioli of merlan and Thai basil served in a lemongrass broth, sea bass with truffles and sun-choke puree, or ginger-glazed veal sweetbreads with braised Brussels sprouts. These are best enjoyed with some muscadet or anjou from the excellent cellar stocked mostly with Loire Valley wines. Vegetarian and vegan menus are also available on request.

Centre des Salorges, 16 quai Ernest Renaud. www.restaurant-atlantide.net. ✆ **02-40-73-23-23**. Main course 30€–45€; fixed-price lunch 40€ or dinner 50€–100€. Mon–Sat noon–1:30pm and 7:30–9:15pm. Closed 1st 3 weeks in Aug and Dec 24–26 and 1st week of Jan.

Maison Le Baron-Lefevre ★ TRADITIONAL FRENCH   Located in a former wholesale market building, excellent food traditions are carried on at this locavore restaurant—so local that all the vegetables come from their own garden. Chef Jean Charles Baron sticks to classic dishes to focus on the flavor of the products. His seasonal menu may feature creamy squash soup, sole meunière with *pot à feu* vegetables, or supreme of chicken with new potatoes. Service is very attentive, with personal touches like seasonal fruit or nuts with your coffee. They also sell a range of their preserves and products.

33 rue de Rieux. www.baron-lefevre.fr. ✆ **02-40-89-20-20.** Main course 16.50€–32€; weekday lunch menu 18.50€; dinner 28€. Tues–Sat noon–2pm and 7–11pm.

Shopping

As the bustling regional capital, Nantes overflows with shops and boutiques. The principal shopping streets are rue du Calvaire, rue Crébillon, rue Boileau, rue d'Orléans, rue de la Marne, and rue de Verdun. Most of these encompass the shopping districts around place Graslin, place Royale, the château, and the cathedral. The Passage Pommeraye, a historic gallery that dates back to 1843, houses a small, upscale shopping center.

A handful of antiques shops can be perused on rue Jean Jaures such as Ecritoire Antiquités Poidras, at no. 12 (✆ 02-40-47-78-18), offering 18th- and 19th-century furniture and decorative pieces such as historic mantels. Further historic knickknacks can be picked through every Saturday morning at the flea market in place Viarme.

St-Malo is a great destination for families. Not only is there the beach, but kids will also love exploring the ramparts, the château, and the fort (see p. 305). For some additional family fun nearby, head to the side-by-side **Cobac Parc & Aqua'Fun Park** (www.cobac-parc.com; ✆ 02-99-73-80-16). A day's worth of fun is had zooming down its waterslides, swinging clubs at the mini-golf, and twirling around on its small amusement park rides. Cobac Parc is open daily 10:30am to 6:30pm in July and August and sporadic hours, usually including weekends, April to June and September (consult website calendar); Aqua'Fun is open the same days but from 1pm. A joint ticket for both parks is 23€ for ages 12 and up and 19.50€ for children 11 and under.

Breton history and culture come to life at the **Village de Poul-Fetan** (www.poulfetan.com; ✆ 02-97-39-51-74), a restored hamlet in Quistinic, a 35-min. drive northeast of Lorient. As you amble through the set of stone houses, historical interpreters demonstrate traditional tasks of daily life and arts and crafts. Children can try their hand at spinning wool, test out some rustic games, and even learn a few words of Breton. Admission is 10.80€ for adults, 5€ for children

ages 5 to 15, and free for ages 4 and under; passes for families of 4 are 28.50€. It's open daily April, May, and September 11am to 6:30pm, June 10:30am to 6:30pm, and July and August 10:30am to 7 pm.

One of the regional highlights for families is Nantes's **Les Machines de l'Ile,** 3 rue de l'Hermitage (www.les machines-nantes.fr; ✆ 02-40-69-72-52), a fantastical workshop based on hometown writer Jules Verne's imagined creatures and the mechanical drawings of Leonardo da Vinci. A 12m (147-ft.) elephant, made from 45 tons of wood and steel, takes 50 passengers at a time for a stroll around the premises. Don't leave without a ride on the massive Carrousel des Mondes Marins (Marine Worlds Carousel) that takes 300 "voyagers" at a time on a trip through its three levels representing the ocean, seabed, and abyss. One ticket gives access to the rides, another admits you to the Galerie, where you can see future creations taking shape. Admission is 8.50€ adults, 6.90€ ages 4 to 18; free for children 3 and under. Because the site is a functioning workshop, its opening hours change weekly; check the English pages of their website for details.

For some local gastronomic specialties, start filling your basket at **La Fraiseraie,** 13 rue de la Marne (www.lafraiseraie.com; ✆ 02-51-72-13-18), which sells a variety of jams, juices, and candies made from famous Pornic strawberries. More tasty treats can be picked up at **Gautier Debotte,** 9 rue de la Fosse (✆ 02-40-48-23-19), a historic *chocolatier* established in 1823, and makers of "Le Muscadet Nantais"—a chocolate-covered white grape macerated in local muscadet wine. Other Debotte boutiques are at 2 rue des Hauts Pavé, 3 rue de Budapest, and 15 rue Crébillon (the latter two have tea salons). Finish off your food shopping with some actual bottles of muscadet or other regional wines; a great selection is stocked at the **Maison des Vins de la Loire,** 15 pl. du Commerce (www.vinsvaldeloire.fr; ✆ 02-40-89-75-98).

Nantes Nightlife

When the sun goes down, the town turns into one big party. On place du Bouffay, place du Pilori, and the pedestrian streets in between, you'll find lots of cafes and pubs, many with live music and fun people. A younger crowd rules rue Scribe.

Live music fans can catch blues, jazz, or rock concerts at the speakeasy style **L'Univers Café,** 16 rue Jean-Jacques-Rousseau (*©* **02-40-73-49-55**), while oenophiles won't be disappointed with the wine lists at the modern **Comédie des Vins,** 4 Rue Suffren (www.facebook.com/lacomedie desvins; *©* **02-40-73-11-68**) or the rustic **Café de Provence,** 2 rue Vauban (www.baravinslaprovencenantes.com; *©* **02-40-48-78-71**). On warm summer nights, amble along the Ile de Nantes to the Le Hangar des Bananes (www.hangarabananes.com). These former storage buildings for exotic fruit from the colonies have been converted into a line of bars and restaurants with large terraces.

The hippest location in Nantes, and the town's leading cultural center, is **Le Lieu Unique,** 2 rue de la Biscuiterie (www.lelieuunique.com; *©* **02-51-82-15-00**). Converted from a 19th-century biscuit factory, the venue offers presentations ranging from plays (in French) to art exhibitions. Admission is free to the dimly lit, concrete-floored bar at ground level, frequented by students and artists who pack the dance floor. The restaurant here also has the same vibe. The bar is open Monday 11am to 8pm, Tuesday and Wednesday 11am to 1am, Thursday 11am to 2am, Friday and Saturday 11am to 3am, and Sunday 3 to 8pm.

For dancing, head to the stylish **Le Royal Club Privé,** 7 rue des Salorges (www.leroyal.fr; *©* **02-40-69-11-10**). Be sure to dress up, avoid jeans and sneakers, and be prepared to pay 15€ to 20€.

9

THE CHAMPAGNE REGION

by Victoria Trott

G eographical luck—both good and bad—has played a large part in the history of Champagne. Warm enough to grow grapes in, but cold enough for snow in winter, the climate frustrated early winemakers by causing an uneven fermentation that resulted in bubbles—a "fault" that led to one of France's most famous luxury products. In 2015, Champagne Hillsides, Houses and Cellars were inscribed onto UNESCO's World Heritage List. On the less-good side, the region's position between the Western Front and Paris meant that the 20th century saw many of its buildings destroyed, especially during the First World War.

Champagne's major tourist towns are easily reached by train from Paris in under 90 min. Travelers with their own wheels, however, will get the most out of the winding roads, vineyard-draped hills, deciduous forests, and farmland that lend themselves to this area's natural beauty.

REIMS ★★

143km (89 miles) E of Paris; 29km (18 miles) N of Epernay

Blessed with a gorgeous cathedral, site of royal coronations for a thousand years, Reims (pronounced "rahns") is the largest city in the region and the unofficial capital of that deliciously fizzy nectar known as champagne. While it was almost obliterated by bombing during World War I, parts of the historic center have survived, including the above-mentioned cathedral, which, as well as the Basilique St-Rémi, Palais du Tau and St-Nicaise hill (vineyards), is a UNESCO World Heritage Site. If it is not as quaint as other French cities, Reims is an interesting place to visit, with a large pedestrian-only shopping district and some attractive Art Deco architecture. The Christmas market is considered one of the best in France.

The main draw though, aside from the cathedral, is bubbly. Some of the most famous names in champagne are found here, notably Lanson, Mumm, Pommery, Ruinart, Taittinger and Veuve Clicquot; all offer tours and tastings. Reims makes a good base for exploring the Champagne region and is just a short hop from Epernay.

Essentials

ARRIVING High-speed, direct **TGV trains** leave for Reims from Paris's Gare de l'Est several times per day (trip time: 45 min.). For information,

FACING PAGE: **Champagne vineyards**

visit www.oui.sncf or call ☏ **36-35** (.40€/min.). It's about 15 min. walk southeast of the station to the cathedral. Alternatively, you'll find taxis and trams (see www.citura.fr for public transport; a day travel pass "*ticket journée*" is available for 4€ from ticket machines) in front of the station. If you are **driving** from Paris, take the A4 east.

VISITOR INFORMATION The main **Tourist Office** is by the cathedral, 6 rue Rockefeller (www.reims-tourisme.com; ☏ **03-26-77-45-00;** open daily). An office is also outside the train station.

Exploring Reims

Basilique St-Rémi ★★ CHURCH   This 11th-century church, about a 20-min. walk south of the cathedral, is one of the best examples of Romanesque religious architecture in Northern France. Within the complex is the former royal abbey of St-Rémi—the Bishop of Reims who converted Clovis, King of the Franks, to Christianity around A.D. 496; it now houses an extensive collection covering the city's history, military history, and regional archaeology including some fine Roman mosaics. The church contains St. Rémi's tomb and a collection of 12th-century stained glass windows.

Basilique: pl. Chanoine Ladame. www.reims.fr/musee-saint-remi. ☏ **03-26-85-31-20.** Free admission. Daily 8am–7pm (or nightfall in winter). **Musée:** 53 rue Simon. ☏ **03-26-35-36-90.** Admission 5€ adults; free for students 25 and under and children 18 and under. Mon–Fri 2–6:30pm; Sat–Sun 2–7pm. Bus stop: St-Rémi.

Basilica St-Rémi

Cathédrale Notre-Dame de Reims ★★★ CATHEDRAL   This mighty cathedral has survived the centuries (it was damaged but left standing when the city was bombed to smithereens in World War I) and today draws tourists (and the faithful) from far and wide who come to admire its magnificent Gothic architecture and elaborate statuary, not to mention some stunning stained-glass windows, including three by Marc Chagall in the axial chapel. The official setting for royal coronations for a thousand years, perhaps its most dramatic moment was the one engineered by Joan of Arc. Instructed by voices, the teenage shepherdess made it her mission to get Charles VII back on the throne, and to get the English out of France. Though she accomplished the first here at Reims in 1429, she was unfortunately burned at the stake before she could complete the second.

Back in the 5th century, France's first king, Clovis I, was baptized by St-Rémi in a small church on this site, giving the sit a royal reputation that would follow it through the centuries. The current cathedral dates from the 13th century, and harbors 2,303 statues carved into its facades and decorating its interior. Its western and northern facades are graced with elaborate portals carved with hundreds of saints and angels. Inside, the narrow nave reaches 38 meters (125 ft.) giving the impression that the soaring arches reach all the way to heaven.

Pl. Cardinal Luçon. www.cathedrale-reims.com. ℂ **03-26-47-55-34.** Free admission. Daily 7:30am–7:30pm.

Musée des Beaux-Arts ★★ MUSEUM   This fine arts museum has a remarkable collection that stretches from the 15th to 20th centuries. On the ground floor are decorative arts from Art Nouveau to Art Deco, while upstairs highlights include a charming collection of animal portraits by Jacques-Raymond Brascassat (1804-67), some fine works by well-known artists from the beginnings of modern art, and the largest collection in Europe of Franco-Japanese painter and printmaker Léonard Foujita (1886-1968); the museum ticket also gives entry to the chapel Foujita built in 1966 in the gardens of Mumm champagne house.

8 rue Chanzy. www.musees-reims.fr. ℂ **03-26-35-36-00.** Admission 5€ adults; free for students 25 and under and children 18 and under. Wed–Mon 10am–noon and 2–6pm.

Musée de la Reddition ★ HISTORIC SITE/MUSEUM   This humble site, a former technical school north of the train station, was the setting for one of the 20th century's turning points: the surrender of the Germans to the Allies, which ended World War II. General Eisenhower himself was on hand on the fateful day, May 7, 1945, and the room hasn't changed since the papers were signed. The exhibit includes an extensive collection of military uniforms, original US newspaper cuttings, German streets signs from Reims, and a short film in French, German, and English.

12 rue Franklin Roosevelt. www.musees-reims.fr. ℂ **03-26-47-84-19.** Admission 5€ adults; free for students 25 and under and children 18 and under. Wed–Mon 10am–6pm. Tram stop: Schneiter.

Palais du Tau ★ MUSEUM   On the southern side of the cathedral lies the former Archbishop's Palace which now houses a museum dedicated to the royal coronations that took place next door. The collection includes eerie statuary and items from the cathedral's treasury, including St. Rémi's 12th-century coronation chalice and the Sainte-Ampoule, a holy flask that held the oil used to anoint new kings. The terrace of the new ground-floor tearoom is a nice spot to relax in summer.

2 pl. Cardinal Luçon. www.palais-du-tau.fr. ℂ **03-26-47-81-79.** Admission 8€ adults; free for children 18 and under. May–Aug Tues–Sun 9:30am–6:30pm; Sept–Apr Tues–Sun 9:30am–12:30pm and 2–5:30pm.

Exploring the Champagne Cellars ★★

Underneath Reims is a vast network of tunnels left over from centuries of chalk extraction. The former quarries turned out to be perfect for storing champagne, and today some 200km (124 miles) of champagne cellars lie 20 to 40m (65–131 ft.) under the city, holding millions of bottles of

Reims

To Laon **1**

To Rethel →

av. de Laon

rue F. Roosevelt

r. du Mont d'Arène

r. du Champs de Mars

Cimetière
du Nord

bd. Jamin

Jaurès

To Rethel →

r. C. Lenoir

Jean

bd. Carteret

r. du Mont d'Arène

rue de bd. Joffre

Porte
Mars

rue
du Temple

r. Lundy
Andrieux

av.

rue

de

Cernay

Gare de
Reims

bd. Foch

rue Thiers

r. J.-J. Rousseau

place A.
Briand

rue

bd. de St-Brice

r. de St-Brice

cours J.-B. Langlet

r. J.-J. Rousseau

rue Cérès

pl. du Forum

4

place
Royale

rue G. Laurent

rue de Cernay

bd. L. Roederer

pl. Drouet d'Erlon

r. Chativesle

r. Buirette

des Elus

place
Carnot

rue G. Laurent

St. Marceaux

bd. du Gén. Leclerc

de Talleyrand

Condorcet

r. Trésor

Notre-Dame
de Reims

Voltaire

8 **9**

Palais
du Tau

rue de la Paix

5 **6** **7**

Centre des
Congrès

← To Epernay

ERLON

r. de Thillois

Vesle

de

i

FRANCE

Paris ★ Reims

HINCMAR

rue Libergier

Chanzy

r. de l'Université

bd. de la Paix

← **10**
To Soissons

av. du Général de Gaulle

chaussée Bocquaine

bd. P. Doumer

autoroute de l'Est

r. Clovis

rue du Jard

r. Lt. Herduin

r. Gerbert

r. du Ponsardin

bd. Pasteur

Sillery

r. de

LA BARBÂTRE

**LES
COUTURES**

av. To Paris

rue des Capucins

rue de Venise

Gambetta

Barbâtre

bd. Victor Hugo

bd. Henry

bd. Pommery

r. des Crayères

To Paris

des Moulins

Ancien
Collège des
Jésuites

13

r. Vasnier

12

Vesle

bd. Docteur Herrot

r. du Ruisselet

du Grand Cerf

FLECHAMBAULT

bd. Dieu Lumière

r. Simon

des Salines pl. St-Nicaise

11
Basilique
St-Rémi

bd. Diancourt

14

A4

place des
Droits-de-
l'Homme av. du Gén. Giraud

To Verdun

Information **i**

Post Office ✉

ATTRACTIONS		HOTELS
Basilique St-Rémi **11**		Les Crayères **14**
Cathédral Notre-Dame de Reims **8**		Les Telliers **4**
Mumm **2**		**RESTAURANTS**
Musée de la Reddition **1**		L'Alambic **5**
Musée des Beaux Arts **7**		L'Assiette Champenoise **10**
Palais du Tau **9**		Le Bouillon des Halles **3**
Ruinart **13**		Le Café du Palais **6**
Villa Demoiselle **12**		

bubbly in various stages of fermentation. Most of the top champagne *maisons* (houses) offer daily tours of their operations; many insist you reserve in advance. Below are three different experiences; for a complete listing of available tours in both **Reims** and **Epernay** (a 30-min. drive south on the D951), visit the official site of the **Union des Maisons de Champagne** (www.maisons-champagne.com).

Mumm ★ WINERY One of the most venerable names in champagne, the Mumm family started this enterprise in 1827. The 1-hr., 15 min. visit includes a descent into the tunnels and a tour of the museum,

Champagne house of Mumm

accompanied by an introduction to champagne basics and a glass of Cordon Rouge. Reservations required.

34 rue du Champ-de-Mars. www.mumm.com. ℂ **03-26-49-59-70.** Tours (in English) from 20€ adults; 5€ ages 11–17; free for children 10 and under. Mar–Oct daily 9:30am–1pm and 2–6pm; Nov–Dec Wed–Sun (Jan–Feb Wed–Sat) 10am–1pm and 2–5:30pm.

Ruinart ★★ WINERY   Founded in 1729, the oldest and most prestigious champagne house is the perfect option for those looking for something special. The small-group 2-hr tours explore the listed chalk cellars and end with a tasting of two prestigious *cuvées*. Art is also a passion here and the house regularly collaborates with internationally renowned artists to create works for the site. Reservations required.

4 rue des Crayères. www.ruinart.com. ℂ **03-26-77-51-51.** Admission 70€ adults; free for children 17 and under. Mid-Mar to mid-Nov Tues–Sat 9:30am–5:30pm.

Villa Demoiselle ★★ WINERY   A 90-min. tour, "La Rêve d'Henry Vasnier" (a local artist and philanthropist), combines a visit to the well-known Pommery cellars with a scout around this stunning Art Nouveau/Art Deco villa. Bought and restored by Pommery's owner Paul-François Vranken in the 2000s, the villa's own cellars now house rare vintages. The visit ends with a glass of the specially created Champagne Demoiselle. Reservations required (inquire about villa tours in English).

56 bd. Henry Vasnier. www.champagnevranken.com/en/champagne-vranken/villa-demoiselle. ℂ **03-26-35-80-50.** Admission 35€ adults; 13€ children ages 10–18; free for children 9 and under. Fri–Sat 10am–1pm and 2–6pm, Sun until 5pm.

Where to Stay

Les Crayères ★★★   This palatial neoclassic château is one of the region's most desirable accommodations. Located in a 7-hectare (17-acre) park, think lush, classically French decor, rich fabrics, ornate paneling and opulent details. The guest rooms range from the "Premium" category to two splendid "Prestige" suites; some rooms are located in a cottage in the grounds. The restaurant, **Le Parc,** is equally exquisite, complete with two Michelin stars (lunch menu 69€–90€; dinner menus 130€–280€). **Le Jardin,** the brasserie, is a more casual option (fixed-price menus 31€–47€). The elegant bar **La Rotonde** has 600 champagnes on offer.

64 bd. Henri-Vasnier. www.lescrayeres.com. ✆ **03-26-24-90-00.** 20 units. 380€–755€ double. Breakfast 31€. Free parking. Closed last week in Dec through first 2 weeks of Jan. **Amenities:** 2 restaurants; bar; babysitting; concierge; laundry service; room service; tennis court; free Wi-Fi.

Les Telliers ★★   Much of Reims was destroyed during World War I and rebuilt in the years thereafter. This cozy B&B on a narrow, quiet street a 5-min. walk northwest of the cathedral is in a typical 1920s townhouse. You'll need to be fit as the two en-suite rooms, "Les Anges" and "Les Jumeaux", are on the two upper floors; both have high ceilings, original fireplaces and antiques. English-speaking owner Renaud will happily advise on the best places to eat and drink.

18 rue des Telliers. https://telliers.fr. ✆ **09-53-79-80-74.** 2 units. 80€–121€ double; 117€–163€ family suite. Breakfast included. Parking 9€. **Amenities:** Free Wi-Fi.

Where to Eat

L'Alambic ★★ FRENCH   This restaurant in a low-ceilinged, window-free champagne cellar might not appeal if you're claustrophobic, but you'd be missing out on a unique experience and delicious French food. The desserts, such as the homemade lemon tart, are particularly good and the *plat du jour* is excellent value at 11€.

63 bis rue de Chativesle. www.restaurant-lalambic.fr ✆ **03-26-35-64-93.** Main course 17€–24€; fixed-price menus 15.80€–42€. Wed–Fri noon–2pm; Mon–Sat 7–9pm. 5 min. walk southwest of train station.

L'Assiette Champenoise ★★★ MODERN FRENCH   With three Michelin stars, this ultra-stylish restaurant in a 19th-century half-timbered manor house in a suburb of Reims, was voted 13th best restaurant in the world by La Liste (www.laliste.com) in 2018. Chef Arnaud Lallement cooks up creative dishes using the finest French seasonal ingredients, such as scallops from Brittany with Périgord truffles. Make a night of it by booking a room or suite (245€–780€) in the attached five-star hotel.

40 av. Paul Vaillant-Couturier, Tinqueux. www.assiettechampenoise.com ✆ **03-26-84-64-64.** Fixed-price lunch 95€ or dinner 185€–315€. Thurs–Mon noon–1:30pm and 7:30–9:30pm. Closed mid-Feb to mid-Mar and first 2 weeks of Aug. 2km (1.25 miles) west of the cathedral via the D980.

Le Bouillon des Halles ★ FRENCH FUSION   On the west side of the curved Art Deco indoor market, this contemporary restaurant is the perfect place for a buzzy lunch, dinner, or Sunday brunch (25€).

TINY bubbles

The difference between champagne and other wines is a second, in-the-bottle fermentation. Once the wine has completed its first fermentation in tanks, it is blended, bottled, sugar and yeast are added, and the bottles sealed with metal caps. Placed horizontally, the bottles are then inverted and turned at regular intervals, allowing the yeast to settle in the neck. This process (called *remuage*, or "riddling") is mostly done by machines now, but some houses still employ *remueurs*, professionals who can hand-turn up to 40,000 bottles per day. Next, the bottles are dipped neck-first into a freezing agent to create an easily removed plug containing the sediment (*dégorgement*). Finally, they are topped up with a mixture of wine and sugar syrup (the *dosage*), the classic corks are inserted, and the finished product goes to the caves, where it ages anywhere from two to 10 years.

Market-fresh produce creates the likes of scallops roasted with mango and passion fruit or pork fillet with truffle polenta. Also here is the city's longest champagne bar, with a glass from 7.90€.

18 rue du Temple. www.bouillondeshallesreims.fr. *©* **03-26-77-08-55.** Main course 13.50€–22.90€; fixed-price menus 18.95€–33€. Mon–Sat noon–2pm and 7–10pm, Sun 11am–3pm.

Le Café du Palais ★★ FRENCH   Reims has some lovely examples of Art Deco architecture, not least this attractive café run by the same family since 1930. The *grandes assiettes* are a popular choice: "La Champenoise" consists of *jambon de Reims* (coarsely cut ham terrine) and local Chaource cheese accompanied by boiled potatoes and salad. Snacks and cakes are served outside mealtimes.

14 pl. Myron Herrick. www.cafedupalais.fr. *©* **03-26-4752-54.** Main course 19€–24€; fixed-price menus 35€–39€. Tues–Fri 8:30am–8:30pm (lunch only), Sat 9am–9:30pm (lunch and dinner).

Shopping

To purchase some bubbly, head to **Trésors de Champagne,** 2 rue Olivier Métra (www.boutique-tresors-champagne.com; *©* **03-26-48-28-42**), where you can also enjoy a tasting. *Biscuits roses* (pink biscuits) are traditionally eaten with champagne; you can get them from **Fossier,** 25 cours Langlet (www.fossier.fr; *©* **03-26-47-59-84**). For a good selection of local products, including mustard, **Terroir des Rois,** 8 rue du Préau (www.terroirdesrois.fr; *©* **03-26-88-34-95**), is your best bet.

Nightlife

Reims has the most vibrant nightlife in the region. For lively bars and clubs head to **place Drouet-d'Erlon.** Locals call it simply "place d'Erlon". At no. 9 you'll find the sophisticated champagne bar **Golden**

Bulles (☎ **03-26-36-68-18**; Tues–Sun 4–10pm). Wine bar **Le Vintage** at 16 pl. du Forum (☎ **03-26-05-89-94;** Tues–Thurs 6–12:30pm, Fri & Sat until 1:30am) offers a similar experience. If you're around in summer, head up to the rooftop bar of the **Holiday Inn,** 46 rue Buirette (☎ **03-26-78-99-99**; Mon–Sat 4–11pm), for panoramic views across the cathedral and city.

Day Trips from Reims
AMIENS
170km (105 miles) NW of Reims.

Is it worth the drive from Reims Cathedral to see yet another one? If that cathedral is in Amiens, the answer is absolutely. **Amiens,** the capital of Picardy, has been a textile center since medieval days. Its old town is a warren of jumbled streets and canals, branching off from the south bank of the Somme River. The main draw is the boldly Gothic **Cathédrale Notre-Dam' d'Amiens,** pl. Notre-Dame (www.cathedrale-amiens.fr; ☎ **03-22-80-03-41**), France's largest cathedral. The dazzling, UNESCO-protected cathedral was started in 1220 to house the head of St. John the Baptist (still visible today), brought back from the Crusades in 1206. One of the biggest Gothic cathedrals ever constructed, it's 113m (370 ft.) tall

Cathédrale Notre-Dam' d'Amiens

9

The **Routes Touristiques du Champagne** are five itineraries developed by tourist offices to show motorists the best their region has to offer. From 70km up to 220km (45–136 miles), they wind their way through vineyards, villages, and sites of interest, clearly marked by black and white road signs. One of the shortest, and prettiest, is the route dedicated to the Montagne de Reims, which is not really a mountain at all but a forested plateau between Reims and Epernay.

Along this route, as with the others, you'll pass dozens of small champagne producers, sometimes as small as in a residence or garage. Tourist offices can give you a list of those open to tastings or where English is spoken; sometimes you'll happen along one with a drop-in policy. Champagne being the livelihood of most of these producers, it's polite to buy at least one bottle in exchange for their time, but you'll likely pay less than you would for two flutes in a restaurant.

For more information, visit any tourist office or see www.tourisme-en-champagne.co.uk/champagne-trail.

with a girth of 200,000 cubic meters (more than 7 million cubic feet). On its south side, hip bistro **Big Ben,** 12 rue Cormont (www.restaurant-bigben.fr; ✆ **03-74-11-66-04**; Tues noon–2:30pm, Wed–Sat noon–2:30pm and 7–10pm) is a good spot for lunch.

From the cathedral, head to the city's **Quartier St-Leu.** Just below the cathedral, across the water, the quarter used to be a thriving medieval craft center, bustling with water mills. Today its narrow streets contain art galleries, bookshops, and antiques boutiques, making the area a wonderful place to wander. During the Saturday morning market on the quayside, farmers from the nearby Hortillonnages—the 300 hectares (741 acres) of floating gardens in the town center—hawk their products.

While in Amiens, be sure to also visit the **Maison de Jules Verne,** 2 rue Charles Dubois (✆ **03-22-45-45-75;** 7.50€ adults, 4€ children ages 6–17, free for EU residents age 25 and under; mid-April to mid-Oct Mon and Wed–Fri 10am–12:30pm and 2–6:30pm, Sat and Sun 11am–6:30pm, Tues 2–6:30pm; mid-Oct to mid-April same as above, except closures are at 6pm and closed Tues), a stately townhouse where the author plunged himself into his imaginary worlds. Period rooms convey how the house would have looked in Verne's day, and a collection of more than 700 objects reveals the author's inspiration.

To get to Amiens, the quickest and easiest option is by car. Take the A26 north to St. Quentin, and then head west on the A29 to Amiens (total about 1 hr., 45 min.). By train, you have to change in Paris and the journey takes around 2 hr., 30 min. The **tourist office** (www.visit-amiens.com; ✆ **03-22-71-60-50**) is on the north side of the square in front of the cathedral.

SEDAN

106km (65 miles) NE of Reims.

In the French Ardennes, the 16th-century **Château Fort de Sedan** (www.chateau-fort-sedan.fr; ✆ **03-24-29-98-80;** daily) is said to be the largest castle in Europe. Set over seven floors and with an area of 35,000 sq. meters (376,736 sq. ft.), the castle took over 150 years to build and, in its heyday, housed more than 4,000 men. You can take a tour and even stay here in the onsite four-star **hotel,** which has a very nice **restaurant.** The castle also hosts a medieval festival on the last weekend in May.

Several trains a day leave from Reims (trip time: 1 hr., 20 min.) or you can drive there in about 1 hr., 10 min. via the A34.

EPERNAY ★

140km (87 miles) E of Paris; 26km (16 miles) S of Reims

Although it has ⅙ the population of Reims, Epernay produces nearly as much champagne, with an estimated 322km (200 miles) or more of cellars and tunnels. Day-trippers also find it more doable, as the town center and major champagne houses are within walking distance of the train station. Unlike urban Reims, it has a quieter, yet monied, atmosphere.

Invading armies have destroyed or burned Epernay nearly two dozen times—this explains a somewhat disappointing lack of architectural character. The stately 1km-long avenue de Champagne, a UNESCO World Heritage Site, helps make up for it though, with neoclassical villas housing the headquarters of Mercier, Moët et Chandon, Perrier-Jouet, and Pol Roger, among others.

Essentials

ARRIVING If you're **driving** to Epernay from Reims, head south on the E51. From Paris, take the A4. By **train** from Paris Gare de l'Est, you'll need to change at Reims (total journey can take up to 2 hr.). From Reims, there are approximately two trains per hour (trip time: 30 min.) on weekdays, fewer at weekends. For information, visit www.oui.sncf or call ✆ **36-35** (.40€/min.). For information on bus services linking Epernay to other towns in Champagne, visit www.vitici.fr.

VISITOR INFORMATION The **Office de Tourisme** is at 7 av. De Champagne (www.ot-epernay.fr; ✆ **03-26-53-33-00;** closed Sun mid-Oct to mid-Apr).

Exploring Epernay

The center of town and shopping district radiate out from the **place Hugues Plomb** and its fountain. Gourmet foodstuffs can be found in and around the iron-and-glass **Halle Saint-Thibault** near the place d'Europe (a very seductive food market is held inside on Wednesday and Saturday mornings).

For champagne, you can go to the individual houses along the avenue de Champagne or one of the shops representing a variety. Both **La Cave Salvatori,** 11 rue Flodoard (✆ **03-26-55-32-32;** Mon–Sat 9am–noon and 2–7pm, Sun 9am–noon), and **520,** 1 av. Paul Chandon (www.le520.fr; ✆ **03-26-54-36-36**), stock a wide array of labels and vintages.

For wine-themed items such as champagne buckets and flutes, try **Home,** 12 rue du Professeur Langevin (www.home-boutique.fr; ✆ **03-26-51-83-83**).

Champagne de Castellane ★★★ WINERY

De Castellane gives you a more comprehensive view of how champagne is actually produced than the two houses recommended below. You see workers doing it all—corking, labeling, even removing sediment. The on-site museum may be a bit dull, but the climb to the tower (237 steps) for a panoramic view of the area is not. The tower is from 1904 and has become an Epernay landmark.

57 rue de Verdun. www.castellane.com. ✆ **03-26-51-19-11.** Admission 14€; free for children age 12 and under. Mid-Mar to mid-Dec daily 10–11am and 2–5pm.

Mercier ★★ WINERY

Mercier is near Moët et Chandon, and you can visit them both on the same day. Mercier conducts tours in English of its 18km (11 miles) of tunnels from laser-guided trains—reached by an elevator that descends past rudimentary champagne-themed dioramas. The

Old Moët et Chandon signs and vineyards

caves contain one of the world's largest wooden barrels, with a capacity of more than 200,000 bottles. No reservation is necessary if there are fewer than 10 in your group, though you may want to call ahead for the schedule of English tours.

70 av. de Champagne. www.champagnemercier.fr. ✆ **03-26-51-22-22.** Admission 16€–25€; 8€ children ages 10–17; free for children 9 and under. Mid-Mar to mid-Nov daily 9:30–11:30am and 2–4:30pm.

Moët et Chandon Champagne Cellars ★★ WINERY   One of the most prestigious champagne houses runs an informative tour, describing the champagne-making process and filling you in on champagne lore: Napoleon, a friend of Jean-Rémy Moët, used to stop by for thousands of bottles on his way to battle. The only time he didn't take a supply was at Waterloo—and look what happened there. The basic tour includes a glass of champagne; more expensive tickets entitle you to more glasses.

20 av. de Champagne. www.moet.com. ✆ **03-26-51-20-20**. Admission 25€–40€; 10€ children ages 10–17; free for children 9 and under. Apr–Dec daily 9:30–11:30am and 2–4:30pm.

Where to Stay

Le Clos Raymi ★   Another 19th-century mansion, this one formerly owned by Monsieur Chandon (of "Moët et" fame). The decor, however, harks back to the 1930s and contemporary artworks adorn the walls. Rooms, with original fireplaces, are individually furnished and possess some nice luxury touches for a three-star hotel, such as dressing gowns and organic toiletries. It's a short (10-min.) walk west of the town center.

30 rue Joseph de Venoge. www.closraymi-hotel.com. ✆ **03-26-51-00-58.** 7 units. 120€–195€ double. Breakfast 18€. Free parking. **Amenities:** Free Wi-Fi.

La Villa Eugene ★★   This charming 19th-century mansion which once belonged to the Mercier family offers excellent value for money for a five-star hotel. And it's just a short walk west to the major champagne houses. The rooms are light and spacious and elegantly decorated in a variety of styles, from colonial to Louis XVI. Breakfast is served in a grand glass conservatory, complete with cherub-painted ceiling, overlooking the garden.

82-84 av. de Champagne. www.villa-eugene.com. ✆ **03-26-32-44-76.** 15 units. 145€–245€ double. Breakfast 21€. Free parking. **Amenities:** Outdoor pool; free Wi-Fi.

Where to Eat

Les Berceaux ★★★ FRENCH   In the only restaurant in Epernay with a Michelin star, chef Patrick Michelon creates delicious, beautifully presented dishes made from local and national seasonal ingredients, often with international flavors. Take, for example, the grilled scallops with physallis butter on a bed of endives. Unsurprisingly, the wine list is excellent. For a less-fancy meal, Bistro Le 7 (open daily, in same building) has fixed-price menus 29€–35€ and wines and champagnes by the glass.

Upstairs are 28 guest rooms, where a double with a tub/shower costs from 99€.

13 rue des Berceaux. www.lesberceaux.com. ✆ **03-26-55-28-84.** Fixed-price menus 45€–95€. Wed–Sun noon–2pm and 7–9pm.

La Cave à Champagne ★ FRENCH   This traditional, family-run restaurant with typical dark-wood furniture, will give you a real taste of Epernay, thanks to its excellent list of champagnes. Try baked eggs with Chaource cream for starters followed by partridge with grapes. The light lunch (main course, drink, and coffee), served on weekdays, is good value at 17€.

16 rue Léon Gambetta. www.la-cave-a-champagne.com. ✆ **03-26-55-50-70.** Main course 12€–25€; fixed-price menus 21.90€–40€. Daily noon–2pm and 7–9pm. Closed Thurs eve.

La Table Kobus ★★ FRENCH   Just behind the church of Notre Dame, this stylish Belle Époque brasserie is noted for its *bistronomique* cuisine: refined dishes made with high-quality seasonal products. The menu offers a seasonal selection of creative dishes such as pheasant with salsify stewed in port or veal roasted with bay leaves on crushed potatoes with preserved lemons. The wine list features several dozen local champagnes as well as top-notch French AOCs.

3 rue Docteur Rousseau. www.la-table-kobus.fr. ✆ **03-26-51-53-53.** Main course 24€; fixed-price menus 26.50€–61€. Tues–Sun noon–2pm and 7:30–9:30pm. Closed Thurs and Sun eve.

Nightlife

As you'd imagine, Epernay has its fair share of champagne bars. The smartest is undoubtedly **Chez Georges** (www.georgescartier.com;

℗ **03-26-32-06-22;** Wed–Sat 6pm–2am, Sun 4pm–midnight) at **Champagne Georges Cartier**, 9 rue Jean Chandon Moët. A DJ spins on Friday and Saturday evenings and you can enjoy the outside terrace in summer. The tasting bar **C Comme**, 8 rue Gambetta (*℗* **03-26-32-09-55**) is open daily until 10pm. Plan a *soirée* around discovering excellent but little-known champagnes by the glass (a four-glass sampler costs around 27€; you can also order cheese and charcuterie plates).

TROYES ★★★

143km (89 miles) SE of Paris; 108km (67 miles) S of Reims

In the southwestern part of Champagne bordering Burgundy, the old center of Troyes is an architectural delight. The underwhelming approach past outlet malls and apartment-filled suburbs might tempt you to turn around and leave—but don't. In store is a walk-through history lesson, thanks to one of the largest remaining medieval residential quarters in France.

Troyes was known in Roman times as Augustobona and served as a meeting point between major roads. What's left of the Agrippa Way, linking Milan and Boulogne-sur-Mer on the northern coast, is buried 3m (10 ft.) under the current rue de la Cité. Stone from the ancient ramparts, long since destroyed, serves as foundations for some of the city's buildings, including the former Bishop's palace, now the Museum of Modern Art.

Gorgeously-restored, half-timbered 16th-century houses are the real showstopper here. A project to bring them back to life, using antique engravings as a guide, began fifty years ago; today the jewel-colored dwellings are well on their way to earning UNESCO World Heritage status.

Essentials

ARRIVING Troyes is a 2-hr. **drive** southeast from Paris on the A104, then A105 and A5/E54 autoroutes. It's most easily reached by **train**, with departures out of Paris's Gare de l'Est nearly every hour (trip time: 1.5 hr.). Unfortunately, from Reims and Epernay you must go back through Paris. For information, visit www.oui.sncf or call *℗* **36-35** (.40€/min.). For information on **bus** service linking Troyes to other towns in Champagne, visit www.vitici.fr. A direct bus to Reims several times a day (trip time: 2 hr.) is much quicker than getting the train.

VISITOR INFORMATION The **Maison de Tourisme** is situated in a beautiful half-timbered building at 16 rue Aristide-Briand (www.tourisme-troyes.com; *℗* **03-25-82-62-70**; closed Sun Nov–Easter).

Exploring Troyes

Keep your head up and camera ready: Wandering the ancient streets you'll find surprises around every corner, such as the **Ruelle des Chats** (Cats'

Old town of Troyes

Alley) between 30 and 32 rue Champeaux. The buildings on either side lean so close that a cat can easily jump from one roof to the other. Sit on one of the benches in front of the **Carrousel des Temps Modernes** (Carrousel of the Modern Age), pl. de Hôtel de Ville, to admire its remarkable animals, chariots, and hand-painted depictions of 20th-century inventions and innovators.

Cathédrale St-Pierre et St-Paul ★★ CATHEDRAL   The spectacular stained-glass windows in this cathedral—180 of them—helped Troyes earn its nickname, the "Holy City of Stained Glass." Arguably the building's main claim to fame is that the Order of the Knights Templar was founded here in 1128/9 by St. Bernard of Clairvaux, whose remains are kept here in an exquisite reliquary casket.

Pl. St. Pierre. www.cathedraledetroyes.com. Free admission. Mon–Sat 9:30am–12:30pm and 2–5pm; Sun 2–5pm.

Maison de l'Outil et de la Pensée Ouvrière (Museum of the Tool and Workers' Thought) ★ MUSEUM   This unusual museum contains 10,000 hand tools, which, although fascinating to some, will have limited appeal to most. Save your money and just enter the leafy courtyard of the 16th-century Renaissance-style building, Hôtel de Mauroy, to admire the architecture.

7 rue de la Trinité. www.mopo3.com. ✆ **03-25-73-28-26.** Admission 7€; 3.50€ ages 12–18; free for children 11 and under. Apr–Sept daily 10am–6pm, Oct–Mar Wed–Mon 10am–6pm. Closed Dec 25 and Jan 1.

Musée d'Art Moderne ★★★ MUSEUM   Housed in the former Bishop's Palace, the collection of textile magnates Pierre et Denise Lévy is one of the most interesting regional art exhibitions we've come across, aided by its atmospheric 16th-century surrounds. Among the works, from the mid-19th century to the 1960s, are paintings by Picasso, Modigliani, Matisse, Derain, and Cézanne; and sculptures by Degas and Maillol. Of particular interest is the Art Deco glasswork of Maurice Marinot (1882–1960), as well as some African artworks, whose style inspired many of the modern artists.

pl. St. Pierre. www.musee-troyes.com. ✆ **03-25-76-26-80.** Admission 5.50€; free for children ages 18 and under (free for all Nov–Mar). Apr–Oct Tues–Sun 10am–1pm and 2–6pm; Mar–Nov Tues–Sun until 5pm. Closed Jan 1, May 1, Nov 1 & 11, and Dec 25.

Where to Stay

Best Western Hôtel De La Poste & Spa ★★   In keeping with its origins as a coaching inn, this four-star hotel has been renovated with an equestrian theme. Standard rooms are decorated in contemporary style, but the two "senior suites" under the roof have added character thanks to exposed beams and skylights (they are accessed by a short staircase, as the elevator stops one floor below). A welcome addition is the new Nuxe Spa, where guests and the public can enjoy face and body treatments as well as a sauna and hammam.

35 rue Emile Zola. www.hotel-de-la-poste.com. ✆ **03-25-73-05-05.** 32 units. 99€–374€ double. Breakfast 16€. Parking 10€. **Amenities:** Bar; spa; free Wi-Fi.

La Champ des Oiseaux ★★★   Walking down the medieval street south of the cathedral to this four-star hotel feels like you're stepping back in time. The 14 rooms are set around a quiet courtyard in three buildings from the 15th and 16th century, which have been carefully restored by master craftsmen. Decor is rustic and cozy, and the "suite Loft," under the eaves, is the stuff of fairytales. The small restaurant is open on Tuesday to Saturday evenings (around 80€ per person).

20 rue Linard Gonthier. www.champdesoiseaux.com. ✆ **03-25-80-58-50.** 14 units. 169€–429€ double. Breakfast 23€. Parking 20€. **Amenities:** Bar; hot tub; outdoor pool; free Wi-Fi.

Les Comtes de Champagne ★   This budget hotel in a half-timbered house oozes character. The en-suite rooms, most with exposed bricks and beams, range from the basic "comfort" option to "charm", which feature the likes of a four-poster bed. Apartments are also available across the road. The vast beam across the bar ceiling "holds up the whole house," according to the receptionist. Breakfast can be taken in the courtyard in summer.

54–56 rue de la Monnaie. www.troyes.brit-hotel.fr ✆ **03-25-73-11-70.** 45 units. 65€–105€ double. Breakfast 10€. Parking 7€. **Amenities:** Bar; free Wi-Fi.

Where to Eat

Au Jardin Gourmand ★★ FRENCH   Troyes is famous for its *andouillette* (chitterling sausage), and this is a very good place to try one—if you're an adventurous eater—especially in Chablis sauce (there are 11 sauces to choose from). Menu favorites include vanilla-scented salmon and chicken with dark chocolate and coffee. The interior is a bit cramped, so ask for a table in the pretty courtyard in summer.

31 rue Paillot de Montabert. ℂ **03-25-73-36-13.** Main course 19€–28€; fixed-price menu 24€–36€. Mon 7:30–10pm, Tues–Sat noon–1:30pm and 7:30–10pm. Closed 2 weeks in Mar and 3 weeks in Sept.

Chez Félix ★★ FRENCH   In the quaintest "street" in town, this quirky, vintage-style bistro with young staff is a good choice for lunch or dinner. Try the lamb coated with local honey for a main course and leave room for vanilla ice cream doused in *prunelle de Troyes* (see "Shopping," below). Champagnes from the *département* and *vins* from nearby Burgundy dominate the wine list. The outdoor terrace is in an attractive leafy courtyard bordered by half-timbered houses.

5 ruelle des Chats. www.chez-felix.fr. ℂ **03-10-94-03-03.** Main course 16€–25€; fixed-price lunch Mon–Fri 10€–18€. Daily noon–1:30pm and 7–9:30pm.

L'Illustré ★ FRENCH   Housed in a former newspaper office (hence the name), this buzzy restaurant, with a gorgeous wooden ceiling and staircase, has a good-value two-course lunch menu at 15.50€, as well as an excellent choice of local wines and champagnes. Try a *champagne gourmand* (glass of champagne with a selection of small desserts) to finish. In the evening, the downstairs vaulted cellar turns into a cocktail bar.

8 rue Champeaux. www.lillustre.com. ℂ **03-25-40-00-88.** Main course 15€–32€; fixed-price menu 29€–37€. Sun–Wed noon–11:30pm, Thurs and Fri until 1am, Sat until 2am.

Shopping

Troyes is home to one of the most renowned *pâtissier-choc-olatier*s in the world. **Pascal Caffet** has taken first place in a half dozen international pastry and chocolate competitions—

> **Did you know?**
>
> The biggest export market for champagne is the United Kingdom (31 million bottles), followed by the United States (22 million bottles).

he's even been decorated by the French government for his cultural contribution. Caffet's sleek, eponymous shop, 2 rue de la Monnaie (www.maison-caffet.com; ℂ **03-25-73-35-73**), captivates the eyes and anyone with a sweet tooth in equal measure.

Opposite the cathedral, **Le Cellier St. Pierre,** 1 pl. St. Pierre (www.celliersaintpierre.fr; ℂ **03-25-80-59-25**), has been open since 1840 and is the oldest continuously running shop in Troyes. It's also a distillery, where *prunelle de Troyes,* a prune-based liqueur, is still made and for sale along with dozens of wines in every price category.

Nightlife

As well as the cocktail bar at **L'illustré** (p. 358), the best option for a few drinks is **Chez Philippe** (www.bullesetdouceurs.com; ℂ **03-25-43-17-96**) at 11 rue Champeaux. This stylish champagne bar specializes in single origin bubbles from the commune of Celles-sur-Ource in the Côte des Bar; you can also get snacks here

Day Trips from Troyes

ESSOYES

60km (37 miles) SE of Troyes.

This small village on the border with Burgundy is on the map thanks to its artistic connections: Essoyes was the birthplace of Aline Charigot who went on the become Mme. Auguste Renoir. The couple bought a house here in 1896 and in 2017 it opened to the public as the **Maison des Renoir.** You buy a ticket in the Espace Renoir, 9 pl. de la Mairie (www.renoir-essoyes.fr; ℂ **03-25-29-10-94**; 14€ adults, 7€ children 17 and under; Mar Sat and Sun 10am–12:30pm and 1:30–5pm; April–May and Sept–Oct Wed–Sun 10am–12:30pm and 1:30–6pm, June–Aug Wed–Mon 10am–12:30pm and 1:30–6pm, mid-July to mid-Aug 10am–6pm, Nov Sat and Sun 10am–12:30pm and 1:30–5pm), where you can browse an exhibition and watch a film on the artist's life before going on to visit the family home, garden, and his light-filled studio. A nice spot for lunch, notably grilled meat, is **La Guinguette des Arts,** 4 bis quai de l'Ource (www.laguinguettedesarts.fr; ℂ **03-25-29-70-59;** Wed–Mon noon–2pm and 7–9pm) next to the river. The easiest and cheapest way to get to Essoyes is by car, which takes around 50 min. on the A5.

NOGENT-SUR-SEINE

52km (32 miles) NW of Troyes.

Most famous for being the lover and student of Auguste Rodin, Camille Claudel (1864–1943) was one of the unsung artists of the 19th century until recent years. Now, as well as having works on show at the Musée Rodin in Paris, as of 2017 Claudel's birthplace is open to the public with an attached museum, **Musée Camille Claudel,** 10 rue Gustave Flaubert (www.museecamilleclaudel.fr; ℂ **03-25-24-76-34;** 7€, free for ages 26 and under, free to all first Sun of month; Apr–Oct Tues–Fri 11am–6pm, Sat and Sun until 7pm, Nov–Mar Wed–Sat 11am–6pm and Sun until 7pm). Here, 43 of her works are exhibited alongside some of her contemporaries, including Rodin and Bourdelle, to celebrate this rich period of French sculpture. A short walk south is wine bar **Au Numéro Vins,** 5 rue de l'Étape au Vin (ℂ **03-25-25-73-47;** daily), where you can savor traditional French dishes or platters of cheese and charcuterie.

From Tropes, several direct TER trains a day run (trip time: 30 min.), or by car it's about 50 min. along the D442.

ALSACE-LORRAINE

By Lily Heise

10

The easternmost regions of France, Alsace and Lorraine, with ancient capitals at Strasbourg and Nancy, were the object of a centuries-old dispute between Germany and France. In fact, they were annexed by Germany between 1870 until after World War I and from 1940 to 1944. Though they've remained part of France since the end of World War II, Alsace especially is still reminiscent of the Black Forest, with its flower-laden half-timbered houses and traditional *winstub* taverns serving *choucroute* and sausage.

With this cultural mélange, it's not surprising Strasbourg became the base of the European parliament. Whereas Lorraine, with its rolling landscape and regal architecture, appears and feels more distinctly French in character and is even the homeland of one of the country's greatest heroines: Joan of Arc. Ponder these local traits while wandering through the quaint towns of the Alsatian Wine Road or through the natural splendor of the Vosges Mountains.

STRASBOURG ★★★

483km (300 miles) SE of Paris; 217km (135 miles) SW of Frankfurt

Situated about 483km (300 miles) southeast of Paris and tucked in the elbow of northwest France, Strasbourg ping-ponged between Germany and France for centuries. Today this capital of wine-growing Alsace blends Teutonic might with a cosmopolitan flair. With the majestic gothic Cathédrale Notre-Dame and its astronomical clock, the maze of cobbled streets, half-timbered houses and the poetic canals of La Petite France, this UNESCO World Heritage Site on the River Ill weaves fairy-tale charm with the European Parliament's political clout.

Essentials

ARRIVING   The **Strasbourg-Entzheim Airport** (Aéroport International Strasbourg; www.strasbourg.aeroport.fr; ⓒ **03-88-64-67-67**), 15km (9.25 miles) southwest of the city center, receives daily flights from many European cities, including Paris, London, Rome, Amsterdam, and Moscow. The **shuttle train** (look for the signs to pedestrian footbridge connecting the airport to the station platform) whisks you to Strasbourg main station in 9 min. The shuttles run every 15 min. from 5:30am until 10pm Monday through Friday, once or twice an hour on Saturday between 6:30am and

FACING PAGE: **The historic town of Colmar**

10pm, and Sundays between 8:30am and 10:30pm. The one-way cost is 4.30€ and includes connection to the municipal tram system. For information, see the "Access" tab on the airport website or call ✆ **03-88-77-70-70.**

The superfast TGV **train** makes round-trips from Paris to Strasbourg, cutting travel time nearly in half to 1 hr., 45 min.. At least 15 **trains** a day arrive from Paris's Gare de l'Est; the one-way fare is 53€ to 93€. For information and schedules, visit www.oui.sncf or call ✆ **36-35** (.40€/min.).

By **car,** the giant A35 crosses the plain of Alsace, with occasional references to its original name, the N83. It links Strasbourg with Colmar and Mulhouse.

VISITOR INFORMATION   The **Office de Tourisme** is on 17 pl. de la Cathédrale (www.otstrasbourg.fr; ✆ **03-88-52-28-28**). A second branch is inside the main train station (same telephone number).

STRASBOURG PASS   If you plan to do several tourist activities or museums, you can save with the Strasbourg Pass. Valid for three days, it grants free entrance to cathedral towers, the clock, one museum, a free boat cruise ticket, a half-day free bike rental, a 50 percent discount on a second museum and other discounts; 21.50€ for adults and 15€ for children 13 to 17 and 10€ for children 4 to 12, available at the tourist office.

SPECIAL EVENTS   The Classical Music Festival runs for two weeks in June, and the Festival Jazzdor runs in early June (both http://strasbourg-festival.com; ✆ **03-88-36-30-48**). They feature international artists and

La Petite France, Strasbourg

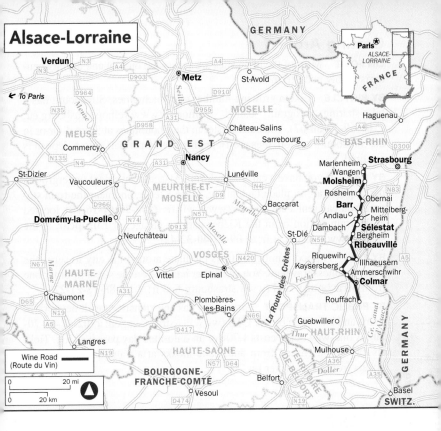

draw large crowds. Ticket prices range from 24€ to 75€ and go on sale in mid-April. **Wolf Music,** 24 rue de la Mésange (www.wolfmusique.com; ℓ **03-88-32-43-10**), arranges ticket sales for these festivals. The **Association Musica** (www.festivalmusica.org; ℓ **03-88-23-46-46**) organizes the Festival International des Musiques d'Aujourd'hui. It takes place from the end of September to the first week of October and combines contemporary concerts with movies and modern opera performances. Tickets (8€–22€) go on sale late June.

In late November and December, the place de Cathédrale erupts with the city's world-famous **Marché de Noël** (Christmas Market), where you can purchase handmade ornaments and gifts and warm up with hot *vin chaud* (mulled wine).

CITY LAYOUT   The center of Strasbourg is mainly located on **Grand Ile,** a large island hugged by two branches of the Ill River. **Petit France** is the area between these two branches; with its crooked streets and half-timbered houses, it's a major visitor destination.

Getting Around

ON FOOT Most of the main sites are accessible on foot and the city center is highly pedestrianized.

BY BICYCLE Like a growing number of French cities, Strasbourg has a bike-sharing program called **Vélhop** (www.velhop.strasbourg.eu; ✆ **09-69-39-36-67**). You can register in their boutiques at 3 rue d'Or or in the Strasbourg station; fees are 1€ per hour or 5€ per half day. A deposit is required.

BY CAR If you have a car for exploring Alsace, convenient underground parking lots are in place Gutenberg, place Kléber, and near the train station. You can rent a car at **Avis** (www.avis.fr; ✆ **08-20-61-16-98**), located at the train station or in the Kléber parking garage, or **Europcar,** at the station (www.europcar.fr; ✆ **09-77-40-32-42**).

BY TAXI A good number of taxis circulate around the city to serve the many business travelers. You can either hail one on the street or order one from **Strasbourg Taxi** (www.strasbourg-taxi.fr; ✆ **03-88-12-21-22**).

BY PUBLIC TRANSPORT Strasbourg has an extensive transit network of trams and buses run by the **CTS** (www.cts-strasbourg.eu; ✆ **02-47-66-70-70**). A one-way ticket costs 1.70€ or an unlimited day pass is 4.30€. Tickets can be purchased from automatic kiosks at a tram station or single tickets from a bus driver for 2€.

[Fast FACTS] STRASBOURG

ATMs/Banks   The city center has plenty of banks; you'll definitely find one around place Kléber.

Doctors & Hospitals   **Hopitaux Universitaires de Strasbourg,** 1 pl. de l'Hopital (www.chru-strasbourg.fr; ✆ **03-88-11-67-68**).

Internet Access   Look out for Wi-Fi signs in many central cafes or enjoy some of seriously good coffee while you surf at **Oh My Goodness Café,** 13 rue de la Première Armée (www.ohmygoodnesscafe.fr; ✆ **09-50-52-08-61**).

Mail & Postage   **La Poste,** 5 pl. du Château (✆ **36-31**).

Pharmacies   **Pharmacie de l'Homme de Fer,** 2 pl. de l'Homme de Fer (✆ **03-88-32-55-55**).

Exploring Strasbourg

Despite World War I and World War II damage, much remains of Old Strasbourg, including covered bridges and towers from its former fortifications, plus many 15th- and 17th-century dwellings with painted wooden fronts and carved beams.

The city's traffic hub is **place Kléber ★**, dating from the 15th century. Sit here with a tankard of Alsatian beer and get to know Strasbourg.

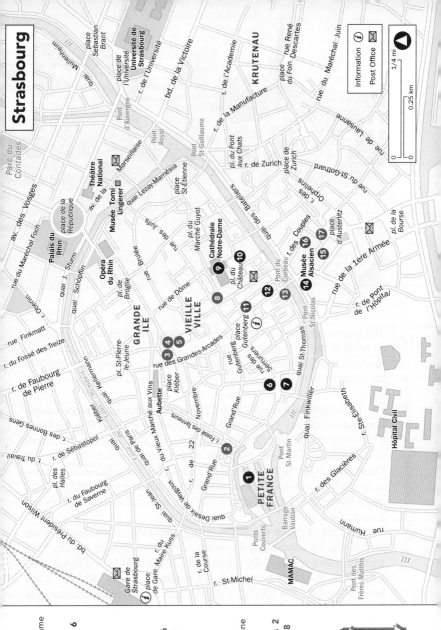

Strasbourg

Parc du Contades

Théâtre National

Musée Tomi Ungerer

Palais du Rhin

Opéra du Rhin

place de la République

GRANDE ILE

VIEILLE VILLE

Aubette

place Kléber

Cathédrale Notre-Dame

KRUTENAU

PETITE FRANCE

Barrage Vauban

Ponts Couverts

MAMAC

Hôpital Civil

Gare de Strasbourg

ATTRACTIONS

Cathédrale Notre-Dame de Strasbourg **9**
Église St-Thomas **7**
Hôtel du Commerce **6**
Musée Alsacien **14**
MAMC **1**
Musée de l'Oeuvre Notre Dame **12**
Palais de Rohan **10**

HOTELS

Cour du Corbeau **16**
Hôtel Gutenberg **11**
Romantik Hôtel Beaucour **15**

RESTAURANTS

Au Crocodile **4**
Brasserie de l'Ancienne Douane **13**
Chez Yvonne **5**
Maison des Tanneurs **2**
Maison Kammerzell **8**
VertuOse **17**
Winstub Le Clou **3**

Information (i)
Post Office ✉

1/4 mi
0.25 km

FRANCE
Strasbourg
Paris

365

Place Kleber, Strasbourg

The bronze statue in the center is J. B. Kléber, born in Strasbourg in 1753; he became one of Napoleon's most noted generals and was buried under the monument. Apparently, his presence offended the Nazis, who removed the statue in 1940. This Alsatian bronze was restored to its proper place in 1945.

From here, take rue des Grandes-Arcades southeast to **place Gutenberg,** one of the city's oldest squares. The central statue (1840), by David d'Angers, is of Gutenberg, who perfected his printing press in Strasbourg in the winter of 1436 and 1437. The former town hall, now the **Hôtel du Commerce,** was built in 1582 and is one of the most significant Renaissance buildings in Alsace. The neighborhoods within a few blocks of the city's **Notre Dame Cathedral** are loaded with medieval references and historical charm.

La Petite France ★★ is Strasbourg's most interesting quarter. A virtual island, it's surrounded by scenic canals on four sides, and its 16th-century houses reflect in the waters of the Ill River. In "Little France," old roofs with gray tiles have sheltered families for ages, and the cross-beamed facades with roughly carved rafters are in typical Alsatian style. For a good view, walk along rue des Moulins, branching off from rue du Bain-aux-Plantes.

Cathédrale Notre-Dame de Strasbourg ★★★ CATHEDRAL
The city's crowning glory is an outstanding example of Gothic architecture, representing a transition from the Romanesque. Construction began in 1176. The pyramidal tower in rose-colored stone was completed in 1439; at 141m (462 ft.), it's the tallest one from medieval times. This cathedral is still in use; religious ceremonies, particularly on feast days,

meld perfectly with the architectural majesty. Individual tourists can visit the tower only in the summer (you may have to wait to climb it). The Office de Tourisme (see above) organizes tours for groups; call for the schedule.

Four large counterforts divide the **main facade ★★★** into three vertical parts and two horizontal galleries. Note the **rose window,** which looks like stone lace. The facade is rich in decoration: On the portal of the south transept, the *Coronation and Death of the Virgin* in one of the two tympanums is the finest such medieval work. In the north transept, see also the facade of the **Chapelle St-Laurence,** a stunning achievement of the late Gothic German style.

A Romanesque **crypt** lies under the chancel, which is covered with square stonework. The stained-glass window is the work of Max Ingrand. The **nave** is majestic, with windows depicting emperors and kings on the north Strasbourg aisle. Five chapels cluster around the transept, including one built in 1500 in the Flamboyant Gothic style. In the south transept stands the **Angel Pillar ★★**, illustrating the Last Judgment, with angels lowering their trumpets.

The **astronomical clock ★** was built between 1547 and 1574. It stopped during the Revolution, and from 1838 to 1842, the mechanism was replaced. Each day at 12:30pm, crowds gather to see its show of allegorical figures. On Sunday, Apollo drives his sun horses; on Thursday, you see Jupiter and his eagle. The body of the clock has a planetarium based on the theories of Copernicus. Close-up views of the clock are available Monday to Saturday from noon to 12:30pm; tickets (3€ adults, 2€ ages 5–18 and students) are on sale in the mornings at the post-card stand or from 11:45am at a kiosk in the south portal.

pl. de la Cathédrale. ℂ **03-88-32-75-78** for times of services. www.cathedrale-strasbourg.fr. **Cathedral:** Free admission. Daily 9:30–11:15am and 2pm–5:45pm. **Tower:** ℂ **03-88-43-60-40.** Admission 5€ adults; 3.50€ children 17 and under and students; free to all the 1st Sun of the month. Apr–Sept daily 9am–7:15pm (July until 9:45pm, early Aug until 8:45 and late Aug 7:45pm); Oct–Mar daily 10am–5:15pm.

Stained-glass rose window, Cathédrale Notre-Dame de Strasbourg

STRASBOURG BY boat

Floating through Strasbourg on a boat excursion on the Ill River from the Palais de Rohan is one of the best ways to see the city. The 70-min. cruises cost 13€ for adults and 7.50€ for children and includes a free audio guide in various languages. From March to early November, rides depart at 30-min. intervals daily between 9:30am and 9pm, with hours extended to 10pm May to September. In November, departures are at 10:30am and 1, 2:30, and 4pm; from December to February, rides depart every 30 min. from 9:45am to 5pm, and in July and August an additional cruise at 8:45pm sails to view the spectacular sound-and-light show (15€ for adults and 10€ for children). For information, call **Batorama,** 9 rue de Nantes (www.batorama.fr; ℂ **03-88-84-13-13**).

Eglise St-Thomas ★ CHURCH   Built between 1230 and 1330, this Romanesque church was one of the first converted to Protestantism when the movement arrived in Alsace in 1524. It contains the **mausoleum** ★★ of Maréchal de Saxe, a masterpiece of French art by Pigalle (1777), and a magnificent 12th-century sarcophagus of Archbishop Aledoch.

Rue Martin-Luther (along rue St-Thomas, near pont St-Thomas). www.strassburg.eu/en/saint-thomas-church. ℂ **03-88-32-14-46.** Free admission. Apr–Oct daily 10am–6pm; Nov–Dec and Mar daily 10am–5pm. Closed Jan to mid-Feb.

Musée Alsacien ★ MUSEUM   Housed in three mansions from the 16th and 17th centuries, this lovely museum takes visitors on a voyage through the ages of Alsatian history via its impressive collection of paintings, furniture, and other decorative arts.

23 quai St-Nicolas. www.musees.strasbourg.eu. ℂ **03-88-52-50-01.** Admission 6.50€ adults; 3.50€ students and seniors; free for children 17 and under. Wed–Mon 10am–6pm.

Musée de l'Oeuvre Notre-Dame ★★★ MUSEUM   This museum, located in excellently restored buildings from the era, illustrates the art of the Middle Ages through the Renaissance and the beginnings of the Reformation, making it a perfect stop for fans of ecclesiastic art and medieval history. The collection displays many pieces that were previously displayed in the cathedral (where copies have since been substituted). The most celebrated is a stained-glass head of Christ from about the 11th century. Other noteworthy works are the 13th-century sculpture hall with the wise and foolish virgins from 1280, the winding Renaissance staircase, and 16th- and 17th-century artifacts by Strasbourg goldsmiths.

3 pl. du Château. www.musees.strasbourg.eu. ℂ **03-88-52-50-00.** Admission (includes free audio guide) 6.50€ adults; 3.50€ students ages 24 and under and seniors; free for children 17 and under. Tues–Sun 10am–6pm.

Museum of Modern and Contemporary Art (MAMC) ★ MUSEUM   In the heart of La Petite France, this is Strasbourg's showcase of modern European art from 1870 to the present. While it's not quite the level of the Orsay or Pompidou in Paris, it's worth a meander for true art lovers. The collection itself was started in 1919 and has grown thanks to donations from local arts patrons. The layout of the museum starts with a historical section tracing the emergence of modern art and going forward to the 21st century, including works by Rodin, Monet, Picasso, and Kandinsky. It also has an art library, a museum shop, and a cafe-restaurant on the terrace.

1 pl. Jean-Hans Arp. www.musees.strasbourg.eu. ✆ **03-88-23-31-31.** Admission 10€ adults; 6.50€ students 24 and under and seniors; free for children 17 and under. Tues–Sun 10am–6pm.

Palais de Rohan ★★ PALACE   This palace south of the cathedral was built from 1732 to 1742 for the Prince-Bishop of Strasbourg, the illegitimate son of Louis XIV. Echoing Parisian Rococo style, it is noted for its facades and sumptuous interior, making it one of the crowning design achievements in eastern France. Impressive works by Rubens, Rembrandt, Van Dyck, Goya, and Renoir are displayed on the first floor fine-arts museum (Musée des Beaux-Arts). On the main floor is a decorative-arts museum featuring ceramics and the original machinery of the cathedral's first astronomical clock. An archaeological museum on site has precious artifacts excavated from nearby digs, with a focus on art and utilitarian objects from the Roman and early medieval eras.

2 pl. du Château. ✆ **03-88-52-50-00.** Admission 6.50€ adults; 3.50€ students; free for children 17 and under. Wed–Mon noon–6pm.

Where to Stay

Cour du Corbeau ★★★   Originally opening in the 17th century, this is one of the oldest hotels in all of France and certainly the most enchanting one in Strasbourg. Though situated in the heart of the historic center, its traditional half-timbered architecture makes you feel like you're at a country inn. The interior has mostly been redone and features classy contemporary furnishings; however, some rooms have wooden beams and lovely old-fashioned windows that bring out its heritage. They have a number of deluxe rooms and 18 spacious suites. In the evening you can enjoy a cocktail at the swanky bar.

5 rue des Bouchers. www.cour-corbeau.com. ✆ **03-90-00-26-26**. 63 units. 197€–375€ double; 277€–450€ suite. Parking 2€. **Amenities:** Babysitting; bar; free Wi-Fi.

Hôtel Gutenberg ★   This is a great-value, centrally located hotel with character. From the street, admire the former 18th-century mansion's elegant facade. Once inside, you've entered the 21st century. Guest rooms have been redone with Scandinavian design, a testament to Strasbourg's espousement of Europe. Other modern features include flatscreen TVs and recently refitted, yet small bathrooms.

31 rue des Serruriers. www.hotel-gutenberg.com. ✆ **03-88-32-17-15.** 42 units. 150€–280€ double. **Amenities:** Free Wi-Fi.

Romantik Hôtel Beaucour ★★   For a restful night's sleep in the boisterous city-center, book at this peaceful hotel. Hidden away on a private street a few blocks from the cathedral, it's hard to imagine that this charming 17th-century building with timbered ceilings used to be an umbrella factory. The welcome is as warm as the foyer's toasty fireplace. Alsatian hospitality and character are sprinkled throughout, so expect a small dose of gingham and hearts. Rooms are on the large size for European hotels and another plus is the presence of whirlpool tubs. The generous breakfast buffet will prep you for your next day of touring.

5 rue des Bouchers. www.hotel-beaucour.com. ℂ **03-88-76-72-00.** 49 units. 164€–209€ double; 224€–269€ suite. Parking 16€. **Amenities:** Babysitting; free Wi-Fi.

Where to Eat

For a quick good-value meal, stop in at the **Brasserie de l'Ancienne Douane,** 6 rue de la Douane. (www.anciennedouane.fr; ℂ **03-88-15-78-78**), a large brasserie serving Alsatian specialties like "sauerkraut of the Customs officers" and foie gras of Strasbourg. Alternatively, try **Maison Kammerzell,** 16 pl. de la Cathédrale (www.maison-kammerzell.com; ℂ **03-88-32-42-14**). Conveniently located on the main square, this fairytale gingerbread-house is a marvel for young and older palates.

For a *choucroute*-free lunch, track down **VertuOse,** 19 rue d'Austerlitz (www.vertuose.eu; ℂ **03-88-23-63-32**); their daily specials, salads, and inventive "Schpeck'Nini" sandwiches please both carnivores and vegetarians.

Au Crocodile ★★★ MODERN ALSATIAN   No, exotic meats are not a specialty here as its name might suggest, notwithstanding, this is easily the most innovative restaurant in Strasbourg. Originally a 14th-century Benedictine monastery, it was converted into an *auberge* in 1801 by a captain of Napoleon's army on his return from the Egyptian campaign (he brought the infamous crocodile, now stuffed and on display, with him). Its brilliant chefs have earned three Michelin stars and have served major French celebrities and heads of state (notably Barack Obama). Current chef Philippe Bohrer's creations could include confit skate wings drizzled in veal juice and served with artichokes *à la barigoule* and hazelnut butter or roasted roebuck with beets, candied grapefruit and pepper sauce.

10 rue de l'Outre. www.au-crocodile.com. ℂ **03-88-32-13-02.** Main course 48€–65€; fixed-price lunch 58€–72€ or dinner 98€–138€. Tues–Sat noon–1:30pm and 7:30–9:30pm. Closed last 3 weeks of July and Dec 24–29.

Chez Yvonne ★★ FRENCH/ALSATIAN   Opened in 1873, this is one of the oldest and most charming *winstub* in town. Located near the cathedral, it is frequented by journalists and political dignitaries. With its neat lines of tables and red-checked curtains, it's a mix of bourgeois home and sophisticated bistro. The menu features refined versions of some of the best regional cuisine such as *maennerstolz* (smoked beef and pork sausage), *Strasbourgeoise* sauerkraut with different cuts of pork, and the house specialty coq au Riesling with spaëtzle pasta.

10 rue du Sanglier. www.chez-yvonne.net. ✆ **03-88-32-84-15.** Main course 14€–27€. Daily noon–2:15pm and 6pm–midnight.

Le Buerehiesel ★★★ MODERN FRENCH   Also known as Le Restaurant Westermann, Buerehiesel is famous for its *cuisine moderne* and for its prime location in l'Orangerie, a park at the end of the allée de la Robertsau planned by the landscape artist Le Nôtre, who gave the park to Josephine during her marriage to Napoleon. The decor is swank with its richly grained wooden ceilings. The kitchen recycles heirloom recipes in innovative and exciting ways. Of special merit are the shredded crab with lime, quinoa, crisp vegetables, and shellfish jelly; *royale*-style Alsatian hare with butternut squash, wild mushrooms, and spaëtzle, and braised free-range goose with root vegetables draped in thick braising sauce. Reservations required.

4 parc de l'Orangerie. www.buerehiesel.fr. ✆ **03-88-45-56-65.** Main course 35€–49€; fixed-price lunch 37€ or 72€–104€ dinner. Tues–Sat noon–2pm and 7–10pm. Closed 1st 2 weeks of Jan, 2 weeks in early Mar and 1st 3 weeks of Aug.

Maison des Tanneurs ★ ALSATIAN   Locals call this place "la Maison de la Choucroute" as it serves the best sauerkraut-and-pork in town. Set in a former tannery dating from 1572, this antiques-filled restaurant opened in 1949. It sits idyllically on the water, its terrace opening onto the canal. If you're not tempted by its signature dish, the chef also prepares veal kidneys with local white wine, the Belle Strabourgeoise foie gras or the stuffed guineafowl on a bed of choucroute. Save room for the Kougelhopf glazed with sweet Gewürztraminer liqueur or the Alsatian fruit tart.

42 rue du Bain-aux-Plantes. www.maison-des-tanneurs.com. ✆ **03-88-32-79-70.** Main course 20€–25€; fixed-price lunch 24€–26€. Tues–Sat noon–1:45pm and 7–10pm (also Sun noon–2pm in Dec). Closed first 2 weeks in Jan.

Winstub Le Clou ★ ALSATIAN   Warmth and hearty Alsatian goodness exude from this great-value, authentic *winstub*. Wood-paneled walls, folkloric artwork, and communal tables add to its charm. They specialize in typical regional fare, like Alsatian snails, *bibeleskas* (thick cream sauce) with country-style potatoes, or a house favorite Pinot Noir–braised *wädele* (Alsatian sauerkraut with hearty knuckle of ham).

3 rue de Chaudron. www.le-clou.com. ✆ **03-88-32-11-67.** Main course 16€–27€; fixed-price menu 17€–26€. Daily 11:45am–2:00pm and 5:30pm–midnight.

Shopping

Strasbourg overflows with antiques shops, artisans, craftspeople, and beer makers. Every well-accessorized home in Alsace owns some of the napkins, aprons, tablecloths, and tea and bath towels of the Beauvillé textile mills. **Nappes d'Alsace,** 6 rue Mercière, near the cathedral (nappesd alsace.free.fr; ✆ **03-88-22-69-29**), has one of the widest selections of textiles in town.

Bastian, 22–24 pl. de la Cathédrale (www.antiquites-bastian.com; ✆ **03-88-32-45-93**) has been a family affair since 1861. They specialize in 18th- and 19th-century ceramic tureens that Alsace produced in abundance. They also have a selection of Louis XV and Louis XVI furniture, crafted in the region during the 18th and 19th centuries following Parisian models from the same era.

One of the most appealing shops in Strasbourg is **Arts et Collections d'Alsace,** 4 pl. du Marché aux Poissons (www.arts-collections-alsace.com; ✆ **03-88-14-03-77**), which sells copies of art objects and utilitarian ware from museums and private collections throughout Alsace in addition to upscale gift items for the home and fabric by the yard.

A name in pottery that you're likely to encounter is **Soufflenheim,** a provincial rococo pattern—usually in blues and reds—named after the Alsatian village north of Strasbourg where the style originated. To get there, take N63 north of the center of Strasbourg for 24km (15 miles). Ceramics and pottery have been made in the village since the Bronze Age. Soufflenheim is home to at least a dozen outlets selling cake molds, tureens, saucers and cups, dinnerware, and more, usually in rustic patterns. One of the most prominent retailers is **Gérard Wehrling,** 64 rue de Haguenau (www.poterie-wehrling.fr; ✆ **03-88-86-65-25**), known for pottery that can withstand the rigors of modern ovens, microwaves, and refrigerators.

Strasbourg Nightlife

A hub of outdoor entertainment is **place de la Cathédrale,** with its assortment of performers and artists. Dancers perform spontaneously against the illuminated cathedral. From mid-July to early August, folk dances take place in La Petite France on Monday night in place des Tripiers, Tuesday in place Benjamin Zix, and Wednesday in place du Marché aux Cochons de Lait. For dates, check with the Office de Tourisme (www.otstrasbourg.fr; ✆ **03-88-52-28-29**) for a schedule.

THE PERFORMING ARTS   For opera and ballet, seek out the **Opéra du Rhin,** 19 pl. Broglie (www.operanationaldurhin.fr; ✆ **03-88-75-48-23**); tickets cost 12€ to 90€. The **Orchestre Philharmonique de Strasbourg** performs at the Palais de la Musique et des Congrès, pl. de Bordeaux (www.philharmonique-strasbourg.com; ✆ **03-69-06-37-00**). Tickets cost 6€ to 55€. The **Théâtre National de Strasbourg** plays a busy schedule at 1 av. de la Marseillaise (www.tns.fr; ✆ **03-88-24-88-00**). Tickets cost 6€ to 28€.

BARS & CLUBS   The streets surrounding place de la Cathédrale, in particular rue des Frères, rue des Soeurs, and rue de la Croix, are bustling with cafes and bars. **Jeannette et les Cycleux,** 3 rue des Tonneliers (www.facebook.com/Jeannette.et.les.Cycleux; ✆ **03-88-23-02-71**), is a quirky retro bar filled with trendy young locals sipping on wine or nibbling at their tasty *planchettes.*

Despite being known for its white wines, Alsace is also the number one beer-producing region of France, not surprising due to its historical links and proximity to Germany. This tradition is being maintained at the artisan brewery **Au Brasseur,** 22 rue des Veaux (www.aubrasseur.fr; ✆ **03-88-36-12-13**); additionally, a wide variety of local and international pints can be sampled at **Les Freres Berthom,** 18 rue des Tonneliers (www.lesberthom.com; ✆ **03-88-32-81-18**).

For a late night with the stylish 20-to-35 strasbourgeois, go underground at **Le Seven,** 25 rue des Tonneliers (www.lesevenstrasbourg.com; ✆ **03-88-32-77-77**), and groove to the beats of contemporary dance and electro music.

LA ROUTE DU VIN (WINE ROAD) ★★★

The fastest route between Strasbourg and Colmar, 68km (42 miles) south, is N83. But if you have time, the famous Route du Vin, the oldest "wine road" in France established in 1950, makes a rewarding experience. It rolls through 60 charming villages and is flanked by the Vosges foothills, with medieval towers and feudal ruins evoking faded pageantry. The vine-covered slopes sometimes reach a height of 435m (1,427 ft.), and an estimated 20,000 hectares (49,400 acres) of vineyards line the road. Some 30,000 families earn their living tending the grapes.

Route du Vin, the oldest wine road in France

biking THE WINE ROAD

A lovely way to experience the Wine Road is to leisurely breeze through the vines and villages by bicycle. The Strasbourg tourist office provides maps showing bike routes that fan out from the city into the countryside, with emphasis on cycle lanes (*les pistes cyclables* in French) that prohibit cars. One of these is a 27km- (17 mile-) stretch that runs southwest from Strasbourg to the wine hamlet of Molsheim. It has a forest on one side,

the banks of the Brûche River (a tributary of the Rhine) on the other, and little car traffic. You can rent bikes from **Esprit Cycles,** 18 rue Jacques Krutenau (www.espritcycles.com; ℂ **03-88-36-18-41**). Their rates start at 12€ per day, 18€ for the weekend, and 42€ weekly. It's open Monday to Friday 9am to 7pm, and on Saturdays 9am to 6pm from April to October and from 10am to 6pm November to March.

Serious oenophiles will want to select specific vineyards to visit; however, the picturesque scenery and quaint towns are a highlight for any visitor to the region. The best villages are described below; charming Kaysersberg is a convenient place for lunch, while most overnights are done in the largest town, Colmar. The best time to go is for the harvest in September and October for the festivals throughout the area (especially in Ribeauvillé). Useful additional information can be found at **https://www.alsace-wine-route.com**.

Mittelbergheim

The loveliness of Mittelbergheim, 43km (27 miles) from Strasbourg, has earned the town a place on the list of "most beautiful villages of France." Houses in the Renaissance style border its **place de l'Hôtel-de-Ville.** Around town are a number of medieval wells and ancient wine presses.

Andlau

This gardenlike resort, 42km (26 miles) from Strasbourg, was the site of an abbey founded in 887 by the disgraced wife of Emperor Charles the Fat. It has now faded into history, but a church remains that dates from the 12th century. In the tympanum are noteworthy Romanesque carvings. The **Office de Tourisme,** 5 rue du Général-de-Gaulle (www.pays-de-barr.com; ℂ **03-88-08-22-57**), is open in summer Monday to Saturday 9am to noon and 2pm to 6pm and Sunday 2pm to 6pm.

Dambach ★

One of the delights of the Wine Road, Dambach (48km/30 miles from Strasbourg) is the largest wine-producing village in Alsace. One of the finest Alsatian wines, the Grand Cru Frankstein, comes from here. The town, formally Dambach-la-Ville, has ramparts and three fortified gates and was once protected by the medieval Bernstein castle, today in ruins above the town. Its timbered houses are gabled with galleries, and many contain oriels. Wrought-iron signs still tell you if a place is a bakery or a butcher shop. A short drive from the town is the **Chapelle St-Sebastian,** with a 15th-century ossuary. The **Office de Tourisme** (www.dambach-la-ville.fr; ✆ **03-88-92-61-00**) is in La Mairie (town hall), pl. du Marché.

Between Dambach and Ribeauvillé is the region's most impressive castle: **Château Haut Koenigsbourg ★★.** Clinging to the mountainside, it has a sprawling view of the whole valley. Presumed to date from the 12th century, it has typical medieval fortress features including thick defensive walls, turrets, and a tall keep. It was highly damaged and subsequently abandoned during the Thirty Years' War. It was eventually restored under German Emperor Wilhelm II in the early 20th century, although the accuracy of the restoration is somewhat dubious; nonetheless, it's a spectacular site. Entrance is 9€ adults, 5€ children 6 to 17 and free for 5 and under. It's open daily November to February 9:30am to noon and 1 to 4:30pm; March and October 9:30am to 5pm, April, May, and September 9:15am to 5:15pm and June to August 9:15am to 6pm (www.haut-koenigsbourg.fr; ✆ **03-69-33-25-00**).

Ribeauvillé ★★

At the foot of vine-clad hills dotted with castle ruins, Ribeauvillé (87km/54 miles from Strasbourg) is picturesque, with old shop signs, pierced balconies, turrets, and flower-decorated houses. The town is noted for its Riesling and Gewürztraminer wines. See its Renaissance fountain and **Hôtel de Ville,** pl. de la Mairie, which has a collection of silver-gilt medieval and Renaissance tankards known as *hanaps.* For information, go to the tourist office at 1 Grand' Rue (www.ribeauville-riquewihr.com; ✆ **03-89-73-23-23**).

Also of interest in Ribeauvillé is the **Tour des Bouchers** (Butcher's Tower), built in stages from the 13th to the 16th century.

Every year on the first weekend in September, visitors fill the town for its **Pfifferdaj** or **Jour des Menetriers (Day of the Minstrels),** the oldest festival in Alsace dating back to the Middle Ages. A medieval market, building illuminations, public dances, and other activities take place all weekend, however, the real event is Sunday at 3pm when a parade of flute players from Alsace, the rest of France, Switzerland, and Germany, and as many as 600 parade participants make their way through town. You can stand anywhere to watch the spectacle, but seats on the medieval stone benches line each side of the parade route.

Kaysersberg ★★

Once a free city of the empire, Kaysersberg (93km/58 miles from Strasbourg) lies at the mouth of the Weiss Valley, between two vine-covered slopes; it's crowned by a castle ruined in the Thirty Years' War. From one of the many ornately carved bridges, you can see the city's medieval fortifications along the top of one of the nearby hills. Many of the houses are Gothic and Renaissance, and most have half-timbering, wrought-iron accents, leaded windows, and multiple designs carved into reddish sandstone.

In the cafes, you'll hear a combination of French and Alsatian. The age of the speaker usually determines the language—the older ones remain faithful to the dialect of their grandparents.

Dr. Albert Schweitzer, who received the 1952 Nobel Peace Prize for his philosophy of "Reverence for Life," was born here in 1875; his house is near the bridge over the Weiss. You can visit the **Musée du Albert Schweitzer,** 126 rue du Général de Gaulle (© **03-89-47-36-55**), from April to November daily from 9am to noon and 2 to 6pm. Admission is 2€ adults and 1€ for students and children 11 and under.

The **Office de Tourisme** is at 39 rue du Général-de-Gaulle (www. kaysersberg.com; © **03-89-78-22-78**).

Ammerschwihr

Ammerschwihr, 9km (5.25 miles) north of Colmar (79km/49 miles from Strasbourg), is a good stop to cap off your Wine Road tour. Once a free city of the empire, the town was almost destroyed in 1944 and has been reconstructed in the traditional style. More and more travelers visit to sample the wine, especially Käferkopf. Check out the town's gate towers, 16th-century parish church, and remains of early fortifications.

Rouffach

Rouffach is south of Colmar. One of the highest of the Vosges Mountains, Grand-Ballon shelters the town from the winds that bring rain, which makes for a dry climate and a special grape. Make a beeline for the excellent vineyard **Clos St-Landelin** (www.mure.com; © **03-89-78-58-00**), on the Route du Vin, at the intersection of RN83 and route de Soultzmatt. A clerical estate from the 6th century until the Revolution, it has been celebrated over the centuries for the quality of its wine. Clos St-Landelin covers 21 hectares (52 acres) at the southern end of the Vorbourg Grand Cru area. Its steep slopes call for terrace cultivation.

The soil that produces these wines is anything but fertile. Loaded with pebbles, sand, and limestone, the high-alkaline earth produces low-yield, scraggly vines whose fruit goes into superb Rieslings, Gewürztraminers, and pinot noirs. Members of the Muré family have owned these vineyards since 1648. In their cellar is a 13th-century wine press, the oldest in Alsace, and one of only three like it in France. (The other two are in Burgundy.) The family welcomes visitors who want to tour the cellars and ask about the wine, which is for sale. It's open Monday to Friday 8am to 6:30pm, and Saturday 10am to 1pm and 2 to 6pm.

Where to Stay & Eat along la Route du Vin

If you don't opt for one of the detailed entries below, a tasty pit stop can be made in Andlau at the unpretentious bistro **Au Boeuf Rouge,** 6 rue du Dr. Stoltz (www.andlau-restaurant.com; ✆ **03-88-08-96-26**), serving up hearty standard classics.

If you're visiting Ribeauvillé, you can satisfy hungry bellies of all ages at quaint **La Flammerie,** 9 Grand Rue (www.winstub-ribeauville. com; ✆ **03-89-73-61-08**); as the name indicates, they have excellent flammekueche tarts, in addition to a wide range of traditional dishes and even some salads, a rarity in Alsace.

The most authentic way to experience the Alsatian Wine Road is to actually sleep amongst the vines, something you can do at one of the area's many charming **B&Bs.** You can peruse an extensive list and book directly on the regional tourism website, **www.alsace-wine-route.com**.

Le Chambard ★★★   The refined regional cuisine here is so good, it's worth planning a stop. However, with the chic two-Michelin starred **64°** **Le Restaurant** and a traditional Winstub, it will be difficult to decide which one to choose. To truly tantalize your palate, opt to dine on chef Olivier Nasti's sophisticated gastronomic delights which have also earned him the prestigious title of *Meilleur Ouvrier de France.* His creative, seasonal menu could include local roebuck pie served on a bed of young greens and drizzled in truffle juice or their signature cauliflower with smoked haddock topped with Tsar Imperial caviar. Whereas over in the rustic **Winstub** you could enjoy a heartier meal of homemade game paté, "Chambord" sauerkraut served with various pork cuts, Munster cheese from the Valley, and finally traditional Alsatian cake *(kugelhof)* with cinnamon-flavored ice cream. In either venue, the cellar is stocked with the best local vintages. Reservations are required.

Next to the restaurant is a stylish hotel annex (with an elegant spa) with 32 recently refurbished rooms. A double goes for 224€ to 329€, a suite from 395€.

9–13 rue du Général-de-Gaulle, Kaysersberg. www.lechambard.com. ✆ **03-89-47-10-17. 64° Le Restaurant:** Main course 50€–120€; fixed-price menu 132€–188€; Thurs–Sun noon–2pm; Tues–Sun 7–9pm. **La Winstub:** Main course 17.50€–27.50€; fixed-price menu 27€–32€; daily noon–2pm and 7–9pm.

Clos St-Vincent ★★★   This is one of the most elegant choices along the Route du Vin. Most of the individually decorated guest rooms have a balcony or terrace, but you get much more than a view of the Haut-Rhin vineyards and summer roses. The rooms, ranging from medium to large, are furnished with grand comfort; each has a bed covered in fine linen and a bathroom with state-of-the-art plumbing and tub/shower. Some have air-conditioning. The Chapotin family's cuisine is exceptional: hot duck liver with nuts, turbot with sorrel, roebuck (in season) in hot sauce, and veal

kidneys in pinot noir. The wines are smooth, especially the popular Riesling and Gewürztraminer.

Rte. de Bergheim, Ribeauvillé. www.leclossaintvincent.com. ✆ **03-89-73-67-65.** 24
units. 170€–260€ double; 315€–335€ suite. Closed mid-Dec to late-Mar. **Amenities:**
Restaurant (dinner only Wed–Mon); bar; babysitting; Jacuzzi; indoor pool; room service; sauna; free Wi-Fi.

La Cour de Bailli ★   Enjoy an authentic Alsatian *auberge* experience
without breaking the bank at this historic hotel and spa. In the heart of
picturesque Bergheim, this traditional half-timbered building, decked out
in colorful geraniums, exudes storybook charm. Decor is simple yet comfortable in their double rooms, studios with kitchenettes, and multi-room
apartments with balconies or terraces—perfect for families or travelers on
a budget who might like to prepare a picnic lunch for the vineyards. That
said, it would be a shame to miss out on the hotel's great value and delicious restaurant set in 16th-century wine cellars or the pretty courtyard in
summer. The menu includes traditional Alsatian dishes like Munster tarte
flambée or the more gourmet queen's steak with Königinpastete potato
dumplings. Save room for an iced Kougelhopf with Marc de Gewurztraminer liqueur.

57 Grand Rue, Bergheim. www.cour-bailli.com. ✆ **03-89-73-73-46.** 34 units. 89€–
134€ double; 109€–205€ suites. Parking 4€. **Amenities:** Restaurant; bar; indoor pool;
Jacuzzi; sauna; free Wi-Fi. Annual closures first 2 weeks Jan. **Restaurant:** Main
course 7.50€–22€; fixed-price lunch 14€ or dinner 24€–35€; children's menu 9.50€.
Daily noon–2pm and 6:30–9:30pm. Closed mid-Nov to Jan.

Hostellerie Schwendi ★★   Nestled in the tiny medieval village of
Kientzheim, next to popular Kaysersberg and surrounded by rolling vines,
is one of most charming, excellent value inns of the Wine Route. For three
generations, the Schillé-Gisie family have been running this hotel-restaurant
in a completely renovated 18th-century mansion. Guestrooms are divided
between the main house and an equally delightful annex. Each room features Alsatian character, exposed wooden beams, exposed stonewalls,
solid wooden furniture, and colorful decorative elements. Six rooms in
the main building have recently refitted bathrooms with either large showers or tubs.

The restaurant mirrors the hotel's attractive Alsatian appeal. The
menu of sophisticated French and regional classics includes foie gras with
Beraweka fruit conserve or *choucroute royale*, which go perfectly with
the family's own wines. On warm days, savor a leisurely lunch on their
lovely terrace surrounded by bright flowers and storybook houses.

2 pl. Schwendi, Kientzheim. www.schwendi.fr. ✆ **03-89-47-30-50.** 29 units. 88€–120€
double; 117€–156€ family room. Free parking. **Amenities:** Restaurant; free Wi-Fi.
Restaurant: Main course 13€–30€; fixed-price menu 26€–55€. Fri–Mon noon–2pm
and Thurs–Tues 7–9pm. Both restaurant and hotel closed Jan–mid Mar.

Winstub Gilg ★   Located in the center of the scenic village of Mittelbergheim, this is one of the best bargains for a meal or overnight along the

Wine Road. Started in 1614, the comfy inn features a two-story stone staircase which is classified as a historic monument. Furnishings are simple and slightly dated, yet rooms are warmly decorated. Some have exposed beams and stone walls, and all have modern bathrooms with a tub/shower. Locals faithfully flock to its restaurant, where chef Vincent Reuschlé prepares regional specialties with creative flare such as the house specialty "wine-maker's" ham puff pastry, saddle of rabbit with mixed mushrooms and cocotte of veal sweetbreads with späetzle dumplings (menus 37.50€–56€, restaurant closed Tues and Wed).

1 route du Vin, Mittelbergheim, Barr. www.hotel-gilg.com. © **03-88-08-91-37.** 15 units. 68€–98€ double. **Amenities:** Restaurant; free Wi-Fi. Hotel and restaurant closed Jan and from late June to early July.

COLMAR ★★★

440km (273 miles) SE of Paris; 140km (87 miles) SE of Nancy; 71km (44 miles) SW of Strasbourg

One of the most attractive towns in Alsace, Colmar is a must for any visitors to the region. Colmar has been so well restored, you'd never guess it was hard hit in two world wars. You can't help but be charmed by its medieval and early Renaissance buildings, half-timbered structures, gables, and gracious loggias. Tiny gardens and washhouses surround many of the homes. Its old quarter looks more German than French, filled with streets of unexpected twists and turns. The third-largest town in Alsace, its geographic location makes it a natural gateway to the Rhine country, near the vine-covered slopes of the southern Vosges.

Essentials

ARRIVING If you're **driving,** take N83 from Strasbourg; trip time is 1 hr. Because of the narrow streets, we suggest that you park and walk. Leave the car in the Champ-de-Mars, or in the underground place Rapp for a fee of around 1.50€ per hour, northeast of the railway station, and then walk a few blocks east to the old city; or park in the lot designated parking vieille ville, accessible from rue de l'Est at the edge of the Petite Venise neighborhood, and walk a few blocks southeast to reach the old city. **Trains** link Colmar to Nancy, Strasbourg, and Mulhouse, as well as to Germany via Strasbourg, across the Rhine. The new TGV lines to Strasbourg have also led to a quicker access to Colmar on one of the 20 daily trains arriving from Paris's Gare de l'Est (trip time now between 2 hr., 15 min. and 2 hr. 30 min.); the one-way fare is 36€ to 102€. For information, see www.oui.sncf or call © **36-35** (.40€/min.).

VISITOR INFORMATION The **Office de Tourisme** is at 4 rue Unterlinden (www.tourisme-colmar.com; © **03-89-20-68-92**). For information on wines, vintages, and winery visits, contact the **CIVA** (Alsace Wine Committee), Maison du Vin d'Alsace, 12 av. de la Foire-aux-Vins (www.

vinsalsace.com; © **03-89-20-16-20**). It's usually open Monday to Friday 8am to noon and 2 to 5pm. Make tour arrangements far in advance.

SPECIAL EVENTS Alsatian **folk dances** on place de l'Ancienne-Douane begin around 8:30pm on Tuesday from mid-May to mid-September. If you want to listen to classical music, visit during the first two weeks in July for the **Festival International de Musique de Colmar** (www.festival-colmar.com), which schedules 24 concerts in venues around the city, such as churches and public monuments. Tickets cost 10€ to 15€. The city also plays host to the **Colmar fête le Printemps** (www.printemps-colmar.com), a 3-week festival celebrating springtime

Balcony of Maison Pfister in Colmar

through music, art exhibits, and a handicraft market, held late March through mid-April. The year comes to a colorful close during the city's annual **Marché de Noël,** voted one of Europe's best Christmas markets and taking place late November through the end of December (www.noel-colmar.com). You can get complete information on any of the events in town at the Office de Tourisme or by calling © **03-89-20-68-92**.

[Fast FACTS] COLMAR

ATMs/Banks You'll find ATMs in place de la Cathédrale or at the intersection of rue Kléber, av. de la République and rue Stanislas.

Doctors & Hospitals **Hopitaux Civils de Colmar,** 39 av. de la Liberté (www.ch-colmar.fr; © **03-89-12-40-00**).

Mail & Postage **La Poste,** 34 av. de la République (© **36-31**).

Pharmacies **Pharmacie du Cygne,** 31 rue des Têtes (© **03-89-41-30-09**).

Exploring Colmar

Colmar is rich with historic houses, many half-timbered and, in summer, accented with geranium-draped window boxes. One of the most beautiful is **Maison Pfister,** 11 rue des Marchands, at the corner of rue Mercière, a 1537 building with wooden balconies. On the ground floor is a wine boutique, **Vinium.** If you take pont St-Pierre over the Lauch River, you'll have an excellent view of Old Colmar and can explore **Petite Venise,** which is filled with canals.

Eglise des Dominicains ★ CHURCH   This deconsecrated church contains one of Colmar's most famous treasures: Martin Schongauer's painting *Virgin of the Rosebush,* or *Vierge au buisson de rose* (1473), all gold, red, and white, with fluttering birds. It's found in the choir and well worth the small entrance fee.

pl. des Dominicains. © **03-89-24-46-57.** Admission 1.50€ adults; 1€ students; .50€ ages 12–16; free for children 11 and under. Mar–Nov daily 10am–1pm and 3–6pm, Dec 9am–6pm.

Eglise St-Martin ★★ CHURCH   In the heart of Old Colmar is this Gothic collegiate church, considered the most beautiful in town. Begun in 1235, it was built on the site of former Carolingian and Romanesque churches. Its 70m (230 ft.) steeple beacons visitors from afar, whereas its spacious interior features soaring pointed arches, delicate medieval statuary and a choir erected by William of Marburg in 1350.

pl. de la Cathédrale. © **03-89-41-27-20.** Free admission. Daily 8am–6:30pm (until 7pm May–Oct). Closed to casual visitors during Mass and Sun mornings.

Musée Bartholdi ★ MUSEUM   American history buffs and New Yorkers should stop here to pay homage to Frédéric-Auguste Bartholdi, sculptor of the Statue of Liberty. This museum is located in the house where he was born in 1834. The display focuses on his masterpieces, especially the Statue of Liberty, with scale models, plans, and documents linked to its construction. A reconstruction of Bartholdi's Paris apartment, with furniture and memorabilia, gives insight into the artist's life and inspirations. Also of note are rooms dedicated to paintings of Egypt that Bartholdi amassed during his travels in 1856 and another with a fine collection of Jewish art.

30 rue des Marchands. www.musee-bartholdi.com. © **03-89-41-90-60.** Admission 6€ adults; 4€ students and seniors; free for children 17 and under. Wed–Mon 10am–noon and 2–6pm. Closed Jan–Feb and national holidays.

Musée d'Unterlinden (Under the Linden Trees) ★★★ MUSEUM
This former Dominican convent (1232), the chief seat of Rhenish mysticism in the 14th and 15th centuries, became a museum around 1850, and it's been a treasure house of the art and history of Alsace ever since. An ambitious project to double the exhibition space to show off its modern and contemporary art collection includes the neighboring former municipal baths, an Art Nouveau building, and a new structure designed by Swiss architects Herzog and de Meuron.

The jewel of its collection is the **Issenheim Altarpiece (Le Retable d'Issenheim)** ★★★, created by Würzburg-born Matthias Grünewald, "the most furious of realists," around 1515. His colors glow, and his fantasy will overwhelm you. One of the most exciting works in German art, it's an immense altar screen with two-sided folding wing pieces—

designed to show the Crucifixion, then the Incarnation, framed by the Annunciation and the Resurrection. The carved altar screen depicts St. Anthony visiting the hermit St. Paul; it also shows the Temptation of St. Anthony, the most beguiling part of a work that contains some ghastly birds, weird monsters, and loathsome animals. The demon of the plague is depicted with a swollen belly and purple skin, his body blotched with boils; a diabolical grin appears on his horrible face.

Other attractions include the magnificent altarpiece (dating from 1470) of Jean d'Orlier by Martin Schongauer, a large collection of religious woodcarvings and stained glass from the 14th to the 18th centuries, and Gallo-Roman lapidary collections, including funeral slabs. The armory collection contains ancient arms from the Romanesque to the Renaissance, featuring halberds and crossbows.

1 rue d'Unterlinden. www.musee-unterlinden.com. ℂ **03-89-20-15-58.** Admission 13€ adults; 8€ students under 30 and children 12–17; free for children 11 and under. Apr–Oct Wed–Mon 9am–6pm (Thurs until 8pm); Nov–Mar Wed–Mon 10am–6pm (Thurs until 8pm). Closed national holidays.

Where to Stay

Rooms are also available in **La Maison des Têtes** (see "Where to Eat," below).

Le Colombier ★ New York meets Colmar at this revamped historic home. The facade, old beams, and spiral staircase are virtually all that's left of the 16th century, for the rooms have all been redone with sleek contemporary furnishings and art. They come in a variety of shapes due to the age of the building; ceilings are high, but often slanted. Modern comfort is accentuated with cushy beds covered in fine linens. Bathrooms are small and only have showers. Request a room with a view of the canals or the timbered courtyard.

7 rue Turenne. www.hotel-le-colombier.fr. ℂ **03-89-23-96-00.** 46 units. 144€–225€ double; 229€–340€ suite. Parking 23€. **Amenities:** Bar; room service; free Wi-Fi.

Hostellerie Le Maréchal ★★ Alsatian charm shines brightly at this hotel located in three 16th-century houses in the heart of la Petite Venice. Guestrooms are named after different composers and you'll discover decorative references to them throughout the hotel. Rooms are on the small side and are roughly divided between classical or modern style, some with canopy beds. Most bathrooms have been redone with contemporary fittings and tiles; the more expensive doubles and both suites have Jacuzzi tubs. The east annex is less desirable with a timbered, sloping ceiling and no Internet. It's worth reserving at its gastronomic restaurant where you can enjoy duck breast with caramelized potatoes and turnips beside the fireplace or in summer, fish cooked in Riesling samosas on its canal-side terrace.

4–6 pl. des Six-Montagnes-Noires. www.hotel-le-marechal.com. ℂ **03-89-41-60-32.** 30 units. 115€–230€ double; 250€–305€ suite. Parking 15€. **Amenities:** Restaurant; room service; free Wi-Fi.

Where to Eat

Le JY'S ★★ MODERN FRENCH   Take in Colmar's best views and most inventive cuisine at this stylish double Michelin-starred restaurant. You'll leave behind tradition as soon as you walk through the door of this 18th-century building and into the contemporary dining room of Jean-Yves Schillinger's temple of cutting edge French gastronomy. This talented chef combines daring and exotic flavors in his tantalizing menu. Possibilities include gravlax salmon marinated in beets, horseradish and hibiscus, duck from Challans in a pepper crust and served with smoked sweat potato purée, and bok choy stuffed with duck leg confit, and bergamot cheesecake with citrus compote and meringue. In summer dine on the terrace overlooking Colmar's "Petite Venise," to achieve the ultimate dining experience in this charming town.

17, Rue de la Poissonnerie. www.jean-yves-schillinger.com. ℂ **03-89-21-53-60.** Main course 40€–55€; fixed-price lunch 46€ or dinner 78€–124€. Tues–Sat noon–1:45pm and 7pm–9:45pm. Closed 3 weeks late Feb to mid-Mar.

La Maison des Têtes ★★★ TRADITIONAL FRENCH   The beauty of this historic building will capture your eye, and the chef's exceptional skills will quickly entice your palate at one of the top restaurant-hotels in town. Take your lunch here after visiting the Unterlinden Museum or stop in for a romantic dinner set in a unique, centrally located 17th-century house. The elegant dining room is surrounded by aged-wood beams and paneling and lit by lovely Art Nouveau lighting fixtures. Dishes include homemade *paté en croute*, soufflé pike quenelle with Riesling sauce, and a sophisticated version of traditional Alsatian Baeckeoffe, a casserole of sliced potatoes confit in a marinade of beef, pork, and lamb. Paired with Alsatian wines, it's sheer culinary perfection.

They have also recently added the gastronomic **Restaurant Girardin,** presenting more refined contemporary dishes served in a slick designer dining room. Among their inventive menus is the "Journey in the Vegetable World" showcasing the region's seasonal produce. Prices at their more stylish branch come with an appropriately higher price tag, though reasonable for the exquisite quality.

You can also stay in one of the 21 rooms featuring crisp modern furniture juxtaposed against the charming historic features of the building—the suites even have Jacuzzis. Rates are 190€ to 320€ for a double, 220€ to 360€ for a suite.

In the Hôtel des Têtes, 19 rue des Têtes. www.la-maison-des-tetes.com. ℂ **03-89-24-43-43.** Main course 18€–32€; fixed-price lunch 19.50€ or dinner 45€–75€. Tues–Sun noon–1:30pm; Tues–Sat 7–9:30pm. Closed Feb.

Winstub Le Cygne ★★ ALSATIAN   Hidden from the tourist masses down an obscure side street, this is a best *winstub* in town. Savor authentic Alsatian specialties in the cozy wood-paneled dining room bustling with locals. You might need to bring your Alsatian dictionary to decipher the excellent value menu items such as *fleischschnackas* (regional pot-au-feu soup), *jambonneau à l'ancienne* (leg of pork), and *lawerknaepfla* (quenelle dumplings of various meats). For the less courageous, they prepare a variety of reliable and tasty *flammekueche* tarts. To complete your experience, order a portion of Muster or Roquefort cheese. The kitchen is open until midnight.

17 rue Edouard Richard. www.winstublecygne.fr. ✆ **03-89-23-76-26.** Main course 8€–18€. Sun–Fri noon–2pm; Tues–Sat 7pm–midnight.

Where to Stay & Eat Nearby

Die-hard gourmets flock to **Illhaeusern** to dine at the Auberge de l'Ill, one of the greatest restaurants in all of France. It's situated on a well-signposted route 18km (11 miles) from Colmar, east of the N83 highway.

Auberge de l'Ill ★★★ MODERN FRENCH Alsatian cuisine is not all choucroute and pork, especially not at the region's best restaurant. The Haeberlin family opened their first *auberge* over a hundred years ago, gradually building up their reputation to obtain a first Michelin star in 1952 and 15 years later, their third. With incredible finesse and foreign flare, Chef Marc Haeberlin transforms Alsatian traditions into *la grande cuisine*. His exquisite creations vary from sautéed bass and Beluga black lentil makis with lime emulsion to caramelized veal sweetbreads in a chestnut crust with malt, foie gras, and leak ravioli, in addition to the local filet of roebuck with mango compote and bubespitzle (German-style gnocchi). Some dishes may require 24 hours' notice, so check when you make reservations.

To enjoy your meal without having the worry of driving back into town, stay at their **Hôtel des Berges.** It has 13 rustic but regal rooms overlooking the Ill River. The splurge-worthy rates are 310€ to 360€ for a double, 420€ to 580€ for a suite, and 500€ for a cottage.

Rue de Collonges, Illhaeusern. www.auberge-de-l-ill.com. ✆ **03-89-71-89-00.** Main course 46€–189€; fixed-price lunch Sat and Sun 132€, dinner 188€. Wed–Sun noon–2pm and 7–9pm. Closed 1st week of Jan and Feb.

Shopping

The best shopping can be achieved in the old town of Colmar, particularly rue de Clefs, Grand' Rue, rue des Têtes, and rue des Marchands.

ANTIQUES Antiques abound in Colmar and shops that deserve particular attention include **Geismar Dany,** 32 rue des Marchands (✆ **03-89-23-30-41**), specializing in antique painted furniture, and **Antiquités Guy Caffard,** 56 rue des Marchands (www.caffard-antiquites.com; ✆ **03-89-41-31-78**), with its mishmash of furniture, postcards, books, toys, bibelots, and the like. Also worth noting are **Lire & Chiner,** 36 rue des Marchands (www.lire-et-chiner.fr; ✆ **03-89-24-16-78**), and **Antiquité Arcana,** 13 pl. l'Ancienne Douane (✆ **03-89-41-59-81**).

WINERIES   With Colmar being at the heart of the wine-producing Rhine country, local wine is one of the best purchases you can make here. If you don't have time to visit the vineyards along the Wine Road, stop in **Vinum** in **la Maison Pfister,** 11 rue des Marchands (www.vinum.pro; ✆ **03-89-41-33-61**), owned by a major Alsace winegrower, **Muré,** proprietor of the vineyard Clos St-Landelin. A vast selection of wines and liqueurs from the region and the rest of France is available at the **Cave du Musée,** 11 rue Kléber (✆ **03-89-23-85-29**).

You can drive to one of the most historic vineyards in Alsace-Lorraine. **Domaines Schlumberger** (www.domaines-schlumberger.com; ✆ **03-89-74-27-00**) lies 26km (16 miles) southwest of Colmar in Gueb-willer. The cellars, established by the Schlumberger family in 1810, are an unusual combination of early-19th-century brickwork and modern stainless steel. These grapes become such famous wines as Rieslings, Gewürz-traminers, muscats, sylvaners, and pinots (blanc, gris, and noir). Views of the vineyards and tasting rooms are available without an appointment, but group tours of the cellars are conducted only when a staff member is available, so call before you go. The vineyard is only open to tastings Monday to Thursday 8am to 6pm and to 5pm on Fridays. They may also have reduced hours in August and the end of December (varies each year—call for details).

LA ROUTE DES CRÊTES ★★

From Basel, Switzerland, to Mainz, Germany, a distance of some 242km (150 miles), the Vosges Mountains stretch along the west side of the Rhine Valley, bearing a similarity to the Black Forest of Germany. Many German and French families spend their summer vacation exploring the Vosges. Travelers with less time may want to settle for a quick look at the ancient mountains that once formed the boundary between France and Germany. They are filled with tall hardwood and fir trees, and a network of twisting roads with hairpin curves traverses them. The depths of the mountain forests are the closest France comes to wilderness.

Exploring the Area

You can explore the mountains by heading west from Strasbourg, but a more interesting route is from Colmar. The French High Command created **La Route des Crêtes** (Crest Road) during World War I to carry supplies over the mountains. It begins at **Col du Bonhomme,** west of Colmar, and descends south through the **Regional Natural Park of the Ballons des Vosges** (www.parc-ballons-vosges.fr) until the village of Cernay. From Col du Bonhomme, you can strike out on this magnificent road, once the object of bitter fighting but today a series of panoramic vistas, including one of the Black Forest.

By **Col de la Schlucht,** 62km (38 miles) west of Colmar, you'll have climbed 1,472m (4,828 ft.). Schlucht is a summer and winter resort and one of the most beautiful spots in the Vosges, with a panoramic view of the Valley of Münster and the slopes of Hohneck. As you skirt the edge of this glacier-carved valley, you'll be in the midst of a land of pine groves with a necklace of lakes. You may want to turn off the main road and go exploring in several directions as the scenery is that tempting. But if you're still on the Crest Road, you can circle **Hohneck,** one of the highest peaks, at 1,590m (5,215 ft.), dominating the Wildenstein Dam of the Bresse winter-sports station.

At **Markstein,** you'll come to another resort. From here, take N430 and then D10 to **Münster,** where the namesake savory cheese is made. You'll go via the Petit-Ballon, a landscape of forest and mountain meadows with grazing cows. Finally, **Grand-Ballon,** at 1,400m (4,592 ft.), is the highest point you can reach by car in the Vosges. Get out of your car and go for a walk; if it's a clear day, you'll be able to see the Jura, with the French Alps beyond.

NANCY ★★★

370km (229 miles) E of Paris; 148km (92 miles) W of Strasbourg

Nancy, in France's northeast corner, was the capital of old Lorraine. The city was built around a fortified castle on a rock in the swampland near the Meurthe River. A canal a few blocks east of the historic center connects the Marne to the Rhine.

The city is serenely beautiful, with a history, cuisine, and architecture all its own. It once rivaled Paris as the center for the design and production of Art Nouveau. Nancy has three faces: the medieval alleys and towers around the old Palais Ducal where Charles II received Joan of Arc, the rococo golden gates and fountains, and colorful Art Nouveau architecture from the turn-of-the-20th-century heyday of the Ecole de Nancy.

With a population of more than 100,000, Nancy remains the hub of commerce and politics in Lorraine. Home to a large university, it's a center of mining, engineering, metallurgy, and finance. Its 30,000 students, who have a passion for *le cool jazz,* keep Nancy jumping at night.

Essentials

ARRIVING The fast **TGV train** from Paris's Gare de l'Est arrives in Nancy after just 90 min., making the city a virtual commute from Paris. Many Parisians now visit for *le weekend.* The one-way fare ranges between 32€ and 82€. Trains from Strasbourg arrive in Nancy every hour, a one-way fare costing 27€. For information and schedules, see www.oui.sncf or call ✆ **36-35** (.40€/min.). If you're **driving** to Nancy from Paris, follow N4 east (trip time: 4 hr.).

VISITOR INFORMATION The **Office de Tourisme** is at pl. Stanislas (www.ot-nancy.fr; ✆ **03-83-35-22-41**).

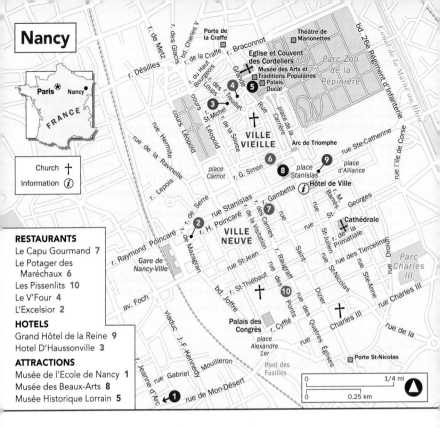

Nancy

Paris • Nancy

FRANCE

Church ✝
Information ⓘ

RESTAURANTS
Le Capu Gourmand **7**
Le Potager des
 Maréchaux **6**
Les Pissenlits **10**
Le V'Four **4**
L'Excelsior **2**

HOTELS
Grand Hôtel de la Reine **9**
Hotel D'Haussonville **3**

ATTRACTIONS
Musée de l'Ecole de Nancy **1**
Musée des Beaux-Arts **8**
Musée Historique Lorrain **5**

NANCY CITY PASS & PASSE-MUSÉE   The Nancy City Pass is perfect for active travelers who want to thoroughly explore the city on foot, bike, and public transit. It's available at the tourist office and costs 16€ per person and includes a guide booklet, a 24-hr. transit pass, an audio guide for the city (or a guided tour, but only offered in French), and 50 percent discount off the city's VelOstan bike-share system (see below). Museum-goers will also want to get the Passe-Musée which allows you free entrance into the six museums in town, all for a net price of 15€ per person. You can acquire the pass at any participating museum. *Note:* Many museums are free on the first Sunday of the month.

SPECIAL EVENTS   Serious jazz lovers come to town for two weeks in October to attend **Jazz Pulsations** (www.nancyjazzpulsations.com; ℡ **03-83-35-40-86**). Some kind of performance takes place every night around sundown in a tent in the Parc de la Pépinière, a very short walk from the place Stanislas. Some performances are free, others charge varying rates from 10€ to 35€.

Getting Around

ON FOOT The train station is a 10-min. walk to the heart of the city and many main sites are within walking distance.

BY BICYCLE You can rent bikes from **VelOstan,** at the Nancy station in the Thiers entrance (www.grand-nancy.org/velostanboutic; ✆ **06-08-05-16-43**). Their reasonable rates are 2.50€ half-day and 3.50€ full day.

BY CAR You can park your car right at the station or south of place Stanislas at the **Vinci Parking,** 6 rue Claude Charles. Car rentals are at the train station at **Avis** (www.avis.fr; ✆ **08-20-61-17-03**), or just outside the station at **Europcar** (www.europcar.fr; ✆ **08-25-35-83-58**).

BY TAXI Taxis are always outside the train station and some circulate around town. You can order one in advance from **Nancy Taxis** (www.taxis-nancy.com; ✆ **03-83-37-65-37**).

BY PUBLIC TRANSPORT Nancy has a well-serviced bus and tram system called the **Reseau Stan** (www.reseau-stan.com; ✆ **03-83-30-08-08**). A one-way ticket costs 1.30€ when purchased from automatic kiosks at a tram station or 1.50€ directly from a bus driver.

[FastFACTS] NANCY

ATMs/Banks   The city center has scores of ATMs, several are along rue Saint-Jean or Saint-Dizier.

Doctors & Hospitals   **Hopital Central de Nancy,** 29 av. du Maréchal de Lattre de Tassigny (www.chu-nancy.fr; ✆ **03-83-85-85-85**).

Mail & Postage   **La Poste,** 10 rue Saint-Dizier (✆ **36-31**).

Pharmacies   **Pharmacie du Point Central,** 35 rue Saint-Dizier (✆ **03-83-32-08-57**).

Exploring Nancy

The most monumental square in eastern France, and the heart of Nancy, is **place Stanislas ★★★,** named for Stanislas Leszczynski, the last of the ducs de Lorraine, ex-king of Poland, and father-in-law of Louis XV. His 18th-century building programs transformed Nancy into one of Europe's most palatial cities. The square stands between Nancy's two most notable neighborhoods: the **Ville Vieille** (old town), in the medieval core, centered on the cathedral, Grande Rue, and the labyrinth of narrow meandering streets that funnel into it; and the **Ville Neuve,** in the southwest. Built in the 16th and 17th centuries, when streets were laid out in straight lines, Ville Neuve centers on rue St-Jean.

Place Stanislas was laid out from 1752 to 1760 according to the designs of Emmanuel Héré. Its ironwork gates are magnificent. The square is fabled for the brilliant and fanciful railings, the work of Jean

Place Stanislas in historical center of Nancy, a UNESCO World Heritage Site

Lamour. His gilded railings with flowery decorations and crests evoke Versailles. The entire plaza is an all-pedestrian zone.

The **Arc de Triomphe,** constructed by Stanislas from 1754 to 1756 to honor Louis XV, adjoins the place de la Carrière, a tree-lined promenade leading to the 1760 **Palais du Gouvernement.** This governmental palace adjoins the **Palais Ducal,** built in 1502 in the Gothic style with Flamboyant Gothic balconies.

Musée des Beaux-Arts ★★ MUSEUM Housed in an 18th-century building on place Stanislas, this outstanding regional museum dates back to the Revolution. Its collection is built on local bequeaths such as Mme. Henri Galilée's donation of 117 modern works, from Bonnard to Modigliani. On display is a remarkable Manet portrait of the wife of Napoleon III's dentist—remarkable for its intensity and luminosity. Other highlights are by Tintoretto, Caravaggio, Rubens, and Delacroix.

3 pl. Stanislas. http://mban.nancy.fr. © **03-83-85-30-72.** Admission 7€ adults; 4.50€ students 12–25; free for children 11 and under and for all first Sun of the month. Wed–Mon 10am–6pm.

Musée de l'Ecole de Nancy ★★ MUSEUM In a building from the époque is a fascinating museum on the city's famous Art Nouveau movement. It features glasswork, furniture, and ceramics from the school's leading artists. Highlights include Emile Gallé's "Dawn and Dusk" bed, and "Mushroom Lamp," Eugène Vallin's oak entrance door and dining room set. Afterwards, amble through the garden in search of the intriguing stained-glass "aquarium" pavilion.

36–38 rue Sergent-Blandan. www.ecole-de-nancy.com. © **03-83-40-14-86.** Admission 6€ adults; 4€ students ages 12–17; free for children 11 and under and for all first Sun of the month. Wed–Sun 10am–6pm.

Musée Historique Lorrain ★★★ MUSEUM   This is one of France's great museums, covering the art and history of the Lorraine region from ancient times. The first floor devotes an entire room to Jacques Callot, an engraver born in Nancy in 1592; it includes a famous yet dark series on *the Miseries and Misfortunes of War* (a later inspiration for Goya). Galerie des Cerfs displays tapestries. You'll see a collection of 17th-century masterpieces by Jacques Bellange, Jacques Callot, Georges de la Tour, and Claude Deruet, dating from when the duchy was known as a cultural center.

Until the Revolution, this was a Franciscan convent. Franciscans were known as Cordeliers—hence the name of the church that adjoins the museum. The Flamboyant Gothic **Eglise des Cordeliers** ★ is the burial site of the dukes of Lorraine. The most notable of the burial monuments are those of René II (1509; attributed to the sculptor Mansuy Gauvain) and a reclining statue of his second wife, Philippa of Gueldres, by Ligier Richier. The limestone rendering of Philippa is one of Nancy's most stunning examples of Renaissance portraiture. The octagonal Chapel of the Dukes (1607) holds the baroque sarcophagi. The rest of the display tells the story of the daily life of the area's country folk with artwork, rooms from period homes, and farming equipment. At the time of print the museum was closed for extensive renovations and expansion. It's scheduled to reopen in 2023. However, some works, including Georges de La Tour's "La Femme à la Puce," will be on display at the **Musée des Beaux-Arts** and the **Eglise des Cordeliers** will remain open and free of charge.

In the Palais Ducal, 64 Grande-Rue. www.musee-lorrain.nancy.fr. ℭ **03-83-32-18-74.** Admission 6€ adults; 4€ students and children ages 12–18; free for children 11 and under and for all on the first Sun of each month. Combo ticket for Palais Ducal and Eglise des Cordeliers. Tues–Sun 10am–12:30pm and 2–6pm.

Where to Stay

Grand Hôtel de la Reine ★★   Right on place Stanislas, a royal stay is assured at Nancy's grandest hotel. Constructed along with the harmonious square in the mid-18th century, it was formerly a splendid private mansion. While the rooms might be a little dated, they are regally appointed in Louis XV–style furniture and drapery with Venetian chandeliers and gilt-framed mirrors. All guestrooms have spacious bathrooms with tub/showers. Your noble experience is complete with a room facing the square; however, they come at a princely supplement. There is a comfortable bar with leather sofas, a lounge hung with portraits of local aristocrats, and an elegant restaurant serving classic and modern dishes.

2 pl. Stanislas. www.hoteldelareine.com. ℭ **03-83-35-03-01.** 51 units. 119€–280€ double; 265€–320€ suite. **Amenities:** Restaurant; bar; babysitting; room service; free Wi-Fi.

Hotel D'Haussonville ★★   Set in a 15th-century classified historic mansion, this is a special find in the elegant former capital of the Duchy of Lorraine. Close to the beautiful Eglise Saint Epvre, the townhouse has a unique gothic balcony and a Renaissance balustrade. The wings surround a quaint courtyard adorned with flowers and a fountain. Each of the seven rooms and suites has its own international theme. Most have high ceilings, luxurious bathrooms, and the best have views of the church.

9 rue Mgr. Trouillet. www.hotel-haussonville.fr. ✆ **03-83-35-85-84.** 7 units. 149€–239€ double. **Amenities:** Breakfast room.

Where to Eat

A range of restaurants line rue des Maréchaux, nicknamed Gourmet Street. At no. 25 is **Le Potager des Maréchaux** (✆ **07-82-54-04-16**), the "vegetable patch," serving up salads, quiches or paté Lorraine. For great market-based cuisine walk a little further to the tiny **Le V'Four,** 10 rue St-Michel (www.levfour.fr; ✆ **03-83-32-49-48**), where you can get a special fixed-price lunch for 21€ and dinner from 32€ to 75€.

You might end your day of sightseeing by calling at the century-old brasserie **L'Excelsior,** 50 rue Henri Poincare (www.brasserie-excelsior-nancy.fr; ✆ **03-83-35-24-57**), which is an amazing period piece from 1911 with stained-glass windows and polished brass chandeliers. Just a block from the rail station, it serves Lorraine specialties with fresh oysters, a delight in season.

Le Capu Gourmand ★★ MODERN FRENCH   You can taste a perfect mix of Nancy's classicism and artistic pizzazz in the town's leading restaurant, located a mere 5-min. walk from place Stanislas. The dining room has a sophisticated flair in greys and mauves with flashes of magentas and purples in the seating. The menu adds rebellious twists to traditional dishes such as foie gras flavored with black chocolate, tartare of salmon with Gewurztraminer jelly, red mullet on a salad of Granny Smith apples, pistachios drizzled with balsamic vinaigrette or the roasted pineapple with acacia honey and lavender cream.

31 rue Gambetta. www.lecapu.com. ✆ **03-83-35-26-98.** Main course 24€–34€; fixed-price weekday lunches 29€ or dinner 38€–62€. Tues–Fri and Sun noon–2pm; Tues–Sat 7:30–10pm.

Les Pissenlits (The Dandelions) ★ TRADITIONAL FRENCH   At this cost-conscious brasserie, the food is simple but flavorful and artfully prepared. Chef Jean-Luc Mengin's specialties are likely to include dandelion salad with fried bacon and creamy meurotte vinaigrette, veal kidneys following Grandma's recipe served with homemade späetzle noodles and matelote of freshwater zander with shallots cooked with local gris de Toule wine. The chef's wife, Danièle, is one of the few accredited female wine stewards in France. Art Nouveau antiques, many of them crafted in Nancy, fill the dining room. They also run the wine bar and cellar next door, **Vins et Tartines** (www.vins-et-tartines.com).

27 bis rue des Ponts. www.les-pissenlits.com. ✆ **03-83-37-43-97.** Main course 10.50€–22€; fixed-price menu 22.50€–40€. Tues–Sat 11:45am–2pm and 7:15–10:30pm.

The Other Centre Pompidou

Since 2010 the vast collections of Paris's Centre Pompidou have been shared with its much-talked-about satellite in Metz, the capital city of Alsace's neighboring region, Lorraine. Located in a building more avant-garde than the art on the walls, you can peruse rotating masterpieces from the main museum's huge collection in addition to thematic temporary exhibits. Film screenings and guest lectures can extend your visit to a full day. Metz is a 30- to 35-min. train ride from Nancy; trains run every 20 min. (11€ one-way). The **museum** is at 1 parvis des Droits de l'Homme (www.centrepompidou-metz.fr; ✆ **03-87-15-39-39;** admission 7€–12€ adults depending on the exhibit, free for seniors and visitors 26 and under). Open Monday and Wednesday to Friday 11am to 6pm, Saturday 10am to 6pm, and Sunday 10 to 6pm.

Shopping

The famous French *macaron* almond flour cookie is said to have been invented in Nancy by Benedictine nuns. **Maison des Soeurs Macarons,** 21 rue Gambetta (www.macaron-de-nancy.com; ✆ **03-83-32-24-25**), follows the original recipe. Another good place to acquire them in addition to another traditional Nancy specialty, Bergamotte candies, is at the pretty shop **Lefèvre Lemoine,** 7 rue Henri Poincaré (✆ **03-83-30-13-83**).

Though larger and more expensive, Art Nouveau antiques also make excellent souvenirs of Nancy. Visit **Denis Rugat,** 13 rue Stanislas (✆ **03-83-35-20-79**), for the best pieces. It stocks Lalique crystal, brightly colored vases, and enameled boxes made with a technique known locally as *les émaux de Longwy,* plus an assortment of glass-shaded lamps.

You'll find more glass and crystal by **Daum,** at more reasonable prices than virtually anywhere else in France. The company's premier outlet is **Boutique Daum,** 14 pl. Stanislas (✆ **03-83-32-21-65**), where the most perfect specimens from the Daum factory are sold at prices that are usually about 30 percent less than what you'd pay in other glass galleries in France. Or for savings of 30 to 40 percent less than what's sold in the above-mentioned boutique, you can seek out Daum's factory outlet, **Magasin d'Usine Daum,** 17 rue Cristallerie (✆ **03-83-30-80-24**), a 5-min. walk from the place Stanislas; its pieces are slightly flawed.

Nancy Nightlife

As night approaches, most of the student population heads to the Old Town. Young *Nancéiens* start their night with a drink at **Le Pinocchio,** 9 pl. Saint Epvre (✆ **03-83-35-55-95**); its terrace facing the Saint Epyre church is the best place to enjoy a pint or glass of chilled wine in summer.

Nancy's most popular dance club is **Les Caves,** 9 pl. Stanislas (www.facebook.com/lescavesnancy; ✆ **03-83-35-24-14**), where a techno crowd flails around in a chrome-and-metallic space. It's open Wednesday noon to 4am and Thursday to Saturday noon to 5am.

10

Nancy

ALSACE-LORRAINE

Work up a more casual sweat at **LNVRS,** 1 ter rue du Général-Hoche (www.facebook.com/lnvrs.nancy; ✆ **06-43-19-76-87**). Formerly known as L'Envers, this self-proclaimed "rockothèque" has two underground rooms, one usually playing rock, the other techno or hip hop. It's open Thursday 11pm to 4am and Friday and Saturday 11pm to 5am. Entrance varies from 3€ to 15€ and if you come before 1am on Saturdays, the cover charged is waived.

DOMRÉMY-LA-PUCELLE

443km (275 miles) SE of Paris; 10km (6.25 miles) NW of Neufchâteau

Most often visited on a day trip, Domrémy is a plain village that would have slumbered into obscurity, but for the fact that Joan of Arc was born here in 1412. Today it's a pilgrimage center attracting fans of the heroine from all over the world.

Essentials

ARRIVING If you're **driving,** take N4 southeast of Paris to Toul, and then A31 south toward Neufchâteau/Charmes. Then take N74 southwest (signposted in the direction of Neufchâteau). At Neufchâteau, follow D164 northwest to Coussey. From there, take D53 into Domrémy.

Domrémy does not have a railway station—you must take one of four **trains** daily going to either Nancy or Toul, where you can make bus and rail connections to Neufchâteau, 9.5km (6 miles) away. You can also take a **taxi,** MBM Assistance 88 (✆ **03-29-06-12-13**), for about 100€ each way.

Discovering Joan's Legacy

Her four-room family's house is known as **Maison Natale de Jeanne d'Arc,** 2 rue de la Basilique (✆ **03-29-06-95-86**). Here you can see the chamber where she was born. The **Centre Johannique,** a museum beside the house, illustrates the life and times of St. Joan. The house is open April to September Wednesday to Monday 10am to 6pm, and October to March Wednesday to Monday 10am to 1pm and 2 to 5pm. Admission is 4€ for adults, 2.50€ for children 13 to 18 and free for children 12 and under. The house is closed in mid-December through January.

Adjacent to the museum, on rue Principale, is **Eglise St-Rémi;** repairs and partial reconstructions from the 19th century have masked its 12th-century origins. All that remains from the age of Joan of Arc are a baptismal font and some stonework. On a slope of the Bois-Chenu 1.5km (1 mile) uphill from the village is a monument steeped in French nationalism, the **Basilique du Bois-Chenu,** built on the spot Joan is said to have heard the voices. Made of local Vosges pink granite and decorated with mosaic and monumental statues celebrating the saint, it was begun in 1881 and consecrated in 1926. To reach it, follow signs from the center and along rue de la Basilique.

VERDUN ★★

261km (162 miles) E of Paris; 66km (41 miles) W of Metz

Built on both banks of the Meuse and intersected by a series of canals, Verdun has an old section, the Ville Haute, on the east bank, which includes the cathedral and Episcopal palace. Today stone houses on narrow cobblestone streets give Verdun a medieval appearance. However, most visitors come to see the famous World War I battlefields, 3km (1.75 miles) east of the town, off N3 toward Metz. With the centennial anniversary of the Great War from 2014–18, many special events and exhibits will be commemorating this at the various sites throughout the region.

Essentials

ARRIVING Two **trains** arrive daily from Paris's Gare de l'Est; you'll have to change at Châlons-en-Champagne. Several daily trains also arrive from Metz, after a change at Conflans. The one-way fare from Paris is 22€ to 50€; from Metz, it's 16€. For train information and schedules, see www.oui.sncf or call ☎ **36-35** (.40€/min.). **Driving** is easy; Verdun is several miles north of the Paris-Strasbourg autoroute (A4).

VISITOR INFORMATION The **Office de Tourisme** is on place de la Nation (www.verdun-tourisme.com; ☎ **03-29-84-14-18**). It's closed on bank holidays.

Verdun Memorial Museum, built on the site of the 1916 battle

ALSACE-LORRAINE FOR kids

One of the best family sites in the region is the **Ecomuseum in Ungersheim** between Colmar and Mulhouse (www.ecomusee-alsace.fr; ℂ **03-89-62-43-00**). It's a reconstructed turn-of-the-20th-century Alsatian village of over 70 buildings, including houses, farms, and traditional artisanal workshops. Kids can watch a potter at work, learn about bee-keeping, poke their heads into a schoolroom or take a ride on a horse-drawn cart. Entrance is 15€ adults, 10€ children 4 to 14, free to children 3 and under. Open daily 10am to 6pm, though it may have alternative hours in December and is closed most of November, January, and February.

The Vosges mountains have plenty of activities for outdoor adventurers, especially the **Regional Natural Park of the Ballons des Vosges** (p. 385). You can discover this incredibly beautiful protected ecosystem hiking, biking, canoeing, horseback riding, or at one of the park's many heritage sites from farms to former mills. For a less strenuous tour of the area, take a ride on the historic **Abreschviller train,** 2 pl. Norbert Prévot, Abreschviller (train-abreschviller.fr; ℂ **03-87-03-71-45**). Started in 1884 for logging, today old-fashioned steam or diesel trains take visitors on a 6km (4-mile) circuit around the area. The round-trip journey takes 90 min. It runs in April and October on Wednesday, Sunday and holidays at 3pm, and more frequently May to September; check the website for a timetable. Tickets are 7€ adult one-way and 13€ round-trip, for children it's 5€ and 9.50€ respectively.

For a family break in Lorraine, stop in at the **Muséum-Aquarium de Nancy**, 34 rue Sainte-Catherine (www.museum aquariumdenancy.eu; ℂ **03-83-32-99-97**), with 57 aquariums and a display of 600 preserved animal and archaeological specimens. Open daily 10am to noon and 2 to 6pm. Admission is 5€ adults; 3€ seniors, students and children 12 to 17; free to children 11 and under and all visitors the first Sunday of the month.

Touring the Battlefields

At this garrison town in eastern France, Marshal Pétain proclaimed, "They shall not pass!" And they didn't. Verdun is where the Allies held out against a massive assault by the German army in World War I. Near the end of the war, 600,000 to 800,000 French and German soldiers died battling over a few miles along the muddy Meuse between Paris and the Rhine. Two monuments commemorate these tragic events: Rodin's *Defense* and Boucher's *To Victory and the Dead.*

The local tourist office provides maps for two tours of the brutal and bloody battlefields that helped define World War I. The "Circuit Champs de Bataille Rive Droite" encompasses the better-known battlegrounds on the River Meuse's right bank. It's a 4-hr., 32km (20-mile) route, and takes in **Fort Vaux,** where Raynal staged a heroic defense after sending his last message by carrier pigeon.

After passing a **French cemetery** of 16,000 graves—an endless field of crosses—you arrive at the **Ossuaire de Douaumont** (www.verdun-douaumont.com; ℂ **03-29-84-54-81**), where the bones of those blown to

A soldier plays bugle in the ceremony of Armistice Day, Douaumont Ossuary

bits were embedded. Nearby, at the **Fort de Douaumont,** the "hell of Verdun" was unleashed. From the roof, you can look out at a vast field dotted by the corroded tops of the tiny "pillbox" guard posts. Then you proceed to the **Tranchée des Baïonettes (Trench of Bayonets).** Bayonets of French soldiers entombed by a shell seem to burst forth from this unique memorial.

Within a few paces of the Tranchée des Baïonettes, you'll see the **Mémorial de Verdun,** Fleury Devant Douaumont (www.memorial-de-verdun.fr; © **03-29-84-35-34**). Originally built in 1967, the museum recently underwent 2 years of renovation which were unveiled in 2016. The sleek new exhibition space chronicles the savage battle through thematic displays of weapons, uniforms, vehicles, and archival material.

The second self-guided tour, known as **"Circuit Champs de Bataille Rive Gauche"** (or "Circuit de l'Argonne"), requires about 4 hr. to cover its 97km (60 miles). The tour focuses on mostly outdoor sites. It takes in the **Butte de Montfaucon,** a hill on which Americans erected a memorial tower, and the moving **Cimetière Américain at Romagne** (www.abmc. gov/cemeteries-memorials), the largest American cemetery in Europe with over 14,000 graves. Because public transportation is inadequate, only visitors with cars should attempt to make these circuits. The British Battlefield Tours Research Society offers group and private tours of the area (www.battlefieldtours.co.uk).

BURGUNDY

By Victoria Trott

Bordered by the River Saône to the east and the River Loire to the west, Burgundy is an agricultural region famed for its wines: The major growing areas are Chablis, Côte de Nuits, Côte de Beaune, Côte Chalonnaise, and Mâconnais. In 2015 *Les Climats du Vignoble de Bourgogn* (Burgundy vineyards) became a UNESCO World Heritage Site. Needless to say, good food plays a large part, too. Cistercian monasteries and medieval churches mark the landscape, along with centuries-old honey-colored villages. Several canals cross the Burgundy countryside, making it a popular destination for water-based holidays, while walkers and cyclists can explore miles of towpaths and routes through the vines. From 1032 until 1477, when it was annexed by France, the Duchy of Burgundy was an independent province whose territory included Luxembourg, Belgium, and the Netherlands; its legacy is a rich cultural heritage.

The Côte d'Or evokes mythical Premier Cru appellations such as Richebourg and Vosne-Romanée, while the region's grassy agricultural plains are home to mouth-watering offerings such as Charolais beef, garlic-infused snails, and pungent Époisses cheese. Sleepy historic towns and villages have been awoken by the appeal of Michelin-starred restaurants: La Côte Saint Jacques in Joigny, Le Relais Bernard Loiseau in Saulieu, and Maison Lameloise in Chagny. Today Burgundy offers many opportunities for wine tourism, from free tastings to private tours.

DIJON ★★★

312km (193 miles) SE of Paris; 320km (198 miles) NE of Lyon

Located in the north of the region, Dijon is the capital of Burgundy. Founded by the Romans, this city of 155,000 residents has undergone a 400 million-euro facelift since 2010, including a new tramway, an Olympic-size swimming pool, pedestrianized shopping streets, and restored landmark squares.

On the doorstep of the illustrious Côte d'Or wine region, Dijon combines world-class wines with good food, including four restaurants with Michelin stars. These important assets will be celebrated in the new **Cité**

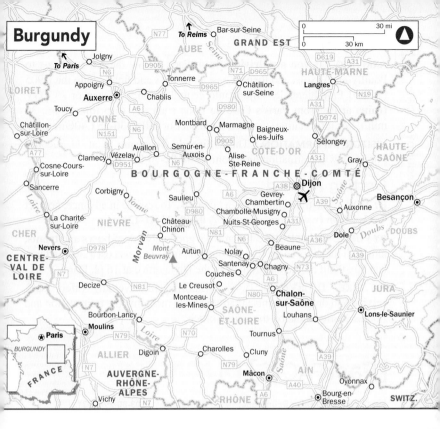

Internationale de la Gastronomie et du Vin (www.citedelagastrono mie-dijon.fr), which is due to open in 2019. The new complex will house a cultural center celebrating French food and wine, as well as a cooking and oenology school. As well as being famed for its mustard, the city is also the home of *Kir* (a mix of white Aligoté wine and Crème de Cassis blackcurrant liqueur, named after former Dijon mayor Canon Félix Kir). After admiring the city's impressive Gothic churches and the sumptuous Palais des Ducs et des États de Bourgogne, make time to get lost in Dijon's medieval heart: Here you'll happen upon extravagant *hôtels particuliers* (private mansions), some of which have colorful roof tiles, a practice that dates back to the 14th century and is found throughout the region.

The city has some interesting events throughout the year; pick up an agenda from the tourist office. In May, vintage motorbike fans arrive for the **Coupes Moto Légende** to race their bikes around the Prenois race track. Every two years, the **Fêtes de la Vigne** celebrate local life and traditions on the last weekend in August (next one 2018). In November, the city hosts one of France's largest food fairs, the **Foire internationale et gastronomique de Dijon.**

Essentials

ARRIVING   If you are **driving,** from Paris follow the A6 southeast to Pouilly-en-Auxois, and then go east along A38 and finally onto the D905 (around Plombières-lès-Dijon) into central Dijon. A dozen or so TGV **trains** arrive from Paris's Gare de Lyon each day (trip time: 1 hr., 35 min.). For information, visit www.oui.sncf or call ☏ **36-35** (.40€/min.).

VISITOR INFORMATION   The **Office de Tourisme** is at 11 rue des Forges (www.destinationdijon.com; ☏ **08-92-70-05-58**).

Getting Around

BY TAXI   The train station has a taxi rank. To reserve in advance, contact **Taxis Dijon** (www.taxis-dijon.fr; ☏ **03-08-41-41-12**).

BY PUBLIC TRANSPORT   Dijon has a good network of **buses** and **trams,** although the city is easy to get around on foot. Tickets cost 1.30€ and you can buy them on the bus/tram or in the Divia office at 16 pl. Darcy.

BY BIKE   **Divia**Vélodi (www.divia.fr/page/diviavelodi) offers self-service and drop-off points all around town including the train station and Forges-Notre Dame by the tourist office.

[Fast FACTS] DIJON

Hospital   **CHU Dijon Bourgogne,** 14 rue Paul Gaffarel; ☏ **03-80-29-30-31.**

Pharmacy   Dijon's pharmacies take turns staying open after hours. Ask at the police station in place Suquet (☏ **03-80-44-55-00**). **La Pharmacie de la Libert**é, 42 rue de la Liberté (☏ **03-80-30-41-69**), is open 8am to 8pm Monday to Saturday.

Exploring Dijon

One of the most historic buildings in this ancient province is the **Palais des Ducs et des États de Bourgogne,** which symbolizes the independent (or semi-independent, depending on the era) status of this fertile region. Capped with an elaborate tile roof, the complex is arranged around a trio of courtyards. The oldest section, only part of which you can visit, is the **Ancien Palais des Ducs de Bourgogne,** erected in the 14th and 15th centuries. The newer section is the **Palais des États de Bourgogne,** constructed in the 17th and 18th centuries for the Burgundian parliament; check out the **Chapelle des Élus** (free access via the tourist office), which dates from 1738 and was designed by Jacques Gabriel, Louis XV's architect. Today the palace is *la mairie* (the town hall); all of its newer section and much of its older section are reserved for the municipal government and not open to the public. However, fabulous views can be had from the top of **Tour Philippe le Bon** (316 steps; 3€ adults; days and times vary); the fine museum, the **Musée des Beaux-Arts** (see below) is also found here.

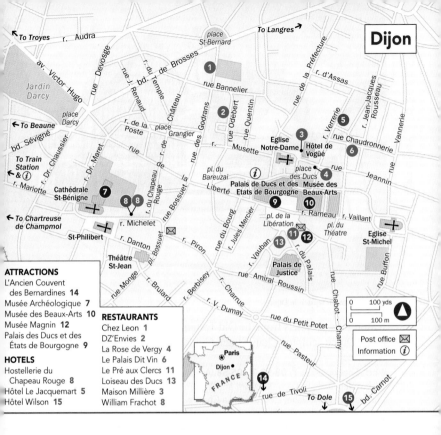

ATTRACTIONS

L'Ancien Couvent
  des Bernardines **14**
Musée Archéologique **7**
Musée des Beaux-Arts **10**
Musée Magnin **12**
Palais des Ducs et des
  États de Bourgogne **9**

HOTELS

Hostellerie du
  Chapeau Rouge **8**
Hôtel Le Jacquemart **5**
Hôtel Wilson **15**

RESTAURANTS

Chez Leon **1**
DZ'Envies **2**
La Rose de Vergy **4**
Le Palais Dit Vin **6**
Le Pré aux Clercs **11**
Loiseau des Ducs **13**
Maison Millière **3**
William Frachot **8**

The **Musée Archéologique,** 5 rue du Docteur Maret (https://archeo logie.dijon.fr; ✆ **03-80-48-83-70**), housed in a medieval abbey, contains finds from the area, including the abbey itself. Admission is free, and it's open Wednesday to Monday 9am to 12:30pm and 2 to 6pm; from November to March, the museum is open Wednesday, Saturday, and Sunday.

A medieval nunnery, **L'Ancien Couvent des Bernardines,** 15–17 rue Ste-Anne (✆ **03-80-48-80-90**), is home to two museums. The chapel holds the **Musée d'Arts Sacrés** (https://art-sacre.dijon.fr), devoted to art from regional churches, and the cloister contains the **Musée de la Vie Bourguignonne** (https://vie-bourgignonne.dijon.fr), which exhibits folkloric costumes, farm implements, and some 19th- and early-20th-century storefronts from Dijon's center. Admission is free to both museums (Wed–Mon 9:30am–12:30pm and 2–6pm).

Chartreuse de Champmol ★ MONASTERY   Although the fancy tombs of the dukes of Burgundy are in what is now the Musée des Beaux-Arts, their bodies are actually buried in this charterhouse at the western edge of Dijon. Now a psychiatric hospital, it's still possible to visit: The main sights are the church portal and magnificent Well of Moses, which

A colorful town square in Dijon

features six prophets from the Old Testament; both were the work of influential Dutch sculptor Claus Sluter. Guided tours are available via the tourist office.

1 bd. Chanoine-Kir. ℓ **08-92-70-05-58.** Admission 3.50€ adults; free for children 18 and under. Daily 9:30am–12:30pm and 2–6pm (Apr–Oct until 4:30pm). Bus 3 direction Fontaine d'Ouche; stop at CH La Chartreuse.

Musée des Beaux-Arts ★★★ MUSEUM   The area of the ducal palace housing France's fifth most important national art collection has been undergoing a 60€-million renovation since 2008, due to be completed in 2019. The museum showcases exceptional sculpture, ducal kitchens from the mid-1400s (with great chimney pieces) and a collection of European paintings and sculptures from the 14th to the 21st centuries (however, works dating from the 17th to 21st centuries have been removed for restoration and will return in 2019). Take special note of the Salle des Gardes, the banquet hall of the old palace built by Philip the Good (Philippe le Hardi). The tomb of Philip the Bold was created between 1385 and 1411 and is one of the best in France: a reclining figure rests on a slab of black marble, surrounded by 41 mourners. The courtyard bar is perfect for a drink or a snack on fine days (Wed–Mon 8am–9pm).

In the Palais des Ducs et des États de Bourgogne, cour de Bar. https://beaux-arts. dijon.fr. ℓ **03-80-74-52-09.** Free admission; audio guides 4€. Mon and Wed–Fri 10am–6:30pm; Sat and Sun 10:30am–7pm.

Musée Magnin ★★ MUSEUM   Housed in a handsome 17th-century *hôtel particulier,* this museum boasts an impressive collection of around 2,000 artworks by lesser-known French, Italian, and Flemish artists from the 14th to the 19th centuries. Some of the paintings, like the Italian landscapes by Anne-Louis Girodet (1767–1824), a pupil of Jacques-Louis David, are exquisite. The collection was bequeathed to the state in 1938 by Maurice and Jeanne Magnin and are displayed around the house, their family home, like an amateur collector's "cabinet of curiosities" in accordance with the couple's wishes.

4 rue des Bons-Enfants. www.musee-magnin.fr. ✆ **03-80-67-11-10.** Admission 3.50€ adults; free for citizens of the EU ages 26 and under. Tues–Sun 10am–12:30pm and 1:30–6pm.

Where to Stay

Like most cities, boutique-style self-catering apartments have sprung up in Dijon, including **Les Appartements à Part** (www.appartements-a-part.com; ✆ **06-81-00-50-77**) from 105€ per night and **Au Nid Douillet** (www.gite-nid-douillet.fr; ✆ **03-80-66-75-71**) from 50€ per night. There is even a water-side **campsite** a 20-min. walk from the town center (www.camping-du-lac-dijon.com; ✆ **03-80-30-54-01**), open from April to mid-October.

Hostellerie du Chapeau Rouge ★★ Instantly recognizable by its pink façade and white shutters, the four-star "Hotel Red Hat" is our favorite luxury abode in Dijon for its style and friendly staff. It's only a 10-min. walk from the train station, too. Most of the rooms in this 19th-century building have had a contemporary makeover; others, notably the Initial and Superior rooms, have a more traditional style. After a hard day's sightseeing, the sauna, hammam, and hydromassage showers (all free) in the basement spa are a welcome respite, and a small range of treatments for face and body are on the menu. Speaking of menus, the hotel restaurant, overseen by William Frachot, is the best in town with two Michelin stars.

5 rue Michelet. www.chapeau-rouge.fr. ✆ **03-80-50-88-88.** 28 units. 102€–309€ double. Breakfast 18€. Valet parking 16€. Fixed-price lunch Tues–Fri 55€ or dinner 90€–150€. **Amenities:** Restaurant; bar; concierge; room service; spa; laundry service; free Wi-Fi.

Hôtel Le Jacquemart ★ If you're looking for budget accommodation in the center of Dijon then this is the place to come. Housed in an 18th-century building in the middle of the antiques district, two-star Le Jacquemart (named after the bell-clanging automaton on the top of the city's Église Notre Dame), has three *économique* rooms with shared bathrooms (42€). You can also choose from standard and premium rooms and a family suite, which have all had a stylish, contemporary makeover. However, original features such as marble fireplaces add to their charm.

32 rue Verrerie. www.hotel-lejacquemart.fr. ✆ **03-80-60-09-60.** 33 units. 42€–75€ double; 75€–89€ family rooms. Breakfast 7.50€. Parking 6€. **Amenities:** Bar; free Wi-Fi.

Hôtel Wilson ★★ This three-star former coaching inn, dating back to the 17th century, is the ideal stop for drivers as it's on the southeast edge of town. Rooms have oodles of character with exposed beams, stone walls and Louis Philippe and Louis XIII furniture, while the bathrooms have been renovated in white contemporary style. Enjoy a hearty buffet breakfast by the stone fireplace before embarking on the 15-min. walk into the town center. In the evening, if you're feeling flush, head to the Michelin-starred restaurant of Stéphane Derbord next door (see "Where to Eat," below).

1 rue de Longvic. www.wilson-hotel.com. ⟨℡⟩ **03-80-66-82-50.** 27 units. 90€–134€ double; 135€–215€ family rooms. Breakfast 13.50€. Parking 10€. **Amenities:** Bar; beauty treatments; room service; free Wi-Fi.

Where to Eat

In addition to the restaurants below, we heartily recommend (and so does Michelin) Loiseau des Ducs, 3 rue Vauban (www.bernard-loiseau.com; ⟨℡⟩ 03-80-30-28-09), which has one star and where lunch menus start at 25€; and William Frachot at Hostellerie du Chapeau Rouge (see "Where to Stay," above), who has two stars. For a snack head to rue de la Chouette and the very quaint Maison Millière (www.maison-milliere.fr; ⟨℡⟩ 03-80-30-99-99) at no. 10–14 or La Rose de Vergy (www.rosedevergy.com; ⟨℡⟩ 03-80-61-42-22) at no.1.

Chez Léon ★★ BURGUNDIAN/FRENCH   Take a step back in time, sit elbow-to-elbow with your neighbor, and savor some French dishes like *grand-mère* used to make. Chalked on the blackboard of this rustic restaurant, where family photos adorn the walls, you'll find the likes of succulent homemade terrines, goats' cheese salad, veal kidneys in mushroom sauce and *tarte tatin* (apple tart). The wine list is Burgundy heavy, with a small selection from the Rhône valley.

20 rue des Godrans. www.restochezleon.fr. ⟨℡⟩ **03-80-50-01-07.** Fixed-price lunch 15.90€–19.90€ or dinner 26€–31€. Tues–Sat noon–1:30pm and 7:30–9pm.

DZ'Envies ★★ BURGUNDIAN/FUSION   You won't find any beams or exposed stonework in this white, minimalist restaurant opposite Les Halles, but you will encounter plenty of locals. Chef David Zuddas used to have a Michelin star at his previous establishment but decided to open a new "bistrogastro" in the city center to give himself more creative freedom. The lunch menu changes daily: expect the likes of scallops with sweet potato and bok choy for starters, beef cheeks in red Burgundy for main, followed by pain d'épices panna cotta with red fruit marmalade. In the evening you can choose from three to five *envies* ("desires" aka dishes).

12 rue Odebert. www.dzenvies.com. ⟨℡⟩ **03-80-50-09-26.** Main course 17€–22€; fixed-price lunch 17€–21€ or dinner 32€–40€. Mon–Sat noon–2pm and 7–10pm.

Le Palais Dit Vin ★★ BURGUNDIAN/MODERN FRENCH   In the antiques district, this simple restaurant serves reasonably priced dishes made with products sourced from local suppliers. Lunch might be cream of potato soup with chorizo (from a nearby Spanish deli) and chicken in Dijon mustard sauce with rice, followed by chocolate panna cotta with passion fruit. The "Menu Bourgogne" (32€) features Charolais steak. Wines come from small vineyards in the region, such as Christian Gros, who works 13 hectares (32 acres) of Côte de Beaune and Côte de Nuits. This is a good example of a 21st-century "traditional" French bistro.

24 rue Chaudronnerie. www.palaisditvin.fr. ✆ **03-80-66-88-03.** Main course 13€–23€; fixed-price menus 14.90€–38€. Tues–Sat noon–2:30pm and 7–9:30pm.

Le Pré aux Clercs ★★ BURGUNDIAN/FRENCH In an 18th-century house across from the Palais des Ducs, this smart restaurant has been given a new lease on life since it was taken over in 2017 by Georges Blanc, who has a small chain of upmarket hotel-restaurants in the region. The new menu has some interesting dishes, such as

Boeuf bourguignon, a Burgundy specialty

quenelle de homardine (pike dumpling with lobster sauce), venison in pepper sauce, and *brioche perdu au jus de Cassis* (French toast with blackcurrant liqueur). In summertime, make sure you book a table outside on the pedestrianized crescent with its privileged view over the magnificent Palais des Duc. Five well-equipped guestrooms with contemporary decor, from 110€, are available to those who decide to stay the night.

13 pl. de la Libération. www.lepreauxclercs.fr. ✆ **03-80-38-05-05.** Main course 14€–42€; fixed-price menus 18€–32€. Daily noon–10pm.

Stéphane Derbord ★★★ BURGUNDIAN/FRENCH This Michelin-starred restaurant is one of the most sought-after eating places in the area, thanks to the chef's creative take on Burgundian cuisine. Charolais beef *tartare* is served with mustard ice cream, Vougeot cheese and radishes; pigeon is rubbed with vanilla seeds and its thighs are caramelized with shallots. The lunch menu is a "surprise" and depends upon what Derbord finds in the market that day. Reservations required.

10 pl. Wilson. www.restaurantstephanederbord.fr. ✆ **03-80-67-74-64.** Main course 38€–46€; fixed-price lunch 30€ and dinner 55€–105€. Tues–Sat noon–1:45pm and 7:30–9:15pm. Closed 1 week in Jan and 2 weeks in Aug.

Where to Stay & Eat Nearby

La Gentilhommière ★ BURGUNDIAN/FRENCH About a 20-min. drive south of Dijon on the A31 is Nuits-St-Georges, world famous for its legendary wines such as Romanée-Conti. On the way into this sweet little town is "The Gentleman's Residence," a three-star family-run hotel and gourmet restaurant, Le Chef Coq, in a former hunting lodge surrounded by fields and forest. On the menu you'll find the likes of partridge with beetroot and celery purée, and also blue shark steak with a preserved lemon; we particularly like the Campari sorbet with orange mousse for dessert. You'll find top-quality local wines on the wine list and the "house" Kir is a must for an aperitif, next to the stone fireplace in winter. The contemporary-design rooms are in two separate 1980s blocks.

13 vallée de la Serrée, Nuits-St-Georges. www.lagentilhommiere.fr. © **03-80-61-12-06.** 31 units. 115€–250€ double. Breakfast 18€. Free parking. Main course 24€–33€; fixed-price lunch Tues–Fri 25€ or dinner 32€–59€. Daily noon–2pm and 7–9pm. Restaurant closed Tues eve and Sat lunch. Hotel closed mid-Dec to Feb. **Amenities:** Restaurant; bar; children's playroom; parkland; outdoor pool; tennis court; free Wi-Fi.

Restaurant des Gourmets ★★ BURGUNDIAN/FRENCH   Romain Détot's imaginative cuisine is reason enough to journey to a charming medieval village 6km (3.75 miles) south of Dijon. One of his signature dishes is *oeufs en meurette* (eggs poached in red wine with bacon, a traditional Burgundian dish). The menu changes with the seasons and, in a modern room overlooking a garden, you can enjoy such delights as trout with lemon and thyme and pears poached in blackcurrant liqueur. The cellar contains more than 600 wines; many are burgundies from lesser-known, small-scale wineries.

8 rue du Puits de Têt, Marsannay-la-Côte. www.restaurant-lesgourmets.com. © **03-80-52-16-32.** Main course 24€–36€; fixed-price lunch Wed–Fri 20€; dinner menus 32€–52€. Wed–Sun noon–1:30pm and 7:45–11:30pm. Closed 2 weeks in Aug. Drive 9.5km (6 miles) south of Dijon on D122, following the signs for Beaune and then Marsannay-la-Côte.

Shopping

Your shopping list may include regional wines, mustard, antiques, *pain d'épices* (spiced bread), and the blackcurrant liqueur, Crème de Cassis. The best shopping streets are rue de la Liberté, rue du Bourg, rue Bossuet, place Grangier for designer shops, and rue Verrerie for antiques. The market at **Les Halles,** rue Odebert, sells fruit, vegetables, and foodstuffs on Tuesday, Thursday, and Friday from 8am to noon, and Saturday from 8am to 5pm.

Dijon has several great *fromageries* (cheese shops) including **Le Chalet Comtois,** 28 rue Musette (© **03-80-30-48-61**); look out for the regionally made semi-soft Cîteaux, made by monks in the abbey of the same name, and pungent, unctuous Époisses. For bread, look no further than **Tartin'art,** 8 rue Musette (www.tartinart.com; © **03-80-30-97-31**), which also offers sandwiches, quiches, and salads. For wine, we like **Dr. Wine,** 5 rue Musette (www.drwine.fr; © **03-80-53-35-16**); they also have a good restaurant and do delicious platters of ham and cheese. You won't be able to pass **Carbillet,** 58 rue des Forges (www.chocolat-carbillet.com; © **03-80-30-38-82**) without going in to buy some cakes or chocolates. At **La Boutique Maille,** 32 rue de la Liberté (© **03-80-30-41-02**), you can purchase many varieties of the world-famous mustard while

Mulot et Petitjean (their ornately paneled flagship store is at 13 pl. Bossuet; www.mulotpetitjean.fr; ✆ **03-80-30-07-10**) is the place to go for homemade *pain d'*épices. You can find out how the product is made at their factory at 6 bd. de l'Ouest (✆ **03-80-66-30-80;** Tues–Sat 10am–12:30pm and 2–6:30pm; 8€ adults).

For antiques and interiors, head to the half-timbered streets around rue Verrerie. Southeast of the city center, **Le Consortium,** 37 rue de Longvic (www.leconsortium.fr; ✆ **03-80-68-45-55**), is Dijon's most interesting modern-art gallery.

For the last 30 years, **Le Baldaquin,** 13 rue Verrerie (www.le-baldaquin-dijon.fr; ✆ **03-80-30-59-69**), has been a children's treasure trove of wooden toys and mobiles.

Nightlife

Housed in an atmospheric vaulted cellar, Latin bar-restaurant **La Salsa Pelpa,** 1 rue Marceau (www.lasalsapelpa.fr; ✆ **03-80-73-20-72**), offers a lively night out. The barge **Péniche Cancale,** 14 av. Jean Jaurès (www.penichecancale.com; ✆ **03-80-43-15-72**), is open Wednesday to Saturday 7pm to 2am and provides an intimate setting for an eclectic program of music concerts. It also has a seafood restaurant on board.

Café-gallery **Alchimia,** 13–15 rue Auguste Comte (✆ **03-80-46-10-42;** Tues–Sat 5:30pm–2am), is a hip spot to enjoy a cocktail or craft beer surrounded by contemporary artworks; they also have bands playing occasionally. Also in the antiques district, **Chez Bruno,** 80 rue J-J Rousseau (✆ **03-80-66-12-33;** Tues–Sat 6–11pm), is a popular wine bar with around 850 labels on the menu.

The opera season (www.opera-dijon.fr; ✆ **03-80-48-82-82**) in Dijon stretches from October to May. Operas, dance recitals, and concerts are held in two venues: **Grand Théâtre de Dijon,** pl. du Théâtre (where you can pop by anytime Tues–Sat 11am–6pm to buy tickets) and **L'Auditorium,** pl. Jean Bouhey (that opens just 1 hr. before each performance). Although it's a good idea to buy tickets in advance online.

Several cinemas show films in their original version including **Eldorado,** 21 rue Alfred de Musset (https://cinemaeldorado.wordpress.com; ✆ **03-80-66-51-89**), and **Devosge,** 4–6 rue Devosge (www.cinedevosge.fr; ✆ **03-80-30-74-79**).

AUXERRE ★★

154km (95 miles) SE of Paris; 148km (92 miles) NW of Dijon

On a hill overlooking the River Yonne, Auxerre (pronounced Ausserre) was founded by the Gauls and enlarged by the Romans; at the bottom of rue des Pêcheurs you can see the remains of a Gallo-Roman tower underneath the medieval one. Joan of Arc spent several days in the town in 1429 and Napoleon Bonaparte stopped here on his return from Elba in 1815.

Restored half-timbered houses, Auxerre

Although these days it's arguably best known for its soccer team, Auxerre's AOC wines produced on the surrounding hills are renowned, too: Try Irancy and Chitry.

The city, which has around 40,000 inhabitants, is a pleasant place to spend a couple of days exploring the narrow, cobbled streets admiring the 700 or so beautifully preserved *colombage* (half-timbered) buildings. The most charming district is the Quartier St-Nicolas, the old fishermen's quarter. However, the main reason to visit is to see the rare crypt murals (see "Exploring Auxerre" below).

Auxerre has a full events calendar. In June, the three-night **Catalpa** world music festival includes the French air guitar championships. In July and August, the **Garçon la note!** festival presents free music concerts Monday to Saturday (9–11:30pm) in the city's bars and restaurants. A market takes place every Tuesday and Friday morning in place de l'Arquebuse.

Essentials

ARRIVING   Visitors often **drive** here because Auxerre is near A6/E15 (the Autoroute du Soleil) motorway from Paris. TER **trains** run every hour from Paris (Gare de Bercy; trip time: 1 hr., 45 min.). For train information, visit www.oui.sncf or call ✆ **36-35** (.40€/min.).

VISITOR INFORMATION   The **Office de Tourisme** is at 1–2 quai de la République (www.ot-auxerre.fr; ✆ **03-86-52-06-19**).

Getting Around

BY TAXI   If you're arriving by train you might want to book a taxi as the train station is about 1.5km (1 mile) from the main sights in the historic center. Contact ✆ **03-86-46-91-61.**

BY BIKE   You can rent bikes from **La Maison du Vélo,** pl. Achille Ribain (www.maison-velo.jimdo.com; ✆ **03-86-46-24-99**). Prices range from 4€ per hour to 80€ for 5 days.

Exploring Auxerre

The railway station is at the eastern edge of town, about 1.5km (1 mile) from the historic center. Most of Auxerre is on the western bank of the Yonne. Its heart is between place du Maréchal-Leclerc (near the Hôtel de Ville [city hall]) and the Cathédrale St-Etienne. A little electric bus, the *Voyager*, takes visitors on a 45-min. guided tour daily in July and August (Sat–Sun only Apr–June and Sept) from 10am–5:30pm for 5€; it's particularly useful for families with small children or those with reduced mobility, due to the hilly nature of some of the streets.

You could also while away quite a few hours "messing about on the river" from April to October, either in your own rented electric boat (ask at the tourist office), which is fun for families, or during a cruise aboard *L'Hirondelle II* (www.bateaux-auxerrois.com; ✆ **06-30-37-66-17**); every Thursday in July and August at 5pm the boat offers a gourmet cruise showcasing regional food and wine (18€ adults, 12€ children ages 4–12).

Abbaye St-Germain ★★★ ABBEY   This Benedictine abbey was founded in the 5th century by St-Germain, a former bishop of Auxerre, after whom it is named; he is buried here. Its school was once reputed throughout Christendom. The main reason to visit is to see the **crypt murals** depicting the stoning of St. Stephen, which date back to the 9th century and are the oldest in France. The lovely 17th-century cloister hosts art exhibitions and concerts in summer. Also here is the town's archaeology museum, whose exhibits include artifacts dating from prehistoric times.

2 bis pl. St-Germain à Auxerre. ✆ **03-86-18-02-90.** Guided tours of crypt 7€ adults; free for children under 16 and students 25 and under; free admission to museum. Wed–Mon Apr–Sept 9am–noon and 2–6pm (guided tours of crypt hourly 9–11am and 2–6pm); Oct–Mar 9am–noon and 2–5pm (guided tours of crypt hourly 9–11am and 2pm–4pm).

Cathédrale St-Etienne ★★ CATHEDRAL   Dominating the River Yonne, this Gothic cathedral, the city's most emblematic sight, is also one of its most interesting. The stained-glass windows, which date from the 13th to the 16th century, are some of France's finest while the crypt protects a rare 11th-century **mural** of Christ on a horse.

Pl. St-Etienne. ✆ **03-86-51-29-20.** Admission to crypt 3€ adults; free for children 11 and under. Cathedral: daily Apr–Oct 8:45am–7pm and Nov–Mar until 6pm. Crypt: Apr–Oct Mon 9am–noon, Tues–Fri 9am–6pm, Sat noon–6pm.

Where to Stay

Hôtel Le Maxime ★★   This former salt storehouse on the banks of the River Yonne is our favorite hotel in town. The style is classical and elegant from the public areas to the rooms; book one at the front for a view of the water. Their themed weekends, including wine tastings, cycling along the canal and exploring Chablis in a 2CV, are particularly popular. Though it doesn't have a restaurant, plenty of eating places are nearby. Relax with a local tipple in the bar of the vaulted cellar or book an in-room massage.

2 quai de la Marine. www.lemaxime.com. ✆ **03-86-52-14-19.** 26 units. 86€–145€ double; 138€–275€ suite. Breakfast 14€. Parking 10€. **Amenities:** Bar; in-room massage; laundry service; room service; free Wi-Fi.

Le Seignelay ★   On the western edge of town, this two-star former coaching inn dating from the 18th century is a good budget option and it's got a well-regarded traditional restaurant, too. Rooms are basic but bright and cheerful and individually decorated; some have original fireplaces. The owner is passionate about motorbikes and, as a result, the hotel has facilities for those touring on two wheels. Another particularity is that they sell wines from producers in the north of Burgundy.

2 rue du Pont. www.leseignelay.com. ✆ **03-86-52-03-48.** 17 units. 63€–72€ double. Breakfast 7.50€. Parking 7.50€. Closed Feb. **Amenities:** Restaurant; free Wi-Fi.

Where to Eat

Le Saint-Pèlerin ★★ BURGUNDIAN   It's well worth making a pilgrimage to "The Holy Pilgrim" for good-quality, good-value Burgundian food. The centerpiece is a wood-fired grill, where pretty much everything is cooked. We're mad about the beef slow-cooked in Irancy red wine (aka *boeuf bourgignon*) accompanied by one of the house potato dishes (like creamy mash served in its skin). The cheese board is laden with regional favorites like Époisses and all dishes are homemade, including the bread and ice cream. In summer there's an outside terrace in the narrow street, a block away from the river.

56 rue Saint-Pèlerin. www.restaurantlesaintpelerin.yonne-france.fr. ✆ **03-86-52-77-05.** Main course 12€–25€; fixed-price menu 14.90€–29€. Tues–Sat noon–2pm and 7:15–10pm. Closed 1 week in May and 2 weeks at Christmas and New Year.

Where to Stay & Eat Nearby

La Côte Saint Jacques ★★★ BURGUNDIAN   This is one of the top Relais & Châteaux members in France. On the banks of the River Yonne, the five-star, family-friendly hotel has recently been renovated in cream and beige tones creating a "contemporary luxe" vibe. The decadence continues in the spa spread over two floors, where you'll find an indoor pool, a Jacuzzi, and beauty treatments on offer.

About a 45-min. drive southwest of Auxerre on the D965 then D955 (48km/29 miles), in a disused quarry deep in the countryside, about 40 master craftsmen are building a medieval château using 13th-century tools, materials and techniques. Started in 1997 and due to be completed in 2023, the team work closely with archaeologists and historians. Visitors to **Guédelon** (www.guedelon.com; ✆ **03-86-45-66-66**; 14€ adults, 12€ children ages 14–17, 11€ children ages 5–13, children 4 and under free; Mar 19–31 daily 10am–5:30pm, Apr–June daily 10am–6pm [Sat until 7pm], July & Aug daily 10am–7pm, Sept & Oct Thurs–Tues 10am–5:30pm [Sat & Sun until 6pm]) can watch the craftsmen at work in their traditional outfits and are encouraged to ask questions; you can even apply to join a working holiday to undertake their "master builder" course if you speak French. Along with the castle-in-progress, also on site is the village where the workers and their animals live, a flour mill, and a medieval tavern serving food from the era. Guided tours in English take place every day in summer. While in the area, you might also want to visit St-Fargeau (www. chateau-de-st-fargeau.com; ✆ **03-86-74-05-67**), a 17th-century Renaissance château which was the inspiration for the Guédelon castle.

But the main reason to come here is for the Michelin-two-star cuisine of Jean-Michel Lorain. Each recipe is a work of art: foie gras with endives and sweetcorn in a consommé of Lapsang souchong and coconut bavarois with jasmine cream and exotic fruits are just two dishes that display Lorain's love of mixing flavors from around the world. A more relaxed, more affordable bistro is here too (Wed–Sun 12:30–2pm), with the emphasis on healthy eating.

14 Faubourg de Paris (N6), Joigny (30km/19 miles NW of Auxerre on the D606). www. cotesaintjacques.com. ✆ **03-86-62-09-70.** 22 units. 320€–640€. Breakfast 29€. Free parking. Fixed-price lunch (from Wed–Sat) 79€ and 94€; dinner 168€–238€. Restaurant Wed 7:30–9:45pm, Thurs–Sun 12:15–2pm and 7:30–9:45pm. Hotel and restaurant closed Mon and Tues. **Amenities:** 2 restaurants; fitness room; indoor pool; kids' playroom; babysitting; cooking classes; wine tasting; sauna; shop; spa; free Wi-Fi.

VÉZELAY ★★

217km (135 miles) SE of Paris; 52km (32 miles) S of Auxerre

Vézelay, a living museum of French antiquity, stands frozen in time. For many, the town is the high point of a trip through Burgundy. During the 12th century, it was one of the great pilgrimage sites of the Christian world as it contained the alleged tomb of St. Mary Magdalene, that "beloved and pardoned sinner."

Today the medieval charm of Vézelay is widely known throughout France, and visitors virtually overrun the town in summer. The hordes are especially thick on July 22, the official day of homage to La Madeleine.

Essentials

ARRIVING If you're **driving** from Paris, take A6 south to Auxerre, then continue south along N6 to Givry and then D951 to Vézelay. Eight **trains** a day travel from Paris Gare de Bercy to Sermizelles, taking 2 hr., 30 min. For train information, visit www.oui.sncf or call *℃* **36-35** (.40€/min.). You'll need to take a taxi or the shuttle bus into town (details on tourist office website).

Alternatively, you might like to arrive on foot or by mountain bike. A new 84-km (52-mile) signposted route (GR213 A) links Vézelay with the UNESCO-listed **Fontenay Abbey** (www.abbayedefontenay.com; *℃* **03-80-92-15-00**), the world's oldest-preserved Cistercian site in Montbard.

VISITOR INFORMATION The **Office de Tourisme** is at 12 rue St-Etienne (www.vezelaytourisme.com; *℃* **03-86-33-23-69**).

Exploring Vézelay

On a hill surrounded by countryside, Vézelay is one of France's most spiritual places as its basilica (see below) is said to house the remains of Mary Magdalene; both it and the hill are UNESCO World Heritage Sites. The town, which is known for its sculptured doorways, mullioned windows, and corbelled staircases, began as an abbey founded in 858 by Girart de Roussillon, Comté de Bourgogne.

It's also classed as one of France's most beautiful villages.

On March 31, 1146, St. Bernard preached the Second Crusade here; in 1190, the town was the rendezvous point for the Third Crusade, drawing such personages as Richard the Lion-hearted and King Philippe-Auguste of France. Later, St. Louis IX came here several times on pilgrimages.

Park outside the town hall and walk through the medieval streets lined with 15th-, 16th-, and 18th-century houses and flower-filled gardens. Download a free guided tour to your smartphone from www.guidigo.com to help you get around. **Musée Zervos** at 14 rue St-Etienne (www.musee-zervos.com; *℃* **03-86-32-39-26**; admission 5€, free for ages 25 and under; July–Aug daily 10am–6pm, closed Tues

Old house in Vézelay

rest of year and mid-Nov to mid-Mar), is worth a look for its fine collection of modern art, including works by Picasso.

If you're in the mood to shop, head for rue St-Etienne and rue St-Pierre; you'll find an assortment of stores selling religious books and statuary. For a bottle or two of Vézelay wine go to **Cave Henry de Vézelay,** 4 route de Nanchèvres, St-Père-sous-Vézelay (www.henrydevezelay.com; ℭ **03-86-33-29-62**). A brewery, **Brasserie de Vézelay,** on rue du Gravier (www.brasseriedevezelay.com; ℭ **03-86-34-98-38**) about 2km (1.4 miles) east of the town, makes organic and gluten-free beer.

Basilique Ste-Madeleine ★★★ CHURCH   Visible for miles around due to its hilltop location, the basilica was founded in the 9th century and then restored by architect Viollet-le-Duc in the 19th century, who famously also renovated Notre Dame de Paris. This Romanesque jewel is at its most atmospheric when the monks sing during the daily services (see website for details). To get the most out of your visit it's advisable to go on a guided tour led by one of the brothers. In the crypt are the supposed remains of Mary Magdalene, which attract pilgrims from around the world; many are en route to Santiago de Compostela. Most of them stay in one of the basilica's three guest houses (https://hotellerie-vezelay.fr; 25€), and you could too.

pl. de la Basilique. www.basiliquedevezelay.org. ℭ **03-86-33-39-50.** Free admission; tours 3.60€. Daily 7am–8pm. Guided 1-hr. visits Easter–Oct Sun at 2:30pm.

Where to Stay

Hotel de la Poste et du Lion d'Or ★★   On the main square at the bottom of the hill, this three-star hotel in a former coaching inn is our favorite in Vézelay. The whole place has undergone renovation in recent years, completed in 2017. Rooms are calm and spacious with traditional wooden furniture; some overlook the village, while others have a view of the Morvan countryside. The latest addition is a gourmet restaurant, *L'Éternel*, where creative Burgundian/French dishes are beautifully presented (fixed-price menus 28€–48€). The light and airy bar, with its summer terrace, is the perfect spot to sample the local wines.

Pl. du Champ de Foire. www.hplv-vezelay.com. ℭ **03-73-53-03-20.** 39 units. 80€–240€ double. Breakfast 14€. Parking nearby. Closed Jan–Feb. **Amenities:** Restaurant; bar; garden; babysitting; free Wi-Fi.

Where to Eat

A La Fortune du Pot ★★ BURGUNDIAN/FRENCH   Don't let the name "Pot Luck" turn you off. You can be sure of good-value Burgundian cooking in this old village house at the bottom of the hill: like *boeuf bourguignon,* slow-cooked lamb shank with beans and eggs poached in red wine. Everything is homemade, even the organic bread. We particularly like the prunes in red Burgundy for dessert, served with vanilla ice cream. The wine list is small but perfectly formed of regional producers; try the

AOC Bourgogne-Vézelay (white only). The ambiance is good too, whether in the rustic dining room or the plant-filled terrace.

6 pl. du Champ de Foire. www.fortuntedupot.com. ☎ **03-86-33-32-56.** Main course 14.50€–16.50€; fixed-price menus 19.50€–25€. Thurs–Mon noon–2pm and 7–9pm.

AVALLON ★

214km (133 miles) SE of Paris; 52km (32 miles) SE of Auxerre; 96km (60 miles) NW of Dijon

This fortified town sits behind ancient ramparts, upon which you can stroll. A medieval atmosphere permeates Avallon, where you'll find many 15th- and 16th-century houses. At the town gate on Grande Rue Aristide-Briand is a 1460 clock tower. The Romanesque **Collégiale St-Lazare** dates from the 12th century and has fantastic doorways, an artfully lit interior, and impressive woodwork. The church, open daily from 8am to 7pm, is said to have received the head of St. Lazarus in A.D. 1000, thus turning it into a pilgrimage site. A good day to visit is Saturday for the local produce market in place Général de Gaulle, which attracts foodies from miles around. While you're there, stock up on artisan tea, coffee, and hot chocolate from **Dame Jeanne,** 59 Grande Rue Aristide Briand (www. damejeanne.fr; ☎ **03-86-34-58-71**), which also has a charming tearoom.

Essentials

ARRIVING   If you're **driving,** travel south from Paris along A6 past Auxerre to Avallon. **Trains** arrive daily from Paris Gare de Bercy every 2 hr. (trip time: almost 3 hr.). For train information, visit www.oui.sncf or call ☎ **36-35** (.40€/min.). **Bus** service 49 from Dijon takes 2 hr. and costs 1.50€ one-way; purchase tickets on the bus.

VISITOR INFORMATION   The **Office de Tourisme** is at 6 rue Bocquillot (www.avallon-morvan.com; ☎ **03-86-34-14-19**).

Where to Stay

Château de Vault de Lugny ★★★   This fairytale château is the place to stay if you want to feel like a king or queen for a few days. In fact, there is even a suite called "Le Roy" which was set aside for the kings of France, complete with monumental fireplace, four-poster bed, double bath tub, and Gothic chairs; the other rooms are a bit more sedate and two are in a cottage. The grounds offer plenty to do, from exploring the parkland to taking a dip in the indoor pool, located in the vaulted cellar, or booking a wine tasting. The gourmet restaurant, which marries French cuisine with Mauritian influences (the chef was born in Mauritius), is housed in the 17th-century former kitchen. And, of course, the wine list is composed of the best vintages from the region.

11 rue du Château, Vault-de-Lugny (6km/4 miles west of Avallon on the D606 then D128). www.lugny.fr. ☎ **03-86-34-07-86.** 15 units. 140€–450€ double. Breakfast 18€– 32€. Free parking. Closed mid-Nov to Apr. Take D957 from Avallon, turn right in

Pontaubert (after the church) and follow signs; Vault-de-Lugny is about 3km (1.75 miles) away. **Amenities:** Babysitting; bar; butler; indoor pool; mountain bikes; restaurant; room service; tennis court; valet parking; free Wi-Fi.

Moulin des Ruats ★   In a wooded valley at the gates of the Morvan Regional Natural Park, this 18th-century water mill is now a cosy three-star hotel. The rooms, some of which have balconies overlooking either the garden or the river, are individually decorated in either contemporary or traditional style with the odd antique. The well-regarded restaurant, overlooking the forest and river, celebrates the local *terroir*; meals can be enjoyed outside in summer. Massage treatments and wine tastings are also available. This is the perfect spot for a relaxing break.

23, rue des Isles Labaumes. (4km/3 miles west of Avallon on the D427). www.moulin-desruats.com. ✆ **03-86-34-97-00.** 25 units. 93€–145€ double; 165€ suite. Breakfast 15€. Free parking. Closed mid-Nov to mid-Feb. Take D427 3km (1.75 miles) west outside town. **Amenities:** Restaurant; bar; lounge; free Wi-Fi.

Where to Eat

Le Vaudésir ★★ BURGUNDIAN   Award-winning chef Cécile Riotte-Jeanne worked in several top restaurants, including Joël Robuchon in Monaco, before returning to her native Burgundy in 2012. This well-established smart bistro specializes in good-value *cuisine de terroir* such as duck pie topped with mashed potato or Charolais steak in red wine sauce; the fruit and veg comes from the chef's garden and the other pro-duce from within a 20km (12 mile) radius. You can eat on the terrace on fine days and enjoy the views over the countryside as you sip wine from a local vineyard.

84 rue de Lyon. www.restaurant-levaudesir.com. ✆ **03-86-34-14-60.** Main course 16€–28€; fixed-price menu 20€–38€. Mon and Thurs–Sat noon–2pm and 7–9pm; Tues and Wed noon–2pm.

SAULIEU ★

250km (155 miles) SE of Paris; 76km (47 miles) NW of Beaune

Saulieu is interesting, but its food put it on the international map. The town (pop. 3,000) has enjoyed a reputation for cooking since the 17th century and is one of France's *Sites Remarquables du Goût* for its Fête du Charolais (festival of Charolais cows) in August; a food festival, Les Journées Gourmandes, also takes place here at the end of May. If you're in town on Thursday or Saturday morning, take a stroll around the market then have a drink in the **Café Parisien,** 4 rue du Marché (www.cafe parisien.net), the oldest cafe in Burgundy (1832) and a historic monument.

The main sight is the 12th-century **Basilique St-Andoche,** pl. Docteur Roclore, which has some interesting decorated capitals. Next door, in the **Musée François-Pompon** (✆ **03-80-64-19-51;** 3€ adults, free for children 12 and under; Apr–Sept Mon 10am–12:30pm, Wed–Sat 10am–12:30pm and 2–6pm, Sun 10:30am–noon and 2:30–5pm; Oct–Dec

Charolais cows

and Mar Mon 10am–12.30pm, Wed–Sat 10am–12:30pm and 2–5:30pm, Sun 10:30am–noon and 2:30–5pm, closed Jan and Feb), you can see works by François Pompon (d. 1933), the well-known sculptor of animals; his large statue of a bull stands on a plaza off the N6 at the entrance to town. Also in the museum are archaeological remnants from the Gallo-Roman era, sacred medieval art, and a room dedicated to France's great chefs including Bernard Loiseau (see "Where to Stay & Eat" below).

Essentials

ARRIVING If you're **driving,** head along A6 from Paris or Lyon. The **train** station is northeast of the town center. Passengers coming from Paris sometimes opt to take the TER from Paris Bercy, getting off in Montbard, 48km (30 miles) to the north. There are about six trains a day to Montbard and the journey takes over 2 hr. From Montbard, a series of **buses** timed to the arrival of the trains carry passengers on to Saulieu for a one-way fare of 1.50€. For bus information, contact **Transco** (www.mobigo-bourgogne.com); for rail information, visit www.oui.sncf or call ☏ **36-35** (.40€/min.).

VISITOR INFORMATION The **Office de Tourisme** is at 24 rue d'Argentine (www.saulieu-morvan.fr; ☏ **03-80-64-00-21**).

Where to Stay & Eat

Le Relais Bernard Loiseau ★★★ This five-star hotel is home to one of France's great restaurants, named after the late chef who created it. It's now run by his wife, along with satellite restaurants in Dijon, Beaune, and Paris, while the Michelin-three-star cuisine is overseen by Patrick Bertron, who has worked in the kitchen since 1982. His cooking showcases the finest products from Brittany, his birthplace, and the forests of Morvan, where he lives. Wine connoisseurs can choose from 900 top labels. The decor throughout is "rustic luxury" with wooden beams and Burgundy-tile floors. The standard or "confort" rooms are spacious and good value and even have their own balconies. In 2017, the hotel opened a new multi-sensory, hi-tech spa with a health-food restaurant. Children are well catered for: They have their own games room and gourmet menu.

2 rue Argentine. www.bernard-loiseau.com. ℂ **03-80-90-53-53.** 23 units. 165€–295€ double; 435€–605€ suite. Breakfast 28€. Free parking. Menus 75€–245€. Check website for closing times and dates. **Amenities:** Restaurant; bar; exercise room; indoor and outdoor pools; kids' playroom; pétanque; room service; sauna; shop; spa; free Wi-Fi.

La Tour d'Auxois ★★ Opposite Le Relais Bernard Loiseau, this three-star hotel in a 17th-century convent is a good option for those who want to experience Saulieu's foodie delights without breaking the bank. Rooms are comfortable, traditionally furnished and rustic, while the six suites have wooden beams. As you'd expect from a *Maître Restaurateur* (Master Chef, an official label designating that the food is homemade), the "modern French" dishes are made with local, seasonal products including snails, charcuterie, and cheese. Thankfully, the outdoor pool is inviting enough to help you work off some calories. Then you can re-tox with some wine in the vaulted-cellar bar.

2 rue d'Argentine. www.tourdauxois.com. ℂ **03-80-64-36-19.** 29 units. 85€–145€ double. Breakfast 13€. Free parking. Main course 16€–28€. Fixed-price menus 29€–52€. Closed mid-Dec to mid-Feb. **Amenities:** Restaurant; bar; lounge; outdoor pool; free Wi-Fi.

AUTUN ★★

293km (182 miles) SE of Paris; 85km (53 miles) SW of Dijon; 48km (30 miles) W of Beaune; 60km (37 miles) SE of Auxerre

Autun is one of the oldest towns in France. Founded by the Romans, it was called Augustodunum: "the other Rome." Some relics still stand, including a section of its ramparts, which date from 1 B.C. Also here are the remains of the largest theater in Gaul, the Théâtre Romain (free admission). It was nearly 150m (492 ft.) in diameter and could hold some 20,000 people. In July and August, it hosts a magnificent *son et lumière* with a 1,000-strong cast recounting the turbulent relationship between the Gauls and the Romans.

Temple of Janus in Autun

Autun is a thriving provincial town of 16,000, but because it's off the beaten track, the hordes go elsewhere. Still, it has its historical associations—Napoleon Bonaparte studied here in 1779 at the military academy (today the Lycée Bonaparte). Don't miss the Passage Balthus, a 19th-century neo-Renaissance arcade with its original features.

Essentials

ARRIVING If you're **driving,** take A6 south until reaching A38, then turn onto N81 towards Autun. Rail links to Autun are awkward. Six high-speed TGV **trains** a day from Paris's Gare de Lyon run to Le Creusot-Montceau, 40km (25 miles) south of Autun taking under 1 hr., 30 min.. From there, take a 30-min. bus connection to Autun. In Autun, **buses** (1.50€ one-way) arrive at a parking lot by the railway station on avenue de la République. For bus information, visit www.mobigo-bourgogne.com/bourgogne_en. For railway information, visit www.oui.sncf or call ✆ **36-35** (.40€/min.).

VISITOR INFORMATION The **Office de Tourisme** is at 13 rue Général Demetz (www.autun-tourisme.com; ✆ **03-85-86-80-38**).

Exploring Autun

Autun was an important Roman link on the road from Lyon to Boulogne. A legacy of that period is the 17m (56-ft.) high **Porte d'Arroux,** once the city's northern gate, which has two archways now used for cars and smaller ones used for pedestrians. Also exceptional is the **Porte St-André (St. Andrew's Gate),** northwest of the Roman theater. Rising 20m (66 ft.), it has four doorways and is surmounted by a gallery of 10 arcades.

Cathédrale St-Lazare ★★ CATHEDRAL   Built in the 12th century to house the relics of Lazarus (who turned out to be the bishop of Aix and not the one that rose from the dead, as was originally believed), this cathedral is one of France's finest examples of Romanesque architecture and was inspired by the famous Cluny Abbey. The steeple, however, dates from the 1460s. Its main attractions are the carving of the Last Judgment on the west tympanum, and the capitals, whose carvings depict the three Magi, the flight to Egypt, and the suicide of Judas (amongst others). It is fortunate that they all survived as the canons here in the 18th century covered them with plaster, thinking them ugly. At the entrance to the sacristy is *The Martyrdom of Saint Symphorian*, by Dominique Ingres. Opposite the cathedral is the **Espace Gislebertus** (free admission; daily July–Sept 10am–7pm), an information center on the town's heritage, where you can watch a 12-min. film, "Revelation: The Great Door of Autun," which explores the cathedral's *Last Judgment* tympanum in high-definition 3-D. pl. St-Louis. Free admission. Daily 8am–7pm.

Musée Rolin ★ MUSEUM   Housed in the 15th-century birthplace of Nicolas Rolin, founder of the Hospices de Beaune (see p. 422), this museum has a rich collection of artefacts from the Gallo-Roman era to the Middle Ages, as well as French and European paintings from the 17th to the 20th centuries. Highlights include mosaics from ancient Augustodunum; the 15th-century polychrome *Autun virgin* and paintings by Maurice Denis and Joan Miró. The building is equally as impressive as the collection.

3 rue des Bancs. ✆ **03-85-52-09-76.** Admission 6.20€ adults; 3.60€ students and children. Feb–Mar and mid-Oct–Nov Wed–Mon 10am–noon and 2–5pm, Sun 2–5pm; Apr–mid-June 9:30am–noon and 1:30–6pm; mid-June to mid-Oct 10am–1pm and 2–6pm. Closed May 1, Nov 1 and 11, and Dec–Jan.

Where to Stay & Eat

La Tête Noire ★   Decorated in warm tones throughout, this three-star family-run hotel offers the best value stay in Autun. From some bedrooms you can see the cathedral and from others the surrounding countryside; all have a shower or bath, and some have air conditioning. The focus of the menu, naturally, is the dishes and produce of Burgundy: We were particularly impressed by the excellent-value four-course "Menu Tête Noire" (23.50€) featuring Charolais steak in mustard sauce.

3 rue de l'Arquebuse. www.hoteltetenoire.fr. ✆ **03-85-86-59-99.** 31 units. 88€–106€ double; 105€ family room. Breakfast 11.50€. Free parking nearby. Fixed-price menus 16.50€–49€. **Amenities:** Restaurant; free Wi-Fi.

BEAUNE ★★★

316km (196 miles) SE of Paris; 39km (24 miles) SW of Dijon

Beaune is the perfect base for exploring the **Côte d'Or** wine region that stretches to the north and south of the city. Burgundy's most influential wine merchants are all based here: Louis Jadot, Joseph Drouhin, and Bouchard Père et Fils, to name but a few. Beaune was a Gallic sanctuary, then a Roman town and some of its ramparts are still intact; you can even walk on them. Until the 14th century, Beaune was the residence of the ducs de Bourgogne. When the last duke, Charles the Bold, died in 1477, Louis XI annexed the town. The main sight is the **Hôtel-Dieu des Hospices Civils de Beaune** (p. 422), also known as the Hospices de Beaune. The Swiss-born Chevrolet brothers, who moved to the U.S. and created one of the world's best-known car brands, were brought up here.

A taste **OF THE CÔTE D'OR**

Beaune is the epicenter of Burgundian winemaking with many of the world's most coveted and expensive wine appellations within a 1 hr. drive. In 2015, Les Climats du vignoble de Bourgogne (Burgundy vineyards) became a UNESCO World Heritage Site. To the north lies the **Côte de Nuits,** famed for its red Pinot Noir vineyards with legendary appellations such as **Romanée-Conti** and **Richebourg.** To the south lies **Côte de Beaune,** home to the great names of white chardonnay wines such as **Meursault** and **Chassagne-Montrachet.** You may want to start your wine tour in Beaune with a visit to the **Maison des Climats** (at the tourist office; same hours; free), a discovery center, to get an overview of the wine-producing area and find out why it got listed by UNESCO. Beaune is where many of Burgundy's *négociants* (wine merchants who process and bottle the produce of smaller winemakers and then sell under their own name) have their bases. As well as being able to simply turn up with no appointment, you'll often be able to taste a wider variety of appellations than at an individual vineyard. **Patriarche**

Père et Fils (www.patriarche.com; ℂ **03-80-24-53-78**) offers 1-hour visits to its fabulous 13th- to 14th-century vaulted tasting cellars where millions of bottles are held along 5km (3 miles) of underground cellars; it's open daily from 9:30 to noon and 2 to 5:30pm; admission is 17€. **Bouchard Père et Fils,** 15 rue du Château, (www.bouchard-pereet-fils.com; ℂ **03-80-24-80-45**) has cellars in the 15th-century Castle of Beaune, a former royal fortress. A guided tour in English and tasting is available by reservation and costs 49€ or 99€. Just opposite the celebrated Hôtel-Dieu, the **Marché aux Vins** (www.marcheauxvins.com; ℂ **03-80-25-08-20**) is housed in a former Cordeliers church. With over 100 hectares (247 acres) of vineyards, this wine *négociant* offers a wide range of appellations to taste. Tastings of four wines cost 10€ and six wines cost 13€. It's open daily April to November from 10am to 7pm; November to March from 10am to noon and 2 to 7pm. On the northern outskirts of town on the D18, **Maison Louis Jadot** (www.louisjadot.com; ℂ **03-80-26-31-98**), is open for free tastings Monday to Friday from 3 to 7pm

Essentials

ARRIVING If you're **driving,** note that Beaune is a few miles from the junction of three highways—the A6, A31, and A36. Beaune has good railway connections with Dijon, Lyon, and Paris. From Paris's Gare de Lyon are several TGV **trains** per day (trip time: just over 2 hr.), with many more possibilities via a change in Dijon. For train information and schedules, visit www.oui.sncf or call ℂ **36-35** (.40€/min.).

VISITOR INFORMATION The **Office de Tourisme** is at 6 bd. Perpreuil (www.beaune-tourisme.fr; ℂ **03-80-26-21-30**).

Getting Around

BY TAXI The train station is a 15-min. walk from the town center so you might want to get a taxi to your accommodation. Try **Taxi Franon** ℂ **06-07-77-77-55.**

and Saturday from 11am to 5:30pm. You can also pre-book a tasting and a visit to its modern cellars (20€) Monday to Friday at 3pm and Saturdays at 10am.

If you fancy visiting vineyards outside Beaune, head south along D974 to the **Château de Pommard,** 15 rue Marey Monge (www.chateaude pommard.com; © **03-80-22-07-99**), the largest privately-owned estate in the Côte d'Or. Built for Messire Vivant de Micault, equerry and secretary of Louis XVI in 1726, this castle was bought in 2014 by the Carabello-Baum family from San Francisco. You can pre-book one of several "experiences," from the hour-long introduction to Burgundy's *climats* and their wine (25€) to learning the basics of being a sommelier (2 hr.; 125€). Next, you can head farther along the D974 to the **Château de Meursault** (www.meursault.com; © **03-80-26-22-75**). This domaine owns over 60 hectares (148 acres) of vineyards covering appellations such as Aloxe Corton, Pommard, Puligny-Montrachet, and of course Meursault. You can turn up without prior reservation for a visit to the cellars of this fabulous 19th-century castle, followed

by a tasting of seven wines in the art gallery for 21€. It is open daily 10am to noon and 2 to 6pm (no lunchtime closure May to September). You may like to stop for a wine-tasting lunch along the way at **La Table d'Olivier Leflaive,** 10 pl. du Monument in Puligny-Montrachet (www.olivier-leflaive.com; © **03-80-21-37-65**), which costs 65€–90€, depending on the accompanying wines.

For those who'd like to visit independent, family winegrowers but don't know where to start, **Burgundy by Request** (www.burgundybyrequest.com; © **06-85-65-83-83**), run by English expat Tracy Thurling, should be your first port of call. Cristina Otel of **Burgundy Wine School** (www.burgundy-wineschool.com; © **06-68-84-24-28**), is a highly qualified winemaker whose courses and tours offer a more in-depth knowledge of the local AOCs. A good introduction to grape varieties is also offered by **Vin Sensation** at 1 rue d'Enfer in Beaune (www.sensation-vin. com; © **03-80-22-17-57**) during their "Essential Burgundy" session, Sunday to Friday at 2:30pm, that lasts 1 hr., 30 min. and costs 37€.

BY BIKE   The best way to see this vine-planted land is by bike. Near Beaune train station, **Bourgogne Randonnées,** 7 av. du 8 septembre (www.bourgogne-randonnees.fr; © **03-80-22-06-03**), rents bikes for 19€ per day.

Exploring Beaune

Known as "the daughter of Cluny," the **Collégiale Notre-Dame,** pl. du Général Leclerc, is a Romanesque church dating from 1120. Some remarkable 15th-century tapestries illustrating scenes from the life of the Virgin Mary are on display in the sanctuary and you can view them from April to mid-November (days and times vary). Admission is 3€ for adults, 2€ for children 12 to 18, and free for children 11 and under.

Dalinéum, 26 pl. Monge (© **03-80-22-63-13;** 7€ adults, 5€ ages 12–18; free for children 11 and under; Apr–Nov Mon–Sat 2–6:30pm, Sun

11am–6:30pm; Dec–Mar Sat 2–6:30pm, Sun 11am–6:30pm), is a permanent private collection of 150 works by Salvador Dalí.

The best **shopping** streets are rue de Lorraine, rue d'Alsace, rue Maufoux, and place de la Madeleine. For smaller boutiques, stroll down the pedestrian rue Carnot and rue Monge. You'll encounter plenty of designer labels, vintners, and antiques dealers.

Every Wednesday and Saturday morning, the streets around place de la Halle and place de Fleury are chock-a-block with Burgundy's liveliest market. The most serious meat and cheese producers have their stalls in Les Halles. Consider taking a tour with American expat chef Marjorie Taylor of **The Cook's Atelier** (www.thecooksatelier.com; ℭ **06-84-83-16-18**), then making your own lunch under her supervision. And be sure to visit **Edmond Fallot** at 31 rue du Faubourg (www.fallot.com; ℭ **03-80-22-10-10**) on the southwestern outskirts of town to buy mustard and have a look around the factory.

Hôtel-Dieu des Hospices Civils de Beaune ★★★ HISTORIC MONUMENT

Famous for its excellent wines, produced by vineyards bequeathed to it by grateful patients over the years, this hospital was founded in 1443 by Nicolas Rolin (p. 419), chancellor to the Duke of Burgundy, and his wife Guigone. The sick are now treated in a state-of-the-art building on the outskirts of town, built and maintained thanks to money earned from the hospital's annual wine auction, which takes place on the

third weekend of November, the *Vente des Vins des Hospices de Beaune*. The interesting sights are many, including the colorful tiled roof, the vast "room of the poor," and *The Last Judgment* polyptych by Flemish artist Roger van der Weyden. An audio guide, included in the entrance fee, provides an entertaining and informative commentary by "Nicolas" and "Guigone."

Rue de l'Hôtel-Dieu. www.hospices-de-beaune.com. ℭ **03-80-24-45-00.** Admission 7.50€ adults, 5.50€ children ages 10–18, free for children 9 and under. Mid-Mar to mid-Nov daily 9am–6:30pm; mid-Nov to mid-Mar daily 9–11:30am and 2–5:30pm.

Hôtel-Dieu, Beaune

Musée des Beaux-Arts ★★ ART MUSEUM   Renovated in 2017, complete with new display, this museum has an eclectic collection of local history, with a rich Gallo-Roman section, and, also, art from the 17th to 20th century including pieces by Beaune-born Félix Ziem, such as *Les Flamants Roses* (Flamingoes), and lithographs by Picasso and Le Corbusier.

6 bd. Perpreuil (Porte Marie de Bourgogne). ✆ **03-80-24-56-92.** Admission 5.80€ adults, 3.80€ students and children 11–18, free for children 10 and under. June–Sept Wed–Mon 10am–1pm and 2–6pm; Oct–Apr Wed–Sun until 5pm.

Musée du Vin de Bourgogne ★ MUSEUM   To be honest, the most interesting aspects of this museum are the building itself, the former home (14th–18th century) of the Dukes of Burgundy, and the collection of Aubusson tapestries depicting vineyard scenes. Other than that, it's a somewhat dry display of tools, bottles, presses, and wine-making life through the ages.

Rue d'Enfer. ✆ **03-80-24-56-92.** Admission 5.80€ adults, 3.80€ students and children 11–18, free for children 10 and under. Apr–Sept Wed–Mon 10am–1pm and 2–6pm; Mar, Oct, and Nov Wed–Sun 10am–1pm and 2–5pm.

Where to Stay

Beaune also has some lovely B&Bs, from the luxury **Côté Rempart** (www.coterempart.com; ✆ **03-80-21-72-57**), with five rooms ranging from 180€ to 210€ in a lovely 18th-century townhouse on a quiet back street, to the charming **Les Planchottes,** (www.lesplanchottes.fr; ✆ **03-80-22-83-67**), an old wine producer's house a short walk northwest of the city center, which has two pretty rooms costing 100€. Accommodation under 70€ per night is hard to find in Beaune, but the municipal four-star campsite, **Les Cent Vignes** (✆ **03-80-22-03-91**), open from Easter to October, has 116 pitches, hot showers, a tennis court, and a restaurant.

Hôtel Le Cep ★★★   Beaune and its surrounds have their fair share of luxury accommodation and this is our favorite. Five-star Le Cep, which takes its name from the roots of a vine, is created from several adjoining *hôtels particuliers* dating from the 16th century (Louis XIV stayed in one). The atmosphere here is of old-fashioned luxury with first-class service to match. The 29 suites, each individually designed in traditional French style and furnished with antiques, have Nespresso machines and a Night Cove, which helps guests to sleep and wake up naturally. Its spa, Marie de Bourgogne, has won international awards and the restaurant, Loiseau des Vignes (see "Where to Eat," below), has a Michelin star. Top class all round.

27 rue Jean-Francois Maufoux. www.hotel-cep-beaune.com. ✆ **03-80-22-35-48.** 65 units. 159€–575€ double. Breakfast 21€. Parking 21€. **Amenities:** Restaurant; bar; concierge; fitness room; spa; room service; free Wi-Fi.

Les Remparts ★★   Less than a 10-min. walk west of the train station, this three-star hotel is one of the most characterful lodgings in town. The

17th-century mansion, backed up against the 5th century ramparts, has two gorgeous inner courtyards where you can have your breakfast on warm days. Each of the rooms is individually decorated in simple, traditional style but fitted with all modern amenities; the one on the third-floor of the tower (no lift), under the rafters, is particularly charming. Original features, such as stone fireplaces and staircases, add to the bygone atmosphere.

48 rue Thiers. www.hotel-remparts-beaune.com. ✆ **03-80-24-94-94.** 22 units. 99€–179€ double. Breakfast 13€. Parking 9€. **Amenities:** Bar; laundry service; lounge; bike rental; babysitting; airport/train station transfers; wine tours and tastings; free Wi-Fi.

Where to Eat

21 Boulevard ★★ BURGUNDIAN/FRENCH   This chic restaurant housed in a 15th-century wine cellar is the place to go if you're looking to make a night of it, as they also have an attached piano bar and club (Thurs–Sat) open until 2am. The menus are inspired by the seasons and naturally there's a "Menu Bourgignon" (28€) with the usual snails, *oeufs en meurette*, local cheeses, and a pudding made with *pain d'épices*. The wine list is superb, solely comprising Burgundy vintages, but also has a good selection of champagnes.

21 bd. St-Jacques. www.21boulevard.com. ✆ **03-80-21-00-21.** Main course 20€–38€; fixed-price menus 28€–48€. Tues–Sat noon–2pm and 7–10:30pm.

Le Comptoir des Tontons ★ FRENCH   This wine bar/restaurant/vintner on the south-eastern outskirts of town, with a traditional French cafe vibe, is instantly recognizable by its bright red facade. Equally bright and breezy is Pépita the chef who is keen to use local organic produce as much as possible, to make hearty dishes such as Bresse chicken with cauliflower compote. The wine list is a tour of French vineyards, with dozens from Burgundy. You could also just stop in for a glass and a platter of cheese or charcuterie.

22 rue du Faubourg Madeleine. www.lecomptoirdestontons.com. ✆ **03-80-24-19-64.** Main course 25€; fixed-price menu 38€–48€. Tues–Sat 6–10:30pm.

Loiseau des Vignes ★★★ MODERN FRENCH   Part of Hôtel Le Cep (see "Where to Stay," above) and a satellite of the Relais Bernard Loiseau in Saulieu (p. 417), this Michelin-star restaurant is one of our favorites in Burgundy. Sure, the food is superb, but it's all about the wine here. This was the first restaurant in Europe to serve wines solely by the glass (5€–45€). And what a choice: around 70 labels, mostly from the region, and some you won't find anywhere else. The two-course lunch menu is accessible at 25€ and features local products enhanced by international flavors, as chef Mourad Haddouche is a keen traveler. Come on a warm day and you'll be able to eat at a table in the gorgeous courtyard.

31 rue Maufoux. www.bernard-loiseau.com. ✆ **03-80-24-12-06.** Main course 45€–76€; fixed-price lunch 25€–35€ or dinner 59€–119€. Tues–Sat noon–2pm and 7–10pm. Closed Feb.

Where to Stay & Eat Nearby

Les Charmes ★★ Meursault is a lovely spot for a break. In the heart of the village, this family-run three-star hotel in a 18th-century winegrower's house offers a stylish and relaxing stay that won't break the bank. The five spacious "Grands Crus" rooms are in the main house and individually decorated in traditional style, while the seven "Villages" rooms in the renovated outbuildings overlooking the courtyard are more contemporary and slightly cheaper. A large, tree-dotted garden with a swimming pool is a welcome oasis in summer. Though the hotel lacks a restaurant, plenty of good eating places are in the area, such as **La Goutte d'Or** (www.lagouttedor-meursault.fr; ✆ **03-80-20-94-05**), not to mention plenty of wineries for tastings. You might also like to visit the spa at nearby château-hotel **La Cueillette** (www.laceuillette.com; ✆ **03-80-20-62-80**).

10 pl. Murger, Meursault (9km/6 miles southwest of Beaune on the D973). www.hoteles charmes.com. ✆ **03-80-21-63-53**. 13 units. 95€–140€ double. Breakfast 13€. Free parking. **Amenities:** Bar; laundry; reading room; room service; outdoor pool; free Wi-Fi.

Maison Lameloise ★★★ BURGUNDIAN Not only does it have three Michelin stars, but this gourmet eating place, housed in a coaching inn dating from the 15th century, was voted the world's third best restaurant in Trip Advisor's Travelers' Choice Restaurant Awards in 2017. Chef Eric Pras has worked in the kitchens of some of France's greatest chefs and since 2008 he's been creating exquisite dishes showcasing Burgundian produce: duck with salsify and turnips, or venison seasoned with fir tree powder, for example. The 16 rooms are comfortably furnished but maybe not as luxurious as you'd expect, and a bit overpriced. Nonetheless, if you're a foodie, this place is one for the bucket list.

36 pl. d'Armes, Chagny (16km/10 miles southwest of Beaune on the D974). www.lameloise.fr. ✆ **03-85-87-65-65**. 16 units. 160€–380€ double. Breakfast 26€. Fixed-price lunch 82€ or dinner 145€–215€. Thurs–Mon noon–1:30pm and 7:30–9:30pm (summer lunch daily). Closed mid-Dec to mid-Jan.

MÂCON

397km (247 miles) SE of Paris; 127km (79 miles) S of Dijon; 87km (54 miles) S of Beaune.

On the banks of the River Saône, in the south of Burgundy, Mâcon is a workaday town whose historic center is a pleasant place to spend a day just strolling around the narrow streets and along the quayside. Founded by the Celts and developed by the Romans, Mâcon is famous for being the birthplace of Romantic poet and politician Alphonse de Lamartine (see "Exploring Mâcon" below). A good time to visit is during the **Vin'Estival** wine festival at the end of April, which includes a competition to find France's best *grand vin;* the surrounding area is famous for its Mâconnais and Beaujolais wines. The town is particularly lively from mid-June until the end of August when the **Eté Frappé** festival takes place, featuring music concerts, open-air cinema, and children's entertainment.

Essentials

ARRIVING   If you're **driving,** take A6 south past Beaune and onto Mâcon. Six direct TGV **trains** a day from Paris's Gare de Lyon run to Mâcon Loche TGV station (7km/4 miles outside Mâcon and connected to the center by shuttle bus Mon–Sat) taking 1 hr., 30 min. For railway information, visit www.oui.sncf or call ✆ **36-35** (.40€/min.).

VISITOR INFORMATION   The **Office de Tourisme** is at 1 pl. Saint-Pierre (www.macon-tourism.com; ✆ **03-85-21-07-07**).

Exploring Mâcon

Mâcon has two churches worth a visit: the Neo-Roman Église Saint Pierre on place St-Pierre, the town's largest church, and 19th-century Cathédral Saint Vincent on Square de la Paix. The **Musée des Ursulines** at 5 rue de la Préfecture (✆ **03-85-39-90-38;** 2.50€ adults, free or ages 26 and under; Tues–Sat 10am–noon and 2–6pm, Sun 2–6pm), named after the 17th-century convent in which it is based, has archaeological finds from the area, a first floor dedicated to local life along with a space devoted to Lamartine's life and work, and, on the second floor, an exhibition of artworks tracing the evolution of paintings over the last 5 centuries. From May to September, you can take boat trips along the River Saône for an afternoon or a day (book at the tourist office). However, the most interesting sights are within a 30 min. drive of the town.

Where to Stay

Best Western Plus Hôtel d'Europe et d'Angleterre ★★   Renovated in 2017 with a stylish new look, this three-star hotel is our favorite place to stay in town. Dating from 1800, anyone who is anyone has stayed here over the years from Winston Churchill to Catherine Deneuve, and even the first giraffe to set foot on European soil (Zarafa, in 1827). Rooms are decorated in a chic dove grey, complemented by dashes of silver and white. Most overlook the courtyard, but we like the deluxe rooms, which have a river view (104€–165€). Breakfast features organic produce including award-winning jams, and the lobby bar has a good selection of local wines accompanied by tapas.

92–109 quai Jean Jaurès. www.hotel-europeangleterre-macon.com. ✆ **03-85-38-27-94.** 37 units. 78€–175€ double. Breakfast 14.50€. Parking 12€. **Amenities:** Babysitting; bar; bikes; terrace; laundry service; packed lunches; free Wi-Fi.

Where to Eat

Mâcon has a clutch of good restaurants, with young chefs serving up quality French and Bourgignon cuisine. Notably **L'Ardoise,** 19 rue Franche (✆ **03-85-31-62-26;** Tues–Sat noon–1:30pm and 7–9:30pm), **Ma Table en Ville,** 5 rue de Strasbourg (www.matableenville.fr; ✆ **03-85-30-99-91;** daily 11:45am–1:30pm and 7:30–9pm), and, on the other side of the river,

A wine theme park

Deep in Beaujolais country, the **Hameau Duboeuf** "wine village" created by well-known wine merchant Georges Duboeuf, is an interesting day out for the family. Visitors can learn about the evolution of wine over 2,000 years via entertaining films and automated puppet shows; you can even "fly" over the surrounding countryside. See p. 420 for more information. It's just 17km (11 miles) south of Mâcon on the D906.

Le Saint Laurent, 1 quai Bouchacourt (www.lespritblanc.com; ℭ**03-85-39-29-19;** daily noon–1:30pm and 7–10pm); all have lunch menus for less than 25€ with main courses between 18€ and 40€.

Restaurant Pierre ★★★ FRENCH   This Michelin-star restaurant is a top pick in the region. While chef Christian Gaulin produces deftly executed French and Bourgignon dishes using seasonal produce, his wife Isabelle takes charge in the rustic-chic dining room. Christian's twist on classic regional dishes such as Charolais beef tournedos with foie gras or pigeon cooked in two ways, is seen in his choice of imaginatively matched sauces and accompaniments. Leave room for the Grand Marnier soufflé with orange sorbet. In summertime, nab a table on the terrace on the pedestrianized street. There's a well-priced lunch menu at 29€. Reservations required.

7-9 rue Dufour. www.restaurant-pierre.com. ℭ **03-85-38-14-23.** Fixed-price menus 54€–98€. Wed–Sat noon–1:30pm and 7:30–9pm; Sun lunch only.

Day Trips from Mâcon

A fun way to explore the vineyards is on foot or by bike, which can be hired from the old train station (now a tourist office; ℭ **03-85-21-07-14**) at Charnay-lès-Mâcon, a 10-min. drive from town on the D54. The former railway line is now a "green route." If driving, you might like to stop off at **Terres Secrètes** at 158 rue des Grandes Vignes in Prissé (www.terres-secretes.com; ℭ **03-85-37-64-89**) to buy some wine and local produce.

Grand Site Solutré-Pouilly-Vergisson ★★★ NATURAL SITE   Dominating the Pouilly-Fuissé vineyards, the Rock of Solutré and its environs, including the Rock of Vergisson, have been inhabited by man for 57,000 years. In 2013, the area received the label "Grand Site de France." Visitors can find out more about the site's history in the **Musée Départemental de Préhistoire,** at the base of the Rock of Solutré, before walking to the top for panoramic views (493m/1,617 ft.; takes about 30 min.). Be sure to arrive early for a car parking space in summer.

71960 Solutré-Pouilly (10km/6miles west of Mâcon on the D54). www.rochedesolu tre.com. ℭ **03-85-35-82-81.** Admission 5€ adults; free for children 18 and under. Museum: Daily Apr–Sept 10am–6pm; Oct–Mar 10am–5pm. Closed mid-Dec to mid-Jan.

Where to Stay & Eat Nearby

Four generations of Blanc chefs have dominated the restaurant scene around Mâcon. The original Mère Blanc's Bresse chicken in a cream sauce with basmati rice is so legendary that this free-range chicken has become a Blanc trademark. The Blanc restaurant empire now extends from Lyon to its postcard-perfect hub in the village of Vonnas (www. georgesblanc.com).

Some of the gorgeous B&B accommodations in this area include **Domaine la Source des Fées** (www.lasourcedesfees.fr; ℂ 03-85-35-67-02) in Fuissé, where double rooms start at 128€; the magnificent **Château de Pierreclos** in the village of Pierreclos (www.chateaudepierreclos.com; ℂ 03-85-35-73-73), which has five rooms starting at 165€; and **Fleur de Vignes** (www.fleurdevignes.com; ℂ 03-85-35-67-41), two sweet rooms (63€) in a wine producer's house in Loché. **Camping du Lac** (www. lac-cormoranche.com; ℂ 03-85-23-97-10) is a four-star campsite next to a lake in Cormoranche-sur-Saône.

La Courtille de Solutré ★★   In an idyllic location in the middle of the Pouilly-Fuissé vineyards, beneath the Rock of Solutré, is this gourmet "restaurant with rooms." Contemporary and original features work well together in this old stone village inn. On the menu you'll find traditional French dishes often enhanced by Spanish flavors, such as snails with chorizo and scallops with Basque ham; look out for the AOC Mâconnais: a hard, mild goats' cheese. The wine list has a good selection from the village and immediate area, including their own vineyard, Domaine du Chatelet in St-Amour. The six stylish rooms are each individually and tastefully decorated in whites and neutrals, with the odd antique; all but two have views over the vines.

71960 Solutré-Pouilly (10km/6 miles west of Mâcon on the D54). www.lacourtillede solutre.fr. ℂ **03-85-35-80-73.** 6 units. 90€–110€ double. Breakfast 12€. Free parking. Fixed-price lunch 24€–28€ or dinner 39.50€–43€. Restaurant closed Sun eve–Tues. **Amenities:** Bar; terrace; free Wi-Fi.

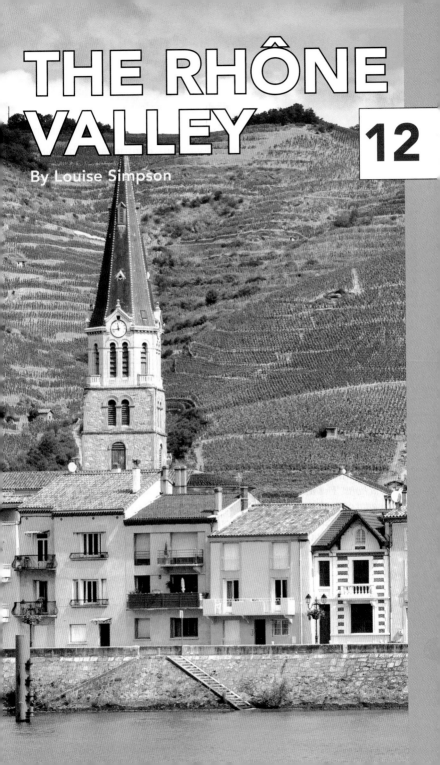

THE RHÔNE VALLEY

12

By Louise Simpson

T he Rhône Valley is France's heartland of gastronomy and heritage. British novelist Anthony Horowitz has described its capital, Lyon, as a "noble city for the people" whose UNESCO-classified architectural roots date back to Roman times when it was the most important region in north-western Europe and the birthplace of two emperors. The region's Prehistoric heritage is celebrated in the Ardèche, while Medieval architecture is dotted all over the region from Troubadour castles to picture-perfect Beaujolais villages.

Limestone hills and forests forge the countryside with vineyards, chestnut orchards, lentil fields, and free-range poultry farms that bring fresh produce straight to the plates of the region's Michelin-starred restaurants. Wine connoisseurs beat a path to prestigious Cru vineyards throughout the Rhône Valley from Côte-Rôtie and Hermitage in the Northern Rhône to Fleurie and Morgon in Beaujolais. Summer is the time for jazz festivals in Vienne and Lyon, for Segway tours around the Northern Rhône vineyards, and for canyoning in the Ardèche gorges.

LYON ★★★

431km (267 miles) SE of Paris; 311km (193 miles) N of Marseille

France's third-largest city is the French gastronomic capital with a culinary spirit that pervades from Michelin-starred restaurants to modest *bouchons*. The forks of the River Sâone and River Rhône converge in this elegant city where Roman ruins meet UNESCO-classified medieval lanes, baroque squares, and contemporary icons such as the new Musée de la Confluence ethnology museum. Lyon is the perfect city break as it's only 2 hr. by train from Paris.

Essentials

ARRIVING   One of the easiest ways to reach Lyon is by train. From central London, you can take the Eurostar via Lille or Paris in under 6 hr. It's a good stopover en route to the Alps or the Riviera with the high-speed TGV from Paris takes only 2 hr. from Paris. One-way fares from Paris start around 55€, although cheaper deals can be found online at the SNCF website: www.oui.sncf. Alternatively, you can call ✆ **36-35** (.40€/min.). If you're arriving from the north by **train,** don't get off at Lyon's first

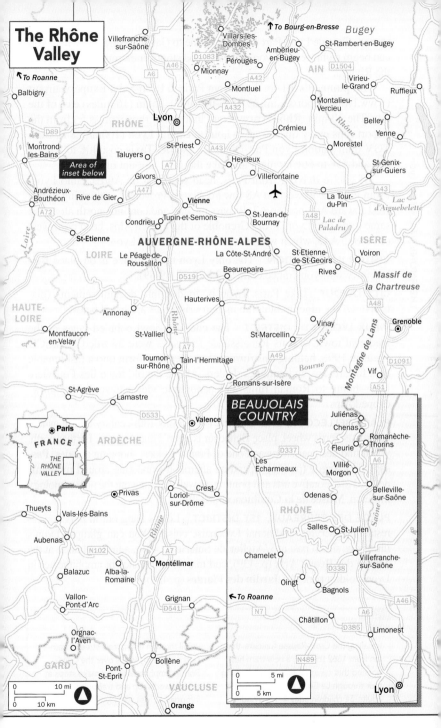

The Rhône Valley

↑ *To Roanne*

Villefranche-sur-Saône

Villars-les-Dombes

↑ *To Bourg-en-Bresse* Bugey

Pérouges

St-Rambert-en-Bugey

Ambèrieu-en-Bugey

AIN

D1083

A46

A6

Mionnay

A42

Montluel

A432

Virieu-le-Grand

D1504

Ruffieux

Balbigny

Lyon

RHÔNE

Montalieu-Vercieu

Belley

Yenne

D89

Montrond-les-Bains

Taluyers

St-Priest

Crémieu

Morestel

Area of inset below

Heyrieux

St-Genix-sur-Guiers

Givors

A7

Villefontaine

A43

Andrézieux-Bouthéon

Rive de Gier

A47

Vienne

St-Jean-de-Bournay

La Tour-du-Pin

A48

Lac de Paladru

A72

Loire

Condrieu

Tupin-et-Semons

AUVERGNE-RHÔNE-ALPES

ISÈRE

Lac d'Aiguebelette

St-Etienne

LOIRE

Le Péage-de-Roussillon

La Côte-St-André

St-Etienne-de-St-Geoirs

Voiron

Massif de la Chartreuse

D519

Beaurepaire

Rives

HAUTE-LOIRE

Hauterives

Annonay

Rhône

Vinay

Grenoble

Montfaucon-en-Velay

St-Vallier

St-Marcellin

Isère

A7

A49

Montagne de Lans

Tournon-sur-Rhône

Tain-l'Hermitage

Bourne

St-Agrève

Lamastre

Romans-sur-Isère

Vif

D1091

A51

D533

Valence

BEAUJOLAIS COUNTRY

Juliénas

★ **Paris**

FRANCE

ARDÈCHE

THE RHÔNE VALLEY

Chenas

Fleurie

Romanèche-Thorins

D337

Les Echarmeaux

Villié-Morgon

A6

Privas

Loriol-sur-Drôme

Crest

Belleville-sur-Saône

Thueyts

Vais-les-Bains

Odenas

RHÔNE

Saône

Aubenas

N102

Salles

St-Julien

Balazuc

Alba-la-Romaine

Montélimar

Chamelet

Villefranche-sur-Saône

Vallon-Pont-d'Arc

Grignan

D338

Oingt

Bagnols

A46

Orgnac-l'Aven

D541

← *To Roanne*

N7

A6

GARD

Bollène

Châtillon

D385

Limonest

Pont-St-Esprit

N489

Lyon

VAUCLUSE

0 10 mi

0 10 km

0 5 mi

0 5 km

Orange

431

station, Gare de Lyon Part-Dieu; continue to Gare de Perrache, where you can begin sightseeing. Lyon makes a good stopover en route to the Alps or the Riviera.

By **plane,** it's a 1-hr. flight from Paris to Lyon-Saint Exupéry airport (www.lyonaeroports.com; © **0426-007-007**), 25km (16 miles) east of the city. The 30-min. **Rhônexpress** tram link (www.rhonexpress.fr) from the airport runs every quarter of an hour to central Lyon (100m/328 ft. from TGV train station Lyon Part-Dieu) for 14.70€. **Taxis** cost 40€ to 45€ by day and 55€ to 60€ by night and take the same amount of time.

If you're **driving** from Paris, head southeast on A6/E15 into Lyon. From Nice, head west on A8 toward Aix-en-Provence, continuing northwest toward Avignon on A7. Bypass the city and continue north along the same route into Lyon. From Grenoble or the French Alps, head northwest on A48 to A43, which will take you northwest into Lyon.

VISITOR INFORMATION   The only Lyon tourist office is on place Bellecour (www.lyon-france.com; © **04-72-77-69-69**).

CITY LAYOUT   Like Paris, Lyon is divided into arrondissements (districts). Of the nine in total, the main tourist areas are listed below.

VIEUX LYON, 5TH DISTRICT   The cheek-by-jowl cobbled lanes of the medieval town with its Renaissance *traboules* were awarded UNESCO status in 1998, helping this former slum area transform into a fashionable area for artisans and antiques dealers. Above the old town lies Fourvière Hill—home to Roman ruins and panoramic views towards the snow-capped Alps.

PLACE BELLECOUR, 2ND DISTRICT   With its 18th-century buildings and enormous Ferris wheel, place Bellecour is Lyon's finest square. Further north, you'll find designer shops and one of France's oldest shopping arcades, **Passage de l'Argue** (p. 446). Spend an afternoon wandering around museums devoted to decorative arts and printing, as well checking out the new ethnology museum, **Musée de la Confluence** (p. 439).

PLACE DES TERREAUX, 1ST DISTRICT   Locals hang out in *bouchons*—restaurants serving traditional Lyonnaise cuisine. You can glimpse Lyon's illustrious silken past at **L'Atelier de Soierie** (p. 446), admire Matisse at the **Musée des Beaux Arts** (p. 439), and marvel at the ancient amphitheater in Lyon's oldest park, the **Jardin des Plantes** (p. 438).

Lyon City Tram

Recalling the Croix-Rousse funicular that ran from 1862 to 1967, a new tram has opened that takes tourists on a 1-hr.-long tour through La Croix Rousse district (9€ adults, 5€ children ages 4–11). Winding uphill through the narrow streets, tram-riders can enjoy views over the Gallo-Roman amphitheater and make stops at the silk workshop and *traboules*. For more information, visit www.lyoncitytour.fr.

Lyon

4e

pl. de la Croix-Rousse
Croix-Rousse
To Geneva ↑

rue Barrème
 **17**

bd. de la Croix-Rousse
r. de Crimée

pont de Lattre de Tassigny

r. des Chartreux
rue de la
r. du Bon Pasteur
place Colbert

rue Dusquesne
av. du Maréchal Foch
rue de Vendôme
rue de Créqui

1er
r. P. Dupont
r. P. Blanc
r. de la Tourette
rue de Tables Claudiennes
rue Burdeau **1**

Croix-Paquet

quai A. Lasagne
rue Malesherbes
rue de Serbie

cours du Gén. Giraud
r. Terme
r. des Capucins

place Louis Pradel

pont Morand

6e
cours F. Roosevelt
Foch
rue de Sèze

quai
St-
r. de la Martinière
2
Vincent
r. d'Algerie
pl. des Terraux
r. du P. Gaillot
r. Jos. Serlin **3**

quai de Gén. Sarail
rue de Gén. Molière
rue P. Corneille
av. du Mar.l de Saxe
rue de Vendôme

Saône
quai de Pierre Scize
Eglise St-Paul
r. St-Paul
q. de
4 M Hôtel-de-Ville

ST-PAUL
pont de la Feuillée
r. du Bât d'Argent
quai J. Moulin
passerelle du Collège
pont Lafayette

5e
Bondy
quai de la Pêcherie
r. Gentil
7

cours Lafayette

FOURVIERE
VIEUX LYON
6
r. du Boeuf
rue St-Jean
5
quai St-Antoine
r. de Brest
Cordeliers M
rue Grenette

rue Rabelais

8
Jardin du Rosaire
funiculaire
r. de la Bombarde
9
10
quai Romain Rolland
pont Juin
r. E. Herriot
rue Carnot
cours de Bonnel
rue de la Liberté
av. du Maréchal de Saxe
rue P. Corneille

11
pl. E. Commette
quai des Célestins
place des Jacobins
place de la République
pont Wilson

12
montée St- Barthélemy
pont Bonaparte
r. E. Zola
r. du Prés. E. Herriot
quai V. Augagneur
cours de la Liberté

3e

13
ST-JEAN ✝
passarelle St-Georges
Tilsitt
place Bellecour
Bellecour M ⓘ
r. de la Barre
pont de la Guillotière

RIVE-GAUCHE

funiculaire
pl. des Minimes
quai Fulchiron
PRESQU'ILE
place Antoine Poncet ✉
r. P. Bert
rue de Chaponnay
r. Villeroy

ST-GEORGES
quai
rue de Vaubecourt
rue Ste-Hélène
rue Sala
Charité
rue Auguste-Comte
quai du Docteur Gailleton
quai C. Bernard
cours Gambetta
r. de Guillotière
16

To Dijon ←
Ampère M
14
2e
la
rue de Marseille

pont Kitchener Marchand
rue Franklin
q. Maréchal Joffre
AUGUSTE COMTE
de
Condé
pont de l'Université
7e
UNIVERSITÉ DE LYON
rue de l'Université

cours Verdun
place Carnot
M Perrache
rue Chevreul

quai Rambaud
Bus Station
15
pont Gallieni
To Grenoble ↘

To St-Etienne ↙

Church ✝
Information ⓘ
Post Office ✉

0   1/4 mi
0   0.25 km
△

Paris ✱
FRANCE
Lyon •

Place des Terreaux, Lyon

GETTING AROUND   A network of Métro lines, trams, and buses branches out to serve the city. A *plan de poche* (pocket map) is available at any office of **TCL** (www.tcl.fr; ✆ **04-26-10-12-12**), which handles all forms of mass transport. Tickets are valid on all forms of public transport, costing 1.80€ for the average ride or else 16.60€ for a *carnet* of 10 tickets. You can buy tickets from tram drivers or at machines at metro stations (although the machines don't accept notes or some international credit cards, so it's best to use coins). Most short-time visitors may want to purchase a **Ticket Liberté** day pass for 5.60€, 11€ for a 48-hr. pass or 15€ for a 72-hr. pass. Trams run from 5am (from 6am on Sun) to 11:45pm with trams every 5 to 15 min. depending upon the line.

Renting and then parking a car is an expensive waste of time as Lyon has one of the most efficient city taxi services we've ever discovered: call **Taxi Radio de Lyon** (www.taxilyon.com) on ✆ **04-72-10-86-86** and you'll be surprised at the speed with which a taxi is winging its way to your door. That said, it's worth renting a car if you're planning on visiting the wine countries north and south of the city. You can rent cars at the train station Lyon Part Dieu including **Avis** (✆ **08-20-61-16-58**); **Hertz** (✆ **08-25-80-01-14**); **Europcar** (✆ **0825-00-25-22**); **Sixt** (✆ **04-78-18-92-01**); and **Budget** (✆ **08-21-23-05-92**). The best way to get around the narrow streets of the old town is by foot, while the easiest way to reach Fourvière Hill is by **Funicular Railway** (p. 436).

SPECIAL EVENTS   Festivals take place practically every day, especially in summer. See box **"Melody Maker"** (p. 438). For 4 days around December 8, the spectacular **Fête des Lumières** lights up Lyon's churches, monuments, and neighborhoods.

[FastFACTS] LYON

ATMs/Banks   ATMs are widespread. Lyon also has several branches of international bank HSBC including at 1 pl. de la Bourse (📞 **04-78-52-25-48**) and 18 pl. Bellecour (📞 **04-78-42-78-15**).

Dentists   Dr. Joseph Benamran, 25 rue Bugeaud, (📞 **04-78-52-25-48**) or **Dr. Alexandre Baroud,** 74 rue Pierre Corneille (📞 **04-78-60-36-68**).

Doctors & Hospitals   For non-urgent medical attention, adults should try Dr. Dominique Faysse, 25 rue Garibaldi (📞 **04-78-93-13-25**), while families should contact **Dr. François Payot,** 51, rue Waldeck Rousseau (📞 **04-78-24-85-09**). The central number for most hospitals in Greater Lyon is: 📞 08-25-08-25-69 including Hôpital Edouard Herriot, 5 pl. d'Arsonval, and **Hôpital de la Croix-Rousse,** Centre Livet, 103 grande rue de la Croix-Rousse. For more information, go to **www.chu-lyon.fr**.

Embassies & Consulates   Lyon has an **Embassy of the United States of America** at 1 quai Jules Courmont (📞 **01-43-12-48-60**), Monday to Friday 9:30am to 5:30pm.

Internet Access   **Allo Phone,** 12 pl. Gabriel Péri (📞 **04-72-71-31-39**).

Mail   A branch of **La Poste** is near place Bellecour at 10 pl. Antonin Poncet.

Pharmacies   **Grande Pharmacie Lyonnaise** is on 22 rue de la République (📞 **04-72-56-44-00**). It's open Monday to Saturday 8am to 11pm; Sunday 7am to 11pm.

Exploring Lyon

A cost-effective way to explore the city is with a Lyon City Card (www.lyoncitycard.com). It costs 25€ per day (or 35€ for 2 days) including transport and access to 38 attractions including museums, riverboats and guided tours.

IN VIEUX LYON ★★★

On the left bank of the Sâone River lies the neo-classical **Palais de Justice**, a.k.a. the "Palace of 24 columns". Around the corner from here is the entrance to the UNESCO-certified cobbled streets of Vieux Lyon. This medieval district is the perfect place to start exploring Lyon. Try to spot Gothic facades such as 15th-century **Maison Thomassin,** 2 pl. du Change, and the 16th-century **Maison du Chamarier,** 37 rue St-Jean, where Mme. de Sévigné lived. You can admire these buildings from the outside, but you are not allowed to enter.

Musée d'Histoire de Lyon (Musée Gadagne) ★ MUSEUM   The Italian banking family who resided here in the 16th century was so famed for their wealth that the Lyonnais phrase "riche comme Gadagne" was coined. Nowadays it's a museum housing 80,000 objects that chart the history of Lyon in every aspect from politics to culture. If you're short on time, skip this section and head straight to the **Musée des Marionnettes du Monde** where you'll see fun puppets by Laurent Mourguet, creator of

Guignol, the best-known French marionette character. The museum has a cafe with a pretty garden overlooking the rooftops of Vieux Lyon.

1 pl. du Petit Collège. www.gadagne.musees.lyon.fr. ✆ **04-78-42-03-61.** Admission to both museums 8€ adults; free for children 17 and under. Wed–Sun 11am–6:30pm.

Primatiale St-Jean ★★ CATHEDRAL   With its exterior restored recently to its original creamy glory, this majestic Gothic cathedral is well worth a visit. Built over the foundations of at least five former churches, the current cathedral was built in the Middle Ages. Paintings around the cathedral belonged to Napoleon's uncle, Cardinal Fesch. A magical time to visit is towards the end of a summer afternoon when the western sun shines through the 14th-century rose window, bathing the nave in an ethereal white light. The most extraordinary feature is a 16th-century astronomical clock whose mechanism includes a perpetual calendar, a religious calendar, and all the saints' days up until 2019 (a new clock is planned for 2020). It announces the hour daily at noon, 2, and 3pm with rooster crows and angels heralding the event.

Pl. St-Jean. ✆ **06-60-83-53-97.** Free admission. Daily 8:15am–7pm (Mon to Fri closes at 7:45pm). The cathedral is closed to tourists for mass during the week and on Sun mornings.

IN FOURVIÈRE HILL ★★★

A trip to Fourvière Hill will take you back to Lyon's ancient roots with Gallo-Roman remains including France's oldest theater. From Vieux Lyon, take the 19th-century **funicular railway** up to the **Colline de Fourvière** (www.fourviere.org). The funicular railway ride is priced at 1.80€ each way; the cable-driven funiculars run every 10 min. between 6am and 10pm. After extensive renovation works, the funicular railway is due to reopen in July 2018. Should there be delays, take the St. Just funicular railway and a replacement bus.

Enthroned on the hill's summit is the monumental 19th-century **Basilique Notre-Dame de Fourvière,** 8 pl. de Fourvière (✆ **04-78-25-13-01**), rising fortress-like with four octagonal towers and crenellated walls. The interior decorations are renovated frequently to ensure that visitors can enjoy the Byzantine mosaics and frescos in their brightly colored original glory. Lyonnais architect Bossan designed the basilica in eclectic styles that combine as a poem to the Virgin Mary. From the outside, spot the gold-leafed Virgin Mary that was inaugurated on December 8, 1852—a date now celebrated annually with the **Fête des Lumières.** Admission is free; open daily 7am to 7pm.

Nearby, an altar dedicated to a bull cult and a marble goddess statue is on display in the **Musée Gallo-Romain,** 17 rue Cléberg (✆ **04-72-38-49-30**). With a staircase that recalls the Guggenheim Museum, the museum houses a fine collection of Gallo-Roman artifacts. The site is open Tuesday through Sunday 10am to 6pm. Admission is 7€ adults, free for ages 17 and under and for everyone on the first Sunday of the month.

Amazing Alleys

Hundreds of secret passageways connect the winding streets of Vieux Lyon. Derived from the Latin "trans-ambulare" (to pass through), *traboules* date back to the 4th century as a way of providing quicker access to the city's fresh water source. Forty of them are open to the public: If you wander around the old town, you'll find each one marked with an identifying bronze seal. Dirty brown doors open unexpectedly into flower-ringed courtyards with balconies perching atop medieval columns, or onto vaulted ceilings and spiral stairs. The longest *traboule* runs between 54 rue Saint-Jean and 27 rue du Bœuf, while one of the prettiest (featuring a six-story external staircase) lies between 9 pl. Colbert and 14 bis montée Saint-Sébastien. Alternatively, you can go on a 2-hr. guided tour on Saturday mornings (call the tourist office in advance for times).

Rather than trekking all the way down to the **Théâtres Romains** (Roman theaters) at 6 rue de l'Antiquaille (℡ **04-72-38-49-30**), you'll have a bird's eye view over this impressive Roman theater-odeum complex from a viewing point on the left of the Musée Gallo-Romain. The Grand Theater is the most ancient in France, built by order of Augustus and expanded during the reign of Hadrian to seat up to over 10,000 people. Reserved for elite society, the smaller odeum seated up to 3,000 people for musical, oratory, and poetry performances. France has only two odeums like this—the other is in Vienne. Its orchestra floor still contains mosaics of marble and porphyry. The site is open from 7am until sunset, and admission is free. The most scenic way back to Vieux Lyon is by foot through the **Jardin du Rosaire,** a minute away from the **Musée Gallo-Romain** and next to the Conservatoire music school where you'll often hear music trickling from the windows. In late spring, you can enjoy roses and cherry trees in bloom as well as panoramic views over Lyon.

2ND ARRONDISSEMENT

The second arrondissement features elegant Haussmann architecture, wide avenues and numerous shops, museums, and workshops dedicated to Lyon's industrious past in printing, silk, and decorative arts. From Vieux Lyon, walk across Bonaparte bridge to the east bank of the River Saône. Begin your tour of the 2nd district at 18th-century **place Belle-cour,** one of France's largest and most charming squares where you can take a ride on the huge Ferris wheel.

Musée de l'Imprimerie de Lyon ★ MUSEUM   Occupying a 15th-century mansion, this museum is devoted to Lyon's role in the world of printing. Exhibits include a page from a Gutenberg Bible, as well as *incunabula*, books printed before Easter 1500.

13 rue de la Poulaillerie. www.imprimerie.lyon.fr. ℡ **04-78-37-65-98.** Admission 6€ adults; 4€ students; free for children 17 and under. Wed–Sun 10:30am–6pm. Métro: Cordeliers.

Musée des Tissus et des Arts Décoratifs ★★ MUSEUM   The decorative arts are housed in the Lacroix-Laval mansion by Soufflot (architect of Paris' Panthéon). Among the furniture and *objets d'art* is a five-octave harpsichord by Donzelague, the 18th-century creator of musical instruments. The collection next door in the **l'Hôtel de Villeroy** takes you through 2,000 years of priceless fabrics from around the world. Look for the partridge-motif brocade from Marie Antoinette's bedchamber and a 150-color brocaded satin woven for Queen Victoria.

34 rue de la Charité. www.mtmad.fr. ℰ **04-78-38-42-00.** Admission 10€ adults; 7.50€ ages 12–25; free for children 11 and under. Tues–Sun 10am–6pm (ticket booth closes at 5:30pm). Métro: Ampère Victor Hugo.

1ST ARRONDISSEMENT

North of the 2nd Arrondissement and below the Croix-Rousse hill lies the 1st arrondissement with its interesting architectural medley from Gallo-Roman remains to modern wall murals such as the **Fresque des Lyonnais** (2 rue de la Martinière) with illustrations of famous Lyonnais residents including Paul Bocuse and Antoine de Saint-Exupéry. Nearby, check out **place des Terreaux** dominated by one of Europe's most splendid city halls, the 17th-century **Hôtel de Ville,** and by the elaborate **Fontaine Bartholdi.** Designed by Frédéric Auguste Bartholdi, who also sculpted the iconic **Statue of Liberty** in New York, this historic fountain depicts France as a female on a chariot controlling four wild horses representing the four great French rivers.

Amphithéâtre des Trois-Gaules ★ RUINS   Constructed in A.D. 19 at the base of the Croix Rousse hill, this Roman amphitheater held up to 20,000 spectators. It became the site of gatherings for the 60 Gallic tribes, for gladiatorial combats and later for the Christian persecutions in 177. Classified as a historic monument in 1961, it is now integrated into Lyon's oldest park, the **Jardin des Plantes.** Although you can't wander around the grounds, you can view the amphitheater from the outside.

Rue Lucien Sportisse. Métro: Croix Paquet.

Musée des Beaux-Arts ★★ ART MUSEUM   Housed in a former Benedictine abbey, this museum has an outstanding collection of paintings and sculpture including Etruscan, Egyptian, Phoenician, Sumerian, and Persian art. The top floor holds one of France's richest 19th-century collections, with works by artists from Veronese, Tintoretto, and Rubens to Matisse, Monet, and Picasso. Be sure to see Joseph Chinard's bust of **Mme. Récamier,** the Lyon beauty who charmed Napoleonic Paris by merely reclining, and the Fantin-Latour masterpiece *La Lecture* (The Reading).

20 pl. des Terreaux. www.mba-lyon.fr. ℭ **04-72-10-17-40.** Admission 8€ adults; free for children 17 and under. Wed–Mon 10am–6pm (Fri from 10:30am). Métro: Hôtel de Ville-Louis Pradel.

ELSEWHERE AROUND THE CITY

L'Institut & Musée Lumière ★ HISTORIC HOME   Film buffs from all over the world head to this living museum of cinema dedicated to the famous Lumière family, who once lived in Lyon. They invented the Lumière process of color photography and produced films, including "La Sortie de L'Usine Lumière," released in 1895 and considered the first movie.

25 rue du Premier Film. www.institut-lumiere.org. ℭ **04-78-78-18-95.** Admission 7.50€ adults; 6€ adults over 60, students, and children ages 7–18 (with proof of age); free for children 6 and under. Tues–Sun 10am–6:30pm. Métro: Monplaisir-Lumière.

Musée de la Confluence ★ MUSEUM   With its strategic location between the Saône and Rhône rivers, this ethnology museum is a futuristic architectural feat dreamt up by Austrian architects Coop Himmelb(l) au. It charts humanity's history and geography going all the way from the Big Bang. A hallmark of its success is that over a million visitors from 69 countries have flocked here since its 2015 opening.

86 quai Perrache. www.museedesconfluences.fr. ℭ **04-28-38-11-90.** Admission 9€ adults; 6€ arrival after 5pm; free for students 25 and under and for children 17 and under. Tues–Fri 11am–7pm (Thurs until 10pm); Sat and Sun 10am–7pm. Métro: Musée des Confluences.

Parc de la Tête d'Or ★★★ PARK/GARDEN   France's largest public park goes from strength to strength. As well as a newly installed *Only Lyon* contemporary sculpture, work is now afoot in the zoo for an Asian

---

Games of Senses: Best New Technology

The latest craze in interactive gaming has hit the city with the recent opening of **Omescape,** 36 rue du Plat (www.ome scape.fr; ℭ **04-72-15-71-19**). Physically trapped in an enclosed space for 1 hr., a group of players have to use all their senses to find an escape. Aviation fans may prefer **I-Way,** 4 rue Jean Marcuit (www.i-way.fr; ℭ **04-37-50-28-70**), a fighter plane simulator in 9th *arrondissement* that has only been available to professional pilots until now. A visual system composed of a spherical screen piloted by five video projects and seven computers enables apprentice pilots to experience the sensations of a life-size air battle.

Best for Sport

A new Olympic park with a 58,000-seat stadium has opened on the outskirts of Lyon. **Le Grand Stade des Lumières,** Chemin du Montout, Décines-Charpieu (www.olweb.fr; ℂ **08-92-69-69-69**), hosts not only football matches, but also international pop stars such as Rihanna and Will.I.am. As well as an adjoining leisure center, the complex includes shops, hotels, and restaurants such as **Brasserie Bocuse.** In 7th arrondissement, the **Tony Bertrand Watersports Centre,** 8 quai Claude Bernard (ℂ **04-78-69-68-62**), has had a recent facelift: It's now possible to bathe all year in water at 27°C (80°F) in this Olympic pool beside the Rhône.

forest with Cambodian temple-inspired architecture where 25 threatened species will be housed from 2020. On the right bank of the Rhône, this 117-hectare (289-acre) park has a magnificent lakeside setting with deer wandering freely around the grounds. The **Zoological Park** (www.zoo. lyon.fr; ℂ **04-72-69-47-78;** daily 9am–5pm) hosts some 1,000 animals including rose-pink flamingos and Senegalese dwarf goats, while the **Botanical Garden** (www.jardin-botanique-lyon.com; ℂ **04-72-69-47-60;** daily 9am–4:30pm) features 15,000 plants including carnivorous plants and orchids. Families will be kept busy with pony rides, carousels, and pedal boats on the lake.

Pl. du Général Leclerc. Entrances on bd. des Belges, quai Charles de Gaulle and av. Verguin. www.loisirs-parcdelatetedor.com. Free admission. Daily 6:30am–8:30pm (until 10pm mid-Apr to mid-Oct). Métro: Masséna.

Where to Stay

With recent openings at both the luxury and inexpensive ends of the hotel market, there has never been a better time to stay in Lyon. Accommodation in Lyon needs to be chosen carefully. Staying in the heart of **Vieux Lyon** is the most convenient place for a whirlwind tour of the city's UNESCO-classified sites. However, guests should beware of high prices, narrow streets, and some street noise (ask for rooms facing internal courtyards). Otherwise, lighter and more spacious accommodation can be found across the Bonaparte Bridge from Vieux Lyon in the nearby **2nd arrondissement**. Here the most sought-after hotels overlook elegant squares such as place Bellecour and place des Célestins. Alternatively, active guests who don't mind a steep uphill walk (or a Funicular railway ride) will be rewarded on **Fourvière Hill** with panoramic city views. For the sake of less-mobile visitors or those with heavy suitcases, we've noted hotels that don't have an elevator.

EXPENSIVE

Cour des Loges ★★   It's hard not to be impressed by this UNESCO-protected landmark. Among its allures are a magnificent loggia-ringed courtyard, a Michelin-starred restaurant, and a spa with indoor pool.

Though this five-star hotel has breathtakingly lavish decor, guests should come prepared for low lighting and small bedrooms. Classic bedrooms often have an open-plan bathroom in the bedroom. The staff, Lyon's savviest, is courteous and efficient.

6 rue du Boeuf. www.courdesloges.com. ✆ **04-72-77-44-44.** 61 units. 200€–410€ double; 340€–520€ suite. Parking 35€. Métro: Vieux Lyon. **Amenities:** 2 restaurants; bar; room service; spa (with fitness room, indoor pool, and sauna); free Wi-Fi.

Le Royal Lyon ★   Place Bellecour provides a suitably grand setting for this Haussmann-style mansion that has welcomed numerous famous faces from Sophia Loren to the Beatles. Fine fabrics by Pierre Frey and Ralph Lauren adorn every corner of this five-star hotel that is now part of the Sofitel group. Decorated with *toile de jouy* wall coverings, the bedrooms vary enormously in size. It's worth upgrading from a Classic room to a Superior room as it's almost double the size. Its cooking-school restaurant, **L'Institut** (p. 445), has fast become a Lyonnaise institution.

20 pl. Bellecour. www.lyonhotel-leroyal.com. ✆ **04-78-37-57-31.** 74 units. 125€–245€ double; 250€–650€ suite. Parking 19€. Métro: Bellecour. **Amenities:** Restaurant; cooking school; bar; tea room; free Wi-Fi.

Villa Florentine ★★★   This 17th-century convent has been converted into a five-star, Relais & Châteaux hotel and our favorite place to stay in Lyon. Up on Fourvière Hill, the hotel's verdant landscaped terraces offer panoramic views over Vieux Lyon. The Italianate accommodations are spacious and comfortable. The annex offers modern and slightly larger rooms.

25 montée Saint Barthélémy. www.villaflorentine.com. ✆ **04-72-56-56-56.** 28 units. 290€–490€ double; from 590€ suite. Métro: Vieux Lyon, then funicular railway to Fourvière Hill. **Amenities:** Restaurant; bar; baby-sitting; exercise room; heated outdoor pool; room service; sauna; mini spa; free Wi-Fi.

MODERATE

Artelit ★   Housed in Lyon's original **Tour de la Rose** (not to be confused with the overpriced, shabby hotel next door) in Vieux Lyon, this exceptional B&B is like an art-museum-cum-antiques-shop. Charming

---

Budget meets Boutique: Best Backpacker hotels

Lyon's new-generation hostels are a far cry from their threadbare predecessors. Now these backpacker hotels come complete with stencil art, designer furnishings, and healthy cuisine. Our favorites are: **Slo Living Hostel**, 5 rue Bonnefoi (www.slo-hostel.com; ✆ 04-78-59-06-90), in Saxe Gambetta with four or six-bed dormitories as well private double rooms; **Away Hostel & Coffee Shop**, 21 rue Alsace Lorraine (www.awayhostel.com;

✆ 04-78-98-53-20), on the slopes of Croix-Paquet, with dorms sleeping four to eight and private doubles with *Nespresso* coffee machines; and **Ho36 Hostel** (www.ho36hostels.com) with two Lyon outlets: **Lyon Guillotière,** 36 rue Montesquieu (✆ 04-37-70-17-03) and **Lyon Opéra,** 9 rue Sainte Catherine (✆ 04-78-28-11-01), offering mixed and women-only (in Lyon Opéra only) dormitories as well as private family rooms and doubles.

owner Frédéric Jean is a renowned Lyonnais photographer. This place is for art lovers who don't mind the slightly rustic approach to hospitality such as ladders to reach the bed and occasional low ceilings. *Note:* There's no elevator and no air conditioning.

16 rue du Boeuf. www.dormiralyon.com. © **04-78-42-84-83.** 4 units. 100€–180€ double; 125€–250€ suite. Métro: Vieux Lyon. **Amenities:** Free Wi-Fi.

Hôtel Carlton ★★

Hôtel Carlton continues to be a fail-safe place to stay in the 2nd district. Part of the Mgallery by Sofitel group, this four-star hotel combines 19th-century architecture with contemporary comfort and reliable service. Adults will appreciate the Cinq Mondes spa, while families will like connecting rooms and cartoon TV channels.

4 rue Jussieu. www.accorhotels.com. © **04-78-42-56-51.** 80 units. 152€–223€ double; 314€–366€ suite. Métro: Cordeliers. **Amenities:** Bar; hammam; room service; free Wi-Fi.

Hôtel des Célestins ★

Seconds from the place des Célestins with its splendid 18th-century theater, this discreet three-star hotel has quietly established itself as one of the best mid-range hotels in Lyon. The secret to their success lies in its homely atmosphere, with bedrooms containing bookshelves lined with well-worn books.

4 rue des Archers. www.hotelcelestins.com. © **04-72-56-08-98.** 27 units. 92€–152€ double; 192€–202€ suite. Métro: Bellecour. **Amenities:** Breakfast room; free Wi-Fi.

Mama Shelter ★

For those who prize style above location, this well-known hipster hotel with furnishings by Philippe Starck could be the ticket. Prices vary from fair to outrageously overpriced depending upon how much in advance you book so it's best to find early online deals. A big plus is the restaurant with its tasty menu dreamt up by Michelin-starred Parisian chef Guy Savoy.

13 rue Domer. www.mamashelter.com. © **04-78-02-58-00.** 156 units. 60€–600€ double; from 209€ suite. Métro: Jean Macé. **Amenities:** Restaurant; business corner; indoor parking; free Wi-Fi.

INEXPENSIVE

Hôtel Bayard Bellecour ★★

With its enviable location overlooking the majestic place Bellecour, three-star Hôtel Bayard Bellecour offers exceptional value. This 16th-century townhouse has beautifully outfitted rooms that vary from contemporary to traditional. Most of the compact

---

Permission to Board

Romantics who fancy a different Lyonnaise perspective should try a houseboat stay. **Péniche Barnum,** 3 quai Sarrail (www.peniche-barnum.com; © **09-51-44-90-18**), offers two pristine-clean modern bedrooms: the Admiral's cabin (150€) and the smaller, but prettier Captain's cabin (from 120€. You will find the boat moored near Pont Morand in central Lyon.

Rooms with a View

New hotels have opened on Fourvière Hill where accommodation comes complete with panoramic city views. **Fourvière Hotel,** 23 rue Radisson (www.fourviere-hotel.com; 𝒞 **04-74-70-07-00**), is a former convent. This historic hotel features 36-arched cloisters, an interior garden, and a beautiful reception area created out of the 19th-century chapel. Japanese designer Stella Work dreamt up the restaurant where vintage telephones enable diners to place their order by telephone. Nearby, **Villa Maïa,** 8 rue Professeur Pierre Marion (www.villa-maia.com; 𝒞 **04-78-16-01-01**), is a Japanese-inspired boutique hotel designed by Jacques Grange. The best feature is the pretty garden with ancient vaults and a spa positioned over the original Roman thermal baths.

For luxury on Fourvière Hill, it's hard to beat the long-established **Villa Florentine** (see below). Meanwhile, the best bargain is **Centre Jean Bosco,** 14 rue Roger Radisson (www.centrejeanbosco.com; 𝒞 **04-78-25-40-90**). The accommodation is Spartan, but you'll find hotel rooms with mini-sized private bathrooms that rival hostel prices (35€ single and from 46.30€ double). Wherever you choose to stay on Fourvière Hill, don't miss the last funicular railway from Vieux Lyon at 10pm or you'll have to trek uphill for about 300m (984 ft.).

bathrooms have showers and tubs. Classic rooms are somewhat cramped. *Note:* There's no elevator.

23 pl. Bellecour. www.hotelbayard.fr. 𝒞 **04-78-37-39-64.** 22 units. 79€–329€ double. Parking 20€ (call ahead). Métro: Bellecour. **Amenities:** Free Wi-Fi.

Hôtel Saint-Paul ★★   If you want to stay in Vieux Lyon on a budget in peak season, this friendly hotel is your best option. Rooms are plainly furnished; more expensive rooms have bathtubs.

6 rue Lainerie. www.hotelsaintpaul.eu. 𝒞 **04-78-28-13-29.** 20 units. 75€–82€ double. Métro: Vieux Lyon/Hôtel de Ville. **Amenities:** Free Wi-Fi.

Where to Eat

The Lyonnais take their cuisine seriously. Michelin stars and culinary associations abound in this gastronomic hub that produces many of France's top chefs. Vieux Lyon's **rue du Boeuf** has become the city's most Michelin-starred street with Jérémy Galvan, La Cour des Loges' Anthony Bonnet, and the newly relocated Tsuyoshi Arai. Make sure you fit in a trip to a traditional Lyonnais bistro *bouchon* where you'll likely dine at a gingham-clothed table on dishes such as *quenelles de brochet* (creamed pike) and *andouillettes Lyonnaises* (course-grained pork sausages in an onion sauce).

EXPENSIVE

Au 14 Février ★★★ FRANCO-JAPANESE   Celebrated chef Tsuyoshi Arai has gone from strength to strength with his Valentine-inspired dining concept. Around the corner from his old restaurant, his new Vieux Lyon establishment wows diners with its contemporary furnishings and

Raymond Peynet romantic drawings. The eight-course dinner menu is a feat of trompe-l'oeil Franco-Japanese cuisine served either with wines by the glass or with Alain Milliat's wonderful juices. Arai also runs a sister restaurant in Beaujolais, the aptly named **Saint-Amour Bellevue** (✆ **03-85-37-11-45**).

36 rue du Boeuf. www.ly-au14fevrier.com. ✆ **04-78-92-91-39.** Fixed-price dinner 92€. Sat noon–1pm; Tues–Sat 8–9pm. Métro: Vieux Lyon.

Jérémy Galvan ★ MODERN LYONNAISE Chef Jérémy Galvan picked up a Michelin star in 2017 for his cozy restaurant in the heart of Vieux Lyon. His wife Nadia welcomes diners with her efficient team into two contrasting dining rooms: one brightly warm with stonewalls, the other elegantly somber. With a choice of five- to seven-course menus, you may want to eat lightly before a visit here. As many as 40 wines are available by the glass.

29 rue du Boeuf. www.jeremygalvanrestaurant.com. ✆ **04-72-40-91-47.** Fixed-price menus 65€–105€. Tues, Thurs, and Fri noon–1:30pm; Tues–Sat 7:30–9pm. Métro: Vieux Lyon.

Mère Brazier ★★★ MODERN LYONNAISE The only two-Michelin-starred restaurant in central Lyon, this legendary institution is run by the charismatic darling of French food critics, Mathieu Viannay. In a striking Art-Deco setting, you can taste Mère Brazier classics (such as Bresse chicken poached with truffles) that have been reworked by Viannay, as well as Renée Richard cheese accompanied by fine Rhône red wines.

12 rue Royale. www.lamerebrazier.fr. ✆ **04-78-23-17-20.** Main course 55€–90€; fixed-price lunch 57€–70€ or dinner 95€–140€. Mon–Fri noon–1:30pm and 7:45–9:15pm. Métro: Croix Paquet.

MODERATE

Brasserie Georges ★ TRADITIONAL FRENCH Founded in 1836, this bustling Lyonnais institution serves up to 450 diners. You can ask for a table that is identified with a plaque for hosting Ernest Hemingway or Edith Piaf. Specialties include roast beef and snails in garlic butter.

30 cours de Verdun. www.brasseriegeorges.com. ✆ **04-72-56-54-54.** Main course 14.50€–26.50€; fixed-price menus 22.50€–27.50€. Daily 11:30am–11pm (Fri–Sat until 12:15am). Closed May 1. Métro: Perrache.

Notes from South America: Best Newcomer

Since opening in 2016, **Miraflores,** 60, rue Garibaldi (www.restaurant-miraflores. com; ✆ **04-37-43-61-26**), has taken Lyon by storm with his Franco-Peruvian cuisine. Young chef Carlos Camino focuses on organic, seasonal produce and plentiful herbs alongside Peruvian ingredients to conjure up dishes such as ox tongue with white quinoa and drum-fish ceviche. The restaurant's location near the Parc de la Tête d'Or recalls the pretty tree-lined neighborhood, Miraflores, in Lima where Camino studied. In 2017, Camino won his first Michelin star.

Mum's the Word

Lyonnaise cuisine was born through women. Generations ago, hard-working women set up low-priced bistros, known as *bouchons*, to feed the local workers with meat-oriented fare such as duck pâté and *andouillettes Lyonnaise* (course-grained pork sausages in an onion sauce). Nowadays these *bouchons* are so famed in Lyon that an official association has been set up to protect the 20 or so official certified *authentiques bouchons Lyonnais* from the numerous fakes that parade around the old town. Nowadays most of these gingham-clothed *bouchons* are run by men, but some pay tribute to their Lyonnais foremothers such as the Michelin-starred **Mère Brazier** (p. 447). Our favorites include **Daniel et Denise** (℃ **04-78-60-66-53**) at 156 rue de Créqui; **Les Adrets** (℃ **04-78-38-24-30**) at 30 rue du Boeuf; **Le Musée**, 2 rue des Forces (℃ **04-78-37-71-54**); long-established **Café des Fédérations** (www.lesfedeslyon.com; ℃ **04-78-28-26-00**) at 8-10 rue Major-Martin; **Le Garet**, 7 rue du Garet (℃ **04-78-28-16-94**) famously frequented by Jean Moulin, hero of *La Résistance*; and newly opened **Bouchon des Cordeliers** (www.bouchondes cordeliers.com; ℃ **04-78-03-33-53**) at 15 rue Claudia.

A bouchon in Lyon

L'Institut ★ MODERN FRENCH This stylish restaurant is run by the well-reputed catering school **L'Institut Paul Bocuse.** You can marvel at the sight of head chef Cyril Bosviel guiding future celebrity chefs in the glassed-in kitchen—part of a lavish design by Pierre-Yves Rochon. Cooking classes in English are offered at the school upstairs.

20 pl. Bellecour. ℃ **04-78-37-23-02.** Fixed-price starters 15€; fixed-price main course 27€. Tues–Sat noon–1pm and 7:30–9:30pm. Métro: Bellecour.

Pléthore et Balthazar ★ INTERNATIONAL This lavish restaurant is frequented by a young Lyonnais crowd. Chef Morgane Testud is behind the stove producing tasty international fare, though the food is second to the hip ambience.

72 rue Mercière. www.plethoreet balthazar.com. ℃ **04-72-16-09-21.** Main course 23€–35€; fixed-price lunch 17€–23€ or dinner 30€–39€. Daily 11:30am–1am. Métro: Cordeliers.

Made in the USA

If you're feeling homesick, comfort yourself with a burger at **Hippolyte**, 22 rue Hippolyte Flandrin (℃ **04-78-27-75-59**). This newly opened American bistro is decorated from floor to ceiling with *Made in the USA* memorabilia.

Shopping

Each district in Lyon has different shopping hours. While shops in Vieux Lyon tend to be open on Sundays and closed on Mondays (also Tues and even Wed in low season), shops in the 2nd district tend to have more traditional Monday or Tuesday to Saturday openings with lunchtime and Sunday closures.

Vieux Lyon is home to art galleries and one-off boutiques. With its dazzling array of *tartes au praline*, the best baker in the area is **Boulangerie du Palais,** 8 rue du Palais (✆ **04-78-37-09-43**), where you'll always find a queue of locals on weekends. **Antic Wine** is one of the best and most amusing wine shops in France, at 18 rue du Boeuf (✆ **04-78-37-08-96**).

The wide avenues of the 2nd district focus upon designer and high-street brands. The densest concentrations of retail shops lie in the streets leading north of place Bellecour. The southern end of rue du Président Edouard Herriot is home to sought-after international brands from **Louis Vuitton** to **Mont Blanc.** Around the corner lies our favorite shopping street in Lyon: **rue des Archers.** Here you'll find chic Parisian clothes brands for adults and children, as well as two of Lyon's award-winning chocolate shops: **Bouillet** at no. 14 (www.chocolatier-bouillet.com; ✆ **04-78-42-98-40**) and **Bernard Dufoux** at no. 15 (www.chocolats dufoux.com; ✆ **04-72-77-57-95**). Linking rue du Président Edouard Herriot with rue de la République, the historic **Passage de L'Argue,** designed by architect Farge in 1827, houses long-established merchants of hats, umbrellas, knives, and shaving brushes. Fit in a visit to cheese specialist **La Crémerie de Charlie** at 9 rue du Plat just off place Bellecour (www. lacremeriedecharlie.com; ✆ **04-78-60-11-24; **Tues–Sat 9am–1pm and 3–7:30pm) where you can taste a wide selection including Ardoise and Savoie cheeses.

The largest shopping center in Lyon is the **Centre Commercial La Part-Dieu,** 17 rue du Dr. Bouchut in the 3rd district (www.centrecommercial-partdieu.com; ✆ **04-72-60-60-62**) with more than 235 boutiques.

Best Workshop-boutiques

Scattered around the city are workshop-boutiques that produce and showcase Lyon's artistic talents. Lyon's silken past is explored at **L'Atelier de Soierie,** 33 rue Romarin (www.atelierdesoierie.com; ✆ **04-72-07-97-83**), where you watch silk *carrés* being printed using traditional Lyonnais techniques before browsing the scarves on display in the neighboring boutique. Meanwhile, our favorite workshop is the new **LafabriQ,** 106 montée de la Grande Côte (www.lafabriq.fr; ✆ **04-26-02-07-77**) that brings together the talents of five creators: jeweler Noémie who brings humor to her **Him&Herz** silver and brass collection; Pascaline who crochets her **Honey&Milk** decorative objects and accessories; Laurène who designs contemporary jewelry; Julia who makes tote bags and stationery; and Anne-lise who produces paintings and brightly-colored jewelry.

Les Halles Paul Bocuse ★★★ On weekends, local gourmands crowd this covered food market to stock up on high-quality Lyonnais specialties: sausage-filled brioche, *Cervelle de Canut* cream cheese, and marzipan *coussins de Lyon* (cushions carried by the Aldermen during the 1643 Plague), as well as soups and *quenelles à brochet* (creamed pike) from **Giraudet** (p. 450). Numerous cafes offer a well-priced lunch.

102 cours Lafayette. www.hallespaulbocuse.lyon.fr. © **04-78-62-39-33.** Mon–Sat 7am–10:30pm; Sun 7am–1pm. Métro: Brotteaux/Part Dieu.

Lyon Nightlife

From opera to house music, Lyon has an eclectic nightlife to suit all tastes. A good start is to pick up a copy of the weekly listings guide "Lyon-Poche" from any newsstand.

The most established haunt for young Lyonnais is the mini-chain of microbreweries **Ninkasi** (www.ninkasi.fr), which now has 10 nighttime venues where you'll find live music, fresh beer, and burgers. Most live concerts are free, although there is sometimes a cover charge for well-known bands playing at the brewery headquarters, **Ninkasi Gerland.** To keep things simple, each venue is named after the nearest metro station. Our favorites are **Gerland,** 267 rue Marcel Mérieux (© **04-72-76-89-00**), and **Cordeliers,** 22 rue Ferrandière (© **04-72-77-91-47**). Most venues are open Monday to Saturday non-stop from lunchtime to evening but check the website for precise opening times.

Wine lovers can start the evening with a glass or two at the diminutive **Mère Brazier Wine bar,** 14 rue Royale (www.lamerebrazier.com; © **04-78-23-17-20;** Mon–Fri 12–2pm and 7:45–10pm), with its wall-to-wall wooden wine racks. Alternatively, you hang out at one of the city's oldest wine bars in Vieux Lyon, **La Cave des Voyageurs,** 7 pl. Saint-Paul (www.lacavedesvoyageurs.fr; © **04-78-28-92-28;** Tues–Sat 5pm–1am).

If you're feeling homesick, you can head to the Anglophone pub **Smoking Dog,** 16 rue Lainerie (© **04-78-28-38-27**), with its bookshelf-lined walls, billiard table, and eight beers on tap. It's a popular place to watch international sports matches on T.V. Open daily from 5pm to 1am (from 2pm on weekends).

Near place des Terreaux, **La Maison M.,** 21 pl. Gabriel Rambaud (www.mmlyon.com; ✆ **04-72-00-87-67;** Métro: Hôtel de Ville), has become a popular nighttime fixture. This bar and late-night club (Wed–Sat 7:30pm–4am) offers an eclectic musical program from soul to rock and hip-hop including live concerts. Another live music and arts venue is **Le Sucre,** 50 quai Rambaud (www.le-sucre.eu; Métro: Perrache), on the rooftop of a 1930s warehouse in the fashionable Confluence district. It's open Friday to Sunday 11pm to 5am.

In summertime, locals flock to the quays along the Rhône. The best of the former cargo boats parked on the Rhône is **Péniche Le Sirius,** Berges du Rhône, 4 quai Victor Augagneur (www.lesirius.com; ✆ **04-78-71-78-71;** Métro: Guillotière). The ship is packed with an under-35 crowd sipping Belgian beers and dancing to the sounds of Lyon's best DJs on the lower-level floor. It's open daily from 5pm to 3am (until 10pm on Sun).

One of Lyon's largest nightclubs is the renamed **F&K Bistroclub,** 13/14 pl. Jules Ferry (www.f-and-k.fr; Métro: Brotteaux), whose house music and chic decor attract a young, kitten-heeled 20s to 30s crowd. Housed in the Brotteaux old railway station, the club has room for 500 people, yet you should expect a strict door policy. It's open Wednesday to Saturday from 6:30pm until 5am (the restaurant is open from 6:30–11pm). The most popular gay bar and club is the long-standing **La Ruche,** 22 rue Gentil (✆ **04-78-37-42-26;** Métro: Cordeliers; Tues–Thurs 5pm–1am; Fri and Sat until 3am; Sun 6–11pm, and Mon 5–11pm). Meanwhile, the gay dance party **Factory Club,** 73 rue Bourbonnais (www.factory-lyon.fr; ✆ **07-56-80-56-52**), takes place every Saturday night (11:30pm–7am) with DJs, go-go dancers, drag queens, and laser shows.

Opera buffs head to the **Opéra National de Lyon,** pl. de la Comédie (www.opera-lyon.com; ✆ **04-69-85-54-54;** Métro: Hôtel de Ville-Louis Pradel; ticket office open Tues–Sat 12–7pm and Mon during performances), while **La Halle Tony Garnier,** 20 pl. des Docteurs Charles et Christophe Mérieux (www.halle-tony-garnier.com; ✆ **04-72-76-85-85;** Métro: Perrache or Debourg), is a popular venue for international pop concerts and dance shows as it seats up to 17,000 visitors.

DAY TRIPS FROM LYON

It's worth taking time to explore the countryside around Lyon. Some places such as **Vienne,** the **Ardèche,** and the wine countries of the **Northern Rhône** and **Beaujolais** will fill several days; others such as **Bourg-en-Bresse** and **Pérouges** make ideal day trips. If you're really pressed for time, you could consider half-day trips to attractions within Greater Lyon such as Bocuse in Collonges au Mont d'Or and Mini World Lyon in Vaulx-en-Velin.

Bourg-En-Bresse ★

37km (23 miles) E of Mâcon; 425km (264 miles) SE of Paris; 61km (38 miles) NE of Lyon

There are two reasons to visit the ancient capital of Bresse: The first is to explore the intensely romantic national historic monument **Brou Monastery,** as well as arguably the best-preserved **apothecary** in France; the second is to dine on the only free-range chickens in the world to have their own *appellation d'origine contrôlée* (certificate of origin).

ESSENTIALS

GETTING THERE If you're driving down the A6 from Paris, head east out of Mâcon on the A40 towards Bourg-en-Bresse. If **driving** from Lyon, take A42 north, before turning onto A40 for the 70-min. trip. Bourg-en-Bresse is accessible by **train** from Lyon Perrache (about 1 hr.); over 20 trains arrive per day. For information, visit www.oui.sncf or call ℂ **36-35** (.40€/min.).

VISITOR INFORMATION The **Office de Tourisme** is at 6 av. Alsace Lorraine (www.bourgenbressetourisme.fr; ℂ **04-74-22-49-40**).

EXPLORING BOURG-EN-BRESSE

Apothecary ★★ HISTORIC LANDMARK This 18th-century pharmacy and laboratory is chock-a-block with fascinating relics: 17th-century alembic distillers, medicine boxes filled with licorice pills and powdered deer antler, and Fleur-de-Lys pots that were hidden during the French Revolution. Visits to this hidden gem need to be organized in advance with the tourist office.

Hôtel de Dieu, 47 bd. de Brou. Guided visits every Sat afternoon and during summer every Tues; contact the tourist office for more information.

Royal Monastery of Brou ★★★ MONASTERY This huge Gothic mausoleum is France's most extravagant love token. The ill-fated Margaret of Austria built it after her husband, Philibert the Handsome, died at the age of 24 from catching a cold on a hunting expedition. You can visit the secret passageway designed for the mourning Margaret to access her chapel from her monastery residence without being seen by the public. She organized her own tomb beside her husband.

63 bd. de Brou. www.monastere-de-brou.fr. ℂ **04-74-22-83-83.** Admission to church, cloisters, and museum 8€ adults; free for children 17 and under if accompanied by an adult. July–Sept daily 9am–6pm; Apr–June daily 9am–12:30pm and 2–6pm; Oct–Mar daily 9am–noon and 2–5pm. Closed Jan 1, May 1, Nov 1 and 11, and Christmas.

Gulliver's Choice

France's first animated miniature park, **Mini World Lyon,** 2 rue Jacquard (www.mini-world-lyon.com; ℂ **04-78-52-90-88**), has recently opened in nearby Vaulx-en-Velin. Explore French city, countryside, and mountain landscapes that are reproduced with miniature buildings, roads, vehicles, and characters.

WHERE TO EAT & SHOP

No trip to Bourg-en-Bresse is complete without visiting the **covered food market** in avenue du Champ de Foire. Every Wednesday and Saturday morning, you'll be able to browse the myriad stalls for flowers, fruit, vegetables, cheese, and even live chickens. Chocoholics are catered for with no less than seven chocolate shops: one of the best is **Chocolaterie Monet,** 14 rue Bichat (✆ **04-74-23-47-42**), where you'll find excellent truffles and seasonally themed chocolates.

Boutique Giraudet ★ Since 1910, Giraudet's *quenelles à brochet* (creamed pike) have been the gold standard of Rhône cuisine. It is one of the last manufacturers that still produce certain quenelles by hand. This smart boutique offers over 40 different quenelles with matching sauces as well as sweet and savory soups made from classic recipes.

21 rue Maréchal Joffre. www.giraudet.fr. ✆ **04-74-22-45-85.** Tues–Sat 9am–12:30pm and 2–7pm.

La Table Ronde ★ TRADITIONAL FRENCH Across the street from the Brou Monastery, this restaurant is a reasonably priced alternative to the celebrated, but expensive **Auberge de Bressane** along the same street. You'll find plenty of hearty French dishes to fill you up such as Bresse chicken with creamy dauphinoise potatoes, frogs' legs, and foie gras. Summertime dining is on the terrace facing the Hôtel de Dieu park.

126 bd. de Brou. ✆ **04-74-23-71-17.** Main course 17€–23.50€; fixed-price menus 29€–45€. Mon–Fri noon–2pm and Mon–Sat 7:30–9pm.

Pérouges ★★

464km (288 miles) SE of Paris; 35km (22 miles) NE of Lyon

Photogenic Pérouges sits on a hilltop throne northeast of Lyon. Ever since "The Three Musketeers" film put medieval Pérouges on the international map in 1961, this thousand-person village has attracted tourists and movie crews. Tourism has caused excessive prices in local restaurants so consider taking a picnic instead. You may also want to bring a pair of comfortable walking shoes; the cobblestone streets are slippery when it rains and from the train station, it is a 20-min. walk into central Pérouges.

Ancient house in Pérouges

The Godfather of Lyonnaise Cuisine

All France mourned the 2018 passing of Paul Bocuse, a.k.a. the Godfather of Lyonnaise cuisine. Foodies from all around the globe are now making a pilgrimage to his culinary headquarters in Collonges au Mont d'Or while his international restaurant empire still stands. Take the N433 north of Lyon to **Restaurant Paul Bocuse,** 40 quai de la Plage, Collonges au Mont d'Or (www.bocuse.fr; ✆ **04-72-42-90-90**) so you can feast on his legendary black-truffle soup. The late Bocuse was the only chef in the Lyon area to boast an unbroken run of 50 years of three Michelin stars. Be warned that you have to book months in advance to be sure of a table.

ESSENTIALS

GETTING THERE   **Trains** serve **Mérimieux-Pérouges** from Lyon Part Dieu taking 30 min.; for information, visit www.oui.sncf or call ✆ **36-35** (.40€/min.). If you **drive** to Pérouges, beware that the signs for the town, especially at night, are confusing. From Lyon, take A42/E611 northeast and exit near Merimieux.

VISITOR INFORMATION   The **Tourist Office** is at 9 route de la Cité (www.perouges.org; ✆ **09-67-12-70-84**).

EXPLORING PÉROUGES

Wander down the rue des Princes to place des Tilleuls where you'll find the **Arbre de la Liberté** (Tree of Liberty) planted in 1792 to commemorate the Revolution. Nearby the 14th-century **Maison des Princes de Savoie,** houses the **Musée du Vieux-Pérouges** (✆ **04-74-61-00-88**), with its panoramic watchtower and perfectly tended 13th-century knot garden. The museum is open June to August daily 10am to noon and 2 to 6pm; off season, weekends 10am to noon and 2 to 6pm. Admission is 4€ for adults, free for children ages 10 and under.

WHERE TO STAY & EAT

Hostellerie du Vieux-Pérouges ★ REGIONAL FRENCH   Run by the town mayor Thibaut, this 13th-century timbered inn is chock-a-block with antiques, from iron lanterns to dressers lined with pewter plates. You can soak up the medieval atmosphere over an unashamedly old-fashioned lunch of Bresse chicken with creamed morels. With prices from 136€–257€ for a double, the bedrooms are rather overpriced. If you do decide to stay, go all out for a *lit à baldaquin* (four-poster bedroom) in Le Manoir or St Georges, as Pavillion rooms lack charm.

pl. du Tilleul. www.hostelleriedeperouges.com. ✆ **04-74-61-00-88.** Main course 24€–35€; menus from 39€–67€. Daily noon–2pm and 7–9pm.

BEAUJOLAIS COUNTRY ★★★

This postcard-pretty wine region punches above its diminutive size. Not only does it produce an impressive 190 million bottles of wine every year, but it also boasts more castles owned by aristocratic dynasties than Bordeaux.

Beaujolais rose to international fame through its barely fermented *vin en primeur*. The craze for **Beaujolais Nouveau** table wine started in Paris 3 decades ago. Nowadays, Beaujolais Nouveau counts for just ⅓ of the annual production of Beaujolais wine. Wine drinkers are gradually becoming aware of the potential of the Gamay grape to produce red wines of finesse, yet light enough to pair with white meat and even fish.

Though wine lovers tend to include this wine-producing region as part of Greater Burgundy, geographically speaking, Beaujolais belongs to the Rhône region. From north of Lyon and to south of Mâcon, the narrow strip of Beaujolais country branches out with no defined wine route. Luckily the road signs are clear so you can branch off easily in any direction from the A6 highway. If you're in doubt, simply follow the signs to the region's capital and commercial center, Villefranche-sur-Saône.

Southern Beaujolais

With its warm-hued stone architecture, Southern Beaujolais has been dubbed "Land of the Golden Stones". It's the most attractive place to use as a base for exploring both Northern and Southern Beaujolais. Capital of Beaujolais, Villefranche-sur-Saône is a businesslike base to start, but you'll probably want to stay in one of the 39 *villages dorés*.

ESSENTIALS

GETTING THERE **Villefranche-sur-Saône** is accessible by **trains** from Lyon. It's a 25-min. journey from Lyon Part Dieu station at 7.70€. For information, visit www.oui.sncf or call ✆ **36-35** (.40€/min.). However, the most practical way of exploring Southern Beaujolais is by car. If you're driving from Lyon, take the A6 north to Villefranche.

VISITOR INFORMATION The **Office de Tourisme** is at 96, rue de la Sous-Préfecture, Villefranche-sur-Saône (www.villefranche-beaujolais. fr; ✆ **04-74-07-27-40**).

EXPLORING SOUTHERN BEAUJOLAIS

Go to Villefranche-sur-Saône tourist office, not far from the marketplace for a booklet on Beaujolais country. It includes a map, itineraries, and lists the wine-tasting cellars open to the public. It also lists and details some 30 villages.

Any tour of Southern Beaujolais should include the pedestrianized, medieval village of **Oingt**—officially designated as one of the most beautiful villages in France. Only the tower remains of the medieval castle, but it's worth climbing for the panoramic views over Beaujolais. A good place to stock up on local Beaujolais wine is **Terroir des Pierres Dorées** (www.vignerons-pierres-dorees.fr; ℭ **04-78-15-91-07**), at place de Presberg on the edge of the pedestrianized center.

Another pretty village is **St-Julien-Sous-Montmelas,** 11km (6.75 miles) northwest of Villefranche (take D35). Claude Bernard, the father of physiology, was born here in 1813. His small stone house—the **Musée Claude-Bernard** (ℭ **04-74-67-51-44**)—exhibits the scholar's mementos, instruments, and books. The museum is open from April to October, Wednesday to Sunday 10am to 12:30pm and 2 to 6pm; admission is 5€ or free for children 12 and under.

If you like fairy-tale castles, you should visit **Château de Montmelas** (www.chateau-montmelas.com; ℭ **04-74-67-32-94**) in Montmelas-Saint-Sorlin. Known locally as Sleeping Beauty castle, it has been home to descendants of the same aristocratic family since the Middle Ages. From this hilltop castle, you'll find breathtaking views towards the distant Mont Blanc. The castle interiors are only open to the public on the first Saturday of the month at 11am (unless you're willing to pay 175€ for a private visit), but you can telephone in advance for a wine tasting in the cellars with the charming Comtesse d'Harcourt, Delphine. Award-winning red and white table wines, and even sparkling wines are produced by the Comte himself. If you'd like to stay, two four-bedroom *gîtes* are available for 2 nights or more. From St. Julien, take the D19 west and then the D44 towards the castle.

WHERE TO STAY & EAT

Château de Bagnols ★★★   Fresh from winning a Michelin star for chef Jean-Alexandre Ouaratta's gastronomic French cuisine, Château de Bagnols has upped its game. Europe's best fairytale castle-hotel comes complete with a moat, landscaped gardens, a spa, and a fabulous glassed-in courtyard. Prices are competitive considering the antiques, paintings, and art that fill the mansion. Guest suites are generously sized with antique beds, period velvets, and Parisian designer Hermès toiletries.

pl. du Château, Bagnols. www.chateaudebagnols.com. ℭ **04-74-71-40-00.** 21 units. From 200€ suite. To reach Bagnols, head west out of Villefranche on D338. **Amenities:** Restaurant; heated outdoor pool; lounge; room service; spa; free Wi-Fi.

La Grande ★ TRADITIONAL FRENCH   This homey address has been keeping local diners happy with traditional French dishes such as Burgundy snails, Quercy foie gras and Beaujolaise *andouillettes* (blood sausage) for decades. Also available is a market-fresh fish of the day. Cheerful owner Florence provides swift service.

322 rue de Belleville, Villefranche. www.restaurant-lagrande.com. ℭ **04-74-60-65-81.** Main course 13€–15€; fixed-price menus 21€–31€. Tues–Fri noon–1:30pm and 7–8:30pm.

La Maison Troisgros ★★★ FRENCH   It's all change for one of France's leading chefs, Michel Troisgros. Following the recent success of his foray into the Roannaise countryside with La Colline du Colombier featuring his *cadoles* (designer cabins), Troigros has now moved his flagship restaurant and hotel to a countryside estate in Ouche. Only his café-épicerie Le Central remains in his native Roanne. The new Maison Troigros is housed in a stone farmhouse that has been cleverly converted with the addition of a wall-to-wall glass dining room that plays with the illusion of outdoor dining. Thankfully one thing never changes: Troigros' culinary genius. Taste exceptional flavors such as caramelized rack of lamb or pineapple-infused mackerel before retiring to one of the luxurious contemporary bedrooms (from 300€). It's the perfect place for a weekend getaway.

728 route de Villerest, Ouche. www.troisgros.fr. © **04-77-71-66-97.** Main course 85€–110€; fixed-price menus 150€–270€. Wed–Sun noon–1:15pm and 7:30–9:30pm. Closed Jan.

Northern Beaujolais

Wine connoisseurs head straight to Northern Beaujolais where the serious Cru appellation wines are grown. Most of the 10 **Beaujolais Crus** (certified as the region's best wines that are more nuanced in flavor and capable of aging longer) are within a short drive of **Belleville-sur-Saône,** the largest town in Northern Rhône. From Lyon or Villefranche-sur-Saône, drive north on the A6.

ESSENTIALS

GETTING THERE **Belleville-sur-Saône** is accessible by **trains** from Lyon. It's a 35-min. journey from Lyon Part Dieu station at 9.70€. For information, visit www.oui.sncf or call © **36-35** (.40€/min.). However, the most practical way of exploring Northern Beaujolais is by car. If you're **driving** from Lyon, take the A6 north to Belleville.

VISITOR INFORMATION The **Office de Tourisme** is at 27, rue du Moulin, Belleville-sur-Saône (www.beaujolaisvignoble.com; © **04-74-66-44-67**).

EXPLORING NORTHERN BEAUJOLAIS

Caveau du Cru Morgon ★ WINERY A good place to start exploring Northern Beaujolais is at this cellar in the basement of the 18th-century Château de Fontcrenne, next to the Hôtel de Ville. Here you can taste red wines from the well-regarded Beaujolais Cru Morgon. Caveau du Cru Morgon produces and bottles wines under its own label, using grapes from local independent wine growers.

Rue du Château Fontcrenne, Villié-Morgon. www.morgon.fr. © **04-74-04-20-99.** From Belleville, head north on the A6, then west on the D9. Daily 10am–noon, 2:30–6pm in winter; 9:30am–noon, 2:30–7pm in summer. Closed first 3 weeks of Jan.

Hameau Duboeuf ★ MUSEUM/WINERY/ADVENTURE PARK Families and wine virgins will enjoy a trip to Europe's premier wine adventure park run by the godfather of Beaujolais wine, George Duboeuf.

The wine museum takes you through 2,000 years of wine history, while the original town train station has been converted into a wine transport exhibition. Interactive games and holograms keep your kids amused as you take a video-animated wine tour through Beaujolais and onto the winery with its cutting-edge technology. In summer, stroll around the Beaujolais garden, ride on the mini train, and play a round of adventure golf (April to mid-Oct); also on site is an excellent cafe. You could easily spend a day here and include the zoo nearby, **Touroparc** (www.touroparc.com; ☎ **03-85-35-51-53**).

796 route de la gare, Romanèche-Thorins. www.hameauduvin.com. ☎ **03-85-35-22-22**. From Belleville, head north on D906, then west on D32 to the Hameau Duboeuf. Admission to wine center, gardens, and adventure golf: 18€ adults; 6€ children ages 7–15; free for children 6 and under. Daily 10am–6pm. Closed Jan.

> ### Château de la Chaize
>
> Fresh from a top-to-bottom renovation of its cellars, this 17th-century castle is re-opening for wine tastings and garden visits in summer 2019. Home of the Marquise de Roussy de Sales, **Château de la Chaize,** Odenas (www.chateaudelachaize.com; ☎ **04-74-03-41-05**), is a fairy-tale setting to taste the sought-after wines of Brouilly. The immaculate grounds are complete with a topiary garden and star-formed vegetable patch.

WHERE TO EAT

L'Auberge du Cêp ★ GASTRONOMIC FRENCH   A popular address for gastronomes since the 1970s, this dining institution has been through a rough couple of years after losing its Michelin star in 2015. Thankfully, new chef Aurélien Merot and his wife Camille stepped in to save the restaurant from bankruptcy. Along with a name change (adding "auberge"), Merot has brought his own twist to the traditional French fare with signature dishes such as hot oysters and sweetbreads with Jerusalem-artichoke cream. He has also introduced competitively priced set menus.

Pl. de L'Eglise, Fleurie. www.aubergeducep.com. ☎ **04-74-04-10-77.** Fixed-price lunch 20€ or dinner 32€–58€. Tues–Sun 12:30pm–2pm and Tues–Sat 7:30–9pm.

VIENNE ★★

Exploring Vienne

Fresh from celebrating its 50th anniversary, the **Musée Gallo-Romain,** Route Départementale 386, Saint-Romain-en-Gal (www.musee-site.rhone.fr; ☎ **04-74-53-74-01**), is a must for visitors to Vienne. This 7-hectare (17-acre) archaeological site merely scratches the surface of the myriad Roman remains that still exist beneath the foundations of modern Vienne. As you take a tour around the remains of Roman houses and public baths, you'll marvel at their sophistication. Inside the museum, you'll see mosaic floors, frescos, and household items. The museum is open Tuesday to Sunday 10am to 5:45pm (Nov–Mar closes at 5pm). Tickets are 6€ for adults; free for kids under 18.

Temple d'Auguste et de Livie.

Back in central Vienne, you can wonder around some Roman sites for free. In place du Palais Charles de Gaulle, you'll find one of the best-preserved Roman remains in France: the **Temple d'Auguste et de Livie,** built on the orders of the Roman emperor Claudius and turned into a "temple of reason" during the French Revolution. Another outstanding monument is **La Pyramide** (rue Fernand Point, next to the Michelin-starred restaurant) part of the Roman circus rising 16m (52 ft.) and resting on a portico with four arches. Nicknamed the "tomb of Pilate", the pyramid was allegedly built over the grave of Pontius Pilate, who was exiled to Gaul after the death of Jesus.

At the foot of Mont Pipet lies one of the most impressive remains: the **Théâtre Antique (Roman Theater)** ★, 7 rue du Cirque (✆ **04-74-85-39-23**) where well-known bands play summertime concerts for up to 7,500 people (for concert information, visit www.theatreantiquevienne.com). You can visit November to March Tuesday to Friday 9:30am to 12:30pm and 2 to 5pm, weekends 1:30 to 5:30pm; April to August daily 9:30am to 12:30pm and 1:30 to 6pm; September to October Tuesday to Sunday 9:30am to 12:30pm and 1:30pm to 6pm. Admission is 3€.

As well as Roman remains, you'll find many religious buildings. If you have to choose just one during a busy itinerary, we'd recommend the **Cloitre de Saint-André-Le-Bas** (✆ **04-74-78-71-06**) in Cour Saint-André-Le-Bas near the river. With its Romanesque stone carvings, columns, and ornately carved capital stones, this church and cloister are all that remains of the 12th-century abbey. You can visit November to March Tuesday to Friday 9:30am to 12:30pm and 2 to 5pm, weekends 1:30 to 5:30pm; April to October Tuesday to Sunday 9:30am to 1pm and 2pm to 6pm. Admission is 3€.

Where to Stay & Eat

Domaine de Clairefontaine ★★★   Surrounded by a dreamy 3-hectare (7-acre) park, this luxurious hotel is our favorite choice for Vienne and the Northern Rhône wine region. After wandering around the violet-carpeted forest and the peacock aviary, you can dine on trout from the freshwater pond in the Michelin-starred restaurant run by chef/owner Philippe Girardon. Well-priced accommodation is provided in the manor, the former stables and Le Cottage (that houses an informal bistro).

105 Chemin des Fontanettes, Chonas-L'Amballan. www.domaine-de-clairefontaine. fr. ✆ **04-74-58-81-52.** 35 units. 61€–130€ double; 280€ apartment. **Amenities:** Restaurant, bar, garden, tennis court, free Wi-Fi. Closed mid-Dec to mid-Jan.

L'Estancot ★ FRENCH   With its bare-stone walls and bistro-style furnishings, this Bib Gourmand restaurant is famed for chef Bruno Ray's *criques*. Served with a simple green salad, these grated potato *rostis* come in all guises from *Gourmandine* (scallops and king prawns) to *Strate de Boeuf* (Charolais beef and spinach).

4 rue de la Table Ronde. ✆ **04-74-85-12-09.** Main course 16.50€–25€; fixed-price menus 20€–51€. Tues–Sat noon–2pm and 7:30–9:30pm. Closed early Sep and early Jan.

La Pyramide ★★ MODERN FRENCH   Chef Patrick Henriroux's contribution to French cuisine was noted in 2016 with a *chevalier de la legion d'honneur* award. La Pyramide is one of the most famous restaurants in the Rhône Valley. It's where Parisians-in-the-know stop over on their annual pilgrimage to holiday in the Riviera. It was once home to the historic chef, Fernand Point, who died in 1955. Current owner-chef Patrick Henriroux has preserved many of Point's secrets, especially his sauces. Gourmands should try the lobster prepared three ways or the Aubrac beef with foie gras cooked like a burger. The excellent bistro **Espace PH3** is a reasonably-priced alternative. A recent renovation has brought a contemporary look to the 19 spacious bedrooms (doubles 200€–240€).

14 bd. Fernand Point. www.lapyramide.com. ✆ **04-74-53-01-96.** Main course 59€–99€; fixed-price menus 66€–198€. Thurs–Mon noon–1:30pm and 8–11:30pm. Closed mid-Feb to mid-Mar and 1 week in mid-Aug.

The Mailman's Palace

Fit in a side trip to one of the world's strangest pieces of architecture in Hauterives (south of Vienne). **Palais Idéal du Facteur Cheval,** 8 rue du Palais, Hauterives (www.facteurcheval.com; ✆ **04-75-68-81-19**), is the lifelong work of French postman Ferdinand Cheval. Built of stone and concrete and elaborately decorated with clamshells, it's a monumental tribute to one man's whimsical imagination. The work was finished in 1912, when Cheval was 76. You can visit December to January 9:30am to 4:30pm; February, March, October, and November until 5:30pm; April to June and September until 6:30pm; July and August until 7pm. Admission is 7.50€ adults; 5€ kids ages 3 to 16; free for kids 2 years and under.

Where to Shop

Every Saturday, the streets around central Vienne play host to one of the Rhône Valley's largest **food markets.** This is a great place to stock up on fresh fruit and vegetables as well as regional products such as pear-infused *Eau de Vie* (colorless fruit brandy). Check out **rue Testé du Bailler** for art galleries and **Yves Caire Créations,** 7 rue Boson (✆ **04-74-85-20-72**) for artisanal jewelry.

NORTHERN RHÔNE WINE COUNTRY ★★★

Curving around the River Rhône from Vienne to Valence, the Northern Rhône has been growing wine since Gallo-Roman times. Sought-after reds hail from **Côte Rôtie** and **Hermitage** where steep hillsides with golden-hued stone terraces are tilled by hand with horse-drawn ploughs. This photogenic region is also home to aromatic white wines such as **Condrieu.** This must-see region can be twinned easily with a visit to the Ardèche or Vienne.

Tupin et Semons

Heading out of Vienne on the route national 86 (D386), you'll pass the mythical vineyards of Côte-Rôtie that cling to steep escarpments up to 60 percent gradient. The names of famous wine producers, such as Guigal and Chapoutier, are hewn into the hillside. The small village of Tupin et Semons lies at the heart of Côte-Rôtie. A little-known treasure of this appellation is **Le Domaine de Corps de Loup,** 2 route de Lyon (www.corpsdeloup.com; ✆ **09-53-87-84-64**), where energetic young vintner Tristan Daubrée has taken over the family domaine. You can call in advance for a tour around the vineyard and the 15th-century cellar before a tasting in the ancient chapel-turned-tasting-room. Nearby, you'll find the far grander **La Maison Vidal-Fleury,** RD 386, 48 route de Lyon (www.vidal-fleury.com; ✆ **04-74-56-10-18**). Founded in 1781, Vidal-Fleury is the oldest continuously operating wine producer in the Rhône Valley. A long-standing US connection started with Thomas Jefferson dining there in 1787. The domaine is now owned by renowned wine producer Guigal and produces over 1 million bottles per year. After a tour of

---

Best Wine Markets

Seasonal wine markets bring together all the appellations of the Northern Côtes du Rhône and provide the perfect way to taste these cru wines: **Ampuis** on the last week-end in January; **Tain l'Hermitage** on the last weekend in February; **Saint Péray** on the first weekend in September; and **Cornas** on the first weekend in December. For more information, contact **Hermitage Tournonais** tourist office, 6 av. du 8 mai 1945, Tain L'Hermitage (www.hermitage-tournonais-tourisme.com; ✆ **04-75-08-10-23**).

Segway to the Vines

From Segway tours to electric bikes and 4x4, the latest vineyard tours make light of the steep hillsides of the Northern Rhône vineyards. These tours also provide an introduction to the geography and *terroir* of this prestigious wine-growing region. Our favorites are:

Terres de Syrah (www.terresdesyrah.com), a collaboration between Les Sens Ciel and the Cave de Tain with tours including "sur les pas de Gambert" Hermitage walking trails, electric bikes, and Segway tours.

Domaine Colombo (www.vinscolombo.fr) including a 4x4 vineyard tour.

Fabien Louis (www.ausommelier.com; ✆ 04-75-08-40-56 or 06-70-11-09-18), a sommelier-turned-wine-merchant whose electric cycle tour of the Hermitage vineyards is followed by a visit to his shop, **Des Terrasses du Rhône** (22 rue des Bessards) which sells more than 600 different Rhône Valley wines at vineyard prices.

the bottling plant and the enormous vaulted cellars, you can enjoy tasting some of the 22 different wines.

WHERE TO STAY & EAT

Hôtel Le Beau Rivage ★   The best thing about this four-star hotel in nearby Condrieu is its restaurant overlooking the majestic River Rhône. The fixed-price menus (40€–107€) are expensive, but the rich French fare served on Limoges porcelain plates comes complete with *amuses-bouches* and a tray of chocolates to end your meal. There's also a well-stocked wine list. The rooms are old-fashioned, but generously sized—look for special deals on the hotel website.

2 rue Beau Rivage, Condrieu. www.hotel-beaurivage.com. ✆ **04-74-56-82-82.** 30 units. 169€–229€ double; 299€ suite. Free parking; garage 13€. On southern outskirts of Condrieu, look for signs on the left. **Amenities:** Bar, restaurant; free Wi-Fi.

Tain-L'Hermitage

Drive south from Tupin et Semons along the D4 and then A7 towards Tain-L'Hermitage. A good place to start finding out about Northern Rhône wines is at celebrated wine producer Michel Chapoutier's **wine school,** 18 av. Dr Paul Durand (www.chapoutier.fr; ✆ **04-75-08-92-61**), where you can turn up for free wine tastings (groups over 5 need to book in advance) or pre-book one of his many wine-themed workshops. It's a great way to learn about Côtes du Rhône wines as his expansive range covers appellations throughout the Northern and Southern Rhône Valley. Finally, gourmands of all ages will enjoy a visit to **La Cité du Chocolat, 12 av. du Président Franklin Roosevelt** (www.citeduchocolat.com; ✆ **04-75-09-27-27**). This chocolate emporium is run by commercial chocolatier, Valrhona, who has been producing chocolate for the world's finest pastry chefs since 1922. More recently, they have developed a range of consumer chocolate bars. Rather than a fact-heavy history, you're taken on a sensorial experience through the stages of chocolate making from collecting pods to a live factory-line replica, complete with plentiful chocolate tasting along the way.

WHERE TO STAY & EAT

Hôtel Les Deux Côteaux ★ This tidy bed-and-breakfast is a convenient stopover for wine enthusiasts on the Rhône Valley trail. With views over the River Rhône, its 18 rooms have wooden floors and smart furnishings. Shower rooms are very small. No dinner is served, but **Brasserie Le Quai** (✆ **04-75-07-05-90**) with its riverside terrace, is next door. Breakfast is copious with plentiful fresh fruit and homemade jams. *Note:* There's no elevator.

18 rue Joseph Peala. www.hotel-les-2-coteaux.com. ✆ **04-75-08-33-01.** 18 units. 85€–88€ double. **Amenities:** Free Wi-Fi.

Tain l'Hermitage vineyards in Rhone Valley

Le Mangevins ★★★ FRENCH   This village restaurant not only got a change of address but also a Michelin Bib Gourmand (like a Michelin star, but for restaurants in a more reasonable price range). The buzz of animated local diners fills this stylish, contemporary restaurant. While owner Vincent welcomes diners, his Japanese wife Keiko is busy in the kitchen. For a chef with no formal training, Keiko shows a hint of genius, cooking dishes such as yellow tuna and Iberica Bellota pork to perfection. The small menu changes daily and is excellent value, while the extensive wine list includes wines by the glass.

7 rue des Herbes, Tain-L'Hermitage. ✆ **04-75-08-00-76.** Fixed-price lunch 28€ or dinner 32€–35€. Mon–Fri noon–2pm and 8–10pm.

Maison Gambert ★ FRENCH   Chef Mathieu Chartron has taken over this ancient farm-turned-restaurant in a dreamy setting surrounded by Hermitage vineyards. Fine French dining is the order of the day with dishes such as snails and *magret de canard* (duck breast).

2 rue de la Petite Pierrelle, Route de Chantemerle les Blés, Tain-L'Hermitage. www.maisongambert.com. ✆ **04-75-09-19-85.** Fixed-price menu 28€. Wed–Sun noon–2:30pm and 7–11pm.

VALENCE

671km (416 miles) SE of Paris; 100km (62 miles) S of Lyon

Follow the Rhône river south from Lyon and you'll reach this grey market town whose identity is now inextricably linked to its star attraction: Anne-Sophie Pic, France's only female three-star Michelin chef. A former Roman colony, it later became the capital of the Duchy of Valentinois, set up by Louis XII in 1493 for Cesare Borgia. Today Valence is a market town and distribution point for Rhône Valley fruit and vegetable producers. It's fitting that François Rabelais, who wrote of gargantuan appetites, spent time here as a student. Valence is a convenient day trip from Vienne or stopover on your way further South to Provence.

Essentials

GETTING THERE **Trains** take 1 hr. from Lyon. For information, visit www.oui.sncf or call *②* **36-35** (.40€/min.). If you're **driving** from Lyon, take A7 south. If you're travelling to Valence from Lyon by train, beware the TGV station: a 20-min. taxi ride costs between 33€ to 43€. It will be quicker and cheaper to take a regional TER train straight to Valence's city center.

VISITOR INFORMATION The **Office de Tourisme** is at 11 bd. Bancel (www.valence-romans-tourisme.com; *②* **04-75-44-90-40**).

Exploring Valence

Gastronomy is the essential draw of Valence, but we'd recommend visiting the **Musée de Valence Art et Archaéologie,** place des Ormeaux (www.museedevalence.fr; *②* **04-75-79-20-80**), that has been tastefully renovated by architect Jean-Paul Philippon. A fusion of ancient and modern architecture, the museum focuses on landscapes, with collections spanning 16th-century to contemporary art. The newest wing is topped by a 360-degree panorama over the Rhône valley towards the Vercors mountains. Open Tuesday to Sunday 10am to 6pm (Tues from 2pm); admission to permanent collections is 6€ adults; free for children under 18.

Where to Stay, Eat & Shop

It's unusual for a small market town to have a Michelin-starred restaurant, but Valence has three: the intimate **Flaveurs,** 32 Grande Rue (*②* **04-75-56-08-40**); the well-regarded **La Cachette,** 16 rue des Cévennes (*②* **04-75-55-24-13**); and the world-famous **Maison Pic** (see below). Check out Anne-Sophie Pic's **Scook,** 243 av. Victor Hugo (www.scook.fr; *②* **04-75-44-14-14**), a cooking school and shop selling kitchen utensils, cookbooks, and aprons—ideal souvenirs from this gastronomic hub.

Maison Pic ★ FRENCH As one of the world's most celebrated female chefs, Pic occasionally lets fame go to her head. Luckily, you'll forget the blown-up portraits in the entranceway as soon as you reach the plush dining room. An army of staff is on hand to serve you course after course from specially commissioned cutlery. Don't miss her celebrated *berlingots* (filled sachets). The new on-site brasserie is the perfect alternative for those on a budget: **André** delivers Pic cuisine at sensible prices in a Parisian bistro-style setting with an open-plan kitchen and leather banquettes. Room prices are punchy: from 280€ to 360€ for a double. Ask for a quieter room facing the garden.

285 av. Victor-Hugo. www.anne-sophie-pic.com. ℃ **04-75-44-15-32. Restaurant:** Fixed-price menus 110€–330€. Wed–Sun noon–1:30pm; Wed-Sat 7:30–9:30pm. **Brasserie:** Fixed-price menu 32€–108€; daily noon–2pm and 7:30–10pm.

THE ARDÈCHE ★★

43km (27 miles) W of Montélimar; 138km (86 miles) SW of Lyon

Since the opening of the world's largest replica cave in 2015, the Ardèche has been rebranding itself as France's number one destination for prehistoric heritage. The region is chock-a-block with history from Paleolithic caves and standing stones (dolmens and menhirs) to Troubadour castles. Of course, no visitor should miss the famous gorges, though you may want to avoid staying in tourist-swarmed Vallon Pont d'Arc.

Essentials

GETTING THERE   Vallon-Pont-d'Arc is accessible by **trains** from Lyon connecting in Valence. It's a 3-hr. journey from Lyon at about 40€ or 2 hr. 15 min. from Valence TGV station at about 20€. For information, visit www.oui.sncf or call ℃ **36-35** (.40€/min.). However, the Ardèche is best explored by car. If you're **driving** from Lyon, take the A7 south, then N7 at Montélimar Sud towards Pierrelatte. Head west on D13, then D59 and finally D4 to Vallon-Pont-d'Arc.

VISITOR INFORMATION   The **Office de Tourisme** is at 1 pl. de l'Ancienne Gare, Vallon-Pont-d'Arc (www.vallon-pont-darc.com; ℃ **04-75-88-04-01**).

Exploring the Ardèche

The Ardèche Gorges ★★ CANYON   Hewn over centuries by the River Ardèche, a 60m (197-ft.) high natural limestone arch is the emblem of the Ardèche gorges. France's fastest-flowing river has carved a 30km

(19-mile) path through limestone cliffs that ascend up to 300m (984 ft.) high. Visitors have been able to canoe down the gorges since 1932. Of the dozens of kayak rental companies, one of the best is **Aventure Canoës,** 1 pl. Allende Neruda (www.aventure-canoes.fr; ✆ **04-75-37-18-14**). The best time for kayaking is April to late November when the waters are green and sluggish and safer than during winter months. Alternatively, you can drive around the gorges on a well-marked route between Vallon-Pont-d'Arc and Pont St-Esprit. Watch out for careless drivers too busy taking snapshots to look where they are going. A good spot for a reliable snack in Vallon Pont d'Arc is **Le Chelsea,** 45 bd. Peschaire Alizon, Vallon-Pont-d'Arc (www.lechelsea.com; ✆ **04-75-88-01-40**), with its shaded terrace.

Vallon-Pont-d'Arc to Pont St-Esprit.

Le Grand Site de L'Aven Orgnac ★★★ MUSEUM/CAVE   This is
the perfect wet-weather attraction as the limestone caves are most beautiful when it rains. Discovered in 1939, the *grotte* is one of the largest in France with a dazzling array of stalactites and stalagmites. The adjacent archaeological museum, **Cité de la Préhistoire,** houses ancient artifacts that have been brought alive through child-friendly exhibits, 3-D animations, and drawings by artist-cum-archaeologist Benoit Clarys. This imaginatively developed archaeological experience leaves visitors of all ages with palpable ideas of how prehistoric men lived in Paleolithic to Iron Age times.

Route de l'Aven, Orgnac-L'Aven. www. orgnac.com. ✆ **04-75-38-65-10.** Admission 13€ adults; 10.40€ students and adults with three or more children; 8.50€ children ages 6–14; free for children 5 and under. Daily Feb and Mar 10am–12:30pm and 2–6pm; Apr–Sept 9:30am–7pm; Oct to mid-Nov 9:30am–1pm and 2–6pm. Check website for special opening hours during school and bank holidays.

Grotte Chauvet Pont d'Arc ★
MUSEUM   Since its opening in 2015, the world's largest replica cave hasn't been without controversy. Some complain that it's an overpriced fake; the original 36,000-year-old cave, that has been awarded UNESCO World Heritage site status, sadly cannot be visited for fear of being damaged by

Vallon-Pont-d'Arc, a natural bridge in the Ardèche

troupes of tourists. However, this 29-hectare (71-acre) site provides an interesting depiction of life in Upper Paleolithic times through paintings, drawings, and engravings as well as life-size fauna and interactive workshops. Guided visits are available in English. The onsite cafe has wonderful views over the Ardèche mountains.

Plateau du Razal, Vallon Pont d'Arc. www.cavernedupontdarc.fr. ☎ **04-75-94-39-40.** Admission 15€ adults; 7.50€ children ages 10–17; free for children 9 and under. Daily wintertime 10:30am–5:30pm (except Jan to mid-Feb Wed–Fri noon–5pm and weekends 11am–4pm); summertime 9:30am–6pm. Check website for special opening hours during school and bank holiday openings.

Where to Stay & Eat

Château de Balazuc ★★★   It's unsurprising that this B&B has won awards. With views over exquisite Balazuc and the Ardèche, the setting is exceptional. Home to courtly troubadours and writers since the Middle Ages, this bed-and-breakfast is owned aptly by two Parisian ex-journalists. Luc and Florence imbibe the castle with a convivial ambience greeting guests with evening cocktails and serving a communal dinner on Saturdays. The contemporary designed rooms show attention to detail such as in-room *Nespresso* machines. The narrow outdoor pool is aptly described as a swimming lane. Guests can now enjoy massages in a vaulted castle room. Due to the number of stone steps, the castle is unsuitable for children or elderly guests.

Balazuc. www.chateaudebalazuc.com. ☎ **09-51-39-92-11.** 3 units. 170€–180€ double. **Amenities:** Jacuzzi; outdoor pool; massage room; free Wi-Fi.

Régis et Jacques Marcon ★★★ MODERN FRENCH   This Relaix & Châteaux eco hotel is home to a famous three-Michelin-starred restaurant run by the Marcon culinary dynasty. With its idyllic location on the hillside plateau of Saint-Bonnet-Le-Froid, this grass-roofed hotel maximizes natural light with wall-to-wall terrace windows. Its 10 large suites feature handmade wooden furniture and bathrooms with huge whirlpool tubs. The gastronomic cuisine (menus 132€–207€) focuses on local ingredients such as chestnuts

---

Table Wines of the Ardèche

The Ardèche is often overlooked as a wine region. Though it may not have the elite crus of the Côtes du Rhône, many well-priced table wines come from this region. A good place to start exploring the region's wines is at a wine festival: the 2-day **Festivin** in Bourg Saint Andéol during first week of December showcases over 30 producers with conferences and wine auctions, while wine estates open their doors for wine tastings and vineyard tours in April during the region-wide **From Farm to Farm** (www.defermeenferme.com) festival. Meanwhile, wine beginners and families can learn about wine at **Néovinum,** bd. de L'Europe Unie, Ruoms (www.neovinum.fr; ☎ **04-75-39-98-08**), a wine museum with interactive exhibits and easy-to-understand explanations.

L'Auberge Rouge

Balzac would laugh at this gruesome tourist attraction in the Ardèche village of Lanarce. Locals tell the tale of notorious criminals Pierre and Marie Martin who owned this local inn, **Auberge de Peyrebeille,** route nationale 102, Peyrebeille (© **04-66-69-47-51;** Mon–Wed and Fri 9am–8pm), in the 19th century. They were charged finally with murder after 50 guests were killed and then fed to other guests. Eponymously titled L'Auberge Rouge after Balzac's infamous novel, the inn is now a museum.

and mushrooms grown in the nearby forests, while the wine list is dedicated to French wines from the 45,000-bottle cellar. The four-star hotel has a neighboring spa where guests can enjoy beauty treatments, saunas, and whirlpools while enjoying majestic mountaintop views. *Note:* Cheaper stays can be organized at the Marcon's three-star sister hotel with bedrooms from 125€.

Larsiallais, Saint-Bonnet-Le-Froid. www.regismarcon.fr. © **04-71-59-93-72.** 10 units. 385€ suite (includes spa entry). **Amenities:** Restaurant; spa; cooking school; free Wi-Fi.

13

THE FRENCH ALPS

by Simon Willmore

N o part of France has more dramatic scenery than the Alps. The majestic western ramparts of the mountains and their foothills stretch along the southeastern flank of France, from the Rhine River and Lake Geneva spanning the France-Switzerland border, south to the shimmering sun of the Mediterranean. The skiing in the French Alps is truly the best in Europe. Some of the resorts are legendary, such as **Chamonix–Mont Blanc,** the capital of Alpine skiing, with its 19km (12-mile) Vallée Blanche run. Mont Blanc, at 4,810m (15,777 ft.), is the highest mountain in Western Europe. From January to March, skiers flock to Chamonix–Mont Blanc, Megève, Val d'Isère, and Courchevel; from July to September, spa fans head to Évian-les-Bains.

Most of this chapter covers the area known as the Savoy (La Savoie), taking in the French lake district and the largest Alpine lake, Lac Léman (Lake Geneva).

ÉVIAN-LES-BAINS ★★★

576km (357 miles) SW of Paris; 42km (26 miles) NE of Geneva

On the château-dotted southern shore of Lac Léman (Lake Geneva), Évian-les-Bains is one of the leading spa resorts in France. Its lakeside promenade, lined with trees and lawns, has been fashionable since the 19th century. Évian's waters became famous in the 18th century, and the first spa buildings were built in 1839. Bottled Evian is considered useful in everything from spa products to salt-free diets and is seen as a treatment for gout and arthritis.

In the days when Marcel Proust came to enjoy the Belle Epoque grandeur, Évian was the haunt of the very rich. Proust modeled his "Balbec baths" on Évian's. Today the spa, with its promenade and elegant casino, attracts a broader range of guests—it's no longer just for the rich.

Évian, thanks to its imposing Ville des Congrès (Convention Hall) and numerous meetings facilities at its hotels, has earned the resort the title of "City of Conventions." From late April to September, the lakeside **Nautical Center** (www.lacitedeleau.com; ⓒ **04-50-75-02-69**) is a popular attraction; it has a 115m (377-ft.) pool with a diving stage and water slide, solarium, restaurant, bar, and children's paddling pool.

FACING PAGE: **Skier in Valle Blanche**

Driving Route des Grandes Alps

Crescent-shaped Lake Geneva (Lac Léman) is the largest lake in central Europe. Covering about 362 sq. km (141 sq. miles), the lake is formed by the Rhône River and is noted for its exceptional blue color. As such, the major excursion from Évian is a boat trip on the lake offered by the **Compagnie Générale de Navigation (CGN;** www.cgn.ch**),** a Swiss outfit whose agent is in Évian. Call the port office directly at © **04-50-70-73-20.** A round-trip ticket from Évian to Lausanne in Switzerland costs 34€, 17€ for children 6 to 16. Contact the company or head for the Office de Tourisme (see "Visitor Information," below) for other prices and hours. If you want to see it all, you can tour both Haut-Lac and Grand-Lac. The most popular trip is the crossing from Évian to Lausanne-Ouchy, Switzerland (the port for Lausanne), on the north side.

Essentials

GETTING THERE The best way to approach Évian-les-Bains by **train** from the French Alps is to the gateway city of Annecy via Annemasse. (Many trains from other parts of France and Switzerland require transfers to the railway junction of Bellegarde.) The one-way fare from Annecy is 17.50€. For train information and schedules, visit www.oui.sncf or call © **36-35** (.40€/min.).

Popular **ferries (CGN)** leave Geneva from quai du Mont-Blanc, at the foot of the rue des Alpes, or from Le Jardin Anglais. From May 28 to September 21, one ferry a day departs Geneva at 9am, arriving in Évian at 11:45am. The return trip leaves Évian at 5:50pm daily and reaches Geneva at 8:45pm. A first-class, one-way ticket costs 59€, a second-class ticket

The French Alps

42€. For ferry information and schedules, visit www.cgn.ch or call ☎ **+41-900-929-929** (calling to Switzerland).

If you're **driving** from Geneva (trip time: 50 min.), take N5 east along the southern rim of the lake. From Paris, take A6 south. Before Mâcon, you'll see signs pointing to the turnoff for Thonon-Évian. From Thonon, N5 leads to Évian. Trip time is about 5.5 hr., which can vary depending on traffic.

VISITOR INFORMATION   The **Office de Tourisme** is on place d'Allinges (www.eviantourism.com; ☎ **04-50-75-04-26**).

Driving the Route des Grandes Alpes

Évian can be a starting point for the 741km (459-mile) drive to Nice along the **Route des Grandes Alpes ★★★**. One of Europe's great drives, it links Lake Geneva with the Riviera, crossing 35 passes along the way. Leaping from valley to valley, it's open from end to end only in summer (many passes are closed in winter).

You can make the drive in two days, but why hurry? The charm of this journey involves stopping at scenic highlights along the way, including Chamonix, Megève, and Val d'Isère. The most dramatic pass is the **Galibier Pass (Col du Galibier),** at 2,645m (8,676 ft.), which marks the dividing line between the northern and southern parts of the French Alps.

En route to Nice, you'll pass to such towns as **St-Veran** (1,959m/6,426 ft.), the highest community in Europe; Entrevaux, once a fortress town marking the border between Upper Provence and the Alps; and **Touet-sur-Var,** a village filled with tall, narrow houses constructed directly against the towering rocky slope.

Taking the Waters at Évian

The clear, cold waters at Évian, legendary for their health and beauty benefits, used to be the sole privilege of a clientele that possessed both the time and the money to appreciate them. Some of this hydro-grandeur is still to be found at the Évian Resort's hotels. Both **Hôtel Royal,** bd. de Royal (www.evianresort.com; ℂ **04-50-26-50-50**), and **Hôtel Ermitage,** av. du Léman (see below) ★★★, maintain private spa facilities, open only to well-heeled guests, offering the most expensive packages and are adept at pampering patrons' bodies, souls, and egos.

More reasonably priced are the spa facilities at **Les Thermes Evian,** pl. de la Libération (www.lesthermesevian.com; ℂ **04-50-75-02-30**). This public spa is adjacent to Débarcadère (the dock), just uphill from the edge of the lake. The hotel spas are more likely to emphasize beauty regimes and stress therapies; the public facility offers a broader range of services, including tanning, massage, and skin and beauty care, plus a well-equipped gym but no facilities for overnight guests.

You can indulge yourself with a daylong *thermale,* which provides access to exercise rooms and classes, saunas, steam baths, water from the Évian springs, and two massage sessions. Depending on the program you select, you will spend 120€ to 180€. You can also spend up to 130€ extra per day on additional massage, health, and beauty regimes. The spa is open Monday to Saturday, usually from 9am to 7pm.

Where to Stay

The **Hôtel-Restaurant Le Bourgogne** (see below) also rents rooms.

Hôtel Ermitage ★★★   This grand Anglo-Normand-Savoyard-style residence is set within 19 hectares (47 acres) of private wooded grounds. Of the 80 rooms on offer, half have lake views—ask for a room with a *loggia* (enclosed balcony space) to be sure to enjoy the vistas whatever the weather. The luxury continues from the rooms to the golf course to the La Table restaurant (offering a three-course 60€ Market Menu).

1230 av. du Léman. www.hotel-ermitage-evian.com. ℰ **04-50-26-50-50.** 80 units. 179€–290€ double; 357€–553€ suite. **Amenities:** Restaurant; bar; golf; indoor pool; spa; room service; free Wi-Fi.

Hôtel de la Verniaz et ses Chalets ★★★　This glamorous country house stands on a hillside with a view of woods, water (Lac Léman), and the Alps. Antiques fill the main house and the separate chalets; the chalets have their own gardens and more privacy but cost a small fortune. Throughout the hotel, you'll find comfortable, even plush accommodations. Main courses in the hotel restaurant run from 25€ to 30€; fixed-price menus, 25€ to 75€.

av. D'Abondance, à Neuvecelle Eglise. www.verniaz.com. ℰ **800/735-2478** in the U.S. and Canada, or 04-50-75-04-90. 36 units. 110€–295€ double; 269€–370€ suite; 285€–610€ chalet. Closed mid-Nov to mid-Feb. **Amenities:** Restaurant; bar; babysitting; outdoor pool; room service; free Wi-Fi.

Where to Eat

Hôtel-Restaurant Le Bourgogne ★ TRADITIONAL FRENCH
Come here for a delectable meal, impeccable service, an attractive setting, and excellent wine. Featured regional wines are Crépy and Rousette. Menu choices in the restaurant are likely to include escalope of fried homemade foie gras, beef entrecote served with morels, and a poached version of *omble chevalier* (tiny local whitefish) with whiskey sauce. Reservations required.

The inn also offers 30 neat, individual rooms for 75€ to 110€ for a double.

73 rue Nationale. www.hotel-le-bourgogne-evian-les-bains.com. ℰ **04-50-75-01-05.** Main course 23€–28€; fixed-price menu 17€–19€. Tues–Sun noon–2pm; Tues–Sat 7–10pm. Closed Jan.

ANNECY ★★★

538km (334 miles) SE of Paris; 56km (35 miles) SE of Geneva; 140km (87 miles) E of Lyon

Lac d'Annecy is the jewel of the Savoy Alps. The resort city of Annecy, which is the region's capital, makes the best base for touring the Haute-Savoie. Once a Gallo-Roman town, the seat of the comtes de Genève until the 15th century, Annecy opens onto one of the best views of lakes and mountains in the French Alps. Since the 1980s, Annecy has become a booming urban center that has managed to preserve its natural setting. In summer, its lakefront promenade is crowded and active.

Essentials

GETTING THERE　If you're **driving,** Annecy is near several highways: From Paris, take A6 southeast to Beaune and connect with A6/N6 south to

Old town of Annecy

Mâcon-Nord. Then follow A40 southeast towards Neydens, connecting with A41 going southeast to Annecy. Allow at least 5 hr. From Geneva, follow D1201 south toward Annecy, crossing the border near Archamps. Trip time is 30 min.

A car is useful but not essential in the Alps. Annecy has rail links with Paris and Lyon. **Trains** arrive hourly from Lyon via Chambery (trip time: 2.5 hr.), with a one-way fare costing 28€ to 42€. Six trains arrive daily from Paris's Gare de Lyon (trip time: around 5 hr., transfer at Lyon or Aix Les Bains); the fare is 85€ to 166€ one-way. For information, visit www. oui.sncf or call ✆ **36-35** (.40€/min.).

The nearby **airport** (www.annecy.aeroport.fr; ✆ **04-50-27-30-06**) is in the hamlet of Meythet (Aéroport Annecy-Haute-Savoie-Mont-Blanc), with service on Air France from Paris's Orly airport.

VISITOR INFORMATION The **Office de Tourisme** is at 1 rue Jean-Jaurès (www.lac-annecy.com; ✆ **04-50-45-00-33**).

Exploring Annecy

Built around the river Thiou, Annecy has been called the Venice of the Alps because of the canals that cut to the old part of town, **Vieil Annecy.** You can explore the arcaded streets where Jean-Jacques Rousseau arrived in 1728.

After seeing Annecy, consider a trek to the **Gorges du Fier** ★★ (www.gorgesdufier.com; ✆ **04-50-46-23-07**), a dramatic river gorge 9.5km (6 miles) to the west. To reach it, take a train or bus from Annecy's rail station to Poisy. From the station, go about 1.5km (1 mile), following the clearly marked signs. This striking gorge is one of the most interesting sights in the French Alps. A gangway takes you to a gully three to 10m (9.75–33 ft.) wide, cut through the rock by torrents of water; you'll hear the roar of the river at the bottom. Emerging from this labyrinth, you'll be greeted by a huge expanse of boulders. You can visit the gorge from June 15 to September 10 daily 9:30am to 7:15pm (last trip at 6:15pm), and from March 15 to June 14 and September 11 to October 15 daily 9:30am to 6:15pm (last trip at 5:15pm). The site is closed October 16 to March 14. A hike to its well-signposted depths takes less than 1 hr. and costs 5.70€ for adults, 3€ for children 7 to 15; it's free for kids 6 and under.

You can also take a cruise on the ice-blue lake for which the town is famous. Tours of **Lac d'Annecy,** conducted from February to December, last 1 hr. and cost 14.40€. An English-speaking guide points out the sights. Tours depart between one and six times a day, depending on the season. Inquire at the Office de Tourisme (see above), or call the **Compagnie des Bateaux du Lac d'Annecy** (www.annecy-croisieres. com; ✆ **04-50-51-08-40**).

Château de Montrottier ★★ CASTLE   Within walking distance of the gorges, in the hamlet of Montrottier, is the 13th- and 14th-century Château de Montrottier. A one-time feudal citadel partially protected by the rugged geology around it, the château's tower offers a panoramic view of Mont Blanc. A small museum features items collected by a local dilettante, showcasing pottery, Asian and African costumes, armor, tapestries, and lace antiques, as well as some bronze bas-reliefs from the 16th century.

Lovagny. www.chateaudemontrottier.com. ✆ **04-50-46-23-02.** Admission 8€ adults; 7€ students; 6€ children 5–15; free for children 4 and under. Apr–June and Sept Wed–Sun 10am–6pm; July–Aug daily 10am–7pm.

Musée Château d'Annecy ★★★ MUSEUM   This forbidding gray-stone monument, whose 12th-century pinnacle is known as the Queen's Tower, dominates the city. The château contains a museum of regional artifacts that include Alpine furniture, religious art, oil paintings, and

---

Annecy for Kids: The Lure of the Hills

The Office de Tourisme (see above) distributes free pamphlets that describe about a dozen easy, family-oriented hiking and biking excursions in the forests around Annecy. More experienced hikers may wish to pick up a free map with a detailed set of challenging walks.

Excursions in both categories last 2 to 6 hr. Some begin in the center of Annecy; others require a trip by car or bus from one of several towns in the area—such as **Saint-Jorioz** or **Sevrier,** to the west, or **Talloires,** to the east (see below)—to the trailhead. A travel agency in Annecy, **Trans Dev Haute Savoie,** pl. de la Gare (www.transdevhautesavoie. com; ✆ **04-50-51-74-62**), sells bus tickets to the destinations around Annecy and Lac d'Annecy and Lac Léman. It also arranges minibus excursions to panoramic sites in July and August.

modern works. One section is devoted to the geology and marine life of the region's deep, cold lakes. pl. du Château. http://musees.agglo-annecy.fr/Chateau-d-Annecy. © **04-50-33-87-30.** Admission (combined ticket with Palais de l'Ile) 7.20€ adults; 3.50€ ages 12–25; free for children 11 and under. June–Sept daily 10:30am–6pm; Oct–May Wed–Mon 10am–noon and 2–5pm.

A summer day on Annecy Lake

Le Palais de l'Ile ★★★ PALACE This is the town's most potent and most frequently photographed visual symbol. Built before the 18th century and connected to the "mainland" of Annecy via a bridge, it resembles a miniature château, surrounded by water, despite its long-term use as a prison (and certainly a very cold one) for local malefactors.

3 passage de l'Ile. musees.agglo-annecy.fr. © **04-50-33-87-30.** Admission (combined ticket with Musée Château d'Annecy) 7.20€ adults; 3.20€ ages 12–25; free for children 11 and under. June–Sept daily 10:30am–6pm; Oct–May Wed–Mon 10am–noon and 2–5pm.

Where to Stay

La Maison de Marc Veyrat (see "Where to Eat," below) also rents rooms.

Best Western Plus Hotel Carlton ★★ The obvious selling point of this hotel is the proximity to the train station, which is just on the other side of Square Verdun. However, each of the rooms has individual and chic decor which hits the right balance between vibrant and elegant. Some of the rooms have large balconies with castle and mountains views and the lakeside and old town are less than a 10-min. walk away.

5 rue Des Glieres. www.bestwestern-carlton.com. © **04-50-10-09-09.** 55 units. 90€–141€ double. Parking 15€. **Amenities:** Bar; room service; free Wi-Fi.

Hôtel du Nord ★ A government-rated two-star hotel in the center of Annecy, minutes from the train station and Lac d'Annecy, the du Nord is one of the town's better bargains. Guests appreciate the modernity of the soundproof rooms; 20 come with showers only, others with tub and shower. The helpful staff speaks English and can direct you to reasonably priced restaurants nearby. Breakfast is the only meal served.

24 rue Sommeiller. www.annecy-hotel-du-nord.com. © **04-50-45-08-78.** 30 units. 75€–95€ double. **Amenities:** Free Wi-Fi.

Where to Eat

Le Belvédère ★★ FRENCH/SEAFOOD This is one of the most appealing reasonably priced restaurants in town. On a belvedere above Annecy, about 1.5km (1 mile) west of the town center, it provides views that extend up to 8km (5 miles) over mountains and lakes. Menu items include a salad of Breton lobster with freshwater crayfish, langoustine *a la plancha* with courgette ravioli, and an unusual pairing of foie gras with a purée of figs and vanilla-flavored bourbon sauce. Dessert may be a selection of tropical-flavored sorbets.

The 10 simple guest rooms are much less opulent than the restaurant. Rooms go for 145€ to 170€ for a double and 190€ to 215€ for a suite.

7 chemin du Belvédère. www.belvedere-annecy.com. ✆ **04-50-45-04-90.** Fixed-price lunch 32€ or 78€–125€ dinner. Thurs–Tues 12:15–1:30pm; Mon and Thurs–Sat 7:30–9:30pm. Closed Jan. From downtown Annecy, follow signs leading uphill to Le Semnoz.

La Maison des Bois, Marc Veyrat ★★★ MODERN FRENCH Famous throughout France for owner Marc Veyrat-Durebex's excellent and unusual cuisine, this world-class and eye-wateringly priced restaurant occupies a romanticized version of a Savoyard château at the edge of a lake in the village of Veyrier-du-Lac, 1.5km (1 mile) south of Annecy. Guests dine in a posh room with ceiling frescoes.

The chef has been dubbed *l'enfant terrible* of upscale Alpine cuisine. He offers a unique dining experience, marked by an almost ritualistic etiquette, and dishes include non-sensical delights such as "virtual foie gras," "wild meadowsweet bonbons," and "the no-mind plate".

The *company* rents expensive and beautifully furnished rooms, just off the *domaine*—about a mile away, in the direction of Manigod. Rates are 750€ for a double; 1,200€ for a suite; 1,560€ for a chalet.

13 vieille rte. des Pensières, Veyrier-du-Lac. www.marcveyrat.fr. ✆ **04-50-60-24-00.** Main course 75€–138€; fixed-price dinner 295€–750€. Sat–Sun noon–1:30pm; Wed–Sun 7:30–9pm. Closed Nov to mid-June. From Annecy's lakefront boulevard, follow signs to Veyrier-du-Lac, Chavoires, and Talloires.

Annecy Nightlife

In the old town, you'll find bars, cafes, pubs, and (in warmer months) street dances, fairs, and even carnivals. A calmer alternative is an evening of theater or dance at the **Théâtre d'Annecy,** 1 rue Jean-Jaurès (www.bonlieu-annecy.com; ✆ **04-50-33-44-00**); tickets cost 18€ to 50€.

If a long day has left you thirsty, try the traditional Irish pub **Le Captain Pub,** 11 rue Pont-Morens (www.captain-pub.fr; ✆ **04-11-88-99-80**), with hearty ales on tap. **Le Vieux Necy,** 3 rue Filaterie (✆ **04-50-45-01-57**), attracts a younger, more boisterous crowd.

The best piano bar in town is **Le Duo,** 104 av. de Genève (✆ **04-50-57-01-46**). It's ideal for quiet conversation. For the most elegant evening on the town, head to the **Casino de l'Impérial,** Allée de l'Impérial

(✆ **04-50-09-30-00**), part of the Belle Epoque–style Impérial Palace hotel on a peninsula jutting into Lac d'Annecy. Entrance to the gaming rooms is free; you must present a passport. The casino is open Sunday to Thursday noon to 2am, and Friday and Saturday noon to 4am.

TALLOIRES ★★

551km (342 miles) SE of Paris; 32km (20 miles) N of Albertville; 13km (8 miles) S of Annecy

The charming village of Talloires, which dates from 866, is old enough to appear on lists of territories once controlled by Lothar II, great-grandson of Charlemagne. Chalk cliffs surround a bay, and at the lower end a promontory encloses a port. An 18-hole golf course, **Golf Club du Lac d'Annecy** (www.golf-lacannecy.com; ✆ **04-50-60-12-89**), and watersports such as boating, swimming, water-skiing, and fishing make this a favorite vacation spot. Talloires also has one of France's great restaurants, Auberge du Père-Bise, and a Benedictine abbey founded in the 11th century, now the deluxe Hôtel de l'Abbaye.

Essentials

GETTING THERE   From Annecy, you can reach Talloires by **driving** south along D909 for 13km (8 miles). About eight daily **buses** connect Annecy to Talloires, which take 35 min. In Talloires, buses stop in front of the post office. For bus information, visit Trans Dev in Annecy (www.transdevhautesavoie.com; ✆ **04-50-51-08-51**).

VISITOR INFORMATION   The **Office de Tourisme** is at 27 rue André-Theuriet (www.talloires.fr; ✆ **04-50-66-76-54**).

Where to Stay

Auberge du Père-Bise and **La Villa des Fleurs** (see below) also rent rooms.

Hôtel de l'Abbaye ★★   This 16th-century Benedictine monastery has been a hotel since the French Revolution. It's one of the grand inns of the Alps. With close-up views of the lake, it doesn't equal the cuisine or the luxury of the Auberge du Père-Bise (see below), but it's a lot more affordable. The hotel is rich with beamed ceilings, antique portraits, leather chairs, gardens, and carved balustrades. The great corridors lead to converted guest rooms, of which no two are alike. The furnishings include all the Louis periods, as well as Directoire and Empire. In summer, the restaurant expands onto a shaded lakefront terrace. Overall, this is an extremely pleasant escape from urban life.

Chemin des Moines. www.abbaye-talloires.com. ✆ **04-50-60-77-33**. 33 units. 144€–521€ double; 324€–792€ suite. Closed mid-Nov to mid-Feb. **Amenities:** Restaurant; bar; room service; sauna; spa; free Wi-Fi.

Where to Eat

Auberge du Père-Bise ★★★ FRENCH   Since the 1950s, when it attracted starlets and millionaires, Auberge du Père-Bise has radiated style and charm. A chalet built in 1901, it's one of France's most acclaimed—and expensive—restaurants. In fair weather, you can dine under a vine-covered pergola and enjoy the view of mountains and the lake. The kitchen, helmed by chef Jean Sulpice, excels at dishes such as roe deer with beetroot, Char Lake fish, and celeriac risotto. Reservations required.

The inn also offers 23 guest rooms. Rates are 229€ to 429€ for a double and start at 779€ for a suite. Reserve at least two months in advance, especially in summer.

Rte. du Port, bord du Lac. www.perebise.com. ℰ **04-50-60-72-01**. Main course 43€–104€; fixed-price menu 98€–210€. Daily noon–2pm and 7–9pm. Closed mid-Nov to mid-Feb.

La Villa des Fleurs ★★★ TRADITIONAL FRENCH   This *restaurant avec chambres* should be better known, because it's the best place in Talloires for the price. The wonderful meals served here may include *salade landaise* with foie gras and filet of fera (a local fish) with sage sauce. The dining room overlooks the water. Reservations required.

Eight simply furnished rooms with Victorian-era decor are at the top of a winding staircase—there's no elevator. Doubles cost 118€ to 155€.

779 rte. du Port, Talloires 74290. www.lavilladesfleurs.com; ℰ **04-50-60-71-14**. Main course 22€–55€. Tues–Sun noon–2pm; Tues–Sat 7–9pm.

GRENOBLE

567km (352 miles) SE of Paris; 55km (34 miles) S of Chambéry; 103km (64 miles) SE of Lyon

The ancient capital of the Dauphine, Grenoble is the commercial, intellectual, and tourist center of the Alps. It's a major stop for travelers, including those driving between the Riviera and Geneva.

A sports capital in winter (it hosted the 1968 Winter Olympic Games) and summer, it attracts many foreign students; its university has the largest summer-session program in Europe. Founded in 1339, the University of Grenoble has a student body of some 55,000. The metropolitan area, the *agglomération grenobloise* (pop. 660,000) is also home to four other universities with a large contingent of English and American students, giving the city a cosmopolitan air.

Essentials

GETTING THERE   Grenoble is the region's gateway and lies 35 min. by car from the Grenoble–St-Geoirs airport, 40 min. from the Lyon-Satolas international airport, and 90 min. from Geneva's Cointrin airport. Flights arrive to Grenoble from London and Bristol (England). **easyJet** and

British Airways fly only in the ski season, but **Ryanair** also flies in summer. For more information, contact Grenoble's **Aéroport Grenoble-Isère** (www.grenoble-airport.com; ✆ **04-76-65-48-48**), 41km (25 miles), often known as Saint-Geoirs airport, northwest of the city center. A shuttle bus meets every flight and takes passengers to and from Grenoble's center; the cost is 14.50€ each way (alps-airport-transfer.co.uk). A taxi (✆ **06-81-51-97-12**) to the town center costs 80€ to 110€.

For information on flying into Lyon, see chapter 12. **Ouibus** (www.ouibus.com) meets most flights at the Lyon airport and takes passengers to Grenoble. Travel time is 1 hr.; the fare is 9.90€ each way.

An important rail and bus junction, Grenoble is easily accessible from Paris and all the cities in this chapter. About 13 **trains** per day arrive from Paris Gare de Lyon (trip time: 3.5 hr.); the one-way fare is 74€ to 97€. Trains arrive almost every hour from Chambéry (trip time: 30 min.; 12€ one-way). For information, visit www.oui.sncf or call ✆ **36-35** (.40€/min.).

The city is on the Chambéry-Geneva motorway (A41) and connected to the Paris-Lyon-Marseille motorway (A6/A7) in the west via the A48. If you're **driving,** take A6 from Paris to Lyon and then continue on A48 into Grenoble. Depending on conditions, the drive should take 6 to 7 hr.

VISITOR INFORMATION The **Office de Tourisme** is at 14 rue de la République (www.isere-tourisme.com; ✆ **04-76-42-41-41**). For information about public transportation in Grenoble, visit **Transports de l'agglomération grenobloise** (TAG)'s website www.tag.fr (✆ **04-76-20-66-66**).

Exploring Grenoble

Grenoble lies near the junction of the Isère and Drac rivers. Most of the city is on the south bank of the Isère, though its most impressive monument, the **Fort de la Bastille,** stands on a rocky hilltop on the north bank. The center of Grenoble's historic section is around the **Palais de Justice;** the more modern part of town is southeast, centered on the **Hôtel de Ville** (town hall) and the nearby **Tour Perret** lookout, affectionately known as the "tower to look at the mountains."

Begin at **place Grenette,** where you can enjoy a drink or an espresso at a cafe. Don't miss the **place aux Herbes** and the **place St-André,** in the very heart of the *centre ville.* Place St-André, dating from the Middle Ages, is the most evocative square in old Grenoble, with the Palais de Justice on one side and the Eglise St-André on the other. The Palace of Justice was built in many stages. The brick church went up in the 13th century. Two great streets for strolling and browsing are rue de la Poste, in the medieval core, and rue J.-J.-Rousseau, a 5-min. walk southwest of the city.

Enjoy a ride on the **Téléphérique-Grenoble-Bastille** (www.bastille-grenoble.fr; ✆ **04-76-44-33-65**), cable cars that take you from the south bank of the Isère River to the top of the fort (closed Jan for annual

Grenoble's cable cars

maintenance). Check the website for the cable car's operating hours. A round-trip ticket costs 5.60€ for adults and 3.20€ for ages 5 to 15. At the belvedere where you land, you'll have a view of the city, the mountains, and the remains of the Fort de la Bastille. Come for the view, not the fort. You can walk up in 1 hr. or so if you're a real athlete; the beginning of the route is signposted to the west of place St-André. We suggest you take the *téléphérique* to the top and then stroll down along the footpath, Montée de Chalmont, that winds to Alpine gardens and past old ruins before reaching a cobblestone walk that leads to the old town.

Musée Archéologique Grenoble ★★★ MUSEUM   At the foot of the Bastille lies the former Romanesque Saint-Laurent church, built on the remains of a Gallo-Roman necropolis. The church was originally deconsecrated in 1983 to become an archaeological dig; in 1986 it became a museum. A huge renovation finishing in 2011 turned the museum into the impressive sight it is today. Upon entering, visitors stand on a platform high above the restored remains of the nave, with colored illuminations to show which section of the building was built during each of the many phases of construction and renovation, dating from the early Middle Ages through to the 19th century. The centerpiece of the museum is the crypt which dates from the original construction of the 6th century cruciform funerary church.

pl. Saint-Laurent. www.musee-archeologique-grenoble.fr. ✆ **04-76-44-78-68.** Free admission. Wed–Mon 10am–6pm.

Musée Dauphinois ★ MUSEUM   Housed in the original 17th-century convent Ste-Marie-d'en-Haut and enhanced by the convent's cloister, gardens, and baroque chapel, this museum lies across the Isère on the way up to La Bastille. A collection of ethnographic and historical mementos of the Dauphine region is on exhibit, along with folk arts and crafts. This place is a quick course on life in the Alps: No other museum gives such a detailed view of the people. Furnishings, tools, artifacts, and replicas of Alpine settings are on display. Check out the special display on pop music, following an interactive exhibit around a space stylized like a cartoon house, where visitors learn how sound effects our daily lives.

30 rue Maurice-Gignoux. www.musee-dauphinois.fr. ✆ **04-57-58-89-01.** Free admission. June–Aug Wed–Mon 10am–7pm; Sept–May Wed–Mon 10am–6pm.

Musée de Grenoble ★★★ MUSEUM Founded in 1796, this is one of the country's oldest art museums. It was the first French museum outside of Paris to focus on modern art, a fact appreciated by Picasso, who donated his *Femme Lisant* in 1921. The collection includes Flemish and Italian Renaissance works, but the Impressionist paintings generate the most interest. Note Matisse's *Intérieur aux aubergines* and Léger's *Le Remorqueur.* Ernst, Corot, Klee, Bonnard, Gauguin, Monet—they're all here. On display are a small number of older paintings and sculptures, along with artifacts and relics from Greek, Egyptian, and Roman times, including a well-preserved mosaic. The artistic highlight is a sculpted door panel from the 1400s, depicting Jacob and his sons. A collection of 20th-century sculptures occupies the François Mitterrand Esplanade and the Albert Michallon Park surrounding the museum.

5 pl. de Lavalette. www.museedegrenoble.fr. ✆ **04-76-63-44-44.** Admission 8€ adults; 5€ seniors and students; free for children 17 and under; free for everyone 1st Sun of each month. Wed–Mon 10am–6:30pm.

Where to Stay

Hôtel d'Angleterre Tulip Inn Grenoble ★★★ In the center of town, this hotel features tall windows and wrought-iron balconies that open onto the pleasant Place Victor Hugo with its huge chestnut trees. The stylish salons boast wood-grained walls and ceilings and tropical plants. Some guest rooms look out on the Vercors Massif. Most of the small to midsize units are comfortably furnished and come with shower-only bathrooms; some have Jacuzzi tubs. Breakfast is the only meal served.

5 pl. Victor-Hugo. www.hotel-angleterre-grenoble.com. ✆ **04-76-87-37-21.** 62 units. 79€–89€ double; 99€ family room. Free parking. **Amenities:** Room service; free Wi-Fi.

Mercure Grenoble Centre Président ★★ Walking distance from the city center but far enough out to enjoy an easy drive out of town to the mountains, this business-focused hotel with nine meeting rooms has enough to keep leisure guests happy with a sauna, gym, and whirlpool. The L'Instant M restaurant, looking out over the pool, serves a buffet breakfast (included) and traditional French cuisine for dinner, and the Sirius bar serves cocktails in a space with more stylish decor than you might expect.

11 rue Général Mangin. www.accorhotels.com. ✆ **04-76-56-26-56.** 105 units. 72€–100€ double; from 176€ suite. Free parking. Tram: C to Foch-Ferrié. **Amenities:** Restaurant; bar; babysitting; room service; free Wi-Fi.

Park Hôtel MGallery by Sofitel ★★ This is one of the most opulent and prestigious hotels in Grenoble, a government-rated four-star venue overlooking Parc Paul-Mistral that welcomes most of the important politicians and entertainment-industry moguls who visit the region. Since it was taken over by AccorHotels, its prices have become pretty competitive, too. On the lower floors of a mid-1960s tower mostly devoted to private condominiums, it's a short drive south of Grenoble's commercial center and close to City Hall. Each guest room is decorated differently, with a blend of dignified (sometimes antique) furniture, state-of-the-art lighting, and modern red fittings and upholstery.

10 pl. Paul-Mistral. www.park-hotel-grenoble.fr. ☎ **04-76-85-81-23.** 50 units. 100€–105€ double; from 200€ suite. Parking 16€. Tram: A to Chavant. **Amenities:** Restaurant; bar; babysitting; room service; free Wi-Fi.

Where to Eat

Auberge Napoleon ★★★ FRENCH   No other restaurant in France boasts as intense an association with Napoleon Bonaparte, but that's less important to diners than the fact that the restaurant is the area's finest. In 1815, Napoleon spent the night here at the beginning of a 100-day reign that ended with his defeat by Wellington at the Battle of Waterloo. You'll find enough references to the history of France, from the Revolution to around 1820, to keep even a student of French history busy. The restaurant seats only 23, in a plush, manicured dining room. We'd vote the bouillabaisse here as the best in the Alps. Try velvety-smooth crayfish-and-shrimp cream soup or duck foie gras terrine. The chef makes a superb filet of beef in game sauce.

7 rue de Montorge. www.auberge-napoleon.fr. ☎ **04-76-87-53-64.** Main course 24€–38€; fixed-price menu 35€–72€. Mon–Sat 7:30–10pm. Closed May 1–15, July 13–14, and Aug 10–25.

Café de la Table Ronde ★★ FRENCH   This is the second-oldest cafe in France, after the more famous Procope in Paris. Founded in 1739, the cafe has attracted such luminaries as Stendhal and Sarah Bernhardt. It is said to be the spot where Pierre Choderlos de Laclos conceived the plot for his 1784 novel "Les Liaisons Dangereuses." The menu offers both regional and national cuisine—the ingredients always fresh and the portions always huge. We gravitate to *le poisson du jour* (fresh fish of the day), although the *fondue Savoyarde* with charcuterie is a winter delight, as is the Alpine ham. The cafe conducts concerts and poetry readings. It's always busy so book a table early and be prepared to wait.

7 pl. St-André. www.restaurant-tableronde-grenoble.com. ☎ **04-76-44-51-41.** Main course 10€–23€; fixed-price menus 25€–33€. Daily 9am–1am.

La Ferme à Dédé ★★★ FRENCH   Owning the most popular Savoyarde restaurant in the Gateway to the Alps is a bold claim but "Dédé" is able to make it with confidence. The central location and Alpine-inspired design (the cash till is situated on a traditional wooden wagon), not to mention the brilliant fondues, raclettes, enormous charcuterie platters, and good choice of local craft beer ensure this place fills up fast even on weekdays. Try to book ahead, but if it's full try your luck at the door, as the staff—always rushed off their feet but unfalteringly happy to help—will try to squeeze you in if your group is four or less; if you're really stuck, a sister venue near the train station.

24 rue Barnave. www.restaurantlafermeadede.com. ☎ **04-76-54-00-33.** Main course 14€–23€. Daily noon–2:30pm and 7–11:30pm.

Grenoble Nightlife

To get things started, walk to **place St-André, place aux Herbes,** or **place de Gordes.** On a good night, these squares overflow with young people, and the energy level builds in anticipation of an explosion of dancing and partying. Join fun-loving crowds of European students at **Le Couche Tard,** 1 rue Palais (✆ **04-76-44-18-79**), the **London Pub,** 11 rue Brochene (✆ **04-76-44-41-90**), and Le Bukana, 1 Quai Créqui (✆ **04-76-46-41-04**).

Le Vieux Manoir, 52 rue Saint-Laurent (✆ **04-76-42-00-68**), is often smelly and always packed. Attuned to cutting-edge music from such centers as London and Los Angeles, guests expect a mix of hip-hop, R&B, soul, and techno, but are prepared for anything.

The town's most animated gay disco is **Le Georges V,** 124 cours Berriat (✆ **06-62-06-16-23**), which is open Wednesday from 9pm, Thursday to Sunday from 11:30pm (free before 1am; closing times vary).

COURCHEVEL 1850 ★★

633km (392 miles) SE of Paris; 52km (32 miles) SE of Albertville; 97km (60 miles) SE of Chambéry

Courchevel has been called a resort of "high taste, high fashion, and high profile," a chic spot where multimillion-dollar chalets sit on pristine pine-covered slopes. Skiers and geographers know it as part of Les Trois Vallées, sometimes called "the skiing supermarket of France." The resort, with 150km (93 miles) of ski runs in Courchevel and 604km (374 miles) of ski runs in the Trois Vallées around it, employs as many workers in summer as in winter, many of whom do nothing more than manicure and maintain the slopes. Courchevel 1850 has excellent resorts and hotels—with price tags to match—so it draws the super-rich. Travelers on average budgets should avoid it and head for more reasonably priced resorts, especially Chamonix (p. 486).

Courchevel consists of four planned ski towns, each designated by its elevation in meters. They are, in order of increasing height, prestige and price: Courchevel 1300 (Le Prez), Courchevel 1550, Courchevel 1650, and, crowning

Cafe in Les Trois Vallées region in Courchevel 1850

them all, Courchevel 1850. Courchevel maintains three ski schools with a staff of 700 instructors, a labyrinth of chairlifts, and more than 200 ski runs, which are excellent in the intermediate and advanced categories

Courchevel 1850 is the most attractive ski mecca in the French Alps. It's also the focal point of a chair-hoist network crisscrossing the Les Trois Vallées region. At the center of one of the largest ski areas in the world, Courchevel sits at the base of a soaring amphitheater whose deep snowfalls last longer than those at most other resorts because it faces north. Expect reliable snow conditions, perfectly groomed runs, vertical cliffs, and enough wide runs to appease the intermediate skier. The glacier skiing draws experts from around the world.

Essentials

GETTING THERE If you're **driving** from Paris, take A6 to Lyon, then A43 to Chambéry, and then A430 to Albertville. At Albertville, take N90 to Moutiers and then follow the narrow roads D915 and D91A into Courchevel. Courchevel 1850 is the last stop on a steep Alpine road that dead-ends at the village center. Roads are open year-round, but driving can be treacherous during snowstorms. To go any higher, you'll have to take a cable car from the center of town. Most visitors drive here (you might need snow tires and chains), but the area has a very good **bus** network linking all four ski towns to each other and the railway junctions farther down the mountain.

The nearest **train** station is in Moutiers Salins. From Paris's Gare de Lyon, five trains per day leave for Moutiers. The high-speed TGV covers the distance from Paris to Chambéry in about 3 hr. (www.oui.sncf; ✆ **36-35** at .40€/min.). In Chambéry, transfer for Moutiers. From the station in Moutiers, a 1-hr. **bus** trip completes the journey to Courchevel. There are five buses per day Monday to Friday and 15 per day on Saturday and Sunday, costing from 12€ to 18€.

The nearest **airports** are in Grenoble and Geneva; buses are timed to coincide with flight arrivals and run to Moutiers, costing around 80€ from either city and both taking around 4 hr. From the airport at Lyon, three to five buses a day go to Courchevel; the 4-hr. trip costs 65€ one-way.

VISITOR INFORMATION The **Office de Tourisme,** at La Croisette in the heart of town (www.courchevel.com; ✆ **04-79-08-00-29**), provides information on skiing and each of the four Courchevel ski towns.

SKI PASSES You can buy ski passes and lift tickets online in advance at www.skipasscourchevel.com or at one of the ski offices, located at each level (1300, 1650, and 1850) and at La Tania. A 1-day pass (lift ticket) for Courchevel costs 52€ (41.60€ for children ages 5–13), and a 1-day pass for all Les Trois Vallées goes for 61€ (48.80€ per child). A 3-day pass costs 153€ (122.40€ per child) for Courchevel, 180€ (144€ per child) for Les Trois Vallées. For groups, you'll need to buy a pass for at least 6 days (from 205€ for a family pass to Courchevel).

EN ROUTE TO geneva

If you're leaving France and headed toward western Switzerland, specifically Geneva, consider a final R & R stopover at **Jiva Hill Park Hotel** ★, route d'Harée, Crozet 01170 (www.jivahill.com; ✆ **04-50-28-48-48**). Set on 28 hectares (69 acres) of parkland, it's within France, but only a 10-min. drive from the Geneva airport. This frontier region of the Alpine foothills, where Voltaire was exiled by the French monarchs, seems more closely tuned to Switzerland (especially Geneva) than to the rest of France. Isolated and peaceful, with only 33 rooms, the hotel bills itself as "a boutique resort."

Angular and avant garde, it has interiors by Jean-Philippe Nuel, the famous French hotel designer. Each unit is accented with exposed wood and touches of wrought iron, and manages to be minimalist, stylish, and ultra-comfortable at the same time. On the premises is a highly rated deluxe spa, decorated like the rest of the hotel, with a spectacular collection of contemporary art and state-of-the-art equipment. Other amenities include a gourmet restaurant, bar, heated indoor pool, two tennis courts, and nearby golf course. Rates range from 261€ to 288€ for a double or start at 378€ for a junior suite.

Where to Stay

Le Chabichou ★★   This is one of the town's finest hotels, within easy walking distance of many bars and clubs, and boasting a superb restaurant of the same name (see below). Most of the guest rooms in the gingerbread-trimmed chalet are large and well furnished; their daring modern design may not appeal to everyone, however. Beds offer grand Alpine comfort, with quality mattresses and fine linens.

90 route des Chenus. www.chabichou-courchevel.com. ✆ **04-79-08-00-55.** 42 units. 470€–830€ double; from 600€ suite. Rates include half-board. Parking 30€. Closed May–June and Sept to mid-Dec. **Amenities:** Restaurant; bar; babysitting; exercise room; room service; sauna; spa; free Wi-Fi.

Hôtel Bellecôte ★★   This seven-story chalet, with direct access to the slopes, is known for its collection of unusual antiques. Bored with traditional Alpine motifs, the founder scoured the bazaars of Afghanistan and the Himalayas for objects that lend exotic warmth to the wood-sheathed walls and ceilings. Guest rooms are outfitted with lots of varnished paneling, plush accessories, and carved wooden objects from the Far or Middle East. The hotel has its own ski shop and rental services.

Full meals in the elegant dining room include cassoulet of sweetbreads with flap mushrooms, frogs' legs Provençal, and chicken with morels.

rue de Bellecôte. www.lebellecote.com. ✆ **04-79-08-10-19.** 54 units. 430€–510€ double; 750€ suite. Rates include half-board. Closed mid-Apr to mid-Dec. **Amenities:** Restaurant; bar; babysitting; exercise room; Jacuzzi; indoor pool; room service; sauna; free Wi-Fi in lobby.

Hôtel Le Strato ★★★   Not only is this one of the Alps' great hotels, it is indeed one of the great hotels in all of France's. This palatial property, named after the iconic skis by Rossignol, features individually decorated rooms and suites including duplexes that look out over the slopes. The ostentatious luxury continues through to the enormous spa (800 sq. m/8,611 sq. ft.), Michelin-starred Baumanière restaurant that serves sea urchins and lamb shoulder confit, and the helipad for guests' private helicopter transfers.

rue de Bellecôte. www.hotelstrato.com. ✆ **04-79-41-51-60.** 25 units. 830€ double; from 1,060€ suite. **Amenities:** Restaurant; bar; indoor pool; spa; room service; free Wi-Fi.

Where to Eat

Le Chabichou ★★★ MODERN FRENCH   On the second floor of the hotel of the same name, with large windows showcasing a view of the slopes, Le Chabichou's cuisine includes a number of superlative dishes, such as soup made from "fish from the lake," magret of duckling with honey sauce, divine lobster salad, red mullet with vinaigrette sauce, and velvety risotto with giant prawns. Reservations required.

In Le Chabichou hotel, 90 route des Chenus. www.chabichou-courchevel.com. ✆ **04-79-08-00-55.** Main course 42€–60€; fixed-price lunch 70€ or dinner 110€. Daily 12:30–2pm and 7:15–9:30pm. Closed May–June and Sept–Nov.

Chalet des Pierres ★★★ FRENCH/SAVOYARD   This is the best of the lunch restaurants scattered across the slopes. Accented with weathered planking and warmed by open hearths, it sits in the middle of the Des Verdons ski slope, a few paces from the path of whizzing skiers. Lunch can be served on a terrace, but most visitors gravitate to the two-story interior, where blazing fireplaces, hunting trophies, and a hip international crowd contribute to the place's charm. Items include air-dried Alpine meat and sausages, the best french fries in Courchevel, pepper steak, and *fondue Savoyarde.* Two appealing dishes are the Beaufort cheese tart and a leg of lamb that's suspended, the traditional way, from a string in the chimney and left to slowly cook in the smoke from the smoldering fire. Reservations required.

rue de Jardin Alpin, Piste des Verdons. www.chaletdepierres.com. ✆ **04-79-08-18-61.** Main course 37€–55€. Daily noon–4:30pm. Closed late Apr to mid-July and mid-Aug to early Dec.

Courchevel Nightlife

A chic but seasonal resort, Courchevel offers nightlife that roars into the wee hours in midwinter but melts away with the snow. The area around **La Croisette** (the departure point for most of the lifts) contains lots of restaurants, bars, and clubs that come and go. For guaranteed atmosphere, head to place du Tremplin, where guests can either relax to live DJs at **Polar Cafe** (✆ **04-79-22-63-51**), enjoy international beers and cocktails at **La Luge** (www.la-luge.com; ℰ **04-79-08-78-68**), or live the high life at **Le Strato's piano bar** (www.hotelstrato.com; ℰ **04-79-41-51-80**).

For a big afternoon out, or a dancing break between ski sessions, **La Folie Douce** (www.lafoliedouce.com; ℰ **04-79-00-58-31**) is the place to be seen.

CHAMONIX–MONT BLANC ★★★

613km (380 miles) SE of Paris; 82km (51 miles) E of Annecy

At an altitude of 1,027m (3,369 ft.), Chamonix is the historic capital of Alpine skiing. This is the resort to choose if you just so happen to not be a millionaire. Site of the first Winter Olympic Games, in 1924, Chamonix is in a valley almost at the junction of France, Italy, and Switzerland. Skiers the world over know its 20km (12-mile) **Vallée Blanche run,** one of the most rugged, and the longest, in Europe. With exceptional equipment—gondolas, cable cars, and chairlifts—Chamonix is among Europe's major sports resorts, attracting an international crowd with lots of English and Swedish skiers. Thrill seekers also flock here for mountain climbing and hang gliding late May to mid-September. An old-fashioned mountain town, Chamonix has a breathtaking backdrop, **Mont Blanc ★★★**, Western Europe's highest mountain, at 4,734m (15,528 ft.).

The 11km (6.75-mile) **Mont Blanc Tunnel** has made Chamonix a major stop along one of Europe's busiest highways. The tunnel is the easiest way to the mountains to Italy; motorists stop here even if they aren't interested in skiing or mountain climbing. For vehicles originating in France, the round-trip toll for a car and its passengers is 44.40€ one-way, 55.40€ round-trip. The return half of the round-trip ticket must be used within seven days of issue. For information, call ℰ **04-50-55-55-00.**

Chamonix sprawls in a narrow strip along both banks of the Arve River. Its casino, rail, and bus stations, and most restaurants and nightlife are in the town center. Cable cars reach into the mountains from the town's edge. Locals refer to Les Praz, Les Bossons, Les Moussoux, Argentière, and Les Pélerins as satellite villages within greater Chamonix, although, technically, Chamonix refers to only a section around place de l'Eglise.

Essentials

GETTING THERE Most (but not all) **trains** coming from other parts of France or Switzerland require a transfer in such nearby villages as St-Gervais (in France) or Martigny (in Switzerland). Passengers change trains in either of these villages before continuing on by train to Chamonix. Passengers from Aix-les-Bains, Annecy, Lyon, Chambéry, Paris, and Geneva pass through those villages. There are six daily connections from Paris (trip time: 6 hr.); the one-way fare is 91€ to 141€. From Lyon are six relatively complicated rail links per day (trip time: 4 hr.): a one-way fare costs 44€, with transfers at Annecy and St-Gervais. For more information

Mont Blanc

and schedules for trains throughout France, visit www.oui.sncf or call ℰ **36-35** (.40€/min.).

Year-round, two to six **buses** a day run from the Geneva airport; the one-way fare ranges from 19€ to 24€. Buses arrive and depart from a spot adjacent to the railway station. For information, call **Cie S.A.T.** (www. sat-montblanc.com; ℰ **04- 50-78-05-33**).

If you're **driving,** you probably won't have to worry about road conditions. Because Chamonix lies on a main road between Italy and the Mont Blanc Tunnel, conditions are excellent year-round. Even after a storm, roads are quickly cleared. From Paris, follow A6 toward Lyon, and then take A40 toward Geneva. Before Geneva, turn south along A40, which runs to Chamonix.

GETTING AROUND Within Chamonix, a local network of small buses (*navettes,* usually painted yellow and blue) make frequent runs from points in town to many of the *téléphériques* (cable cars) and villages up and down the valley. For information, contact **Chambus** (www.chamonix-bus.com; ℰ **04-50-53-05-55**).

VISITOR INFORMATION Chamonix's **Office de Tourisme** is at 85 pl. du Triangle-de-l'Amitié (www.chamonix.com; ℰ **04-50-53-00-24**).

SKI PASSES To buy passes online, go to www.chamonix.com; many ski offices in the area sell same-day tickets. The ski offices are dotted around Chamonix, for example at the Brevent or Montenvers lift entrances or further afield in Les Houches. Daily ski passes cost 43.50€ for Les Houches only (37€ per child; 134.90 for a family); 52.50€ for Chamonix (43.80€ per child; 134.90 for a family); and 63.50€ (54€ per child; 196.90€ for a family) for "Mont Blanc Unlimited."

Skiing

With the highest mountain in Western Europe, this is an area for the skilled skier. Regrettably, the five main ski areas are not connected by lifts (you must return to the resort and take a different lift to ski a different area), and lines at the most popular areas are the longest in the Alpine world. Weather and snow conditions create crevasses and avalanches that may close sections for days and even threaten parts of the resort.

Skiing is not actually on Mont Blanc, but on the shoulders and slopes across the valley facing the giant. Vertical drops can be spectacular, with lift-serviced hills rising to as high as 3,150m (10,332 ft.). Glacier skiing begins at 3,740m (12,267 ft.). This is not for beginners or timid intermediate skiers, who should head for Les Houches or Le Tour. World-class skiers come here to face the challenges of the high snows of Brévent, La Flégère, and especially Les Grands Montets, a fierce north-facing wall of snow about three city blocks wide.

Exploring Chamonix

The belvederes accessible from Chamonix by cable car or mountain railway are famous. For information, contact **Compagnie du Mont-Blanc,** 35 pl. de la Mer de Glace (www.compagniedumontblanc.fr; ℂ **04-50-53-22-75**).

In town, you can board a cable car for the **Aiguille du Midi** ★★★ and on to Italy—a harrowing full-day journey. The first stage, a 9-min. run to Plan des Aiguilles at an altitude of 2,263m (7,423 ft.), isn't so alarming. But the second stage, to the Aiguille du Midi station at 3,781m (12,402 ft.), may make your heart leap, especially when the car rises 600m (1,968 ft.) between towers. At the summit, you'll be about 100m (328 ft.) from Mont Blanc's peak. You'll have a commanding view of the aiguilles of Chamonix and Vallée Blanche, the largest glacier in Europe (15km/9.25 miles long and 6km/3.75 miles wide), and of the Jura and the French, Swiss, and Italian Alps.

You leave the tram station along a chasm-spanning narrow bridge leading to the third cable car and the glacial fields beyond. Or you can end your journey at Aiguille du Midi and return to Chamonix; this excursion takes half a day. Generally, the cable cars operate year-round: in summer daily 7am to 5pm, leaving at least every 10 min., and in winter daily 8:30am to 3:30pm, leaving every 10 min. The first stage, to Plan de L'Aiguille, is free. The complete round-trip from Chamonix to Aiguille du Midi goes for 49.50€.

You can also cross over high mountains and pass jagged needles of rock and ice bathed in dazzling light. The final trip to **Pointe Helbronner,** Italy—at 3,407m (11,175 ft.)—does not require a passport if you want to leave the station and descend on two more cable cars to the village of Courmayeur. From there, you can go to nearby Entrèves to dine at **La Maison de Filippo** (ℂ **01-65-86-97-97**), a "chalet of gluttony." The round-trip from Chamonix to Pointe Helbronner is 49.50€; the cable car operates from mid-May to mid-October only.

Another cableway takes you up to **Le Brévent ★★★**, at 2,485m (8,151 ft.). From here, you'll have a first-rate view of Mont Blanc and the Aiguilles de Chamonix. The round-trip excursion takes about 1.5 hr. Cable cars operate year-round from 8am to 5pm. Summer departures are at least every 15 min. A round-trip costs 32.50€.

Another journey takes you to **Le Montenvers ★★★** (*©* **04-50-53-12-54**), at 1,883m (6,176 ft.). Access is not by cable car, but on a **rack and pinion railway** known as the **Train Montenvers–Mer de Glace.** It departs from the Gare Montenvers–Mer de Glace, behind Chamonix's Gare SNCF, near the center of town. At the end of the run, you'll have a view of the 6.5km-long (4-mile) *mer de glace* ("sea of ice," or glacier). Immediately east of the glacier, Aiguille du Dru is a rock climb notorious for its difficulty. The trip takes 1.5 hr., including a return by rail. Departures are 8am to 6pm in summer, until 4:30pm in the off season; service usually operates year-round. The round-trip fare is 31.50€.

You can also visit a cave, **La Grotte de Glace,** hollowed out of the *mer de glace;* a cable car connects it with the resort of Montenvers, and the trip takes 3 min. The train, cable car, and visit to the cave cost 24€.

Where to Stay

A large selection of AirBnB options are available in central Chamonix and Les Houches; the value for your money increases quickly as you move down the mountain. Try the picturesque villages of Combloux, Domancy, and St-Gervais-Les-Bains, all less than a 30-min. drive away.

Hôtel Le Faucigny ★★★ This place defines contemporary mountain chic. After a massive renovation, the Le Faucigny promptly set itself apart from the rest of the herd. The common areas boast comfortable sofas flanking natural wood benches and tables scattered about. Rooms are soothing muted greys and simple modern furnishings (think IKEA style, but top quality) and more natural wood accents. The state-of-the-art on-site spa is decked out on oodles of slate and the decadent terrace offers views of the Mont Blanc. Family rooms sleep up to four people so you can maximize your budget. In ski and other busy periods the hotel often requires a 2- or 3-night minimum stay.

118 pl. de l'Eglise. www.hotelfaucigny-chamonix.com. *©* **04-50-53-01-17.** 28 units. 117€–260€ double; 340€ family room. **Amenities:** Bar; spa.

Where to Eat

Bartavel ★ ITALIAN The place is a sporty, informal pizzeria and brasserie. Service is a bit rough, but that's part of its style. Decorated much like a tavern in Italy, this restaurant serves a range of pastas, salads, soups, and rib-sticking platters designed to go well with cold air and high altitudes. Beer and wine flow liberally. Bartavel attracts many outdoor enthusiasts who appreciate its copious portions and reasonable prices.

26 cours du Bartavel. ℂ **04-50-53-97-19.** Main course 16€–30€; pasta and pizzas 9.50€–12€. Daily 11:30am–11:30pm.

Le Chaudron ★ TRADITIONAL FRENCH   You'll find fancier places in town, but for good value, honest cooking, and fine mountain ingredients, Le Chaudron is near the top of our list. Chef Stephan Osterberger cooks in front of you, and you're sure to appreciate his specialties, which include house-style sweetbreads, rabbit stew with juniper berries, and fondues. The cellar is filled with well-chosen wines, including Château Mouton-Rothschild and Château Latour.

79 rue des Moulins. www.le-chaudron-chamonix.com. ℂ **04-50-53-40-34.** Main course 18.50€–34€; fondue savoyarde (min. 2 persons) 19€ each; fixed-price menu 38€. Daily 7–10:30pm. Closed May–June and Oct–Nov.

Restaurant Albert 1er ★★★ MODERN FRENCH   This stalwart features a trio of cozily decorated dining rooms, with bay windows opening onto views of Mont Blanc and walls accented by rustic artifacts and antique farm implements. Begin with a broth (*fumet*) of wild mushrooms garnished with ravioli stuffed with foie gras. Main courses include bison steak with green-peppercorn sauce, superb pan-fried scallops with risotto and lobster sauce, and foie gras with truffled chicken rillettes. In summer, dine alfresco in the garden with a Petite Fête Gourmande du Marché, a small gourmet festival of the market.

In the Hameau Albert 1er hotel, 38 rte. du Bouchet. www.hameaualbert.fr. ℂ **04-50-53-05-09.** Main course 54€–65€; fixed-price lunch 42€ or dinner 66€–92€. Fri–Mon 12:30–2pm; Thurs–Tues 7:30–9:30pm. Closed mid-May to early June and early Nov to early Dec.

Chamonix Nightlife

Nightlife in Chamonix runs the gamut from classical to riotous. You'll find the most bars and pubs along rue des Moulins and rue Paccard. **Monkey,** 81 pl. Edmond Desailloud (monkeychamonix.com; ℂ **04-50-96-64-34),** is open daily, serving stylish street food such as tacos and burritos washed down with craft beer and agave-based cocktails. Clientele here could include just about anyone, reflecting the changing hordes of skiers and mountaineers who swarm to Chamonix at regular intervals. The **casino,** 12 pl. H.-B.-de-Saussure (www.casino-chamonix.fr; ℂ **04-50-53-07-65**), has slot machines and roulette and blackjack tables.

14

PROVENCE

Kathryn Tomasetti

T he ancient Greeks left their vines, the Romans their monuments, but it was the 19th-century Impressionists who most shaped the romance of Provence today. Cézanne, Gauguin, Chagall, and countless others were drawn to the unique light and vibrant spectrum brought forth by what van Gogh called "the transparency of the air." Modern-day visitors will delight in the region's culture, colors, and world-class museums. And from the markets of the Luberon to the street-eats of buzzing Marseille, they will certainly dine well, too.

Provence, perhaps more than any other part of France, blends past and present with an impassioned pride. It has its own language and customs, and some of its festivals go back to medieval times. The region is bounded on the north by the Dauphine River, on the west by the Rhône, on the east by the Alps, and on the south by the Mediterranean. In chapter 15, we focus on the part of Provence known as the Côte d'Azur, or the French Riviera.

AVIGNON ★★★

691km (428 miles) S of Paris; 83km (51 miles) NW of Aix-en-Provence; 98km (61 miles) NW of Marseille

In the 14th century, Avignon was the capital of Christendom. What started as a temporary stay by Pope Clement V in 1309, when Rome was deemed too dangerous even for clergymen, became a 67-year golden age. The cultural and architectural legacy left by the six popes who served during this period makes Avignon one of Europe's most alluring medieval destinations.

Today this walled city of some 95,000 residents is a major stop on the route from Paris to the Mediterranean. In recent years, it has become known as a cultural center, thanks to its annual international performing-arts festivals and wealth of experimental theaters and art galleries.

Essentials

ARRIVING Frequent TGV **trains** depart from Paris's Gare de Lyon. The ride takes 2 hr., 40 min. and arrives at Avignon's modern TGV station 10 min. from town by shuttle bus. The one-way fare is around 80€ depending on the date and time, although it can also be as cheap as 25€ if booked well in advance. Regular trains arrive from Marseille (trip time: 60 min.;

PREVIOUS PAGE: **Lavender field in Valensole, Provence**

Provence

493

15€ one-way) and Arles (trip time: 20 min.; 8€ one-way), arriving at either the TGV or Avignon's central station. Hourly trains from Aix-en-Provence (trip time: 20 min.; 25€ one-way) shuttle exclusively between the two towns' TGV stations. For rail information, visit www.oui.sncf or call ✆ **36-35** (.40€/min). The regional **bus** routes (www.info-ler.fr; ✆ **08-21-20-22-03**) go from Avignon to Arles (trip time: 1 hr., 10 min.; 7.10€ one-way) and Aix-en Provence (trip time: 1 hr., 15 min.; 17.40€ one-way). The bus station at Avignon is the **Gare Routière,** 5 av. Monclar (✆ **04-90-82-07-35**). If you're **driving** from Paris, take A6 south to Lyon, and then A7 south to Avignon.

VISITOR INFORMATION   The **Office de Tourisme** is at 41 cours Jean-Jaurès (www.avignon-tourisme.com; ✆ **04-32-74-32-74**).

CITY LAYOUT   Avignon's picturesque Old Town is surrounded by 14th-century ramparts. Within the walls is a mix of winding roads, medieval townhouses, and pedestrianized streets. To the west of the city is the Rhône River, and beyond, Villeneuve les Avignon. Just south of the Old Town sits the Gare d'Avignon Centre train station.

SPECIAL EVENTS   The international **Festival d'Avignon** (www.festival-avignon.com; ✆ **04-90-14-14-14**), held for three weeks in July, focuses on avant-garde theater, dance, and music. Tickets are 12€ to 40€. Prices for rooms skyrocket during this period, so book yours well in advance. An edgier alternative festival, the **Avignon OFF** (www.avignonleoff.com; ✆ **04-90-85-13-08**), takes place almost simultaneously in July, with theater performances in various improbable venues.

Getting Around

ON FOOT   All of Avignon's major sights—as well as its infinitely enchanting back streets—are easily accessible on foot. The helpful tourist office's free maps show four easy walking routes, ideal for getting a feel for the city.

BY BICYCLE & MOTOR SCOOTER   The **Vélopop** bicycle-sharing scheme (www.velopop.fr; from 1€ per day) lets registered riders borrow any of the city's 200 bikes for up to 30 min. at a time for free. To get out of town and explore the surrounding countryside, **Provence Bike,** 7 av. St-Ruf (www.provence-bike.com; ✆ **04-90-27-92-61**), rents different models for around 12€ to 40€ per day. It's possible to reserve a bike online.

BY CAR   Traffic and a labyrinthine one-way system means it's best to park once you've arrived in Avignon's town center. Around the city are seven fee-paying parking lots and two free ones.

BY TAXI   **Taxis Avignon** (www.seeprovence.com/taxis/avignon-city-taxis-avignon-656923; ✆ **04-90-82-20-20**).

BY PUBLIC TRANSPORT   Eco-friendly **Baladine** vehicles (www.tcra.fr; Mon–Sat 10am–12:30pm and 2–6pm; July–Aug daily 10am–8pm) zip around within the city walls for 0.50€ per ride.

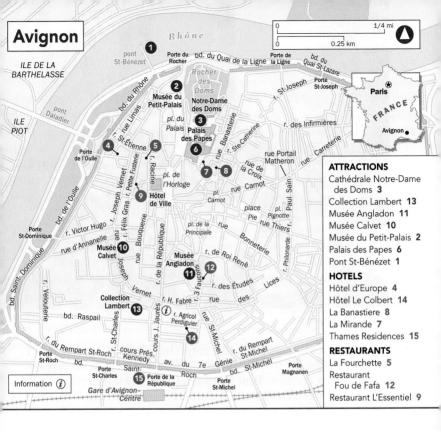

Avignon

Rhône

ILE DE LA
BARTHELASSE

ILE
PIOT

ATTRACTIONS
Cathédrale Notre-Dame
  des Doms **3**
Collection Lambert **13**
Musée Angladon **11**
Musée Calvet **10**
Musée du Petit-Palais **2**
Palais des Papes **6**
Pont St-Bénézet **1**

HOTELS
Hôtel d'Europe **4**
Hôtel Le Colbert **14**
La Banastiere **8**
La Mirande **7**
Thames Residences **15**

RESTAURANTS
La Fourchette **5**
Restaurant
  Fou de Fafa **12**
Restaurant L'Essentiel **9**

[FastFACTS] AVIGNON

ATMs/Banks   Avignon's town center is home to banks aplenty, including three along cours Jean-Jaurès.

Doctors & Hospitals   **Hôpital Général Henri Default,** 305 rue Raoul Follereau (www.ch-avignon.fr; ✆ **04-32-75-33-33**).

Internet Access   **Cyberphone,** 16 rue Paul Pamard (✆ **04-90-25-65-50**).

Mail & Postage   **La Poste,** 4 cours Président Kennedy (✆ **36-31**).

Pharmacies   **Pharmacie des Halles,** 52 rue Bonneterie (✆ **04-90-82-54-27**).

Exploring Avignon

Avignon is undoubtedly one of the prettiest towns in France. From its impressively imposing skyline to the verdant Ile de la Barthelasse opposite, it's a delight to simply amble along aimlessly, perhaps stopping at a sidewalk cafe or two en route. Countless hidden gems crop up along the way, including the sun-dappled courtyard of the **Hôtel d'Europe** (www.heurope.com). This luxury hotel has been in operation since 1799, welcoming luminaries from Charles Dickens to Jacqueline Kennedy.

Avignon theater festival

Every French child knows the ditty *"Sur le pont d'Avignon, l'on y danse, l'on y danse"* ("On the bridge of Avignon, we dance, we dance"). The bridge in question, **Pont St-Bénézet ★★** (www.palais-des-papes. com; ☏ **04-90-27-51-16**), was constructed between 1177 and 1185. Once spanning the Rhône and connecting Avignon with Villeneuve-lèz-Avignon, it is now a ruin, with only four of its original 22 arches remaining (half of it fell into the river in 1669). On the third pillar is the **Chapelle St-Nicolas** (www.avignon-pont.com), its first story in Romanesque style, the second in Gothic. The remains of the bridge are open daily, June 9am to 8pm, August until 8:30pm, March through June, September, and October until 7pm, and November through February 9:30am to 5:45pm. Admission to the bridge is 5€ for adults, 4€ for seniors and students, and free for children 7 and under. Entrance to the chapel is included.

Cathédrale Notre-Dame des Doms ★ CATHEDRAL   Near the Palais des Papes, this majestic 12th-century cathedral contains the elaborate tombs of popes Jean XXII and Benoît XII. Crowning the top is a 19th-century gilded statue of the Virgin. From the cathedral, enter the **Promenade du Rocher-des-Doms** to stroll its garden and enjoy the view across the Rhône to Villeneuve-lez-Avignon.

pl. du Palais des Papes. ☏ **04-90-82-12-21.** Free admission. Daily 8am–6pm. Hours may vary according to religious ceremonies.

Collection Lambert ★★ MUSEUM   This contemporary art space is housed within an 18th-century private home that once belonged to collector and gallery owner Yvonne Lambert. It stages three groundbreaking exhibitions each year. Works may range from video and photography to conceptual installations. Previous exhibitions have included major artists such as Anselm Kiefer, Jenny Holier, and Cy Tomboy, as well as an acclaimed Keith Haring show in 2017.

5 rue Violate. www.collectionlambert.fr. ℰ **04-90-16-56-20.** Admission changes according to exhibition; free for children 5 and under. July–Aug daily 11–7pm; Sept–June Tues–Sun 11–6pm.

Musée Angladon ★★ MUSEUM   Haute-couture designer Jacques Doucet (1853–1929) didn't limit himself to the appreciation of finely cut fabrics. His former home is now a showcase for the international artworks that he and his wife collected over their lifetimes—from 16th-century buddhas and Louis XVI chairs to Degas's famous dancers and canvases by Cézanne, Sisley, and Modigliani. Temporary exhibitions may showcase works by Pierre Bonnard or Henri de Toulouse-Lautrec, while events in 2018 were dedicated to David Hockney and Vincent Van Gogh.

5 rue Laboureur. www.angladon.com. ℰ **04-90-82-29-03.** Admission 8€ adults; 6.50€ students and children ages 13–17; 1.50€ children ages 7–12; free for children 6 and under. Tues–Sat 1–6pm; summer daily.

Musée Calvet ★ MUSEUM   Housed in what was formerly an 18th-century private home, the Musée Calvet is Avignon's top fine art museum. Native son Esprit Calvet bequeathed to the city upon his death a lifetime's worth of acquired art, including works by Verne, David, Corot, Manet,

Pont St-Bénézet

and Soutine, plus a collection of ancient silverware. Recent additions include a garden wing dedicated to local archaeology.

65 rue Joseph-Verne. www.musee-calvet-avignon.com. ℓ **04-90-86-33-84.** Admission 6€ adults; 3€ students; free for children 12 and under. Wed–Mon 10am–1pm and 2–6pm.

Musée du Petit-Palais ★ MUSEUM   An ideal complement to the Palais des Papes' architectural austerity, this museum's artworks were originally part of a collection belonging to 19th-century art lover Giampietro Campania. As a quirk of history, the palace was nationalized and sold off during the French Revolution, and became a secondary school, before reopening as a museum in the 1970s. Today the museum exhibits a myriad of paintings from the Italian and Provençal schools of the 13th to 16th centuries. Botticelli's *Madonna with Child* is a particular highlight.

Palais des Archevêques, pl. du Palais des Papes. www.petit-palais.org. ℓ **04-90-86-44-58.** Admission 6€ adults; 3€ students; free for children 11 and under. Wed–Mon 10am–1pm and 2–6pm.

Palais des Papes ★★★ PALACE   Dominating Avignon from a hilltop is one of the most famous, or notorious, palaces in the Christian world. Headquarters of a schismatic group of cardinals who came close to destroying the authority of the popes in Rome, this fortress is the city's most popular monument. Because of its massive size, you may be tempted

Palais des Papes

to opt for a guided tour—but these can be monotonous. The detailed audio guide, included in the price of admission, will likely suffice. In late 2017 the palace also introduced augmented reality iPad-style tablets (also included in ticket price) which reveal historic incarnations of each room you visit—in all their papal glory.

A highlight is the **Chapelle St-Jean,** known for its frescoes of John the Baptist and John the Evangelist, attributed to the school of Matteo Giovanetti and painted between 1345 and 1348. The **Grand Tinsel (Banquet Hall)** is about 41m (134 ft.) long and 9m (30 ft.) wide; the pope's table stood on the south side. The walls of the **Pope's Bedroom,** on the first floor of the Tour des Anges, are painted with foliage, birds, and squirrels. The frescoes of hunting scenes in the **Studium (Stag Room)**—the study of Clement VI—date from 1343. The **Grande Audience (Great Receiving Hall)** contains frescoes of the prophets, also attributed to Giovanetti and painted in 1352.

Note that the 12th-century **Cathédrale Notre-Dame des Doms cathedral,** just next door on the main square, contains the elaborate tombs of popes Jean XXII and Benoît XII.

Pl. du Palais des Papes. www.palais-des-papes.com. ℂ **04-32-74-32-74.** Admission (including audio guide) 12€ adults; 10€ seniors and students; free for children 7 and under. Daily Nov–Feb 9:30am–5:45pm; Mar 9am–6:30pm; Apr–June and Sept–Oct 9am–7pm; July 9am–8pm; Aug 9am–8:30pm.

OUTLYING ATTRACTIONS IN VILLENEUVE-LEZ-AVIGNON ★

While the popes lived in exile, cardinals built palaces, or *livers,* just across the Rhône in sleepy Villenueve-lez-Avignon. Many visitors prefer to stay or dine here—it's quieter and less modernized, while still convenient to Avignon's major attractions. Take bus no. 5, which crosses the larger of the two relatively modern bridges, the **Pont Daladier.**

Avignon's **Office de Tourisme** can provide further information, as can the local branch in place Charles David (www.tourisme-villeneuve lezavignon.fr; ℂ **04-90-25-61-33**).

Musée Pierre de Luxembourg (Musée de Villeneuve-lez-Avignon) ★ ART MUSEUM Villeneuve's most important museum occupies a 14th-century "urban palace" constructed for a local cardinal. Since its designation as a museum in 1986, it's been the richest repository of medieval painting and sculpture in the region. The remarkable *Coronation of the Virgin,* by Enguerrand Charonton, painted in 1453, depicts the denizens of hell supplicating the eternally calm mother of Christ. Equally important is a rare 14th-century ivory statue of the Virgin by an unknown sculptor; it's one of the finest of its type anywhere. For French speakers, in-depth tours courtesy of knowledgeable guides are available at 3€ per person.

2 rue de la République. www.museepierredeluxembourg.gard.fr. ℂ **04-90-27-49-66.** Admission 3.80€ adults; free for children 18 and under. Mar–Oct Tues–Sun 10am–12:30pm and 2–6pm; Nov–Dec and Feb 2–5pm. Closed Jan, Nov 1, Nov 11, Christmas, and Dec 26.

St-André Abbey Gardens ★★ GARDENS   Clustered around the 17th-century Benedictine Abbaye St-André, these spectacular gardens include a rose-trellis colonnade, fountains flecked with lily pads, and an olive orchard. They also offer unbeatable views over the Rhône Valley and Avignon's skyline beyond. Fort St-André (separate entrance fee, 5.50€), founded in 1360 by Jean-le-Bon to serve as a symbol of might to the pontifical powers across the river, is adjacent to the monastery.

Fort Saint-André, rue Montée du Fort. www.abbayesaintandre.fr. ✆ **04-90-25-55-95.** Admission 7€ adults; 6€ students and ages 13–18; free for children 12 and under. Mar and Oct Tues–Sun 10am–1pm and 2–5pm, Apr 10am–1pm and 2–6pm, May–Sept 10am–6pm. Closed Nov–Feb.

Tour Philippe le Bel ★ RUINS   Philippe the Fair built this tower in the 13th century, when Villeneuve became a French possession; it was a gateway to the kingdom. If you have the stamina, climb to the top for a view of Avignon and the Rhône Valley.

Rue Montée-de-la-Tour. ✆ **04-32-70-08-57.** Admission 2.60€ adults; free for children 18 and under. May–Oct Tues–Sun 10am–12:30pm and 2–6pm; Nov–Apr Sun 2–5pm. Closed May 1 and Nov 1 and 11.

Val de Bénédiction Chartreuse ★ MONASTERY   France's largest Carthusian monastery, built in 1352, comprises a church, three cloisters, cells that housed the medieval monks, and a 12th-century graveyard where Pope Innocent VI is entombed. Part of the complex houses the *Centre National d'Ecritures du Spectacle,* a residence for artists and playwrights who live rent-free for up to a year to deepen their crafts. Art exhibitions, concerts, and theater take place throughout the year.

58 rue de la République. www.chartreuse.org. ✆ **04-90-15-24-24.** Admission 9€ adults; 5.50€ students and under 25; free for children 17 and under. Apr–Sept daily 9:30am–6:30pm; Oct–Mar daily 10am–5pm.

Where to Stay

For travelers on a budget, the friendly **Hôtel Le Colbert** (www.avignon-hotel-colbert.com) is an excellent town center option.

La Banasterie ★   This oh-so-pretty B&B is situated in a 16th-century property just opposite the Palais des Papes. It's owned by gregarious chocolate lover Tanguy—and his candy-fueled passion permeates throughout, from the Nespresso coffee machines to the Missoni bath products. The traditionally decorated bedrooms (exposed stone walls, sumptuous fabrics) are named for varieties of chocolate, and decadent cups of cocoa are on offer at bedtime. Four living rooms throughout the building are decked out in Hermès textiles and designer furnishings. The indulgent breakfast alone (included in the rate) makes this spot unmissable. Note that there is no elevator.

11 rue de la Banasterie. www.labanasterie.com. ✆ **06-87-72-96-36.** 5 units. 125€–175€ double; 165€–245€ suite. Parking 10€. **Amenities:** Free Wi-Fi.

La Mirande ★★★   La Mirande was once a 14th-century cardinal's palace from the adjoining Palais des Papes. It now boasts an additional 7 centuries of fixtures and features in one gloriously palatial package. The hotel's owners are not from the hotel industry, and it shows. Guestrooms are no-expense-spared collections of locally sourced antique furniture, Carrara marble, authentic Chinoiserie, and Murano chandeliers. The courtyard chairs, for example, used to belong in the Musée d'Orsay in Paris. Yet traditional meets modernity at every turn. Head chef Florent Pietravalle proposes a 5-course, completely vegan menu every day, alongside seasonal and organic ingredients sourced from local meat and vegetable producers. All-organic afternoon tea—featuring homemade madeleines, thick hot chocolate, and kombucha—is served daily on the patio or terrace.

4 pl. de l'Amirande. www.la-mirande.fr. ✆ **04-90-14-20-20.** 27 units. 290€–540€ double. Parking 25€. **Amenities:** Restaurant; bar; concierge; room service; free Wi-Fi.

ALTERNATIVE ACCOMMODATIONS

Thames Résidences ★★   This handful of suites and superbly equipped apartments lies a short stroll from both the train station and Avignon's city center. Decor is Provençal-themed, and each room boasts either its own private balcony or panoramic views over the town's medieval ramparts. As well as speedy Wi-Fi and unlimited free telephone calls abroad, some of the residences also possess kitchenettes and sleek Nespresso espresso machines. Host Philippe is also a mine of information on local restaurants and sights. *Note:* Apartments may also be rented (at a discount) by the week.

36 bd. Saint Roch. www.thames-residences.com. ✆ **04-32-70-17-01.** 9 units. 169€–259€ 2-person apartments. Free parking. **Amenities:** Free Wi-Fi.

Where to Eat

La Fourchette ★★ PROVENÇAL   Set a block back from the bustling place de l'Horloge, this upscale bistro has been a local favorite since it opened its doors in 1982. Philippe Hilly, the sixth generation in his family's long line of chefs, dishes up a cuisine that's sophisticated yet hearty on a short no-nonsense menu: Think saffron-infused salt cod *brandied* and served with crusty bread, or ravioli of Provençal *brousse* cheese atop a saffron-spinach bed. Walls are adorned with an eclectic collection of antique cutlery (*la fourchette* translates as "the fork"), making the ambience as alluring as the food. Just don't drop by at the weekend: The restaurant is closed Saturday and Sunday.

17 rue Racine. www.la-fourchette.net. ✆ **04-90-85-20-93.** Main course 21€; fixed-price menu 38€. Mon–Fri 12:15–1:45pm and 7:15–9:45pm. Closed 3 weeks in Aug.

Restaurant Fou de Fafa ★★ FRENCH/PROVENÇAL   It may be British-owned, but this cozy little restaurant dishes up authentic local cuisine—often with a contemporary twist—that truly hits its mark. Delicious combinations may include pear and Roquefort salad with caramelized walnuts, or sea bream in saffron cream paired with Camargue rice. Be sure to save space for desserts, including the definitively non-French but delightful banoffee pie. *Note:* The monthly menu is very short and highly seasonal.

17 rue des Trois Falcons. ℂ **04-32-76-35-13.** Fixed-price menu 27€–33€. Tues–Sat 6:30–11pm. Closed Dec–Jan.

Restaurant L'Essentiel ★★ PROVENÇAL   When hotel concierges recommend an offbeat place to eat, they insist on this relaxed eatery inside an ancient family home. The mini menu at L'Essentiel shouts France at every turn: Seared back of cod with shallots and fennel oil, or a beef cheek slow-cooked in red wine. Somewhat lighter, seasonal fare is served on the courtyard terrace in summer.

2 rue Petite Fusterie. www.restaurantlessentiel.com. ℂ **04-90-85-87-12.** Main course 19€–24€; fixed-price menus 36€–48€. Tues–Sat noon–2pm and 7–9:45pm.

Shopping

The chain boutique **Souleiado,** 19 rue Joseph-Verne (ℂ **04-90-86-32-05**), sells reproductions of 18th- and 19th-century Provençal fabrics by the meter or made into clothing and linens. It is also has a large selection of housewares and gifts.

Hervé Baume, 19 rue Petite Fusterie (ℂ **04-90-86-37-66**), is the place to buy a Provençal table—or something to put on it. A massive inventory includes French folk art and hand-blown hurricane lamps. **Jaffier-Parsi,** 42 rue des Fourbisseurs (ℂ **04-90-86-08-85**), is known for copper saucepans from the Norman town of Villedieu-les-Poêles, which has been making them since the Middle Ages.

A covered market with 40 different merchants is **Les Halles,** pl. Pie, open Tuesday through Sunday (6am–1:30pm). The **flower market** is on place des Carmes on Saturday (8am–1pm), and the **flea market** occupies the same place each Sunday morning (6am–1pm).

Nightlife

Avignon's beautiful people frequent **Les Ambassadeurs,** 27 rue Braincase (www.clublesambassadeurs.fr; ℂ **04-90-86-31-55**), an upscale dance club. For wine **Le Bar à Vin,** part of the **Carré du Palais** (www.carredupalais.fr; ℂ **04-65-00-01-01**) viticulture school that opened in 2017, is by far the best bet in town. Purchase a 20€ *carte de dégustation* (a credit card pre-loaded with wine credit), then pour one of 50 wines by the glass from an electronic kiosk. The stunning city center establishment hosts 700 other vintages, plus a wine-centric **Bistrot** that serves a 3-course lunch for 29€. **83 Verne,** 83 rue Joseph Vernet (www.83vernet.com; ℂ **04-90-85-99-04**), switches from restaurant into dance club mode around 10pm, under the high-ceilinged hallways and stone courtyards of a former 1363 Benedictine convent.

Behind the Hôtel d'Europe, disco-bar **L'Esclave,** 12 rue du Limas (ℂ **04-90-85-14-91**), is a focal point of the city's gay scene.

DAY TRIPS FROM AVIGNON

Orange ★

31km (19 miles) N of Avignon

Antiquities-rich Orange was not named for citrus fruit, but as a dependency of the Dutch House of Orange-Nassau during the Middle Ages. It is home to two UNESCO World Heritage sites: Europe's third-largest **triumphal arch** and its best-preserved **Roman theater.** Louis XIV, who once considered moving the theater to Versailles, claimed: "It is the finest wall in my kingdom." The Théâtre Antique is now the site of **Les Choragi's d'Orange** (www.choregies.fr), a summertime opera and classical music festival.

Just 10km (6 miles) south along the D68 is **Châteauneuf-du-Pape,** a prestigious appellation known for its bold red wines. Spend an afternoon visiting the village's numerous tasting rooms, winding your way up to the ruins of a castle that served as a summer residence for Pope John XXII.

ESSENTIALS

Trains (trip time: 20 min.; www.oui.sncf; ✆ **36-35** at .40€/min.; 8.50€ one-way) and **buses** (www.sudest-mobilites.fr; ✆ **04-32-76-00-40;** trip time: 1 hr.; 2.10€ one-way) connect Avignon and Orange. If you're **driving** from Avignon, take A7 north to Orange. The **Office de Tourisme** is at 5 cours Aristide-Briand (www.otorange.fr; ✆ **04-90-34-70-88**).

EXPLORING ORANGE & AROUND

The carefully restored **Théâtre Antique ★★★**, rue Madeleine Roch (www.theatre-antique.com; ✆ **04-90-51-17-60;** daily Nov–Feb 9:30am–4:30pm; Mar and Oct until 5:30pm; Apr, May, and Sep 9am–6pm; June–Aug 9am–7pm), dates from the days of Augustus. Built into the side of a hill, it once held 9,000 spectators in tiered seats. It stands at nearly 105m (344 ft.) long and 37m (121 ft.) high. Admission (which includes a free audio guide) is 9.50€ adults, 7.50€ students and children 8 to 17, and free for children 7 and under.

Across the street, at the site of a ruined temple, the **Musée d'Art et d'Histoire d'Orange,** pl. du Théâtre-Antique (✆ **04-90-51-17-60**), displays paintings, friezes, and artifacts from local archaeological digs. A ticket to the theater also admits you to the museum. Hours are October to March 9:45am to 12:30pm and 13:30 to 4:30pm (Mar and Oct until 5:30pm); April, May, and September 9am to 6pm; and June to August 9am to 7pm.

The imposing **Arc de Triomphe ★**, av. de lark-de-Triomphe, comprises a trio of arches held up by Corinthian columns embellished with military and maritime emblems. Also built during the reign of Augustus, it was once part of the original town's fortified walls.

The hilltop park on the **Colline St-Eutrope,** accessible by stairs behind the theater, offers a panoramic view of Orange and the surrounding landscape.

WHERE TO EAT

At **Au Petit Patio,** 58 cours Aristide Briand (✆ **04-90-29-69-27**), contemporary Provençal cuisine is served on a petite outdoor terrace. Sample honey-glazed sea bass or summery strawberry tartare. Market-fresh menus start at 19€; open Monday to Saturday for lunch, Monday, Tuesday, Friday, and Saturday for dinner.

Vaison-la-Romaine ★★

50km (31 miles) NE of Avignon

Part medieval village, part Roman ruins, and all crowned by a 13th-century castle, Vaison-la-Romaine sits in the fertile northern reaches of Provence. Well off this region's traditional tourist trail, the combination of history and low-key allure makes for an exquisite escape. To the east of Vaison-la-Romaine towers Mont Ventoux, a monolith of a mountain (1,900m/6,300 ft.) famed for its bogeyman role in the annual Tour de France cycle race.

ESSENTIALS

Frequent **trains** (trip time: 20 min.; www.oui.sncf; ✆ **36-35** at .40€/min.); 6.40€ one-way) connect Avignon and Orange. From Orange, hop aboard bus no. 4 (www.vaucluse.fr; trip time: 45 min.; 2€ one-way). If you're **driving** from Avignon, take A7 north, veering northeast onto D977.

The **Office de Tourisme** is at place du Chanoine Sauté (www.vaison-ventoux-tourisme.com; ✆ **04-90-36-02-11**).

Cyclists climb Mont Ventoux in the Tour de France

SHOPPING FOR brocante IN PROVENCE

In France, there's a wide gap between true antiques and old knickknacks, and it's wise to know the difference. For serious purchases, stick to well-established *antiquaires,* found in almost every town and city. If you're looking for more affordable treasures and enjoy flea markets, what you really want is a *brocante.* These are usually held outside on specific days (the markets in Cannes are a good example; see chapter 15). Furniture and objects can also be found in warehouses known as *depot-ventes.*

A village that specializes in *brocante* is **Isle-sur-la-Sorgue,** situated 23km (14 miles) east of Avignon, 11km (6.75 miles) north of Cavaillon, and 42km (26 miles)

south of Orange. The **Déballage Brocante** is held on Sundays; the activity starts at 9am and finishes around 6pm. From 8am to 2pm, there's also a Provençal food market. If you're driving, try for a parking space in the Parking Portalet or Parking Allele des Muriers (both free). The *brocante* is concentrated in the southern part of town, where you'll find warehouses filled with dealers and loot—although plenty of small stalls are dotted throughout the pedestrianized town center, too.

Isle-sur-la-Sorgue's **Office de Tourisme** is at place de la Liberté (www.oti-delasorgue.fr; $\mathcal{C}$ **04-90-38-04-78**).

EXPLORING VAISON-LA-ROMAINE & AROUND

Ancient capital to the Voconce people, Vaison-la-Romaine is home to two important archaeological sites, **Puymin** and **La Vilasse** (www.provence romaine.com; $\mathcal{C}$ **04-90-36-50-48**). Both are peppered with ancient Roman residences, the remains of thermal baths, statues, and mosaics. The sites are open daily November, December, and February 10am to noon and 2 to 5pm; March and October 10am to 12:30pm and 2 to 5:30pm; April and May 9:30am to 6pm; and June to September 9:30am to 6:30pm. From January to early February both sites are closed. Admission (which includes a free audio guide and is valid for 24 hr.) is 9€ adults, 4€ students and children 12 to 18, and free for children 11 and under.

For more detailed information about Vaison-la-Romaine's history, visit the **Musée Archéologique Théo Desplans,** located within Puymin (entrance valid with same ticket, same opening hours), which focuses on local and regional discoveries.

The oldest part of Vaison-la-Romaine itself—the Cité Médiévale—is a medieval wonderland, crisscrossed by winding alleyways and splashed with pretty squares. To the south sits its **Roman bridge,** dating from the 1st century A.D., which spans the Ouvèze River. If possible, time your visit to coincide with the town's superb regional market (Tues, 8am–1pm, held around town).

Every three years, Vaison-la-Romaine holds the 10-day **Chorales,** or Choral Festival, in August (www.choralies.fr, next edition 2019). Visitors also descend on the town annually for **Vaison Dances** (www.vaison-danses. com), a prestigious dance festival held every July.

WHERE TO EAT

Head to **Restaurant le Bateleur,** pl. Théodore Subpanel (www.restaurant-lebateleur.com; ☎ **04-90-36-28-04;** Wed–Sun lunch 12:15pm or dinner 7:30pm; during high season, also Sun and Tues lunch and Tues dinner) for one of their seasonal lunchtime menus (two courses for 19€). The cuisine makes the most of local ingredients, from wild mushrooms and Mediterranean bonito to free-range chicken from nearby Monteux and heirloom tomatoes.

GORDES ★★★

720km (446 miles) S of Paris; 38km (24 miles) E of Avignon; 77km (48 miles) N of Aix-en-Provence; 92km (57 miles) N of Marseille

Hilltop Gordes is a supremely chic rocky outcrop deep in Provence. From afar, this gorgeous *village perches* (perched village) is a pastiche of beiges, grays, and terra cotta that blushes golden at sunrise and sunset. The place also served as a backdrop for the love affair between Marion Cotillard and Russell Crowe in the movie "A Good Year."

Essentials

ARRIVING Gordes is difficult to reach via public transportation. The closest train station is Cavaillon, where trains arrive from Avignon's central station (trip time: 35 min.; www.oui.sncf; ☎ **36-35** .40€/min.; 7€ one-way). From here, bus no. 15.3 departs three times daily for place du Château in Gordes (www.sudest-mobilites.fr; trip time: 35 min.; 2€ one-way). Another option is to take a 1-day coach tour from either Avignon or Aix-en-Provence. **Autocars Lieutaud** (www.excursionprovence.com; ☎ **04-90-86-36-75;** from 55€ per person) offers this service in Avignon, as does the Aix-en-Provence tourist office (www.aixenprovencetourism.com; ☎ **04-42-16-11-61;** from 60€ per person). By car, Gordes is a 38km (24-mile) drive east of Avignon via D900.

Gordes

VISITOR INFORMATION The **Office de Tourisme** is at Le Château (www.gordes-village.com; ☎ **04-90-72-02-75**).

[FastFACTS] GORDES

Mail & Postage   **La Poste,** pl. du Jehu de Boules (✆ **36-31**). Note that the post office also offers an ATM.

Pharmacies   **Pharmacie de Gordes,** 2 rue de l'Eglise (✆ **04-90-72-02-10**).

Exploring Gordes

Gordes is best explored on foot. Its primarily pedestrianized streets unwind downhill from the Château de Gordes, the Renaissance rehabilitation of a 12th-century fortress. Its windows still bear grooves from bows and arrows used to protect Gordes during Gallo-Roman times, when it was a border town. Today Gordes is more likely to be invaded by easels. Its austere beauty has drawn many artists, including Marc Chagall and Hungarian painter Victor Vasarely, who spent summers here gathering inspiration for his geometric abstract art.

Caves du Palais St. Firming ★ RUINS   Steep Gordes lacks an abundance of surface area, so early settlers burrowed into the rock itself, creating an underground network of crude rooms and stairways over seven levels. Over the centuries, these rooms have housed the village's production of olive oil and grain. Though the tunnels are adequately lit, children are provided with a small headlamp to let them feel like true explorers. The views from the cave gardens are immense.

Rue du Belvédère. www.caves-saint-firmin.com. ✆ **04-90-72-02-75.** Admission 6€ adults; 4.50€ students and children ages 5–15; free for children 4 and under. Free audio guide. May–Sept Wed–Mon 10am–6pm. Oct–Apr by reservation only.

Château de Gordes ★ HISTORIC HOME/ART MUSEUM   Access to the ancient château is reserved for visitors of its small museum, dedicated to contemporary Flemish painter Pol Mara (1920–98), a former resident of Gordes. More than 200 of the artist's works are on display, along with temporary shows. As one might expect, the castle grants spectacular panoramas over Gordes and the surrounding countryside.

Pl. Genty Pantaly. ✆ **04-90-72-98-64.** Admission 4€ adults; 3€ children 10–17; free for children 9 and under. Daily 10am–1pm and 2–6:30pm.

Outlying Attractions

Abbaye Nôtre Dame de Sénanque ★★★ MONASTERY   One of the prettiest sights in the Luberon—indeed, in all of Provence—is the Abbaye Nôtre Dame de Sénanque, even more so when the lavender is in bloom. Five kilometers (3 miles) down the road from Gordes, it was built by Cistercian monks in 1148. Just a handful of monks continue to live on the premises today. The structure is noted for its simple architecture and unadorned stone—though standing in a sea of lavender purple, from June to late July, it's dramatic indeed. The walk from the car park is arduous if stunningly beautiful, as it winds through lavender plants and plane trees.

THE LAST HOME OF albert camus

Author of "The Stranger," among many other works, Algerian-born Albert Camus (1913–60) moved to France at the age of 25. Member of the French Resistance, political journalist, and philosopher, he was awarded the Nobel Prize for Literature in 1958 "for his important literary production, which with clear-sighted earnestness illuminates the problems of the human conscience in our times."

That same year, drawn by its "solemn and austere landscape despite its bewildering beauty," Camus and his wife moved to Lourmarin, 30km (18 miles) southeast of Gordes along D36. Just two years later, Camus was killed in a car accident near Paris. According to his wishes, he was buried in Lourmarin's cemetery.

In 1999, former French president Nicolas Sarkozy—with whom Camus would have had little in common philosophically or politically—proposed moving the writer's ashes to the Pantheon in Paris, to rest aside such literary giants as Alexander Dumas, Victor Hugo, and Emile Zola. His descendants politely declined.

A gift shop sells items made by the resident monks, as well as lavender honey.

D177. www.senanque.fr. ✆ **04-90-72-05-86.** Admission 7.50€ adults; 5€ students and ages 19–25; 3€ children 6–18; 20€ families; free for children 5 and under. Hours vary; call or see website.

Village des Bories ★ RUINS   Bories are beehive-shaped dwellings made of intricately stacked stone—and not an ounce of mortar. They date back as far as the Bronze Age and as recently as the 18th century in Provence. An architectural curiosity, their thick walls and cantilevered roofs beg the question: How did they do that? The Village des Bories is the largest group of these structures in the region, comprising 30 huts grouped according to function (houses, stables, bakeries, silkworm farms, and more). Traditional tools are on display, along with an exhibit on the history of dry-stone architecture in France and around the world.

1.5km (1 mile) west of Gordes on the D15. www.levillagedesbories.com. ✆ **04-90-72-03-48.** Admission 6€ adults; 4€ children 12–17; free for children 11 and under. Daily 9am to sundown.

Where to Stay

Domaine de Fontenille ★★★   A château, working vineyard, and farm-to-table dining experience par excellence. Outside nearby Lourmarin, the Domaine de Fontenille was opened in 2015 by the owner of Parisian fashion label Comptoir des Cotonniers—and it shows. Modern art graces the walls. The grounds are manicured to look like a Provençal photoshoot for Vogue. And best of all, guests may stroll the Domaine's 35-hectare (86-acre) all-organic vineyard and farm, then sample the goods in a Michelin-starred restaurant run by the region's hottest young chef.

The price? This isn't St Tropez, so rates are far keener than you might expect.

Route de Roquefraiche, Lauris. www.domainedefontenille.com. ℂ **04-13-98-00-00.** 17 units. 158€–264€ double; 318€–454€ suite, breakfast included. Free parking. **Amenities:** Restaurant; bar; outdoor pool; free Wi-Fi.

La Ferme de la Huppe ★★ This combination bed-and-breakfast, and its superb Provençal restaurant (also open to non-guests), spills over a pristinely renovated 18th-century farmhouse, with a handsome and recently renovated swimming pool area. Country-style guest rooms are named after their former functions, such as Hay Loft or Wine Cellar, and all boast cute modern bathrooms. An abundant buffet breakfast (croissants, fresh juices, local cheeses) is served on the poolside terrace. La Ferme's location, just down the road from Gordes itself, makes it perfectly positioned for exploring the wider Luberon region, including the gorgeous villages of Bonnieux and Roussillon.

R.D. 156, Les Pourquiers. www.lafermedelahuppe.com. ℂ **04-90-72-12-25.** 10 units. 145€–225€ double. Breakfast included; half-board available. Free parking. Closed Nov–Feb. **Amenities:** Restaurant; outdoor pool; free Wi-Fi.

Hotel Le Petit Palais d'Aglaé ★ A timeless stone mas (Provençal farmhouse) reopened as a charming inn with 16 boutique bedrooms in 2016. Like many establishments in this foodie corner of Provence, it

Sénanque Abbey and lavender fields

offers half-board deals at its seasonal restaurants, where the ingredients are mostly sourced from the hotel's organic garden. Rooms are a little too 21st-century, given the historic setting, in our opinion. Finally, the valley views from the infinity pool perched over a cliff face are immense.

Route de Murs. www.petitpalaisdaglae-gordes.com.com. ✆ **04-32-50-21-02.** 10 units. 155€–276€ double. Half-board available. Free parking. Closed Nov–Feb. **Amenities:** Restaurant; outdoor pool; free Wi-Fi.

Where to Eat

L'Artegal ★ PROVENÇAL A standout venue among Gordes' handful of eateries, this family-run restaurant prides itself on its creative local cuisine. Well-conceived dishes include lentil and salmon tartare or rich lamb stew. At lunchtime, salads are the order of the day, topped with seasonal asparagus and melon from nearby Cavaillon, or the restaurant's own generous adaptation of duck-heavy *salade Landaise.* Tucked into the shadow of the Château de Gordes, L'Artegal is a romantic spot to dine, particularly in the evening when the town's day-trippers have disappeared.

Pl. du Château. ✆ **04-90-72-02-54.** Main course 17€–26€; fixed-price lunch 28€ or dinner 38€. Thurs–Tues noon–1:45pm; Thurs–Mon 7:15–8:45pm. Closed mid-Jan to mid-Mar.

DAY TRIP FROM GORDES

Gordes is part of the **Parc Naturel Régional du Luberon** (www.parcdu luberon.fr) made up of three mountain ranges and their common valley. Author Peter Mayle brought attention to the area with his "A Year in Provence" series extolling the virtues of picturesque villages such as Bonnieux, Lourmarin, and Menderes, where Mayle restored his first French home. Most of these are within 12km (7.5 miles) of each other, making the Luberon well worth an afternoon's exploration.

For avid cyclists, **Vélo Loisir en Luberon** (www.veloloisirluberon. com) has marked hundreds of kilometers of bike routes throughout the region's vineyards and lavender fields. See the website for maps and rental agencies, as well as a great selection of bucolic dining spots en route.

Roussillon ★

10km (6 miles) E of Gordes

The remarkable town of Roussillon is perched atop undulating terrain, stained by the region's unique ochre earth. Vineyards and forests cleave the countryside, revealing stunning stripes of this natural pigment, each one ranging from amber gold to a deep scarlet. A hundred years ago, dozens of quarries mined the much-coveted Provençal ochre from the surrounding area and used it to add color to paints and textiles.

ESSENTIALS

Two daily **buses** (www.vaucluse.fr; trip time: 30 min.; 1.50€ one-way) connect Gordes and Roussillon. If you're **driving** from Gordes, take D2 east to Roussillon.

The **Office de Tourisme** is at place de la Poste (www.tourisme-pays-roussillonnais.fr; ✆ **04-90-05-60-25**).

EXPLORING ROUSSILLON

Begin with an amble through Roussillon itself. The town's compact center is trimmed by multicolored homes, each facade tinted in warm ochre hues. Every Thursday morning, **place du Pasquier** is given over to a large Provençal market. Then it's time to explore the otherworldly landscape that surrounds the town. Follow the signposts from Roussillon center about a 5-min. walk out of town to the **Sentier des Ocres de Roussillon** (Ochre Footpath), where the remains of century-old quarries expose the neon orange countryside. The footpath is open daily July and August 9am to 7:30pm; June until 6:30pm, May and September 9:30am to 6:30pm; April 9:30am to 5:30pm; March 10am to 5pm; October 10am to 5:30pm; first 2 weeks of November 10am to 4:30pm, mid-November to December and last 2 weeks of February 11am to 3:30pm. Admission is 2.50€ and free for children 9 and under. The short walk takes around 35 min., and the longer walk around 50 min.

WHERE TO EAT

Head to **Le Piquebaure,** Les Estrayas (✆ **04-90-05-79-65;** fixed-price menu 25€–29€; Thurs–Tues lunch and dinner), for a modern take on Provençal classics, such as grilled beef entrecôte, followed by lavender crème brûlée. The seasonal ingredients are locally sourced.

ST-RÉMY-DE-PROVENCE ★

710km (440 miles) S of Paris; 24km (15 miles) NE of Arles; 19km (12 miles) S of Avignon; 10km (6.25 miles) N of Les Baux

Though the physician and astrologer Nostradamus was born here in 1503, most associate St-Rémy with Vincent van Gogh, who committed himself to a local asylum in 1889 after cutting off part of his left ear. *Starry Night* was painted during this period, as were many versions of *Olive Trees* and *Cypresses.*

Come to sleepy St-Rémy not only for its history and sights, but also for an authentic experience of daily Provençal life. The town springs into action on Wednesday mornings, when stalls bursting with the region's bounty, from wild-boar sausages to olives, elegant antiques to bolts of French country fabric, huddle between the sidewalk cafes beneath the plane trees.

Essentials

ARRIVING   A regional bus, the Cartreize, runs four to nine times daily between Avignon's Gare Routière and St-Rémy's place de la République (trip time: 45 min.; 3.80€ one-way). For **bus** information, see www.cartreize.com or call *©* **08-10-00-13-26. Drivers** can head south from Avignon along D571.

VISITOR INFORMATION   The **Office de Tourisme** is on place Jean-Jaurès (www.saintremy-de-provence.com; *©* **04-90-92-05-22**).

[FastFACTS]
ST-RÉMY-DE-PROVENCE

ATMs/Banks   **Société Marseillaise de Crédit,** 10 bd. Mirabeau (*©* **04-90-92-74-00**).

Mail & Postage   **La Poste,** 5 rue Roger Selangor (*©* **36-31**).

Pharmacies   **Pharmacie Cenders,** 4 bd. Mirabeau (*©* **04-32-60-16-43**).

Exploring St-Rémy

St-Rémy's pale stone Old Town is utterly charming. Scattered among its pedestrianized streets are 18th-century private mansions, art galleries, medieval church towers, bubbling fountains, and Nostradamus's birth home. Note that St-Rémy's two major sites (listed below) lie around 1km (0.6 miles) south of the town center.

Saint Paul de Mausole ★ MONASTERY   This former monastery and clinic is where Vincent Van Gogh was confined from 1889 to 1890. It's now a psychiatric hospital for women, which specializes in art therapy. You can't see the artist's actual cell, but there is a reconstruction of his room, which makes for the perfect Instagram update. The Romanesque chapel and cloisters are worth a visit in their own right, as Van Gogh depicted their circular arches and beautifully carved capitals in some of his paintings. Twenty-one reproductions of Van Gogh's paintings from the period he resided here dot a marked path between the town center and the site (east of av. Vincent Van Gogh).

Chemin Saint-Paul. www.saintpauldemausole.fr. *©* **04-90-92-77-00.** Admission 5€ adults; 3.50€ students; free for children 12 and under. Apr–Sept daily 9:30am–6:30pm; Oct–Mar daily 10:15am–4:30pm.

Le Site Archéologique de Galbanum ★★ RUINS   Kids will love a scramble around this bucolically sited Gallo-Roman settlement, which thrived here during the final days of the Roman Empire. Its monuments include a triumphal arch (across the street and separated from the main ruins) from the time of Julius Caesar, all garlanded with sculptured fruits and flowers. Another interesting feature is the baths, which had separate

Courtyard of Saint Paul de Mausole, St-Rémy-de-Provence.

chambers for hot, warm, and cold. Visitors can see entire streets and foundations of private residences from the 1st-century town, plus the remains of a Gallo-Greek town of the 2nd century B.C.

Route des Baux-de-Provence. http://glanum.monuments-nationaux.fr. ℰ **04-90-92-23-79.** Admission 8€ adults; 6.50€ students; free for EU nationals ages 18–25 and children 17 and under. Apr–Sept daily 9:30am–6pm; Oct–Mar Tues–Sun 10am–5pm.

Where to Stay

Château des Alpilles ★★★ A former castle situated at the heart of magnolia-studded parkland, Château des Alpilles was constructed by the Picot family in 1827. Françoise Bon converted the mansion in 1980, creating luxurious double rooms inside the castle itself, with additional private accommodation in the property's former chapel, farmhouse, and washhouse. Decor throughout encompasses a confident mix of antiques (plush upholstery, local artworks) and cool amenities (deep travertine-trimmed bathtubs, smartphone docks). It's 2km (1.25 miles) from the center of St-Rémy, with sprawling grounds that give it the feel of a countryside retreat.

Route de Rougadou. www.chateaudesalpilles.com. ℰ **04-90-92-03-33.** 21 units. 220€–340€ double; 370€–470€ suite; 370€–400€ apartment. Free parking. Closed Jan to mid-Mar. **Amenities:** Restaurant; bar; outdoor pool; room service; sauna; 2 tennis courts; free Wi-Fi.

Mas Serafini ★★★ In 2018 award-winning British restaurateurs Doug and Glen turned their love for France into this fabulous *chambres d'hôtes* homestay. It's set in an organic orchard of lemon trees, apricots,

513

pines, and plane trees, a few minutes' stroll from St-Rémy's buzzing town center. Inside, classic Provence touches and high ceilings pair with contemporary art and Nespresso machines. Guests may also explore the gardens or pour their own rosé from the honesty bar.

Av. Théodore Subpanel. www.mas-serafini.com. ⓒ **04-90-92-82-82.** 4 units. 100€–140€ double. Breakfast included. Free parking. **Amenities:** Bar; free Wi-Fi.

Where to Eat

L'Estagnol ★★ MEDITERRANEAN This popular eatery (which translates as "little pond" in the regional dialect) is owned and operated by the Meynadier family, third-generation restaurateurs. Hearty local cuisine ranges from Camargue bull hamburger topped with goat cheese to Provençal gazpacho with basil sorbet. Dining takes place either in the ancient *orangerie* (private greenhouse) or in the sun-dappled courtyard adjacent. A chalkboard advertises local wine vintages from 3.50€ per glass.

16 bd. Victor Hugo. www.restaurant-lestagnol.com. ⓒ **04-90-92-05-95.** Main course 14€–32€; fixed-price lunch 14.50€ or dinner 27€–34€. Tues–Sun noon–2pm and 7:15–9:30pm.

Shopping

St-Rémy is a decorator's paradise, with many antiques shops and fabric stores on the narrow streets of the Old Town and surrounding boulevards. **Broc de Saint Ouen,** route d'Avignon (ⓒ **04-90-92-28-90**), is a 6,000-sq.-m (64,583-sq.-ft.) space selling everything from architectural salvage to vintage furniture. The town's famous Provençal market is held Wednesday mornings.

Nightlife

Live music bar **Le Rex,** 17 pl. de la République (ⓒ **06-82-11-61-08**), hosts a fabulous selection of Provence wines, many of them organic. It is open Thursday to Saturday from 6pm until 1am.

LES BAUX ★★★

720km (446 miles) S of Paris; 18km (11 miles) NE of Arles; 85km (53 miles) N of Marseille

Les Baux de Provence's location and geology are extraordinary. Cardinal Richelieu called the massive, 245m (804-ft.) high rock rising from a desolate plain "a nesting place for eagles." A real eagle's-eye view of the outcropping would be part moonscape, dotted with archeological ruins and a vast plateau, with boxy stone houses stacked like cards on the rock's east side. The combination is so cinematic that it seems like a living, breathing movie set.

Baux, or *bayou* in Provençal, means "rocky spur." The power-thirsty lords who ruled the settlement took this as their surname in the 11th century, and by the Middle Ages had control of 79 other regional fiefdoms.

Les Baux

After they were overthrown, Les Baux was annexed to France with the rest of Provence, but Louis XI ordered the fortress demolished. The settlement experienced a rebirth during the Renaissance, when structures where restored and lavish residences built, only to fall again in 1642 when, wary of rebellion, Louis XIII ordered his armies to destroy it once and for all. Today the fortress compound is nothing but ruins, but fascinating ones.

Now the bad news: Because of its dramatic beauty, plus a number of quaint shops and restaurants in the village, Les Baux is often overrun with visitors at peak times, so time your visit wisely.

Essentials

ARRIVING   Les Baux is best reached by **car.** From St-Rémy, take D27 south; from Arles, D17 east. Alternatively, on weekends in June and September, and every day during July and August, **bus** no. 59 (35 min.; 2.40€ one-way) runs between Arles and St-Rémy, stopping at Les Baux en route. For bus information, see www.lepilote.com or call ✆ **08-10-00-13-26.** You can also book 1-day coach tours through **Autocars Lieutaud** (www.excursionprovence.com; ✆ **04-90-86-36-75;** from 55€ per person) in Avignon.

VISITOR INFORMATION   The **Office de Tourisme** (www.lesbaux deprovence.com; ✆ **04-90-54-34-39**) is at Maison du Roy, near the northern entrance to the old city.

FAST FACTS   Note that you'll need to head to the nearby town of Maussane-les-Alpilles for access to a bank, pharmacy, or post office.

Exploring Les Baux

Les Baux's windswept ruins, **Château des Baux** ★★★ (www.chateau-baux-provence.com; ℭ **04-90-54-55-56**), cover an area of 7 hectares (17 acres), much larger than the petite hilltop village itself. Consider visiting them early in the morning before the sun gets too strong.

The medieval compound is accessed via the 15th-century **Hôtel de la Tour du Brau.** Beyond this building are replicas of wooden military equipment that would have been used in the 13th century. Built to scale—that is to say, enormous—are a battering ram and various catapults capable of firing huge boulders. From April to August, these are fired every day at 11am and 1:30pm, 3:30pm, and 5:30pm, with an extra show during July and August at 6:30pm. Medieval jousting demonstrations (noon, 2:30, and 4:30pm) are held in summer.

Other stopping points include the **Chapel of St-Blaise** (where you can watch a film of aerial views of Provence) include a windmill, the skeleton of a hospital built in the 16th century, and a cemetery. The **Tour Sarrazin,** so named because it was used to spot Saracen invaders coming from the south, yields a sweeping view. Alongside each of the major points of interest, illustrated panels show what the buildings would have originally looked like and explain how the site has evolved architecturally.

Admission to the Château (including audio guide) is 8€ adults, 6€ children 7 to 17 from September to March. The rest of the year, it costs 10.50€ adults, 8.50€ children 7 to 17 (daily Apr–June and Sept 9am–7:15pm; July and Aug 9am–8:15pm; Mar and Oct 9:30am–6:30pm; Nov–Feb 10am–5pm).

Carrières de Lumières ★★ EXHIBITION SPACE   A 10-min. stroll downhill from Les Baux, this awe-inspiring temporary exhibition space occupies the site of a former limestone quarry. It's here that images of modern artworks (such as audiovisual exhibitions dedicated to Monet, Renoir, Van Gogh, or Gauguin) are projected against the 7m to 9m (23- to 30-ft.) columns. The museum's Cubist-style entrance featured in Jean Cocteau's final film, "The Testament of Orpheus."

Route de Maillane. www.carrieres-lumieres.com. ℭ **04-90-54-47-37.** Admission 12€ adults; 10€ children ages 7–17; free for children 6 and under. Daily Apr–Sept 9:30am–7pm; Oct–Jan and mid- to late Mar 10am–6pm. Closed Feb to mid-Mar.

Yves Brayer Museum ★ ART MUSEUM   Born in Versailles, figurative painter Yves Brayer (1907–90) was enchanted with the landscapes of Provence. This compact museum, located within Les Baux's 16th-century Hôtel de Porcelet, showcases the artist's oils, watercolors, and drawings of everyday life, created during the first half of the 20th century. Each summer, the museum also hosts a small temporary exhibition, such as 2018's homage to Paul Signac, the pointillist who painted St. Tropez.

Intersection of rue de la Calare and rue de l'Eglise. www.yvesbrayer.com. ℭ **04-90-54-36-99.** Admission 5€ adults; free for children 18 and under. Apr–Sept daily

10am–12:30pm and 2–6:30pm; Oct–Dec and Mar Wed–Mon 11am–12:30pm and 2–5pm. Closed Jan and Feb.

Where to Stay & Eat

Baumanière ★★★ PROVENÇAL   Baumanière is the name of the cluster of fabulous inns, guesthouses, and authentically Provençal hotel accommodation dotted around the medieval town. Each section of the diverse hotel boasts kitchen gardens and swimming pools, amid scenes of bucolic bliss reminiscent of a French movie set. In terms of dining, Chef Michel Hulin of **La Cabro d'Or** (set menus 33€–85€) delivers intelligent, innovative Provençal cuisine with a lightness of touch. Diners savor the unctuousness of Mediterranean langoustines, the crispness of roasted red mullet, the froth of fresh pea velouté, and the crunch of slow-cooked suckling pig. The main **Oustau de Baumanière** (set menus 100€–165€) building has hosted the likes of Queen Elizabeth and Johnny Depp and also purveys an even more acclaimed (and more expensive) restaurant than the Cabro d'Or site nearby.

Mas de Baumanière. www.baumaniere.com. ✆ **04-90-54-33-07.** 52 units. 203€–338€; 304€–642€ suite. **Amenities:** Restaurant; bar; outdoor pool; room service; sauna; tennis courts; free Wi-Fi.

ARLES ★★

744km (461 miles) S of Paris; 36km (22 miles) SW of Avignon; 92km (57 miles) NW of Marseille

On the banks of the Rhône River, Arles (pop. 53,000) attracts art lovers, archaeologists, and historians. To the delight of visitors, many of the vistas van Gogh painted remain luminously present today. Here the artist was even inspired to paint his own bedroom (*Bedroom in Arles*, 1888).

Julius Caesar established a Roman colony here in the 1st century. Constantine the Great named Arles the second capital of his empire in A.D. 306, when it was known as "the little Rome of the Gauls." The city was incorporated into France in 1481.

Arles's ancient streets are not as pristinely preserved as, say, Avignon's, but are stunningly raw instead, with excellent restaurants and summer festivals to boot. Its position on the river makes it a gateway to the Camargue, giving the town a healthy dose of Spanish and gypsy influence.

Essentials

ARRIVING   **Trains** run almost every hour between Arles and Avignon (trip time: 20 min.; www.oui.sncf; ✆ **36-35** at .40€/min; 6€ one-way) and Marseille (trip time: 1 hr.; 18€). Be sure to take local trains from city center to city center, not the TGV, which, in this case, takes more time. If **driving,** head south along D570N from Avignon.

VISITOR INFORMATION   The **Office de Tourisme** is on bd. des Lices (www.arlestourisme.com; ℂ **04-90-18-41-20**).

SPECIAL EVENTS   Arles's world-beating photographic event, **Les Recontres d'Arles** (www.rencontres-arles.com; ℂ **04-90-96-76-06**), held from early July until late September, focuses on contemporary international images from nature to warzones. Some exhibitions are free, although passes for all key shows also available from 25€ when booked online. The ticket office is located in place de la République for the duration of the festival.

[FastFACTS] ARLES

ATMs/Banks   Downtown Arles has more than a dozen banks, including three in place de la République.

Internet Access   **CyberSaladelle Informatique Arles,** 17 rue de la République (www.cybersaladelle.fr; ℂ **04-90-93-13-56**).

Mail & Postage   **La Poste,** 5 bd. des Lices (ℂ **36-31**).

Pharmacies   **Pharmacie des Arènes,** 17 rue du 4 Septembre (ℂ **04-90-96-02-77**).

Exploring Arles

The **place du Forum,** shaded by plane trees, stands around the old Roman forum. The Terrace du Café le Soir, immortalized by Van Gogh, is now the square's Café Van Gogh. Visitors keen to follow in the footsteps of the great artist may pick up a **Van Gogh walking map** (1€; available at the tourist office), which takes in 10 important sites around the city. On a corner of place du Forum sits the legendary, if slightly faded, **Grand Hôtel Nord-Pinus** (nord-pinus.com/en/): Bullfighters, artists, and A-listers have all stayed here. Three blocks south, the **place de la République** is dominated by a 15m (49-ft.) tall red granite obelisk.

One of the city's great classical monuments is the Roman **Théâtre Antique** ★, rue du Cloître (ℂ **04-90-49-59-05**). Augustus began the theater in the 1st century; only two Corinthian columns remain. The *Venus of Arles* (now in the Louvre in Paris) was discovered here in 1651. The theater is open May through September daily 9am to 7pm; March, April, and October until 6pm; and November through February daily 10am to 5pm. Admission is 6.50€ adults, 5€ students, and free for children

> ### Les Taureaux
>
> Bulls are a big part of Arlesien culture. It's not unusual to see bull steak on local menus, and *saucisson de taureau* (bull sausage) is a local specialty. The first bullfight, or *corrida*, took place in the amphitheater in 1853. Appropriately, Arles is home to a bullfighting school (the **Ecole Taurine d'Arles**). Like it or loathe it, *corridas* are still held during the Easter Ferias and in September, during the Ferias du Riz.

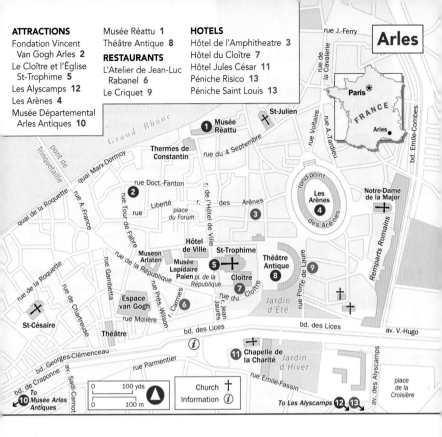

Arles

17 and under. The same ticket admits you to the nearby **Amphitheater (Les Arènes)** ★★, rond-pont des Arènes (✆ **04-90-49-59-05;** same opening hr.), also built in the 1st century. Sometimes called Le Cirque Romain, it seats almost 25,000. For a good view, climb the three towers that remain from medieval times, when the amphitheater was turned into a fortress.

Les Alyscamps ★ RUINS   Perhaps the most memorable sight in Arles, this once–Roman necropolis became a Christian burial ground in the 4th century. Mentioned in Dante's "Inferno," it has been painted by both Van Gogh and Gauguin. Today it is lined with poplars and studded with ancient sarcophagi. Arlesiens escape here with a cold drink to enjoy a respite from the summer heat.

Avenue des Alyscamps. ✆ **04-90-49-59-05.** Admission 3.50€ adults; 2.60€ students; free for children 17 and under. Daily May–Sept 9am–7pm; Mar, Apr, and Oct 9am–noon and 2–6pm; Nov–Feb 10am–noon and 2–5pm.

Le Cloître et l'Eglise St-Trophime ★ CHURCH   This church is noted for its 12th-century portal, one of the finest achievements of the southern Romanesque style. Frederick Barbarossa was crowned king of Arles here in 1178. In the pediment, Christ is surrounded by the symbols

A sidewalk cafe in Arles

of the Evangelists. The pretty cloister, in Gothic and Romanesque styles, possesses noteworthy medieval carvings: During July's Les Recontres d'Arles festival, contemporary photographs are also exhibited here.

East side of pl. de la République. ℂ **04-90-49-59-05.** Free admission to church; cloister 3.50€ adults, 2.60€ students, free for children 17 and under. Church daily 10am–noon and 2–5pm; cloister May–Sept daily 9am–7pm; Mar, Apr, and Oct daily 9am–6pm; Nov–Feb daily 10am–5pm.

Fondation Vincent Van Gogh Arles ★★ EXHIBITION SPACE

This permanent home for the Van Gogh Foundation (founded more than 3 decades ago) is housed in the 15th-century private mansion Hôtel Léautaud de Donines. Highlighting the connection between Arles and Van Gogh, it stages a variety of temporary exhibitions, seminars, and interactive debates. The Foundation's exhibitions included "Soleil chaud, soleil tardif" in 2018: a celebration of 20th century artists including Van Gogh, Pablo Picasso, and Alexander Calder. Check the website for the current program.

35 ter rue du Docteur Fanton. www.fondation-vincentvangogh-arles.org. ℂ **04-90-93-08-08.** Admission 9€ adults; 7€ seniors; 4€ students and children 12–18; free for children 11 and under. Admission may vary depending on temporary exhibition. Daily 11am–6pm (Apr–Oct until 9pm). Closed 3 weeks in Sept.

Musée Départemental Arles Antiques ★★ MUSEUM

Set within a sleek compound around 1km (.5 mile) south of Arles' town center, this archaeological museum has finds uncovered throughout the region's rich territories. Vast, airy rooms present Roman sarcophagi, sculptures, mosaics, and inscriptions from ancient times through the 6th century. Some temporary exhibitions, such as 2017's show dedicated to Egyptian pharaoh Ramesses II, are conducted in collaboration with the Musée du Louvre in Paris.

Avenue 1ere Division France Libra, presqu'île du Cirque Romain. www. avignon-et-provence.com/en/museum/arles-antique-departmental-museum. ℂ **04-13-31-51-03.** Admission 8€ adults; 5€ visitors ages 65 and over; free for children 17 and under. Wed–Mon 10am–6pm.

Musée Réattu ★★ ART MUSEUM

Exhibited over the labyrinthine rooms of the 15th-century Grand Priory of the Order of Malta, this museum opened in 1868 to showcase artworks previously owned by local painter Jacques Réattu. Over the past 150 years, the collection has swollen with donations and annual acquisitions—attracting the likes of prestigious visitors, including Van Gogh in 1888—and now includes dozens of Picasso drawings and close to 4,000 photographs. The building's former archives room is now dedicated to the history of the Order of the Knights Hospitaller. The museum also stages some three temporary exhibitions each year.

10 rue du Grand-Prieuré. www.museereattu.arles.fr. © **04-90-49-37-58.** Admission 8€ adults; 6€ students; free for children 17 and under. Tues–Sun Mar–Oct 10am–6pm, Nov–Feb 10am–5pm.

Outlying Attractions

Abbaye de Montmajour ★★ MONASTERY

This medieval monastery, founded in the leafy countryside 6km (3.5 miles) northeast of Arles during the 10th century, is now an innovative exhibition venue. Temporary shows, ranging from a Christian Lacroix installation to annual photographic displays as part of Les Recontres d'Arles, are dotted throughout the atmospheric ruins. A wonderful outdoor restaurant is tucked under the trees at the back of the parking lot opposite.

Route de Fontvieille. http://montmajour.monuments-nationaux.fr. © **04-90-54-64-17.** Admission 6€ adults; 5€ students; free for children 17 and under. July–Sept daily 10am–6:30pm; Apr–June daily 9:30am–6pm; Oct–Mar Tues–Sun 10am–5pm.

Where to Stay

Hôtel de l'Amphithéâtre ★★

This delightful hotel is a firm favorite with regular visitors to Arles. Tucked into the heart of the Old Town, the main building itself was originally constructed in the 17th century and retains its historical atmosphere, with slightly more modern decor in the building opposite. Guest rooms feature reproduction Provençal furniture

---

Mistral, Two Ways

Born just north of Arles, Frédéric Mistral (1830–1914) dedicated his life to defending and preserving the original Provençal language known as Occitan. The poet won the Nobel Prize for his epic work "Mirèio" and his overall contributions to French literature. Mistral joined six other Provençal writers in 1854 to found Félibrige, an association for the promotion of Occitan language and literature. He is the author of "Lo Tremor *dóu Félibrige*," the most comprehensive dictionary of the Occitan language to this day. Many think Mistral lent his name to the notorious glacial wind that roars through Provence every year. However, in this case, *mistral* is the Occitan word for "master"—and those who experience the phenomenon regularly say it's a cruel one. Tearing through the Rhône River Valley toward the Mediterranean, the mistral reaches speeds of 100km (62 miles) per hour and can blow up to 100 days per year. Most of these occur in winter, but it is also common in the spring and, in unlucky years, can persist until early summer.

and some—including the bright Belvedere Suite, surrounded by windows on all four walls—offer views over the terra-cotta roofs of historic Arles. The hotel frequently proposes discounted rates out of season.

5–7 rue Diderot. www.hotelamphitheatre.fr. ℂ **04-90-96-10-30.** 33 units. 80€–139€ double; 89€–149€ triple; 119€–179€ quadruple; 129€–139€ suite. Parking 8€. **Amenities:** Free Wi-Fi.

Hôtel du Cloître ★★

Perfectly positioned in Arles' Old Town, midway between Les Arènes and place de la République, Hôtel du Cloître is a unique medley of ancient stone features and funky 1950s furnishings. Each room is individually decorated in bright tones, with wooden ceiling beams, mosaic floors, and designer knickknacks. Free bikes are available for guest use, and the communal lounge is packed with tomes on local arts and history. Organic breakfast is served up on the rooftop terrace, alongside views over the city's Saint-Trophime Church.

18 rue du Cloître. www.hotelducloitre.com. ℂ **04-88-09-10-00.** 19 units. 95€–180€ double. Parking 10€. **Amenities:** Bar; free Wi-Fi.

Hôtel Jules César ★★

The colonnaded Hôtel Jules César has long been one of Arles' landmark hotels, with a prestigious guest book that includes Pablo Picasso. The former 17th-century convent has been entirely renovated, a project undertaken in collaboration with born and bred local designer Christian Lacroix. Today, the hotel's rooms and suites are thoroughly refreshed, with Lacroix focusing on rustic decor inspired by the nearby Camargue region. The top-notch Lou Marquès restaurant, serving classic Provençal cuisine, is also on site. The hotel's location, opposite the Old Town and next door to the tourist office, is ideal for easy access to Arles' major sights.

9 bd. des Lices. www.hotel-julescesar.fr. ℂ **04-90-52-52-52.** 52 units. 149€–254€ double; 297€–416€ family-sized suite. Parking 10€. **Amenities:** Restaurant; outdoor pool; free Wi-Fi.

Péniche Risico and Péniche Saint Louis ★★

Péniche are motorized historic barges that once ferried wine and other goods up the Rhône River. Both these boats are permanently moored near the drawbridge that Van Gogh painted in the 1880s, a sleepy 1.6km (1 mile) walk along a leafy canal away from the center of Arles. **Péniche Risico** (www.peniche-risico.com; ℂ **06-03-31-81-18**) was built in Holland in 1911 and is kitted out with funky private bathrooms and a wooden communal sunbathing deck. Double rooms overlook the rippling water and cost just 80€ per night including breakfast. Italian-owned **Péniche Saint Louis** (http://penichearles.jimdo.com; ℂ **06-19-11-81-69**) was built in Germany in 1931. The boat's solitary double room has large glazed windows that peer over the waterway, plus a private bathroom. The rate is 70€ per night including breakfast.

Rue Jean Charcot (both). **Amenities:** Free Wi-Fi.

A day out **IN THE CAMARGUE**

A marshy delta south of Arles, the Camargue is located between the Mediterranean and two arms of the Rhône. With the most fragile ecosystem in France, it has been a nature reserve since 1970. You cannot drive into the protected parts, and some areas are accessible only to the Gardians, the local cowboys. Their ancestors may have been the first American cowboys, who sailed on French ships to the port of New Orleans, where they rode through the bayous of Louisiana and east Texas, rounding up cattle—in French, no less.

The Camargue is also cattle country. Black bulls are bred here both for their meat and for the regional bullfighting arenas. The whitewashed houses, plaited-straw roofs, plains, sandbars, and pink flamingos in the marshes make this area different, even exotic. There's no more evocative sight than the snow-white horses galloping through the marshlands, with hoofs so tough that they don't need shoes. The breed was brought here by the Arabs long ago, and it is said that their long manes and bushy tails evolved over the centuries to slap the region's omnipresent mosquitoes. Exotic flora and fauna abound. The

birdlife here is among the most luxuriant in Europe. Looking much like the Florida Everglades, the area is known for its colonies of pink flamingos *(flamants roses)*, which share living quarters with some 400 other bird species, including ibises, egrets, kingfishers, owls, wild ducks, swans, and ferocious birds of prey. The best place to see flamingo colonies is at the **Parc Ornithologique de Pont de Gau**, D570 (www.parcornithologique. com; © **04-90-97-82-62**), 4km (3 miles), north of Camargue's capital, Stes-Maries-de-la-Mer.

You can explore the Camargue's rugged terrain by boat, bike, jeep, or horse. The latter can take you along beaches and into the interior, fording waters to places where black bulls graze and wild birds nest. Dozens of stables are located along the highway between Arles to Stes-Maries. Virtually all charge the same rate (around 40€ for 2 hr.). The rides are aimed at the neophyte, not the champion equestrian.

For details, visit Arles' Office de Tourisme (p. 518) or head to the **Office de Tourisme**, 5 av. Van Gogh, Ste-Maries-de-la-Mer (www.saintesmaries.com; © **04-90-97-82-55**).

Where to Eat

L'Atelier Jean-Luc Rabanel ★★★ MODERN PROVENÇAL Put simply, this is the finest restaurant that one of the authors of this book has ever had the pleasure of experiencing. And that's saying something. Double-Michelin-starred chef Jean-Luc Rabanel pairs organic ingredients from his own garden with locally reared bull, pork, and game (and even herbs, mushrooms, and flowers). Delivery combines the deftness of touch of a Japanese samurai (an Asian influence pervades Rafael's set menus) with the creative vision of a Parisian fashion designer. A wine-accompaniment option offers a unique and passionate oenophile's tour of France. Wow. The chef also purveys an adjoining restaurant, **Bistro A Côté** (www.bistro-acote.com; © **04-90-47-61-13**), which is softer on the wallet and serves Provençal classics on a 32€ fixed-price menu.

Rabanel also operates his "Suites Confidentielles". This luxury accommodation (designed by the chef) is reserved for guests dining at one of his restaurants. Prices range from 200€ to 295€, with special packages comprising breakfast, dinner and/or lunch also available.

7 rue des Carmes. www.rabanel.com. ✆ **04-90-91-07-69.** Fixed-price lunch 55€–125€ or dinner 95€–185€. Wed–Sun noon–1:30pm and 8–9pm.

Le Criquet ★ MODERN PROVENÇAL   Tiny, charming, and worth reserving well in advance, Le Criquet is a classic local restaurant on the back streets of Arles. Friendly service meets unpretentious dishes like *bourride* of salt cod and spices, duck breast in honey sauce, and stew made from local Camargue bull. Sit outside amid a romantic street setting or in the rather cramped—but with its exposed stone walls, undeniably cozy—interior.

21 rue Porte de Laure. ✆ **04-90-96-80-51.** Main course 13€–22€; fixed-price menus 24€–28€. Tues–Sun noon–1:30pm and 7–9pm.

Nightlife

Because of its relatively small population, Arles doesn't offer as many nightlife options as Aix-en-Provence, Avignon, or Marseille. The town's most appealing spot is the organic wine and tapas bar–cafe **L'Ouvre-Boîte,** 22 rue du Cloître (no phone). Open June to September only, it's set under a majestic canopy of trees in one of the Old Town's loveliest squares.

AIX-EN-PROVENCE ★★

760km (471 miles) S of Paris; 84km (52 miles) SE of Avignon; 34km (21 miles) N of Marseille; 185km (115 miles) W of Nice

One of the most surprising aspects of Aix is its size. Guidebooks frequently proclaim it the very heart of Provence, evoking a sleepy town filled with flowers and fountains, which it is—in certain quarters. But Aix is also a bustling university town of around 143,000 inhabitants (the Université d'Aix dates from 1413).

Founded in 122 B.C. by Roman general Caius Sextius Calvinus, who conveniently named the town Aquae Sextiae, after himself, Aix originated as a military outpost. Aix's most celebrated son, Paul Cézanne, immortalized the Aix countryside in his paintings. Just as he saw it, the **Montagne Sainte-Victoire** looms over the town today.

Time marches on, but there are still plenty of decades-old, family-run shops on the narrow streets of the Old Town. A lazy summer lunch at one of the bourgeois cafes on the **cours Mirabeau** is an experience not to be missed.

Essentials

ARRIVING   **Trains** arrive frequently from Marseille (trip time: 40 min.; 8.30€ one-way) and Nice (trip time: 3 hr.; www.oui.sncf; ✆ **36-35** at .40€/min.; 36€ one-way). High-speed TGV trains—from Paris as well as

Aix-en-Provence

ATTRACTIONS
Atelier de
Cézanne **1**
Cathédrale
St-Sauveur **4**
Musée Granet **10**

HOTELS
Hotel Cézanne **9**
Hotel du Globe **3**
Villa Gallici **2**

RESTAURANTS
Brasserie des
Deux Garcons **8**
Le Mille Feuille **6**
Mickaël Féval **7**
Mitch **5**

Marseille and Nice—arrive at the modern station near Vitrolles, 18km (11 miles) west of Aix. Bus transfers to the center of Aix cost 4.30€ one-way. **Buses** arrive from Marseille, Avignon, and Nice; for information, see www.lepilote.com or call ✆ **08-10-00-13-26.** If you're **driving** to Aix from Avignon or other points north, take A7 south to A8 and follow the signs into town. From Marseille or other points south, take A51 north.

VISITOR INFORMATION   The **Office de Tourisme** is at Les Allées Provençales, 300 av. Giuseppe Verdi (www.aixenprovencetourism.com; ✆ **04-42-16-11-61**).

CITY LAYOUT   Aix's **Old Town** is primarily pedestrianized. To the south, it's bordered by the grand **cours Mirabeau,** flanked by a canopy of plane trees. The city was built atop thermal springs, and 40 fountains still bubble away in picturesque squares around town.

SPECIAL EVENTS   The **Festival d'Aix,** created in 1948 (www.festival-aix.com; ✆ **08-20-92-29-23**), mid-June through late July, features music and opera from all over the world.

[FastFACTS] AIX-EN-PROVENCE

ATMs/Banks   Downtown Aix has scores of banks, including three along cours Mirabeau.

Internet Access   **Brasserie Les Deux Garçons,** 53 cours Mirabeau, (*℃* **04-42-26-00-51**).

Mail & Postage   **La Poste,** pl. de l'Hôtel de Ville (*℃* **36-31**).

Pharmacies   **Pharmacie Victor Hugo,** 16 av. Victor Hugo (*℃* **04-42-26-24-93**).

Exploring Aix-en-Provence

Aix's main street, **cours Mirabeau ★**, is one of the most beautiful boulevards in Europe. A double row of plane trees shades it from the Provençal sun and throws dappled daylight onto its rococo fountains. Shops and sidewalk cafes line one side; 17th- and 18th-century sandstone *hôtels particuliers* (private mansions) take up the other. Stop into **Brasserie Les Deux Garçons,** 53 cours Mirabeau, for a coffee or a glass of rosé. The brasserie was founded in 1792 and frequented by the likes of Emile Zola, Cézanne, Picasso, and Sir Winston Churchill. Boulevard Carnot and cours Sextius circle the heart of the old quarter (Vieille Ville), which contains the pedestrian-only zone.

One fun way to check out the lay of the land is aboard an eco-friendly **Diabline** (www.la-diabline.fr; Mon–Sat 8:30am–7:30pm; 0.60€/ride). These vehicles operate three routes along cours Mirabeau and through most of the Old Town.

Cours Mirabeau, Aix-en-Provence

Aix through the Eyes of Cézanne

One of the best experiences in Aix is a walk along the well-marked *route de Cézanne.* From the east end of cours Mirabeau, take rue du Maréchal-Joffre across boulevard Carnot to boulevard des Poilus, which becomes avenue des Ecoles-Militaires and D17. The stretch between Aix and the hamlet of Le Tholonet is full of twists and turns where Cézanne used to set up his easel. The route also makes a lovely 5.5km (3.5-mile) stroll. Le Tholonet has a cafe or two where you can refresh yourself while waiting for one of the frequent buses back to Aix.

Atelier de Cézanne ★★ MUSEUM   A 10-min. (uphill) stroll north of Aix's Old Town, Cézanne's studio offers visitors a unique glimpse into the artist's daily life. Because the building remained untouched for decades after Cézanne's death in 1906, the studio has remained perfectly preserved for close to a century. Note the furnishings, vases, and small figurines on display, all of which feature in the modern master's drawings and canvases. Cézanne aficionados will also enjoy both **Jas de Bouffan,** the artist's family manor, which reopens after refurbishment in 2019, and the inspirational Cubist landscape of the **Bibémus Quarries.** The **Aix-en-Provence City Pass** (25€ for 24 hours or 34€ or 48 hours) allows entry to all three sites, plus 11 other essential must-sees, Diabaline rides, and guided tours.
9 av. Paul-Cézanne. www.cezanne-en-provence.com. ℂ **04-42-21-06-53.** Admission 6.50€ adults; 3.50€ students and children ages 13–25; free for children 12 and under. Jun–Sept daily 10am–6pm, English tour at 5pm; Apr–May daily 10am–noon and 2–6pm, English tour at 5pm; Oct–Mar daily 10am–12:30pm and 2–5pm, English tour at 4pm. Closed Sun Dec–Feb.

Cathédrale St-Sauveur ★ CATHEDRAL   The cathedral of Aix is dedicated to Christ under the title St-Sauveur (Holy Savior or Redeemer) and dates from the 4th and 5th centuries. Its pièce de résistance is a 15th-century Nicolas Froment triptych, *The Burning Bush.* One side depicts the Virgin and Child; the other, Good King René and his second wife, Jeanne de Laval.
34 pl. des Martyrs de la Résistance. ℂ **04-42-23-45-65.** Free admission. Daily 8am–noon and 2–6pm. Mass Sun 10:30am and 7pm.

Musée Granet ★★ MUSEUM   One of the South of France's top art venues, this popular museum displays a permanent collection of paintings and sculpture ranging from 15th-century French canvases to 20th-century Giacometti sculptures. However, it's the large-scale temporary exhibitions that truly impress, such as 2018's "Cézanne at Home," which featured rarely seen sketches by the great impressionist.
Pl. Saint Jean de Malte. www.museegranet-aixenprovence.fr. ℂ **04-42-52-88-32.** Admission 5.50€ adults; 4.50€ students and children 13–25; free for children 12 and under. Additional fee for temporary exhibitions. Tues–Sun June–Sept 10am–7pm; Oct–May noon–6pm.

Where to Stay

Hôtel Cézanne ★★ This super-chic—and enormously friendly—boutique hotel is best suited to guests seeking a more unusual spot to snooze. Conceived by the designers behind the sophisticated (and more expensive) Villa Gallici, the Cézanne is a mélange of colorful decor and hip designer touches. Baroque furnishings, unique artworks, and an honesty bar all add to the atmosphere. The hotel's location—midway between the train station and Aix's Old Town—makes it ideal for visitors planning day trips farther afield. And, unusually for France, the gourmet breakfasts of truffle omelettes, pancakes, and eggs benedicts are both ample and delicious.

40 av. Victor Hugo. www.hotelaix.com. ✆ **04-42-91-11-11.** 55 units. 99€–190€ double; 150€–205€ junior suite; 200€–340€ suite. Parking 17€. **Amenities:** Bar; free Wi-Fi.

Hôtel du Globe ★ In a city where expensive is the norm, the Hôtel du Globe is Aix's finest no-frills budget option. Ideally located just west of the Old Town, the hotel's rooms are basic yet bright—although definitely on the small side—and staff are as welcoming as they come. Breakfast is served on the roof terrace in summertime; the backdrop ranks among the best photo opportunities in the entire city. All in all, a most pleasant spot to bed down.

74 cours Sextius. www.hotelduglobe.com. ✆ **04-42-26-03-58.** 46 units. 45€–79€ single; 94€–104€ double; 110€–129 triple. Parking 15€. **Amenities:** Free Wi-Fi.

La Villa Gallici ★★★ This 18th-century Provençal house is one of Aix's most luxurious getaways. It also boasts a 3-hectare (7-acre) garden and a gastronomic restaurant on-site. It may be just a 5-min. stroll from the town center, yet the countrified ambience makes it feel miles away. Guest rooms are swathed in pastel-printed fabrics, while suites have their own private patios. Days may be spent lounging by the terracotta–trimmed pool; candlelit dinners are served alfresco under the stars. The villa also has a new wine cellar, where guests may taste up to 330 different châteaus alongside a sommelier.

Av. de la Violette. www.villagallici.com. ✆ **04-42-23-29-23.** 22 units. 280€–465€ double; from 535€ suite. Free parking. Closed Jan. **Amenities:** Restaurant; bar; babysitting; outdoor pool; room service; free Wi-Fi.

To the Markets We Will Go

Aix offers the best markets in the region. Place Richelme holds a **fruit and vegetable market** every morning from 8:30am to 12:30pm. Come here to buy exquisite products such as olives, lavender honey, and local cheeses. A daily **flower market,** with the same hours, is at place de l'Hôtel de Ville (Tues, Thurs, and Sat) or place des Prêcheurs (Mon, Wed, Fri, and Sun). The **fish market** takes place every morning on the south side of place Richelme.

Flowers and produce at an Aix open-air market

Where to Eat

Mickaël Féval ★★ FRENCH   For good reason was chef Mickaël Féval awarded a Michelin star for his modernistic French creations in 2017. Lunch is a light and inexpensive affair, with market-fresh carpaccios of sea bass plus local wild duck on his 26€ set menu. Join serious gastronomes for dinner. Deer, scallops, and giant bass from Corsica are seared in respectively seasonal stocks of forest fruit, oyster reduction, and mandarin. Mickaël's wife, Olivia, presides over front-of-house.

11 petite rue St Jean. www.mickaelfeval.fr. © **04-42-93-29-69.** Main course 16€–21€; fixed-price lunch 26€–35€ or dinner 63€–87€. Tues–Sat noon–2:30pm and 7:30–10:30pm.

Le Mille Feuille ★ PROVENÇAL   Nestled into a quiet corner of Aix's Old Town, this excellent eatery stands out against the often-average local dining scene. Little surprise, as the restaurant is the brainchild of chef Nicolas Monribot and sommelier Sylvain Sendra, both former staff at the famous Baumanière in Les Baux. The market-fresh menu may include yellow and green zucchini crumble with *cœur de bœuf* tomatoes, slow-cooked Sisteron lamb served with homemade gnocchi, or their signature vanilla bourbon *millefeuille* pastry. You can dine either on the small outdoor terrace or indoors, where the classy decor features crimson walls and chartreuse upholstered furnishings.

8 rue Rifle-Rafle. www.le-millefeuille.fr. © **04-42-96-55-17.** Main course 18.50€–24€; fixed-price lunch 24€–30€ or dinner 37€–43€. Wed–Sat noon–2pm and 8–9:30pm.

Mitch ★★ FRENCH There's a reason why Mitch isn't big on social media. Regular dinner guests are reluctant to share this gourmet homage to Southern French cuisine with anyone else. Heirloom tomatoes from France's southern shoreline blend with Mediterranean scallops and red mullet. Then Mitch and his in-the-know staff, all of whom speak excellent English, deliver heftier dishes of monkfish and steaks, each paired with more fragrantly intense ingredients from Provence and the Languedoc interior. A dinnertime triumph.

26 rue des Tanneurs. ✆ **04-42-26-63-08.** Main course 18€–27€; fixed-price dinner 39€–59€. Mon–Sat 7:30–10pm.

Shopping

Opened more than a century ago, **Béchard,** 12 cours Mirabeau (✆ **04-42-26-06-78**), is the most famous bakery in town. It specializes in the famous *Calissons d'Aix,* a candy made from ground almonds, preserved melon, and fruit syrup. **Chocolaterie de Puryicard,** 7 rue Rifle-Rafle (www.puyricard.fr; ✆ **04-42-21-13-26**), creates sensational chocolates filled with candied figs, walnuts, or local lavender honey.

Founded in 1934 on a busy boulevard just east of the center of town, **Santons Fouque,** 65 cours Gambetta (www.santons-fouque.com; ✆ **04-42-26-33-38**), stocks close to 2,000 traditional *santons* (crèche figurines).

For a range of truly useful souvenirs, including copper pots and pocket knives by famous French forgers such as Laguiole, try **Quincaillerie Centrale,** 21 rue de Monclar (✆ **04-42-23-33-18**), a hardware/housewares store that's been offering a little bit of everything since 1959.

Nightlife

Open daily from 8am until 2am, **La Rotonde,** 2A pl. Jeanne d'Arc (www.larotonde-aix.com; ✆ **04-42-91-61-70**), is a bar, cafe, and historic hangout.

Under-30s who like thumping beats should head for **Le Mistral,** 3 rue Frédéric Mistral (www.mistralclub.fr; ✆ **04-42-38-16-49**), where techno and house pumps long and loud for a cover charge of around 10€ to 20€.

For jazz produced by a changing roster of visiting musicians, head for the **Scat Club,** 11 rue de la Verrerie (✆ **04-42-23-00-23**), a preferred venue for more mature local patrons.

Last but certainly not least is the **Joïa Glam Club** (✆ **06-80-35-32-94**), chemin de l'Enfant, in the hamlet of Les Milles, 8km (5 miles) south of Aix (follow the signs to Marseille). A shuttle bus connects from La Rotonde in Aix proper—probably a safer bet. On site is a restaurant, several bars, an outdoor swimming pool, and indoor/outdoor dance floor. Be forewarned that long lines are common on Fridays (when females get in free) and Saturdays. Entrance usually costs around 20€, unless you're a star or self-confident enough to schmooze the doorman.

MARSEILLE ★★

776km (481 miles) S of Paris; 203km (126 miles) SW of Nice; 32km (20 miles) S of Aix-en-Provence

Marseille, with nearly 1.5 million inhabitants, is the second-largest city in France. It's also the country's oldest metropolis, founded as a port by the Greeks in the 6th century B.C.

Author Alexandre Dumas called teeming Marseille "the meeting place of the entire world." It's a working city with many faces, both figuratively and literally. A view from high up reveals the colorful Vieux Port, with its elegant old buildings, boat-filled harbor, and the Mediterranean beyond. The city is sprawling but it's also a cosmopolitan nexus of vibrant sounds, smells, and sights—unlike any other place in France.

Marseille's age-old problems may include unemployment, the Mafia, and racial tension (around a quarter of the population is of North African descent, with significant Armenian, Jewish, and Asian communities, too), but civic pride is strong, and the city is firmly focused on the future, evidenced by the ongoing **Euroméditerranée urban regeneration project** (www.euromediterranee.fr). Marseille proudly held the title of **European Capital of Culture** in 2013, sparking the construction of a flurry of new cultural venues, the creation of landmark museums, and the completion of long-term architectural projects, particularly in the old docklands neighborhood west of the Vieux Port. Further new sites will follow as Marseille hosts the Olympic marina and sailing competition for the 2024 Paris Olympiad, plus soccer games in its landmark 67,000-seat Stade

Fort Saint-Jean, on the Marseille waterfront

Vélodrome stadium. More than anywhere else, Marseille is the nation's foodie go-to, with street food so good that tourism bosses regularly host food bloggers ready to Instagram the city's eats. France's second city has finally come of age.

Essentials

ARRIVING **Marseille-Provence Airport** (www.marseille-airport.com; ✆ **04-42-14-14-14**), 27km (17 miles) northwest of the city center, receives international flights from all over Europe. From the airport, shuttle buses (*navettes;* www.navettemarseilleaeroport.com; ✆ **08-92-70-08-40**) make the trip to Marseille's St-Charles rail station, near the Vieux-Port, for 8.30€, 5.80€ passengers 12 to 26, and 4.15€ children 11 and under. The shuttle buses run daily every 20 min. from 5am until midnight; the trip takes 25 min.

Marseille has **train** connections from all over Europe, particularly to and from Nice, and on to Italy. The TGV bullet train also links it to Paris, with departures almost every hour from the Gare de Lyon (trip time: 3 hr., 20 min.; www.oui.sncf; ✆ **36-35** at .40€/min.; 30€–125€ one-way). **Buses** serve the **Gare Routière,** rue Honnorat (✆ **04-91-08-16-40**), adjacent to the St-Charles railway station. Several buses run daily between Aix-en-Provence and Marseille (www.navetteaixmarseille.com; trip time: 40 min.; 6€ one-way). If you're **driving** from Paris, follow A6 south to Lyon, and then continue south along A7 to Marseille. The drive takes about 8 hours. From Provence, take A7 south to Marseille.

VISITOR INFORMATION The **Office de Tourisme** is at 11 la Canebière (www.marseille-tourisme.com; ✆ **08-26-50-05-00;** Métro: Vieux-Port).

CITY LAYOUT Marseille is a large metropolis, although most sights are concentrated around the Vieux Port. If you're keen to explore different parts of the city, you'll need to take advantage of its comprehensive public transport or have a strong set of legs.

NEIGHBORHOODS IN BRIEF The major arteries divide Marseille into 16 *arrondissements.* Like Paris, the last two digits of a postal code tell you within which *arrondissement* an address is located. Visitors tend to spend most of their time in four main neighborhoods. The first is the **Vieux Port,** the atmospheric natural harbor that's a focal point for the city center. From here, the wide La Canebière boulevard runs eastwards, bisected by Marseille's most popular shopping avenues. To the north lies **Le Panier,** the original Old Town, crisscrossed by a pastel network of undulating alleyways. This neighborhood's western edge is trimmed by former docklands, which have been completely redeveloped over the past few years. Southeast of the Vieux Port, the alternative neighborhood around **cours Julien** is home to convivial restaurants and one-off boutiques aplenty. And come summertime, action shifts to the **Plages du Prado,** a strip of beaches due south of the city center.

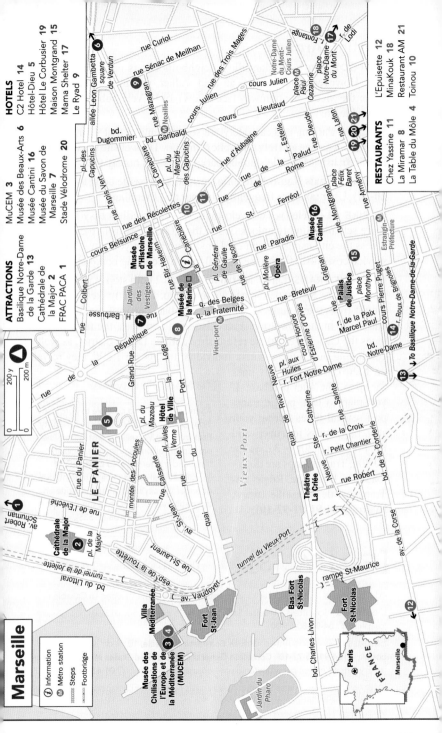

Marseille

Legend:
- ⓘ Information
- Ⓜ Métro station
- Steps
- Footbridge

0 — 200 y
0 — 200 m

LE PANIER

Vieux-Port

FRANCE
Paris ✵
Marseille ●

533

Getting Around

ON FOOT Each of Marseille's neighborhoods is easily navigable on foot. However, unless you're an avid walker, you may want to rely on either the Métro, the tramway (see below), or Le Vélo public bikes, to zip around town.

BY CAR Parking and car safety are so problematic that your best bet is to park in a garage and rely on public transport. The website **www.parking-public.fr** lists Marseille's public parking lots and hourly fees.

BY TAXI **Taxis Radio Marseille** (www.taximarseille.com; ✆ **04-91-02-20-20**). Uber taxis are frequently cheaper and friendlier.

BY BIKE **Le Vélo** (www.levelo-mpm.fr) is Marseille's easy-to-use bike share scheme. Simply unlock one of the 1,000 bikes from the 130 stands across the city using a credit card or sign up before you travel. The 7-day service costs just 1€ with the first 30 min. of pedaling completely free.

BY PUBLIC TRANSPORT **Métro** lines 1 and 2 both stop at the main train station, Gare St-Charles, place Victor Hugo. Line 1 makes a U-shaped circuit from the suburbs into the city and back again; Line 2 runs north and south in the downtown area. Also with two lines, the **tramway** services the Canebière and the refurbished Joliette Docks district, as well as continuing out to the suburbs. Individual tickets are 1.60€; they're valid on Métro, tram, and bus lines for up to 1 hr. after purchase. If you plan to take public transport several times during your stay, buy a **pass journée,** valid for 1 day for 5.20€ or 3 days for 10.80€. Transit maps are downloadable from the Régie des Transport de Marseille (www.rtm.fr; ✆ **04-91-91-92-10**).

> ### Marseille City Pass
>
> Alternatively, it's also possible to purchase a 1-day (24€), 2-day (26€), or 3-day (41€) **City Pass** from the Marseille Tourist Office. The pass covers all public transport, including the round-trip ferry trip to **Château d'If** (p. 538), as well as entrance to more than a dozen of the city's museums and a ride on the *petit-train* (p. 539) up to the **Basilique Notre-Dame-de-la-Garde** (p. 535).

[Fast FACTS] MARSEILLE

ATMs/Banks Marseille's banks are plentiful, including several along La Canebière.

Doctors & Hospitals **Hopital Saint Joseph,** 26 bd. de Louvain (www.hopital-saint-joseph.fr; ✆ **04-91-80-65-00**).

Embassies & Consulates **British Consulate Marseille,** 10 pl. de la Joliette (www.gov.uk; ✆ **04-91-15-72-10**); **Consulate General of the United States Marseille,** pl. Varian Fry (https://fr.usembassy.gov/embassy-consulates/marseille/; ✆ **01-43-12-48-85**).

Internet Access Marseille's municipality hosts 50 free Wi-Fi hotspots around the city. Central locations (including Jardin du Pharo, the square outside the Hôtel de Ville, and La Vieille Charité) are indicated on the free maps distributed by the tourist office.

Mail & Postage   **La Poste,** 1 cours Jean Ballard (✆ **36-31**).

Newspapers & Magazines   Bilingual **"COTE Magazine"** (www.cotemagazine.com) offers a good selection of tried-and-true Marseille tips, as well as local interviews and recent openings.

Pharmacies   **Leader Santé,** 37 la Canebière (✆ **04-91-91-32-06**).

Safety   As in any big city, it's wise to keep a close eye on your belongings and avoid poorly lit areas at night.

Exploring Marseille

Immerse yourself in local life with a wander through Marseille's busy streets, including along the famous **La Canebière.** Lined with hotels, shops, and restaurants, it used to be a very seedy street indeed, saturated with sailors from every nation. With Marseille's ongoing urban regeneration, however, it has become the heart and soul of a world-class city.

La Canebière joins the **Vieux Port ★★**, dominated at its western end by the massive neoclassical forts of St-Jean and St-Nicolas. The harbor is filled with fishing craft and yachts and ringed by seafood restaurants. For a panoramic view, head to the **Jardin du Pharo,** a promontory facing the entrance to the Vieux-Port. From the terrace of the Château du Pharo, built by Napoleon III, you can clearly see the city's old and new cathedrals, as well as the recently redeveloped docklands, now the **Cité de la Méditerranée,** which includes **Fort Saint-Jean** and the architectural wonder that is **MuCEM** (Museum of European and Mediterranean Civilizations).

North of the old port is **Le Panier,** Marseille's Old Town. Small boutiques and designer ateliers now populate these once-sketchy streets. To the south, the **corniche Président-J.-F.-Kennedy** is a 4km (2.5-mile) promenade. You'll pass villas and gardens facing the Mediterranean, before reaching the popular **Plages du Prado.** Patrolled by lifeguards in the summer, these spacious sandy beaches have children's playgrounds, sun loungers, and waterside cafes. Serious hikers can continue south of here into the **Parc Nationale des Calanques** (www.calanques-parcnational.fr), France's newest national park (p. 547). This series of stunning limestone cliffs, fjords, and rocky promontories stretches along the coast for 20km (12 miles) southeast of Marseille.

Basilique Notre-Dame-de-la-Garde ★ CHURCH   This landmark church crowns a limestone rock overlooking the southern side of the Vieux-Port. It was built in the Romanesque-Byzantine style popular in the 19th century and topped by a 9.7m (32-ft.) gilded statue of the Virgin. Visitors come for the views (best at sunset) from its terrace. Spread out before you are the city, the islands, and the shimmering sea.

rue Fort-du-Sanctuaire. www.notredamedelagarde.com. ✆ **04-91-13-40-80.** Free admission. Daily Apr–Sept 7am–7:15pm, Oct–Mar 7am–6:15pm. Métro: Estrangin-Préfecture. Bus: 60.

Cathédrale de la Major ★ CATHEDRAL One of the largest cathedrals (some 135m/443 ft. long) built in Europe during the 19th century, this massive structure has almost swallowed its 12th-century predecessor, built on the ruins of a temple of Diana. Its striped exterior is a bastardized Romanesque-Byzantine style with domes and cupolas; the intricate interiors include mosaic floors and red-and-white marble banners. The cathedral's architecture is particularly arresting now that it overlooks Marseille's redeveloped port and dockland areas. It also provides shady respite from sightseeing on a summer's day.

Esplanade de la Major. © **04-91-90-53-57.** Free admission. Hours vary. Head west of Le Panier district. Métro: Vieux-Port. Bus: 49, 60, or 82.

FRAC PACA (Fonds Régional d'Art Contemporain Provence-Alpes-Côte d'Azur) ★ MUSEUM Formerly located in Le Panier, FRAC PACA, Marseille's regional contemporary art museum, is now situated squarely in the up-and-coming Joliette Docks district. The museum's mosaic-like recycled glass structure was designed by Japanese architect Kengo Kuma. It's a fitting tribute to the FRAC's thousand-strong collection of artworks. It was inaugurated—like so many cultural spaces in this city—in 2013. Within the museum itself, exhibitions spread over two galleries. There's also a restaurant, two terraces, artists' residences, a performance hall, and a bookstore.

20 bd. de Dunkerque. www.fracpaca.org. © **04-91-91-27-55.** Admission 5€ adults; 2.50€ students ages 18–25 and seniors; free for children 17 and under. Wed–Sat 10am–6pm, Sun 2–6pm. Métro: Joliette. Tram: Joliette. Bus: 35, 49, 55, or 82.

MuCEM (Museum of European and Mediterranean Civilizations) ★★★ MUSEUM Opened in 2013, the long-anticipated MuCEM is the first national gallery in France to be located outside of Paris. More than 250,000 objects collected from throughout the Mediterranean region are exhibited here, along with local prints, photographs, and historical postcards. Temporary exhibitions focus on anything from Mediterranean football to Arabian graffiti, while the most eye-catching event of 2018 was the exhibition by Chinese dissident artist Ai Weiwei. The premises encompass the 12th-century **Fort Saint-Jean,** its suspended gardens, and Michelin-starred-chef Gérard Passédat's primarily organic restaurant, **La Table du Môle** (p. 542).

1 esplanade du J4. www.mucem.org. © **04-84-35-13-13.** Admission 9.50€ adults; 5€ seniors and students; 14€ family ticket, free for children 17 and under. Additional fee for temporary exhibitions. Sept–June Wed–Mon 11am–7pm (until 6pm Nov–Apr); Jul and Aug Wed–Mon 10am–8pm. Métro: Vieux-Port. Bus: 49, 60, or 82.

Musée des Beaux-Arts ★ MUSEUM The 150-year-old Museum of Fine Arts is Marseille's oldest exhibition venue. Its venue, the Palais Longchamp, is gloriously grand—the palace took 30 years to build and its high ceilings and marble floors still astound today. The museum reopened its permanent collection to the public in 2014, after an incredible 9 years of renovations. Exhibits range from 16th-century Italian works to 19th-century French masterpieces, including Rodin's sculpture *La Voix Intérieure* ("The Inner Voice").

Palais Longchamp. http://musee-des-beaux-arts.marseille.fr. ✆ **04-91-14-59-30.** Admission 6€ adults; 3€ students and seniors; free for children 17 and under. Additional fee for temporary exhibitions. Tues–Sun 10am–6pm. Métro: Longchamp. Tram: Longchamp.

Musée Cantini ★ ART MUSEUM   This 17th-century *hôtel particulier* (private mansion) organizes an outstanding modern art show. Better still, current visitors will be the first to see the latest exhibitions, as the museum reopened after lengthy renovations in 2018 with a blockbuster Courbet, Degas, and Cézanne exposition. The museum also houses a permanent collection, particularly strong on masterpieces (by Picasso, Dufy, de Staël, Ernst, and others) created during the first half of the 20th century.

19 rue Grignan. http://musee-cantini.marseille.fr. ✆ **04-91-54-77-75.** Admission 6€ adults; 3€ students and seniors; free for children 17 and under. Tues–Sun 10am–6pm. Métro: Estrangin/Préfecture.

Musée du Savon de Marseille ★ MUSEUM   Marseille's newest museum opened in 2018 to celebrate the city's most famous industry: Savon de Marseille soap. The city's official soap recipe was fixed in 1688 to feature 72 percent olive oil plus seawater and ashes. Bars bearing the stamp "72% extra pur" were exported worldwide and used by salty sailors on their voyages from Marseille, France's most important port. Alongside a history lesson, a workshop allows customers to produce their own slab of bona-fide Marseille soap to take home. The temporary exhibition space opened with a "Bathroom of the Future" show, which highlighted a Japanese electronic toilet and an app that pours a bath—with not-so-subtle latherings of Savon de Marseille shown alongside.

1 rue Henri Fiocca. www.musama.fr. ✆ **04-91-14-59-30.** Admission 12€ adults; 6€ seniors and students; free children 17 and under. Additional fee for soapmaking workshop exhibitions. Tues–Sun 10am–6pm. Métro: Vieux-Port.

Stade Vélodrome ★★ ATTRACTION   Soccer fans should make a beeline for Marseille's recently-reopened (2016) Olympique de Marseille (OM) football stadium, home to one of France's most popular soccer teams and a key site in European football. After more than 4 years of renovations, the modern Stade is now one the largest soccer grounds in France, with 67,000 seats. Which means it's more than perfectly placed to host matches throughout the upcoming **2024 Paris** Olympiad, as well as weekly games in France's premier soccer league. Behind-the-scenes tours of the grounds and the stadium are also offered three times each week. See the Stade Vélodrome website for details.

rue Raymond Teisseire, bd. Michelet. www. orangevelodrome.com. ✆ **08-26-10-40-44.** Stadium tours 13€ adults; 8€ students; 6€ schoolchildren. Métro: Rond-point du Prado.

La Marseillaise

Few know that France's national anthem was actually composed in Strasbourg. Originally titled "War Song of the Army of the Rhine," it was written in a single night by army captain Claude-Joseph Rouget de Lisle in 1792. That same year, revolutionaries from Marseille (who had been given printed copies) marched into Paris singing it. In their honor, the song became known as "La Marseillaise" and was quickly adopted as the rallying cry of the French Revolution. It was officially declared the national anthem of France in 1795, only to be banned by Napoleon during the Empire, Louis XVIII in 1815, and Napoleon III in 1830. The anthem was reinstated for good in 1879.

Outlying Attractions

You can take a 25-min. ferry ride to the **Château d'If** (if.monuments-nationaux.fr), a national monument built by François I as a fortress to defend Marseille. Alexandre Dumas used it as a setting for the fictional adventures of "The Count of Monte Cristo." The château is open October to March 10am to 5pm (closed Monday); April to September daily 10am to 6pm. Entrance to the island is 6€ adults, free for children 17 and under. Boats leave approximately every 45 to 60 min., depending on the season; the round-trip transfer is 10.80€. For information, contact the **Frioul If Express** (www.frioul-if-express.com; ✆ **04-96-11-03-50;** Métro: Vieux-Port).

North of Marseille proper, **L'Estaque** was once a picturesque seaside village (although it now looks out over the city's more urban skyline). It was painted by Provence's artistic greats—including Cézanne, Renoir, and Braque—between the 1860s and 1920s. Today, visitors can tread these legendary footsteps and easel sites, following the "Painters' Path" signposted around town (strolling time around 2 hr.). L'Estaque's seafront stalls sell popular local snacks, including *chichi frégi* (sugar-topped fritters flavored with orange blossom water) and *panisses* (savory chickpea flour fritters). You can reach L'Estaque via bus no. 35 from Marseille's place de la Joliette (journey time around 30 min). Between April and September, *navette* ferry service runs from the Vieux Port to L'Estaque for 3€ (journey time 40 min).

Organized Tours

One of the easiest ways to see Marseille's centrally located monuments is aboard the fleet of open-top **Le Grand Tour Buses** (www.marseillele grandtour.com; Métro: Vieux-Port). You can hop off at any of 13 different stops en route and back on to the next bus in the day's sequence, usually arriving between 1 and 2 hours later, depending on the season. The buses run four to eight times a day during each month except January. A 1-day pass costs 18€ adults and 16€ seniors and students with ID; the fare for children ages 4 to 11 is 8€. Two-day passes are also available for just a few euros more.

The motorized **Trains Touristiques de Marseille** (www.petit-train-marseille.com; © **04-91-25-24-69;** Métro: Vieux-Port), or *petit-trains,* make circuits around town, too. Year-round, train no. 1 drives a 75-min. round-trip to Basilique Notre-Dame-de-la-Garde and Basilique St-Victor. From April to mid-November, train no. 2 makes a 65-min. round-trip of old Marseille by way of the cathedral, Vieille Charité, and the Quartier du Panier. Both trains make a 30-min. stop for sightseeing en route. The trains depart from the quay just west of the Hôtel de Ville. The fare for both trains is 1 is 8€ adults and 4€ children.

Marseille's Office de Tourisme offers two bilingual tours of the city center. The first explores the **Vieux Port and Le Panier** (Sat 2:00pm; included with purchase of a City Pass, p. 534). The second meanders its way around **cours Julien's contemporary art galleries and street art** (1 Sat per month at 3:30pm; 10€). In 2014, the Office de Tourisme also began leading bilingual guided tours of Le Corbusier's **Cité Radieuse,** site of Hôtel le Corbusier (p. 539). Taking place from Tuesday to Saturday at 2:30pm and 4:30pm, tours cost 10€ per person and can be reserved through the tourist office. Private walking tours of the city's historic, architectural, and foodie hotspots are run by the supremely well-informed Benedicte Sire, whose **Urban Walks** (www. urbanwalks.eu) cost from 35€ per person.

Boat tours to the **Parc National des Calanques** are popular. Many tour operators with different prices and formulas (for example, three Calanques in 2 hr./22€, or eight in 3 hr./28€) can be found on the quai des Belges at the Vieux-Port. For more information about visiting the Calanques from nearby Cassis, see p. 544.

Where to Stay

Although slightly removed from the city center, the iconic **Hôtel le Corbusier** (www.hotellecorbusier.com) is a must for architecture aficionados. In 2013, local French designers transformed the hotel's rooftop gym into a hip contemporary art space, **MAMO** (www.mamo.fr).

C2 Hotel ★★   Marseille's uber-cool option, the five-star C2 was launched in 2014. Twenty luxurious, light-filled rooms spill over a 19th-century merchant family mansion typical of this portside quarter, each one decked out in exposed brick walls and designer furnishings. Some have a private hammam steam bath. The superb Filorga Spa onsite has an indoor pool and Jacuzzi, as well as a cocktail bar. But the hotel's *pièce de résistance*? That would have to be C2's beach on the private Mediterranean island of Île Degaby. Pack a picnic and castaway.

48 rue Roux de Brignoles. www.c2-hotel.com. © **04-95-05-13-13.** 20 units. 199€–449€ double. Free valet parking. Métro: Estrangin-Préfecture. **Amenities:** Bar; private beach; concierge; spa; free Wi-Fi.

Hôtel-Dieu ★★   The luxurious Hôtel-Dieu is perched just behind Marseille's Hôtel de Ville, overlooking the Vieux Port from Le Panier. This five-star hotel occupies what was once an 18th-century hospital—and history oozes from every pore. It's now managed by the InterContinental Group with aplomb. As well as modern, minimalist guest rooms with superb views, guests may enjoy the indoor pool and sea view bistro **Les Fenêtres.** Pick of the eateries is gastronomic restaurant **Alcyone,** where Michelin-starred superchef Lionel Levy invented the Milkshake de Bouillabaisse, a new take on the classic Marseille dish.

1 pl. Daviel. www.ihg.com. ✆ **04-13-42-42-42.** 194 units. 230€–455€ double; from 550€ suite. Parking 25€. Métro: Vieux-Port. **Amenities:** Restaurant; bar; business center; fitness center; indoor pool; room service; spa; free Wi-Fi.

Maison Montgrand ★★   This bargain concept hotel shouts Marseille at every turn. Sited in two sister apartment blocks, simple new rooms share a massive communal space in the reception townhouse. This funky area features a nail bar, a perfumery, an outdoor restaurant, and a pour-your-own-Provençal wine dispenser. The mostly organic breakfast is served in a hipster tearoom. And it's all just a block from the port's nighttime noise and bustle.

35 rue Montgrand. www.hotel-maison-montgrand.com. ✆ **04-91-00-35-20.** 37 units. 75€–170€ double. Métro: Vieux-Port. **Amenities:** Restaurant; bar; room service; free Wi-Fi.

Mama Shelter ★★   Tucked into the hipster cours Julien district, this unique hotel is the brainchild of designer Philippe Starck. Rooms are bright and cool, from the modular furnishings to the wall-mounted Macs offering dozens of free on-demand movies. Downstairs, Egyptian graffiti artist Tarek has tagged the industrial-chic restaurant's ceiling. Super chef Guy Savoy has recently revamped the menu, and the space now hosts a stage set up for live performances. And outdoors, Mama Shelter's yellow-striped courtyard hosts a pastis bar where guests can sip their way through more than four dozen variants of the city's beloved anise-flavored tipple. This is an excellent bet for a contemporary taste of France's second city.

64 rue de la Loubière. www.mamashelter.com. ✆ **04-84-35-20-00.** 126 units. 69€–109€ double; 129€ family room; 199€ suite. Parking 19€. Métro: Notre Dame du Mont. **Amenities:** Restaurant; bar; free Wi-Fi.

Le Ryad ★   Marrakech-meets-Marseille at this Moorish inspired backstreet hotel. Styled by its former Moroccan owner, the 11 rooms are now presided over by a kindly French proprietor who remains a fountain of local knowledge. Breakfasts are a cornucopia of Arabian sweets, North African breads, and mint tea. From spring onwards, morning meals are served outdoors in the oasis-like garden. Rooms have a faded grandeur and less expensive ones overlook a bustling street. Family suites peek out over the garden and can comfortably sleep four.

16 rue Sénac de Meilhan. www.leryad.fr. ✆ **04-91-47-74-54.** 11 units. 69€–129€ double; from 129€ family rooms. Métro: Noailles. **Amenities:** Restaurant meals prepared by order; free Wi-Fi.

Where to Eat

The **Noailles** district is street food central. Stroll down rue d'Aubagne to sample Tunisian *leblebi* soup joints, Ivorian *alocco* fish grills, and stalls stocking Egyptian *mahjouba* pancakes. Bites start from 1€ apiece. Or perch on a stool for a glass of Moroccan mint tea or Syrian falafel.

For diners interested in re-creating Marseille's famous *bouillabaisse* fish stew at home, **Miramar Restaurant** (www.lemiramar.fr) offers cooking classes (112€/5-hr. lesson including lunch). Contact the tourist office for details.

Chez Yassine ★ SEAFOOD   Come here for the best example of the migrant street food synonymous with the bustling Noailles neighborhood. Chez Yassine serves the unctuous Tunisian creations of three North African brothers, including spicy *lablabi* chickpea soup and *brik a l'oeuf* egg pastry. For the remaining cooking pots of the untranslatable delights, simply point and order. Pair with mint tea or the establishment's home-made lemonade. 8 rue d'Aubagne. ✆ **09-80-83-39-13.** Main course 6€. Daily 11am–9pm. Métro: Noailles.

L'Epuisette ★★ SEAFOOD/MEDITERRANEAN   This Michelin-starred option is undoubtedly the premier place in Marseille to sample bouillabaisse stew. Bring your appetite: Fresh fish is poached in saffron-infused soup; the final product is served as two separate courses, accompanied by *rouille,* a mayonnaise-like sauce flavored with garlic, cayenne pepper, and saffron. Or visit during wintertime to sample the restaurant's exquisite truffle menu, a selection of courses which may feature scallops in truffle sauce, or a truffle-infused chocolate mousse (165€). The setting is as sublime as the cuisine: A seaside dining room overlooks Château d'If from the picturesque fishing port of Vallon des Auffes, 2.5km (1.5 miles) south of Marseille's Vieux Port. Vallon des Auffes. www.l-epuisette.fr. ✆ **04-91-52-17-82.** Main course 18€–65€; fixed-price dinner 75€–125€. Tues–Sat noon–1:30pm and 7:30–9:30pm. Closed Aug. Bus: 83.

MinaKouk ★ ALGERIAN   This contemporary Algerian eatery and tea shop sits on a narrow backstreet in Marseille's cours Julien district. All bright colors and modern furnishings, Mina is ideal for wallet-friendly *chorba* soup, savory *beurek* pastries, *tajine* bakes, and couscous come lunchtime. Mid-afternoon, attention is given over to steaming pots of mint tea and towering trays of traditional North African sweets. A neighborhood favorite. 21 rue Fontange. www.minakouk.com. ✆ **04-91-53-54-55.** Main course 11.50€–23€; fixed-price menu 11.50€–13€. Tues–Sat 8am–7pm, open later Fri and Sat. Métro: Notre-Dame du Mont-Cours Julien.

Restaurant AM ★★★ MODERN MEDITERRANEAN   The city's latest must-eat won its first Michelin star in 2016. Here inspirational chef Alexandre Mazzia spins the flavors from the migrant cultures that make up Marseille—including Turkish sumac and Arabian harissa—into a multiple award-winning cuisine. Highlights include seaweed chips layered with sweet potato jelly then topped with grated roe. Dishes are also inspired by Mazzia's complex roots: In a tale typical of this melting pot city, he was born in Congo to Italian and Corsican parents, before washing up in Marseille at the age of 15. Book as far in advance as you can.

9 rue Rocca. www.alexandremazzia.com. (C) **04-91-24-83-63.** Fixed-price menus 39€–110€. Tues–Sat noon–1:30pm and 7:30–9:30pm. Closed Aug. Metro: Rond-Point du Prado. Bus: 19, 44, or 83.

La Table du Môle ★★★ MODERN MEDITERRANEAN   Triple Michelin-starred-chef Gérard Passédat's most accessible restaurant, this "chic bistro" sits atop the MuCEM (p. 535). Much like the MuCEM exhibits themselves, stellar dishes herald from across the Mediterranean, including seafood tart served with a creamy ginger jus, crab paired with spicy harissa, or grilled turbot with truffled potatoes. Top chef Passédat's modern take on bouillabaisse stew is gloriously inventive. All is served against a sweeping backdrop of Marseille's port and the Mediterranean Sea. Note that it's also possible to dine at Le Môle's lower-key (and cheaper) sister restaurant, **La Cuisine** (lunch only), also located at the MuCEM.

MuCEM, 1 esplanade du J4. www.passedat.fr. (C) **04-91-19-17-80.** Reservations online only. Main course 38€; fixed-price lunch 55€ or dinner 75€. Wed–Mon 12:30–2:30pm; Wed–Sat and Mon 7:30–10:30pm. Métro: Vieux-Port. Bus: 49, 60, or 82.

Toinou ★★ SEAFOOD   For the veritable seafood aficionado, there is no better place to dine in Marseille than this landmark restaurant. Platters are piled high with dozens of varieties of mussels, oysters, clams, and this region's famous sea urchins, as well as sea snails of all shapes and sizes. Doing a bustling local business for nearly 60 years, the seafood dished up here is sublime. Want your fish with a sea view? Choose your own selection of shellfish from the restaurant's kiosk out front, then head down to the coast for a beachside picnic. In a nod to modernity, this classic eatery now allows guests to order oysters from Bouzigues and Oléron online.

3 cours St-Louis. www.toinou.com. (C) **08-11-45-45-45.** Shellfish by the half dozen 2.60€–9€; fixed-price platters 16.50€–91€. Daily 11:30am–11:30pm. Métro: Vieux-Port or Noailles.

Shopping

Only Paris and the French Riviera can compete with Marseille for its breadth and diversity of merchandise. Your best bet is a trip to the streets just southeast of the **Vieux-Port,** crowded with stores of all kinds.

Rue Paradis and **rue Saint Ferréol** have many of the same upscale fashion boutiques found in Paris, as well as a Galeries Lafayette, France's largest chain department store. For more bohemian wear, try **cours Julien** and **rue de la Tour** for richly brocaded and beaded items on offer in North African boutiques. **Le Panier** is now home to a vibrant range of unique boutiques. Try ceramics store with adjoining restaurant **Ahwash Concept**

Store, 56 rue de Lorette (✆ **04-91-44-04-60**), or **Les Baigneuses,** 3 rue de l'Eveche (www.lesbaigneuses.com; ✆ **09-52-68-67-64**), which sells a gorgeous range of retro-styled swimwear.

For unique souvenirs, head to **Ateliers Marcel Carbonel,** 49 rue Neuve-Ste-Catherine (www.santonsmarcelcarbonel.com; ✆ **04-91-13-61-36**). This 80-year-old business specializes in *santons,* clay figurines meant for Christmas nativities. In addition to personalities you may already know, the carefully crafted pieces depict Provençal common folk such as bakers, blacksmiths, and milkmaids. The figurines sell for around 12.60€ and up.

Navettes, small cookies that resemble boats, are a Marseillaise specialty. Flavored with secret ingredients that include orange zest and orange flower water, they were invented in 1791 and are still sold at **Le Four des Navettes,** 136 rue Sainte (www.fourdesnavettes.com; ✆ **04-91-33-32-12**), for around 10€ per dozen.

One of the region's most authentic fish markets at **Quai des Belges** (daily 8am–1pm), on the old port, is partially sheltered under the Norman Foster–designed Ombrière mirrored canopy. On **cours Julien,** you'll find a market with fruits, vegetables, and other foods (Tues, Thurs, and Sat 8am–1pm); exclusively organic produce (Wed 8am–1pm); stamps (Sun 8am–1pm); and secondhand goods (3rd Sun of the month 8am–1pm). The cheapest buys are in the photogenic **Noailles** neighborhood, where stores of 50 nationalities from Algerian to Vietnamese vend spices, spring rolls, jewelry, and homeware.

Nightlife

For an amusing and relatively harmless exposure to the town's saltiness, walk around the **Vieux-Port,** where cafes and restaurants angle their sightlines for the best view of the harbor.

L'Escale Borély, av. Pierre Mendès France, is 20 min. south of the town center (take bus no. 83). With a dozen animated bars and cafes, plus restaurants of every possible ethnicity, you'll be spoiled for choice.

Marseille's dance clubs are habitually packed out, especially **Trolley Bus,** 24 quai de Rive-Neuve (www.letrolley.com; ✆ **04-91-54-30-45;** Métro: Vieux-Port), known for techno, house, hip-hop, jazz, and salsa. Equally buzzing is **l'Exit,** 12 quai de Rive-Neuve (✆ **06-42-59-96-24;** Métro: Vieux-Port), a bar/disco with a terrace that profits from Marseille's sultry nights and two floors of seething nocturnal energy (happy hour starts at 5pm and runs all night on Thursdays). The **New Can Can,** 3–7 rue Sénac (www.newcancan.com; ✆ **04-91-48-59-76;** Métro: Noailles), is a lively, sprawling bar and disco that identifies itself as a gay venue but attracts many straight folks too. It's open Friday through Sunday midnight until 7am. **Le Funiculaire,** 11 rue Poggioli (www.lefuniculaire.fr; ✆ **04-91-37-77-98;** Métro: Notre Dame du Mont) is an organic wine bar that holds weekly jazz, samba, and Brazilian music events.

For jazz right on the port, head to **La Caravelle,** 34 quai du Port (www.lacaravelle-marseille.com; ℭ **04-91-90-36-64;** Métro: Vieux-Port), an aperitif bar and dinner club that offers a different musical flavor almost every night, including *manouche,* the French gypsy style most associated with guitarist Django Reinhardt.

CASSIS ★★

806km (501 miles) S of Paris; 128km (80 miles) SE of Avignon; 50km (31 miles) S of Aix-en-Provence; 32km (20 miles) E of Marseille

Cassis is unarguably the prettiest coastal town in Provence. The settlement dates from Ancient Greek times—that's as far back as both Marseille and Nice—but its fame rose in the early 20th century, when famous personalities like Virginia Woolf and Sir Winston Churchill guzzled its crisp white wines. The resort recently found a new outdoor-oriented audience as the capital of France's first mainland National Park since 1979.

Essentials

ARRIVING Cassis Station is a cinch to reach by rail. Half-hourly **trains** arrive from Marseille (trip time: 25 min.; www.oui.sncf; ℭ **36-35** at .40€/min.; 6.30€ one-way). Sound easy? It's not, as Cassis Station is then a

The colorful harbor at Cassis

3km (1.75 miles) downhill walk from Cassis town center. Walk down, grab one of the waiting taxis (10€), or catch the Marcouline city bus (.80€) every 30 min.

VISITOR INFORMATION   The helpful **Office de Tourisme** is on the beachfront quai des Moulins (www.ot-cassis.com; ✆ **08-92-39-01-03**).

[FastFACTS] CASSIS

Mail & Postage   **La Poste,** 3 rue Arène (✆ **36-31**). Note that the post office also offers an ATM.

Pharmacies   **Pharmacie Trossero,** 11 av. Victor Hugo (✆ **04-42-01-70-03**).

Exploring Cassis

The deliciously beautiful center of Cassis is best explored on foot. The coastal path winds from the wide expanse of Grande Plage beach past restaurant terraces and boutiques all the way to Plage du Bestouan and the start of the Parc Nationale des Calanques. Each August the entire town comes alive for a series of literary festivals, fireworks shows, and sea jousting tournaments (yes, involving lances and motor boats).

Cassis Snorkeling Tour ★ TOUR   As you might expect from a town that borders a massive marine and land National Park, Cassis is awash with diving schools. These include **Cassis-Plongée** (www.cassis-calanques-plongee.com) and **Narval Plongée** (www.narval-plongee.com). Novice divers may also scuba or snorkel along the **Sentier Sous-Marin de Cassis,** or underwater trail. This self-guided 30-min. swim route begins on the Promenade des Lombards. Four buoys mark marine life discovery spots along the way. Be aware that a mineral water source (as in thousands of bottles of chilled Evian) seeps from the limestone cliffs into Cassis harbor, so sea temperatures are often chilly!

Cassis Wine Tour ★ WALKING TOUR   White wines from Cassis (www.vinsdecassis.fr) are so superb that they were protected as an AOC region in 1936 (along with Châteauneuf-du-Pape, p. 503, outside of Avignon). Most vintages are infused with flowery Marsanne from the Rhône Valley, and herby Clairette from Provence. Just a dozen small, mostly organic producers tend their ocean-facing vineyards that are planted from the port up to the Cassis train station. All can be toured (with free tasting sessions to those who wish to purchase a bottle or three) by foot or by bicycle using the free Vineyard Tour map from the Cassis Tourist Office. A final fact for your friends at home: AOC Cassis is the only appellation to be entirely included within a National Park. Au natural never tasted so good.

Cassis environs. www.vinsdecassis.com.

Outlying Attractions

In 2012 Cassis was declared the capital of the new **Parc Nationale des Calanques** (p. 547). The calanques are towering cliffs created 120 million years ago. They were then split apart by rising sea levels and bleached white by the Provençal sun. Each calanque crashes into the azure sea from heights of up to 565m (nearly 2,000 ft.). Like Norway's fjords, they surround a series of boat-only bays that stretch for 32km (20 miles) from Cassis to Marseille. So sturdy is the snow-white stone from Calanque Port-Miou, a creek within walking distance of Cassis, that it was used to build the base of the Statue of Liberty in New York.

The main public pathway through the park is the GR51, a long-distance hiking trail known as the "Balconies of the Mediterranean." This *grande randonnée* route links Marseille with Monaco. Those visitors without Ironman thighs (or without a spare 3 weeks of vacation) may hike along a score of shorter marked paths instead, passing lonely islands, rocky passes, secret beaches, and gaping creeks. Park maps are available from Cassis's ever-helpful Tourist Office.

A more relaxed way to tour the park is by **boat.** Head down to Cassis' harbor, where a well-signposted kiosk sells tickets for regular daily boat trips. Opt to take in three calanques (45 min.; 16 € adults, 9.50€ children 9 and under), five calanques (65 min.; 19.50€ adults, 13.50€ children) or nine calanques (2 hr.; 29€ adults, 17€ children). A particular favorite is

Boaters and swimmers explore Parc Nationale des Calanques

The **Parc Nationale des Calanques** (www.calanques-parcnational.fr) is the seventh National Park in mainland France—and the first since 1979. Some 50,000 hectares (193 sq. miles) of land, coastline and sea are now protected forever more, including the wildlife, flora, and 60 species of fish that reside therein. Cars, scooters, jet skis, and speedboats are prohibited in the National Park, so tranquility is assured.

Southern French travelers hoping to hike further off the beaten track are spoiled for choice. On their doorstep is the **Port-Cros National Park** (www.port-crosparcnational.fr; see "Exploring Ile de Port-Cros," below), which covers a series of sub-tropical islands. The **Mercantour National Park** (www.mercantour.eu), a haven for wolves, deer, and butterflies, sits just north of Nice.

Calanque de Sugiton, which crumbles into an island-strewn bay. The postcard-perfect **Calanque d'En Vau** is also well worth seeking out. As non-official motorboats are banned from the National Park, try paddling under the calanques by kayak or SUP instead. For equipment, contact **Cassis Sport Loisirs Nautiques** (www.cassis-kayak.com).

Where to Stay

L'Avila ★★   This impossibly romantic B&B sits a 10-min. hike from the seafront promenade on the way to Cassis train station. It is managed by amiable French-Cuban couple Corinne and Humberto. Five modernist guestrooms (with interior touches from the likes of Starck and Kartell) are set across a 1920s villa. The top rooms boast a panoramic sea view. From Easter onwards, designer sun loungers are positioned in the fragrant gardens beside the outdoor pool.

15 av. Joseph Liautaud. www.lavila-cassis.com. *✆* **04-42-03-35-37.** 5 units. 130€–230€ double. Breakfast included. Free parking. **Amenities:** Outdoor pool; free Wi-Fi. Closed Nov to mid-Mar.

Hotel La Rade ★   The pick of Cassis's mid-range hotels, La Rade gazes out over the ocean, a 3-min. walk from the pedestrian only quays. Its enviably tranquil position is also convenient for strolls west to plage du Bestouan and into the Calanques National Park beyond. In summer, the hotel's locally sourced breakfast—think Cassis jams and Provençal *saucisson*—is served by the swimming pool. It's not only the only sea view *piscine* in town, but heated too, which means it's open year-round. The hotel terrace is justly popular with artists. Indeed, Sir Winston Churchill honed his painting skills at the Camargo Foundation (www.camargofoundation.org) artist residency just across the street.

1 av. des Dardanelles. www.bestwestern-cassis.com. *✆* **04-42-01-02-97.** 28 units. 99€–159€ double. Breakfast 16€ per person. **Amenities:** Restaurant; outdoor pool; free Wi-Fi.

Where to Eat

Bar de la Marine ★ BISTRO   This harborside eatery won't feature in the Michelin guide or any other French foodie bible. And thank heavens for that. This no-nonsense bar and bistro has been dishing up hearty breakfasts, *steak-frites*, *salade Niçoise*, and seafood salads to tired fishermen for close to 5 decades. In season, its proximity to Cassis's working port makes it a prime spot to try sea urchins, the local delicacy. Simply order a platter from the septuagenarian street vendor to be delivered to your table. Like almost every other restaurant in Cassis, Bar de la Marine boasts rustic service and age-old tableware.

5 quai des Baux. ℂ **04-42-01-76-09.** Main course 10€–17€. Daily noon–2:30pm and 7–10:30pm.

Poissonnerie Laurent ★★ SEAFOOD   The Giannettini family have been serving harbor-fresh seafood at this portside emplacement since 1940. They've had 75 years to perfect their simple recipes. My goodness they're good. Grilled sardines, octopus salad, and the special house spicy aïoli share the menu with local sea urchins (in season) and oysters from near Marseille. Bouillabaisse, the famed seafood stew from Marseille, may be ordered in advance.

6 quai Barthélémy. ℂ **04-42-01-71-56.** Main course 11€–24€. Tues–Sun noon–1:30pm; Jun–Sept Tues–Sat 7:30–10pm. Closed Jan.

ILES D'HYÈRES ★★

39km (24 miles) SE of Toulon; 119km (74 miles) SW of Cannes

Bobbing off the French Riviera in the Mediterranean Sea, a small group of islands encloses the eastern boundary of Provence. During the Renaissance, they were coined the Iles d'Or (Golden Islands), named for the glow the rocks give off in sunlight. As might be expected, their location only 30 min. from the French coast means the islands are often packed with tourists in summer—but its breathtaking beaches still have space for everyone.

If you have time for only one island, choose the beautiful, lively **Ile de Porquerolles.** The **Ile de Port-Cros** is quieter—and perhaps better for an overnight stay to take advantage of the great hiking, exploring, and snorkeling that would be too rushed for a 6-hr. day trip. As for the **Ile du Levant,** 80 percent belongs to the French army and is used for missile testing; the remainder is a nudist colony.

Essentials

GETTING TO ILE DE PORQUEROLLES   Ferries leave from several points along the Côte d'Azur. The most frequent, cheapest, and shortest trip is from the harbor of La Tour Fondue on the peninsula of Giens, a 32km (20-mile) drive east of Toulon. Depending on the season, there are 5 to 19

View of Porquerolles Island marina

departures per day. The round-trip fare for the 15-min. crossing is 19.50€ adults and 16.80€ children ages 4 to 10. For information, contact **TLV-TVM,** La Tour Fondue, Giens 83400 (www.tlv-tvm.com; ℰ **04-94-58-21-81**). **Bateliers de la Côte d'Azur** (www.bateliersdelacotedazur.com; ℰ **04-94-05-21-14**) and **Les Vedettes Ile d'Or** (www.vedettesilesdor.fr; ℰ **04-94-71-01-02**) also offer services from La Londe-les-Maures and Le Lavandou respectively.

GETTING TO ILE DE PORT-CROS The most popular ferry route to the island is the 35-min. crossing that departs from Le Lavandou 3 to 7 times daily, depending on the season (round-trip 28€ adults, 22.60€ children 4–12). For information, contact **Les Vedettes Ile d'Or & Le Corsaire** (see above). The **TLV-TVM** and **Bateliers de la Côte d'Azur** (see above) also service Ile de Port-Cros. Some of the former's services travel onwards to Ile de Levant.

VISITOR INFORMATION Other than temporary, summer-only kiosks that distribute brochures and advice near the ferry docks in Porquerolles and Port-Cros, the islands do not have tourist bureaus. For further information, contact the **Office de Tourisme de Hyères, Bureau de Porquerolles,** Rotonde du Park Hôtel, av. de Belgique, Hyères (www.hyeres-tourisme.com; ℰ **04-94-01-84-50**). Information can also be found at www.porquerolles.com and www.portcrosparcnational.fr.

MAIL/POSTAGE & MONEY The post office, **La Poste,** pl. d'Armes, Porquerolles (ℰ **36-31**), also has an ATM, but it's best to bring petty cash. Most establishments accept credit cards.

Exploring Ile de Porquerolles ★★

Ile de Porquerolles is the largest and westernmost of the Iles d'Hyères. It has a rugged south coast, but the northern strand, facing the mainland, boasts a handful of pristine white-sand beaches. The island is about 8km (5 miles) long, 2km (1.25 miles) wide, 4.8km (3 miles) from the mainland. The permanent population is only 400.

The island is said to receive 275 days of sunshine annually. The landscape is one of rocky capes, pine forests twisted by the mistral, sun-drenched vineyards, and pale ochre houses. It's best explored on foot or by bike (look for plenty of bike-rental agencies just behind the harbor). The **place d'Armes,** former site of the garrison, is home to several quaint cafes—your best bet for lunch if you're here for a day trip.

The island has a history of raids, attacks, and occupation by everyone from the Dutch and the English to the Turks and the Spaniards. Ten forts, some in ruins, testify to its fierce past. The most ancient is **Fort Ste-Agathe,** built in 1531 by François I. In time, it was a penal colony and a retirement center for soldiers of the colonial wars.

In 1971, the French government purchased a large part of the island and turned it into a national park. Indigenous trees such as fig, mulberry, and olive are protected, as well as plants that attract butterflies.

WHERE TO STAY & EAT

Hotel et Residence Les Medes (www.hotel-les-medes.fr) also offers good-value guest rooms and apartments.

Mas du Langoustier ★★   This Provençal-style hotel is far and away Porquerolles' most luxurious accommodation. Located on the island's western tip, it's set in a 40-hectare (99-acre) park laced with bougainvillea, shaded by eucalyptus and Aleppo pines, and overlooking a lovely pine-ringed bay. Elegant rooms have a truly traditional feel and are decorated with classic local textiles; many have their own private patio. Even better, come evening time, there's no need to leave paradise. The onsite **Restaurant L'Olivier** (open to non-guests) is Michelin-starred: Prepare for unique pairings like steamed crayfish and fig ravioli or foie gras with hibiscus jelly.

83 400 Île de Porquerolles. www.langoustier.com. ✆ **04-94-58-30-09.** 50 units. 340€–600€ double; from 560€ suite. Rates include half-board for two people. Closed Oct to late Apr. **Amenities:** 2 restaurants; bar; babysitting; outdoor pool; tennis court; free Wi-Fi.

Exploring Ile de Port-Cros ★★

The most mountainous island of the archipelago, Port-Cros has been France's smallest national park since 1963. It's just 5km (3 miles) long and 2km (1.25 miles) wide. It's blanketed with beautiful beaches, pine forests, and subtropical vegetation (birders flock here to observe nearly 100 different species). A hiker's paradise, it also has a number of

Ile de Port-Cros

well-marked trails. The most popular and scenic is the easy, 1-hr. *sentier des plantes*. The more adventurous and athletic take the 10km (6.25-mile) *circuit de Port-Man* (and pack their lunch). There is even a 274m (899-ft.) "underwater trail" along the coast where you can snorkel past laminated signs identifying the plants and fish you'll see.

WHERE TO STAY & EAT

Le Manoir de Port-Cros ★ Port-Cros's only hotel is within an 18th-century whitewashed building. Accommodation may be simple—crisp white sheets, oversized copper vases, terra-cotta tiled floors—but guests stay here to truly switch off. Paddle in the pool, head out for a hike, or simply amble the surrounding palm and eucalyptus-studded gardens. Rates are half-board, although plenty of day trippers visit for the restaurant's hearty three-course lunch (66€), which can include monkfish medallions with kaffir lime, and local rockfish soup.

Route du Barrage. www.hotel-lemanoirportcros.com. ℂ **04-94-05-90-52.** 21 units. 165€–265€ double; 210€–240€ family room; 230€–265€ bungalows for 4. Closed Nov–Mar. **Amenities:** Restaurant; bar; outdoor pool; room service; free Wi-Fi in common areas.

15

THE
FRENCH
RIVIERA

By Tristan Rutherford

T
he fabled real estate known as the French Riviera, also called the Côte d'Azur (Azure Coast), ribbons for 200km (125 miles) along the sun-kissed Mediterranean. The region has long attracted artists and jet-setters alike with its clear skies, blue waters, and carefree cafe culture. Chic, sassy, and incredibly sexy, the Riviera can be explored by bus, train, boat, bike, Segway, electric car, or in a dozen novel ways.

A trail of modern artists captivated by the region's light and setting has left a rich heritage: Matisse at Vence, Cocteau at Villefranche, Léger at Biot, Renoir at Cagnes, and Picasso at Antibes and seemingly everywhere in between. The finest collection of modern artworks is at the Fondation Maeght in St-Paul-de-Vence. Museums dedicated to Jean Cocteau in Menton and Pierre Bonnard near Cannes also offer a vivid introduction to the Riviera's storied art scene.

A century ago, winter and spring were considered high season on the Riviera. In recent decades, July and August have become the most crowded months, and reservations are imperative. The region basks in more than 300 days of sun per year, and even December and January are often pleasant and sunny.

The ribbonlike corniche roads stretch across the western Riviera from Nice to Menton are scenic stars in scores of films including Cary Grant's "To Catch a Thief" and Robert de Niro's "Ronin", as well as the 2017 British blockbuster series, "Riviera". The lower road, the 32km (20-mile) Corniche Inférieure (often referred to as the Basse Corniche), takes in the resorts of Villefranche, Cap-Ferrat, Beaulieu, Monaco, and Cap-Martin. The 31km (19-mile) Moyenne Corniche (Middle Road) winds in and out of mountain tunnels and passes the picture-perfect village of Èze. Napoleon built the Grande Corniche—the most panoramic roadway—in 1806. La Turbie is the principal town along the 32km (20-mile) stretch, which reaches more than 480m (1,574 ft.) high at Col d'Èze.

ST-TROPEZ ★★★

874km (542 miles) S of Paris; 76km (47 miles) SW of Cannes

While this sun-kissed town has a well-known air of hedonism, Tropezian style is blissfully understated—it's not in-your-face. St-Tropez attracts artists, musicians, models, writers, and an A-lister movie colony each summer, with a flamboyant parade of humanity trailing behind. In winter

FACING PAGE: **Antibes, one of the French Riviera's oldest resorts**

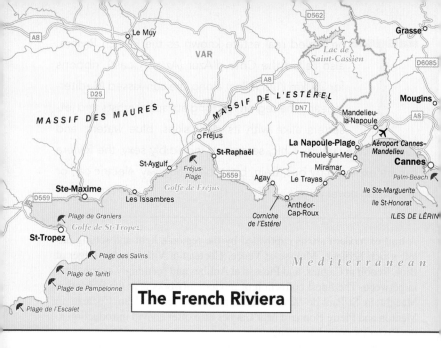

The French Riviera

it morphs back into a boho fishing village, albeit one with modern art galleries and some of the best restaurants along the coast.

The 1956 Brigitte Bardot movie "And God Created Woman" put St-Tropez on the tourist map. Droves of decadent tourists baring almost all on the peninsula's white-sand beaches trailed in her wake. Two decades ago, Bardot pronounced St-Tropez dead, "squatted by a lot of no-goods, drugheads, and villains". But even she returned, followed in recent years by international celebrity A-listers, from David Beckham and Beyoncé to Vanessa Paradis and Kourtney Kardashian.

Essentials

ARRIVING   The nearest rail station is in St-Raphaël, a neighboring coastal resort. **Boats** depart (www.bateauxsaintraphael.com; ⓒ **04-94-95-17-46**) from its Vieux Port for St-Tropez (trip time: 1 hr.) five times a day in high summer, reducing to once- or twice-daily sailings in winter. The one-way fare is 15€. Year-round, 10 to 15 Varlib **buses** per day leave from the Gare Routière in St-Raphaël (www.varlib.fr; ⓒ **04-94-44-52-70**) for St-Tropez. The trip takes 1.5 to 2 hr., depending on the bus and the traffic, which during midsummer is usually horrendous. A one-way ticket is 3€. Buses also run from Toulon train station, 56km (35 miles) away.

If you **drive,** note that parking in St-Tropez is tricky, especially in summer. For parking, follow the signs for **Parking des Lices** (ⓒ **04-94-97-34-46**), beneath place des Lices, or **Parking du Nouveau Port,** on

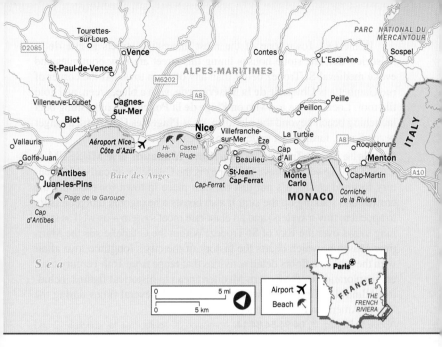

waterfront avenue Charles de Gaulle (📞 **04-94-97-74-99**). To get here from **Cannes,** drive southwest along the coastal highway (D559), turning east when you see signs to St-Tropez.

VISITOR INFORMATION   The **Office de Tourisme** is on quai Jean-Jaurès (www.sainttropeztourisme.com; 📞 **08-92-68-48-28**). Note that they charge 2€ for a town map. Meanies. Alternatively, for 3€ you can rent an iPod from them and explore the town via an interactive self-guided tour.

[FastFACTS] ST-TROPEZ

ATMs/Banks   **Crédit Agricole,** 17 pl. des Lices (📞 **32-25**).

Internet Access   The St-Tropez's **Tourist Office** (see above for details) has free Wi-Fi.

Mail & Postage   **La Poste,** rue de la Poste (📞 **36-31**).

Pharmacies   **Pharmacie du Port,** 9 quai Suffren (📞 **04-94-97-00-06**).

Exploring St-Tropez

During summertime, St-Tropez's pleasure port is trimmed with super-yachts, each one berthing stern-to after a day of hedonistic excess at nearby Plage de Pampelonne. Yacht owners, their lucky guests, specta-tors, and celebrity-seekers all intermingle along the chic quays.

In the Old Town, one of the most interesting streets is **rue de la Miséricorde.** The stone houses lining this street are now boutiques and evoke medieval St-Tropez better than any other in town. At the corner of rue Gambetta is **Chapelle de la Miséricorde,** with a blue, green, and gold tile roof. Locals come to swim on **Plage de la Ponche,** an old fishing boat launching beach beyond the old town, or at **Plage des Graniers,** a longer beach 5 min. farther east underneath the Citadelle.

Citadelle de St-Tropez & Maritime Museum ★★ MUSEUM & CASTLE   Towering above St-Tropez is the Citadelle, an early 17th-century fortified castle. It's not just the best place in town for escaping the crowds and soaking up the sun. It also boasts a hexagonal dungeon (sure to appeal to tiny travelers) and an elaborate moat system—as well as stunning views over the Bay of St-Tropez. Within the Citadelle sits the Maritime Museum, which charts the history of the city's longtime love affair with the sea. Two floors detail activities that range from 16th-century traders' exploration of the eastern Mediterranean to historical figures including Admiral Suffren, who whupped the British several times during the War of American Independence.

Above St-Tropez. 🕿 **04-94-54-84-14.** Admission 3€ adults; free for children 12 and under. Apr–Sept daily 10am–6:30pm; Oct–Mar daily 10am–12:30pm and 1:30-5:30pm.

Sunset over St-Tropez

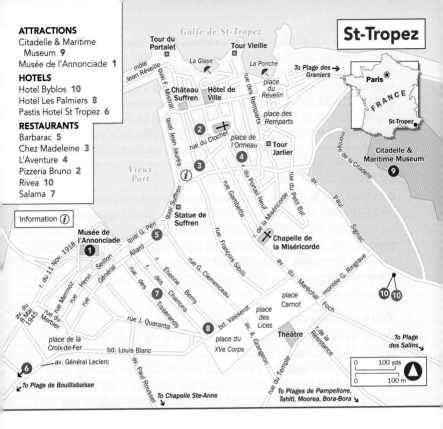

ATTRACTIONS
Citadelle & Maritime
  Museum **9**
Musée de l'Annonciade **1**

HOTELS
Hotel Byblos **10**
Hotel Les Palmiers **8**
Pastis Hotel St Tropez **6**

RESTAURANTS
Barbarac **5**
Chez Madeleine **3**
L'Aventure **4**
Pizzeria Bruno **2**
Rivea **10**
Salama **7**

Information (i)

Musée de l'Annonciade (Musée St-Tropez) ★★★ MUSEUM   If you leave town without seeing this spellbinding museum, you've missed a colorful part of St-Tropez's past. Showcasing superb post-Impressionist paintings (1890–1950), this collection is displayed throughout the interior of a 16th-century chapel just off of St-Tropez's harbor. In 1892, it was St-Tropez's adopted son, Paul Signac, who kick-started the wave of painters who flooded to this picturesque seaside town. Many of the artists featured—including Signac—painted the port of St-Tropez, a backdrop that lies right outside the building. The museum includes such masterpieces as Matisse's *La Femme à la fenêtre, Nice,* as well as artworks by Bonnard, Braque, Dufy, Marquet, and Derain. Temporary shows are held on the ground floor.

Pl. Grammont. © **04-94-17-84-10.** Admission 6€ adults; 4€ children 11 and under. Tues–Sun 10am–1pm and 2–6pm. Closed Nov.

Outdoor Activities

BEACHES   The hottest Riviera beaches are at St-Tropez. The best for families are closest to the center, including **Plage de la Bouillabaisse** and **Plage des Salins.** More daring and infinitely more famous is the 5km

(3-mile) crescent of **Plage de Pampelonne,** about 10km (6.25 miles) from town. Here, around 35 hedonistic beach clubs dot the sand. Overtly decadent is **Club 55** (www.club55.fr; ℂ **04-94-55-55-55**), a former Bardot hangout, while the American-run **Nikki Beach** (www.nikkibeach.com; ℂ **04-94-79-82-04**) is younger and more understated, if painfully chic. Gay-friendly **Aqua Club** (ℂ **04-94-79-84-35**) and bare-all **Plage de Tahiti** (www.tahiti-beach.com; ℂ **04-94-97-18-02**) are extremely welcoming.

You'll need a car, bike, or scooter to get from town to Plage de Pampelonne. Parking is around 10€ for the day. More than anywhere else on the Riviera, topless bathing is the norm.

BOATING   In St-Tropez port, **Octopussy** (www.octopussy.fr; ℂ **04-94-56-53-10**) rents boats 5 to 16m (16–52 ft.) long. Larger ones come with a captain at the helm. Prices begin at 350€ per day.

DIVING   Multilingual scuba training and equipment rental is available from the **European Diving School** (www.europeandiving.com; info@europeandiving.com), on Plage de Pampelonne. Regular dives, including all equipment, cost 42€.

Where to Stay

Hôtel Byblos ★★★   Opened in 1967 on a hill above the harbor, this hamlet of pastel-hued, Provençal-style houses is opulence personified. Inspired by the legendary Phoenician city of the same name, Byblos is decked with bubbling fountains and ancient olive trees, and is favored by visiting celebrities, rock stars, and aristocrats. Rooms range in size from medium to mega; some units have such special features as four-posters with furry spreads or sunken whirlpool tubs. The breakfast is superb: Served up around the swimming pool, it's a cornucopia of chocolate fountains, hand-baked pastries, organic granola, and unique teas from across the globe. Later on, guests can while away an afternoon at the hotel's Spa by Sisley, indulge at super chef Alain Ducasse's onsite restaurant, Rivea, or dance among the world's über-rich and famous at nightclub Caves du Roy.

20 av. Paul Signac. www.byblos.com. ℂ **04-94-56-68-00.** 91 units. From 480€ double; from 910€ suite. Breakfast 40€–48€. Parking 40€. Pets 90€. Closed Nov to mid-Apr. **Amenities:** 2 restaurants; bar; nightclub; babysitting; concierge; exercise room; massage; outdoor pool; room service; sauna; spa; free Wi-Fi.

Hôtel Les Palmiers ★   In a town packed with pricey accommodation options, this friendly, family-run hotel is a real find. Not only is its location fantastic—directly astride place des Lices in the center of St-Tropez—but Les Palmiers also boasts pretty Provençal-colored rooms and a top-notch contemporary courtyard garden with dark wicker furnishings, bold cushions, and sun-dappled corners, ideal for sipping a glass or two of local rosé. Part of the hotel dates from the late 18th century, giving the place a cozy, vintage feel.

34 bd. Vasserot (pl. des Lices). www.hotel-les-palmiers.com. ℂ **04-94-97-01-61.** 25 units. 90€–288€ double. Breakfast 14€. **Amenities:** Bar; free Wi-Fi.

A beach at St-Tropez

Pastis Hôtel St Tropez ★★   This portside Provençal house feels more like a sophisticated, eclectic home than a hotel—albeit one decorated with a phenomenal eye for design. British owners John and Pauline Larkin have arranged their private collection of Matisse prints, vintage photographs, 1970s framed album artwork, and Provençal antiques in both the guest-only lounge and inspired guestrooms surrounding the courtyard swimming pool. Bathrooms are stocked with niche Sicilian toiletries by Ortigia, while each guestroom hosts its own selection of quirky books, magazines, and DVDs. Each unique unit is spacious yet intimate and possesses its own balcony or breakfast terrace.

75 av. du Général Leclerc. www.pastis-st-tropez.com. © **04-98-12-56-50.** 10 units. 200€–850€ double. Free parking. Closed Nov–Feb. **Amenities:** Bar; outdoor pool; free Wi-Fi.

Where to Eat

St-Tropez's dining scene is both expensive and exclusive, particularly during the summer season. Reserve well in advance or be prepared to dine very early or very late. In addition to the suggestions below, the long-established Moroccan restaurant **Salama,** 3 rue Tisserands (www.restaurant-salama.com; © **04-94-97-59-62**), cooks up a fine selection of couscous, pastilla, and tajines; **Chez Madeleine,** 14 pl. aux Herbes (© **06-85-91-03-76**), behind the fish market, is renowned for its oyster bar, and also serves stellar seafood platters; and **Barbarac,** 2 rue Général Allard (www.barbarac.fr; © **04-94-97-67-83**), has been scooping up the finest artisanal ice cream in town since it opened in 1986.

L'Aventure ★ MODERN PROVENÇAL   A backstreet St-Tropez eatery beloved of locals and visitors alike, L'Aventure serves globally inspired market-fresh cuisine: think classic French ingredients like snails, Provençal lamb, and harbor-fresh fish. But flavors run the gamut, from pesto and honey to ginger and preserved lemons. Affable owner Ayala is even happy to cater for special diets given 48 hours' notice. This place is blessedly unpretentious, right down to the authentically battered tables on the petite terrace.

31 rue du Portail-Neuf. ✆ **04-94-97-44-01.** Main course 25€–38€; fixed-price menu 40€. Tues–Sun 7:30–10pm.

Pizzeria Bruno ★ ITALIAN   Proving that not all good meals in St-Tropez have to break the bank, this casual joint has been turning out thin, crispy, wood-fired pizzas since 1959. Even Bardot was a regular. The menu includes a handful of creative salads, pasta dishes, and grilled meats. Note that the restaurant's copious wood-paneled and overly snug seating isn't the comfiest—and hearty eaters may find the pizzas a little on the small side—but the atmosphere is among the liveliest in town.

6 rue de l'Eglise. ✆ **04-94-97-05-18.** Main course 12€–20€. Daily noon–2pm and 7–11pm. Closed Oct–Apr.

Rivea ★★ MODERN PROVENÇAL   Set downstairs from the Hotel Byblos and across a palm-shaded terrace, Alain Ducasse's sleek restaurant has wow-factor in spades. Head chef Vincent Maillard uses ingredients sourced exclusively from the French and Italian Rivieras to create

St-Tropez Harbor

tapas-style appetizers, including *vitello tonnato* (veal in a creamy tuna sauce), *daube provençale* beef ravioli, and porcini mushroom fritters. Both the crisp house salad (a medley of artichokes, fennel, zucchini flowers, and tomato croutons), and Maillard's signature dish, marinated sea bream and eggplant, are unmissable.

27 av. Maréchal Foch. www.alain-ducasse.com. ② **04-94-56-68-20.** Main course 25€–44€; fixed-price menus 71€–98€. Daily 7pm–12:30am. Closed mid-Oct to mid-Apr.

Shopping

St-Tropez is awash in stylish shops. The merchandise is Mediterranean, breezy, and sophisticated. Dotted throughout the town's *triangle d'or,* the rough triangle formed by place de la Garonne, rue François Sibilli and place des Lices, chic labels include Hermès, Sonia Rykiel, and Louis Vuitton. Every summer, a Chanel summer pop-up shop occupies the old Hotel la Mistralée at 1 av. du Général Leclerc, while nearby, Michelin-starred chef Yannick Alléno dishes up delights at **Dior des Lices,** 13 rue François Sibilli, the fashion house's own summertime pop-up eatery. Scores of unique boutiques are around the Vieille Ville (Old Town), including **Vachon Saint-Tropez,** 33 av. Paul Roussel (② **04-94-97-23-90**), which has been purveying fashionable swimwear, tunics, and hats since 1919; **Titamàlà,** 53 rue Portail Neuf (www.titamala.com; ② **06-25-59-47-32**), an atelier and boutique that creates locally-inspired bijoux jewelry; and **K. Jacques,** 25 rue Allard (www.kjacques.fr; ② **04-94-97-41-50**), with its iconic *tropéziennes* sandals. Place des Lices hosts an excellent **outdoor market,** Marché Provençal, with food, clothes, and *brocante,* on Tuesday and Saturday mornings.

Nightlife

On a lower level of the Hôtel Byblos' grounds, **Les Caves du Roy,** 20 av. Paul-Signac (www.lescavesduroy.com; ② **04-94-56-68-00**), is the most self-consciously chic nightclub in St-Tropez. Entrance is free, but drink prices are eye-wateringly high. It's open from 11:30pm until dawn

15

THE FRENCH RIVIERA

St-Tropez

HEAD TO THE hills

Unfurling along the shores between St-Tropez and Cannes is a scarlet stretch of coastline known as the Esterel. It's both regional nature reserve and a cluster of mountains (the Massif de l'Esterel), the latter renowned for their ethereal crimson hue. Hiking trails criss-cross the area and the tiny turquoise beaches are perfect for private picnics. Best of all, the Esterel receives just a fraction of the tourists that congregate along the Riviera's more popular seaside resorts. Regular trains run from Cannes to Théoule-sur-Mer, a village in the center of the park. One-way tickets cost 2.70€, and journey time is around 10 min. The **Théoule-sur-Mer Tourist Office,** 2 bd. de la Corniche d'Or (www.theoule-sur-mer.org; ✆ **04-93-49-28-28**), distributes walking and cycling maps of the region.

Fridays and Saturdays from Easter to June, nightly from June through August, and Fridays and Saturdays from September to early October. Open from mid-May through mid-October is **White 1921,** pl. des Lices (www.white1921.com; ✆ **04-94-45-50-50**), a champagne and cocktail bar set within a jasmine-cloaked courtyard garden. The legendary venue Le Papagayo—a hotspot for international A-listers since the 1960s—has recently transformed into **Gaïo,** 4 av. du 11 Novembre 1918 (www.gaio. club; ✆ **04-94-97-89-98**). A combination restaurant and club with an Asian-inspired menu and similar decor, it remains as celebrity-studded as ever. Adjacent to Gaïo is **Le VIP Room,** in the Résidence du Nouveau-Port (www.st-tropez.viproom.fr; ✆ **04-94-97-14-70**), a younger yet similarly chic version of Les Caves du Roy. Paris Hilton and Snoop Dogg have been known to drop by. Cocktails hover around the 20€ mark.

Le Pigeonnier, 19 rue de la Ponche (✆ **06-33-58-92-45**), rocks, rolls, and welcomes a mostly gay and lesbian crowd between 20 and 50. **L'Esquinade,** 2 rue de Four (✆ **04-94-56-26-31**), equally gay-friendly, is the habitual sweaty follow-up club.

Below the Hôtel Sube in the port, **Café de Paris** (www.cafedeparis.fr; ✆ **04-94-97-00-56**), is one of the most popular—and friendly—hangouts in town. It has 1900s-style globe lights, masses of artificial flowers, and a long zinc bar. **Café Sénéquier,** quai Jean Jaurès (www.senequier.com; ✆ **04-94-97-20-20**), is historic, venerable, snobbish by day, and off-puttingly stylish by night.

CANNES ★★★

905km (561 miles) S of Paris; 163km (101 miles) E of Marseille; 26km (16 miles) SW of Nice

When Coco Chanel came here and got a suntan, returning to Paris bronzed, she shocked the milk-white society ladies—who quickly began to copy her. Today the bronzed bodies, clad in nearly nonexistent swimsuits, line the beaches of this chic resort and continue the late fashion designer's example. A block back from the famed promenade de la Croisette are the boutiques, bars, and bistros that make Cannes the Riviera's capital of cool.

Essentials

ARRIVING By **train,** Cannes is 10 min. from Antibes, 30 min. from Nice, and 45 min. from Monaco. The TGV from Paris reaches Cannes in an incredibly scenic 5 hr. The one-way fare from Paris is 43€ to 131€, although advance purchase bargains can be had for as low as 26€. For rail information and schedules, visit www.oui.sncf or call ✆ **36-35** (.40€/ min). **Lignes d'Azur** (www.lignesdazur.com; ✆ **08-10-06-10-06**) provides bus service from Cannes' Gare Routière (pl. Bernard Cornut Gentille) to Antibes every 20 min. during the day (trip time: 25 min.). The one-way fare is 1.50€.

The **Nice International Airport** (www.nice.aeroport.fr; ✆ **08-20-42-33-33**) is a 30-min. drive east. **Bus** no. 210 picks up passengers at the airport every 30 min. during the day (hourly at other times) and drops them at Cannes' Gare Routière. One-way is 22€, round-trip is 33€.

By **car** from Marseille, take A51 north to Aix-en-Provence, continuing along A8 east to Cannes. From Nice, follow A8 or the coastal D6007 southwest to Cannes.

Promenade de la Croisette and beach, Cannes

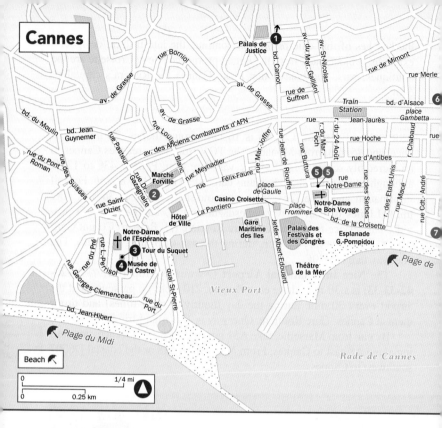

VISITOR INFORMATION The **Office de Tourisme** is at 1 bd. de la Croisette (www.cannes-destination.fr; ☏ **04-92-99-84-22**).

SPECIAL EVENTS Cannes is at its most frenzied in mid-May during the **International Film Festival** (www.festival-cannes.com) at the Palais des Festivals, on promenade de la Croisette. It attracts not only film stars (you can palm the cement molds of their handprints outside the Palais des Festivals), but also seemingly every photographer in the world. You have a better chance of being named prime minister of France than you do attending one of the major screenings, although if you're lucky, you may be able to swing tickets to screenings of one of the lesser films. (Hotel rooms and tables at restaurants are equally scarce during the festival.) But the people-watching is absolutely fabulous!

Getting Around

ON FOOT Cannes' small town center is a labyrinth of one-ways and serious traffic—which makes it best explored on foot.

BY BICYCLE & MOTOR SCOOTER Despite the summertime commotion, the flat landscapes between Cannes and satellite resorts such as La Napoule and Juan-les-Pins are well suited for bikes and motor scooters.

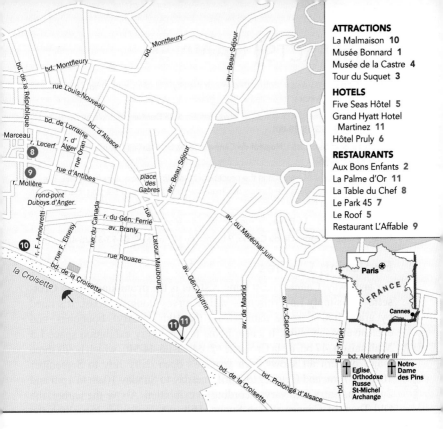

ATTRACTIONS

La Malmaison **10**
Musée Bonnard **1**
Musée de la Castre **4**
Tour du Suquet **3**

HOTELS

Five Seas Hôtel **5**
Grand Hyatt Hotel
 Martinez **11**
Hôtel Pruly **6**

RESTAURANTS

Aux Bons Enfants **2**
La Palme d'Or **11**
La Table du Chef **8**
Le Park 45 **7**
Le Roof **5**
Restaurant L'Affable **9**

At **Daniel Location,** 12 rue Montaigne (www.daniel-location-cannes. com; ☏ **04-93-99-90-30**), *vélos tout terrain,* or VTT (mountain bikes) cost 18€ a day. Motorized bikes and scooters cost from 30€ per day. For larger motorbikes, you must present a valid driver's license. Another bike shop is **Mistral Location,** 4 rue Georges Clémenceau (www.mistral-location. com; ☏ **04-93-39-33-60**), which charges 20€ per day for bikes, and also offers scooters and motorcycles from 30€ per day.

BY CAR   The Cannes Tourist Office website (see above) offers a downloadable document (under "Cannes Practical," then "Useful Information") listing all of the town's **public parking lots** and their hourly fees.

BY TAXI   **Allô Taxi Cannes** (www.allo-taxis-cannes.com; ☏ **04-93-99-27-27**).

BY PUBLIC TRANSPORT   **Palm Bus** (www.palmbus.fr; ☏ **08-25-82-55-99**) operates all public transport in and around Cannes. There's little need for public transport in the city center—although the open-top no. 8, which runs along the seafront from the port in the west to the Pointe Croisette peninsula in the east, makes for a fun and scenic ride. Tickets cost 1.50€ and can be purchased directly aboard any bus.

[FastFACTS] CANNES

ATMs/Banks   Banks are dotted throughout the city, including more than a dozen along the central rue d'Antibes.

Dentists   For emergency dental services, contact **SOS Dentaire** (http://sos-dentaire-cannes.fr; ✆ **04-93-68-28-00**).

Doctors & Hospitals   **Hopital de Cannes,** 15 av. Broussailles (www.ch-cannes.fr; ✆ **04-93-69-70-00**).

Internet Access   Cannes is in the process of blanketing the city with free Wi-Fi. The first area with coverage is the Jardins de l'Hotel de Ville, just behind the port; the network is "Cannes sans fil."

Mail & Postage   **La Poste,** 22 rue Bivouac Napoléon (✆ **16-31**).

Pharmacies   **Pharmacie du Casino,** 9 bis square Mérimée (✆ **04-93-39-25-48**).

Exploring Cannes

Far and away, Cannes' most famous street is the **promenade de la Croisette**—or simply La Croisette—which curves along the coast. It's lined by grand hotels (some dating from the 19th century), boutiques, and exclusive beach clubs. It's also home to temporary exhibition space **La Malmaison,** 47 bd. de la Croisette (✆ **04-97-06-44-90**), which holds three major modern art shows each year. It's open daily July to September 10am to 7pm, and October to April Tuesday to Sunday 10am to 1pm and 2 to 6pm. Entry fees vary according to exhibition. Above the harbor, the Old Town of Cannes sits on Suquet Hill, where visitors can climb the 14th-century **Tour de Suquet.**

Musée Bonnard ★★ ART MUSEUM   The only museum in the world dedicated to the Impressionist painter Pierre Bonnard is 3km (1.75 miles) north of Cannes, in the suburb of Le Cannet. Portraits, sculptures, and sketches on display in this petite museum date from primarily between 1922 and 1947, the period during which the artist was a local resident. Temporary exhibitions, such as 2018's celebration of the 150 years that have passed since Bonnard's birth, offer unqiue opportunities for a peek at privately owned paintings on loan from around the globe. The museum's audio guide comes courtesy of an iPod Touch (1€) or can be downloaded in advance onto your smartphone (free).

16 bd. Sadi Carnot, Le Cannet. www.museebonnard.fr. ✆ **04-93-94-06-06.** Admission 5€–7€ adults; 3.50€–5€ ages 12–18; free for children 11 and under. July–Aug Tues–Sun 10am–8pm (Thurs until 9pm); Sept–June Tues–Sun 10am–6pm. Closed 3 weeks in Jan. Bus no. 1 and 4 from Cannes city center.

Musée de la Castre ★ MUSEUM   Perched above Cannes' Old Town within the medieval Château de la Castre, this museum focuses primarily on ethnographic finds from around the world. Spears from the South Seas and Tibetan masks are interspersed with Sumerian cuneiform tablets and

19th-century paintings of the Riviera. There's also a collection of international instruments on display in the museum's Sainte-Anne Chapel. Many visitors, however, will be most impressed by the astounding views from the museum's viewing tower—accessed via 109 steep steps—which offers glorious views over Cannes, the Mediterranean coastline, and the Lerins Islands beyond. The shady gardens, just outside the museum's entrance, are a welcome respite for tired sightseers.

Le Suquet. ✆ **04-89-82-26-26.** Admission 6€ adults; 3€ ages 18–25; free for children under 17. July–Aug daily 10am–7pm (Wed until 9pm); Sept and Apr–June Tues–Sun 10am–1pm and 2–6pm (June and Sept Wed until 9pm); Oct–Mar Tues–Sun 10am–1pm and 2–5pm.

Organized Tours

One of the best ways to get your bearings in Cannes is to climb aboard the **Petit Train touristique de Cannes** (www.cannes-petit-train.com; ✆ **06-22-61-25-76**). The vehicles operate daily from 9 or 10am to between 7 and 11pm, depending on the season. The three itineraries offered are: Modern Cannes, with a ride along La Croisette and its side streets (35 min.); Historical Cannes, which weaves through the narrow streets of Le Suquet (35 min.); or the Big Tour, a combination of the two (1 hr.). All trains depart from the Palais des Festivals every 30 to 60 min. Shorter tours cost 7€ for adults and 3€ for children 3 to 10; the Big Tour costs 10€ for adults and 5€ for children 3 to 10.

Outdoor Activities

BEACHES Going to the beach in Cannes has more to do with exhibitionism than actual swimming. **Plage de la Croisette** extends between the Vieux Port and the Port Canto. The beaches along this billion-dollar stretch of sand are *payante,* meaning entrance costs between 15€ to 30€. You don't need to be a guest of the Martinez (p. 569), say, to use the beaches associated with a high-end hotel, and Cannes has heaps of buzzing beach clubs, including sassy **3.14 Beach** (www.314casino.com; ✆ **04-93-94-25-43**). Why should you pay an entry fee at all? Well, the fee includes a full day's use of a mattress, a chaise lounge (the seafront is more pebbly than sandy), and a parasol, as well as easy access to freshwater showers. There are also outdoor restaurants and bars (some with organic menus, others with gourmet burgers and sushi) where no one minds if you dine in your swimsuit. Every beach allows topless bathing. Looking for a free public beach without chaises or parasols? Head for **Plage du Midi,** just west of the Vieux Port, or **Plage Gazagnaire,** just east of the Port Canto. Here you'll find families with children and lots of RV-type vehicles parked nearby.

BOATING Several companies around Cannes's Vieux Port rent boats of any size, with or without a crew, for a day, a week, or even longer. An outfit known for short-term rentals of small motorcraft is **Boat Evasion,**

Plage de la Croisette, Cannes

Port du Béal, 110 bd. du Midi (www.boatevasion.com; ℰ **06-26-59-10-77**). For kayak rental and guided tours of the coastline, try **SeaFirst,** pl. Franklin Roosevelt (www.seafirst.fr; ℰ **06-63-98-20-53**).

GOLF Ten golf courses ring Cannes and almost all are within a 20-min. drive of the city. The **Old Course,** 265 route de Golf, Mandelieu (www. golfoldcourse.com; ℰ **04-92-97-32-00**), is a leafy gem dating from 1891. Greens fees start at 90€, with big reductions for lunch deals and afternoon tee-offs. The prestigious **Royal Mougins Golf Club,** 424 av. du Roi, Mougins (www.royalmougins.fr; ℰ **04-92-92-49-69**), also boasts a gourmet restaurant and spa. Greens fees start at 180€, including cart hire; it's half-price for 9 holes. Discounts are available from mid-November through mid-April.

PADDLEBOARDING Like the rest of the world, Cannes has fallen in love with stand-up paddleboarding (SUP). Rent your own from **Cannes Standup Paddle Location,** Plage du Mouré Rouge, bd. Gazagnaire, Palm Beach (www.cannesstanduppaddle.fr; ℰ **06-82-17-08-77**). Fees start at 12€ per hr.

TENNIS Some resorts have their own courts. The city of Cannes also maintains 16 synthetic courts and six clay-topped courts at the **Garden Tennis Club,** 99 av. Maurice Chevalier (ℰ **04-93-47-29-33**). You'll pay from 8€ to 20.20€ per hr., plus 3.80€ per hr. for floodlights.

Where to Stay

Five Seas Hôtel ★★ The coolest hotel in Cannes harks back to a Gatsby era of Art Deco furnishings and no-limits lavishness. The style is Louis Vuitton meets vintage ocean liner. The furniture design is based on classic traveling cases, albeit with Apple computers and Nespresso machines thrown into the mix. Popular with both guests and non-residents is the hotel's **Cinq Mondes & Carita Spa.** The top-floor terrace features a small infinity pool, a cocktail bar, and linen-shaded sun loungers. It's also the location of the acclaimed **Le Roof** modern Mediterranean restaurant (✆ **04-63-36-05-06;** main course 34€–59€; lunch and dinner daily, buffet brunch on Sundays) under the direction of head chef Arnaud Tabarec. And boy, what a view it has. Desserts come courtesy of former World Pastry Champion Jérôme de Oliveira, who also maintains **Intuitions** (p. 573), a tea and pastry shop on the ground floor. For zipping around town, the hotel offers guests the use of bikes or a chauffeured electric cart.

1 rue Notre Dame. www.fiveseashotel.com. ✆ **04-63-36-05-05.** 45 units. 152€–805€ double; from 448€ suite. **Amenities:** Restaurant; bar; concierge; outdoor pool; room service; spa; free Wi-Fi.

Grand Hyatt Hotel Martinez ★★★ The Martinez has been the socialite hub of the South of France for a century. The great and good have marched through its revolving doors including recent guests Eva Longoria, Nicole Kidman, and Steven Spielberg. This Art Deco masterpiece—refreshed following a complete renovation in early 2018, with guestrooms that now boast a contemporary twist courtesy of interior designer Pierre-Yves Rochon—is more than just an ultra-luxe hotel. Non-guests can mingle with celebrities in the **l'Amiral** cocktail bar, bathe next to A-listers in the **ZPlage** beach club, or dine alongside minor royalty in one of the finest restaurants in the South of France, **La Palme d'Or** (p. 570). The hotel also offers a popular bicycle-sharing scheme—and what deliciously cool bikes they are.

73 bd. de la Croisette. http://cannesmartinez.grand.hyatt.com. ✆ **04-93-90-12-34.** 409 units. From 240€ double; from 1,960€ suite. Parking 45€. **Amenities:** 3 summer restaurants, 2 winter restaurants; bar; babysitting; private beach; free bikes; children's center; concierge; exercise room; outdoor pool; room service; sauna; spa; free Wi-Fi.

Hôtel Pruly ★★ Just behind Cannes' train station, this delightful hotel spills out from a renovated century-old townhouse. Charming rooms are decorated in bright colors and Provençal textiles; some boast traditional terra-cotta *tomette* floors or private balconies. An afternoon nap on a sun lounger in the hotel's palm-splashed private garden is a welcome respite from Cannes' summertime crowds. Depending on the season, the hotel may require a minimum stay of 3 to 7 nights.

32 bd. d'Alsace. www.hotel-pruly.com. ✆ **04-93-38-41-28.** 14 units. 85€–270€ double; 110€–320€ triple. **Amenities:** Garden; free Wi-Fi.

Where to Eat

Cannes' dining scene is all-encompassing: expect to stumble across everything from Michelin-starred gastronomy to traditional Provençal peasant cuisine. Restaurants are scattered across the city center, with a particularly heavy concentration around Le Suquet, Cannes' Old Town.

EXPENSIVE

La Palme d'Or ★★★ MODERN FRENCH   Double-Michelin-starred chef Christian Sinicropi has presided over this theater of fine dining—also thoroughly renovated in early 2018—for more than a decade. His level of innovation knows no bounds. Think algae lollipops, flavored smoke, and herb perfume. Guests are greeted at the table by the man himself, then taken on an intensely seasonal 5- to 10-course gastronomic journey. Sinicropi not only creates his own quirky ceramic tableware, he also serves the Cannes Film Festival jury a special set dinner each spring. Spellbinding dishes created for recent festival presidents, like Tim Burton and Woody Allen, can be sampled from the menu. Unforgettable.

In the Grand Hyatt Hotel Martinez, 73 bd. de la Croisette. http://cannesmartinez. grand.hyatt.com. ☎ **04-92-98-74-14.** Jacket and tie recommended. Main course 68€–84€; fixed-price menu 78€–210€. Wed–Sat 12:30–2pm and 8–10pm. Closed Jan–Feb.

Le Park 45 ★★★ MEDITERRANEAN   One of the most inventive— and least expensive—Michelin-starred restaurants on the Riviera is run by baby-faced chef Sébastien Broda. Nicknamed the "Petit Prince de la Croisette," Broda scooped up his first Michelin star before the age of 30, after a career at La Palme d'Or in Cannes and L'Amandier in Mougins, two dens of fine Riviera dining. Locally sourced vegetables and seafood—

Sailboats at harbor, Cannes

from stuffed baby squid to Mediterranean octopus—sparkle with additions of yuzu condiment, ponzu cream, Parmesan bouillon, and zingy Granny Smith apple *jus*. Surrounding Le Park 45 is the modernist splendor of **Le Grand Hotel** (www.grand-hotel-cannes.com; ✆ **04-93-38-15-15**). Originally the first hotel on the Croisette, this current 1960s incarnation boasts the best sea views in Cannes and perfectly preserved period features—from funky plastic telephones to Art Deco lampshades. Prices run 180€ to 570€ for a double and from 520€ for a suite, including free Wi-Fi.

In Le Grand Hotel, 45 bd. de la Croisette. www.grand-hotel-cannes.com. ✆ **04-93-38-15-45.** Main course 38€–62€; fixed-price lunch 55€ or dinner 55€–140€. July–Aug daily noon–2pm and 7:30–10pm; Sept–June Tues–Sat noon–2pm and 7:30–10pm.

MODERATE

Restaurant L'Affable ★★ MEDITERRANEAN   Chef Jean-Paul Battaglia's menu may be petite, but his creations are as innovative and contemporary as can be. The frequently changing selection of dishes may be classically French, but it has plenty of modern twists too. Look out for pumpkin soup with foie gras foam, ceviche "Grenoble-style" drizzled with capers and lime, or tartare of scallops and oysters served with lemon Chantilly cream. Be sure to save space for Battaglia's signature *soufflé au Grand-Marnier*. Note that the ambiance at lunch is vibrant, while evenings are more formal. The service is consistently superb—making L'Affable a good choice for a special occasion.

5 rue Lafontaine. www.restaurant-laffable.fr. ✆ **04-93-68-02-09.** Main course 40€–44€; fixed-price lunch 25€–29€ or dinner 46€. Mon–Sat 12:30–2pm and 7–10pm (closed Sat lunch). Closed Aug.

La Table du Chef ★ FRENCH/PROVENÇAL   Just off Cannes' premier shopping street, rue d'Antibes, this unassuming little bistro serves up some of the city's tastiest cuisine. Chef Bruno Gensdarme (who spent almost 20 years working alongside superchef Guy Savoy in Paris) puts his own spin on traditional French dishes, such as Muscadet-infused rabbit terrine, or eggplant *millefeuilles* drizzled in goat's cheese cream and olives. Picky eaters beware: Waitstaff will take on any dietary requirements at the start of your meal, but from that point onwards, your taste buds are left to the whims of the chef's delectable (and surprising!) set menus.

5 rue Jean Daumas. ✆ **04-93-68-27-40.** Fixed-price menu 26€–45€. Mon–Sat noon–2pm; Thurs–Sat 7–10pm.

INEXPENSIVE

Aux Bons Enfants ★ PROVENÇAL   You could easily miss this old-fashioned eatery, tucked among a crowd of mediocre tourist-targeted restaurants. But what an oversight that would be. Family-run for three generations—since 1935—the authentic Aux Bons Enfants today is headed up by Chef Luc Giorsetti. Dishes are traditional: *daube de canard;*

zucchini flower fritters; or house-cured salmon gravlax. Some are even defiantly retro: think slow-cooked *duck à la niçoise;* veal with a side of macaroni *gratin*; followed by a tower of citrusy grapefruit pavlova. Seasonal ingredients are sourced each morning from Marché Forville. *Note:* The restaurant has no telephone and does not accept reservations or credit cards.

80 rue Meynadier. www.aux-bons-enfants-cannes.com. No phone. Main course 16€–23€; fixed-price menus 27€–34€. Tues–Sat noon–2pm and 7–10pm.

Shopping

Cannes achieves a blend of resort-style leisure, glamour, and media glitz more successfully than many of its neighbors. You'll see every big-name designer you can think of, plus a legion of one-off designer boutiques and shoe stores. There are also real-people shops; resale shops for star-studded castoffs; flea markets for funky junk; and a fruit, flower, and vegetable market.

BOOKS Ciné-Folie, 14 rue des Frères-Pradignac (✆ **04-93-39-22-99**), is devoted entirely to film. Called "La Boutique du Cinema," it is the finest film bookstore in the south of France; vintage film stills and movie posters are also for sale. The newly opened **Autour d'un Livre,** 11 rue Bivouac Napoleon (✆ **04-93-68-01-99**), is a combination bookshop and cafe with a small selection of English language novels and travel guides.

DESIGNER SHOPS Most of the big fashion names line promenade de la Croisette, the main drag along the sea. Among the most prestigious are **Dior,** 38 La Croisette (✆ **04-92-98-98-00**), and **Hermès,** 52 La Croisette (✆ **04-93-39-08-90**). The stores stretch from the Hôtel Carlton almost to the Palais des Festivals, with the top names closest to the **Gray d'Albion,** 38 rue des Serbes (www.lucienbarriere.com; ✆ **04-92-99-79-79**), both a mall and a hotel (how convenient). Near the train station, department store **Galeries Lafayette** has all the big-name labels crammed into one small-ish space at 6 rue du Maréchal-Foch (www.galerieslafayette.com, ✆ **04-97-06-25-00**).

Young hipsters should try **Bathroom Graffiti,** 52 rue d'Antibes (✆ **04-93-39-02-32**), for sexy luggage, bikinis, and designer houseware. The rue d'Antibes is also brilliant for big-brand bargains (Zara and Max-Mara), as well as one-off boutiques.

FOOD The Marché Forville (see below) and the surrounding streets are unsurprisingly the best places to search for picnic supplies. For bottles of Côtes de Provence, try **Cave du Marché,** 5 pl. Marché Forville (✆ **04-93-99-60-98**). It also serves up glasses of local rosé and olive crostini on tables outside. **La Compagnie des Saumons,** 12 pl. Marché Forville (✆ **04-93-68-33-20**), brims with caviar, bottles of fish soup, and slabs of smoked salmon. Local cheese shop **Le Fromage Gourmet,** 8 rue des Halles (✆ **04-93-99-96-41**), is a favorite of celebrated chef Alain Ducasse.

Closer to the seafront, World Pastry Champion Jérôme Oliveira creates fairy-tale desserts in bite sizes—from flower-topped tarts to a pastel rainbow of *macarons*—at **Intuitions,** 22 rue Bivouac Napoléon (www. patisserie-intuitions.com; ℰ **04-63-36-05-07**).

MARKETS   The **Marché Forville,** in place Marché Forville just north of the Vieux Port, is a covered stucco structure with a few arches but no walls. From Tuesday to Sunday, 7am to 1pm, it's the fruit, vegetable, and flower market that supplies the dozens of restaurants in the area. Monday (8am–6pm) is *brocante* day, when the market fills with dealers selling everything from Grandmère's dishes and bone-handled carving knives to castaways from estate sales. Tuesdays to Sundays, 8am to 12:30pm, the small **Marché aux Fleurs** (Flower Market) takes place outdoors along the edges of the allée de la Liberté, across from the Palais des Festivals.

Nightlife

BARS & CLUBS   A strip of sundowner bars stretches along rue Félix Faure. Most are chic, some have happy-hour cocktails, and several have DJs after dinner. Wine bar **Le Bouche à Oreille,** 7 rue des Gabres (www. lebouchaoreille.com; ℰ **04-93-39-97-90**), is a convivial spot to sample more unusual South of France wines. For an aperitif with history, the **Bar l'Amiral,** in the Hôtel Martinez, 73 La Croisette (ℰ **04-93-90-12-34**), is where deals have always gone down during the film festival. The bar comes complete with the nameplates of stars that once propped it up, Humphrey Bogart among them. Alternatively, head to **Le 360,** Radisson Blu 1835 Hotel & Thalasso, 2 bd. Jean Hibert (www.restaurant-le-360. com; ℰ **04-92-99-73-04**), a panoramic rooftop terrace overlooking the port that's idyllic for a cocktail as the sun sets. Continue the party at **Chrystie,** 22 rue Macé (www.chrystie.com; ℰ **04-93-99-66-91**), with a choice of dozens of impeccably-created sexy cocktails on offer (Daïkiri Red Lips, anyone?), luxurious nibbles (try the truffle pizza), plus live pop, international DJs, and cabaret. At **Le Bâoli,** Port Pierre Canto, La Croisette (www.baolicannes.com; ℰ **04-93-43-03-43**), Europe's partying elite, from Prince Albert of Monaco to Jude Law, dance until dawn. Dress to the nines to slip past the über-tight security and into this Asian-inspired wonderland.

CASINOS   Cannes is invariably associated with easygoing permissiveness, filmmaking glitterati, and gambling. If the latter is your thing, Cannes has world-class casinos (you must present a passport for entry) loaded with high rollers, voyeurs, and everyone in between. The better established is the **Casino Barrière Cannes Le Croisette,** in the Palais des Festivals, 1 espace Lucien Barrière (www.lucienbarriere.com; ℰ **04-92-98-78-00**). A well-respected fixture in town since the 1950s, a collection of noisy slot machines it is most certainly not. Its main competitor is the **3.14 Casino,** 5 Rue François Einesy, (www.314casino.com;

ⓒ 04-97-06-36-90). It attracts a younger crowd with private games rooms, a beach club, two restaurants, and a juice bar. The casino also pulls in daytime visitors with tasty Middle Eastern mezze (from 8€) and its set menu lunches (14€–21€). Both casinos maintain slots that operate daily from lunchtime to around 4am. Smarter dress is expected for the *salles des grands jeux* (blackjack, roulette, craps, poker, and chemin de fer), which open nightly 8pm to 4am.

DAY TRIPS FROM CANNES
Iles de Lérins ★★
Short boat ride from Cannes

Floating in the Mediterranean just south of Cannes' southern horizon, the Lérins Islands are an idyllic place to escape the Riviera's summertime commotion. Head for Cannes port's western quai Laubeuf, where ferryboats by **Trans-Côte d'Azur** (www.trans-cote-azur.com; ⓒ 04-92-98-71-30) offer access to Ile Ste-Marguerite. To visit Ile St-Honorat, head for the same quay, to the **Transports Planaria** (www.cannes-ilesdelerins.com; ⓒ 04-92-98-71-38) ferryboats. Both companies offer frequent service to the islands daily at intervals of between 30 and 90 min. depending on the season. Round-trip transport to Ile Ste-Marguerite costs 15€ per adult and 9.50€ for children 5 to 10; round-trip transport to Ile St-Honorat costs 16.50€ per adult, 13€ for children 13 to 18, and 8.50€ for children 8 to 12 (although a 10 percent discount on tickets is offered to those who book in advance online). Travel to both islands is free for children 4 and under. As dining options on the islands are limited, pack up a picnic lunch from Cannes' Marché Forville before you set off. To preserve nature, mountain bikes, spear fishing, and drones are completely banned.

EXPLORING ILE STE-MARGUERITE

Ile Ste-Marguerite is one big botanical garden—cars, cigarettes, and all other pollutants are banned—ringed by crystal-clear sea. From the dock, you can stroll along the island to Fort Royal, built by Spanish troops in 1637 and used as a military barracks and parade ground until World War II. The infamous "Man in the Iron Mask" was allegedly imprisoned here, and you can follow the legend back to his horribly spooky cell.

Musée de la Mer, Fort Royal (ⓒ 04-93-38-55-26), traces the history of the island, displaying artifacts of Ligurian, Roman, and Arab civilizations, plus the remains discovered by excavations, including paintings, mosaics, and ancient pottery. The museum is open June to September daily from 10am to 5:45pm, and Tuesday to Sunday October to May 10:30am to 1:15pm and 2:15 to 4:45pm (closing at 5:45pm Apr–May). Admission is 6€ for adults, 3€ for visitors 25 and under, and free for children 17 and under.

EXPLORING ILE ST-HONORAT ★★

Only 1.6km (1 mile) long, Ile St-Honorat is much quieter than neighboring Ste-Marguerite. But in historical terms, it's much richer than its island sibling and is the site of a monastery whose origins date from the 5th century. The **Abbaye de St-Honorat ★** (www.abbayedelerins.com; ✆ **04-92-99-54-00**) is a combination of medieval ruins and early-20th-century ecclesiastical buildings and is home to a community of about 25 Cistercian monks. Most visitors content themselves with a wander through the pine forests on the island's western side, a clamber around the ruined monastery on the island's southern edge, and a bathe on its seaweed-strewn beaches.

The monks also transform the island's herbs, vines, and honey into a wealth of organic products, including lavender oil and wine. All can be purchased in the monastery shop. There is also an excellent lunch-only seafood restaurant, **La Tonnelle** (www.tonnelle-abbayedelerins.fr; ✆ **04-92-99-54-08**). It's closed from November to mid-March. And no, it's not the monks who cook, but they can organize a wine-tasting or small island tour if arranged in advance. In particular, a new option is an 18€ wine tour, which includes 15 min. for strolling the island vineyards and a taste of two wines, as well as a round-trip ferry ticket to the island.

Grasse ★

18km (11 miles) N of Cannes

Grasse, a 20-min. drive from Cannes, has been renowned as the capital of the world's perfume industry since the Renaissance. It was once a famous resort, attracting such royals as Queen Victoria and Princess Pauline Borghese, Napoleon's lascivious sister.

Today some three-quarters of the world's essences are produced here from thousands of tons of petals, including violets, daffodils, wild lavender, and jasmine. The quaint medieval town, which formed the backdrop for the movie "Perfume," has several free perfume museums where visitors can enroll in workshops to create their own scent.

ESSENTIALS

Trains run to Grasse from Cannes, depositing passengers a 10-min. walk south of town. From here, a walking trail or shuttle bus leads visitors into the center. One-way train tickets cost 5.30€ from Cannes, and journey time is around 30 min. For further train information, visit www.oui.sncf or call ✆ **36-35** (.40€/min.).

Buses pull into town every 10 to 60 min. daily from Cannes (trip time: 50 min.), arriving at the Gare Routière, pl. de la Buanderie (✆ **04-93-36-37-37**), a 5-min. walk north of the town center. The one-way fare is 1.50€. Visitors arriving by **car** may follow RN85 from Cannes. The **Office de Tourisme** is at place du cours Honoré Cresp (www.grassetourisme.fr; ✆ **04-93-36-66-66**). For a guided 35-min. glide around town, ride the

Petit Train Touristique (www.petit-train-grasse.fr; ✆ **06-35-47-11-66**). This electric vehicle that buzzes around all the top sites daily from 11am to 6pm; tickets cost 6€ for adults, and 3.50€ for children aged between 3 and 12.

EXPLORING GRASSE

Musée International de la Parfumerie ★ MUSEUM

This comprehensive museum chronicles both Grasse's fragrant history, as well as worldwide perfume development over the past 4,000 years, is the only one of its kind in the world. Wander among raw materials, ancient flasks (including Marie Antoinette's 18th-c. toiletry set) and scented soaps, all set against a backdrop of temporary exhibitions and contemporary artworks. Kids age 7 and older have their own dedicated pathway, lined with interactive exhibits to touch—and, of course, smell. The museum recently hosted a conference run by famous industry "nose" Julie Massé.

2 bd. du Jeu-de-Ballon. www.museesdegrasse.com. ✆ **04-97-05-58-00.** Admission (depending on exhibition) 4€–6€ adults; 2€–3€ students; free for children under 18. Apr–Sept daily 10am–7pm; Oct–Mar Wed–Mon 10:30am–5:30pm. Closed Nov.

Parfumerie Molinard FACTORY TOUR

This firm is well known in the United States, where its products are sold at Saks, Neiman-Marcus, and Bloomingdale's. In the factory, you can witness the extraction of the essence from the flowers, understand the distillation process completed in copper tanks designed by Gustave Eiffel of tower fame, and even make your own scent. You'll also learn all the details of the process of converting flowers into essential oils. You can admire a collection of antique perfume bottle labels and see a rare collection of perfume *flacons* by Baccarat and Lalique. The nearby **Parfumerie Fragonard factory**, 20 bd. Fragonard, offers a similar experience.

60 bd. Victor Hugo. www.molinard.com. ✆ **04-93-36-01-62.** Free admission. Daily 9:30am–6:30pm (until 7pm July–Aug).

Villa Musée Fragonard ★ HISTORIC HOME/ART MUSEUM

The setting is an 18th-century aristocrat's town house with a magnificent garden in back. The collection displayed here includes the paintings of Jean-Honoré Fragonard, who was born in Grasse in 1732; his sister-in-law, Marguerite Gérard; his son, Alexandre; and his grandson, Théophile. Alexandre decorated the grand staircase. Curiously, this is the least-visited museum in town but is surely one of the loveliest.

23 bd. Fragonard. ✆ **04-97-05-58-00.** Admission 2€ adults; free for children under 18. May–Sept daily 10am–7pm; Oct–Apr Wed–Mon 11am–6pm. Closed Nov.

WHERE TO EAT

For light lunch or an afternoon snack, pop into **Les Delicatesses de Grasse,** 7 rue Marcel Journet (✆ **09-81-76-59-29**), a combination restaurant with terrace, traditional food store, and charcuterie. Try the platters of local sausage and tapenade, plus rosé wines from St-Tropez.

La Bastide St-Antoine (Restaurant Chibois) ★★★ FRENCH/
PROVENÇAL   La Bastide St-Antoine offers one of the grandest farm-
to-table culinary experiences along the Riviera. In a 200-year-old Provençal farmhouse, top chef Jacques Chibois sources dishes from the
surrounding by 2.8 hectares (7 acres) of orchards, cottage gardens, and
olive groves, which diners can stroll through before they eat. Exquisite
examples include roasted pigeon smoked with girolles mushrooms. Desserts may include strawberry soup with spice wine or ice cream made
with olives and a hint of olive oil. Reservations are required.

You can stay in the attached five-star accommodation of nine rooms
and seven suites, decorated in upscale Provençal style. Outside there's a
pool, jogging track, and boules court. Doubles cost 187€ to 390€, suites
from 391€.

48 av. Henri-Dunant. www.jacques-chibois.com. ℰ **04-93-70-94-94.** Main course
70€–90€; fixed-price lunch Mon–Sat 66€–205€ or dinner 105€–205€. Daily noon–2pm
and 8–9:30pm.

Golfe-Juan & Vallauris ★

7km (4.5 miles) NE of Cannes

Napoleon and 800 men landed at Golfe-Juan in 1815 to begin his march
to Paris and famous Hundred Days in power; the pint-sized general meet
his Waterloo against the combined forces of Britain and Continental
Europe a few months later. Today it's a family resort known for its beaches
and a once noteworthy restaurant, Chez Tétou. Until French authorities
closed the eatery in 2018 for beach infringements, it attracted every
Cannes Film Festival attendee from Steven Spielberg to Angelina Jolie –
although the owners recently applied to rebuild the restaurant in a plot
across the street.

The 2km-long (1.25-mile) RN135 leads inland from Golfe-Juan to
Vallauris. Once simply a stopover along the Riviera, Vallauris's ceramics
industry was in terminal decline until it was "discovered" by Picasso just
after World War II. The artist's legacy lives on both in snapshots of the
master in local galleries and in his awesome *La Paix et La Guerre* fresco.

ESSENTIALS

You can **drive** to Golfe-Juan or Vallauris on any of the Riviera's coastal
highways. Although route numbers are not always indicated, city names
are clear once you're on the highway. From Cannes or Antibes, N7 east is
the fastest route. From Nice or Biot, take A8/E80 west.

Golfe-Juan's rail station, on avenue de la Gare, is linked to Cannes,
Juan-les-Pins, Antibes, and Nice every 30 min. A one-way ticket to
Cannes costs 2.10€. For railway information, visit www.oui.sncf or call
ℰ **36-35** (.40€/min). **Buses** operated by Envibus (www.envibus.fr;
ℰ **04-89-87-72-00**) make frequent trips from Cannes; the 20-min. trip
costs 1€ each way.

EXPLORING GOLFE-JUAN & VALLAURIS

Because of its position beside the sea, Golfe-Juan long ago developed into a warm-weather resort. The town's twin strips of beach are **Plage du Soleil** (east of the Vieux Port and the newer Port Camille-Rayon) and **Plage du Midi** (west of those two). Each stretches 1km (.5 mile) and charges no entry fee, with the exception of small areas administered by concessions that rent mattresses for between 20€ and 25€ for a day's use. Like everywhere else on the Riviera, Golfe-Juan indulges bathers who choose to remove their bikini tops.

In Vallauris, Picasso's *l'Homme au Mouton* (Man and Sheep) is the outdoor statue at place Paul Isnard in front of which Prince Aly Kahn and screen goddess Rita Hayworth were married. The local council had intended to enclose this statue in a museum, but Picasso insisted that it remain on the square, "where the children could climb over it and dogs piss against it."

Musée Magnelli, Musée de la Céramique & Musée National Picasso La Guerre et La Paix ★★ ART MUSEUM

Three museums in one, this petite cultural center developed from a 12th-century chapel where Picasso painted *La Paix* (Peace) and *La Guerre* (War) in 1952. Visitors can physically immerse themselves in this tribute to pacifism. Images of love and peace adorn one wall; scenes of violence and conflict the other. Also on site is a permanent exposition of works by Florentine-born abstract artist Alberto Magnelli, as well as a floor dedicated to traditional and innovative ceramics from regional potters.

Pl. de la Libération. www.musee-picasso-vallauris.fr. ✆ **04-93-64-71-83.** Admission 5€ adults; 2.50€ for visitors 16–25; free for children 15 and under. July–Aug daily 10am–12:45pm and 2:15–6:15pm; Sept Wed–Mon 10am–12:15pm and 2–5pm.

WHERE TO EAT & SHOP

Join the locals for lunch at **Le Clos Cosette,** 1 av. du Tapis Vert (www.le-clos-cosette-restaurant-vallauris.com; ✆ **04-93-64-30-64**). The restaurant's menu proposes an excellent home-made terrine (10€), which also features on the daily 17.50€ lunchtime set menu. For souvenirs, head around the corner to avenue Georges-Clemenceau, lined with small shops selling brightly glazed, locally made ceramics. Picasso's former ceramics studio, **Galerie Madoura,** rue Georges et Suzanne Ramié, is open to well-dressed tourists (the sort that look interested in buying some pottery at the same time).

Le Bistrot du Port ★★ SEAFOOD   With the demise of Chez Tétou in 2018, visiting celebrities in search of seafood book tables at this ocean-front eatery. The Allinei brothers, Thomas and Mathieu, serve simple, modern creations including tuna tartare, and John Dory seared on a hot stone. Most seafood is locally sourced. The restaurant purveys a superb array of rosé wines, including Le Clos Saint Joseph from the hills above Nice. The 3-course weekday lunchtime menu for 26.50€ is a particular steal.

53 av. des Frères-Roustan, Golfe-Juan. ℮ **04-93-63-70-64.** www.bistrotduport.com. Main course 28€–36€; fixed-price menu 45€. Tues–Sun noon–2pm and 7–10pm.

Mougins ★★

7km (4.5 miles) N of Cannes

A fortified hill town, Mougins preserves the quiet life in a postcard-perfect manner. The town's artsy legacy—Picasso, Jean Cocteau, Paul Eluard, Fernand Léger, Isadora Duncan, and Christian Dior were all previous residents—has blessed the town with must-see galleries. Real estate prices are among the highest on the Riviera, and the wealthy residents support a dining scene that also punches well above its weight. The **Etoile des Mougins food festival** (www.lesetoilesdemougins.com), held each June, is a highbrow gastronomic love-in featuring Michelin-starred chefs from across the globe.

ESSENTIALS

From Cannes, the best way to get to Mougins is to **drive** north of the city along D6285. By bus, **Société Tam** (www.cg06.fr; ℮ **08-00-06-01-06**) runs bus no. 600 from Cannes to Val-de-Mougins, a 10-min. walk from the center of Mougins. One-way fares cost 1.50€. The **Office de Tourisme** is at 18 bd. Courteline (www.mougins-tourisme.fr; ℮ **04-93-75-87-67**).

Etoile des Mougins food festival

EXPLORING MOUGINS

Picasso discovered Mougins' tranquil maze of flower-filled lanes in the company of his muse, Dora Marr, and photographer Man Ray, in 1935. The Vieux Village's pedestrianized cobblestone streets—each corner prettier than the last—have changed little over the decades since. The setting is so romantic that, according to locals, former French President François Hollande wined and dined his former first lady, Valérie Trierweiler, in one of the restaurants listed below. He then proceeded to indulge his mistress, Julie Gayet, in the same establishment. Classy guy.

Chapelle Notre-Dame de Vie ★ RELIGIOUS SITE The most romantic site in Mougins is surely this medieval chapel. It lies 1.5km (1 mile) southeast of Mougins. It was built in the 12th century and reconstructed in 1646. Its tree-dappled grounds inspired local resident Picasso and were once painted by Sir Winston Churchill. More importantly, the priory next door was once Picasso's studio and private residence for the last 12 years of his life. On his death in 1973, the art collection inside was worth in excess of $1 billion. More prosaically, in 2017 his sprawling estate was sold to a merchant banker from London.

Chemin de la Chapelle. Admission free.

Musée d'Art Classique de Mougins ★★ MUSEUM The newest addition to Mougins' art scene is wonderfully quirky: Egyptian, Greek, and Roman artifacts are juxtaposed alongside similarly themed modern artworks, including sculptures, drawings, and canvases from Matisse, Dufy, Cézanne, Dalí, and Damien Hirst. A personal favorite pairing matches an ancient statue of Venus with Yves Klein's neon-blue *Venus* sculpture.

32 rue Commandeur. ✆ **04-93-75-18-22.** www.mouginsmusee.com. Admission 12€ adults; 7€ students and seniors; 5€ children 10–17; free for children 9 and under. Daily 10am–6pm (July–Sept until 8pm).

Musée de la Photographie André Villers ★ ART MUSEUM Picasso's close friend, photographer André Villers, chronicled the artist's Mougins years in black-and-white photos. Images line the walls of an ancient medieval home: Some are hilarious, such as the photo showing Picasso sitting down for breakfast in his trademark Breton shirt, pretending he has croissants for fingers. Additional portraits by Villars—including snaps of Dalí, Catherine Deneuve, and Edith Piaf—are frequently on display. Additional images in the museum were taken by top photographers like Robert Doisneau, who shot the famous "couple kissing in Paris" shot.

Porte Sarrazine. ✆ **04-93-75-85-67.** Free admission. Daily 10am–12:30pm and 2–6pm (June–Sept until 7pm). Closed Jan.

WHERE TO EAT

Mougins is a global dining capital so you can't go far wrong, wherever you choose to dine. Pick of a very good bunch is **Paloma,** 47 av. du

Moulin-de-la-Croix, (www.restaurant-paloma-mougins.com; © **04-92-28-10-73;** menus 49€–155€). If you only allow yourself a single splurge of a (2-star Michelin) lunch, do it here. Overlooking a verdant valley, chef Nicolas Decherchi steers a fine line between fabulous ingredients (local frogs' legs, coastal scallops) and innovative flavors (honey ice-cream, crab pincer consommé).

For a more budget-friendly option, try the traditional bistro **Le Resto des Arts,** 2 rue Maréchal Foch (© **04-93-75-60-03**), which dishes up hearty specials like basil-spiked *soupe au pistou,* red mullet doused in tomato sauce, or seared steak with morel mushrooms.

JUAN-LES-PINS ★★

913km (566 miles) S of Paris; 9.5km (6 miles) S of Cannes

Just west of the Cap d'Antibes, this Art Deco resort burst onto the South of France scene during the 1920s, under the auspices of American property developer Frank Jay Gould. A decade later, Juan-les-Pins was already drawing a chic summer crowd, as the Riviera "season" flipped from winter respites to the hedonistic pursuit of summer sun, sea, and sensuality. It has been attracting the young and the young-at-heart from across Europe and the U.S. ever since. F. Scott Fitzgerald decried Juan-les-Pins as a "constant carnival." His words ring true each and every summer's day.

Essentials

ARRIVING Juan-les-Pins is connected by **rail** to most nearby coastal resorts, including Nice (trip time: 30 min.; 5.20€ one-way), Antibes, and Cannes. For further train information, visit www.oui.sncf or call © **36-35** (.40€/min). A **bus** (www.envibus.fr; © **04-89-87-72-00**) leaves for Juan-les-Pins from Antibes' Gare Routière (bus station) daily every 20 min. and costs 1€ one-way (trip time: 10 min.). To **drive** to Juan-les-Pins from Nice, travel along coastal D6007 south; from Cannes, follow the D6007 north.

VISITOR INFORMATION The **Office de Tourisme** is at 51 bd. Charles-Guillaumont (www.antibes-juanlespins.co.uk; © **04-97-23-11-10**).

SPECIAL EVENTS The town offers some of the best nightlife on the Riviera. The action reaches its peak during the annual 10-day **Festival International de Jazz** (www.jazzajuan.com) in mid-July. It attracts jazz, blues, reggae, and world music artists who play nightly on the beachfront Parc de la Pinède. Recent performers have included George Benson and Norah Jones, while the 2018 event showcased Melody Gardot and Lenny Kravitz. Tickets cost 25€ to 75€ and can be purchased at the Office de Tourisme in both Antibes and Juan-les-Pins, as well as online.

[FastFACTS] JUAN-LES-PINS

ATMs/Banks   **BNP Paribas,** 14 av. Maréchal Joffre (☎ **08-20-82-00-01**).

Internet Access   **News Café,** 60 chemin des Sables (☎ **04-83-14-68-04**).

Mail & Postage   **La Poste,** 1 av. Maréchal Joffre (☎ **36-31**).

Pharmacies   **Pharmacie Provençale,** 144 bd. Président Wilson (☎ **04-93-61-09-23**).

Exploring Juan-les-Pins

Spilling over from Antibes' more residential quarter, Juan-les-Pins is petite—which makes it best navigated on foot. Be sure to swing by the shady square known as **La Pinède** (square Frank Jay Gould) to check out the legions of local *pétanque* players. Nearby, the town's long-awaited **Palais des Congrès,** or Convention Center (www.antibesjuanlespins-congres.com) recently opened to much fanfare. With the perennial success of year-round conferences in nearby Cannes, Juan-les-Pins' local municipality is hoping to shift some of the business action here.

Most of us, however, would rather stroll the long, beachside promenade to Golfe-Juan where Napoleon kicked off his march to Paris and famous Hundred Days in power in 1815. Alternatively, pick a beach bar, order a glass of rosé, and watch the sun drop over the Iles de Lérins.

Outdoor Activities

BEACHES   Part of the reason people flock to Juan-les-Pins is for the town's wealth of sandy beaches, all lapped by calm waters. The town also basks in a unique microclimate, making it one of the warmest places on the Riviera to soak up the sun, even in winter. **Plage de Juan-les-Pins** is the most central beach, although quieter stretches of sand wrap around the Cap d'Antibes and include family-friendly **Plage de la Salis** and chic **Plage de la Garoupe.** If you do want to stretch out on a sun lounger, go to any of the beach-bar concessions that line the bay, where you can rent a mattress for around 15€ to 20€. Topless sunbathing and overt shows of cosmetic surgery are the norm.

WATERSPORTS   If you're interested in scuba diving, try **Easy Dive,** bd. Edouard Baudouin (www.easydive.fr; ☎ **04-93-61-26-07**). A one-tank dive costs 30€ to 60€, including all equipment. **Sea kayaking, pedalos,** and **paddleboarding** are available at virtually every beach in Juan-les-Pins but are best booked at **Cap Kayak** (www.capkayak.fr; ☎ **06-62-28-09-54**), a friendly establishment that knows all the secret ocean spots. **Waterskiing** was invented at the Hôtel Belles-Rives in the 1920s, and it's still a great place to try out the sport.

Where to Stay

Le Grand Pavois ★★   Nestled in an unbeatable location between the base of the Cap d'Antibes and Juan-les-Pins' center, this Art Deco edifice is literally a 2-min. walk to the beach. The elegant period lobby has been perfectly restored, and a live pianist often graces the ground-floor **La Rotonde** bar with jazzy tunes. Guestrooms are simply decorated with Provençal furnishings; many possess private balconies and sea views, while families can ask for a free baby's cot. Breakfast is served in the palm-fringed garden outside. Sun-seekers can ride the elevator to the rooftop solarium, which has fabulous views over the annual Festival International de Jazz in the neighboring park.

5 av. Saramartel. www.hotelgrandpavois.fr. © **04-92-93-54-54.** 60 units. 61€–159€ double; 90€–199€ suite. Parking 10€. **Amenities:** Bar; restaurant; room service; free Wi-Fi.

Hôtel Belles-Rives ★★★ This luxurious hotel is one of the Riviera's most fabled addresses. It started life in 1925 as a holiday villa rented by Zelda and F. Scott Fitzgerald (as depicted in Fitzgerald's semi-autobiographical novel "Tender Is the Night"). Today, 90 years after her grandparents first opened the Belles-Rives' doors, the elegant Madame Estène-Chauvin owns and oversees this waterside gem. Guestrooms are sumptuous yet eclectic—each one its own unique size and shape. The lower terraces hold garden dining rooms, an elegant bar and lounge, as well as a private jetty. Also on site is the superb **La Passagère** restaurant run by Michelin-starred chef Aurélien Véquaud, who was poached from St-Tropez's three-star eatery La Vague d'Or in 2017. Lunch overlooking the shimmering Mediterranean costs 55€ for three courses. If you're daring, you can even try waterskiing at the waterside aquatic club where, almost a century ago, the sport was invented.

33 bd. Edouard Baudoin. www.bellesrives.com. © **04-93-61-02-79.** 43 units. 170€– 780€ double; from 650€ suite. Parking 30€. Closed Jan–Mar. **Amenities:** 2 summer restaurants; winter restaurant; 2 bars; private beach; room service; free Wi-Fi.

Where to Eat

Cap Riviera ★★ FRENCH One of Juan-les-Pins' most appealing attributes is its endless ripple of beachside restaurants, all peering out over the picturesque Iles de Lérins. And Cap Riviera is undoubtedly one of this resort's finest. Cuisine is seafood-based with a squeeze of French sophistication. Think shrimp flambéed in pastis, lemon-infused sardine *rillettes*, or *sole meunière*; staff are charming and attentive. It's well worth popping by in advance to select your own special sea-facing table. Lunchtime diners can also indulge in a new 28€ 3-course menu, which includes rockfish soup and flash-fried tuna.

13 bd. Edouard Baudoin. www.cap-riviera.fr. © **04-93-61-22-30.** Main course 16€– 28€; fixed-price lunch 28€ or dinner 42€. Daily noon–3pm and Mon–Sat 8–10pm. Closed Nov to mid–Dec and Jan.

Le Capitole ★ CLASSIC FRENCH This restaurant's decor and menu has hardly changed since its inception in the 1950s. And that's no bad thing. Expect impeccable service—with limited English—in a mirrored dining room filled with more lamps, boxes, and *objets d'art* than The Great Gatsby's mansion. Classic French fare is a delight. Menu items may include smoked herrings with potatoes, *steak-frites*, snails in garlic, and créme caramel. Best value of all is the 16€ early dining menu. Arrive for dinner before 8pm for three bargain courses, with coffee and wine included in the deal. Service spills outside onto a sunny street terrace from May onwards.

22 av. Amiral Courbet. ✆ **04-93-61-22-44.** Main course 10€–16€; fixed-price lunch 16€ or dinner 22€–39€. Wed–Sun noon–2pm and 7–10pm.

Le Perroquet ★ PROVENÇAL   One of the best restaurants in Juan-les-Pins, Le Perroquet attracts both casual visitors and longtime locals. The *assortiment de poissons grillés*—grilled sea bream, John Dory, giant prawns, and red mullet—is an excellent introduction to the best of the Mediterranean; a good-value fixed-price lunch changes daily. The pretty sidewalk seating looks out over La Pinède's Aleppo pines.

Av. Georges-Gallice. www.restaurantleperroquet.fr. ✆ **04-93-61-02-20.** Main course 16€–32€; fixed-price lunch 18€ or dinner 34€–42€. Daily noon–2pm and 7–10pm. Closed Nov–Dec.

Nightlife

For a faux-tropical-island experience, head to **Le Pam Pam,** 137 bd. Wilson (www.pampam.fr; ✆ **04-93-61-11-05**), a time-honored "rhumerie" where guests sip rum and people-watch while reggae beats drift around the bar. More modern is **La Réserve,** av. Georges Gallice (✆ **04-93-61-20-06**), where a younger crowd sips rosé on leopard-print seats.

If you prefer high-energy partying, you're in the right place. The entire Riviera descends upon Juan-les-Pins' discos every night in summer, and it's best to follow the crowds to the latest hotspot. **Le Village,** 1 bd. de la Pinède (✆ **04-92-93-90-00**), is one of the more established clubs and boasts an action-packed dance floor with DJs spinning summer sounds from salsa to soul. The cover charge is usually 16€ including one drink; more for themed evenings. For top jazz, head to **Le New Orleans,** 9 av. Georges Gallice (✆ **04-93-67-41-71**), a relatively new addition to the local live music scene.

ANTIBES & CAP D'ANTIBES ★★

913km (566 miles) S of Paris; 21km (13 miles) SW of Nice; 11km (6.75 miles) NE of Cannes

Antibes has a quiet charm unique to the Côte d'Azur. Fishing boats and pleasure yachts fill its harbor. The likes of Picasso and Monet painted its oh-so-pretty streets, today thronged with promenading locals and well-dressed visitors. A pedestrianized town center makes it a family-friendly destination as well, and a perfect place for an evening stroll. An excellent covered market is also located near the harbor, open every morning except Mondays.

Spiritually, Antibes is totally divorced from Cap d'Antibes, a peninsula studded with the villas of the super-rich. But the less affluent are welcome to peek at paradise, and a lovely 6km (3.75 miles) coastal path rings the headland, passing picnic and diving spots en route.

Essentials

ARRIVING **Trains** from Cannes arrive at the rail station, pl. Pierre-Semard, every 20 min. (trip time: 15 min.); the one-way fare is 3.10€. Around 25 trains arrive from Nice daily (trip time: 20 min.); the one-way fare is 4.80€. For further train information, www.oui.sncf or call ℂ **36-35** (.40€/min). The **bus** station, or Gare Routière, pl. Guynemer (www.cg06.fr or www.envibus.fr; ℂ **04-89-87-72-00**), offers bus service throughout Provence. Bus fares to Nice, Cannes, or anywhere en route cost 1.50€ one-way.

To **drive** to Antibes from Nice, travel along coastal D6007 south; from Cannes, follow the D6007 north. The Cap d'Antibes is clearly visible from most parts of the Riviera. To drive here from Antibes, follow the coastal road south—you can't miss it.

VISITOR INFORMATION   The **Office de Tourisme** is at 11 pl. du Général de Gaulle (www.antibesjuanlespins.com; ℂ **04-97-23-11-11**).

[Fast FACTS] ANTIBES

ATMs/Banks   Among others, there are half a dozen banks dotted along av. Robert Soleau.

Internet Access   **Le Happy Face Bar,** 13 rue Auberon (ℂ **06-20-43-77-10**).

Mail & Postage   **La Poste,** 2 av. Paul Doumer (ℂ **36-31**).

Pharmacies   **Grande Pharmacie d'Antibes,** 2 pl. Guynemer (ℂ **04-93-34-16-12**).

Exploring Antibes

Antibes' largely pedestrianized Old Town—all pale stone homes, weaving lanes, and window boxes of colorful flowers—is easily explored on foot. The highlights are undoubtedly a dip into Picasso's former home, now a museum, and a stroll along the bling-tastic pleasure port, where artist Jaume Plensa's giant *Nomad* sculpture shimmers in the night.

The town is also skirted by wonderful walking trails. It's an easy stroll around the ancient walls of the 16th-century **Fort Carré,** just north of Antibes's port. Alternatively, like all of the prominent peninsulas on the French Riviera, the Cap d'Antibes boasts a scenic hiking trail around its perimeter. Highlights include the rustic coastal path south of Plage de la Garoupe, as well as a stop—if you can time it correctly—at the **Villa Eilenroc,** 460 av. L.D. Beaumont (ℂ **04-93-67-74-33**). The latter is where Woody Allen directed "Magic in the Moonlight," the Riviera romp staring Emma Stone and Colin Firth. The garden and villa, which reopened after

Fishing boats, yachts, and sailboats at Antibes' harbor

renovations in 2018, are currently open to the public on Wednesday from 2 to 5pm, and the 1st and 3rd Saturday of the month from 2 to 5pm; but check the tourism office website before you visit. Admission is 2€, free for children 11 and under.

Espace du Littoral et du Milieu Marin ★ MARITIME CENTER

Located within this stone-sided fort and tower on the Cap d'Antibes, built in stages as a coastal gunnery battery the 17th and 18th centuries, is a child-friendly space showcasing a permanent Jacques Cousteau exhibition. Prominent displays range from models of Costeau's research vessel, the Calypso, as well as the explorer's intimidating shark cage. Visitors keen to escape the crowds will revel in the center's seaside park (which overlooks the grounds of the ultra-exclusive Hôtel du Cap–Eden-Roc!). The center also organizes fun, **scientific snorkeling trips** (20€ per person; www.graillon-aquarando.com) and **kayak tours** (same price) around the pristine Cap d'Antibes.

Bd. J.F. Kennedy. ✆ **04-93-61-45-32.** Free admission. Tues–Sat 10am–4:40pm.

Musée Picasso ★★ ART MUSEUM

Perched on the Old Town's ramparts, the 14th-century Château Grimaldi was home to Picasso in 1946, when the Spanish artist lived and worked here at the invitation of the municipality. Upon his departure, he gifted all the work he'd completed to the château museum: 44 drawings and 23 paintings, including the famous *La Joie de Vivre*. In addition to this permanent collection inside the kooky building, which emerged from a fresh renovation in 2018, contemporary artworks by Joan Miró, Arman, and Modigliani, among many others, are also on display.

Château Grimaldi, pl. Mariejol. ✆ **04-92-90-54-28.** Admission 6€ adults; 3€ students and seniors; free for children 17 and under. Mid-June to mid-Sept Tues–Sun 10am–6pm; mid-Sept to mid-June Tues–Sun 10am–1pm and 2–6pm.

Where to Stay

Hôtel du Cap–Eden-Roc ★★★ This legendary hotel was first launched in 1887, serving as a Mediterranean getaway for visitors seeking winter sunshine. Over the intervening years, it's played host to the world's most famous clientele, from the Duke and Duchess of Windsor (who escaped here after the former king's abdication) to the Hollywood superstars who cavort at the Vanity Fair Cannes Film Festival party, which welcomed Jessica Chastain, Jake Gyllenhall, and Kendall Jenner in 2017. Surrounded by a maze of manicured gardens, accommodation is among the most sumptuous on the Riviera. Guests lounge by the seawater swimming pool, carved from natural basalt rock, while evenings are spent at the panoramic **Restaurant Eden-Roc** or the **Bellini Bar.** Looking to splurge? Pick up an exclusive Eden-Roc-label beach sarong. Alternatively, signature treatments at the onsite spa come courtesy of luxury Swiss brand La Prairie.

Bd. J.F. Kennedy. www.hotel-du-cap-eden-roc.com. ℂ **04-93-61-39-01.** 118 units. From 580€ double. Closed mid-Oct to mid-Apr. **Amenities:** 2 restaurants; 2 bars; babysitting; exercise room; massage; outdoor pool; room service; spa; tennis, free Wi-Fi.

La Villa Fabulite ★★ A fabulously friendly hotel a 5-min. stroll from the Hôtel du Cap–Eden-Roc… without the 1,000€ price tag. This leafy estate with wild gardens and naturally heated pool is housed on the site of a former diving school. That means it's close to all the Cap d'Antibes' elite—yet publically accessible—beaches. Rooms aren't large but they are chic and functional, with a private terrace apiece. Better still is wide range of activities, including mountain biking and paddleboarding around the peninsula for 15€ per person.

150 Traverse des Nielles, Cap d'Antibes. www.fabulite.com. ℂ **04-93-61-47-45.** 10 units. 90€–291€ double; 300€–629€ suite. Parking 10€. **Amenities:** Garden; bar; massage; restaurant; free Wi-Fi.

Where to Eat

The Zelda and Scott Fitzgeralds of today head for the **Restaurant Eden-Roc** at the Hôtel du Cap-Eden-Roc for grand service and grand cuisine. Alternatively, the excellent **Restaurant de Bacon,** bd. de Bacon (www.restaurantdebacon.com; ℂ **04-93-61-50-02**), has served the best seafood around

The Old Town, Antibes

for more than 6 decades. For light bites and unusual local wines, stop into **Entre 2 Vins,** 2 rue James Close (© **04-93-34-46-93**).

Bistro Le Rustic ★ FRENCH/PIZZA   For hearty local dishes on a budget, it's hard to beat family-run Le Rustic, where granny still tends the open fire. The pizzas emerge baked to perfection from inside this roaring oven. The specialty, honey-glazed duck, is also cooked in the oven, shoved into the hearth on the tip of a spade. Find other Riviera classics (fish soup, a fresh shrimp platter, fried red mullet) too. The restaurant is located at the heart of Antibes' Old Town, with spacious (and kid-friendly) outdoor seating in the square.

33 pl. Nationale. © **04-93-34-10-81.** Main course 10€–18€; fixed-price menu 16€–22€. Daily noon–3pm and 7–11pm.

Chez Helen ★ VEGETARIAN   Whether you're a vegetarian on the road or simply seeking a little bit of lighter fare—despite the fact that Southern French food already tends to eschew butter, cream, and heavier meats—this petite restaurant is a delight. All ingredients are organic and locally sourced. Expect subtle dishes like roasted tomato salad with basil *pistou* and mustard leaves, or spinach and feta stuffed Tunisian-style *brik*. Afternoon tea and a homemade pastry (7.50€) is another delightful option. The 12€ half-liter pitchers of wine are also all-organic.

35 rue des Revennes. www.chezhelen.fr. © **04-92-93-88-52.** Main course 12€; fixed-price menu 13€–16€. Tues–Sat noon–5pm.

DAY TRIP FROM ANTIBES
Biot ★
6.5km (4 miles) NW of Antibes

Biot has been famous for its pottery since merchants began to ship earthenware jars to Phoenicia and throughout the Mediterranean. It's also where Fernand Léger painted until the day he died, leaving a magnificent collection of his work on display just outside town.

ESSENTIALS
Bus no. 10 from Antibes's Gare Routière, pl. Guynemer (www.envibus.fr; © **04-89-87-72-00**), runs to Biot's town center. Tickets cost 1.50€. To **drive** to Biot from Antibes, follow D6007 east, then head west on the D4.

Biot's **Office de Tourisme** is at 46 rue St-Sébastien (www.biot-tour isme.com; © **04-93-65-78-00**).

EXPLORING BIOT
Exploration of Biot's small historic center begins at **place des Arcades,** where you can see the 16th-century gates and the remains of the town's ramparts. The **Musée d'Histoire et Céramique Biotoise,** 8 rue St-Sebastien (www.musee-de-biot.fr; © **04-93-65-54-54**), has assembled the best works from local artists, potters, ceramists, painters, and silver- and goldsmiths.

Hours are mid-June to mid-September Wednesday to Sunday 10am to 6pm, and mid-September to mid-June Wednesday to Sunday 2 to 6pm. Admission is 4€, 2€ for seniors and students, and free for children 16 and under.

Outside of town, the excellent **Musée National Fernand Léger,** 316 chemin du Val de Pôme (www.musees-nationaux-alpesmaritimes.fr/fleger; ☏ **04-92-91-50-20**), displays a comprehensive collection of the artist's colorful creations, from 1930s Cubist ladies to circus scenes of the 1950s. Some 400 sq. m (4,305 sq. ft.) of mosaics, while modernistic stained-glass windows pour light inside. Hours are Wednesday to Monday May to October 10am to 6pm, November to April 10am to 5pm. Admission is 5.50€, 4€ for students and seniors, and free for ages 25 and under. Also on site are temporary exhibitions and a cafe garden.

The very zen **Musee du Bonsaï,** 299 chemin du Val de Pôme (www.museedubonsai-biot.fr, ☏ **04-93-65-63-99**), is located just around the corner. Cultivated by father and son team Jean and Karol Okonek, more than 1,000 sq. m (1,076 sq. ft.) of Japanese-style gardens are dedicated to bonsai trees collected from as far afield as Australia and China. It's open Wednesday to Monday from 10am to noon and from 2 to 6pm. Admission is 4€, 2€ for students and seniors. Note that the museum is closed from early January until the third week of February.

WHERE TO EAT & SHOP

For a Provençal take on crêpes—such as summery tomato, olive tapenade with basil or the house specialty, crêpe-pizza—stop in to **Crêperie Auberge du Village,** 29 rue Saint Sébastien (www.creperie-aubergeduvieuxvillage.com; ☏ **04-93-65-72-73**). This low-key lunch spot sits at the northern end of Biot's main shopping street.

In the late 1940s, local glassmakers created a bubble-flecked glass known as *verre rustique.* You'll easily spot its brilliant cobalts and emeralds while window shopping in town.

ESPECIALLY FOR KIDS

Just south of Biot sits a kid-tastic complex of theme parks. **Aquasplash** (www.marineland.fr) has more than 2km (1.25 miles) of waterslides, including toboggan-style Rainbow Cannon and the Side Winder. **Adventure Golf** is criss-crossed by two dinosaur-dotted miniature golf courses. And, newest of the bunch, **Kid's Island** caters to animal-loving little ones, with pony rides and a petting zoo, plus plenty of jungle gyms and a Magic River. Admission is as follows: Aquasplash 29€, 23€ children between 3 and 12; Adventure Golf 11.50€, 10€ children between 3 and 12; and Kid's Island 14€, 11€ children between 3 and 12. All are free for children 2 and under. Aquasplash, Adventure Golf, and Kid's Island all have varying opening hours, which stretch right into the evening in summer. In all cases, booking a ticket online before you visit saves around 30 percent on the same day ticket.

ST-PAUL-DE-VENCE ★★

926km (574 miles) S of Paris; 23km (14 miles) E of Grasse; 28km (17 miles) E of Cannes; 31km (19 miles) N of Nice

Of all the hilltop villages of the Riviera, St-Paul-de-Vence is by far the most famous. It gained popularity in the 1940s and '50s, when artists including Picasso, Chagall, and Matisse frequented the town, trading their paintings for hospitality at the Colombe d'Or inn. Art is now the town's principal attraction, and the winding streets are studded with contemporary galleries and museums. Circling the town are magnificent old ramparts (allow about 30 min. to walk the full loop) that overlook flowers and olive and orange trees.

Essentials

ARRIVING   The nearest **rail** station is in Cagnes-sur-Mer. Some 20 **buses** per day (no. 400) leave from central Nice, dropping passengers off in St-Paul-de-Vence (1.50€ one-way, trip time: 1 hr.), then in Vence 10 min. later. For information, contact **Lignes d'Azur** (www.lignesdazur.com; ✆ **08-10-06-10-06**). If you're **driving** from Nice, take either the A8 highway or the coastal route du Bord du Mer west, turn inland at Cagnes-sur-Mer, and follow signs north to St-Paul-de-Vence.

VISITOR INFORMATION   The **Office de Tourisme** is at 2 rue Grande (www.saint-pauldevence.com; ✆ **04-93-32-86-95**).

Getting Around

St-Paul's Old Town is entirely pedestrianized, and most of the narrow streets are paved in cobblestones. Since driving a car here is prohibited, except to drop off luggage at an Old Town hotel by prior arrangement only. The Fondation Maeght is around half a mile out of town.

[FastFACTS] ST-PAUL-DE-VENCE

ATMs/Banks   **BNP Paribas,** rd-pt Sainte Claire (✆ **08-20-82-00-01**).

Mail & Postage   **La Poste,** rd-pt Sainte Claire (✆ **36-31**).

Pharmacies   **Pharmacie Saint Paul,** rd-pt Sainte Claire (✆ **04-93-32-80-78**).

Exploring St-Paul

Perched at the top of the village, the **Collégiale de la Conversion de St-Paul ★** was constructed in the 12th and 13th centuries and has been much altered over the years. The Romanesque choir is the oldest part, containing some remarkable stalls carved in walnut in the 17th century. Look to the left as you enter: You'll see the painting *Ste-Cathérine d'Alexandrie*, which has been attributed to Tintoretto. The **Trésor de l'Eglise** is one of

Art galleries in St-Paul-de-Vence

the most beautiful in the Alpes-Maritimes, with a spectacular ciborium. Look also for a low relief of the *Martyrdom of St-Clément* on the last altar on the right. It's open daily 9am to 6pm (to 7pm July–Aug). Admission is free.

Just around the corner is the light-flooded **Chapelle des Pénitents Blanc** ★★ (℗ **04-93-32-41-13**). The artist Jean-Michel Folon, who worked on this masterpiece until his death in 2005, decorated the church with modern stained-glass windows, shimmering mosaics, and rainbow-hued frescos—the 17th century meets the 21st. It's open May to September daily 10am to 12:30pm and 2 to 6pm, and October and December to April daily from 10am to 12:30pm and 2 to 4pm. Admission is 4€ adults, 3€ students and children 6 to 18, and free for children 5 and under.

Fondation Maeght ★★★ ART MUSEUM   A museum you would travel thousands of miles to visit. Established by Parisian art dealers Aimé and Marguerite Maeght in 1964, this avant-garde building houses one of the most impressive modern art collections in Europe. It was Spanish architect José Luis Sert who designed the pagoda-like exhibition space, ensuring the artwork it displays sits in perfect harmony with the surrounding pine-studded woods. In the gardens, colorful Alexander Calder installations are clustered with skinny bronze sculptures by Alberto Giacometti. A rotating selection of artworks is displayed over the various levels inside, showcasing key pieces by artists like Matisse, Chagall, Bonnard, and Léger. Each year the museum stages a large seasonal show, including "Is This How Men Live" in 2018, which featured works from Joan Miró, Vassily Kandinsky, and Francis Bacon.

623 chemin des Gardettes, outside the town walls. www.fondation-maeght.com. ℗ **04-93-32-81-63.** Admission 15€ adults; 10€ students and ages 10–18; free for children 9 and under; 5€ fee for photographs. July–Sept daily 10am–7pm; Oct–June daily 10am–6pm.

Organized Tours

With advance booking, the local tourist office offers 10 different walking tours of the town's historic core and outskirts. **Themed tours** (7€, free for children under 12) last around 1 hr. They include following in the footsteps of former resident Marc Chagall, trying your hand at the beloved Provençal pastime of *pétanque* (also known as *boules*) under the instruction of accomplished locals, or guided tours of the Fondation Maeght. Almost all tours are given in both English and French.

In nearby La Colle sur Loup, culinary legend Alain Llorca offers cooking workshops for adults and children at the **Ecole de Cuisine** (www.alainllorca.com; 60€–170€ per person). Lessons are in French and English and are often followed by an informal dinner.

Where to Stay

La Colombe d'Or rents deluxe rooms (see "Where to Eat," below). Note that Vence's hotels make an accessible base for exploring St-Paul-de-Vence, too.

Le Mas de Pierre ★ The most relaxed five-star on the St-Paul scene is a vision of Provençal elegance, with a dash of boutique charm thrown in. It's about 2km (1.25 miles) from the village center—walkable but a taxi home after a night of rosé and fine dining is recommended. Thanks to the hotel's family-friendly vibe, eating in jeans and a jacket inside the superb Table de Pierre restaurant, or outside on its poolside terrace, is completely acceptable. Many guestrooms were renovated in 2017. The surrounding gardens loop around the pool and are dotted with wooden cabanas, each one with a linen canopy roof that can be pulled shut for a sneaky snooze.

2320 route de Serres. www.lemasdepierre.com. © **04-93-59-00-10.** 48 units. 195€–330€ double; from 331€ suite. Free parking. **Amenities:** Restaurant; bar; outdoor pool; spa; free Wi-Fi.

La Vague de Saint-Paul ★★★ La Vague filled a glaring gap in the St-Paul accommodations market when it opened earlier this decade: an affordable hotel for art lovers seeking country tranquility and wow-factor design. The wavelike main hotel building was originally conceived by far-out architect André Minangoy in the 1960s. Color-coded guestrooms now look out onto a vast garden complete with *pétanque* run, tennis court, bar, and pool. The attached (almost 100 percent organic) restaurant delivers five daily starters and mains on 22€ and 29€ set menus. The complex sits a short walk from the Fondation Maeght contemporary art museum—and a longer stroll through the forest to St-Paul-de-Vence village via a secret trail. Check the website for fabulous low season offers, with rates for 3 nights for the price of 2.

Chemin des Salettes. www.vaguesaintpaul.com. © **04-920-11-20-00.** 37 units. 160€–240€ double; from 210€ suite. Free parking. **Amenities:** Restaurant; bar; concierge; outdoor pool; room service; spa; tennis; free Wi-Fi.

Where to Eat

St-Paul's petite size means that dining options are limited and may also be pricey. That said, the views and the ambience of pretty much any local eatery often make up for these shortcomings.

La Brouette ★ SCANDINAVIAN   It's a brave move to include a Scandinavian restaurant in a destination as classic as St-Paul-de-Vence. But La Brouette pairs local ingredients with foodie mores, including gluten-free breads and seasonal citrus emulsions. In true Danish style, fish comes smoked not grilled. Wine is served, *bien sur*, but many patrons can be seen sipping jam jar smoothies containing lavender honey and kefir.

830 route de Cagnes. ✆ **04-93-58-67-16.** Fixed-price lunch 21€ or dinner 35€. Daily noon–2pm and 7:30–10pm.

La Colombe d'Or ★★ PROVENÇAL   This celebrated restaurant opened its doors in 1920. At the time it was little more than a scattering of tables overlooking an overgrown artichoke patch. It was Paul Roux, the restaurant's art-adoring owner, who encouraged the era's struggling artists, such as Raoul Dufy, Paul Signac, and Chaime Soutine, to swap a canvas or two for generous room and board. Picasso, Braque, and Miró followed—and today La Colombe d'Or's private art collection is one of the finest in the world. For a peek at these masterpieces, you'll need to dine here, either indoors beneath works by the likes of Signac, Matisse, and Braque or outdoors on the fig-trimmed terrace. The colorful handwritten menu, which has barely changed in a century, is famous for its selection of fresh starters (such as *crudités* with *anchoïade,* a traditional anchovy dip), and crispy roast chicken. It also offers 25 luxurious accommodations in the original 16th-century stone house and the two 1950s wings. Prices are 250€ for a double, 430€ for a suite.

1 pl. du Général-de-Gaulle. www.la-colombe-dor.com. ✆ **04-93-32-80-02.** Main course 20€–44€. Daily noon–2pm and 7:30–10pm. Closed late Oct to 3rd week of Dec and 10 days in Jan.

Shopping

The pedestrian-only **rue Grande** is St-Paul's most evocative street, running the length of the town. Most of the stone houses along it are from the 16th and 17th centuries, and several still bear the coats of arms placed there by the original builders. Today many of the houses are antiques shops, arts-and-crafts galleries, and souvenir and gift shops; some are still artists' studios.

    Galerie du Vieux Saint-Paul, 16–18 rue Grande (www.galeries-bartoux.com; ✆ **04-93-32-74-50**), is the place to pick up serious art, from sculptures by local artist Arman to bronze works by Salvador Dalí. Just down the road, **Galerie Capricorne,** 64 rue Grande (www.galeriecapricorne.com; ✆ **04-93-58-34-42**), offers a colorful array of prints, including a selection by Marc Chagall. Nearby **Atelier Silvia B,** 11 pl. de la Mairie (www.silvia bertini.com; ✆ **04-93-32-18-13**) is packed with bright collages of St-Paul.

VENCE ★

926km (574 miles) S of Paris; 31km (19 miles) N of Cannes; 24km (15 miles) NW of Nice

Often bypassed in favor of nearby St-Paul-de-Vence, the pretty village of Vence is well worth a detour. Its pale stone Old Town is atmospheric yet untouristy, splashed with shady squares and pavement cafes. The highlight is undoubtedly Matisse's Chapelle du Rosaire, set among a countryside studded with cypresses, olive trees, and oleanders.

Essentials

ARRIVING   Frequent **buses** (no. 94 or 400) originating in Nice take 65–80 min. to reach Vence, passing the nearest **rail** station in Cagnes-sur-Mer, about 10km (6.25 miles) southwest from Vence, en route. The one-way fare is 1.50€. For bus information, contact **Lignes d'Azur** (www.lignesdazur.com; ✆ **08-10-06-10-06**). For train information, visit www.oui.sncf or call ✆ **36-35** (.40€/min). To **drive** to Vence from Nice, take D6007 west to Cagnes-sur-Mer, and then D36 north to Vence. Visitors with sturdy legs can also hike mostly downhill from Vence to St-Paul-de-Vence; but it's tough going in the opposite direction.

VISITOR INFORMATION   The **Office de Tourisme** is on place due Grand-Jardin (www.vence-tourisme.com; ✆ **04-93-58-06-38**).

[FastFACTS] VENCE

ATMs/Banks   Vence has many banks, including **BNP Paribas,** 28 pl. du Grand-Jardin (✆ **08-20-82-00-01**).

Internet Access   Look for the free **WIFI VENCE** network at a dozen locations around town, including pl. Clemenceau and around Matisse's Chapelle du Rosaire.

Mail & Postage   **La Poste,** pl. Clemenceau (✆ **36-31**).

Pharmacies   **Pharmacie du Grand-Jardin,** 30 pl. du Grand-Jardin (✆ **04-93-58-00-39**).

Exploring Vence

Vence's medieval **Vieille Ville (Old Town)** is compact, making it easy to explore on foot. A poke around its picturesque squares reveals place du Peyra's bubbling **Vieille Fontaine (Old Fountain),** while nearby the **Château de Villeneuve/Fondation Emile Hugues,** 2 pl. du Frêne (www.vence.fr; ✆ **04-93-58-15-78**), is a temporary exhibition space dedicated to 20th-century art. In 2018, Vence's mayor inaugurated a new **permanent Matisse collection** of items owned by city hall. Hours are Tuesday to Sunday 11am to 6pm. Admission is 6€ for adults, 3€ for students, and free for children under 12. Also in the Old Town is **place Godeau,** where the **mosaic** *Moses Saved from the Nile* by Marc Chagall adorns the 11th-century **cathedral**'s baptistery (free).

Vence's main draw, however, lies just outside the fortified main town. The Chapelle du Rosaire represents one of Matisse's most remarkable achievements.

Chapelle du Rosaire ★★ RELIGIOUS SITE From the age of 47, Henri Matisse made Nice his home. But Vence held a special place in the artist's heart: It was his place of residence during World War II, as well as home to Dominican nun Sister Jacques-Marie, Matisse's former nurse and muse. So in 1947, when Matisse discovered that the sisters were planning the construction of a new chapel, he offered not only to design it, but fund the project as well. Matisse was 77 at the time. Not to mention an atheist too.

The Chapelle du Rosaire was completed in 1951. A beautifully bright space, it offers the exceptional possibility of stepping into a three-dimensional artwork. As Sir Nicholas Serota, former director of London's Tate gallery claimed: "It has to be one of the great works made anywhere at any time. Sistine Ceiling or Vence Chapel? I wouldn't want to choose between the two."

From the front of the chapel, you may find the structure unremarkable and pass it by—until you spot a 12m (39-ft.) crescent-adorned cross rising from a blue-tile roof. Within, dozens of stained-glass windows shimmer cobalt blue (symbolizing the sea), sapphire green (the landscape), and golden yellow (the sun). Most remarkable are the 14 black-and-white-tile Stations of the Cross, featuring Matisse's self-styled "tormented and passionate" figures.

The bishop of Nice came to bless the chapel in the late spring of 1951; Matisse died 3 years later.

466 av. Henri-Matisse. ℂ **04-93-58-03-26.** Admission 7€ adults; contributions to maintain the chapel are welcome. Mon, Thurs, and Fri 10am–noon and 2–6pm; Wed and Sat 2–6pm; until 5pm in winter. Closed mid-Nov to mid-Dec.

Where to Stay

Note that St-Paul-de-Vence's hotels also make an excellent base for exploring Vence, and vice versa.

Cantermerle Hotel ★ Just south of Vence's Old Town, this hotel, restaurant, and spa is set within 1.2 hectares (3 acres) of lush gardens. Spacious guestrooms feature terra-cotta tile floors and Provençal fabrics; many also boast their own private terrace. At the gourmet restaurant **La Table du Cantemerle,** chef Jérôme Héraud dishes up grilled Aveyron lamb in a parsley crust and lobster ravioli in the elegant dining room or outdoors alongside the pool. Best value is the 27€ 2-course weekday lunch menu (more expensive in the evening and on weekends). Use of the spa's heated indoor pool, mosaic Turkish baths, and fitness area is complimentary for guests. The hotel website sells spa packages, which include massages and breakfast, often selling for 100€ extra per night.

258 chemin Cantemerle. www.cantemerle-hotel-vence.com. ℂ **04-93-58-08-18.** 27 units. 145€–265€ double; 353€–565€ suite. Closed Nov–Mar. **Amenities:** Restaurant; 2 bars; outdoor pool; spa; free Wi-Fi.

Château Saint-Martin & Spa ★★★ Just 20 min. from the Nice airport, amid 14 hectares (35 acres) of enchanting gardens, lies one of the world's most sumptuous hotels. Take, for example, the spa. In addition to massages, it offers La Prairie signature treatments, yoga lessons, color chromotherapy, and a wellness shower than can emulate the misting breeze of a tropical rainstorm. Moreover, the hotel complex is shared by a mere handful of guests, who revel in the vast infinity pool, the outdoor **Oliveraie** grill restaurant set in an ancient olive grove, and mammoth château suites that overlook the shimmering sea below. Six independent villas are larger and more luxurious still. The Michelin-starred restaurant under accomplished chef Franck Ferigutti switches from modern French fare to infused foam creations and desserts chilled with nitrogen steam. And it sits atop a wine cellar worth far more than the average Riviera mansion. Finally, a new promotion allows château guests who reserve 2 nights to sojourn around the pool (and take a complimentary lunch) at sister hotel, the ultra-glamorous Hotel du Cap-Eden-Roc.

2490 av. des Templiers. www.chateau-st-martin.com. ✆ **04-93-58-02-02.** 39 units, 6 villas. 390€–650€ double; 520€–780€ suite. Rates include breakfast. Closed Oct to mid-Apr. **Amenities:** 3 restaurants; bar; babysitting; outdoor pool; room service; sauna, spa; tennis; free Wi-Fi.

Where to Eat

Vence's unpretentious attitude is also evident in the local cuisine. It tends to be traditional and tasty, occasionally Michelin-starred, and often dished up in a sublime setting.

Les Bacchanales ★★ PROVENÇAL A short stroll from the Chapelle du Rosaire, Les Bacchanales is located inside a century-old villa, overlooking chef Christophe Dufau's enchanting kitchen garden. The creative menu uses almost exclusively local ingredients, transforming them into strikingly innovative versions of traditional Provençal cuisine. Mediterranean bream may be paired with apricots and Italian Taggiasche olives; sweet cantaloupe melon is grilled and served with fresh almonds and Corsican *brousse* cheese. The market-fresh weekly menu is limited to a mere handful of ultra-seasonal meat or fish dishes: Diners may simply select their preferred number of courses (4 to 5 at lunch, or up to 7 at dinner). The restaurant holds one Michelin star.

247 av. de Provence. www.lesbacchanales.com. ✆ **04-93-24-19-19.** Fixed-price menus 65€–115€. Tues and Thurs–Sun 12:30–2pm and 7:30–9:30pm. Closed last 2 weeks of Dec and 3 weeks in Jan.

Les Lavandes ★ PROVENÇAL This handsome eatery describes itself as a *restaurant fusionnel.* That's because chef-patron Robert worked at some of Bangkok's best hotel kitchens, and dishes like frogs' legs with Thai basil sauce, and scallops flambéed in pastis with green pepper, are 90 percent French, 10 percent Asian. Vegetarian and vegan dishes are plentiful. The bargain wine list (from 22€ per bottle) is almost all completely organic.

8 rue du Marché. © **04-93-32-61-52.** Main course 17€–45€; fixed-price lunch 21€ or dinner 34€. Thurs–Mon noon–10pm.

NICE ★★★

929km (576 miles) S of Paris; 32km (20 miles) NE of Cannes

Nice is known as the "Queen of the Riviera" and is the largest city on this fabled stretch of coast. It's also one of the most ancient, founded by the Greeks, who called it Nike (Victory). By the 19th century, Russian aristocrats and the British upper class—led by Queen Victoria herself—were sojourning here. These days, however, Nice is not as chi-chi as Cannes or St-Tropez. In fact, of all the major French resorts, Nice is the most down-to-earth, with an emphasis on fine dining and high culture. Indeed, it has more museums than any other French city outside Paris.

It's also the best place to base yourself on the Riviera, especially if you're dependent on public transportation. Getting around is now easier than ever. From 2018 a new tram whizzed from Nice Airport right into the city center and Port. Also from the airport, which is the second busiest in France, you can travel by train or bus along the entire coast to resorts such as Antibes, Juan-les-Pins, and Monaco. It's also possible to catch a train

Beachfront promenade des Anglais, Nice

to San Remo, a glamorous town over the Italian border, have lunch, then return to Nice by nightfall. Daytrips to expensive destinations like St-Tropez and Cannes are also on the cards.

Because of its brilliant sunshine and liberal attitude, Nice has long attracted artists and writers, among them Dumas, Nietzsche, Flaubert, Hugo, Sand, and Stendhal. Henri Matisse, who made his home in Nice, said, "Though the light is intense, it's also soft and tender." The city averages 300 sunny days a year.

Essentials

ARRIVING   **Trains** arrive at the city's main station, Gare Nice-Ville, avenue Thiers. From here you can take trains to Cannes for 7.20€, Monaco for 4.10€, and Antibes for 4.80€, with easy connections to Paris, Marseille, and anywhere else along the Mediterranean coast. For more information, visit www.oui.sncf or call ☎ **36-35** (.40€/min).

Buses (www.lignesdazur.com; ☎ **08-10-06-10-06**) to towns east, including Monaco (no. 100) depart from place Garibaldi; to towns west, including Cannes (no. 200) from Jardin Albert I.

Transatlantic, intercontinental, European, and domestic flights land at **Aéroport Nice–Côte d'Azur** (www.nice.aeroport.fr; ☎ **08-20-42-33-33**). From there, municipal bus nos. 98 and 99 depart at 20-min. intervals for the Port and Gare Nice-Ville, respectively; the one-way fare is 6€. **Official taxis** are not cheap. A ride from the airport to the city center costs around 50€; **Uber taxis** are less than half the price. Trip time is about 20 min.

Ferryboats operated by **Trans-Côte d'Azur** (www.trans-cote-azur.com; ☎ **04-92-00-42-30**), on quai Lunel on Nice's port, link the city with Ile Ste-Marguerite (p. 574) (40€) and St-Tropez (65€) from May to September.

VISITOR INFORMATION   Nice maintains four **tourist offices.** The largest is at 5 promenade des Anglais, near place Masséna (www.nicetourisme.com; ☎ **08-92-70-74-07**). Additional offices are in the Promenade du Paillon city center park, in the arrivals hall of the Aéroport Nice–Côte d'Azur, and outside the railway station on avenue Thiers.

CITY LAYOUT   The city is divided into five main neighborhoods: the Italianate Old Town; the vintage port; the commercial city center between place Masséna and the main train station; the affluent residential quarter known as the Carre d'Or, just inland from the promenade des Anglais; and hilltop Cimiez. All are easy to navigate on foot, with the exception of Cimiez. For more, see "Exploring Nice," p. 601.

SPECIAL EVENTS   The **Nice Carnaval** (www.nicecarnaval.com), known as the "Mardi Gras of the Riviera," runs from mid-February to early March, celebrating the return of spring with three weeks of parades, *corsi*

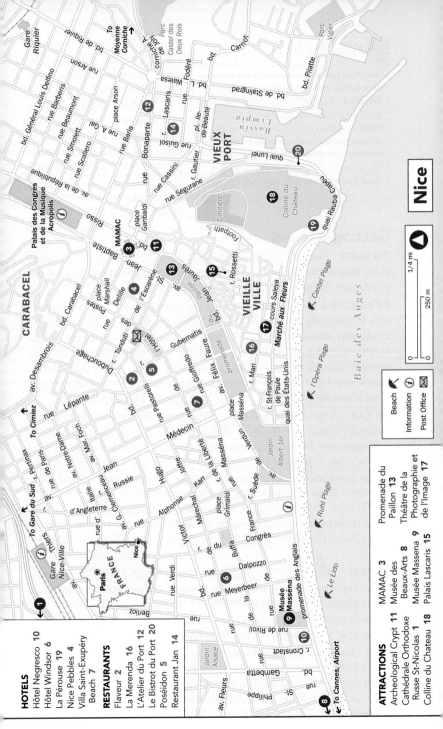

Nice

HOTELS
Hôtel Negresco 10
Hôtel Windsor 6
La Pérouse 19
Nice Pebbles 4
Villa Saint-Exupéry
Beach 7

RESTAURANTS
Flaveur 2
La Merenda 16
L'Atelier du Port 12
Le Bistrot du Port 20
Poséidon 5
Restaurant Jan 14

ATTRACTIONS
Archeological Crypt 11
Cathédrale Orthodoxe
Russe St-Nicolas 1
Colline du Chateau 18

MAMAC 3
Musée des
Beaux-Arts 8
Musée Massena 9
Palais Lascaris 15

Promenade du
Paillon 13
Théâtre de la
Photographie et
de l'Image 17

Beach
Information
Post Office

1/4 mi
250 m

599

Post-2016 Nice

Like other European cities hit by the scourge of terrorism, including London, Paris and Barcelona, Nice quickly rebounded from the tragic attack that occurred here in July 2016. Niçois are proud of their centuries-old tourism industry and have introduced even more activities—combined with beefed up security on the boardwalk—to make guests feel more welcome, and safe, than ever before.

(floats), *veglioni* (masked balls), confetti, and battles in which young women toss flowers at the audience.

The **Nice Festival du Jazz** (www.nicejazzfestival.fr) runs for a week in mid-July, when jazz, funk, and reggae artists perform in the Jardins Albert I near the seafront. The 2018 event included British trip hop artists Massive Attack.

Getting Around

ON FOOT　Nice is very walkable, and no point of interest downtown is more than a 10-min. walk from place Massena, including the seafront promenade des Anglais, Old Town, and harbor.

BY BICYCLE & MOTOR SCOOTER　Like many French cities, Nice has its own bike-sharing scheme, **Vélo Bleu** (www.velobleu.org). You can register directly at one of Nice's 175 bike stands (difficult) or online (much easier); fees range from 1€ for 1 day to 5€ for a week. Alternatively, you can rent bikes (from 16€ per day) and scooters (from 26€ per day; driver's license and deposit required) from **Holiday Bikes,** 23 rue de Belgique and 6 rue Massenet (www.motorbike-rentals.com; ✆ 04-93-16-01-62).

BY CAR　A novel addition to the Nice transport scene is **Auto Bleue** (www.auto-bleue.org; ✆ 09-77-40-64-06). The scheme allows visitors to rent an electric Peugeot car from one of 50 vehicle stands around Nice for 45€ per day, inclusive of electricity, parking, and insurance. Sign-up online in advance. Cooler cats may rent an E Type Jaguar or Ford Mustang from **Rent A Classic Car** (www.rentaclassiccar.com; ✆ 09-54-00-29-33) from 329€ per day. The coolest, newest addition to Nice's car hire scene is **NiceCar** (www.nice-car.fr; ✆ 04-93-16-90-36). For 50€ per half-day, visitors can drive one of their three-wheeled, GPS-guided cabriolet cars.

BY TAXI　**Taxis Nice** (www.taxis-nice.fr; ✆ 04-93-13-78-78) will pick up within 5 min. across town. Alternatively, call a **Cyclopolitain** (nice.cyclopolitain.com; ✆ 04-93-81-76-15) electronic tricycle for a ride around town (until 7pm, maximum two passengers, from 5€ per ride).

BY PUBLIC TRANSPORT　Most local buses leave from the streets around place Masséna. Municipal **buses** charge 1.50€ for rides within the entire Alpes-Maritime province, even as far as Monaco or Cannes. The same ticket can also be used on Nice's **tramway,** which connects the Old Town with Gare Nice-Ville, Nice Airport, the Allianz Riviera stadium, and northern Nice. Tickets, day passes (5€), and week passes (15€) can be bought directly onboard buses (although not trams) or at electronic kiosks around the city (where 10€ carnets of 10 tickets can also be purchased). For further information, see www.lignesdazur.com.

[FastFACTS] NICE

ATMs/Banks   Nice is home to dozens of banks; **LCL Banque,** 15 av. Jean Médecin (© **04-93-82-84-61**), is one of the most central.

Dentists   **SOS Dentaire** (www.ordre-chirurgiens-dentistes-06.com; © **04-93-01-14-14**).

Doctors & Hospitals   **Hôpital Lenval,** 57 av. de la Californie (www.lenval.org; © **04-92-03-03-92**).

Embassies & Consulates   **U.S. Consular Agency Nice,** 7 av. Gustave V (© **04-93-88-89-55**); **Consulate of Canada,** 2 pl. Franklin (© **04-93-92-93-22**).

Internet Access   Various public squares and streets (such as the cours Saleya) throughout Nice offer free Wi-Fi.

Local Information   The **"Riviera Reporter"** (www.rivierareporter.com) both cover news, art, culture, and events in and around Nice. Alternatively, **"Angloinfo French Riviera"** (http://riviera.angloinfo.com) is an invaluable resource.

Mail & Postage   **La Poste,** 6 rue Louis Gassin (© **36-31**).

Pharmacies   **Pharmacie Masséna,** 7 rue Masséna (© **04-93-87-78-94**).

Safety   Nice is generally a very safe place. However, as in any big city, it's important to keep an eye on your valuables, in particular anywhere that's crowded. Avoid poorly lit streets at night, including in Nice's Old Town. Shortchanging in shops across Nice is the commonplace, so overtly count your change.

Exploring Nice

In 1822, Nice's orange crop had an awful year. The workers faced a lean time, so the English residents employed them to build the **Promenade des Anglais** ★★, today a wide boulevard fronting the bay that stretches for 7km (4.25 miles), all the way to the airport. Along the beach are rows of grand cafes, the Musée Masséna, and the city's most glamorous hotels.

Crossing this boulevard in the tiniest bikinis are some of the world's most attractive bronzed bodies. They're all heading for the **beach.** Tough on tender feet, *le plage* is made not of sand, but of pebbles (and not small ones, either).

Rising sharply on a rock at the eastern end of the promenade is the **Colline du Château.** Once a fortified bastion, the hill has since been turned into a wonderful public park complete with a waterfall, cafes, and a giant children's play area, as well as an incredibly ornate cemetery. Head up aboard an elevator from the quai des Etats-Unis; more athletic visitors can walk up one of five sets of steep steps. The park is open daily from 8am to dusk.

Marché aux Fleurs (flower market) at cours Saleya

Continuing east of the Colline, you reach the **Vieux Port,** or harbor, where locals fill the restaurants. While lingering over a drink at a sidewalk cafe, you can watch the ferries depart for Corsica and the yachts for St-Tropez. Just inland, the neighborhood around rue Bonaparte and place Garibaldi has become one of the hippest in town: head here for authentic eateries, hip bars, and the superb **MAMAC** (Museum of Contemporary Art; see below).

The **Vieille Ville ★★**, or Old Town, begins at the foot of the Colline and stretches to place Masséna. Sheltered by red-tiled roofs, many of the Italianate facades suggest 17th-century Genoese palaces, including the free museum **Palais Lascaris** (see below). The Old Town is a maze of narrow streets teeming with local life, flower-strewn squares, and traditional *boulangeries:* sample a Niçois-style onion pizza *(pissaladière)* here. Many of the buildings are painted a faded Roman gold, and their banners are laundry flapping in the sea breeze.

From Tuesday through Sunday (8am–1pm), the Old Town's main pedestrianized thoroughfare, the **cours Saleya,** is crowded with local producers selling seasonal fruits and vegetables, cured meats, and artisanal cheeses. At the market's western end is the **Marché aux Fleurs.** A rainbow of violets, lilies, and roses, the market operates Tuesday to Sunday from 8am to around 6pm. On Monday (8am–6pm) the cours Saleya is occupied by a superb **antiques market,** with vendors carting wares in from across France and Italy.

Nice's centerpiece is **place Masséna,** with rococo buildings and bubbling fountains, as well as the new **Promenade du Paillon** parkway that stretches from the MAMAC down to the **Jardin Albert-1er.** With palms and exotic flowers, this pedestrian-only zone is one of the prettiest places in town. During renovations, the city authorities discovered an **Archeological Crypt** near place Garibaldi, place Jacques Toja (www.nice.fr/culture; ✆ **04-92-00-41-90;** 5€ adults, 2.50€ children under 16; closed Tues, Thurs, and Fri). The site can now be visited on a 60-min. guided tour.

Cathédrale Orthodoxe Russe St-Nicolas à Nice ★ CATHEDRAL Ordered built by none other than Tsar Nicholas II, Russia's last emperor, this recently renovated cathedral is the most beautiful religious edifice of the Orthodoxy outside Russia. It dates from the Belle Epoque, when some of the Romanovs and entourage turned the Riviera into their stomping ground. Everyone from grand dukes to ballerinas arrived on the reinstated direct train from Moscow (it takes two days, crosses eight countries, and costs from 300€ one way), then paraded their tiaras on the promenade. The cathedral is richly ornamented and decorated with icons. You'll spot the building from afar because of its collection of ornate onion-shaped domes.

Av. Nicolas II (off bd. Tzaréwitch). ℂ **04-93-83-94-08.** www.cathedrale-russe-nice.fr. Free admission. Guided tour 10€ adults; free for children 9 and under. Apr–Oct daily 9am–noon and 2–6pm; Nov–Mar daily 9:30am–noon and 2–5:30pm. From the central rail station, bus no. 71, or head west along av. Thiers to bd. Gambetta, and then go north to av. Nicolas-II.

Musée d'Art Moderne et d'Art Contemporain ★★ MUSEUM

Nice's Modern and Contemporary Art Museum (or MAMAC) is a visionary display of art, architecture, and color. The building itself is boldness personified. It comprises two stone blocks clad in shimmering Cararra marble, with a glass walkway winding around the top. Stride around in winter to see snow on the Alps to the north as sunshine glitters on the Mediterranean to the south. Of the 10 main salons, three permanent collections stand out. The first is the American Pop Art display featuring Tom Wesselmann, Robert Indiana, and Andy Warhol, which includes the latter artist's rejection letters from the New York MoMA. The second is the European New Realist display of César, Arman, and Niki de Saint Phalle. The third unique collection is the School of Nice room of locally acclaimed artists including Sacha Sosno and Ben. The MAMAC also puts on exhibitions at the Galerie des Ponchettes (an old fishermen's lodge) on the Promenade des Anglais.

Pl. Yves Klein (adjoining pl. Garibaldi). www.mamac-nice.org. ℂ **04-97-13-42-01.** Admission 6€ adults; free for children aged 18 and under. Tues–Sun 10am–6pm.

Musée des Beaux-Arts ★★ ART MUSEUM

Housed in the fabulous former residence of the Ukrainian Princess Kotchubey, this fine collection of 19th- and 20th-century art includes works by Rodin and Dufy, as well as works by a dynasty of painters, the Dutch Vanloo family. One of its best-known members, Carle Vanloo, born in Nice in 1705, was Louis XV's premier *peintre.* High drama hit the museum in 2007, when armed robbers broke into the museum on a quiet summer Sunday, stealing priceless canvases by Monet and Sisley. The artworks were recovered less than a year later in Marseille.

33 av. des Baumettes. www.musee-beaux-arts-nice.org. ℂ **04-92-15-28-28.** Admission 6€ adults; free for children aged 13 and under. Tues–Sun 10am–6pm. Bus: 3, 9, 10, 22, or 38.

Musée Masséna ★★★ MUSEUM

Riviera aficionados will adore this astounding history museum. Located within an imposing Belle Epoque villa, it exhibits a quirky range of objects charting local life in

Nice and its surrounds, from the first Victorian visitors through the roaring 1920s. Elegantly printed menus, train tickets from London to Nice, period maps, and snapshots of the promenading rich on vacation bring the past to life. Of additional note are the paintings and *objets d'art* donated by the Masséna family, a noble set of locals who constructed the villa. Botanist Edouard Ardre, who also designed the verdant greenery in front of the Casino de Monte-Carlo, landscaped the museum's neatly manicured gardens.

65 rue de France or 35 promenade des Anglais. ℂ **04-93-91-19-10.** Admission 6€ adults; free for children aged 16 and under. Wed–Mon 10am–6pm (from 11am Nov–May).

Palais Lascaris ★★ PALACE   The baroque Palais Lascaris in the city's historic old town is associated with the Lascaris-Vintimille family, whose recorded history dates back over seven centuries. Built in the 17th century, it contains elaborately detailed ornaments and suits of armor. An intensive restoration by the city of Nice in 1946 brought back its original beauty, and the palace is now classified as a historic monument. From 2018, the venue started to exhibit contemporary art within the baroque setting. The most elaborate floor, the *étage noble,* retains many of its 18th-century panels and plaster embellishments.

15 rue Droite. www.palais-lascaris-nice.org. ℂ **04-93-62-72-40.** Admission 6€ adults; free for children aged 16 and under. Wed–Mon 10am–6pm (from 11am Oct–Mar).

Théâtre de la Photographie et de l'Image ★★ PHOTOGRAPHY MUSEUM   Nice's brand-new photography exhibition space houses world-beating photography displays. Spectacles have included homages to Riviera photographer Jean Gilletta, Paris chronicler Brassaï, as well as images from Nice in the roaring 1920s. The Théâtre also held an acclaimed retrospective of National Geographic photographer Steve McCurry, whose most captivating image was of a green-eyed Afghan refugee girl taken in 1984. In 2018, the venue hosted a show on Franco Fontana, the Italian photographer whose color-rich work has been used in advertising campaigns by Fiat, Versace, and Canon.

1 pl. Pierre Gautier. www.tpi-nice.org. ℂ **04-97-13-42-20.** Admission 6€ adults; free for children aged 16 and under. Wed–Mon 10am–6pm (from 11am Nov–May).

Outlying Attractions in Cimiez

In the once-aristocratic hilltop quarter of Cimiez, 5km (3 miles) north of Nice, Queen Victoria wintered at the Hôtel Excelsior. Half the English court traveled down from Calais with her on a luxurious private train. To reach this suburb and its attractions, take bus no. 15 from bd. Dubouchage.

Monastère de Cimiez (Cimiez Convent) ★ CONVENT   The convent embraces a church that owns three of the most important works by the locally prominent Bréa brothers, who painted in the late 15th century. In a restored part of the convent where some Franciscan friars still live,

17th-century frescoes decorate the Musée Franciscain. Some 350 documents and works of art from the 15th to the 18th centuries are on display. The magnificent gardens are a photographer's dream, and there's rarely a tourist in sight. Panoramic views pan over Nice and the Baie des Anges. Artists Matisse and Dufy are buried in the cemetery nearby, and their graves are modern day pilgrimage spots; Matisse's in particular is scattered with flowers and letters from aspiring artists.

pl. du Monastère. *©* **04-93-81-00-04.** Free admission. Museum Mon–Fri 8:30am–12:30pm and 2:30–6:30pm. Church daily 9am–6pm.

Musée Matisse ★★ ART MUSEUM

In 1963, this beautiful old Italian villa was transformed into a museum honoring Henri Matisse, one of the 20th century's greatest painters. Matisse came to Nice for the light and made the city his home, living in the Hotel Beau Rivage and on the cours Saleya, and dying in Cimiez in 1954. Most of the pieces in the museum's permanent collection—including *Nude in an Armchair with a Green Plant* (1937) and *Blue Nude IV* (1952)—were created in Nice. Artworks are interspersed with Matisse's personal possessions, such as ceramic vases and antique furniture, as well as scale models of his architectural masterpiece, Vence's **Chapelle du Rosaire** (p. 595).

164 av. des Arènes de Cimiez. www.musee-matisse-nice.org. *©* **04-93-81-08-08.** Admission 6€ adults; free for children aged 16 and under. Wed–Mon 10am–6pm (from 11am Oct–Jun).

Musée National Message Biblique Marc Chagall ★★ ART MUSEUM

Surrounded by pools and a garden, this handsome museum is devoted to Marc Chagall's treatment of biblical themes. Born in Russia in 1887, Chagall became a French citizen in 1937 and painted with astonishing light and color until his death in St-Paul-de-Vence in 1985. This museum's focal set of artworks—12 large paintings, illustrating the first two books of the Old Testament—was originally created to adorn the central cathedral in Vence. The church's high humidity nixed the artist's original plans, and Chagall assisted in planning this purpose-built space instead. Big-hitting temporary exhibitions include *The Weightless World of Marc Chagall* in 2018, which highlighted the flying figures within the topsy-turvy universe of the artist's mind.

Av. du Dr. Ménard. www.musee-chagall.fr. ✆ **04-93-53-87-20.** Admission 10€ adults; 8€ students; free for children 17 and under. May–Oct Wed–Mon 10am–6pm; Nov–Apr Wed–Mon 10am–5pm.

Organized Tours

One of the most enjoyable ways to quickly gain an overview of Nice is aboard a **Nice Open Top** (www.nice.opentour.com; ✆ **04-92-29-17-00**) double-decker bus. Between 10am and 6pm year-round, one of a flotilla of this company's buses departs from a position adjacent to the Jardin Albert I. The panoramic 90-min. tour takes in the harbor, the museums of Cimiez, the Russian church, and the promenade. Per-person rates for the experience are 22€ adults, 18€ students, and 5€ for children 4 to 11. Participants can get off at any of 12 stops en route and re-board any other buses, which follow at 30- to 60-min. intervals, depending on the season. Advance reservations aren't necessary, and commentary is piped through to headsets in seven different languages. For just 3€ more, visitors can purchase a 2-day pass.

Another easy way to see the city is by the small **Train Touristique de Nice** (www.trainstouristiquesdenice.com; ✆ **06-08-55-08-30**), which also departs from the promenade des Anglais, opposite Jardin Albert I. The 45-min. ride passes many of Nice's most-heralded sites, including place Masséna, the Old Town, and the Colline du Château. Departing every 30 min., the train operates daily 10am to 5pm (Apr–May and Sept until 6pm and June–Aug until 7pm). The round-trip price is 10€ adults and 5€ children 4 to 12.

Possibly the coolest way to get around Nice is by Segway, the two-wheeled electronic scooters. **Mobilboard,** 2 rue Halévy (www.mobilboard.com; ✆ **04-93-80-21-27**) runs tours. Children 14 (minimum age) to 17 must be accompanied by an adult. A 1-hr.-long tour of Nice costs 30€ per person. More energetic guests may join **Nice Cycle Tours** (www.nicecycletours.com; ✆ **06-19-99-95-22**), 3-hr. bike voyages around the city. Tours cost 35€ per person, and the friendly team also run food tours and eBike expeditions. More professional cyclists can join Danish biker Tina Baltzer at **Lifesparkz** (www.lifesparkz.net; ✆ **06-40-52-94-39**). Her trips (from 40€ person) run along the Tour de France and Ironman routes that ribbon across the French Riviera. Alternatively, **2CV Escapade,** 7 pl. Ile de Beauté (www.2cv-escapade.com; ✆ **06-52-01-30-40**), in Nice Port, offers multilingual city tours in a classic Citroën convertible from 60€ per group of two or three persons.

Outdoor Activities

BEACHES   Along Nice's seafront, beaches extend uninterrupted for more than 7km (4.25 miles), going from the edge of Vieux-Port (the old port, or harbor) to the international airport. Tucked between the public areas are several rather chic private beaches. Many of these beach bars provide mattresses and parasols for around 20€ to 25€ per day. The coolest club, **Castel Plage** (www.castelplage.com; ✆ **04-93-85-22-66**), is a celebrity hangout in summer.

SCUBA DIVING   Of the many diving outfits in Nice harbor, **Nice Diving,** 13 quai des Deux Emmanuel (www.nicediving.com; ✆ **06-14-46-04-06**), offers bilingual instruction and *baptêmes* (dives for first-timers) around Nice and Cap-Ferrat. A dive for experienced divers, equipment included, costs around 50€; diver's certification is required.

Where to Stay

EXPENSIVE

Hôtel Negresco ★★   For more than a century, the Negresco has been Nice's most iconic hotel. Its flamingo-pink dome crowns the promenade des Anglais, its Belle Epoque facade turned towards the sea. Guestrooms—a mix of Louis XIV antiques and state-of-the-art bathrooms—have hosted each era's most noted celebrities, from the Beatles and Salvador Dalí to Michael Jackson. An exceptional collection of private art decorates the public areas. Dining includes the exquisite **Chantecler,** which held two Michelin stars until its head chef quit in 2018. The restaurant has been allowed to keep its stars during the transition period and odds are that this gourmet restaurant will win them back in earnest soon. Check the hotel website for deals like the **summer package,** which includes access to the private beach club Neptune Plage.

37 promenade des Anglais. www.hotel-negresco-nice.com. ✆ **04-93-16-64-00.** 117 units. 165€–600€ double; from 620€ suite. Parking 28€. **Amenities:** 2 restaurants; bar; babysitting; exercise room; massage; room service; free Wi-Fi.

MODERATE

Hôtel Windsor ★★   The coolest, funkiest, and most friendly hotel in Nice is also one of its best-value lodgings. This *maison bourgeoise* was built by disciples of Gustav Eiffel in the 1890s and has remained a family-run hotel for three generations. Current owner Mme. Payen-Redolfi has ushered in an artsy era where a different acclaimed artist decorates another guest room each year. The hotel currently has over 30 contemporary-art rooms, including one painted entirely in gold leaf by Claudio Parmigiani. Art and color stream outside into the **WiJungle** bamboo garden—location for the alfresco breakfast as well. Back indoors, **WiLounge** serves dinner and chilled rosé. **WiZen** is the fifth-floor health club, hammam, sauna, and meditation zone. The Windsor is a founder of **Botox(s)** (www.botoxs.fr), which guides visitors around the smaller private galleries of Nice, Cannes, and Antibes.

11 rue Dalpozzo. www.hotelwindsornice.com. ℰ **04-93-88-59-35.** 57 units. 95€–260€ double. Parking 15€. **Amenities:** Restaurant; bar; babysitting; health club; outdoor pool; room service; sauna; free Wi-Fi.

La Pérouse ★★ Once a prison, La Pérouse has been reconstructed into a spectacular and unique Riviera hotel. Set on a cliff, it's built right in the gardens of the ancient château hill, with a secluded swimming pool almost carved out of the rock to the rear. No hotel aside from the adjoining (and slightly less expensive) Hotel Suisse affords a better view over both the old city and the Baie des Anges. Inside it resembles an old Provençal home, with low ceilings, white walls, and antique furnishings. The lovely, spacious rooms are beautifully furnished, often with Provençal fabrics. Most have balconies overlooking the bay. Guests who book directly online also receive a complimentary breakfast.

11 quai Rauba-Capéu. www.hotel-la-perouse.com. ℰ **04-93-62-34-63.** 64 units. 119€–425€ double. **Amenities:** Bar; babysitting; restaurant; room service; outdoor pool; free Wi-Fi.

INEXPENSIVE

Villa Saint Exupéry Beach ★ Welcome to what has been voted the best hostel accommodation in France. Travelers of all ages adore the dormitory-style beds and private twin rooms, which are painted in homage to great French artists. Introduced in 2018 were a number of pod-style individual beds with curtains, lights, and storage next to each bunk. For an extra 5.50€, guests may graze on an abundant buffet breakfast; use of a communal kitchen and gym with sauna is free. Finds also include daily happy hour drinks prices (beers are only 1.50€) and quality meals at backpacker prices. A popular free addition is the daily art tour, which meanders past Matisse's old house in Cimiez.

6 rue Sacha Guitry. www.villahostels.com. ℰ **04-93-16-13-45.** 60 units. 25€–60€ per person in a single or twin-bedded room; 16€–47€ per person for dormitory bed. Rates include continental breakfast, sheets, and towels. **Amenities:** Bar; cooking facilities; computers; luggage room; TV lounge; free Wi-Fi.

ALTERNATE ACCOMMODATIONS

Nice Pebbles ★★★ A short-term rental of one of these holiday apartments allows you time to truly immerse yourself in local life, from cooking up morning-market bounty to sipping sunset aperitifs on your private terrace. More than 150 carefully selected properties (from studios to 10-bed homes) are dotted throughout the city's central neighborhoods, including the Old Town and harbor and along the promenade des Anglais. Apartments boast first-class amenities (Netflix and designer bathrooms are common) yet weigh in at just a fraction of the price of a hotel room. Demand is high, so book well in advance.

20 rue de l'Hotel des Postes. www.nicepebbles.com. © **04-97-20-27-30.** 90€–350€ per apartment per night. **Amenities:** Free Wi-Fi.

Where to Eat

The combined regions of Provence and the Riviera boast 110 Michelin stars across 90 restaurants (as of 2018)—that's an incredible statistic amounting to more than almost anywhere else on the planet. The Riviera's regional capital of Nice teems with exquisite restaurants, from the high end to the downright local. Excellent eateries are scattered across the city—although beware of many of the Old Town's careless offerings, keen to lure in tourists for a single night only. In addition to the suggestions below, the portside **Le Bistrot du Port,** 28 quai Lunel (© **04-93-55-21-70**), is where the Orsini family has been dishing up top-quality fish and creative seafood concoctions for over 30 years.

EXPENSIVE

Flaveur ★★★ MODERN FRENCH As the Hotel Negresco finds itself in a transition period after its head chef left, Flaveur is Nice's must-eat. As of 2018, this restaurant can now boast of having two Michelin stars. Brothers Mickaël and Gaël Tourteaux (whose last name, almost unbelievably, translates as "cake") are a pair of very talented chefs. They may be relatively young—late 30s and early 40s respectively—yet they've already spent decades in the kitchens of the Riviera's top restaurants. A childhood growing up on the tropical islands of Réunion and Guadeloupe means their modern Michelin-starred cuisine is laced with exotic flavors: Plump scallops seasoned with Japanese *gomasio;* artistically displayed lemongrass and bubbles of lemon caviar sit atop risotto. Meals are variations on fixed-price menus only; there's no ordering à la carte, although lunchtime menus allow for gourmet bites on a relative budget.

25 rue Gubernatis. www.flaveur.net © **04-93-62-53-95.** Fixed-price lunch 62€ or dinner 85€–145€. Tues–Fri noon–2pm and 7:30–11pm; Sat 7:30–11pm. Closed early Jan.

Restaurant Jan ★★★ MODERN MEDITERRANEAN The winner of Nice's newest Michelin star is this Franco–South African gourmet restaurant. Situated in the city's new dining district a block behind Nice Port, both decor and service (under the watchful eye of Maître d' Philippe Foucault, formerly of the Negresco and Grand Hotel du Cap-Ferrat) are akin to being a guest in a French Presidential retreat. The inventive cuisine of South African chef Jan Hendrik van der Westhuizen blends regional ingredients (line-caught seabass, Charolais beef) with African spice (Madagascar vanilla, rooibos jelly) and Italian style (Parmesan shavings, prosciutto chips). True foodies book Jan's new private dining room, named Maria, across the street. The gourmet experience costs 179€ per person and includes wine pairing, valet parking, and a six-course tasting menu cooked by the man himself.

12 rue Lascaris. www.restaurantjan.com. © **04-97-19-32-23.** Main course 28€–43€; fixed-price lunch 55€ or dinner 98€. Fri–Sat noon–2pm and Tues–Sat 7:30–10pm.

MODERATE

L'Atelier du Port ★★ NIÇOIS   This is a design-heavy restaurant that mixes sleek contemporary furniture with an open kitchen and indoor citrus garden . . . and gets it completely right. Two of this guidebook's authors live around the corner from this establishment and are devoted regulars. Chalkboard menus chart locally sourced daily delights including squid from the Italian border, lemons (for various desserts) from Menton, and stuffed ricotta tortelli from Nice Old Town's finest pasta store, **Barale** (7 rue Saint Réparate). In a final toast to modernism, reservations are accepted via Facebook, and fairly priced Provençal wines can be purchased by the *pichet* (carafe).

45 rue Bonaparte. © **09-83-03-88-44.** Main course 14€–23€. Daily noon–3:30pm and 7–11pm.

Caju ★★ VEGAN   A vegan restaurant so good it makes you embarrassed that you're still eating meat and dairy. Their "Beauty and the Beets" burger with "slaw lights up the palate with texture, flavor, and zing." Homemade potato chips with nut mayo make for an easy snack, alongside a freshly pressed juice (all 5.50€). As long as you like hemp seeds, cocoa, and unaffectedly enthusiastic service, you're in the right place.

12 rue Sainte-Claire. www.cajuvegan.fr. © **04-22-16-28-58.** Main courses 11€–15€. Wed–Sun 10:30am–8pm.

La Merenda ★★ NIÇOIS   Top chef Dominique Le Stanc left the world of *haute cuisine* far behind to take over this tiny, traditional, family-run bistro. And how lucky we all are. La Merenda is now one of the most authentic and unpretentious eateries along the French Riviera. Market-fresh specials scribbled on a small chalkboard depend on the season and may include stuffed sardines, tagliatelle drenched in delicious basil pesto, or a delectable *tarte au citron*. **Note:** The restaurant has no phone, so you'll need to make reservations in person.

4 rue Raoul Bosio. No phone. www.lamerenda.net. Main course 14€–29€. No credit cards. Mon–Fri noon–2pm and 7:30–10pm.

INEXPENSIVE

Poséidon ★ MODERN FRENCH   This is the bargain seafood offshoot from Michelin-starred Japanese chef Keisuke Matsushima. While dinner at his other high-end restaurant will easily top a hundred euros, here a lunch of *soupe de poisson* and sea bass with citrus oils will set you back a mere 18€. Though the food is far from Asian, Matsushima slices oysters, red mullet, and other seafood with a Japanese precision, resulting in rave reviews.

17 rue Gubernatis. www.poseidon-nice-06.com. © **04-93-85-69-04.** Main course 17€; fixed-price lunch 18€ or dinner 45€. Tues–Sat noon–2pm and 7:30–9:30pm.

Shopping

CLOTHES   Clustered around **rue Masséna** and **avenue Jean-Médecin** is Nice's densest concentration of fashionable French labels. For more high-end couture, the streets around **place Magenta,** including **rue de Verdun, rue Paradis,** and **rue Alphonse Karr** are a credit card's worst nightmare. A shop of note is **Cotelac,** 12 rue Alphonse Karr (✆ **04-93-87-31-59**), which sells chic women's clothing. Men should try **Façonnable,** 7–9 rue Paradis (www.faconnable.com; ✆ **04-93-88-06-97**). This boutique is the original site of a chain with several hundred branches worldwide; the look is conservatively stylish. For more unusual apparel, **Lucien Chasseur,** 2 rue Bonaparte (✆ **04-93-55-52-14**), is the city's coolest spot for Italian-designed shoes, scarves, and soft leather satchels. In the Old Town, rue de la Prefecture is home to far-out fashion stores including **Michel Negrin** (no.17), for women, and **Antic Boutik** (no.19), for men.

FOOD   The winding streets of Nice's Old Town are the best place to find local crafts, ceramics, gifts, and foodie purchases. If you're thinking of indulging in a Provençale *pique-nique,* **Nicola Alziari,** 14 rue St François de Paule (www.alziari.com.fr; ✆ **04-93-62-94-03**), will provide everything from olives, anchovies, and pistous to aiolis and tapenades. For an olive-oil tasting session—and the opportunity to buy the goods afterward—check out **Oliviera,** 2 rue Benoit Bunico (www.oliviera.com; ✆ **04-93-11-06-45**), run by the amiable Nadim Beyrouti. In the port, **Confiserie Florian,** 14 quai Papacino (www.confiseriefflorian.com; ✆ **04-93-55-43-50**), has been candying fruit, chocolate-dipping roasted nuts, and crystallizing edible flowers since 1949.

SOUVENIRS   The best selection of Provençal fabrics is at **Le Chandelier,** 7 rue de la Boucherie (✆ **04-93-85-85-19**), where you'll see designs by two of the region's best-known producers of cloth, Les Olivades and Valdrôme. Nearby, seek out **L'Atelier des Cigales,** 17 rue du Collet (✆ **04-93-85-70-62**), for Provençal platters and smart local handicrafts. For antiquarian books, contemporary art, kitsch, and comic books, wander north of place Garibaldi to **rue Delille** and **rue Defly,** just past the MAMAC modern art gallery. For art deco *objets d'art* from the 1930s to 1960s, hit **Harter,** 36 rue Ségurane (✆ **04-93-07-10-29**)—prices are not cheap but the items are museum-quality.

Nightlife

Nice has some of the most active nightlife and cultural offerings along the Riviera. Big evenings out usually begin at a cafe or bar, take in a restaurant, opera, or film, and finish in a club. The website **riviera.angloinfo. com** lists all the week's English-language movies in VO, or *version originale.*

The major cultural center on the Riviera is the **Opéra de Nice,** 4 rue St-François-de-Paule (www.opera-nice.org; ✆ **04-92-17-40-00**), built in

Cours Saleya, a daytime and nighttime hotspot in Nice

1885 by Charles Garnier, fabled architect of the Paris Opéra. It presents a full repertoire, with emphasis on serious, often large-scale operas, such as "Tristan and Isolde" and "La Bohème," as well as a *saison symphonique* dominated by the Orchestre Philharmonique de Nice. The opera hall is also the major venue for concerts and recitals. Tickets are available right up until the day of performance. You can show up at the box office (Mon–Thurs 9am–5:30pm; Fri until 7:45pm; Sat until 4:30pm) or, more easily, buy tickets in advance online. Tickets run from 10€ to 86€.

A chic gaming spot is the **Casino in the Palais de Mediterranée,** 15 promenade des Anglais (www.casinomediterranee.com; ✆ 04-92-14-68-00), which offers a similar experience daily from 10am for slot machines, 8pm for gaming tables.

Within the cool-kitsch decor of a former garage in the port area, talented staff serves up fruity cocktails and organic local wines at **Rosalina,** 16 rue Lascaris (✆ 04-93-89-34-96). Around the corner, gay-friendly **Comptoir Central Electrique,** 10 rue Bonaparte (✆ 04-93-14-09-62), has been the place Garibaldi neighborhood's epicenter of cool since opening in 2013. Also on the same street, **Deli Bo,** 5 rue Bonaparte (✆ 04-93-56-33-04), is a hip spot for ladies who lunch.

The party spirit is best lapped up in the alfresco bars on the **cours Saleya.** Otherwise, head a block inland to **Wayne's Bar,** 15 rue de la Préfecture (www.waynes.fr; ✆ 04-93-13-46-99), where dancing on the tables to raucous cover bands is the norm. For excellent house tunes, nonstop dancing, and heaps of understated cool, head to **Bliss,** 12 rue de l'Abbaye (✆ 04-93-16-82-38).

Day Trips from Nice

CAGNES-SUR-MER ★
7km (4 1/2 miles) W of Nice

The orange groves and fields of carnations of the upper village of **Haut-de-Cagnes** provide a beautiful setting for the narrow flower-filled streets and 17th- and 18th-century homes. Head to the top, where you can enjoy the view from **place du Château** and have lunch or a drink at a pavement cafe. The old fishing port and beach resort of **Cros-de-Cagnes** is known for its 4km (2.5 miles) of pebbly beach. For years Cagnes-sur-Mer attracted the French literati, such as Simone de Beauvoir. Great Impressionist painter Renoir said the village was "the place where I want to paint until the last day of my life." His former home (see below) is the highlight of a visit here.

Frequent no. 200 buses (1.50€) and trains (3.10€) zip along the coast between Nice and Cagnes-sur-Mer. The climb to hilltop Haut-de-Cagnes is strenuous; a free minibus runs daily about every 15 min. year-round from place du Général-de-Gaulle in the center of Cagnes-sur-Mer to Haut-de-Cagnes. Cagnes' **Office de Tourisme** is at 6 bd. Maréchal Juin, Cagnes-sur-Mer (www.cagnes-tourisme.com; ✆ **04-93-20-61-64**).

In Haut-de-Cagnes, the ever-popular **Josy-Jo,** 2 rue du Planastel (www.restaurant-josyjo.com; ✆ **04-93-20-68-76**), was the home and studio of painters Modigliani and Soutine during their hungriest years. The menu features Niçois specialty *petits farcis* (tiny stuffed vegetables), grilled lamb from the Hautes-Alpes, and a variety of homemade desserts. In Cros-de-Cagnes, chef Jacques Maximin dishes up fresh fish at the seafront **Bistrot de la Marine,** 96 promenade de la Plage (www.bistrotdelamarine.com; ✆ **04-93-26-43-46**). The best seafood deal is their daily lunchtime three-course special for 29€.

Château-Musée Grimaldi (Musée de l'Olivier & Musée d'Art Moderne Méditerranéen) ★ HISTORIC HOME/MUSEUMS
Château-Musée was a fortress built in 1301 by Rainier Grimaldi I, a lord of Monaco and a French admiral (his portrait is in the museum). In the early 17th century, the castle was converted into a gracious Louis XIII château, which now contains two museums. The Museum of the Olive Tree shows the steps involved in cultivating and processing the olive. The Museum of Mediterranean Modern Art displays works by Kisling, Carzou, Dufy, Cocteau, and Seyssaud, plus temporary exhibits. In one salon is an interesting *trompe l'oeil* fresco, *La Chute de Phaeton.* The tower affords a view of the Côte d'Azur.

7 pl. Grimaldi, Haut-de-Cagnes. ✆ **04-92-02-47-30.** Admission to both museums 4€ adults and free for visitors 26 and under; double ticket to museum plus the Musée Renoir 8€. Jul–Aug Wed–Mon 10am–1pm and 2–6pm; Apr–Jun and Sept Wed–Mon 10am–noon and 2–6pm; Oct–Mar Wed–Mon 10am–noon and 2–5pm.

ROYA VALLEY & THE MERCANTOUR NATIONAL PARK

The timeless Roya Valley and the Mercantour forests (one of only seven National Parks in mainland France) are a train hop away from Nice. The entire area was once the private hunting ground of Italy's Turin-based kings. It only became part of France in 1947, and the Italianate train stations and tumbling hill villages remain. Thankfully, a lot of wildlife is left, too, in the form of wolves, marmots, ibex, eagles, and deer.

The **Train de Merveilles** (tendemerveilles.com), climbs up into the Roya Valley from Nice-Ville station up to six times daily. A stunning stop is **Sospel,** 45 min. from Nice. This age-old village is sliced in two by a raging river, and is a center for mountain biking, horseback riding, and alpine hikes.

Further north up the valley, the village of **Breil-sur-Roya** has stolen a few hearts, too. It lies at the nexus of several hiking paths, one of them leading downhill to Sospel.

The large ex-Italian town of **Tende,** 2 hr. from Nice, is the train's final stop. The names above its stores, on its churches, and in its rococo graveyard are distinctly non-French. It's also the gateway to the **Mercantour National Park** (www.parc-mercantour.eu). Before partaking in the park's 100 hiking routes, make a visit to Tende's **Musée des Merveilles** (www.museedesmerveilles.com; © **04-93-04-32-50**), which highlight's the area's prehistory, cave paintings, and fairytale geography.

Lovers of *la bella italia* may continue on to Cuneo in Italy using a locals-only train that runs from Tende towards Turin several times each day.

Musée Renoir & Les Collettes ★★ HISTORIC HOME/MUSEUM
Built in 1907 in an orange grove, this was the Impressionist master's home for 12 years. The terrace of Mme. Renoir's bedroom faces stunning views over Cap d'Antibes and Haut-de-Cagnes. On a wall hangs a photograph of one of Renoir's sons, Pierre, as he appeared in the 1932 film "Madame Bovary." Although Renoir is best remembered for his paintings, in Cagnes he began experimenting with sculpture, a form he found easy to manage, given his growing arthritis. The museum has 20 portrait busts and portrait medallions, most of which depict his wife and children. For many, the orange groves, olive plantation, and unkempt gardens that so inspired the artist are a definite highlight. Be aware the museum is poorly signposted. Following a cellphone marker on Google Maps is strongly advised.

19 chemin des Collettes. © **04-93-20-61-07.** Admission (includes admission to Château-Musée Grimaldi) 6€ adults; 2€ students; free for ages 26 and under. Jul–Aug Wed–Mon 10am–1pm and 2–6pm; Apr–Jun and Sept Wed–Mon 10am–noon and 2–6pm; Oct–Mar Wed–Mon 10am–noon and 2–5pm.

VILLEFRANCHE-SUR-MER ★★

935km (580 miles) S of Paris; 6.5km (4 miles) E of Nice

Just east of Nice, the coastal Lower Corniche sweeps inland to reveal Villefranche, its medieval Old Town tumbling downhill into the shimmering sea. Paired with a dazzling sheltered bay set against picturesque Cap-Ferrat beyond, it's little wonder than countless artists made this beachy getaway their home—or that it's served as the cinematic backdrop for numerous movies including "Dirty Rotten Scoundrels". Hit British TV soap opera "Riviera," which follows various art, crime, and seduction scandals across the South of France, filmed its second series here through 2018.

Essentials

ARRIVING   **Trains** arrive from all the Côte d'Azur's coastal resorts from Cannes to Monaco every 30 min. or so. For rail schedules, visit www.oui. sncf or call ✆ **36-35** (.40€/min). **Lignes d'Azur** (www.lignesdazur.com; ✆ **08-10-06-10-06**) maintains a **bus** service at 5- to 15-min. intervals aboard line no. 100 from Nice to Monte Carlo via Villefranche. One-way fares cost 1.50€. Buses deposit passengers just above the Old Town, almost directly opposite the tourist information office. Many visitors **drive** via the Basse Corniche (Lower Corniche).

VISITOR INFORMATION   The **Office de Tourisme** is on Jardin François-Binon (www.villefranche-sur-mer.com; ✆ **04-93-01-73-68**).

[FastFACTS] VILLEFRANCHE

ATMs/Banks   **LCL Banque,** 6 av. du Maréchal Foch (✆ **04-93-76-24-01**).

Internet Access   **Chez Net,** 5 pl. du Marché (www.cheznet.com; ✆ **04-89-08-19-43**).

Mail & Postage   **La Poste,** 6 av. Albert 1er (✆ **36-31**).

Pharmacies   **Pharmacie Laurent,** 2 av. du Maréchal Foch (www.pharmacielaurent.com; ✆ **04-93-01-70-10**).

Exploring Villefranche

Villefranche's long arc of golden sand, **plage des Marinières,** is the principal attraction for most visitors. From here, **quai Courbet** runs along the sea to the colorful Old Town past scores of bobbing boats; it's lined with waterside restaurants.

Old-town action revolves around **place Amélie Pollonnais,** a delightful square shaded by palms and spread with the tables of six easygoing restaurants. It's also the site of a Sunday antiques market, where people from across the Riviera come to root through vintage tourism posters, silverware, 1930s jewelry, and ex-hotel linens.

Alfresco dining at Villefranche-sur-Mer

The painter, writer, filmmaker, and well-respected dilettante Jean Cocteau left a fine memorial to the town's inhabitants. He spent a year (1956–57) painting frescoes on the 14th-century walls of the Romanesque **Chapelle St-Pierre,** quai Courbet (*©* **04-93-76-90-70**). He presented it to "the fishermen of Villefranche in homage to the Prince of Apostles, the patron of fishermen." In the apse is a depiction of the miracle of St. Peter walking on the water, not knowing that an angel supports him. Villefranche's busty local women, in their regional costumes, are honored on the left side of the narthex. Admission is 3€ for adults, free for children 14 and under. In spring and summer, it is open Wednesday to Monday 10am to noon and 3 to 7pm; fall and winter hours are Wednesday to Monday 10am to noon and 2 to 6pm. It's closed from mid-November to mid-December.

A short coastal path leads from the car park below place Amélie Pollonnais to the **16th-century citadelle.** This castle dominates the bay, and its ramparts are open for leisurely wandering. Inside the citadel sits a cluster of small, locally focused **museums** (*©* **04-93-76-33-27**), including the **Fondation Musée-Volti,** a collection of voluptuous female sculptures by Villefranche artist Volti (Antoniucci Voltigero) and **Le Musée Goetz-Boumeester,** featuring around 50 artworks by Dutch artist Christine Boumeester. Opening hours are July and August, Monday and Wednesday to Saturday 10am to noon, Wednesday to Monday 3 to 7pm; June and September, Monday and Wednesday to Saturday 9am to noon, Wednesday to Monday 3 to 6pm; and October and December to May, Monday and Wednesday to Saturday 10am to noon, Wednesday to Monday 2 to 5pm. Admission is free.

Where to Stay

Hotel Villa Patricia ★   This petite seaside hotel really does offer some of the Riviera's cheapest double rooms during the height of summer. A 5-min. stroll from the water, it also boasts a shared garden sheltered by lemon trees. As one might expect for the price, some rooms are small, while others are oddly shaped, but all are stylish, smart, and exceptionally clean, and share a large lounge area complete with book swap, outdoor sofas, and a piano. It's a gentle 10-min. stroll from Villefranche, Beaulieu, and Cap-Ferrat.

310 av. de l'Ange Gardien. www.hotel-patricia.riviera.fr. ✆ **04-93-01-06-70.** 10 units. 65€–89€ double; 89€–119€ triple; 80€–119€ suite. Free parking. Closed Dec–Jan. **Amenities:** Free Wi-Fi.

Hôtel Welcome ★★   Villefranche's most prestigious hotel, the Welcome sits in the center of town and has been home to Riviera artists since the 1920s, including author and filmmaker Jean Cocteau (in room 22). Every one of the modern hotel's midsize-to-spacious rooms possesses a balcony and sea views. The wine bar spills out onto the quay in warm weather. The Welcome offers a *petit déjeuner famille* option for breakfast: 48€ for all the family instead of 18€ per person.

3 quai Amiral Courbet. www.welcomehotel.com. ✆ **04-93-76-27-62.** 35 units. 149€–296€ double; 226€–539€ suite. Parking 46€. **Amenities:** Bar; babysitting; room service; free Wi-Fi.

Where to Eat

Le Mayssa ★ MEDITERRANEAN   A little-known rooftop restaurant overlooking the yachts in the Bay of Villefranche? Yes, please. On linen-covered tables a sea-sourced cornucopia of crab salads and scallop risottos are served in style. The establishment sits atop the town's Gare Maritime boat office and is owned by the family behind **Paloma Plage** (www.paloma-beach.com; ✆ **04-93-01-64-71**), the coolest beach club on Cap-Ferrat.

pl. Wilson. www.mayssabeach.fr. ✆ **04-93-01-75-08.** Main course 14€–25€. Daily noon–2:30pm and 7–11pm.

ST-JEAN-CAP-FERRAT ★★

942km (584 miles) S of Paris; 9.5km (6 miles) E of Nice

Of all the oases along the Côte d'Azur, no other place has the snob appeal of Cap-Ferrat. It's a 15km (9.25-mile) promontory sprinkled with luxurious villas and outlined by sheltered bays, beaches, and sun-kissed coves. In the charming port of St-Jean, the harbor accommodates yachts, fishing boats, and a dozen low-key eateries.

It's worth mentioning that Cap-Ferrat is seriously wealthy. As in seriously, seriously rich. Stars like David Niven and Gregory Peck called "Le Cap" home before a new generation of Russian oligarchs and Hollywood

A-listers moved in. It's all very hush-hush, but we can tell you that Madonna is a regular visitor and Brad Pitt enjoys dinner on Paloma Plage, the best of St-Jean-Cap-Ferrat's beach clubs. The world's most expensive property, Villa Leopolda, went on sale here a few years back for a cool half-billion dollars. The BBC recently confirmed that the peninsula is the second most expensive location in the world (since you ask, Monaco came first). A wonderful coastal path loops past many of the world's richest residents' private homes.

Essentials

ARRIVING   **Trains** connect Beaulieu with Nice, Monaco, and the rest of the Côte d'Azur every 30 min. Many visitors then take a **taxi** to St-Jean from Beaulieu's rail station; alternatively, it's a 30-min. walk along Cap-Ferrat's promenade Maurice Rouvier to St-Jean village. For **rail** information, visit www.oui.sncf or call ✆ **36-35** (.40€/min). **Bus** line no. 81 connects Nice with St-Jean every hour. One-way fares costs 1.50€. For bus information and schedules, contact **Lignes d'Azur** (www.lignes dazur.com; ✆ **08-10-06-10-06**). By **car** from Nice, take D6098 (the *basse corniche*) east.

VISITOR INFORMATION   St-Jean's **Office de Tourisme** is on 59 av. Denis-Séméria (www.saintjeancapferrat-tourisme.fr; ✆ **04-93-76-08-90**).

[Fast FACTS] ST-JEAN

ATMs/Banks   **Banque Populaire Côte d'Azur,** 5 av. Claude Vignon, St-Jean 06230 (✆ **04-89-81-11-42**).

Mail & Postage   **La Poste,** 51 av. Denis Séméria, St-Jean 06230 (✆ **36-31**).

Pharmacies   **Pharmacie Pont Saint Jean,** 57 bd. Dominique Durandy, St-Jean 06230 (✆ **04-93-01-62-50**).

Exploring St-Jean

One way to enjoy the area's beautiful backdrop is to stroll the public pathway that loops around Cap-Ferrat from Beaulieu all the way to Villefranche. The most scenic section runs from **plage de Paloma,** near Cap-Ferrat's southernmost tip, to **pointe St-Hospice,** where a panoramic view of the Riviera landscape unfolds. Allow around 3 hr. to hike from St-Jean to family-friendly **plage Passable,** on the northwestern "neck" of the peninsula.

Villa Ephrussi de Rothschild ★★ HISTORIC HOME/MUSEUM   If Jay-Z and Beyoncé were born a century before, this is where they would live. The winter residence of Baronne Béatrice Ephrussi de Rothschild, this Italianate villa was completed in 1912 according to the finicky specifications of its ultra-rich owner. Today the pink edifice preserves an

St-Jean-Cap-Ferrat

eclectic collection, gathered over her lifetime: 18th-century furniture, Tiepolo ceilings, tapestries from Gobelin, a games table gifted from Marie-Antoinette (Ephrussi's hero) to a friend, and tiny seats for her beloved poodles. The nine themed gardens, from Florentine to Japanese, are a particular delight. The attractive tea salon, which overlooks the Bay of Villefranche, is run by Aude Filipowski, a chef who learnt her trade at the Grand Hôtel du Cap-Ferrat. For 31€ visitors can expect a superb lunch, including coffee and wine, as well as the price of an entrance ticket. An additional new family ticket welcomes two adults plus two children under 17 for the combined price of 46€.

1 av. Ephrussi de Rothschild. www.villa-ephrussi.com. ✆ 04-93-01-33-09. Admission 14€ adults; 11€ students and children 7–17; free for children 6 and under. July–Aug daily 10am–7pm; Mar–June and Sept–Oct daily 10am–6pm; Nov–Feb Mon–Fri 2–6pm and Sat–Sun 10am–6pm.

Villa Santo Sospir ★★ HISTORIC HOME/MUSEUM   In 1950, the Parisian socialite Francine Weisweiller invited artist Jean Cocteau to her Cap-Ferrat villa. The canny Cocteau didn't just stay the evening: he sojourned for the next 11 years, frescoing the entire property in dreamy wall-sized paintings. Today the villa is preserved in situ—it's like a party for Cocteau's friends Picasso, Man Ray, and Greta Garbo has been paused midway through. The property's bilingual guide and caretaker is Eric Marteau. A genial host, he worked as Weisweiller's nurse before becoming a trusted friend to her daughter, Carole, the current owner of this one-of-a-kind villa. Advance bookings with Eric are both necessary and simple to arrange.

14 av. Jean Cocteau. www.santosospir.com. ✆ 04-93-76-00-16. Admission 14€. By appointment only via visits@santosospir.com.

CAP-FERRAT'S HOMES OF THE rich & famous

The global aristocratic, business, and cultural elite have long favored Cap-Ferrat. As you wander around keep your eyes out for these four key villas. **Lo Scoglietto** is a rococo pink edifice looking out towards Monaco from the promenade Maurice Rouvier coastal path. Once owned by Charlie Chaplin, it later passed to fellow British actor David Niven. More famous still is **Villa Mauresque** at the Cap's southern tip. In 1928 it was acquired by British author Somerset Maugham. The writer took up residence again after World War II to find that the liberating Allies had bombed his ornamental garden and the occupying Italians had raided his wine cellar. More modernist is **Villa La Voile.** This yacht-shaped mansion has "sails" that draw across the property each day to diffuse the Riviera sun. To lend an idea of Cap-Ferrat's worth, that particular project was overseen by Lord Norman Foster, the architect responsible for the world's biggest airport (in Beijing). Peek over the fence between Villefranche and Cap-Ferrat at the **Villa Nelcotte.** Once owned by Count Ernst de Brulatour, a secretary of the American embassy in France, then by Samuel Goldenberg, a wealthy American survivor of the Titanic, it was rented in 1971 by reprobate rocker Keith Richards. That summer the Rolling Stones recorded the album "Exile on Main Street" in the villa's sweaty basement. John Lennon and Eric Clapton dropped by, as did half the personalities of the Riviera underworld.

Where to Stay

Four Seasons Resort: Grand Hôtel du Cap-Ferrat ★★★   Put simply, this grande dame of a hotel is the greatest building on Europe's richest peninsula. It's sumptuous, stylish, and incredibly sexy. Set on nearly 7 hectares (17 acres) of tropical trees and manicured lawns, it's been the exclusive retreat of the international elite since 1908. The **Le Spa** wellness center spills outside into curtained cabanas, where you can indulge in massages and other treatments. Aside from the modernist guestrooms, the coolest place to hang out is the seaside **Club Dauphin** beach club (non-guests can gain access for 90€ per day). It's reached by a funicular rail pod that descends from the hotel. The children of many visiting celebrities, including the Kennedys and Paul McCartney, have learned to swim in the Olympic-size infinity pool. The concierge can also organize private dinners at the nearby Villa Santo Sospir, the former home of Jean Cocteau.

71 bd. du Général-de-Gaulle. www.fourseasons.com/capferrat. ℂ **04-93-76-50-50.** 73 units. From 350€ double; from 1,090€ suite. Closed Dec–Feb. **Amenities:** 3 restaurants; bar; babysitting; beach club; bikes; Olympic-size heated outdoor pool; room service; spa; tennis; free Wi-Fi.

Hôtel Brise Marine ★   An Italianate villa constructed in 1878, the Brise Marine is tucked into a quiet residential neighborhood south of

St-Jean. Rooms are simply furnished and sunny, with enchanting sea views. During breakfast on the rose-twined terrace, you can almost imagine you're aboard one of the luxury super-yachts bobbing off Paloma Plage.

58 av. Jean-Mermoz. www.hotel-brisemarine.com. ℭ **04-93-76-04-36.** 16 units. 160€–229€ double; 190€–259€ triple. Parking 16€. Closed Nov–Feb. **Amenities:** Bar; room service; free Wi-Fi.

Where to Eat

La Cabane de L'Ecailler ★★ SEAFOOD   Cap-Ferrat is all about seafood—and this is the peninsula's best. La Cabane is the only establishment in the area to purchase directly from Arnaud, the last remaining working fisherman on the Cap. House specials include wild red mullet and vast platters of sea urchins and oysters. The simple port-side terrace overlooks the local yachts—not the billionaire gin palaces—in the new pleasure port.

Nouveau Port de Plaisance. www.lacabanedelecailler.com. ℭ **04-93-87-39-31.** Main course 16€–27€; fixed-price lunch 24€. Daily noon–2:30pm and 7–10:30pm. Closed Nov–Feb.

Capitaine Cook ★ PROVENÇAL/SEAFOOD   Perhaps the peninsula's most beloved eatery, Capitaine Cook is run by husband-and-wife team Lionel and Nelly Pelletier. Dine outdoors on the leafy terrace or indoors within the ruggedly maritime dining room. The menu is particularly strong on hearty yet imaginative fish dishes, from Cap-Ferrat style bisque to salmon ravioli. A timeless classic.

11 av. Jean-Mermoz. www.restaurantcapitainecook.fr. ℭ **04-93-76-02-66.** Main course 19€–29€; fixed-price menu 28€–32€. Fri–Tues 12:30–2pm and Thurs–Tues 7:30–10:30pm. Closed mid-Nov to Dec.

BEAULIEU-SUR-MER ★

941km (583 miles) S of Paris; 9.5km (6 miles) E of Nice

Cradled on the mainland just east of Cap-Ferrat, the Belle Epoque resort of Beaulieu-sur-Mer has long attracted *bons vivants* with its casino and fine restaurants. Its genteel environs once sheltered Sir Winston Churchill. Its palm-backed beaches and alfresco restaurants now welcome visiting celebrities from Bono to Sylvester Stallone.

Essentials

ARRIVING   **Trains** connect Beaulieu with Nice, Monaco, and the rest of the Côte d'Azur every 30 min. For **rail** information, visit www.oui.sncf or call ℭ **36-35** (.40€/min). **Bus** line no. 100 from Nice to Monte Carlo passes through Beaulieu. One-way fares costs 1.50€. For bus information and schedules, contact **Lignes d'Azur** (www.lignesdazur.com; ℭ **08-10-06-10-06**). By **car** from Nice, take D6098 (the *basse corniche*) east.

VISITOR INFORMATION   Beaulieu's **Office de Tourisme** is on place Georges Clémenceau (www.otbeaulieusurmer.com; ℭ **04-93-01-02-21**) adjacent to the train station.

[FastFACTS] BEAULIEU

ATMs/Banks   **Banque Populaire Côte d'Azur,** 40 bd. Marinoni (✆ **04-89-81-10-56**).

Mail & Postage   **La Poste,** pl. Georges Clemenceau (✆ **36-31**).

Pharmacies   **Pharmacie Anglaise,** 45 bd. Marinoni (✆ **04-93-01-00-35**).

Exploring Beaulieu

Beaulieu has popular public beaches at both ends of town. The beaches aren't as rocky as those in Nice or other nearby resorts, but they're still closer to gravel than sand. The longer of the two is **Petite Afrique,** just past the yacht harbor. It has a submerged diving platform, a beach bar, and a family-friendly atmosphere. The shorter is **Baie des Fourmis,** which lies beneath the casino at the foot of Cap Ferrat.

The town is home to an important church, the late-19th-century **Église de Sacré-Cœur,** a quasi-Byzantine, quasi-Gothic mishmash at 13 bd. du Maréchal-Leclerc (✆ **04-93-01-01-46**). It's open daily 8am to 7pm.

As you walk along the seafront promenade, you can see many stately Belle Epoque villas that evoke the days when Beaulieu was the height of fashion. Although you can't go inside, you'll see signs for **Villa Namouna,** which once belonged to Gordon Bennett, the owner of the "New York Herald," and **Villa Léonine,** former home of the marquess of Salisbury.

For a memorable 90-min. walk, start north of boulevard Edouard-VII, where a path leads up the Riviera escarpment to **Sentier du Plateau St-Michel.** A belvedere here offers panoramic views from Cap d'Ail to the Estérel. A 1-hr.-long alternative is the stroll along **promenade Maurice-Rouvier.** The promenade runs parallel to the water, stretching from Beaulieu to St-Jean. On one side you'll see the most elegant mansions in well-landscaped gardens, including the pink palace of former resident David Niven on place Niven; on the other, views of the Riviera landscape and the peninsular point of St-Hospice.

Villa Kérylos ★★ HISTORIC HOME/MUSEUM   This replica ancient Greek residence, constructed between 1902 and 1908, was painstakingly designed by archaeologist and devoted Hellenophile Theodore Reinach. Both indoors and out, the villa is a fastidiously flawless copy of a second-century Greek home. All period furniture was re-created using traditional Greek methods, while various rooms incorporated 20th-century conveniences, such as running water in the villa's *balaneion,* or thermal baths. The bucolic waterside gardens, dotted with olive and pomegranate trees, offer sweeping vistas over nearby Cap-Ferrat. Little wonder the site now doubles as a wedding venue for ultra-high net worth individuals, aided by the villa's proximity to five-star hotels like the Royal Riviera and Grand Hôtel du Cap-Ferrat.

Impasse Gustave Eiffel. www.villa-kerylos.com. ✆ **04-93-01-01-44.** Admission 11.50€ adults; 8€ students and children 7–17; free for children 6 and under. May–Aug daily 10am–7pm; Sept–Apr daily 10am–5pm.

Where to Stay

Le Havre Bleu ★   You could easily spend a fortune on a luxury hotel. Or you could check into this Riviera stalwart that underwent a recent design overhaul and blow your money in boutiques and beach clubs instead. Le Havre Bleu has a variety of accommodation options, including triples and family rooms, some with terraces and patios, that rarely rise above 100€ per night year-round. Breakfast (10€) is served on the sunny communal terrace, where guests may sip a rosé or a café au lait any time of day. The train station, Villa Kérylos, and Villa Ephrussi de Rothschild are all within strolling distance.

29 bd. Maréchal Joffre. www.lehavrebleu.com. *℃* **04-93-01-01-40.** 19 units. 70€–89€ double. Parking 12€. **Amenities:** Bar; free Wi-Fi.

Royal Riviera ★★   At last, a bona-fide Riviera luxury hotel with all the trappings, yet none of the pretention. The palatial splendor of the Royal Riviera's interior is paired with contemporary elegance inside the light, airy guestrooms. Rooms in the ancient Orangerie annex are even cooler, calmer, and quieter. The hotel's low-key friendliness extends to kids, too, who may enjoy treasure hunts on the hotel's private beach, waterskiing lessons, and pottery workshops while grown-ups lounge at the gigantic pool, which is heated in winter. This is one of the few Beaulieu hotels to open year-round, with low-season delights that include a Bistrot Lunch in its **La Table du Royal** restaurant for 48€.

3 av. Jean Monnet. www.royal-riviera.com. *℃* **04-93-76-31-00.** 94 units. 180€–815€ double; from 705€ suite. Parking 15€. **Amenities:** 2 restaurants; bar; babysitting; concierge; exercise room; indoor and pool; private beach; room service; spa; free Wi-Fi.

Where to Eat

The African Queen ★ FRENCH/INTERNATIONAL   A lively mix of yachties, celebrity patrons, and excellent cuisine makes this portside restaurant perennially popular. Wood-fired pizzas are superb; the finely chopped *salade Niçoise* is dressed at your table; the sole *meunière* is a buttery classic. Service can be erratic, but both the menu and the atmosphere are a delight. Celebrity-spotting opportunities abound all summer long at this unassumingly high-end option. Just don't fixate on the yachts bobbing a few feet from the dining tables. The rental price tag on most of them starts at around 100,000€ per week.

Port de Plaisance. www.africanqueen.fr. *℃* **04-93-01-10-85.** Pizzas 14€; main course 18€–40€. Daily noon–midnight. Closed some holidays.

Pignatelle ★ FRENCH   This neighborhood favorite spills out from a rustic dining room onto a simple, sunny terrace. La Pignatelle's à la carte selection and bargain fixed-price menus don't do pretention. Solid yet sublime starters include buckwheat crêpes, baked bone marrow, and garlic-laced escargot. Mains won't earn a Michelin star but have already won the hearts of local French diners: think veal kidneys with Dijon mustard, and cod with aïoli Provençal.

10 rue de Quincenet. www.lapignatelle.fr. ℂ **04-93-01-03-37.** Main course 19€–22€; fixed-price menus 27€–37€. Mon, Wed, and Thurs noon–2pm; Fri–Sun noon–2pm and 7–10pm.

ÈZE & LA TURBIE ★★

942km (584 miles) S of Paris; 11km (6.75 miles) NE of Nice

The hamlets of Èze and La Turbie, 6.5km (4 miles) apart, are picture-perfect hill villages that literally cling to the mountains. Both have forti-fied medieval cores overlooking the coast, and both were built during the early Middle Ages to stave off raids from Saracen pirates. In Èze's case, it's now tour buses that make daily invasions into town. Impossibly cute streets contain galleries, boutiques, and artisans' shops. La Turbie is much quieter, offering a welcome respite from the summertime heat.

Essentials

ARRIVING **Trains** connect Èze-sur-Mer with Nice, Monaco, and the rest of the Côte d'Azur every 30 min. You may take a taxi from here up 427m (1,400 ft.) to Èze; alternatively, bus no. 83 connects the rail station with the hilltop village. For rail information, visit www.oui.sncf or call ℂ **36-35** (.40€/min). **Bus** line no. 82 runs between Nice and Èze around every 90 min., while five to seven daily buses (no. 116) connect Nice and La Turbie. Both journeys take 40 min. One-way fares cost 1.50€. For all bus information and schedules, contact **Lignes d'Azur** (www.lignesda-zur.com; ℂ **08-10-06-10-06**). By **car** from Nice, take the spellbindingly pretty D6007 (the *moyenne corniche*) east.

VISITOR INFORMATION Èze's **Office de Tourisme** is on place du Général-de-Gaulle, Èze-Village (www.eze-tourisme.com; ℂ **04-93-41-26-00**). La Turbie's small **tourist information point** is at 2 pl. Detras, La Turbie (www.ville-la-turbie.fr; ℂ **04-93-41-21-15**).

[FastFACTS] ÈZE & LA TURBIE

ATMs/Banks   **Société Générale,** pl. de la Colette, Eze (ℂ **04-92-41-51-10**); **BNP Pari-bas,** 6 av. Général de Gaulle, La Turbie 06360 (ℂ **08-20-82-00-01**).

Mail & Postage   **La Poste,** av. du Jardin Exotique, Èze; **La Poste,** pl. Neuve, La Turbie 06360; both ℂ **36-31.**

Pharmacies   **Pharmacie Lecoq,** pl. Colette, Èze (ℂ **04-93-41-06-17**); **Pharmacie de La Turbie,** 6 av. Général de Gaulle, La Turbie 06360 (ℂ **04-93-41-16-50**).

On the western side of Monaco, reachable by a picturesque coastal trail cut into the coastline's rocks, is the **Villa les Camélias**, 17 av. Raymond Gramaglia, Cap d'Ail (www.villalescamelias.com; *②* **04-93-98-36-57**). A local history museum, albeit one with astounding sea views and a private swimming pool, the villa charts the history of this Monaco suburb by way of photographs, handwritten notes from regular visitor Sir Winston Churchill, and even a calling card from a glamorous local bordello. It's open from April to October Tuesday to Friday 9:30am to 12:30pm and 2 to 6pm, and Sunday 11am to 6pm; and from November to March Tuesday to Friday 9:30am to noon and 1:30 to 4:30pm, and Sunday 10am to 4pm. Admission is 9€ adults, 5€ for children aged 12 to 18, and free for children 11 and under.

Exploring Èze & La Turbie

Aside from its pretty lanes, the leading attraction in Èze is the **Jardin d'Èze ★**, 20 rue du Château (*②* **04-93-41-10-30**). Here exotic plants are interspersed with feminine sculptures by Jean Philippe Richard, all perched atop the town at 427m (1,400 ft.; 6€ adults, 2.50€ students and ages 12–25, and free for children 11 and under). In July and August, it's open daily 9am to 7:30pm; the rest of the year it opens daily at 9am and closes between 4 and 7pm, depending on the time of sunset.

La Turbie boasts an impressive monument erected by Roman emperor Augustus in 6 B.C., the **Trophée des Alps (Trophy of the Alps) ★**. Still partially intact today, it was created to celebrate the subjugation of the French Alpine tribes by the Roman armies. The nearby **Musée du Trophée d'Auguste,** cours Albert-1er de Monaco (*②* **04-93-41-20-84**), is an interactive mini-museum containing finds from digs nearby, a historical 3-D film, and details about the monument's restoration. Both the ruins and the museum are open Tuesday to Sunday mid-May to mid-September 9:30am to 1pm and 2:30 to 6:30pm, and mid-September to mid-May 10am to 1:30pm and 2:30 to 5pm. Admission to both sites is 6€ adults and free for children 17 and under.

Where to Stay

Château de la Chèvre d'Or ★★★   No hotel better sums up the glamour and grace of the French Riviera than La Chèvre d'Or. This resort hotel is built into and around the elegant hilltop town of Èze. Each sumptuously decorated suite is a grand apartment with a panoramic view of the coastline. It's a habitual favorite of royalty and A-listers, and recent makeovers have made it popular with vacationing families and young hipsters as well. The 38 terraced gardens drip down the hill towards the Mediterranean to ensure absolute privacy—indeed there's a ratio of one garden and three staff members to each room or suite. The best thing about La Chèvre d'Or? That would be the eponymous double-Michelin-starred **restaurant** overseen by top chef Arnaud Faye (fixed-price menus 85€–240€). Experimental dishes include a vegan square decorated with an edible garden of herbs and flowers; San Remo shrimp wrapped in oyster-infused gossamer-thin pasta; and roast lamb served with chickpea pancakes and lemon leaves.

Rue du Barri. www.chevredor.com. ℂ **04-92-10-66-66.** 37 units. 277€–409€ double; from 790€ suite. Parking 20€. Closed Dec–Feb. **Amenities:** 4 restaurants; bar; babysitting; exercise room; outdoor pool; room service; sauna; free Wi-Fi.

Where to Eat

Gascogne Café ★ FRENCH/ITALIAN On the main road just outside of Èze's fortified Old Town, this bustling eatery is a friendly spot to sample authentic local fare. The menu ranges from traditional flavors (homemade lasagna, sea bass on a bed of ratatouille) to more creative offerings (Asian-style rolls stuffed with snails and garlic cream). Tasty pizzas are also available. Ambience is decidedly casual.

151 av. de Verdun, pl. de la Collette. ℂ**04-93-41-18-50.** Main course 11€–27€; fixed-price menus 19€–31€. Daily noon–3pm and 7:30–10pm.

La Table de Patrick Raingeard ★★ MODERN FRENCH Cap Estel is the most secret of Riviera hotels. Jutting out from a peninsula of land in Èze-sur-Mer, below the raised village of Èze, its brass gates ward off beady paparazzi. While starlets prefer Cannes, older A-listers check in here (from 510€ per night). That said, casual visitors are welcomed with open arms to Patrick Raingeard's Michelin-starred restaurant, which commands the glorious seafront gardens. Food becomes theater by way of zucchini flowers on verbena ice cream and crayfish atop Gewürztraminer wine jelly. Just beware the initial offer of Champagne, which clocks in at 25€ or more per glass.

Inside the Hotel Cap Estel, 1312 ave. Raymond-Poincaré. www.capestel.com. ℂ **04-93-76-29-29.** Fixed-price lunch 52€; fixed-price dinner 125€–160€. Tues–Sat noon–2pm and 7:30–10pm (Jun–Aug also open Sun). Closed Oct to mid-Mar.

MONACO ★★

939km (582 miles) S of Paris; 18km (11 miles) E of Nice

This sunny stretch of coast became the property of the Grimaldi clan in 1297, when one Francesco Grimaldi tricked his way into the fortress protecting the harbor. The dynasty has maintained something resembling independence ever since. In recent decades the family has turned Monaco into the world's chicest city-state with its own mini-airport (with direct helicopter links to Nice and St-Tropez, no less).

Hemmed in by France on three sides and the Mediterranean on the fourth, this feudal anomaly harbors the world's greatest number of

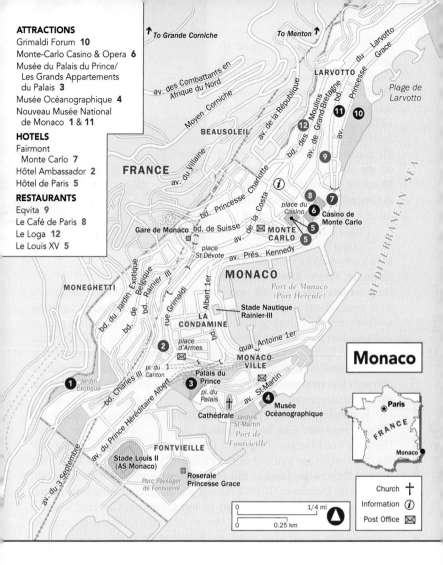

billionaires per capita. And as almost everybody knows, the Monégasques do not pay taxes. The tax regime attracts celebrity exiles as well—including racing driver Lewis Hamilton and tennis player Novak Djokovic (who owns the city-state's hottest new restaurant, Eqvita, p. 636). Nearly all of Monaco's revenue comes from banking, tourism, and gambling. Better still, in an astute feat of cunning, local residents aren't allowed to gamble away their inheritance, so visitors must bring a passport to play in the Principality's famed casino.

Monaco, or, more precisely, its capital of Monte Carlo, has for a century been a symbol of glamor. The 1956 marriage of Prince Rainier III to actress Grace Kelly enhanced its status. She met the prince while in Cannes to promote "To Catch a Thief." Their daughter, Caroline, was born in 1957; a son, Albert, in 1958; and a second daughter, Stephanie, in 1965. The actress's life and times were recently relived on the silver screen in "Grace of Monaco." Starring Nicole Kidman as Grace Kelly, the movie opened at the 2014 Cannes Film Festival.

The Principality of Monaco

Prince Rainier was nicknamed the "Builder Prince" as he expanded Monaco by building into the Mediterranean. Prince Albert took over from his late father in 2005 and burnishes his "Eco-Prince" credentials with pride. Newer, more environmentally conscious land-reclamation schemes near the Fairmont Hotel started in 2017. The $2.5 billion project will transport hundreds of thousands of tons of sand from Sicily to create an extra six hectares (15 acres) of land. Work should be complete by 2028. The Principality also has its own green car manufacturer, Venturi—although this marquee specializes in a typically Monégasque market for all-electric supercars.

Fortunately for the Grimaldi line, Albert married his girlfriend, South African swimmer Charlene Wittstock, in July 2011, now Her Serene Highness The Princess of Monaco. Despite rumors of a pre-wedding fall-out, the couple are idolized in the Principality, especially following the birth of their twins, Jacques and Gabriella, who will celebrate their fifth birthday in December 2019. Following a hasty course in both Monégasque dialect and European court protocol, Princess Charlene is now a familiar sight at society events. The royal family's official portrait has pride of place in every bar, hotel, and bakery in the land.

Essentials

ARRIVING   Monaco has rail, bus, highway—and helicopter—connections from other coastal cities, particularly Nice. There are no border formalities when entering Monaco from France. The 19km (12-mile) **drive** from Nice takes around 30 min. and runs along the N7 Moyenne Corniche. The pretty D6098 coast road takes a little longer. **Lignes d'Azur** (www.lignesdazur.com; ℂ **08-10-06-10-06**) runs a **bus** service at 15-min. intervals aboard line no. 100 from Nice to Monte Carlo. One-way bus transit from Nice costs 1.50€. **Trains** arrive every 30 min. from Cannes, Nice, Menton, and Antibes (www.oui.sncf; ℂ **36-35** (.40€/min). Monaco's underground railway station (*gare*) is on place St. Devote. A system of pedestrian tunnels, escalators, and elevators riddle the Principality, and such an underground walkway links the train station to Monte Carlo. The scheduled **chopper** service to Nice Airport costs 120€ via **Heli Air Monaco** (www.heliairmonaco.com; ✆ **92-05-00-50**). By **bus** it's just 22€ (www.niceairportxpress.com; ✆ **04-97-00-07-00**).

VISITOR INFORMATION The **Direction du Tourisme et des Congrés** tourist office is at 2A bd. des Moulins (www.visitmonaco.com; ✆ **92-16-61-16**).

CITY LAYOUT The second-smallest state in Europe (Vatican City is the tiniest), Monaco consists of four parts. The Old Town, **Monaco-Ville,** is on a rocky promontory 60m (197 ft.) high. It's the seat of the Prince's Palace and the government building, as well as the Oceanographic Museum. To the west, **La Condamine** is at the foot of the Old Town, forming its ritzy harbor and port sector. This area also has an open-air daily market. Up from the port (Monaco is seriously steep) is **Monte Carlo,** the playground of royalty and celebrity, and the setting for the casino, the Tourist Office, and various luxurious hotels. The fourth part, **Fontvieille,** is an industrial suburb housing the Monaco Football club, which was purchased by Russian billionaire Dmitry Rybolovlev. Thanks to the Russian's financial backing, the club was promoted to the French premier league in 2013 and won the title in 2017.

SPECIAL EVENTS Two of the most-watched **car-racing events** in the world take place here in January (**Le Rallye**) and May (the **Grand Prix**); see www.acm.mc and www.formula1monaco.com. The **Monte-Carlo Masters** ATP tennis tournament (www.monte-carlorolexmasters.com) takes place in April. The **Monte-Carlo International Fireworks Festival** lasts all summer long. The skies above the harbor light up several times a week as millions of euros go up in smoke, courtesy of those who can assuredly afford it.

> ### Earth to Monaco
>
> To call Monaco from within France, dial 00 (the access code for all international long-distance calls from France); followed by the **country code, 377;** and then the eight-digit local phone number. (Don't dial 33; that's the country code for France.)

[Fast FACTS] MONACO

ATMs/Banks   Among many others, several banks are along boulevard Albert 1er behind the Port of Monaco.

Internet Access   **Bilig Café,** 11 rue Princesse Caroline (✆ **97-98-20-43**).

Mail & Postage   **La Poste,** pl. de la Mairie in Monte-Carlo (✆ **36-31**).

Pharmacies   **Pharmacie Internationale,** 22 rue Grimaldi (✆ **04-93-50-35-99**).

Getting Around

BY FOOT   Aside from two very steep hills, the world's second-smallest country is **pedestrian-friendly.** Hardy local Jean-Marc Ferrie at **Monaco Rando** (www.monaco-rando.com; ✆ **06-30-12-57-03**) organizes **guided hikes** around his hometown from 12€ per person with an interpreter in-tow.

BY TAXI   **Taxis** wait outside Monaco train station, or call ✆ **08-20-20-98-98.**

BY PUBLIC TRANSPORT   **CAM** (www.cam.mc; ✆ **97-70-22-22**) runs buses inside the Principality. Line nos. 1 and 2 link Monaco-Ville with the casino area. CAM's **solar-powered shuttle boat** hops between the banks of Monaco's port every 20 min. The ride is great for kids and connects the casino area with the foot of Monaco-Ville. All CAM tickets cost 2€.

BY OPEN-TOP BUS   **Monaco–Le Grand Tour** (www.monacolegrand tour.com; ✆ **97-70-26-36**) open-top minibuses allow visitors to hop on and hop off at the Principality's 12 main sights. Day passes cost 22€ adults; 8€ children between 4 and 11; free for children 3 and under.

BY ELECTRIC CAR   It may be the land of the gas-guzzling Grand Prix, but Monaco is a global pioneer in green technology and is justly proud of its eco-credentials. Join the club with **Mobee** (www.mobee.mc), Monaco's sexy car-sharing service based around the **Renault Twizy,** a super-tiny electric car. Prices are 30€ per hour or 75€ for 3 hr.—enough time to whiz to some secret beaches and all the Monaco sights. These electric cars enjoy complimentary parking in 14 public spaces across Monaco, with distribution points high-lighted on an app.

> ## Getting Around by Luxury Car
>
> Of course, nothing shouts Monaco more than a rented **Ferrari California** (1,100€ per day) or a **Lamborghini Huracan** (1,600€ per day). Reserve your ride with **Elite Rentacar** (www.eliterent.com; ✆ **97-77-17-37**).

Exploring Monaco

Monaco's main sights—including its glamorous port, casino, and hotels—are clustered around the pedestrianized place du Casino. Its principal museums, including the Prince's Palace and Oceanographic Museum, are situated on the history-laden rock of Monaco-Ville.

Les Grands Appartements du Palais ★ PALACE   The home of Monaco's royal family, the Palais du Prince dominates the Principality from the Rock. A tour of the Grands Appartements—with audio tour recorded by none other than Prince Albert himself—allows visitors to glimpse the Throne Room and artworks by Bruegel and Holbein. The palace was built in the 13th century, and some of it dates from the Renaissance. The ideal time to arrive is 11:55am, so you can watch the 10-min. **Relève de la Garde (Changing of the Guard).** Summer concerts by the

Place du Casino

Monte-Carlo Philharmonic Orchestra are held outside in the court-yard. Fancy a Facebook post? Forget it—taking photos inside the Prince's palace is strictly prohibited.

Pl. du Palais. www.palais.mc. ✆ **93-25-18-31.** Admission 8€ adults; 4€ children 8–14; free for children 7 and under. Daily Apr–Oct 10am–6pm. Closed Nov–Mar.

Musée Océanographique de Monaco ★ AQUARIUM This mammoth oceanfront museum was founded by Albert I, great-grandfather of the present prince, in 1910. It's now a living, breathing science lesson covering the world's oceans by way of a Mediterranean aquarium, tropi-cal tanks, and a shark reserve. A delight for budding marine scientists is the 18m-long (60-ft.) whale skeleton that washed up on a local beach a century ago. Equally as compelling are the scientific specimens brought up from the ocean depths over the past 100 years. Princess Charlene hosted the third birthday party of twins Jacques and Gabriella here in 2017. Be aware that during the wintry low season (through most of Nov until Mar), entry prices are reduced by 5€.

Av. St-Martin. www.oceano.mc. ✆ **93-15-36-00.** Admission 16€ adults; 12€ children 4–18; free for children 3 and under. Daily Apr–June and Sept 10am–7pm; July–Aug 9:30am–8pm; Oct–Mar 10am–6pm.

Nouveau Musée National de Monaco ★★ ART MUSEUM Over the past decade Monaco has touted its cultural credentials to attract a sav-vier, younger, and more artistically aware crowd. The Villa Sauber and Villa Paloma museums are two stunning art spaces set in palatial former homes across the city from one another. Both bring in global culture vul-tures by way of contemporary-art exhibitions and shows covering

Museums are all well and good, but to survey the soul of Monaco you need a credit card, a suntan, and a late-morning wake-up call. Early-evening glamour revolves around the bars that surround the historic port. Here, locally based luxury yacht agencies like **Y.CO** (www.y.co; © 93-50-12-12) charter 50m-long (262 ft.) sailing craft for around $200,000 per week. At sundown the action moves uphill to place du Casino, where **Buddha Bar** (© 98-06-19-19) is bedecked with chinoiserie, Asian statues, and a raised DJ booth. For sheer class, the **Crystal Bar** (© 98-06-98-99) inside the Hôtel Hermitage pulls out all the stops. Patrons may sip 22€ glasses of Perrier-Jouët Champagne until 2am. **Le Bar Américain** (© 98-06-38-38), in the Hôtel de Paris, is far more raucous, with chillingly expensive cocktails and nightly jazz. Near Plage du Larvotto, the timeless superclub **Jimmy'z** (© 98-06-36-36),

open nightly 11:30pm until dawn, has attracted stars from Farrah Fawcett to George Clooney. But it's the mythical **Casino de Monte-Carlo** (www.monte carlocasinos.com; © 98-06-21-21) that lends the square its name. The casino's marble-floored Atrium is open to all (for 10€ plus the presentation of a valid passport) from 2pm. Gamers can shoot slots or play blackjack in the hallowed Salle des Amériques or try their luck at roulette in the Salle Europe. For roulette, *trente et quarante*, and Texas Hold'em visit the private areas of rococo Salon Touzet and Salon Médecin. Entrance to Les Salons Supers Privés is by invitation only (heh, they've got our number!) and requires smart dress and nerves of steel. Another great summer addition is the Casino de Monte-Carlo **alfresco** terrace. Here visitors may play roulette and poker overlooking the moonlit Mediterranean. Now *that's* glamorous.

sculpture, architecture, photography, and the French Riviera's glamorous history. The villas are amazing in themselves; the Sauber is a belle époque home built by the developers of the Casino de Monte-Carlo, while Villa Paloma was constructed by an American, Edward N. Dickerson, who adored the view across the Bay of Monaco.

Villa Sauber, 17 av. Princess Grace; Villa Paloma, 56 bd. du Jardin Exotique. www.nmnm.mc. © **98-98-16-82.** Admission to both 6€ adults; free for visitors 26 and under. June–Sept daily 11am–7pm; Oct–May daily 8am–6pm.

Opéra de Monte-Carlo ★ OPERA HOUSE Monaco takes music seriously. The Principality's lavish Opera House sits next to the casino, where its Salle Garnier hosts rock, pop, classical, and opera events—and even hosted the wedding reception of Prince Albert and Charlene Wittstock. Naturally, when guests attend the Opera House for events like 2018's season of Peter Grimes by Benjamin Britten, they dress to impress. For big-hitting pop and DJ events, try the **Grimaldi Forum,** 10 av. Princesse-Grace (www.grimaldiforum.com; © **99-99-20-00**).

Pl. du Casino. www.opera.mc. © **98-06-28-28.** Year-round admission prices 20€–120€ adults; reduced entrance for visitors 26 and under.

Outdoor Activities

BEACHES   Just outside the border on French soil, the **Monte-Carlo Beach Club** adjoins the **Monte-Carlo Beach Hotel,** 22 av. Princesse-Grace (www.monte-carlo-beach.com; ✆ **93-28-66-66**), a five-star sister establishment of the ultra-elegant Hôtel de Paris. Princess Grace used to frolic here, and today it's an integral part of Monaco social life. It now has an Olympic-size swimming pool, a La Prairie spa, cabanas, a poolside fine dining restaurant, and a low-key Mediterranean restaurant. Beach activities include inner tubes, jet skis, and parachute rides. As the temperature drops in late October, the beach closes for the winter. The admission charge of 60€ to 150€, depending on the season, grants you access to changing rooms, toilets, restaurants, and bar, along with use of a mattress for sunbathing.

More low-key swimming and sunbathing is at **Plage du Larvotto,** off avenue Princesse-Grace. Part of this popular man-made strip of sand is public. The other part contains private beach clubs with bars, snacks, and showers, plus a kids' club. A jogging track runs behind the beach.

SPA TREATMENTS   The century-old **Thermes Marins,** 2 av. de Monte-Carlo (www.thermesmarinsmontecarlo.com; ✆ **98-06-69-00**), embodies wellness at its most chic. Spread over four floors is a pool, Turkish *hammam* (steam bath), healthy restaurant, juice bar, tanning booths, fitness center, beauty center, and private treatment rooms. A day pass, giving access to the sauna, steam rooms, fitness facilities, and pools is 150€. Therapies include a seaweed body wrap for 80€. In 2018 Camille Marie Kelly Gottlieb, daughter of Princess Stephanie and grand-daughter of Grace Kelly, got into hot water by posting suggestive Instagram shots of her inside the spa.

SWIMMING   Overlooking the yacht-studded harbor, the **Stade Nautique Rainier-III,** quai Albert-1er, at La Condamine (✆ **93-30-64-83**), a pool frequented by the Monégasques, was a gift from Prince Rainier to his subjects. It's open May to October daily 9am to 6pm (June–Aug until 8pm). Admission costs 5.70€ per person. Between November and March, it's an ice-skating rink.

TENNIS & SQUASH   The **Monte Carlo Country Club,** 155 av. Princesse-Grace, Roquebrune-Cap Martin, France (www.mccc.mc; ✆ **04-93-41-30-15**), has 21 clay and two concrete tennis courts. The 47€ fee provides access to a restaurant, health club with Jacuzzi and sauna, putting green, beach, squash courts, and well-maintained tennis courts. Guests of the hotels administered by the Société des Bains de Mer (Hôtel de Paris, Hermitage, Monte Carlo Bay, and Monte Carlo Beach Club) pay half-price. It's open daily 8am to 8 or 9pm, depending on the season.

ATTACKING THE plastic

If you insist on the likes of Hermès, Gucci, and Lanvin, you'll find them cheek by jowl near the Hôtel de Paris and the Casino de Monte-Carlo. But the prize for Monaco's hippest store goes to **Lull,** 29 rue de Millo (✆ 97-77-54-54), awash in labels like Dries Van Noten and Levi's Made & Crafted. Almost next door, **Une Femme à Suivre** (✆ 97-77-10-52) sells French classics from the likes of Tara Jarman and Mariona Gen. Just west of place du Casino, **Pretty You,** 5 pl. Saint James (✆ 97-70-48-08), vends Oscar de la Renta and Elie Saab. Just east of this piazza, **Galeries du Métropole** is packed with high fashion and specialty stores. As well as Dunhill and Gant, try **McMarket** (✆ 97-77-12-12). Serious labels in this fashion emporium include Balenciaga, Louboutin, and Jimmy Choo. **Fnac** (✆ 08-25-02-00-20) is recommended for English-language novels, Monaco history books, and the latest electronics. Heading east from place du Casino, **boulevard de Moulins** sells "everyday" Monaco labels. We're talking **Baby Dior,** no. 31 (✆ 97-25-72-12) and swimwear-to-the-stars brand **Erès,** also at no. 31 (✆ 97-70-76-50). For Repetto ballet slippers and Michael Kors satchels try **La Botterie,** no. 14 (✆ 97-25-80-55). For real-people shopping, stroll **rue Grimaldi,** the Principality's most commercial street, near the fruit, flower, and food market at **place des Armes,** which is open daily from 7:30am until noon.

Where to Stay

Fairmont Monte Carlo ★★ This five-star hotel is easily Monaco's most fun. It combines fine-dining restaurants, a spa, and a rooftop pool with an unstuffy attitude; albeit one backed by a legion of ever-smiling, mostly Italian, staff. Of course, this vision of modern opulence is also one of the most valuable pieces of real estate on the Côte d'Azur. It dips into the Mediterranean from behind the Casino de Monte-Carlo—indeed, a private passageway runs to the casino's rear entrance—and guests may combine the endless breakfast with the best sea views in the Principality. Formula 1 fans should also note that the fastest part of the Monaco Grand Prix zips right beneath the basement. In 2017, Prince Albert inaugurated a suite dedicated to racing legend Ayrton Senna—it's one of four super-sized guestrooms that overlook the Grand Prix circuit. The Fairmont also has a partnership with four local beach clubs, where families are dropped off with towels, mineral water, and sun spray, then picked up on demand. Diners are in for a treat, too. At Japanese atelier **Nobu** guests enjoy half-price cocktails from 6 to 8pm.

12 av. des Spélugues. www.fairmont.com/montecarlo. ✆ 93-50-65-00. 602 units. 254€–479€ double; from 519€ suite. Parking 50€. **Amenities:** 3 restaurants; 2 bars; babysitting; concierge; health club; outdoor pool; room service; spa; free Wi-Fi.

Hôtel Ambassador ★ A 5-min. stroll from the main Monaco action, the Ambassador makes a bargain base from which to explore the Principality. Elegant guestrooms benefit from a style overhaul. Dimensions are tiny, however (but the entire country occupies 202 hectares/less than 1 sq.

mile, so little wonder). A buffet breakfast (included in the price) is offered next door in the cheap and tasty **P&P** restaurant and pizzeria. Patrons also receive a 10 percent discount off all meals at the same establishment.

10 av. Prince Pierre. www.ambassadormonaco.com. ☎ **97-97-96-96.** 35 units. 90€–210€ double. Breakfast included. Parking 20€. **Amenities:** Bar; free Wi-Fi.

Hôtel de Paris ★★★   Never has so much history and glamour been suffused into 158 effortlessly chic guest rooms. Sir Winston Churchill was also a regular. La Prairie products and free access to the **Thermes Marins spa** (p. 633) come as standard in all of them. Accommodation culminates in a series of super suites, including the Princess Grace suite, launched in 2018, which has a bargain price tag of 41,000€ per night. The former British Prime Minister used to sneak along a secret rooftop passageway from his suite to **Le Grill,** which has a special 55€ lunch menu—a relative bargain in Monaco. It's one of three award-winning restaurants in the hotel (see also the Louis XV, below). If that isn't enough, the Hôtel de Paris boasts several sister hotels, including the five-star family friendly **Monte-Carlo Beach Hotel** (www.monte-carlo-beach.com; ☎ **93-28-66-66**)—whose **Restaurant Elsa** received the region's first 100 percent organic certificate—and the imposingly elegant **Hôtel Hermitage** (www.hotelhermitagemontecarlo.com; ☎ **98-06-40-00**), just around the corner.

Pl. du Casino. www.montecarloresort.com. ☎ **98-06-30-00.** 15 units. From 446€ double; from 680€ suite. Valet parking 40€. **Amenities:** 3 restaurants (see Le Louis XV, p. 636); bar; babysitting; concierge; exercise room; large indoor pool; room service; sauna; Thermes Marins spa offering thalassotherapy; free Wi-Fi.

Where to Eat

Pinch yourself. This postcard-sized Principality boasts a total of eight Michelin stars, and includes the most highly rated eatery on the entire Mediterranean, Le Louis XV.

Le Café de Paris ★ MODERN FRENCH   Pricey, pretentious, and ever-popular, this Parisian-style restaurant-cafe on place du Casino has a location to die for. The menu has taken on an even more classic edge under new head chef Franck Lafon, who started working in the Hôtel de Paris across the street when he was just 17 years old. Simple starters like garlic escargot and *croque-monsieur* share the menu with more innovative mains like filet of plaice (a North Sea fish) with pumpkin purée or steak tartare. Best value is the bistro-style weekday dish of the day, which may include braised beef cheeks with polenta on Mondays and scallop risotto with lemon on Fridays.

Pl. du Casino. ☎ **98-06-76-23.** Main course 18€–53€. Daily 8am–2am.

Le Loga ★ MEDITERRANEAN   This locals-only find is one of the best—not to mention cheapest—places to find *barbajuans*, the Monégasque national dish of ravioli stuffed with ricotta and chard. A tea room-cum-bistro, it's ever popular with ladies who lunch (and shop) on the boulevard des Moulins. Le Loga's Italian chef busts out home-made saffron gnocchi, brésaola pressed beef, and carpaccio of local seabass with crispy hazelnuts. Dine inside the hipster tearoom interior or outside on the south-facing street terrace.

25 bd. des Moulins. www.logarestaurant.com. ℭ **93-30-87-72.** Main course 13€–28€; fixed-price lunch 22€ or dinner 38€. Mon, Tues, Thurs–Sat 8am–11pm.

Le Louis XV ★★★ MEDITERRANEAN   Within the Hôtel de Paris, the Louis XV offers one of the finest dining experiences on the Riviera, and thus the world. Superstar chef Alain Ducasse oversees the refined but not overly adorned cuisine that has three Michelin stars to its name. The restaurant reopened after a mammoth renovation in 2017 with a menu lighter, and more contemporary, than ever before. Head chef Dominique Lory presides over the painstakingly sourced yet awesomely executed starters like San Remo shrimp on a bed of rockfish jelly with caviar. Everything is light and attuned to the seasons, with intelligent, modern interpretations of Provençal and northern Italian dishes. The old-school service, decor (the frescoed ceiling includes the portraits of Louis XV's six mistresses), and the sheer amount of cutlery used makes for a memorable evening.

In the Hôtel de Paris, pl. du Casino. ℭ **98-06-88-64.** Jacket and tie recommended for men. Main course 114€–160€; fixed-price lunch 165€ or dinner 240€–360€. Thurs–Mon 12:15–1:45pm and 8–9:45pm. Closed first 2 weeks Mar.

Eqvita ★★ VEGAN   When global tennis champ Novak Djokovic met vegetarian chef Erik Božic at Wimbledon he discovered how good gluten-free, dairy-free, and refined sugar-free dishes can taste. That's right, in ostentatious Monaco, the hottest new eatery is vegan, albeit owned and frequented by one of the world's most recognizable sporting celebrities. Ingredients are carefully sourced then flipped into naked burgers (wild rice, beetroot, and tomato patties) and cashew gazpacho (with cider vinegar, avocado, and radish sprouts). This edible bargain will keep you sightseeing for far longer than a platter of beef bourguignon.

7 rue Portier. www.eqvitarestaurant.com. ℭ **97-77-07-49.** Main course 15€–18€; fixed-price lunch 22€. Daily 8am–10pm.

ROQUEBRUNE & CAP-MARTIN ★★

Roquebrune: 953km (591 miles) S of Paris, 7km (4.5 miles) W of Menton, 58km (36 miles) NE of Cannes, 3km (1.75 miles) E of Monaco. Cap-Martin: 4km (2.5 miles) W of Menton, 2.5km (1.5 miles) W of Roquebrune.

Roquebrune, along the Grande Corniche, is a charming mountain village with vaulted streets. The views over the Mediterranean rival the village of Èze and are equally immense. Artists' workshops and boutiques with their pricey merchandise line rue Moncollet.

Down the hill from Roquebrune, Cap-Martin is a pine-covered peninsula, long associated with the rich and famous since the empress Eugénie wintered here in the 19th century. In time, the resort was honored by

The view over Roquebrune and Cap-Martin

the presence of Sir Winston Churchill, who came here often in his final years. The long, pebbly plage de la Buse lies underneath Roquebrune-Cap-Martin train station. Its tranquility is disturbed only by the odd paraglider looping down to the beach from Roquebrune village.

Essentials

GETTING THERE   To **drive** to Roquebrune and Cap-Martin from Nice, follow N7 east for 26km (16 miles). Cap-Martin has **train** and bus connections from the other cities on the coast, including Nice and Menton. For **railway** information and schedules, www.oui.sncf or call ℓ **36-35** (.40€/min). To reach Roquebrune, you'll have to take a **taxi** or follow the hiking signs for 30 min. uphill. For bus information, contact the Gare Routière in Menton (ℓ **04-93-28-43-27**).

VISITOR INFORMATION   The **Office de Tourisme** is at 218 av. Aristide-Briand, Roquebrune (www.rcm-tourisme.com; ℓ **04-93-35-62-87**).

More than any other municipality in the region, Roquebrune and Cap-Martin have at least three guided walking tours of its attractions. The most popular of the three is a 90-min. guided tour of the old town, priced at 8€ for adults and 4€ for students. Tours depart whenever there are enough (at least 5) participants to justify it.

Exploring Roquebrune & Cap-Martin

ROQUEBRUNE

Exploring Roquebrune will take about 1 hr. You can stroll through its colorful streets, which retain their authentic feel. **Château de Roquebrune** (ℓ **04-93-35-07-22**) was originally a 10th-century Carolingian castle; the present structure dates in part from the 13th century, although it was jazzed up by its wealthy British owner, Sir William Ingram, nearly a century ago. From the towers is a panoramic view along the coast. The interior is open in February to May daily 10am to 12:30pm and 2 to 6pm; June to September daily 10am to 1pm and 2 to 7pm; and October to January daily 10am to 12:30pm and 2 to 5pm. Admission is 5€ for adults, 4€ for seniors, 3€ students and children 7 to 11, and free for children 6 and under.

Rue du Château leads to place William-Ingram. Cross this square to rue de la Fontaine and take a left. This leads you to the **Olivier millénaire** (millenary olive tree), one of the oldest in the world—it's at least 1,000 years old.

CAP-MARTIN

Once the exclusive domain of Belgian despot King Leopold II, Cap-Martin is still a fabulously rich spit of land. At its base, you can see the ruins of the **Basilique St-Martin,** a ruined priory constructed by the monks of the Lérins Islands in the 11th century. After pirate raids in later centuries, notably around the 15th century, it was destroyed and abandoned. Privately owned, it is not open to visitors.

You can also take one of the most scenic walks along the Riviera here, lasting about 2 hr. The coastal path, **Sentier Le Corbusier ★**, extends between Pointe du Cap-Martin to the eastern (meaning, the closest) frontier of Monaco. If you have a car, you can park it in the lot at avenue Winston-Churchill and begin your stroll. A sign labeled promenade le corbusier marks the path. See box on p. 639.

MENTON ★★

963km (559 miles) S of Paris; 30km (19 miles) E of Nice

Pack your shades, for the Belle Époque resort of Menton is the sunniest place in all France. It's no surprise that this balmy locale hosts both a winter lemon festival and the finest botanical gardens in the country. Liberal sprinklings of sun, sand, and citrus also attracted artists by the dozens, among them Picasso, Matisse, and Jean Cocteau. The brand-new Musée Cocteau dedicated makes the town worth visiting alone.

The aptly named Promenade du Soleil runs in front of Menton's Old City, port, and casino. Game guests may follow this seaside boulevard all the way into Monaco—provided they have a spare 90 min. and a sturdy set of legs.

Essentials

ARRIVING   **Trains** run to Menton from Nice, Monaco, the rest of the Côte d'Azur en route, and right into Italy every 30 min. For **rail** information, visit www.oui.sncf or call ✆ **36-35** (.40€/min). **Bus** line no. 100 to Nice runs every 15 min. until 8pm. One-way fares costs 1.50€. For bus information and schedules, contact **Lignes d'Azur** (www.lignesdazur.com; ✆ **08-10-06-10-06**). By **car** from Nice, take D6098 (the *basse corniche*) east.

LE CORBUSIER AND EILEEN GRAY on cap martin

Cap-Martin is the fabulously rich spit of land between Monaco and Menton. Not as glitzy as Cap-Ferrat nor as fabled as Cap d'Antibes, its beauty lies in a 2-hr.-long coastal trail that loops past the gardens of countless billionaires. This seaside path is as historical as it is beautiful. It was named after Le Corbusier, the zany French architect who built an urban utopia in Marseille before constructing a coastal retreat here.

Pride of place goes to Le Corbusier's **Cabanon** log cabin. It was created by the architect to showcase his love of low-impact prefabricated living spaces. Even more fun is the row of five teeny-tiny **Holiday Cabins** nearby. Le Corbusier designed these 9 sq. m (97 sq. ft.) seaview escapes to prove that vacations should be about simplicity, not all-out luxury. Each one fits two beds, windows, storage, and sinks. Best of all is **Villa E-1027,** designed by Le Corbusier's one-time muse, the furniture designer Eileen Gray. Splashed with frescoes and beset with period furnishings, it's among the world's finest visions of art deco design. The rooftop garden is pretty special too.

Guided visits to all three sites are compulsory for all visitors. Contact **Cap Moderne** (www.capmoderne.com; ✆ **06-48-72-90-53;** admission 18€ adults, 10€ children aged 7–17, 2€ for children ages 6 and under).

The **Sentier le Corbusier** path extends between Pointe du Cap-Martin to the eastern frontier of Monaco. If you have a car, you can park it in the lot at av. Winston-Churchill and begin your stroll. A sign labeled PROMENADE LE COR-BUSIER marks the path. As you hike along, you'll take in a view of Monaco set in a natural amphitheater. In the distance, you'll see Cap-Ferrat and, high above, Roquebrune village.

The scenic path ends at Monte-Carlo Beach and passes several secret sandy coves en-route. Walkers may then take the line no. 100 bus back to their rough starting point. An alternative is to return on foot from either Monte-Carlo Beach or Roquebrune-Cap-Martin train station, following the walking signs back through the Parc des Oliviers, which occupies the central spine of Cap-Martin.

VISITOR INFORMATION   The **Office de Tourisme** occupies a magnificent Belle Époque building near the train station at 8 av. Boyer (www.tourisme-menton.fr; ✆ **04-92-41-76-76**).

[Fast FACTS] MENTON

ATMs/Banks   **Crédit Mutuel,** 24 rue de la République (✆ **32-25**).

Internet Access   For free Wi-Fi, hit **Menton Tourist Office,** which maintains its own wireless hotspot.

Mail & Postage   **La Poste,** 2 cours George V (✆ **36-31**).

Pharmacies   **Pharmacie Otto,** pl. St Roch (✆ **04-93-35-70-16**).

Exploring Menton

Mentonnaise are lucky devils. They can choose to hang out in the historic Old Town, on a very long beach, or on the seaside boulevard (the Promenade du Soleil). The resort's world-famous gardens all lie just behind this ocean walk. Meanwhile, Jean Cocteau's artist legacy is spread out along the seafront.

Jardin Val Rahmeh ★★★ GARDEN   Even if you loathe botanical gardens, and even if you only visit one in Menton, we beg you to come here. Menton's microclimate has reared a leafy wonderland within its protective walls. Fragrant paths weave past giant Amazon water lillies, Buddha's Hand citruses from Thailand, and flowering *toromiro* trees from Easter Island. The scene is most magical within the black bamboo plantation, where sunlight dapples a babbling brook. Menton's other botanical gardens include **Serre de la Madone.** They were designed and owned by American heir Lawrence Johnston, whose family made their fortune in the Klondike gold rush.

Route St Jacques. www.menton.fr. © **04-93-35-86-72.** Admission 7€ adults; 5€ for children 16 and under. Apr–Sept Wed–Mon 9:30am–12:30pm and 2–6pm; Oct–Mar Wed–Mon 9:30am–12:30pm and 2–5pm.

Musée Jean Cocteau ★★★ MUSEUM   When not judging the Cannes Film Festival or chasing ballet dancers from the Monaco stage, *bon viveur* Jean Cocteau turned his artistic hand to painting on a grand scale. Many of his finest works were displayed in this oceanfront museum. Most of the 1,800 exhibit pieces were donated by Belgian-American collector Séverin Wunderman. These include canvases by Cocteau's friends Picasso, Modigliani, and Miró, plus movies shot by the Frenchman at the Villa Santo Sospir on Cap-Ferrat. Architecture fans may note that the curvy, light-filled building that houses the Musée Jean Cocteau was designed by Rudy Ricciotti, who also styled the new MuCEM European and Mediterranean Museum in Marseille (p. 535). It's so serene that, from 2017, twice-weekly Tai-Chi lessons (18€) have been offered in the museum cafe. A few blocks away, Cocteau's life-size love scenes inside Menton's **Salle des Marriages** (marriage office, pl. Ardoïno; adults 2€, free to children 17 and under; Mon–Fri 8:30am–noon and 2–4:30pm) earned him honorary citizenship of the town in 1958. Three years after Cocteau's death in 1963, the **Musée du Bastion** (Tues–Sun 10am–6pm) opened on Menton's seafront to showcase his final period of work.

2 quai de Monléon. www.museecocteaumenton.fr. © **04-89-81-52-50.** Admission 8€ adults; free for children 18 and under. Wed–Mon 10am–6pm.

Outdoor Activities

BEACHES   The all-public Plage du Soleil pans west from Menton to Cap Martin. Private beach clubs are on Plage du Garavan just east of town. All-day sun loungers at **Panama Plage** (© **04-92-10-92-60**) and **Plage Les Sablettes** (© **07-76-14-18-32**) cost around 15€ per day.

BIKING   The verdant hills around Menton are the training ground for several Tour de France cyclists. Lesser mortals may still peddle along the seafront from Italy to Monaco on a rented mountain bike (from 14€ per day) or electric bike (from 25€ per day) from **Bike Trip,** 1 av. Carnot (www.rent-bike.fr, ✆ **04-94-96-48-93**), which also offers self-guided tour maps of the Menton Riviera.

SAILING   From the end of April until October visitors may bob around the Bay of Menton on a paddleboard, kayak, or sailing dinghy available for rent from the **Centre Nautique de Menton** (www.voile-menton.fr, ✆ **04-93-35-49-70**), beside beach bar La Pergola.

Where to Stay

Hôtel Napoléon ★★★   It's hard to find a hotel this perfect on the entire French Riviera. Guestrooms at this Cocteau-themed delight were designed by Jean-Philippe Noel, an artist usually found creating 7-star hotels in Dubai. Yet prices at the Napoléon couldn't be keener for such a stunning beachfront location. The hotel also boasts a private beach club, a solar-powered heated swimming pool, and a leafy garden. And, as many guests stay in order to dine at top gourmet restaurant **Mirazur** nearby, the Napoléon offers a concessionary Gourmet Stay package with guaranteed table booking. Leaving such a cocoon of fine linen and original art for anything less is a painful experience.

29 porte de France. www.napoleon-menton.com. ✆ **04-93-35.89.50.** 44 units. 95€–330€ double. Parking 12€. **Amenities:** Bar; concierge; outdoor pool; free Wi-Fi.

Hôtel Palm Garavan ★   The prize for the friendliest hotel in Menton goes to the Palm Garavan. Superior rooms boast cracking views over the resort's botanical gardens, while guests may also gaze at Italy in their bathrobes. The spotless modern accommodation boasts touch-sensitive lights and ice-white decor. A top touch is the 3.50€ express breakfast, offering early-bird guests a croissant and cappuccino before they hit the resort's gardens, art museums, and beach.

3 porte de France. www.hotel-menton-garavan.fr. ✆ **04-93-78-80-67.** 19 units. 75€–160€ double. Parking 10€. **Amenities:** Bar; free Wi-Fi.

Hôtel Royal Westminster ★   A grand hotel without the grand prices, the venerable Westminster has a plum emplacement, facing due south towards the shimmering Mediterranean in the epicenter of town. Attracting an older clientele, guests may relax in the genteel front gardens or in the various lobby bars. On permanent display in the hotel are works by 150 different artists, many inspired by the sun-kissed climate of Menton. The hotel boasts a library and billiards room, too.

28 av. Félix Faure. www.hotel-royal-westminster.com. ✆ **04-93-28-69-69.** 92 units. 78€–215€ double. Breakfast included. Parking 15€. **Amenities:** Restaurant; bar; concierge; library; free Wi-Fi.

15

THE FRENCH RIVIERA

Menton

Where to Eat

A mere mile from the Italian border, Menton does pizza and pasta with aplomb. For more exotic fare laced with Menton lemons and offerings from the Ligurian fishing fleet, sail in to one of the eateries below.

La Rotonde ★ MEDITERRANEAN   La Rotonde is a seaside restaurant par excellence. Franco-Italian chef Sandro dishes up simple Italian starters (buffalo mozzarella with pesto) and mains (linguine with calamari) on the sunniest boardwalk in all of France. The restaurant also scoops up Menton's social media prize: 12€ lunch specials are posted on La Rotonde's Facebook page each morning.

1360 Promenade du Soleil. www.rotonde-menton.fr. ℃ **04-93-44-60-88.** Main course 14€–24€; fixed-price lunch 12€. Wed–Mon noon–3pm and 7–11:30pm.

Restaurant Mirazur ★★ MODERN MEDITERRANEAN   The awards have rolled in for Mirazur's young Argentine chef Mauro Colagreco, not least of all a place on San Pellegrino's World's 5 Best Restaurants list. The restaurant also held two stars in 2018's Michelin Guide. The watchword on Colagreco's multiple fixed-price menus (which range from a moderately priced lunchtime "Discover" to the wallet-crunching "Signature") is élan, not experimentation. This is sleepy Menton after all. Expect tuna carpaccio with raspberries and almonds, langoustine decorated with edible flowers, and a heady volley of desserts topped with homemade marshmallows. Graceful service and a panoramic sea view over Menton Port complete this priceless picture.

30 av. Aristide Briand. www.mirazur.fr. ℃ **04-92-41-86-86.** Fixed-price menus 80€–210€. Wed–Sun noon–2pm and 7:30–10pm. Closed mid-Nov to mid-Feb.

Al Vecchio Forno ★ ITALIAN   As authentic as a Neapolitan scooter, this established eatery serves Menton's Italian neighbors from just across the border. If the dress and dialect of its patrons shouts "Godfather," the pizza is just as genuine. Seasonal artichokes and *funghi* come from Italy, as does the mozzarella and sea bream. The latter is seared crisp alongside the pizzas in the wood-fired oven.

39 quai Bonaparte. ℃ **04-92-10-04-78.** Main course 9€–19€. Daily 7–11pm.

Shopping

Menton has an Italian heart, with the taste buds to match. The best place to start is the pedestrian-only **rue Saint Michel.** Try **Maison Larnicol** at no. 28 (℃ **04-93-97-80-92**) for chocolates; **Famille Mary** at no. 10 (℃ **04-92-09-19-43**) for flowery honey; or Menton-based **Oliviers & Co** at no. 5 (℃ **04-89-74-19-76**) for olive oil tastings. The town's most venerated product, its home-grown lemons, are served by two rival stores at no. 22 and no. 27. From the former, **Au Pays du Citron** (www.aupaysducitron.fr, ℃ **04-92-09-22-85**), purchase lemon soap and citrus liqueur. From the latter, **Coté Citron** (℃ **04-89-74-19-76**), find limoncello and marmalade. One of Menton's most charming stores is **Maison Herbin,** 2 rue Vieux Collège (www.confitures-herbin.com, ✆ **04-93-57-20-29**). Visitors can see local citrus turned into jams, chutneys, and candies in their adjoining sweet factory.

Nightlife

Sunny Menton hosts the highest number of retirees in France, so the resort doesn't exactly dance until dawn. However, the town buzzes all August during the **Menton Music Festival** (www.festival-musique-menton.fr), where evening classical concerts occupy almost every Old Town square. Gamblers may also test their luck at the **Menton Casino,** at 2 av. Félix Faure (www.casinosbarriere.com; ✆ **04-92-10-16-16**). It boasts a traditional poker room as well as a vast seaview gaming terrace.

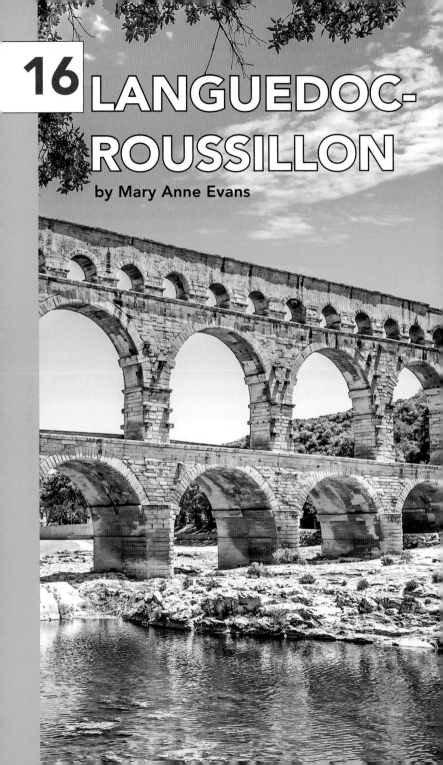

16
LANGUEDOC-ROUSSILLON

by Mary Anne Evans

L anguedoc-Roussillon in the south of France includes the cities of Montpellier, Nîmes, Toulouse, and Carcassonne. One of the leading wine-producing areas of the world, it's also known for its impressive Roman heritage and the 240km- (149 mile-) long Canal du Midi.

Both Languedoc and Roussillon are old provinces of France, the first named for the language *(langue)* spoken by its occupants, called Occitan, and the second from the Roman name Ruscino. Languedoc covers the present-day *départements* of Lozère, Gard, Hérault, and Aude, and Roussillon covers the Pyrénées Orientales, on the border with Spain. To the west, the city of Toulouse is in the Haute-Garonne *département* of the Midi-Pyrénées region.

The coast of Languedoc-Roussillon, from Montpellier to the Spanish frontier, might be called France's "second Riviera" (after the Côte d'Azur). This land of ancient cities has an almost continuous strip of sand stretching west from the Rhône toward the Pyrénées, adored by sun lovers in July and August. But it's a far more relaxed region than its eastern rival, particularly out of season when the beaches empty, the cities return to their inhabitants and the crowds disappear.

The area around the regional capital of Perpignan is French Catalonia. From the 13th to the 17th centuries, it passed between the kings of Aragón, Majorca, and France. In 1659, it became part of Louis XIV's centralized kingdom. Though officially French today, cultural links with Spain are strong, and the high-speed rail link to Barcelona has brought the two Catalan cities even closer.

As for wine, Hérault, Aude, and Garde are some of the largest wine producers in the world. Huge investment over the years has led to a new reputation for the region's wines and many have now been granted an Appellation d'Origine Contrôlée. It's become an area to discover small, boutique producers, biodynamic and organic experts, unknown labels and the local co-operatives. Look for Fitou in the Hautes-Corbières district near Narbonne, Minervois, north of Carcasssonne, Gaillace west of Albi, and Blanquette de Limoux, south of Carcassonne.

NÎMES ★★★

713km (443 miles) S of Paris; 43km (27 miles) W of Avignon

Nîmes, originally Nemausus, is an extraordinarily rich city for Roman relics, with one of the best-preserved Roman amphitheaters in the world plus a near-perfect Roman temple. During the reign of Caesar Augustus (27

FACING PAGE: **Pont du Gard, near Nîmes**

NÎMES EVENTS

The Roman Games in the ancient Arena in April take you back to the city's Roman roots with battles, gladiators, and chariot races. At Pentecost (Whitsun and seven weeks after Easter), the five-day **Féria de Pentecôte** is one of Europe's most popular festivals. Along with the bull fights, the city hosts plenty of street entertainment, while the bodegas offer plenty of drinking, dancing, and Spanish food. A second *féria*, **Féria des Vendanges,** celebrating the grape harvest, takes place the third weekend of September.

Every Thursday night during July and August, Nîmes' squares fill with jazz and rock, classic and salsa musicians and stalls selling books, crafts, works of art, and bric-a-brac.

B.C.–A.D. 14) Nîmes became an important city on the vital chariot route between Spain and Rome.

Like many cities, its fortunes waxed and waned particularly after Arles took over as the local capital. By 1860, the togas of Nîmes' Roman citizenry had long given way to denim, the cloth *de Nîmes.* An Austrian immigrant to Nîmes, Levi Strauss, exported the heavy fabric to California to make into work pants for gold-rush prospectors. The rest, as they say, is history.

The city is more like Provence than Languedoc in feel. You might notice a touch of Pamplona, Spain, in the festivals of the *corridas* (bullfights) at the arena and the flamenco festivals. But Nîmes has also championed modern architecture; the latest contemporary building is the Musée de la Romanité opened in June 2018.

Essentials

GETTING THERE   Nîmes has bus and train services from the rest of France and is near several autoroutes. It lies on the main **rail** line between Marseille and Bordeaux. Regular TGV trains arrive daily from Paris's Gare de Lyon; the one-way fare is from 24€ and the journey takes 2 hr., 51 min. The station is a 5-min. walk from the old center. Train information and schedules are on www.oui.sncf or call ✆ **36-35** (.40€/min.). If you're **driving,** take A7 south from Lyon to Orange and connect to A9 into Nîmes.

VISITOR INFORMATION   The **Office de Tourisme** is at 6 rue Auguste (www.ot-nimes.fr; ✆ **04-66-58-38-00**).

CITY LAYOUT   All the main attractions, both ancient and modern are in a small central area, originally the Roman city.

GETTING AROUND   The center of Nîmes is traffic free, but five car parks surround the center, so park and walk.

Languedoc-Roussillon

Exploring Nîmes

It's worth getting the **Nîmes romaine** combined ticket, valid for one month and sold online and at the ticket counter of each site. It covers the three main ancient sites that are all close together: Maison Carrée, les Arènes de Nîmes, and Tour Magne. The fee is 18.50€ for adults, 14€ for children aged 7 to 17, and free for children 6 and under. More information is available from **Culturespaces** (www.arenes-nimes.com; ℂ **04-66-21-82-56**).

The pride of Nîmes is the **Maison Carrée ★★★**, pl. de la Maison Carrée (www.arenes-nimes.com; ℂ **04-66-21-82-56**). Founded around A.D. 3 by the Emperor Augustus, it's the only completely preserved ancient Roman temple in Europe. It may be small but it's perfectly proportioned: 26m (85 ft.) long by 15m (49 ft.) wide and 15m (49 ft.) high. It inspired the builders of La Madeleine in Paris, and Thomas Jefferson's Virginia Capitol building. It makes a perfect start to a Nîmes visit with a film showing the founding of the city from its Celtic roots through the fortunes of a fictional family from 55 B.C. to A.D. 90. Admission is 6€ for adults or 5€ for students and children (free for ages 7 and under). Open March and October daily 10am to 1pm and 2 to 6pm; April, May, and September daily 10am to 6:30pm; June daily 10am to 7pm; July and August daily 10am to 8pm; and November through February daily 10am to 1pm and 2 to 4:30pm.

Across the square stands its modern-day twin, the **Carré d'Art ★★**, whose understated design by Norman Foster was inspired by (but doesn't overpower) the ancient monument. Inside, the **Musée d'Art Contemporain** (www.carreartmusee.com; ℂ **04-66-76-35-70**), has a permanent collection of art from 1960 to the present day as well as temporary exhibitions that take in both past masters like Picasso and the work of contemporaries like photographer Wolfgang Tillmans. Renovation at the beginning of 2018 gave it more exhibition space. It's open Tuesday through Sunday 10am to 6pm. The permanent collection is free; changing exhibitions cost 6€ for adults and are free for anyone aged 25 and under and for everybody on the first Sunday of each month.

Scholars call it **Amphithéâtre Romain de Nîmes ★★★**; locals refer to it as **Les Arènes.** No matter what you call it, the monument at place des Arènes (www.arenes-nimes.com; ℂ **04-66-21-82-56**), is spectacular. It's a better-preserved twin of the one at Arles, and far more complete than Rome's Colosseum. Two stories high—each floor has 60 arches—it was built by master Roman engineers who fitted the huge stones together without mortar. It once held over 20,000 spectators who entered through arched entrances (*vomitaria;* coming from the Latin for "to spew") ringing the building to see gladiatorial combat and chariot races. Today it's used for everything from ballet recitals to bullfights, and the Roman games, when it is closed for visits; check the website before you visit. Admission is 10€ for adults and 8€ for students and children from 7 to 17

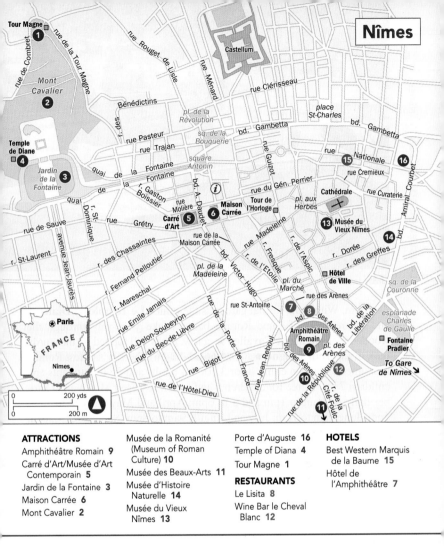

Nîmes

ATTRACTIONS

Amphithéâtre Romain **9**
Carré d'Art/Musée d'Art Contemporain **5**
Jardin de la Fontaine **3**
Maison Carrée **6**
Mont Cavalier **2**

Musée de la Romanité (Museum of Roman Culture) **10**
Musée des Beaux-Arts **11**
Musée d'Histoire Naturelle **14**
Musée du Vieux Nîmes **13**

Porte d'Auguste **16**
Temple of Diana **4**
Tour Magne **1**

RESTAURANTS

Le Lisita **8**
Wine Bar le Cheval Blanc **12**

HOTELS

Best Western Marquis de la Baume **15**
Hôtel de l'Amphithéâtre **7**

years, free for children 6 years old and under. Open March and October daily 9am to 6pm; April, May, and September daily 9am to 6:30pm; June 9am to 7pm; July and August daily 9am to 8pm; and November through February daily 9:30am to 5pm.

One of the most beautiful gardens in France, the **Jardin de la Fontaine ★★**, at the end of quai de la Fontaine, was laid out in the 18th century around a centerpiece of ruins of a Roman shrine. It was France's first public park and is a godsend on a baking hot summer's day with its shady paths and fountains. The garden is open from April to September daily 9:30am to 6:30pm, and from October to March daily 9:30am to 1pm and

Jardin de la Fontaine

2 to 6pm. Within the formal garden is the ruined **Le Temple de Diane** ★ and the remains of some Roman baths. Make your way through the wooded paths to **Mont Cavalier** ★, a low, rocky hill topped by the sturdy bulk of the **Tour Magne** ★ (✆ **04-66-21-82-56**), the city's oldest Roman monument. You can climb it for 3.50€ for adults and 3€ for students and children 7 to 17, free for children 6 and under. It's open March and October daily 9:30am to 1pm and 2 to 6pm; April and May daily 9:30am to 6pm; June 9am to 7pm; July and August 9am to 8pm; September 9:30am to 1pm and 2 to 6:30pm; and November through February 9:30am to 1pm and 2 to 4:30pm.

Nîmes has a good variety of museums, augmented by the opening in June 2018 of the **Musée de la Romanité (Museum of Roman Culture)** ★★★, 16 bd. des Arènes, (www.museeromanite.com; ✆ **06-19-61-56-58**). Using the latest technology in its displays, this is one of the big openings of 2018 in France. The futuristic building opposite Les Arènes is clad in a translucent glass facade that sinuously covers the museum. A remarkable and wide collection of art and artifacts fills the galleries while interactive displays lead you through ancient Rome. The **Musée des Beaux-Arts** ★, rue Cité Foulc (www.nimes.fr; ✆ **04-66-28-18-32**), contains French paintings and sculptures from the 17th to the 20th centuries, as well as Flemish, Dutch, and Italian works from the 16th to the 18th centuries. Some unexpected masterpieces here include Rubens' *Portrait of a Monk* and the masterpiece of G. B. Moroni, *La Calomnie d'Apelle.* With the opening of the Museum of Roman Culture in this ancient city, the first thing to see should be the huge Gallo-Roman mosaic showing the mythical marriage of Admetus. The museum is open Tuesday to Sunday 10am to 6pm. Admission is free for the permanent collection. Exhibitions are from 3€ for adults and free for those under 25. Free admission the first Sunday of the month.

If time allows, visit the **Musée du Vieux-Nîmes ★**, pl. aux Herbes (𝄐 **04-66-76-73-70**), to the north of Les Arènes and housed in an Episcopal palace from the 1700s. Its rich collection covers antiques, antique porcelain, and workday objects from the 18th and 19th centuries. It also covers the all-important textile industry here from the silk shawls that were the must-have item of the 18th century to the story of denim. Admission is free for the permanent collection and 5€ for exhibitions; open Tuesday to Sunday 10am to 6pm.

About 45m (148 ft.) east you come to the **Musée d'Histoire Naturelle ★** (𝄐 **04-66-76-73-45**) at 13 bis bd. l'Amiral-Courbet with a strange and quirky collection of masks, spears, and taxidermy animals. Items from the archaeology museum formerly here are now on display in the new Museum of Roman Culture. Admission is free; hours are Tuesday to Sunday 10am to 6pm. From here, you can walk north along one of the city's busiest thoroughfares, **boulevard de l'Amiral-Courbet,** to the **Porte d'Auguste (Porte d'Arles)**—the remains of a gate built by the Romans during the reign of Augustus.

Le Temple de Diane

Outlying Attractions

Outside the city, 27km (16 miles) northeast, the great **Pont du Gard ★★★** spans the Gardon River. The great bridge with its huge stones, fitted together without mortar, stands as one of France's most vivid reminders of ancient glory. The top tier of the three tiers of arches in graceful symmetrical patterns carried water to the growing city of Nîmes. Probably constructed in the 1st century, this masterpiece of engineering stands 50m (164 ft.) high and measures 360m (1,181 ft.) at its longest point. If you can, tour the upper tier and the water canal giving panoramic views over the countryside.

The Site du Pont du Gard visitors' complex gives the best introduction to the monument. The interactive museum, **Le Musée ★** (www.pontdugard.fr; 𝄐 **04-66-37-50-99**), shows ancient building techniques and the complex construction of the Pont du Gard, how it worked during the Middle Ages, and its status through the centuries as a symbol of the architectural savvy of ancient Rome. Working models, films, and interactive displays are centered around different themes, with the all-precious water taking center stage. A film takes you through the history. You can wander through the **Mémoires de Garrigue** garden of nature trails and take the children to the interactive Ludo center. The large site also has a restaurant, cafe, and gift shop. It's open May and June daily 9am to 9pm, July and August 9am to 11:30pm, September 9am to 8pm, April and October 9am to 6pm, January to March and November to December 9am to 5pm. A Discovery Pass of the main sites is 8.50€ for adults, 6€ for children ages 6 to 16 and is worth it if you plan to spend a half or full day here. Guided tours are extra.

To get here, take the highway D6086 from Nîmes to a point 3km (1.75 miles) from the village of Remoulins, then follow signs to the site.

During July and August, artificial beaches and small shelters are installed on the right bank of the Gardon near the bridge for **"Rendez-vous à la Rivière,"** with lifeguards overseeing river swimming.

Where to Stay

Best Western Marquis de La Baume ★★   Originally built for the de la Baume family in the 17th century, this central hotel happily mixes old and new. The old comes with the magnificent stone staircase with columns and greenery in the interior courtyard, stone-flagged floors, wooden beamed ceilings, and chandeliers. The new bedrooms are bang up-to-date with contemporary fittings, padded headboards above the large comfortable beds, and bold colored textiles. Tiled bathrooms are well designed with lighted mirrors, though some come with a bathtub only. A nice touch is the in-room Nespresso machine. Ask for a room at the back to avoid any noise from the street.

21 rue Nationale. www.hotel-marquis-de-la-baume-nimes.com. ✆ **04-66-76-28-42.** 34 units. 90€–250€ double; 170€–400€ junior suite. **Amenities:** Bar; room service; free Wi-Fi.

Hôtel Amphithéâtre ★★   Perfectly placed in a square near Les Arènes, this unpretentious, comfortable three-star hotel offers great value for your money. It has good-sized bedrooms decorated in soft greys, pinks, and warm browns and modern tiled bathrooms with either a shower or bath. Ask for a room looking onto the square to watch the action at the bars and restaurants (which are not noisy). The affable English owner Marcus Reeves and his French wife Ghislaine are always there to offer help and advice. They serve an excellent breakfast and have a small boutique for last-minute gifts.

4 rue des Arènes. www.hoteldelamphitheatre.com. ✆ **04-66-67-28-51.** 14 units. 75€–90€ double. **Amenities:** Breakfast room; boutique; free Wi-Fi.

Where to Eat

Le Lisita ★★ FRENCH   With views over the Roman Arena from the open-air terrace and impressive classic cooking, this is the place to go. The chef and sommelier, Olivier Douet and Stéphane Debaille, met at Le Gavroche in London and opened this charming restaurant in 1998. With the emphasis on local products, expect asparagus from the Camargue and truffles from Uzès. Inventiveness comes in the combination of ingredients and spicing: a starter of green lentil creamy soup with duck foie gras foam and small pieces of smoked ham, then roast honey-marinated duck with orange puréed carrots and a Cajun spiced sauce. The well-selected wine list emphasizes local wines.

28 bd. des Arènes. www.lelisita.com. ⓒ **04-66-67-29-15.** Main course 20€; fixed-price menus 29€–58€. July and Aug daily noon–2pm and 7–10pm; rest of the year Wed–Sun noon–2pm and 7–10pm.

Wine Bar le Cheval Blanc ★ FRENCH   It's easy to see why this historic wine bar is the place where the locals gather. The vaulted restaurant has brown leather banquettes and bare wooden tables; a ham ready for carving sits pride of place on the bar, and the waiters work swiftly carrying loaded trays above their heads. Part-brasserie, part-bodega, you can take a quick lunch of Bigorre ham and a glass of wine, be more serious with the likes of Bresse chicken with mushroom sauce or go for the special grilled fish. Owner Michel Hermet knows his wines; he comes from a family of wine makers so try some of the 300 varieties of wine in stock, with 13 to 15 available by the glass each day. In summer eat and sip on the outdoor terrace.

1 pl. des Arènes. www.winebar-lechevalblanc.com. ⓒ **04-66-76-19-59.** Main course 11€–28€; fixed-price lunch 15€; Ardoise menu 26€. Mon–Sat noon–2pm and 7–11pm (Fri and Sat until midnight).

Shopping

Head to the center of town and **rue du Général-Perrier, rue des Marchands, rue du Chapître,** and the pedestrian **rue de l'Aspic** and **rue de la Madeleine.** A Friday **flea market** runs from 8am to 1pm in boulevard Jean Jaurès in the town center and a daily food market daily is in **Les Halles**.

If you have a sweet tooth, go to any pastry shop and ask for the regional almond-based cookies called *croquants*, or visit **Maison Villaret,** 13 Rue de la Madeleine (www.maison-villaret.com), specialists in croquants since 1775. *Santons,* wood or clay figurines sculpted into characters from Provençal country life and often used at Christmas, can be found at **Boutique Provençale,** 10 pl. de la Maison Carré (www.laboutique provencale.fr; ⓒ **04-66-67-81-71**).

Nîmes Nightlife

In the warm weather, the arena hosts many events, including open-air concerts and theater. The Office de Tourisme has a complete listing.

If you like hanging out with the locals any time from 7am to midnight, head to the famous **Café Le Napoleon,** 46 bd. Victor-Hugo (✆ **04-66-67-20-23**). **O'Flaherty's,** 26 bd. Amiral-Courbet (✆ **04-66-67-22-63**), apart from British beer (seven on tap), serves up great Irish, country, and bluegrass music on Thursdays.

Sexy, hip **Le First Club,** 28 rue Jean-Reboul (✆ **06-37-12-31-63**), is hands-down the best for dancing and attracts a crowd of youthful dance-aholics. A little less flashy, but great fun, **Lulu Club,** 10 impasse de la Curaterie (www.lulu-club.com; ✆ **04-66-36-28-20**), is the gay and lesbian stronghold in Nîmes with a straight following as well. It's open Friday and Saturday. A youth-oriented contender is **Le Club Kafé Fashion-CKF,** 20 rue de l'Etoile (✆ **04-66-21-59-22**), open Thursday to Saturday at 11pm, it rocks 'n' rolls to music from L.A. to London.

Streets to explore on virtually any night of the week include **place de la Maison Carrée** and **boulevard Victor-Hugo.** For nightlife try **rue Fresque**, **rue Saint-Antoine,** and **rue de l'Etoile.**

AIGUES-MORTES ★★

750km (465 miles) SW of Paris; 53km (33 miles) NE of Séte; 44km (27 miles) E of Nîmes; 43km (26 miles) SW of Arles

South of Nîmes in Provence lies the Camargue with its marshes and great saltwater lagoons. To the west of this great nature reserve you come across Aigues-Mortes, the city of the "dead waters." This is France's most perfectly preserved walled town, impossibly romantic but also horribly crowded during the high season. In the 13th century, Louis IX and his crusaders set forth from Aigues-Mortes, then a thriving port, the first in France on the Mediterranean. Then the Rhône silted up, leaving the city 6.5km (4 miles) inland from the sea. The **ramparts ★★**, which still enclose the town, were constructed between 1272 and 1300. The **Tour de Constance ★★** (www.monuments-nationaux.fr; ✆ **04-66-53-61-55**), is a model castle of the Middle Ages. Take the lift to the top for panoramic view of the marshes. Admission is 8€ for adults, 4.50€ for visitors 18 to 25, and free for children 17 and under. The monument is open May to August daily 10am to 7pm, and September to April daily 10am to 5:30pm.

Aigues-Mortes' main appeal is the medieval atmosphere that permeates virtually every building, rampart, and cobble-covered street. The city's religious centerpiece is the **Eglise Notre-Dame des Sablons ★**, rue Jean-Jaurès. Constructed of wood in 1183, it was rebuilt in stone in 1246 in the ogival style. The church is open May to September daily 8:30am to 6pm, and October to April daily 10am to 5pm.

Essentials

GETTING THERE   Six **trains** per day connect Aigues-Mortes and Nîmes. Trip time is from 41 min., costing 8.30€. The station is a 5-min. walk to the old town. **Taxis:** ☎ **06-11-56-20-12** or 04-66-53-40-04. Train information and schedules are on www.oui.sncf or call ☎ **36-35** (.40€/min.). If you're **driving** to Aigues-Mortes, take D979 south from Gallargues, or A9 from Montpellier or Nîmes.

VISITOR INFORMATION   The **Office de Tourisme** is at place St-Louis (www.ot-aiguesmortes.com; ☎ **04-66-53-73-00**).

Where to Stay

Hôtel Les Templiers ★   This 18th-century former merchant's house by the medieval ramparts offers a peaceful stay at reasonable rates. The ambience is chic, with stone-flagged floors and wood-beamed high ceilings in the main rooms. Bedrooms are comfortable and some have old fireplaces. Decorated in country style with modern pictures on the walls and shelves of books, Provençal pottery, and colorful textiles in each room, this hotel has a pleasant home away from home feel. Relax by the pool hidden from the street by a high wall and tall cypress trees. You can take your breakfast in the pretty courtyard; the restaurant serves traditional food.

23 rue de la République. www.hotellestempliers.fr. ☎ **04-66-53-66-56.** 14 units. 125€– 190€ double. **Amenities:** Restaurant; bar; outdoor pool; room service; free Wi-Fi.

Yelloh! Village La Petite Camargue ★   If you've got a family or you're on a budget a good bet is this campsite just 3.7 km (2.5 miles) outside Aigues-Mortes and 3.5 km (2.3 miles) from the sea. You can rent a mobile home or take your own caravan or tent. With a bar, restaurant, food market, swimming pool, sports and even horse-riding available on site you might find it difficult to move the kids away.

Rte de Cacharel. www.yellohvillage.co.uk. ☎ **04-66-53-98-98.** 553 sites. 39€–299€ mobile homes; 61€ caravan/tent. **Amenities:** Bar, restaurant; outdoor pool; free Wi-Fi (for one device; fee for additional devices); free internet area.

Where to Eat

Hôtel Les Templiers (see above) is also a good choice for dining.

L'Atelier de Nicolas ★★ MODERN FRENCH   The building is nearly as old as the nearby fortifications, but inside it's a modern, industrial-style space. The cooking may be based on classic French dishes, but again this is a modern take with added Asian influences that subtly enhance the flavors. Start with *gyozas* (dumplings) stuffed with wild shrimp and a sauce of sautéed mushrooms, onions, and parsley accompanied by a Thai sauce, then move on to more conventional sweet scallops with a Nantais sauce. The chef uses organic products where possible and is particularly careful on allergies. Tucked down a side street, this is a great find away from the main tourist spots, and usually full of locals. Reservations are recommended in high season.

28 Rue Alsace Lorraine. © **04-34-28-04-84.** Main course 26€–30€; fixed-price menu 22.90€–34€. July–Aug daily noon–2pm and 7:30–9:30pm; Sep–June Fri–Tues noon–2pm and 7:30–9:30pm. Closed first 2 weeks in Jan.

MONTPELLIER ★★

750km (466 miles) SW of Paris; 170km (105 miles) NW of Marseille; 56km (34 miles) SW of Nîmes

Montpellier is one of France's most exciting cities with architecture that mixes old and new and a university that has brought a dynamic edge to Montpellier life. Its renowned medical school was founded in the 13th century. Nostradamus qualified as a doctor here, and Rabelais studied at the school. A medieval, not a Roman city, its oldest buildings date back to the 15th century. Today Montpellier is a bustling metropolis with a population of 272,000, one of southern France's fastest-growing cities.

Cars are banned from the center which is the largest pedestrianized area in France; the excellent public transport system is great for getting around outside this area. The city has a handsome core, with tree-flanked promenades, broad avenues, and historic monuments.

Essentials

GETTING THERE The fastest way to get to Montpellier is to fly from Paris's Orly or Charles de Gaulle airports to **Aéroport Montpellier Méditerranée** (www.montpellier.aeroport.fr; © **04-67-20-85-00**), 8km (5 miles) southeast of Montpellier (trip time 1 hr., 17 min.). Taxis (© **04-30-96-60-60**) from the airport to the center cost from approximately 17€. The airport shuttle no. 120 goes to place Europe and costs 1.60€. Trains arrive regularly daily from Avignon (trip time: from 1hr., 8 min.; one-way fare is from 17.70€), from Marseille (trip time: 1.5 hr.; one-way fare is from 16€), from Toulouse (trip time: 2 hr., 12 min.; one-way fare is from 26€), and from Perpignan (trip time: 1.5 hr.; one-way fare is from 27.20€). Fourteen TGV trains arrive daily from Paris Gare de Lyon, taking less than 3.5 hr. The one-way fare is from 75€. Train information and schedules are on www.oui.sncf or call © **36-35** (.40€/min.).

If you're **driving**, Montpellier lies off A9.

> ### A SUMMER DANCE FESTIVAL IN MONTPELLIER
>
> From June 24 to July 7 (approximately), classical and modern dancers leap into town for the **Festival International Montpellier Danse.** Tickets for performances range from free to 35€ and are available from the box office, 18 rue Ste-Ursule (www.montpellier danse.com; © **08-00-60-07-40.**

VISITOR INFORMATION The **Office de Tourisme** is at 30 Allée Jean de L. de Tassigny (www.montpellier-fr.com; © **04-67-60-60-60**).

Place de la Comédie

LAYOUT OF THE CITY   The compact, pedestrianized old town lies north and west of the heart of Montpellier, the place de la Comédie.

Exploring Montpellier

The expansive **place de la Comédie** is the living room of Montpellier, a square full of bars and cafes where the 18th-century "Fountain of the Three Graces," takes pride of place in front of the 19th-century opera. The former military parade ground, champ du Mars, spreads out from here, where you'll find the **Tourist Office, Musée Fabre,** and **Le Corum** convention and arts venue. Head up **rue de la Loge** to explore the old town.

Walk west along the **Rue Foch** past the Arc de Triomphe and into the park. The formal arch was erected in 1691 to celebrate the victories of Louis XIV whose equestrian statue you pass on your way up to the 17th-century **promenade du Peyrou ★★** with views of the Cévennes and the Mediterranean. The lofty classical-style pavilion, **Château d'Eau ★** is a monument to 18th-century classicism, built as the terminus of an aqueduct carrying water to the city from a nearby source. Just to the northeast lie the cathedral and botanical gardens.

Cathédrale St-Pierre ★ CATHEDRAL   Originally a monastery church founded in 1364, it was mainly rebuilt in the 17th-century after the Wars of Religion. You enter though an odd structure of a projecting porch held up by two solid towers into a light-filled nave. If you're lucky, at certain times you can hear the splendid restored 18th-century organ being played.

Pl. St-Pierre. www.cathedrale-montpellier.fr. ℂ **04-67-66-04-12.** Free admission. Mon–Sat 9:30am–noon and 2:30–7pm; Sun 9am–noon.

Le Jardin des Plantes ★ PARK/GARDEN   Paul Valéry met André Gide in the Jardin des Plantes, the oldest such garden in France. The botanical garden, filled with exotic plants and a handful of greenhouses, opened in 1593.

163 rue Auguste-Broussonnet (enter from 1 bd. Henri-IV). ℂ **04-67-63-43-22.** Free admission. Jun–Sept Tues–Sun noon–8pm; Oct–May Tues–Sun noon–6pm.

Musée Fabre ★★★ MUSEUM   One of France's great provincial art galleries occupies the splendid former Hôtel de Massilian. The collection has over 800 works from the Renaissance to the 20th century and includes works by Rubens and Reynolds, Delacroix and Dufy. It began when Napoleon sent Montpellier an exhibition from the Académie Royale in 1803 then expanded with a donation of its most important works from François Fabre, a Montpellier painter, in 1828. Other donated works have made the collection strong on French art including Poussin's *Venus and Adonis* and works by Delacroix, David, and Dufy. An entire wing is devoted to abstract expressionist Pierre Soulages. For a glimpse at aristocratic 18th and 19th century living, visit the **Hôtel Cabrières** opposite with its ornate furniture and luxurious textiles with the same ticket.

39 bd. Bonne Nouvelle. http://museefabre.montpellier3m.fr. ℂ **04-67-14-83-00.** Admission 7€ adults; 5€ ages 6–26; free for children 5 and under and for all the 1st Sun of the month. Tues–Sun 10am–6pm; Hôtel Cabrières Tues–Sun 2–6pm.

Where to Stay

Best Western Hôtel Le Guilhem ★   Two former residences in the Old Town have been converted into this comfortable hotel. It's well located in a street that leads to the charming Jardin des Plantes and just a 10-min. walk from the station. Rooms are all individually decorated running from pretty country chintz to a stone-vaulted room with bright textiles. Some rooms look towards the cathedral; others onto small gardens. Bathrooms are modern, and the larger ones have double basins. Begin the day with breakfast on the terrace. The location in the old town makes it an ideal base for sightseeing.

18 rue Jean-Jacques-Rousseau. www.leguilhem.com. ℂ **04-67-52-90-90.** 35 units. 87€–130€ double. Nearby parking 7.50€. **Amenities:** Room service; free Wi-Fi.

Grand Hôtel du Midi ★★★   If you want the best, book in this aptly named grand hotel opposite the Opera House. The three-story hotel was built in 1876 in Second Empire style and much of the original stained glass, molded ceilings and columns remain intact. A redecoration in 2015 brought a more contemporary style and a bold color palette to the bedrooms. The bathrooms are equally as dramatic, with Italian showers, though you'll have to book a suite if you want a bath. All bedrooms have a small balcony. The excellent breakfast is served in a room with dark purple tiling and original stained glass. There's a bar and an outside terrace for a drink or a coffee watching the world go by.

22 bd. Victor-Hugo. www.grandhoteldumidimontpellier.com. ℂ **04-67-92-69-61.** 44 units. 113€–260€ double. Public parking nearby at reduced rate. **Amenities:** Bar; business center; room service; free Wi-Fi.

Hôtel du Palais ★★ Built in the late 18th century at the top of the old town in a delightful neighborhood, this three-star hotel is housed in a warm stone building with wrought-iron balconies. It's a real find: good value for money and charming as well. Different sized bedrooms have traditional furniture and light Provençal curtains and bed coverings. The bathrooms are old-fashioned rather than state-of-the-art but have everything you need. Enjoy your breakfast either in the pretty downstairs cafe or out on the terrace in front of the hotel.

3 rue du Palais des-Guilhem. www.hoteldupalais-montpellier.fr. ℂ **04-67-60-47-38.** 26 units. 95€–130€ double. Public parking nearby. **Amenities:** Room service; free Wi-Fi.

Where to Eat

Le Grillardin ★★ FRENCH Located in a busy, shaded square where restaurant tables spill out into the surrounding terraces, it's difficult to know which to choose. Go for Le Grillardin where chef Mickaël Diore makes the most of local seasonal ingredients, changing his dishes daily. Grilled meat and fish are specialties here and free-range chicken and filet de boeuf are all on offer. Unusually for France, a note on the menu encourages you to ask for a doggy bag. The restaurant has a bistro decor of wooden tables and chairs but harks back to the past with its stone walls and wood ceiling. Sit on the heated terrace until late on a summer evening.

2 pl. de la Chapelle Neuve. www.restaurantlegrillardin.com. ℂ **04-67-66-24-33.** Main course 17€–23€; fixed-price lunch (weekdays) 24€ or dinner 45€. Wed–Sat noon–2pm and 7–11pm; Tues 7–11pm.

Le Petit Jardin ★★★ FRENCH In the historic old town with a view of the cathedral from the spacious garden, this pretty restaurant makes you feel you've made a discovery, even though it's a favorite with locals and visitors in the know. Regional ingredients go into starters like Cevennes onion tart with goat cheese and sharp endive, while mains like mildly spiced pork belly cooked in honey with mashed potatoes keep the cold at bay. The bistro is the place for a more casual menu with an excellent set lunch of one course plus a café gourmand at 21€ and a three-course menu at 32€.

20 rue Jean-Jacques Rousseau. www.petitjardin.com. ℂ **04-67-60-78-78.** Main course 47€–82€; fixed-price menu 39€–55€. Tues–Sat noon–1:30pm and 7:30–9:30pm. Closed last week of Dec and first week of Jan.

La Réserve Rimbaud ★★ FRENCH The oldest restaurant in Montpellier, founded in 1835, delights locals and visitors with its lovely riverside position on the banks of the Lez. This one-star Michelin restaurant is light and spacious inside with pale grey and white furnishings and has a large terrace for summer dining directly overlooking the gently flowing river. Passionate about local ingredients, chef Charles Fontès produces imaginative cooking. Start with the likes of roast scallops with beetroot carpaccio then take in sole menunière with cauliflower in curry sauce. Desserts are superb; try the lemon ice cream scented with rosemary coming in a lemon shell.

820 av. Saint-Maur. www.reserve-rimbaud.com. ☎ **04-67-72-52-53.** Main course 39€–45€; fixed-price lunch 32€–40€ or gourmet menu 95€. Tues–Fri and Sun noon–2pm, Tues–Sat 7:30–10pm.

Les Vignes ★ PROVENÇAL/LANGUEDOCIENNE This restaurant in the old town champions regional and local ingredients and cuisine. Choose from two spaces to dine: a 13th-century arched dining room and an interior courtyard. Bull from the Camargue, sweet lamb from Provence, veal from the Aveyron, and fish from the Mediterranean appear on a monthly changing menu of classic dishes. The wine list is similarly regional with wines from Collioure to Provence and a good selection from Languedoc vineyards.

2 rue Bonnier d'Alco. www.lesvignesrestaurant.com. ☎ **04-67-60-48-42.** Main course 16€–22€; fixed-price lunch 16€–21€; other fixed-price menus 26€–49€. Tues–Sat noon–1:30pm; Thurs–Sat 7:45–9:45pm.

Montpellier Nightlife

After the sun sets, head for **place Jean-Jaurès, rue des Ecoles Laïques, place St Ravy,** or the more sophisticated area around **rue du Palais de Guilhems.**

The large student population means Montpellier has its fair share of great bars. **Fitzpatricks,** 5 pl. St-Côme (www.fitzpatricksirishpub.com ☎ **04-67-60-58-30**), serves Irish beer and has an Irish music evening on Fridays. It's open daily noon to 1am. **La FaBRik,** 12 rue Boussairolles (☎ **09-60-37-86-45**) is friendly, crowded, and noisy and showing TV sports and live music during the week.

Rockstore, 20 rue de Verdun (www.rockstore.fr; ☎ **04-67-06-80-00**), has 1950s rock memorabilia, a Cadillac embedded in its front entrance, live concerts, several bars, and a disco. No cover, but charges for music nights. For the best jazz and blues in town, check out **JAM,** 100 rue Ferdinand-de-Lesseps (www.lejam.com; ☎ **04-67-58-30-30**). Regular concerts in the noisy, industrial-style space average 10€ to 25€.

Students gather in crowds at **Cargo,** 5 rue du Grand St-Jean (☎ **04-67-29-96-85**) for its Tuesday night Latin parties and great bars. Otherwise expect blues, funk, soul, and Latin from their DJs. **Le Coxx,** 5 rue Jules Latreilhe (☎ **04-99-66-77-61**), is one of the most popular hangouts for mainly gay men. Good bar plus karaoke nights and dancing are the main attractions here.

NARBONNE ★

787km (489 miles) SW of Paris; 61km (38 miles) E of Carcassonne; 93km (58 miles) S of Montpellier

In 118 B.C., Narbonne was the first town outside Italy to be colonized by the Romans. At that time, it was an important port and in the 12th and 13th century had a prestigious Jewish university. In the 14th century the river silted up and Narbonne became a backwater while the surrounding countryside transformed into prime vine-growing territory.

Around 50,500 Narbonnais live in this sleepy backwater, and while some vineyards have been torn up for holiday homes, others are raising the profile of their estates. You can visit vineyards in the surrounding area (the tourist office will advise you). If you want to go to the beach, head to the nearby village of **Gruisson** and its adjoining beach, Gruisson-Plage, or to the suburb of **St-Pierre la Mer** and its adjoining beach, Narbonne-Plage. Both are 15km (9.25 miles) south of Narbonne. Buses from the town are frequent, each marked with its destination.

Essentials

GETTING THERE Narbonne has rail, bus, and highway connections with other cities on the Mediterranean coast and with Toulouse. Rail travel is the best way to get here, with regular daily **trains** from Perpignan (trip time: 35 min.; one-way from 13€), 13 per day from Toulouse (trip time: 1.25 hr.; one-way fare from 19€), and 42 per day from Montpellier (trip time: from 58 min.; one-way fare is 17.40€). From Paris, the TGV runs directly to Narbonne (trip time: 4.5 hr.; one-way from 76€). Train information and schedules are on www.oui.sncf or call ✆ **36-35** (.40€/min.). If you're **driving,** Narbonne is at the junction of A61 and A9, easily accessible from either Toulouse or the Riviera.

VISITOR INFORMATION The **Office de Tourisme** is at 31 rue Jean Jaurès (www.narbonne-tourisme.co.uk; ✆ **04-68-65-15-60**).

GETTING AROUND La Citadine is a free shuttle around the town center. Taxi: ✆ **06-73-22-33-78.**

Exploring Narbonne

The **Canal de la Robine,** which connects to the **Canal du Midi,** bisects the town. The old town, which contains all the sights, is compact and easy to navigate.

Start at the oldest site, the **Horreum ★**, 7 rue Rouget de Lisle (✆ **04-68-32-45-30**), an underground warren of granaries and grain chutes built by the Romans in the 1st century B.C. It's in the restored medieval quarter, which is now full of attractive shops and restaurants. In the center of town, dominating the main place de l'Hôtel-de-Ville, the huge palace and cathedral complex, built from the 12th to the 14th centuries, reveals vaunting ecclesiastical ambitions. The **Cathédrale de St-Just et**

Palais des Archevêques

St-Pasteur ★, rue Armand Gautier ★★ (✆ **04-68-32-09-52;** free admission; daily 9am–noon and 2–6pm), is just a section of the original cathedral plan which was never completed, but it is still magnificent, decorated with 14th-century statues, stained glass, and Aubusson tapestries. Cloisters join it to the **Palais des Archevêques** (Archbishops' Palace), which contains the **Archaeology Museum ★** with an impressive collection of Roman artifacts and mosaics, and the **Museum of Art and History** (for all ✆ **04-68-90-30-54**). Additional sights include the **Donjon Gilles-Aycelin,** pl. de l'Hôtel-de-Ville (✆ **04-68-90-30-65**), a watchtower and prison from the late 13th century, where an observation platform looks out at the cathedral, the plain, and the Pyrénées; and the **Maison Charles Trenet,** 13 av. Charles Trenet (✆ **04-68-90-30-66**), birthplace of the singer/songwriter. There are pleasant walks by the canal, which is lined with 18th-century houses and *chais* (wine warehouses).

All Narbonne museums and the Horreum have the same opening hours and prices. Admission to one museum is 4€ (children 9 and under are free); a pass for all museums (the Pass Monuments & Musées), plus the Donjon Gilles-Aycelin, the Cathedral treasure, and Charles Trenet's birthplace is 9€ (6€ students and children ages 10 to 17, children 9 and under free). Attractions are open June to September daily 10am to 6pm, May Wednesday to Sunday 10am to noon and 2 to 5pm.

Where to Stay

La Résidence ★ Ideally placed on a quiet street but near the Cathédrale St-Just, this three-star hotel is housed in a former 19th-century house. The reception area is gracious, lit by chandeliers with a large sweeping staircase. Bedrooms are comfortably furnished with traditional fixtures and pretty textiles and bathrooms are a good size and well equipped. Some have a separate bath. Book a superior room if you want a larger room and larger bed. The hotel has no restaurant but serves breakfast in a striking room where the black-and-white wallpaper, black tables, and silver chairs will give you the morning jolt you need.

6 rue du 1er-Mai. www.hotelresidence.fr. ✆ **04-68-32-19-41.** 26 units. 80€–165€ double. Parking 9€. **Amenities:** Free Wi-Fi.

Will's ★ Conveniently right by the station, two-star Will's occupies a 19th-century townhouse. It's a good value option with neutral-colored rooms furnished with queen-sized beds, bright throws, and a desk in each room. Bathrooms are up to date and a good size for the price. A buffet breakfast is served on the ground floor. It's a popular option, so book in advance.

23 av. Pierre-Semard. www.willshotel-narbonne.com. *©* **04-68-90-44-50.** 17 units. 69€–79€ double; 128€ family room. **Amenities:** Free Wi-Fi.

Where to Eat

La Table St-Crescent ★★★ FRENCH/LANGUEDOCIENNE It's well worth making the excursion just south of the canal to this white-washed, terracotta-tiled restaurant. It's part of the local wine producers' Palais des Vins which promotes and sells the wines of Languedoc-Roussillon. Chef Lionel Giraud produces carefully sourced and beautifully presented dishes using top seasonal ingredients. The freshest fish from the coasts of France goes into dishes like lobster cooked on pine cones with ravioli and an Armganac sauce; free range chicken might come cooked in clay with fresh verbena, and there's always Wagyu beef matured for 60 days. Wines are, as you would expect, exemplary and the sommelier is particularly knowledgeable on local varieties, so tell him your budget and go from there. This is not a cheap option, but it will be a meal to remember.

In the Palais des Vins, 68 av. Général Leclerc, rte. de Perpignan. www.la-table-saint-crescent.com. *©* **04-68-41-37-37.** Main course 25€–40€; fixed-price lunch Tues–Fri 35€ or dinner 60€–90€. Wed–Sun noon–3pm; Tues–Sat 8–midnight. Closed May 1 to 23.

COLLIOURE ★★

882km (548 miles) SW of Paris; 28km (17 miles) SE of Perpignan

This town on the Côte Vermeille was established as a trading port by the Greeks but was invaded by neighboring factions through the centuries. It's a picturesque place, still with its ports, and best known as the place that became the summer home of the Fauvists who included Derain, Dufy, and Matisse. Collioure manages to retain some of the charm of a pre-Bardot St-Tropez.

Essentials

GETTING THERE Collioure has frequent **train** and **bus** service, especially from Perpignan (trip time: 22 min.). Train information and schedules are on www.oui.sncf or call *©* **36-35** (.40€/min.). There's a good **drive** along the coastal road (RN114) leading to the Spanish border.

VISITOR INFORMATION The **Office de Tourisme** is on place du 18-Juin (www.collioure.com; *©* **04-68-82-15-47.**

GETTING AROUND In high season, park your car for free at Cap Dourats (2km to the east) and take the free shuttle bus into town.

Shopping in the narrow streets of Collioure

Exploring Collioure

Two beaches sit on either side of the 13th-century **Château Royal ★**, pl. de 8-Mai-1945 (① **04-68-82-06-43**). Originally built for the Templars, it was later used by the Kings of Mallorca and Aragon. It's a massive building with formidable medieval fortifications that hark back to its past. In summer it hosts changing exhibitions by contemporary artists. Entrance costs the same regardless of whether there's an exhibition: 4€ for adults, 2€ students and children 10 to 18, and free for children 9 and under. Open June 1 to September 30 10am to 6pm, July 1 to August 30 10am to 7pm, October 1 to May 31 9am to 5pm.

The **Eglise Notre-Dame-des-Anges ★**, rue de l'Eglise (① **04-68-82-06-43**), is the town's most famous monument. The church with a tower that once acted as the lighthouse, looks austere from the outside, but inside features a floor-to-ceiling altarpiece dripping with gilt. The church is open daily from 9am to noon and 2 to 6pm. Also try to visit the **Modern Art Museum ★**, founded by Jean-Peské in the Villa Pams, rue de Port-Vendres (① **04-68-82-10-19**), home to works by artists who painted in Collioure. It's open daily June to September 10am to noon and 2 to 6pm and from October to May it has the same hours but is closed on Tuesdays. Admission is 3€ for adults, 2€ for children 12 to 16 and students, and free for children 11 and under. The **Chemin du Fauvisme** is a walking trail with 19 stops where you can see reproductions of paintings by Matisse,

Dérain, and other Fauvists beside the actual scene they painted. Pick up a map at the tourist office.

Where to Stay

Casa Païral ★ This pleasant family-run hotel is rightly popular. A short walk to the port and the beach, the 150-year old house has delightful, well-sized rooms furnished in different styles. The colors of the Matisse room will remind you of his famous cut-outs. Loft rooms have high ceilings and wooden beams while the best rooms come with a small sitting room and balcony with typical south of France views over red-tiled rooftops and the sea. Take breakfast in the pretty parlor or on the shaded patio where a fountain keeps the air cool. There's a delightful swimming pool for hot days.

Impasse des Palmiers. www.hotel-casa-pairal.com. ℂ **04-68-82-05-81.** 27 units. 79€–220€ double. Parking 16€. **Amenities:** Outdoor pool; room service; free Wi-Fi.

Relais des 3 Mas ★★ Collioure's best hotel and restaurant has wonderful harbor views and rooms that are simple but elegant with red Provençal tiled floors, pale wood, and white painted furniture. Deluxe rooms have balconies, one has a pretty grass terrace or take the suite with a garden. Bathrooms are large and have Jacuzzis. La Balette restaurant has a Michelin star and majors in fish as well as offering meat from local producers. Fixed-price menus run from 35€ at lunch on weekdays to a gastronomic feast at 105€.

Rte. de Port-Vendres. www.relaisdestroismas.com. ℂ **04-68-82-05-07.** 23 units. 100€–340€ double; 180€–500€ suite. Free parking. Closed Dec–mid-Feb. **Amenities:** Restaurant; babysitting; outdoor pool; room service; sauna; free Wi-Fi.

Where to Eat

Restaurant La Balette, at the Relais des 3 Mas (see above), is the best hotel dining room in town.

Le Neptune ★★ FRENCH/CATALAN This delightful restaurant in a tiered garden just above the beach looks over to the port to the castle. This is the place for toying with a dozen oysters and drinking the local sparkling wine while looking out over the deep blue Mediterranean. A market-based menu concentrates on fish, taking in a terrine of potatoes in olive oil with herring, quail egg, and vegetable pickles in winter, a pot au feu of seasonal fish, and for carnivores, dishes like lamb roasted in an herb and thyme crust with cabbage stuffed with foie gras. A good wine list contains some notable organic varieties.

9 rte. de Porte-Vendres. www.leneptune-collioure.com. ℂ **04-68-82-02-27.** Main course 27€–49€; fixed-price lunch 29€; other fixed-price menus (including vegetarian menu) 39€–99€. Apr–Oct daily noon–2pm and 7:30–10pm; Nov–Mar Wed–Mon noon–1:30pm and 7–9:30pm.

PERPIGNAN ★★

849km (527 miles) SW of Paris; 318km (197 miles) NW of Marseille; 64km (40 miles) S of Narbonne

Perpignan is a flourishing city with several grand new renovation projects and buildings. The former capital of the kingdom of Majorca and second city of Catalonia is just 45 min. from Barcelona, making it a Catalan cultural and business hub and confirming its multi-cultural status. Perpignan's new Espace Méditerranée neighborhood around the Théâtre de l'Archipel arts complex was designed by France's favorite architect, Jean Nouvel.

Perpignan retains the relaxed pace it is famous for. At night things heat up as it embodies the late-night culture and love of partying of its Spanish neighbors.

This is one of the sunniest places in France, but during summer afternoons in July and August, it's a cauldron. That's when many locals catch the 9.5km (6-mile) ride to the beach resort of Canet-en-Roussillon. Bus no. 6 runs from the center of Perpignan every 30 min. in the summer and costs 4€. A young scene brings energy to Perpignan, especially along the flower-decked quays of the Basse River, site of impromptu nighttime concerts, beer drinking, and tapas eating, a tradition adopted from nearby Barcelona.

Essentials

GETTING THERE   Regular TGV **trains** per day arrive from Paris mostly from Gare de Lyon and some from Austerlitz (trip time: from 5 hr.); others change at Montpellier; the one-way fare starts at 61€. Trains run regularly from Marseille (trip time: from 3 hr., 5 min., depending on the route; from 20.50€ one-way). Train information and schedules are on www.oui.sncf or call ☎ **36-35** (.40€/min.). If you're **driving** from the French Riviera, take the A9 west to Perpignan.

VISITOR INFORMATION   The **Office Municipal du Tourisme** is in place Francois-Arago (www.perpignantourisme.com; ☎ **04-68-66-30-30**).

GETTING AROUND   The free shuttle **P'tit Bus** runs around the old town and to the station. Taxis: ☎ **04-68-35-15-15** or **04-68-83-83-83.**

Exploring the City

A 2-hr. guided **walking tour** is a good way to see the attractions in the town's historic core. Tours begin at 5pm on Monday and Wednesday in July and August. The rest of the year, they start at 3:30pm on Saturdays only. They depart from in front of the Palmarium tourist information point on place Arago and cost 7€ per person. Check which are in English. Popular themed walks are on different days. For more details, contact the tourist office (see above).

Events in Perpignan

Perpignan is the only city in France to celebrate Holy Week in the same way as Spain: with remarkable processions of penitents dressed in hooded gowns. The **Procession de la Sanch** leaves from Eglise St-Jacques on Good Friday morning and moves through the city center, accompanied by chants and the beating of drums. In the heat of July, **Les Jeudis de Perpignan** (www.perpignantourisme. com; ✆ 04-68-66-30-30) takes over the city with an international cultural festival of street arts.

During the first two weeks of September, Perpignan is host to the most famous celebration of photojournalism in the industry, **Visa pour l'Image** (www. visapourlimage.com; ✆ 04-68-62-38-00). Photographs are exhibited in at least 10 sites of historical (usually medieval) interest. Entrance to the shows is free, and an international committee awards prizes.

Most of the major sites are concentrated in the compact, pedestrianized old town. The huge Palais des Rois de Majorque dominates the southern side of town. West of the river lies the new town.

Place de la République is at the heart of the pedestrianized city center, whose inviting streets make it a good town for shopping. Catalan is the style indigenous to the area, seen in the textiles, pottery, and furniture. A good selection of Catalan-inspired home-decorating items is found at **La Maison Quinta,** 3 rue Grands-des-Fabriques (www.maison-quinta.com; ✆ **04-68-34-41-62**).

Try the outdoor market **Marché Cassanyes,** pl. Cassanyes, for fruit, vegetables, preserves, and cheap clothes. It happens daily from 7:30am to 1:30pm. The **Halles Vauban** is a new covered market in refurbished old buildings opened at the end of 2017. It's full of organic food stalls, fruit, and vegetables but is also a great place for a snack or light lunch at the many cafes. It's at Quai Vauban and is open Tuesday to Sunday 8am to 8pm. For one of the best selections of Catalan ceramics from several makers, visit **Centre Sant-Vicens,** rue Sant-Vicens (www.santvicens.fr; ✆ **04-68-50-02-18**). It's 4km (2.5 miles) south of the town center; follow signs to Enne and Collioure.

Cathédrale St-Jean ★ CATHEDRAL The city's cathedral was started in 1324 but not completed until the late 16th century and built in Catalan gothic style which is very different from classic French gothic. The impressive columned nave is wide, with side chapels retaining ornate 16th and 17th-century retables (altarpieces). Leave through the south door to see the chapel with the polychrome wooden *Devost-Christ* (Devout Christ), a magnificent 14th-century woodcarving depicting the suffering of Jesus on the cross.

pl. Gambetta/rue de l'Horloge. ✆ **04-68-51-33-72.** Free admission. June–Sep daily 8am–7pm, Oct–May 8am–6pm.

Le Castillet ★ MONUMENT/MUSEUM This crenelated red-brick building is a combination gateway and fortress and the only surviving fortification from the 14th-century town walls. Climb its bulky tower for a view of the town and the surrounding narrow streets. It houses the **Musée des Arts et Traditions Populaires Catalans** (also known as La Casa Païral), with exhibitions of Catalan regional artifacts and folkloric items, including typical dress.

pl. de Verdun. ℂ **04-68-35-42-05.** Admission 2€ adults; free for children 18 and under. June–Sept daily 10:30am–6:30pm; Oct–May Tues–Sun 11am–5:30pm.

Musée d'Art Hyacinthe Rigaud ★★★ MUSEUM A huge expansion over three years has given this museum a new look and new space. Housed in two 18th-century *hôtels particuliers,* just off the cafe-lined place Arago, the museum displays the history of art from the 15th to 20th centuries, concentrating on those artists who lived or passed through Perpignan. The original collection was from native son Hyacinthe Rigaud, the official court artist of Versailles who painted Louis XIV and Louis XV. The collection, and temporary exhibitions, show works from the likes of Aristide Maillol, Picasso, Dufy, Jean Lurçat, and Miró as well as Catalan ceramics and contemporary artists.

16 rue Mailly. www.musee-rigaud. ℂ **04-68-66-19-83.** Admission 8€ adults; 6€ students and children ages 12–18; free for children 11 and under. June–Sept daily 10:30am–7pm; Oct–May Tues–Sun 11am–5:30pm.

Palais des Rois de Majorque (Palace of the Kings of Majorca) ★★ CASTLE At the southern end of the old city, the massive Spanish citadel encloses the now restored former Palace of the Kings of Majorca. Built in the 13th and 14th centuries around a 2-story courtyard encircled by arcades, this is Perpignan's most famous building. Entering via a huge ramp wide enough to take several horsemen side by side, you walk into a park with the castle ahead. From the courtyard you climb to the first-floor king's and queen's apartments. The square tower with its double gallery gives panoramic views of the Pyrénées. A free guided tour, in French only, departs at 11am and 3pm.

Rue des Archers. ℂ **04-68-34-96-29.** Admission 4€ adults; 2€ students and children 12–18; free for children 11 and under. June–Sept daily 10am–6pm; Oct–May daily 9am–5pm.

Where to Stay

La Villa Duflot ★★★ If you want the best in the region, book here where prices are reasonable for the luxury on offer. In a suburb 4km (2.5 miles) from Perpignan between the city center and the airport, the two-story, pink-washed building looks out onto gardens abundant with orange and olive trees, mimosa, and eucalyptus. You can sunbathe around the pool and order drinks from the outdoor bar. The good-size bedrooms are bright with stylish Art Deco interiors and have views over the gardens. All have king size beds and good bathrooms. The restaurant is reason enough to stay, using ingredients from regional suppliers (minutely detailed on the menu) for dishes like foie gras with pear and gingerbread, Charolais beef, and fish of the day with fricassée of mushrooms. It's open daily noon to 2pm and 8 to 11pm, with main courses from 24€ to 32€, and fixed-price menus at 25€ and 33€.

Rond-Point Albert Donnezan, Perpignan. www.villa-duflot.com. ℂ **04-68-56-67-67.** 24 units. 131€–197€ double; 210€–344€ suite. From central Perpignan, follow signs to Perthus–Le Belou and A9, 3km (1.75 miles) south. Just before you reach A9, you'll see the hotel. **Amenities:** Restaurant; 2 bars; outdoor pool; room service, free Wi-Fi.

Hotel de la Loge ★★ In the center of the old town, this good-value hotel is tucked away in a small street in a lovely 16th-century building. A wrought-iron staircase leads up to the bedrooms (there is an elevator as well) and a small bar and breakfast room are on the ground floor. Bedrooms are surprisingly spacious with pale walls, bright fabrics, and glass-topped desks. Bathrooms have tubs and some rooms have small terraces overlooking place de la Loge. There's a pretty courtyard and prices include a light breakfast.

I rue Fabriques d'En Nabot. www.hoteldelaloge.com. ℂ **04-68-34-41-02.** 22 units. 59€–89€ suite. **Amenities:** Bar; room service; free Wi-Fi.

Where to Eat

La Villa Duflot (see above) has a good restaurant.

Le Divil ★ CATALAN   Near Le Castillet, this bull-themed restaurant fits perfectly into Perpignan's love affair with all things bovine. There are brick walls, stone floors, decorative bulls' heads on the walls, and a cold meat store full of steaks. The popular outside terrace fills up quickly in summer. It's fun, full of locals, and laid back. Starters include truffled eggs, and fish options, but this is a beef restaurant so you'd do best to order their grilled beef fillet, burgers or steaks, all of which come with perfect fries. Set menus are devised with a nutritionist and dietician.

9 rue Fabriques d'En Nabot. www.restaurant-le-divil-66.com. ℂ **04-68-34-57-73.** Main course 18€–28€; fixed-price lunch 14€–18€. Mon–Sat noon–2pm and 7–10pm.

Le Saint Jean ★ FRENCH/CATALAN   This highly regarded restaurant is right beside the cathedral so you can eat on the large terrace looking at the ancient flying buttresses. Beautifully illuminated at night, this is great for a romantic summertime meal. Chef Yann Auger describes the restaurant as a bistro, but his cooking is more sophisticated. Try a rillette of ray with crisp vegetables, and a creamy prawn risotto for a light meal, or duck confit with dried fruits then filet mignon with spaghetti squash, hazelnuts, and Banyuls juice. Some of the wines from the well-thought-out list of Roussillon wines come from the chef's vineyards.

1 rue cité Bartissol. www.lesaint-jean.com. ℂ **04-68-51-22-25.** Main course 22€–28€; fixed-price lunch 15€–19€ or dinner 32€–41€. Mid-June–mid Sept Mon–Sat noon–2pm and 7–10:30pm. Mid-Sept to mid-June Mon–Fri noon–2pm and Thurs–Sat 7pm–10:30pm.

Perpignan Nightlife

Perpignan's cultural life is centered around the **Théâtre de l'Archipel**, av. Maréchal Leclerc (www.theatredelarchipel.org; ✆ **04-68-62-62-00**) which holds multi-cultural events all year round.

Perpignan shows its Spanish and Catalan side at night, getting lively after other cities have gone to bed. Nightclubs in Perpignan open around 11pm. The streets around **place de la Loge** and **avenue Maréchal Leclerc** buzz after dark with bars and clubs.

Begin at **Le Habana Bodegita,** 5 rue Grande-des-Fabriques (✆ **04-68-34-11-00**), where salsa and merengue play and Cuban cocktails flow. **Le O'Flaherty's,** 27 av. Marechal Leclerc (www.oflahertys-perpignan.com) is a good Irish bar with Irish beer on draft and DJs to keep you dancing from 5pm onwards. **Le Cosy Club,** 4 rue du Théâtre (✆ **04-68-66-02-57**), is a discotheque which rings the changes with jazz, electro, and soul on different nights washed down with cocktails.

During summer, the beachfront strip at the nearby resort of **Canet-Plage,** 12km (7.5 miles) east of Perpignan's historic core, lights up with seasonal bars and dance clubs that come and go with the tourist tides.

CARCASSONNE ★★★

770km (479 miles) SW of Paris; 94km (59 miles) SE of Toulouse; 105km (65 miles) S of Albi

The greatest fortress city of Europe stands out against the background of the Pyrénées. Seen from afar, this glorious citadel surrounded by fortified walls suggests fairy-tale magic, but in its heyday in the Middle Ages, it was very different. Shattering the peace and quiet were battering rams, grapnels, a mobile tower (inspired by the Trojan horse), catapults, flaming arrows, and the mangonel (a type of catapult) as the forces of the French King fought the heretical Cathars.

Today the city that is used for movies (most notably as a backdrop for the 1991 movie "Robin Hood, Prince of Thieves"), is overrun with visitors. But the elusive charm of Carcassonne emerges in the evening, when the day-trippers have departed and floodlights bathe the ancient monuments.

Essentials

GETTING THERE Carcassonne is a major stop for **trains** between Toulouse and destinations south and east. Seventeen trains per day arrive from Toulouse (trip time from 48 min.; 16.50€ one-way), 16 per day from Montpellier (trip time: 1.5 hr.; from 26€ one-way), and 10 per day from Marseille (trip time: from 3 hr.; from 36.30€ one-way). Train information and schedules are on www.oui.sncf or call ✆ **36-35** (.40€/min.). If you're **driving,** Carcassonne is on A61 south of Toulouse.

VISITOR INFORMATION   The **Office de Tourisme** has locations: 28 rue de Verdun (www.carcassonne-tourisme.com; ☏ **04-68-10-24-30**) and in the medieval town at Porte Narbonnaise (☏ **04-68-10-24-36**).

Exploring Carcassonne

Carcassonne consists of two towns: the **Bastide St-Louis** ★★ (also known as Ville Basse, or "Lower City"), and the UNESCO World Heritage Site upper town, or medieval **Cité ★★★**, which is among the major attractions in France. The impressive fortifications here consist of inner and outer walls, a double line of ramparts with walkways between them called *les lices.* The city began in the 6th century B.C., was later settled by the Romans and Visigoths, then became the main city of the Languedocian family, the Trencavels and its prosperity was ensured.

The epic medieval poems "Chansons de Geste" tell how the city got its name. During a siege by Charlemagne when the city was under Muslim rule, the starving populace was near surrender until a local noblewoman, Dame Carcas, reputedly gathered up the last of their grain, fed it to a sow, and tossed the pig over the ramparts. The pig burst, scattering the grain. Dame Carcas then demanded a parley and cried, *"Carcas te sonne!"* ("Carcas is calling you!") The Franks, concluding that Carcassonne must have unlimited food supplies, ended their siege. Like all such stories, it is not checkable and almost certainly apocryphal.

Carcassonne's walls were further fortified by the *vicomtes* de Trencavel in the 12th century but the town was taken during the Albigensian Crusade by anti-Cathar troops under Simon de Montfort. In 1249 the city passed to Louis IX who laid out the *ville basse.* It was razed to the ground in 1355 by the English Black Prince during the Hundred Years War, then rebuilt by the citizens. By the mid-17th century, the city had lost its position as a strategic frontier, and the ramparts were quarried for their stones. But interest in the Middle Ages revived, and the government ordered Viollet-le-Duc (the restorer of Notre-Dame in Paris) to repair and, where necessary, rebuild the walls. He took considerable license when rebuilding

---

Events in Carcassonne

The town's nightlife sparkles during its summer festivals. During the **Festival de Carcassonne** (www.festivaldecarcassonne.com) from mid-July to mid-August, concerts, modern and classical dance, operas, and theater fill the city, with international stars appearing at the **Théâtre Jean Deschamps,** an amphitheater seating 5,000 in La Cité. Tickets run 9€ to 73€. To purchase call

☏ **04-68-11-59-15** or go online. On July 14, **Bastille Day,** one of the best fireworks spectacles in France lights up the skies at 10:30pm. Over six weeks in July and August, the merriment and raucousness of the Middle Ages take over the city during the **Spectacles Medievaux,** in the form of jousts, food fairs, and street festivals. For information, contact the **Office de Tourisme** (see above).

the citadel to incorporate various very un-medieval features. But what does that matter? Carcassonne casts its spell on all who come here.

In the highest part of the Cité, on rue Cros Mayrevielle, you'll find the **Château Comtal ★**, pl. du Château (www.carcassonne.monuments-nationaux.fr; ✆ **04-68-11-70-72**), a restored 12th-century fortress defended by Raymond Trencavel then surrendered to the Crusaders in 1209. It's open April through September daily 10am to 6:30pm, October through March daily 9:30am to 5pm. Entrance includes an obligatory 45-min. guided tour, in French and broken English but it's the only way to climb onto the city's inner ramparts. You see the archaeological remnants discovered on-site, and an explanation of the 19th-century restorations. Entry is 9€ for adults, 7€ ages 18 to 25, and free for children 17 and under.

The major church, **Basilique St-Nazaire ★**, pl. de l'Eglise (✆ **04-68-25-27-65**), dates from the 11th to the 14th centuries and contains some beautiful stained-glass windows including two exceptional rose windows. It has other attractions: a soaring Romanesque nave, a gothic choir and transept, and the original tombstone of Simon de Montfort. The 16th-century organ is one of the oldest in southwestern France. The basilica is open Monday through Saturday 9am to noon and 2 to 7pm, Sunday 9am to 10:45am and 2 to 5pm. It closes slightly earlier in winter. Mass is celebrated on Sunday at 11am. Admission is free.

Where to Stay

IN THE CITÉ

Hôtel de la Cité ★★★　The best hotel in Carcassonne was originally a palace for the ruling bishops before it was turned into a hotel in 1909. This is where you can escape the crowds, safe behind an enclosed courtyard in the old city. The best bedrooms are straight out of a fairy tale book with paneled walls, wooden or tiled floors; some have friezes running around the top of the walls while others have fireplaces or a four-poster bed. Many rooms look out onto the ramparts or the garden. If you can, book no. 308 with its panoramic view of the city. Drink very expensive and exclusive brandy and cognac in the library bar. The hotel is renowned for its restaurant, **La Barbacane** (p. 673). Take your breakfast on the terrace looking down at the city below you.

Pl. Auguste Pierre Pont. www.hoteldelacite.com. ✆ **04-68-71-98-71.** 60 units. 219€–450€ double; 405€–935€ suite. Parking 16€–20€. **Amenities:** 3 restaurants; bar; babysitting; outdoor pool; room service; free Wi-Fi.

AT THE ENTRANCE TO THE CITÉ

Best Western Le Donjon et Les Remparts ★★　The second hotel within the city walls is big on charm and offers the best value in the moderate price range. The main building has a honey-colored stone exterior with iron bars on the windows. The lobby is cosy with suits of armor and elaborate Louis XIII–style furniture. Bedrooms are modern and very comfortably furnished; some have old exposed stone walls. At the end of the garden a second building has the family rooms and suites, all with a terrace. Bathrooms here have both a tub and a shower. The hotel also runs the adjacent Brasserie Le Donjon. In summer, the garden is the perfect breakfast spot.

2 rue du Comte-Roger. www.hotel-donjon.fr. ⓒ **04-68-11-23-00.** 61 units. 119€–218€ double; 208€–298€ suite. Parking 12€. **Amenities:** Restaurant; bar; room service; free Wi-Fi.

IN VILLE-BASSE

Hotel du Pont Vieux ★★   Near the old bridge (*le vieux pont*) and a 10-min. walk to the citadel, this friendly, family-run two-star hotel is on a lively street of bars, restaurants, and shops. It occupies an 18th-century building which has the advantage of a large courtyard, an internal garden, and a terrace which gives panoramic views of the citadel. The recently renovated bedrooms are simply furnished but pretty with bright fabrics. Pale tiled bathrooms are a good standard; some have rain showerheads. Pick a room on the upper floor for a splendid view. Triple and family rooms are available. Take breakfast either in the small downstairs room or on the terrace.

32 rue Trivalle. www.hotelduvieuxpont.com ⓒ **04-68-25-24-99.** 19 units. 65€–200€ double. Parking 7€–10€. **Amenities:** Lounge; free Wi-Fi.

Where to Eat

Brasserie Donjon, run by Le Donjon et Les Remparts hotel, is also recommended.

L'Escargot ★★ FRENCH   This popular tapas and wine bar is first rate for a light lunch or casual meal. Inside it has stone walls, a big-beamed ceiling and wooden floors and tables; the outside terrace tables fill up quickly. Tapas range from six snails at 5€ to top Iberico ham at 10€. Other dishes include large salads and the excellent value three-course menus include beef on skewers with roast potatoes, salad, and vegetables. Service is fast, fun, and efficient; the central location couldn't be better and it's open until 1am.

7 rue Viollet-le-Duc. www.restaurant-lescargot.com. ⓒ **04-68-47-12-55.** Fixed-price menus 16€–25€. Wed–Tues 11am–3pm and 7pm–1am.

La Barbacane ★★ FRENCH   You'll find this baronial-style restaurant in the Hotel de la Cité. Start with a drink in the majestic Library Bar looking out to the castle. The setting might be medieval but the cooking is bang up to date. Chef Jérôme Ryon uses local ingredients as a base for innovative ideas. A traditional and regional dish like cassoulet might appear as a soup with added truffles; Bresse chicken comes stuffed with mushrooms and crayfish. This is the place for a special meal in a grand setting, with crisp linen on the large tables and a welcoming and knowledgeable staff. Otherwise the fixed-price lunch menu which includes wine and water makes this restaurant a reality for a range of budgets.

In the Hôtel de la Cité, pl. de l'Eglise. www.hoteldelacite.com. ⓒ **04-68-71-98-71.** Main course 45€–70€; fixed-price lunch 39€–45€ or gourmet menu 85€. Thurs–Mon 7:30–9:30pm. Closed Feb–beginning of Mar.

Le Jardin en Ville ★★ FRENCH/CATALAN   Try this unusual restaurant concept: set within a shop selling modern and fairly hip items and occasional exhibition space. Eat inside where the funky interior features mismatched furniture and the likes of a hanging bicycle; or dine on the pretty shaded terrace. Share a platter of Catalan charcuterie then enjoy sliced duck breast with roast potatoes and spiced vegetables or wasabi tuna with rice. Vegetables are picked each morning from the garden; meat comes from local southwest France suppliers.

5 rue des Framboisiers. www.lejardinenville.fr. ℰ **04-68-47-80-91.** Main course 17€–21€; fixed-price lunch 16.50€–18.50€. Tues–Wed noon–2pm; Thurs–Sat noon–2pm and 7–9pm; July and Aug Tues–Sat noon–2pm and 7–9pm.

Shopping

Carcassonne has two distinct shopping areas. In the Lower City, the major streets for shopping, particularly for clothing, are **rue Clemenceau** and **rue de Verdun.** In the walled medieval city, the streets are chock-full of tiny stores and boutiques; many sell gift items such as antiques and local arts and crafts.

In the Cité, visit **Comptoir des Vins,** 3 rue du Conte Roger (ℰ **04-68-26-44-76**), for its wide selection of regional wines. Find a wide range of regional foods at **Le Panier Gourmand,** 1 rue du Plo (ℰ **04-68-25-15-63**). Antiques stores of merit include **Antiquités Safi,** 26 rue Trivalle (ℰ **04-68-25-60-51**), for paintings and art objects; and **Maison du Sud,** 13 porte d'Aude (ℰ **04-68-47-10-06**), for home decoration.

Carcassonne Nightlife

Carcassonne nightlife centers on **rue Omer-Sarraut** in La Bastide and **place Marcou** in La Cité. For a wonderful night time view of La Cité, live music and events, walk up to **La Métairie,** 3 chemin de Montlegun (ℰ **04-68-26-80-38**). It's open daily 6pm to 2am. An enduringly popular and smart disco, 4km (2.5 miles) southwest of town, **Le Black,** route de Limoux (www.complexeleblack.fr; ℰ **04-68-47-37-11**) plays all kinds of dance music from 11pm to 6am Friday and Saturday indoors or outside. Entrance costs 10€ on Saturday only.

CASTRES ★

721km (448 miles) SW of Paris; 42km (26 miles) S of Albi; 78 km (43.5 miles) E of Toulouse

On the bank of the Agout River, Castres is a delightful small town and the gateway for trips to the odd rock formations of the Sidobre granite massif and the mountains of Lacaune. Once a Roman military town, it became a religious center and stop on the pilgrim route to Santiago de Compostela after Benedictine monks arrived with the remains of St. Vincent of Saragossa. Caught up in the Cathar heresy, the first Albigensian martyrs were burnt here in 1209 and it continued its anti-Catholic church stance in the wars of religion in the late 16th century. The Eglise St-Benoît in French baroque style was started in 1677 on the Benedictine site but never finished. Echoes of Castres as a wool-producing town in the 14th century are found in the brightly colored old tanners' and weavers' houses by the river.

Essentials

GETTING THERE   From Toulouse, there are regular **trains** each day (trip time: around 1 hr., 21 min.; one-way fare is 15.70€). Train information and schedules are on www.oui.sncf or call ℭ **36-35** (.40€/min.). Shuttle bus no. 2 runs between the station and the center. If you're **driving,** Castres is on N126 east of Toulouse and N112 south of Albi.

VISITOR INFORMATION   The **Office de Tourisme** is at 2 pl. de la République (www.tourisme-castres.fr; ℭ **05-63-62-63-62**).

Exploring Castres

Jean-Jaurès Museum ★ MUSEUM   Jean-Jaurès, born in Castres, was one of France's most liberal political activists. He supported Dreyfus, founded the communist newspaper "L'Humanité" (still in print today), was leader of the socialist party, and campaigned for causes like abolishing the death penalty. His pacifist beliefs led to his assassination in Paris in July 1914. Though the documentation is in French, the large collection of satirical cartoons and lithographs gives a good picture of political life in France in the 1900s. Temporary exhibitions focus on life in all its aspects—cultural, economic, and social—between 1880 and 1914.

2 pl. Pélisson. ℭ **05-63-62-41-83.** Admission 2€ adults. July–Aug daily 10am–noon and 2–6pm; Oct–May 10am–noon and 2–5pm.

Musée Goya ★ MUSEUM   The museum, also known as the Museum of Hispanic Art, is in the town hall, once the archbishop's palace designed by Louis XIV's chief architect in 1669. A beautiful formal garden designed by Le Nôtre stretches out to the south. Inside the rooms house the second largest collection of Spanish art in France after the Louvre from antiquity to the 20th century. The museum also houses 16th-century tapestries, some outstanding sculpture, and paintings by Spanish artists from the 15th to the 20th centuries including works by Velázquez and Murillo. Despite the museum's name, only a few works by Francisco Goya are on display. Pierre Briguiboul, son of the Castres-born artist Marcel Briguiboul, donated these to the town in 1894. On show are portraits, including the famous *Self-portrait with Glasses.*

In the Jardin de l'Evêché. ℭ **05-63-71-59-27.** Admission 5€ adults; 2.50€ visitors 18–26; free for children 17 and under. July–Aug daily 10am–6pm; Oct–Mar Tues–Sat 9am–noon and 2–5pm, Sun 10am–noon and 2–5pm.

Where to Stay

Hôtel Renaissance ★   This charming 4-star hotel in the old town is housed in a red-brick, half-timbered 17-century building that started life as a grand family home. Bedrooms are decorated with differing styles: try the large traditional room with a half tester bed and wooden beamed ceiling; others have brightly patterned fabrics and walls which range in color from lime green to deep red—one has a wall of fabric depicting elephants. It's not for those with minimal tastes but it's great fun if you like something different. Public rooms are equally exuberant in decor with comfortable fuschia and purple armchairs and a welcoming fire in an elaborate hearth. Plus, there's a cosy bar. The hotel serves a good breakfast and although it doesn't have a restaurant, room service is available.

17 rue Victor-Hugo. www.hotel-renaissance.fr. ⓒ **05-63-59-30-42.** 20 units. 79€–100€ double; 100€–207€ suite. Parking 10€. **Amenities:** Bar; room service; free Wi-Fi.

Where to Eat

Le Bistrot des Saveurs ★★ FRENCH   Englishman Simon Scott worked in the kitchens of the Ritz and Savoy hotels in London before moving to France with his French wife and opening this Michelin-rated restaurant. It's a smart, modern restaurant with comfortable leather chairs, wooden floor and stone vaults. Like the decor, the classically based cooking has a chic contemporary touch. The menu changes weekly or every 10 days according to the seasons and the markets. A typical menu might include black pudding with squash foam and apple chutney followed by grilled beef with carrots fresh from the garden. At lunch a glass of wine and coffee comes at a mere 4€ extra. Beautiful desserts, a good wine list and charming staff complete the package.

5 rue Sainte-Foy. ⓒ **05-63-50-11-45.** Fixed-price lunch 19€–25€ or dinner 35€–45€. Mon–Fri noon–2:30pm and 7:30–9:15pm.

Le Cercle 81 ★ FRENCH   This chic restaurant is simply decorated with pale walls, dark chairs, and striking pictures on the walls of different world cities. A small outside terrace beckons in summer. Chef Xavier Bories takes classic dishes and elevates them to gourmet tastes. Starters like rillettes are beautifully prepared by the kitchen; rumpsteak is cooked to perfection; desserts are like works of art. The menu is brief in its description, so ask the friendly staff to elaborate. Prices are very reasonable with starters from 9.50€ to 11.50€, even when including expensive ingredients like foie gras.

52 rue Emile Zola. ⓒ **09-80-78-10-44.** Main course 17.50€–20.50€; fixed-price weekday lunch from 16.90€; other fixed-price menus 27.50€–59€. Tues–Sat noon–2:30pm; Thurs–Fri noon–2:30pm and 7:30–9:30pm; Sat 7:30–9:30pm.

ALBI ★★★

697km (432 miles) SW of Paris; 76km (47 miles) NE of Toulouse

Albi straddles both banks of the Tarn River and is dominated by its 13th-century cathedral, the heart of the remarkable Episcopal city. The whole of this medieval city center was added to UNESCO's World Heritage List in 2010. Albi is known as the "red city," its major remarkable buildings constructed from red bricks. Toulouse-Lautrec was born in the Hôtel Bosc in Albi; it's still a private home and not open to visitors, but a plaque is on the wall of the building, on rue Toulouse-Lautrec in the town center. Naturally, one of the town's major attractions is the Toulouse-Lautrec museum with a world-class collection of the artist's work.

Essentials

GETTING THERE Twenty **trains** per day link Toulouse with Albi (trip time: from 1 hr.; the one-way fare is 14.10€). Train information and schedules are on www.oui.sncf or call ✆ **36-35** (.40€/min.). If you're **driving** from Toulouse, take A68 northeast.

VISITOR INFORMATION The **Office de Tourisme** is in place Ste-Cécile (www.albi-tourisme.fr; ✆ **05-63-49-48-80).**

Exploring Albi

The old town with the major sights is a delightful mix of narrow streets near the cathedral and south of the river Tarn. Lovers of fashion should dive into the **Musée de la Mode ★**, 17 rue de la Souque (www.musee-mode.com; ✆ **05-63-43-15-90**), for its annual exhibitions of clothes and accessories through history from its 1,000-strong collection. The old town is also a good area for shops.

Cathédrale Ste-Cécile ★★ CATHEDRAL   Fortified with ramparts and parapets, this extraordinary 13th-century cathedral dominates the city. It was started as a building to strike fear into the hearts of the Albigensian heretics, 50 years after their defeat but it took 200 years to complete. It holds three records: it is the largest brick-built cathedral in the world, and it has the oldest medieval depiction of the Last Judgment (complete with devils and grimacing souls), and the largest surface area of Italian Renaissance frescos in France. It also has an exceptional restored 15th-century rood screen with unique polychromatic statues from the Old and New Testaments. It's worth getting to the cathedral on Wednesdays at 5pm and Sundays at 4pm in July and August for a free organ recital.

Place Ste-Cecile. ✆ **05-63-43-23-43.** Cathédrale: Free admission. Choir and Treasury: 6€ including audio guide; free for children 12 and under. May–Oct daily 9am–6:30pm; Nov–Apr daily 9:30am–noon and 2–6:30pm.

Musée Lapérouse ★★ MUSEUM   On the opposite bank of the Tarn from the bulk of Albi's medieval core (take the Pont-Vieux), this museum tells the story of the Albigeois Jean-François de Lapérouse. Louis XVI was so impressed by the sea-faring captain that he sent him on a mission with two frigates and 225 sailors and scientists to map and chart the coastlines of Alaska, California, and China at a time of commercial rivalry with England over overseas colonies. In 1788 they reached the Salomon

Islands, then vanished without trace. The museum tries to unravel the mystery.

Square Botany Bay. www.laperouse-france.fr. ℂ **05-63-49-15-55.** Admission 4€ adults; 2.50€ students and ages 13–25; free for children 12 and under. Mar–June and Sept–Oct Tues–Sun 9am–noon and 2–6pm; July–Aug Mon–Fri 9am–noon and 2–6pm, Sat–Sun 10am–noon and 2–7pm; Nov–Feb Tues–Sun 10am–noon and 2–5pm.

Palais de la Berbie: Musée Toulouse-Lautrec ★★★ MUSEUM

The Palais de la Berbie dating from the 13th century was the fortified residence of the Archbishops. Today it houses the Toulouse-Lautrec museum containing the world's most important collection of the 19th-century artist's paintings and works, more than 1,000 in all. It follows the life of the aristocratic Albigeois from his teenage years to those famous drawings (563 of them), 219 oil paintings, 183 lithographs, and 31 posters depicting the raffish demi-monde of turn-of-the-century Paris. For an art buff or Toulouse-Lautrec fan, this is a must-see museum. The top floor displays work by other French artists: Degas, Bonnard, Matisse, Utrillo, and Rouault. Another gallery focuses on Albi's Episcopal city.

Pl. Ste-Cécile. www.musee-toulouse-lautrec.com. ℂ **05-63-49-48-70.** Admission 8€ adults; 4€ students; free for children 14 and under. Jan–Mar daily 10am–noon and 2–5:30pm; Apr–May 10am–noon and 2–6pm; first 3 weeks in Jun 9am–noon and 2–6pm; mid-Jun–end of Sept 9am–6pm; Oct–Mar Wed–Mon 10am–noon and 2–5pm. Closed Jan 1, May 1, Nov 1, and Dec 25.

Where to Stay

Alchimy ★★★ This is a spectacular boutique hotel that you might expect to find in central Paris rather than Albi. With five junior suites and two large bedrooms, it is the inspiration of two professional interior designers so expect rooms individually decorated with panache. Furnishings are super comfortable with armchairs, matching fabrics and colors and one-off accessories carefully sourced to match the feel of each room. Public areas are equally sophisticated, including an elegant outdoor terrace. Alchimy is really a restaurant with rooms; the brasserie is another must-see venue with columns, mirrors, a glass roof, and modern chandelier. This is the restaurant of choice for chic locals. A la carte main dishes range from 18.90€ to 32.90€ but order the fixed-price menus for great food superbly cooked. Lunch menus run from 15€ to 27.90€.

50 rue Séré-de-Rivières. www.alchimyalbi.fr. ℂ **05-63-76-18-18.** 7 units. 130€–162€ double; 170€–250€ suite. **Amenities:** Restaurant; bar; room service; free Wi-Fi.

Hôtel Chiffre ★ Originally a coaching inn, this city-center hotel remains a good choice for travelers. Today's renovated version offers good-sized rooms with fabric-covered or wall-papered walls and old-fashioned, comfortable furniture; some overlook the inner courtyard. It's a good-value option with super friendly staff on a quiet street just 10 min.

from the cathedral. The hotel restaurant offers fixed-price menus from 25€ to 27€ per person.

50 rue Séré-de-Rivières. www.hotelchiffre.com. ℂ **05-63-48-58-48.** 39 units. 51€–136€ double. Parking 9€. **Amenities:** Restaurant; bar; room service; free Wi-Fi.

Hotel St-Antoine ★★   One of the oldest hotels in France, this former monastery was rebuilt as an inn in 1734. The same family has owned it for five generations; today Jean-François Rieux manages the hotel just a 10-min. walk from the Episcopal City. Some of the bedrooms are traditional with classic furniture and antiques while others are bright with modern drapes and fabrics. Ask for a room with a view over the garden where you can sit on a balmy day. Downstairs, the public rooms are bright and airy, with a cozy bar and casual restaurant looking out at the greenery.

17 rue St-Antoine. www.hotel-saint-antoine-albi.com. ℂ **05-63-54-04-04.** 44 units. 75€–168€ double; 126€–228€ suite. Parking 7€. **Amenities:** Restaurant; bar; babysitting; room service; free Wi-Fi. Closed Dec–Apr.

Where to Eat

For a gourmet meal in chic surroundings book at **Alchimy.** Both **La Hostellerie St-Antoine** and the **Hôtel Chiffre** are good choices. See "Where to Stay," above.

Jardin des Quatre Saisons ★★ MODERN FRENCH   Owner and chef Georges Bermond believes that the market should dictate the menu, so for 33 years he has been using the best local and seasonal ingredients. Menus take in carpaccio of beef with Thai spices and a tomato sorbet; pork confit with seasonal mushrooms, and pigeon with foie gras. The small brick-walled restaurant is full of everyday objects and has a fireplace that gives it a homely feel. It's an excellent value and popular with locals.

5 rue de la Pompe. www.le-jardin-des-quatre-saisons.com. ℂ **05-63-60-77-76.** Fixed-price weekday lunch 17€; other fixed-price menus 29€–41€. Tues–Sun noon–2:30pm; Tues–Wed and Fri–Sat 7:30–10pm.

La Planque de l'Evêque ★★ MODERN FRENCH   All the dishes that you would hope to find in a restaurant where modern touches have revitalized traditional French cooking are found here. Try the likes of a soup of Jerusalem artichokes and nuts with poached egg and peppered olive oil, then fish cooked in Parmesan pastry with leeks, followed by a chestnut-flavored crème brûlée. But an equally compelling reason to cross the river is the spectacular view you get of the cathedral complex from the summer terrace. It's far enough off the main tourist track that you feel you have really made a discovery.

1 rue de Lamothe. www.laplanquedeleveque.com. ℂ **05-63-56-89-49.** Main course 15€–20€; fixed-price lunch Tues–Fri 14€–16€; other fixed-price menus 20€–28€. Tues–Sat noon–1:30pm and 7:30–9:15pm. Closed 3 weeks in Jan.

CORDES-SUR-CIEL ★★

651km (404 miles) SW of Paris; 25km (16 miles) NW of Albi

This remarkable site is like an eagle's nest on a hilltop looking out onto the Cérou valley. The fortified town, or bastide, circled by several medieval walls, makes a spectacular place at sunrise. Stand on the ramparts when the air is soft and the colors muted before the crowds arrive to swell a population of under 1,000 to 10,000.

Founded in 1222 by Count Raymond VII of Toulouse during the war between his Cathar subjects and the French king, its prosperity came from its leather, textile, and silk industries. Today, it's an arts-and-crafts city with artisans occupying many of the old houses on the narrow streets—blacksmiths, enamellers, graphic artists, weavers, engravers, sculptors, and painters.

Essentials

GETTING THERE   If you're **driving,** take A68 northeast from Toulouse to Gaillac, turning north at exit 9 on D922 to Cordes-sur-Ciel. Park outside and then pass under an arch leading to the old town. If you're coming by **train,** get off in Cordes-Vindrac and walk, rent a bicycle, or take a taxi the remaining 5km (3 miles) to Cordes. Train information and schedules are on www.oui.sncf or call ✆ **36-35** (.40€/min.). For taxis or a **minibus,** call Taxi Barrois (✆ **05-63-56-14-80**). There's no regular bus service.

VISITOR INFORMATION   The **Office de Tourisme** is at Maison Gaugrin, 38-42 Grand-Rue (www.cordessurciel.fr; ✆ **05-63-56-00-52**).

Exploring Cordes-sur-Ciel

Sometimes called "the city of a hundred Gothic arches," the winding narrow streets are full of *maisons gothiques* ★★ of pink sandstone. The **Grande Rue Raymond VII,** also called **rue Droite,** is lined with houses, distinguished by 13th- and 14th-century pointed arches over the doors and windows. The old citadel or "upper town" runs along the ridge; the "lower town" hugs the eastern end of the old town.

You get to the upper town via the steep Grand-Rue de l'Horloge from the **Maison de Pays** (8 pl. Jeanne Ramels-Cals), which organizes the Saturday market in place de la Bouteillerie and sells good regional products. Walk along the Rue St-Michel past the **St-Michel Church,** dating from the 13th century but much modified in the intervening centuries. Its organ was brought from Notre-Dame in Paris in 1842.

Musée Charles-Portal ★ MUSEUM   Small and quirky, this somewhat sleepy museum is near a pass-through (Painted Gate) in the fortifications surrounding the city's medieval center. Inside reveals the story of Cordes and the surroundings with photographs, films, local textiles and

Cordes-sur-Ciel

embroidery, and medieval artifacts. Climb to the top-floor terrace for stunning views.

Porte des Ormeaux. www.museecharlesportal.fr. ℮ **09-72-87-07-95.** Admission 3€ adults; 2.50€ ages 12–25; free for children 11 and under. June–Aug Wed–Mon 2:30–6:30pm; Sept–Nov and Apr–May only Fri–Sun 2:30–6pm.

Where to Stay & Eat

Hostellerie du Parc ★ TRADITIONAL FRENCH   Just outside Cordes and set in its own park, this 19th-century mansion is a restaurant with rooms. Eat in the pretty, rather formal wood-paneled dining room with a baronial fireplace, or in the shaded garden surrounded by tall trees. The hearty dishes by chef Claude Izard use local ingredients and suppliers where possible. You might choose a starter of duck with foie gras, mains of tender pink roast lamb with garlic, local cheeses and apple croustade. Reservations are recommended.

The hotel offers 13 comfortable and well-furnished rooms, some with terraces; a double costs 70€ to 80€. You might consider half board (dinner, bed, and breakfast) from 80€ to 90€ per person.

Les Cabannes. www.hostellerie-duparc.com. ℮ **05-63-56-02-59.** From the town center, take rte. de St-Antonin (D600) for about 1km (.5 mile) west. Main course 28€–32€; fixed-price menu 26€–55€. June–Oct daily noon–2pm and 7–9:30pm; off season Fri–Sun noon–2pm, Fri–Sat 7–10pm. Closed 3 weeks in Jan. **Amenities:** Bar; restaurant; room service; free Wi-Fi.

Hostellerie du Vieux Cordes ★★ MODERN FRENCH   This warm mellow stone hotel in the center of town was once a 14th-century monastery. Today the wisteria-clad Logis de France, has simply decorated, decent sized rooms overlooking the Cerou valley. Some have the original stone walls and old beams; others are modern. Good southwest French cuisine with a modern twist produces starters like snails on a bed of ravioli and mushrooms, mains of daily caught steamed fish with tagliatelle and pesto sauce. Eat in the pretty restaurant, or in summer on the terrace, shaded by trees or the patio which looks out over the countryside.

21 rue St-Michel. www.vieuxcordes.fr. © **05-63-53-79-20.** 18 units. 68€–118€ double; 148€ suites. Main course 14€; fixed-price menu 25.50€–45€. Wed–Sat noon–2pm and 7:30–9pm; Sun noon–2pm. Closed Christmas and Jan to mid-Feb. Free parking. **Amenities:** Restaurant; bar; free Wi-Fi.

TOULOUSE ★★★

677km (420 miles) SW of Paris; 245km (152 miles) SE of Bordeaux; 94km (59 miles) W of Carcassonne

The old capital of Languedoc, and now the capital of the new Occitanie region, Toulouse (known as *La Ville Rose*), is France's fourth-largest city. It's lively and cosmopolitan and filled with spacious squares and gardens. Most of Toulouse's fine old mansions date from the Renaissance, when this was one of the richest cities in Europe. Today Toulouse is an artistic and cultural hub and a high-tech center, home to two huge aircraft makers—Airbus and Aerospatiale. Also making the city tick is its large student population: the university is France's third largest.

A city with a distinguished past, Toulouse is also a city of the future with the National Center for Space Research making its headquarters here since 1968. The first regularly scheduled airline flights from France took off from the local airport in the 1920s. Today Airbus planes are assembled in a gargantuan hangar in the suburb of Colombiers.

Essentials

GETTING THERE The Toulouse-Blagnac international **airport** lies in the city's northwestern suburbs, 10km (6 miles) from the center; for flight information, go to www.toulouse.aeroport.fr or call © **00-8-25-38-00-00** from abroad or 08-25-38-00-00 in France. **Air France** (www.airfrance.fr; © **09-69-39-02-15**), has about 25 flights a day from Paris and flies to Toulouse from London twice a day in high season. easyJet flies from the UK to Toulouse. The regular shuttle bus from the airport to the bus station takes 20 min. and costs 8€ one way.

Five TGV **trains** per day arrive from Paris Montparnasse (trip time: 5.5 hr.; from 65€ one-way), 14 trains (TGV and local) from Bordeaux (trip time from 2 hr., 4 min.; from 21€ one-way), and eight from Marseille (trip time: from 3 hr., 42 min.; from 35€ one-way). Train information and schedules are on www.oui.sncf or call © **36-35** (.40€/min.). The **drive** from Paris takes 6 to 7 hr. Take A10 south to Bordeaux, connecting to A62 to Toulouse. The Canal du Midi links many of the region's cities with Toulouse by waterway.

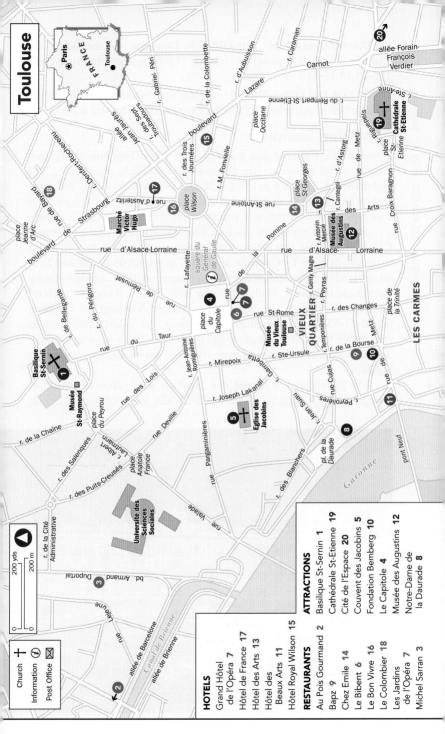

VISITOR INFORMATION The **Office de Tourisme** is in the Donjon du Capitole in the Square de Gaulle (www.toulouse-tourisme.com; ✆ **5-40-13-15-31**).

LAYOUT OF THE CITY The old town contains the main sights, encircled by large boulevards which follow the city's former defensive walls.

Exploring Toulouse

If you're here for more than a day, buy the **Passe Tourisme** giving free entry to major museums, free transport, and discounts on shopping and entertainment. The cost is 15€ for 24 hr.; 22€ for 2 days, and 29€ for 3 days. The slightly more expensive Premium Pass adds tourist trains and boat trips. More information is available from the tourist office (see above).

Start at the impressive place du Capitole, the heart of the old town. Cafes on the west side offer great views over the square that fills with market stalls daily. **Le Capitole ★**, pl. du Capitole (✆ **05-61-22-34-12**), is an outstanding achievement of civic architecture with its columns of pink marble and brickwork. Built in baroque style in 1753, it houses the **Hôtel de Ville** (City Hall), as well as the **Théâtre National du Capitole** (✆ **05-61-63-13-13**), which presents operas and ballets. Admission is free; group tours allow access to the theater. It is open Monday through Saturday 8:30am to 7pm, and from 10am to 7pm on Sundays and public holidays.

The gothic brick **Couvent des Jacobins ★★**, parvis des Jacobins (ww.jacobins.toulouse.fr; ✆ **05-61-22-23-82**), west of the place du

Place du Capitole

Capitole in the narrow streets of the old town, dominates its surroundings. Founded in 1230 by the Dominicans to fight the Cathar heresy, the convent and church formed the center of a powerful monastery complex that includes a peaceful cloister, sacristy, chapter house, and refectory. Inside the 13th century church, look up at its "palm tree" ceiling of delicate fan vaults supported by seven huge columns. The chapelle de la Vierge contains richly embroidered ceremonial robes. The old refectory now houses temporary exhibitions. The complex is open Tuesday to Sunday 10am to 6pm, admission to the church and chapelle is free; the rest costs 4€, free on first Sunday of the month and for those 18 years and under.

Small and dating mostly from the 18th century, **Notre-Dame de la Daurade** ★, 1 pl. de la Daurade (✆ **05-61-21-38-32**), sits to the west of the place du Capitole beside a riverside park from where you can take a boat cruise. Built on the site of a pagan temple, it was once covered in gilding. Its main possession is a statue of the Black Virgin, about 1m (3.25 ft.) tall, believed to cure ailments. The present *Vierge noire*, made in 1807, is a replica of the original destroyed during the French Revolution. Admission is free, and it is open January to June daily 8:30am to 6pm; July to August 8:30am to 7pm and September to December 9:30am to 6pm.

Basilique St-Sernin ★★★ BASILICA   Walk north from the place du Capitole to reach the St-Sernin district. Consecrated in 1096, the basilica is the largest, finest, and purest Romanesque church in Europe, topped by a wedding-cake style bell tower. An important stop on the pilgrimage route to Santiago de Compostela, it was also the burial place of the Counts of Toulouse. The interior may be plain but it impresses with its enormous size and double side aisles. The altar, still used today, was consecrated by Pope Urban II in 1096. The old baroque *retables* (altarpieces) and shrine in the ambulatory around the church have been reset; the relics here are those of the apostles and the first bishops of Toulouse. In the crypt are the body parts of more major Catholic saints, plus a thorn said to be from the Crown of Thorns.

Pl St-Sernin. www.basilique-saint-sernin.fr. ✆ **05-61-21-80-45.** Free admission to church; combined admission to the crypt and ambulatory 2.50€. Church June–Sept Mon–Sat 8:30am–7pm, Sun 8:30am–7:30pm; Oct–May Mon–Sat 8:30am–6pm, Sun 8:30am–7:30pm. Crypt and ambulatory June–Sept Mon–Sat 10am–6pm, Sun 11:30am–6pm; Oct–May Mon–Sat 10am–noon and 2–5:30pm, Sun 2–5:30pm.

Cathédrale St-Etienne ★ CATHEDRAL   Still of rue de Metz, continue east to the place St-Etienne and the cathedral. Because it took so long to build, from the 13th to the 17th centuries, and is smaller than the original plan, this cathedral is an odd mix of proportions and architectural styles. Inside are Renaissance tapestries along the nave and stained-glass windows that go back to the 15th century.

Pl. St-Etienne. Free admission. Mon–Sat 8am–7pm; Sun 9am–7pm.

La Cité de l'Espace ★★★ MUSEUM/PLANETARIUM   It may be out of the center, but with Toulouse being the center of European space exploration, this high-tech attraction is very popular. Offering hands-on experiences, you learn how to program a satellite launch, what life is like on board the Soyuz spacecraft, and look at earth from space with views taken from the weather satellites that update every 3 hr. The IMAX cinema and Planetarium take you into space on spectacular journeys while the Gyro-extreme shows you what it's like to be a real astronaut navigating while your sense of direction is disturbed. It's a great place for children with special play areas and their own planetarium, the Stellarium. In summer on Thursday evenings, the museum stays open late to let you see the stars through massive telescopes before watching fireworks arch into the sky next to the Ariane 5 rocket.

Av. Jean Gonord. www.en.cite-espace.com. ✆ **05-67-22-23-24.** Admission 21€–24.50€ adults; 18.50€ ages 5–18; free for children 4 and under. Open 10am–5pm/6pm/7pm/11pm depending on the season and day of the week. Check the website. Closed Jan. Bus: 37 from Ramonville metro station. Follow N126 from the center of town to the E. Peripheral route and take exit 17.

Fondation Bemberg ★★★ MUSEUM   Walk east along rue de Metz to reach one of the city's most important museums. Housed in the magnificent Hôtel Assézat built in 1555, the museum which opened in 1955 provides an overview of five centuries of world-class European art. The first floor takes you through a series of rooms from Renaissance furniture and works by old masters like Van der Weyden and Lucas Cranach to Boucher's 18th-century landscapes. The 2nd floor offers a wonderful overview of the 19th century with rooms dedicated to the Impressionists, the Fauvists, and Pointillists. German-French collector *extraordinaire* Georges Bemberg started the collection, donating 331 works including works by Pisarro, Matisse, and Monet. Pierre Bonnard's gift of his 28 paintings includes his *Moulin Rouge.*

Pl. d'Assézat, rue de Metz. www.fondation-bemberg.fr. ✆ **05-61-12-06-89.** Admission 10€ adults; 8€ students and children ages 8–26; free for children 7 and under. Tues–Sun 10am–12:30pm and 1:30–6pm (Thurs until 9pm).

Musée des Augustins ★★ MUSEUM   A little further east on the rue de Metz, you come to another monastic order. Originally built for the powerful Augustinians in 1309, the monastery became a museum in 1793, shortly after the French Revolution and is the 2nd oldest in France after the Louvre. The two main collections are in the monastery buildings and the refectory built in the 19th century by Viollet-le-Duc: 17th-to-19th-century paintings and a striking collection of medieval sculpture. The original French gothic cloisters contain the world's most valuable collection of beautifully carved Romanesque capitals. On the upper floors the large painting collection includes works by Rodin, Brueghel, Gérard,

Delacroix, Ingres, and others. The museum also contains several portraits by Antoine Rivalz, a local artist and major talent.

21 rue de Metz. www.augustins.org. ℰ **05-61-22-21-82.** Admission 5€; free for children 18 and under and for all first Sun of the month. Wed 10am–9pm; Thurs–Tues 10am–6pm. Closed public holidays.

Where to Stay

EXPENSIVE

Grand Hôtel de l'Opéra ★★★   If you're after a great location, exuberant decor, luxury as well as comfort, this is the answer. The hotel looks out over the main square and is just a 2-min. walk from the metro. As for the decor, it's a colorful mixture of strong reds, oranges, and blues. Setting this hotel apart are the patterned curtains everywhere, with chandeliers hanging above, mirrors and portraits on the walls, a tented ceiling in the bar, and even a costume from the theater in an alcove on the stairs. Large bedrooms are equally bold with thick carpets and rich dark wood furniture. Some rooms have oversize dramatic pictures behind the bed; others have prints on the walls while bathrooms are marble and dark wood. The hotel restaurant, Michelin-starred Les Jardins de l'Opéra is one of the top Toulouse restaurants so it's expensive, though it has a good value 32€ menu. It also, unusually for France, caters well for people with gluten and lactose intolerances. More modest meals are at the Grand Café de l'Opéra brasserie.

1 pl. du Capitole. www.grand-hotel-opera.com. ℰ **05-61-21-82-66.** 57 units. 109€–330€ double; 119€–395€ suite. Public parking 15€–26€. Métro: Capitole. **Amenities:** Restaurant; brasserie; bar; room service; sauna; Turkish hammam; free Wi-Fi.

MODERATE

Hôtel des Arts ★★   This charming hotel on a quiet street just behind the Musée des Augustins, and just a 5-min. walk from the place du Capitole, offers a quiet oasis. The decor combines old and new: think exposed red brick walls with smart contemporary furniture. Each room takes a different style from comics to photography; each has a glass-topped desk, bright colored cushions and throws on comfortable beds, colored lighting you can control, and good modern tiled bathrooms. The bilingual staff are welcoming and friendly and will carry your luggage (there's no lift). Book breakfast in your room as there is no restaurant or bar.

1 bis rue Cantegril. www.hoteldesartstoulouse.fr. ℰ **05-61-23-36-21.** 12 units. 89€–250€ double; 99€–250€ family room for 4. **Amenities:** Room service; free Wi-Fi.

Hôtel des Beaux-Arts ★★   This is not a hotel for the conventional even though it's housed in a charming 18th-century red brick building by the river Garonne. The decor includes bold purple walls, brightly colored furniture with modernist sofas and a retro Ball chair, a huge wall mirror and chandeliers of mother-of-pearl suspended from a distressed silvered ceiling. Each bedroom was designed by a different artist or design boutique owner and each has a startling piece of art. Choose from the relatively classic rooms to those with swirling patterns on the walls and unconventional furniture. Such daring has to be done well to work, and this hotel has perfected it. Ask for the "Chamber Only You" for its terrace and top view, though all rooms do look over the Garonne River. The hotel serves breakfast and brunch, and the independently run Brasserie Flo Les Beaux-Arts in the same building offers good traditional and regional cooking.

1 pl. du Pont-Neuf. www.hoteldesbeauxarts.com. ✆ **05-34-45-4242.** 18 units. 130€–200€ double; 200€ junior suite. Nearby parking 18€. Métro: Esquirol. **Amenities:** Restaurant; bar; free Wi-Fi.

INEXPENSIVE

Hôtel de France ★ This good value-for-money hotel near place de Wilson with its restaurants, cafes, markets, and shops, has been run by the same family since 1930. It's in a restored historic building from 1890, once the Hôtel des Américains. Bedrooms of varying sizes are comfortable with color schemes from dark greys to reds and purples, with pictures or old photographs of street scenes on the walls; some have small balconies. Bathrooms are travertine-tiled and some have tubs.

5 rue Austerlitz. www.hotel-france-toulouse.com. ✆ **05-61-21-88-24.** 62 units. 79€–109€ double; 115€ quad. **Amenities:** Breakfast room; room service; free Wi-Fi.

Hôtel Royal Wilson ★★ Just off Rue d'Aubuisson and a 2-min. walk to the place Wilson, this 2-star hotel is a real find. Bedrooms vary in size and are comfortable, charmingly decorated in pleasant colors with either a contemporary feel or with antiques. Some look over the theater and have balconies; others open onto a pretty Moorish-style interior courtyard. The bi-lingual staff are welcoming and helpful. Breakfast is made from ingredients bought in the nearby Victor Hugo market. The hotel caters also for bicyclists with an "Acceuil Vélo" (Cyclists Welcome) label and a secure garage for bicycles.

6 rue Labéda. www.hotelroyalwilson-toulouse.com. ✆ **05-61-41-41.** 27 units. 63€–99€ double; 91€–99€ quad. Parking 9€. **Amenities:** Breakfast room; room service; free Wi-Fi.

Where to Eat

The other top Toulouse restaurant is in the **Grand Hotel de l'Opera** (p. 687).

EXPENSIVE

Michel Sarran ★★★ MODERN FRENCH This double Michelin-starred restaurant is rightly regarded as the top restaurant in Toulouse, worth the slight journey west to the University district. Master chef Michel Sarran produces dishes that challenge the norm of modern French cooking using imaginative Asian spicing: a starter of langoustines marinated in miso olive oil with a mango and lemon guacamole and creamy Armagnac beignet, followed by Aubrac beef with carrots and ginger and rice with beef teppanyaki. This is complex cooking done with great skill. Sarran's wife, Françoise, oversees the main dining room decorated in a modern, smart style with strong colored chairs and textured walls. Expect sophisticated dining in a sophisticated setting; reservations are essential.

21 bd. Armand Duportal. www.michel-sarran.com. ℂ **05-61-12-32-32.** Main course 44€–73€; fixed-price lunch 60€; other fixed-price menus 110€–145€. Mon–Fri noon–1:45pm and 8–9:45pm (closed Wed for lunch). Closed Aug and 1 week around Christmas. Métro: Capitole.

Au Pois Gourmand ★★ FRENCH   Set in a mansion with wooden carving and balconies that might have covered a colonial house in an exotic corner of the world, Au Pois Gourmand is run by the Plazotta family. Eat in the elegant, grey-toned dining room or on the large terrace that overlooks the river; it's partially closed and heated so you can dine even on chilly evenings. Three menus are on offer. At lunchtime the 28€ menu might include foie gras lightly cooked with mango, slow cooked venison in a sweet and sour sauce then either local cheeses or a creamy milk chocolate dessert with ice cream. Menus at 55€ and 65€ (add just 10€ for good wines) using more expensive ingredients and offering more complex dishes are very good value for money.

3 rue Emile Heybrard. www.poisgourmand.fr. ℂ **05-34-36-42-00.** Fixed-price lunch 28€ or dinner 55€–75€; special occasion menus 65€–125€. Mon–Fri noon–2pm and Mon–Sat 8–10pm.

MODERATE

Le Bibent ★★★ MODERN FRENCH   Originally opened in 1861, right in the heart of Toulouse in the place du Capitole, Le Bibent is a glorious example of a classic brasserie. The huge room has a vaulted ceiling, painted panels, gilding galore, mirrors, chandeliers, and banquette seating. It was taken over by starred chef Christian Constant in 2011 and he's still wooing contented locals and visitors with the ambience, long opening hours (from 7am–11pm), and a menu that takes in breakfast, Caesar salad or croque-monsieur for lunch, and a full-blown dinner of classics like a satisfying beef daube for winter and scallops roasted in herbs. Dine outside on the terrace in summer dining.

5 pl. du Capitole. www.maisonconstant.com. ℂ **05-32-30-18-37.** Main course 26€–38€; fixed-price menus 45€–75€. Daily 7am–11pm. Métro: Capitole.

Chez Emile ★ TOULOUSIAN   This delightful restaurant fits the bill if you're looking for good French cooking and a relaxed atmosphere. It's in a traditional red-brick house in a busy square that has a pleasant small town local feel. Eat upstairs or down and make for the terrace in summer. Chef Christophe Fasan keeps to southwest France with ingredients like lamb from the Pyrénées and dishes like Catalan seafood stew with mussels, freshwater ling, calamari, and prawns. But if you're hungry and after a classic dish, order the cassoulet of the original chef, cooked in duck fat, which customers have been ordering for over 50 years. There's a good wine list where you can go for a local Fitou or Corbières, or push the boat out with a Bordeaux at 2,950€.

13 pl. St-Georges. www.restaurant-emile.com. ℂ **05-61-21-05-56.** Telephone reservations only. Main course 23€–35€; fixed-price lunch 22€; other fixed-price menus 32€–60€. Tues–Sat noon–2pm and 7–10:30pm. Closed Dec 23–Jan 8. Métro: Capitole or Esquirol.

Le Colombier ★★ TOULOUSIAN   Walls of alternating strands of red brick and stone and a wood-beamed ceiling take you back to the origins of this popular restaurant. You're in the former stables of the Capitole where Alain Lacoste has been delighting locals and visitors since 2007 with his robust southwest France-inspired dishes. But the greatest of these, as every Toulousian will tell you, is his cassoulet, slow cooked for 8 hours. This is a dish for the hearty: it's made of white beans, pork, Toulouse sausage, and confit goose leg. Or try foie gras with sweetbreads and mushrooms, followed by scallops cooked with a Provençale sauce. Take tradition to the nth degree with crêpes flamed in Grand Marnier.

14 rue Bayard. www.restaurant-lecolombier.com. ℂ **05-61-62-40-05.** Main course 24€–26€; fixed-price lunch 19€–23.50€ or dinner 27.50€–39€. Tues–Fri noon–2pm and Mon–Sat 7:15–10pm. Métro: Jeanne d'Arc.

INEXPENSIVE

Bapz ★ CAFE/TEA ROOM   Dainty china, silver teapots that your grandmother might have used, and a collection of odd artifacts suggest an English tea room but undeniable French influences are palpable here (***Note:*** Tea at 5pm is 1 hr. late for the true enthusiast). But try brunch and the generous quiches and salads and you can forgive any lapse of etiquette at this pretty, welcoming place.

13 rue de la Bourse. www.bapz.fr. ℂ **05-61-23-06-63.** Brunch 17.50€; lunch 11.50€. Tues–Sat noon–7pm; Oct–Mar Sun noon–7pm. Metro: Esquirol.

Le Bon Vivre ★ SOUTHWESTERN FRENCH   This popular, welcoming and bustling bistro is also known as Café Cantine du Bon Vivre. Locals simply call this place Huguette after the founder, Huguette Meliet, who now runs it with her daughter, Cathy. It's the place for good, honest, southwest France food, and an honest appetite. Ingredients come from the Midi-Pyrénées and particularly from Gers in Gascony. Try cassoulet, Toulouse sausages, duck, and Bigorre black pork. Look for dishes the likes of beef tartare, confit of duck cooked in a wok with seasonal vegetables, and fish caught in Saint Jean de Luz with salad and frites. For dessert, go for a top ice cream like salted caramel with caramelized peanuts. The renovated restaurant is simple with a wooden floor, tables and chairs in pinks, greens, and blues, and banquette seating along the walls. It's in an 18th-century mansion next to the Town Hall, the perfect spot.

15 bis pl. Wilson. www.lebonvivre.com. ℂ **05-61-23-07-17.** Main course 15€–36€; fixed-price lunch 15€–18€. Daily 11am–11pm. Métro: Capitol.

Shopping

Head for the streets north and west of **place St-Etienne** for top high street names. You'll find more boutiques in the **rue Croix-Baragnon, rue des Arts,** and rue **St-Antoine de T** (including The Kooples, originally from Toulouse). The newly renovated **Reflets Compans** (www. reflets-compans.com), to the north of the old town, offers mid-range high street brands. Antique lovers head for **rue Fermat.** More down-market antiques spread out each Saturday 6am to 1pm during the weekly **flea market** by the place Saint-Aubin. The Square Charles De Gaulle holds an **organic market** on Tuesday and Saturday mornings and around Eglise St-Aubin on Sunday mornings. The three main covered markets, all filled with food stalls, restaurants, and cafes, are the 126-year old **Les Carmes** (pl. des Carmes), the large **Victor Hugo** (pl. Victor Hugo) with 100 stalls, and **Saint-Cyprien** at place Rouguet. They all have late night openings (check times with the Tourist Office). For superb chocolates and cakes, try **Maison Pillon,** 2 rue Ozenne, 2 rue d'Austerlitz, and 23 rue du Languedoc.

Violets grow in abundance in meadows near Toulouse. Two shops selling items like violet-scented perfume and patterned-violet clothes and accessories include **Violettes & Pastels,** 10 rue St-Pantaléon (© **05-61-22-14-22**), and **La Maison de la Violette,** a boat on the Canal du Midi opposite 2 bd. Bonrepos (© **05-61-99-01-30**).

Toulouse Nightlife

Toulouse's theater, dance, and opera are often on a par with those found in Paris. It's also a city of festivals throughout the year from a world-famous **Piano aux Jacobins** in the cloister of the Jacobins to rock and world music. Contact the Tourist Office for detailed information.

PERFORMING ARTS

The city's most notable theaters are **Théâtre du Capitole,** pl. du Capitole (www.theatreducapitole.fr; © **05-61-63-13-13**), which specializes in operas, operettas, and works from the classical French repertoire; and **Halle aux Grains,** 1 pl. Dupuy (www. onct.toulouse.fr; © **05-61-63-13-13**), home of the Orchestre National du Capitole de Toulouse and the venue for mostly classical concerts. **Théâtre Garonne,** 1 av. du Château d'Eau (www. theatregaronne.com; © **05-62-48-56-56**), stages plays, dance from classic to flamenco, and a wide variety of music. Another important venue is the **Zénith de Toulouse,** 11 av. Raymond-Badiou (www.zenith-toulouse metropole.com; © **05-34-31-10-00**), one of France's biggest rock music venues with variety acts and musical comedies from other European cities as well. Another venue, with a roughly equivalent mix of music, theater, and entertainment, is **Théâtre National de Toulouse,** 1 rue Pierre Baudis (www.tnt-cite.com; © **05-34-45-05-05**).

BARS & CLUBS

The liveliest squares to wander after dark are **place du Capitole, place St-Georges, place St-Pierre,** and **place Wilson.**

The best wine bar, possibly in France, is **N5 Wine Bar**, 5 rue de la Bourse (www.n5winebar.com; ✆ **05-61-38-44-51**), which has over 3,600 bottles to choose from. For bars and pubs, **La Tantina de Burgos,** 27 rue de la Garonette (www.la-tantina-de-burgos-bodega.com; ✆ **05-61-55-59-29**), has a Latin flair popular with students. The busiest English-style pub in town, **Le Frog & Le Roast Beef,** 14 rue de l'Industrie (✆ **05-61-99-28-57**), has its own microbrewery, hosts quiz nights, shows football, and is usually crowded with the city's English-speaking community. **The iBar,** 3 rue Gabrielle-Peri (www.i-bar.fr; ✆ **05-61-62-08-07**), with restaurant, bar, and club lounge, is the smart place for tapas and cocktails before dancing to the DJs' tunes.

L'Ubu Club, 16 rue Saint Rome (✆ **05-61-23-26-75**), in the heart of town is a series of cellars with a restaurant and a discotheque that notches up the beat later.

The oldest and most deeply entrenched LGBT bar in Toulouse is Le **Shanghai Club,** 12 rue de la Pomme (✆ **05-61-23-37-80**), a man's dance domain playing the latest in techno. Entrance is free, and it's open every night.

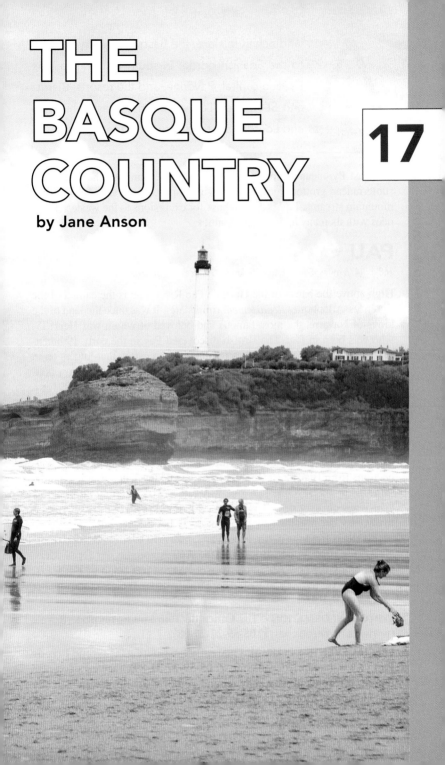

THE BASQUE COUNTRY

by Jane Anson

A land rich in folklore, the Basque Country extends to the Spanish border in southwest France. The Basque capital, Bayonne, and the resorts, Biarritz and St-Jean-de-Luz, are on the coast, while Pau and Lourdes are the gateway to the Pyrénées.

The vast Pyrenean region is a land of glaciers, summits, thermal baths, subterranean grottoes and caverns, winter-sports centers, and trout-filled mountain streams. **Pau** is a good base for excursions to the western Pyrénées with its many hiking opportunities.

PAU ★★★

768km (476 miles) SW of Paris; 196km (122 miles) SW of Toulouse

High above the banks of the Gave de Pau River, Pau is the capital of the Pyrénées-Atlantiques *département* (ministate). It was once the land of the kings of Navarre, the most famous and beloved of whom was Henri IV, who was born in Pau. The British discovered Pau in the early 19th century, launching such practices as fox hunting, a custom that lingers on in the form of the Pau Hunt. Even if you're just passing through, follow boulevard des Pyrénées, an esplanade erected on Napoleon's orders, for a famous panoramic view.

Essentials

GETTING THERE   **Pau-Uzein airport** is 12km (7.5 miles) north of town; call ✆ **05-59-33-33-00** for flight information. There are good **train** connections from Biarritz (three direct per day, taking 1 hr., 40 min. and the same again via Bayonne); the one-way fare is 21€. For train information, visit www.oui.sncf or call ✆ **36-35** (.40€/min.). **Driving** to Pau is relatively easy because the new A65 motorway has dramatically speeded up access times from the north. From Paris, take A10 south to Bordeaux, the N230 ring road around Bordeaux, the A62 Autoroute des Deux Mers, until joining the new A65 motorway at Langon just south of Bordeaux, which runs all the way to Pau. Alternatively, from Toulouse, the smaller N117 runs to Pau.

VISITOR INFORMATION   The **Office de Tourisme** is on place Royale (www.tourismepau.com; ✆ **05-59-27-27-08**).

SPECIAL EVENTS   In late May and early June, during the **Grand Prix de Pau** (www.grandprixdepau.com; ✆ **05-59-27-31-89**), race cars compete for speed records in what may remind you of a small-scale and slightly less glamorous Monaco Grand Prix.

PREVIOUS PAGE: **Biarritz beach**

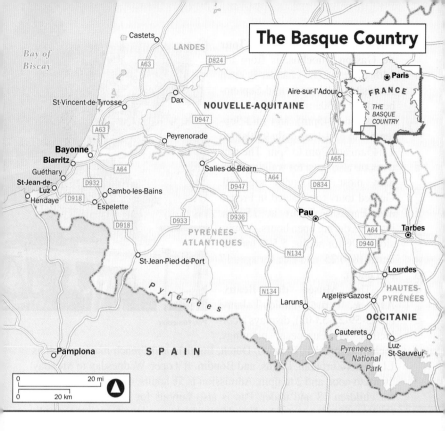

Exploring Pau

The city center is 30m (98 ft.) up from the river and the railway station, and if you arrive by train, you'll have the pleasure of ascending in its historic **Funicular** from near the station to place Royale. Restored in 2010 and more than a century old, it runs Monday to Saturday from 6:45am to 9:40pm and on Sundays from 1:30 to 8:50pm; admission is free. Place Royale is in the center of the 2km-long (1.25-mile) **boulevard des Pyrénées,** a popular promenade since the 19th century for its views over palm-landscaped slopes to the distant mountains. At the eastern end is Parc Beaumont, where the **Palais Beaumont** (www.pau-congres.com; ✆ 05-59-11-20-00), built as a casino and winter garden, now hosts concerts, theater performances, and exhibitions; and at the western end is the **Château de Pau ★**, 2 rue du Château (www.musee-chateau-pau.fr; ✆ 05-59-82-38-00), dating from the 12th century and steeped in the Renaissance spirit of the bold Marguerite de Navarre, who wrote the bawdy novel *Heptaméron* at age 60. Inside are many relics from the age, including a crib made of a single tortoiseshell for Henri de Navarre, who was born here, and a splendid array of Flemish and Gobelin tapestries.

The great rectangular tower, **Tour de Gaston Phoebus,** is from the 14th century. The château is open for visits mid-June to mid-September daily 9:30am to 6:45pm (last admission 5:45pm), and mid-September to mid-June daily 9:30am to 11:45am and 2pm to 5pm. The gardens are also open for walking from 8am most days until nightfall. Guided tours (conducted in French and English) depart at 15-min. intervals during open hours. Admission is 7€ for adults, 5.50€ for students 18 to 25, and free for ages 17 and under.

The **Musée des Beaux-Arts ★**, 1 rue Mathieu-Lalanne (✆ **05-59-27-33-02**), displays a collection of European paintings,

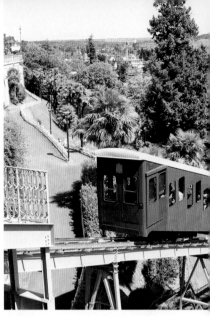

Pau funicular

including Spanish, Flemish, Dutch, English, and French masters such as El Greco, Zurbarán, Degas, and Boudin. It's open Wednesday to Monday 10am to noon and 2 to 6pm. Admission is 5€ adults, 4€ students, and free for children 18 and under. Pau is also famous for its **Haras National** (National Stud), created by Napoléon, which is no longer open to the public but does hold some wonderful race and jumping events throughout the year that are worth attending if you are in the area. It's situated south of the Gave de Pau at 1 rue du Maréchal Leclerc (www.haras-nationaux.fr; ✆ **05-59-06-98-37**).

A little further out of town, heading towards the foothills of the Pyrénées, the **Zoo d'Asson** is an excellent place for children, with over 500 species of animals, kept in large, open spaces and carefully-maintained enclosures. Of particular interest are the white tigers and the kangaroo sanctuary, one of the biggest in Europe. In total, the zoo covers 5 hectares (12 acres); the entrance is at 6 Chemin du Brouquet, Asson (www.zoo-asson.org; ✆ **05-59-71-03-34**). It's open daily April to September 10am to 7pm, and the rest of year from 10am to 6pm. Admission is 14€ adults, 9€ children ages 3 to 11, and free for children ages 2 and under.

Where to Stay

Hotel Parc Beaumont ★★   This is a Sofitel hotel that offers some of the best accommodation in the city. Most of the rooms have views over Parc Beaumont or the upmarket residential area of Trespoey (worth a wander round if you have time). The hotel offers good-sized beds and a balcony in every room. The Jeu de Paume restaurant is particularly recommended.

1 av. Edouard VII. www.hotel-parc-beaumont.com. ℂ **05-59-11-84-00.** 75 units. 165€–275€ double. Free parking. **Amenities:** Bar; restaurant; indoor pool; room service; free Wi-Fi.

Le Fer à Cheval ★   Around 10 min. from the center of Pau, in Lons, this unflashy but thoroughly lovely hotel is worth discovering. The well-decorated and luxurious-feeling bedrooms each have a different theme. You'll have good access from here to various walking routes and the hotel has an excellent restaurant on site.

1 av. des Martyrs du Pont Long. www.hotel-leferacheval.com. ℂ **05-59-32-17-40.** 10 units. 70€–100€ double. **Amenities:** Bar; restaurant; free Wi-Fi.

Where to Eat

Au Fin Gourmet ★★ BASQUE   This restaurant makes a regular appearance in the Michelin guide, and is well located in the Joantho gardens near the bottom of the funicular, with floor to ceiling windows looking out over the greenery, and a terrace for summer days. Brothers Patrick and Laurent Ithurriague have done a good job of updating the menu while retaining its traditional focus on local Pyrénées ingredients.

24 av. Gaston-Lacoste. www.restaurant-aufingourmet.com. ℂ **05-59-27-47-71.** Main course 22€–25€; fixed-price lunch 28€–76€ or dinner 38€–74€. Tues–Sun noon–2pm; Tues–Sat 7–10pm.

Au Grain du Raisin ★ FRENCH/WINE BAR   One of an increasing number of wine bars that is helping liven up Pau's nightlife, this is right in the center of town. The food is mainly tasting plates and tapas (French-style, which means charcuterie and cheese), and the wine list excellent, focusing as you would hope on southwest France. On most weekends, the restaurant hosts small, relaxed live music sessions.

11 rue Sully, Quartier du Château. www.baravin-pau.com. ℂ **05-59-82-98-44.** Tasting plates 15€. Mon–Sat 5pm–midnight.

Les Halles ★ Food market   Fairly discreet from the outside, this is one of the most enjoyable places to eat like a local in Pau. This lively food market is full of local foodstuffs, from cured hams and charcuterie and Basque cheeses, to fruits, vegetables, and delicious patisseries, all direct from the producers. Buy a Pass Gourmand which gives you coupons to exchange for food (also in other shops around town) and pull up a chair at one of the market's many counters.

Pl. de la République. www.pau.fr/marches. Tasting pass 12€. Mon–Fri 6am–1pm and 3:30–7:30pm, and Sat 5am–2pm.

Shopping

Pau's shopping doesn't quite live up to its surrounding scenery and cultural attractions, but it does offer regional specialties such as chocolates, sweet jams, and Basque antiques. The pedestrian **rue Serviez** and **rue des Cordeliers** harbor an array of boutiques and shops that carry these items, as do **rue Louis-Barthou** and **rue du Maréchal-Foch,** which are all around the central **place Georges Clemenceau.**

Pau has some of the region's best antiques shops, such as **Antiquités Delan,** 4 rue Gassion (www.delanpatrick.com; ✆ **05-59-27-45-62**).

One of the best-known shops in Pau is **La Féerie Gourmande,** 46-48 rue du Maréchal Joffre (✆ **05-59-27-69-51**). The owner, M. Francis Miot, has been voted best jam and candy maker in France several times. If you're interested in seeing where his confections are made, head for the suburbs of Pau, about 1.5km (1 mile) southeast of the center, to the residential hamlet of Uzos. Here you'll find **Musée de la Confiture** (www.francis-miot.com; ✆ **05-59-35-05-56**), where exhibits display the history of jams from medieval times to the present, as well as offering numerous workshops and tastings detailing his techniques. It's open Monday to Saturday 10am to noon and 2 to 6pm; admission is 4.60€ adults and 3€ ages 3 to 12; closed in December. It has a special price of 3€ adults, 2€ ages 3 to 12 during July and August.

Pau Nightlife

Nightlife in Pau has always centered on **Le Triangle,** an area in the town center that's flanked by the rue Emile Garet, rue Lespy, and rue Castetnau. In recent years, a few new bars along **boulevard des Pyrénées** near place Clemenceau have augmented Pau's nightlife.

Within the borders of Le Triangle, **Le Garage Bar,** at 47 rue Emile Garet (www.legaragebar.com; ✆ **05-59-83-75-17**), has been going strong since 1993. Set within an old auto repair shop, it retains many of its original industrial-looking fixtures, plus a collection of antique traffic lights, road signs, and mopeds hanging from chains in the ceiling. It's open Monday to Friday noon to 1:30am, Saturday and Sunday 3pm to 1:30am.

Near Parc Beaumont is **L'Adresse,** 20 rue des Orphelines (✆ **06-82-33-73-99**), offers tapas, cocktails, and music that goes late. Student night is every Thursday. It's open Wednesday to Saturday 6pm to 2am, with DJs from 10pm.

BAYONNE ★★

770km (477 miles) SW of Paris; 184km (114 miles) SW of Bordeaux

Bayonne is the leading port and pleasure-yacht basin of the Côte Basque, divided by the Nive and Adour rivers. A cathedral city and the capital of the Pays Basque, it's characterized by narrow streets, quays, and ramparts. Enlivening the scene are bullfights (although protests against them are on the rise in France and Spain), *pelote* (jai alai), and street dancing at annual fiestas. You may want to buy some of Bayonne's famous chocolate at one of the arcaded shops along rue du Port-Neuf, and then enjoy coffee at a cafe along place de la Liberté, the hub of town.

Essentials

17

GETTING THERE Four TGV **trains** per day link Bayonne and Paris (trip time: 5 hr., 10 min.; 95€ one-way). Nine trains per day arrive from Bordeaux (trip time: 1 hr., 50 min.; 22€ one-way). For train information and schedules, visit www.oui.sncf or call ✆ **36-35** (.40€/min.).

A **bus** service connects to Biarritz, 15 min. away. Bus no. 1 departs from Biarritz at 12-min. intervals throughout the daylight hours, depositing passengers on place de la Mairie in Bayonne; the one-way fare is 1€, and tickets can be bought on the bus. Bus service also connects Bayonne and outlying towns and villages not serviced by train. For bus information in Bayonne, call ✆ **05-59-59-04-61.**

Bayonne is near the end of the N117 roadway, easily accessible by **car** from Toulouse and other cities in the south of France. From Paris, take A10 south to Bordeaux, and then the N10 and A63 down the Atlantic coast towards Bayonne.

VISITOR INFORMATION The **Office de Tourisme** is on place des Basques (www.bayonne-tourisme.com; ✆ **05-59-46-09-00**).

SPECIAL EVENTS During the 4-day **Fête de Bayonne,** the last week in July, a frenzy of outdoor concerts and dancing fills the streets. The celebration is intense. For **free concerts** on fair-weather Thursday evenings in July and August, head to the gazebo on place de Gaulle, where styles range from jazz to traditional Basque. Contact the Office de Tourisme (see above) for more information. As of 2017, October in Bayonne sees a new street art festival. Held over 5 days, **Points de Vue** (www.pointsdevuefest.org) sees several prominent city walls given over to graffiti artists, with sculptures and live performances going on throughout the city.

Fête de Bayonne

Exploring Bayonne

Vieux Bayonne, the old town, is inside the ramparts, on the left bank of the Nive. The early-13th-century **Cathédrale Ste-Marie** (www.cathedrale-bayonne.fr; ✆ **05-59-59-17-82**) dominates this part of town on rue d'Espagne and rue des Gouverneurs. The spiny 19th-century steeples are the best-known landmarks in Bayonne. The cathedral is worth 30 min. of your time and is a good retreat on a hot day. It was begun in 1258 when Bayonne was under English rule; it fell to the French in 1451. Don't miss the gorgeous 14th-century cloisters. They're like a secret garden from the Middle Ages. The cathedral is open Monday through Sunday 8am to 12:30pm and 5pm to 6.30pm (Sunday until 8pm); admission is free.

Atelier de Chocolat de Bayonne Andrieu ★★ FACTORY TOUR
Bayonne's chocolate tradition began with the Jewish community that fled here from the Spanish Inquisition. Come to this always-popular place for an insight into history and ingredients for one of the world's most sought-after confections, followed, of course, by a tasting. Expect to spend around 1.5 hr.

7 allée de Gibéléou, Zone Artisanale Sainte-Croix. www.atelierduchocolat.fr. ✆ **05-59-55-70-23.** Entrance 6€ adults; 3€ children 4–12. July–Aug Mon–Sat 10am–6:30pm; Sept–June Mon–10am–12:30pm and 2–6pm. The chocolate makers stop work at 4pm and only work Monday to Friday.

Jardin Botanique ★★ PARK
After stocking up on information and maps at the tourist office, wander through these lovely Japanese-style gardens next door.

Allée de Tardies. ✆ **05-59-46-60-93.** Free admission. Apr 15–Oct 15 Tues–Sat 9:30am–noon and 2–6pm.

Musée Basque ★★ MUSEUM
You don't have to spend long in the Basque region to realize how proud the locals are of their culture— and quite rightly so. This is the place to find out more about the origins of the region's distinctive architecture, music, textiles, and local crafts. It's also had major internal renovations over recent years, making it a beautiful place to visit, with the exhibits clearly and carefully laid out, and plenty of interactive displays.

37 quai des Corsaires. www.musee-basque.com. ✆ **05-59-59-08-98.** Admission 7.50€ adults; free for visitors 26 and under and for all first Sun of each month. July–Aug Wed 10am–9:30pm, Thurs–Tues 10am–6:30pm; Sept–June Tues–Sun 10am–6pm.

Musée Bonnat-Helleu ★★ MUSEUM
The city's modern art museum has been closed for renovations since 2011 and is due to open in 2019 with more than double the current floor space—and poised to transform the art scene in the city.

5 rue Jacques Lafitte. http://mbh.bayonne.fr. ✆ **05-59-55-70-23.** See website for opening details.

Plaine d'Ansot et Musée d'Histoire Naturelle ★★ MUSEUM
Set in a conservation area just outside of the city, this is the only museum of its kind in France. You can head off along the walking and bike paths, all laid out around lakes, open spaces and rivers over 89 hectares (220 acres) of parkland. The Maison Barthe is the official museum space set at the entrance to the park, with information on activities, as well as

temporary exhibits. A traditional Natural History museum forms a separate building.

Plaine d'Ansot. www.ansot.bayonne.fr. ℰ **05-59-42-22-61.** Free admission. Maison Barthe mid-Apr to mid-Oct Tues–Sun 10:30am–12.30pm and 1:30–6pm, rest of year 1:30–5pm; Museum Tues–Sun 10:30am–12.30pm and 1:30pm–6pm (Thurs during term time for school groups only); rest of park 9am–7pm. Rest of the year, Museum Mon–Fri 1:30pm–5pm and Sat–Sun 11am–12:30pm; park Mon–Fri 9am–5:30pm and Sat–Sun from 9:30am. Closed May 1, 1 week at Christmas, 1 week in Jan, 1 week during Fête de Bayonne, last week of July.

Where to Stay

Hotel les Basse Pyrénées ★ Fully (and beautifully) renovated in 2015, this is a lovely hotel on the Vauban ramparts, a few minutes from the cathedral and the pedestrianized old town. Two suites (at a higher price) are in the stone tower, and an excellent restaurant offers local food. The cosy bar offers a good range of wines also.

1 pl. des Victoires. www.hotel-bassespyrenees-bayonne.com. ℰ **05-25-70-88-00.** 27 units. 70€–300€ double. Parking 10€. **Amenities:** Restaurant; bar; room service; free Wi-Fi.

La Villa Bayonne ★★ If you can manage to get a room here, you'll enjoy a dreamy setting and the owners' personal touch. On a hill overlooking the River Nive, 900m (.25 mile) from the town center, this lovely 1905 villa, surrounded by an Italianate garden, offers a peaceful stay. The rooms are decorated in muted colors and feel fairly traditional but are comfortable and well-maintained.

12 Chemin de Jacquette. www.bayonnne-hotel-lavilla.com. ℰ **05-59-03-01-20.** 10 units. 60€–150€ double. Free parking. **Amenities**: Free Wi-Fi.

Where to Eat

Bistro Itsaki ★ BASQUE   Head to this relaxed, contemporary-styled bistro for delicious local Basque products matched to a wide array of wines from around the world. The menu changes regularly, depending on the season and what the chef found in the market that morning. The chef can also cater to gluten free diners but do ask ahead of time.

43 quai Amiral Jaureguiberry. www.lebistrotitsaski.com. ℰ **05-59-46-13-96.** Main course 16.50€–20€; fixed-price menu 15€–25€. Thurs–Sun noon–2pm; and 7–9:30pm.

La Table de Pottoka ★★ BASQUE   Just down the road from Bistro Itsaki but an entirely different feeling, this utterly gorgeous restaurant, that is worth the travel to Bayonne alone. Sebastien Gravé presides over seasonal, local ingredients, beautifully and imaginatively presented. Gravé also has a Paris restaurant.

21 Quai Amiral Dubourdieu. http://pottoka.fr. ℰ **05-59-46-14-94.** Main course 22€; fixed-price menu 39€; tasting menu 50€. Tues–Sun noon–2:30pm and 7:30–10:30pm.

Shopping

Most of Bayonne's specialty shops and boutiques lie inside the ramparts of the old town, Grand Bayonne. The pedestrian streets of **rue Port Neuf** (aptly nicknamed the "street of chocolate shops"), **rue Victor-Hugo,** and **rue de la Salié** are major shopping destinations. For antiques, walk along the **rue des Faures** and the edges of **place Montaut,** behind the cathedral. Most of the modern shops and French chain stores are on **rue Thiers** and **quai de la Nive,** outside the old town. Visit the **Maison Jean Vier** shop, carrefour Cinq Cantons (www.jean-vier.com; ✆ **05-59-51-33-24**), to get your Basque bathroom, kitchen, and bed linens. Do not miss a visit to **Cazenave,** 19 rue Port Neuf (www.chocolats-bayonne-cazenave.fr; ✆ **05-59-59-03-16**), pretty much the only place left that still works directly with cacao in its raw form and specializes in turning it into *chocolats de Bayonne.* Stop in the tearoom here for a warm chocolate mousse.

The accessories of one Basque tradition have become something of a fine art. In olden days, the *makhila* was used as a walking stick, a cudgel, or—when equipped with a hidden blade—a knife. Today carved *makhilas* are sold as collectors' items and souvenirs. For safety's sake, they almost never come with a blade. One of the best outlets in town is **Makilas-Leoncini,** 37 rue Vieille Boucherie (✆ **05-59-59-18-20**). Another famous product of the Basque country is *jambon de Bayonne,* cured hams, which taste best shaved into paper-thin slices and consumed with one of the region's heady red wines. An establishment that prepares and sells these hams is **Saloir et Séchoire à Jambon Pierre Ibaialde,** 41 rue des Cordeliers (www.pierre-ibaialde.com; ✆ **05-59-25-65-30**), where they are sold either whole or in thin slices. Also available is an impressive roster of sausages, pâtés, and terrines.

Bayonne Nightlife

Nightlife centers on the neighborhood known as Petit Bayonne, the town's historic core. **Rue des Tonneliers, rue Pannecau,** and **rue des Cordeliers** are the liveliest areas after dark. **Le Caveau des Augustin,** 7 rue des Augustins, is a good choice for live music and jam sessions, and its vaulted stone cellars allow excellent acoustics (www.lecaveaudesaugustins.com; ✆ **05-59-25-69-76**). Good choice of tapas and wine is also on offer. For an equally interesting taste of local color, with slightly more traditional music, head to **Le Cabaret La Luna Negra,** also on rue des Augustins (www.lunanegra.fr; ✆ **05-59-25-78-05**). The 6€-to-10€ cover charge includes cabaret, jazz, or blues performances and popular French songs.

BIARRITZ ★★★

779km (483 miles) SW of Paris; 193km (120 miles) SW of Bordeaux

One of the world's most famous seaside resorts, Biarritz was once a fishing village. Empress Eugénie and her husband, Napoleon III, put it on the map and started a constant stream of royal visitors. In the 1930s, the Prince of Wales (before and after his brief reign as Edward VIII) and Wallis Simpson did much to make Biarritz more fashionable as they headed south with these instructions: "Chill the champagne, pack the pearls, and tune up the Bugatti." Although those legendary days are long gone, the resort is still fashionable and has become France's surf capital, so expect rows of surf shops and snack bars along the beach front.

Essentials

GETTING THERE More than 20 **trains** arrive daily from Bayonne (trip time: 10 min.), which has rail links with Paris and other cities in the south of France. The one-way fare is 2.90€. The rail station is 3km (1.75 miles) south of the town center, in La Négresse. For information, www.oui.sncf or call ✆ **36-35** (.40€/min.). Bus no. 2 carries passengers from the station to the center of Biarritz; the one-way fare is 1€. You can also take a cab for around 15€ to 20€. If you're **driving,** Biarritz is at the end of the N117 roadway, the major thoroughfare for the Basque country. From Paris, take A10 south to Vierzon, and then N20 south to Limoges. Continue on N21 south to Tarbes, and then head west on N117.

VISITOR INFORMATION The **Office de Tourisme** is on square d'Ixelles (www.biarritz.fr; ✆ **05-59-22-37-10**).

SPECIAL EVENTS If you're in town in mid-September, check out the modern dance and ballet performances during the 9-day festival **Le Temps d'Aimer** (www.letempsdaimer.com). Tickets cost 90€ for admission to six performances, with reduced rates for children, students, and families. For reservations and ticket sales for the festival, contact the tourist office above. At the end of September, the **Festival Biarritz Amérique Latine** (www.festivaldebiarritz.com) is the world's most important Latin American film festival. It's much more laid-back than Cannes—you'll find yourself rubbing shoulders or even doing the salsa with top Latin directors in the casino, where most events are held. Entry to the whole week's films is 65€, and single-film entry is 6.50€.

Biarritz is the surfing capital of France, and each year dozens of competitions are held through the summer months, usually centered on the waves offshore from La Plage de la Côte Basque. For more information, contact the tourist office. Biarritz also has 10 golf courses within a short drive of the town. A good practice setting is the **Center d'Entraînement d'Ilbarritz-Bidart,** av. du Château, Bidart 64210 (www.golfilbarritz. com; ✆ **05-59-43-81-30**); you can play nine holes for 25€ to 38€. The **Biarritz Cup** is a nationwide competition attended by mostly French golfers in the third week in July at the Golf du Phare, av. Edith-Cavell (www.biarritz-cup.com; ✆ **05-59-03-41-08**). Information on both festivals is available from the tourist office.

Exploring Biarritz

Eglise St-Martin, rue St-Martin (✆ **05-59-23-08-36**), is one of the few vestiges of the port's early boom days. In the 12th century, Biarritz grew prosperous as a whaling center. The mammals' departure from the Bay of Biscay marked a decline in the port's fortunes. The church dates from the 1100s and was restored in 1541 with a flamboyant Gothic chancel. It's in the town center between two of Biarritz's major arteries, rue d'Espagne and avenue de Gramont, and is open daily 8am to 7pm. Admission is free.

Biarritz's turning point came with the arrival of Queen Hortense, who spent lazy summers here with her two daughters. One of them, Eugénie, married Napoleon III in 1853 and prevailed on him to visit Biarritz the next year. The emperor fell under its spell and ordered the construction of the **Hôtel du Palais.** The hotel remains the town's most enduring landmarks. When Biarritz's star started to wane in the 1950s, the municipality showed a great deal of foresight in buying the hotel and the equally monumental casino, the essence of Biarritz's fading glamour. In a commanding spot on Grande Plage, the hotel is worth a visit even if you're not a guest. Grab a drink in one of the bars or even head over for breakfast after you have stayed somewhere a little less pricey.

Across from the Hôtel du Palais, the **Eglise Orthodoxe Russe,** 8 av. de l'Impératrice (✆ **05-59-24-16-74**), was built in 1892 so that wintering Russian aristocrats could worship when they weren't enjoying champagne, caviar, and Basque prostitutes. It's noted for its gilded dome, the interior of which is the color of a blue sky on a sunny day. It can be visited only on weekends: Saturday 3 to 6pm and Sunday 4 to 7pm. After you pass the Hôtel du Palais, the walkway widens into **quai de la Grande Plage,** Biarritz's principal promenade. This walkway continues to the opposite end of the resort, where a final belvedere opens onto the southernmost stretch of beach. This whole walk takes about 3 hr. At the southern edge of Grande Plage, steps will take you to **place Ste-Eugénie,** Biarritz's most gracious old square. Right below place Ste-Eugénie is the colorful **Port des Pêcheurs** (fishers' port). Crowded with fishing boats, it has old wooden houses and shacks backed up against a cliff, along with small harborfront restaurants and cafes.

The rocky **plateau de l'Atalaye** forms one side of the Port des Pêcheurs. Carved on orders of Napoleon III, a tunnel leads from the plateau to an esplanade. Here a footbridge stretches over the sea to a rocky islet that takes its name, **Rocher de la Vierge (Rock of the Virgin),** from the statue crowning it. Alexandre-Gustave Eiffel (designer of the tower) directed construction of the footbridge. The walk out onto the edge of the rock, with crashing surf on both sides, is the most dramatic in Biarritz. You can see all the way to the mountains of the Spanish Basque country, far to the south.

Here you can visit the **Musée de la Mer,** 14 plateau de l'Atalaye (www.museedelamer.com; ✆ **05-59-22-75-40**), which has recently doubled its aquarium space from 3,500-sq. m (37,673 sq. ft.) to 7,000-sq. m

(75,347 sq. ft.). The seals steal the show at their daily 10:30am and 5pm feedings, while the sharks follow suit on Monday, Wednesday, Friday, and Saturdays at 2:30pm during school holidays only. Admission is 14.90€ adults, 11.90€ students, 10.50€ children 4 to 12, and free for children 3 and under. It's open in July and August daily 9:30am to midnight, April to June, September, and October daily 9:30am to 8pm, and November to March 9:30am to 7pm. Don't miss the other space in Biarritz dedicated to the sea: the **Cité de L'Océan,** just around the corner at 1 av. de la Plage (www.citedelocean.com; © **05-59-22-75-40**). A spectacularly designed building that—of course—overlooks the Atlantic and explains pretty much everything you might want to know about the seas and oceans of the world. You can even take a virtual surfing class. Admission is 12.50€ adults, 8.50€ children ages 6 to 12. Or combine both the aquarium and the Cité de l'Océan for 22.50€ adults, 13.90€ children 6 to 12, and 17.90€ students.

A Day at the Beach

Along the seafront facing the Casino is the **Grande Plage.** During the Belle Epoque, this was where Victorian ladies promenaded under parasols and wide-brimmed veiled hats. Today's bathers are more likely to be in wetsuits or surfy combos.

The Grande Plage in Biarritz

Promenade du Bord de Mer, along the coast within the city limits, is still a major attraction. The paths are often carved into cliffs, and sections have been designed as rock gardens with flowers, turning the area into a public park. From here, you can head north to Pointe St-Martin, where you'll find more gardens and a staircase (look for the sign descente de l'ocean) leading you to allée Winston-Churchill, a paved path going along Plage Miramar.

La Perspective de la Côte des Basques, a walk that goes up to another plateau, leads to one of the wildest beaches in France: Plage de la Côte des Basques, with breakers crashing at the base of the cliffs. This is where serious surfers head. It's easy to hire a surfboard for a few hours or to get a lesson, but if you don't want to surf yourself, find a cafe and enjoy a few hours people watching.

If you like calmer beaches, the safest is the small, horseshoe-shaped Plage du Port-Vieux, along the path from plateau de l'Atalaye. Its tranquil waters, protected by rocks, make it a favorite with families.

Where to Stay

Biarritz has a lot of holiday rentals and summer houses, as well as options available through AirBnB, so it's always worth comparing prices.

Le Beaumanoir ★★★   It is hard not to love this converted traditional Basque house set in around 1.25 hectares (around 3 acres) of grounds just over a mile from the Grande Plage in downtown Biarritz. Views over the Atlantic coast and surrounding countryside, a lovely snug bar, marble bathrooms, crystal chandeliers—this is Baroque-style luxury delivered with a tongue-in-cheek charm. You can even indulge in a free Rolls Royce transfer from the airport.

10 av. de Tamamès. www.lebeaumanoir.com. ☎ **05-59-24-89-29.** 8 units. 250€–500€ double; from 750€ suite. Closed Jan to mid-April. Free parking. **Amenities:** Bar; spa; outdoor pool; free Wi-Fi.

Hotel de Silhouette ★★   The Les Halles district of Biarritz is great for eating and drinking, making this hotel a particularly good choice. Fully restored, this is actually one of the oldest buildings in the city, but it manages to pull off that difficult trick of retaining period features while delivering a luxury, contemporary feel. It is just a few minutes to the beach.

30 rue Gambetta, Quartier des Halles. www.hotel-silhouette-biarritz.com. ☎ **05-59-24-93-82.** 20 units. 102€–340€ double. Parking 15€. **Amenities:** Restaurant; bar room service; free Wi-Fi.

Maison Garnier ★   A good value and well-located hotel converted from a spacious 1870s villa. The hotel does not offer suites, but the largest room is 35 sq. m (376 sq. ft.) and feels beautifully airy. Though there is no parking, you can easily get around downtown on foot, so this is handy if you are traveling without a car.

1 av. de l'Impératrice. www.hotel-biarritz.com. ☎ **05-59-01-60-70.** 7 units. 70€–185€ double. Breakfast 13€. **Amenities:** Free Wi-Fi.

Where to Eat

Chez Albert ★★ BASQUE/FRENCH   It's fun just to wander down to the Port des Pêcheurs, just a little bit further along the promenade from the Casino, where you'll find a number of different restaurants offering fresh seafood. This is one of the classics, with a large terrace and big, well-spaced dining room. It gets busy so book ahead.

51 allée Port des Pêcheurs. ℂ **05-59-24-43-84.** Main course 15€–40€ each; fixed-price menu 40€–72€. Thurs–Tues 12:15–2pm and 7:30–10pm; July and Aug daily.

Saline Ceviche Bar ★ SOUTH AMERICAN   You're going to love this place for its laid-back beach vibe and its brilliant food. Thankfully, it is in a particularly good spot along rue Gambetta where you can find dozens of tiny restaurants with their own atmosphere, so don't worry too much if you haven't booked ahead. As the name suggests, the specialty is super fresh ceviche and poke dishes made with local fish. True to their Peruvian roots, you can even get a Pisco sour.

62 rue Gambetta. ℂ **05-59-443-65-98.** Main course 12€–16€; fixed-price lunch 15€. Tues–Sat noon–2:30pm and two seatings in the evening starting at 7:30 and 10pm. Daily July and Aug. Closed 2 weeks Nov.

Shopping

The major boutiques, with all the big designer names from Paris, are on **place Clemenceau** in the heart of Biarritz. From this square, fan out to **rue Gambetta, rue Mazagran, avenue Victor-Hugo, avenue Edouard-VII, avenue du Maréchal-Foch,** and **avenue de Verdun.** Look for the exceptional Biarritz chocolates and confections, and textiles from the Basque country.

The finest chocolatiers are **Pariès,** 1 pl. Bellevue (www.paries.fr; ℂ **05-59-22-07-52**), where you can choose from seven kinds of *tourons* (nougats), ranging from raspberry to coffee; and **Henriet,** pl. Clemenceau (www.chocolaterie-henriet.com; ℂ **05-59-24-24-15**), where the house specialty is *rochers de Biarritz* (morsels of candied orange peel and roasted almonds covered in dark chocolate). At the other end of the gastronomic spectrum, try **Mille et Un Fromages,** 8 rue Victor Hugo (ℂ **05-59-24-06-87**), specializing in, as the name suggests, French cheeses, as well as a host of hearty wines to accompany them.

Virtually every souvenir shop and department store in the region sells **espadrilles,** the canvas-topped, rope-bottomed slippers which originate from the Pyrénées. A simple off-the-shelf model begins at around 15€, and made-to-order versions (special sizes and colors) rarely top 70€.

Biarritz Nightlife

Start the night with a stroll around **Port des Pêcheurs,** an ideal spot for people-watching, with its sport fishermen, restaurants, and fascinating crowds. Especially lively will be the area around Les Halles market, or in a wine bar like **L'Art Dit Vin,** 15 av. de Verdun (© **05-59-23-73-74**). Closing times are flexible here—owner Laurent Lacouture says, "if there's a crowd, I won't close up!" Tapas-style food is on offer also, but the real draw is the 300-strong wine list at extremely good prices, with a particular focus on Spain. Another perfect mid- to late-evening hangout is **The Beach House,** a little further up the road in Anglet but worth the trip. At 26 av. des Dauphins (http://beachhouseanglet.com; © **05-59-15-27-17**), it is a bar and restaurant right on the beach. It is open over April to December, but at its height in July and August the aperitifs start at 6pm and things can go pretty late.

Fortunes have been made and lost at **Le Casino Municipal,** 1 av. Edouard-VII (© **05-59-22-37-08**). The less formal section, containing only slot machines, is open daily 10am to 3am (Sat until 4am). Entrance is free, no ID is required, and there's no dress code. The more elegant section (for *les jeux de table,* or table games) is open Sunday to Thursday 8pm to 3am, Friday and Saturday 8pm to 4am. This section requires a passport or photo ID and more formal attire (no shorts of flip-flops).

You'll find a few good nightclubs in Biarritz, including **Le Caveau,** 4 rue Gambetta (www.caveau-biarritz.com; © **05-59-24-16-17**), where a well-dressed and attractive crowd of gay and straight people mingle. **Le Carré Coast,** 21 av. Edouard VII (www.lecarrecoast.com; © **05-59-24-64-64**), is open June to September nightly 7:30pm and 4am, but closed Sunday to Wednesday the rest of the year. It combines a view of the sea, an outdoor terrace, a minimalist decor with lots of burnished steel, and a dance floor. Entrance is free, but a whiskey with soda begins at around 10€.

ST-JEAN-DE-LUZ ★★

791km (490 miles) SW of Paris; 15km (9.25 miles) S of Biarritz

This tuna-fishing port and beach resort is ideal for a seaside vacation. St-Jean-de-Luz lies at the mouth of the Nivelle, opening onto the Bay of Biscay, with the Pyrénées in the background. Tourists have been flocking here since the 1920s, when H. G. Wells, Aldous Huxley, and friends "discovered" the town.

Essentials

GETTING THERE   Twenty-five daily **trains** arrive from Biarritz (trip time: 11 min.; from 3.40€ one-way), and seven per day arrive from Paris (trip time: 5 hr., 40 min.; from 95€ one-way). For train information and schedules, visit www.oui.sncf or call © **36-35** (.40€/min.). **Buses** pulling into town from other parts of the Basque country arrive at the Gare Routière (© **05-59-26-06-99**), in front of the railway station. St-Jean-de-Luz is a short **drive** from Biarritz along N10 south.

VISITOR INFORMATION   The **Office de Tourisme** is on 20 bd. Victor Hugo (www.saint-jean-de-luz.com; © **05-59-26-03-16**).

St-Jean-de-Luz

SPECIAL EVENTS In July and August on Wednesday after 10:30pm and Sunday after 10:30pm, people pile into place Louis-XIV to take part in **Toro de Fuego,** a celebration of the bull. Revelers take to the streets to dance and watch fireworks. The highlight of the festivities is a snorting papier-mâché bull carried around place Louis-XIV. During the second half of June, the city celebrates the **Festival of St-Jean** *(Fêtes Patronales de la Saint Jean)* with concerts and a series of food kiosks along the harborfront. For four days during the first half of October, the **Festival International du Film** (www.fifsaintjeandeluz.com; ℂ **05-59-85-80-81**), has grown more ambitious over recent years. For information about festivals, contact the Office de Tourisme (see above).

Fun on & off the Beach

The major draw here is the gracefully curving stretch of the white-sand **La Grande Plage St-Jean-de-Luz;** it's one of the best beaches in France and, consequently, very crowded in July and August. The beach lies in a half-moon-shaped bay between the ocean and the source of the Nivelle River. Lifeguards are on-duty daily in July and August from 11am to 7:30pm and until 7pm in June and September. You can also hire parasols and deck chairs. All of St-Jean-de-Luz's other beaches have lifeguards from 11am to 7pm in July and August only.

St-Jean-de-Luz is also a **working port,** where garishly painted fishing boats jut right up to the shopping streets. Eating seafood recently plucked from the sea is one of the reasons to visit, especially when Basque chefs transform the big catch into intriguing platters. This port's many narrow streets flanked by old houses are great for strolling. For one of the best views, climb the **Colline de Saint-Barbe,** a large hill at one end of the waterfront. It has a walking path and lovely views over the city.

Exploring St-Jean-de-Luz

In the town's principal church, the 13th-century **Eglise St-Jean-Baptiste** ★★, at the corner of rue Gambetta and rue Garat (ℂ **05-59-26-08-81**), Louis XIV and the Spanish Infanta, Marie-Thérèse, were married in 1660. The interior is stunning: Look out for the altar with its statue-studded gilded *retable* (altarpiece). The interior is open to visitors Monday to Saturday 9am to noon and 2 to 6pm, and Sunday 3 to 6:30pm.

Two houses are associated with the couple. **La Maison Louis XIV,** place Louis XIV (www.maison-louis-xiv.fr; ℭ **05-59-26-27-58**), was the scene of the royal wedding night. Built of chiseled gray stone between 1644 and 1648 beside the port, it is richly furnished with antiques and mementos. It's open daily for guided tours in July and August at 10:30am and 12:30, 2:30, and 6:30pm; and from April to June and September to October at 11, 3, and 4pm. Entrance is 6.50€. **La Maison de l'Infante,** 1 rue de l'Infante (ℭ **05-59-26-36-82**), is where the Infanta lived at the time of her marriage. It was designed and built by wealthy weapons merchant Johannot de Haraneder. Its pink façade, made from bricks and local stones, evokes an Italian palazzo. Inside is a "grand" reception room with a 17th-century fireplace and ceiling beams richly adorned and painted. It is open June to October 15, and October 25 to November 11, Tuesday to Saturday from 11am to 12:30pm and 2:30 to 6:30pm, and Sunday and Monday from 2:30 to 6:30pm. Entrance is 2.50€.

Where to Stay

A wide range of options are available here, from the **Camping Ferme Erromardie** on the Erromardie breach, 40 Erromardie (www.camping-erromardie.com; ℭ **05-59-26-34-26**) with its cabins and lodges as well as pitching spots, to a number of good AirBnB listings.

Le Casa Valerie ★   At this traditional Basque house overlooking the port of Saint Jean de Luz, you get exposed stone walls and plenty of quiet nooks and crannies to relax. The house has just two guest rooms so book ahead (and prices can be slightly cheaper if you ask for breakfast to not be included).

16 rue Pocalette. http://lacasadevalerie.com. ℭ **05-59-26-35-36.** 2 units. 130€–170€ double. Breakfast included. **Amenities:** Free Wi-Fi.

La Réserve ★★   Palm trees, wide lawns, and blue skies (more often than not) all set off the lovely white walls and tiled roof of this hotel, complete with a gorgeous view of the ocean. The newly renovated Residence has studios and apartments for rent, with terraces overlooking the Atlantic which is a good option for larger families, but plenty of normal hotel rooms and suites are available as well. The beaches of St. Jean de Luz are accessible by a (fairly steep) coastal path.

1 rue Gaëtan de Bernoville. http://hotel-lareserve.com. ℭ **05-59-51-32-00.** 47 units hotel, 44 Residence units. Closed Nov–Mar. 118€–280€ double; 325€–578€ suite; 135€–586€ Residence apartments from two to six people. Free parking. **Amenities:** Restaurant; bar; spa; tennis court; free Wi-Fi.

Where to Eat

Chez Kako ★ BASQUE   An oldie but a goodie. This is a St-Jean-de-Luz institution but manages to keep on delivering, so we keep on recommending. It's well located in Les Halles also, so even if every table here is

exploring BASQUE VILLAGES

The entire Basque region is dotted with atmospheric, beautifully-preserved villages. From Saint-Jean-de-Luz, the most easily reached is **Guéthary,** 3km (1.9 miles) away either on the main N10 road to Biarritz, or along the pretty coastal backroads. A traditional fishing village which has become something of a gourmet center and artistic refuge, the old town is laid out around the lovely church and fishing port, and a walk takes you along the headland, past some dramatic coves. Heading the other way from Saint-Jean-de-Luz, along the D932 up into the hills of the Pyrénées, both **Saint-Jean-Pied-de-Port** and **Espelette** are unmissable. They epitomize the traditional Basque village—classic half-timbered houses in red, white, and green, shops offering local cheeses and hams, Irouléguy wines, and other specialties, all with the mountains rising dramatically behind. Espelette is known for its tiny red peppers, often seen strung outside the houses around the main square like cheerful garlands, while Saint-Jean-Pied-de-Port has a 17th century citadel along banks of the pretty river Nive.

Saint-Jean-Pied-de-Port on the Camino de Santiago

full (and that happens fairly often), plenty of other places stacked with the best fresh Basque produce are just around the corner. Take your pick of the choice selection of wines and ciders also.

18 rue du Maréchal Harispe at the pl. des Halles. www.saint-jean-de-luz.com/1098-kako-etxea. ℂ **05-59-85-10-70.** Main course 18€–52€; fixed-price menu 37€. Tues–Sat noon–2:15pm and 7:30–10pm (Fri–Sat until 11pm). Open Mon in summer.

La Guingette d'Erromardie ★ BASQUE   Follow the surfing crowd to this lunch spot that turns into a tapas and cocktail bar at night. You'll get good fresh seafood, with dishes like oysters, mussels, and breaded calamari, topped off by amazing views and always a musical backdrop, sometimes live bands.

Plage Erromardie. ℭ **05-59-43-97-66.** Main course 10€–25€. Wed–Sun noon until late. Closed Nov–Mar.

Ostalamer ★ BASQUE/FRENCH   Amazing views and brilliant food make this place hard to beat. Just outside town overlooking Lafitenia beach, the best thing to order here is shellfish or fresh fish and lots of it. The *chipirones à la plancha,* one of the most traditional Basque ways of serving squid, is hard to beat. This place also has a sister restaurant-farm-BnB called **Ostalapia** (www.ostalapia.fr) a little further into the Pyrénées mountains

160 route des Plages. ℭ **05-59-85-84-71.** Main course 22€–65€. Daily noon–2:30pm and 7:30–10pm. Closed Jan.

Shopping

You'll find the best shopping along pedestrian **rue Gambetta** and around the Eglise St-Jean-de-Luz. You can find anything here from clothes and leather handbags to books and chocolates, dishes and linens.

You can also ramble around the port, sip pastis in a harborfront cafe, and debate the virtues of the beret. Then scout out **Maison Adam,** 49 rue Gambetta (www.macarons-adam.com; ℭ **05-59-26-03-54**), which has sold almond-based confections from this boutique since 1660. For quality tablecloths, throws, bedding, and other gorgeous linen, the traditional **Mendiburutegia Tissus,** 3 rue Renau-d'Elissagaray (http://decotextile basque.com; ℭ **05-59-26-02-63**), is hard to beat.

St-Jean-De-Luz Nightlife

Start by taking a walk along the promenade to watch the sunset. Around place Louis-XIV, you'll find a hotbed of activity at the cafes and bars. If you're here over the summer, head to **Chez Renauld,** 4 bd. Victor Hugo (ℭ **05-59-51-31-30**), a pop-up bar from June to October. There might not be too many more seasons here for this fun bar, as there are plans to develop the spot. Another summer pop-up that is almost certain to stick around a little longer is **Le Middle,** from chef Jean-Pascal Lacoste, up on Chemin de la Digue, Pointe Sainte Barbe (ℭ **06-24-48-11-83**). DJs or live music most evenings over the summer provide the backdrop to incredible views over the bay. Excellent food is available during the day, but this is pretty much the perfect spot as the sun goes down.

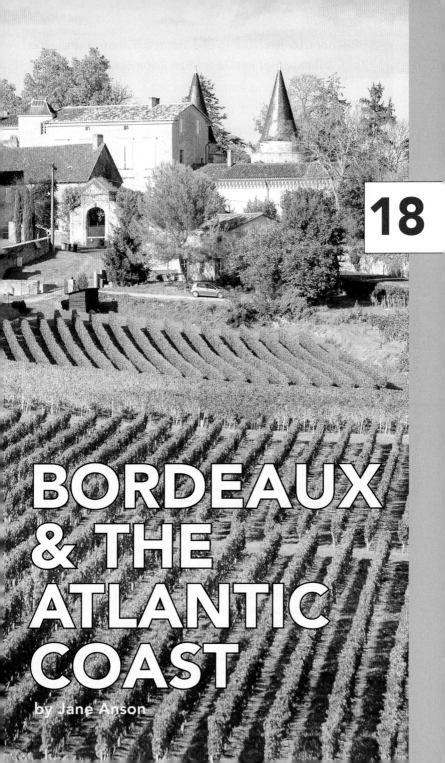

BORDEAUX & THE ATLANTIC COAST

by Jane Anson

Ffrom La Rochelle to the Bordeaux wine district, the southwest of France is often just a quick stopover for visitors driving from Paris to Spain. However, this area is well worth a more in-depth visit for its Atlantic beaches, medieval and Renaissance ruins, Romanesque and Gothic churches, vineyards, and the increasingly dynamic city of Bordeaux. A new high-speed rail link from Paris to Bordeaux has cut travel times down to this corner of France substantially.

This intriguing region merits a detour inland to sample cognac in Cognac and to visit nearby art cities such as Poitiers and Angoulême. If you can manage it, allow a week here—enough time to sample the wine, savor the cuisine, and see some of the sights.

BORDEAUX ★★★

578km (358 miles) SW of Paris; 549km (340 miles) W of Lyon

No longer called *La Belle Endormie* ("Sleeping Beauty"), today Bordeaux is one of the most vibrant cities in France, with property prices overtaking Lyon and regularly listed as the city that most French people would like to move to. Its renaissance started around 15 years ago, coinciding with the arrival of mayor Alain Juppé. First the **historic city center** was cleaned up, revealing the splendors of its harmonious 18th-century architecture. Then a sleek tramway (streetcar) system was installed, and cars were banished from most of the historic center. Finally, the **quays of the Garonne River** were given an extensive overhaul and are now lined with public gardens, fountains, and playgrounds. The city has reconnected with the river, as best symbolized by the stunning 18th-century **place de la Bourse,** which opens directly on the banks and is now scrubbed down and bedecked with a "water mirror," a long, shallow fountain that you can walk and splash around in on sunny days.

As you move away from the center, elegant streets give way to narrow cobbled streets, ancient churches, and a more youthful, funky Bordeaux. Home to 87,000 students, bringing the average age of the population down sharply when class is in session, they fuel a lively nightlife scene. The recent urban overhaul has bled into former working-class neighborhoods like **Chartrons,** where you can find galleries, bars, and restaurants.

PREVIOUS PAGE: **Vineyards of St-Emilion**

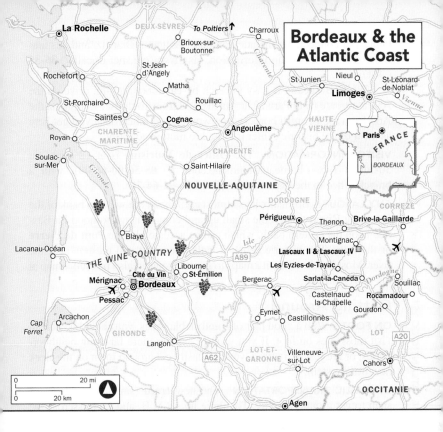

Bordeaux & the Atlantic Coast

Bordeaux, of course, is also a wine capital. Not only does it make a great base for exploring **thousands of wine estates,** you can also taste many of the region's wares right here, particularly if you stop in at the **Ecole du Vin** (p. 727) or at the **Cité du Vin** (p. 722), or one of the dozens of wine bars that have opened in recent years.

Essentials

ARRIVING Bordeaux–Mérignac **airport** (www.bordeaux.aeroport.fr; ℂ 05-56-34-50-50 for flight information) is 15km (9.25 miles) west of the city in Mérignac, and as of March 2018 is one of easyJet's French hubs, increasing the number of flights to here from around Europe. A **shuttle bus** (Jet'Bus) runs from the airport to the train station every 30 min. (trip time: 55 min.). The one-way trip is 8€ adults, 7€ for passengers 25 and under, free children under 5. A **taxi** (ℂ 05-56-96-00-34) from the airport to the train station costs about 45€.

Some 15 to 30 high-speed TGV **trains** arrive from Paris each day; the trip takes 2 hr., 5 min. with the new high-speed link and a one-way fare is 77€ to 94€, although cheaper fares exist if you are booking in advance.

Other rail connections include Toulouse, Avignon, Biarritz, and destinations in Spain. For train information, visit www.oui.sncf or call © **36-35** (.40€/min.).

While Bordeaux is easy to reach by **car** (about a 6-hr. drive on the A10 autoroute from Paris; 2 hr. via the A62 from Toulouse; 15 min. on the A63 from the Spanish border), you won't use it much once you get here as most of the historic center is closed to motorized traffic.

VISITOR INFORMATION The **Office de Tourisme** is at 12 cours du 30-Juillet (www.bordeaux-tourisme.com; © **05-56-00-66-00**), with a branch office in the Gare St-Jean (© **05-56-91-64-70**).

CITY LAYOUT Bordeaux lays almost entirely on the western bank of the **Garonne River,** though the small up-and-coming neighborhood La Bastide is on the eastern bank, which can be accessed by the **Pont de Pierre** or the ferry. The historic center is rather compact and clusters near the river. Most hotels offer city maps to guests; you can also pick up a map at the tourist office.

Getting Around

ON FOOT With a good pair of comfortable shoes, you should be able to visit most sites on foot. If you want to explore more far-flung neighborhoods, or are just plain tired, you can easily get around town on the sleek new tram system.

BY PUBLIC TRANSPORTATION The new **tram** (streetcar) makes it a snap to get around the city. The three lines (A, B, and C) crisscross the town; line D is due to open in 2019. The tram runs daily from 5am to 1am. Tickets (called "Tickarte") are good on the tram, the **city bus,** and the **ferry** that crosses the river, and cost 1.60€, transfers included during a 1-hr. period. You can get a 5-ticket card for 6.70€, a 10-ticket card for 12.90€, as well as 1-day pass for 4.60€ and a 7-day pass for 13.40€. You can buy tickets at the tram stops or at the Transport Bordeaux Métropole (TBM) outlets at place Quinconces, Gare St. Jean or place Gambetta, or online at www.infotbm.com. Weekly passes are sold in numerous *tabacs* across the city. Don't forget to validate your ticket once you are on board; failure to do so can result in a fine. For information, maps, and a phone app, visit www.infotbc.com or call © **05-57-57-88-88. Bicycles** for hire by the hour or day are available for pick up from 174 stations around the city (www.infotbm.com/en/bicycles-vcub).

BY TAXI As mentioned above, parts of the city center are car-free, so taxis are only practical for longer distances. You must hail a taxi from a taxi stand, which can be found at the place Gambetta, the Grand Théâtre, the Hôtel de Ville, and the place de la Victoire. Or call **Taxi-Tele** at © **05-56-96-00-34.** Uber is also an option and, since traditional taxis are relatively expensive, can save a lot of money.

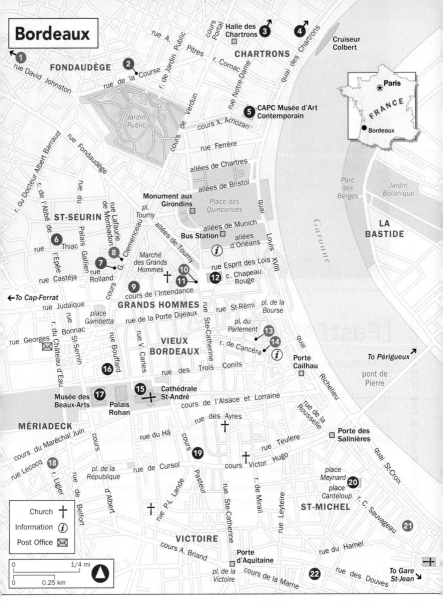

Bordeaux

FONDAUDÈGE

rue David Johnston

rue A.
cours Portal

Halle des
Chartrons **3**

4

Cruiseur
Colbert

rue de la Course
rue de Verdun
r. de Jardin Public
Pitres
r. Cornac
r. Notre-Dame
quai des Chartrons

CHARTRONS

2

1

Jardin
Public

cours X. Arnozan

CAPC Musée d'Art
Contemporain **5**

rue Ferrère

allées de Chartres

allées de Bristol

ST-SEURIN

rue Fondaudège
r. du Docteur Albert Barraud
rue de l'Abbé de
Palais Gallien
rue
l'Épée
rue Castéja
rue du
rue Lafaurie
de Monbadon
Clemenceau
G.
rue
Rolland
cours

6 Thiac

8

Monument aux
Girondins
pl.
Tourny

Place des
Quinconces

allées de Tourny

Marché
des Grands
Hommes

7

9

10

11

allées de Munich

allées
d'Orléans

Bus Station

(i)

rue Esprit des Lois
c. Chapeau
Rouge

12

←To Cap-Ferrat

rue Judaïque

GRANDS HOMMES

cours de l'Intendance

place
Gambetta
rue de la Porte Dijeaux

rue St-Rémi

pl. de la
Bourse

Parc
des
Bèrges

Jardin
Botanique

LA
BASTIDE

Garonne

rue Georges
r. du Château d'Eau
rue de Bonnac
rue St-Sernin
rue Boufard
rue V. Carles
rue Ste-Catherine

VIEUX
BORDEAUX

pl. du
Parlement

r. de Cancéra

13

14

(i)

Porte
Cailhau

To Périgueux

pont de
Pierre

Richelieu

quai

rue des Trois Conils

16

Musée des
Beaux-Arts
17
Palais
Rohan

15

Cathédrale
St-André

cours de l'Alsace et Lorraine

rue de la Rousselle

Porte des
Salinières

quai St-Croix

MÉRIADECK

cours du Maréchal Juin

rue Lecocq
r. Ligier
rue de Belfort

18

pl. de la
République

rue du Hâ

rue de Cursol

rue des Ayres

cours
Pasteur
rue Ste-Catherine
r. de Mirail

19

cours Victor Hugo

rue Teulere

rue Leyteire

r. C. Sauvageau

place
Meynard
place
Canteloup

ST-MICHEL

20

21

rue P.L. Lande

d'Albert

VICTOIRE

cours A. Briand

Porte
d'Aquitaine

22

rue du Hamel

To Gare
St-Jean

pl. de la
Victoire

cours de la Marne

rue des Douves

Church †
Information (i)
Post Office ✉

0   1/4 mi
0   0.25 km

FRANCE
★ Paris
● Bordeaux

HOTELS

Hôtel de France **9**
Intercontinental
  Grand Hôtel de
  Bordeaux & Spa **11**
La Course Bordeaux **2**
Le Boutique Hotel **7**
Yndo Hotel **6**

RESTAURANTS

Kuzina **21**
La Grande Maison **1**
La Pâtisserie Essentielle **14**
Le Petit Commerce **13**
Le Pressoir d'Argent **10**
L'Univerre **18**
Peppone **8**

ATTRACTIONS

Basilique St-Michel **20**
CAPC Musée d'Art
  Contemporain **5**
Cathédral St-André **15**
Cité du Vin **4**
Grand Théatre **12**
Marché des Capucins **22**

Musée d'Aquitaine **19**
Musée des Arts
  Décoratifs **16**
Musée des
  Beaux-Arts **17**
Musée du Vin
  et du Négoce **3**

Modern tram on the place de la Comedie, Bordeaux

[FastFACTS] BORDEAUX

ATMs/Banks   The historic center has plenty of banks, including several ATMs on the cours de l'Intendance.

Doctors & Hospitals   **Groupe Hospitalier Pellegrin,** pl. Amélie Raba-Léon (www.chu-bordeaux.fr; ✆ **05-56-79-56-79**).

Embassies & Consulates   **American Presence Post,** 89 quai des Chartrons (http://bordeaux.usconsulate.gov; ✆ **01-43-12-48-65**); **British Consulate Bordeaux,** 353 bd. du President Wilson (www.gov.uk; ✆ **05-57-22-21-10**).

Mail & Postage   **La Poste,** 6 pl. Saint-Projet (✆ **36-31**).

Pharmacies   **Pharmacie des Grands Hommes,** 1 pl. des Grands Hommes (✆ **05-56-15-61-12**). Pharmacy open 24/7: **Pharmacie des Capucins,** 30 pl. des Capucins (✆ **05-56-91-62-66**).

Safety   The area around the Gare Saint Jean train station and place des Victoires can get a little seedy at night.

Exploring Bordeaux

THE HISTORIC CENTER ★★★

At first sight, the 18th-century grandeur of Bordeaux is almost overwhelming. At the very center is the supremely sophisticated "**Golden Triangle,**" defined by three boulevards: Cours Georges Clemenceau, **Cours de l'Intendance,** perhaps the grandest street in the city, and Allées de Tourny. This last street leads down the **place de la Comédie,** the unofficial heart of the city, a large square that is dominated by the **Grand Théâtre,** a colonnaded masterpiece by 18th-century architect Victor Louis, who also designed the Comédie Française.

A quick walk east towards the river brings you to the splendid **place de la Bourse,** a creation of Ange-Jacques Gabriel, King Louis XV's architect. Considered the *ne plus ultra* of French 18th-century architecture, the two wings of the plaza open onto the Garonne River like a giant bird. On warm days, Bordelaise (particularly the youngest ones) come here to splash through the 3,500 sq. m (37,000 sq. ft.) 1-in. deep water, known as the **Miroir d'Eau** (Water Mirror) that lies between the square and the river.

Those suffering from elegance overload will be relieved to find a younger, more accessible version of Bordeaux hiding just behind the grandiose plaza. A warren of small streets and pretty squares extends from **place du Parlement** south-ish to **place Saint Pierre, place du Palais,** and **place Camille-Jullien.** The farther you get from place du Parlement, the less touristy it is, and the better the restaurants get. That amazingly turreted gateway at place du Palais is the **Porte Caihau,** left over from the days when the city was surrounded by ramparts.

Heading back westward, you will no doubt cross **rue Saint Catherine,** which is hyped as the longest pedestrian street in Europe, but you'll find better shopping on rue du Pas-Saint-Georges and Saint James. Further on are the spires of the imposing **Cathedral Saint André** and its separated bell tower, the **Tour Pey-Berland.** Just behind the cathedral are two of the city's best-known museums: the **Musée des Beaux Arts** (www.musba-bordeaux.fr) and the **Musée des Arts Decoratifs.** A little farther to the south lies the **Musée d'Aquitaine,** a regional history museum (p. 720).

Place de la Bourse, Bordeaux

Cathédrale Saint-André de Bordeaux ★★ CHURCH   This towering edifice, originally built in the early 12th century, was where Eleanor of Aquitaine celebrated her first (and ill-fated) marriage to Louis VII. While there have been additions and subtractions over the centuries (during the French Revolution it was used for storing animal feed), the main attraction is the soaring heights of the nave, with its 12th century Plantagenet Gothic arches that reach as high as 29m (95 ft.). The church is also known for its stunning organ, whose sculpted wood case has been declared a historic monument. Outside, are two beautifully sculpted portals: The North Portal, dating from 1250, shows the Judgment of Christ, while the Royal Portal (c. 1330) details the Ascension. Next to the church is the 15th-century **Tour Pey-Berland,** the cathedral's belfry, which is separate because the vibrations from the huge bells could have damaged the cathedral if the tower had been attached. If you can handle climbing the 232 stairs, the tour offers a terrific view from the top.

Pl. Pey Berland. www.cathedrale-bordeaux.fr. ✆ **05-56-52-68-10.** Free admission to the cathedral. Admission to the Tour Pey-Berland: adults 5.50€; free for children 17 and under. **Church:** Mon 2–6pm, Tues–Sat 10am–noon and 2–6pm, Sun 9:30am–noon and 2–6pm. **Tower:** Jun–Sept daily 10am–1:15pm and 2–6pm; Oct–May Tues–Sun 10am–12:30pm and 2–5:30pm. Tram A or B: Hôtel de Ville.

Grand Théâtre ★ THEATER   As soon as it was inaugurated in 1780, everybody who was anybody in the performing arts wanted to perform in this gorgeous theater. Then as now, top names in opera, classical music, and dance grace the stage here. If you don't have time for a show, you can still take a tour on Wednesday and Saturday between 2:30pm and 6:30pm (6€ adults, free for visitors 26 and under), or at least pop in and check out the magnificent staircase.

Pl. de la Comédie. www.opera-bordeaux.com. ✆ **05-56-00-85-95.** Tram B: Grand Théâtre.

Musée d'Aquitaine ★ HISTORY MUSEUM   This museum offers a fascinating look at the growth of Bordeaux from its Gallo-Roman beginnings right up to the outbreak of World War II, passing by its explosive growth as a global port in the 17th, 18th, and 19th centuries. The 20th century section is undergoing expansion and has already hosted some fascinating temporary exhibitions. However, the real draw here is the unflinching permanent exhibition looking at the role that slavery played in the growth of Bordeaux.

20 cours Pasteur. www.musee-aquitaine-bordeaux.fr. ✆ **05-56-01-51-00.** Permanent collections 5€. Tues–Sun 11am–6pm. Tram B: Musée d'Aquitaine.

Musée des Arts Décoratifs ★★ MUSEUM   This is one of the city's best smaller museums and a real insider's secret. Set in the Hôtel de Lalande, a stunning *hotel particulier* built in 1779, much of the sculpture, furniture, and paintings date from the time of the house's construction. The excellent modern exhibits include Art Nouveau, Art Deco, and periodic samplings of contemporary design. The coffee shop is really good and in the summer, you can eat in the cobbled courtyard.

39 rue Bouffard. www.bordeaux.fr. ℭ **05-56-10-14-00.** Admission 5€. Wed–Mon 11–6pm. Tram B: Gambetta.

THE QUAYS ★★★

In the 18th century, the banks of the Garonne were just as elegant as the rest of the city, and wealthy wine merchants lived in limestone mansions on the edge of the river. However, time was not kind to the quays, which became known as a messy array of warehouses, gritty bars, and traffic jams. Fortunately, the city came to the rescue, and after a multi-year overhaul, the banks of the Garonne River have been given a superb makeover. Today, a **stroll along the quays** is Bordeaux's favorite weekend activity. You can start your walk at the vast **Esplanade des Quinconces,** just north of the place de la Bourse. Laid out in the early 1800s, this gargantuan esplanade covers 12 hectares (30 acres). Be sure to admire the huge **Monument to the Girondins.** During the French Revolution, this relatively moderate local faction tried to put the brakes on a revolution that was getting out of hand. They butted heads with the radical Montagnards, who came out on top, resulting in the mass execution of the Girondins and the beginning of the Reign of Terror.

Now stroll northwards along the river, and enjoy the new gardens, skateboard park, and playgrounds that line the **quai Louis XVIII** and the **quai des Chartrons.** At the **quai de Bacalan,** just before the new spaceage **Pont Jacques-Chaban-Delmas** bridge, a few old warehouses were left intact and transformed into a giant outlet center, but one where you can both shop and relax. Among the bargains are spiffy cafes, restaurants, and bars with terraces overlooking the water, as well as plenty of benches to plunk yourself down on. Just beyond the bridge is the new **Cité du Vin** museum (p. 722).

THE CHARTRONS QUARTER ★★

Once the beating heart of the Bordeaux wine trade, where every wine broker worth a cork set up shop, today Chartrons is the hot spot for young and enterprising creative types, especially those with some money to throw around. The neighborhood's hub is the refurbished **Halle des Chartrons,** an erstwhile covered market that is now a cultural center. A block east is **rue Notre Dame,** lined with cafes, clothes shops, and interior design boutiques. The neighborhood is also home to two good museums: on the southern end, the enormous **CAPC Musée d'Art Contemporain;** and up near the skateboard park, the small, but fascinating **Musée du Vin et du Négoce,** 41 rue Borie (www.museeduvinbordeaux.com; ℭ **05-56-90-19-13;** 10€ adults, 5€ students, free for children under 18; daily 10am–6pm; closed Dec 25 and Jan 1; tram B: Chartrons).

CAPC Musée d'Art Contemporain ★★ CONTEMPORARY ART MUSEUM Back in the 19th century, this vast building was a customs depot, where goods from the French colonies were held before being sold off in Northern Europe. Those crusty civil servants would probably faint at the sight of today's holdings, a compendium of avant-garde art from the 1950s up until today. Director María Inés Rodríguez has overseen recent exhibitions from, among others, Beatriz Gonzalez, Daniel Buren, and Judy Chicago. If you are hungry, stop in at the museum's chic cafe, by design maven Andrée Putman.

7 rue Ferèrre. www.capc-bordeaux.fr. ✆ **05-56-00-81-50.** Admission 7€ adults; 4€ students; free for children 17 and under. Tues–Sun 11am–6pm. Tram B: CAPC station.

Cité du Vin ★★ MUSEUM Opened in 2016, this has become the city's most talked-about museum. Not that the designers want you to call it that—they would say it's a cross between a cultural space, a gallery, and a theme park, with interactive exhibits showcasing the entire world of wine. Cafes, a restaurant, and a panoramic bar complete the picture, so allow yourself a good few hours to explore. Oh, and the wine shop also stocks bottles from over 80 countries, as well as holding regular tastings.

134 quai de Bacalan. www.laciteduvin.com. ✆ **05-56-16-20-20.** Admission 20€ (including a tasting); 9€ children 6–17; free for children 5 and under. Thurs–Tues 10am–6pm. Tram C: Cite du Vin.

SAINT MICHEL QUARTER ★

This neighborhood revolves around its church, the **Basilica of Saint Michel.** This lively, working-class quarter is home to Arab, Portuguese, and African immigrants, as well as a good sprinkling of the city's artists and *bobos* (bourgeois bohemians). The main draw here is the wide plaza (**place Duburg**) surrounding the church where the open-air food, clothes and bric-a-brac **market,** known as the Marché Royale, takes place on Saturdays (7am–4pm). The market also invades the nearby quai des Salinières. A drink at one of the cafes on the edge of the square is a post-shopping must. The whole area has been fully renovated in recent years.

Basilique Saint Michel ★★ CHURCH The most stunning thing about this church is its bell tower, which is not even attached to the building. Like the Cathedral of Saint André (p. 719), the vibrations of the bells and the weight of the tower were deemed too much for a church built on marshy land. At 114m (374 ft.), *la fleche* (the arrow), can be seen for miles around. The church itself is nothing to sniff at either. Built between the 14th and 16th centuries, it is lauded for its architectural harmony, its Flamboyant Gothic style, and its organ, which was recently restored. A fantastic view can be had from the top of the tower (May–Oct), if you are up for climbing the 230 stairs to get there.

pl. Canteloup et Meynard. www.bordeaux-tourisme.com. ✆ **05-56-94-30-50.** Free admission to church. Tower: 5€ adults; 3.50€ seniors and students; free for children 12 and under. Church daily 3–6pm. Tower Jun–Sept 2–7pm. Tram C: Saint-Michel.

A tour boat passes under the Saint Pierre bridge on the Garonne River, Bordeaux

Organized Tours & Boat Rides

The Bordeaux Tourist Office (p. 716) organizes a variety of guided tours in both French and English. The most popular is the 2-hr. bilingual **walking tour** of the city center, which leaves the tourist office at 10am, Thursday to Tuesday (12€ adults, 8€ ages 13–17, 2€ ages 5–12 and free children 4 and under). For an extra 3€, they'll throw in a wine tasting at the extremely well-stocked Bar à Vins (see box "Buying Bordeaux in Bordeaux," below). They also offer several **day trips to nearby wineries.** For a complete list of tours, visit the website.

You can also get a riverside view of Bordeaux on a **boat cruise** on the Garonne. You can taste wine, eat, or just gaze at the view, depending on the cruise and your budget. The two best cruise companies are **Crosières Burdigala,** quai Richelieu (www.evolutiongaronne.fr; ✆ **05-56-49-36-88**) which offers a 1.5-hr. cruise of Bordeaux for 15€, and **Bordeaux River Cruise,** quai des Chartrons (www.croisiere-bordeaux.com; ✆ **05-56-39-27-66**) which has a 2-hr. Bordeaux cruise with a winemaker and onboard tasting for 21€. Both also offer much more elaborate tours of Bordeaux and the wine country. The **Bat3** (known as the BatCub; use your public transit Tickarte tickets) is a boat-bus that ferries locals and tourists from one side of the Garonne to the other, between La Bastide, Jean-Jaurès, les Hangars, and Lormont. These run Monday to Friday from 7am to 7:30pm and Saturday and Sunday from 8:45am to 8pm (although times may vary depending on how busy things are, www.infotbm.com should have up to date times).

Where to Stay

EXPENSIVE

Intercontinental Le Grand Hôtel de Bordeaux & Spa ★★★

After decades of neglect, the majestic Grand Hôtel was reborn in 2007, with an exquisite interior makeover by decor-maestro Jacques Garcia. Taking inspiration from its neighbor the Grand Théâtre, the lush decoration hints at 19th century theater trimmings, and the unusual color schemes gracefully blend the old and the new. The top-floor spa goes even farther into the past—ancient Rome, to be exact—with red columns, black trim, and a mosaic pool with a ceiling that opens to the sky. The rooftop bar has a terrific view and is a popular nightspot in the warmer months. There is a bistro as well as a gourmet restaurant, **Le Pressoir d'Argent,** run by Gordon Ramsay (p. 725).

2–5 pl. de la Comédie. www.ghbordeaux.com. ✆ **05-57-30-44-44.** 130 units. 320€–550€ double; from 640€ suite. Parking 35€. **Amenities:** 2 restaurants; 2 bars; business center, concierge; room service; tea room; spa; free Wi-Fi.

Yndo Hotel ★★

The Yndo opened a few years ago and has brought some welcome understated luxury to the hotel scene in Bordeaux. This is really a special experience. You'll find it on a quiet side road only a few minutes stroll from place Gambetta and the lovely shops on rue Judaïque. Owner Agnès Guiot Du Doignon has decorated in beautifully understated but hugely luxuriously style, with wonderful paintings and furniture throughout.

108 rue de l'Abbée de l'Epée. www.yndohotelbordeaux.fr. ✆ **05-56-23-88-88.** 14 units. 220€–600€ double; 780€ suite. Breakfast 18€. Parking 20€. **Amenities:** Restaurant (reserve ahead, for hotel guests only); wine tastings; winery tours; free Wi-Fi.

MODERATE

Le Boutique Hotel ★★

This well-located hotel, right on the doorstep of the Golden Triangle of chic shops, has small but nicely designed rooms (all named after local châteaux). You'll love the inner courtyard garden, that gets fairly busy with locals in the summer months, where you can eat and choose from the pretty good wine list on offer. Parking is available at an underground public car park around the corner at a good rate.

3 rue Lafaurie de Monbadon. http://hotelbordeauxcentre.com/eng. ✆ **05-56-48-80-40.** 27 units. 164€–464€ double. Breakfast 18€. Nearby public parking 2€. **Amenities:** Babysitting; dry-cleaning; free Wi-Fi.

La Course Bordeaux ★★

Right opposite the Jardin Public park, this beautifully appointed luxury *chambre d'hotes* offers a friendly reception, a wine tasting cellar, and easy access to the shops of Chartrons. If you want to push the boat out, the "Under the Stars" suite has a glass roof and private terrace with a small pool (around 5 sq. m/54 sq. ft., so don't get too excited).

69 rue de la Course. www.lacourse-bordeaux.fr. ✆ **05-56-52-28-07.** 7 units. 152€–260€ double; 277€–650€ suite. Breakfast included. **Amenities:** Free Wi-Fi.

INEXPENSIVE

Hôtel de France ★★ Right around the corner from the elegant Cours de l'Intendance, this unpretentious, well-placed hotel manages to make basic accommodation very welcoming. The friendly owners keep their rooms clean and comfortable and will help you find the best local restaurants and bars, all within easy walking distance. Don't expect big rooms, but you'll have everything you need, and it's quiet at night.

7 rue Franklin. www.hotel-france-bordeaux.fr. ℂ **05-56-48-24-11.** 20 units. 94€ double; 99€ triple. **Amenities:** Free Wi-Fi.

Where to Eat

Eating is serious business in Bordeaux, where tantalizing restaurants seem to line every street. Vegetarians rejoice: You'll find today's Bordeaux increasingly caters to your tastes. If you aren't ready for a full meal, fear not. Tapas are currently all the rage; you can even tapas-hop from bar to bar on rue du Parlement-Saint-Pierre. Keep an eye out for tearooms, too—a great option for breakfast or a quick snack. My favorite is **La Pâtisserie Essentielle,** 2 pl. Saint Pierre (ℂ **09-81-28-83-40**), for exquisite pastries and quiches by a young couple of pastry chefs.

EXPENSIVE

La Grande Maison ★★ MODERN FRENCH This hotel in a wonderful 18th century building is also a popular dining spot for la belle Bordelaise. The restaurant is run by chef Pierre Gagnaire, and he brings his experimental style, with inventive takes on local produce. You can peruse what is possibly the best wine list in the city, with every single classified growth from Bordeaux, and a wide range from further afield.

10 rue Labottière. ℂ **05-56-38-16-16.** https://lagrandemaison-bordeaux.com/en/. Main course 90€–200€; fixed-price lunch 135€; tasting menu 195€. Mon–Sat noon–1:30pm and 7–9:30pm. Closed first 2 weeks of Aug.

Le Pressoir d'Argent ★★★ CLASSIC FRENCH/SEAFOOD The gourmet restaurant in the Grand Hotel now has Gordon Ramsay installed as head chef (or rather overseeing the restaurant from his base in London, with Gilad Peled as full-time head chef in Bordeaux). Named after its rare silver lobster press, this gastronomic palace honors seafood from the Atlantic coast but also the best quality produce from around southwest France, such as the celebrated chicken from Les Landes, organic vegetables from the Pays Basque, and many more, depending on the season. Reservations essential.

2-5 pl. de la Comédie. www.ghbordeaux.com. ℂ **05-57-30-44-44.** Main course 42€–135€; tasting menu 185€. Tues–Sat 7:30–10:30pm. Closed last 2 weeks of Aug.

MODERATE

Le Petit Commerce ★★ TRADITIONAL FRENCH/SEAFOOD This unassuming restaurant is so successful it had to open a second dining room across the narrow street. Fish, fish, and more fish is the motto here,

A terrific taste **OF ANOTHER BORDEAUX**

Out in a working-class quarter just east of the place de la Victoire lies Bordeaux's best and largest covered market, **Marché des Capucins** at place des Capucins (Tues–Sat 7am–1:45pm; Sun 9am–3:15pm; tram B: place de la Victoire; tram C: Sainte Croix). The city's chefs head here as soon as it opens, and all food fans will go nuts when they see the vast selection of goodies before them: fresh vegetables, fruits, meats, fish, cheese, bread, charcuterie—not to mention all the delicious prepared foods waiting for you to pounce. You can buy dried sausage, pastries, olives, and salads to take away, or you can treat yourself to one of the dozen or so food stands that serve from their bars or seating areas. On Saturdays, tapas are everywhere and everyone seems to be selling them, from the charcutier to the cheese guy. Other stands serve their treats on a daily basis. Crepes, couscous, and steamed mussels are all on hand. **La Maison de Pata Negra** (www. maisondupatanegra.com; ✆ **05-56-88-59-92**), specializing in the famous Spanish ham but also terrific tapas (1.50€–4€, technically, *pintxos*, served on slices of bread), made with various smoked meat combos as well as grilled bonito, or even sautéed foie gras. Other favorites include **Chez Jean-Mi** (www.facebook.com/chez. jean.mi; ✆ **06-81-20-24-49**) where if you stand too close to the bar, you'll suddenly find yourself savoring a plate of six sparkling fresh oysters with a cold glass of white wine (7€) and the newly-opened **Café Laiton** (✆ **07-82-88-49-59**), where owner Gaëlle serves freshly brewed Columbian, Brazilian, and Kenyan coffees, along with delicious pastries, at the market entrance.

though a steak or veal roast can be found on the menu as well. You can do the tapas thing here, too: Order up a platter of oysters, prawns, grilled sardines, particularly in the early evening where they have an offer for 10€ including a glass of wine. They also have a great two-course lunch deal during the week for 13€. Book ahead, as this is just as popular as ever.

22 rue du Parlement-Saint-Pierre. ✆ **05-56-79-76-58.** Main course 17€–38€; fixed-price lunch 16€; tapas 7€–14€; oysters 18€–26€. Daily noon–midnight.

L'Univerre ★★★ MODERN FRENCH If you like wine, this is the place to come in Bordeaux. You are likely to be sharing the dining room with a wine broker, merchant or a producer or two, as they make the most of a well-priced and wide-ranging list that includes wines from all over France and further afield. You can pick up some brilliant bottles, many organic or biodynamic, at the excellent wine shop. The food focus is on seasonal market produce, although I sometimes find the non-meat options are a bit limited.

40 rue Lecocq. www.univerre-restaurant.com. ✆ **05-56-23-01-53.** Main course 20€–30€. Mon 6–10pm; Tues–Fri noon–10pm. Closed 2 weeks in Aug.

INEXPENSIVE

Kuzina ★ FRENCH/CRETAN Part of Jean-Pierre Xiradakis' gourmet empire (the chef of the famed Tupina restaurant has four restaurants and a bed and breakfast on this same street), this airy restaurant is a homage to his Greek roots. The interior and menu have Mediterranean feel, which highlights simple, fresh fish (and a few meat) dishes. Tzatziki, hummus, gorgeous grilled bread smeared liberally in oregano are perfect to kick off a meal here. It is also worth noting that vegetarians have some excellent options here too.

22 rue Porte de la Monnaie. www.latupina.com. ☎ **05-56-74-32-92.** Main course 10€–17€; fixed-price lunch 18€–27€ or dinner 21€–27€. Wed–Sat noon–2pm; Tues–Sat 7–11pm.

Peppone ★★ ITALIAN   You might think you don't come to Bordeaux for Italian food, but with a queue forming outside this restaurant pretty much every evening you'd be missing out of one of the liveliest and most enjoyable restaurants in town. Take your pick of wood-fired pizza and freshly-made pasta, all beautifully done and served by the friendly staff. My personal favorite pizza is the Saint Pierre de Roma with its fresh basil and mozzarella. The same owners run **Ragazzi di Peppone** down on Quai Richelieu along the waterfront with the same menu, but with an outside terrace.

31 Cours Georges Clemenceau. ☎ **05-56-44-91-05.** Main course 8€–20€. Sat–Sun noon–2:30pm and 7–11pm; Mon–Fri noon–2:15pm and 7–11pm.

Shopping

For chic clothing and designer shops, go to the couture quarter around **place des Grands Hommes** and **cours de l'Intendance.** More high-end goodies, including wine and chocolates, can be found on the **Allées de Tourny.** For shopping that is easier on the budget, stroll down **rue Ste-Catherine,** which claims to be the longest pedestrian street in Europe. On either side of this road are two other good finds: the newish (from 2015)

Buying Bordeaux in Bordeaux

Not surprisingly, wine stores are on just about every corner of the city, many staffed with knowing initiates of the mysteries of the vine. If you want to sigh over rare bottles and legendary vintages, take a spin around **Badie,** 62 allées de Tourny (www.badie.com; ☎ **05-56-52-23-72**) or **La Vinothèque,** 8 cours du 30-Juil-let (www.vinotheque-bordeaux.com; ☎ **05-57-10-41-41**). For a more educational approach, from June to August you can take a **2-hr. class in English** on Saturdays (32€ or 25€ for students; check the website since they usually run only three Saturdays out of four) with the **Ecole du Vin** (Wine School) at the Conseil Interprofessionnel du Vin de Bordeaux (**CIVB**), an industry association representing some 8,000 Bordeaux wine producers and growers. It's easy to find the distinctive flat-iron building at 3 cours du 30-Juillet (www.bordeaux.com; ☎ **05-56-00-22-66**). Their English-language website is a goldmine of information; be sure to check out their "Wine 101" page for a quick overview. Finally, the CIVB is home to the **Bar à Vin,** a chic wine-tasting bar where you can sample the local wares from at least half of the region's 65 appellations.

Promenade Saint Catherine and the quirky boutique-style shops on rue du Pas-St-Georges and rue Saint James. Another good budget option is the pleasant riverside **outlet shops** at the Hangars (also known as the **Quai des Marques,** quai des Chartrons, www.quaidesmarques.com).

Antiques hunters will want to head to **rue Notre-Dame** in the Chartrons quarter, which harbors the **Village Notre-Dame** (https://www.villagenotredame.com/en/; ✆ **05-56-52-66-13**), an indoor antiques market with dozens of stands.

Food hounds can find lots of yummy things at the **Marché des Capucins** (p. 726), as well as **Le Comptoir Bordelais,** 1 bis rue des Piliers de Tutelle (www.lecomptoirbordelais.com; ✆ **05-56-79-22-61**), a terrific gourmet grocery. Chocoholics will feel compelled to pay their respects at **Cadiot-Badie,** 26 Allées de Tourny (www.cadiot-badie.com; ✆ **05-56-44-24-22**), considered the best in the city.

Bordeaux Nightlife

Starting at **place du Parlement,** the tiny nearby streets are filled with night spots and tapas bars, particularly as you approach **place St-Pierre** and **place Camille-Jullian. Place Gambetta** and **place de la Victoire** swarm with students. Night owls in Bordeaux gravitate toward **quai du Paludate,** where restaurants, bars, and discos remain open until the wee hours.

One of the most fun drinking spots in Bordeaux remains **Le Calle Ocho,** 24 rue des Piliers de Tutelle (www.calle-ocho.eu; ✆ **05-56-81-89-99**), a red-and-black enclave of Cuban music, photographs, and mojitos. And the last few years have seen a wave of excellent cocktail bars opening, among the best of which are **L'Alchimiste,** 16 rue Parlement Saint-Pierre (www.lalchimistebordeaux.com) and **Pointe Rouge,** 1 Quai de Paludate (www.pointrouge-bdx.com).

For a more laidback night on the town, **Café Populaire,** 1 rue Kléber (www.cafepop.fr; ✆ **05-56-94-39-06**), is a fun place to have a drink and mix with the locals, as is **Un Château en Ville,** 25 rue Saint-James (www.lestrille.com), a wine shop and bar owned by a local Bordeaux château owner. The best night here is Friday, where they serve up oysters with their Entre deux Mers white wine.

For dancing, try **La Plage,** 40 quai de Paludate (www.laplage-leclub.fr; ✆ **06-82-57-88-37**), with its 1970s decor and just-as-classic 25- to 45-year-old crowd. **La Dame,** Quai A. Lalande (www.facebook.com/ladamebordeaux; ✆ **05-57-10-20-50**), a restaurant-bar-club in a moored boat in the Bassins à Flot, is another good bet for a late night.

Day Trips from Bordeaux

ST-EMILION ★★
40km (25 miles) E of Bordeaux

Surrounded by vineyards, the village of St-Emilion sits on a ridge overlooking the Dordogne Valley. Aside from its famous wine, the town is a treasure in itself: Ancient alleyways lined with centuries-old limestone buildings, half-timbered homes from the Renaissance era, and pleasant cobblestoned plazas draw visitors from all over the world. Sometimes too many—the town can get clogged with tourists in the summer months. Since most come for the day, the best time to visit is in the late afternoon when they are all leaving, and you can enjoy an early evening glass of red in relative peace.

Essentials

Trains from Bordeaux make the 35-mi. trip to St-Emilion 10 to 15 times per day; the one-way fare is 9.50€. Trains from elsewhere in France require transfers in either Bordeaux or Libourne, a 10-min. train ride from St-Emilion. For train schedules visit www.oui.sncf or call ✆ **36-35** (.40€/min.).

The **Office de Tourisme** is on place des Créneaux (http://au.france.fr/en/information/bordeaux-tourism; ✆ **05-57-55-28-28**).

Exploring St-Emilion

At the town's heart is the medieval **place de l'Eglise Monolithe,** which is brimming with outdoor cafes. From here, a knot of cobbled streets and stone houses beckon with gift shops, wine-tasting rooms, and boutiques.

The **Eglise Monolithe ★★**, pl. de l'Eglise Monolithe (✆ **05-57-55-28-28**), was carved into the limestone side of a small hill sometime around the beginning of the 12th century. The largest underground church in Europe, it is dedicated to a saintly hermit named Emilion who frequented the neighborhood in the 8th century. To get in, you'll have to take a tour, which also gets you into the **catacombs,** the 13th-century Chapelle de la Trinité, and its underground grotto—where St-Emilion sequestered himself during the latter part of his life. The 45-min. tour costs 7.50€ for adults, 5.25€ for students, and is free for children 11 and under. Regularly scheduled English tours run April to October.

For a splendid view of the town and its vine-covered environs, climb the 196 steps to the top of the **bell tower** *(clocher)* of the Eglise Monolithe. To get in, you'll need a key, which you pick up from the tourist office for a fee of 1.50€ per person (leave your ID as a deposit). More views can be had from the top of the **Tour du Roi** (✆ **05-57-55-28-28**), a 13th-century castle keep. Open from April through September, this moody tower offers views of the surrounding countryside—on a clear day you can see the Dordogne River. For more medieval thrills, take a stroll around the crenellated **ramparts.**

Where to Stay & Eat

You're not going to find a better welcome in St-Emilion than **Le Pavillon ★★★**, lieu-dit Villemaurine (www.lepavillon-saintemilion.com; info@lepavillon-saintemilion.com). This luxury *chambres d'hotes* is a 3-min. stroll into the medieval town center. Doubles start at 250€ (all king size) including breakfast, complimentary wine, and mineral water. Owners Jules and Nikki Garafano are a wealth of information for where to eat and explore nearby. They would no doubt point you in the direction of **L'Envers du Décor,** 11 rue du Clocher (www.envers-dudecor.com; ✆ **05-57-74-48-31;** daily noon–2:30pm and 7–10:30pm; main courses 21€–23€, fixed-price menus 25.50€–35€), a popular restaurant and wine bar with a courtyard terrace. Also worth trying is **Le Terrasse Rouge,** 1 Château La Dominique (www.laterrasserouge.com; ✆ **05-57-24-47-05;** Tues–Sun noon–3pm, Fri–Sat 7–10:30pm), just 5 min. out of town at Château la Dominique, this laid-back bistro has stunning views over the vineyards.

ARCACHON & CAP FERRET ★★★

40km (25 miles) W of Bordeaux

Arcachon and Cap Ferret are situated at either end of the Arcachon Bay, almost touching each other from either side of the opening to the Atlantic Ocean, but completely different in atmosphere. Arcachon is the once-bustling and now a little sleepy coastal resort that comes with a Casino, plenty of spa hotels and an increasingly smart pocket of hotels based around the town of Pyla (where you can climb Europe's largest sand dune.) Cap Ferret, on the other hand, is all about understated chic, like a dollop of Cape Cod in Western France. Bordeaux châteaux owners and Parisian bankers have their second homes here, but you'd never know, as the dress code is strictly casual. A lovely shaded bike path runs for 200km (125 miles) between the two, tracing the shoreline of the bay and passing through beaches, pine forests, and over a dozen small fishing villages along the way, each one loaded with oyster huts where you can stop for refreshments. Bike hire is also available at pretty much every village, although it can get busy in the summer.

Where to Stay & Eat

Philippe Starck has created a luxurious enclave in Pyla, with two wonderful if pricey hotels that both offer brilliant dining. The original is perhaps still the best **La Co(or)niche,** 46 av. Louis Gaume (www.lacoorniche-pyla.com; ✆ **05-56-22-72-11;** from 390€ double, breakfast included), with incredible ocean and dune views from its chic terrace. This also happens to be the perfect spot for cocktails at sunset.

THE WINE COUNTRY ★★

Certainly France has so many wonderful vineyards that the entire country could be considered "the wine country." Still, when it comes to mystique, nothing says wine like the **Bordelais,** the world's most famous wine-growing region. **Pomerol, St-Emilion, Margaux, St-Estèphe**—this is where you'll find the greatest stars, a sort of oenological Beverly Hills. However, not all of the wine estates are grandiose affairs with names like Mouton-Rothschild and Château d'Yquem. The region has literally thousands of wineries, and many are relatively approachable family affairs

Chateaux and vineyards in Bordeaux

where, if you call ahead, you can drop in for a *dégustation* (wine tasting). But here's the rub: Your hard-working vintners are not always available to show off their estate to tourists. For some of them you will need to book in advance, but increasingly even the most prestigious châteaux offer excellent visits and wine shops, even catering for the smaller members of your party with ideas like grape juice tastings (**Château Kirwan** in Margaux for example; www.chateau-kirwan.com) and garden treasure hunts (**Château d'Agassac** in Haut-Médoc; www.agassac.com).

You'll have several ways to enjoy this beautiful region, whether you are a wine fanatic or just someone who likes wine and would like to learn (and taste) more. The major areas of Bordeaux are the Médoc, Bourg and Blaye, Entre-Deux-Mers, Saint Emilion, Castillon, and Graves and Sauternes. The **Médoc** and **Bourg/Blaye** are both fairly flat, stretching out towards either side of the Gironde estuary. Both are pretty, but you don't come here to sightsee: these are some of the most high-rent vineyards in the country. **Graves** and **Sauternes** is more scenic, but for rolling hills, adorable villages, and photo opportunities, **Entre-Deux-Mers, Saint Emilion,** and **Castillon** are where it's at. The beautiful towns of St-Emilion and Castillon are packed full of medieval treasures, while the Entre-Deux-Mers harbors *bastides* (neatly ordered towns around a central square—strategic urban planning left over from the Hundred Years' War) like **Sauveterre-de-Guyenne** and **Cadillac.**

Visiting the Grand Crus

If you are a serious wine fan, you will no doubt be aching to visit the famous châteaux. You can visit these estates, but in general, you must reserve a visit well in advance. Below are a few of the *grand crus;* for a

Bed & Breakfasting in Wine Country

While you can easily fit your wine country excursion into a day trip from Bordeaux, you could also use it as an excuse to get away from it all. There aren't a lot of hotels to choose from, but there are loads of adorable *gîtes* (vacation cottages) and bed-and-breakfasts. Even more intriguing, many wine producers have **onsite bed-and-breakfasts** and offer their overnight guests tours and tastings. Your best bet is to visit the **Gîtes de France** website: www.gites-de-france.com. This vast network has been around for decades and has very strict standards about cleanliness and comfort. If you want to stay at a vineyard, just search for "Oenology" under the "themed stays" heading on the site's English version. If you can surf in French, go to the **Gîtes de France Gironde** site (www.gites-de-france-gironde.com)

which will give you plenty of options in the Bordeaux region. Aside from vineyards, both sites list restored dovecotes, ancient outbuildings, and country castles, as well as humbler farms and homes. Rates for a double with breakfast run 50€ to 120€ per night, depending on comfort levels. Many bed-and-breakfasts offer a *table d'hôte*, a dinner with other guests for 20€ to 30€. For an enjoyable lunch while out in the vines, stop off at **Café Lavinal** in the village of Bages. This small hamlet has been renovated by Château Lynch Bages, which is closed for renovations until 2019, but the shops and bistro behind the château are still open for business and worth a detour. There is also an upscale hotel-restaurant, the **Cordeillan-Bages** (www.cordeillanbages.com).

more complete listing visit the tourist websites of the individual areas or www.bordeaux.com.

Château Margaux ★ WINE ESTATE Known as the Versailles of the Médoc, this stately Empire-style château was built in the 19th century. The visit includes a tasting, but you can't buy bottles onsite. This estate has had a recent extension by Sir Norman Foster, and there is an interesting architecture exhibition about the old and new building.

On D2, Margaux. www.chateau-margaux.com. ℘ **05-57-88-83-83.** Free admission, by appointment only Mon–Fri. Closed Aug. Tours in English on request.

Château Pichon-Longueville ★ WINE ESTATE A little further north in Pauillac, this 19th-century wonder includes turrets, a reflecting pool, and an excellent onsite wine shop.

Pauillac. www.pichonlongueville.com. ℘ **05-56-73-17-17.** 15€ with tasting. Tours in English on request. By appointment only, daily 9am–12:30pm and 2–6:30pm.

Château Prieuré Lichine ★ WINE ESTATE Although better to make an appointment in advance for the full tour, there is a well-stocked boutique that you can drop into as you drive past.

24 av. de la 5ième Répúbliique, Cantenac. www.prieure-lichine.fr. ℘ **05-57-88-36-28.** Discovery tour including tasting 9€. Tours in English, French, Spanish, Japanese. Mon–Sat 9am–noon and 2–5pm. Closed Aug.

Visiting Smaller Estates

As noted above, the Bordelais has thousands of wine estates, and the smaller, less-hyped wineries are becoming increasingly visitor-friendly. Some have joined up with labels or listings publications. One of the most comprehensive is a booklet entitled **"Itineraires Dans Les Bordeaux,"** which also has a terrific website (where you can download the booklet): www.itineraires-vignobles.fr. They have a huge list of wine estates, including many smaller operations where you can actually drop in (though even they prefer that you call ahead to let them know you are coming). The listings include hours, websites, if they speak English, whether or not you need to reserve—in short, everything you need to know to plan your own wine trip.

Another good strategy is to contact the area's wine association (see "Where to Find the Château of Your Dreams").

Going on a Wine Tour

If you'd like to know more about wine, but are not sure where to begin, or are strapped for time and not up for adventure, an organized tour is a good option. Nonetheless, you could also download the app Bordeaux Wine Trip ★ (www.bordeauxwinetrip.com). For do-it-yourselfers who could use a little help, this useful, free, application (Android and iOS) helps you navigate the wine country, with maps and listings for wineries, restaurants, accommodations, and information on upcoming events.

Bordeaux Tourist Office Tours ★ TOURS Led by guides with ample wine expertise, these tours start with half-day outings including a tasting or two at a top-grade château and perhaps a short walking tour of St-Emilion (70€–85€ per person, reductions for children) and move on to more elaborate full-day tours (120€–160€ per person), which might include a trip down to Sauternes for a visit of Château d'Yquem and lunch at a Michelin-starred restaurant. For a complete list, click on the Wine Tours heading on the website.

12 cours du 30-Juillet, Bordeaux. www.bordeaux-tourisme.com. ℰ **05-56-00-66-00.**

Where to Find the Château of Your Dreams

Each area has its own wine associations that function as information clearinghouses. To find out more about a particular wine area and listings for wine estates, visit the following websites:

Conseil des Vins de Medoc (www.medoc-bordeaux.com)
Conseil du Vin de Saint-Emilion (www.vins-saint-emilion.com)
Maison du Vin de Blaye (www.vin-blaye.com)
Maison du Vin de Entre-Deux-Mers (www.vins-entre-deux-mers.com)
Maison du Vin de Graves (www.vins-graves.com)
Maison du Sauternes (www.maisiondusauternes.com)

Bordovino ★ TOURS   Specializing in wine tours, this well-established company works to open up the sometimes intimidating Bordeaux wine world to non-expert wine fans. A wide variety of tour configurations range from a day-long "wine and bike" tour of St-Emilion and two châteaux (145€ per person), to a 3-day/2-night tour of wine estates with a side trip to Arcachon (from 475€ per person).

3 rue Enghien, Bordeaux. www.bordovino.com. ✆ **05-57-30-04-27.**

Uncorked Wine Tours ★ TOURS   One of the friendliest options for regional wine tours comes care of Caroline Matthews, who does fully tailored tours for a minimum of one day. Prices are flexible depending on what you are looking for.

www.uncorkedwinetours.com. ✆ **06-50-04-28-84.**

POITIERS ★★

333km (206 miles) SW of Paris; 177km (110 miles) SE of Nantes

Poitiers stands on a hill overlooking the Clain and Boivre rivers—a strategic location that tempted many conquerors. Everybody has passed through here—from Joan of Arc to Richard the Lion-Heart. Charles Martel chased out the Muslims in A.D. 732 and altered the course of European civilization. Poitiers was the chief city of Eleanor of Aquitaine, who had her marriage to pious Louis VII annulled, so she could wed England's Henry II (a marriage that effectively launched the modern Bordeaux wine trade).

For history buffs, this is one of the most fascinating towns in France. The Battle of Poitiers, fought on September 19, 1356 between the armies of Edward the Black Prince and King John of France, was one of the three great English victories in the Hundred Years' War, distinguished by the use of the longbow in the skilled hands of English archers.

After decades of slumber, the town came alive with the opening of the **Futuroscope** theme park in 1987, which now gets upward of 3 million visitors per year. The thriving student population (25,000 of Poitiers's 92,000 residents are students) adds vitality as well.

Essentials

GETTING THERE   Frequent **rail** service is available from Paris, Bordeaux, and La Rochelle. Around 15 high-speed TGV trains arrive daily from Paris's Gare Montparnasse (trip time: 78 min.; 20€ one-way), with the new high-speed rail link cutting times by 20 min. since 2017. Another 14 TGVs arrive daily from Bordeaux (trip time: 1.75 hr.; 10€ one-way), and 12 regular trains arrive from La Rochelle (trip time: 1.75 hr.; 18€one-way). For train information, visit www.oui.sncf or call ✆ **36-35** (.40€/min.). **Bus** service from Poitiers is so badly scheduled that it's virtually nonexistent. If you're **driving,** Poitiers is located on the A10 highway; from Paris, follow A10 south through Orléans and Tours, and on to Poitiers.

Place Charles de Gaulle, Poitiers

VISITOR INFORMATION   The **Office de Tourisme** is at 45 pl. Charles de Gaulle (www.ot-poitiers.fr; ✆ **05-49-41-21-24**).

SPECIAL EVENTS   The liveliest time to visit is from mid-June to mid-September during **Poitiers l'Eté,** a festival of free live jazz, theater, opera, rock, and fireworks. Free concerts and theater pieces, both in and out of the streets, take place at various parks and churches around the city. Check with the tourist office for schedules.

Exploring Poitiers

Baptistère St-Jean ★ RELIGIOUS SITE   From the cathedral, you can walk to the most ancient Christian monument in France. It was built as a baptistery in the early 4th century on Roman foundations and extended in the 7th century. It contains frescoes from the 11th to the 13th centuries and a collection of funerary sculpture.

Rue Jean-Jaurès. ✆ **05-49-41-21-24.** Admission 2€ adults; 1€ children 11 and under. July–Aug daily 10:30am–12:30pm and 3–6pm; Sept and Apr–Jun Wed–Mon 10:30am–12:30pm and 3–6pm; Oct–Mar Wed–Mon 2:30–4:30pm.

Cathédrale St-Pierre ★ CATHEDRAL   In the eastern sector of Poitiers is the twin-towered Cathédrale St-Pierre, begun in 1162 by Henry II of England and Eleanor of Aquitaine on the ruins of a Roman basilica. The architecturally undistinguished cathedral was completed much later. The interior, 89m (292 ft.) long, contains some admirable 12th- and 13th-century stained glass.

pl. de la Cathédrale. ✆ **05-49-41-23-76.** Free admission. Daily 8:30am–7:30pm (until 6pm in winter).

Eglise Notre-Dame-la-Grande ★★ CHURCH   This church, built in the Romanesque-Byzantine style and richly decorated, is from the late 11th century. See in particular its western front, dating from the mid-12th century. Surrounded by an open-air market, the facade, carved like an ivory casket, is characterized by pine cone-shaped towers. It was thoroughly cleaned and restored in 1996. Carvings on the doorway represent biblical scenes.

pl. Charles de Gaulle. ℭ **05-49-41-22-56.** Free admission. Mon–Sat 9am–7pm; Sun noon–7pm.

Futuroscope ★★ AMUSEMENT PARK   This multimedia amusement park in a suburb of Poitiers is a wonderland of technology that lets you experience sounds, images, and sensations with the world's most advanced film-projection techniques and largest screens. The architecture is extraordinary—take a peek at the **Kinémax,** a 400-seat cinema shaped like a rock crystal covered with mirrors, or the **Cité du Numérique** (Digital City), a giant glass triangle with a huge white globe sitting in the middle. The site has six IMAX theaters, as well as attractions that use 3-D technology, motion simulators, and sophisticated lighting effects. Attractions let you rocket deep into space, dive under the ocean, or fly up in the air for a virtual sky tour. New rides include a space adventure with Thomas Pesquet, the Extraordinary Voyage where you fly over every conceivable landscape around the world, and the ever-popular Dance with the Robots ride. In July and August every night until 10pm, *les nocturnes* are staged with illuminated fountains, lights, and recorded music, including a new event staged by the team behind Cirque du Soleil.

The park's success is such that it has its own TGV train station with direct connections to Bordeaux, Paris, and other major cities, as well as a selection of hotels and restaurants (detailed on the website).

Jaunay-Clan. www.futuroscope.com. ℭ **05-49-49-30-80.** Admission 40€ adults, 36€ children ages 5–16; free for children 4 and under. Daily 8:30am–10:30pm. Bus: Vitalis line 1 and E direct from Poitiers Centre train station. Driving: From Poitiers, take D910 or A10 autoroute about 12km (7.5 miles) north. Closed Jan to mid-Feb.

Musée Ste-Croix ★ MUSEUM   On the site of the old abbey of Ste-Croix, this museum has extensive art and archeology collections. Exhibits date right back to the Gallo-Roman times, but the really unmissable part for is the fine art section that covers paintings and sculpture from 14th century right up to contemporary art. Works by Bonnard, Sisley, Mondrian, and Moreau are on display, as well as an impressive collection of sculptures, including Maillol, Rodin, and seven statues by Camille Claudel.

3 Bis rue Jean-Jaurès. www.musees-poitiers.org. ℭ **05-49-41-07-53.** Admission 4.50€ adults; 2.50€ Sun; free for children ages 17 and under. June–Sept Tues 10am–8pm and Wed–Sun 10am–6pm; Oct–May Tues–Fri 10am–6pm and Sat–Sun 1–6pm.

Where to Stay

Hôtel de l'Europe ★   Composed of several buildings, one of which dates from the 19th century, this family-owned hotel manages to successfully combine contemporary and fin-de-siècle style. The breakfast room features curlicue moldings and a grand fireplace, while most of the rooms are modern and sleek. Sixty rooms were fully renovated in 2009; the older ones in the main building are smaller (and cheaper) and accessible only by staircase. You can eat or enjoy an aperitif outside in the lovely garden complete with a boules court.

39 rue Carnot. www.hotel-europe-poitiers.com. ✆ **05-49-88-12-00.** 87 units. 58€–99€ double. Parking 6€. **Amenities:** Room service; Wi-Fi.

Hôtel Mercure Poitiers ★★   If you think you don't want to stay in a Mercure, you haven't been to this one. In one of the city's most attractive old buildings, a former Jesuit chapel, with the brilliant Les Archives restaurant directly underneath, this is both inexpensive and well located. Inside you get Gothic windows, vaulted ceilings, pure character everywhere you look, with almost nothing to say you are in a chain hotel. A public car park is just next door for 5€ a day.

14 Edouard-Grimaux. www.mercure.com. ✆ **05-49-50-50-60.** 20 units. 88€–145€ double; 225€–285€ suite. Breakfast 16€. **Amenities:** Restaurant; bar; free Wi-Fi.

La Maison de Marc ★   Small, cosy, and super welcoming, this *chambres d'hôtes* run by Agnes Cognard makes an excellent alternative to the bigger hotels in town. Well-thought out details abound, from luxurious throws on the bed to double sinks in all the bathrooms. Book ahead if you are coming over the summer months.

10-12 rue Bourbeau. www.lamaisondemarc.com. ✆ **05-49-58-58-13.** 4 units. 87€–120€ double; 250€ apartment for 2 nights over the weekend or 480€ for the week. **Amenities:** Free Wi-Fi.

Where to Eat

Alain Boutin ★ FRENCH/SEAFOOD   Chef Boutin and his wife Annick have given this popular restaurant a recent internal renovation, and it remains a cheerful, welcoming place where you get market-fresh cuisine delivered with culinary imagination. The chef works closely with a number of Aquitaine's best-known producers to give an excellent overview of the region's most interesting ingredients, often paired with local wines. Located near the Jardins de Blossac; reservations required.

65 rue Sadi Carnot. www.alainboutin.com. ✆ **05-49-88-25-53.** Main course 16€–30€; fixed-price menus 26€–39€. Tues–Fri noon–1:30pm; Mon–Sat 7:30–9:30pm. Closed 1st week of Sept and 1st week of Jan.

Les Archives ★ MODERN FRENCH   Just below the Hotel Mercure, this is one of the best places to eat in Poitiers, hands down. Set in a beautiful large space with a mezzanine level, this was once the Gésu chapel, and today is a restaurant, bar, tea-room, and sometimes live music space. The food is excellent, with an emphasis on updating French classics with whatever is in season. A good range of vegetarian options are also available, including an excellent coriander and coconut milk risotto. Reservations are required.

14 rue Edouard-Grimaux. www.lesarchives.fr. ✆ **05-49-30-53-00.** Main course 14€–25€; fixed-price lunch 11.50€ or dinner 27€–39€. Daily noon–2 and 7–10pm (Fri–Sat until 10:30pm).

Day Trip from Poitiers

ANGOULÊME ★★
443km (275 miles) SW of Paris; 116km (72 miles) NE of Bordeaux

The old town of Angoulême hugs a hilltop between the Charente and Aguienne rivers. You can visit it on the same day you visit Cognac or take your time and do both separately. The town has been a center for the French paper industry since the 17th century, a tradition that carries on today in the five remaining paper mills. These days, Angoulême (pop. 43,000) is probably best known for something that gets printed on that paper: comics. Authors, artists, and fans come from all over the world to attend the **Festival International de la Bande Dessinée,** one of the largest comic book/graphic novel gatherings on earth. The festival takes over the town for three days in January, when the latest books are presented, prizes awarded, and contracts signed. For more information, contact the festival (www.bdangouleme.com; ☎ **05-45-97-86-50**) or the tourist office (see below). If you miss the festival, you can still explore this graphic world at the **Cité Internationale de la Bande Dessinée et de l'Image (CNBDI);** see "Exploring the Town," below.

GETTING THERE   About two TGV **trains** per hour (trip time: 55 min.) and a handful of regular trains (trip time: 1.5 hr. or 1 hr. high speed) arrive every day from Bordeaux; the one-way fare is 20€. Frequent train service also arrives from Saintes (trip time: 1 hr.) and Poitiers (trip time: 45 min.). From Paris's Montparnasse Station, some 15 TGV trains make the trip daily (trip time: 1 hr., 18 min. with the new high-speed TGV.); the one-way fare is 35€ to 85€. For train information and schedules, visit www. oui.sncf or call ☎ **36-35** (.40€/min.). **Véolia** (www.vtpc.fr; ☎ **05-45-95-95-99**) runs eight buses per day between Cognac and Angoulême. The trip takes 1 hr. and costs 4.50€ each way. If you're **driving** from Bordeaux, take N10 northeast to Angoulême.

VISITOR INFORMATION   The **Office de Tourisme** is at place des Halles (www.angouleme-tourisme.com; ☎ **05-45-95-16-84**).

Exploring the Town

The hub of the town is **place de l'Hôtel-de-Ville.** The town hall was erected from 1858 to 1866 on the site of the palace of the ducs d'Angoulême, where Marguerite de Navarre, sister of François I, was born. All that remains of the palace are the 15th-century Tour de Valois and 13th-century Tour de Lusignan.

    Cathédrale St-Pierre ★, 4 pl. St-Pierre, was built in the 11th and 12th centuries and restored in the 19th. Flanked by towers, its facade has 75 statues, each in a separate niche, representing the Last Judgment. This is one of France's most startling examples of Romanesque-Byzantine style. The 19th-century architect Abadie (designer of Sacré-Coeur in Paris) tore down the north tower and then rebuilt it with the original materials in the same style. In the interior, you can wander under a four-domed ceiling. It's open Monday to Saturday 9am to 6pm, Sunday 10am to 6:30pm.

As the European capital of comic book art, the city is home of the **Cité Internationale de la Bande Dessinée et de l'Image,** 121 rue de Bordeaux (www.citebd.org; ✆ **05-45-38-65-65;** July and Aug Tues–Fri 10am–7pm and Sat–Sun 2–7pm; Sept–June Tues–Fri 10am–6pm and Sat–Sun 2–6pm), which might just be the best resource for graphic art lovers in Europe. It offers a complete history of French and American comics, with over 12,000 original drawings in an exhibition space that also shows audiovisual sequences of the artists drawing their works. A library, book shop, research center, and two cinemas add to the interest. Entrance is 7€ for adults, 5€ for students under 26, 3€ for children ages 10 to 18, and free for children 9 and under.

To get out into the city itself, you can walk along the panoramic **promenade des Remparts ★,** a path that flanks the site of the long-gone fortifications that once surrounded the historic core of Angoulême. The most appealing section of the 3km (1.75-mile) walkway is the 1km (.5-mile) section that connects the cathedral with Les Halles (the covered market). Views from here stretch over the hills that flank the River Charente almost 75m (246 ft.) below. Or stroll the **Circuit des Murs Peints**

Cité Internationale de la Bande Dessinée et de l'Image

(Graffiti Walk). Famous graphic artists such as Florence Cestac and Marc-Antoine Mathieu have created over 20 commissioned pieces of graffiti and street art at various public spots around the city; the tourist office has a walking tour map.

Where to Eat

L'Agape ★★ FRENCH   This classic French restaurant with a contemporary feel has ever-changing menu from an inventive young chef and a wide-ranging wine list. L'Agape represents great value for this quality of cooking; plenty of vegetarian options are available as well. Reservations recommended.

16 pl. du Palet. www.l-agape.com. ℂ **05-45-95-18-13.** Main course 22€–32€, fixed-price menu 16.90€–44€. Thurs–Tues noon–1:30pm and 7:30–9:30pm (closed Tues night).

Les Halles Market ★ MARKET   As in most French cities, the daily market is one of the best places to eat. You'll find plenty of stalls with bars and high stools offering a range of local products, or try restaurant **Le Bistro Bachelier** for more serious refueling if you're really hungry (duck is the speciality here).

Pl. des Halles. Sat–Thurs 8am–1pm and Fri until 6pm.

LA ROCHELLE ★★★

467km (290 miles) SW of Paris; 145km (90 miles) SE of Nantes; 183km (113 miles) N of Bordeaux; 142km (88 miles) NW of Angoulême

La Rochelle is a historic port and ancient sailors' city, formerly the stronghold of the Huguenots. It was founded as a fishing village in the 10th century on a rocky platform in the center of a marshland. Eleanor of Aquitaine gave La Rochelle a charter in 1199, freeing it from feudal dues. After becoming an independent city-state, the port capitalized on the wars between France and England. It was the departure point for the founders of Montreal. From the 14th to the 16th century, La Rochelle was one of France's great maritime cities. It became the principal port between France and the colony of Canada, but France's loss of Canada ruined its Atlantic trade.

As a hotbed of Protestant factions, it armed privateers to prey on Catholic vessels but was eventually besieged by Catholic troops, led by Cardinal Richelieu (with his Musketeers) and Jean Guiton. When Richelieu blockaded the port, La Rochelle bravely resisted. It took 15 months to starve the city into submission, during which time 25,000 citizens perished from hunger. On October 30, 1628, Richelieu entered the city and found only 5,000 survivors.

Today La Rochelle, a city of 77,000, is the cultural and administrative center of the Charente-Maritime *département* (administrative region, now part of the larger Nouvelle Aquitaine). Its famous city lights have earned it the title "City of Light." While many of La Rochelle's sights are old, the city is riddled with high-rise condos and home to the largest pleasure-boat basin in Europe. In summer, the city is overrun with visitors.

Essentials

GETTING THERE   The La Rochelle–Ile-de-Ré **airport** (www.larochelle. aeroport.fr; ✆ **08-92-23-01-03**) is on the coast, 4km (2.5 miles) north of the city. Take bus no. 7 or 47 to reach it; for information and schedules, visit www.rtcr.fr or call ✆ **05-46-34-84-58**. Six to eight **trains** from Bordeaux and Nantes arrive daily (trip time: 2 hr.; 29€–31.50€ one-way). A few direct TGVs arrive from Paris's Gare Montparnasse, although most require a transfer at Nantes (trip time: 3 hr., although this also benefits from the new high-speed rail if you work out the connection times well); the one-way fare is 30€ to 83€. For train information, visit www.oui.sncf or call ✆ **36-35** (.40€/min.). The main **bus** lines in, out, and around the city leave from place de Verdun (✆ **05-46-00-95-15** for information). If you're **driving,** follow A10 south from Poitiers to exit 33 toward La Rochelle/Niort/St-Maixent, and then take N11 west to the coast and La Rochelle.

VISITOR INFORMATION   The **Office de Tourisme** is on Quai Georges Simenon, Le Gabut (www.larochelle-tourisme.com; ✆ **05-46-41-14-68**).

SPECIAL EVENTS   The busiest month is July because the **Festival International du Film de La Rochelle** rolls in at the beginning of the month.

La Rochelle.

Tracing Your Roots

During the French Wars of Religion that raged off and on for much of the 17th century, a large number of both Huguenots and Catholics emigrated from La Rochelle to north America, especially Canada. It is thought that as many as 14,000 emigrants landed in New France (the term referred to French colonies across north America including Québec, Newfoundland, Nova Scotia, and parts of the Great Lakes) in the century up to 1760. Besides the **Musée du Nouveau-Monde** (p. 744), you will also see a sculpture in the Vieux-Port called Globe de la Francophonie by artist Bruce Krebs,

celebrating this global spread of French culture and language. If you are tracing your own roots here, you could start with the **Unicaen Project** run by Caen university (no longer funded, but the information gathered in a research project from 2001-2006 is searchable on www.unicaen.fr/mrsh/prefen/index.php). Open by request only, the **Musée Rochelais d'Histoire Protestante** on 2 Rue Saint-Michel (www.protestantisme-museelarochelle.fr; © 05-46-50-88-03; 4€ adults, 2€ students and visitors 24–18, free for children 17 and under) has some potentially useful archives.

It attracts a huge following of fans, press, actors, directors, and, of course, paparazzi. Screenings are held around town; a pass for 10 screenings costs 48€. For information, contact the festival office, at 10 Quai Georges Simenon (www.festival-larochelle.org; © **05-46-52-28-96** or 01-48-06-16-66). For a week in mid-July, **Les Francofolies,** a festival of French-speaking music, features big names as well as not-so-famous groups, many of them international musicians. The town is overrun with fans, and a party atmosphere prevails. Tickets range from 20€ to 50€. Call © **05-46-28-28-28** for details (www.francofolies.fr).

La Rochelle is also the site of the biggest showcase of boats and yachts in Europe, **Le Grand Pavois–Salon Nautique.** It's a 6-day extravaganza in late-September attracting some 80,000 visitors. The action is based in and around La Rochelle's Port de Plaisance (better known as the Bassin des Yachts, or Yacht Basin). Sellers and buyers of boats and marine hardware, as well as weekend sailors from everywhere, usually attend. For information about dates and venues, check www.grand-pavois.com or call © **05-46-44-46-39.**

Exploring La Rochelle

La Rochelle has two sides: the old and unspoiled town inside the Vauban defenses and the modern and industrial suburbs. The city's **fortifications** have a circuit of 5.5km (3.5 miles), with a total of seven gates. It's an easy city to walk around, or you can use the yellow bicycles (or electric cars), called **Yélo** (https://yelo.agglo-larochelle.fr), that are available for hire from stations around the city. There are even solar-powered boats that chug across the harbor. These cross the La Rochelle channel from Cours des Dames to La Médiathèque and are called by pressing on a button that on the quay side. A 10-trip ticket is 11€, or a single ride is 1.30€, and is also valid on the city's buses. You can also buy a 24-hr. unlimited ticket for 4.50€.

The town, with its arch-covered streets, is great for strolling. The port is a fishing harbor and one of Europe's major sailing centers. If you are here during the summer, try to schedule a visit in time to attend a **fish auction** (called La Criée aux Poissons) at the Marché Central de la Rochelle, starting at 5am every Thursday from mid-June to mid-September (7€ per person booked through the tourist office, see above). You can even learn how to lift the nets like a professional fisherman at the **Lycée Maritime de la Rochelle** during the summer when the full-time students are not around. For information on these 2-hr. introductions, see www.lycee-maritime-larochelle.com or again go through the tourist office. The best streets for strolling, each with a 17th-century arcade, are **rue du Palais, la Rue du Temple, rue Chaudrier,** and **rue des Merciers,** with its ancient wooden houses (seek out the ones at nos. 3, 5, 8, and 17).

The town's 14th-century showcase **Hôtel de Ville** (City Hall) ★ is built in flamboyant Gothic style with battlements. It was heavily damaged in a 2013 fire. Extensive renovations are nearing completion and the building is due reopen in 2019.

Aquarium de La Rochelle ★ AQUARIUM   La Rochelle's blockbuster crowd pleaser, this is one of the biggest aquariums in Europe and has just benefitted from an upgrade, reopening in February 2018. It rises from a portside position near the Port des Minimes, north of the old city. Inside are guided walkways stretching over several floors of massive seawater tanks loaded with some 10,000 species of flora and fauna from the oceans of the world, living in what look like natural habitats. New exhibits look at the ocean's deepest depths, with five large tanks employing light shows and interactive high-definition images to illuminate these little-known corners of the earth, along with the ecosystem of the Atlantic coastline and the stunning array of sea life carried by the Gulf Stream. The jelly fish exhibition remains as beautiful and popular as ever.

Bassin des Grands Yachts, Quai Louis Prunier, Le Vieux Port. www.aquarium-larochelle.com. ✆ **05-46-34-00-00.** Admission 16€ adults; 13.50€ students; 12€ children ages 3–17; free for children 2 and under. English-language audio guide 3€. July–Aug daily 9am–11pm; Apr–June and Sept daily 9am–8pm; Oct–Mar daily 10am–8pm.

Musée des Beaux-Arts ★ ART MUSEUM   This museum is in an Episcopal palace built in the mid–17th century. The 900-strong art collection spans the 15th to the 20th centuries but focuses mainly on 19th century art with works by Gustave Doré, Brossard de Beaulieu, Camille Corot, and Paul Huet, as well as local artists William Bouguereau and Eugène Fromentin.

28 rue Gargoulleau. www.ville-larochelle.fr. ✆ **05-46-41-64-65.** Admission 6€ adults; free for children 18 and under. Oct–Mar Mon and Wed–Fri 9:30am–12:30pm and 1:45–5pm, Sat–Sun 2–6pm; Apr–Sept Mon and Wed–Sat 10:30am–12:30pm and 2–6pm, Sun 2–6pm.

Musée du Nouveau-Monde ★ MUSEUM   In an 18th-century town house named after the Fleuriau family who lived there from 1772 to 1974, this is one of La Rochelle's most intriguing museums. It's rich with evidence of the city's prominent role in the colonization of Canada, as La Rochelle was the primary port in France for voyages to New France (as Québec was known). Exhibits start with LaSalle's discovery of the Mississippi Delta in 1682 and end with the settling of the Louisiana territory. Other exhibits depict French settlements in the West Indies, including Guadeloupe and Martinique. The museum examines the vast cane sugar and tobacco cultivations they ran, as well as the slavery that fueled them. You'll find other examples of the link between La Rochelle and Canada around the city, with many set out along the walking path "Les Chemins du Québec" (map available in the tourist office).

In the Hôtel Fleuriau, 10 rue Fleuriau. ℭ **05-46-41-46-50.** Admission 6€ adults; free for children 18 and under. Mid-Jun to mid-Sept Mon and Wed–Fri 10am–1pm and 1:45–6pm, Sat–Sun 2–6pm; Sept to mid-Jun Mon and Wed–Sat 9:30am–12:30pm and 1:45–5pm and Sun 2–6pm.

Musée Maritime ★ MUSEUM   This museum is comprised of eight permanently docked boats, two of which can be visited: a weather ship that was used in the North Atlantic until the 1980s, and an antique *chalutier de peche* (fishing trawler). The vintage yachts evoke the grand days of La Rochelle as a maritime power and its New World commerce.

Quai Sénac de Meilhan. www.museemaritimelarochelle.fr. ℭ **05-46-28-03-00.** Admission 9€ adults; 6.50€ for students and children 4–16; free for children ages 3 and under. Apr–June and Sept daily 10am–6:30pm; July–Aug daily 10am–7pm.

Muséum d'Histoire Naturelle ★ MUSEUM   One of the hidden treasures of La Rochelle, this lovely museum is set within an enormous (2,500 sq. m/26,910 sq. ft.) mansion in the heart of town and surrounded by lovely botanical gardens. This is truly a museum to get lost in. Expect an array of taxidermied animals, African masks, maps of prehistoric migration patterns, and more. They are all part of the 10,000 or so objects, brought back by La Rochelle's 17th-century traders on their ships. The gardens outside are part of the exhibition, with plants from many of the same far-flung locations.

28 rue Albert 1er. www.museum-larochelle.fr. ℭ **05-46-41-18-25.** Admission 6€; free for children 17 and under. Oct to mid-May Tues–Fri 9am–6pm, Sat–Sun 2–6pm; mid-May to Sept Tues–Fri 10am–7pm, Sat–Sun 2–7pm.

Money-Saving Museum Pass

You can buy a **combination ticket** good for entrance to the Musée des Beaux-Arts, Musée Orbigny-Bernon, Muséum d'Histoire Naturelle, and Musée du Nouveau-Monde. Available at any of the museums and the tourist office, it costs 12€, a big savings.

Tour de la Chaîne ★ HISTORIC SITE   During the 1300s, this tower was built as an anchor piece for the large forged-iron chain that stretched across the harbor, closing it against hostile warships. The exhibits focus on the history of the first migration to Canada.

Quai du Gabut. www.monuments-nationaux.fr. ℂ **05-46-34-11-81.** Admission, see box "Saving Money Tower-Hopping". Oct–Mar daily 10am–1pm and 2:15–6:30pm; Apr–Sept 10am–6:30pm

Tour de la Lanterne ★ HISTORIC SITE Built between 1445 and 1476, this was once a lighthouse but was used mainly as a jail as late as the 19th century. A low rampart connects the cylindrical tower to the Tour de la Chaîne. During the Wars of Religion, 13 priests were tossed from its summit. You climb 162 steps to the top hold; in clear weather, the panoramic view extends all the way to Ile d'Oléron. On the way up, you can still see graffiti scrawled by former prisoners.

Opposite Tour St-Nicolas, quai du Gabut. ℂ **05-46-41-56-04.** Admission, see box "Saving Money Tower-Hopping." Oct–Mar daily 10am–1pm and 2:15–6:30pm; Apr–Sept 10am–6:30pm.

Tour St-Nicolas ★ HISTORIC SITE The oldest tower in La Rochelle, Tour St-Nicolas was built between 1371 and 1382. It originally guarded the town against surprise attacks. From its second floor, you can enjoy a view of the town and harbor; from the top, you can see only the old town and Ile d'Oléron.

Quai du Gabut. ℂ **05-46-41-74-13.** Admission, see box "Saving Money Tower-Hopping." Oct–Mar daily 10am–6:30pm and Apr–Sept 10am–6:30pm.

> ### Saving Money Tower-Hopping
>
> Instead of paying separate admissions to visit each of the three 14th and 15th century historic towers of La Rochelle, you can purchase a three-tower ticket for 8.50€ adults or 5.50€ ages 18 to 25. It allows you to visit all three tours (though usually after two towers, only the most die-hard tower devotees press on). Should you wish to visit only one tower, you'll pay just 6€ for adults and 74€ for ages 18 to 25, free for children 17 and under.

Where to Stay

La Monnaie Art & Spa ★★ Located near to the Tour de la Lanterne, this hotel is in a 17th-century building that has been tastefully restored in a luxurious, contemporary style. All rooms come with flat screen TVs and air conditioning. A word to the wise, the normal doubles are a little small. Also on-site are a small spa with a Jacuzzi and sauna (but no pool). Take a cocktail in the bar or enjoy the beautiful Jardin des Loges outside space.

3 rue de la Monnaie. www.hotelmonnaie.com. ℂ **05-46-50-65-65.** 36 units. 159€–204€ double; 259€–319€ suite. Parking 20€ reserved in advance. **Amenities:** Bar; spa; room service; free Wi-Fi.

Un Hôtel en Ville ★ This great-value option stands out because of its roof terrace with amazing views over the city and its friendly welcome. Centrally located close to the port with its bars and restaurants, every element has been recently redone, introducing welcome touches like high

sailing THE PORTS OF LA ROCHELLE

La Rochelle has always earned its living from the sea and the ships that make its harbor their home. Four distinct harbors have grown up over the centuries, each a world unto itself, rich with local nuance and lore. They include the historic **Vieux-Port,** the **Port de Plaisance** (a modern yacht marina), the **Port de Pêche** (the fishing port), and the **Port de Commerce,** mostly used by large container ships.

The best way to appreciate them is to take a boat tour. Visit the tourist office (see Essentials, earlier in this chapter), which acts as a clearinghouse for the outfitters (Croisières Inter-Iles, Navipromer, Ré Croisières). Tours combine a look at the modern facilities with a waterside view of the historic ramparts which, despite their girth and height, did not protect the city's 17th-century Protestants from starvation and eventual annihilation.

The company with the most frequent departures is the **Croisières Inter-Iles** (www.inter-iles.com; © **05-46-50-55-54**). Every day from April to October, about a half-dozen cruises glide into each of the six ports. In winter, they're offered less frequently, usually only on school vacations. Tours last 70 to 180 min. each, are conducted in French, and average 20€.

Another excellent waterborne outing—but only during the warmer

months—involves taking a **ferry** from the Vieux-Port of La Rochelle to **Ile de Ré.** The island, 26km (16 miles) off the coast of La Rochelle and ringed with 69km (43 miles) of sandy beaches, holds nature preserves crisscrossed with biking and hiking paths, and a number of excellent restaurants in the island's main town, St-Martin-de-Ré. Croisières Inter-Iles (see above) serves the island. If you want to get here during July or August, and if you don't have a car, we recommend taking the ferry for a round-trip fare of 22€. It's worth spending a few days on the island if you have time, joining the many Parisians who escape here during the summer months. The island has many bike rental shops and over 100km (62 miles) of excellent bike paths. Since the island is fairly flat (the highest point only 19m/62 ft.) you can easily do the trip without a car.

You can also drive your car across the bridge that connects the Ile de Ré to the French mainland. It's accessible from a point 3km (1.75 miles) south of La Rochelle. The toll is 17€ in summer, 9€ in winter. The local bus company, **Les Mouettes** (www.lesmouettes-transports.com; © **08-11-36-17-17**), offers 14 round-trips per day year-round (line 3), and charges 4.40€ one-way or 7.40€ round-trip from La Rochelle to several stops along the island.

quality bedding and hearty breakfasts. You snag an excellent deal during the winter months, so do check with them directly.

20 pl. du Maréchal Foch. http://unhotelenville.fr. © **05-46-41-15-75.** 11 units. 79€–129€ double; 124€–159€ suite. Breakfast 12€. **Amenities:** Room service; free Wi-Fi.

Where to Eat

Bar/Bistro André ★ SEAFOOD   This may be the classic La Rochelle restaurant, but we wouldn't be keeping it in here if it wasn't good. Traditional menu items include fish soup, an unusual *cabillaud fumé* (home-smoked codfish) served with garlic-flavored cream sauce, and curried mussels *(mouclade)*. But the best thing to do is simply ask what's come freshly in off the boats that day. Reservations recommended.

5 rue St-Jean du Pérot/pl. de la Chaîne. www.barandre.com. ✆ **05-46-41-28-24.** Main course 19€–32€; fixed-price menus 18€–45€. Daily noon–2:30pm and 7–11pm.

Christophe Coutanceau ★★★ MODERN FRENCH   This is not only the city's most glamorous and prestigious restaurant, but also one of the Atlantic coast's finest. It is worth the expense for a special evening. With stunning views over the Concurrence beach and the bay beyond, the restaurant is contemporary in feel with luxurious touches everywhere. Christophe Coutanceau is both owner and chef (and, as he likes to underline, also a fisherman), and so very much aware of the importance of sustainability in what he catches and serves. For example, no fish on the menu here will be served during its breeding season. If you book far enough ahead, you could snag the Chef's Table, where you can watch the masters at work. The insanely comprehensive wine list has over 1,000 wines listed from a cellar with 22,000 bottles. Reservations required.

Plage de la Concurrence. www.coutanceaularochelle.com. ✆ **05-46-41-48-19.** Main course 65€–95€; fixed-price menus 70€–145€. Mon–Sat 12:15–1:30pm and 7:30–9:30pm.

Prao Resto ★★ MODERN FRENCH   This place is as laid-back as you would hope from a restaurant that focuses on the slow food philosophy. Named after the simple wooden *prao* boats with triangular sails that you find in the Indian Ocean, restaurant features exposed stone walls and heating pipes that give the interior an industrial but creative feel. The menu focuses on local foodstuffs, from oysters to fish to locally-sourced meats. The place is run as a cooperative, so the suppliers are also partners. The Sunday brunch is excellent and the menus always have great vegetarian options. The **Prao Café,** serving salads and hot and cold sandwiches, is at 21 quai Valin.

10 rue Saint-Nicolas. www.prao.biz. ✆ **05-46-41-28-24.** Main course 14€–16€; fixed-price menus 11€–28€. Daily noon–2:30pm and 7:30–11pm; closed Sun nights.

La Rochelle Nightlife

From July to September, head for **quai Duperré, cours des Dames,** and **cours des Templiers.** Once the sun starts to set, this becomes one big pedestrian zone peppered with street performers. It's a fun, almost magical area that sets the tone for the rest of the night. Your early evening should include a stop in at **La Cave de Guignette,** 8 rue Sainte Nicolas (https://la-guignette.fr; ✆ **05-56-41-05-75**), which looks pretty much unchanged since it opened in the 1930s and has on tap la guignette, a blend of white wine, sparkling water, and syrup rarely found outside of La Rochelle (and possibly this bar).

Day Trip from La Rochelle

COGNAC

478km (296 miles) SW of Paris; 37km (23 miles) NW of Angoulême; 113km (70 miles) SE of La Rochelle

The world enjoys 163 million bottles a year of the nectar known as cognac, which Victor Hugo called "the drink of the gods." It's worth a detour to visit one of the château warehouses of the bottlers. Martell, Hennessy, and Otard welcome visits from the public, as well as other worthy *maisons de négoce;* visits usually include free tastings, although increasingly the big houses are charging for visits but making them more interesting in return.

GETTING THERE   Five trains per day arrive from Angoulême (trip time: 40 min., ticket price 10.30€ one-way), and six trains pull in from Saintes (trip time: 20 min., ticket price 5.90€ one-way). For train information and schedules, visit www.oui.sncf or call ☎ **36-35** (.40€/min.). Limited **bus** service arrives from Angoulême; the trip takes 50 min. and costs 4.50€; visit www.vtpc.fr or call ☎ **05-45-95-95-99** for schedules. If you're **driving** to Cognac, the best route from Saintes (which lies along the major route A10) is N141 east.

Exploring the Town

Many visitors don't realize that this unassuming town of some 20,000 people is about more than just a drink. Though the air is perfumed with the sweet scent from the distilleries, business goes on as usual in the cobbled streets, some of which still sport a few half-timbered houses from the Renaissance.

If you'd like to visit a distillery, go to its main office during regular business hours and request a tour, or visit the tourist office for assistance. On a tour, you'll see some brandies that have aged for as long as 50 or even 100 years. You can have a free taste and then purchase a bottle or two. As far as we're concerned, **Otard** offers the most informative and insightful tours, partly because of the sheer majesty of its headquarters, in the late-medieval **Château de Cognac,** 127 bd. Denfert-Rochereau (www.otard.com; ☎ **05-45-36-88-86**). The tour is half historical overview of the castle, half technical explanation of cognac production. Parts of the château are appropriately baronial (King François I was born here). Tours last about 1 hr. and cost 11€ for adults, 5€ for students 12 to 18, and are free for children 12 and under. From April to October, tours depart at frequent intervals daily. During November to March, you need to contact them in advance to arrange the tour. Call the tourist office or the company several days in advance for exact schedules.

Other distilleries that conduct tours include **Hennessy,** 1 quai Hennessy (www.hennessy.com; ☎ **05-45-35-06-44;** 18€; Apr–Oct daily , with regular tours between 9:45am and 5pm; Nov–Mar Tues–Sat tours at 10:45am, 2, and 4pm); **Camus,** 21 rue de Cagouillet (www.camus.fr; ☎ **05-45-32-28-28;** 7€, master sommelier class where you blend your own cognac 160€; May–Sept Mon 2–6pm, Tues–Sat 10:30am–12:30pm and 2–6pm; tours at 11am, 2:30, 3:30, and 4:30pm); and **Maison Rémy Martin,** 20 rue de la Société Vinicole (www.visitesremymartin.com; *℃* **05-45-35-76-66**). Here you can take a variety of tours of the estate, the cellars, a combination of the two, or enjoy various themed tastings. Priced from 20€, the most elaborate package costs 250€ for a 2-hr. class that gives an insight into their iconic Louis XIII cognac. There is also a cocktail making class for 110€. For all tours, call in advance for reservations.

If you're short on time, a good retail outlet is **La Cognathèque,** 8 pl. Jean-Monnet (www.cognatheque.com; *℃* **05-45-82-43-31**), which prides itself on having the widest selection from all the region's distilleries, large and small (some 400 different cognacs).

The **Musée des Arts de Cognac** is in the town center at place de la Salle Verte (www.musees-cognac.fr; *℃* **05-45-36-21-10;** July and Aug Tues–Sun 10am–6:30pm; May, June, and Sept Tues–Friday 11am–6pm, and Sat and Sun 1–6pm; Oct–April Tues–Sun 2–6pm). This takes you through the history of the trade coupled with more modern exhibitions, often incorporating local artists. The museum also has a good boutique. Entrance is 4.50€ for adults, 3€ for students. Admission is free for anyone 17 and under.

Within a 15-min. walk lies the **Musée d'Art et l'Histoire de Cognac,** 48 bd. Denfert-Rochereau (www.musees-cognac.fr; *℃* **05-45-32-07-25;** July and August Wed–Mon 10am–6:30pm; May, June, and Sept Mon and

Cognac at Hennessy.

Wed–Fri 11am–1pm and 2–6pm, and Sat and Sun 1–6pm; Oct–April daily 10am–noon and 2–6pm). Located in a gorgeous building classified as a historic monument, it has exhibits on popular arts and traditions, and a fine art collection. Your ticket to the Musée des Arts de Cognac includes entrance here (and vice versa).

Where to Eat

In downtown Cognac, **Le Bistro de Claude,** 15 rue Grande (www.bistro-de-claude.com; ✆ **05-45-82-60-32;** fixed-price menus 20€–34€; Mon–Fri noon–2pm and 7:30–9:30pm), serves up carefully prepared, well-presented classic French fare along with an excellent Cognac list.

La Ribaudière ★★ MODERN FRENCH   This is perhaps the region's best restaurant, certainly the most acclaimed. Chef Thierry Verrat has been producing the best of the region's cuisine for 23 years. Reservations recommended.

16200 Bourg-Charente. www.laribaudiere.com. ✆ **05-45-81-30-54.** Main course 49€–105€. Wed–Sun noon–2pm and 7–9:30pm; Tues evening only.

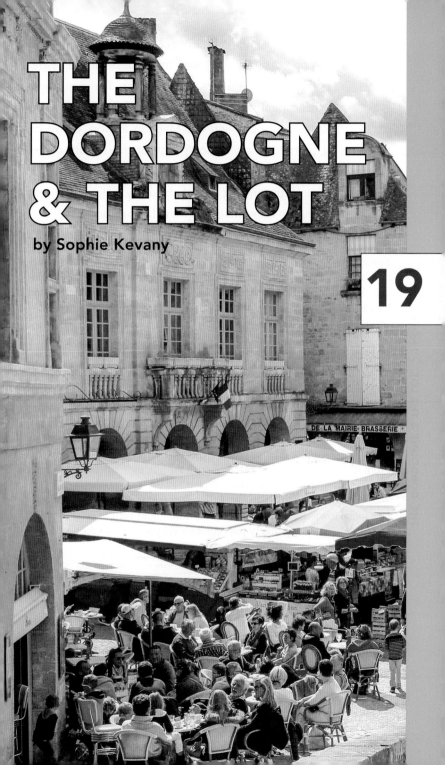

THE DORDOGNE & THE LOT

by Sophie Kevany

19

K
nown for its food and landscapes, the Dordogne and Périgord are much-loved travel destinations, especially for truffle lovers. Our first stop, Périgueux, was the capital of the old province of Périgord. In this region, we can find Cro-Magnon artwork drawn on the walls of prehistoric caves, softly sigh at the beauty of the Dordogne Valley, explore the lofty heights of Rocamadour and, finally, visit Cahors, the ancient capital of Quercy, well known for its robust, deep purple wines made from the Malbec grape.

Though the larger towns are inviting, the countryside is the main attraction here. Villages, carved into the limestone cliffs, overlook the Dordogne River; medieval fortresses peer down from craggy bluffs; and breathtaking cave paintings offer a glimpse of daily, prehistoric life. Allow several days to explore, eat, and simply gaze.

PÉRIGUEUX ★

485km (301 miles) SW of Paris; 85km (53 miles) SE of Angoulême; 113km (70 miles) NE of Bordeaux; 101km (63 miles) SW of Limoges

Capital of the old province of Périgord, Périgueux stands on the Isle River. In addition to its food products (foie gras and truffles reign supreme here), the town is known for its medieval and Renaissance architecture and its Gallo-Roman ruins. The city is divided into three sections: Le Puy St-Front (the medieval town), on the slope of the hill; the Cité (the old Roman town); and, to the west, the modern town.

Though Périgueux (pop. 30,000) is very pretty, it is basically a sleepy provincial town. Its attractions probably won't hold your interest for more than a day, but you'll likely pass through on your way to the Dordogne Valley and the cave paintings at Les Eyzies.

Essentials

GETTING THERE At least a dozen **trains** per day arrive from Paris from either Montparnasse or Gare d'Austerlitz (trip time: 4–5 hr.; 50€–135€ one-way), 11 direct trains from Bordeaux (trip time: 1.5 hr.; 22€ one-way), and one or two direct trains per hour from Limoges (trip time: 1 hr.; 17€ one-way). For train information, visit www.oui.sncf or call ✆ **36-35** (.40€/min.). If you're **driving** from Paris, take A10 south to Orléans and then A20 south to Vierzon, where you'll pick up the A89 to Périgueux.

PREVIOUS PAGE: **Market day in Sarlat-La-Canéda**

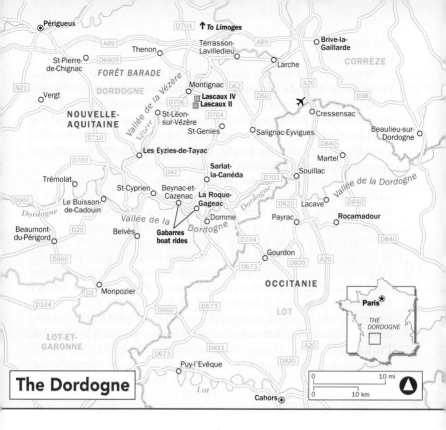

↑ To Limoges

The Dordogne

The new high-speed rail link from Paris to Bordeaux might now make a transfer here the fastest way to get to the Dordogne.

VISITOR INFORMATION   The **Office du Tourisme** is at 9 bis pl. du Coderc (www.tourisme-perigueux.fr; ℂ **05-53-53-10-63**). Among other useful items, they offer an area restaurant guide. You may want to rent a bike and explore the countryside; a map is available at the tourist office. Electric bikes and something to eat can be found at Le **Veloc Café,** 7 av. Daumesnil (ℂ **06-33-48-22-89**); prices start at 20€ per half day. The Vinci car parks also offer free bike hire to their customers.

Exploring Périgueux & Environs

Give yourself the time to amble through the **Puy St-Front,** Périgueux's well-preserved medieval quarter, rich with ancient houses, cobbled alley-ways, and Renaissance facades. It's hard to miss the imposing **Tour Mataguerre,** a 15th-century tower that is all that's left of the city's forti-fications. Follow the winding streets up to the **Cathedral St-Front** (see below) and the **place de Coderc,** once a literal pigsty, and later the admin-istrative center of the medieval town. An outdoor market takes place here and snakes down to place de la Cautre and the Hôtel de Ville on Wednesdays and Saturdays from 8am to 1pm.

Périgueux is a treasure trove of Gallo-Roman antiquities. The most visible is the **Tour de Vésone,** a partially ruined site that stands 26m (85 ft.) tall, just southwest of town beyond the railway station. Here you'll see the remains of a Roman temple dedicated to the goddess Vesuna, but you can't enter the site. The remains of a large 1st-century Gallo-Roman villa were discovered next to the temple, and in 2003, a sleek new museum was opened, **Musée Gallo Romain Vesunna** (see below).

Nearby is the **Jardin des Arènes,** a public garden that holds a few remains of an amphitheater that held as many as 22,000 spectators back in the 2nd century. Near the arena are the ruins of the **Château Barrière,** rue Turenne, built in the 11th or 12th century on Roman foundations.

Gastronomy reigns supreme in Périgueux, especially when it comes to foie gras, or "fat liver", which comes from force-fed geese and ducks. (Vegans may want to skip directly to truffles below.) Stores that sell what some call a delicacy (and others animal cruelty) abound. One is **L'Espace Du Sixième Sens,** 6 pl. Saint-Silain (✆ **05-53-09-24-29**). If you want an adventure, and to see an example of less industrial production methods, head for a goose farm that makes its own foie gras, such as **A la Ferme de Puygauthier,** about 15 min. south of town in Marsaneix (http://www.bienvenue-a-la-ferme.com/aquitaine/dordogne/marsaneix/ferme/ferme-de-puygauthier/307926; ✆ **05-53-08-87-07**). To get there, take the D2 and follow signs to Brive.

Black truffles are another local specialty, and many fans of the delectable mushroom come to the area with only one aim: to eat as many as possible, in as many forms as possible, especially during the **Truffle Festival** (Fête de la Truffe) in mid-December. Truffle markets are held during December to February in place St Louis in Périgueux, and in a few local villages, most notably in Saint Genies and Brantome. In July and August, although not the season for truffles, there is a singing competition in honor of the local delicacy in Périgueux itself.

Cathédrale St-Front ★ CATHEDRAL   This 12th-century cathedral is one of the rare Byzantine-style churches to be found in France. Left in ruins after the Wars of Religion, it was restored with more than a few 19th-century flourishes by Paul Abadie, who, thus inspired, went on to design the Sacre-Coeur in Paris. With its five white domes and colonnaded turrets, St-Front evokes Constantinople. The cathedral's bell tower is one of the only authentic vestiges of the original church. The interior is built on the plan of a Greek cross, unusual for a French cathedral. The recently restored cloisters, which date from the 9th century, can be visited for a fee of 1.50€.

Pl. de la Clautre. www.amiscathedralesaintfront.fr. ✆ **05-53-53-10-63.** Free admission. Daily 8:30am–7pm (in winter until 6pm).

Eglise St-Etienne-de-la-Cité ★★ CHURCH   Périgueux's other remarkable church—this one in the Cité area—was a cathedral until 1669, when it lost its position to St-Front. The church was built in the 12th century but has been much damaged since. It contains a 12th-century bishop's tomb and a carved 17th-century wooden reredos depicting the Assumption of the Madonna.

10 av. Cavaignac. ✆ **05-53-06-48-10.** Free admission. Daily 8am–6pm.

Musée d'Art et d'Archéologie du Périgord ★ MUSEUM   Built on the site of an Augustinian monastery, this museum has one of the most extensive collections of prehistoric relics in France and is an excellent introduction to the wealth of the Périgord region (as most were found from local digs). A smaller collection of medieval and Renaissance treasures is also on offer.

22 cours Tourny. http://musee-perigord.museum.com. ✆ **05-53-06-40-70.** Admission 4€ adults; 2€ students; free for children 17 and under. Apr–Sept Mon and Wed–Fri 10:30am–5:30pm, Sat–Sun 1–6pm; Oct–Mar Mon and Wed–Fri 10am–5pm, Sat–Sun 1–6pm.

Musée Gallo-Romain Vesunna ★ MUSEUM   This fascinating museum presents extensive vignettes of Roman life based on the ruins of a villa, replete with mosaics and many of the workaday artifacts of

Cathédrale St-Front

BIKING & CANOEING DOWN THE
dordogne

The Dordogne's rivers meander through countryside that's among the most verdant and historic in France. This area is underpopulated but dotted with monuments, châteaux, 12th-century villages, and charming churches.

As you bike around, the rural character of the area unfolds before you. No château, hotel, or inn treats you disdainfully if you show up on two rather than four wheels. (*Au contraire,* the staff will probably offer advice on suitable bike routes.) If you're ever in doubt about where your handlebars should lead you, know that you'll rarely go wrong if your route parallels the riverbanks of the Lot, the Vézère, the Dordogne, or any of their tributaries. Architects and builders since the 11th century have added greatly to the visual allure of their watersides.

France's national train service, SNCF, makes it easy to transport a bike on the nation's railways. However, if you don't want to bring your own wheels on the train, the region has plenty of rental shops. (Recommend rentals are in this chapter's sections on Périgueux and Les Eyzies-de-Tayac.)

Exploring the rivers by canoe is another option. Every summer, a flotilla of bathing-suited visitors can be seen paddling down the Dordogne; the Lot and the Vézère get less traffic and are also beautiful. The rivers tend to be shallow and lazy, perfect for a family outing.

Le Comité Départemental du Tourism, 25 rue du Président Wilson, (www.dordogne-perigord-tourisme.fr; ✆ **05-53-35-50-24**), provides information about all the towns in the *département* and will help you organize biking, hiking, kayaking, and canoeing trips. Two of the best outdoors outfitters are **Canoë Loisir,** Vitrac (www.canoes-loisirs.com; ✆ **05-53-31-22-92** or 05-53-28-23-43) and **Adventure Plein Air,** St-Léon sur Vézère (www.canoevezere.com; ✆ **05-53-50-67-71**), or just head to the town of Brantôme which has several places to pick up canoes.

Kayaking on the Dordogne River

everyday life in the ancient Roman provinces. This mainly glass-fronted building was designed by renowned architect Jean Nouvel. A short walk from the center of Périgueux, the site's recent improvements include several interactive displays, including a 3-D movie, and an escape game where players are given 1 hr. to unlock an archaeological mystery.

Rue du 26e Régiment d'Infanterie. www.vesunna.fr. ℂ **05-53-53-00-92.** Admission 6€ adults; 4€ students and children ages 6–25; free for children 5 and under. Oct–March Tues–Fri 9:30am–12:30pm and 1:30–5pm, Sat–Sun 10am–12:30pm and 2:30–6pm; Apr–June and Sept Tues–Fri 9:30am–5:30pm, Sat–Sun 10am–12:30pm and 2:30–6pm; July–Aug daily 10am–7pm. Closed 1st and 2nd week of Jan; closed Mondays except in July and Aug; closed Nov 1 and 11, and Dec 25.

Musée Militaire ★ MUSEUM   This small is unmissable for military buffs. It collections of medals, insignia, flags, military uniforms, helmets, badges, and weaponry are well-worth browsing.

32 Rue des Farges. www.museemilitaire-perigord.fr. ℂ **05-53-53-47-36.** Admission 6€ adults; 3€ students; free for children 11 and under. Daily Mon–Sat 2–6pm.

Where to Stay

The **Château des Reynats** (see "Where to Eat," below) also has rooms.

Hôtel Bristol ★   Périgueux does not have a huge amount of choice for places to stay but this is a good bet if you want to stay central. Fully updated over the past few years, it has comfortable rooms with small but perfectly workable bathrooms. It's only a 5-min. walk to the town's best restaurants and major points of interest.

37–39 rue Antoine Gadaud. www.bristolfrance.com. ℂ **05-53-08-75-90.** 29 units. 70€ double. Free parking. Closed btw. Christmas and New Year's Day. **Amenities:** Room service; free Wi-Fi.

Castel Peyssard ★★   It might be worth heading a little further out of town to find this spa hotel—not too far though, as this is still within easy reach of the main sites, in the middle of a 1-hectare (2.5-acre) park. The hotel has just four bedrooms, each decorated according to a theme from films such as "Cleopatra" or "Out of Africa," with comfortable well-sized beds. The on-site bistro offers lunch and evening meals. It's all a little quirky, certainly, but thoroughly enjoyable.

15 rue Paul Louis Courier. www.castelpeyssard.com. ℂ **05-53-35-91-90.** 4 units. 185€–210€ double. **Amenities:** Bar; restaurant; spa; free Wi-Fi.

Where to Eat

Eating is a major occupation in Périgueux. Stores that sell truffles and foie gras abound, but one of the best known is **L'Espace du Sixième Sens,** 6 pl. Saint Silain (ℂ **05-53-09-24-29**), where visitors can also eat. Fans of the delectable mushroom come from far and wide, especially during the **Truffle Festival** (Fête de la Truffe; www.perigueux-city.com/fete-de-la-truffe-a-perigueux.html), with different events December to February.

Au Bien Bon Tome II ★★ TRADITIONAL FRENCH The name means "at the place that is really good" and this homey restaurant (which has closed and reopened a few times, hence the name Tome II) doesn't disappoint. Hearty portions of *magret de canard* (duck breast in wine sauce), *andouillette* sausage, duck *confit*, and other regional specialties are on the menu, which changes according to what's good at the market that day. Wash it all down with a glass of the local Bergerac wine and you've had a true southwestern experience.

2 rue Montaigne. www.facebook.com/aubienbon. ✆ **09-83-85-09-35.** Main course 10€–14€; fixed-price lunch 11€–15€ or dinner 23€. Tues–Sat noon–2pm, Fri 7:30–9:30pm, Sat 7–9:30pm.

Château des Reynats ★★ MODERN FRENCH This slate-roofed 19th-century manor has a yellow and soft-red Empire dining room in which you can enjoy the finest *cuisine du marché* in the entire region. It also has an interesting history of its own dating from France's disastrous exit from its former department of Algeria, when it functioned as a kind of refugee center for French citizens booted off their estates.

You can also stay in the château or l'Orangerie, a comfortable space but less grand than the château. Doubles in the château range from 132€ to 213€, suites 243€ to 279€, whereas doubles in the guesthouse go for 103€ to 115€.

15 av. des Reynats, Chancelade. www.chateau-hotel-perigord.com. ✆ **05-53-03-53-59.** Main course 24€–52€; fixed-price lunch 38€ or dinner 44€–89€. Mon–Sat 7–9:30pm. Restaurant closed first 3 weeks of Jan.

Le Clos Saint Front ★★ MODERN FRENCH Still going strong and delivering innovative takes on local market food, this makes a good choice if you are just a little tired of duck and truffles and want to find a more contemporary (although almost always still rich) menu. It has a lovely garden for summer months, but this is a year-round destination.

5-7 rue de la Vertu. www.leclossaintfront.com. ✆ **05-53-46-78-58.** Main course 21.50€; fixed-price menu 28.50€, lunch 35€ or dinner 40€–62€. Tues–Sun noon–1:45pm; Tues–Sat 7–9:45pm.

L'Essentiel ★★ MODERN FRENCH Book ahead for a chance to dine at Périgueux's one-star Michelin restaurant. The wine list alone is worth the trip, and the food in this family-run establishment is equally good. Service is attentive, ingredients top quality, and food carefully prepared. Diners can start with a dozen oysters in vegetable jelly with creamed crab and a langoustine tartare, followed by a stuffed, roasted half pigeon with pumpkin or roast pear puree, and finish up with a green lemon tart with bergamot and a calamansi sorbet.

8 rue de la Clarté. www.restaurant-perigueux.com. ✆ **05-53-35-15-15.** Lunch 29€; dinner menu 43€–49€; a la carte 65€–85€. Tues–Sat noon–1:15pm and 7–9:15pm.

Périgueux Nightlife

Begin your evening with a stroll in the streets and alleyways surrounding **place St-Silain, place St-Louis,** and **place du Marché.**

If you're feeling lively, the leading (let's face it the choice isn't extensive) disco is **La Régence,** 16 rue Chancelier de l'Hôpital (✆ **05-53-53-10-55**). It's open Thursday to Saturday from 12:30am to 6am; theme night details are available on their Facebook page (www.facebook.com/DiscothequePerigueuxcentre).

LASCAUX (MONTIGNAC) ★★

496km (308 miles) SW of Paris; 47km (29 miles) SE of Périgueux

The **Caves at Lascaux,** 2km (1.25 miles) from the Vézère River town of Montignac in the Dordogne region, contain the most beautiful and most famous cave paintings in the world. Unfortunately, you can't view the actual paintings (the caves have been closed to the public to prevent deterioration), but a precise replica gives you a clear picture of the remarkable works.

Four boys looking for a dog called Robot discovered the caves in 1940. They opened to the public in 1948, quickly becoming one of France's major attractions and drawing 125,000 visitors annually. However, the hordes of tourists caused atmospheric changes in the caves, endangering the paintings. Scientists went to work to halt the destructive fungus plaguing the paintings, known as "the green sickness," and a detailed facsimile was constructed nearby for visitors. The town of Montignac itself is worth a stop, for its well-preserved medieval streets and houses.

Essentials

GETTING THERE   By far, the easiest way to reach Montignac is to **drive** northeast from Les Eyzies on D706 for 19km (12 miles).

Rail service is to the neighboring hamlet of Condat-Le-Lardin, 9.5km (6 miles) northeast. From there, **taxis** (✆ **05-53-51-80-46**) take visitors to Montignac for 20€. If no taxis are waiting, a railway station employee will call one for you. For train information, visit www.oui.sncf or call ✆ **36-35** (.40€/min.).

VISITOR INFORMATION   For information on Lascaux, visit the website www.lascaux.fr/en or call ✆ **05-53-50-99-10**; the **Office de Tourisme** in Montignac, on place Bertrand-de-Born (www.tourisme-vezere.com; ✆ **05-53-51-82-60**), can also assist. The tourist office does not sell tickets for Lascaux. Online booking is recommended, although for same-day reservations it is best to call Lascaux directly.

Exploring the Caves & Other Attractions

Public visits to the original Lascaux caves ceased in 1963. Permission to visit for research purposes is given only to qualified archaeologists, so unless you've got an advanced degree and good connections, you will have to make do with the replica. That said, Lascaux II is nothing to sniff at. Years of painstaking artistic and scientific labor went into re-creating the cave, including the use of prehistoric painting techniques and natural colorants. While some of the magic is lost, what you see is virtually identical to the real thing. For more virtual reality, you can visit the original cave online at extensive sites set up by the French government: www.lascaux.culture.fr or www.lascaux.fr/en. More recently, the new Lascaux IV has opened (with Lascaux III being a touring exhibit). Somewhat confusingly, the Lascaux website refers to Lascaux IV as The International Centre For Cave Art, something to bear in mind when buying tickets online.

Lascaux IV ★★★ or The International Centre For Cave Art

HISTORIC SITE   Newly opened in January 2018 and very much in demand, the home of the latest replica reveals far more of the cave than previous versions and uses a range of technology to take visitors back 20,000 years. New sections cover the cave's discovery and at its position in relation to cave art more generally. The center took 3 years to create and has been integrated into the surrounding landscape. From the outside, Lascaux IV is a fissure in the landscape, as is the original. In an interview

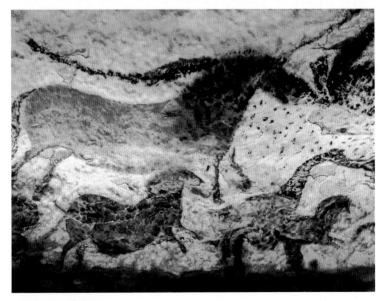

Lascaux cave paintings

with design website "designcurial," one of the exhibit's designers, Roger Mann, of Casson Mann (the same scenographers that designed Bordeaux's Cité du Vin), said he wanted visitors to feel as though they were entering the original cave—something that he has achieved.

2km (1.25 miles) from Montignac, off D706. www.lascaux.fr/en/prepare-your-visit/visit-lascaux/international-centre-for-cave-art. ✆ **05-53-50-99-10.** Admission 17.00€ adults; 13€ children ages 13–17; 11€ children ages 5–12; free for children 4 and under. Daily Jan 22–Mar 30 10am–6pm; Mar 31–July 8 9am–7:30pm; July 9–Aug 8am–9:30pm; September 9am–7:30pm; October 9:30–7pm; Nov–Jan 6 10am–6pm.

Lascaux II ★★ HISTORIC SITE   A short walk downhill from the real cave is the first reproduction of the original, duplicated and molded in concrete to look and feel like the original stone. The 39m-long (128-ft.) tunnel faithfully reproduces the section of the cave harboring 90 percent of the famous paintings, so you will get a good idea of what the "Sistine Chapel of Prehistory" looks like. You'll see majestic bulls, ibex, stags, horses, and deer, the originals of which were painted by Cro-Magnon peoples 15,000 to 20,000 years ago. No one has yet figured out exactly what purpose these paintings served, but the artistry of these prehistoric painters is startling.

2km (1.25 miles) from Montignac, off D706. www.semitour.com or www.lascaux.fr/en/prepare-your-visit/visit-lascaux/lascaux-2. ✆ **05-53-51-95-03.** Admission 13.00€ adults; 8.50€ children. Daily Mar 31–June 30 10am–12:30pm and 2–6pm; July 1 to July 21 9:30am–7pm; July 22 to Aug 25 9am–8pm; Aug 26 to Aug 31 10:00am–12:30pm and 2–6pm; Sept 1 to Nov 4 10am–12:30pm and 2–5:30pm.

Le Thot ★ ZOO/MUSEUM   This attraction includes a zoo with animals that approximate those depicted on the walls of Lascaux, like Przewalski horses and European bison. Projection rooms show short films on the discovery of cave art at Lascaux. After your visit, walk out on the terrace for a view of the Vézère Valley and the Lascaux hills. The zoo is free when you have tickets for Lascaux IV and young children particularly love seeing the real-life version after their Lascaux visit.

Thonac, 7km (4.25 miles) southwest of Montignac along D706 (follow the signs for Les Eyzies). www.semitour.com. ✆ **05-53-50-70-44.** Admission 7€ adults; 4.50€ children 6–12; free for children 5 and under. July–Aug daily 10am–7pm; Oct to mid-Nov daily 10am–6pm; mid-Feb to Mar and mid-Nov to Dec Tues–Sun 10am–12:30pm and 2–5:30pm; Apr–June and Sept daily 10am–6pm. Closed Jan. Ask the ticket office for options on combined tickets with either Lascaux II or Lascaux IV.

Site Préhistorique de Regourdou ★ MUSEUM   About 450m (1,476 ft.) uphill from Lascaux, a minor road branches off and runs through a forest until it reaches this site, discovered in 1954 by Roger Constant when he conducted an archeological dig in front of his house. Among the treasures here is a skeleton of a Neanderthal man and several bear skeletons. The house has been made into an archaeological museum; nearby, six semi-wild bears roam around a naturalized and barricaded habitat. Depending on the time of year, you may be required to take a guided tour (available in English and French, at no extra cost).

www.regourdou.fr. ℂ **05-53-51-81-23.** Admission 6.50€ adults; 3.50€ children 6–12; free for children 5 and under. July–Aug daily 10am–7pm; Sept–Nov and Feb–June daily 11am–6pm. Closed Dec–Jan.

Préhisto Parc ★★ MUSEUM   Around 15km (9 miles) from Lascaux but well worth the detour, this is a child-friendly overview of how Neanderthal and Cro-Magnon man lived. The exhibits are set around a wooded walkway through a 5-hectare (12-acre) park, with recreations of scenes from daily life, such as a Wooly Mammoth hunt, and a family making tools and cooking around an open fire that really bring the history to life. Workshops during school holidays and the summer months teach skills such as fire-making, flint-cutting and spear-throwing. **La Madeleine,** a riverside cave village just a few minutes' drive away, also makes an excellent visit.

La Faure Reignac, Tursac. www.prehistoparc.fr. ℂ **05-53-50-73-19.** Admission 7.50€ adults; 6.50€ students; 4.50€ children 5–13; free for children 4 and under. Mar 31–Nov 4 daily 10am–6pm. Open year-round for adults with booking.

Where to Stay & Eat

Aux Berges de la Vézère ★ MODERN FRENCH/ITALIAN   This is easily one of the best restaurants in the area, without being fussy or over-polished. It sits right on the banks of the river, with views over the medieval streets on the far banks of the Vézère and a large terrace for the summer months. The bistro-style French menu offers a good range of freshly-caught river fish, and a few local surprises such as Périgord bison. Their Italian pizza menu may seem odd, but it is expertly done, with quality touches such as 36-month aged parmesan and 24-month aged Prosciutto ham. Books for children add to the relaxed feeling. In a town where restaurants can be tourist traps in the summer, this is a great choice.

pl. Tourny, Montignac. www.restaurant-montignac.fr. ℂ **05-53-50-56-31.** Main course 8.90€–20€. July–Aug daily noon–2:30pm and 9–11pm; rest of year Tues–Sun noon–2pm and 7pm–9pm.

Hostellerie la Roseraie ★   In the heart of the medieval village, this little charmer is both affordable and cozy, complete with a rose garden out back. It was converted from a comfortable home built for a local merchant in the 19th century on the banks of the Vézère. The bedrooms have individual character and well-kept bathrooms with either a tub or shower. There is a pleasant terrace to enjoy in the summer months. The restaurant serves traditional French cuisine; fixed-price menus cost from 31€ to 59€.

11 pl. d'Armes, Montignac. www.laroseraie-hotel.com. ℂ **05-53-50-53-92.** 14 units. 111€–148€ double; 212€–293€ family apartment. Parking 8€. **Amenities:** Restaurant; bar; outdoor pool; Wi-Fi (in most rooms; 3€ per 2 hr.). Closed Nov–Mar 24.

Restaurant and Hotel de Bouilhac ★★   This four-star, family-run hotel opened in June 2017. The building is an historic monument from the

17th century, typical of the Périgord Noir style, with an excellent restaurant, right in the heart of town. The website declares "Greed, family and culture" are the hotel's keywords (we're thinking they might mean that the food tastes good), and pets are welcome. Fixed menus in the restaurant range from 15€ to 23€.

Av. du Professeur Faurel, Montignac. http://hoteldebouilhac-montignac.fr. ✆ **05-53-51-21-46.** 10 units. 105€ double in low season; up to 230€ for a four-person room in high season. Free parking. **Amenities:** Restaurant; bar; free Wi-Fi.

LES EYZIES-DE-TAYAC ★★★

533km (330 miles) SW of Paris; 45km (28 miles) SE of Périgueux

When prehistoric skeletons were unearthed here in 1868, the market town of Les Eyzies-de-Tayac (known as Les Eyzies) suddenly became an archaeologist's dream. This area in the Dordogne Valley was found to be one of the richest in the world in ancient sites and deposits. Some of the caves contain primitive drawings made 30,000 years ago. The most beautiful and most famous are at Lascaux (see above), but many caves around Les Eyzies are open to the public.

Essentials

GETTING THERE   **Trains** run from Le Buisson, 19km (12 miles) away, and, on the same line, from Périgueux which are more direct. For information, www.oui.sncf or call ✆ **36-35** (.40€/min.). To **drive** from Périgueux, start along D710 southeast to Le Bugue, and then follow the signs to Les Eyzies-de-Tayac.

VISITOR INFORMATION   The **Office de Tourisme** (www.tourisme-vezere.com; ✆ **05-53-06-97-05**) is open year-round at 19 av. la Préhistoire (pl. de la Mairie).

Exploring the Area

Many of the caves in this area limit the number of daily visitors they admit; you can call ahead for reservations up to a year in advance. We recommend that you do so, especially if you plan to visit in summer. The area does not have a permanent bike rental option, but you can try calling **Canoe Loisirs Evasion** (✆ **06-33-00-29-19**), open from April to September (https://canoe24.com/en/welcome/).

Whether you're biking or driving, the loveliest villages in the **Dordogne Valley ★★★** include **Sarlat-la-Canéda,** 17km (11 miles) southeast of Les Eyzies, and **La Roque-Gageac,** 14 km (8.75 miles) south of Sarlat. Smaller villages, including **Beynac-et-Cazenac, Castelnaud, Domme,** and **Montfort,** lie beside the road that meanders through the Dordogne Valley. Throughout the region, routes are country roads marked only with signs leading to the above-mentioned destinations.

Make a special effort to stand in the shadow of the foreboding **Château de Beynac ★★**, Beynac-et-Cazenac (✆ **05-53-29-50-40**), a remarkably intact 12th-century fortress that peers out over the Dordogne Valley from a rocky crag. The fortress played an important role in the 100 Years War and at one point was seized by Richard the Lionheart. The Grosso family, who lived on-site for almost 40 years, did an amazing job of restoration, now handed over to Alberic and Audrey de Mongolfier; the castle has served as a backdrop in several movies, including Luc Besson's "Jean d'Arc". The view alone is worth the hike up hill; fans of knights in shining armor will surely appreciate the visit. It was closed for a while following the death of Denise Grosso, but things should now be back to normal, open April through September daily from 10am to 6:30pm, and October to March daily until 6pm. Free 1-hr. guided tours (in French) begin once or twice an hour. Admission, with or without the tour, costs 8€, 4.50€ ages 12 to 16, and 3.50€ ages 5 to 11. A worthy restaurant is in the nearby **Hôtel Restaurant du Château** (✆ **05-53-29-19-20**), on the river at the base of the château; it is open daily April to October.

Grotte de Font-de-Gaume ★★ HISTORIC SITE   This is the last cave with multicolored prehistoric paintings that is still open to the public (although there are rumors that this too will be closed within a few years, so move fast). Only 78 visitors are allowed per day and you cannot make advance reservations, so the only thing to do is turn up early and be prepared to change your plans. You will be on a 45-min. guided tour (12 per tour make sure to request one in English when you reserve) through a rather narrow cave (claustrophobes beware). Discovered in 1901, the paintings and etchings in the cave date from the Magdalenian period (17,000–9,000 B.C.). While the paintings are not as spectacular as those at Lascaux, here you are seeing the real thing, including depictions of bison, mammoths, horses, and other animals. The knowledgeable guides will point out how prehistoric artists used the shape of the caves walls to make their paintings more lifelike. They may also show some eerie prehistoric hand prints.

On D47, 1.5km (1 mile) outside Les Eyzies. http://eyzies.monuments-nationaux.fr/en. ✆ **05-53-06-86-00**. Admission 10€ adults; 8€ students; free for visitors 24 and under. May 15–Sep 15 Sun–Fri 9:30am–5:30pm; Sep 16–May 14 9:30am–12:30pm and 2pm–5:30pm.

Grotte des Combarelles ★ HISTORIC SITE   Discovered at the turn of the 20th century, this wide cave on the southeast edge of town has over 400 etchings of animals, including musk oxen, horses, bison, and aurochs (prehistoric oxen). Think of it as a gallery of Magdalenian art. Advanced reservations not accepted; purchase tickets at the same office as Font-de-Gaume. Daily visits are limited to 60 people.

On D47, 17km (11 miles) north of Bergerac. http://eyzies.monuments-nationaux.fr/en. ℂ **05-53-06-97-72.** Admission prices and time same as Font-de-Gaume.

Grotte du Grand-Roc ★ NATURAL ATTRACTION   The artistic marvels here are all created by nature, not man; this cave is a geological wonder of crystals, stalagmites, and stalactites. The cave is about 1.5km (1 mile) northwest of Les Eyzies on the left bank of the Vézère (signs point the way on D47). While the venue does not limit to visitor numbers but you might still get stuck in a queue in the summer. Ensure you have a sweater, as it gets chilly underground.

Grotte du Grand-Roc, Les Eyzies. www.semitour.com. ℂ **05-53-06-92-70.** Admission 7.80€ adults; 5.30€ children 5–12; free for children 4 and under. Daily Feb–Mar 10am–12:30pm and 2–5:30pm; Apr–July 10am–1pm and 2–6pm; Sept and Oct 10am–1pm and 2–6pm. Closed Jan.

Musée National de la Préhistoire ★★ MUSEUM   In the shadow of the limestone cliff that hovers above the village, this museum had a major overhaul and is now set in a modern limestone building next to a fortress-castle from the 16th century. One of the largest collections of prehistoric artifacts in Europe ("only" 18,000 of its 5 million objects are on display), this museum traces 400,000 years of human history, from the origins to the end of the Ice Age (around 10,000 B.C.). Highlights include the 15,000-year-old bone **etching of a bison** licking its flank★, **tools** dating back 150,000 years and replicas of the **first-known human footprints,** thought date back about 3.6 million years, as well as a very life-like statue of a Neanderthal man. Teaching workshops are available for children, but these also need booking an advance.

1 rue du Musée, Les Eyzies. www.musee-prehistoire-eyzies.fr. ℂ **05-53-06-45-45.** Admission 6€ adults; 4.50€ ages 18–25; free for visitors 24 under and students; free to all first Sun of month. July–Aug daily 9:30am–6:00pm; Jan–May Wed–Mon 9:30am–12:30pm and 2–5:30pm; June–Sept Wed–Mon 9:30–12.30pm and 2–6pm.

Musée National de la Préhistoire

Where to Stay & Eat

Hôtel Le Moulin de la Beune ★   This hotel offers a good value for staying in a renovated 17th-century mill (complete with working water-wheel) just off the main street. The simple but cozy rooms are nicely decorated with homey touches. Ivy covers the outside of the hotel and the restaurant, **Au Vieux Moulin,** which serves elegant regional classics with set menus starting at 26€. As of 2018 several rooms have been renovated and the restaurant has a new chef who has redone the menus. In good weather, you can dine on a shaded terrace or just laze in a lounge chair next to the babbling brook. The best way to reserve a room is to email (English is not a problem) moulindelabeune@gmail.com.

2 rue du Moulin Bas, Les Eyzies-de-Tayac. www.moulindelabeune.com. ✆ **05-53-06-94-33.** 20 units. 75€–85€ double. Closed Nov–Apr. **Amenities:** Restaurant; free Wi-Fi in common areas only.

Hôtel Les Glycines ★   This hotel has beautiful gardens set among the trappings of the 19th-century building. You get regional cuisine, comfort-able accommodation, and drinks on a veranda with a grape arbor. Rooms are painted in relaxing neutral shades, combining regional charm with designer style. Some rooms look out over the ample grounds, which include a pool and lots of the flowers. Specialties at the restaurants include new twists on foie gras, cèpes, and truffles. Fixed-price menus range from 17€ at lunch to 110€ for the special evening truffle menu. Many ingredi-ents come from the hotel's impressive kitchen garden. The hotel has also opened a new spa and treatments start at 29€ for a half day.

Rte. de Périgueux (D47), Les Eyzies-Tayac-Sireuil. www.les-glycines-dordogne.com. ✆ **05-53-06-97-07.** 25 units. 129€–179€ double; 255€ junior suite. Closed mid-Nov and Dec. **Amenities:** Restaurant; bar; babysitting; outdoor pool; room service; free Wi-Fi.

Restaurant de Laugerie Basse ★ TRADITIONAL FRENCH   This picturesque and large family restaurant is tucked in an interesting setting just under the troglodyte cliff, close to the Grotte du Grand Roc. It offers local basic Périgueux-style food and also welcomes large groups.

Les Eyzies-Tayac-Sireuil. ✆ **05-53-06-97-91**. Fixed-price menus from 17€. Closed weekends Halloween to Easter.

SARLAT-LA-CANÉDA ★★

9.5km (6 miles) E of Les Eyzies-de-Tayac; 530km (329 miles) SW of Paris; 60km (37 miles) NW of Cahors

If Sarlat looks like it could be a movie set, that's because it is so picture perfect that it actually has starred in a dozen or so films, including Luc Besson's "Jean d'Arc," Robert Hossein's "Les Misérables" in 1982, and Peter Hyams' "D'Artagnan." You can't come to the Dordogne and not at least take a quick stroll through its narrow streets, a pristine collection of medieval architecture and delightful squares. Unfortunately, you won't be alone, especially if you come in high season. Traffic can snarl as you enter the town, so try to plan your arrival for early morning, or better yet, late afternoon, when everyone is leaving.

Sarlat grew up around a Benedictine abbey back in the 8th century, but its glory days were in the 14th, when it bustled with artisans, painters, and students. Many of the buildings from that era survived, along with other jewels from the Renaissance and subsequent periods, and the town's beauty was such that it was the first to be officially preserved by French law in the 1960s. The **Old Town (Vieille Ville)** ★★★, which has been carefully restored, is as romantic and historic as ever—if anything, it's been overly cleaned up, giving it a slightly Disney-esque feel. If you ignore the tourist traps and wander off down the tiny medieval streets, you will still fall under the spell of this beautiful place.

Essentials

GETTING THERE About seven direct **train** connections arrive daily from Bordeaux (trip time: 2.5 hr., 25€). Trains from Paris go to Souillac, about 30km (19 miles) by bus from Sarlat; **buses** run fairly frequently (trip time: 40 min.); visit www.ter-sncf.com/Regions/Aquitaine/fr for schedules. For train information and schedules, visit www.oui.sncf or call ℰ **36-35** (.40€/min.). The terminus in Sarlat lies 1km (.5 mile) south of the old town. You can walk it in 15 min. or else take a taxi.

Motorists **drive** the A10 autoroute from Paris, going by way of Poitiers, Angoulême, and Périgueux to reach Sarlat. Or you can take the A89 from Bordeaux. Sarlat lies 180km (112 miles) east of Bordeaux.

VISITOR INFORMATION The **Office de Tourisme,** 3 rue Tourny (www.sarlat-tourisme.com; ℰ **05-53-31-45-45**), sells area maps and offers English-language tours from May to October.

SPECIAL EVENTS In the summer, the streets of Sarlat are bustling with people, many of whom come to attend the **Féstival des Jeux de Théâtre de Sarlat** (www.festival-theatre-sarlat.com; ℰ **05-53-31-10-83**), a theater festival that runs from mid-July to the first week of August. During the month of August and into the first week of September, Sarlat also hosts the **Féstival de Musique du Périgord Noir** (www.festivalduperigord-noir.fr; ℰ **05-53-51-95-17**). The November film festival, **Le Féstival de Film de Sarlat** (www.festivaldufilmdesarlat.com; ℰ **05-53-29-18-13**), is the biggest such event in France after Cannes and Deauville.

Exploring Sarlat-La-Canéda

Start your tour of Old Sarlat at **place du Peyrou** ★ and allow at least 2 hr. to wander around. Opening onto place du Peyrou is the **Cathédral de Saint Sacerdos,** which enjoyed its greatest prestige when it was an Episcopal seat between 1317 and 1790. The cathedral has a Romanesque bell tower, but most of the structure dates from the 16th and 17th centuries

Old town of Sarlat-La-Canéda

with the interior in the late Gothic style. The structure is to the right of the tourist office (see above). Leave by the south doorway.

Behind the cathedral is **Lanterne des Morts,** or "Lantern to the Dead" ★★, which was reputedly built in the 1100s to honor St. Bernard's pilgrimage to Sarlat, and a fine example of early medieval sepulchral architecture.

Also opening on place du Peyrou, **Maison de la Boétie** ★ stands opposite the cathedral. You can admire its facade, as it's the most charming Renaissance house in Sarlat. Dating from 1525, the house has mullioned windows and a painted gable. It was once inhabited by the town's most famous son, Etienne de la Boétie, who was born about the time the house was completed. A criminal magistrate, he had a lifelong friendship with Montaigne, who was at La Boétie's bedside when he died in 1563. That death inspired Montaigne's famous essay "Friendship."

The second square to visit is **place du Marché aux Oies** ★, known for its bronze statue of three geese by Lalanne. For centuries, this market sold live fowl, and the statue commemorates that long-ago role. The most stunning Renaissance facade on this square belongs to the Hotel Chassaing.

One of Sarlat's most colorful medieval streets is **rue des Consuls** ★★, whose greatest buildings include **Hôtel Plamon,** its Gothic windows making it look like a church. Beyond the doorway of Plamon is a series of five arcades on the ground floor opening onto a covered market. A trio of Gothic bay windows on the second floor has been restored to its original appearance.

If you follow **Jardin des Enfeus** (behind the cathedral), you reach **rue Montaigne** ★ where the great 16th-century philosopher was born and once lived. The buildings along this street are extremely photogenic.

Feel free to roam the back streets of Sarlat. You can allow yourself to get lost, as you'll invariably wind up back at **place de la Liberté,** in the center of town, and the 18th-century Hotel de Ville, or City Hall.

Sarlat is celebrated by French gastronomes for its foie gras and truffle market, **Le Marché aux Truffles et au Gras,** held at the bottom of rue Fénelon December to February Saturday from 9am to noon. Sarlat is also known for its wines, and the best selection is found at **Julien de Savignac,** pl. Pasteur (℃ **05-53-31-29-20**).

Château de Milandes ★ MUSEUM   Although very impressive, this château is outshone by the star-power of its former owner, the internationally renowned singer and entertainer, Josephine Baker. Born Freda Josephine McDonald in St. Louis, Missouri, Baker rented the château from 1940 and eventually bought it in 1947. Famous for many things, her active role in the French Resistance (for which she was later honored by the nation), is probably the least well-known part of her history. Able to move freely, thanks to her international reputation, she helped refugees leave the country and acted as an informant and courier. Her musical acts at the time also contained coded messages. The home is worth a visit for the history, architecture, gardens, fencing lessons, and birds of prey demonstrations. It is about 30 min. south of Sarlat-la-Caneda. Allow about 2 hr. minimum for a visit.

On D53, Castelnaud-la-Chapelle. www.milandes.com/gb. ℃ **05-53-59-31-21.** Opening times are many, detailed, and changeable; check the website for specifics.

Gabarres de Benac ★ RIVER RIDE   Another *gabarre* option about 20 min. south of Sarlat-la-Canéda in the village of Beynac-et-Cazenacbout, is Gabarres de Benac. Children go free here on the morning sailings, up to 11:30am and dogs are allowed on board. The departure point is at the end of the car park, opposite the Post Office. A wide range of sailings (up to every 30 min. in high season) are available but much depends on the time of year. Call or check the website for sailing times.

On D46, Beynac-et-Cazenac. www.gabarre-beynac.com. ℃ **05-53-28-51-15.** Admission 8.50€ adults; 4.50€ children 11 and under. Group rates available.

Les Gabarres Norbert ★ RIVER RIDE   About 20 min. south of Sarlat-la-Canéda is La Roque-Gageac. Here, you can take a trip on a *gabarre*, the traditional flat-bottomed boats that used to ply up and down the shallow Dordogne, taking goods from one town to the next. Today they are used for guided river cruises and offer visitors a unique way to experience this unspoiled waterway and dramatic landscape. The trip takes about an hour and takes in several impressive châteaux. In 2018, owner Michel Norbert began offering audio guides in English that provide a historical context to the surrounding landscape.

On D57, La Roque-Gageac. pl. du 8 Mai. www.gabarres.com. ℃ **05-53-29-40-44.** Admission 10€ adults; 8€ children 12 and under. Apr–Nov 1 from 10am, with last boat departing at 6pm; check ahead to confirm availability and sailings.

A Side Trip to Gordka

After a few days exploring the prehistoric and medieval riches of the Dordogne, a trip to **Gorodka-Za village of modern art** ★ (www.gorodka.com; ✆ **05-53-31-02-00** or 06-83-36-77-96), 4km (2 miles) from Sarlat in La Canéda, is a refreshing change. The brainchild of artist Pierre Shasmoukine, you might find exhibits by various artists-in-residence, live theater shows, or sculptures and multimedia exhibits, either dotted around a forest with three separate walkways or within eight art galleries displaying over 500 works. It's a particularly interesting place at night, as many of the works of art start glowing and moving when you least expect them to. The site seems to be constantly threatened by local opposition, but it remains for now one of the most unusual and inspiring sites in the region. Gorodka can be visited daily July and August from 6pm to 11pm and in winter by appointment. Free admission (although certain exhibits have entrance fees).

Where to Stay

Château de Puymartin ★★   The most sumptuous way to live in and around Sarlat is at this château, which rents two elegant guest rooms (a twin and a double). Surrounded by antiques, you get to live like a count (or countess) of medieval times, but with all the modern comforts. Visitors are also welcome and several new public areas have recently opened, including the dungeons and a new salon and bedroom. For those who like ghost stories, this is where the White Lady lives and is often seen wafting past, say members of the family. Legend has it that she was an unfaithful wife, caught by her husband and imprisoned until her death in a small room in the castle. Visits are at 9€ for adults, 6.50€ for students, 4.50€ for children 6 to 12 (Apr–June 10:30am–6pm; July–August 10am–6:30pm; October–Nov 11 2–5:30pm). The rooms are available April through September; reserve at least 2 weeks in advance.

Sarlat-la-Canéda. D47, 8km (5 miles) from Sarlat and 12km (7.5 miles) from Les Eyzies (if you get to Marquay, you have gone too far.) www.chateau-de-puymartin.com. ✆ **05-53-59-29-97.** 2 units. 150€. **Amenities:** Museum.

Les Chambres du Glacier ★   You're going to be popular with your family if you choose this place—especially if they love ice cream. Well located on the pedestrianized place de la Liberté, this *chambres d'hotes* is housed in an 18th century building and is full of character. The well-sized bedrooms have slightly old-fashioned private bathrooms. A brasserie (and ice cream parlor, hence the name) is on the ground floor, making plans easy with children in the evenings.

9 pl. de la Liberte, Sarlat. ✆ **05-53-29-99-99.** www.chambres-du-glacier-sarlat.com. 4 units. 82€ double; 135€ 4-person suite. **Amenities:** Restaurant; ice cream parlor; free Wi-Fi.

Hotel Les Remparts ★   This is one of those well-appreciated, highly central hotels that are incredibly useful when returning for forgotten items, children who need a break, or if you just for a nap. The rooms are slightly small but clean, comfortable, and air-conditioned. The staff is helpful and friendly.

48 av. Gambetta. http://hotel-lesremparts-sarlat.com. ✆ **05-53-59-40-00.** 25 units. 61€–108€ double. Closed Dec to mid-Mar. **Amenities:** Free Wi-Fi.

Where to Eat

Le Bistrot ★ FRENCH   Just in front of the cathedral, in a pretty stone building, Le Bistrot has a simple menu of IGP products (officially labeled as coming from geographically recognized areas known for their production of this particular product, such as the IGP foie gras du Périgord). Other options include beef tartare, fresh fish, and handmade ice cream. A children's menu is available for 10€. Reservations are recommended, although, helpfully, the restaurant has opened a sister establishment about a 5-min. walk from this one, in case it's overbooked.

14 pl. du Peyrou, Sarlat. www.le-bistrot-sarlat.com. ✆ **05-53-28-28-40.** Fixed-price menus 18€–32€. Mid-Mar to mid-Nov daily 9:30am–11 am and 11:30am–9:45pm.

Le Grand Bleu ★★   If you've taken the train to Sarlat, you can tumble out of the station and right into this Michelin-starred restaurant. This might not sound like the best location, but the food here is excellent, with the emphasis, as you would expect, on the many local Périgord ingredients, but given imaginative twists from spices like coriander or ginger, or from techniques like smoking rather than roasting the duck. If you want to go all out, the truffle menu that will knock your socks off.

43 av. de la Gare, Sarlat. www.legrandbleu.eu. ✆ **05-53-31-08-48.** Fixed-price lunch 36€–50€, dinner 54€–70€, truffle menu 100€–125€. Tues–Wed 7:30–9pm, Thurs–Sat 12:30–1:30pm and 7:30–9pm, Sun 12:30–1:30pm. Closed Jan.

ROCAMADOUR ★★★

541km (335 miles) SW of Paris; 66km (41 miles) SE of Sarlat-la-Canéda; 55km (34 miles) S of Brive; 63km (39 miles) NE of Cahors

Rocamadour reached the zenith of its fame and prosperity in the 13th century, when it was one of the most famous pilgrimage sites in Christendom. Countless miracles were said to have taken place here, thanks to the sacred aura of the Chapel of Notre Dame and, specifically, the statue of the Black Madonna. Pilgrims still come here (in significantly smaller numbers), but most visitors are secular tourists who come to admire this spectacular village that seems to be carved into sheer rock. It's definitely worth a detour, even if it's out of your way. The setting is one of the most unusual in Europe: Towers, churches, and oratories rise in stages up the side of a cliff above the usually dry gorge of Alzou.

Only around 600 people live in the village year-round, but in the summer that numbers skyrockets during the day, when crowds of tourists arrive. For obvious logistical reasons, vehicles are prohibited in the town; you'll have a lot of stair climbing to do. The faint of heart or the mobility-impaired can take an elevator from the village at the base of the cliff up to the religious sanctuary, and from the religious sanctuary to the château (see below). It's a short walk from the parking lot to the village.

Rocamadour

Essentials

GETTING THERE   The best way to reach Rocamadour is by **car.** From Bordeaux, travel east along A89 autoroute to Brive-la-Gaillarde, then take the A20 to exit 54 toward Gramat. Then continue on D840 and take the D673 south to Rocamadour.

Rocamadour and neighboring Padirac share a **train** station, Gare de Rocamadour-Padirac, that isn't really convenient to either—it's 4km (2.5 miles) east of Rocamadour on N140. Trains arrive about five or six times a day from Brive in the north and Capdenac in the south; for transport from the station, your only option is to call a **taxi** (phone numbers posted at the station). For train information and schedules, visit www.oui.sncf or call ☎ **36-35** (.40€/min.).

VISITOR INFORMATION   The town maintains two separate **tourist offices,** one in the village Hôtel de Ville, rue Roland-le-Preux (☎ **05-65-33-62-59**), and another well-signposted branch office in l'Hospitalet, a small village in the heights that you will pass through on your way to Rocamadour (www.rocamadour.com; ☎ **05-65-33-22-00**).

Exploring Rocamadour

This gravity-defying **village ★★★** rises abruptly across the landscape. Its single street, lined with souvenir shops, runs along the side of a steep hill. It's best seen when approached from the road coming in from the tiny village of L'Hospitalet. Once in Rocamadour, you will want to get from the lower town (Basse Ville) to the **Cité Réligieuse,** a cluster of chapels and churches halfway up the cliff. The main way of getting from bottom to top is a narrow street/staircase that loops and twists its way upward. Called the *Chemin de la Croix*, or the Stations of Christ, it was the route medieval penitents used to make their way to the sacred chapel—the most penitent did it on their knees.

For the unrepentant, and others who are loath to negotiate the town's steep inclines, the town maintains two elevators. One goes from Basse Ville to Cité Réligieuse, midway up the rocky heights of Rocamadour. The ride costs 2€ one-way, 3€ round-trip. The other goes from Cité Réligieuse to the panoramic medieval ramparts near the hill's summit; it costs 2.50€ one-way, 4€ round-trip. A tourist train also trundles up and down at regular intervals from April to September, for 2.50€ one-way, 3.50€ round-trip.

For a superb **view**, head toward the **Château de Rocamadour,** on a rock spur high above the town center. You can reach it by way of Chemin de la Croix or take the elevator. It was built in the 14th century and restored by the local bishops in the 19th century. Its interior is off-limits, except for guests of the church officials who live and work here. You can, however, walk along its panoramic **ramparts** ★★, which open at 8am daily year-round. Closing times vary, usually just before sunset and no later than 9pm in the summer. Admission to the ramparts costs 2€. *Note:* You must buy your entrance ticket at a machine; be sure to have exact change, or you will have made the trip up for nothing. If possible, try an evening visit when the crowds should have thinned a little.

Cité Réligieuse ★★★

This cluster of chapels and churches is the town's religious centerpiece, visited by both casual tourists and devoted pilgrims. Site of many conversions, with mystical connotations that date to the Middle Ages, it's accessible from the town on the **Grand Escalier,** a stairway of 216 steps. Climbing the weathered steps will lead you to the **parvis des Eglises,** place St-Amadour, with seven chapels. Volunteers conduct free tours; schedules change frequently, according to holidays and church schedules. Two to five 1-hr. tours take place each day (depending on the season); times are prominently posted at the entrance. The most important churches are detailed below.

Basilique St-Sauveur ★ RELIGIOUS SITE   Set against the cliff, this small basilica was built in the Romanesque-Gothic style from the 11th to the 13th centuries. It's decorated with paintings and inscriptions recalling visits of celebrated persons, including Philippe the Handsome.

Free admission; donations appreciated. Suggested donation for tour 6€ adults, 3.50€ children 8–18. Daily winter 8am–6:30pm; summer 7:30am–10pm. Crypt year-round daily 11am–6:30pm.

Chapelle Notre-Dame ★★ RELIGIOUS SITE   This is the *chapelle miraculeuse*, the holy of holies, where St. Amadour is said to have carved out an oratory in the rock (who exactly St. Amadour was, however, is subject of debate). After caving in during the 15th century, it was rebuilt in flamboyant Gothic style, and it underwent various alterations in the 19th century, when it was restored. It shelters the venerated **Black Madonna,** a small sculpture carved out of wood that dates from the 12th century, depicting the Virgin seated with a small Jesus on her knee. Hanging from the roof is a 9th-century **bell** that was rung when a miracle occurred. Outside, above the door leading to the chapel, is an iron sword stuck in the rock that is said to be **Durandal,** the sword of Roland, the legendary 8th-century knight.

Daily winter 8am–6:30pm; summer 7:30am–10pm.

Chapelle St-Michel, Chapelle St. Jean-Baptiste, Chapelle St. Anne ★ RELIGIOUS SITE

Sheltered by an overhanging rock on the outside of this Romanesque chapel are two impressive **12th-century frescoes** representing the Annunciation and the Visitation. More frescoes are inside, though many are damaged.

Admission by guided tour only. Contact Laurence du Peloux. ℓ **06-76-48-05-06.** She also offers tours (in French and English) to all the other religious sites except the crypt.

Where to Stay & Eat

Grand Hôtel Beau-Site ★ This may be Best Western hotel, but its location is pretty unbeatable. The stone walls were built in the 15th century by an Order of Malta commander, Jehan de Valon (1440–1516). Today the rear terrace provides a view of the Val d'Alzou. The reception area has heavy beams and a cavernous fireplace. Rooms (23 of which are in the air-conditioned main building, the rest in a less desirable annex) are comfortable and conservatively decorated; many have beautiful views, and some have spa bathtubs.

The restaurant serves regional cuisine prepared by chef Xavier Menot, whose family has owned the place for generations. Fixed-price menus cost 27€ at lunch, and between 36€ to 58€ for dinner.

Cité Médiévale. www.bw-beausite.com. ℓ **800/528-1234** in the U.S. and Canada, or 05-65-33-63-08. 38 units. 105€–165€ double. Free parking. Pets stay for free. Breakfast 14€. Closed mid-Nov to mid-Feb. **Amenities:** Restaurant; bar; free Internet; outdoor pool; free Wi-Fi.

Hôtel-Restaurant Le Belvedere ★ This is a good option and a good value, well located with views over the streets of Rocamadour, which are particularly beautiful with the illuminations at night. The rooms at La Belvedere are not air conditioned, but just next door the same owners have another hotel called the Bellaroc with air conditioning (45€–71€ double; main course 15€–26€). The Belvedere has a contemporary-styled restaurant, with fixed-price menus from 18€ to 36€. A children's menu is also available at 8.50€. On summer evenings, ask for a table on the terrace.

L'Hospitalet. www.hotel-le-belvedere.fr. ℓ **05-65-33-63-25.** 17 units. 58€–84€ double. Free parking. Closed Jan. **Amenities:** Restaurant; bar; outdoor pool; free Wi-Fi.

Where to Stay & Eat Nearby

Hotel Château de La Treyne ★★★   Built in the 14th and 17th centuries, this superb château sits on the edge of a particularly tranquil bend of the Dordogne River. The owner points out that this is one of the cleanest rivers in France and is itself a UNESCO World Heritage Site and is open for dry and wet fly fishing. Typical catches include pike and trout. This four-star, Relais & Châteaux hotel is blessed with lush grounds of about 120 hectares (300 acres) of forest for hiking and truffle hunting, plus, the estate's own dog to snuffle them out, and a classic French garden. River kayaking, canoeing, and swimming are also on offer. The spacious rooms and even larger suites, which can sleep up to five people, feature Pierre Frey fabrics, antiques, and exposed beams; the more luxurious ones feel like private apartments from another era. The restaurant (Sat–Mon; though dinner is available daily) has been awarded a Michelin star for chef Andrieux's delectable creations. Set menus start at 50€ at lunch and for dinner the five-course set menu is 96€; seven courses for 130€.

Lacave. http://chateaudelatreyne.com. ℂ **05-65-27-60-60.** 17 units. 200€–530€ double; from 600€ suite. Closed mid-Nov to Christmas and Jan to mid-Mar. Take the D43 from Rocamadour to Souillac and you will find Lacave. **Amenities:** Restaurant; bar; heated outdoor pool; tennis court; free Wi-Fi.

Domaine de La Rhue ★★   After raising sheep for 15 years, Eric Jooris picked up his toolbox and virtually single-handedly transformed the 19th-century stables on the family property into a beautiful country inn. Today handed over to his sister Karine and her husband Yannick, this is still a wonderful place to stay. The beams that used to separate the horse stalls have been incorporated into the spacious lobby, and the upper floor has more exposed wooden beams. The rooms are spotless and fresh, with an uncluttered, elegant look, and all you see from the windows are vast fields and open countryside. Hiking trails take you to Rocamadour, or if you are feeling lazy, you could take a hot-air balloon tour.

5km (3 miles) from Rocamadour on the D673, then N140. www.domainedelarhue. com. ℂ **05-65-33-71-50.** 14 units. 95€–135€ double. Studio La Forge 600€ per week. Closed Nov–Easter. **Amenities:** Outdoor pool; free Wi-Fi.

CAHORS ★

541km (335 miles) SW of Paris; 217km (135 miles) SE of Bordeaux; 89km (55 miles) N of Toulouse

The ancient capital of Quercy, Cahors was a thriving university city in the Middle Ages, and many antiquities from its illustrious past remain. Today Cahors is best known for the red wine that's made principally from the Malbec grapes grown in vineyards around this old city. Firm but not harsh, Cahors is one of the most deeply colored fine French wines.

Since the mid-1990s, the city of Cahors has funded the redesign and replanting of at least **21 municipal gardens** most of them laid out in medieval patterns, using historically appropriate plants. The most spectacular of these lie immediately adjacent to Town Hall. Together they function as a magnet for horticultural societies throughout France. In total, 25 gardens are open to the public for visits.

Essentials

GETTING THERE   To **drive** to Cahors from Toulouse, follow the A62 autoroute north to the junction with A20 and continue on A20 north into Cahors.

Trains serve Cahors from Toulouse, Brive, and Montauban. For train information and schedules, visit www.oui.sncf or call ☎ **36-35** (.40€/ min.). Infrequent **bus** service connects some of the outlying villages, several of which are of historical interest, but it's vastly easier to drive.

VISITOR INFORMATION   The **Office de Tourisme** is on place François-Mitterrand (www.tourisme-cahors.com; ☎ **05-65-53-20-65**).

SPECIAL EVENTS   The **Festival du Blues** turns this town upside down for a week in mid-July, when blues groups, including some from the United States, descend. Most of the performances are free outdoor affairs along boulevard Gambetta. Main concerts are usually at the open-air **Théâtre des Verdures,** a courtyard in the heart of the medieval city. Ticket prices vary, but the average is about 40€. For exact dates and information, contact the Office de Tourisme (see above) or visit the site of **Cahors Blues Festival** (www. cahorsbluesfestival.com). You can buy tickets on the website or at any Fnac bookstore (www.fnac.fr). Every other year in April and May (next in 2020), La Diagonale des Arts reunites contemporary artists for exhibitions around the city. Info can be found at http://diagonaledesarts.over-blog.com.

Exploring the Area

The town is on a rocky peninsula almost entirely surrounded by a loop of the Lot River. It grew near a sacred spring that still supplies the city with water. At the source of the spring, the **Fontaine des Chartreux** stands by the side of **Pont Valentré ★★** (also called Pont du Diable), a bridge with a trio of

Pont Valentré

towers. It's a magnificent example of medieval defensive design erected between 1308 and 1380 and restored in the 19th century. The pont, the first medieval fortified bridge in France, is the most eye-catching site in Cahors, with crenelated parapets, battlements, and pointed arches.

Dominating the old town, the **Cathédrale St-Etienne ★**, 30 rue de la Chantrerie (© **05-65-35-27-80**), was begun in 1119 and reconstructed between 1285 and 1500. It was the first cathedral in the country to have cupolas, giving it a Romanesque-Byzantine look. One remarkable feature is its sculptured Romanesque north portal, carved around 1135 in the Languedoc style. It's open daily from 9am to 7pm; in winter the cathedral is closed Sunday mornings. Adjoining the cathedral are the remains of a Gothic cloister from the late 15th century. The admission-free cloister is open during the same hours as the cathedral. The **Musée de Cahors Henri-Martin,** 792 rue Emile Zola (www.mairie-cahors.fr/musee), is also worth a few hours browsing with its extensive range of 18th and 19th century art, however, it is closed for renovations until 2019. Some of the contents might be on temporary display during the closure but it is best to either check at the Tourist Office or call or email them directly (© **05-65-20-88-66;** musee@mairie-cahors.fr).

Where to Stay

Brit Hôtel ★   Hotel choices are limited in Cahors, although the stock has grown recently. First up, the Brit Hotel chain offers two options in the historic center: Le Valentré (two stars) and the Hotel de France (three stars). The two hotels share an entrance and are only about 200m (656 ft.) from the train station.

252 av. Jean-Jaurès. http://cahors-france.brithotel.fr. © **05-65-35-16-76.** 70 units combined. Valentré 59€–67€ double; Hotel de France 69€–87€ double. Parking 5€ outside; 8€ inside. **Amenities**: Baby cots (5€); free Wi-Fi.

Hôtel Chartreuse ★   This hotel on the banks of the River Lot about 5 min. from the town center gives you the choice of hill or river views. Traditional Quercy and French cooking is available in the restaurant (fixed-price menus 15.50€–27€). Pilgrim's Packages are available for those on the Saint-Jacques-de-Compostelle route and have a Pilgrim's Passport.

130 chemin de la Chartreuse. www.hotel-la-chartreuse.com. © **05-65-35-17-37.** 50 units. 142€–152€ double. **Amenities:** Free Wi-Fi.

Hôtel Terminus ★   On the avenue leading from the railway station into the heart of town, this hotel oozes turn-of-the-20th-century character with its original stone construction. Rooms are conservative yet tasteful, with floral prints, fresh flowers, and firm beds. On the premises is Le Balandre, the town's best restaurant, which specializes in regional dishes from the surrounding Périgord-Quercy district. Fixed-price menus are 23€ to 65€at lunch and 30€ to 65€ at dinner. Even if you don't opt for a meal in its quaint dining room or on the outdoor terrace, you may want to stop into the 1920s-style bar for a drink.

5 av. Charles de Freycinet. www.balandre.com. ℂ **05-65-53-32-00.** 21 units. 60€–75€ double; 105€–130€ suite. Free courtyard parking, 7€ in garage. Closed last 2 weeks in Nov. **Amenities:** Restaurant; bar; room service; free Wi-Fi.

Where to Eat

Le Balandre, the restaurant at **Hôtel Terminus** (see above), serves well-recommended cuisine.

Auberge de Vieux Cahors ★ TRADITIONAL FRENCH   Come here for sophisticated regional food in an old brick and stone work building, on the outskirts of the old town, with a small terrace for summer dining. The atmosphere is warm and welcoming and generally busy but accommodating. The wine list focuses on regional wines and there is also some local craft beer. Open Monday nights which is very useful in a country where some many places can be closed.

144 rue Saint-Urcisse. http://aubergeduvieuxcahors.com. ℂ **05-65-35-06-05.** Fixed-price menus 19.50€–36€. Mon and Thurs–Sun noon–3pm and 7–10:30pm.

Le Coin des Halles ★ TRADITIONAL FRENCH   Just a few steps from the main market, right in the center of town, this is one of the less pricey options. The good food here often comes directly from the nearby market. Above the restaurant are also 17 hotel rooms. They are clean and basic and cost 55€ to 97€ for a three- or four-person room.

30 pl. St. Maurice. ℂ **05-65-30-24-27.** Fixed-price menus 13€–25€. Mon–Sat noon–1:30pm and Wed–Sat 7:30–9:30pm.

L'O à la Bouche ★ MODERN FRENCH   One of Cahors's best brasseries is in a restored mansion from the turn of the 20th century in the center of town. Meals at this popular spot might include fresh trout from the Pyrénées served with leeks in vinaigrette, and Quercy lamb flavored with walnuts and Esplette peppers, all depending on what chef Jean-Francois Dive has found locally. The wine list includes an excellent sampling of Cahors vintages but also draws its bottles from further afield in France. Reservations recommended.

56 allée Fénelon. www.loalabouche-restaurant.com. ℂ **05-65-35-65-69.** Fixed-price menu 21.50€–45€. Tues–Sat noon–1:30pm and 7–9:30pm.

LIMOGES ★

396km (246 miles) S of Paris; 311km (193 miles) N of Toulouse; 93km (58 miles) NE of Périgueux

Limoges, the ancient capital of Limousin in west-central France, is world famous for its exquisite porcelain and enamel works. Enamel production is a medieval industry revived in the 19th century and still going strong. In fact, Limoges is the economic capital of western France. Occupying the Vienne's right bank, the town has historically consisted of two parts: La Cité (aka Vieux Limoges), with its narrow streets and old *maisons* on the lower slope, and La Ville Haute (aka "Le Château"), at the summit.

Essentials

GETTING THERE   Limoges has good **train** service from most regional cities, with direct trains from Toulouse, Poitiers, and Paris. Ten trains depart daily from Paris's Gare d'Austerlitz for Limoges (trip time: 3 hr.; prices vary but from about 60€ one-way). About eight trains a day arrive from Périgueux (trip time: 1 hr.; from about 17€ one-way). For complete train information, www.oui.sncf or call ☎ **36-35** (.40€/min.). **Bus** transit in and out of the small towns and villages nearby can be arranged through the **Régie des Transports de la Haute-Vienne,** pl. des Charentes (☎ **05-55-10-31-00;** www.rdthv.com). If you're **driving** from Périgueux, take N21 north for the 1.5-hr. trip. If driving from Cahors, take A20 north for the 2-hour trip.

VISITOR INFORMATION   The **Office de Tourisme** is at 12 bd. de Fleurus (www.limoges-tourisme.com; ☎ **05-55-34-46-87**)

Exploring Limoges

Sadly, the workshops no longer offer opportunities for the public to get their hands dirty. However, you can still admire the result of the rich deposits of kaolin (known locally as "white gold") found near Limoges in

Limoges

the 18th century. More than 30 porcelain manufacturers have set up operations here through the years. Many of the most famous maintain shops that offer good-quality seconds at reduced prices, as well as items from out of date collections, and, of course, the new collections. One of the best is the **Fondation Bernardaud,** 27 av. Albert-Thomas (www.bernardaud. com/fr/la-fondation; ℭ **05-55-10-21-86** or 05-55-10-55-50), where as well as the ceramics, regularly changing exhibitions of "super super contemporary" (as the director said) artistic porcelain are on display. A tearoom adjoins the showroom. Guided visits are available all year (June–Sep 9:45–11:15am and 1:30–4:15pm; for the rest of the year, call in advance to book). Other options are the **Magasin d'usine Raynaud,** 14 ancienne rte. d'Aixe (www.raynaud.fr; ℭ **05-55-01-77-65**), and **Porcelaines Philippe Deshoulières-Lafarge,** 77bis rue Armand Dutreix (www. deshoulieres.com; ℭ **05-55-38-91-38**), which highlights the eco-friendly nature of its raw materials and production processes.

Cathédrale St-Etienne ★★ CATHEDRAL   The cathedral was begun in 1273 and took years to complete. The choir was finished in 1327, but work continued in the nave until almost 1890. The cathedral is the only one in the old province of Limousin built entirely in the Gothic style. The main entrance is through Porte St-Jean, which has carved wooden doors from the 16th century (constructed at the peak of the Flamboyant Gothic style). Inside, the nave appears so harmonious it's hard to imagine that its construction took six centuries. The rood screen is of particular interest, built in 1533 in the ornate style of the Italian Renaissance. The cathedral also contains some bishops' tombs from the 14th to the 16th centuries.

pl. de l'Evêché. ℭ **05-55-34-46-87.** Free admission. Mon–Sat 2:30–5pm, Sun 2:30–6pm.

Eglise St-Michel-des-Lions ★★ CHURCH   Two stone lions guard the entrance to this church. Constructed between the 14th and 16th centuries, it features a typically Limousin bell tower surmounted by a strange copper globe and splendid vaulting supported by slender pillars. Despite its name, the church is the center of the cult of St-Martial, a Limoges hometown bishop who died in the 3rd century. The church is the home of what's reputed to be his skull, stored in an elaborately enameled reliquary. Les Ostensions is a religious pilgrimage, established in 994, that occurs every seven years from February to November. The skull, La Châsse de St-Martial—which some believers credit with healing powers—is removed from storage and exhibited as part of religious processions (which take place all over France, although this is the only one in Limoges) that attract tens of thousands of devout adherents. The next such procession is scheduled for 2023. A smaller ceremony, when the skull is brought out into the church, also takes place every year on the day of St-Martial.

Pl. St-Michel. ℭ **05-55-34-46-87** (Tourist Office) or 05-55-34-18-13 (church). Free admission. Daily 9am–noon and 2–6pm.

Musée des Beaux-Arts de Limoges ★★ MUSEUM

Recently renovated, this museum has an outstanding collection of spectacularly colored enamels (said to be the best in Europe outside those in the Hermitage in St. Petersburg, Russia) and a range of Limoges porcelain from the 12th century to the present day. Other attractions include a 2,000-piece Egyptian collection; archeology finds; and sculptures and fine art, including works by Auguste Renoir, the impressionist painter who was born in Limoges in 1841. The main part of the museum is housed in the 18th-century archbishops' palace with luminous modern galleries for temporary exhibitions. The Jardins de l'Evêché, which offer a view of the Vienne and the 13th-century pont St-Etienne, surround the museum. See the website for an events calendar. One-hour guided tours are available but, for now, only in French. They take between an hour and an hour and a half and cost 3€ to 5€. For families (in French only) there is the "Folio" visit, with a guide and a book that has pictures and games that help to explain the collections.

1 pl. de l'Evêché. www.museebal.fr. ✆ **05-55-45-98-10.** 5€ adults; free for visitors 26 and under, jobseekers, disabled, and other categories with special dispensations; free to all the first Sun of every month. Apr–Sept Wed–Mon 10am–6pm; Oct–Mar Wed–Mon 10–noon and 2–5pm, Sun 2–5pm. Check website for annual closures.

Musée National de la Porcelaine Adrien-Dubouché ★★ MUSEUM

This is the largest museum in Europe for Limoges porcelain, and the largest in in the world on global ceramic history. It has 18,000 pieces, 5,000 of which are on display, which illustrate the history of glassmaking and ceramics (porcelain, earthenware, stoneware, and terra cotta) throughout the ages, starting with Ancient History and moving toward the present. In France, its porcelain collection is second in quantity only to that of Sèvres. It has recently undergone a 15€ million renovation project, that created a new modern building of glass, metal, and porcelain, alongside the traditional 19th-century space, tripling the previous exhibition area to 7,200 sq. m (77,500 sq. ft.). For English speaking visitors, the museum offers iPads with exhibit explanations in English (free). In 2018, they will also launch an app for personal download. The museum expanded shop now sells souvenirs, books, and some porcelain jewelry. The website details a range of temporary exhibitions and events.

8 bis pl. Winston-Churchill. www.musee-adriendubouche.fr/en. ✆ **05-55-33-08-50.** Admission 7€ adults; free for visitors 25 and under and a range of other categories such as jobseekers and teachers. Wed–Mon 10am–12:30pm and 2–5:45pm. Closed Dec 25 and Jan 1.

Parc Victor Thuillat ★ PARK

Besides porcelain, Limoges is one of the greenest cities in France, with numerous open spaces and attractive walks along the river Vienne. Victor Thuillat is one of the largest and most attractive parks, with a large collection of centuries-old sequoia and cypress trees. A *boules* court and children's play area make this a pleasant place to while away a few hours.

Av. Emile Labussiere. ✆ **05-55-45-62-67.** Free admission. Daily dawn to dusk.

Where to Eat

Chez Alphonse ★ FRENCH   This typical Limousin bistro beside the food market, Halles Centrales, is full of locals and a warm and convivial atmosphere. Foodies describe this place as a "gem". Typical dishes include pig's feet, veal, and that classic French pudding, Ile Flottant. Diners who don't speak French may find certain staff members just a tad impatient. Reservations recommended.

5 pl. de la Motte. www.chezalphonse.fr. ℂ **05-55-34-34-14.** Fixed-price lunch 16€–21€; dinner main course 10€–25€. Mon–Sat noon–2pm and 7:30–10:30pm, Fri and Sat until 11pm.

La Tables du Couvent ★ FRENCH   In a former convent, this restaurant is known for its bistro food including veal, terrines, various egg dishes, and a range of Limousin beef. It also offers cooking courses every Wednesday and Saturday, from 3pm to 5pm; an on-site shop sells freshly-made pasta, olive oil, and other goodies including kitchen accessories. Weekly menus depend on seasonal produce, but expect fresh local ingredients put together with imagination and a delicate touch.

15 Rue Neuve des Carmes. www.latableducouvent.com. ℂ **05-55-32-30-66.** Main course 9€–26€; fixed-price weekday lunch 19€–24€ or dinner 32€ and 38€. Tues 7–10pm, Wed–Sat noon–2pm and 7–10pm, Sun noon–2pm.

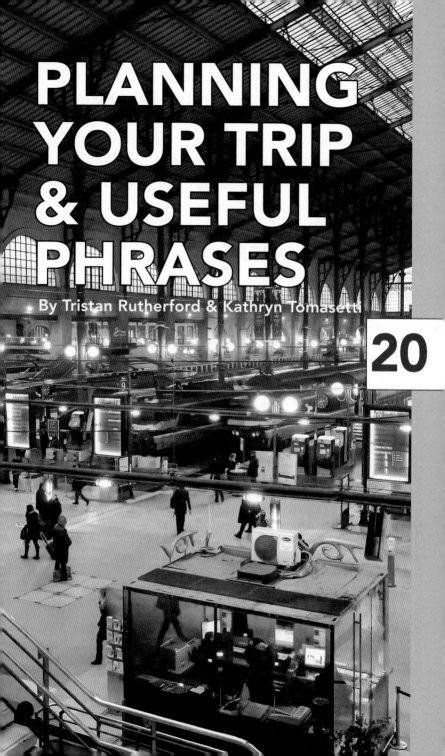

PLANNING YOUR TRIP & USEFUL PHRASES

By Tristan Rutherford & Kathryn Tomasetti

20

O f almost any destination in the world, flying into France is one of the most effortless undertakings in global travel. There are no immunizations to get and no particular safety precautions, and more and more French people now speak English. With your passport, airline or train ticket, and enough money, you just go. In the pages that follow, you'll find everything you need to know to plan your trip: getting around the country, deciding when to go, and much, much more.

GETTING THERE
By Plane

The two Paris airports—**Orly** (airport code: ORY) and **Charles de Gaulle** (airport code: CDG)—are about even in terms of convenience to the city's center. Orly, the older of the two, is 13km (8 miles) south of the center; Charles de Gaulle is 22km (14 miles) northeast. Air France serves Charles de Gaulle (Terminal 2E) from North America. U.S. carriers land at both airports. Flight status and transport information for both airports can be found online (www.aeroportsdeparis.fr). If you're heading to the South of France, **Nice Côte d'Azur** (airport code: NCE; www.nice.aeroport.fr) is served by direct flights from New York.

Most airlines charge their lowest fares between November and mid-March. The shoulder season (Oct and mid-Mar to May) is a bit more expensive, but we think it's the ideal time to visit France.

By Train

Paris is one of Europe's busiest rail junctions, with trains departing from its seven major stations every few minutes. If you are in the U.K., Germany, Holland, Italy, or Spain, our recommendation is to travel to the country by train.

Eurostar (www.eurostar.com; ℂ **800/387-6782** in the U.S.) links London directly with Paris Gare du Nord station from as little as $66 one-way; trip time just over 2 hr. It also runs direct seasonal routes to Disneyland Paris, Avignon, Marseille, and Aix-en-Provence. Better still, trips from London can be booked online to any major station in France. For the best deals, book as tickets become available exactly 3 months in advance (although tickets between London and Paris are available up to 6 months in advance). Highly recommended is train and accommodation specialist

PREVIOUS PAGE: **Gare du Nord train station, Paris**

Great Rail (www.greatrail.com; ✆ **866/711-2858** in the U.S.). Their specialized teams can plan rail journeys throughout France.

By Bus

Paris is a major arrival and departure point for Europe's largest bus operator, **Eurolines** (www.eurolines.fr; ✆ **08-92-89-90-91**). Its rather nasty bus terminal, Gallieni, is a 35-min. Métro ride from central Paris, at the terminus of line no. 3 (Métro: Gallieni). Despite the inconvenience, tickets are cheap, cheap, cheap. Standard singles to London are $29; trip time is around 7 hr.

Long-haul buses are equipped with toilets, and they stop at mealtimes for rest and refreshment. Tickets must be purchased online before you travel.

By Car

The major highways into Paris are A1 from the north (Great Britain and Benelux); A13 from Rouen, Normandy, and northwest France; A11 from Nantes and the Loire valley; and the A6 from Lyon, Provence, the Riviera, and Italy.

By Boat from England

Ferries and hydrofoils operate day and night from the English Channel ports to Normandy. The major routes include at least 12 trips a day between Dover or Folkestone and Calais or Boulogne. Ferries often drop passengers off by the rail junction of each port.

Various ferry operators cross the channel for multiple ports in France. **P&O Ferries** (www.poferries.com; ✆ **0871/664-2121** in the U.K.) operate car and passenger ferries between Dover, England and Calais, France. **Brittany Ferries** (www.brittanyferries.com; ✆ **0871/244-0744**) operates ferry services from Portsmouth to Cherbourg, Caen, Le Havre or St. Malo, France; from Poole, England to Cherbourg, France; and from Plymouth, England to Roscoff, France. **DFDS Seaways** (www.dfds. co.uk; ✆ **0844/576-8836** in the U.K.) sail twice daily between Newhaven and Dieppe; and up to 44 times daily between Dover and Calais and Dover and Dunkirk.

SPECIAL-INTEREST TRIPS & TOURS
Academic Trips & Language Classes

The **Alliance Française,** 101 bd. Raspail, Paris 75006 (www.alliancefr. org; ✆ **01-42-84-90-00**), is a nonprofit French-language teaching organization with a network of 1,040 establishments in 136 countries. The school in Paris is open all year; 3-week courses range from 100€ to 314€.

Just outside Nice, the **Institut de Francais,** 23 av. Général-Leclerc, Villefranche-sur-Mer 06230 (www.institutdefrancais.com; ✆ **04-93-01-88-44**), offers highly acclaimed month-long French immersion courses.

Each day includes 8 hr. of lessons, plus breakfast and lunch taken together with professors. Prices range from 3,260€ to 3,930€.

A clearinghouse for information on French-language schools is **Lingua Service Worldwide** (www.linguaserviceworldwide.com; ✆ **800/394-5327**). Its programs are available in many cities throughout France. Cost ranges from around $200 to close to $6,000 per week, depending on the city, the school, and accommodation.

Adventure Trips

ACTIVE VACATIONS **Bourgogne Escapades** (www.bourgogne-escapades.com; ✆ **06-26-97-01-70**) offers a variety of activity holidays in Burgundy including walking (occasionally accompanied by donkeys), cycling, sailing, wine tours, and golf. In the Beaune area, **Dilivoyage** (www.dilivoyage.com; ✆ **03-80-24-24-82**) specializes in short breaks on the themes of wine tourism, local heritage, and family fun.

Exodus Travels (www.exodustravels.com; ✆ **844/227-9087**) offer adventure travel around France from white water rafting to Alpine hiking. Their six-night Trekking in the French Pyrenees trip costs $1,700.

BARGE CRUISES Before the advent of rail, many crops, building supplies, raw materials, and finished products were barged through France on a series of rivers, canals, and estuaries. Many of these waterways retain their old-fashioned locks and pumps, allowing shallow-draft boats easy access through idyllic countryside.

European Waterways (www.europeanwaterways.com; ✆ **877/879-8808**) operates cruises departing from all around France plus traditional barge hire. Trips include a seven-night tour from Marseille up the Canal du Midi to rural Provence. Fares start for this voyage start at 4,110€ per person (based on double occupancy) including bike tours, vineyards visits, and all meals and drinks.

Viking River Cruises (www.vikingrivercruises.com; ✆ **800/304-9616**) leads one-week tours from Paris through Normandy, with stops in Rouen and at the D-Day beaches, through the wine country of Bordeaux and St-Emilion, and along the Rhône, taking in Arles and Avignon en route. For double occupancy, prices start at $1,356.

Wellness Trips

The luxury hotel **La Cueillette** (www.lacueillette.com; ✆ **03-80-20-62-80**), located in Meursault, Burgundy, offers well-being stays of 3 to 5 nights which include bike rides through the vineyards and spa treatments using products from their own grape-based Fruitithérapie range.

For serious Provençal pampering just outside of Gordes, the five-star **Les Bories Hotel & Spa** (www.hotellesbories.com, ✆ **04-90-72-00-51**) offers two- to five-day treatment programs at their on-site spa, La Maison d'Ennea. Facials, massages, and wraps use locally sourced essential oils, such as lavender and sweet orange.

Plenty of excellent **yoga** and **meditation** retreats are dispersed around the country. A few popular places include **Les Passesroses** (www. passeroses.com), set inside a Charentaise *longere*, or longhouse, northeast of Bordeaux, and **LuxYoga** (www.luxyoga.com), based in a rambling Provence villa above the French Riviera, which serves gluten-free, organic meals based on Ayurvedic principles.

Food & Wine Trips

The famous/infamous Georges Auguste Escoffier (1846–1935) taught the Edwardians how to eat. Today the Hôtel Ritz maintains the **Ecole Ritz Escoffier,** 15 pl. Vendôme, Paris 75001 (www.ritzescoffier.com; ✆ **01-43-16-30-50**), with culinary, cocktail, and pastry workshops, as well as professional-level courses and lessons for kids.

Established in 1895, **Le Cordon Bleu,** 8 rue Léon Delhomme, 75015 Paris (www.cordonbleu.edu; ✆ **01-53-68-22-50**), is the most famous French cooking school, where Julia Child learned to perfect her *pâté brisée* and *mousse au chocolat.* The best-known courses last nine months and cost 28,850€, including equipment and uniform, after which you are awarded a certificate. Many enthusiasts prefer a less intense immersion, opting for a two-day bread-making workshop (from 470€) or a 1- to 2-hr. demonstration class (from 40€).

Less formal but equally enjoyable are the cooking classes offered by **La Cuisine Paris,** 80 quai de l'Hôtel de Ville, 75004 (www.lacuisineparis. com; ✆ **01-40-51-78-18**), a friendly school set up by a Franco-American team. It organizes small classes by professional chefs in both French and English, including the popular French Macaron Class. Prices range from 69€ for a 2-hr. soufflé lesson to 99€ for a 3-hr. poultry cooking class. Alternatively, **Les Caves du Louvre** (www.cavesdulouvre.com; ✆ **01-40-28-13-11**) offers English guided tours of former royal wine cellars (32€ including a *dégustation* of three wines). Plus, serious oenophiles can create their own wines in one of the workshops (75€).

At Home with Patricia Wells (www.patriciawells.com) is a Paris- and Provence-based cooking school taught by Patricia Wells, cookbook author and famed former restaurant critic for the "International Herald Tribune." The extremely popular five-day classes are limited to either seven students (in Paris) or 10 students (in Provence) and cost $6,000 (accommodation not included).

Les Petits Farcis (www.petitsfarcis.com), run by Cordon Bleu–trained Canadian chef Rosa Jackson, offers tours of Nice's colorful produce market, followed by daylong gourmet cooking sessions. Prices begin at 195€ per person and include a four-course lunch with wine.

In Burgundy, **L'Ecole des Vins de Bourgogne** (www.ecoledes vins-bourgogne.com; ✆ **03-80-26-35-10**) in Beaune has courses ranging from 2 hr. to 12 days for both novices and experts to learn about the region's wines. Or explore the market in Beaune on Wednesday or

Saturday morning with American chef Marjorie Taylor and **The Cook's Atelier** (www.thecooksatelier.com; ☏ **06-84-83-16-18**), before preparing and eating your lunch in her chic 16th-century kitchen.

Bordovino (www.bordovino.com) is a specialist in wine tourism in the Bordeaux area, offering everything from 2-hr. intensive tasting classes (45€), to an all-day bike trip to St-Emilion and nearby vineyards (145€). Also in Bordeaux, **Wine Cab** (www.wine-cab.com) conducts behind-the-scenes tours around the city's top vineyards from the back of a decommissioned London black cab. The fleet of three former taxis ply the narrow lanes of the Médoc and St-Emilion, with tasting tours starting at 500€ for three persons. **Uncorked Wine Tours** (www.uncorkedwinetours.com; ☏ **06-50-04-28-84**) offer a wide range of options for getting the inside route into Bordeaux châteaux, courtesy of friendly Irish owner Caroline Matthews. Nationwide wine specialist **Arblaster & Clarke** (www.arblaster andclarke.com; ☏ **888/479-6040**), operate tours from Alsace to the Loire Valley, including a 3-day Champagne tour for $1,095.

Guided Tours

BIKE TOURS Some of the best cycling tours of France are offered by **Butterfield & Robinson** (www.butterfield.com; ☏ **866/551-9090**), which offers some 20 trips through most scenic parts of France. Rides range from a gentle peddle among the Loire's châteaux or skirting Burgundy's legendary vineyards, to a more challenging exploration of the D-Day beaches. Prices start at $3,295 per person, with luxury accommodation and gourmet meals thrown in.

Cycling for Softies (www.cycling-for-softies.co.uk; ☏ **020-7471-7760** in the U.K.) is ideal for easygoing travelers with little cycling experience. Tours cover most of France. Prices vary according to type of tour (both self-guided and small groups are available); buffet breakfasts and gourmet dinners are included.

Fat Tire Bike Tours (http://paris.fattirebiketours.com; ☏ **01-56-58-10-54**) offers a 4-hr. day or night tour of Paris by bike; adult tickets cost 35€. It also organizes cycling tours of Versailles and Giverny.

CHAUFFEURED TOURS **4 Roues Sous 1 Parapluie** (www.4roues-sous-1parapluie.com; ☏ **08-00-80-06-31**) offers chauffeur-driven themed rides around Paris and Versailles in its colorful fleet of Citroën 2CV. Tours for three start at 60€ per person for a 1.5-hr. tour. The fewer people in the car, the more expensive the tour. Or tour Paris in an original 1970s Combi Van, with **Combi Paris** (www.combi.paris; ☏ **06-95-94-39-77**). Depending on the time of day you'll sample breakfast, lunch, or champagne from carefully selected bakeries or winemakers. A 3-hr. tour costs 350€ for up to seven passengers. For small group travel look no further than award-winning agency **France Off The Beaten Path** (www.traveloffthebeatenpath.com; ☏ **877/846-2831**), which operate cozy cooking, cultural, and wine tours in Provence, Bordeaux and the Loire Valley.

SHOPPING TOURS Paris is a dream come true for shopaholics. **Chic Shopping Paris** (www.chicshoppingparis.com; ✆ **06-77-65-08-01**) offers tours designed to give visitors a behind-the-scenes shopping experience. Themed tours include "Chic Consignment" and "Unique Boutique." All of the standard tours are 4 to 4.5 hr. and start at 100€ per person.

GETTING AROUND

Within most major cities—including Paris, Lyon, and Marseille—public transportation is efficient, comprehensive, and cheap. In smaller towns, such as Rouen, Arles, or Antibes, it's easy to navigate the city center on foot. See each chapter for specific details.

By Plane

Air France (www.airfrance.com; ✆ **800/237-2747** in the U.S.), with its low-cost offshoot **HOP!**, is the country's primary carrier, serving around 30 cities in France and 30 more destinations throughout Europe. Air travel time from Paris to almost anywhere in France is about 1 hr. **British Airways** (www.ba.com) links London with Paris, Bordeaux, Chambery, Grenoble, Lyon, Marseille, Montpellier, Nantes, Strasbourg, Toulouse, and Nice. Low-cost airline **easyJet** (www.easyjet.com) also links London with a dozen French cities. The budget airline offers additional internal flights between Paris, Bordeaux, Lyon, Nantes, Toulouse, and Nice, and connects French cities to dozens of other European destinations.

By Car

The most charming châteaux and country hotels always seem to lie away from the main cities and train stations. Renting a car is a good way to travel around the French countryside, especially along the Normandy beaches, the Loire Valley, the vineyards of Bordeaux, and in rural Provence. Day car hire is inexpensive, so visitors may want to rent a vehicle just for a day en route if they wish.

Driving schedules in Europe are largely a matter of conjecture, urgency, and how much sightseeing you do along the way. Driving time is 2.5 hr. from Paris to Rouen, 3.5 hr. to Nantes, and 7 hr. to anywhere in Provence.

RENTALS To rent a car, you'll need to present a passport, a driver's license, and a credit card. You will also have to meet the company's minimum-age requirement: 21 or above at most rental agents. The biggest agencies have pickup spots all over France, including **Budget** (www.budget.com; ✆ **800/472-3325**); **Hertz** (www.hertz.com; ✆ **800/654-3001**); and **Europcar** (www.europcar.com; ✆ **877/940-6900**). We highly recommend AutoSlash.com over other online car rental services. It applies every available coupon on the market to the booking, yielding surprisingly low daily rates. If the cost of a rental drops, it automatically rebooks, again lowering the price.

Note: The best deals are always booked online, in advance. Though the rental company won't usually mind if you drive your car into, say, Germany, Switzerland, Italy, or Spain, it's often forbidden to transport your car by ferry, including across the Channel to England.

In France, **collision damage waiver (CDW)** is usually factored into the overall rate quoted, but you should always verify this before taking a car on the road. At most companies, the CDW provision won't protect you against theft, so if this is the case, ask about purchasing extra theft protection. Automatic transmission is a luxury in Europe. If you prefer it to stick-shift, you must specifically request it—and you'll pay a little extra for it.

GASOLINE Known in France as *essence,* gas is expensive for those accustomed to North American prices, although the smaller cars common in Europe use far less gas. Depending on your car, you'll need either leaded (*avec plomb*) or unleaded *(sans plomb).*

Note: Sometimes you can drive for miles in rural France without encountering a gas station; don't let your tank get dangerously low.

DRIVING RULES Everyone in the car, in both the front and the back seats, must wear seat belts. Children 10 and under must ride in the back seat.

In France, you drive on the right. Drivers are supposed to yield to the car on their right (*priorité a droite*), except where signs indicate otherwise, as at traffic circles. If you violate the speed limit, expect a big fine. Limits are 130kmph (80 mph) on expressways, 110kmph (68 mph) on major national highways, and 90kmph (55 mph) on country roads. In towns, don't exceed 50kmph (31 mph).

Note: It's illegal to use a cellphone while you're driving in France; you will be ticketed if you're stopped.

MAPS While most French drivers are happy with Google Maps, traditional motorists opt for the large **Michelin maps** of the country and regions (www.viamichelin.com) on sale at all gas stations. Big travel-book stores in North America carry these maps as well. GPS navigation devices can be rented at most car-hire stations.

BREAKDOWNS/ASSISTANCE A breakdown is called *une panne* in France. Call the police at ℭ **17** (if calling from a landline) or ℭ **112** (if calling from a mobile phone) anywhere in France to be put in touch with the nearest garage. Most local garages offer towing.

By Train

The world's fastest trains—known as *Train à Grande Vitesse,* or TGVs—link some 50 French cities, allowing you to travel from Paris to just about anywhere else in the country within hours. With 32,000km (20,000 miles) of track and 3,000 stations, **SNCF** (French National Railroads; www.oui.

sncf or call ☎ **36-35** at .40€/min. in France) is fabled for its on-time performance and comfy trains. You can travel in first or second class by day and couchette by night. Most trains have light dining facilities.

For information or reservations, go online (www.oui.sncf). You can also visit any local travel agency. If you have a chip credit card and know your PIN, you can use your card to buy your ticket at the easy-to-use *billetteries* (ticket machines with an English-menu option) in every train station.

> ### OUIGO for Cheaper Train Tickets
>
> **OUIGO** (www.ouigo.com) is a subsidiary of SNCF that offers cheap TGV travel to 19 destinations throughout France. Flat-rate tickets start at 10€ per adult and 5€ per child. Taking a cue from Europe's low-cost airlines, OUIGO charges 5€ per piece of baggage larger than an airline carry on.

RAIL PASSES   Rail passes as well as individual rail tickets are available from **Rail Europe** (www.raileurope.com; ☎ **800/622-8600** in the U.S.). Options include a five-day rail pass usable for a one-month period in First Class for $354. **Eurail** (www.eurail.com) offers regional rail passes throughout Europe, including a France pass for $223, allowing four days of first-class travel within a one-month period in First Class, including a Eurostar trip from London to Paris.

[Fast FACTS] FRANCE

Business Hours   Business hours in France can be erratic. Most banks are open Monday through Friday from 9:30am to 4:30pm. Many, particularly in small towns, take a long lunch break. Hours are usually posted on the door. Most museums close one day a week (often Tues), and they're generally closed on national holidays. Usual hours are from 9:30am to 5pm. In Paris or other big French cities, stores are open from around 10am to 6 or 7pm, with or without a lunch break (up to 2 hr.). Some shops, delis, cafes, and newsstands open at 8am and close at 8 or 9pm; restaurants often have two seatings, one for lunch and a second for dinner, and close in between. Beware seasonal closings for many businesses in regions dependent on seasonal tourism, such as the coastal resorts and Alpine ski areas.

Customs & Etiquette   French value pleasantries and take manners seriously: Say "Bonjour, Madame/Monsieur" when entering an establishment and "Au revoir" when you depart. Always say "Pardon" when you accidentally bump into someone. With strangers, people who are older than you and professional contacts use *vous* rather than *tu* (*vous* is the polite form of the pronoun *you*).

Disabled Travelers   Facilities for travelers in France, and nearly all new or modern hotels, provide disabled access. The TGVs (high-speed trains) are wheelchair accessible; older trains have compartments for wheelchair boarding. If you visit the Paris tourist office website (www.parisinfo.com) and click on "Practical Paris," the section "Practical Information for Disabled Visitors" includes links to a number of websites dedicated to travelers with disabilities. For disabled-access to Paris public transport, see www.infomobi.com.

Doctors   Doctors are listed in the Pages Jaunes (Yellow Pages; www.pagesjaunes.fr) under "Médecins: Médecins généralistes." The minimum fee for a consultation is about 35€—for this rate, look for a doctor who is described as "secteur 1." The higher the "secteur," the higher the fee. **SOS Médecins** (www.sosmedecins.fr; ✆ **36-24**) can make house calls. See also "Emergencies" and "Health," later in this section.

Drinking Laws   As well as bars and restaurants, supermarkets, and cafes sell alcoholic beverages. The legal drinking age is 18, but persons under that age can be served alcohol if accompanied by a parent or guardian. Drinking and driving is illegal and incurs a heavy fine. You can drink in public, but you cannot be drunk in public. Local laws may prohibit drinking at certain times or in certain places.

Electricity   Electricity in France runs on 220 volts AC (60 cycles). Adapters or transformers are needed to fit sockets, which you can buy in branches of Darty or Fnac.

Embassies & Consulates   If you have a passport, immigration, legal, or other problem, contact your consulate. Many are open Monday to Friday, approximately 10am to 5pm. However, call or check online before you visit to confirm. The following offices are all in Paris.

Australian Embassy: 4 rue Jean-Rey, 15e (www.france.embassy.gov.au; ✆ **01-40-59-33-00;** Métro: Bir Hakeim).

Canadian Embassy: 35 av. Montaigne, 8e (www.canadainternational.gc.ca/france; ✆ **01-44-43-29-00;** Métro: Franklin-D-Roosevelt or Alma-Marceau).

Irish Embassy: 4 rue Rude, 16e (www.embassyofireland.fr; ✆ **01-44-17-67-00;** Métro: Argentine).

New Zealand Embassy: 7ter rue Léonard de Vinci, 16e (www.mfat.govt.nz; ✆ **01-45-01-43-43;** Métro: Victor Hugo).

UK/British Embassy: 35 rue du Faubourg St-Honoré, 8e (http://ukinfrance.fco.gov.uk; ✆ **01-44-51-34-00;** Métro: Concorde or Madeleine).

United States Embassy: 2 av. Gabriel, 8e (https://fr.usembassy.gov; ✆ **01-43-12-22-22;** Métro: Concorde).

Emergencies   In an emergency while at a hotel, contact the front desk. If the emergency involves theft, go to the police station in person. Otherwise, call ✆ **112** from a cellphone. The fire brigade can be reached at ✆ **18.** For an ambulance, call ✆ **15.** For the police, call ✆ **17.** SOS Help is a hotline for English-speaking callers in crisis ✆ **01-46-21-46-46** (www.soshelpline.org). Open 3 to 11pm daily.

Health   For travel abroad, non-E.U. nationals should consider buying medical travel insurance. For U.S. citizens, Medicare and Medicaid do not provide coverage for medical costs incurred abroad; check your health insurance before leaving home. U.K. nationals need a **European Health Insurance Card** (**EHIC;** www.ehic.org.uk) to receive free or reduced-cost medical care during a visit to France. If you take regular medication, pack it in its original pharmacy containers, along with a copy of your prescription.

Holidays   Major public holidays are New Year's Day (Jan 1), Easter Sunday and Monday (late Mar/Apr), Labor Day (May 1), VE Day (May 8), Ascension Thursday (40 days after Easter), Pentecost/Whit Sunday and Whit Monday (seventh Sun/Mon after Easter), Bastille Day (July 14), Assumption Day (Aug 15), All Saints' Day (Nov 1), Armistice Day (Nov 11), and Christmas Day (Dec 25).

Hospitals   Dial ✆ **15** for medical emergencies.

LGBT Travelers   France is one of the world's most tolerant countries toward gays and lesbians. Paris boasts a large gay population, with many clubs, restaurants, organizations, and services. For books, DVDs, and local information, visit Paris's best-stocked gay bookstore, **Les Mots à la Bouche**, 6 rue Ste-Croix-de-la-Bretonnerie, 4e (www.motsbouche.com; 🕿 **01-42-78-88-30;** Métro: Hôtel-de-Ville). Both www.paris-gay.com and www.gay-vox.fr have updated listings about the gay and lesbian scene.

Mail   Most post offices in France are open Monday to Friday from 8am to 5pm and every Saturday from 8am to noon. A 24-hr. post office is located in Paris at 52 rue du Louvre 1e (🕿 **36-31**). Allow 5 to 8 days to send or receive mail from home. Stamps are also sold in *tabacs* (tobacconists). For more information, see www.laposte.fr.

Mobile Phones   You can use your mobile phone in France, provided it is **GSM** (Global System for Mobile Communications) and triband or quad-band; just confirm with your operator before you leave.

Using your phone abroad can be expensive, so it's a good idea to get it "unlocked" before you leave. This means you can buy a French SIM card from one of the three main French providers, **Bouygues Télécom** (www.bouyguestelecom.fr), **Orange** (www.orange.fr), or **SFR** (www.sfr.fr). Or do like the locals do and use **Skype** (www.skype.com) or **Whats App** (www.whatsapp.com) for long-distance calls.

Money & Costs   Frommer's lists exact prices in the local currency. The currency conversions quoted here were correct at press time. However, rates fluctuate, so before departing, consult a currency exchange website such as www.oanda.com to check current rates.

It's always advisable to bring a mix of cash and credit cards on vacation. Before you leave home, exchange enough petty cash to cover airport incidentals, tipping, and transportation to your hotel. Alternatively, withdraw money upon arrival at an airport ATM. In many international destinations, ATMs offer the best exchange rates. Avoid exchanging money at commercial exchange bureaus and hotels, which often have the highest transaction fees and terrible exchange rates. ATMs are widely available in France.

Newspapers   The most popular French newspapers are **"Le Monde"** (www.lemonde.fr), **"Le Figaro"** (www.lefigaro.fr), and left-leaning **"Libération"** (www.liberation.fr).

The **"International New York Times"** (www.nytimes.com) has a key office in Paris. Published from Monday to Saturday, it is distributed all over France.

Pharmacies   Spot French *pharmacies* by the green neon cross above the door. If your local pharmacy is closed, a sign on the door should indicate the nearest one open. Alternatively, **Pharmacies de Garde** (www.pharmaciesdegarde.com or www.3237.fr; 🕿 **32-37**) can direct you to the nearest open pharmacy.

Police   In an emergency, call 🕿 **17** (from a land-line) or **112** (from a mobile phone) anywhere in France.

Safety   The most common menace, especially in large cities, is the plague of *pickpockets*. Take precautions and be vigilant at all times: Don't take more money with you than

THE VALUE OF THE EURO VS. OTHER POPULAR CURRENCIES

Euro(€)	US$	C$	UK£	A$	NZ$
1	1.23	1.52	0.87	1.53	1.67

necessary, keep your passport in a concealed pouch or leave it at your hotel, and ensure that your bag is firmly closed at all times. In cafes, bars, and restaurants, it's best not to leave your bag under the table, on the back of your chair, or on an empty chair beside you. Keep it between your legs or on your lap. Never leave valuables or luggage in a car, and never travel with your car unlocked.

In general, Paris is a safe city and it is safe to use the Métro late at night, though it is always best to not drawn attention to the fact you are foreign by speaking loudly in English. Use common sense when taking public transport at night.

Although there is a significant level of discrimination against West and North African immigrants, there has been almost no harassment of African-American tourists to Paris or France itself in recent decades. However, **S.O.S. Racisme,** 51 av. de Flandre, 19e (www.sos-racisme.org; ✆ **01-40-35-36-55**), offers legal advice to victims of prejudice and will even intervene to help with the police.

Female travelers should not expect any more hassle than in other major cities, and the same precautions apply. Avoid walking alone at night and never get into an unmarked taxi. If you are approached in the street or on public transportation, it's best to avoid entering into conversation, and walk into a well-lit, populated area.

Senior Travel Many discounts are available to men and women over 60. Senior citizens do not get a discount for traveling on public transport in Paris, but national trains have senior discounts. Check out www.oui.sncf for more information. Frommers.com offers more information and resources on travel for seniors.

Smoking Smoking is banned in all public places in France, including cafes, restaurants, and nightclubs. It's permitted on outdoor and semi-enclosed terraces.

Student Travel Student discounts are less common in France than in other countries, simply because young people under 26 are usually offered reduced rates. Be on the lookout for the **Ticket Jeunes Week-end** when using the Métro in Paris. It can be used on a Saturday, Sunday, or bank holiday, and provides unlimited travel in zones 1 to 3 for 4.10€. SNCF also offer discounts for under-26-year-olds traveling on national trains (www.oui.sncf).

Taxes As a member of the European Union, France routinely imposes a value-added tax (VAT in English; TVA in French) on most goods. The standard VAT is 20 percent, and prices that include it are often marked TTC (*toutes taxes comprises,* "all taxes included"). If you're not an E.U. resident, you can get a VAT refund if you're spending less than 6 months in France, you purchase goods worth at least 175€ at a single shop on the same day, the goods fit into your luggage, and the shop offers *vente en détaxe* (duty-free sales or tax-free shopping). Give them your passport and ask for a *bordereau de détaxe* (export sales invoice). When you leave the country, you need to get all three pages of this invoice validated by France's Customs officials. They'll keep one sheet, and you must mail the pink one back to the shop. Once the shop receives its stamped copy, it will send you a *virement* (fund transfer) using the payment method you requested. It may take several months. You can also opt to receive a cash VAT refund at some airports for an additional fee.

Telephones Public phones can still be found in France. All require a phone card (known as a *télécarte*), which can be purchased at post offices or *tabacs*.

The country code for France is 33. To make a local or long-distance call within France, dial the person or place's 10-digit number. If you're calling from outside of France, drop the initial 0 (zero).

Mobile numbers begin with 06 or 07. Numbers beginning with 0-800, 0-804, 0-805, and 0-809 are free in France; other numbers beginning with 8 are not. Most four-digit numbers starting with 10, 30, and 31 are free of charge.

TURNING TO THE INTERNET OR APPS FOR A HOTEL discount

It's not impossible to get a good deal by calling a hotel, but you're more likely to snag a discount online and with an app. Here are some strategies:

1. Browse extreme discounts on sites where you reserve or bid for lodgings without knowing which hotel you'll get. You'll find these on **Priceline. com** and **Hotwire.com,** and they can be money-savers, particularly if you're booking within a week of travel (that's when the hotels get nervous and resort to deep discounts). These feature major chains, so it's unlikely you'll book a dump.

2. Review discounts on the hotel's website. Hotels often give the lowest rates to those who book through their sites rather than through a third party. But you'll only find these truly deep discounts in the loyalty section of these sites—so join the club.

3. Use the right hotel search engine. They're not all equal, as we at Frommers.com learned in the spring of 2017 after putting the top 20 sites to the test in 20 destinations around the globe. We discovered that Booking.com listed the lowest rates for hotels in the city center, and in the under $200 range, 16 out of 20 times—the best record, by far, of all the sites we tested. And Booking. com includes all taxes and fees in its initial results (not all do, which can make for a frustrating shopping experience). For top-end properties, again in the city center, both **Priceline.com** and **HotelsCombined. com** came up with the best rates, tying at 14 wins each.

Time   France is on Central European Time, which is 1 hr. ahead of Greenwich Mean Time. French daylight savings time lasts from the last Sunday in March to the last Sunday in October, when clocks are set 1 hr. ahead of the standard time. France uses the 24-hr. clock (so 13h is 1pm, 14h15 is 2:15pm, and so on).

Tipping   By law, all bills in **cafes, bars,** and **restaurants** say *service compris,* which means the service charge is included. However, it is customary to leave 1€ or 2€, depending on the quality of the service; in more upscale restaurants leave 5€ to 10€. **Taxi drivers** usually expect a 5 percent to 10 percent tip, or for the fare to be rounded up to the next euro. The French tip **hairdressers** around 15 percent, and if you go to the theater, you're expected to tip the **usher** about 2€.

Toilets   If you're in dire need, duck into a cafe or brasserie to use the lavatory. It's customary to make a small purchase if you do so. Paris is full of gray-colored automatic street toilets, some of which are free to use, and are washed and disinfected after each use. France still has some hole-in-the-ground squat toilets. Try not to lose your change down the pan!

Visitor Information   Before you go, your best source of information is the **French Government Tourist Office** (www.francetourism.com).

Water   Drinking water is generally safe. If you ask for water in a restaurant, it'll be served bottled (for which you'll pay), unless you specifically request *une carafe d'eau* or *l'eau du robinet* (tap water). Your waiter may ask if you'd like your water *avec gas* (carbonated) or *sans gas* (without bubbles).

GLOSSARY OF FRENCH-LANGUAGE TERMS

A word or two of halting French will often change your hosts' dispositions in their home country. Try to learn at least a few numbers, basic greetings, and—above all—the life raft, *"Parlez-vous anglais?"* Many French speak passable English and will use it liberally if you demonstrate the basic courtesy of greeting them in their language. Go on, try our glossary, and don't be bashful. *Bonne chance!*

BASICS

English	French	Pronunciation
Yes/No	Oui/Non	**wee/nohn**
Okay	D'accord	**dah-*core***
Please	S'il vous plaît	**seel voo *play***
Thank you	Merci	**mair-*see***
You're welcome	De rien	**duh ree-*ehn***
Hello (during daylight hours)	Bonjour	**bohn-*jhoor***
Good evening	Bonsoir	**bohn-*swahr***
Goodbye	Au revoir	**o ruh-*vwahr***
What's your name?	Comment vous appellez-vous?	**ko-*mahn* voo za-pell-ay-*voo*?**
My name is . . .	Je m'appelle . . .	**jhuh ma-*pell* . . .**
Happy to meet you	Enchanté(e)	**ohn-shahn-*tay***
Miss	Mademoiselle	**mad-mwa-*zel***
Mr.	Monsieur	**muh-*syuh***
Mrs.	Madame	**ma-*dam***
How are you?	Comment allez-vous?	**ko-mahn tahl-ay-*voo*?**
Fine, thank you, and you?	Très bien, merci, et vous?	**tray bee-*ehn*, mair-*see*, ay voo?**
Very well, thank you	Très bien, merci	**tray bee-*ehn*, mair-*see***
So-so	Comme ci, comme ça	**kum-*see*, kum-*sah***
I'm sorry/excuse me	Pardon	**pahr-*dohn***
I'm so very sorry	Désolé(e)	**day-zoh-*lay***
That's all right	Il n'y a pas de quoi	**eel nee ah pah duh kwah**

GETTING AROUND/STREET SMARTS

English	French	Pronunciation
Do you speak English?	Parlez-vous anglais?	**par-lay-voo ahn-*glay*?**
I don't speak French	Je ne parle pas français	**jhuh ne parl pah frahn-say**

I don't understand	Je ne comprends pas	**jhuh ne kohm-*prahn* pas**
Could you speak more loudly/more slowly?	Pouvez-vous parler un peu plus fort/plus lentement?	**poo-vay-voo par-lay un puh ploo for/ploo lan-te-*ment*?**
Could you repeat that?	Répetez, s'il vous plaît?	**ray-pay-tay, seel voo *play***
What is it?	Qu'est-ce que c'est?	**kess kuh *say*?**
What time is it?	Qu'elle heure est-il?	**kel uhr eh-*teel*?**
What?	Quoi?	**kwah?**
How? or What did you say?	Comment?	**ko-*mahn*?**
When?	Quand?	**kahn?**
Where is . . . ?	Où est . . . ?	**ooh eh . . . ?**
Who?	Qui?	**kee?**
Why?	Pourquoi?	**poor-*kwah*?**
Here/there	ici/là	**ee-*see*/lah**
Left/right	à gauche/à droite	**a goash/a drwaht**
Straight ahead	tout droit	**too drwah**
I'm American/Canadian/British	Je suis américain(e)/canadien(e)/anglais(e)	**jhe sweez a-may-ree-*kehn*/can-ah-dee-*en*/ahn-glay (*glaise*)**
Fill the tank (of a car), please	Le plein, s'il vous plait	**luh plan, seel voo *play***
I'm going to . . .	Je vais à . . .	**jhe vay ah . . .**
I want to get off at . . .	Je voudrais descendre à . . .	**jhe voo-*dray* day-son-drah ah**
I'm sick	Je suis malade	**jhuh swee mal-*ahd***
airport	l'aéroport	**lair-o-*por***
bank	la banque	**lah bahnk**
bridge	pont	**pohn**
bus station	la gare routière	**lah gar roo-tee-*air***
bus stop	l'arrêt de bus	**lah-*ray* duh boohss**
by means of a bicycle	en vélo/par bicyclette	**ahn vay-low/par bee-see-*clet***
by means of a car	en voiture	**ahn vwa-*toor***
cashier	la caisse	**lah *kess***
cathedral	cathédral	**ka-tay-*dral***
church	église	**ay-*gleez***
dead end	une impasse	**ewn am-*pass***
driver's license	permis de conduire	**per-mee duh con-*dweer***
elevator	l'ascenseur	**lah-sahn-*seuhr***

stairs	l'escalier	**les-kal-*yay***
entrance (to a building or a city)	une porte	**ewn port**
exit (from a building or a freeway)	une sortie	**ewn sor-*tee***
fortified castle or palace	château	**sha-*tow***
garden	jardin	**jhar-dehn**
gasoline	du pétrol/de l'essence	**duh pay-*trol*/de lay-*sahns***
highway to . . .	la route pour	**la root por**
hospital	l'hôpital	**low-pee-*tahl***
museum	le musée	**luh mew-zay**
no entry	sens interdit	**sehns ahn-ter-*dee***
no smoking	défense de fumer	**day-*fahns* de fu-may**
on foot	à pied	**ah pee-*ay***
one-day pass	ticket journalier	**tee-kay jhoor-nall-ee-ay**
one-way ticket	aller simple	**ah-*lay* sam-pluh**
police	la police	**lah po-*lees***
rented car	voiture de location	**vwa-*toor* de low-ka-see-on**
round-trip ticket	aller-retour	**ah-*lay*-re-toor**
slow down	ralentir	**rah-lahn-*teer***
store	le magasin	**luh ma-ga-*zehn***
street	rue	**roo**
subway	le Métro	**le *may*-tro**
telephone	le téléphone	**luh tay-lay-*phone***
ticket	un billet	**uh *bee*-yay**
ticket office	vente de billets	**vahnt duh bee-yay**
toilets	les toilettes/les WC	**lay twa-*lets*/lay vay-*say***

NECESSITIES

English	French	Pronunciation
I'd like . . .	Je voudrais . . .	**jhe voo-*dray* . . .**
a room	une chambre	**ewn *shahm*-bruh**
the key	la clé (la clef)	**la *clay***
I'd like to buy . . .	Je voudrais acheter . . .	**jhe voo-dray ahsh-tay . . .**
aspirin	des aspirines/des aspros	**deyz ahs-peer-*eens*/ deyz ahs-*prohs***
condoms	des préservatifs	**day pray-ser-va-*teefs***
dictionary	un dictionnaire	**uh deek-see-oh-*nare***
dress	une robe	**ewn robe**

envelopes	des envelopes	**days ahn-veh-*lope***
gift (for someone)	un cadeau	**uh kah-*doe***
handbag	un sac	**uh sahk**
hat	un chapeau	**uh shah-*poh***
magazine	une revue	**ewn reh-*vu***
map of the city	un plan de ville	**unh plahn de *veel***
matches	des allumettes	**dayz a-loo-*met***
necktie	une cravate	**eun cra-*vaht***
newspaper	un journal	**uh jhoor-*nahl***
phone card	une carte téléphonique	**ewncart tay-lay-fone-*eek***
postcard	une carte postale	**ewn carte pos-*tahl***
road map	une carte routière	**ewn cart roo-tee-*air***
shirt	une chemise	**ewn che-*meez***
shoes	des chaussures	**day show-*suhr***
skirt	une jupe	**ewn jhoop**
soap	du savon	**dew sah-*vohn***
socks	des chaussettes	**day show-*set***
stamp	un timbre	**uh *tam*-bruh**
trousers	un pantalon	**uh pan-tah-*lohn***
writing paper	du papier à lettres	**dew pap-pee-*ay* a *let*-ruh**
How much does it cost?	C'est combien? / Ça coûte combien?	**say comb-bee-*ehn*?/sah coot comb-bee-*ehn*?**
Do you take credit cards?	Est-ce que vous acceptez les cartes de credit?	**es-kuh voo zaksep-*tay* lay kart duh creh-*dee*?**

NUMBERS & ORDINALS

English	French	Pronunciation
zero	zéro	**zare-*oh***
one	un	**uh**
two	deux	**duh**
three	trois	**twah**
four	quatre	***kaht*-ruh**
five	cinq	**sank**
six	six	**seess**
seven	sept	**set**
eight	huit	**wheat**
nine	neuf	**nuf**
ten	dix	**deess**

eleven	onze	**ohnz**
twelve	douze	**dooz**
thirteen	treize	**trehz**
fourteen	quatorze	**kah-*torz***
fifteen	quinze	**kanz**
sixteen	seize	**sez**
seventeen	dix-sept	**deez-*set***
eighteen	dix-huit	**deez-*wheat***
nineteen	dix-neuf	**deez-*nuf***
twenty	vingt	**vehn**
twenty-one	vingt-et-un	**vehnt-ay-*uh***
twenty-two	vingt-deux	**vehnt-*duh***
thirty	trente	**trahnt**
forty	quarante	**ka-*rahnt***
fifty	cinquante	**sang-*kahnt***
sixty	soixante	**swa-*sahnt***
sixty-one	soixante-et-un	**swa-*sahnt*-et-*uh***
seventy	soixante-dix	**swa-*sahnt*-*deess***
seventy-one	soixante-et-onze	**swa-*sahnt*-et-*ohnze***
eighty	quatre-vingts	**kaht-ruh-*vehn***
eighty-one	quatre-vingt-un	**kaht-ruh-vehn-*uh***
ninety	quatre-vingt-dix	**kaht-ruh-venh-*deess***
ninety-one	quatre-vingt-onze	**kaht-ruh-venh-*ohnze***
one hundred	cent	**sahn**
one thousand	mille	**meel**
one hundred thousand	cent mille	**sahn meel**
first	premier	***preh*-mee-ay**
second	deuxième	***duhz*-zee-em**
third	troisième	***twa*-zee-em**
tenth	dixième	***dees*-ee-em**
twentieth	vingtième	***vehnt*-ee-em**
thirtieth	trentième	***trahnt*-ee-em**
one-hundredth	centième	***sant*-ee-em**

THE CALENDAR

English	French	Pronunciation
Sunday	dimanche	**dee-*mahnsh***
Monday	lundi	***luhn*-dee**

Tuesday	mardi	*mahr-dee*
Wednesday	mercredi	*mair-kruh-dee*
Thursday	jeudi	*jheu-dee*
Friday	vendredi	*vawn-druh-dee*
Saturday	samedi	*sahm-dee*
yesterday	hier	*ee-air*
today	aujourd'hui	*o-jhord-dwee*
this morning/this afternoon	ce matin/cet après-midi	*suh ma-tan/set ah-preh-mee-dee*
tonight	ce soir	*suh swahr*
tomorrow	demain	*de-man*

GLOSSARY OF BASIC MENU TERMS

Note: To order any of these items from a waiter, simply preface the French-language name with the phrase *"Je voudrais"* (jhe voo-*dray*), which means "I would like . . ." *Bon appétit!*

MEATS

English	French	Pronunciation
beef stew	du pot au feu	**dew poht o fhe**
beef braised with red wine	du boeuf à la mode	**dew bewf ah lah mhowd**
chicken	du poulet	**dew poo-lay**
chicken, veal, or fish rolls	des quenelles	**day ke-nelle**
chicken with mushrooms and wine	du coq au vin	**dew cock o vhin**
frogs' legs	des cuisses de grenouilles	**day cweess duh gre-noo-yuh**
ham	du jambon	**dew jham-bohn**
kidneys	des rognons	**day row-nyon**
lamb	de l'agneau	**duh lahn-nyo**
rabbit	du lapin	**dew lah-pan**
sirloin	de l'aloyau	**duh lahl-why-yo**
steak	du bifteck	**dew beef-tek**
pepper steak	un steak au poivre	**uh stake o pwah-vruh**
beef tenderloin	du chateaubriand	**dew sha-tow-bree-ahn**

| sweetbreads | des ris de veau | **day *ree* duh voh** |
| veal | du veau | **dew *voh*** |

FRUITS/VEGETABLES

English	French	Pronunciation
cabbage	du choux	**dew *shoe***
eggplant	de l'aubergine	**duh loh-ber-*jheen***
grapefruit	un pamplemousse	**uh *pahm*-pluh-moose**
grapes	du raisin	**dew ray-*zhan***
green beans	des haricots verts	**day ahr-ee-coh *vaire***
green peas	des petits pois	**day puh-tee *pwah***
lemon/lime	du citron/du citron vert	**dew cee-*tron*/dew cee-tron *vaire***
orange	une orange	**ewn o-*rahnj***
pineapple	de l'ananas	**duh lah-na-*nas***
potatoes	des pommes de terre	**day puhm duh *tehr***
french fried potatoes	des pommes frites	**day puhm *freet***
spinach	des épinards	**dayz ay-pin-*ards***
strawberries	des fraises	**day *frez***

BEVERAGES

English	French	Pronunciation
beer	de la bière	**duh lah bee-*aire***
milk	du lait	**dew *lay***
orange juice	du jus d'orange	**dew joo d'or-*ahn*-jhe**
water	de l'eau	**duh *lo***
red wine	du vin rouge	**dew vhin *rooj***
white wine	du vin blanc	**dew vhin *blahn***
coffee	un café	**uh ka-*fay***
coffee (black)	un café noir	**uh ka-fay *nwahr***
coffee (with cream)	un café crème	**uh ka-fay *krem***
coffee (with milk)	un café au lait	**uh ka-fay o *lay***
coffee (decaf)	un café décaféiné (slang: un déca)	**un ka-fay day-kah-fay-nay (uh *day*-kah)**
coffee (espresso)	un café espresso (un express)	**uh ka-fay e-*sprehss*-o (un ek-*sprehss*)**
tea	du thé	**dew *tay***

Index

A

C

INDEX

PHOTO CREDITS